Ephesians

CONCORDIA COMMENTARY

A Theological Exposition of Sacred Scripture

EPHESIANS

Thomas M. Winger

THE SCRIPTURES
TESTIFY TO ME

Concordia Publishing House
Saint Louis

Library of Congress Cataloging-in-Publication Data

Winger, Thomas M.
    Ephesians / Thomas M. Winger.
       pages   cm. — (Concordia commentary: a theological exposition of sacred scripture)
    Includes bibliographical references and indexes.
    ISBN 978-0-570-06313-1
    1. Bible. Ephesians—Commentaries. I. Title. II. Series.

    BS2695.53.W56   2014
    227'.5077—dc23
                                 20140217996

2 3 4 5 6 7 8 9 10   24 23 22 21 20 19 18 17 16 15

To Roger Winger,
my father in the flesh
and in the Lord

Contents

COMMENTARY

PHOTOS

Editors' Preface

What may a reader expect from the Concordia Commentary: A Theological Exposition of Sacred Scripture?

The purpose of this series, simply put, is to assist pastors, missionaries, and teachers of the Scriptures to convey God's Word with greater clarity, understanding, and faithfulness to the divine intent of the text.

Since every interpreter approaches the exegetical task from a certain perspective, honesty calls for an outline of the presuppositions held by those who have shaped this commentary series. This also serves, then, as a description of the characteristics of the commentaries.

First in importance is the conviction that the content of the scriptural testimony is Jesus Christ. The Lord himself enunciated this when he said, "The Scriptures … testify to me" (Jn 5:39), words that have been incorporated into the logo of this series. The message of the Scriptures is the Good News of God's work to reconcile the world to himself through the life, death, resurrection, ascension, and everlasting session of Jesus Christ at the right hand of God the Father. Under the guidance of the same Spirit who inspired the writing of the Scriptures, these commentaries seek to find in every passage of every canonical book "that which promotes Christ" (as Luther's hermeneutic is often described). They are *Trinitarian*, Christ-centered, and *Christological* commentaries.

As they unfold the scriptural testimony to Jesus Christ, these commentaries expound Law and Gospel. This approach arises from a second conviction—that Law and Gospel are the overarching doctrines of the Bible itself and that to understand them in their proper distinction and relationship to one another is a key for understanding the self-revelation of God and his plan of salvation in Jesus Christ.

Now, Law and Gospel do not always appear in Scripture labeled as such. The palette of language in Scripture is multicolored, with many and rich hues. The dialectic of a pericope may be fallen creation and new creation, darkness and light, death and life, wandering and promised land, exile and return, ignorance and wisdom, demon possession and the kingdom of God, sickness and healing, being lost and found, guilt and righteousness, flesh and Spirit, fear and joy, hunger and feast, or Babylon and the new Jerusalem. But the common element is God's gracious work of restoring fallen humanity through the Gospel of his Son. Since the predominant characteristic of these commentaries is the proclamation of that Gospel, they are, in the proper sense of the term, *evangelical.*

A third, related conviction is that the Scriptures are God's vehicle for communicating the Gospel. The editors and authors accept without reservation that the canonical books of the Old and New Testaments are, in their entirety, the inspired, infallible, and inerrant Word of God. The triune God is the ultimate author of the Bible, and every word in the original Hebrew, Aramaic, and Greek is inspired by the Holy Spirit. Yet rather than mechanical dictation, in the mysterious process by which the Scriptures were divinely inspired (e.g., 2 Tim 3:16; 2 Pet 1:21), God made use of the human faculties, knowledge, interests, and styles of the biblical writers, whose individual books surely are marked by distinctive features. At the same time, the canon of Scripture has its own inner unity, and each passage must be understood in harmony with the larger context of the whole. This commentary series pays heed to the smallest of textual details because of its acceptance of *plenary and verbal inspiration* and interprets the text in light of the whole of Scripture, in accord with the analogy of faith, following the principle that *Scripture interprets Scripture.* The entirety of the Bible is God's Word, *sacred* Scripture, calling for *theological* exposition.

A fourth conviction is that, even as the God of the Gospel came into this world in Jesus Christ (the Word incarnate), the scriptural Gospel has been given to and through the people of God, for the benefit of all humanity. God did not intend his Scriptures to have a life separated from the church. He gave them through servants of his choosing: prophets, sages, evangelists, and apostles. He gave them to the church and through the church, to be cherished in the church for admonition and comfort and to be used by the church for proclamation and catechesis. The living context of Scripture is ever the church, where the Lord's ministry of preaching, baptizing, forgiving sins, teaching, and celebrating the Lord's Supper continues. Aware of the way in which the incarnation of the Son of God has as a consequence the close union of Scripture and church, of Word and Sacraments, this commentary series features expositions that are *ecclesiological* and *sacramental.*

This Gospel Word of God, moreover, creates a unity among all those in whom it works the obedience of faith and who confess the truth of God revealed in it. This is the unity of the one holy Christian and apostolic church, which extends through world history. The church is to be found wherever the marks of the church are present: the Gospel in the Word and the Sacraments. These have been proclaimed, confessed, and celebrated in many different cultures and are in no way limited nor especially attached to any single culture or people. As this commentary series seeks to articulate the universal truth of the Gospel, it acknowledges and affirms the confession of the scriptural truth in all the many times and places where the one true church has been found. Aiming to promote *concord* in the confession of the one scriptural Gospel, these commentaries seek to be, in the best sense of the terms, *confessional, ecumenical,* and *catholic.*

All of those convictions and characteristics describe the theological heritage of Martin Luther and of the confessors who subscribe to the *Book of Concord* (1580)—those who have come to be known as Lutherans. The editors and authors forthrightly confess their subscription to the doctrinal exposition of Scripture in the *Book of Concord.* As the publishing arm of The Lutheran Church—Missouri Synod, Concordia Publishing House is bound to doctrinal agreement with the Scriptures and the Lutheran Confessions and seeks to herald the true Christian doctrine to the ends of the earth. To that end, the series has enlisted confessional Lutheran authors from other church bodies around the world who share the evangelical mission of promoting theological concord.

The authors and editors stand in the exegetical tradition of Martin Luther and the other Lutheran reformers, who in turn (as their writings took pains to demonstrate) stood in continuity with faithful exegesis by theologians of the early and medieval church, rooted in the hermeneutics of the Scriptures themselves (evident, for example, by how the New Testament interprets the Old). This hermeneutical method, practiced also by many non-Lutherans, includes (1) interpreting Scripture with Scripture according to the analogy of faith, that is, in harmony with the whole of Christian doctrine revealed in the Word; (2) giving utmost attention to the grammar (lexicography, phonetics, morphology, syntax, pragmatics) of the original language of the Hebrew, Aramaic, or Greek text; (3) seeking to discern the intended meaning of the text, the "plain" or "literal" sense, aware that the language of Scripture ranges from narrative to discourse, from formal prose to evocative poetry, from archaic to acrostic to apocalyptic, and it uses metaphor, type, parable, and other figures; (4) drawing on philology, linguistics, archaeology, literature, philosophy, history, and other fields in the quest for a better understanding of the text; (5) considering the history of the church's interpretation; (6) applying the text as authoritative also in the present milieu of the interpreter; and (7) above all, seeing the fulfillment and present application of the text in terms of Jesus Christ and his corporate church; upholding the Word, Baptism, and the Supper as the means through which Christ imparts salvation today; and affirming the inauguration, already now, of the eternal benefits of that salvation that is yet to come in the resurrection on the Last Day.

To be sure, the authors and editors do not feel bound to agree with every detail of the exegesis of our Lutheran forefathers. Nor do we imagine that the interpretations presented here are the final word about every crux and enigmatic passage. But the work has been done in harmony with the exegetical tradition that reaches back through the Lutheran confessors all the way to the biblical writers themselves, and in harmony with the confession of the church: grace alone, faith alone, Scripture alone, Christ alone.

The editors wish to acknowledge their debt of gratitude for all who have helped make possible this series. It was conceived at CPH in 1990, and a couple of years of planning and prayer to the Lord of the church preceded its formal launch on July 2, 1992. During that time, Dr. J. A. O. Preus II volunteered his enthusiasm for the project because, in his view, it would nurture and advance the faithful proclamation of the Christian faith as understood by the Lutheran church. The financial support that has underwritten the series was provided by a gracious donor who wished to remain anonymous. Those two faithful servants of God were called to heavenly rest not long after the series was inaugurated.

During the early years, former CPH presidents Dr. John W. Gerber and Dr. Stephen J. Carter had the foresight to recognize the potential benefit of such a landmark work for the church at large. CPH allowed Dr. Christopher W.

Mitchell to devote his time and energy to the conception and initial development of the project. Dr. Mitchell has remained the CPH editor and is also the Old Testament editor. Dr. Dean O. Wenthe has served on the project since its official start in 1992 and is the general editor, as well as a commentary author. Julene Gernant Dumit (M.A.R.) has been the CPH production editor for the entire series. Dr. Jeffrey A. Gibbs, author of the Matthew commentary volumes, served on the editorial board as the New Testament editor from 1999 into 2012. Dr. Curtis P. Giese, author of the commentary on 2 Peter and Jude, joined the board as interim assistant New Testament editor in 2011 and now serves as the New Testament editor.

CPH thanks all of the institutions that have enabled their faculty to serve as authors and editors. A particular debt of gratitude is owed to Concordia Theological Seminary, Fort Wayne, Indiana, for kindly allowing Dr. Dean O. Wenthe to serve as the general editor of the series and to dedicate a substantial portion of his time to it for many years. CPH also thanks Concordia Seminary, St. Louis, Missouri, for the dedication of Dr. Jeffrey A. Gibbs during his tenure as the New Testament editor. Moreover, Concordia University Texas is granting Dr. Curtis P. Giese a reduced load to enable him to carry on as the New Testament editor of the series. These institutions have thereby extended their ministries in selfless service for the benefit of the greater church.

The editors pray that the beneficence of their institutions may be reflected in this series by an evangelical orientation, a steadfast Christological perspective, an eschatological view toward the ultimate good of Christ's bride, and a concern that the wedding feast of the King's Son may be filled with all manner of guests (Mt 22:1–14).

> Now to him who is able to establish you by my Gospel and the preaching of Jesus Christ, by the revelation of the mystery kept secret for ages past but now revealed also through the prophetic Scriptures, made known to all the nations by order of the eternal God unto the obedience of faith—to the only wise God, through Jesus Christ, be the glory forever. Amen! (Rom 16:25–27)

Author's Preface

With the completion of this commentary, my long-term relationship with Ephesians passed its silver anniversary. It began as the tiny seed of an idea in the same year I was joined in marriage to my dear Sara, with whom I recently celebrated a much more significant jubilee! As I was searching for a topic for my upcoming M.Div. treatise, my vicarage supervisor, James Fandrey, pointed me to an intriguing article in the *Concordia Journal*: Henry Hamann's "The Translation of Ephesians 4:12—A Necessary Revision" (1988). This erudite investigation of how and why "the work of (the?) ministry" (Eph 4:12) had become detached from the *office* of the ministry in modern translations of the verse wedded my exegetical interest with a growing desire to investigate the biblical roots of the pastoral office. It resulted in a treatise whose subtitle, "The Question of a Comma," has been the occasion of much friendly teasing over the years.

Nearly a decade later, then general editor of the Concordia Commentary series, Jonathan Grothe, who was part of the body of Christ where the Lord had put me as pastor, proposed that I take on Ephesians. By that time I had developed some thoughts on the baptismal character of the letter, though I protested that a commentary should be written at the *end* of one's exegetical career, not the beginning. Whether through sloth, distraction, or diligence, my seventeen years of labor on the project have brought that prophecy to fulfillment—though one prays this is more the middle than the end of said career.

As teaching is the best path to learning, any credit for insight into this "crown of Paulinism"[1] must be shared with my students at Westfield House, Cambridge, in the seven consecutive years that I led a seminar there on Ephesians. Many an idea fleshed out in these pages began in notes hastily scribbled while young men and women expressed surprisingly mature insights. Though three students returning from the pub may claim to have saved the manuscript by frightening a would-be thief from my study window, the reality is that there was little yet to steal! Turning notes and ideas into readable text happened chiefly in a concentrated half-year sabbatical, thanks to the generosity of Concordia Lutheran Theological Seminary, St. Catharines, Ontario, and Concordia Publishing House.

At an evening social in Cambridge, a chaplain from St. John's College (to whom the host had introduced me so we could "talk theology") expressed his wonder that yet another commentary on Ephesians was warranted. At the time the best answer I could muster was that a Lutheran perspective ought to be distinctive enough to be welcomed into the mix of modern studies. Since that time

---

[1] C. H. Dodd, "Ephesians," in *The Abingdon Bible Commentary* (ed. Frederick Carl Eiselen, Edwin Lewis, and David G. Downey; New York: Abingdon, 1929), 1224–25.

I have pondered the question and venture the following as distinctive features of this commentary.

Firstly, in contrast to both critical commentaries that deny Pauline authorship and conservative volumes that treat the letter as a general epistle or circular, this commentary argues that two isagogical factors are simultaneously true: the apostle *Paul* wrote Ephesians to the Christian community in the city of *Ephesus*. This means, on the one hand, that the record of Acts and Paul's other letters may be used to construct a picture of the historical and ecclesiastical situation addressed by the letter. On the other hand, it also means that both the narrow higher critical and the narrow conservative Protestant pictures of who Paul was and what he could have written need thorough examination and revision—a task taken up in this commentary's admittedly lengthy introduction. This commentary allows the letter to tell us who Paul is and what he thought, rather than critiquing the letter on the basis of a narrow preconception of the so-called "authentic Paul."

Secondly, by anchoring the letter in Paul's ministry (both in Ephesus and later in his arrest and imprisonment), this commentary discerns a number of important themes. *Baptism*, though mentioned by name only once (Eph 4:5), undergirds and permeates the entire letter, with its concern for the unity of the *church* in Christ and its depiction of the church as his *body*. Paul's lengthy ministry in Ephesus both explains and leads to the discernment of a *liturgical* and *sacramental* flavor to a letter written to a church where the apostle had baptized, preached, prayed, and presided at the Lord's Supper. Paul's farewell sermon to the Ephesian presbyters assembled in Miletus (Acts 20:15–38) coheres with his explication of the *office of the ministry* in Ephesians 3–4. And the rather one-sided conflict between the triumphant Gospel of Christ and the polytheistic pagan culture of Ephesus, home of the magnificent temple of the goddess Artemis, provides background to the letter's emphasis on *spiritual warfare* and the opposition between *idolatry* and *true worship*.

Thirdly, flowing from my doctoral research into the *oral* character of Paul's epistles, this commentary pays close attention to the letter as an act of proclamation of Law and Gospel within the context of the Christian Divine Service. Orality theory suggests both microscopic and macroscopic techniques and observations. Its fruits are harvested in the interpretation of phrases, clauses, and larger units that include repetition, lists, and various patterns, for example. But the commentary also draws upon *rhetorical* analysis to uncover Paul's strategies of argumentation and persuasion. Put in churchly terms, it seeks to discern the Christian rhetoric that characterizes the letter as *sermon*. This is an eminently practical endeavor, for the goal of Christian commentary is to facilitate the proclamation of God's Holy Word.

In contrast to many modern commentaries, the present volume is therefore somewhat thin in its reliance on and citation of secondary literature (modern academic studies)—though thick and weighty in the hand! Modeling the classical pattern of sermon preparation, it focuses on careful grammatical analysis of the text within the context of Holy Scripture and in light of classical history and culture. Lexicons, grammars, and concordances (including complex and exhaustive BibleWorks computer searches) have been the primary tools. The exegetical results were then matured in the barrel of patristic interpretation, the Lutheran confessional writings, the sermons of Luther, and the liturgical context of the Word in Christ's church. The final step—application to his flock in one particular place—is left to the wisdom of the preacher, to whom this commentary is respectfully entrusted.

This rigorous textual approach was implanted in me by my first NT professor, Roger Humann; refined by my *Doktorvater*, James Voelz; and matured by constant interaction with my colleagues at Westfield House, Glen Zweck and Reginald Quirk. The desire to integrate all facets of theology, rather than dividing the disciplines, was stirred up by my teachers during graduate studies at Concordia Seminary, St. Louis, Missouri, particularly the Cantabrigians Norman Nagel and Ronald Feuerhahn, as well as OT teachers Paul Schrieber and Horace Hummel. I give thanks to God for my faithful colleagues at Concordia Lutheran Theological Seminary, St. Catharines, who were constant resources for this work, particularly Jonathan Grothe, John Stephenson, Duane Peters, and Wilhelm Torgerson. The Concordia Commentary editors protected me from countless embarrassing errors and filled up what was lacking in my very raw manuscript, for which thanks are due to NT editors Jeffrey Gibbs and Curtis Giese, and especially CPH editors Christopher Mitchell and Julene Dumit. My wife, Sara, and children, Anne and Benjamin, who were constantly in my mind as gifts of God while studying Eph 5:21–6:4, were unfailingly generous in giving me over to this massive task. But final thanks, and a heartfelt dedication, are given to my father in the flesh and in the Spirit, Roger Winger, who with my sainted mother, Della, raised me "in the discipline and instruction of the Lord" (Eph 6:4), who baptized, catechized, married, and ordained me, and who remains my beloved companion in the ministry and in the faith.

The Festival of St. Thomas AD 2014

Principal Abbreviations

Books of the Bible

Gen	2 Ki	Is	Nah	Rom	Titus
Ex	1 Chr	Jer	Hab	1 Cor	Philemon
Lev	2 Chr	Lam	Zeph	2 Cor	Heb
Num	Ezra	Ezek	Hag	Gal	James
Deut	Neh	Dan	Zech	Eph	1 Pet
Josh	Esth	Hos	Mal	Phil	2 Pet
Judg	Job	Joel	Mt	Col	1 Jn
Ruth	Ps (pl. Pss)	Amos	Mk	1 Thess	2 Jn
1 Sam	Prov	Obad	Lk	2 Thess	3 Jn
2 Sam	Eccl	Jonah	Jn	1 Tim	Jude
1 Ki	Song	Micah	Acts	2 Tim	Rev

Apocrypha and Septuagint

1–4 Kgdms	1–4 Kingdoms
1–2 Esdras	1–2 Esdras
Tobit	Tobit
Judith	Judith
Add Esth	Additions to Esther
Wis Sol	Wisdom of Solomon
Sirach	Sirach/Ecclesiasticus
Baruch	Baruch
Ep Jer	Epistle of Jeremiah
Azariah	Prayer of Azariah
Song of the Three	Song of the Three Young Men
Susanna	Susanna
Bel	Bel and the Dragon
Manasseh	Prayer of Manasseh
1–4 Macc	1–4 Maccabees
Ps 151	Psalm 151
Odes	Odes
Ps(s) Sol	Psalm(s) of Solomon

Dead Sea Scrolls and Related Texts

CD	Cairo (Genizah text of the) *Damascus (Document)*
1Q	Qumran Cave 1, followed by the abbreviation or number of a document found there

1QH	*Hodayoth (Thanksgiving Hymns)*
1QM	*Milḥamah (War Scroll)*
1QS	*Serek Hayaḥad (Community Rule)*

Papyri

PGM	*Papyri graecae magicae: Die griechischen Zauber-papyri.* Edited by Karl Preisendanz. Berlin, 1928
P.Oxy.	*The Oxyrhynchus Papyri.* Edited by B. P. Grenfell et al. Vols. 1–67. London: Egypt Exploration Society, 1898–2001
P.Ryl.	*Catalogue of the Greek (and Latin) Papyri in the John Rylands Library.* Edited by A. S. Hunt et al. 4 vols. Manchester, England, 1911–1952
P.Tebt.	*The Tebtunis Papyri.* Edited by B. P. Grenfell et al. 4 vols. London: Egypt Exploration Society, 1902–1976

Reference Works and Scripture Versions

AAT	An American Translation of the Bible
ABD	*The Anchor Bible Dictionary.* Edited by David Noel Freedman. 6 vols. New York: Doubleday, 1992
AC	Augsburg Confession
ACCS	*Galatians, Ephesians, Philippians.* Edited by Mark J. Edwards. Ancient Christian Commentary on Scripture: New Testament 8. Downers Grove, Ill.: InterVarsity, 1999
ACW	*Ancient Christian Writers: The Works of the Fathers in Translation.* Edited by Johannes Quasten et al. 1946–
AE	*Luther's Works.* St. Louis: Concordia, and Philadelphia: Fortress, 1955– [American Edition]
ANF	*The Ante-Nicene Fathers.* Edited by Alexander Roberts and James Donaldson. 10 vols. Repr., Peabody, Mass.: Hendrickson, 1994
Ap	Apology of the Augsburg Confession
APOT	*The Apocrypha and Pseudepigrapha of the Old Testament in English.* Edited by R. H. Charles. 2 vols. Oxford: Clarendon, 1913
BDAG	Bauer, Walter, Frederick William Danker, William F. Arndt, and F. Wilbur Gingrich. *A Greek-English Lexicon of the New Testament and Other Early Christian Literature.* 3d ed. Chicago: University of Chicago Press, 2000
BDF	Blass, F., A. Debrunner, and Robert W. Funk. *A Greek Grammar of the New Testament and Other Early*

	Christian Literature. Chicago: University of Chicago Press, 1961
BELK	*Die Bekenntnisschriften der evangelisch-lutherischen Kirche.* 12th ed. Göttingen: Vandenhoeck & Ruprecht, 1998
BHS	*Biblia Hebraica Stuttgartensia.* Edited by K. Elliger and W. Rudolph. Stuttgart: Deutsche Bibelgesellschaft, 1967/1977
BHT	Beiträge zur historischen Theologie
CBQ	*Catholic Biblical Quarterly*
CCSL	Corpus Christianorum: Series latina. Turnhout, Belgium: Brepols, 1953–
CSEL	Corpus scriptorum ecclesiasticorum latinorum
DBI	*Dictionary of Biblical Imagery.* Edited by Leland Ryken, James C. Wilhoit, and Tremper Longman III. Downers Grove, Ill.: InterVarsity, 1998
Denzinger	Denzinger, Heinrich, original compiler. *Compendium of Creeds, Definitions, and Declarations on Matters of Faith and Morals.* 43d ed. San Francisco: Ignatius, 2012
DNTB	*Dictionary of New Testament Background.* Edited by Craig A. Evans and Stanley E. Porter. Downers Grove, Ill.: InterVarsity, 2000
DPL	*Dictionary of Paul and His Letters.* Edited by Gerald F. Hawthorne, Ralph P. Martin, and Daniel G. Reid. Downers Grove, Ill.: InterVarsity, 1993
Dreves-Blume	Dreves, Guido Maria, and Clemens Blume, eds. *Analecta hymnica medii aevi.* 55 vols. Leipzig: Fues's Verlag and O. R. Reisland, 1886–1922
EDEJ	*The Eerdmans Dictionary of Early Judaism.* Edited by John J. Collins and Daniel C. Harlow. Grand Rapids: Eerdmans, 2010
ESV	English Standard Version of the Bible
ET	English translation, where the verse numbering differs from the MT and/or the LXX, or the Greek NT
FC Ep	Formula of Concord, Epitome
FC SD	Formula of Concord, Solid Declaration
HALOT	Köhler, Ludwig, Walter Baumgartner, and Johann Jakob Stamm. *The Hebrew and Aramaic Lexicon of the Old Testament.* Translated and edited under the supervision of M. E. J. Richardson. Study ed. 2 vols. Leiden: Brill, 2001

HS98 Handbook	*Hymnal Supplement 98: Handbook.* Edited by Paul Grime and Joseph Herl. St. Louis: Commission on Worship, The Lutheran Church—Missouri Synod, 1998
ICC	International Critical Commentary
IDB	*The Interpreter's Dictionary of the Bible.* Edited by George Arthur Buttrick et al. 5 vols. Nashville: Abingdon, 1962, 1976
Joüon	Joüon, Paul. *A Grammar of Biblical Hebrew.* Translated and revised by T. Muraoka. 2 vols. Subsidia biblica 14/1–2. Rome: Editrice Pontificio Istituto Biblico, 1991
JSOTSup	Journal for the Study of the Old Testament: Supplement Series
KJV	King James Version of the Bible
Kolb-Wengert	Robert Kolb and Timothy J. Wengert, eds. *The Book of Concord: The Confessions of the Evangelical Lutheran Church.* Minneapolis: Augsburg Fortress, 2000
LC	Large Catechism of Martin Luther
LCC	Library of Christian Classics. Philadelphia: Westminster, 1953–
LCL	Loeb Classical Library
LCMS	The Lutheran Church—Missouri Synod
Louw-Nida	Louw, Johannes P., and Eugene A. Nida. *Greek-English Lexicon of the New Testament: Based on Semantic Domains.* 2d ed. 2 vols. New York: United Bible Societies, 1989
LSB	*Lutheran Service Book.* St. Louis: Concordia, 2006
LSB Agenda	*Lutheran Service Book: Agenda.* St. Louis: Concordia, 2006
LSB Altar Book	*Lutheran Service Book: Altar Book.* St. Louis: Concordia, 2006
LSJM	Liddell, Henry George, Robert Scott, Henry Stuart Jones, and Roderick McKenzie. *A Greek-English Lexicon.* 9th ed. with rev. supplement. Oxford: Clarendon, 1996
LXX	Septuagint
Moulton-Milligan	Moulton, James Hope, and George Milligan. *The Vocabulary of the Greek Testament.* London: Hodder & Stoughton, 1930. Repr., Grand Rapids: Eerdmans, 1980
MT	Masoretic Text of the Hebrew Old Testament
NA[27]	Nestle, Eberhard and Erwin, Kurt and Barbara Aland, et al. *Novum Testamentum Graece.* 27th ed. Stuttgart: Deutsche Bibelgesellschaft, 1993

NA[28]	Nestle, Eberhard and Erwin, Kurt and Barbara Aland, et al. *Novum Testamentum Graece.* 28th ed. Stuttgart: Deutsche Bibelgesellschaft, 2012
NASB	New American Standard Bible
NEB	New English Bible
NIGTC	New International Greek Testament Commentary
NIV	New International Version of the Bible
NLT	New Living Translation of the Bible
NPNF[1]	*The Nicene and Post-Nicene Fathers.* Series 1. Edited by Philip Schaff. 14 vols. Repr., Peabody, Mass.: Hendrickson, 1994
NPNF[2]	*The Nicene and Post-Nicene Fathers.* Series 2. Edited by Philip Schaff and Henry Wace. 14 vols. Repr., Peabody, Mass.: Hendrickson, 1994
NRSV	New Revised Standard Version of the Bible
NT	New Testament
OED	*The Oxford English Dictionary.* 13 vols. Oxford: Clarendon, 1933
OT	Old Testament
PG	Patrologia graeca. Edited by J.-P. Migne. 161 vols. Paris, 1857–1866
PL	Patrologia latina. Edited by J.-P. Migne. 217 vols. Paris, 1844–1855
RSV	Revised Standard Version of the Bible and Apocrypha
SA	Smalcald Articles
SC	Small Catechism of Martin Luther
Soncino ed.	Hebrew-English Edition of the Babylonian Talmud. Edited by I. Epstein. 30 vols. London: Soncino, 1984–1990
StL	*Dr. Martin Luthers sämmtliche Schriften.* Edited by Johann Georg Walch. New revised stereotyped ed. 23 vols. in 25. St. Louis: Concordia, 1880–1910 [St. Louis ed.]
Str-B	Strack, Hermann Leberecht, and Paul Billerbeck. *Kommentar zum Neuen Testament aus Talmud und Midrasch.* 6 vols. in 7. Munich: Beck, 1922–1961
TDNT	*Theological Dictionary of the New Testament.* Edited by Gerhard Kittel and Gerhard Friedrich. Translated by Geoffrey W. Bromiley. 10 vols. Grand Rapids: Eerdmans, 1964–1976

TDOT	*Theological Dictionary of the Old Testament.* Edited by G. Johannes Botterweck, Helmer Ringgren, and Heinz-Josef Fabry. Translated by John T. Willis et al. 15 vols. Grand Rapids: Eerdmans, 1974–2006
TEV	Good News Bible, the Bible in Today's English Version
θ	Theodotion's Greek translation of the OT
TLH	*The Lutheran Hymnal.* St. Louis: Concordia, 1941
TLSB	*The Lutheran Study Bible.* Edited by Edward A. Engelbrecht et al. St. Louis: Concordia, 2009
Treatise	Treatise on the Power and Primacy of the Pope
TRENT	Instone-Brewer, David. *Traditions of the Rabbis from the Era of the New Testament.* Vol. 1: *Prayer and Agriculture.* Grand Rapids: Eerdmans, 2004
Triglotta	*Concordia Triglotta: The Symbolical Books of the Ev. Lutheran Church.* St. Louis: Concordia, 1921
UBS⁴	*The Greek New Testament.* 4th rev. ed. Stuttgart: Deutsche Bibelgesellschaft and United Bible Societies, 1994
WA	*D. Martin Luthers Werke: Kritische Gesamtausgabe.* 73 vols. in 85. Weimar: Böhlau, 1883– [Weimarer Ausgabe]
WA DB	*D. Martin Luthers Werke: Kritische Gesamtausgabe. Die Deutsche Bibel.* 12 vols. in 15. Weimar: Böhlau, 1906–1961 [Weimarer Ausgabe Deutsche Bibel]

Icons

These icons are used in the margins of this commentary to highlight the following themes:

Trinity

Temple, Tabernacle

Incarnation

Passion, Atonement

Death and Resurrection,
Theology of the Cross,
the Great Reversal

Christus Victor,
Christology

Baptism

Catechesis,
Instruction, Revelation

Lord's Supper

Ministry of Word and Sacrament,
Office of the Keys

The Church,
Christian Marriage

Worship

Sin, Law Breaking,
Death

Hope of Heaven,
Eschatology

Justification

Bibliography

Patristic Works

Chrysostom, John. *Homilies on Ephesians.* PG 62:9–176; *NPNF*[1] 13:49–172; and *Interpretatio omnium epistolarum Paulinarum*, 4:104–419. Oxford, J. H. Parker, 1852.

Tertullian. *Adversus Marcionem [Against Marcion].* Edited and translated by Ernest Evans. 2 vols. Oxford: Clarendon, 1972. Ephesians is treated particularly in 5.17–18.

Theodore of Mopsuestia. *Commentary on Galatians.* PG 66:897–926; and H. B. Swete, *Theodori episcopi mopsuesteni in epistolas B. Pauli commentarii*, 1:112–96. Cambridge: Cambridge University Press, 1880.

Luther's Sermons

Luther, Martin. "First Sermon at the Baptism of Bernhard von Anhalt, Matthew 3:1–12." April 1, 1540. AE 51:313–29; WA 49:111–24.

———. "Second Sermon at the Baptism of Bernhard von Anhalt, Matthew 3:13–17." April 2, 1540. WA 49:124–35.

———. "Second Wedding Sermon on Ephesians 5:22–33." Easter 1536, wedding of Caspar Creuziger. StL 12:2018–31.

———. "Sermon for the Feast of St. Michael, Revelation 12:7–12." September 29, 1544. WA 49:570–87.

———. "Sermon for the Twentieth Sunday after Trinity, Ephesians 5:15–20." October 18, 1545. AE 58:294–302; WA 51:60–67.

———. "Sermon for the Twenty-first Sunday after Trinity, Ephesians 6:10–17." October 25, 1545. AE 58:303–12; WA 51:67–76.

———. "Sermon for the Twenty-first Sunday after Trinity, Ephesians 6:10–17." November 6, 1530. StL 12:1626–31.

———. "Sermon on the Christians' Armor and Weapons, Ephesians 6:10–17." October 20, 1532. StL 9:810–57; WA 34/2:371–406.

———. "Sermon on the Festival of Christ's Epiphany: On the Baptism of Christ." 1546. StL 12:1130–45.

———. *Sermons of Martin Luther [Church Postils].* Edited by John Nicholas Lenker. Translated by John Nicholas Lenker et al. 8 vols. Grand Rapids: Baker, 1983. See 8:259–80 ("Sermon for the Sixteenth Sunday after Trinity, Ephesians 3:13–21," printed in 1525); 8:281–91 ("Sermon for the Seventeenth Sunday after Trinity, Ephesians 4:1–6"); 8:304–16 ("Sermon for the Nineteenth Sunday after Trinity, Ephesians 4:22–28," October 22, 1536); 7:150–161 ("Sermon for the Third Sunday in Lent, Ephesians 5:1–9"); 8:317–28 ("Sermon for the Twentieth Sunday after Trinity, Ephesians 5:15–21," October 29, 1536). For the German text, see, respectively, StL 12:868–89; 12:888–899; 12:910–23; 12:450–61; 12:924–35.

————. *Sermons of Martin Luther: The House Postils*. Edited by Eugene F. A. Klug. Translated by Eugene F. A. Klug et al. Grand Rapids: Baker Books, 1996. See 2:112–25 ("First Sermon for the Day of Christ's Ascension, Acts 1:1–11 and Psalm 68:19," 1534). For the German text, see StL 13b:2002–19.

Excerpts from some of Luther's sermons are translated in *Day by Day We Magnify Thee: Daily Meditations from Luther's Writings Arranged according to the Year of the Church*. Compiled and translated by Margarete Steiner and Percy Scott. Repr., Philadelphia: Fortress, 1982.

Modern Studies

Abbott, Thomas Kingsmill. *A Critical and Exegetical Commentary on the Epistles to the Ephesians and to the Colossians*. International Critical Commentary. Edinburgh: T&T Clark, 1897.

Aland, Kurt, and Barbara Aland. *The Text of the New Testament: An Introduction to the Critical Editions and to the Theory and Practice of Modern Textual Criticism*. Translated by Erroll F. Rhodes. Rev. ed. Grand Rapids: Eerdmans, 1989.

Allan, John A. "The 'In Christ' Formula in Ephesians." *New Testament Studies* 5 (1958–1959): 54–62.

Arnold, Clinton E. *Ephesians*. Zondervan Exegetical Commentary on the New Testament 10. Grand Rapids: Zondervan, 2010.

————. *Power and Magic: The Concept of Power in Ephesians*. Repr., Eugene, Oreg.: Wipf & Stock, 2001.

Aune, David E. *The New Testament in Its Literary Environment*. Library of Early Christianity 8. Philadelphia: Westminster, 1987.

Bales, William. "The Descent of Christ in Ephesians 4:9." *Catholic Biblical Quarterly* 72.1 (January 2010): 84–100.

Barth, Markus. *Ephesians*. 2 vols. Anchor Bible 34–34A. New York: Doubleday, 1974.

Baugh, Steven M. "Cult Prostitution in New Testament Ephesus: A Reappraisal." *Journal of the Evangelical Theological Society* 42.3 (September 1999): 443–60.

————. "A Foreign World: Ephesus in the First Century." Pages 13–38 in *Women in the Church: An Analysis and Application of 1 Timothy 2:9–15*. Edited by Andreas J. Köstenberger and Thomas R. Schreiner. 2d ed. Grand Rapids: Baker Academic, 2005.

Baur, Ferdinand Christian. *Paul, the Apostle of Jesus Christ: His Life and Works, His Epistles and Teachings: A Contribution to a Critical History of Primitive Christianity*. 2 vols. London: Williams & Norgate, 1873–1875. Translation of *Paulus, der Apostel Jesu Christi: Sein Leben und Wirken, seine Briefe und seine Lehre: Ein Beitrag zu einer kritischen Geschichte des Urchristenthums*. Stuttgart: Becher & Müller, 1845.

Best, Ernest. *A Critical and Exegetical Commentary on Ephesians*. International Critical Commentary. Edinburgh: T&T Clark, 1998.

————. *Essays on Ephesians*. Edinburgh: T&T Clark, 1997.

————. "The Use of Credal and Liturgical Material in Ephesians." Pages 53–69 in *Worship, Theology and Ministry in the Early Church: Essays in Honor of Ralph P. Martin*. Edited by Michael J. Wilkins and Terence Paige. Sheffield: Sheffield Academic, 1992.

————. "Who Used Whom? The Relationship of Ephesians and Colossians." *New Testament Studies* 43 (1997): 72–96.

Black, David Alan. "The Peculiarities of Ephesians and the Ephesian Address." *Grace Theological Journal* 2 (1981): 59–73.

Brown, Raymond E. *An Introduction to the New Testament*. New York: Doubleday, 1997.

Bruce, F. F. *The Epistles to the Colossians, to Philemon, and to the Ephesians*. New International Commentary on the New Testament. Grand Rapids: Eerdmans, 1984.

Burton, Ernest DeWitt. *Syntax of the Moods and Tenses in New Testament Greek*. 3d ed. Edinburgh: T&T Clark, 1898.

Cabié, Robert. "Christian Initiation." Pages 11–100 in *The Sacraments*. Vol. 3 of *The Church at Prayer: An Introduction to the Liturgy*. Edited by Aimé George Martimort. Translated by Matthew J. O'Connell. New ed. Collegeville, Minn.: Liturgical Press, 1988.

————. *The Eucharist*. Vol. 2 of *The Church at Prayer: An Introduction to the Liturgy*. Edited by Aimé George Martimort. Translated by Matthew J. O'Connell. New ed. Collegeville, Minn.: Liturgical Press, 1986.

Cadbury, Henry J. "The Dilemma of Ephesians." *New Testament Studies* 5 (1958–1959): 91–102.

Caird, G. B. *The Language and Imagery of the Bible*. London: Duckworth, 1980.

Carson, D. A., Douglas J. Moo, and Leon Morris. *An Introduction to the New Testament*. Leicester: Apollos, 1992.

Charles, R. H., ed. *The Apocrypha and Pseudepigrapha of the Old Testament in English*. 2 vols. Oxford: Clarendon, 1913.

Charlesworth, James H., ed. *The Old Testament Pseudepigrapha*. 2 vols. New York: Doubleday, 1983, 1985.

Classen, C. Joachim. "St Paul's Epistles and Ancient Greek and Roman Rhetoric." Pages 265–91 in *Rhetoric and the New Testament: Essays from the 1992 Heidelberg Conference*. Edited by Stanley E. Porter and Thomas H. Olbricht. Journal for the Study of the New Testament: Supplement Series 90. Sheffield: Sheffield Academic, 1993.

Collins, John N. *Deacons and the Church: Making Connections between Old and New*. Leominster, England: Gracewing, 2002.

————. *Diakonia: Re-interpreting the Ancient Sources*. Oxford: Oxford University Press, 1990.

Comfort, Philip. *Encountering the Manuscripts: An Introduction to New Testament Paleography and Textual Criticism*. Nashville: Broadman & Holman, 2005.

Connolly, R. Hugh, trans. and ed. *Didascalia Apostolorum*. Oxford: Clarendon, 1929.

Coutts, John. "Ephesians I.3–14 and I Peter I.3–12." *New Testament Studies* 3 (1956–1957): 115–27.

———. "The Relationship of Ephesians and Colossians." *New Testament Studies* 4 (1957–1958): 201–7.

Cross, F. L., ed. *Studies in Ephesians*. London: Mowbray, 1956.

Dahl, Nils Alstrup. *Studies in Ephesians: Introductory Questions, Text- and Edition-Critical Issues, Interpretation of Texts and Themes*. Edited by David Hellholm, Vemund Blomkvist, and Tord Fornberg. Tübingen: Mohr Siebeck, 2000. The following essays are particularly useful:

- "The Particularity of the Pauline Epistles as a Problem in the Ancient Church," 165–78.
- "Benediction and Congratulation," 279–314.
- "Das Proömium des Epheserbriefes," 315–34.
- "Cosmic Dimensions and Religious Knowledge (Eph 3:18)," 365–88.
- "Kleidungsmetaphern: Der alte und der neue Mensch," 389–411.
- "The Concept of Baptism in Ephesians," 413–39.
- "Gentiles, Christians, and Israelites in the Epistle to the Ephesians," 441–49.

D'Amato, Raffaele. *Arms and Armour of the Imperial Roman Soldier: From Marius to Commodus, 112 BC–AD 192*. Illustrated and with an introduction by Graham Sumner. Barnsley, England: Frontline, 2009.

Danby, Herbert, trans. *The Mishnah*. Oxford: Oxford University Press, 1933.

Daniélou, Jean. *The Bible and the Liturgy*. Notre Dame, Ind.: University of Notre Dame Press, 1956.

Das, A. Andrew. *Galatians*. Concordia Commentary. St. Louis: Concordia, 2014.

Daube, David. *The New Testament and Rabbinic Judaism*. London: Athlone, 1956.

Davis, Casey Wayne. *Oral Biblical Criticism: The Influence of the Principles of Orality on the Literary Structure of Paul's Epistle to the Philippians*. Journal for the Study of the New Testament: Supplement Series 172. Sheffield: Sheffield Academic, 1999.

Davis, John Jefferson. "Ephesians 4:12 Once More: 'Equipping the Saints for the Work of Ministry?'" *Evangelical Review of Theology* 24 (2000): 167–76.

Deissmann, Adolf. *Light from the Ancient East*. Translated by Lionel R. M. Strachan. 4th ed. Grand Rapids: Baker, 1978.

Derrett, Duncan M. *Law in the New Testament*. London: Darton, Longman & Todd, 1970.

Deterding, Paul E. *Colossians*. Concordia Commentary. St. Louis: Concordia, 2003.

Dinkler, Erich. "Die Taufterminologie in 2 Kor. i 21 f." Pages 173–91 in *Neotestamentica et Patristica: Eine Freundesgabe, Herrn Professor Dr. Oscar Cullmann zu seinem 60. Geburtstag überreicht*. Edited by W. C. van Unnik. Leiden: Brill, 1962.

Donfried, Karl P. "Ministry: Rethinking the Term *Diakonia*." *Concordia Theological Quarterly* 56 (1992): 1–15.

Doty, William G. *Letters in Primitive Christianity*. Philadelphia: Fortress, 1973.

Elert, Werner. *The Structure of Lutheranism*. Translated by Walter A. Hansen. St. Louis: Concordia, 1962.

Elowsky, Joel C. "The Ministry in the Early Church." *Concordia Theological Quarterly* 76 (2012): 295–311.

Fischer, Karl Martin. *Tendenz und Absicht des Epheserbriefes*. Göttingen: Vandenhoeck & Ruprecht, 1973.

Funk, Robert W. *Parables and Presence: Forms of the New Testament Tradition*. Philadelphia: Fortress, 1982.

Franzmann, Martin H. *The Word of the Lord Grows*. St. Louis: Concordia, 1961.

Gamble, Harry. *The Textual History of the Letter to the Romans*. Grand Rapids: Eerdmans, 1977.

Gibbs, Jeffrey A. *Matthew 1:1–11:1*. Concordia Commentary. St. Louis: Concordia, 2006.

———. *Matthew 11:2–20:34*. Concordia Commentary. St. Louis: Concordia, 2010.

Gibson, Jack J. "Ephesians 5:21–33 and the Lack of Marital Unity in the Roman Empire." *Bibliotheca sacra* 168 (2011): 162–77.

Giese, Curtis P. *2 Peter and Jude*. Concordia Commentary. St. Louis: Concordia, 2012.

Gnilka, Joachim. *Der Epheserbrief*. 2d ed. Freiburg: Herder, 1977.

Goodspeed, Edgar J. *An Introduction to the New Testament*. Chicago: University of Chicago Press, 1937.

———. *The Key to Ephesians*. Chicago: University of Chicago Press, 1956.

———. *The Meaning of Ephesians*. Chicago: University of Chicago Press, 1933.

Gordon, T. David. "'Equipping' Ministry in Ephesians 4?" *Journal of the Evangelical Theological Society* 37 (1994): 69–78.

Grothe, Jonathan F. *The Justification of the Ungodly: An Interpretation of Romans*. 2 vols. St. Catharines, Ontario, 2005.

———. "The Mysteries and the Ministry." Pages 55–65 in *Mysteria Dei: Essays in Honor of Kurt Marquart*. Edited by Paul T. McCain and John R. Stephenson. 2d ed. Fort Wayne, Ind.: Concordia Theological Seminary Press, 2000.

Guthrie, Donald. *New Testament Introduction*. Rev. ed. Downers Grove, Ill.: InterVarsity, 1990.

Hamann, Henry P. "Church and Ministry: An Exegesis of Ephesians 4:1–16." *Lutheran Theological Journal* 16 (1982): 121–28.

———. "The Translation of Ephesians 4:12—A Necessary Revision." *Concordia Journal* 14 (1988): 42–49.

Harris, Horton. *The Tübingen School.* Oxford: Oxford University Press, 1975.

Harstad, Adolph L. *Joshua.* Concordia Commentary. St. Louis: Concordia, 2004.

Harvey, John D. *Listening to the Text: Oral Patterning in Paul's Letters.* ETS Studies 1. Grand Rapids: Baker, 1998.

Heine, Ronald E., trans. *The Commentaries of Origen and Jerome on St. Paul's Epistle to the Ephesians.* New York: Oxford University Press, 2002.

Hoehner, Harold W. *Ephesians: An Exegetical Commentary.* Grand Rapids: Baker Academic, 2002.

Hofius, Otfried. "Gemeinschaft mit den Engeln im Gottesdienst der Kirche: Eine traditionsgeschichtliche Skizze." *Zeitschrift für Theologie und Kirche* 89 (1992): 172–96.

Hughes, Frank Witt. *Early Christian Rhetoric and 2 Thessalonians.* Journal for the Study of the New Testament: Supplement Series 30. Sheffield: Sheffield Academic, 1989.

Hummel, Horace D. *Ezekiel 21–48.* Concordia Commentary. St. Louis: Concordia, 2007.

Jasper, R. C. D., and G. J. Cuming. *Prayers of the Eucharist: Early and Reformed.* 3d ed. New York: Pueblo, 1987.

Jenkins, Ian. *Greek Architecture and Its Sculpture.* London: British Museum Press, 2006.

Jewett, Robert. "Following the Argument of Romans." Pages 265–78 in *The Romans Debate.* Edited by Karl P. Donfried. Rev. ed. Edinburgh: T&T Clark, 1991.

Johnson, Luke Timothy. *The First and Second Letters to Timothy.* Anchor Bible 35A. New York: Doubleday, 2001.

Jurgens, W. A., trans. and ed. *The Faith of the Early Fathers: A Source-Book of Theological and Historical Passages from the Christian Writings of the Pre-Nicene and Nicene Eras.* 3 vols. Collegeville, Minn.: Liturgical Press, 1970.

Käsemann, Ernst. "Ephesians and Acts." Pages 288–97 in *Studies in Luke-Acts.* Edited by Leander E. Keck and J. Louis Martyn. Philadelphia: Fortress, 1980.

Kelly, J. N. D. *A Commentary on the Pastoral Epistles: I Timothy, II Timothy, Titus.* London: Black, 1963.

———. *Early Christian Creeds.* 3d ed. Harlow: Longman, 1972.

Kennedy, George A. *New Testament Interpretation through Rhetorical Criticism.* Chapel Hill: University of North Carolina Press, 1984.

Kirby, John C. *Ephesians: Baptism and Pentecost: An Inquiry into the Structure and Purpose of the Epistle to the Ephesians.* London: SPCK, 1968.

Klauck, Hans-Josef. *Ancient Letters and the New Testament: A Guide to Context and Exegesis.* Waco: Baylor University Press, 2006.

Kleinig, John W. *Leviticus.* Concordia Commentary. St. Louis: Concordia, 2003.

———. "The Mystery of Doxology." Pages 129–47 in *Mysteria Dei: Essays in Honor of Kurt Marquart*. Edited by Paul T. McCain and John R. Stephenson. 2d ed. Fort Wayne, Ind.: Concordia Theological Seminary Press, 2000.

———. "Ordered Community: Order and Subordination in the New Testament." *Lutheran Theological Review* 17 (Academic Year 2004–2005): 45–59.

———. "Sharing in God's Holiness." *Lutheran Theological Review* 8.1–2 (Fall/Winter 1995–Spring/Summer 1996): 105–18.

Koester, Helmut, ed. *Ephesos: Metropolis of Asia: An Interdisciplinary Approach to Its Archaeology, Religion, and Culture*. Valley Forge, Pa.: Trinity Press International, 1995.

Lampe, G. W. H. *The Seal of the Spirit: A Study in the Doctrine of Baptism and Confirmation in the New Testament and the Fathers*. 2d ed. London: SPCK, 1967.

Lessing, R. Reed. *Isaiah 40–55*. Concordia Commentary. St. Louis: Concordia, 2011.

———. *Isaiah 56–66*. Concordia Commentary. St. Louis: Concordia, 2014.

———. *Jonah*. Concordia Commentary. St. Louis: Concordia, 2007.

Lincoln, Andrew T. *Ephesians*. Word Biblical Commentary 42. Dallas: Word, 1990.

Lockwood, Gregory J. *1 Corinthians*. Concordia Commentary. St. Louis: Concordia, 2000.

MacDonald, Margaret Y. *Colossians and Ephesians*. Sacra Pagina 17. Collegeville, Minn.: Liturgical Press, 2000.

Mack, Burton L. *Rhetoric and the New Testament*. Minneapolis: Fortress, 1990.

Merklein, Helmut. *Das kirchliche Amt nach dem Epheserbrief*. Munich: Kösel, 1973.

Metzger, Bruce M. *A Textual Commentary on the Greek New Testament*. 2d ed. New York: United Bible Societies, 1994.

Metzger, Bruce M., and Bart D. Ehrman. *The Text of the New Testament: Its Transmission, Corruption, and Restoration*. 4th ed. Oxford: Oxford University Press, 2005.

Middendorf, Michael P. *Romans 1–8*. Concordia Commentary. St. Louis: Concordia, 2013.

Mitchell, Christopher W. *The Meaning of* BRK *"To Bless" in the Old Testament*. Atlanta: Scholars, 1987.

———. *The Song of Songs*. Concordia Commentary. St. Louis: Concordia, 2003.

Mitchell, Margaret M. "New Testament Envoys in the Context of Greco-Roman Diplomatic and Epistolary Conventions: The Example of Timothy and Titus." *Journal of Biblical Literature* 111 (1992): 641–62.

Mitton, C. Leslie. *The Epistle to the Ephesians: Its Authorship, Origin and Purpose*. Oxford: Oxford University Press, 1951.

Moe, John M. "Εὐαγγελιστής: Evangelist?" *Logia* 2.3 (Holy Trinity/July 1993): 4–5.

Moule, C. F. D. *An Idiom Book of New Testament Greek*. 2d ed. Cambridge: Cambridge University Press, 1959.

Moule, H. C. G. *Ephesian Studies*. London: Hodder & Stoughton, 1900.

Moulton, James Hope. *Prolegomena*. Vol. 1 of *A Grammar of New Testament Greek*. Edinburgh: T&T Clark, 1906.

Moulton, James Hope, and Wilbert Francis Howard. *Accidence and Word-Formation*. Vol. 2 of *A Grammar of New Testament Greek*. Repr., Edinburgh: T&T Clark, 1986.

Mounce, William D. *Pastoral Epistles*. Word Biblical Commentary 46. Nashville: Thomas Nelson, 2000.

Murphy-O'Connor, Jerome. *St. Paul's Ephesus: Texts and Archaeology*. Collegeville, Minn.: Liturgical Press, 2008.

Nineham, Dennis E. "The Case against the Pauline Authorship." Pages 21–35 in *Studies in Ephesians*. Edited by F. L. Cross. London: Mowbray, 1956.

Nordling, John G. *Philemon*. Concordia Commentary. St. Louis: Concordia, 2004.

———. "Research Notes [on Eph 5:21]." *Concordia Theological Quarterly* 77 (2013): 327–34.

O'Brien, Peter T. *The Letter to the Ephesians*. Grand Rapids: Eerdmans, 1999.

Oster, Richard. "The Ephesian Artemis as an Opponent of Early Christianity." *Jahrbuch für Antike und Christentum* 19 (1976): 24–44.

Parker, David C. *An Introduction to the New Testament Manuscripts and Their Texts*. Cambridge: Cambridge University Press, 2008.

Patzia, Arthur G. *Ephesians, Colossians, Philemon*. Repr., Grand Rapids: Baker, 2011.

Percy, Ernst. *Die Probleme der Kolosser- und Epheserbrief*. Lund: Gleerup, 1946.

Peters, Albrecht. *Commentary on Luther's Catechisms*. Vol. 1: *Ten Commandments*. Translated by Holger K. Sonntag. St. Louis: Concordia, 2009.

Pieper, Francis. *Christian Dogmatics*. 4 vols. St. Louis: Concordia, 1950–1957.

Porter, Stanley E. "The Theoretical Justification for Application of Rhetorical Categories to Pauline Epistolary Literature." Pages 100–22 in *Rhetoric and the New Testament: Essays from the 1992 Heidelberg Conference*. Edited by Stanley E. Porter and Thomas H. Olbricht. Journal for the Study of the New Testament: Supplement Series 90. Sheffield: Sheffield Academic, 1993.

Reed, Jeffrey T. "Using Ancient Rhetorical Categories to Interpret Paul's Letters: A Question of Genre." Pages 292–324 in *Rhetoric and the New Testament: Essays from the 1992 Heidelberg Conference*. Edited by Stanley E. Porter and Thomas H. Olbricht. Journal for the Study of the New Testament: Supplement Series 90. Sheffield: Sheffield Academic, 1993.

Reed, Luther D. *The Lutheran Liturgy*. Rev. ed. Philadelphia: Fortress, 1960.

Reicke, Bo. *Re-examining Paul's Letters: The History of the Pauline Correspondence*. Edited by David P. Moessner and Ingalisa Reicke. Harrisburg, Pa.: Trinity Press International, 2001.

———. *The Roots of the Synoptic Gospels*. Philadelphia: Fortress, 1986.

Robertson, A. T. *A Grammar of the Greek New Testament in the Light of Historical Research*. 4th ed. Nashville: Broadman, 1934.

Robinson, J. Armitage. *St Paul's Epistle to the Ephesians*. 2d ed. London: Macmillan, 1909.

Robinson, John A. T. "The One Baptism." Pages 158–75 in *Twelve New Testament Studies*. London: SCM, 1962.

———. *Redating the New Testament*. Philadelphia: Westminster, 1976.

———. "Traces of a Liturgical Sequence in 1 Cor. 16:20–24." *Journal of Theological Studies* 4 (1953): 38–41.

Roosien, Mark. "Putting on Christ: Metaphor and Martyrdom in John Chrysostom's *Baptismal Instructions*." *Studia Liturgica* 43 (2013): 54–67.

Royse, James R. *Scribal Habits in Early Greek New Testament Papyri*. Leiden: Brill, 2008.

Sampley, J. Paul. *"And the Two Shall Become One Flesh": A Study of Traditions in Ephesians 5:21–33*. Cambridge: Cambridge University Press, 1971.

Sanders, J. N. "The Case for the Pauline Authorship." Pages 9–20 in *Studies in Ephesians*. Edited by F. L. Cross. London: Mowbray, 1956.

Sanders, Jack T. "Hymnic Elements in Ephesians 1–3." *Zeitschrift für die neutestamentliche Wissenschaft* 56 (1965): 214–32.

Sasse, Hermann. "Intersynodical Exegetical Theses [Jn 17:20–23; Eph 4:1–6]." Unpublished and undated manuscript.

———. "Selective Fellowship." *Australian Theological Review* 28.3 (September 1957): 45–62.

Scharlemann, Martin H. "The Pastoral Office and Divorce, Remarriage, Moral Deviation." *Concordia Journal* 6.4 (July 1980): 141–50.

———. "The Secret of God's Plan: Studies in Ephesians." *Concordia Theological Monthly* 40 (1969): 532–44; 41 (1970): 155–64, 338–46, 410–20.

Schlier, Heinrich. *Der Brief an die Epheser: Ein Kommentar*. 2d ed. Düsseldorf: Patmos-Verlag, 1958.

Schnackenburg, Rudolf. *Ephesians: A Commentary*. Translated by Helen Heron. Edinburgh: T&T Clark, 1991.

———. " 'Er hat uns mitauferweckt': Zur Tauflehre des Epheserbriefes." *Liturgisches Jahrbuch* 2 (1952): 159–83.

Schuchard, Bruce G. *1–3 John*. Concordia Commentary. St. Louis: Concordia, 2012.

Schwindt, Rainer. *Das Weltbild des Epheserbriefes: Eine religionsgeschichtlich-exegetische Studie*. Tübingen: Mohr Siebeck, 2002.

Shuckburgh, Evelyn S., trans. *The Histories of Polybius*. 2 vols. London: Macmillan, 1889.

Smyth, Herbert Weir. *Greek Grammar*. Revised by Gordon M. Messing. Cambridge, Mass.: Harvard University Press, 1956.

Steinmann, Andrew E. *Daniel*. Concordia Commentary. St. Louis: Concordia, 2008.

Stoeckhardt, George. *Ephesians*. Translated by Martin S. Sommer. Concordia Classic Commentary Series. St. Louis: Concordia, 1952. Translation of *Kommentar über den Brief Pauli an die Epheser*. St. Louis: Concordia, 1910.

Stowers, Stanley K. *Letter Writing in Greco-Roman Antiquity*. Philadelphia: Westminster, 1986.

Theron, Daniel Johannes. *Evidence of Tradition*. London: Bowes & Bowes, 1957.

Thomson, Ian H. *Chiasmus in the Pauline Letters*. Sheffield: Sheffield Academic, 1995.

Trebilco, Paul. *The Early Christians in Ephesus from Paul to Ignatius*. Grand Rapids: Eerdmans, 2007.

Turner, Nigel. *Christian Words*. Edinburgh: T&T Clark, 1980.

———. *Grammatical Insights into the New Testament*. Edinburgh: T&T Clark, 1965.

———. *Syntax*. Vol. 3 of *A Grammar of New Testament Greek*. By James Hope Moulton. Edinburgh: T&T Clark, 1963.

Van Roon, A. *The Authenticity of Ephesians*. Supplements to Novum Testamentum 39. Leiden: Brill, 1974.

Vermes, Geza. *The Complete Dead Sea Scrolls in English*. London: Penguin, 1997.

Voelz, James W. *Fundamental Greek Grammar*. 3d rev. ed. St. Louis: Concordia, 2011.

———. *What Does This Mean? Principles of Biblical Interpretation in the Post-Modern World*. 2d ed. St. Louis: Concordia, 2003.

Wallace, Daniel B. *Greek Grammar Beyond the Basics: An Exegetical Syntax of the New Testament*. Grand Rapids: Zondervan, 1996.

Warnach, V. "Taufwirklichkeit und Taufbewusstsein nach dem Epheserbrief." *Liturgie und Mönchtum* 33/34 (1963–1964): 46–51.

Watson, Duane F. "Paul's Speech to the Ephesian Elders (Acts 20.17–38): Epideictic Rhetoric of Farewell." Pages 184–208 in *Persuasive Artistry: Studies in New Testament Rhetoric in Honor of George A. Kennedy*. Edited by Duane F. Watson. Journal for the Study of the New Testament: Supplement Series 50. Sheffield: Sheffield Academic, 1991.

Weinrich, William. " 'It Is Not Given to Women to Teach': A *Lex* in Search of a *Ratio*." Fort Wayne: Concordia Theological Seminary Press, 1993.

Whiston, William, trans. *The Works of Josephus*. Buffalo, N.Y.: Beardsley, 1895.

Whitaker, E. C., ed. *Documents of the Baptismal Liturgy*. 2d ed. London: SPCK, 1970.

Wilder, Terry L. *Pseudonymity, the New Testament, and Deception: An Inquiry into Intention and Reception*. Lanham, Md.: University Press of America, 2004.

Williams, R. R. "Logic *versus* Experience in the Order of Credal Formulae." *New Testament Studies* 1 (1954–1955): 42–44.

Winger, Thomas M. "From Apostolic Witness to Christian Confession: I John 4:1–6." *Lutheran Theological Review* 11 (Academic Year 1998–1999): 69–89.

———. "The Office of the Holy Ministry according to the New Testament Mandate of Christ." *Logia* 7.2 (Eastertide 1998): 37–46.

———. " 'One Baptism' and the Purpose of Ephesians." Pages 247–70 in *Teach Me Thy Way, O Lord: Essays in Honor of Glen Zweck on the Occasion of His Sixty-fifth Birthday*. Houston: Zweck Festschrift Committee, 2000.

———. "Orality as the Key to Understanding Apostolic Proclamation in the Epistles." Th.D. dissertation. St. Louis: Concordia Seminary, 1997.

———. "The Priesthood of All the Baptized: An Exegetical and Theological Investigation." S.T.M. thesis, Concordia Seminary, St. Louis, 1992.

———. "Rhetoric and Media in the Judgement of St Paul." *Lutheran Theological Review* 16 (Academic Year 2003–2004): 47–58.

———. "*Simul justus et peccator*: Did Luther and the Confessions Get Paul Right?" *Lutheran Theological Review* 17 (2004–2005): 90–108.

———. "The Spoken Word: What's Up with Orality?" *Concordia Journal* 29 (2003): 133–51.

Wright, N. T. *Paul: In Fresh Perspective*. Minneapolis: Fortress, 2005.

Yonge, C. D., trans. *The Works of Philo: Complete and Unabridged*. New updated ed. Peabody, Mass.: Hendrickson, 1993.

Zerwick, Maximilian. *Biblical Greek: Illustrated by Examples*. Translated and edited by Joseph Smith. 9th reprint. Rome: Pontifical Biblical Institute, 2011.

Zuntz, Günther. *The Text of the Epistles: A Disquisition upon the Corpus Paulinum*. London: Oxford University Press, 1953.

Introduction

Why Study Ephesians?

Ephesians is out of fashion. As inappropriate as it may seem, each age has its favorites. The ancients with their attachment to St. Matthew would be dismayed to observe how the Gospel of Mark has displaced it in university curricula today. This is owing, of course, to the wholesale shift in scholarly opinion from Matthean to Markan priority. No one is interested in what appears to be secondary or derivative. So also Ephesians has suffered in modern times by its relegation to the category of "deutero-Pauline." If Ephesians were merely the product of a second-generation disciple of Paul, if it represented the stagnant institutionalization of a once-vibrant theology, thinly veiled by borrowed catchphrases from Paul's authentic works, then it would thoroughly deserve early retirement.

While one ought to reserve judgment about its authenticity until the evidence is heard,[1] it is well worth considering the higher appraisals of an earlier era. Far from being at odds with the theology of the undisputed Pauline epistles (Romans, Galatians, 1 Corinthians, Philippians), Ephesians was once thought to be a veritable compendium of Pauline thought. J. Armitage Robinson famously dubbed it "the crown of St Paul's writings."[2] C. H. Dodd echoed him with "the crown of Paulinism."[3] Church fathers drew Paul's iconic symbol, "the sword of the Spirit" (*Spiritus gladius*), from this letter (6:17). John Chrysostom has left us with sermons on its every word. Though he never lectured on it at length, Luther included Ephesians among the chief evangelical writings of the NT:

> In a word St. John's Gospel and his first epistle, St. Paul's epistles, especially Romans, Galatians, and Ephesians, and St. Peter's first epistle are the books that show you Christ and teach you all that is necessary and salvatory for you to know, even if you were never to see or hear any other book or doctrine.[4]

The church's historic evaluation of Ephesians thus stands starkly opposed to current fashion, as Raymond Brown recently reaffirmed: "Among the Pauline writings only Rom can match Eph as a candidate for exercising the most influence on Christian thought and spirituality."[5]

---

[1] See "Authorship" below.

[2] J. Armitage Robinson, *St Paul's Epistle to the Ephesians* (2d ed.; London: Macmillan, 1909), vii.

[3] C. H. Dodd, "Ephesians," in *The Abingdon Bible Commentary* (ed. Frederick Carl Eiselen, Edwin Lewis, and David G. Downey; New York: Abingdon, 1929), 1224–25.

[4] Martin Luther, *Prefaces to the New Testament* (1522), AE 35:362.

[5] Brown, *An Introduction to the New Testament*, 620. Cf. "The Influence of the Epistle throughout History" in Schnackenburg, *Ephesians*, 311–42; Dahl, "Interpreting Ephesians: Then and Now," in *Studies in Ephesians*, 461–63. Dahl, 463, suggests that Ephesians made a greater

A brief tour of the epistle's highlights swiftly demonstrates why this was so. In Ephesians we hear of

- the reconciliation of the cosmos and our eternal election in Christ (1:3–14);
- Christ's exaltation to the right hand of God (1:20–23);
- salvation by grace through faith apart from works (2:8–10);
- the equality of Jew and Gentile in Christ (2:11–22);
- the mystery of the salvation of the Gentiles (3:1–13);
- "one Lord, one faith, one Baptism" (4:4–6);
- the gift of the office of the ministry (4:7–12);
- the church as Christ's body (1:23; 2:16; 3:6; 4:4, 12–16; 5:23, 30);
- the Christological meaning of marriage (5:22–33);
- the Christological meaning of all vocations (6:1–9); and
- the resplendent armor of God (6:10–17).

How much poorer the church would be without these teachings!

If the value of studying Ephesians is not apparent from its historic value and the strength of its content, consider its place in the church's liturgy. Most of the epistle was read in the historic Western lectionary and even more is now included in the one- and three-year lectionaries commonly in use among Lutherans. In the Sundays after Pentecost in series B, a *lectio continua* of Ephesians spans eight Sundays,[6] giving the pastor ample opportunity to preach these texts. In addition, the detailed description of the office of the ministry in chapter 4 holds a key place in Lutheran ordination rites.[7] Likewise, chapter 5 is the appointed epistle for the Lutheran rite of holy marriage, even as it had adorned most Christian marriage rites until modern secular sensibilities began to shy away from it.[8] If it was through liturgical reading that Ephesians first gained place in the canon of Scripture,[9] then its continued place in the ἀνάγνωσις, the "public reading," surely commends it to our study.

---

impact on the theology of the Eastern Orthodox Church than on the West, which owed more to Romans and Galatians from Augustine onward—though he pays due deference to the role of Eph 2:5, 8, "by grace … through faith," in the Reformation (in addition to Eph 4:5–6 in defining the true unity of the church).

[6] See *LSB*, xvii.

[7] See, for example, *LSB Agenda*, 164. Luther's ordination rite (1539) cites Paul's words to Timothy in Ephesus (1 Tim 3:1–7) and his sermon to the Ephesian pastors (Acts 20:28–31), but not Ephesians 4 specifically (AE 53:124–25).

[8] See, for example, *LSB Agenda*, 66–67. Luther's 1529 marriage rite quotes from Ephesians 5 (AE 53:114), as does Thomas Cranmer's rite in the *Book of Common Prayer* (1549 et al.) and virtually all other historic Christian marriage rites.

[9] While apostolic authorship and agreement with the rule of faith were two basic *criteria* by which texts were judged for inclusion in the canon, it was liturgical reading that first presented texts to the church for such judgment. Placing them alongside the inspired OT in the liturgy accorded them the same divine status. Those texts that created and sustained faith in Jesus Christ commended themselves. In addition, widespread liturgical reading was part of the evidence that was considered, as it represented the broad consensus of the church on the apostolicity and faithfulness of the text. Texts were tested because they were being read; use

The Lutheran *Book of Concord* cites Ephesians sixty-six times. Nearly every major article of faith finds a *sedes doctrinae* in this chief letter of Paul. Not surprisingly, "by grace you have been saved through faith" (2:8) features prominently in explaining justification apart from works (AC 20:11; Ap 4:73, 93; 15:6; FC Ep 3:10; 4:7). Good works are placed in their proper sequence following justification by Eph 2:10 (FC SD 4:7; 6:12). "One faith, one Baptism, one God and Father" (Eph 4:5–6) explains the true unity of the church (AC 7:4), as also does Christ's unique headship over his churchly body (Eph 1:22–23; 5:25–27; Ap 7:5, 7). The work of the devil in the sons of disobedience (Eph 2:2) explains original sin and the lack of free will (Ap 7:16; 18:5; FC SD 1:6; 2:7), while only rebirth in Christ can overcome them (Eph 2:5; FC Ep 2:3). That the office of the ministry is a gift to the *whole* church and not the possession of the pope alone (Treatise, 67) is proved from "when he ascended he gave gifts to men …" (Eph 4:8, 11, 12). The role of the Word in Baptism is taught by Eph 5:26 (SA 3:5.1). Christ's session in power at the right hand of God, above all things (Eph 4:10; see also Eph 1:21–22), demonstrates that he can indeed give his body and blood in the Sacrament (FC Ep 8:16–17; FC SD 8:27–29). The true doctrine of our eternal election is affirmed on the basis of Eph 1:4 (FC Ep 11:7; FC SD 11:5). Luther cites approvingly Paul's observation that the Fourth Commandment is the first with a promise (Eph 6:2; LC 1:133; Ap 4:197). He also points to Eph 5:21–33 in defense of the Sixth Commandment (LC 1:220). Luther cites Ephesians 6 four times in the Small Catechism's Table of Duties (SC 9:8–11), and in the preface of the Large Catechism, he uses the armor of God passage (Eph 6:10–17) to highlight the value of learning the catechism (LC, Preface, 14; cf. LC 3:104). For our Lutheran forefathers, then, Ephesians was an indispensable compendium of theology.

Ultimately, it is the letter's self-testimony that must cause the reader/hearer to recognize its value. At a theological level this is so because the Holy Spirit alone can bring the conviction of faith through the reading of the words he has inspired. But it is also true that a literary work of any kind must be evaluated according to the purposes for which it was produced. Ephesians is apostolic proclamation for the church. The letter must not only be studied, but also heard. Or better said, one studies it in order to proclaim and hear it more clearly.

Orality and the Interpretation of the Epistles: A Brief Introduction

Oral Traditionalism

Prior to the modern era, no reader would have been startled by the contention that Paul's epistles are to be proclaimed orally and heard. But the explosive

---

preceded canon. Those that passed such tests were approved for continued liturgical use, and thus the canon arose. See Brevard S. Childs, *The New Testament as Canon: An Introduction* (Philadelphia: Fortress, 1985), 31–32; Bruce M. Metzger, *The Canon of the New Testament: Its Origin, Development, and Significance* (Oxford: Clarendon, 1987), 253.

appearance of the printing press led to a profound cultural shift that introduced as normative the isolated reader surrounded by all the books that might content his heart.[10] As this shift took hold in the Enlightenment era, texts lost their character as communal products to be read aloud by one person to others. Ancient texts, therefore, were no longer received in a context approximating what their authors intended and often became objects of scientific criticism in the silence of the scholar's study.[11]

Granted, it was in this early period of biblical criticism that oral theories concerning the background and development of the Gospels were first promulgated. But such theories were products of the romantic and evolutionary mind-set of the time. According to such scholars, "orality" applied to that primitive, first-generation period in which the sayings and deeds of Jesus were passed on with varying degrees of accuracy and were developed in accord with the needs of the church (the *Sitz im Leben*) until the authors of a later generation manufactured "mature," written Gospels from the fragmentary oral building blocks. Thus, while they were keen to discover the historical Jesus' obscure origins by looking "through" the written text, and while they certainly held a romantic attachment to the oral period in the way that nineteenth-century Victorians were fascinated by "primitive" native peoples, there was no doubt that they considered the oral tradition unreliable as a medium for transmitting the true story of Jesus.[12]

In the twentieth century such skepticism toward oral tradition has been challenged particularly by the Uppsala School, which investigated Jewish methods of memorization and oral transmission, demonstrating the remarkable ability of well-trained ancient peoples to maintain the verbal accuracy of oral traditions.[13] But in Gospel studies the fundamental dichotomy between speech and text has been generally maintained, with "orality studies" entailing the discernment of the original context of each individual unit as it was composed *prior* to entering the written Gospels. Rarely have interpreters asked how the *written*

---

[10] See the classic study by Elizabeth L. Eisenstein, *The Printing Press as an Agent of Change: Communication and Cultural Transformations in Early Modern Europe* (2 vols.; Cambridge: Cambridge University Press, 1979).

[11] Thomas E. Boomershine, "Biblical Megatrends: Towards a Paradigm for the Interpretation of the Bible in Electronic Media," in *Society for Biblical Literature 1987 Seminar Papers* (Atlanta: Scholars, 1987), 146–47, refers to this stage as "the culture of silent print," when texts begin to serve merely "as documentary sources for the establishment of either historical facticity … or theological truths or ideas."

[12] Though source critics in the eighteenth through nineteenth centuries uniformly accepted this proposition, in recent times it is perhaps Werner Kelber who most forcefully posited a radical divide between the oral and written stages of Gospel transmission: *The Oral and the Written Gospel: The Hermeneutics of Speaking and Writing in the Synoptic Tradition, Mark, Paul, and Q* (Philadelphia: Fortress, 1983).

[13] See, for example, Birger Gerhardsson, *Memory and Manuscript: Oral Tradition and Written Transmission in Rabbinic Judaism and Early Christianity* (Uppsala: Boktryckeri Aktiebolag, 1961); Birger Gerhardsson, *The Origins of the Gospel Traditions* (Philadelphia: Fortress, 1979).

Gospels themselves function when they are read aloud (although this question is sometimes addressed by receptor-oriented [e.g., reader-response] critics[14]).

For the same reason, the oral character of the epistles, which presumably were not assembled from primitive oral components, has been mostly ignored. The present author's doctoral dissertation thus entered somewhat uncharted territory when it proposed that the epistles should be examined as the script for an oral production—in other words, that writing not be viewed as a replacement for speaking, but as its companion and aid.[15] This dissertation's title perhaps engaged in hyperbole by calling orality "*the* key to understanding apostolic proclamation in the epistles." The present commentary does not pretend to engage in "oral criticism" at the expense of a thorough, well-rounded treatment of the text. But the insights of an oral approach recur with sufficient frequency that the reader deserves at least a brief introduction.

Reading in the Ancient World

The first clue that one ought not drive a wedge between orality and textuality when interpreting ancient texts is the surprising observation that ancient peoples almost always vocalized their reading, whether or not any listeners were present. Nearly a century ago a seminal study[16] pointed to the extraordinary surprise expressed by St. Augustine when he first encountered Bishop Ambrose of Milan reading *silently*:

> I was excluded from his ear and from his mouth by crowds of men with arbitrations to submit to him, to whose frailties he ministered. When he was not with them, which was a very brief period of time, he restored either his body with necessary food or his mind by reading. When he was reading, *his eyes ran over the page and his heart perceived the sense, but his voice and tongue were silent*. He did not restrict access to anyone coming in, nor was it customary even for a visitor to be announced. Very often when we were there *we saw him silently reading and never otherwise*. After sitting for a long time in silence (for who would dare to burden him in such intent concentration?) we used to go away. We supposed that in the brief time he could find for his mind's refreshment, free from the hubbub of other people's troubles, he would not want to be invited to consider another problem. We wondered if he read silently perhaps to protect himself in case he had a hearer interested and intent on the matter, to whom he might have to expound the text

---

[14] See, for example, Robert M. Fowler, *Let the Reader Understand: Reader-Response Criticism and the Gospel of Mark* (Minneapolis: Fortress, 1991); Winger, "Orality as the Key to Understanding Apostolic Proclamation in the Epistles," 5–20. Note that not all reader-response approaches address the *hearing* of a text; many simply focus on what the reader brings to the text.

[15] See Winger, "Orality as the Key to Understanding Apostolic Proclamation in the Epistles," summarized in Winger, "The Spoken Word: What's Up with Orality?" It is intriguing that two similar doctoral studies were published independently of one another around the same time: Harvey, *Listening to the Text* (1998), and Davis, *Oral Biblical Criticism* (1999).

[16] Josef Balogh, " 'Voces paginarum': Beiträge zur Geschichte des lauten Lesens und Schreibens," *Philologus* 82 (1927): 84–109, 202–40.

being read if it contained difficulties, or who might wish to debate some difficult questions. If his time were used up in that way, he would get through fewer books than he wished. Besides, the need to preserve his voice, which used easily to become hoarse, could have been a very fair reason for silent reading. Whatever motive he had for his habit, this man had a good reason for what he did.[17]

Augustine was not alone in his surprise. While ancient texts rarely commented on what was common practice—reading out loud—there are dozens of examples of observers who noted an unusual circumstance that led to silent reading: whether to steal information or keep a secret, whether from shock or emotional ecstasy. Benedict's Rule confirms normal practice by his exceptional appeal to the monks to read silently, lest the cramped study spaces become a cacophony of individual readers. Thus, the first impetus to oral criticism is the observation that ancient texts were written with the assumption that they would be read aloud. This means that the interpreter ought to be on the lookout for oral structuring and patterns.

More surprising to modern readers, however, is a second observation: that ancient Greek and Roman authors often expressed a certain skepticism about written texts, believing that the personal presence of the author brought distinct advantages. Socrates (himself a legendary dialogical teacher who left no teachings written in his own hand[18]) expressed through his student Plato this common preference for the spoken word:

> He who thinks, then, that he has left behind him any art in writing, and he who receives it in the belief that anything in writing will be clear and certain, would be an utterly simple person, and in truth ignorant of the prophecy of Ammon, if he thinks written words are of any use except to remind him who knows the matter about which they are written.[19]

From Plato's perspective in the fifth/fourth centuries BC, writing was a relative newcomer that had not yet proved its ability to compete with oral rhetoric and dialectic.[20] He expresses the concern that writing is easily misunderstood and is unable to respond to clarifying questions from the reader. At most, writing is useful as an *aide-mémoire*. As Galen the physician would later argue, a

---

[17] Augustine, *Confessions*, 6:3.3 (trans. Henry Chadwick, *Confessions* [Oxford: Oxford University Press, 1991], 92–93; emphasis added).

[18] Thomas Aquinas, *Summa*, 3, question 42, compares Socrates in this regard to Christ, noting that Christ did not write down his oral teachings but left this task to his inspired apostles. In highlighting the spoken word of Christ, Aquinas gives evidence that this ancient perspective persisted well into the Middle Ages.

[19] Plato, *Phaedrus*, 275d (trans. Harold North Fowler, LCL).

[20] Eric A. Havelock, *Preface to Plato* (Oxford: Blackwell, 1963), gives extensive evidence that the Greeks experienced a lengthy period of illiteracy between the twelfth and seventh centuries BC. Perhaps more important, the Greek alphabet introduced only centuries before Plato was a far more capable instrument than the cumbersome pictorial and syllabic systems that preceded it. See also Winger, "Orality as the Key to Understanding Apostolic Proclamation in the Epistles," 36–55.

textbook is useful in the hands of an apprentice who has the living voice of the mentor always available to him, but it cannot teach anything useful on its own.[21] For this reason even Papias, who had the written epistles and Gospels handed down from the apostles, nonetheless sought to hear from the eyewitnesses: "For I did not suppose that information from books would help me so much as the word of a living and surviving voice [τὰ παρὰ ζώσης φωνῆς καὶ μενούσης]."[22]

Christians would rightly object that Holy Scripture ("what is written") stands as an obvious exception to this oral preference.[23] The OT people of God treasured the *writings* of the prophets as the very Word of God. When the NT cites the OT with such formulas as "it is written [γέγραπται]" (e.g., Mt 2:5; Rom 1:17), the author is wielding the text's divine authority. Yet God's people did not view the text as a silent witness, but as his living Word. The NT is conscious that the OT texts are records of the prophetic voice that continues to speak through the written Word:

- "Moses says [Μωϋσῆς λέγει]" (Rom 10:19).
- "For Moses said [Μωϋσῆς γὰρ εἶπεν]" (Mk 7:10; cf. Acts 3:22; Heb 7:14).
- "They have Moses and the prophets; let them hear [ἀκουσάτωσαν] them" (Lk 16:29).
- "This is the one who was spoken of [ὁ ῥηθείς] by Isaiah the prophet" (Mt 3:3; cf. 21:4; 27:9).
- "About whom does the prophet say this?" (Acts 8:34).
- "Another Scripture says [λέγει]" (Jn 19:37; cf. Rom 4:3).
- "Do you not hear the Torah [τὸν νόμον οὐκ ἀκούετε]? For it is written [γέγραπται] that Abraham …" (Gal 4:21–22).
- "Isaiah cries out [κράζει, present tense]" (Rom 9:27).[24]

---

[21] Galen's disclaimer at the beginning of his own medical text: *De compositione medicamentorum secundum locos*, 6.

[22] From Papias' preface to his *Collection of Dominical Sayings*, recorded by Eusebius, *Ecclesiastical History*, 3:39.4 (trans. Kirsopp Lake, LCL). See Loveday Alexander, "The Living Voice: Scepticism towards the Written Word in Early Christian and in Graeco-Roman Texts," in *The Bible in Three Dimensions* (ed. David J. A. Clines, Stephen E. Fowl, and Stanley E. Porter; JSOTSup 87; Sheffield: Sheffield Academic, 1990), 221–47.

[23] One might also object that the culture of first-century AD Palestine and the Greco-Roman world had long ago crossed the divide from orality to literacy. However, the transition cannot be viewed as instantaneous. Most orality scholars describe a period of transition, of "oral residue," lasting many centuries, indeed well beyond the close of the Middle Ages. See, for example, Harvey, *Listening to the Text*, 37–40.

[24] The oral character of prophecy explains the seemingly bizarre imagery of eating a scroll (Ezek 2:8–3:3; Rev 10:9–10). The prophet internalized the words before proclaiming them. His writing was not for the eye, but for the ear and the mouth.

In addition, the NT writers rarely address their "readers" directly[25] and more frequently use the language of speaking and hearing than reading and writing:[26] for example, "I, Paul, say to you" (Gal 5:2); "listen, my beloved brethren" (James 2:5); "we saw it and testify to it and proclaim to you" (1 Jn 1:2). Such examples illustrate the twofold judgment of Demetrius' ancient handbook concerning the style of letter writing:

> Artemon, the editor of Aristotle's *Letters*, says that a letter should be written in the same manner as a dialogue; the letter, he says, is like one of the two sides to a dialogue. There is perhaps some truth in what he says, but not the whole truth. The letter should be a little more formal than the dialogue, since the latter imitates improvised conversation, while the former is written and sent as a kind of gift (δῶρον).[27]

The Mandate to Proclaim Scripture

From the time of Moses, author of the Torah and the Scriptures' first named author, God mandated the oral proclamation of their content. Moses read the Torah aloud to the people after he first received it, that they might assent to its contents and become parties to God's covenant (Ex 24:7). Through Moses, God committed it in written form to Israel and decreed that it be read aloud to all the people every seven years (Deut 31:10–11).[28] Joshua fulfilled this command when they entered the promised land (Josh 8:34–35). Neglected for many generations, the Torah was rediscovered during renovations of the temple by Hilkiah the high priest, read aloud by Shaphan to King Josiah (2 Ki 22:8–10), and then proclaimed to all Israel to initiate religious reform (2 Ki 23:1–3). Likewise, when Israel returned from exile centuries later, Ezra the scribe initiated a new phase of obedience to God by reading the Torah to the people over eight days during the Feast of Booths (Neh 8:1–3, 18; 9:3). Thus, the public reading of Scripture was a divinely mandated practice intended to maintain God's covenant relationship with the people, and it was the central act of every reformation.

The NT records no examples of the public reading of the Torah in worship at the Jerusalem temple or at a "covenant renewal ceremony." However, it contains the earliest documented evidence of Scripture reading in the synagogue (Lk 4:16–21; Acts 13:15; 15:21; 2 Cor 3:15), as well as private, vocalized reading of Scripture (Acts 8:29–30). It would have been quite natural for early Christians to maintain this established practice in their liturgy, while also supplementing

---

[25] References to the act of reading are found in Paul's letters, but most likely refer not to a solitary reader (as in Acts 8:29–30), but to the lector in a public, ecclesial setting. See "The Mandate to Proclaim Scripture" below.

[26] Authors like Luke (Lk 1:3), John (Jn 20:30–31; 21:24–25; 1 Jn 1:4; Rev 22:18–19), Paul (Rom 15:15; 1 Cor 4:14; 5:9; and passim), and Peter (1 Pet 5:12; 2 Pet 3:1) refer explicitly to the writing process. But they *write* in order that their words might be *spoken*.

[27] Demetrius of Phaleron, *On Style*, 223–24, quoted in Klauck, *Ancient Letters and the New Testament*, 185.

[28] See also the mandate and explanation in Josephus, *Antiquities*, 4:209–11.

the reading of the OT with accounts of the work of Jesus, in accord with the mandate of the Father, "listen to him" (Mt 17:5). The interjection "let the reader understand" (Mk 13:14) may well be a reference not simply to the *receiver* of the Gospel text, but to the public *lector* in the Divine Service.[29] This context is made explicit in the opening of Revelation. John was "in the Spirit on the Lord's day" (Rev 1:10)—that is, in the Divine Service—and he expects that his revelation will be read aloud to the assembled congregation in the same context: "blessed is he who reads aloud [ὁ ἀναγινώσκων], and [blessed are] those who hear [οἱ ἀκούοντες] the words of the prophecy" (Rev 1:3). When the Gospel writers include the interjection "he who has ears to hear, let him hear" (Mt 11:15),[30] one might therefore understand it as a reference not to the hearers of Jesus in the first instance, but to the hearers of the text as it is later proclaimed in a liturgical setting. This is all the more likely when the same admonition occurs in John's Revelation (Rev 2:7).[31]

St. Paul both expects and mandates that his epistles be read aloud to the gathered congregation.[32]

> And when this letter has been read aloud among you [ἀναγνωσθῇ παρ' ὑμῖν ἡ ἐπιστολή], have it read aloud [ἀναγνωσθῇ] also in the church of the Laodiceans; and see that you read aloud [ἀναγνῶτε] also the letter from Laodicea. (Col 4:16)

> I place you under oath by the Lord [!] that this letter be read aloud to all the brothers [ἀναγνωσθῆναι τὴν ἐπιστολὴν πᾶσιν τοῖς ἀδελφοῖς]. (1 Thess 5:27)

Paul includes this task in his threefold mandate to Pastor Timothy concerning the ministry of Word, in which the public reading of Scripture notably ranks alongside preaching and teaching, indeed preceding them:

> Until I come, devote yourself to the public reading of Scripture [τῇ ἀναγνώσει], to exhortation/preaching [τῇ παρακλήσει], to teaching [τῇ διδασκαλίᾳ]. (1 Tim 4:13)[33]

This mandate arises from Paul's firm belief that faith comes from hearing the Word of God (Rom 10:14–18) and that Scripture is the chief tool in the pastor's equipment (2 Tim 3:16–17). Thus, Paul's statement "when you read this [ἀναγινώσκοντες]" (Eph 3:4) likely refers to the proclamation of his letter to the congregation (cf. 2 Cor 1:13).

---

[29] BDAG, s.v. ἀναγινώσκω, b.

[30] See also Ezek 3:27; Mt 13:9, 43; 25:29 (variant reading); Mk 4:23; 7:16 (variant reading); Lk 8:8; 12:21 (variant reading); 14:35; 21:4 (variant reading).

[31] See also Rev 2:11, 17, 29; 3:6, 13, 22; 13:9.

[32] In addition to previously cited literature, see Harry Gamble, "The Uses of Early Christian Books," chapter 5 in *Books and Readers in the Early Church: A History of Early Christian Texts* (New Haven, Conn.: Yale University Press, 1995), 203–41.

[33] Note how in the synagogue "preaching" (παράκλησις, Acts 13:15) followed upon, and was based on, the public reading of Scripture (Lk 4:20–21; Acts 13:15).

The reading of the NT writings alongside the OT as the Scripture of the Christian church (cf. 2 Pet 3:16) is confirmed by the earliest witnesses to liturgical practice, most clearly expressed by Justin Martyr:

> And on the day called Sunday there is a meeting in one place of those who live in cities or the country, and the memoirs of the apostles [τὰ ἀπομνημονεύματα τῶν ἀποστόλων] or the writings of the prophets are read [ἀναγινώσκεται] as long as time permits. When the reader [ὁ ἀναγινώσκων] has finished, the president [ὁ προεστώς] in a discourse urges and invites [us] to the imitation of these noble things.[34]

His phrase "as long as time permits" is not only a sober reminder to us moderns of the greater patience that ancient peoples had for lengthy recitation, but it also suggests that the reading of Scripture itself was given a higher priority than it may appear to have in our modern liturgy. Our brief lectionary excerpts followed by lengthy sermons may give the impression that the Scripture readings are merely pretexts for the "real" work done in the sermon, rather than the effective activity of God's Spirit in and of themselves.

The Liturgical Context of the New Testament Epistles

Indeed, it is reasonable to assume that the NT epistles were meant to be read in their entirety (at least on the first hearing). While Paul's epistles (and to a certain extent the Catholic Epistles that follow his pattern) are certainly longer than other letters in ancient times,[35] nearly all his letters can be read aloud in fifteen minutes or less. Where the recipients of the letter were the original audience to whom Paul directed his letter, the epistle would have functioned as both Scripture reading and sermon inasmuch as it was the application of God's Word to their specific situation. This supposition is supported by a number of liturgical features in the epistles, such as the (presumed) quotation of creedal[36] and hymnic[37] material that would echo or at least find a natural home in the Divine Service. Paul makes explicit reference to hymn singing by the gathered congregation (1 Cor 14:26; Eph 5:18–20; Col 3:16). Doxologies and the frequent interjection of "amen" (whether in the text or in variants) likewise suggest a liturgical setting.[38] Paul's prayers within his epistles frequently bear the marks

---

[34] Justin Martyr, *First Apology*, 67 (*Early Christian Fathers* [trans. and ed. Cyril C. Richardson; New York: Collier, 1970], 287). For the Greek, see PG 6:429.

[35] There were, of course, various kinds of letters in the ancient world. Both private and official letters were usually no longer than one sheet of papyrus. But philosophical treatises and public orations may have been sent in written form and may have been similar in length to Paul's epistles. See Doty, *Letters in Primitive Christianity*; Stowers, *Letter Writing in Greco-Roman Antiquity*.

[36] E.g., Rom 3:30; 1 Cor 8:4, 6; 12:3, 12–13; Eph 4:4–6; 1 Tim 2:5–6; 3:16; James 2:19; 1 Pet 3:18–22.

[37] E.g., Eph 5:14; Phil 2:5–11; Col 1:15–20.

[38] See the textual notes and the commentary on 1:14; 3:14–21; 6:24.

of public, even eucharistic, praying,[39] to which he sometimes refers explicitly (1 Cor 14:16). He knows that the congregation is gathered on the first day of the week (1 Cor 16:2).

Paul's consciousness that his letters will be read aloud in the setting of the Divine Service may be evidenced by certain features of their opening and closing. The greeting "grace to you and peace [χάρις ὑμῖν καὶ εἰρήνη]" (e.g., Eph 1:2) in the name of God the Father and his Son, Jesus Christ, found with little variance at the beginning of Paul's every letter, transcends the secular greeting χαίρειν, "rejoice," by combining the OT priestly blessing of peace (Num 6:22–27) with the uniquely Christian vocabulary of grace (see the first textual note on Eph 1:2). Early Christian liturgical rites connected the blessing of grace intimately with the gift of the Lord's Supper, frequently using the apostolic blessing (2 Cor 13:13 [ET 13:14]) as the opening words of the Preface. Likewise, the closing sections of Paul's letters contain a significant number of parallels to the liturgical language and practice of early Christian Communion rites, including eucharistic praying, exclusion of the unbaptized and impenitent, the kiss of peace and other expressions of fellowship, and the pastor's blessing of his flock.[40] The clearest example of this may be the close of 1 Corinthians, in which J. A. T. Robinson discerned parallels with the Communion rite of the very early document the *Didache*:[41]

---

[39] E.g., 2 Cor 1:3–4; Eph 1:3–14; 3:14–21. See the textual notes and the commentary on the Ephesian passages.

[40] See the commentary on 6:18–24. Sasse, "Selective Fellowship," 53–54, writes of the concluding greetings:

> They are solemn expressions of the existing unity, declarations or reaffirmations of the *communicatio in sacris* ["communion in the holy things"], as the admonition to greet one another with the "holy kiss" (Rom. 16:16; 1 Cor. 16:20), the "kiss of charity" (1 Peter 5:14), the *Pax*, as it was later called. This kiss, expressing the full peace and unity of the Church, had its place at the beginning of "Holy Communion" already in the apostolic age, as the fact shows that the formula "The grace of our Lord Jesus Christ be with you" (1 Cor. 16[:23]; Rev. 22:21) or its trinitarian form (2 Cor. 13:13 [ET 13:14]) has remained in the Eastern Church the beginning of the dialogue leading to the Preface and Sanctus. The "Pax" is already in the New Testament connected with the "Anathema" of those who do not love the Lord (schismatics), 1 Cor. 16:22; or who "cause divisions and offences contrary to the doctrine" of the apostles (heretics), and therefore must be avoided, Rom. 16:17f.; comp. the corresponding warnings Gal. 1:8; 1 Tim. 6:3–6, 20; Titus 3:10; 1 John 4:1ff; 2 John 10f.

[41] Robinson, "Traces of a Liturgical Sequence in 1 Cor. 16:20–24," 38–39. The division into versicle and response is Robinson's analysis. He writes:

> This exchange of versicle and response comes at the end of the prayer "after you are satisfied." The probability is that the reference is to the Agape and that the dialogue forms the introduction to the Eucharist proper, which presupposes (*Did.* 14.1) prior confession of sin and mutual reconciliation. *Maranatha* … is then a prayer to Christ to stand among his own in his *parousia* (anticipated in the real presence of the Eucharist).

> I suggest that in 1 Cor. 16[22] Paul is quoting a similar liturgical sequence already current in the Corinthian Church. He is visualizing the context in which his closing words will reach his listeners. His letter has been read out in the *ecclesia* … , the Christian assembly gathered for worship. As the *synaxis* comes to an end, dispositions for the Eucharist

Didache 10:6	1 Cor 16:20–24
Versicle: Let grace come and let this world pass away.	[20]All the brothers greet you. Greet one another with a holy kiss.
Response: Hosanna to the God of David.	[21]This greeting is with my (Paul's) own hand.
Deacon (?): If any man is holy, let him come; if any be not, let him repent.	[22]If anyone does not love the Lord, let him be accursed [ἀνάθεμα]. Our Lord, come [μαράνα θά]!
Versicle: Maranatha.	[23]The grace of the Lord Jesus be with you.
Response: Amen.	[24]My love be with you all in Christ Jesus. [Amen.]

If this is correct, it means that Paul envisioned his letter being read in the liturgy at the point of the Scripture readings and sermon, with the rite of Holy Communion taking place immediately afterward. Paul injects himself into the church's liturgy. He enters into his recipients' fellowship—not only as a brother Christian, but as their father in Christ, God's minister in their service. For churches like that in Ephesus, where Paul had been a founding missionary figure and spent a lengthy period of time in ministry among the people, he is, through his epistle, stepping back into the pulpit and behind the altar, once more presiding over the liturgy among them as he had so often done before.[42] Thus, his letter to them is part of his pastoral work; in it he expresses what he would proclaim if he were with them in person.[43] His letters, therefore, are to be *heard* today as apostolic proclamation to the church.[44]

Oral Patterning in Paul's Epistles

The reader of—or rather, the *listener to*—Paul's epistles ought therefore to be presensitized to the oral characteristics with which these ancient letters

---

begin. Mutual greetings and the kiss of peace are exchanged—to which, in autograph, Paul adds his own.

[42] See "Liturgical Context" in "Authorship" below and the commentary on 6:18–24.

[43] See the commentary on 1:1–2; 6:18–24. Ancient theorists such as Demetrius stressed that a letter was intended to create *parousia* (transforming bodily absence into spiritual presence) and *homilia* (personal conversation). See Klauck, *Ancient Letters and the New Testament*, 189–93. Turpilius described letters as "the only means of making absent people present" (fragment 215, in Jerome, *Epistles*, 8:1 [quoted in Klauck, 191]); Cicero defines a letter as "the communion of friends in absence" (*Philippics*, 2:4.7 [quoted in Klauck, 192]); and Libanius explains that "one will speak in it as though one were in the company of the absent person" (*Epistolary Styles*, 2 [quoted in Klauck, 193]).

[44] Hebrews is often thought of as a homily in letter form, but it is not unique. The absence of a traditional epistolary opening and close has merely provoked recent commentators to recognize its homiletical character. The author refers to what he has written as παράκλησις "exhortation/preaching": "Now I exhort [παρακαλῶ] you, brothers, listen willingly to this message of exhortation [τοῦ λόγου τῆς παρακλήσεως], for I have written to you rather briefly" (Heb 13:22).

are richly endowed. Naturally, Ephesians will serve as the source of examples cited below (while the detailed explanation of the same must be sought in the textual notes and commentary proper).

Rhetoric

As rhetoric was the ancient art of public speaking, the handbooks produced by its greatest practitioners and teachers are a gold mine of information about how Paul might have composed his letters. Aristotle's five-step method of creating a speech—invention, arrangement, style, memory, and delivery—included oral considerations at each point. The art's influence on the invention (proofs) and arrangement (structure) of Ephesians will be considered in detail later in this introduction. Paul's establishment of his apostolic character (1:1, 16; 3:1–13), for example, parallels the rhetorical advice first to establish one's *ethos* in order to lead the audience to trust the message. His customary thanksgiving (1:15–23) generates *pathos*, capturing their goodwill. Other rhetorical skills are in evidence in the letter, and the following brief survey of oral features in Ephesians might be subsumed in its entirety under the heading of "rhetoric."

Commonplaces

Rhetorical masters prepared "commonplace" books that included stock phrases, illustrations, and vocabulary for talking about common topics (τόποι in Greek, *loci* in Latin). Paul's preaching of the Law is the most likely place to seek them. His virtue and vice lists (e.g., 4:25–32; 5:3–5), while fundamentally dependent on the Decalogue, may also have drawn on these standard compendia, for example:

- πᾶσα πικρία καὶ θυμὸς καὶ ὀργὴ καὶ κραυγὴ καὶ βλασφημία ἀρθήτω ἀφ᾽ ὑμῶν σὺν πάσῃ κακίᾳ, "let all bitterness and rage and anger and shouting and slander be taken away from you, with all malice" (4:31)

- πορνεία δὲ καὶ ἀκαθαρσία πᾶσα ἢ πλεονεξία μηδὲ ὀνομαζέσθω ἐν ὑμῖν, καθὼς πρέπει ἁγίοις, καὶ αἰσχρότης καὶ μωρολογία ἢ εὐτραπελία, ἃ οὐκ ἀνῆκεν, "but let not sexual immorality and all uncleanness or lust even be named among you, as is fitting for saints, nor shamefulness and foolish talk or coarse joking, which are not fitting" (5:3–4)

Alliteration

The repetition of initial sounds in a sequence of words holds little semantic value, but captivates the hearer and maintains his attention. In such cases, the exegete must be careful not to overinterpret a particular choice of vocabulary or the distinction between synonyms, as the reason may chiefly be sound. Examples:

- ἁγίους καὶ ἀμώμους, "holy and without blemish" (1:4; cf. 5:27)

- τὸ πλήρωμα τοῦ τὰ πάντα ἐν πᾶσιν πληρουμένου, "the fullness of the one who fills all things in all" (1:23)

- συγκληρονόμα καὶ σύσσωμα καὶ συμμέτοχα, "fellow heirs and fellow members of the body and fellow partakers" (3:6)

13

- ἐν ᾧ ἔχομεν τὴν παρρησίαν καὶ προσαγωγὴν ἐν πεποιθήσει διὰ τῆς πίστεως αὐτοῦ, "in whom we have boldness and access in confidence through faith in him" (3:12)
- μετὰ πάσης ταπεινοφροσύνης καὶ πραΰτητος, μετὰ μακροθυμίας, ἀνεχόμενοι ἀλλήλων ἐν ἀγάπῃ, "with all humility and meekness, with patience, bearing with one another in love" (4:2)
- διὰ πάσης προσευχῆς … προσευχόμενοι ἐν παντὶ καιρῷ ἐν πνεύματι, "through all prayer … praying at every opportune time in the Spirit" (6:18)

Rhythm

Paul's penchant in Ephesians for groups of three may reflect an underlying Trinitarian thought pattern,[45] but often it simply appears to be his natural, oral rhythm:

- the threefold petition: τίς … τίς … τίς, "*what* is … *what* is … *what* is" (1:18–19)
- the threefold purpose of the ministry: πρὸς … εἰς … εἰς, "*for … for … for*" (4:12)
- the threefold result of its work: εἰς … εἰς … εἰς, "*for … for … for*" (4:13)
- πορνεία δὲ καὶ ἀκαθαρσία πᾶσα ἢ πλεονεξία, three Greek nouns (the second modified by an adjective), "but *sexual immorality* and all *uncleanness* or *lust*" (5:3)
- πᾶς πόρνος ἢ ἀκάθαρτος ἢ πλεονέκτης, three Greek substantives, "every *sexually immoral* or *unclean* or *lustful person*" (5:5)
- the three-line hymn stanza (5:14)
- ψαλμοῖς καὶ ὕμνοις καὶ ᾠδαῖς πνευματικαῖς, three Greek nouns, "*psalms* and *hymns* and *songs* of the Spirit" (5:19)
- three main participial clauses describing the work of the Spirit (5:18–21)
- εἰρήνη … καὶ ἀγάπη μετὰ πίστεως, three Greek nouns, "*peace* … and *love* with *faith*" (6:23)

Repetition

A reader of written material has the luxury of slowing down when encountering complex sentences or thoughts. He can also back up and reread what perplexes him. The writer is fully aware of this situation and may thereby excuse lengthy, complicated sentences by placing responsibility on the reader to work them out. The speaker cannot make the same assumption about the hearers. In oral delivery everything must either be immediately clear or be repeated in the same or varied wording until it is understood.[46] Such emphatic repetition may also mark the major themes of the letter:

- the repetition of the adjective πᾶς, "all, every," which occurs fifty-two times in Ephesians, marks it as a major emphasis of the letter; note especially its fourfold occurrences in 4:6 and in 6:18, and its six occurrences in 1:21–23
- εὐλογητὸς ὁ θεὸς καὶ πατὴρ … , ὁ εὐλογήσας ἡμᾶς ἐν πάσῃ εὐλογίᾳ πνευματικῇ, "blessed be the God and Father … , who has blessed us with every blessing of the Spirit" (1:3)

---

[45] E.g., 1:3; 1:3–14 as a whole; 1:16–17; 3:14–17; 4:4–6; 5:18–20.

[46] See Harvey, *Listening to the Text*, 43–44.

- εἰς ἔπαινον δόξης τῆς χάριτος αὐτοῦ ἧς ἐχαρίτωσεν ἡμᾶς ἐν τῷ ἠγαπημένῳ ... κατὰ τὸ πλοῦτος τῆς χάριτος αὐτοῦ, "to the praise of his glorious <u>grace</u>, which he '<u>graced</u>' upon us in the Beloved ... according to the riches of his <u>grace</u>" (1:6–7)

- τὸ <u>πλήρωμα</u> τοῦ τὰ <u>πάντα</u> ἐν <u>πᾶσιν</u> <u>πληρουμένου</u>, "the <u>fullness</u> of the one who <u>fills</u> all things in all" (1:23; note also the alliteration, as four words begin with π)

- ἵνα <u>πληρωθῆτε</u> εἰς <u>πᾶν</u> τὸ <u>πλήρωμα</u> τοῦ θεοῦ, "that you may be <u>filled</u> up to all the <u>fullness</u> of God" (3:19; note also the alliteration, as three words begin with π)

- seven occurrences of "one" (εἷς, μία, ἕν) in the creedal, baptismal hymn (4:4–6)

- διὰ τοῦτο ἀναλάβετε τὴν πανοπλίαν τοῦ θεοῦ, ἵνα δυνηθῆτε <u>ἀντιστῆναι</u> ἐν τῇ ἡμέρᾳ τῇ πονηρᾷ καὶ ἅπαντα κατεργασάμενοι <u>στῆναι</u>. <u>στῆτε</u> οὖν, "for this reason take up the full armor of God, that you may be able to <u>withstand</u> in the evil day, and having accomplished all things to <u>stand</u>. <u>Stand</u>, therefore" (6:13–14)

- the most significant repetition may be ἐν Χριστῷ, "in Christ," with its variations ἐν αὐτῷ, "in him"; ἐν ᾧ, "in whom"; etc., which dominates the opening *Berakah* prayer (1:3–14) and recurs throughout the letter (see the fifth textual note on 1:3)[47]

Some cases of repetition occur more for pragmatic than for semantic reasons. In other words, the repetition does not necessarily serve to ensure that the *meaning* is caught, but may, like alliteration, be *artistic*; it may be intended to catch the listener's attention and highlight the significance of a statement or engender an emotional response.[48] One example is the repetition or patterning of grammatical features as in homoioptoton, when several words are of the same gender or inflection or have the same case ending. Sometimes Paul forms or chooses words with a common prefix (homoiarchon) or a common ending (homoioteleuton):

- <u>συνε</u>ζωοποίησεν τῷ Χριστῷ ... καὶ <u>συν</u>ήγειρεν καὶ <u>συν</u>εκάθισεν ἐν τοῖς ἐπουρανίοις ἐν Χριστῷ Ἰησοῦ, "he made [us] alive <u>together</u> with Christ ... and he raised [us] <u>together</u> and seated [us] <u>together</u> in the heavenly places in Christ Jesus" (2:5–6)

  cf. <u>συγ</u>κληρονόμα καὶ <u>σύσ</u>σωμα καὶ <u>συμ</u>μέτοχα, "<u>fellow</u> heirs and <u>fellow</u> members of the body and <u>fellow</u> partakers" (3:6); <u>συν</u>αρμολογούμενον καὶ <u>συμ</u>βιβαζόμενον, "being jointed <u>together</u> and knit <u>together</u>" (4:16)

- τὸ πλάτ<u>ος</u> καὶ μῆκ<u>ος</u> καὶ ὕψ<u>ος</u> καὶ βάθ<u>ος</u>, four Greek nouns that end with -ος, "[its] breadth and length and height and depth" (3:18)

- <u>εἷς</u> κύριος, <u>μία</u> πίστις, <u>ἓν</u> βάπτισμα, "<u>one</u> Lord, <u>one</u> faith, <u>one</u> Baptism" (4:5)— the numeral "one" is repeated with the grammatical variation masculine first, then feminine, then neuter

- εἷς θεὸς καὶ πατὴρ <u>πάντων</u>, ὁ ἐπὶ <u>πάντων</u> καὶ διὰ <u>πάντων</u> καὶ ἐν <u>πᾶσιν</u>, "one God and Father of <u>all</u>, who is over <u>all</u> and through <u>all</u> and in <u>all</u>" (4:6)

- further examples may be seen above under "Rhythm," where three feminine singular nouns (5:3) occur in sequence or words like τίς, "what," are repeated to place clauses into parallel

---

[47] Davis, *Oral Biblical Criticism*, 93, identifies ἐν Χριστῷ, "in Christ," as "a personal Pauline formula" of an oral nature. He compares it to a recurring musical theme in a song (92).

[48] Quintilian, *Institutio oratoria*, 9:3.66, speaks of the Gorgian figure of speech, "which attracts the ear of the audience and excites their attention by some resemblance, equality, or contrast of words" (quoted in Davis, *Oral Biblical Criticism*, 81).

Parallelism

It is well-known that the OT, as much as a third of which is composed of Semitic poetry, is marked by a love of parallelism. The heightened frequency of this feature in the NT is certainly a sign of Semitic (particularly OT) influence, but nonbiblical Greek is not unfamiliar with parallelism. It is a form of repetition,[49] by which ideas (rather than words themselves) are stressed and explored through synonymous rephrasing or the statement of opposites, using grammatical or rhythmic patterning to highlight the parallel.[50] These are examples from Ephesians:

- ἀπὸ θεοῦ πατρὸς ἡμῶν καὶ κυρίου Ἰησοῦ Χριστοῦ, "from *God our Father* and *the Lord Jesus Christ*" (1:2)
- ἐν ᾧ ἔχομεν τὴν ἀπολύτρωσιν διὰ τοῦ αἵματος αὐτοῦ, τὴν ἄφεσιν τῶν παραπτωμάτων, "in whom we have *redemption* through his blood, the *forgiveness* of trespasses" (1:7)
- ἀνακεφαλαιώσασθαι τὰ πάντα ἐν τῷ Χριστῷ, τὰ ἐπὶ τοῖς οὐρανοῖς καὶ τὰ ἐπὶ τῆς γῆς ἐν αὐτῷ, "that all things might be brought together in Christ, *the things in heaven* and *the things on earth* in him" (1:10)
- ἀκούσαντες τὸν λόγον τῆς ἀληθείας, τὸ εὐαγγέλιον τῆς σωτηρίας ὑμῶν, "having heard *the Word* of truth, *the Gospel* of your salvation" (1:13)
- ἐγείρας αὐτὸν ἐκ νεκρῶν καὶ καθίσας ἐν δεξιᾷ αὐτοῦ ἐν τοῖς ἐπουρανίοις, "by *raising* him from the dead, and by *seating* [him] at his right hand in the heavenly places" (1:20)
- οὐ μόνον ἐν τῷ αἰῶνι τούτῳ ἀλλὰ καὶ ἐν τῷ μέλλοντι, "not only *in this age* but also *in the one to come*" (1:21)
- καὶ ὑμᾶς ὄντας νεκροὺς … καὶ ἡμεῖς πάντες … καὶ ὄντας ἡμᾶς νεκρούς, "and *you* being dead … also *we all* … and *all of us* being dead" (2:1, 3, 5)
- νυνὶ δὲ ἐν Χριστῷ Ἰησοῦ ὑμεῖς οἵ ποτε ὄντες μακρὰν ἐγενήθητε ἐγγὺς ἐν τῷ αἵματι τοῦ Χριστοῦ, "but now in Christ Jesus you who at one time were *far off* have become *near* by the blood of Christ" (2:13)

Chiasm and *Inclusio*[51]

Modern written languages can avail themselves of a significant number of techniques to mark out units and highlight words and phrases visually. Punctuation is the chief tool: commas and full stops identify smaller subunits, while paragraph divisions mark larger thought units for the reader. Typographic conventions such as *italics* and **boldface** accomplish the task borne by intonation

---

[49] See Harvey, *Listening to the Text*, 44–46.

[50] Hebrew parallelism was traditionally divided, following Bishop Lowth (*De sacra poesi Hebraeorum*, 1753), into synonymous, antithetical, and synthetic kinds, but recent authors have analyzed it more rigorously. See, for example, James L. Kugel, *The Idea of Biblical Poetry: Parallelism and Its History* (New Haven, Conn.: Yale University Press, 1981), and Adele Berlin, *The Dynamics of Biblical Parallelism* (rev. ed.; Grand Rapids: Eerdmans, 2008).

[51] See particularly Thomson, *Chiasmus in the Pauline Letters*; also Kenneth E. Bailey, *Poet and Peasant and Through Peasant Eyes: A Literary-Cultural Approach to the Parables in Luke* (combined ed.; Grand Rapids: Eerdmans, 1983).

of the voice in an oral culture. The writing conventions of Greek in the NT era were significantly less helpful. The lector (or person preparing to make a public delivery of a writing) needed to spend considerable time with the text working out where the divisions lay and what stresses the author intended him to convey.[52] What markers could the author use to give help to the lector?

Chiasm,[53] named for the Greek letter X (*chi*) that a diagram of the technique resembles, consists of an "inside-outside" parallelism of words or ideas in a sentence or clause: AB–B'A' or

While chiasms carry out all the functions of the parallelisms noted above—stressing the ideas they repeat, enticing the hearer with artistic beauty,[54] and aiding the memory—they additionally mark the limits of the sentence, clause, or thought: i.e., when the reader/hearer reaches the repetition (A') of the initial idea (A), he knows that the unit is complete.[55]

Inclusio is chiasm wrought large[56] and therefore serves as a paragraphing technique. *Inclusio* may be as simple as framing a unit with a repeated word or idea: Ephesians begins with "grace and peace" (1:2) and ends with "peace" and "grace" (6:23–24). An external *inclusio* occurs when one or the other repetition is not part of the unit itself, but marks its beginning and end nonetheless: for example, τούτου χάριν, "for this reason" (3:1, 14).[57] But Ephesians also

---

[52] See Thomson, *Chiasmus in the Pauline Letters*, 20–21, who describes the fourfold method of analyzing a text before reading it that was taught in Greek schools.

[53] The term "chiasm" is not found in ancient rhetoricians prior to the fourth century AD, but the figure of speech known as *commutatio* is described by both Quintilian and Cicero. See Thomson, *Chiasmus in the Pauline Letters*, 14; Kennedy, *New Testament Interpretation through Rhetorical Criticism*, 28–29.

[54] Thomson, *Chiasmus in the Pauline Letters*, 34–35: "Chiasmus functioned as an art form lending beauty as well as a pleasing sound to a passage and giving variety, particularly in language types where there exists the possibility of exploiting flexibility of word order."

[55] Thomson, *Chiasmus in the Pauline Letters*, 35: "Chiasmus functions in the text as a structuring device that helps to divide one section of material from another." While some scholars have questioned the hearer's ability to discern these patterns on first hearing and thereby realize that the unit has reached its completion, Thomson, 36–37, argues, first, that the ancient mind was more attuned to these patterns than moderns, and, second, that Paul would not necessarily have expected everything to be apparent on first reading. His epistles were meant to be saved and savored.

[56] The simplest forms of *inclusio* (repetition at the beginning and end of a unit) are not strictly speaking chiastic, but most examples do contain some form of inversion. Thomson, *Chiasmus in the Pauline Letters*, 33, notes: "An *inclusio* may indicate that further analysis will reveal greater symmetry. Likewise, a sudden change in a unit of text may turn out to be the shift and reversion at the centre of a chiasm."

[57] The initial τούτου χάριν, "for this reason," in 3:1 begins the unit that consists of 3:1–13. The repetition of τούτου χάριν, "for this reason," in 3:14 marks the start of the next unit (3:14–21) and therefore implies that the preceding unit (3:1–13) had ended with 3:13.

contains *inclusio* patterns that are much more elaborate, often called ring compositions or inversion patterns.[58] In such cases the *inclusio*, which contains a chiasm that goes beyond a simple AB–B'A', may highlight a large-scale, intricate parallelism in which each element of the first half is matched in regressive order by an element in the second, for example, ABCDE–F–E'D'C'B'A'.[59] Step by step the hearer's brain is prepared for and begins to anticipate the counterpart of each item.[60]

In the two best examples of chiastic *inclusio* in Ephesians (2:1–10; 2:11–22), the regression pattern corresponds to a Law-Gospel, "then-now" theology: Paul builds up a devastating picture of the sinful, prebaptismal life and then demonstrates how it is overturned point by point in the work of Christ, by the grace of God.[61] The chiasm thus serves the Gospel by exploring the transformative nature of baptismal renewal. But, perhaps most significantly, *the chiasm usually points to its center as the turning point and/or central thought.*[62] This crucial insight is of immense exegetical significance in the interpretation of the two aforementioned pericopes (2:1–10 and 2:11–22). The following structural paraphrase, for example, illustrates the function of the chiastic *inclusio* in 2:1–10:

---

[58] Thomson, *Chiasmus in the Pauline Letters*, 23, refers to these units as "chiasmus of intermediate length" (ten to twenty elements in seven to fifteen verses), which he locates between the four-member "micro-chiasmus" and the "macro-chiasmus" (which could span an entire work or a major division thereof). P. S. Cameron, "The Structure of Ephesians," *Filologia Neotestamentaria* 3 (1990): 3–17, claims that the entire letter is "palistrophic" (chiastically structured), with pairs of units balanced around a midpoint at 4:15–16 (the body of Christ). His vocabulary-based argument, which deliberately ignores other criteria, is founded on many of the same patterns discovered in the present commentary, but is on the whole unconvincing.

[59] Thomson, *Chiasmus in the Pauline Letters*, 25, defines chiasm in the broad sense as "a device that employs bilateral *symmetry*." He expands this definition as follows:

Chiasmus may be said to be present in a passage if the text exhibits bilateral symmetry of four or more elements about a central axis, which may itself lie between two elements, or be a unique central element, the symmetry consisting of any combination of verbal, grammatical or syntactical elements, or, indeed, of ideas and concepts in a given pattern. (25–26)

[60] Davis, *Oral Biblical Criticism*, 88: "Word repetition in the form of inclusio and chiasm is the most common oral method of signifying structure." Eric A. Havelock comments: "All oral narrative is in structure continually both prophetic and retrospective. … The narrative is not linear but turns back on itself in order to assist the memory to reach the end by having it anticipated somehow in the beginning" ("Oral Composition in the *Oedipus Tyrannus* of Sophocles," *New Literary History* 16 [1984]: 183, quoted in Davis, *Oral Biblical Criticism*, 99).

[61] Thomson, *Chiasmus in the Pauline Letters*, 39: "The use of chiasmus may be particularly appropriate in a passage, say, where a series of antitheses are being developed, or in which there is a circular sweep of movement of thought."

[62] Davis, *Oral Biblical Criticism*, 100; Thomson, *Chiasmus in the Pauline Letters*, 27, 43. Thus, for example, in 2:1–10 the pericope's chief point is not at the end (good works), but in the middle (grace). At the same time, the author "may well wish to make more points in a passage than that which is highlighted by the central elements" (Thomson, 38).

A   You Gentiles were dead <u>in sins,</u> <u>walking</u> according to the age of this world,

   B   following this evil spirit, who is at <u>work</u> in the disobedient sons,

      C   among whom also we [Jews] were, following the lusts of the <u>flesh and thoughts</u>;

         D   thus, we [Jews], too, <u>by nature</u> deserved God's <u>wrath</u> like the rest of mankind;

            E   but God, <u>rich</u> in mercy, so loved us that

               [A] even us, who were dead in sins,

                  F   God made us alive <u>together</u> with <u>Christ,</u>

                     G   —by grace you have been saved—

                  F'   God raised us and seated us <u>together</u> in heaven in <u>Christ,</u>

               E'   that he might show the <u>richness</u> of his grace in Christ.

         D'   For <u>by grace</u> you have been <u>saved</u> through faith;

      C'   this is not from <u>yourselves,</u> but it is God's gift,

   B'   not from your <u>works,</u> lest anyone should boast.

A'   God has re-created us <u>in Christ</u> to <u>walk</u> in good works.

The central thought highlighted by the structure at point H, *sola gratia*, is the pivot in the lives of the Gentiles whose walk is thereby transformed from demonic subjection to new life in Christ.

The location of the main theme in the center is also illustrated by the marriage pericope (5:21–33), the structure of which is chiastic:

A   wives

   B   husbands

      C   marriage/Christ

   B'   husbands

A'   wives

Within that structure we find this AB–B'A' pattern in 5:21–24:

A   wives

   B   husband/Christ

   B'   church/Christ

A'   wives

Lists

Modern writers use commas, semicolons, colons, full stops, and (now increasingly) bullets to divide items in a list, group them, and mark when the list has drawn to a close. Lacking such tools, ancient Greeks made use of variety in conjunctions and particles to accomplish the same task.[63] Frequently in the NT the beginning of a list will be marked with one conjunction (such as μέν, "on the one hand" [but often left untranslated]); the list may continue with another (such as δέ, "on the other hand" [but often left untranslated]); and its end will be indicated by switching to another (such as καί, "and"; see 4:11 in

---

[63] See Winger, "Orality as the Key to Understanding Apostolic Proclamation in the Epistles," 274–77.

the fourth bullet below). Groupings within lists may be marked by a change of conjunction (perhaps εἴτε, "either, or") or grammatical structure (e.g., Rom 12:6–8; 1 Cor 3:21–23). A sequence of nouns connected by καί, "and," may be concluded by an "etc." phrase, for example, καὶ τὰ ὅμοια τούτοις, "and things like these" (Gal 5:21), perhaps followed by an adversative. For example:

- ὑπεράνω πάσης ἀρχῆς <u>καὶ</u> ἐξουσίας <u>καὶ</u> δυνάμεως <u>καὶ</u> κυριότητος <u>καὶ</u> <u>παντὸς</u> <u>ὀνόματος ὀνομαζομένου</u> <u>οὐ μόνον</u> ἐν τῷ αἰῶνι τούτω <u>ἀλλὰ καὶ</u> ἐν τῷ μέλλοντι, "far above every ruler <u>and</u> authority <u>and</u> power <u>and</u> lordship, <u>and</u> [etc. phrase:] *<u>every name that is named</u>*, <u>not only</u> in this age <u>but also</u> in the coming one" (1:21)

- τί τὸ πλάτος <u>καὶ</u> μῆκος <u>καὶ</u> ὕψος <u>καὶ</u> βάθος, γνῶναί <u>τε</u> τὴν ὑπερβάλλουσαν, "what is [its] breadth <u>and</u> length <u>and</u> height <u>and</u> depth, and <u>also</u> to know …" (3:18–19)

- in 5:3–4 we find two lists of three that each shift from καί, "and," to ἤ, "or," to mark their conclusions:

  ❖ πορνεία δὲ <u>καὶ</u> ἀκαθαρσία πᾶσα <u>ἢ</u> πλεονεξία, "but sexual immorality <u>and</u> all uncleanness <u>or</u> lust" (5:3)

  ❖ καὶ αἰσχρότης <u>καὶ</u> μωρολογία <u>ἢ</u> εὐτραπελία, "and shamefulness <u>and</u> foolish talk <u>or</u> coarse joking" (5:4)

Inattention to the "punctuation" function of such conjunctions or grammatical shifts has often led the exegete astray. This insight features greatly in this commentary's analysis of the fivefold (not fourfold!) office of the ministry Paul delineates in 4:11, in which the shift from δέ, "and," to καί, "and," is explained *not* as grouping the last two items together (i.e., "pastors and teachers" would describe one office, "pastors who teach"), but as merely marking the end of the list (i.e., "pastors" and "teachers" are two distinct offices):

- καὶ αὐτὸς ἔδωκεν τοὺς <u>μὲν</u> ἀποστόλους, τοὺς <u>δὲ</u> προφήτας, τοὺς <u>δὲ</u> εὐαγγελιστάς, τοὺς <u>δὲ</u> ποιμένας <u>καὶ</u> διδασκάλους, "and he himself gave [here μὲν is untranslated] the apostles <u>and</u> [δέ] the prophets <u>and</u> [δέ] the evangelists <u>and</u> [δέ] pastors <u>and</u> [καί] teachers" (4:11)

Formulae as Structural Markers

While all language is filled with conventional expressions, oral cultures in particular use formulae to mark the beginning and end of units in a story or speech.[64] Paul's epistolary conventions are not simply a habit, but they also allow the listener to keep track of where he is in the progress of the letter. Such functions are all the more important in Paul's letters, which are significantly longer than others in antiquity.[65]

- The salutation, while varying slightly in content, inevitably includes these items in this order: "Paul, apostle of Christ Jesus," "to the saints in _____," and "grace to you and peace from God our Father and the Lord Jesus Christ" (1:1–2).

- Most of Paul's epistles continue with a thanksgiving, marked by characteristic verbs, such as οὐ παύομαι εὐχαριστῶν ὑπὲρ ὑμῶν μνείαν ποιούμενος ἐπὶ τῶν

---

[64] Davis, *Oral Biblical Criticism*, 101–2.

[65] Paul J. Achtemeier, "*Omne verbum sonat*: The New Testament and the Oral Environment of Late Western Antiquity," *Journal of Biblical Literature* 109 (1990): 22.

προσευχῶν μου, "I do not cease giving thanks for you, making remembrance of you at the time of my prayers" (1:16).

- The epistolary conclusion is marked by a sequence of formulae, including a request for prayer, the bestowal of peace, the commendation of the letter carrier, greetings, the holy kiss, a reference to the writing process, a doxology, and a blessing (see 6:18–24).

Some analysts would add the doxology (3:14–21) as marking the conclusion of the letter's doctrinal half (chapters 1–3), and the clause παρακαλῶ οὖν ὑμᾶς, "therefore I exhort you" (4:1), as marking the inception of its ethical half (chapters 4–6). This commentary will take issue with that analysis, but does not deny that such expressions can be significant oral formulae. These are other formulae that serve as structural markers in Ephesians:

- the phrases εἰς ἔπαινον δόξης τῆς χάριτος αὐτοῦ, "to the praise of his gracious glory" (1:6), and εἰς ἔπαινον (τῆς) δόξης αὐτοῦ, "to the praise of his glory" (1:12, 14), which divide the opening Trinitarian prayer (1:3–14) into three stanzas
- the parallel use of an articular noun (functioning as a vocative) followed by an imperative that marks out the distinct sections of the *Haustafel*, as the speaker addresses each group in turn: αἱ γυναῖκες, "wives" (5:22); οἱ ἄνδρες, "husbands" (5:25); τὰ τέκνα, "children" (6:1); οἱ πατέρες, "fathers" (6:4); οἱ δοῦλοι, "slaves" (6:5); and οἱ κύριοι, "masters" (6:9)
- transitional words and phrases that mark the beginning and end of units: διὰ τοῦτο, "for this reason" (1:15; 5:17; 6:13); διό, "therefore" (2:11; 4:25); τούτου χάριν, "for this reason" (3:1, 14); οὖν, "therefore" (4:1, 17; 5:1, 15)
- τοῦ λοιποῦ, "finally" (6:10), which signals that the orator has reached his *peroratio*, the summation of the argument

The preceding summary has perhaps begun to sensitize the reader to the oral qualities that are present in Paul's epistles as documents intended to be read aloud to the gathered Christian congregation. This cross-cultural leap from the modern text-based world of silent reading to the ancient, lively, rhetorical environment is critical if today's reader is to understand Paul's writings as he meant them and as the Spirit inspired them. Insights based on oral analysis will frequently come to bear in this commentary on Ephesians as part of the interpreter's toolbox to understand the grammar and semantics of a given text from the perspective of an ancient listener. But if this primer on orality has only provided another set of hermeneutical tools, it has fallen somewhat short of its goal. One hopes that the reader is inspired to take up the Scriptures' own mandate to read them aloud as God's proclamation and to listen to them as the living voice of Christ through his apostles and prophets.

Authorship

While no Christian writer prior to the eighteenth century expressed any doubt that Ephesians was written by the apostle Paul, in modern times this letter has become a great battlefield of contested ground lying between the well-defended homeland of the so-called "undisputed Pauline letters" and the lost territory of the Pastoral Epistles.[66] The breadth of opinion found among twentieth-century scholars is staggering. To the right stand stalwart defenders of the church's historic judgment such as F. F. Bruce, who calls Ephesians "the quintessence of Paulinism,"[67] and Markus Barth, whose monumental two-volume Anchor Bible commentary parries every critical blow. In the middle stands the remarkably ironic proposition of C. H. Dodd that, "whether the Epistle is by Paul or not, certainly *its thought is the crown of Paulinism*."[68] To the left stand arrayed some 80 percent of current critical scholars according to the estimate of Raymond Brown in 1997.[69] The venerable American Quaker theologian Henry Cadbury once commented: "The persistent and widely shared doubt of Paul's authorship of Ephesians creates an embarrassment to our profession."[70] Cadbury's face flushed red not from any polite concern for Paul's reputation, but for his own—the fact that the industry of NT criticism cannot produce a reliable consensus on the question calls into doubt the basic competence of its machinery and workforce. Or to return to the military metaphor, Ephesians is, as Goodspeed put it, "the Waterloo of commentators."[71]

To subject the authorship of a NT epistle to vigorous scrutiny is not in itself a surrender to the skeptical agenda of higher criticism. It is, on the contrary, an

---

[66] The seven letters generally accepted by critical scholars as authentically Pauline are Romans, Galatians, Philippians, 1 and 2 Corinthians, 1 Thessalonians, and Philemon. The others are disputed.

[67] F. F. Bruce, *Paul: Apostle of the Free Spirit* (Exeter: Paternoster, 1977), 424. Note that it is not merely "conservative" exegetes who have defended Pauline authorship in recent times. The notoriously liberal former bishop of Woolwich, J. A. T. Robinson, was not persuaded by the arguments against Pauline authorship, citing also the example of Armitage Robinson (*St. Paul's Epistle to the Ephesians* [London: Macmillan, 1903]), "who was in close touch with Harnack and contemporary German scholarship and certainly not conservative for his day" (Robinson, *Redating the New Testament*, 63).

[68] C. H. Dodd, "Ephesians," in *The Abingdon Bible Commentary* (ed. Frederick Carl Eiselen, Edwin Lewis, and David G. Downey; New York: Abingdon, 1929), 1224–25.

[69] Brown, *An Introduction to the New Testament*, 620. Barth, *Ephesians*, 1:38, provides a summary list of where major scholars in the last century stood. Hoehner, *Ephesians*, 6–20, disputes the contention that the majority of NT scholars have rejected Pauline authorship. He demonstrates that only in the period after 1971 has the anti-Pauline position even gained a majority hold and then only 51 percent.

[70] Cadbury, "The Dilemma of Ephesians," 93. He continues:

Persons who otherwise agree on critical questions often sharply differ here. They may feel the strength of the arguments on each side, but are ashamed to make no choice. So they answer the question one way or the other, more because of their unwillingness to admit indecision than out of clear conviction. The same arguments are quite differently appraised by advocates of the same side. In the pressure to arrive at some decision, now one, now another minor matter is given undeserved weight. Perhaps the individual scholar himself vacillates in his opinion, or over the years shifts from one side to the other. The book on the question that he has read most recently may move him, but not always as the author intended.

[71] Goodspeed, *The Meaning of Ephesians*, 15. One wonders whether Goodspeed himself noted the irony of placing the modern higher critical establishment into the role of the brutal tyrant Napoléon and the genuine Paul of Ephesians into the boots of the noble Field Marshal Wellington.

age-old concern of the Christian church, for which biblical "authority" cannot be separated from "*author*ship." Certainly, the authority of Scripture, the Word of *God*, derives fundamentally from its heavenly Author. Yet the Holy Spirit has chosen in his wisdom to work through certain called spokesmen, chiefly the prophets of the Old Testament and the apostles of the New (Eph 2:20; 3:5; cf. Neh 9:30; Zech 7:12; Acts 1:2). Christ promised that the apostles would speak for him in the age between his ascension and second coming ("he who hears you hears me," Lk 10:16; cf. Lk 24:46–48; Acts 1:8; 26:16; Gal 1:11–12). The apostle Paul was therefore most concerned to establish the authenticity of his writings in a society populated with false prophets and imposters (Gal 6:11; Col 4:18; 2 Thess 2:2; 3:17). What is written by an apostle carries the weight of his office, that is, the authority of the One who sent him (see the first textual note and the commentary on Eph 1:1). To the church, it really does matter whether or not Ephesians was written by the apostle Paul.

But the authorship question is not satisfied with a simple yes/no answer—and this is why it is so interesting. What emerges from a review of the scholarly debate over the authorship of Ephesians is that there is significant disagreement on who Paul was and how he thought, matters on which so much depends. For one's conception of Paul may well determine whether one accepts that he could have written Ephesians. Furthermore, one's picture of the "Paul" who did or did not write Ephesians will necessarily influence the way the epistle is interpreted. For this reason, the authorship question is crucial even for those who accept Pauline authorship a priori.

The interrelatedness of authorship and interpretation may be illustrated by a few examples. In each case, a caricature of Paul derived from an exaggerated reading of some of his letters is placed in opposition to an exaggerated reading of others. If it is assumed that the "authentic Paul" believed Christ would return in his own lifetime, then the perspective of Ephesians presents some challenges. Whereas the Paul of Galatians, Romans, and 1 Corinthians appears to champion complete freedom from the rituals and institutions of religion, Ephesians 3–4 envisions a well-established church with an ordered ministry that is prepared to function over the long haul. Whereas Paul in 1 Corinthians 7 advocates celibacy for Christians in view of Christ's imminent return, Ephesians 5–6 lays down guidelines for Christians to marry and raise children in the faith. Scholars have responded to these issues in a variety of ways. Some accept this view of the "authentic Paul" and this interpretation of Ephesians and conclude that Paul could not have written it (the result, in simplistic terms, is a "liberal, high-church" reading). Others accept this view of Paul, yet are convinced that he wrote Ephesians, and therefore are compelled to interpret the letter accordingly (resulting in a "conservative, low-church" reading).

Innumerable permutations are pursued in the literature, but what is common to all is an uncritical acceptance of the "Paul" constructed by liberal German

Protestantism of the nineteenth century.[72] This Paul is a caricature painted to comply with a particular evolutionary theory of early Christianity and assembled from data drawn exclusively from as few as four supposedly "authentic" letters.[73] The interpretation of Ephesians is then either squeezed into conformity with this authorial caricature or set up in opposition to it. One ironically surprising result of this situation is that the commentators who deny Pauline authorship (e.g., Andrew Lincoln, Rudolf Schnackenburg) frequently provide more helpful exposition of the text itself, since they feel no need to compress it into their narrow view of Paul.[74] In any case, neither the "liberal, high church" nor the "conservative, low church" perspective provides a completely satisfactory reading of Ephesians.

What is in order is a fundamental reevaluation of the authorship and interpretation of Ephesians. In the traditional way, we shall first consider the internal evidence of the epistle (its self-testimony to its author) and the historical or external testimony from the first centuries of its use. It should not prejudice the case to note already that these data point unambiguously to Paul as the author. The case against Pauline authorship will then be summarized, consisting mainly in matters of literary style and theology. We will then consider whether these arguments are compelling enough to overturn the external data. However, as important as the conclusion is, the process itself will be immensely profitable. For in the course of evaluating these arguments, we shall already be many steps along the road to understanding the epistle.

---

[72] Barth, *Ephesians*, 1:46–47, quips with ironic seriousness: "The question must be raised whether this understanding of Paul, based as it is upon selected passages from Galatians and Romans, can claim that infallibility which among Protestants is denied the Pope and the Papal Bible Commission, but is *de facto* claimed for 'objective,' scholarly, historical-critical research."

[73] The theory of *Frühkatholizismus* will be discussed in further detail below (see "Incipient Catholicism" in "Arguments against Pauline Authorship" and "Incipient Catholicism" in "Evaluation of the Case," both below in "Authorship")—though it should already be obvious that an anti-Catholic bias is at work in these liberal German Protestants. Also obvious is the circularity of the argument: the authenticity of epistles is determined by comparison with those which have been predetermined to be authentic.

[74] The case of Heinrich Schlier is even more intriguing. In his early life as a liberal Lutheran NT scholar (indeed, one of Bultmann's most gifted students), he denied Pauline authorship of Ephesians owing to its "incipient Catholic" features. Having later converted to Roman Catholicism, he penned a commentary on Ephesians that robustly defended Pauline authorship, for he now found the Paul of Ephesians to be more compatible with his own faith. See Heinrich Schlier, "A Brief Apologia," in *We Are Now Catholics* (ed. Karl Hardt; trans. Norman C. Reeves; Cork: Mercier, 1958), 193–215; cf. Lincoln, *Ephesians*, lx (Lincoln himself confesses to making the opposite journey with respect to Pauline authorship, citing also Nils Dahl and Rudolf Schnackenburg); and Bruce, *The Epistles to the Colossians, to Philemon, and to the Ephesians*, 240. Schnackenburg, *Ephesians*, 24, n. 16, suggests that Schlier may later have expressed a renewal of doubt about Pauline authorship.

The Case for Pauline Authorship

Internal Evidence

The opening words of Ephesians, in a fashion consistent with Hellenistic letter-writing practice, name the author: Παῦλος ἀπόστολος Χριστοῦ Ἰησοῦ, "Paul, apostle of Christ Jesus" (1:1). The opening verse of each of the thirteen letters in the Pauline corpus explicitly names Paul, with only four (Philippians, 1 and 2 Thessalonians, Philemon) failing to call him "apostle." The continuation διὰ θελήματος θεοῦ, "through the will of God" (Eph 1:1), is identical to the wording of 1 and 2 Corinthians, Colossians, and 2 Timothy and accords in content with the lengthier apology in Gal 1:1. Thus, the self-identification of the author is fully consistent with Pauline practice and bears no marks of slavish or unsophisticated imitation; there is no immediate reason to doubt its claim. The author again names himself as Paul in 3:1,[75] at which point he also claims to be ὁ δέσμιος τοῦ Χριστοῦ [Ἰησοῦ] ὑπὲρ ὑμῶν τῶν ἐθνῶν, "the prisoner of Christ [Jesus] for the sake of you Gentiles" (cf. 3:13; 4:1; 6:20). This claim is in agreement with the record of Acts, which narrates Paul's arrest at the instigation of hostile Jews on the charge that he was teaching Gentiles not to observe the distinctively Jewish provisions of the Torah or to attend the temple's worship (Acts 21:27–28). In the "you/we" sections of Ephesians, which address the distinction between Jew and Gentile, the author identifies himself with the Jewish side (1:12; 2:3); he prays like a Jew (1:3–14; 3:14–21) and applies Jewish exegetical techniques to the OT.[76] The author also calls himself διάκονος, "minister," of the Gospel (3:7), and τῷ ἐλαχιστοτέρῳ πάντων ἁγίων, "quite the least of all the saints" (3:8)—probably an allusion to Paul's persecution of the first disciples.[77] He is aware of the Ephesians' circumstances (1:15), as they are of his (3:13). He remembers them and prays for them regularly (1:16–23; 3:14–19). He knows they have heard the Gospel, have been baptized (1:13), and have been catechized (4:20–21).

Thus, the data of Ephesians portray a figure entirely consistent with Paul: a Jewish man who once persecuted the church but has now been given the grace of apostleship with the particular mission to proclaim the Gospel of Christ to the Gentiles, and has been imprisoned for doing so.[78] In addition, there is no doubting that its *structure* conforms to the Pauline pattern (and differs somewhat

---

[75] Lest it be thought artificial for the author to assert his name as "Paul" within the body of the letter, note the parallels to Eph 3:1 with "Paul" in 2 Cor 10:1; Gal 5:2; Col 1:23; 1 Thess 2:18; Philemon 9.

[76] E.g., Eph 1:22; 2:13–17; 4:8, 25–26; 5:30–33; 6:1–4, 10–17.

[77] Acts 7:58; 8:1, 3; 9:1–2; 1 Cor 15:8–10; Gal 1:13, 23; Phil 3:6; 1 Tim 1:15.

[78] It is therefore apropos to note the irony of Schnackenburg's conclusion about who the *pseudonymous* author of Ephesians must be:

His way of analyzing Scripture (especially 2.17; 4.8; 5.31) reveals a similarity to the Jewish Midrash although it is applied in a Christian manner, and the way the quotations from Scripture are so easily introduced (4.26; 5.2, 18; 6.3, 14–17) betrays knowledge of and familiarity in dealing with Scripture. … *We should have to define him more*

from the epistles of Peter, John, James, and Jude): opening greeting, prayers and thanksgiving,[79] didactic and paraenetic material, concluding greetings and salutation. And though critics today will dispute the *content* of the epistle (see "Thought/Theology" in "Arguments against Pauline Authorship" below), no theologian of the premodern era found its theology inconsistent with Paul—indeed, it was often thought to be a compendium of Pauline theology.

External Evidence

No early author disputed Pauline authorship, and as even the skeptical Dennis Nineham admits, "as far as external attestation goes, Ephesians is unassailable."[80] The *appreciation* of such early Christian attestation, however, varies quite dramatically. On the one hand is the traditional respect accorded by Abbott's classic ICC commentary, which finds significant testimony in explicit claims of Pauline authorship and allusions to Ephesians in early patristic sources:

> The earliest express reference to the Epistle as St. Paul's is that of Irenaeus; but inasmuch as, if [Ephesians were] not genuine, it must be much later than St. Paul, evidence of acquaintance with it on the part of early writers is important. When we add to this the fact that it professes to be St. Paul's, we are fairly justified in saying that evidence of its reception is evidence of its genuineness.[81]

Contrast that sober historical confidence with Andrew Lincoln's cavalier dismissal of external evidence:

> It should be noted in passing that although Ephesians appears to have been an uncontested part of the canon of Paul's letters since the time of Marcion and it was clearly accepted as being by Paul since the time of Irenaeus and Tertullian, we know nothing about how this situation came about. Therefore, this cannot be a decisive factor in discussion of the original authorship.[82]

Between 1909 (Abbott) and 1990 (Lincoln) a postmodern shift occurred that led to this devaluation of historical data in favor of an exclusive reliance on the "soft" evidence of stylistic, theological, and other criteria of internal probability. There is nothing scientific in this preference, and the suspicion arises that the external evidence is dismissed not because it is weak but because it is inconvenient. This

---

closely as a Jewish-Christian with a Hellenistic education who was receptive to his spiritual and intellectual surroundings. (*Ephesians*, 36; emphasis added)
This sounds suspiciously like Paul!

[79] Although Ephesians is the only Pauline letter to include both a *Berakah* prayer (1:3–14) and a thanksgiving section (1:15–23), 2 Corinthians contains the former, nine other Pauline epistles contain the latter, and Galatians and Titus include neither. Thus, the structure of Ephesians falls within the parameters of Pauline practice.

[80] Nineham, "The Case against the Pauline Authorship," 22.

[81] Abbott, *The Epistles to the Ephesians and to the Colossians*, ix. Subsequent to this introduction, Abbott provides five pages of testimony to Pauline authorship from the first and second centuries.

[82] Lincoln, *Ephesians*, lxii. Consequently, Lincoln *does not even cite the evidence*.

commentary, by contrast, takes the position that historical evidence is primary and can only be overturned by *unassailable* internal evidence to the contrary.

Lincoln's contention that "we know nothing about how this situation came about" is not defensible. As Tertullian testifies (below), the early church was certainly capable of mounting a historical investigation to see whether the churches to which the epistles were originally addressed could attest to their authenticity. Second-century authors provide such proof (see below). As Abbott contends, however, one need not merely be satisfied with direct statements of authorship.[83] As heirs of the OT, the early Christians knew the difference between authoritative and non-authoritative writings; they knew when they could say, "It stands written." When the earliest fathers *used* Paul's writings in the same way that they used the OT Scriptures—in quotation, paraphrase, and allusion, as proof and example—this is evidence that they already had a sense of Christian *canon*. And as the *authority* of a writing derived from its *authorship*, the use of any Pauline writing in the manner of authoritative Scripture counts as attestation to a belief that it was truly from Paul.[84]

Consider, then, the following places in which early postapostolic authors from the turn of the first century cite or allude to Ephesians:[85]

---

[83] Abbott's ICC replacement, Ernest Best, though drawing the opposite conclusion to his illustrious predecessor, nevertheless soberly contends: "It should not be assumed that those who used Ephesians prior to Irenaeus did not believe it was by Paul; it was not customary in Christian literature of the period to identify sources" (*Ephesians*, 14).

[84] The device of pseudepigraphy will be explored in more detail below; see "Pseudepigraphy?" in "Evaluation of the Case" in "Authorship." Suffice it to say, however, that the canonical *use* of Ephesians is at the very least testimony to a *belief*—mistaken or not—that it is Pauline. The significance of apostolic authorship as a fundamental criterion for canonicity is borne out by second- and third-century suspicion against the Gospels of Mark and (to a lesser extent) Luke (who were not apostles and whose authority was ultimately derived from Peter and Paul, respectively), as well as against the seven antilegomena enumerated by Eusebius' *Ecclesiastical History* (3:25).

[85] Translations are by the present author. Best, *Ephesians*, 14, cautions about such parallels:

> Care is necessary here since a similarity between Ephesians and another writing may have come about because both writings are independently indebted to oral, creedal, catechetical or liturgical tradition, or even other written material. It is also not sufficient to show in respect of a phrase from Ephesians that there are parallels to it; it needs also to be shown that other parallels to the phrase in a wider literature are rare.

The examples provided would seem to satisfy these criteria to the extent it is possible, in that they involve unique expressions from Ephesians not attested in any other early literature.

Didache	Ephesians
ὑμεῖς δὲ οἱ δοῦλοι ὑποταγήσεσθε τοῖς κυρίοις ὑμῶν ὡς τύπῳ θεοῦ ἐν αἰσχύνῃ καὶ φόβῳ but you slaves, be subordinate to your lords/masters as to a representative of God in reverence and fear (4:11; cf. *Barnabas*, 19:7)	οἱ δοῦλοι, ὑπακούετε τοῖς κατὰ σάρκα κυρίοις μετὰ φόβου καὶ τρόμου ἐν ἁπλότητι τῆς καρδίας ὑμῶν ὡς τῷ Χριστῷ slaves, heed your fleshly lords/masters with fear and trembling in the sincerity of your heart, as to Christ (6:5)

1 Clement	Ephesians
διὰ τούτου ἠνεῴχθησαν ἡμῶν οἱ ὀφθαλμοὶ τῆς καρδίας through whom the eyes of our heart were opened (36:2; cf. 59:3)	πεφωτισμένους τοὺς ὀφθαλμοὺς τῆς καρδίας [ὑμῶν] the eyes of [your] heart having been enlightened (1:18)
καὶ ὑποτασσέσθω ἕκαστος τῷ πλησίον αὐτοῦ and let each be subordinate to his neighbor (38:1)	ὑποτασσόμενοι ἀλλήλοις ἐν φόβῳ Χριστοῦ being subordinate to one another in the fear of Christ (5:21)
ἢ οὐχὶ ἕνα θεὸν ἔχομεν καὶ ἕνα Χριστὸν καὶ ἓν πνεῦμα τῆς χάριτος τὸ ἐκχυθὲν ἐφ᾽ ἡμᾶς; καὶ μία κλῆσις ἐν Χριστῷ; or do we not have one God and one Christ and one Spirit of grace who was poured out upon us? and one calling in Christ? (46:6)	ἓν σῶμα καὶ ἓν πνεῦμα, καθὼς καὶ ἐκλήθητε ἐν μιᾷ ἐλπίδι τῆς κλήσεως ὑμῶν· εἷς κύριος, μία πίστις, ἓν βάπτισμα, εἷς θεὸς καὶ πατὴρ πάντων one body and one Spirit—just as you were also called in the one hope of your calling—one Lord, one faith, one Baptism, one God and Father of all (4:4–6)
ὅτι μέλη ἐσμὲν ἀλλήλων for we are members of one another (46:7)	ὅτι ἐσμὲν ἀλλήλων μέλη for we are members of one another (4:25)
ὁ ἐκλεξάμενος τὸν κύριον Ἰησοῦν Χριστὸν καὶ ὑμᾶς δι᾽ αὐτοῦ εἰς λαὸν περιούσιον [God] who chose the Lord Jesus Christ and you through him for a specially possessed people (64:1)	καθὼς ἐξελέξατο ἡμᾶς … διὰ Ἰησοῦ Χριστοῦ … εἰς ἀπολύτρωσιν τῆς περιποιήσεως just as he chose us … through Jesus Christ … for the redemption of [his] special possession (1:4, 5, 14; cf. Acts 20:28)

28

2 Clement	Ephesians
οὐκ οἴομαι δὲ ὑμᾶς ἀγνοεῖν, ὅτι ἐκκλησία ζῶσα σῶμά ἐστιν Χριστοῦ· λέγει γὰρ ἡ γραφή· ἐποίησεν ὁ θεὸς τὸν ἄνθρωπον ἄρσεν καὶ θῆλυ· τὸ ἄρσεν ἐστὶν ὁ Χριστός, τὸ θῆλυ ἡ ἐκκλησία now I suppose you are not ignorant that the living church is the body of Christ; for the Scripture says, "God made man male and female" [Gen 1:27]; the male is Christ, the female is the church (14:2)	τῇ ἐκκλησίᾳ, ἥτις ἐστὶν τὸ σῶμα αὐτοῦ for the church, which is his body (1:22–23); cf. the application of Genesis 2 to Christ and the church in Eph 5:22–33
ἐσκοτίσμεθα τὴν διάνοιαν we were darkened in understanding (19:2)	ἐσκοτωμένοι τῇ διανοίᾳ ὄντες [the Gentiles] being darkened in their understanding (4:18)
Ignatius	**Ephesians**
ἀγαπᾶν τὰς συμβίους ὡς ὁ κύριος τὴν ἐκκλησίαν to love their wives as the Lord [loves] the church (*To Polycarp*, 5:1)	οἱ ἄνδρες, ἀγαπᾶτε τὰς γυναῖκας, καθὼς καὶ ὁ Χριστὸς ἠγάπησεν τὴν ἐκκλησίαν husbands, love [your] wives, just as also Christ loved the church (5:25)
τὸ βάπτισμα ὑμῶν μενέτω ὡς ὅπλα, ἡ πίστις ὡς περικεφαλαία, ἡ ἀγάπη ὡς δόρυ, ἡ ὑπομονὴ ὡς πανοπλία let your Baptism remain as [your] armor, faith as [your] helmet, love as [your] spear, endurance as [your] full body armor (*To Polycarp*, 6:2)	Compare to 6:10–17.
ἐν ἑνὶ σώματι τῆς ἐκκλησίας αὐτοῦ in the one body of his church (*To the Smyrnaeans*, 1:2)	ἓν σῶμα one body (4:4) τῇ ἐκκλησίᾳ, ἥτις ἐστὶν τὸ σῶμα αὐτοῦ for the church, which is his body (1:22–23; cf. 5:23)
προσκαλεῖται ὑμᾶς ὄντας μέλη αὐτοῦ. οὐ δύναται οὖν κεφαλὴ χωρὶς γεννηθῆναι ἄνευ μελῶν he calls you who are his members; therefore the head is not able to be born without its members (*To the Trallians*, 11:2)	αὐξήσωμεν εἰς αὐτὸν τὰ πάντα, ὅς ἐστιν ἡ κεφαλή, Χριστός that we might grow up in all things into him, who is the head, Christ (4:15; cf. 4:16) μέλη ἐσμὲν τοῦ σώματος αὐτοῦ we are members of his body (5:30; cf. 3:6; 4:25)

Polycarp, *To the Philippians*	**Ephesians**
εἰδότες, ὅτι χάριτί ἐστε σεσῳσμένοι, οὐκ ἐξ ἔργων, ἀλλὰ θελήματι θεοῦ διὰ Ἰησοῦ Χριστοῦ knowing that by grace you have been saved, not from works, but by the will of God through Jesus Christ (1:3)	τῇ γὰρ χάριτί ἐστε σεσῳσμένοι διὰ πίστεως· καὶ τοῦτο οὐκ ἐξ ὑμῶν, θεοῦ τὸ δῶρον· οὐκ ἐξ ἔργων for by grace you have been saved through faith; and this is not from yourselves; it is the gift of God, not from works (2:8–9; cf. 1:5; 2:5)
ἀναζωσάμενοι τὰς ὀσφύας ὑμῶν having girded your loins (2:1)	περιζωσάμενοι τὴν ὀσφὺν ὑμῶν having girded your loins (6:14)
ὑποτασσομένους τοῖς πρεσβυτέροις καὶ διακόνοις ὡς θεῷ καὶ Χριστῷ being subordinate to the presbyters and deacons as to God and to Christ (5:3)	ὑποτασσόμενοι ἀλλήλοις ἐν φόβῳ Χριστοῦ, αἱ γυναῖκες τοῖς ἰδίοις ἀνδράσιν ὡς τῷ κυρίῳ being subordinate to one another in fear of Christ: wives to their own husbands as to the Lord (5:21–22; cf. 4:11–12)
omnes vobis invicem subiecti estote all of you be subordinate to one another (10:2)	ὑποτασσόμενοι ἀλλήλοις being subordinate to one another (5:21)
irascimini et nolite peccare, et sol non occidat super iracundiam vestram "be angry and do not sin" and "do not let the sun go down on your anger" (12:1)	This precise combination of Ps 4:5 (ET 4:4) with a paraphrase of Deut 24:13, 15 is first made in Eph 4:26.
Shepherd of Hermas	**Ephesians**
ἀλήθειαν ἀγάπα καὶ πᾶσα ἀλήθεια ἐκ τοῦ στόματός σου ἐκπορευέσθω love truth and let all truth proceed from your mouth (*Mandates*, 3:1)	λαλεῖτε ἀλήθειαν ἕκαστος … πᾶς λόγος σαπρὸς ἐκ τοῦ στόματος ὑμῶν μὴ ἐκπορευέσθω each one of you speak truth … let no harmful word proceed from your mouths (4:25, 29)
καὶ πονηρὰν συνείδησιν μετὰ τοῦ πνεύματος τῆς ἀληθείας μὴ κατοικεῖν μηδὲ λύπην ἐπάγειν τῷ πνεύματι τῷ σεμνῷ καὶ ἀληθεῖ and [it is necessary] that an evil conscience not dwell with the Spirit of truth and that grief not come upon the holy and true Spirit (*Mandates*, 3:4) λυπεῖ τὸ πνεῦμα τὸ ἅγιον grieves the Holy Spirit (*Mandates*, 10:2.2)	καὶ μὴ λυπεῖτε τὸ πνεῦμα τὸ ἅγιον τοῦ θεοῦ and do not grieve the Holy Spirit of God (4:30)

καὶ οἱ πιστεύσαντες τῷ κυρίῳ διὰ τοῦ υἱοῦ αὐτοῦ καὶ ἐνδιδυσκόμενοι τὰ πνεύματα ταῦτα ἔσονται εἰς ἓν πνεῦμα, ἓν σῶμα, καὶ μία χρόα τῶν ἱματίων αὐτῶν	ἓν σῶμα καὶ ἓν πνεῦμα, ... εἷς κύριος, μία πίστις, ἓν βάπτισμα
and those who believe in the Lord through his Son and are clothed with these spirits will become one spirit, one body, and their garments will be of one color (*Similitudes*, 9:13.5) (The word "garments" appears to be a reference to the white baptismal robes.)	one body and one Spirit ... one Lord, one faith, one Baptism (4:4–5)
ἔσται ἡ ἐκκλησία τοῦ θεοῦ ἓν σῶμα, μία φρόνησις, εἷς νοῦς, μία πίστις, μία ἀγάπη the church of God shall be one body, one understanding, one mind, one faith, one love (*Similitudes*, 9:18.4)	
πάντα τὰ ἔθνη τὰ ὑπὸ τὸν οὐρανὸν κατοικοῦντα, ἀκούσαντα καὶ πιστεύσαντα ἐπὶ τῷ ὀνόματι ἐκλήθησαν [τοῦ υἱοῦ] τοῦ θεοῦ. λαβόντες οὖν τὴν σφραγῖδα μίαν φρόνησιν ἔσχον καὶ ἕνα νοῦν, καὶ μία πίστις αὐτῶν ἐγένετο καὶ μία ἀγάπη, ... καὶ γενέσθαι ἓν σῶμα	ἀκούσαντες τὸν λόγον τῆς ἀληθείας, τὸ εὐαγγέλιον τῆς σωτηρίας ὑμῶν, ἐν ᾧ καὶ πιστεύσαντες ἐσφραγίσθητε τῷ πνεύματι τῆς ἐπαγγελίας τῷ ἁγίῳ
all the nations that were dwelling under heaven, having heard and believed on the name [of the Son] of God, were called; therefore, when they had received the seal, they had one understanding and one mind, and their one faith became also one love; ... and they became one body (*Similitudes*, 9:17.4–5)	having heard the Word of truth, the Gospel of your salvation, in whom, having also believed, you were sealed with the promised Holy Spirit (1:13)
Barnabas	**Ephesians**
ἡμερῶν οὖν οὐσῶν πονηρῶν καὶ αὐτοῦ τοῦ ἐνεργοῦντος ἔχοντος τὴν ἐξουσίαν since, therefore, the days are evil and the one who is at work [in the world] has authority (2:1)	ὅτι αἱ ἡμέραι πονηραί εἰσιν for the days are evil (5:16; cf. 6:13)
	τὸν ἄρχοντα τῆς ἐξουσίας τοῦ ἀέρος, τοῦ πνεύματος τοῦ νῦν ἐνεργοῦντος ἐν τοῖς υἱοῖς τῆς ἀπειθείας the ruler of the authority of the air, the spirit of the one now working in the sons of disobedience (2:2)

This is an extensive and persuasive accumulation of evidence demonstrating, at the very least, that Ephesians was widely known and used by AD 90.[86] To this collection can be added the even more extensive correspondences with Ignatius' own letter to the Ephesians (cited below in "Ignatius to the Ephesians" in "Addressees"). The evidence that 1 Peter is dependent on Ephesians is weaker,[87] but if accepted, adds the weight of apostolic imprimatur to the letter.

By the second century one finds unanimous, direct attestation to Pauline authorship of Ephesians, from both friendly sources and hostile ones (the Valentinians and Marcion):

- Irenaeus: "Even as the blessed Paul declares in his Epistle to the Ephesians, that 'we are members of His body [Eph 5:30], of His flesh, and of His bones.' "[88] Irenaeus attributes Ephesians to Paul repeatedly in this writing.[89]

- Hippolytus tells us that the Valentinians quote Eph 3:14–18 as γραφή, "Scripture."[90]

- Clement of Alexandria, having quoted 1 Cor 11:3, 8, 11 and Gal 5:16–17, 19–23 with "the apostle says," adds: "Therefore also in the epistle to the Ephesians he writes [γράφει], 'Being subject to one another in the fear of God …' [Eph 5:21–29]."[91]

- Tertullian: "Let us consider what milk it was that Paul gave the Corinthians to drink, by the line of what rule the Galatians were again made to walk straight, what the Philippians, the Thessalonians, and the Ephesians are given to read."[92]

- Tertullian, again: "On the Epistle to the Laodiceans. By the church's truth we have it that this epistle was sent to the Ephesians, not the Laodiceans: Marcion has been at pains some time to falsify its title, in this matter too an industrious discoverer of new ways. But the title is of no concern, since when the apostle [Paul] wrote to some he wrote to all, and without doubt his teaching in Christ was of that God to whom the facts of his teaching rightly belong."[93]

- Muratorian Fragment (Canon): "As for the epistles of Paul, they themselves make clear to those desiring to understand, which ones they are, from what place, or for what reason they were sent. First of all, to the Corinthians, … next, to the Galatians, … then to the Romans he wrote at length. … It is necessary for us to

---

[86] Best, *Ephesians*, 15, is skeptical that *1 Clement* is dependent on Ephesians. Nevertheless, he draws a firm conclusion about dating: "This examination of the Apostolic Fathers shows there is a fair possibility that either Ignatius or Polycarp or both knew Ephesians; it may then have been known by AD 110 and therefore must have been written some time prior to that. This would suggest a date prior to AD 90" (17).

[87] See Guthrie, *New Testament Introduction*, 503–4, 796.

[88] Irenaeus, *Against Heresies*, 5:2.3 (*ANF* 1:528).

[89] Irenaeus, *Against Heresies*, 1:3.4; 1:8.4, 5; 2:2.5; 3:18.3; 4:20.2; 4:27.4; 4:32.1; 4:37.4; 5:8.1; 5:14.3; 5:24.4; 5:31.1.

[90] Hippolytus, *Refutation of All Heresies* (*Philosophoumena*), 6:29.

[91] Clement of Alexandria, *Stromata*, 4:8. His quotation of Eph 4:13–15 in *The Instructor*, 1:5, is similarly attributed to "the apostle."

[92] Tertullian, *Against Marcion*, 4:5.1 (trans. Evans).

[93] Tertullian, *Against Marcion*, 5:17.1 (trans. Evans). The fact that Marcion included it in his canon means by definition that he, too, accepted it as Pauline. The dispute was over its addressees, not its author.

discuss these one by one, since the blessed apostle Paul himself, following the example of his predecessor John, writes by name to only seven churches in the following sequence: To the Corinthians first, to the Ephesians second, …"[94]

At the close of the second century, therefore, the unanimous testimony of the church was that Paul wrote the epistle to the Ephesians.

Arguments against Pauline Authorship

The earliest scholar to publish doubts about Pauline authorship of Ephesians was Evanson (1792), followed by Usteri (1824) and de Wette (1826).[95] It was de Wette who made a significant impression on F. C. Baur (1845), who formulated most of the arguments that characterize critical Pauline studies today. Doubtless, both diligent critics and apologists will be less than satisfied with the following brief overview of the case against Pauline authorship. Standard NT introductions like Donald Guthrie's present both sides fairly. The case for the prosecution is most forcefully and thoroughly presented by Andrew Lincoln and Ernest Best. Markus Barth exhaustively pursues the case for the defense.[96] The evidence will strike the reader as somewhat piecemeal; there is no "smoking gun" or trump card. The prosecutors accept this reality, but contend nonetheless:

> First, it is not claimed that Ephesians has many—or even any—characteristics *flagrantly* incompatible with Pauline authorship. Rather the case against Pauline authorship—well-nigh overwhelming though it is, in my opinion— rests upon the *cumulative* force of a number of considerations, none of which would be decisive, or even perhaps readily attract notice, by itself.[97]

There is a weakness in this contention—and Pauline defenders have identified here an unwillingness on the part of the critics to accept a careful examination of their evidence point by point[98]—but it is not inherently illogical to accept the notion of cumulative evidence.[99] Whether the strength of the overall case is weakened when its individual strands are cut remains to be seen.

---

[94] Translation from http://www.catholicscripture.net/enchiridion/Muratorian.html.

[95] This triumvirate is regularly cited in the commentaries. Edward Evanson, *The Dissonance of the Four Generally Received Evangelists and the Evidence of Their Respective Authenticity Examined* (Ipswich: George Jermyn, 1792); Leonhard Usteri, *Entwicklung des paulinischen Lehrbegriffs* (Zürich: Orell, Füssli und Compagnie, 1824), 2–8; W. M. L. de Wette, *Lehrbuch der historisch-kritischen Einleitung in die kanonischen Bücher der Neuen Testaments* (Berlin: Reimer, 1826), 254–65.

[96] See Lincoln, *Ephesians*, lix–lxxiii; Best, *Ephesians*, 6–36; Barth, *Ephesians*, 1:4–50; see also Nineham, "The Case against the Pauline Authorship"; Sanders, "The Case for the Pauline Authorship."

[97] Nineham, "The Case against the Pauline Authorship," 23.

[98] Guthrie, *New Testament Introduction*, 509.

[99] Lincoln, *Ephesians*, lxix.

Style

No careful reader can fail to notice the distinctive character of Ephesians in comparison to Galatians or Romans, especially as it is concentrated in the very first chapter. Without any prejudice, Erasmus first commented on its dissonant style;[100] Baur found it incompatible with his experience of Paul.[101] Sanday and Headlam, while offering no comment on authenticity, graphically portrayed the difference: in comparison to the "rapid, terse, incisive" style of Romans, in Ephesians "we have a slowly-moving onwards-advancing mass, like a glacier working its way inch by inch down the valley."[102] This impression is generated by the following features, which might be summed up as "he rarely uses one word when two will do"![103]

Unusually Long Sentences

Ephesians begins with the longest sentence in the NT (1:3–14, comprised of 204 Greek words), followed on its heels by the second longest (1:15–23; 169 words). The rest of the letter is dominated by long sentences which, though individually comparable to some long sentences in Paul's other letters, are notable for their frequency in Ephesians (e.g., 2:1–7; 3:1–7; 4:11–16).

Lengthy, Often Redundant Genitive Constructions

This is perhaps the letter's most distinctive linguistic feature. Examples:

- εἰς ἔπαινον δόξης τῆς χάριτος αὐτοῦ, literally, "to the praise of the glory of the grace of him" (1:6; cf. 1:12, 14)
- ὁ πλοῦτος τῆς δόξης τῆς κληρονομίας αὐτοῦ, literally, "the richness of the glory of the inheritance of him" (1:18)
- τὸ ὑπερβάλλον μέγεθος τῆς δυνάμεως αὐτοῦ, literally, "the surpassing greatness of the power of him" (1:19)
- τὴν ἐνέργειαν τοῦ κράτους τῆς ἰσχύος αὐτοῦ, literally, "the working of the strength of the might of him" (1:19)
- τὸ μεσότοιχον τοῦ φραγμοῦ, literally, "the dividing wall of the fence" (2:14)

---

[100] Erasmus, *Annotationes in Novum Testamentum* (Basel, 1519), 413: "Certe stilus tantum dissonat a ceteris Pauli epistolis, ut alterius videri possit, nisi pectus atque indoles Paulinae mentis hanc prorsus illi vindicarent" (quoted in Schlier, *Epheser*, 18, n. 3). "For sure, the way of writing is so different to Paul's other letters, that it would seem to be the work of someone else, if the thoughts and manners of Paul's mind did not so thoroughly prove it to be his" (trans. Edward Naumann). Lincoln, *Ephesians*, lxii, incorrectly asserts that Erasmus "had doubts about the letter's authenticity because of its style."

[101] Baur, *Paul, the Apostle of Jesus Christ*, 2:35: "In its heavy long-drawn periods, laden with far-fetched and magniloquent expressions, we miss both the lively dialectical process and the wealth of thought for which the apostle is distinguished."

[102] William Sanday and Arthur C. Headlam, *A Critical and Exegetical Commentary on the Epistle to the Romans* (5th ed.; International Critical Commentary; Edinburgh: T&T Clark, 1902), lv. So also Käsemann, "Ephesians and Acts," 289: "The freshness and vitality of the Pauline language stands in contrast with Ephesians which, like the Fourth Gospel, has a remarkable hieratic style which often sounds turgid in our ears."

[103] Best, *Ephesians*, 8. This is sometimes called a "pleonastic" style.

- εἰς πάσας τὰς γενεὰς τοῦ αἰῶνος τῶν αἰώνων, literally, "into all the generations of the age of the ages" (3:21)
- ἐν τῷ κράτει τῆς ἰσχύος αὐτοῦ, literally, "in the strength of the might of him" (6:10)

It is particularly noteworthy that so many of these genitive chains feature genitives of quality—a Hebraic construction that has greater impact than an adjectival phrase (also used when Hebrew lacks an appropriate adjective) (cf. 2:2; 4:16, 22; 5:6, 8).[104]

Frequent, Redundant Association of a Cognate Noun and Verb[105]

- τῆς χάριτος αὐτοῦ ἧς ἐχαρίτωσεν ἡμᾶς, literally, "his grace that he graciously bestowed on us" (1:6)
- παντὸς ὀνόματος ὀνομαζομένου, "every name that is named" (1:21)
- τὴν πολλὴν ἀγάπην αὐτοῦ ἣν ἠγάπησεν ἡμᾶς, "his great love with which he loved us" (2:4)
- τὴν δωρεὰν ... τῆς δοθείσης μοι, "the gift ... that was given to me" (3:7; cf. 4:7)
- τῆς κλήσεως ἧς ἐκλήθητε, "the calling by which you were called" (4:1; cf. 4:4)

Synonyms Connected by καί, "And"

- ἁγίους καὶ ἀμώμους, "holy and without blemish" (1:4; cf. 5:27)
- ἀρχῆς καὶ ἐξουσίας καὶ δυνάμεως καὶ κυριότητος, "ruler and authority and power and lordship" (1:21)
- τοῖς παραπτώμασιν καὶ ταῖς ἁμαρτίαις, "trespasses and sins" (2:1)
- ξένοι καὶ πάροικοι, "strangers and sojourners" (2:19)
- ἐρριζωμένοι καὶ τεθεμελιωμένοι, "rooted and founded" (3:17)
- κλυδωνιζόμενοι καὶ περιφερόμενοι, "tossed to and fro and carried about" (4:14)
- προσφορὰν καὶ θυσίαν, "offering and sacrifice" (5:2)
- ψαλμοῖς καὶ ὕμνοις καὶ ᾠδαῖς, "psalms and hymns and songs" (5:19)
- ἐκτρέφει καὶ θάλπει, "nourishes and cherishes" (5:29)

Frequent and Lengthy Prepositional Phrases

- ἐν ἀγάπῃ προορίσας ἡμᾶς εἰς υἱοθεσίαν διὰ Ἰησοῦ Χριστοῦ εἰς αὐτόν, κατὰ τὴν εὐδοκίαν τοῦ θελήματος αὐτοῦ, literally, "in love having predestined us for adoption as sons through Jesus Christ for him, according to the good pleasure of the will of him" (1:4–5)
- κατὰ πρόθεσιν τοῦ τὰ πάντα ἐνεργοῦντος κατὰ τὴν βουλὴν τοῦ θελήματος αὐτοῦ, "according to the purpose of the One who accomplishes all things according to the plan of his will" (1:11)
- διὰ πάσης ἁφῆς τῆς ἐπιχορηγίας κατ᾽ ἐνέργειαν ἐν μέτρῳ ἑνὸς ἑκάστου μέρους τὴν αὔξησιν τοῦ σώματος ποιεῖται εἰς οἰκοδομὴν ἑαυτοῦ ἐν ἀγάπῃ,

---

[104] Barth, *Ephesians*, 1:5, n. 4. Best, 29, notes that Semitisms are many times more frequent in Ephesians than in the rest of Pauline literature.

[105] See also "Repetition" in "Oral Patterning in Paul's Epistles" in "Orality and the Interpretation of the Epistles: A Brief Introduction" above.

literally, "through every ligament of provision, in accord with [his] activity in the apportioning of each single part, makes growth of the body toward its building up in love" (4:16)

Preference for Relative Clauses and Participial Constructions

As one would expect, this feature is most prominent in the book's lengthy sentences (particularly 1:3–14; 1:15–23). While Paul has a fondness for attaching a string of participles to a main verb, in Ephesians this penchant reaches epic proportions (see also 2:1–7; 2:14–16; 3:2–7; 3:8–12; 3:14–19; 4:11–16; 5:15–21; 5:25–28; 6:18–20).

Rich Use of Adjectives and Adjectival Phrases

Just as the letter is characterized by frequent and lengthy genitive constructions, many of which are adjectival in nature, so also the author is reluctant to leave any noun unmodified.

- πάσῃ εὐλογίᾳ πνευματικῇ, literally, "every *Spiritual* blessing" (1:3)
- τὸ ὑπερβάλλον μέγεθος τῆς δυνάμεως αὐτοῦ, "the *surpassing* greatness of *his* power" (1:19)
- τὸ ὑπερβάλλον πλοῦτος τῆς χάριτος αὐτοῦ ἐν χρηστότητι, "the *surpassing* richness of *his* grace *in kindness*" (2:7)
- τὸν νόμον τῶν ἐντολῶν ἐν δόγμασιν, "the Law *of commandments in decrees*" (2:15)
- τὸν καινὸν ἄνθρωπον τὸν κατὰ θεὸν κτισθέντα ἐν δικαιοσύνῃ καὶ ὁσιότητι τῆς ἀληθείας, "the *new* man who has been created *according to God's [likeness] in true righteousness and holiness*" (4:24)
- τοῖς ἔργοις τοῖς ἀκάρποις τοῦ σκότους, "the *fruitless* works *of darkness*" (5:11)
- ἵνα παραστήσῃ αὐτὸς ἑαυτῷ ἔνδοξον τὴν ἐκκλησίαν, μὴ ἔχουσαν σπίλον ἢ ῥυτίδα ἤ τι τῶν τοιούτων, ἀλλ᾽ ἵνα ᾖ ἁγία καὶ ἄμωμος, "that he himself might present to himself a *glorious* church, not having a *spot* or *wrinkle* or any *of such things*, but that she might be *holy* and *without blemish*" (5:27)

Vocabulary

Today there is consensus that Ephesians has no greater number of unique words than is average for Pauline letters. However, this observation is usually qualified by a pair of secondary observations. "It contains 40 *hapax legomena* for the NT and 51 further words not found in the undisputed Pauline letters," notes Lincoln.[106] In other words, while its vocabulary (by this measure) differs no more from the rest of the NT than other Pauline epistles, it appears also to differ from the undisputed Pauline letters as a group more than they do from one another. Furthermore, such unique vocabulary tends to find parallels first in

---

[106] Lincoln, *Ephesians*, lxv, citing Ernst Percy, *Die Probleme der Kolosser- und Epheserbriefe* (Lund: Gleerup, 1946), 179–80. A search in BibleWorks 8 turns up thirty-five NT hapax legomena in Ephesians and five words occurring twice in Ephesians but not elsewhere in the NT.

the Pastoral Epistles and second in early postapostolic literature.[107] While those who hold to Pauline authorship of the Pastorals would be unconcerned by this observation, the majority of scholars who reject the same find that such parallels with late first-century Christian vocabulary cast doubt on Pauline authorship. This is another example of circular reasoning: the argument against Pauline authorship of Ephesians is supposedly bolstered by the letter's linguistic similarity to the Pastoral Epistles. But the critical judgment that the Pastorals are not Pauline is itself based (at least partly) on dubious linguistic analysis. And who is to say that the postapostolic fathers did not derive their characteristic vocabulary from Paul's own writings? This is a fragile house of cards. The following are examples of rare terms in Ephesians that appear to align it with non-Pauline writings:[108]

- διάβολος, "devil" (4:27; 6:11), which is used elsewhere in Paul only in the Pastorals, where it occurs six times; Paul more often uses Σατανᾶς, "Satan" (ten times, including twice in the Pastorals)
- ἀσωτία, "debauchery" (5:18; elsewhere in the NT only in Titus 1:6; 1 Pet 4:4)
- πολιτεία, "commonwealth" (2:12; elsewhere in the NT only in Acts 22:28)
- χαριτόω, "show grace" (1:6; elsewhere in the NT only in Lk 1:28); Paul elsewhere uses δίδωμι χάριν, "give grace" (e.g., Rom 12:3; 1 Cor 1:4)

In addition, there are a number of unusual phrases in Ephesians:

- ἔργα ἀγαθά, "good works" (2:10; this plural phrase occurs elsewhere in the NT only in Acts 9:36; 1 Tim 2:10)[109]
- ἐν τοῖς ἐπουρανίοις, literally, "in the heavenlies" occurs five times in Ephesians (1:3, 20; 2:6; 3:10; 6:12) and not elsewhere in the NT[110]
- ὁ ἠγαπημένος, "the Beloved" (1:6); only here in the NT is this term used of Christ, while it is so used perhaps twelve times in the Apostolic Fathers[111]

Aside from unusual vocabulary, there are unique emphases in Ephesians. It is claimed that the prepositions ἐν, "in," and κατά, "according to," occur more frequently (on a proportionate basis) in this book than in other writings by

[107] Lincoln, *Ephesians*, lxv, with Schnackenburg, *Ephesians*, 26, n. 19, cites the following examples: ἄθεος, "without God" (2:12); ἄσοφος, "unwise" (5:15); ἑνότης, "unity" (4:3, 13); εὔνοια, "willingness" (6:7); εὔσπλαγχνος, "tenderhearted" (4:32); κληρόω, "to appoint" (1:11); μέγεθος, "greatness" (1:19); ὁσιότης, "holiness" (4:24); and συνοικοδομέω, "to build up together" (2:22). This list, however, is scarcely persuasive as many of these terms are cognate with common Pauline words. Cannot a man who often writes σόφος, "wise," also occasionally write ἄσοφος, "unwise"?

[108] See Best, *Ephesians*, 28–29.

[109] The singular phrase ἔργον ἀγαθόν (or ἀγαθόν ἔργον), "good work," occurs eleven times in the Pauline corpus: Rom 2:7; 13:3; 2 Cor 9:8; Phil 1:6; Col 1:10; 2 Thess 2:17; 1 Tim 5:10; 2 Tim 2:21; 3:17; Titus 1:16; 3:1.

[110] Paul, however, does use the adjective ἐπουράνιος, "heavenly," quite frequently: also 1 Cor 15:40 (twice), 48 (twice), 49; Phil 2:10; 2 Tim 4:18. Elsewhere it occurs six times in Hebrews and once in John (3:12).

[111] But the Gospels use ὁ ἀγαπητός, "the Beloved One," of Christ (e.g., Mt 3:17; 12:18; 17:5), and Paul frequently speaks of Christians as "beloved" (ἀγαπητοί and ἠγαπημένοι).

Paul—which is consistent with the frequency of prepositional phrases in general (see "Frequent and Lengthy Prepositional Phrases," above in "Authorship") and also Ephesians' thematic emphasis on being "in Christ."[112] Most stark, however, is the frequent occurrence of the adjective πᾶς, "all." Its fifty-two (!) occurrences in Ephesians ranks it behind only Colossians in the NT on a percentage basis.[113]

Thought/Theology

Werner Kümmel's standard critical introduction to the NT baldly asserts: "The theology of Eph makes the Pauline composition of the letter completely impossible."[114] The following factors are usually cited in support of such a view.

View of the Apostolic Ministry

The assertion that the church is "built up upon the foundation of the apostles and prophets, the cornerstone being Christ Jesus himself" (2:20) is thought to be at variance with how Paul diminishes the apostles in his first letter to the Corinthians: "For no one is able to lay another foundation than that which is laid, which is Jesus Christ" (1 Cor 3:11; cf. 1 Cor 1:13). Second, calling the apostles "holy" and pairing them with the "prophets" (Eph 3:5)[115] is thought to reflect a stage after the death of the apostles (cf. Rev 18:20; 21:14).[116] Third, the description of the apostles as gifts to the church from the ascended Christ (Eph 4:10–11) is considered to be arrogant if from the hand of Paul, but characteristic of a later period in which the apostles have become revered historical figures. Finally, one might add that the letter's similarly high regard for other officeholders in the church, including "pastors and teachers" (4:11), is often

---

[112] Lincoln, *Ephesians*, lxv. Such claims can now be easily tested via computer. ἐν certainly occurs *most* frequently on a percentage basis in Ephesians and Colossians (particularly because of their emphasis on "in Christ"), but not significantly more often than in the rest of Paul; the statistics on κατά are even less persuasive.

[113] As a percentage of total words, πᾶς counts for 2.147 percent of Ephesians; only Colossians exceeds it at 2.467 percent (thirty-nine times). One must note, however, that Philippians isn't far behind (2.026 percent of its words are πᾶς, "all"). By raw numbers, the total of fifty-two occurrences of πᾶς, "all," in Ephesians is equaled in the Pauline epistles by 2 Corinthians and bettered by 1 Corinthians (one hundred twelve times) and Romans (seventy times), though those three are significantly longer letters. If NT books are ranked by their percentage of words that are πᾶς, "all," eleven of the top fifteen are Pauline epistles. In other words, though Ephesians ranks near the top in its frequent use of πᾶς, "all," this *is* Pauline style!

[114] Werner Georg Kümmel, *Introduction to the New Testament* (17th [rev.] ed.; trans. Howard Clark Kee; Nashville: Abingdon, 1975), 360.

[115] Käsemann, "Ephesians and Acts," 291: "The fact that in vs. 5 the holy apostles and prophets are mentioned points to a past period whose representatives are, in a redemptive-historical perspective, separated not only from earlier generations but are also, as recipients of revelation, set apart from the rest of mankind in general."

[116] Baur, *Paul, the Apostle of Jesus Christ*, 2:32:

> But the chief point is that this designation is not found in any other passage of an apostolical letter, but becomes a standing predicate of the apostles in a later age, which the greater the distance from them, looked up to them with the humbler reverence. The author of the Epistle, then, seems here to have made a slip, and to have betrayed himself involuntarily as a different man from the apostle, and as living in a later age.

thought to reflect the supposedly more highly structured, institutional church of the postapostolic era.[117]

Ecclesiology

Ephesians uses the noun ἐκκλησία, "church," exclusively of the universal church;[118] other Pauline letters, critics claim, use ἐκκλησία more frequently of the local "church" or congregation. It is also claimed that Ephesians has a shift in emphasis, even in comparison with its twin, Colossians: rather than Christ (the church's Head), the church itself becomes the center of attention.[119] In addition, the relationship of Jew and Gentile within the church is viewed by the author as a settled question, while in other Pauline letters it appears to remain a live debate.[120] Thus, the church has reached a "catholic" settlement in which the unity of the church, as the highest goal, has been achieved.[121] Some would contend that Eph 2:11–22 alludes to the destruction of the temple (AD 70), which would place the letter's writing after the death of Paul (ca. AD 64–68).

Christology

Critics discern a shift in the letter's depiction of Christ compared to the undisputed Pauline epistles. They maintain that Ephesians does not mention the incarnation (though perhaps in 4:9); it does not describe Christ's work with the vocabulary of "justification" (see below); and the cross is not central. When Ephesians does mention the cross, it is simply as the means by which Jew and

---

[117] The classic expression of this view is Helmut Merklein, *Das kirchliche Amt nach dem Epheserbrief* (Munich: Kösel, 1973). In the same year, a "charismatic" alternative was presented by Karl Martin Fischer, *Tendenz und Absicht des Epheserbriefes* (Göttingen: Vandenhoeck & Ruprecht, 1973).

[118] Eph 1:22; 3:10, 21; 5:23, 24, 25, 27, 29, 32.

[119] E.g., Best, *Ephesians*, 33; cf. Goodspeed, *The Key to Ephesians*, v. Käsemann, "Ephesians and Acts," 290: "Closely related to this is the fact that the church itself more and more becomes the content of theology. For Ephesians as for Acts, it is the 'center of time,' i.e., the exclusive place and means of salvation—in this regard the eschatological phenomenon per se."

[120] Guthrie, *New Testament Introduction*, 505; Lincoln, *Ephesians*, lxiii; Nineham, "The Case against the Pauline Authorship," 33.

[121] Ferdinand Christian Baur, *Geschichte der christlichen Kirche* (3rd ed.; 5 vols.; Tübingen: Fues, 1863–1877), 1:120:

Es ist, wenn wir uns in die Anschauungsweise dieser Briefe hineinversetzen, schon ein ächt katholisches Bewusstsein, das sich in ihnen ausspricht, und wenn wir sie einerseits mit dem Hebräerbrief, andererseits mit den pseudoclementinischen Schriften zusammenstellen, so erhalten wir drei verschiedene Grundanschauungen des Christentums, in welchen dasselbe Streben nach Einheit seinen höchsten Ausdruck und dogmatischen Anknüpfungspunkt zu finden sucht.

If we immerse ourselves in the viewpoint of these letters, [we find] it is already a genuinely Catholic consciousness that is expressed in them. And if we read them alongside the letter to the Hebrews on the one hand, and the pseudo-Clementine writings on the other, we obtain three different fundamental perspectives on Christianity, in which [nevertheless] the very same striving after unity seeks its highest expression and dogmatic point of contact.

Gentile are reconciled to each other (2:16).[122] In place of these typical Pauline emphases, Ephesians gives a central place to Christ's ascension, session at the right hand of God, and glorification (1:20–21; 2:6; 4:8–10). In contrast to Romans 6, the Christian is not said to die with Christ, but rather to rise and ascend with him (Eph 2:5–6). The divinity of Christ is more prominent:[123] Ephesians ascribes to Christ divine activities such as reconciliation (2:16) that Paul elsewhere ascribes to God the Father (2 Cor 5:19; cf. Rom 5:11; Col 1:20). So also the officeholders in the church are said to be Christ's gifts (Eph 4:10–11) rather than God's (1 Cor 12:28).

Gnosticism

A major platform of Baur's argument was the discernment of Gnostic elements in the letter. He contended that Ephesian concepts like the church as the body of Christ, the church's marriage with Christ, his descent into hell, his ascension above the layers of spiritual powers, and the language of "mystery" were evidence of Gnostic thinking. At great length he identified vocabulary held in common with the Valentinians.[124] He concluded that these data "make us think that the Epistle to the Ephesians especially is of post-apostolic origin, and dates from a time when the Gnostic ideas were just coming into circulation, and still wore the garb of innocent Christian speculations."[125] One must acknowledge that this particular feature of Baur's argument has lost considerable ground. No one today would suggest that Ephesians was actually written in the second century when Gnosticism became an identifiable school of thought. However,

---

[122] This observation is usually coupled with the previously noted assertion about its ecclesiology: that the unity of the church is the utmost concern. Thus, Baur, *Geschichte der christlichen Kirche*, 1:116:

> Auch sie [Ephesians and Colossians] ringen nach einer Auffassung des Christenthums, in welcher der Unterschied der Judenchristen und Heidenchristen in der concreten Anschauung einer über den Gegensätzen stehenden Einheit von selbst ein verschwindendes Moment des gemeinsamen religiösen Bewusstseins wird. Allgemeine Versöhnung, Vereinigung des Getrennten und Entzweiten ist die höchste durch den ganzen Inhalt der beiden Briefe hindurchgehende Idee, auf welche sich alles bezieht, und deren höchster Ausdruck die Christologie dieser Briefe ist. Alles im Himmel und auf Erden soll in Christus Eins werden.

> These [Ephesians and Colossians], too, strive for a conception of Christianity in which the distinction between Jewish Christians and Gentile Christians, in the concrete perspective of a unity that transcends these contrasts in and of itself, becomes but an insignificant element of a common religious consciousness. Universal reconciliation, unification of what is separated and divided, is the highest idea permeating the entire content of the two letters. Everything relates to that point, and its highest expression is the Christology of these letters. Everything in heaven and on earth shall become one in Christ.

[123] Baur, *Geschichte der christlichen Kirche*, 2:35, first spoke of "higher views of the person of Christ."

[124] The shared vocables include πλήρωμα, "fullness"; σῶμα, "body"; σοφία, "wisdom"; αἰών, "age"; μυστήριον, "mystery"; κοσμοκράτωρ, "world ruler"; and φῶς, "light" (see Baur, *Paul, the Apostle of Jesus Christ*, 2:9–22).

[125] Baur, *Paul, the Apostle of Jesus Christ*, 2:22. Baur, 2:22–26, also finds elements consistent with later Montanism, especially the use of πνεῦμα, "Spirit," and the role of prophets.

many critics still contend that Ephesians bears the marks of a later Christian *Sitz im Leben*, when proto-Gnostic ideas were beginning to trouble the church.[126]

Soteriology

Several factors characterize the claim that the soteriology of Ephesians differs from that of the undisputed Pauline letters. First, the vocabulary of "justification" (δικαιόω and cognates) is supposedly lacking or less prominent.[127] Related to this is Baur's contention that the letter weakens its otherwise stellar presentation of salvation by grace through the intimate and consistent attachment of good works.[128] Second, then, the letter seems to give the cross and death of Christ a diminished role (see "Christology," above in "Authorship"). Third, the statement that Christ has nullified the Law (2:15) would seem to be at variance with Paul's claim that he does not abolish the Law (Rom 3:31). Finally, salvation is described as a present reality for the baptized (2:5, 8), while Paul more regularly speaks of it as a future event.[129]

Sacramental Theology

While many commentators do not see a strong sacramental focus in the letter[130] and the Lord's Supper does not feature in any direct way,[131] the appeal to Baptism as the source of the church's unity in the context of a creedal

---

[126] The two most prominent proponents of the Gnostic interpretation of Ephesians in the twentieth century were Heinrich Schlier, *Christus und die Kirche im Epheserbrief* (BHT 6; Tübingen: Mohr, 1930), and Ernst Käsemann, *Leib und Leib Christi: Eine Untersuchung zur paulinischen Begrifflichkeit* (BHT 9; Tübingen: Mohr, 1933).

[127] While there are four such occurrences in Ephesians (δικαιοσύνη or δίκαιος in 4:24; 5:9; 6:1, 14), critics will contend that the word group is used of right behavior rather than justification; that interpretation is challenged in our commentary.

[128] Baur, *Paul, the Apostle of Jesus Christ*, 2:39: "The writer of the Epistle to the Ephesians cannot, as a true follower of Paul, degrade the Pauline doctrine of justification from the position which belongs to it; yet hardly has he mentioned faith, when he appears, although unconsciously, to be unable to refrain from going on to speak of works or love." Baur cites 2:8–10; 3:17–18; 6:23 and suggests that 2:10 is "adopted from the doctrine of James." He continues:

> Works are thus to go by the side of faith, but instead of faith being alleged to be the foundation of them, they are placed by the side of faith as the final purpose of the creation of men. … By setting faith and love in this relation to each other, justice is to be done to both parties; and we see that in these Epistles [Ephesians and Colossians], Gentile and Jewish Christians are placed side by side, as equally privileged members of the Christian Church. (2:40)

> The deeper reason of the difference [between Ephesians and the "genuine Pauline view"] is, that the peculiar Pauline conception of faith is not familiar to these Epistles. They know nothing of faith as an inward process in the consciousness, the most essential part of which is a personal conviction and experience of the impossibility of justification through the law. Hence the object of this faith, the death of Christ, remains purely external to them. (2:41)

[129] Rom 5:9; 10:9–10, 13; 13:11; Phil 2:12; 1 Thess 5:9.

[130] E.g., Lincoln, *Ephesians*, lxxix: "The single mention of the term 'baptism' (4:5) in a context devoted not to baptism but to unity, and a few metaphors, behind which a baptismal reference may lie, make it unlikely that baptism itself was a major concern in the writing of the letter."

[131] This commentary sees allusions to the Lord's Supper, however, in 1:7; 4:4; 5:3–20, 29–31; 6:18–24 and to eucharistic praying in 1:3–14; 3:14–21.

formulation (4:4–6) is often thought to represent a theology too developed for Paul. At the very least, the letter's view of Baptism is considered to have more in common with the Apostolic Fathers than with Paul.[132]

Eschatology

While Paul's letters maintain a tension between "now" and "not yet," directing the Christian both to the present reality of justification and to the imminent rescue of salvation on the Last Day at the return of Christ, certain features of Ephesians suggest to critics that the dynamic has been weakened. Not only salvation (2:5, 8; see above) but also resurrection and ascension are viewed as present realities for the baptized (2:5–6). Paul, by contrast, once warned of those false teachers who claimed that there was no resurrection yet to come (1 Cor 15:12; cf. 2 Tim 2:18). The letter's positive view of marriage, not only as an institution in which the traditional roles of husband and wife are maintained but also as a positive portrayal of the Gospel (5:21–33), allegedly contrasts with Paul's skepticism of its value in light of the imminent return of Christ (1 Cor 7:25–40). In fact, the letter supposedly has no interest in the second coming,[133] but describes a church that is resigned to "hunkering down for the long haul"[134] by assigning roles to everyone from pastors (4:11–12) to husbands/wives, parents/children, and masters/slaves (5:21–6:9). Ernest Best calls this "fully realised soteriology."[135]

Incipient Catholicism

The German term *Frühkatholizismus* ("incipient Catholicism") sums up the theological features we have noted above. Raymond Brown defines this as "the initial stages of high ecclesiology, sacramentalism, hierarchy, ordination, and dogma," and notes:

> At the beginning of the 20th century A. von Harnack suggested that there was no early Catholicism in the NT; rather, such theology and church organization were a development that began in the 2d century under the influence of the Greek spirit, distorting the pristine evangelical character of Christianity (to which the Reformation returned). In a challenge to that position E. Käsemann has been prominent in contending that there is "Early Catholicism" in the NT itself, but that these developments were not necessarily normative for Christianity. He resorted to the principle of "the canon within the canon."

---

[132] Baur, *Paul, the Apostle of Jesus Christ*, 2:42: "This statement that Christian baptism was to have the same meaning with Jewish circumcision [Col 2:11–12; cf. Eph 2:5, 11; 4:5] is one we meet with elsewhere in post-Apostolic writings."

[133] Schnackenburg, *Ephesians*, 27, considers it un-Pauline that the letter speaks only of an "inheritance" in heaven (1:14, 18; 5:5). The view is thus "turned upwards," not ahead. However, these passages describe an inheritance that is not yet attained.

[134] Käsemann, "Ephesians and Acts," 290: "Thereby, one takes a step away from early Christianity which understands itself eschatologically and moves toward the early Catholicism which regards itself as a force in history. Ephesians as well as Acts marks the moment of this transition."

[135] Best, *Ephesians*, 52.

> Just as Paul distinguished between the letter and the Spirit (II Cor 3), so the Christian cannot make an infallible authority out of the canonical NT but must distinguish the real Spirit within the NT.[136]

In other words, Käsemann wished not only to use the marks of *Frühkatholizismus* to identify those documents that were later and inauthentic but also to exclude them from the body of biblical literature whose authority he would recognize.

Käsemann's discernment of "incipient Catholicism" in Ephesians,[137] Luke, and Acts arises from an evolutionary, Hegelian model of NT development found, once again, in F. C. Baur.[138] Baur applied Hegel's dialectical interpretation of history to the apostolic period. In Gal 2:11 (cf. 1 Cor 1:12) he discerned the trace of an open conflict between two forms of Christianity represented by Peter and Paul, the former advocating a Judaic Christianity that maintained the ceremonial precepts of the Torah while confessing Christ as the Messiah, and the latter proclaiming a Law-free Christianity without ritual, dogma, or hierarchy. In the Apostolic Council of Acts 15, Baur saw the victors (re-)writing the history, presenting a calm reconciliation between the Petrine and Pauline visions of Christianity in a Catholic settlement under the headship of the bishop of Jerusalem. This was an example of Hegel's classic "thesis meets antithesis, conflicts, and results in synthesis":[139]

---

[136] Brown, *An Introduction to the New Testament*, 625–26. Käsemann's essay "Ephesians and Acts" is apropos. Bruce, *The Epistles to the Colossians, to Philemon, and to the Ephesians*, 237, focuses on ecclesiology: "Chief among the elements of incipient catholicism, so far as Ephesians is concerned, is the conception of the church throughout the world as a unity."

[137] Käsemann, "Ephesians and Acts," 288: "In the New Testament it is Ephesians that most clearly marks the transition from the Pauline tradition to the perspectives of the early Catholic era." See also his essay "Paul and Early Catholicism," in Ernst Käsemann, *New Testament Questions of Today* (Philadelphia: Fortress, 1969), 237–50.

[138] Baur, *Paul, the Apostle of Jesus Christ*, 2:38: "All this carries us to that period when, not without the ferment and commotion of conflicting elements, the Christian church was coming to realize herself and to achieve her unity." He identifies this period as "the immediately post-apostolic age." Lincoln, *Ephesians*, lxiv: "The concentration on this sort of ecclesiology with its vision of the universal Church as one (4:4), holy (5:26, 27), catholic (1:22, 23), and apostolic (2:20) in all probability reflects a stage beyond that of the ministry of Paul."

[139] Thanks to my Westfield colleague Glen Zweck for the visualization of Baur's application of Hegelian dialectic to the NT. Harris, *The Tübingen School*, 181–82, affirms this connection:

> The cornerstone of this new approach was found in the opposition between Pauline and Jewish Christianity. … According to Baur, this bitter confrontation between Gentile and Jewish Christianity, between Paul and the other apostles, between the universalism of the gospel and the bondage of the law not only dominated the apostolic age, but continued after Paul's death late into the second century. Only at the end of this century did the opposition diminish, when in the face of dangers from outside the Church a conciliatory movement gained ascendancy which brought the two hostile parties together, both being finally absorbed into the higher unity of the emerging catholic Church.

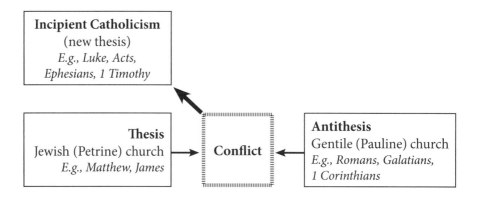

In another context, one might continue the process by introducing a new antithesis in the early history of the church (e.g., Marcionism), resulting in a new conflict, this time with incipient Catholicism, resulting in a new synthesis, and so on and so on. But for present purposes it is sufficient to note the influence that Baur's Hegelian analysis continues to have on the debate over Pauline authorship of Ephesians. Based on this principle, documents are dated according to where they fall along the presumed evolutionary process from the Pauline-Petrine conflict to the early Catholic resolution.[140]

The Literary Relationship between Ephesians and Other Pauline Epistles

The distinctive style, vocabulary, and thought of Ephesians in comparison to the undisputed Pauline letters has generated skepticism that the same apostle Paul could have written it. But the flipside of the Ephesian coin is its uncanny similarity to some Pauline letters, particularly Colossians. The "synoptic problem" resulting from the intense parallels between Ephesians and its fraternal twin, Colossians, has likewise raised doubt that one man could have written both. First, the statistics of their similarity are striking: (1) It is thought that a fourth of the *words* in Ephesians are found in Colossians, while a third of the words in the shorter letter Colossians are found in its longer twin.[141] (2) Between a third and half of the *verses* of Ephesians are parallel to

---

[140] Harris, *The Tübingen School*, 183–84, summarizes:

> Here [in Galatians] the bitter dispute with the Judaizers was at its height and Baur assumed that this hostility was to be found everywhere among the Jews to whom Paul carried the gospel. Nor did this hostility abate, but continued with undiminished intensity throughout the whole of Paul's life. To his gospel of freedom from the law was opposed the Jewish-Christian fanaticism for keeping the law, and the authentic Paulinism, according to Baur, was to be found where the opposition between the two factions was most evident. Where no evidence of such a struggle was to be seen in the writings of the early Church, the conclusion was to be drawn that such writings dated from a later period. Thus in Baur's view the only genuine letters from the hand of Paul were Romans, Galatians, 1 and 2 Corinthians; all other letters traditionally accepted as Pauline were unauthentic.

[141] Guthrie, *New Testament Introduction*, 501.

Colossians.[142] What complicates the relationship is the relative lack of a "synoptic outline"; that is, while such a large number of verses are parallel, they appear scattered in different locations in the parallel work. Critics allege, therefore, that one or the other is the product of a copyist who has excerpted almost at random from his source without being conscious of its inner coherence and logic. Substantial illustrations of this will be provided when Ephesians and Colossians are compared in more detail below and a proposed solution to this synoptic problem will be provided.[143] But one parallel text cited by Dennis Nineham serves as a representative example:

καὶ πᾶν ὅ τι ἐὰν ποιῆτε ἐν λόγῳ ἢ ἐν ἔργῳ, πάντα <u>ἐν ὀνόματι κυρίου Ἰησοῦ</u>, εὐχαριστοῦντες τῷ θεῷ πατρὶ δι' αὐτοῦ	εὐχαριστοῦντες πάντοτε ὑπὲρ πάντων <u>ἐν ὀνόματι τοῦ κυρίου ἡμῶν Ἰησοῦ Χριστοῦ</u> τῷ θεῷ καὶ πατρί
and everything whatsoever you do in word or in deed, [do] all things <u>in the name of the Lord Jesus</u>, giving thanks to God the Father through him (Col 3:17)	giving thanks always for all things <u>in the name of our Lord Jesus Christ</u> to [our] God and Father (Eph 5:20)

Nineham notes that the phrase "in the name of the Lord Jesus" serves a different function in the two texts. In Colossians (presumed to be the original) it appears to modify ποιῆτε, "you do," while in Ephesians it modifies εὐχαριστοῦντες, "giving thanks"—suggesting to Nineham that the second author has borrowed the phrase without understanding the grammatical structure of the text he was copying.[144]

Second, certain key vocabulary held in common between the two writings is allegedly used in rather different ways:

- In Ephesians (1:22; 4:15; 5:23) Christ is the κεφαλή, "Head," of his body, the church; in Colossians (2:10) he is the "Head" of the cosmic powers.
- In Ephesians (3:3, 4, 9) the content of the μυστήριον, "mystery," is how God will save the Gentiles through Christ; in Colossians (1:27; 2:2) the "mystery" is Christ himself.[145]

---

[142] Brown, *An Introduction to the New Testament*, 627.

[143] See "Relationship to Colossians" below.

[144] Nineham, "The Case against the Pauline Authorship," 30, citing Mitton, *Ephesians*, 253.

[145] Nineham, "The Case against the Pauline Authorship," 28: "In Colossians Paul seems to have made it [μυστήριον, 'mystery'] into something of a technical term to describe that which God had hitherto concealed from all eternity but now revealed; and the content of the *mystery* in Colossians is Christ himself, and particularly the amazing fact of his indwelling in his people of all sorts and kinds. ('Christ in you the hope of glory' [Col 1:27].)"

- In Ephesians οἰκονομία refers to God's "plan" or "strategy" (1:10; 3:9); in Colossians (1:25) it retains its more usual Pauline meaning of "entrusted task" (cf. 1 Cor 9:17).[146]

Critics find it difficult to conceive of an author making such changes in terminology when writing two letters in a presumably rapid succession.[147]

When Ephesians is compared to the other letters of the Pauline corpus, additional significant parallels appear. Some critics argue that Ephesians borrows from stellar passages in the Pauline corpus in a way that differs from the ordinary parallels found among the Pauline letters.[148] Since the argumentation and themes of Ephesians are most like Romans, the select examples in the chart on the next page are illustrative.[149] Such an exercise can be fruitfully repeated with other Pauline epistles to which Ephesians has significant parallels, particularly 1 Corinthians, Galatians, and 1 Timothy. Surely one must admit, however, that this is among the weakest of the arguments in the critics' arsenal: that Ephesians cannot be by Paul because it has too much in common with his major writings!

Raymond Brown expresses the conclusion that most critics have drawn from the above data:

> A plausible theory, then, would be that on the basis of the undisputed Pauline letters and especially of Col (which had been composed in the school earlier) someone in the Ephesian school of Paul's disciples produced Eph as an encouraging portrayal of aspects of Pauline thought.[150]

---

[146] Barth, *Ephesians*, 1:4, adds to these a list of other words supposedly used in an un-Pauline sense in Ephesians: κληρονομία, "inheritance" (1:14, 18; 5:5); περιποίησις, "possession" (1:14); πλήρωμα, "fullness" (1:10, 23; 3:19; 4:13); ἀνακεφαλαιόω, "to sum up" (1:10); and σῴζω, "to save" (2:5, 8).

[147] E.g., Lincoln, *Ephesians*, lxvii: "It is one thing for a writer to reproduce the same ideas in the same words or even in different words, but it is quite another for a writer within a short period of time to reproduce the same words and phrases to express different ideas" (cf. Nineham, "The Case against the Pauline Authorship," 27–28).

[148] Nineham, "The Case against the Pauline Authorship," 34, following Mitton, *Ephesians*, 108–9 (cf. Guthrie, *New Testament Introduction*, 503), claims that Ephesians has parallels to the Pauline corpus in 32.7 percent of its words, while Philippians, for example, has relatively fewer (15.2 percent). He also suggests that Ephesians gravitates toward "purple passages," while the parallels between other Pauline letters are more subtle. (By "purple passages," Nineham is referring to "striking and memorable" phrases, to use Mitton's terminology [113].) In other words, the author of Ephesians allegedly viewed the writings of the genuine Paul as a treasure trove to draw upon. Here Nineham takes the ironic position that Ephesians cannot be genuine because it is *too much* like Paul's letters.

[149] Lincoln, *Ephesians*, lviii, writes: "Ephesians makes greater use of Romans than any other letter, even when the latter's length is taken into consideration." Yet, while Ephesians seems to borrow extensively from Romans, Nineham, "The Case against the Pauline Authorship," 31, notes that it differs significantly in style: for example, while Romans is characterized by frequent rhetorical questions (every 6.5 lines), Ephesians contains only one question in the entire letter (4:9).

[150] Brown, *An Introduction to the New Testament*, 630.

Ephesians	Romans	Parallel Language or Thought
1:3–12	8:28–30	God's plan, predestination, and election of the saints
1:20–23; 2:4–8	8:29–30	Christ's glorification is connected to the glorification of every Christian in him
2:1–3, 11–12	1:18–3:20	a unity between Jew and Gentiles is found in their common failure to fulfill the Law of God
4:17	1:21	the depiction of the old idolatrous Gentile life as futile
1:21; 3:18–19	8:38–39	multidimensional depiction of Christ's love and his victory over hostile powers for the Christian
2:5–6	6:1–11	the baptized have died and risen with Christ
2:11–22	9:1–11:36	Jews and Gentiles are united in Christ
2:18	5:1–5	the access we have to the Father through Christ
3:17	11:18	the Christian is rooted in Christ
4:1–16	12:3–8	the gifts given by Christ to his body, the church
4:22–24; 5:3–14; 6:10–17	13:11–14	the transition from darkness to light in the life of the baptized and their clothing with the armor of Christ

Evaluation of the Case

In presenting the data adduced by those who dispute Pauline authorship of Ephesians, we have mostly refrained from raising any challenge. As we now turn to such an examination, we would remind the reader of the twofold goal with which we embarked on this exercise. First, exposing the evidence to scrutiny demonstrates the weakness of the case when it is held up against the uniform internal testimony of the letter and the unanimous external witness of the early church. But, second, *a close reading of the evidence also discloses the unique characteristics of Ephesians and moves the reader a significant way along the path toward understanding the letter.* In other words, much of the supposed evidence against Pauline authorship is nothing of the sort, but serves to put more substantial flesh onto the bones of the undisputed Paul and deepens our insight into his thought as expressed in Ephesians.

Style/Vocabulary

On the scales of judgment, the contention that the style of Ephesians is incompatible with Pauline authorship must be weighed against the universal acknowledgment that the letter's *structure* is thoroughly consistent with normal Pauline practice (see "Internal Evidence" in "The Case for Pauline Authorship," above in "Authorship"). The facts of the matter are, therefore, significantly different from those of Hebrews, for example. Not only does Hebrews lack any *claim* to Pauline authorship, but it is also not *structured* like a Pauline letter.[151] Thus, it is only partly true to say that the style of Ephesians differs from Paul's.

Certainly one cannot and ought not dispute the observation (beginning with Erasmus) that the letter's *linguistic* style is distinctive; the examples and analyses above mark out its contours. Such data, however, merely demonstrate that Paul did not *normally* write this way; they do not stand conclusively against Pauline authorship unless it could be proved that Paul *could not* have written in such a way. The data may simply be "evidence of Paul's versatility."[152] Whether there are enough data in Ephesians to determine that this style is impossible for Paul has been seriously questioned for two reasons.

First, statistical analysts have suggested that the amount of material from Paul's hand is too small to make a valid study.[153] There are only 2,422 words in Ephesians and a total of 32,407 words in the full thirteen-letter Pauline corpus. If the Pauline corpus were restricted to the seven more-or-less undisputed letters (excluding Ephesians, Colossians, 2 Thessalonians, and the Pastorals), the word count is only 24,092.[154] By either count, the full Pauline corpus is smaller than Luke-Acts and only slightly larger than the Johannine writings. For comparison's sake, the thirty-eight plays of Shakespeare contain a total of 884,647 words.[155] The entire Pauline corpus is thus similar in size to just *one* of Shakespeare's plays—and repeated attempts to attribute some of his plays to a different author have often faltered on the *small* size of the corpus.

Second, statistical analysis of style and vocabulary can only be truly scientific if one has other writings by the purported second author with which to

---

[151] Hebrews differs from the Pauline structure in its *opening*, but its *close*, with its request for prayer, its mention of peace, its final exhortation, its greetings, and its bestowal of grace, is quite Pauline.

[152] Guthrie, *New Testament Introduction*, 510. Further he contends: "The differences in usage must be shown to be incompatible in one mind at one period of time, and they must further be inconceivable in the works of the writer to whom they are attributed" (514).

[153] See William D. Mounce, *Pastoral Epistles* (Word Biblical Commentary 46; Nashville: Thomas Nelson, 2000), cxiii–cxvii. George Udny Yule, *The Statistical Study of Literary Vocabulary* (Cambridge: Cambridge University Press, 1944), 2, 281, warns that a text needs to be at least ten thousand words long to be a valid subject for statistical study. No Pauline letter satisfies this criterion. The total vocabulary (number of unique words) in Paul's letters is also far too small.

[154] These statistics are based on the Greek text of NA[27] via BibleWorks 8. Ironically, the present introduction to Ephesians, exceeding fifty thousand words, is longer than the entire Pauline corpus!

[155] See Marvin Spevack, *A Complete and Systematic Concordance to the Works of Shakespeare* (9 vols.; Hildesheim: Olms, 1968–1980).

compare the disputed work.[156] In other words, if it were claimed that Ephesians had been written by, say, Barnabas, and one had other writings by Barnabas, then one could make a reasoned comparison of the two corpora. But to date no critic has proposed that the alleged pseudonymous author of Ephesians is also the author of an extant body of other writings.

These observations are not intended to minimize the significance of the distinctive Ephesian style. Rather, they illustrate how difficult it would be to say with any certainty that it is un Pauline, in light of the very small size of Paul's body of writings, and how tenuous it would be to attribute Ephesians to another author in the absence of any extant contenders.

Hapax Legomena

The statistical problem applies in the same measure to questions of vocabulary. It has already been noted that Ephesians does not contain any more hapax legomena than Pauline letters of a similar size.[157] Raymond Brown himself admits: "The vocabulary argument that Eph has some eighty words not found in the undisputed Pauline letters loses much of its force when we know that about the same number may be found in Gal, which matches Eph roughly in length and in the number of diverse words it uses."[158]

The claim that the unique terms in Ephesians are frequently found in the postapostolic fathers is no more persuasive, for three reasons. First, consider that the gap between the traditional dating of Ephesians in the mid 50s and the earliest parallels in *1 Clement* in the mid 90s, for example, is only forty years (one or two generations). The time is too short to suggest that the vocabulary of Ephesians demonstrates a late date; to date the letter so precisely on the grounds of a few common words is quite unreasonable. Second, even if the claimed parallels of vocabulary with the early postapostolic fathers were deemed valid, the explanation need not be that the letters arose from *authors* in the same time period. It is just as likely that the commonalities are owing to a similar *audience* (as Ignatius, for example, also wrote his letters to Ephesus and other locations in Asia Minor) and/or to similar *topics* (as churches in the same area might have been united by common problems and needs). Third, there may be many quite sensible reasons why Ephesians very quickly became a *favorite* Pauline writing

---

[156] See Cadbury, "The Dilemma of Ephesians," 100–101. Cadbury, 95–96, frames the dilemma:

> In dealing with the possibility of the pseudonymous origin of Ephesians both sides are handicapped by the absence from Christian antiquity of cases where we can compare the spurious with the genuine writings of the same author. … Until we can discover an instance where close adherence to a known master's style has been aimed at in a definitely spurious composition it must be regarded as doubtful whether any imitator of Paul would or would not either strive for or unconsciously achieve the degree of stylistic similarity which exists between Ephesians and the Pauline *homologoumena*.

[157] P. N. Harrison, *The Problem of the Pastoral Epistles* (London: Oxford University Press, 1921), 20, notes that Ephesians has on average 4.6 hapax legomena per page, which is in line with the Pauline average (e.g., 5.6 in 2 Corinthians, and 6.2 in Philippians). Cited in Carson, Moo, and Morris, *An Introduction to the New Testament*, 308. By "page" Harrison is presumably referring to a standard critical edition of his day.

[158] Brown, *An Introduction to the New Testament*, 628.

among the early fathers and therefore influenced their vocabulary more than his other letters did. Certainly the parallels between Ephesians and Ignatius' letter to the Ephesians (see "Ignatius to the Ephesians" in "Addressees" below) illustrate all three of these phenomena.

Finally, one must give due weight to the significance of *subject matter* for the choice of vocabulary. Nowhere else does Paul speak in such detail of the armor of God (6:10–17), for example.[159] The hapax legomena and other unique vocabulary of the letter may, therefore, tell us less about authorship than about the letter's *themes*. The following list, therefore, helps focus the reader on the letter's *unique* themes (though not necessarily its *chief* themes). This list consists of forty words in Ephesians, thirty-five of which are NT hapax legomena, and five of which occur twice in Ephesians but nowhere else in the NT.[160]

NT Hapax Legomena and Other Terms Unique to Ephesians		
κληρόω	1:11	to appoint by lot, obtain an inheritance
προελπίζω	1:12	to hope before, be the first to hope
μέγεθος	1:19	size, greatness
ἄθεος	2:12	without God, godless
μεσότοιχον	2:14	a middle wall, dividing wall
συμπολίτης	2:19	a fellow citizen
συναρμολογέω (twice)	2:21 (also 4:16)	to fit or join together
συνοικοδομέω	2:22	to build (up) together
σύσσωμος	3:6	of the same body
συμμέτοχος (twice)	3:6 (also 5:7)	sharing with, partaking with
πολυποίκιλος	3:10	many-sided, manifold

[159] Best, *Ephesians*, 28, who denies Pauline authorship, nevertheless admits:

Hapax legomena are often counted as a help in determining authorship; they are in fact rarely a good guide since subject-matter affects the choice of words. Thus a considerable number of the *hapax legomena* in Ephesians are found in 6.14–17, a passage relating to military equipment, a subject to which Paul does not refer elsewhere in such detail. In fact the number of *hapax legomena* in Ephesians is not exceptional and therefore tells us nothing in respect of its authorship in relation to Paul.

[160] The list of words and their English glosses (provided merely for the convenience of the reader, without necessarily approving them) are drawn from the BibleWorks 8 flashcard module, from which the statistics were also drawn.

NT Hapax Legomena and Other Terms Unique to Ephesians		
ἐξισχύω	3:18	to be able, be strong enough
ἑνότης (twice)	4:3 (also 4:13)	oneness, unity
αἰχμαλωτεύω	4:8	to capture, take captive
κατώτερος	4:9	lower
καταρτισμός	4:12	equipment, equipping
ἑνότης (twice)	4:13 (also 4:3)	oneness, unity
κλυδωνίζομαι	4:14	to be tossed here and there by waves
κυβεία	4:14	craftiness, trickery
μεθοδεία (twice)	4:14 (also 6:11)	scheming, craftiness
συναρμολογέω (twice)	4:16 (also 2:21)	to fit or join together
ἀπαλγέω	4:19	to become callous, become dead to feeling, be despondent
ἀνανεόω	4:23	to renew, become young again
ἐπιδύω	4:26	to set, go down
παροργισμός	4:26	irritation, anger
αἰσχρότης	5:4	shamefulness, obscenity, filthiness
εὐτραπελία	5:4	coarse jesting
μωρολογία	5:4	foolish or silly talk
συμμέτοχος (twice)	5:7 (also 3:6)	sharing with, partaking with
κρυφῇ	5:12	secretly
ἐπιφαύσκω	5:14	to arise, appear, shine
ἄσοφος	5:15	unwise, foolish
ῥυτίς	5:27	a wrinkle
ἐκτρέφω (twice)	5:29 (also 6:4)	to nourish, rear, bring up
μακροχρόνιος	6:3	long-lived
ἐκτρέφω (twice)	6:4 (also 5:29)	to nourish, rear, bring up

NT Hapax Legomena and Other Terms Unique to Ephesians		
εὔνοια	6:7	favor, affection, goodwill
μεθοδεία (twice)	6:11 (also 4:14)	scheming, craftiness
κοσμοκράτωρ	6:12	a world ruler
πάλη	6:12	a struggle, fight
ἑτοιμασία	6:15	readiness, preparation
βέλος	6:16	an arrow
θυρεός	6:16	a shield
προσκαρτέρησις	6:18	perseverance, steadfastness
ἄνοιξις	6:19	an opening

The *clumping* of the unique terms in certain pericopes (marked in gray) is significant, for it illustrates how the frequency of hapax legomena can be dictated by subject matter. These terms exemplify the letter's unique concern for exposing and condemning the pagan life, extolling the unity derived from dying and rising with[161] Christ and the holiness resulting from new birth into his body, warning against evil forces, and pointing Christians to the weapons by which Christ defends them.

Equally interesting is the brief list of special vocabulary provided by Sakae Kubo. These are terms that occur more than five times in Ephesians, but fewer than fifty times in the entire NT. Thus, they mark the letter's unique emphases. It is perhaps surprising that only three words fall into this category: γνωρίζω, "make known" (six times in Ephesians and twenty-five in the entire NT); μυστήριον, "mystery" (six times in Ephesians; twenty-eight in the NT); and ποτέ, "formerly" (six times in Ephesians; twenty-nine in the NT).[162] Yet these

---

[161] Note that five of the forty occurrences mapped here are compounds formed from συν-, "together with." These readily understandable terms were most likely coined by the author for the unique subject matter at hand and therefore should be excluded from any statistical analysis for the purpose of determining authorship. In other words, one should not expect that the author would be in the habit of using these newly minted words elsewhere. One might place into this same category a few other compound words in the list that are simple variations of common NT vocabulary, for example, μακροχρόνιος, ἐκτρέφω, ἄσοφος, ἀνανεόω, ἐξισχύω, ἄθεος, and προελπίζω.

[162] See Sakae Kubo, *A Reader's Greek-English Lexicon of the New Testament and a Beginner's Guide for the Translation of New Testament Greek* (Grand Rapids: Zondervan, 1975), 181. The significance of these special-vocabulary lists for exposing a letter's themes can be illustrated by the list for Galatians (175): δικαιόω, "justify" (eight times in Galatians; thirty-nine times in the entire NT); ἐλεύθερος, "free" (six in Galatians; twenty-three in the NT); περιτέμνω, "circumcise" (six in Galatians; seventeen in the NT); and περιτομή, "circumcision" (seven in Galatians; thirty-six in the NT).

few words encapsulate succinctly the letter's stress on the revelation of the mystery that the Gentiles, who formerly were not included in God's family, have now been incorporated into Christ.

Liturgical Context

There is a simple explanation for the distinctive *style* that manifests itself in lengthy sentences, complicated subordinate clauses, lengthy and redundant genitive constructions, and lavish use of adjectives. Heinrich Schlier comments succinctly: "The 'liturgical' character of the language and style of our letter has been quite correctly pointed out."[163] The term "liturgical" may be open to some misunderstanding, as it is so often used today of a particular order of service (rite) or style of worship (high ceremony). The Lutheran Confessions point to the classical meaning of λειτουργία, *leitourgia*, as "public service" (that is, a work done by a wealthy citizen for the benefit of society) in order to identify the essence of the liturgy as God giving out his gifts of Word and Sacrament through the office of the ministry to his people (Ap 24:79–80). Ephesians is certainly "liturgical" in this sense, stressing the preached Gospel that produces faith (1:13; 4:20–21), the office of the ministry (4:7–12), and Baptism (1:13; 4:4–6; 5:26), and alluding to the Eucharist (1:7; 4:4; 5:3–20, 29–31; 6:18–24).

But the adjective "liturgical" is also commonly used to refer to the church's public worship that is conducted with a reverence and dignity befitting a recognition of the Lord's real presence. Ephesians includes at least five features that suit such a context. First, it is one of the most *prayerful* writings in the NT. It opens with a lengthy prayer that bears great resemblance to the Jewish *Berakah* pattern characteristic of synagogue worship and early Christian Eucharistic prayers (1:3–14; see the commentary). Paul continues by noting his regular habit of praying for all the saints (1:15–23). His contemplation of the mystery drives him onto his knees in prayer (3:14–19). And he closes with a call to public prayer for himself (6:18–20).[164] Second, responding to the revelation of the mystery, Paul breaks out in *doxology* (3:20–21). Third, the letter contains quotations that might derive from *creeds* or *hymns* of the early church (4:4–6; 5:14).[165] Fourth, it directs the Ephesians to *sing* "psalms and hymns and songs

---

[163] Schlier, *Epheser*, 18: "Man hat mit Recht auf den 'liturgischen' Charakter von Sprache und Stil unseres Briefes hingewiesen." Goodspeed, *An Introduction to the New Testament*, 234, calls the style "reverberating and liturgical, not at all the direct, rapid Pauline give-and-take."

[164] Barth, *Ephesians*, 1:5: "[Percy, *Die Probleme der Kolosser- und Epheserbrief*, 179–252] has shown that precisely the same style is characteristic of such passages in the homologoumena [undisputed Pauline epistles] in which Paul employs the language of prayer and adoration (e.g. Rom 8:38–39; 11:33–36), and of all the Thanksgivings which except in Galatians are found at the beginning of Paul's letters." Barth notes that Ephesians consists of one prayer running into another, "a combination of prayers (cf. I Thess 1:2–3:16; also Col 1:2–23; Philip 1:3–11)," and calls the style "hymnodic" (1:5–6).

[165] Barth, *Ephesians*, 1:9–10, notes: "Stanley considers it almost certain that all Christological hymns in the NT were composed before Paul's letters were written, i.e. before about A.D. 50. It may be observed that the vocabulary of Ephesians is strange to Paul particularly in

of the Spirit" (5:19). Fifth and finally, it concludes with a series of elements that likely allude to the goings on in *the service of Holy Communion* (6:18–24).

At each of these points, the present commentary argues that Paul is interposing himself and his letter into the public liturgy of the Ephesian congregation, echoing in his writing what they would have been saying and doing at the time of its reading. There are two very good reasons why he would have done so. First, he intended that his letters be read aloud to the assembled congregation (Col 4:16; 1 Thess 5:27), which most likely would have been in the context of the Divine Service (see the commentary on Eph 6:18–24). Second, Paul had a unique relationship with the Ephesian congregation. For Ephesus was one of only two places where he spent a lengthy period of "parish"[166] ministry (the other being Corinth). In his three-year pastorate there (Acts 20:31), it is almost certain that he would have instituted the Divine Service on each Lord's Day (Acts 20:7; cf. Rev 1:10) and been himself the preacher and presider.[167] *It would therefore have been entirely natural for him to adopt the language and style of the liturgy when writing to the Ephesians.*[168]

Contextual/Rhetorical Factors

Not only ought one give heed to the unique content of a letter such as Ephesians, but one also ought to take note of its *addressees*. This means, for example, that one should not be surprised to find vocabulary and style that matches 1 Timothy, as that letter was written to Timothy at the very same Ephesian congregation. It will be argued below that, despite an early textual variant, Ephesians was indeed originally addressed to the church in Ephesus. But even if (in accord with widespread opinion) it was originally a circular letter to many churches in Asia Minor, the relevance of the addressees for its style remains significant. First, the language (like that of Colossians) is likely influenced by the need to combat an incipient form of Jewish Gnosticism prevalent in that area. This would explain Ephesians' attacks on spiritual forces (1:21;

---

those passages which contain hymns or other traditional material" (citing David M. Stanley, "Carmenque Christo quasi Deo dicere," *CBQ* 20 [1958]: 173–91).

[166] The term "parish" (from the Greek παροικία, "place of sojourning," via the French *paroisse*) derives from a later, Constantinian context in which all residents of a certain geographical area were considered members of the church in that place, under the care of its parish priest, and came together for worship in one or more church buildings located there. By speaking of Paul's "parish" ministry, we mean no more than to identify his settled, congregational work in distinction from his itinerant missionary labors.

[167] It should not be surprising that Paul's lengthy discussion of the conduct of the Lord's Supper is located in his first letter to the Corinthians, among whom he also had a lengthy pastorate. "For I received from the Lord what I also delivered to you, that the Lord Jesus on the night when he was betrayed took bread …" (1 Cor 11:23).

[168] Barth, *Ephesians*, 1:6: "The peculiar substance of Ephesians required a specific style. Since a large part of the content is a public prayer to God, the diction of the epistle resembles that of contemporary Jewish and some pagan prayers and of the extant examples of the prayers of Paul. Thus, the vocabulary and style of Ephesians neither demonstrate nor preclude Pauline authorship." Best, *Ephesians*, 9, though denying Pauline authorship, believes that the author "may have been accustomed to lead in worship and this may have influenced his style."

2:2; 6:12), its appeal to true knowledge (4:13, 20), and its revelation of God's mysterious plans (1:9–10; 3:3–6, 9; cf. 1 Cor 2:6–7).[169] One need not presume (with Baur[170]) that the letter is a second-century production to recognize its challenge to such common Jewish and Greek thought. Second, Paul may have consciously adapted his style to the preferences of his audience in a part of the world that was accustomed to a "high style." Bo Reicke notes:

> From a historical point of view, independent of theology, one should ask whether the peculiarity of these epistles [1 Timothy, Titus, Colossians, Ephesians] was not due to the intended readers, residents of Asia Minor, where a heavy baroque style called Asianism was the rhetorical ideal. It is possible that Paul, who could be a Jew among Jews and a Greek among Greeks (1 Cor. 9:20), was able to adapt himself to his Hellenistic colleagues Timothy and Titus as well as to the Hellenistic believers in Colossae and Ephesus.[171]

Thus, the unique style and vocabulary of Ephesians can be attributed to topical, liturgical, and contextual factors without the need to resort to theories of pseudonymity, and the identification of these unique features helps the reader to understand the purposes for which the letter was written.

Thought/Theology

View of the Apostolic Ministry

Rudolf Schnackenburg's identification of a postapostolic *Sitz im Leben* to explain Ephesians is a typical example of the concern many critics have with the letter's view of the apostolic office:

> If we look closely at the section 4.11–16 with its emphatic reference to the offices given to the Church which should serve to strengthen Christ's Body, we might suspect a "crisis of leadership" which is connected with the dying-out of the "apostles and prophets" and the transition to the post-apostolic period.[172]

Schnackenburg contends that this situation led to a twofold emphasis in the letter: on the "holy" (3:5) status of the revered, past generation of apostolic leaders, and on the authority of "pastors and teachers" (4:11) as their successors in representing Christ to the postapostolic church. Schnackenburg continues by pointing to other supposedly late NT writings that evidence this same concern for the apostolic foundation, the tradition, and the need to combat false doctrine: 1 and 2 John, Jude, the Pastorals, and the speech to the Ephesian pastors (Acts 20:18–35; he cites also 2 Thess 2:11; Jude 11; 1 Jn 4:6; 2 Pet 2:18; 3:17)![173] The list is quite stunning in its comprehensiveness, raising a significant logical prob-

---

[169] Schlier, *Epheser*, 19.

[170] See "Gnosticism" in "Arguments against Pauline Authorship," above in "Authorship."

[171] Reicke, *Re-examining Paul's Letters*, 52–53; see also 119. On the rhetorical characteristics of the "Second Sophistic" period, see Anthony C. Thiselton, *The First Epistle to the Corinthians* (NIGTC; Grand Rapids: Eerdmans, 2000), 13–15.

[172] Schnackenburg, *Ephesians*, 34.

[173] Schnackenburg, *Ephesians*, 34, including n. 45.

lem: if the fabric of Ephesians is deemed to be cut from the same cloth as such a large swath of the NT, at what point does the postapostolic argument become circular and self-defeating?

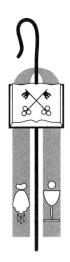

While there is a superficial case to be answered in comparing Eph 2:20 with 1 Cor 3:11 (is the church built on the apostles or on Christ?), the assertion that the church has an apostolic foundation is a widespread NT teaching. While some critics would claim that the apparently late appearance of the idea in Revelation (21:14) supports their case, the Gospel of Matthew (16:18) places it on the lips of Jesus, and the critic is compelled to deem this, too, to be inauthentic. None would doubt that Paul wrote Galatians, in which he refers to the reputation of the apostles as the "pillars" of the church (Gal 2:9). Paul claims to have laid a foundation like a skilled master builder (1 Cor 3:10)—a role elsewhere attributed, without contradiction, to God (Heb 11:10). Indeed, the fundamental error of the critics is to overlook what Paul asserts of his apostolic office at the beginning of every letter: that it was bestowed directly by God through his encounter with the risen Christ, such that Paul now speaks for Christ himself. If Ephesians' view of the apostolic office is deemed too high for Paul, then Galatians 1–2 and 2 Corinthians 10–12 would likewise need to be excised from his corpus.

The critics are guilty of their own anachronism when they contend that Paul would not have referred to the apostles and prophets as "holy" (3:5). For Paul does not intend to call them "saints" in the medieval sense of the term, as if to separate them from the rest of Christ's body. Not only does Ephesians itself call the apostles and prophets ἅγιοι, "holy" (3:5), but it also repeatedly applies the very same adjective to the entire Ephesian congregation, calling the Ephesians "saints" together with all those who have been cleansed by the blood of Christ.[174] Shortly after calling the apostles and prophets "holy," the apostolic author not only includes himself in the body of Christ but also refers to himself as "quite the least of all the saints" (3:8)—hardly putting himself on a pedestal! So, then, neither should the reader be surprised by the designation of the prophets—whether OT or NT—as "holy" (cf. Lk 1:70; 2 Pet 3:2). This is what the church is made of: "saints and apostles and prophets" (Rev 18:20).

If one were to find in Ephesians the hierarchical structure characteristic of second-century Christianity, with the regularized terminology of bishop, presbyter, and deacon, then one might have cause to consider the possibility of a relatively late date. But of this structure there is not a trace.[175] Neither, of course, do the Pastoral Epistles display any trace of a monarchical episcopate or a threefold office, and the somewhat cloudy twofold distinction they make between ἐπίσκοπος/πρεσβύτερος, "overseer [bishop]/elder [presbyter]," and διάκονος, "assistant minister [or deacon]" (1 Tim 3:1–13; see also Titus 1:5–9),

---

[174] See ἅγιοι, "saints," in 1:1, 4, 15, 18; 2:19; 3:8, 18; 4:12; 5:3; 6:18; and ἅγιος, "holy," in reference to the church in 2:21; 5:27.

[175] Even Schnackenburg, *Ephesians*, 33, admits that "a tension between 'apostolic' and 'episcopal' Church organisation can not be detected in Eph."

does not in any way go beyond the uncontested words of Paul (Phil 1:1). Paul's application of the term διάκονος, "minister," to himself (Eph 3:7) ought to dispel any notion that Ephesians is working with a later terminology or structure. Likewise, when Paul names five subcategories within the office of the ministry as given by the ascended Christ (4:11), he does not include any of the three terms characteristic of later usage, but instead identifies the inhabitants of the ongoing ministry as "pastors and teachers." In lumping these "lower" officers together with "the apostles and the prophets and the evangelists," the author of Ephesians does quite the opposite of what the critics contend; and in calling the lot of them "gifts" of the ascended Christ (4:8, 11), he says no more than the undisputed words of Paul (Rom 12:6–8; 1 Cor 12:28–30). Thus, far from denigrating what Paul says about the office of the ministry in Ephesians 2, 3, and 4, the sensible interpreter ought to recognize here a view of the divinely instituted office that is entirely consistent with Paul's other writings and with the words of Christ himself (particularly Lk 10:16; see also Mt 16:18–19; 28:16–20; Jn 20:21–23).[176]

Ecclesiology

The letter's consistent use of the term ἐκκλησία, "church," to refer to the universal church (rather than to the local congregation) can be recognized without conceding that it is inconsistent with Pauline habit. A careful reading of the NT demonstrates that the term ἐκκλησία is used in three ways: (1) one local congregation;[177] (2) an aggregate of local congregations in a city or region, i.e., a "diocese";[178] and (3) the church universal, across the earth and in heaven.[179] In the footnoted examples Pauline usage is quite evenly spread across these three categories.[180] Paul is quite accustomed to speaking of the universal church, even in his undisputed letters.[181] If one considers the social situation of apostolic Christianity—that Christians would have normally gathered for worship

---

[176] See Winger, "The Office of the Holy Ministry according to the New Testament Mandate of Christ."

[177] E.g., Mt 18:17; Rom 16:5; 1 Cor 11:18; 14:23, 28, 34–35; 16:19; Col 4:15; Philemon 2.

[178] E.g., Acts 8:1; 9:31; 11:22, 26; 13:1; 15:22; 18:22; 20:17; Rom 16:1, 23; 1 Cor 1:2; 2 Cor 1:1; Col 4:16; 1 Thess 1:1; 2 Thess 1:1; Revelation 1–3 (in which all the house churches in each city are addressed as a single "church"); and possibly Heb 10:25, where τὴν ἐπισυναγωγήν means "the trans-parochial gathering." See also the use of ἐκκλησία, "church," in the plural to refer to an aggregate of churches in 1 Cor 16:1, 19; 2 Cor 8:1; Gal 1:2; 1 Thess 2:14.

[179] Mt 16:18; Rom 16:4, 16; 1 Cor 10:32; 12:28; 15:9; Gal 1:13; Eph 1:22; 3:10, 21; 5:23–32; Phil 3:6; Col 1:18, 24; 1 Tim 3:15.

[180] The alternation of referent between house church, diocese, "all the churches of the Gentiles," "all the churches of Christ," and "the whole church," is significant in the close proximity of Rom 16:1, 4, 5, 16, 23, demonstrating that Paul is comfortable with all three uses of the term. The diversity of usage in Paul's epistles is illustrated by a comparison between Romans (in which ἐκκλησία, "church," does not occur prior to the final greetings, Rom 16:1, 4, 5, 16, 23) and 1 Corinthians (in which it occurs twenty-two times throughout the epistle).

[181] One might also note the occasions when he refers to the universal church without actually using the term ἐκκλησία: Rom 12:5–8; 1 Cor 1:2; 12:12–31; Eph 4:1–6; Col 1:13.

in homes capable of accommodating only a few dozen people—it is likely that large cities like Ephesus, Corinth, and Rome would have contained numerous such "house churches." Phrases like "the church of God that is in Corinth" (1 Cor 1:2; cf. Rom 16:23) almost certainly do not refer to a single local congregation, but embrace aspects of the second and third categories above. It may, in fact, be fair to say that Paul *more often* speaks of the diocesan and universal church than he does of an individual local congregation[182] and therefore that his concentration in Ephesians on the third common usage of ἐκκλησία (the church universal) is not at all unusual for him.

The distinction between the three uses is probably overwrought. In many places Paul alternates in quick succession between "church" (singular) and "churches" (plural),[183] closely relating the phenomenon of the local worshiping community to the larger aggregates of the diocese and the church universal. It is probably better to speak of the church (singular) as an entity that manifests itself in local forms. This is Paul's ecclesiology. It is inconceivable, for example, that Paul's "body of Christ" ecclesiology in Romans 12 and 1 Corinthians 12 be restricted to the local congregation, as if Christ's body were divided into various places; these passages form the background to Paul's development of the theme in Ephesians.[184] Indeed, it is inaccurate to suggest that Ephesians has a different *ecclesiology* in comparison to the other letters. For, in addition to his exaltation of the church universal, Paul frequently refers to the local congregation(s) in Ephesus as he

- addresses the local congregation as "the saints ... who are in Ephesus" (1:2);
- refers to them as those who have heard and believed the Gospel (1:13);
- has heard a positive report of their "faith in the Lord Jesus and love toward all the saints" (1:15);
- encourages them to maintain the unity of the faith into which they were baptized (4:1–6);

---

[182] See also Jeffrey J. Kloha, "The Trans-Congregational Church in the New Testament," *Concordia Journal* 34 (2008): 172–90.

[183] In the following sets of verses, singular and plural forms of ἐκκλησία, "church," alternate:

- 1 Cor 11:16, 18, 22
- 1 Cor 14:33, 34, 35
- 1 Cor 16:19 (singular and plural in this single verse)
- Gal 1:13, 22

The same dynamic can occur when Paul uses vocabulary other than ἐκκλησία, "church." In 1 Cor 1:2, for example, Paul follows up the singular phrase "the church of God that is in Corinth" with the plural reference to "all those who call upon the name of our Lord Jesus Christ in every place."

[184] Eph 1:22–23; 2:16; 3:6; 4:12, 16; 5:23, 30. Bruce, *The Epistles to the Colossians, to Philemon, and to the Ephesians*, 238:

To Paul's way of thinking Christ could no more be divided among the several congregations than he could be divided among the factions within the congregation at Corinth. The explicit teaching about the church universal in Ephesians is a corollary of Paul's understanding of the phrase "in Christ" and all that it implies.

- refers to the pastors who serve them, describing the saints as a body being knit together in unity (4:7–16);
- alludes to their catechesis in the truth of Christ (4:20–21);
- and, as noted above, alludes frequently to their liturgical gathering (e.g., 1:3–14; 6:18–24).

Thus, Paul develops in Ephesians his normal ecclesiology of the church as the body of Christ that is manifested in localities where the saints gather together for the Divine Service. The only thing lacking in Ephesians is the explicit application of the term ἐκκλησία, "church," to this local gathering.

Christology

The broad contours of the Ephesian Christology have been painted above, and the contention that any of its features are un-Pauline is quite puzzling. The incarnation does not feature prominently in Paul's epistles (but see, e.g., Rom 1:3), and when Ephesians refers to it (4:9), the language of descent from above is consistent with Paul elsewhere (e.g., Rom 10:6). The vocabulary of the "cross" (σταυρός) and "crucifixion" (σταυρόω) features in only some of Paul's letters (being notably absent from Romans,[185] 1 and 2 Thessalonians, and the Pastorals) and is especially prominent only in 1 Corinthians (a total of six instances of the two words) and Galatians (six instances). The single reference to Christ's "cross" in Ephesians (2:16) compares favorably with the two instances each in Philippians (2:8; 3:18) and Colossians (1:20; 2:14), and the resulting reconciliation of men with each other and with God "through the cross" (Eph 2:16) is a Pauline notion (2 Cor 5:18–19).

Certainly, Ephesians draws one's attention to the ascension and glorification of Christ. But to refer to this as a change in Christology (compared to the undisputed Pauline epistles) is to miss the point. These themes come to the fore in Ephesians because of the theme of divine warfare that it addresses: when Christians are confronted with demonic adversaries (Eph 6:12), they need to hear that Christ has ascended far above these foes and has triumphed over them. While the ascension does not feature explicitly in Paul's other letters, to deny that it could be significant for Paul would entail denying the importance of his Damascus road encounter with the ascended Lord (Acts 9:3–5; Gal 1:11–16; cf. 2 Cor 12:2)! So also, while Eph 2:5–6 does not speak of *dying* with Christ, but only *rising* and *ascending* with him, Paul had already asserted that we were dead in our sins (Eph 2:1), and our rising with Christ is not absent from Romans (6:11, 13). Thus, rather than seeing these distinctive Christological features in Ephesians as a departure from Paul, we ought note them as highlighting the themes that Ephesians uniquely addresses.

---

[185] Romans prefers to speak of the "death" of Christ (θάνατος, Rom 5:10; 6:3, 5) and his "dying" (ἀποθνήσκω, Rom 5:6, 8; 6:10; 8:34; 14:9, 15; cf. Rom 6:9), language admittedly absent from Ephesians.

Gnosticism

As noted previously, present-day critical scholarship has lost enthusiasm for the idea that Ephesians addresses second-century Gnostic ideas.[186] Yet one occasionally comes across lingering sentiments that Ephesians' language so resonates with later Gnostic terminology that it must be at least post-Pauline. Perhaps it is best simply to note that Gnosticism was a heresy synthesized from strands of thought deeply rooted in the Greek (and Jewish) philosophical and religious tradition. If Paul was to confront the environment in which the Ephesians lived, he would have been bound to use similar language. This perspective is pursued most vigorously—to a fault—by Heinrich Schlier's commentary. Working from the conviction that Paul *did* write Ephesians, he nevertheless argues that it is replete with challenges to proto-Gnosticism and that Paul deliberately takes up and uses their vocabulary.[187] Insofar as these ideas were an inescapable part of first-century Jewish speculative writings and were related to commonalities of Greek philosophical thinking, there is no need to deny that Ephesians might address them, no matter what its date or authorship.

Soteriology

The vocabulary of "justification" (δικαιόω and cognates) is supposedly absent from Ephesians. In fact, this is not true, as δικαιοσύνη, "righteousness," occurs three times (4:24; 5:9; 6:14), and δίκαιος, "righteous," once (6:1).[188] Statistically, this is in line with the majority of Paul's epistles. Only in Romans (sixty-four times) and Galatians (thirteen times) does the vocabulary of justification feature more prominently. Markus Barth has warned against making

---

[186] Markus Barth, who quite thoroughly examines and refutes Baur's view (1:12–18 and passim), summarizes the state of the question:

> It is today commonly accepted that Ephesians is not dependent upon any of the classical Christian-heretic Gnostic systems. But no agreement exists as yet regarding the question whether or not specific elements in Jewish Wisdom literature and apocalyptic books, in Philo, in Matt 11:25–29; Col 1:15–20, and also in the Johannine and the unquestioned Pauline writings deserve to be labeled Gnostic, or proto-Gnostic. It is not impossible that before the second century, maybe even before the Christian era, several proto-Gnostic elements had been combined to form the pattern of a religious world view, and found expression in fabulous myths. If not the full-blown myth of the Aion-Prime-Anthropos, at least several of its constitutive features may have been known to the author of Ephesians. (*Ephesians*, 1:13)

Guthrie, *New Testament Introduction*, 506, likewise contends that the Gnostic Redeemed-Redeemer myth as collated by Mani is far too late to have influenced Ephesians and Colossians. Arnold, *Power and Magic*, 11–13, challenges the existence of a Gnosticized Judaism in the first century AD. Deterding, *Colossians*, 7–12, provides a helpful summary of Gnostic teaching and its relationship to Colossians, concluding that the letter does indeed address an early form of Gnosticism.

[187] Schlier, *Epheser*, 19: Ephesians' "language stands without a doubt under the influence of the Jewish-Christian 'Gnosis,' to which he [Paul] is opposed." Schlier finds proto-Gnosticism under every stone in the Ephesian landscape and is manifestly overzealous in his pursuit of it.

[188] The commentary proper will treat each of these passages in detail and examine the contention that they address not passive justification (by faith) but active righteousness (in good works).

justification language a criterion of authenticity—though one might question whether he accords justification the prominence that Lutherans would.[189] It is more helpful to recognize—with no little caution—that "justification" is in some senses a figure of speech (law court imagery) to describe a divine act that can be expressed in other ways without loss of substance.[190] Thus, Ephesians is able to describe the same act as

- the forgiveness of sins, redemption by the purchase price of Christ's blood (1:7; 4:32);
- a result of hearing and believing the Gospel (1:13);
- resurrection to new life in Christ (2:5–6; 5:14);
- salvation by grace through faith apart from works (2:5, 8–9), i.e., God's work (2:10);
- reconciliation with God and one another by the cross of Christ (2:16);
- partaking in the promise of the Gospel (3:6);
- an act of grace by the gift of Christ (4:7);
- renewal in the spirit of the mind, being clothed with Christ, and re-created in God's image (4:23–24);
- the result of Christ's self-sacrifice, which was accepted by God (5:2);
- a cleansing by water and the Word (5:26).

Thus, though Ephesians does not express the forensic image of "justification" in a detailed manner (and the verb δικαιόω is lacking), it presents the same theology of justification in the language of slavery/redemption, rescue/salvation, re-creation/new life, grace/gift, and cultic cleansing. How can one possibly read this great declaration of *sola fide*, "by grace you have been saved through faith; and this is not from yourselves; it is the gift of God, not from works, lest anyone should boast" (2:8–9), and find it inconsistent with the Pauline teaching on justification?

The use of the perfect passive participle σεσῳσμένοι, "have been saved," to describe the Christian's *present* saved condition (2:5, 8) certainly differs from Paul's normal use of "salvation" vocabulary to describe the rescue from this world that Christ will bring on the Last Day. Yet, as the commentary on 2:5, 8 will note, Paul *can* speak of salvation as something already achieved (e.g., Rom 8:24).[191] The addition of the qualifiers "by grace" and "through faith" (Eph 2:8) not only give the efficient and instrumental causes of that salvation, but they also indicate *in what sense* it can be said that Christians are saved already now. Salvation in the present life contrasts with salvation on the Last Day in that it

---

[189] Barth, *Ephesians*, 1:48: "Ephesians may force extreme Paulinists of all times to revise their prejudices. Certainly the apostle's teaching and preaching was much more politically, socially, ethically oriented than his individualizing and existentialist interpreters have been willing to acknowledge." This is not the perspective of the present commentary!

[190] See, for example, Jacob A. O. Preus, *Just Words: Understanding the Fullness of the Gospel* (St. Louis: Concordia, 2000).

[191] Cf. Rom 11:11; 1 Cor 1:18; 15:2; 2 Cor 2:15; 6:2; 2 Tim 1:9; Titus 2:11; 3:5.

remains hidden and is perceivable only by faith. The tension between the two views—"now" versus "not yet"—is not at all out of character for Paul, who wrestles with similar paradoxes such as *simul justus et peccator* (Romans 6–7) and Law versus Gospel (passim!).

So, too, it would be simplistic to posit that the words "nullifying the Law [τὸν νόμον … καταργήσας] of commandments in decrees" (2:15) contradict "Do we then abolish the Law [νόμον … καταργοῦμεν] through faith? May it never be! But we uphold the Law" (Rom 3:31). Ephesians uses καταργέω (2:15) not in the sense of "destroy," but rather "nullify," and applies it quite specifically to the Law's power to divide and condemn Christians within the body of Christ (a prominent teaching also in Romans, e.g., 8:1, 34). Rom 3:31 addresses a quite different question: does the righteousness of God in Christ invalidate the νόμος as "Torah," as "God's Word"? In the context of his investigation of Abraham and David (Romans 3–4), Paul insists that even the OT proclaims justification through faith alone and therefore the OT is not nullified by the Gospel.[192]

Sacramental Theology

The letter's prominent appeal to Baptism as the source and focus of Christian unity cannot be seriously opposed to Paul's teaching elsewhere. For the language of Eph 4:1–6 is thoroughly in harmony with 1 Cor 12:13 and Gal 3:26–28. The typological association of baptismal death and resurrection with circumcision—a teaching of Col 2:11–12 that is echoed in Eph 2:5–6 (see the textual notes on those verses)—is scarcely different from Paul's teaching of the Christian's death with Christ in Baptism (Rom 6:1–11) and his rejection of external circumcision in favor of one wrought internally by the Spirit (Rom 2:28–29; Phil 3:3).[193] Ephesians, indeed, gives Baptism a significant and prominent place (1:13; 4:5; 5:26). Once again, critics have rightly marked a unique feature of Ephesians, but they fail to prove that it is un-Pauline.

Eschatology

There are four basic flaws in the argument that places the eschatological perspective of Ephesians in opposition to that of Paul's other letters. First, its supposedly settled, institutional view of the church and the Christian life is not entirely absent from the rest of Paul's epistles. Its teaching that the church is well served by officeholders who are gifts of the ascended Christ (4:11–16) echoes Paul's regular appeal to his own apostolic authority and his view that the office of the ministry is instituted by Christ (see "View of the Apostolic Ministry" in "Evaluation of the Case," above in "Authorship"). Likewise, its teaching of order in Christian marriage and the home (5:21–6:9) is consistent with the headship

---

[192] A most thorough explanation is given by Jonathan Grothe, "Romans 3:31 and Ephesians 2:15," in *The Justification of the Ungodly*, 229–32.

[193] Compare the language of circumcision as a "seal" (Rom 4:11) with "sealed" in Eph 1:13 and 2 Cor 1:22.

principles espoused in 1 Cor 11:3–16 and 14:33–36.[194] Second, it is not true to assert that Ephesians teaches an *exclusively* realized eschatology. It speaks of an inheritance yet to be received,[195] a redemption yet in store, wrath yet to come against the unrighteous, and the hope of a glorious, heavenly future (1:14, 18; 4:30; 5:5–6; 6:8). Third, there are prominent examples of proleptic, realized eschatology in Paul's other writings (see "Soteriology" in "Evaluation of the Case," above in "Authorship"). Finally, such a view again oversimplifies Paul's thinking and does not allow him to wrestle with the difficult tension between the proleptic and future aspects of eschatology. Clearly, Eph 2:5–6 does *not* teach that resurrection and ascension have been experienced by the Christian in such a way that there is nothing left to come, for the Ephesians were well aware that their bodies were still rooted firmly on this earth. The Pauline warning against false teachers who claimed that the resurrection had already happened (1 Cor 15:12; 2 Tim 2:18) does not target the truth that *sacramentally* and *by faith* we glimpse the hidden reality that we are already in the bosom of the Father in heaven (cf. Col 3:1–4). The church was able to maintain such tensions for eighteen hundred years before critics raised the claim that it was impossible.

The cumulative effect of the critics' arguments is not at all what the critics intend. For when examined point by point, the supposed contradictions of Pauline thought turn out either to be quite harmonious with Paul's usual manner of speaking or to highlight unique themes of this letter that complement his other writings. Donald Guthrie concludes quite rightly: "The special plea for cumulative consideration of this evidence rather than analytical approach amounts to an admission of its weakness."[196] One might, in fact, be impressed by the complex manner in which this letter relates to the rest of Paul's writings. Markus Barth sees this as a mark of authenticity:

> Not though but *because* some typically Pauline words have a slightly different, perhaps unique, meaning in Ephesians, and *because* deviations from a straight party-line Paulinism are indisputable, Ephesians may have to be considered authentic. Only a foolish plagiarist or editor would have been unaware of the changes, additions, corrections he made. … Paul himself is the man who could best afford to write in a non-Paulinistic way, even under his own name.[197]

Incipient Catholicism

In the preceding analysis, we have opined (on the basis of considerable evidence) that none of these features of Ephesians are in conflict with Pauline

---

[194] Eph 5:21–6:9 is also consistent with the headship principles espoused in 1 Tim 2:7–15; 5:14; 6:1–2; Titus 2:1–15, though critics would not accept these as Pauline.

[195] Surely, contra Schnackenburg, *Ephesians*, 27, the inheritance in heaven is not simply "above," but also *future*!

[196] Guthrie, *New Testament Introduction*, 522; cf. Nineham, "The Case against the Pauline Authorship," 23.

[197] Barth, *Ephesians*, 1:49.

thought as expressed in his other letters—and the burden of proof that Paul could not have spoken this way remains on the critics. Yet it would seem that more is going on when critics apply the label *Frühkatholizismus*, "incipient Catholicism." This is not an objective debate about balance of probability. "Catholic" is, in most Christian circles, not a neutral term; it (ironically, in that it refers to the universal quality of the church) draws a line between camps, inviting either loyalty or contempt. These human factors cannot be discounted in analyzing opinions on Pauline authorship.[198]

F. F. Bruce, the academic doyen of English-speaking Evangelicalism for most of the twentieth century's second half, serves as a notable example. After brilliantly demonstrating that the Ephesian teaching on the universal character of the church is fully compatible with Pauline parallels in 1 Corinthians and Romans, Bruce quite vehemently distances himself from what he identifies as the *Catholic* interpretation of the letter:

> When incipient catholicism is discerned in NT documents, it is implied that those features are present which were to characterize the life and theology of the later church, the church itself being viewed as the locus of salvation. But the universal church is far from being presented in Ephesians as a cultic institution, with a priesthood mediating the means of grace to the rank and file of the faithful. Not even in the latest NT documents has it come anywhere near that stage of development. The church's ministry in Ephesians is still mainly charismatic: it is not regulated as it is in the Pastorals. The apostles and the prophets of Eph. 4:11 constitute foundation ministries (as in Eph. 2:20); as for the evangelists, pastors, and teachers, they do not reserve the ministry to themselves but are given to the church by the ascended Lord that they may enable all its members to discharge their respective ministries, each member functioning for the health and growth of the whole body.[199]

Three points can be made on the basis of this notable quotation. First, Bruce chooses heavily freighted words to express his disdain for what he believes to be the Catholic corruption of the church, e.g., "cultic," "priesthood," and "mediating." Second, while he is quite correct that Ephesians does not speak of the ministry as a "priesthood" or as "mediating,"[200] he goes too far in rejecting the letter's clear *cultic* (liturgical/sacramental) language. Paul does indeed describe the church as the place where Christ cleanses his bride through water and the Word by the power of his blood in order to present her holy to the Father, making her into a spiritual temple (1:4, 7; 2:13–22; 5:2, 26–27). The church

[198] Barth, *Ephesians*, 1:46, concurs: "To this way of thinking, … Ephesians is forgiven its baroque language, its Gnostic elements, its dependence upon Colossians and other letters of the NT, yet it is not forgiven its 'Early Catholicism.' The image of Paul cultivated among those Protestants does not permit being dragged into any morass, least of all the ecclesiastical."

[199] Bruce, *The Epistles to the Colossians, to Philemon, and to the Ephesians*, 238–39.

[200] Neither of these terms is used for the office of the ministry in Ephesians. Yet, if the ministry represents the ascended Christ and distributes his gifts (Eph 4:7–16), then language of mediation need not be discounted (cf. 2 Cor 5:20: "God making his appeal through us").

(believers gathered around the means of grace [AC 7]) *is*, therefore, "the locus of salvation."[201] Bruce's diminution of the office of the ministry is rooted in his own theological position, not in what Paul actually teaches in chapter 4. Third, then, it is ironic that Bruce has *accepted* the evolutionary pattern laid down by the proponents of *Frühkatholizismus*. For he concurs that there is a line of progressive development in the NT from an early, charismatic period (1 Corinthians) to a later, institutional and structured church (Pastorals), effectively denying that the office of the ministry derives from the mandate and institution of Christ himself. Thus, *the only essential difference between Bruce and the proponents of incipient Catholicism is that Bruce places Ephesians earlier in the development and believes that its culmination in the Pastoral Epistles could have happened within Paul's lifetime.*

We noted Käsemann's argument that Ephesians represents the point of transition from the supposedly charismatic early Pauline version of Christianity to the later, Catholic institutionalism.[202] Käsemann identifies Ephesians (together with Luke-Acts and the Pastorals) as incipiently Catholic not only in order to date them late and question their authenticity, but also to reject their authority. This, too, is no objective assessment. While he is quite right to align Pauline authorship with apostolic authority, as the early church did when recognizing NT writings as canonical (i.e., normative), it is quite clear that Käsemann does not *want* to accept these writings as authoritative *because* he discerns in them traces of the Catholicism to which he personally objects.[203] Anyone familiar with contemporary German Lutheranism will understand the implications of declaring, "*Das ist katholisch!*" For the radically liberal German Protestants of the nineteenth century (and their only slightly less radical twentieth-century successors), the antipathy toward all things Catholic was even stronger. In the JEDP analysis of the Pentateuch, they expressed this antipathy in their preference for the supposedly earlier "ethical monotheism" of pious individuals in J over the later "priestly cult" intended to deal with the corporate guilt of Israel in P. So also among Paul's letters they instinctively preferred those writings in which they found Gospel freedom and the justification of the individual

---

[201] One must, of course, qualify this by explaining that *no one particular church body* can be identified as the locus of salvation to the exclusion of all others. In this way, Luther subverts the Roman church's traditional claim to be the sole locus of salvation when he interprets "church" in the expression "outside the church there is no salvation" as any place where the Gospel is purely taught and the Sacraments are administered in accord with the Gospel (LC 2:54–56; see also AC 7:1–4, citing Eph 4:4–5).

[202] See "Incipient Catholicism" in "Arguments against Pauline Authorship," above in "Authorship."

[203] Note L. T. Johnson's comment on the subjectivity of the enterprise: "De Wette makes explicit a theological agenda that is operative throughout the debate over authenticity: the quest for a usable Paul" (*The First and Second Letters to Timothy*, 44–45, citing W. M. L. de Wette, *Kurze Erklärung der Brief an Titus, Timotheus und die Hebräer* [Leipzig: Weidmann'sche Buchhandlung, 1844], vii and passim). "Usable" means "fitting my personal vision of Christianity."

(coupled with ethical admonitions) and deprecated those letters which presented the church as a corporate body in which the ministry dispensed God's grace through Word and Sacraments.

Grasping this polar opposition between liberal Protestantism and institutional Catholicism in nineteenth-century Germany is vital to understanding F. C. Baur, the architect of the edifice of present-day NT studies. Horton Harris, in writing the most thorough study of Baur's "Tübingen School," writes in his introduction (with some hyperbole):

> The Tübingen School was not of merely minor importance for theology. It was *the most important theological event in the whole history of theology from the Reformation to the present day*. Within the two decades of its existence the whole course of Biblical and especially New Testament criticism was fundamentally changed. Indeed, it would not be too much to say that all modern exegesis and interpretation of the Bible find their roots and origins in the Tübingen School.[204]

If this is true, then one must understand Baur in order to understand present-day arguments about the Pauline authorship of Ephesians. We have noted Baur's Hegelian, dialectical analysis of the NT's historical development (see "Incipient Catholicism" in "Arguments against Pauline Authorship," above in "Authorship").[205] It is crucial to add that his choice of Pauline and Petrine factions as the parties in the initial conflict was also influenced by two fundamental presuppositions.

First, Baur shared the anti-Catholic sentiment of his German Protestant culture. When, for example, Johann Adam Möhler of the Catholic faculty of theology at Tübingen wrote a book seeking to bridge the gap between Catholics and Protestants (1825) and a second describing their basic differences (1832), Baur reacted with two published responses (1833/1834) delineating the profound differences between Lutheranism and Catholicism; the second response was particularly vicious.[206] Second, Baur was a pantheist who denied anything supernatural or revelatory in Scripture.[207] Harris comments on the significance of this fact:

---

[204] Harris, *The Tübingen School*, v.

[205] Harris, *The Tübingen School*, 26–27:

> In this year [1833], in his long refutation of Möhler's [anti-Lutheran] book, Baur explicitly confessed himself a Hegelian. ... In the work itself, however, there is little to indicate a convinced adoption of the Hegelian viewpoint and it would appear that not until the winter of 1834/5 ... did Baur really make an intensive study of the speculative philosophy. ...

> From this time on, Baur set himself under the banner of Hegel, and there were few whose understanding of the Master surpassed his own.

> For a thorough critique of Baur's reconstruction of early Christianity, see Craig C. Hill, *Hellenists and Hebrews: Reappraising Division within the Earliest Church* (Minneapolis: Fortress, 1991).

[206] Harris, *The Tübingen School*, 23–25.

[207] Harris, *The Tübingen School*, 19–21.

If one had to sum up the aim and object of the Tübingen School in a single statement it would be that the Tübingen School made the first comprehensive and consequent attempt to interpret the New Testament and the history of the early Church from a non-supernatural (indeed, anti-supernatural) and non-miraculous standpoint. …

The fundamental axiom of Baur's whole historical investigation was that the New Testament writings are not trustworthy historical documents. This axiom followed logically from the rejection of the supernatural and miraculous element in Christianity.[208]

The consequence of this anti-supernaturalistic presupposition was that Baur did not accept the book of Acts as a reliable depiction of the history of the apostolic age.[209] His personal reconstruction of the history on the basis of his dialectical thinking replaced the record of Acts, and he dated each NT writing according to its apparent amount of catholicizing development.[210] His anti-supernaturalism was a ready-made companion for his anti-Catholicism. For him the early church was a thoroughly naturalistic institution marked by the power struggles and conflicts of human ambition, entirely devoid of divine intervention or guidance.

The use of *Frühkatholizismus*, "incipient Catholicism," as a diagnostic tool for dating or authenticating NT documents is therefore well past its expiration date. One cannot ignore the culture from which it arose.[211] Nor can one ignore the anachronism involved in applying polemical terms from the Reformation era to the first and second centuries of Christian history, as if the errors Luther opposed could be identified with the contents of the Pastoral

---

[208] Harris, *The Tübingen School*, 255–56.

[209] Harris, *The Tübingen School*, 259–60, notes in passing that William Ramsay's famous defense of the historicity of Acts (*St. Paul the Traveller and the Roman Citizen* [London: Hodder & Stoughton, 1895]) began as an investigation of the Tübingen theory and ended by comprehensively refuting it.

[210] Harris, *The Tübingen School*, 258:

Baur concluded that Simon [Magus] was to be identified with Paul [in the narrative in Acts 8:9–24]. Thus in order to strengthen his case for the historical framework which he had adduced, Baur simply grasped at every straw he could find. The date and authorship of each New Testament book was then determined according to how it fitted into this historical framework (the tendency approach). "Fitted" is the wrong word. Baur *forced* the books into the framework by manipulating the facts and distorting the evidence, by emphasizing the details which harmonized with his views while omitting everything which did not.

[211] N. T. Wright's *Paul: In Fresh Perspective* presents the Hulsean Lectures, which the present author was privileged to hear in Cambridge. Wright challenges the consensus on non-Pauline authorship of Colossians and Ephesians as a "fixed point" of scholarship:

But our suspicions ought to be aroused by the fact that such consensus as there has ever been on the subject came from the time when the all-dominant power in New Testament scholarship lay with a particular kind of German existentialist Lutheranism for whom any ecclesiology other than a purely functional one, any view of Judaism other than a purely negative one, any view of Jesus Christ other than a fairly low Christology, any view of creation other than a Barthian "Nein," was deeply suspect. The false either/or, as I would see it, of justification *or* the church, of salvation *or* creation, hovered as a brooding presence over the smaller arguments (which are in any case always unconvincing, given the very small textual base) from style. (18)

Epistles, Ignatius, or Clement of Rome![212] The sober exegete ought to distinguish carefully between his personal prejudices and what Paul (under divine inspiration and following the tradition handed down from Christ) could have written. Put another way, the exegete is bound to submit his judgment to the teachings of the text. If Ephesians teaches that the church as the body of Christ is a universal entity spanning heaven and earth, that the risen and ascended Christ exercised a divine prerogative by bestowing on his church ministers to give out his gifts, that he works through Word *and* Sacrament to cleanse his bride, and that Christians gather around these gifts in liturgical assemblies to be built up toward their heavenly goal, then one ought not kick against the goads (Acts 26:14) by denying Paul the right or ability to teach the same.[213]

The Literary Relationship between Ephesians and Other Pauline Epistles

The critical case concerning the relationship between Ephesians and other Pauline epistles falls into two parts: the unique case of its fraternal twin, Colossians, and the rest of the Pauline corpus. The overall relationship of Ephesians to Colossians will be treated in more detail below,[214] but for the present purpose we must address the charge that Ephesians uses three key terms from Colossians in a manner that departs significantly from their "original" meaning.

1. The claim that Christ's headship has a different meaning in the two epistles does not bear up under scrutiny. For although Col 2:10 identifies Christ as "the Head [ἡ κεφαλή] of all rule and authority," Ephesians makes the same assertion in related terms: God's plan was that "all things might be brought together [under headship, ἀνακεφαλαιώσασθαι][215] in Christ" (1:10). The teaching that even the spiritual forces are brought under Christ's headship is also taught by his ascension above them (1:21) and the subsequent assertion that he is "Head [κεφαλή] over all things for the church" (1:22). Likewise, the chief Ephesian emphasis on Christ as the Head of the *church* is also taught expressly in Col 1:18. Both letters teach that Christ is Head of all things *and*, in a unique way, Head of the church.

---

[212] The term "catholic," when used in the second century by church fathers like Ignatius, Tertullian, and Clement of Alexandria, does not mean "*Roman* Catholic." Nor do well-informed Lutherans subscribe to the "gap theory," by which it is supposed that the church was corrupt from the end of the apostolic age right up till the Reformation. Luther himself believed that the Roman Catholic Church in which he grew up had only been corrupt for some three hundred years (e.g., AE 27:165–66; 31:337; 36:31; he was probably thinking of the Fourth Lateran Council, 1215).

[213] Heinrich Schlier submitted his will to Ephesians when he accepted that Paul could have written such things about the church and forsook his earlier judgment that it was inauthentic (see the footnote about Schlier near the beginning of this section, "Authorship"). Living in the context of radically liberal Bultmannian Lutheranism, Schlier found it necessary to convert to Roman Catholicism as a necessary consequence of this submission. It is unfortunate that he did not recognize the compatibility of Ephesian teaching with historic, confessional Lutheranism.

[214] See "Relationship to Colossians" below.

[215] The verb ἀνακεφαλαιόω, so difficult to render in English, is built on the root κεφαλή, "head," and implies gathering things together under one "heading."

2. The contention that the term "mystery" (μυστήριον) has a different meaning in the two epistles is not only theologically false but also linguistically confused. The *meaning* of the term μυστήριον is the same: something hidden that has been revealed. The question is whether its *referent* in the two epistles is the same.[216] Colossians certainly asserts that the "mystery" is (or refers to) Christ himself (Col 2:2). But it also teaches that the "mystery" is "Christ *in you, the hope of glory*" (Col 1:27). Thus, in Colossians the "mystery" includes the way in which Christ works salvation. The use of "mystery" in Ephesians to refer to the revelation of God's plan to save the Gentiles in Christ (3:3, 4, 9) is therefore not so different. Every NT occurrence of "mystery" (μυστήριον) has Christ at its heart.[217]

3. Finally, the contention that Ephesians gives a unique meaning to οἰκονομία, "stewardship; administration," is flawed. In Col 1:25 this noun refers in normal Pauline fashion to the "stewardship" of Paul's apostolic office. First, in two of its three Ephesian appearances (1:10; 3:9), it is far from certain that it means "plan"; "stewardship/administration" remains an option.[218] Second, in the third Ephesian occurrence (3:2), it refers to Paul's apostolic office in precisely the same way that it does in Col 1:25!

Thus, the assertion that Ephesians and Colossians use key terms in different senses fails on two counts: first, it can be shown that the two letters use the terms in a more similar manner than critics propose, and second, one finds that the terms vary somewhat in usage within Ephesians itself. No author is so rigid that he cannot or will not use polysemous words in more than one sense or with diverse referents in very close proximity.[219]

The parallels between Ephesians and other Pauline epistles such as Romans (as noted above[220]), far from casting doubt on Pauline authorship, surely

---

[216] See Caird, *The Language and Imagery of the Bible*, 54–55.

[217] Lincoln, *Ephesians*, liv: "Without repudiating that the mystery centers in Christ, Ephesians can develop the significance of the mystery within a new frame of reference by highlighting different implications of what has happened in Christ, particularly the one Church out of Jew and Gentiles that has resulted." Arnold, *Power and Magic*, 128: "Thus, there are not a number of 'mysteries' with limited applications, but one supreme 'mystery' with a number of applications." Markus N. A. Bockmuehl, *Revelation and Mystery in Ancient Judaism and Pauline Christianity* (Tübingen: Mohr, 1990), 202, while denying Pauline authorship of Ephesians, dismisses the notion that its definition of "mystery" is incompatible with Paul's: "It would not be correct to consider that this notion of the incorporation of the Gentiles is an innovation which in Ephesians completely displaces the more comprehensive idea of the mystery. ... We are merely dealing with a change in emphasis, seconded by a concomitant shift ... in the presentation of the gospel, viz. from a christological (Gal 1:12, 15) to an ecclesiological focus [in Ephesians]."

[218] As Lincoln, *Ephesians*, liv, proposes; but, as he notes, "a term can be used differently in different contexts."

[219] Bruce, *The Epistles to the Colossians, to Philemon, and to the Ephesians*, 231, is completely comfortable with the notion that Paul might adapt his vocabulary to his unique themes: "This change of perspective from Christ [in Colossians] to the church [in Ephesians] may go far to account for the different nuances which have been discerned in the use of such terms as 'fullness' and 'mystery' in Ephesians as compared with Colossians."

[220] See the chart comparing the thought of Ephesians with that of Romans in "The Literary Relationship between Ephesians and Other Pauline Epistles" in "Arguments against Pauline Authorship," above in "Authorship."

demonstrate how utterly Pauline it is.[221] The body of the present commentary finds parallel passages in Romans to be the best and most frequent expositors of Ephesians. One might suggest (with some support from patristic commentators) that Ephesians, as a compendium of Pauline theology, is a florid digest of the longer, but more rhetorically Spartan, letter to the Romans. The argument in Eph 2:1–3 that Jews and Gentiles are united in their sinfulness prior to justification in Christ relies upon the detailed argumentation in Romans 1–3. The sinner's death and resurrection with Christ through Baptism and justification by grace through faith (Eph 2:4–8) as well as reconciliation through Christ's cross (2:13–18) relies on the more developed argument in Romans 4–7, just as predestination in Christ (Eph 1:3–14) has been gloriously proclaimed in Romans 8. The unity of Jews and Gentiles in Christ asserted in Eph 2:4–10 and 2:11–22 builds on the more rigorous exploration undertaken in Romans 9–11. The presentation of Paul as the apostle to the Gentiles (Rom 11:13; 15:15–21) is assumed by Ephesians (3:1, 8, 13). These and further extensive parallels (as noted above[222]) include virtually no word-for-word parallels that might be evidence of a copyist's hand, but are better explained as the developing thought of a single author.

Major themes in Ephesians are developments of ideas in Paul's earlier writings. His presentation of Christ as the Head and the church as his body is an expansion of Romans 12 and 1 Corinthians 12. The Ephesian teaching on baptismal unity with Christ and one another via the Spirit arises from 1 Corinthians 10 and 12 and Romans 6 (compare 1 Cor 12:13 with Eph 4:1–7; 2 Cor 1:22 with Eph 1:13; and Rom 6:4–5 with Eph 2:5–6). Galatians, too, though often alleged to be the polar opposite of Ephesians,[223] is in complete harmony at key points. Its opening salvo against those who would attack Paul's apostleship asserts that he received it directly from Christ (Gal 1:11–16), just as Paul claims in Eph 3:1–13. The key theme of Ephesians—that Jew and Gentile are one in Christ on the basis of their common Baptism by one Spirit—is encapsulated succinctly in the famous passage Gal 3:28. Far from having a weak position on justification by faith alone apart from works, Eph 2:5–9 proclaims precisely the same message as Gal 2:16. The extensive coherence of Ephesians with the core Pauline writings of Romans, 1 and 2 Corinthians, and Galatians, is acknowledged even by the opponents of Pauline authorship of Ephesians.[224] Further parallels to

---

[221] See Bruce, *The Epistles to the Colossians, to Philemon, and to the Ephesians*, 229–33. Wright, *Paul: In Fresh Perspective*, 18–19, contends: "The extremely marked stylistic difference between 1 Corinthians and 2 Corinthians is far greater than that between, say, Romans and Ephesians, but nobody supposes for that reason that one of them [1 Corinthians or 2 Corinthians] is not by Paul."

[222] See the chart comparing the thought of Ephesians with that of Romans in "The Literary Relationship between Ephesians and Other Pauline Epistles" in "Arguments against Pauline Authorship," above in "Authorship."

[223] See Bruce, *The Epistles to the Colossians, to Philemon, and to the Ephesians*, 232.

[224] Best, *Ephesians*, 26–27, extensively details the parallels, but he can only draw the conclusion that that anonymous author of Ephesians was deeply familiar with Paul's writings!

1 Timothy might be adduced, though opponents of Pauline authorship would claim that such parallels support their own argument!

There is a profound (and stubborn) illogic to the critical position that both similarities to Pauline thought *and* divergences from it give evidence of the inauthenticity of Ephesians. But we might well pose in return the question that the undecided Henry Cadbury once tossed into the ring: "Which is more likely—that an imitator of Paul in the first century composed a writing ninety or ninety-five per cent in accordance with Paul's style or that Paul himself wrote a letter diverging five or ten per cent from his usual style?"[225] In light of the strength of the unanimous historical evidence in favor of Pauline authorship, the answer to this dilemma should be clear.

Pseudepigraphy?

"In the first Christian centuries neither moral nor literary standards condemned writing under an assumed name or impersonating a well-known character."[226] With these words Henry Cadbury succinctly defines what is euphemistically called "the literary device of pseudonymity."[227] "Pseudepigraphy" (ψευδής, "false, lying," + ἐπιγραφή, "superscription, title") and "pseudonymity" (ψευδής, "false, lying" + ὄνομα, "name") are equivalent technical terms that mask the thoroughly negative implications of the underlying Greek: someone has made a false claim of authorship.

There is some evidence that in Greco-Roman culture the practice of falsely attributing writings to a famous historical figure did not always carry a negative moral stigma. Students in a school of philosophy may have attributed their own writings to their master in order to honor his ownership of the ideas.[228] In some works of fiction, an author assumed the identity of a historical person for artistic purposes, inviting the reader to suspend disbelief; the device was rather transparent and did not necessarily stem from an intention to deceive.[229]

But there are also copious examples of attempts to mislead the reader. Letters supposedly written by famous historical figures were a popular genre

---

[225] Cadbury, "The Dilemma of Ephesians," 101. Cf. "Imitation and Its Detection" in Guthrie, *New Testament Introduction*, 1022–23.

[226] Cadbury, "The Dilemma of Ephesians," 94.

[227] Lincoln, *Ephesians*, lxx. In Lincoln's words: "This was a widespread and accepted literary practice in both Jewish and Greco-Roman cultures." For a comprehensive treatment of epistolary pseudepigraphy, see Wilder, *Pseudonymity, the New Testament, and Deception*; Guthrie, *New Testament Introduction*, 1012–28; and Carson, Moo, and Morris, *An Introduction to the New Testament*, 367–71.

[228] E.g., Porphyry, the neo-Platonist, identified two hundred eighty books in the Pythagorean corpus, but contended that two hundred of them were written by "mature men who belong to the group of Pythagoras, to his party and to the heritage of his knowledge" (quoted in Wilder, *Pseudonymity, the New Testament, and Deception*, 55).

[229] C. S. Lewis' *The Screwtape Letters* is a modern-day Christian equivalent: a novel using the device of pseudepigraphical letters. But Lewis surely did not intend the reader to believe the letters were *actually* exchanged between two demons (Screwtape and Wormwood)! Nor did he claim any ecclesiastical authority for his writing.

in the Greco-Roman world. There were two common motives for producing them: to lend the figure's authority to the writer's views or merely to satisfy the public's interest in celebrity lives.[230] While it would be difficult to prove that the reader recognized the deception and was nevertheless unfazed, a lack of moral outrage would not be particularly surprising, given the culture's diminished standards of morality.

Critics usually cite such Greco-Roman examples in support of the notion that later Christian writers attributed their own letters to Paul (or Peter or Jude) without believing that they had violated their community's morality. One instinctively objects that early Christians must have held higher moral standards than their pagan neighbors. But critics will then appeal to the presence of pseudonymous writings in Judaism.[231] It is true that Jewish apocryphal writings were routinely attributed to famous OT persons, perhaps because of the widespread belief that true prophecy had ceased after the death of Malachi,[232] for example, *1 Enoch, 2 Enoch, Testament of Moses, Testament of Abraham, Testaments of the Twelve Patriarchs.*[233] Inasmuch as such supposedly ancient documents are mostly extant only in Greek (not the Hebrew or Aramaic of the OT) and appeared quite suddenly and "miraculously" on the eve of the NT era, not even the most conservative Jew or Christian would claim authenticity for them. The most sensible conclusion is that these popular writings were recognized to be pious fiction. While they were certainly meant to convey spiritual truths and uplift the reader, there is no evidence that they were accepted as authoritative—evidenced precisely by the fact that they do not appear in the OT canon. Thus, these pseudonymous Jewish writings are in quite a different category from the NT writings under consideration.

Certainly, some critics will claim that there *are* pseudonymous writings within the OT canon itself. Andrew Lincoln, for example, pronounces:

> In the Hebrew Bible, writings are attributed to great names such as Moses, David, Solomon, and Isaiah. Such writings must have been produced after these figures had died, and in them earlier authoritative traditions were elaborated and contemporized but attributed to the figures at their source.[234]

---

[230] Frederik Torm, *Die Psychologie der Pseudonymität im Hinblick auf die Literatur des Urchristentums* (Gütersloh: Bertelsmann, 1932), as cited in Guthrie, *New Testament Introduction*, 1012. Bruce M. Metzger, "Literary Forgeries and Canonical Pseudepigrapha," *Journal of Biblical Literature* 91 (1972): 3–24, offers nine possible motives.

[231] Many critics claim that early (first-century) Jewish Christians understood the device of pseudonymity, while second-century Gentile Christians lost sight of the concept. Thus, these critics claim, pseudonymous writings were accepted into the NT at its inception, while the church of the next century, ignorant of this fact, rejected new instances of the same practice. See Wilder, *Pseudonymity, the New Testament, and Deception*, 166.

[232] As claimed in Talmud, *Sanhedrin*, 11a.

[233] For an introduction and the text of these writings, see Charlesworth, *The Old Testament Pseudepigrapha*, vol. 1.

[234] Lincoln, *Ephesians*, lxx.

But there are two flaws in such an appeal. First, it involves *petitio principii*, "begging the question." Lincoln assumes without demonstration that some OT writings were not authored by the persons to whom they are attributed and then he uses that assumption as proof that God's people in OT times accepted the practice.[235] Second, *if* it were true that the traditional authors of these books were not entirely responsible for their final form, this would nevertheless not be pseudonymity in entirely the same sense as the term is applied to the Pauline letters. For these books do not make precisely this explicit claim. Some portions of the Pentateuch (such as Deuteronomy 34 or comments ending "to this day") may not have come from Moses' hand—and do not make that claim. The prophecies uttered by Isaiah might conceivably have been written down or compiled by someone else. The psalms of David and Solomon were almost certainly compiled into the canonical book by a later hand. But the epistles of Paul are quite a different matter: if they were not written in precisely this form by the apostle Paul, then one cannot escape the fact that they make a false claim for themselves.

When it comes to pseudepigraphical *letters* in Jewish tradition, the data are meager.[236] (The paucity of examples may itself demonstrate that the Jews held to a stricter moral standard than their Greco-Roman neighbors.) There are, in fact, only two viable cases: the *Epistle of Jeremiah* and the *Letter of Aristeas*. Yet neither of these is entirely applicable to the Pauline question. In the case of the *Epistle of Jeremiah*, like the apocryphal writings (see above), it first appears on the scene hundreds of years after its supposed context and in a language (Greek) not spoken by its supposed author. The readers would have recognized its inauthenticity and read it simply as a pious homily, or perhaps some would have naïvely accepted it for what it claimed to be. But if the *author* had intended the latter, that is, intended to deceive, then his purpose would have been accomplished only if the deception had worked and the *audience* truly believed the letter came from the ancient prophet. There is no logic to the oft-claimed *via media* that the readers could have recognized it as inauthentic and nonetheless have accepted it as authoritative. The *Letter of Aristeas*, if it indeed was not written by the person it claims, is simply irrelevant to the Pauline question. For "Aristeas" is not a famous historical figure whose authority might have been claimed for the teaching contained in the "letter" (which is, in any case, not formally a letter).[237]

---

[235] NT scholars regularly make the same error as they use the supposedly proven case of 2 Peter as justification for seeking other pseudonymous letters in the NT. On the authorship of 2 Peter, see, for example, Giese, *2 Peter and Jude*, 6–11.

[236] Wilder, *Pseudonymity, the New Testament, and Deception*, 78: "Many pseudepigraphical epistles were composed in Greco-Roman antiquity, but relatively few pseudonymous letters exist in the religious literature of the Jews and Christians. One is indeed hard pressed to find *any* pseudonymous epistles from antiquity to which the disputed NT letters are entirely comparable."

[237] On Jewish pseudepigraphy, see Guthrie, *New Testament Introduction*, 1012–15.

This is, indeed, the crucial question: did the early Christian church accept the practice of pseudepigraphy as a valid way to apply apostolic authority to issues arising in the postapostolic church?[238] The NT itself gives evidence that some people had produced letters in Paul's name with the intent to deceive. This can be deduced from Paul's warning against accepting "a letter purporting to come from us" (δι᾽ ἐπιστολῆς ὡς δι᾽ ἡμῶν, 2 Thess 2:2)[239] and from his use of commended letter carriers and personal annotations to authenticate his writings (Gal 6:11; 2 Thess 3:17).[240] There is also evidence that pseudepigraphy was practiced in Christian circles in the second century—but in every case, when the ruse was uncovered, the documents were rejected as forgeries.[241] The closing words of the NT impose the harshest stricture ("plagues") on anyone who would think to add to or take away from the words of the book's prophecy (Rev 22:18–19). This evidence indicates that pseudepigraphy was thoroughly rejected by the apostolic and early postapostolic church—at least when it was a tool in the hand of false teachers.

But what if the motive was more honorable? Could a student of Paul write a letter in his teacher's name, believing that the Christian church would accept its contents as apostolic even though they were aware that Paul did not write it?[242] Scholars frequently answer yes by appealing to the words of Tertullian: "It is allowable that that which pupils publish should be regarded as their masters' work."[243] This apparently conclusive testimony seems to settle the question. But

---

[238] The most recent thorough study, Wilder, *Pseudonymity, the New Testament, and Deception*, 49–52, 123–63, answers no.

[239] Wilder, *Pseudonymity, the New Testament, and Deception*, 51, notes that the anarthrous ἐπιστολή, "*a* letter" (2 Thess 2:2), means Paul is not simply condemning *one* letter as a forgery, but *any* letter that falsely claims to be from him.

[240] See the interpretation of "Tychicus" in the commentary on Eph 6:21.

[241] Guthrie, *New Testament Introduction*, 1015, notes six "noteworthy examples" of pseudepigraphical epistles among the NT Apocrypha. See also Best, *Ephesians*, 11–12. Among these only two are pseudo-Pauline letters. The *Third Letter to the Corinthians* was contained in the *Acts of Paul*, which the second-century church exposed as a forgery; see the quotation of Tertullian about the *Acts of Paul* below. The *Letter to the Laodiceans* is either the one the Muratorian Canon declared to be forged or a much later letter (fourth century AD?) that cannot inform the early postapostolic era. Thus, there is no evidence here that the early church *accepted* such letters. Those in the Middle Ages who accepted the *Letter to the Laodiceans* did so because they believed it was a genuine letter by Paul. See Wilder, *Pseudonymity, the New Testament, and Deception*, 132–35.

[242] A related question is whether the ancient world had a legal or moral concept of literary intellectual property. Though this has frequently been answered in the negative, Terry Wilder offers substantial evidence to the contrary. Wilder, *Pseudonymity, the New Testament, and Deception*, 50, cites evidence from Eusebius' *Preparation for the Gospel*, 10:2–3, which quotes (among others) Clement of Alexandria, *Stromata*, 6:2:

> And not only have they been detected pirating and paraphrasing thoughts and expressions, as will be shown; but they will also be convicted of the possession of what is entirely stolen. For stealing entirely what is the production of others, they have published it as their own. (*ANF* 2:486)

[243] Tertullian, *Against Marcion*, 4:5.4, quoted by Lincoln, *Ephesians*, lxxii; cited also by Best, *Ephesians*, 13. Likewise, Kirby, *Ephesians: Baptism and Pentecost*, 40, proposes that the

one wonders how many scholars have uncritically reproduced the citation without taking the time to read it in context. For, it appears that *Tertullian means to say quite the opposite of what the critics think.*

In writing against Marcion and his truncated NT canon, Tertullian is concerned to defend the authority and authenticity of every NT writing. His demonstration of authenticity arises from an understanding of historical verification that even modern scholars would approve. He proposes that each writing that claims to be apostolic be investigated by visiting the community to which it was written or where it was preserved:

> To sum up: if it is agreed that that has the greater claim to truth which has the earlier priority, and that has the priority which has been so since the beginning, and that has been since the beginning which was from the apostles, there will be no less agreement that that was handed down by the apostles which is held sacred and inviolate in the churches the apostles founded.[244]

On this basis Tertullian claims that the letters to the Corinthians, Galatians, Philippians, Thessalonians, Ephesians (!), and Romans are genuinely apostolic because there is ancient testimony to each letter in each of those respective places. Likewise, he asserts the genuineness of John's Revelation, and the Gospels of John and Matthew, for the churches founded by those apostles, as well as "all those which are in alliance with them in the fellowship of the mystery [i.e., the Gospel],"[245] testify that these Gospels go all the way back to their apostolic authors.

But when Tertullian comes to Luke and Mark he has a slight problem, for these Gospels were not written by apostles. Undeterred, Tertullian explains how they, nevertheless, came to bear apostolic authority—and here we find the contentious sentence reproduced in context:

> That same authority of the apostolic churches will stand as witness also for the other gospels, which no less than Luke's we possess by their agency and according to their text—I mean John's and Matthew's, though that which Mark produced is stated to be Peter's, whose interpreter Mark was. Luke's narrative also they usually attribute to Paul. *It is permissible for the works which disciples published to be regarded as belonging to their masters.*[246]

In other words, in the second century some people had doubts about the authority of the Gospels of Luke and Mark precisely because they were *not* written by

---

ancients not only *accepted* the practice but also *praised* it: "It was considered highly laudatory in the ancient world for a disciple to publish his own work under his teacher's name, as Tertullian tells us."

[244] Tertullian, *Against Marcion*, 4:5.1 (trans. Evans). Serapion of Antioch likewise writes (ca. AD 190) concerning a church that was using a *Gospel of Peter*: "We receive both Peter and the other Apostles as Christ; but as experienced men we reject the writings falsely inscribed with their names, since we know that we did not receive such from our fathers" (quoted by Guthrie, *New Testament Introduction*, 1020). Cf. Wilder, *Pseudonymity, the New Testament, and Deception*, 135–39.

[245] Tertullian, *Against Marcion*, 4:5.2 (trans. Evans).

[246] Tertullian, *Against Marcion*, 4:5.3–4 (trans. Evans; emphasis added).

apostles. Tertullian responds by rooting their authority in Paul and Peter. *But this is not a case of pseudepigraphy!* For neither Gospel claims to be written by Paul or Peter. In fact, neither claims to be written by Luke or Mark, but they were attributed to these men by the earliest witnesses on the basis of presumably sound evidence.[247] Tertullian's point is that Luke and Mark ought to be accepted by the church because the authors were companions and disciples of the apostles. That is, Luke and Mark did not write their own words and attribute them to the apostles, but instead recorded the apostolic testimony for the sake of the church.

Thus, the actual evidence from Tertullian proves the very opposite of what the proponents of pseudepigraphy would have us believe: no writing could gain acceptance in the early church unless it could be demonstrated that it came from the hand of an apostle.[248] The Gospels of Luke and Mark were the exceptions that proved the rule. In fact, in his treatise *On Baptism*, Tertullian actually refers to a case of pseudepigraphy and describes the church's response to the scandal:

> But if certain Acts of Paul, which are falsely so named, claim the example of Thecla for allowing women to teach and to baptize, let men know that in Asia the presbyter who compiled that document, thinking to add of his own to Paul's reputation, was found out, and though he professed he had done it for love of Paul, was deposed from his position.[249]

This intriguing text addresses every element of the supposed "literary device of pseudonymity." The motives claimed by the pseudepigrapher were noble, for he hoped to add to Paul's reputation. Yet the church did not accept these noble motives, and when it was determined that the writing was forged ("falsely so named"[250]), not only was the writing rejected, but the presbyter himself was even defrocked for his crime.

Authenticity and authority therefore cannot be separated. It is for this reason that the investigation of the Pauline authorship of Ephesians is a critical endeavor. Paul's writings hold authority for the church because he was

---

[247] See Eusebius, *Ecclesiastical History*, 3:24.7 and 3:39.15 (quoting Papias). Critics regularly fail to make this distinction between a writing's own claim to authorship and later attributions of authorship by the early church. For example, Best, *Ephesians*, 11, writes: "Though for centuries Hebrews was assumed to be by Paul, the realisation that it was not did not lessen the respect for it; what is important is its content. Were Ephesians not by Paul its content might still be true and helpful to believers." The difference, of course, is that Hebrews does not claim to be written by Paul, while Ephesians does. The early church's attribution of Pauline authorship to Hebrews is evidence that apostolic authorship—not just agreeable content— *did* matter.

[248] For further evidence of this requirement, see Wilder, *Pseudonymity, the New Testament, and Deception*, 126–28, 165–216.

[249] Tertullian, *On Baptism*, 17 (trans. Ernest Evans, *Tertullian's Homily on Baptism* [London: SPCK, 1964], 37).

[250] This phrase indicates that it was not simply the false doctrine in the document that was objectionable but also the act of forgery itself and the non-apostolic origin that it evidenced. The second-century Muratorian Canon uses similar language: "There is extant also [an epistle] to the Laodiceans, and another to the Alexandrians, forged in the name of Paul according to the heresy of Marcion. There are also many others which cannot be received in the General Church, for gall cannot be mixed with honey" (trans. Theron, *Evidence of Tradition*, 111).

authorized by Christ as his apostle to speak for him in teaching his church. If Paul did not write Ephesians, its value as a pious and beautiful Christian writing might not diminish, but it would have no place in the Christian Scriptures[251] and could claim no authority over the faith and life of its readers.[252] It would be deeply ironic if a writer falsely claiming to be the apostle Paul would have written: "Therefore, since you have put off *falsehood*, 'each one of you speak *truth* with his neighbor,' for we are members of one another" (Eph 4:25).[253]

Addressees

The letter titled "To the Ephesians" apparently claims in its first line that Paul wrote "to the saints who are *in Ephesus*" (τοῖς ἁγίοις τοῖς οὖσιν [ἐν Ἐφέσῳ], 1:1)—a church quite familiar to the Christian reader from the accounts of Paul's missionary work in the book of Acts. Yet the accuracy of that claim has been challenged in modern times as much as Pauline authorship itself, albeit on rather different grounds. For while the critical denial of Pauline authorship is a relatively recent phenomenon, the original destination of the letter has been in doubt since ancient times, and on the basis of hard textual evidence.

The Textual Variant "in Ephesus" in Ephesians 1:1

The absence of the phrase "in Ephesus" in the letter's address (1:1) in some early Greek manuscripts is one of the most famous text-critical problems in the NT. Even the layperson stumbles upon it in the footnotes of most

---

[251] See E. Earle Ellis, "Pseudonymity and Canonicity of New Testament Documents," in *Worship, Theology and Ministry in the Early Church: Essays in Honor of Ralph P. Martin* (ed. Michael J. Wilkins and Terence Paige; Sheffield: Sheffield Academic, 1992), 212–24. As Tertullian and the Muratorian Canon demonstrate, apostolic authorship was the chief criterion for canonicity. Lincoln's view is therefore illogical: "Whether written by Paul or by a follower, Ephesians is now canonical; it has the same authoritative and foundational status for the Church's teaching and life as, for example, one of the gospels or Paul's letter to the Romans" (*Ephesians*, lxxiii). If a scholar were to determine that the early church was mistaken in believing a letter was written by Paul, then that scholar's integrity should lead him to exclude the letter from his present-day canon. Bart Ehrman, at least, has the honesty to admit as much in *Forged: Writing in the Name of God—Why the Bible's Authors Are Not Who We Think They Are* (New York: HarperOne, 2011).

[252] Lincoln, *Ephesians*, lxxiii, represents the opposite position: "There should be no suggestion that to decide that Ephesians is pseudonymous is somehow to detract from the validity or authority of its message as part of the NT canon. This could be said to be committing the 'authorial fallacy,' that is, to set more store by who wrote a document than by what it says."

The danger in Lincoln's position is subjectivism: if the authority of the document does not derive from its origin (inspired author), then the reader determines whether a document belongs in the canon according to how it resonates with his own views and accords with his preselected mini-canon. This subjectivism is the essence of the critical position.

[253] Cf. appeals to "truth" in Eph 4:15; 6:14; Col 3:9; 2 Thess 2:10–12. Lincoln objects that this argument entails "a confusion of literary and moral categories" (*Ephesians*, lxxi), though this objection has the anachronistic ring of postmodernism. Best, *Ephesians*, 12, likewise insists that early Christians and Jews operated with a different standard of truth and honesty than we do today (!)—that "deception" was acceptable when it was exercised not for personal gain, but for the common good. For the contrary view, see Guthrie, *New Testament Introduction*, 1021; Wilder, *Pseudonymity, the New Testament, and Deception*, passim.

English translations. The implications for interpreting Ephesians are immense and affect a major premise of the present commentary. The lengthy treatment that follows deals not with a minor textual problem, but speaks directly to the question of the letter's addressees, content, and purpose. If this letter was not written to the Ephesian church, then what we can learn about Ephesus in the Acts of the Apostles is not directly relevant to its interpretation. Those who follow that route treat Ephesians as a general epistle that, in contrast to Paul's usual practice, does not deal with any specific problems among its addressees. By corollary, if the traditional Ephesian address is upheld, then one stands to gain a great deal from reading the letter against the background of Paul's experience in Ephesus during his third missionary journey (Acts 18:24–20:38).

The Manuscript Evidence

The evidence for and against the inclusion of ἐν Ἐφέσῳ, "in Ephesus," is best read in conjunction with the other variants in the immediate context. The following chart collates four distinct readings, progressing from shortest to longest, noting a few major manuscripts in support of each:[254]

1	𝔓46	τοῖς ἁγίοις to the saints			οὖσιν being		καὶ πιστοῖς ἐν Χριστῷ Ἰησοῦ and faithful in Christ Jesus
2	ℵ·, B·	τοῖς ἁγίοις to the saints		τοῖς the	οὖσιν being		καὶ πιστοῖς ἐν Χριστῷ Ἰησοῦ and faithful in Christ Jesus
3	B², D, 𝔐, latt, sy, co	τοῖς ἁγίοις to the saints		τοῖς the	οὖσιν being	ἐν Ἐφέσῳ in Ephesus	καὶ πιστοῖς ἐν Χριστῷ Ἰησοῦ and faithful in Christ Jesus
4	ℵ², A	τοῖς ἁγίοις to the saints	πᾶσιν all	τοῖς the	οὖσιν being	ἐν Ἐφέσῳ in Ephesus	καὶ πιστοῖς ἐν Χριστῷ Ἰησοῦ and faithful in Christ Jesus

To summarize the evidence:

- The earliest manuscript extant for the Pauline epistles, 𝔓46 (ca. AD 200),[255] omits "in Ephesus," though it nevertheless titles the letter "To the Ephesians."

---

[254] Full evidence is available in the critical editions. Note that the blank spaces in the chart are not meant to indicate blank space in the original manuscripts (an issue that will be significant later in the discussion). The blank spaces merely aim to help the reader see which words change in the progression from the shortest to the longest reading.

[255] Comfort, *Encountering the Manuscripts*, 134–39, discusses the possibility that 𝔓46 is much older, dating perhaps to the last decade of the first century, but finally settles on the likelihood of the mid second century.

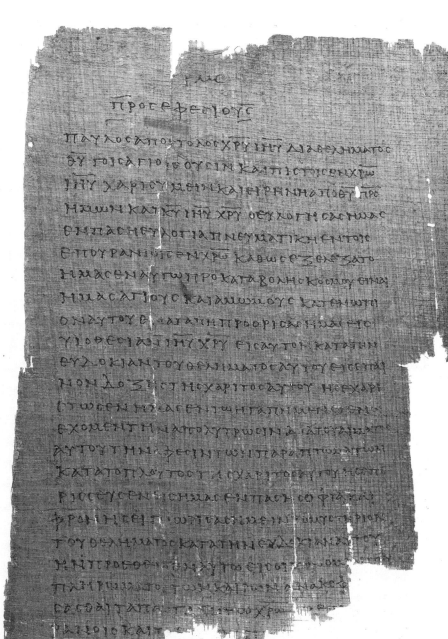

$\mathfrak{P}^{46}$ showing Ephesians 1:1–11.

- Two major fourth-century manuscripts, Sinaiticus (‭א‬) and Vaticanus (B), omit "in Ephesus" in their first hand, but a corrector later adds it. Their first hand differs from 𝔓⁴⁶ merely in the addition of the definite article τοῖς, "the," before the participle οὖσιν, "being."
- Almost all later manuscripts[256] include "in Ephesus," with a minor disagreement over the presence or absence of πᾶσιν, "all."

Three further comments are relevant to the text's external evidence:

- All three early manuscripts that omit the place name are part of what has traditionally been called the Alexandrian text-type (though 𝔓⁴⁶ itself predates the differentiation of text-types).[257] If there is a geographical or genealogical connection between them, the evidence might represent a single ancestor.
- 𝔓⁴⁶, though carrying great respect as one of the earliest papyrus texts of the NT, is often found to be in disagreement with the best reading in a given instance.[258]

---

[256] Some late, medieval manuscripts (6 424ᶜ 1739) also omit "in Ephesus," suggesting either that they were copied from an ancient manuscript in the 𝔓⁴⁶ tradition or that they omitted the addressees independently (for the same reason as their ancient forebears). The tenth-century minuscule 1739, which Kurt and Barbara Aland call "outstanding" (*The Text of the New Testament*, 317), frequently stands with 𝔓⁴⁶ in a unique reading. See Royse, *Scribal Habits in Early Greek New Testament Papyri*, 205–6; Parker, *New Testament Manuscripts and Their Texts*, 261–63. Comfort, *Encountering the Manuscripts*, 315, comments:

> The relationship between 𝔓⁴⁶ and 1739 is noteworthy because 1739 is a tenth-century manuscript that was copied from a fourth-century manuscript of excellent quality. According to a colophon, the scribe of 1739 for the Pauline epistles followed a manuscript which came from Caesarea in the library of Pamphilus and which contained an Origenian text. The three manuscripts, 𝔓⁴⁶ B and 1739, form a clear textual line: from 𝔓⁴⁶ (second century) to B (early fourth century) to 1739 (tenth century based on fourth century).

[257] While few modern textual scholars any longer affirm the theory that an Alexandrian text-type arose from deliberate editorial work in Egypt (i.e., the Hesychian recension), the familial relationship of the great early manuscripts 𝔓⁴⁶, ‭א‬, and B is undeniable. It suggests a carefully preserved manuscript tradition. See Royse, *Scribal Habits in Early Greek New Testament Papyri*, 204–5; Parker, *New Testament Manuscripts and Their Texts*, 165, 171–74, 307; and Eckhard J. Schnabel, "Textual Criticism: Recent Developments," in *The Face of New Testament Studies: A Survey of Recent Research* (ed. Scot McKnight and Grant R. Osborne; Grand Rapids: Baker Academic, 2004), 65–69.

[258] In NA²⁷ the editors' chosen text differs from 𝔓⁴⁶ on forty occasions in Ephesians (by the present author's count). Admittedly, this is a rough and unscientific measure of the reliability of 𝔓⁴⁶, but it is instructive, nonetheless. Kurt and Barbara Aland, *The Text of the New Testament*, 57, note: "Until their [the Bodmer papyri's] discovery it was thought on the basis of 𝔓⁴⁵ and 𝔓⁴⁶ that the second/third century text was generally characterized by considerable irregularity. 𝔓⁶⁶ seemed to confirm this. But 𝔓⁷⁵ proved this to be wrong, because its text was so closely similar to that of Codex Vaticanus that it could even be suspected of being its exemplar." Thus, they label 𝔓⁴⁶ a " 'free' text" in comparison to the "strict" text of 𝔓⁷⁵, the "normal" text of 𝔓⁴⁷, and the "paraphrastic" text of the later 0171 (pp. 59, 93, 95). Zuntz, *The Text of the Epistles*, is a thorough study of the characteristics of 𝔓⁴⁶ in the epistles. He concludes about its tendency to standardize the liturgical/lectionary address, ἀδελφοί [μου], "[my] brothers": "In this detail, then, the text of the papyrus is about as bad as it could be" (179). A more recent study of 𝔓⁴⁶ notes the manuscript's tendency to omit rather than add, but does not deal specifically with the addressees of Ephesians: Royse, *Scribal Habits in Early Greek New Testament Papyri*, 199–358. Royse concludes:

- Both of the fourth-century manuscripts Sinaiticus (א) and Vaticanus (B) had the words "in Ephesus" added by a corrector's hand. Since correctors typically worked on the basis of another ancient manuscript, thought (by definition) to hold equal authority to the master manuscript, this *may* be evidence that other early manuscripts (no longer extant) included the words.[259]

Playing this game by traditional text-critical rules leads to a draw. In favor of the omission of "in Ephesus" is the antiquity of the three major manuscripts and the traditional nod given to the Alexandrian family, as well as the text critic's preference for the *lectio brevior* (shorter reading).[260] In favor of the inclusion of "in Ephesus" is the antiquity of the versions (Old Latin, etc.) and the great geographical distribution of manuscripts that include it. This stalemate led the textual committee to enclose "in Ephesus" in square brackets in UBS[4] (as also in NA[27]) and express their uncertainty by giving it a "C" grade.[261]

Let us consider the two major options in more detail. Most commentators and many modern translations favor the omission of the place name "in Ephesus" on the grounds of its omission being the supposedly oldest and best reading. Such an automatic preference for the papyri and the traditional Alexandrian text-type is increasingly under suspicion among modern textual critics. But in this case, the most compelling argument against this conclusion may be the grammar itself. The absence of the place name in $\mathfrak{P}^{46}$ produces a reading that is nonsensical: τοῖς ἁγίοις οὖσιν καὶ πιστοῖς ἐν Χριστῷ Ἰησοῦ, "to the saints being and/also faithful in Christ Jesus." The problem is the participle οὖσιν, "being": if Paul had wished to say that his addressees were both "saints and faithful," the participle would not have been necessary.[262] The parti-

---

The scribe makes a number of errors that result in nonsense, despite frequent correction by him of his text. Many of these seem to arise from his faulty understanding of what he is copying, resulting in a high density of nonsense in context readings. …

The scribe has a very marked tendency to omit portions of the text, most often only one word but longer phrases also. Some of these are due to scribal leaps, but most seem to have arisen from simple oversight or carelessness. (358)

[259] Metzger and Ehrman, *The Text of the New Testament*, 67, note concerning Sinaiticus:

At a later date (probably sometime about the sixth or seventh century), a group of correctors working at Caesarea entered a large number of alterations into the text of both the Old and New Testaments. These readings, designated by the siglum א[ca] or א[cb], represent a thoroughgoing effort to correct the text to a different standard, which, according to a colophon at the end of the books of Esdras and Esther, is stated to have been "a very ancient manuscript that had been corrected by the hand of the holy martyr Pamphilus."

[260] Recent specialized study of the papyri has challenged the traditional view that a shorter reading in a papyrus manuscript is always to be preferred. H. A. G. Houghton, "Recent Developments in New Testament Textual Criticism," *Early Christianity* 2 (2011): 256, summarizes: "Material is more commonly omitted than added in extant papyri, reinforcing the fact that the text-critical canon of *lectio brevior potior* must not be applied indiscriminately." See also "The Shorter Reading?" in Royse, *Scribal Habits in Early Greek New Testament Papyri*, 705–36.

[261] Metzger, *A Textual Commentary on the Greek New Testament*, 532.

[262] Turner (*Syntax*, 151–52) finds a number of parallels for this "redundant" use of the participle (Acts 5:17; 13:1; 14:13 [D]; Rom 13:1), thus asserting that the $\mathfrak{P}^{46}$ reading "need not be

ciple requires some sort of predicate completion ("the saints being _____") that is absent in this text. The conjunction καί, "and," interrupts the syntax and makes it difficult to accept that πιστοῖς, "faithful," might be the expected predicate completion ("the saints being and/also faithful").[263] In other words, *the participle makes sense only if it is followed by the words ἐν Ἐφέσῳ, "in Ephesus," or if it were followed immediately by πιστοῖς, "faithful."* While it might seem that the omission of "in Ephesus," which is the *lectio brevior* ("shorter reading"), is therefore also the *lectio difficilior* ("the more difficult reading," the one that explains the creation of the others), the peculiar grammar is not just difficult, but impossible.[264]

By contrast, the reading of the majority of manuscripts that include "in Ephesus" is grammatically difficult, but *not* impossible, and is consistent with Pauline usage. In the address of three other letters Paul uses the same articular participle (τοῖς οὖσιν) to introduce a place name with the preposition ἐν, "in":

- τοῖς οὖσιν ἐν Ῥώμῃ, "to the ones being in Rome" (Rom 1:7)
- τοῖς οὖσιν ἐν ὅλῃ τῇ Ἀχαΐᾳ, "to the ones being in all Achaia" (2 Cor 1:1)
- τοῖς οὖσιν ἐν Φιλίπποις, "to the ones being in Philippi" (Phil 1:1)

Note also that Ignatius addresses his letter to the Ephesians in precisely the same way:

τῇ ἐκκλησίᾳ τῇ ἀξιομακαρίστῳ τῇ οὔσῃ ἐν Ἐφέσῳ τῆς Ἀσίας

to the church, the deservedly most blessed, the one being in Ephesus of Asia (Preface)[265]

---

rejected." Yet none of these parallels reproduces the real difficulty of the case in Eph 1:1, where the participle is immediately followed by καί. Best, *Ephesians*, 99–100, proposes omitting the participle *and* the place name, but has no manuscript evidence for his conjecture. The participle is unused in Col 1:2, τοῖς ἐν Κολοσσαῖς ἁγίοις καὶ πιστοῖς ἀδελφοῖς ἐν Χριστῷ, "to the in-Colossae saints and faithful brothers in Christ," which is grammatically more sensible than the reading of 𝔓[46] in Eph 1:1.

[263] A creative explanation for the καί has been proposed by van Roon, *The Authenticity of Ephesians*, 72–85, and taken up by Lincoln, *Ephesians*, 3–4. They argue that the καί is evidence of the omission of *two* place names: those mentioned in Col 4:13. Their proposed reading is: τοῖς ἁγίοις τοῖς οὖσιν ἐν Ἱεραπόλει καὶ ἐν Λαοδικείᾳ, πιστοῖς ἐν Χριστῷ Ἰησοῦ, "to the saints who are in Hierapolis and Laodicea, faithful in Christ Jesus." Note the presence of the comma before "faithful," which solves the grammatical difficulty by making the second adjective, πιστοῖς, "faithful," an appositive (as is ἀγαπητοῖς in Rom 1:7). If ἐν Ἱεραπόλει καὶ ἐν Λαοδικείᾳ were original, it would explain Marcion's belief that the letter was written to Laodicea. But the theory founders on a complete lack of manuscript evidence and compounds the problem by postulating the loss of not one but *two* place names.

[264] BDF, § 413 (3) asserts: "The ptcp. ὤν can only be used when there are other adjuncts to the predicate: A 28:17 τοὺς ὄντας τῶν Ἰουδαίων πρώτους … ; otherwise it must be omitted … ; therefore E 1:1 τοῖς ἁγίοις οὖσιν καὶ πιστοῖς (𝔓[46]; D adds ἐν Ἐφέσῳ, which satisfies the rule) *is impossible* (ὁ ὤν 'the existing one or thing' is different §474(5c))" (emphasis added).

[265] Ignatius begins his letters to the Magnesians, Trallians, Philadelphians, and Smyrnaeans with the same grammatical structure: articular (usually dative) participle of εἰμί + ἐν ("in") + the place name.

Thus, it makes perfect sense that Paul should write here τοῖς ἁγίοις τοῖς οὖσιν ἐν Ἐφέσῳ, "to the saints being in Ephesus." What makes this reading difficult nonetheless is the addition of the phrase καὶ πιστοῖς ἐν Χριστῷ Ἰησοῦ, "and faithful in Christ Jesus." For "in Ephesus" and "in Christ" are not parallel ideas (the first is a geographical location, while the second is spiritual), and the additional phrase makes the preceding articular participle τοῖς οὖσιν, "the ones being/those who are," more difficult. This grammatical problem is explored in more detail in the fourth textual note on 1:1, where the following analysis is tentatively proposed:

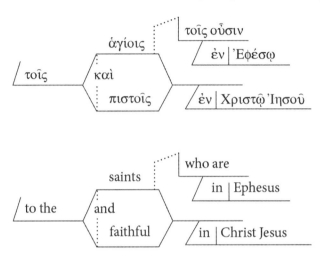

This uneasy solution implies that Paul has combined two sentence structures into one. The main sentence is this: "to the saints and faithful in Christ Jesus." Into this Paul inserts his usual way of describing the recipients' geographical location: "the ones being/those who are in Ephesus." What confuses matters is that he inserts it immediately after the first substantive, ἁγίοις, "saints." This syntax would be more shocking if it were not observed that his description of his epistolary addressees frequently demonstrates this kind of grammatical disorder (see Rom 1:7; 2 Cor 1:1; Phil 1:1 in their entirety). Thus, what Paul writes to the Ephesians ought to be understood in the same way as what he writes to the Colossians:

τοῖς ἐν Κολοσσαῖς ἁγίοις καὶ πιστοῖς ἀδελφοῖς ἐν Χριστῷ

to the in-Colossae saints and faithful brothers in Christ (Col 1:2)

Hence, the best reading of the grammar of Eph 1:1 is "to the saints and faithful ones in Christ Jesus who are in Ephesus."

Evidence from the Fathers

The patristic evidence reflects the confusion in the manuscripts. Origen knows our epistle as Paul's letter to the Ephesians but interprets a text that omits the words "in Ephesus"; he discusses the difficult grammar at length.[266] Marcion, who claimed that our letter was written "to the Laodiceans," provides ambiguous evidence. Did he change the *title* of the letter for some reason in support of his heretical agenda? Or does his use of an alternate title indicate that his copy of our letter omitted the place name in the *text* of 1:1? Our knowledge of Marcion comes from Tertullian's emphatic retorts:

> I forbear to treat here of another epistle to which we give the title *To the Ephesians*, but the heretics *To the Laodiceans*.[267]

> On the Epistle to the Laodiceans. By the church's truth we have it that this epistle was sent to the Ephesians, not the Laodiceans: Marcion has been at pains some time to falsify its title, in this matter too an industrious discoverer of new ways. But the title is of no concern, since when the apostle [Paul] wrote to some he wrote to all, and without doubt his teaching in Christ was of that God to whom the facts of his teaching rightly belong.[268]

It is intriguing that Tertullian claims Marcion falsified the *title*, not the *text*. Does this mean that Tertullian's own copy of our letter did *not* include the words ἐν Ἐφέσῳ, "in Ephesus," in 1:1? For if it did include them, Tertullian might have appealed to the text itself. Whether or not this is true about the text, Tertullian provides emphatic (albeit indirect) testimony that the universal early church knew the letter as from Paul to the Ephesians. Irenaeus, the Muratorian Canon, and Clement of Alexandria give similar testimony.[269]

The idea that there was a letter of Paul to the Laodiceans was persistent in the early and medieval church. The Muratorian Canon speaks of an early forgery, and a later text that circulated under that name is also clearly a fake. The origin of these suppositions and fabrications is most likely the words of Paul himself:

> And when the letter has been read among you, have it read also in the church of the Laodiceans, and see that you also read the letter from Laodicea [τὴν ἐκ Λαοδικείας]. (Col 4:16)[270]

---

[266] Origen, *Ephesians*, on Eph 1:1 (cf. Origen, *Against Celsus*, 3:20). Origen takes the participle οὖσιν, "being," as absolute, interpreting τοῖς οὖσιν to mean "those called out of non-existence into real existence through participation in the one who is Being itself" (Lincoln, *Ephesians*, 2). Basil, *Against Euonius*, 2:19, repeats Origen's explanation, indicating that he, too, was aware of an ancient text or texts lacking the place name (Schwindt, *Das Weltbild des Epheserbriefes*, 56).

[267] Tertullian, *Against Marcion*, 5:11.12 (trans. Evans).

[268] Tertullian, *Against Marcion*, 5:17.1 (trans. Evans).

[269] Irenaeus, *Against Heresies*, 1:3.4; 1:8.4; Clement of Alexandria, *Stromata*, 4:8.

[270] Nils A. Dahl, "Adresse und Proömium des Epheserbriefes," *Theologische Zeitschrift* 7 (1951): 242–43, believes that Marcion did not possess a manuscript with the words "in Laodicea" in Eph 1:1, but that his title "to the Laodiceans" was merely an educated guess (presumably on the basis of Col 4:16). This is a common proposal.

The letter "*from* Laodicea" may or may not have been a letter of Paul *to* Laodicea. In light of the common Pauline origin of Ephesians, Colossians, and Philemon and their common movement with Tychicus the letter carrier (Eph 6:21; Col 4:7; cf. 2 Tim 4:12), it is more likely that the letter being read *in* Laodicea was Ephesians and that Paul desired the Colossians to read this letter as well (Col 4:16). Paul may, therefore, have given Tychicus precise instructions about sharing the two letters, Ephesians and Colossians, while he stayed in the area of the two nearby cities of Colossae and Laodicea.[271]

Theories about "in Ephesus"

If the words "in Ephesus" are original, what might explain their subsequent omission? If they are not original, what might explain their insertion? A number of explanations have been offered.

Accidental Omission

The possibility that a scribe was asleep at the switch while copying the very first sentence of the letter must be dismissed as absurdly remote. Nor are there any appropriate factors (such as homoioteleuton) in play that might have caused the eye to skip the words.

Critical Change

The proposition that the letter's contents do not align with Paul's relationship to the Ephesian church will be considered below (see "Internal Evidence" in "Addressees"). Yet, even if the letter be adjudged to contain few clear references to its intended audience, it beggars belief that a scribe would have taken upon himself to dispute the veracity of the letter's opening line and change it.

Circular Letter

Here we encounter the most widespread explanation. Adjudging that the letter displays little detail connecting it specifically to Ephesus (see "Internal Evidence," below in "Addressees"), most scholars believe that the letter was originally a circular. This opinion is held by critics who reject Pauline authorship and postulate that the letter was written by a disciple of Paul to summarize his message for a generic audience in Asia Minor. It is also promulgated by conservative scholars who hold to Pauline authorship but accept the evidence for the omission of the place name in the manuscript tradition. By this theory, Paul (or an unknown author) had a number of copies of his letter produced, which Tychicus was to deliver to a series of churches along his route, perhaps working his way along the Lycus and Meander Valleys from Colossae, Hierapolis,

---

[271] Note the connection between Colossae and Laodicea in Col 2:1; 4:13, 16. Carson, Moo, and Morris, *An Introduction to the New Testament*, 310, object: "Ephesians and Colossians are so like one another that one wonders why the churches should go through the process of exchanging them." Yet there *are* differences between these two letters, and it would make sense that the area churches should read both of them. The churches were not so awash in apostolic writings that they would have declined to receive one.

and Laodicea to Ephesus. The mechanics of the circular letter theory have been described in two distinct ways:

1. The name of a particular church destination was written on the outside of each scroll, but the letters were otherwise identical. The text of Eph 1:1 reads as in number 1 or 2 in the chart in "The Manuscript Evidence" (above in "Addressees"), lacking the place name.[272] At a later date the place name of the addressees migrated into the text itself—but only in the case of the copy sent to the Ephesians.

2. Each letter copy was produced with a blank space in the first verse so that Tychicus could fill in the place name of the addressees as he came to each church, but the letters were otherwise identical.[273] The assumption is that Paul did not prescribe which particular churches ought to get a copy and gave Tychicus the authority to personalize them. What survived subsequently were only the copy to the Ephesians and a leftover copy with no place name.

The circular letter theory is fraught with at least five difficulties.[274] First, we have a number of examples in the NT itself of how an apostle would write a circular letter. The address is either generic enough to suit the entire audience (Galatians, 1 Peter, Hebrews), or individual messages are contained within one larger letter (Revelation 1–3). Thus, Paul could have written "to the churches of Asia" (cf. Rev 1:4) or "to the churches of the Lycus and Meander Valleys." Second, Col 4:16 indicates that letters could be exchanged without readdressing them. Third, the idea of leaving a blank space to be filled in later is an anachronistic theory arising from the present age of mass reproduction. When scribes are producing each manuscript separately, there is no reason to delay writing the name of the addressee until later.[275] Since Paul traveled through the region on at least three occasions and founded most of its congregations, he would have had no cause to leave the choice of addressees to his letter carrier. Fourth, there is no documentary evidence from antiquity of circular letters leaving blanks for the place name.[276] And if a copy were produced with a blank, it would make sense to include the preposition ἐν, "in," to indicate where the place name went—yet no copy survives with just the preposition and no place

[272] E.g., Franzmann, *The Word of the Lord Grows*, 130; Schnackenburg, *Ephesians*, 29.

[273] This was first suggested by Archbishop James Ussher in the seventeenth century in *Annales Veteris et Novi Testamenti* (London: Crook, 1650–1654), cited in Lincoln, *Ephesians*, 3; see also Brown, *An Introduction to the New Testament*, 627. Schlier, *Epheser*, 32, follows this theory, as do Comfort, *Encountering the Manuscripts*, 345–46, and Zuntz, *The Text of the Epistles*, 228–29, 276–77.

[274] Nineham, "The Case against the Pauline Authorship," 25–26, offers five objections to the circular letter theory that are substantially the same as ours.

[275] Carson, Moo, and Morris, *An Introduction to the New Testament*, 310:

If the whole had to be handwritten, there seems no reason for omitting the two words for the name of the individual church. The saving in time would be miniscule. It is also to be borne in mind that the copies with the omission lack "in" as well as the place name: surely "in" would remain in each copy of the circular. It is further urged that it would be very curious if no copy of a circular survived other than that to one particular church: even those MSS that lack "in Ephesus" do not have another name inserted.

[276] Lincoln, *Ephesians*, 3, citing O. Roller, *Das Formular der paulinischen Briefe: Ein Beitrag zur Lehre vom antiken Briefe* (Stuttgart: Kohlhammer, 1933), 199–212, 520–25.

name.[277] Fifth and finally, there is no adequate explanation for why we should be left with only two versions of the text: one with "in Ephesus" and one with *no* addressee. Why would an unaddressed copy be left over? Why did none of the other copies addressed to other churches survive?[278]

Of the two versions of this theory presented above, while the first option is possible but unlikely, the second is quite certainly to be excluded.

Introduction to a Collection

Mention must be made of Goodspeed's famous, though fanciful, theory.[279] He postulated that a Gentile Christian living in Colossae after Paul's death used Acts as a guide to gathering together the letters of Paul. Noticing the absence of a letter to Ephesus, where Paul had spent the most time (three years), he composed Ephesians on the basis of Colossians, placing it at the head of the collection as its introduction. Goodspeed later postulated that the Gentile might have been Onesimus, onetime slave and spiritual child of Paul, who could have made this first collection when he became bishop of Ephesus.[280] Onesimus might have made Ephesus the addressee of the letter in order to give honor to his diocese, thus rectifying the perceived indignity of the chief Asian city having no letter from Paul. Other scholars have taken up the general outline of Goodspeed's theory, accepting at least that it gained its name when Paul's letters were collected.[281]

In response to this inventive theory, one must first note that it is entirely without foundation in fact or evidence. Second, no ancient collection of Paul's letters has Ephesians in first place.[282] Third, there is no evidence that knowledge of or respect for Paul declined after his death, requiring a creative disciple to restore his fame. Finally, though it is a worthy candidate for the role, most scholars would not find Ephesians to be the most comprehensive introduction to Paul's theology. Romans, which stands first in every collection, is the more obvious candidate.

---

[277] Lincoln, *Ephesians*, 3. Of course, a text with just the preposition would be even more nonsensical than the reading of $\mathfrak{P}^{46}$ and would have invited scribal adjustment.

[278] Guthrie, *New Testament Introduction*, 531. One might add, of course, that no manuscript exists containing a blank space, though it is unlikely that scribes would have preserved the blank space when copying a manuscript with no place name.

[279] Goodspeed, *The Meaning of Ephesians*, 3–17; Goodspeed, *The Key to Ephesians*, xiv–xvi; see Best, *Ephesians*, 65–66; Barth, *Ephesians*, 1:39–40. Barth notes that Goodspeed was following a suggestion first made by Johannes Weiss, *The History of Primitive Christianity* (2 vols.; New York: Wilson-Erickson, 1937), 1:150; 2:684.

[280] For a discussion of the possibility that the runaway slave Onesimus in the book of Philemon is the same Onesimus who became the bishop of Ephesus and was named as such by Ignatius in his epistle to the Ephesians, see Nordling, *Philemon*, 330–32. See also "Ephesus?" in "Location and Date of Writing" below.

[281] E.g., Bruce, *The Epistles to the Colossians, to Philemon, and to the Ephesians*, 250, n. 6.

[282] $\mathfrak{P}^{46}$ has this order: Romans, Hebrews, 1 and 2 Corinthians, Ephesians, Galatians, Philippians, Colossians, 1 Thessalonians (Aland and Aland, *The Text of the New Testament*, 79). But, as Ephesians is actually longer than Galatians, this may simply represent a variation on the traditional ordering by size. See also Parker, *New Testament Manuscripts and Their Texts*, 254.

Generalization/Lectionary Theory

The apostolic writers of the NT epistles intended their letters to be read aloud to the gathered congregation to which they were sent. This contention was explored above in "Oral Traditionalism" in "Orality and the Interpretation of the Epistles: A Brief Introduction" and will be developed in the commentary on 1:1–14 and 6:18–24. As an epistle's liturgical reading was repeated in other churches beyond its original target audience, evidence shows there was a tendency to modify the text, generalizing it for the sake all Christian listeners. The inclusion of the word πᾶσιν, "all [the saints]," in some manuscripts of Eph 1:1 (see the chart in "The Manuscript Evidence," above in "Addressees") may itself be evidence of this tendency.[283] Tertullian made precisely this assertion in response to Marcion's corruption of the letter's title: "When the apostle [Paul] wrote to some he wrote to all."[284] The addition of "amen" after 6:24 in many later manuscripts demonstrates the effect that liturgical reading could have on the text that is transmitted.[285]

There is concrete evidence for this phenomenon in other Pauline letters. On the one hand, Paul himself appears to have anticipated it with his expansion of the addressees of 1 Corinthians:

> τῇ ἐκκλησίᾳ τοῦ θεοῦ τῇ οὔσῃ ἐν Κορίνθῳ, ἡγιασμένοις ἐν Χριστῷ Ἰησοῦ, κλητοῖς ἁγίοις, σὺν πᾶσιν τοῖς ἐπικαλουμένοις τὸ ὄνομα τοῦ κυρίου ἡμῶν Ἰησοῦ Χριστοῦ ἐν παντὶ τόπῳ, αὐτῶν καὶ ἡμῶν
>
> to the church of God, the one being in Corinth, those sanctified in Christ Jesus, called saints, *together with all those who call upon the name of our Lord Jesus Christ in every place*, their [Lord] and ours (1 Cor 1:2)[286]

---

[283] It may also be the result of unconscious harmonization to other texts that use the common expression "*all* the saints" in their epistolary salutations (2 Cor 1:1; Phil 1:1; cf. Rom 1:7; 1 Cor 1:2) and elsewhere (Rom 16:15; 2 Cor 13:12 [ET 13:13]; Eph 1:15; 3:8, 18; 6:18; Phil 4:22; Col 1:4; 1 Thess 3:13; Philemon 5).

[284] Tertullian, *Against Marcion*, 5:17.1 (trans. Evans). See "Evidence from the Fathers," above in "Addressees," where Tertullian is quoted in greater length. Cf. the Muratorian Canon: "But although he [Paul] wrote twice to the Corinthians and Thessalonians, for reproof, it is nevertheless obvious that one church is known to be dispersed throughout the whole globe of the earth. For John also, while he wrote in the Apocalypse to seven churches, nevertheless speaks to all" (translation adapted from Theron, *Evidence of Tradition*, 111). On this generalizing tendency, see Black, "The Peculiarities of Ephesians and the Ephesian Address," 67–69; Dahl, "The Particularity of the Pauline Epistles as a Problem in the Ancient Church," in *Studies in Ephesians*, 165–78; Gamble, *The Textual History of the Letter to the Romans*, especially 114–26.

[285] The insertion of "my brothers" in Eph 6:10 in some manuscripts may also represent a tendency in liturgical reading to engage the listeners, or it may indicate that a new pericope was begun here. See Zuntz, *The Text of the Epistles*, 175–80; Best, *Ephesians*, 589. Cadbury, "The Dilemma of Ephesians," 94, writes: "The deletion of an original local reference if there was one may have been due to the tendency to make the several Pauline letters more suitable for general reading."

[286] In the early papyrus 𝔓⁴⁶, the phrase "those sanctified in Christ Jesus" occurs before "the one being in Corinth" so that the first part of the salutation reads "to the church of God, those sanctified in Christ Jesus, the one being in Corinth" (1 Cor 1:2a). This evidence led Dahl to propose that one or the other of these phrases, "the one being in Corinth" and "those sanctified in Christ Jesus," was missing in some early manuscripts, was then written in the margin, and

In the case of Romans, there is manuscript evidence. First, there is the famous problem of the peregrinating doxology. The letter's doxological conclusion (Rom 16:25–27) appears in two other locations in the manuscript tradition: after chapter 14 and after chapter 15.[287] Each variation may be evidence that the final chapters of Romans were omitted from reading in public worship because the discussion of Paul's travel plans and the lengthy final greetings were deemed inapplicable to other audiences. In other words, the lector would skip to the doxology, and so copies of the letter prepared for public reading (i.e., lectionaries) may have saved cost by abbreviating the text.[288]

The most compelling and applicable evidence of the tendency to generalize a text for the purpose of liturgical reading emerges in the address of Romans itself. There, in absolute parallel to Eph 1:1, the location of the addressees, ἐν Ῥώμῃ, "in Rome" (Rom 1:7), is omitted in a few manuscripts (G *pc*).[289] While G is a late manuscript (ninth century), the tenth-century minuscule 1739 (which itself in Eph 1:1 omits "in Ephesus"!) notes in its margin that Origen used a text lacking these words in Rom 1:7. Manuscript G repeats the omission in Rom 1:15. *Yet, as far as the present author is aware, no scholar has concluded from this variant that the epistle to the Romans was originally written to a generic audience; most accept that the words "in Rome" were dropped to express the letter's universal applicability for the purpose of liturgical reading.*[290] In the

---

finally found its way into the text—but at the wrong place ("The Particularity of the Pauline Epistles as a Problem in the Ancient Church," in Studies in Ephesians, 173). He concludes that one branch of the manuscript tradition therefore contained no geographical destination (as in Eph 1:1 and Rom 1:7). Following Dahl, Gamble draws the logical conclusion that the addressee had been omitted at an early stage to make the letter applicable for reading in other early Christian communities (Harry Y. Gamble, *Books and Readers in the Early Church: A History of Early Christian Texts* [New Haven: Yale University Press, 1995], 98). This sort of generalizing tendency led Johannes Weiss to conjecture (without manuscript evidence; see the NA[27] apparatus) that 1 Cor 1:2b ("together with all those …") was itself not original to the text but added for liturgical reading (*Der erste Korintherbrief* [Göttingen: Vandenhoeck & Ruprecht, 1910], 4). Note also the generalizing address of the *Martyrdom of Polycarp*, 1:1: "the church of God which sojourns at Smyrna, to the church of God sojourning in Philomelium, and to all the congregations of the holy and catholic church in every place."

[287] Note that 𝔓[46] places the doxology after chapter 15, again demonstrating a tendency in this significant papyrus to modify texts for liturgical reading.

[288] See Grothe, *The Justification of the Ungodly*, 22, 871–75, who suggests that the composition and addition of the doxology might have postdated Paul's writing of Romans—whether or not it was Paul himself who wrote and added it.

[289] The NA[27] abbreviation *pc* (*pauci*) suggests that "a few" other, unspecified manuscripts agree with G in omitting the words ἐν Ῥώμῃ, "in Rome." (NA[28] has entirely dropped the abbreviation *pc* as imprecise and misleading.) UBS[4] lists "it[g]" in support of the omission—but this is simply the interlinear Old Latin text of the Greek manuscript G and cannot be taken as a separate witness.

[290] Metzger, *A Textual Commentary on the Greek New Testament*, 446, notes the committee's opinion that the absence of ἐν Ῥώμῃ, "in Rome," in Rom 1:7 occurred "more probably, as a deliberate excision, made in order to show that the letter is of general, not local, application." Gamble, *The Textual History of the Letter to the Romans*, 29–33, 114–24, notes that the two textual issues in Romans are connected: the uncial G, which omits "in Rome" (Rom 1:7, 15), also omits the doxology (though leaving blank space between chapters 14 and 15). Origen

case of Ephesians, theories skeptical of the inclusion of ἐν Ἐφέσῳ, "in Ephesus" (Eph 1:1), have arisen most likely because of an uncritical respect accorded to the early manuscripts 𝔓⁴⁶, ℵ*, and B*.

The hypothesis that lectionaries existed early enough to have influenced 𝔓⁴⁶ at the end of the second century admittedly lacks concrete evidence. Although more than two thousand lectionaries have been catalogued, none can be dated earlier than the fourth century.[291] But it would be foolish to assume that they did not exist any earlier. Inasmuch as (1) the Jews had already divided the OT into lectionary units prior to the first century AD, (2) the NT itself gives both evidence and prescriptions for liturgical reading, and (3) copying only those portions required for public reading would have been cheaper than copying an entire NT, it is highly likely that lectionary editions of NT writings were in existence from early postapostolic times. Indeed, one might argue that, at least in the case of the Gospels, lectionary pericopes may have existed *prior* to the creation of complete Gospels and formed part of the material gathered together by the evangelists (Lk 1:1–4).[292] Kurt and Barbara Aland argue that such lectionaries were bound to have had an effect on the readings of the complete Bibles:

> The fact should not be ignored that even "normal" lectionaries also exercised an influence on continuous text manuscripts because a monastic scribe would be particularly familiar with their readings from constant repetition in worship services. This is particularly true for the beginnings of the pericopes, i.e., of the lessons. A passage read in the worship service would frequently need some adaptation in its introductory phrasing to provide contextual information about who is speaking and to whom, as well as the place and occasion of the event, etc. … Introductory phrases are often altered for stylistic reasons, and concluding phrases adapted or expanded for greater effect.[293]

Thus, it is highly likely that the omission of the words "in Ephesus" (Eph 1:1) in some manuscripts came about in a two-step process: (1) the words were omitted in some early lectionaries or copies of the letter in order to make the letter more

---

worked with a manuscript or manuscripts that omitted "in Rome" (Rom 1:7) and placed the doxology after chapter 14. Parker, *New Testament Manuscripts and Their Texts*, 270, 274, draws the same connection between Rom 1:7, 15; the Romans doxology (Rom 16:25–27); Eph 1:1; and 1 Cor 1:2. Gamble, 115–16, ultimately rejects the idea that Romans 15 and/or Romans 16 was removed for liturgical reading, preferring the related hypothesis that there were deliberate revisions of the text made in order to "catholicize" the letter. He says: "According to evidence, precisely these three letters [Romans, 1 Corinthians, Ephesians] enjoyed the greatest ecclesiastical use in the late first and early second centuries, and so would seem to have called for some resolution of the problem of particularity" (117–18). See also Dahl, "The Particularity of the Pauline Epistles as a Problem in the Ancient Church," in *Studies in Ephesians*, 170–73.

[291] See Aland and Aland, *The Text of the New Testament*, 81–82. See also Carroll Osburn, "The Greek Lectionaries of the New Testament," in *The Text of the New Testament in Contemporary Research: Essays on the Status Quaestionis* (ed. Bart D. Ehrman and Michael W. Holmes; 2d ed.; Leiden: Brill, 2013), 93–114.

[292] This is the theory of Bo Reicke, *The Roots of the Synoptic Gospels*.

[293] Aland and Aland, *The Text of the New Testament*, 169–70.

applicable to a general, Christian audience; (2) a scribe who became familiar with hearing the letter read this way allowed his memory to influence his copying of the text. This process provides a satisfactory explanation for the omission of the addressees in $\mathfrak{P}^{46}$ and the first hand of ℵ and B, while avoiding the difficulties inherent in the more popular circular letter theory.[294]

Internal Evidence

Many scholars have buttressed their belief that this letter was not written to the Ephesian church by referring to three features of its internal content:

1. Paul appears to express doubt about what the Ephesians were taught or ignorance about their present situation:

   - "for this reason, I myself—having *heard* of your faith in the Lord Jesus and [your] love toward all the saints" (1:15)
   - "*if indeed* you have heard of the stewardship of the grace of God that was given to me for you" (3:2)
   - "*if indeed* you heard him and were taught in him" (4:21)

2. The letter does not greet any members of the Ephesian church by name, but gives only a generic blessing at its close (6:23–24).

3. There appears to be no reference to specific problems in Ephesus.[295]

In a lecture in Cambridge in 2005, Professor Morna Hooker expressed the dilemma these factors posed to her mind: "If it's by Paul, then it's not to the Ephesians; if it's to the Ephesians, then it's not by Paul."[296]

This superficially puzzling situation is, on further examination, less than persuasive, particularly when the letter is compared carefully with the rest of

---

[294] Scholars adopting this explanation include Clinton E. Arnold, "Ephesians, Letter to the," in *DPL*, 244; Arnold, *Ephesians*, 28; and Gnilka, *Epheserbrief*, 7. Gnilka notes that Euthalius of Alexandria (fourth century), who in his "Sections" divided the NT into liturgical pericopes and verses, referred to Romans and Ephesians as key catechetical texts (PG 85:704); Gnilka therefore suggests Egypt in the second century as the place where the addressees of both were first omitted for that purpose. (See also Dahl, "The 'Euthalian Apparatus' and the Affiliated 'Argumenta,' " in *Studies in Ephesians*, 231–75.) This is consistent with Gamble's and Dahl's observations that Romans, 1 Corinthians, and Ephesians were the most commonly cited Pauline epistles in the early postapostolic era (see the footnote about them above).

[295] Lincoln, *Ephesians*, 1, expresses this opinion in a succinct and typical manner:

According to the account in Acts, Paul had not only founded the church at Ephesus but had had an extensive ministry there (cf. Acts 18:19–21; 19:1–20:1; 20:17–38). Yet in this letter there are clear indications that Paul does not know the addressees personally (cf. 1:15; 3:2; 4:21) and there is a complete absence of any personal greetings. Certainly this makes an Ephesian address highly unlikely on the assumption of Pauline authorship.

See also Abbott, *The Epistles to the Ephesians and to the Colossians*, iii. Theodore of Mopsuestia (*Commentary on Galatians*) first noted that the letter seemed oddly impersonal and concluded that Paul wrote it before he first visited Ephesus, according to Gnilka, *Epheserbrief*, 6.

[296] As recalled by the present author. The same thought is expressed by Josef Schmid, *Der Epheserbrief des Apostels Paulus* (Freiburg: Herder, 1928), 46, as quoted by Gnilka, *Epheserbrief*, 6.

the Pauline correspondence. The textual notes and the commentary on the above passages discuss the resolution to the problems in detail, but those explanations may be anticipated by the following summary:[297]

1. Paul writes to the Ephesians from prison (probably in Caesarea; see "Location and Date of Writing" below), separated from his beloved Ephesian children by considerable distance. His ministry in Ephesus was cut short by the silversmiths' riot (Acts 20:1). He never visited the church again, but only met briefly with its pastors in Miletus while on his way to Jerusalem (Acts 20:17–38). His sermon to them refers to dangerous false teachers (Acts 20:28–31), and in light of his mandate to Timothy to oppose false teachers and ordain pastors in Ephesus (1 Tim 1:3; 3:1–13), it may be that a serious conflict had occurred there, leading to the expulsion of some pastors and the ordination of new ones. Thus, Paul in prison would have been anxious over the Ephesians' fate and would have rejoiced to receive news from the Ephesian church's emissary to him. That he has heard of their faith and love (1:15) does not therefore mean that he previously knew nothing, but that he was relieved to hear that they had kept the faith in spite of their troubles.

The passages in which Paul uses the expression εἴ γε, "if indeed" (3:2; 4:21), do not necessarily mean that Paul was in doubt about what the Ephesians had been taught—especially since in 4:21 he refers to fundamental teaching of and by Christ himself! The expression is a rhetorical device designed to provoke a response in the hearers: "of course we were taught that!" It is akin to the parent who addresses a child in frustration, "Haven't I ever told you … ?" The answer, of course, is "yes, a thousand times!"

2. The contention that Paul in his concluding greetings ought to name a lot of people when addressing a church where he had served for three years conflicts with the evidence from his other letters, for the opposite seems to be the case. Paul uses extensive greetings to develop a relationship with a church he does *not* know, while being restrained in naming specific people in a place where nearly everyone was his child in the faith. Thus, Romans has the most greetings, though Paul had never been to Rome at the time when he wrote the epistle. Colossians has numerous greetings, and we have no clear record in Acts that Paul had conducted mission work there. Yet at the conclusion of his first letter to Corinth, where Paul had worked for a year and a half, Paul does not name anyone in the Corinthian congregation (but only the prominent figures of Aquila and Prisca). Nor does he greet anyone by name at the close of 2 Corinthians, Galatians, Philippians, or 1 and 2 Thessalonians, places where he himself had founded churches and frequently visited. Thus, it makes perfect sense that Paul would not name anyone in Ephesus, where he had had an extensive ministry, for fear of puffing up some and offending others.

---

[297] The following arguments find considerable support in Black, "The Peculiarities of Ephesians and the Ephesian Address."

3. The argument that Paul does not refer to any particular problems in Ephesians is circular. The vast majority of commentators, proceeding from the assumption that the letter was not written to Ephesus, have set aside the background given in Acts and therefore have missed a significant number of connections. The present commentary will argue that the letter is replete with references to the specific situation of the Ephesian church.

Ignatius to the Ephesians

The Muratorian Canon notes that the Pauline corpus of letters addresses seven churches, suggesting that Paul had imitated his predecessor John with his seven letters to the churches of Asia (Revelation 1–3). The modern reader might be puzzled by the chronology this implies: that John's Revelation was written *before* Paul wrote his epistles. But the parallel holds even if the sequence is reversed. John himself, most likely imprisoned on Patmos after Paul's death, may well have seen himself as taking up apostolic supervision over the churches Paul had founded (including Ephesus [Rev 2:1–11]), even writing to them from prison, like Paul. The phenomenon recurs after John's death in the work of Ignatius, bishop of Syrian Antioch. During persecution sponsored by Trajan, Ignatius was arrested for defying the edict to offer sacrifice to the emperor and then bound in chains and conducted to Rome for his execution. Traveling overland through Asia Minor, he had opportunity (in Smyrna and Troas) to write a total of *seven* episcopal letters. While only the letters to Rome and Ephesus overlap specifically with Paul's, it appears that he saw himself imitating Paul in multiple ways: writing from prison, on his way to Rome, and looking to his probable martyrdom.

Ignatius' letter to the Ephesians is essential reading for anyone studying Paul's letter to the same. The number of parallels between the two is, quite frankly, astonishing. Ignatius was surely aware that he was following in Paul's footsteps, even referring to Paul's own letter to the Ephesians in a grammatically difficult, but undeniable way (Ignatius, *To the Ephesians*, 12:2). Thus, *Ignatius' own way of writing to the Ephesians gives evidence that he believed Paul had written the present letter to them.* His letter, therefore, serves as the earliest external testimony to the Ephesian origin of Paul's letter.[298]

The immense parallels, set out below, serve also as the first commentary on Paul's writing and will be referenced frequently in the present work. Ignatius' letter is a strong appeal for unity, which is also the major focus of Paul's. His emphasis on the bishop in providing unity to the church is similar to what Paul writes about the pastoral office (Eph 4:11–12), though Ignatius expresses it more in the way of the Law. The role of the Eucharist as the focus of unity (Ignatius, *To the Ephesians*, 5:2; 13:1; 20:2) parallels Paul's appeal to Baptism (to which

---

[298] Ignatius clearly had personal knowledge of the Ephesian church, as he had received at least Burrhus and Crocus as their emissaries, and he names three other Ephesian representatives, including Onesimus, their bishop (*To the Ephesians*, 1:3; 2:1; 6:2).

Ignatius also refers in *To the Ephesians*, 17:1; 18:2). Ignatius builds upon the foundation laid by Paul.

Finally, the example of Ignatius also stands in defiant opposition to the critical theory of pseudepigraphy: if a true disciple of Paul wished to honor him, he would not forge a letter in Paul's name, but would, like Ignatius, write a letter in his own name that paralleled, quoted, and evoked Paul at every turn of phrase.[299]

Ignatius' preface seems modeled in almost every detail on the opening prayer of Paul's Ephesians (1:1–14). The stress on God the Father and Jesus Christ, his Son, is perhaps not unique; but the rest of the vocabulary contains stunning parallels, not only to Paul's opening prayer, but also to the rest of his letter to the Ephesians:[300]

Ignatius, *To the Ephesians*, Preface	
Ἰγνάτιος, ὁ καὶ Θεοφόρος, τῇ <u>εὐλογημένη</u> ἐν <u>μεγέθει</u> θεοῦ πατρὸς <u>πληρώματι</u>, τῇ <u>προωρισμένη</u> πρὸ αἰώνων εἶναι διὰ παντὸς <u>εἰς δόξαν</u> παράμονον ἄτρεπτον ἡνωμένη καὶ <u>ἐκλελεγμένη</u> ἐν πάθει ἀληθινῷ, ἐν <u>θελήματι</u> τοῦ πατρὸς καὶ Ἰησοῦ Χριστοῦ τοῦ θεοῦ ἡμῶν, τῇ <u>ἐκκλησία</u> τῇ ἀξιομακαρίστῳ, <u>τῇ οὔσῃ ἐν Ἐφέσῳ</u> τῆς Ἀσίας, πλεῖστα <u>ἐν Ἰησοῦ Χριστῷ</u> καὶ ἐν <u>ἀμώμῳ</u> χαρᾷ <u>χαίρειν</u>.	Ignatius, who is also [called] Theophorus, to the [church] that is <u>blessed</u> in the <u>greatness</u> of God the Father <u>with fullness</u>, the [church] <u>predestined</u> before the ages to be always <u>for</u> an enduring and unchangeable <u>glory</u>, being united and <u>elected</u> in true passion by the <u>will</u> of the Father, and Jesus Christ, our God, to the <u>church</u> that <u>is in Ephesus</u> of Asia, worthily most blessed: abundant <u>greetings in Jesus Christ</u> and in <u>blameless</u> joy.

Ignatius' intimate familiarity with Paul's letter shows through in vocabulary, phrasing, and thought as the letter continues:

---

[299] Note also that Ignatius' allusions to Paul's Ephesians provide a terminus ad quem for its dating (Schnackenburg, *Ephesians*, 33). *1 Clement*, which alludes to Ephesians less obviously, would form an even earlier terminus (see "External Evidence" in "Authorship" above). Best, who is quite reserved about such parallels, nevertheless concludes: "These [parallels] taken together create a fair possibility that Ignatius knew our Ephesians" (*Ephesians*, 15–16).

[300] Schwindt, *Das Weltbild des Epheserbriefes*, 57–60, also cites these extensive parallels in arguing that the canonical Ephesians was surely written to the same addressees. He believes that Ignatius' epistle to the Ephesians gives undeniable testimony that in the late first century Paul's letter bore the title "To the Ephesians." Schwindt does not go so far as to deduce the originality of the place name in Eph 1:1, though he concludes that the letter was, indeed, sent to Ephesus as the chief city and church of Asia Minor.

Ignatius, *To the Ephesians*	Paul, Ephesians
μιμηταὶ ὄντες θεοῦ, "being imitators of God" (1:1; see also 10:3)	5:1
ἵνα ἐν μιᾷ ὑποταγῇ κατηρτισμένοι, ὑποτασσόμενοι τῷ ἐπισκόπῳ καὶ τῷ πρεσβυτερίῳ, "that you may be equipped with one submission, being subordinate to the bishop and to the presbyterate" (2:2) σπουδάσωμεν οὖν μὴ ἀντιτάσσεσθαι τῷ ἐπισκόπῳ, ἵνα ὦμεν θεῷ ὑποτασσόμενοι, "therefore let us be careful not to oppose the bishop, that we might be submitting to God" (5:3)	4:11–12; 5:21–22; 6:1, 5
δέδεμαι ἐν τῷ ὀνόματι, "I am bound in the name" (3:1) ἐν ᾧ τὰ δεσμὰ περιφέρω, "in whom [Christ] I bear my chains" (11:2) δεδεμένος εἰς Ῥώμην ἀπάγομαι, "I am being led away as a prisoner to Rome" (21:2)	3:1; 4:1; 6:20
ἐν ἑνότητι, "in unity" (5:1; 14:1) ἐν ἀμώμῳ ἑνότητι, "in blameless unity" (4:2)	1:4; 4:3, 25; 5:27
μέλη ὄντας τοῦ υἱοῦ αὐτοῦ, "being members of his Son" (4:2; cf. Ignatius, *To the Trallians*, 11:2)	4:25; 5:30
οἰκονομία, "stewardship, plan, administration" (6:1; 20:1)	1:10; 3:2, 9
εἰς οἰκοδομὴν θεοῦ πατρός, "for the building of God the Father" (9:1)	4:12
ἐστε … Παύλου συμμύσται τοῦ ἡγιασμένου, "you share in the mysteries with Paul, the sanctified" (12:2) μυστήρια, "mysteries" (19:1)	1:9; 3:3, 4, 9; 5:32; 6:19
ὑμῶν Ἐφεσίων ἐκκλησίας τῆς διαβοήτου τοῖς αἰῶσιν, "you Ephesians, a church renowned forever" (8:1) ὃς ἐν πάσῃ ἐπιστολῇ μνημονεύει ὑμῶν ἐν Χριστῷ Ἰησοῦ, "who [Paul] makes mention of you in the entire† epistle in Christ Jesus" (12:2)	1:1
οἱ οἰκοφθόροι βασιλείαν θεοῦ οὐ κληρονομήσουσιν, "those who corrupt families shall not inherit the kingdom of God" (16:1)	5:5

†The phrase ἐν πάσῃ ἐπιστολῇ would be translated naturally as "in *every* epistle," yet it makes little sense to assert that Paul referred to the Ephesians in *all* his letters. Moule, *Idiom Book*, 94, notes that πᾶς can mean "whole," even without the article (and one wonders whether the article is more likely to be omitted in a prepositional phrase). "In the entire epistle" is the only way to make sense of the phrase. Even this translation is not without its difficulties, as it involves hyperbole to say that Paul *mentions* them in the entire letter. See Abbott, *The Epistles to the Ephesians and to the Colossians*, ix–xi.

Ignatius, *To the Ephesians*	Paul, Ephesians
ὁ γὰρ θεὸς ἡμῶν Ἰησοῦς ὁ Χριστὸς ἐκυοφορήθη ὑπὸ Μαρίας κατ᾽ οἰκονομίαν θεοῦ ἐκ σπέρματος μὲν Δαυείδ πνεύματος δὲ ἁγίου· ὃς ἐγεννήθη καὶ ἐβαπτίσθη ἵνα τῷ πάθει τὸ ὕδωρ καθαρίσῃ, "for our God, Jesus Christ, was conceived by Mary according to the plan of God, from the seed of David and of the Holy Spirit, who was born and was baptized in order that by his suffering [or submission] he might cleanse the water" (18:2)	οἰκονομία, "stewardship, plan, administration," in 1:10 and allusions to Christ's Baptism in 1:3–10

The conclusion that Paul's letter was indeed originally written to the church of God at Ephesus, that the words "in Ephesus" (Eph 1:1) are original, and that their omission in the later textual tradition occurred because of a tendency to generalize NT writings for liturgical reading forms the basis for the following examination of the context of that great city, Ephesus, and Paul's work there according to the record of Acts.

Ephesus at the Time of Paul

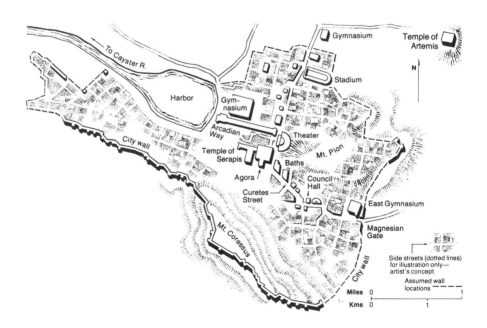

Map of Ephesus. © 1973, 1978, 1984. Used by permission of Zondervan. www.zondervan.com.

The City of Ephesus and Paul's Relationship to It[301]
The City

The great and ancient city of Ephesus, located on the western coast of Asia Minor where the Cayster River empties into the Aegean Sea, was occupied as early as 1400 BC. It was supposedly founded by Amazons, though the Ephesians themselves honored the Greek hero Androclus as their founding father.[302] The well-preserved ruins are found near the modern city of Selçuk, where a small but excellent museum houses the artifacts uncovered by a century of Austrian archaeological work.[303] The city's fortunes under successive conquerors, its repeated destruction by earthquakes, and the silting up of its harbor led to four distinct periods of settlement among the three small hills in the area: Old Ionian, Greek, Hellenistic–Roman–Early Byzantine, and Late Byzantine.[304] For the present purposes, only the third period is strictly relevant.

Alexander the Great took control of the city in 334 BC; his successor, Lysimachus, built a six-mile (nine-kilometer) wall around the city and rebuilt the temple of Artemis.[305] A huge theater seating twenty-five thousand people was built in the Hellenistic period; it features in Paul's story (Acts 19:29–31). Two massive agoras (public squares) were also constructed.[306] In 133 BC, Attalus III of Pergamum bequeathed the city to the Romans. On his ascendency (27 BC), Augustus declared it the capital of the province of Asia.[307] This led to an unprecedented period of prosperity and architectural grandeur. Aqueducts were constructed, streets were paved, and the State Agora was renovated. The city became, as noted on numerous ancient inscriptions, "the first and greatest metropolis of Asia."[308]

The Greek geographer Strabo (64/63 BC–ca. AD 24) highlighted the city's concomitant physical advantages. The city's fine, deep harbor was connected to the Cayster (Kaÿstros) River by a narrow channel, the river then traveling a few miles to the sea, which was made ever more distant by the river's continuous disgorging of silt. Strabo reports that engineers had narrowed the entrance

---

[301] The most comprehensive recent resources are Murphy-O'Connor, *St. Paul's Ephesus: Texts and Archaeology*, and Trebilco, *The Early Christians in Ephesus from Paul to Ignatius*.

[302] Strabo, *Geography*, 11:5.4; 14:1.3–4, 2; Pausanius, *Description of Greece*, 7:4–5; Pliny the Elder, *Natural History*, 5:115.

[303] See Gilbert Wiplinger, Gudrun Wlach, and Kurt Gschwantler, *Ephesus: 100 Years of Austrian Research* (trans. Claudia Luxon; Vienna: Österreichisches Archäologisches Institut, 1996).

[304] Richard E. Oster, Jr., "Ephesus," *ABD* 2:542.

[305] See "The Temple of Artemis Ephesia," below in "The City of Ephesus and Paul's Relationship to It."

[306] The State Agora (later renovated by the Romans) measures 190 x 525 feet (58 x 160 meters). The Square (Commercial) Agora is even larger: 368 x 368 feet (112 x 112 meters; Oster, "Ephesus," *ABD* 2:546).

[307] Dio Cassius, *Roman History*, 51:20.6.

[308] L. Michael White, "Urban Development and Social Change in Imperial Ephesos," in Koester, *Ephesos: Metropolis of Asia*, 34.

to the city's harbor in order to make it more protected, with the unintended consequence that it, too, silted up and became too shallow for large ships to enter![309] Yet, the harbor problems have been exaggerated by some NT scholars. In Roman times it was repeatedly (and successfully) dredged, and the river was diverted; the problem does not seem to have affected the city's commercial prosperity. Strabo comments that Ephesus was located at a crossroads on the principal trans-Anatolian highway, a "common road constantly used by all who travel from Ephesus toward the East."[310] Thus, he could conclude: "The city, because of its advantageous situation in other respects [than the harbor], grows daily and is the largest market (*emporium*) in Asia on this side of the Taurus."[311]

Both its history of being conquered successively by Ionians, Lydians, Greeks, and Romans and its character as a commercial crossroads gave the city a cosmopolitan character with a more culturally diverse population than any other city in the Greek East. In the early third century AD, Philostratus described Ephesus (through the mouth of Apollonius of Tyana) as

> a city which took the beginning of its race from the purest Attic [stock], and which grew in size beyond all other cities of Ionia and Lydia, and stretched herself out to the sea, outgrowing the land on which she is built, and is filled with studious inhabitants, both philosophers and rhetoricians, thanks to whom the city owes her strength not to her cavalry, but to the myriads of humans in whom she inculcates wisdom.[312]

This character seems to have suited Paul, who regularly chose commercially and intellectually vibrant cities as his mission centers. Philostratus' comments on the unique Ephesian interest in philosophy, rhetoric, and wisdom are particularly relevant for Paul's letter to the Ephesians, which displays an elevated rhetorical style of its own and emphasizes God's gift of divine "wisdom" (σοφία, Eph 1:8, 17; 3:10; see also σόφος, "wise," 5:15).

Ephesus was certainly a very large city when Paul lived there. "Apollonius of Tyana said that Ephesus was larger than any cities in Ionia or Lydia."[313]

---

[309] Strabo, *Geography*, 14:1.24. See Heinrich Zabehlicky, "Preliminary Views of the Ephesian Harbor," in Koester, *Ephesos: Metropolis of Asia*, 201–15; Murphy-O'Connor, *St. Paul's Ephesus*, 26–27.

[310] Strabo, *Geography*, 14:2.29, quoted in Oster, "Ephesus," *ABD* 2:543. Trebilco, *The Early Christians in Ephesus from Paul to Ignatius*, 18, notes that "the two great trade-routes from the Euphrates both ended at Ephesus" and that it was host to a Roman communications center for their Asian network.

[311] Strabo, *Geography*, 14:1.24 (trans. Horace Leonard Jones, LCL; quoted in L. Michael White, "Urban Development and Social Change in Imperial Ephesos," in Koester, *Ephesos: Metropolis of Asia*, 35). The rich depiction of merchants and their wares in Rev 18:11–13 could easily describe the city of Ephesus in which John spent his latter years and to which he addressed the first of Revelation's seven letters (Rev 2:1–7).

[312] Philostratus, *Life of Apollonius*, 8:7.8 (trans. F. C. Conybeare, LCL; quoted in L. Michael White, "Urban Development and Social Change in Imperial Ephesos," in Koester, *Ephesos: Metropolis of Asia*, 35). Heraclitus, born ca. 540 BC, was the city's most famous philosopher.

[313] Arnold, *Power and Magic*, 174, n. 7, citing Philostratus, *Life of Apollonius*, 8:7.8.

The great theater, Ephesus, looking down Harbor Street (Arcadian Way) toward the sea.

Photo: © 2014 Thomas M. Winger.

Precisely how large it was is difficult to determine. The usual estimates of 250,000 (including the surrounding countryside) rank it third in the empire, after Rome and Alexandria. Yet this is a late, third-century AD figure, estimated from a report that it had 40,000 male citizens at the time (to which women, children, and slaves would be added). Its population in Paul's day is unknown and may have been only 100,000, ranking it, nonetheless, as a major city of the empire.[314] Ephesus suffered great destruction from an earthquake in AD 60, was grandly reconstructed, and grew rapidly over the next century.[315] The famous and beautiful library of Celsus, for example, not present when Paul lived in the city, was built under Trajan (AD 115–25).[316]

The Religious Scene

The city of Ephesus had a religious scene as diverse as any cosmopolitan city of the Greco-Roman world.

Judaism

There was a large population of Jews,[317] who had obtained legal protection under the Seleucids. At the time of the Roman conquest, their freedom to observe the Sabbath and food laws, to send money to the temple in Jerusalem, and to follow other customs was reaffirmed.[318] Jews holding Roman citizenship gained exemption from military service. These facts indicate that the community was sizable, was culturally and religiously observant, and possessed significant political influence (suggesting that some Jews held high office).[319] But the sources also indicate a perpetual tension between the authorities and the Jews in Asia Minor, who were "mistreated," had their temple tax misappropriated, and suffered "mischief on other particular occasions."[320] Thus, on the one hand, Paul could observe his custom of beginning his mission in Ephesus

---

[314] L. Michael White, "Urban Development and Social Change in Imperial Ephesos," in Koester, *Ephesos: Metropolis of Asia*, 41–49. White suggests that the population may have doubled between AD 50 and 150.

[315] "This growth of Ephesos, although inaugurated under the Julio-Claudian emperors, did not commence until the end of the first century under Domitian, when Ephesos replaced Pergamon as the neokoros ('temple warden') of the imperial cult" (L. Michael White, "Urban Development and Social Change in Imperial Ephesos," in Koester, *Ephesos: Metropolis of Asia*, 35).

[316] Oster, "Ephesus," *ABD* 2:546. The library, dedicated to Tiberius Julius Celsus Ptolemaeanus, proconsul of Asia, contained fifteen thousand volumes—impressive, but small by Hellenistic standards.

[317] On the Jews in Ephesus, see Trebilco, *The Early Christians in Ephesus from Paul to Ignatius*, 37–51.

[318] Josephus, *Antiquities*, 14:262–64; cf. Josephus, *Antiquities*, 12:125–26; 14:223–27; 16:167–68, 172–73; Josephus, *Against Apion*, 2:39.

[319] Cf. the Jewish jealousy when in Thessalonica Paul attracted converts from among the leading women (or wives of the leading men) in Acts 17:4–5, 12.

[320] Josephus, *Antiquities*, 16:160 (trans. Whiston, *The Works of Josephus*).

by engaging the synagogue (Acts 19:8–10).[321] On the other hand, the Jews of Asia Minor were sensitive about their status and rights and would have seen the Christian movement as a serious threat. This tension is evidenced in the account of Acts 19 and in the divide between Jew and Gentile that permeates Ephesians.

Polytheism

Ephesus also housed numerous pagan temples, including dedications to Hestia, Serapis, Zeus, and the Phrygian mother goddess (Cybele). There is documentary evidence of the worship of up to fifty gods, including Greek, Egyptian, and local gods. In addition, historical figures such as Alexander the Great and Androclus, the city's legendary Greek founder, had their cults.[322] But all other religions paled in comparison with the cult of Artemis Ephesia, the Lady of Ephesus.

The Temple of Artemis Ephesia

The magnificent temple of Artemis Ephesia was in its fifth and grandest incarnation when Paul entered the city. The fourth temple, known as the "archaic" Artemision, had been erected in the mid sixth century BC, with the Lydian king Croesus as its chief benefactor.[323] Severely damaged by fire in 356 BC (on the eve of Alexander the Great's birth!), it was being torn down and rebuilt (with financial aid from nearby cities)[324] when Alexander arrived in 334 BC. "Always mindful of his own legend, Alexander offered himself to pay for the completion of the new temple."[325] Perhaps fearful of taking sides with Alexander against the Persians, the Ephesians refused his money, saying (with flattery and irony) that it was improper to take money from one god to serve another.

This fifth temple, the so-called "younger" Artemision, was numbered among the seven wonders of the ancient world.[326] According to Pliny, the monumental temple was 225 by 425 feet (ca. 70 x 130 meters) in area—the largest building in the Greek world and four times larger than the Parthenon. Made entirely of marble, it had 127 columns, each 6 feet (2 meters) in diameter and

---

[321] According to Trebilco, *The Early Christians in Ephesus from Paul to Ignatius*, 43–44, no synagogue has been discovered in Ephesus, but the existence of a synagogue there is attested by Josephus, *Antiquities*, 14:227, and by inscriptions. Eusebius, *Ecclesiastical History*, 4:18.6, tells us that Justin Martyr's *Dialogue with Trypho* was set in Ephesus.

[322] Oster, "Ephesus," *ABD* 2:548; Arnold, *Ephesians*, 33; Schwindt, *Das Weltbild des Epheserbriefes*, 87–103.

[323] Jenkins, *Greek Architecture*, 48–49; Oster, "Ephesus," *ABD* 2:543, 545; Herodotus, *Histories*, 1:92.

[324] Due to fear of the powerful goddess, the temple of Artemis was a completely secure place of asylum and served as a bank for the entire region; no one would dare to violate the site to steal the money (Dio Chrysostom, *Orations*, 31:54–55).

[325] Jenkins, *Greek Architecture*, 60–61.

[326] Antipater of Sidon (ca. 100 BC), *Greek Anthology*, 9:58, said the other six wonders dimmed in comparison (Jenkins, *Greek Architecture*, 47).

60 feet (18 meters) high.[327] Thirty-six of the columns were decorated with base relief carvings, which, placed end to end, would form a frieze 1,640 feet (500 meters) long. The only decorated base to survive can be seen in the British Museum.[328] The temple likely had a double row of columns around the outside, with an open courtyard in the middle, where the massive statue of Artemis Ephesia was located. In front of the temple was an enormous horseshoe-shaped altar of sacrifice (105 x 72 feet; 32 x 22 meters).[329] This temple stood until AD 262, when it fell victim to Gothic plunder and Christian looting. The cult of Artemis had been in decline for some time before.[330]

The temple of Artemis, Ephesus, from the wooden scale model
in the Ephesus Museum, Vienna, Austria.

Photo: © 2014 Thomas M. Winger.

---

[327] Pliny the Elder, *Natural History*, 36:21.95–97. Jenkins, *Greek Architecture*, 55, notes that we cannot be certain of the exact length of the "foot" measure Pliny was using.

[328] Jenkins, *Greek Architecture*, 61–68.

[329] Oster, "Ephesus," *ABD* 2:545.

[330] It began to decline in the second century AD as other oriental religions (e.g., Serapis, Mithras) became more popular than the old religions. This was compounded by climate changes that led to flooding at the temple site—suggesting that she was losing her power. See Dieter Knibbe, "Via Sacra Ephesiaca: New Aspects of the Cult of Artemis Ephesia," in Koester, *Ephesos: Metropolis of Asia*, 146–47. It is believed that a Christian church was later built on the site of the temple. Marble columns and stonework from the temple were used to build the spectacular Basilica of St. John on a nearby hill and also transported to Constantinople for constructing the Hagia Sophia (AD 532–537). Thus, Christianity visibly triumphed over the goddess. Today only some foundation stones and a single reconstructed column can be seen in a soggy field outside the town of Selçuk.

The Cult of Artemis Ephesia

In the record of Acts, the city clerk himself proclaimed to the crowd the common and undeniable knowledge that τὴν Ἐφεσίων πόλιν νεωκόρον οὖσαν τῆς μεγάλης Ἀρτέμιδος καὶ τοῦ διοπετοῦς, "the city of the Ephesians is the temple keeper of the great Artemis and the stone fallen [from heaven]" (Acts 19:35).[331] In Paul's day, the emperors Tiberius and Gaius/Caligula had both declined to institute his imperial cult in the city for fear that it would ever take second place behind hers.[332] It has been calculated that of 524 references to Ephesus in classical literature, fully a third refer to her cult.[333]

Despite the wealth of data, the precise nature of her cult has proved difficult to delineate, though in broad terms it was probably similar to that of other pagan deities.[334] An entire month called Artemisia, probably in the spring, was dedicated to her festivities, including athletic and musical competitions. Uniquely in comparison to contemporary cults, she was honored with great processions, held twice weekly, which stopped at altars and graves along the road through town and out to her temple, followed by a common meal.[335] This may represent a belief that she had power over death, normally associated with the Anatolian mother-earth goddess Cybele. Indeed, one should not interpret the Ephesian goddess entirely on the basis of the Greek name "Artemis." Quite likely, the early Greek immigrants found the cult of the local Ephesian goddess already well established and, as was their habit, assimilated her to Artemis in their pantheon.[336] Clinton Arnold emphasizes:

---

[331] The Greek compound noun νεωκόρος, from νάος (Attic νεώς), "temple," and a derivative of the verb κορέω, "to sweep," literally means "temple sweeper," identifying Ephesus as a sort of corporate custodian of the goddess. Prior to its political elevation under the Romans, Ephesus existed primarily for Artemis' cult.

[332] Tacitus, *Annals*, 4:55. Dio Cassius, *Roman History*, 59:28.1. Yet the imperial cult was still prominent. A temple was dedicated to Dea Roma and Divus Julius in order to venerate Augustus in AD 29 (Dio Cassius, *Roman History*, 51:20.6). Later Domitian (AD 81–96) was honored with a massive temple (112 x 79 feet; 34 x 24 meters) on a massive platform (164 x 328 feet; 50 x 100 meters). A smaller temple was dedicated jointly to Hadrian and Artemis (ca. AD 127). The city hosted more than fifty statues of the emperor. See Oster, "Ephesus," *ABD* 2:544–45, and Trebilco, *The Early Christians in Ephesus from Paul to Ignatius*, 35–37.

[333] Christine M. Thomas, "At Home in the City of Artemis," in Koester, *Ephesos: Metropolis of Asia*, 85.

[334] See Schwindt, *Das Weltbild des Epheserbriefes*, 103–34; and Dieter Knibbe, "Via Sacra Ephesiaca: New Aspects of the Cult of Artemis Ephesia," in Koester, *Ephesos: Metropolis of Asia*, 141–55.

[335] Dieter Knibbe, "Via Sacra Ephesiaca: New Aspects of the Cult of Artemis Ephesia," in Koester, *Ephesos: Metropolis of Asia*, 153–54.

[336] See Hubert M. Martin, Jr., "Artemis," *ABD* 1:464–65, who writes:

> Artemis the virgin huntress paradoxically contained within her personality obvious characteristics of a mother goddess, probably acquired in Asia Minor and from the Creton goddesses Britomartis and Dictynna, with whom she was sometimes identified. She zealously protects the suckling young of all wild animals, nurturing at their birth the very creatures she will later slaughter in the hunt; see, e.g., Aesch[ylus,]

It is important to point out that an equation cannot be made between the Ephesian Artemis and the Artemis known to Greek mythology. The Ephesian divinity appears to be a hybrid of Asian influences—perhaps chiefly from "the Great Mother" (Cybele, Meter, Ma) of Phrygia and Lydia. ... Oster supposes that when the Greeks came to the Ionian coast they imposed the name of the Homeric Artemis upon the indigenous Mother Goddess whom they found there, and thereby gave birth to the Ephesian Artemis.[337]

The Greek Artemis (Roman Diana), daughter of Zeus and Leto, was the twin sister of Apollo. Emerging from her mother as a fully formed adult, she assisted with the birth of her brother; thus, she was called upon for aid in childbirth.[338] She was the perpetually virgin huntress, depicted normally in a short dress carrying a bow and arrow, equipped both for the hunt and to fend off suitors. The ancient novel *The Adventures of Leucippe and Clitophon* by Achilles Tatius applies these attributes of Artemis to the Lady of Ephesus. "Artemis of Ephesos is seen as the champion of chastity, not in ritual context, but in everyday behavior, that is, a supporter of chastity as a moral value, a conventional Greek attitude."[339] In a monologue in the story,

> Thersandros accuses the high priest of Artemis of sullying the reputation of the temple by admitting the two lovers into the sanctuary: "A murderer and adulterer, living in the house of the goddess of purity! Oh, an adulterer dwelling with the Virgin! ... You have made ... the home of Artemis a bedroom for adulterers and whores."[340]

On the basis of this reference, some scholars have asserted that ritual prostitution and immorality were not features of the worship of the Ephesian Artemis[341]—yet

---

    Ag[amemnon,] 134–143, where she is incensed with Zeus' two eagles for devouring a pregnant hare.

[337] Arnold, *Power and Magic*, 26, citing Oster, "The Ephesian Artemis as an Opponent of Early Christianity," 27.

[338] Strabo offers the explanation that "Artemis has her name from the fact that she makes people ἀρτεμέας [safe and sound]" (*Geography*, 14:1.6, quoted in Trebilco, *The Early Christians in Ephesus from Paul to Ignatius*, 21). Luther, LC 1:18, is aware that in ancient times pregnant women called upon Diana (Artemis) for help.

[339] Christine M. Thomas, "At Home in the City of Artemis," in Koester, *Ephesos: Metropolis of Asia*, 96.

[340] Christine M. Thomas, "At Home in the City of Artemis," in Koester, *Ephesos: Metropolis of Asia*, 104–5, quoting Achilles Tatius, *Leucippe and Clitophon*, 8:8.10–11 (trans. Susan A. Stephens and John J. Winkler, *Ancient Greek Novels: The Fragments: Introduction, Text, Translation, and Commentary* [Princeton, N.J.: Princeton University Press, 1995], 275).

[341] Scholars citing this story, who are also skeptical of ritual prostitution on account of a general lack of evidence, include Oster, "The Ephesian Artemis as an Opponent of Early Christianity," and Baugh, "Cult Prostitution in New Testament Ephesus: A Reappraisal"; Baugh, "A Foreign World: Ephesus in the First Century," 23–26. But even Baugh admits: "Nor was Ephesian paganism necessarily as innocent as the inscriptions portray" ("A Foreign World," 26). Karel van der Toorn, "Cultic Prostitution," *ABD* 5:510–13, though sharing their skepticism over evidence for the sacred significance of temple prostitution in the ancient world, is happy to admit that prostitution often featured in temples as a money-raising scheme and that sexual immorality was a normal consequence of drunken temple festivities.

there are reasons to doubt this inference. First, the author of the classical novel hailed from Alexandria and may not have had firsthand experience of the cult in Ephesus. He may have created the above scenario on the basis of the Greek idea of the virgin Artemis. Second, the virginity of Artemis and her priestesses may have been little more than symbolic.[342] "Virgin" priestesses could have been virgins only at the point of their dedication or were called virgins because they served the perpetually virgin goddess; eunuch priests were employed, not because they were necessarily unable to have sexual intercourse, but because there was no danger of pregnancy.[343] Third, an argument from silence—that there is a lack of evidence for ritual prostitution in Ephesus—can as easily run in reverse: in the absence of evidence, one should assume the religious environment was similar to other goddess cults of Asia Minor.

In any case, the distinctive character of the *Ephesian* Artemis is evident from her unique depiction in art.[344] The peculiar image may have arisen from the διοπετής, "stone fallen [from heaven]," referred to in Acts (19:35).[345] Grand statues unearthed at Ephesus present her in a long robe, with her chest covered by row upon row of protuberances. The only ancient sources that refer to these bulbous objects identify them as breasts,[346] suggesting (1) that she was understood as a mother goddess with nourishing power and (2) that she possessed enormous fertility that could be bestowed on the worshiper through ritual action. Recently, this identification has been disputed, with the alternate

---

[342] Re the "virginity" of fertility goddesses, see "Having Put Aside Idolatry (4:17–19)" in the commentary on 4:17–5:2.

The high priesthood of Artemis Ephesia was held by females, and the goddess was served by large ranks of priestesses. See Baugh, "A Foreign World: Ephesus in the First Century." The central role of women in the cult of Artemis Ephesia has important implications for the interpretation of Ephesians 5 and 1 Timothy 2; Paul did not derive his view of the female vocation from the Greco-Roman environment.

[343] Christine M. Thomas, "At Home in the City of Artemis," in Koester, *Ephesos: Metropolis of Asia*, 90–92, discusses the history of eunuch priests at Ephesus. She notes Strabo's comment that eunuch priests *used to* work (imperfect tense) alongside virgin priestesses at Ephesus (*Geography*, 14:1.23). Strabo implies that their ritual castration had undergone a shift in interpretation—from an act of consecration to a mark of sexual purity. In other words, the older and more local Anatolian fertility cult was slowly giving way to the Greek-style Artemesian cult of quiet and honorable chastity. How far this transformation had progressed (and how thorough it was in practice) in the first century AD is the question at issue. Strabo himself writes that "some of the [older] customs are [still] practiced, some are not" (*Geography*, 14:1.23; trans. Thomas, 90).

[344] Early coins (from the third century BC) portray her as the short-skirted virgin huntress. From the second century BC onward, the distinctive cult statue image begins to appear on coins, though its origins are as early as the seventh century BC (Christine M. Thomas, "At Home in the City of Artemis," in Koester, *Ephesos: Metropolis of Asia*, 95).

[345] See Schwindt, *Das Weltbild des Epheserbriefes*, 114. The adjective διοπετής is a combination of a form of Zeus (διο-) and a derivative of πίπτω, "to fall." The stone to which it refers perhaps was a meteorite, either having the form of a woman or later carved to resemble one.

[346] Both the Latin and the Greek mean "many breasts": Minucius Felix, *Octavius*, 21: "mammis multis"; Jerome, *Ephesians*, Preface to Book 1: "πολύμαστον" (Heine, *The Commentaries of Origen and Jerome*, 77; PL 26:441). It is notable that Jerome switches from Latin to Greek when speaking of the "many breasts," indicating that he might be quoting a Greek source.

suggestions that they are eggs or bull's testicles removed from sacrificial victims and attached to her statue in a kind of power renewal ceremony.[347] By either interpretation, the unique depiction of the Artemis Ephesia in statuary suggests that *fertility* was a part of her cult.[348] Ritual prostitution via temple priestesses as a means of achieving unity with the goddess, absorbing her power, and inducing her to grant fertility to people, land, and animals was a standard feature of pagan religion at the time and in the area. It is probable, though not provable, that the cult of Artemis Ephesia (perhaps in distinction from the Greek Artemis) included orgies and sacred prostitution.[349] This provides significant context for Paul's discussion of pagan worship and immorality in Eph 5:3–14 (cf. also "Having Put Aside Idolatry" in the commentary on 4:17–5:2).

In addition to her role as a fertility goddess and her power over the underworld, Artemis Ephesia was thought to be the most powerful of gods and therefore could be appealed to for help in every facet of life. Clinton Arnold's magnificent study *Power and Magic: The Concept of Power in Ephesians* exhaustively demonstrates that her cult is targeted by Paul's strong emphasis on Christ's power and superiority in Ephesians. He notes that she was the most widely worshiped deity in Asia Minor, with satellite sites of worship in the Lycus Valley cities of Colossae, Laodicea, and Hierapolis.[350] This fact has implications for the exchange of Paul's letters (Ephesians and Colossians) among these cities, as what he wrote to one would apply to all. She was πρωτοθρονία, "supreme in divine power and place"[351]—language that Paul trumps in his assertions about Christ in both Colossians and Ephesians. Richard Oster summarizes:

> Her ability to help her worshippers stemmed, in fact, from her awesome power. It was because of her supra-natural powers that she could intercede between her followers and the cruel fate which plagued them. To those who called upon Artemis she was Savior (Σώτειρα), Lord (Κυρία), and Queen

---

[347] Christine M. Thomas, "At Home in the City of Artemis," in Koester, *Ephesos: Metropolis of Asia*, 86–87; Arnold, *Power and Magic*, 25; Schwindt, *Das Weltbild des Epheserbriefes*, 116–19; Trebilco, *The Early Christians in Ephesus from Paul to Ignatius*, 22–23. There are three objections to the "breast" interpretation: (1) it comes only from Christian sources, which may have had no firsthand knowledge of the cult; (2) in the extant statues they are often fashioned from a stone different in color from the flesh of the goddess, suggesting that they are not part of her body; and (3) only in a few late examples do they have nipples. Arnold, *Ephesians*, 35, refers to a theory that they were pouches containing charms, based on a reference in Athenaeus. Yet the breast interpretation remains the only explicit explanation from the ancient world. As to their appearance, there is no reason why the breasts need have been portrayed as *bare*, considering the statue is otherwise covered in a long robe and jewelry.

[348] Dieter Knibbe, "Via Sacra Ephesiaca: New Aspects of the Cult of Artemis Ephesia," in Koester, *Ephesos: Metropolis of Asia*, 142, calls her "the mistress of the earth's fertility, but also the protector of the dead"—the latter being a role taken over from Cybele, the Phrygian great mother goddess. Arnold, *Power and Magic*, 25, concludes: "Most scholars agree that this ornamentation in some way illustrates her well-attested role as goddess of fertility."

[349] Arnold, *Power and Magic*, 27, despite the contrary view in Oster, Baugh, and van der Toorn (cited above).

[350] Arnold, *Power and Magic*, 20.

[351] Arnold, *Power and Magic*, 21.

of the Cosmos (Βασιληῖς κόσμου). She was a heavenly goddess (οὐράνιος θεὸς Ἄρτεμις Ἐφεσία), whose being and character could only be described in superlatives: μεγίστη, ἁγιωτάτη, and ἐπιφανεστάτη ["greatest," "holiest," and "most prominent"].[352]

Her superiority over all other powers may also have been depicted by the signs of the zodiac that ring her neck in the statuary, as well as the frightening wild beasts on her skirt.[353] See the photos below.

The Beautiful Artemis statue discovered at Ephesus,
housed at the Ephesus Museum, Selçuk, Turkey.

Photo: © Valery Shanin/Shutterstock.

---

[352] Oster, "The Ephesian Artemis as an Opponent of Early Christianity," 40, quoted in Arnold, *Power and Magic*, 21.

[353] Arnold, *Power and Magic*, 25; Schwindt, *Das Weltbild des Epheserbriefes*, 123.

Close-up of the astrological signs around Artemis' neck.

Photo: © Valery Shanin/Shutterstock.

An Ephesian Gentile would naturally call upon her name for help in extreme need, even rescue from death. The third-century AD *Acts of John* by Pseudo-Prochorus depicts the worshipers of Artemis praying:

> O Great Artemis of the Ephesians, help! Display your power (δύναμιν) upon this young man who has died. For all the Ephesians know, both men and women, that all things (τὰ πάντα) are governed by you, and that great powers (δυνάμεις μεγάλαι) come to us through you. Give now to your servant what you are able to do in this regard. Raise up your servant Domnos.[354]

One can easily see Paul's letter to the Ephesians as a challenge to such pagan appeals as it places Christ above Artemis by ascribing to him a position above the heavens, above all powers, subordinate only to his Father, who works all things (1:20–23; 2:6–7; 3:10; 4:6, 10).

Magic was strongly associated with the religions of Ephesus. Pliny records that there was an image of the underworld goddess Hekate behind the sanctuary of the temple of Artemis;[355] another stood at the crossroads in the center of town. Hekate was a goddess of witchcraft and sorcery. But Artemis Ephesia herself was also called upon by the practitioners of magic. Pausanias, the Atticist lexicographer, claimed that images of Artemis existed with the "Ephesia Grammata" inscribed on them. No such image survives today, but it is probable that silversmiths like those Paul encountered (Acts 19:24–25) may have made them.[356]

---

[354] Quoted in Arnold, *Power and Magic*, 22.

[355] Pliny the Elder, *Natural History*, 36:4.22.

[356] Arnold, *Power and Magic*, 23.

These so-called "letters" were six secret, ancient, untranslatable words that are well-attested in magic spells contained in the literature of the time: ἄσκιον, κατάσκιον, λίξ, τετράξ, δαμναμενεύς, and αἴσια.[357] These letters, words, or names were thought to have apotropaic power; that is, they were used to ward off demons. They also gave strength and power to their user.[358] They would be written on jewelry (amulets) or spoken as incantations. Although such magical practices were common throughout the ancient world, Ephesus "had a reputation in antiquity as a place where magical practices flourished."[359]

There is recent archaeological evidence from Ephesus of curses uttered in Artemis' name and an inscription fragment referring to a "magician … of the goddess."[360] Paul's clashes with the magicians of Ephesus who tried to use *Jesus'* name (Acts 19:11–20)[361] and his claim that Christ has been lifted "far above every ruler and authority and power and lordship, and *every name* that is *named*" (Eph 1:21), are brightly illuminated by this background. It is also not surprising that Acts identifies the exorcists and magicians as *Jewish* (Acts 19:13–14), for, as the *Testament of Solomon* gives evidence, Jewish folk culture in Asia Minor had absorbed magical practices.[362] Clinton Arnold suggests that Paul's reference to fighting "wild beasts" in Ephesus (1 Cor 15:32), often identified as his *Jewish* opponents, might in fact refer to the *demonic* opposition he faced in the cult of Artemis and the magicians.[363] Whether or not this is what Paul meant, he certainly faced a battle on many fronts as he proclaimed there the powerful Gospel of Jesus Christ.

---

[357] Arnold, *Power and Magic*, 15; Schwindt, *Das Weltbild des Epheserbriefes*, 77–78. Arnold, *Ephesians*, 33, suggests that the words were originally Hittite.

[358] Arnold, *Power and Magic*, 15, quotes the story of the Ephesian wrestler who won repeated victories in Olympia until it was revealed that he had the Grammata on his ankles. Once these were removed, he lost three successive matches. See Eustathius of Thessalonica, *Commentary on Homer*, 19:247.

[359] Arnold, *Ephesians*, 34. Schwindt, *Das Weltbild des Epheserbriefes*, 77, calls Ephesus "a metropolis for magic."

[360] Arnold, *Ephesians*, 36.

[361] The only reference to magic in Ignatius comes in his letter to the Ephesians, 19:3: "Hence, every kind of magic was destroyed [ὅθεν ἐλύετο πᾶσα μαγεία]." Plutarch, *Quaestiones convivales*, 7:5, said that the Ephesian Grammata could drive out demons if spoken in the correct order (quoted in Arnold, *Ephesians*, 35).

[362] The *Testament of Solomon* is thought to have originated in Ephesus. It contains references to the Ephesian Grammata (7:5) and refers to Artemis (8:11), perhaps calling her "the Great One" (7:5). See the references in Arnold, *Ephesians*, 38. Schwindt, *Das Weltbild des Epheserbriefes*, 301, asserts that it reflects magical Jewish folk religion of Asia Minor.

[363] Arnold, *Ephesians*, 39. The *Testament of Solomon*, 18:1, refers to evil spirits as beasts. The robe on the statue of the Beautiful Artemis is ringed with wild beasts under her dominion. Peter calls the devil a roaring lion (1 Pet 5:8). Jerome, *Ephesians*, Preface to Book 3, uses this key to interpret 1 Cor 15:32, saying: "When he [the devil] perceived that the chief city of Asia was snatched from his jaws to the teaching of Paul he gathered all the armies of his attendants and attempted to suppress him" (Heine, *The Commentaries of Origen and Jerome*, 202; cf. PL 26:515).

Paul and Ephesus in Acts

The best preparation for reading Paul's letter to the Ephesians is a close examination of Acts 18–20.[364] According to Luke's record, Paul first visited Ephesus at the end of his second missionary journey (Acts 18:19–21). There he entered the synagogue (as was his custom) to debate with the Jews, presumably to demonstrate that Jesus of Nazareth was the Messiah promised in the OT. He cut his visit short in order to return to Caesarea and meet with the mother church in Antioch (Acts 18:22), but he promised the Ephesians that he would return, "God willing" (Acts 18:21). When he did so (Acts 19:1), Paul remained in Ephesus for nearly three years (Acts 19:8, 10; 20:31). His ministry there may not have spanned a full thirty-six months, but he was in Ephesus at least portions of three consecutive years. It is significant to the interpretation of Ephesians that this was the longest sojourn in Paul's public ministry. Here Paul watched the small group of twelve initial converts (Acts 19:7) increase to a church that likely embraced the large city in multiple places of worship.[365] Here Paul himself likely baptized those who heard and believed his message (Eph 1:13; cf. his baptizing at Corinth, his other place of lengthy pastoral ministry, in 1 Cor 1:13–16). Here he probably presided at the Lord's Supper (as in nearby Troas, Acts 20:7, and in Corinth, 1 Cor 11:23–26) and established patterns of public prayer that are particularly evident in Ephesians (1:3–14; 3:14–21; 6:18–24). Paul's unique liturgical relationship with the Ephesians may be the best explanation for its elevated and rhetorically elaborate style.

Conflict over Baptism and the Spirit (Acts 18:24–19:7)

Prior to Paul's arrival back in Ephesus (Acts 19:1), Luke narrates the background story of Apollos' brief, but eventful, mission work in the city (Acts 18:24–28). We are given a series of significant facts about Apollos:

- He was an Alexandrian (Acts 18:24), presumably a part of the sizable Jewish community in that great city, but Hellenized in language and perhaps philosophy.
- He was ἀνὴρ λόγιος, "an eloquent man" (Acts 18:24), that is, educated and rhetorically skillful—characteristics that would serve him well in Ephesus, which was under the influence of the Second Sophistic and many of whose residents were addicted to high rhetoric.
- He was δυνατὸς … ἐν ταῖς γραφαῖς, "powerful in the Scriptures" (Acts 18:24).
- And he was κατηχημένος τὴν ὁδὸν τοῦ κυρίου, "catechized in the Way of the Lord" (Acts 18:25).

---

[364] Guthrie, *New Testament Introduction*, 504, writes: "There are similarly more parallels between Ephesians and the Acts than is the case for any other Pauline epistle." The relevance is disputed, of course, by those who do not believe that the letter was really written to Ephesus. Käsemann, "Ephesians and Acts," sees the parallels as part of an intricate rewriting of history in the interest of the victorious early Catholic party.

[365] Acts 20:17 speaks of "presbyters/pastors [plural] of the church [πρεσβυτέρους τῆς ἐκκλησίας]." Paul writes to Timothy in Ephesus about proper practice "in every place [ἐν παντὶ τόπῳ]" (1 Tim 2:8). Writing from Ephesus to Corinth, Paul refers to multiple churches in Asia (1 Cor 16:19–20).

The picture that quickly emerges is of a highly educated Hellenistic Jew who had come to understand that Jesus was the promised Messiah. He used his massive skill and knowledge to continue Paul's conversations with the Jews, convincing them that the OT pointed to Jesus. However, Luke adds that there was a significant gap in his Christian catechesis: "he was speaking and teaching accurately the things concerning Jesus, *though he knew only the Baptism of John*" (Acts 18:25). Is it possible that Apollos had himself been baptized by John on a visit to Israel, but in his zeal he had quickly struck out on his travels before his education was complete? Priscilla and Aquila, companions whom Paul left in Ephesus after his first brief visit (Acts 18:18–19), were quick to correct Apollos (Acts 18:26). But one suspects that the damage to his ministry had already been done and that (like many a zealous young seminary graduate) his first "pastorate" was short-lived![366]

Luke clearly expects us to read the story of Paul's second visit to Ephesus against the background of Apollos' rocky ministry there. Having revisited the churches of his first missionary journey in central Asia (Acts 18:23), Paul arrived in Ephesus over land (Acts 19:1). The account of his meeting with the small Christian group there is abridged and is among the most difficult NT passages to interpret. The motive for Paul's abrupt opening question is unclear: "Did you receive the Holy Spirit when you believed [πιστεύσαντες]?" (Acts 19:2; cf. Eph 1:13–14). He seems to have in mind an external, visible or audible manifestation of the Spirit's work, as happened in Jerusalem, Samaria, and Caesarea (Acts 2:1–13; 8:14–17; 10:44–48). In each case, the Lord gave public testimony to the apostolic Word of the Gospel at the opening of a new mission field in accord with his promise, and Paul may have expected the phenomenon to continue to the ends of the earth (Acts 1:8). But the reply from the Ephesians is not at all what he expected: "*But we have not heard that there is a Holy Spirit*" (Acts 19:2). Paul uncovers a defect in their catechesis. But the problem runs deeper, for it calls into question their Baptism: " 'Into what then were you baptized?' And they said, 'Into the Baptism of John' " (Acts 19:3).

Over the past five hundred years this account has caused much strife. It has been used to support either or both of these teachings:

1. that Baptism with water does not give the Holy Spirit, but that he comes through a separate act
2. that John's Baptism and Christian Baptism differed so fundamentally that John's did not give the Holy Spirit (so that all those baptized by John needed a second, "Christian" Baptism to receive the Spirit)

---

[366] We speak of "pastorate" loosely, for the text gives no evidence that Apollos was sent by anyone or called by God—indeed, the account implies that he ran into trouble both because his catechesis was incomplete and because he had entered into a self-chosen work. At the same time, it is worth noting that after Priscilla and Aquila corrected his theology (Acts 18:26), the brothers in Ephesus forgave him and sent him off to Achaia with a letter of commendation (Acts 18:27)—though his time in Corinth was not without its difficulties (1 Cor 1:12).

The first misunderstanding of the text, the Pentecostal postulation of a division between water Baptism and Spirit Baptism, cuts completely across the grain of the context. For Paul's question, "into what then were you baptized?" (Acts 19:3), implies his expectation that, if they had been baptized, they would have received the Spirit. Paul is stunned that they could have been baptized without having received the Spirit and that they did not even know about the Spirit.

The second misunderstanding has been a bit of a storm in a teacup across Christian history, inasmuch as the precise nature of John's Baptism has little ongoing relevance to the Christian church since it ceased with the passing of John himself. But the debate has generated important discussion about Baptism itself. At the time of the Reformation, the Council of Trent issued a condemnation of anyone who "says that the baptism of John had the same power as the baptism of Christ."[367] It is not entirely clear who was the target of this condemnation, inasmuch as Luther himself had occasionally described John's Baptism as greatly inferior to Christ's (e.g., AE 22:175–78). Yet Martin Chemnitz took up the challenge and offered an admirably strong affirmation of the character of John's Baptism as a means of grace.[368] While John's Baptism was clearly not identical to the Trinitarian Baptism carried out by the apostles and their successors under Christ's mandate (Mt 28:19), Chemnitz's arguments have persuaded the present author that great dangers lurk in the arguments used to undervalue it.

Three observations on the basis of the Gospel accounts may help clarify the nature of John's Baptism and its relationship to the Sacrament later instituted by Christ:

First, the Gospel texts in which John declared that he baptized with water while Christ would baptize with the Holy Spirit (Mt 3:11; Mk 1:8; Lk 3:16; Jn 1:33) surely do not refer to a contrast between John's Baptism and Christian Baptism. For that would mean that Christian Baptism is with the Spirit but *not* with water. John may have meant to say, "All I do is pour the water, but the Messiah is the one who gives the Spirit"—thus, not distinguishing two Baptisms, but two actors. For the purpose of John's words was to direct the crowds away from *himself* and toward the coming *Messiah*, not to direct people away from his *Baptism*, which God sent him to administer (Jn 1:33).[369] But

---

[367] Quoted in Martin Chemnitz, *Examination of the Council of Trent* (trans. Fred Kramer; St. Louis: Concordia, 1978), 2:121.

[368] Chemnitz, *Examination of the Council of Trent*, 2:121–36.

[369] Some have suggested that cults of John the Baptist persisted even after the death and resurrection of Christ and have proposed that the existence of these cults is the reason why John's Gospel in particular includes passages designed to dispel the belief that John the Baptizer was himself the Messiah (Jn 1:15, 19–34; 3:25–30; 4:1; 5:33–35); see Helmut Koester, "Ephesos in Early Christian Literature," in Koester, *Ephesos: Metropolis of Asia*, 127. C. K. Barrett, "Apollos and the Twelve Disciples of Ephesus," in *The New Testament Age: Essays in Honor of Bo Reicke* (ed. William C. Weinrich; 2 vols.; Macon, Ga.: Mercer University Press, 1984), 1:37, considers the evidence for such cults "not proved" and "exaggerated." If Apollos himself had not performed the Baptisms in Ephesus, the account may confirm the suggestion that there were cults of John the Baptist in existence in various places. See F. F. Bruce, *New Testament History* (London: Thomas Nelson, 1969), 161–62. But the text of Acts 19 in no

Luke himself provides the best interpretation when he gives us Christ's words: "for John baptized with water, but you will be baptized in the Holy Spirit after not many days" (Acts 1:5; cf. Acts 11:16). In other words, *the contrast is not between John's Baptism and Christian Baptism, but between John's Baptism and Pentecost.*

Second, the texts of the Gospel are quite clear that John had the Spirit and that the Spirit came through his Baptism. John himself was filled with the Spirit even from the womb (Lk 1:15), and the Word of the Lord came to him like a prophet of old (Lk 3:2). Most important, it was through the water of John's hand that the Holy Spirit came visibly upon Jesus at his Baptism (Mt 3:16; Mk 1:10; Lk 3:22; Jn 1:32). What was exceptional in Jesus' Baptism was not the gift of the Spirit, but the *visibility* of the Spirit and the *audibility* of the Father's words. On that special occasion God revealed what happens to every child whom he receives in Baptism (whether that of John or of the apostles), for Christ's Baptism *is* our Baptism (see "Baptism and the Spirit" in "Purpose and Themes" below, and particularly "Baptism in the Prologue" in the commentary on 1:3–14).

Third, the Gospels unanimously testify that John's Baptism was "for the forgiveness of sins [εἰς ἄφεσιν ἁμαρτιῶν]" (Mk 1:4; Lk 3:3; cf. Mt 3:6). While this phrase appears to attribute Gospel power to John's Baptism, many interpret the preposition εἰς, "for, unto," to mean only that it pointed forward to a forgiveness that was yet to come. But the very same phrase (εἰς ἄφεσιν ἁμαρτιῶν) attributes the forgiveness of sins to the preaching of the Gospel (Lk 24:47) and to the blood of Christ in the Lord's Supper (Mt 26:28). Thus, if one interprets this phrase to mean that John's Baptism did not *give* forgiveness, but only *pointed* to it in the future, there are dangerous implications, for this interpretation could imply that none of the means of grace (the Word, Baptism, and the Supper) actually bestow the forgiveness of sins.

This extended discussion of John's Baptism is meant to illuminate the situation Paul confronted in Ephesus. For since the disciples there had received a "Baptism of John" without knowing the Holy Spirit at all (Acts 19:2–3), then it was surely a *false* baptism of John. No conclusions about John's original and authentic Baptism can be drawn from Acts 19, but what we know of John's Baptism from the Gospels can and should be applied to this story. If those twelve disciples (Acts 19:7) were baptized by Apollos (and not already baptized when he arrived [Acts 18:24–25]), it appears that in ignorance Apollos had been carrying out an *illegitimate* Baptism in the name of John—illegitimate for two reasons: (1) Baptism in the Triune name as mandated by Christ (Mt 28:19) had already supplanted John's Baptism, and (2) *only John* had the authority to do "John's Baptism."[370]

---

way implies that these were disciples *of John*; on the contrary, Luke's absolute use of "disciples [μαθητάς]" in Acts 19:1 implies that they were disciples *of Jesus*.

[370] The possibility that these were Jews who had been baptized by John himself (e.g., Murphy-O'Connor, *St. Paul's Ephesus*, 206) seems to be excluded by Paul's own diagnostic questions

These conclusions about the effective nature of John's original Baptism and the illegitimacy of what the twelve disciples at Ephesus received are confirmed by the fact that Apollos, who had presumably received Baptism from the hand of John himself, was not rebaptized but merely properly catechized (Acts 18:26), while those who had received his false washing were given true Baptism "in the name of the Lord Jesus" (Acts 19:5). Paul, responding to this odd situation, demonstrates remarkable pastoral wisdom: he refrains from passing judgment against Apollos or condemning the Ephesians for receiving a false baptism. Instead, he builds on the foundation Apollos laid by directing them beyond John's Baptism to the Christ whom John had served. Then he baptizes them in the name of Christ and lays hands on them so that they receive the Holy Spirit with his visible signs (Acts 19:5–6). Their number, "and there were about *twelve* men in all" (Acts 19:7), signifies a new Israel among the Gentiles.

This story in Acts intersects with Ephesians at a number of points. First, the commentary will discern a number of allusions to Jesus' own Baptism at the hand of John (see particularly "Baptism in the Prologue" in the commentary on Eph 1:3–14). Second, Ephesians is replete with teaching on the Holy Spirit, precisely what had been lacking in the original teaching of Apollos (Acts 18:25; 19:2). Third, the letter insists that there is just "one Baptism" (Eph 4:5). Why this emphasis? Could it be that there was lingering confusion over the experience of the original twelve converts? Did they perhaps brag that they had received *two* Baptisms, John's and Christ's? Or was the problem the reverse: were they denigrated by their brothers for having first received an illegitimate Baptism from Apollos? In either scenario, Baptism had become a point of *division* in the church, and if so, then Paul's response in Ephesians is quite apropos. He locates their *unity* not simply in the shared Sacrament of Baptism, but also in the "*one* Baptism" of Christ at the hand of John. Eph 4:5 does not merely teach that there is "one Baptism" per person, but also that *all Christians share the very same Baptism* and find their unity as they are located in Christ when he enters the Jordan, hangs on the cross, rises from the dead, and ascends to the right hand of God.[371]

Conflict with the Jews (Acts 19:8–10)

For the first three months of his three-year Ephesian ministry, Paul continued to debate with the Jews over the OT's testimony to the Messiah. This work, which he had begun (Acts 18:19–20) and Apollos briefly continued (Acts 18:24–28), initially took place in the synagogue. But "when some became hardened [ἐσκληρύνοντο] and persistently disbelieved [ἠπείθουν], speaking evil [κακολογοῦντες] of the Way before the multitude" (Acts 19:9), Paul withdrew from the synagogue, taking with him those who wished to continue the debate, and relocated to the "Hall of Tyrannus" (Acts 19:9). The exact location

---

(Acts 19:2–3). Why would he have expected a visible manifestation of the Spirit in the later Christian sense during a Johannine Baptism at the Jordan River?

[371] See the commentary on 4:5 and "Baptism in the Prologue" in the commentary on 1:3–14, as well as Winger, " 'One Baptism' and the Purpose of Ephesians."

is unknown, but some (Western) manuscripts add the detail "from the fifth hour until the tenth." In the heat of midday the group probably found a public space in a school of philosophy (or the like) that was quiet and unoccupied.

This brief account of Paul's work among the Jews serves to confirm (1) that the Ephesian church did include some converts from Judaism, but (2) that the majority of the Jews remained hostile to Paul's mission. His reputation among the Jews could not have been helped when the pagan rioters later identified Paul's troublesome cause with theirs (Acts 19:33–34), tarring both with one brush. The imprint of this conflict between Jews and Gentiles can be seen particularly in Ephesians 2, but also in Paul's defense of his mission to the Gentiles in chapter 3 and in his promotion of the baptismal unity of the church in chapter 4.

Conflict with Jewish Exorcists and Pagan Magicians (Acts 19:11–20)

In a series of narrative vignettes, Luke describes a succession of further conflicts that followed upon Paul's initial Jewish mission in Ephesus. Paul himself, writing to the Corinthians from Ephesus, summarizes: "A great and effective door has opened to me, and there are many adversaries [ἀντικείμενοι]" (1 Cor 16:9). We have previously noted that the Ephesian religious scene was pluralistic, and that even the Judaism of Asia Minor had absorbed some pagan elements into its folk culture (see the references to the *Testament of Solomon* in "The Cult of Artemis Ephesia," above in "The City of Ephesus and Paul's Relationship to It"). The incident of the Jewish exorcists illustrates the context well. These seven sons of the chief priest Sceva recognized the power of the name of Jesus from Paul's miraculous deeds (Acts 19:11–14). Perhaps they had been casting out demons by the name of God Most High; perhaps they had used pagan names like the Ephesian Grammata[372] or Artemis' own. But their appropriation of Paul's Jesus scarcely represented a conversion experience!

When the demons themselves overwhelmed the exorcists, confessing the power of Jesus' name, these bumblers ended up unwittingly promoting Paul's mission, as the humorous tale of their fleeing naked from the house of the demon-possessed man became known throughout the region (Acts 19:16–17). The superior power of Jesus' name was so widely acknowledged that the famous magic of Ephesus became quickly antiquated and a riotous book-burning ensued (Acts 19:18–19). Lest the Ephesians ever forget the vast superiority of Jesus over "every name that is named" (Eph 1:21) or power above, Paul's letter reaffirms it at every turn (1:19–23; 2:1–2, 6; 3:8–10; 4:6, 8–10; 6:10–17).

Conflict with the Cult of Artemis Ephesia (Acts 19:21–41)

It was one thing for Paul to embarrass the itinerant Jewish exorcists (the local residents probably cheered) or to prove superior to the cohorts of local magicians (Acts 19:11–19). But as Christ himself experienced, so also his apostle would disturb the chief priests of a great temple at his peril. Once again, it was the "money changers" who were most upset. We have noted above the

---

[372] For these Grammata, see "The Cult of Artemis Ephesia," above in "The City of Ephesus and Paul's Relationship to It."

significance of the unique image of Artemis Ephesia to the local cult.[373] With historic verisimilitude, the account of Acts records what an industry had grown up around the production of silver (and perhaps other) images of Artemis Ephesia and her temple. Artemis Ephesia could tolerate competitors, but Paul's message that gods "made with hands are not gods" (Acts 19:26; cf. ἄθεοι, "godless," in Eph 2:12) was putting a serious dent in that industry's profits (Acts 19:25). The speech of Demetrius the silversmith attests to the preeminence of the Artemis cult in the region, as he cries out: "There is a danger not only that our trade may come into disrepute but also that the temple of the great goddess Artemis may be reckoned as nothing and that she may soon be deposed from her magnificence, she whom all Asia and the inhabited world worship" (Acts 19:27).[374] The crowd will have none of this; their city's wealth and prestige depend on her cult. "Great is Artemis of the Ephesians!" they cry (Acts 19:28). Is it more

Silver coins (cistophors) showing the temple and statue of Artemis (Diana),
second century AD. From the Ephesus Museum, Vienna, Austria.

Photo: © 2014 Thomas M. Winger.

---

[373] See "The Temple of Artemis Ephesia" and "The Cult of Artemis Ephesia," above in "The City of Ephesus and Paul's Relationship to It."

[374] Pausanius proclaimed her cult the greatest in Asia, *Description of Greece*, 4:31.8 (trans. W. H. S. Jones, LCL):

But all cities worship Artemis of Ephesus, and individuals hold her in honor above all the gods. The reason, in my view, is the renown of the Amazons, who traditionally dedicated the image, also the extreme antiquity of this sanctuary. Three other points as well have contributed to her renown, the size of the temple, surpassing all buildings among men, the eminence of the city of the Ephesians and the renown of the goddess who dwells there.

than coincidence, then, that Paul later writes to the Ephesians (1 Tim 1:3) through Timothy: "*Great* is the mystery of *our* religion, [Christ] who was manifested in the flesh ..." (1 Tim 3:16)?

The great riot that ensued, spilling into the massive 25,000-seat theater (Acts 19:29),[375] included two hours of shouting (Acts 19:34). Only when the town clerk suggested that Artemis Ephesia's cult would probably survive this upstart[376] and that the silversmiths' complaint could be taken up in court did the riot subside (Acts 19:35 41). But Paul's public image was so damaged that he had to end his lengthy sojourn in Ephesus, and he departed for Macedonia, perhaps sooner than he had intended (Acts 20:1). Ephesians bears the imprint of the Gospel's battle with this pagan goddess and her cult, particularly in chapter 5, which calls Christians away from fellowship with such darkness and toward the true worship of God through Christ in the Spirit. But those passages that proclaim the elevation of Christ above every power and name that is named (1:19–23; 2:1–2, 6; 3:8–10; 4:6, 8–10; 6:10–17) apply equally to his elevation over her.

Lead statuette of Artemis from the Roman period.
From the Ephesus Museum, Vienna, Austria.

Photo: © 2014 Thomas M. Winger.

---

[375] See the photo of the theater in "The City," above in "The City of Ephesus and Paul's Relationship to It."

[376] The confident claim would prove mistaken. Pliny the Younger, governor of Bithynia, wrote to Trajan (in AD 112) that the spread of Christianity had already put a dent in the temple cult and ritual: "Sacrifices at the temples had been neglected and the sacrificial meat found no buyers" (Helmut Koester, "Ephesos in Early Christian Literature," in Koester, *Ephesos: Metropolis of Asia*, 130, summarizing Pliny, *Epistles*, 10:96).

Paul's Sermon to the Ephesian Pastors (Acts 20:15–38; cf. 1 Timothy)

While in Ephesus Paul wrote his first letter to Corinth, sending it with Timothy as his envoy (Acts 19:22; 1 Cor 4:17); he expected Timothy to return to him in Ephesus (1 Cor 16:8–11). Timothy's role as Paul's emissary continued in their later correspondence, when Paul wrote two letters to Timothy at Ephesus (1 Timothy certainly, according to 1 Tim 1:3, and apparently also 2 Timothy). Higher critical scholars, of course, have for centuries rejected the historical veracity of this situation, arguing on the basis of their construal of the contents that the Pastoral Epistles could not have been written during Paul's lifetime (see "Incipient Catholicism" in "Arguments against Pauline Authorship" in "Authorship" above). Even most conservative scholars, while affirming Pauline authorship, date the letters after the close of Acts, under the assumption that Paul was released from prison and revisited Asia Minor.[377] Yet there is very little evidence for this traditional dating scheme,[378] and it may be that even conservative scholars have been influenced by critical theories of theological development.[379]

If such presumptions are set aside, the opening lines of 1 Timothy align quite directly with the account of Paul and Timothy's movements in Acts and 1 Corinthians:[380]

> As I urged you to remain in Ephesus, when I was going to Macedonia, that you might charge certain men not to teach a different doctrine, nor to devote themselves to myths and endless genealogies, which promote useless speculations rather than the plan [οἰκονομία] of God that is in faith. (1 Tim 1:3–4)[381]

For when the riot in Ephesus had subsided, Paul "bade farewell and departed for Macedonia" (Acts 20:1). The natural interpretation of these two passages is that

---

[377] Re Paul's imprisonment, see "Location and Date of Writing" below.

[378] E.g., Franzmann, *The Word of the Lord Grows*, 149, begins his discussion with an unproved assumption: "*Since* we do not have the help of the Book of Acts for the period in which the writing of the Pastoral Letters falls and must reconstruct the history of this period entirely from hints given in the letters themselves, the order of events must remain somewhat doubtful; even an approximate dating of them is difficult" (emphasis added). Paul's release from prison is postulated on the basis of early (unverified) tradition that he visited Spain (*1 Clement*, 5:7). Clement speaks of "the limits of the west [τὸ τέρμα τῆς δύσεως]," a vague reference that could refer to Rome itself—though from Clement's own perspective it more likely did mean Spain (i.e., the Strait of Gibraltar; see Mounce, *Pastoral Epistles*, lv). Clement may have had access to local tradition about Paul's later journeys, or he may simply have assumed that Paul's planned journey to Spain (Rom 15:24, 28) was fulfilled. Whether or not Paul was released and visited Spain, there are no good reasons for dating the Pastoral Epistles after the close of Acts.

[379] Reicke, *Re-examining Paul's Letters*, 58–59: "Because these instructions [in 1 Timothy] are intended for a church leader, they are more detailed than those in such community addresses as 1 Thessalonians or 1 Corinthians. But this greater specification does not prove that 1 Timothy was composed at a time later than any other Pauline correspondence."

[380] The following reconstruction follows to a great extent Reicke, *Re-examining Paul's Letters*, 48–59, 105–20. Cf. Robinson, *Redating the New Testament*, 82–83; Johnson, *The First and Second Letters to Timothy*, 135–37.

[381] See οἰκονομία also in Ephesians, where it is translated as "administer" (1:10), "administration" (3:9), and "stewardship" (3:2).

Timothy had returned from Corinth to Ephesus and that Paul, shortly after his departure from Ephesus to Macedonia, wrote his first letter back to Timothy in Ephesus.[382] While 1 Timothy is addressed directly to Timothy, there are subtle indications that it was also aimed at the entire church at Ephesus,[383] for whom it served as a letter of commendation for Timothy as Paul's authorized representative.[384] Paul's first letter to Timothy gives insight into the situation in the Ephesian church as Paul left her. The letter deals with the proto-Gnostic, syncretistic philosophical/religious environment of Asia Minor. The opening mandate to deal with certain false teachers in Ephesus (1 Tim 1:3–4) suggests that all was not well within the church—Paul had already dealt with two false teachers (1 Tim 1:20)—and that Ephesians itself may be dealing with false teaching (see Eph 4:14, 25). The central concern of 1 Timothy—that Timothy find men properly suited for the office of the ministry and ordain them (1 Tim 3:1–13)—is capable of two different explanations. Possibly, the church had simply grown to the point where more pastors were needed, and Paul had not had time to appoint them. However, in light of the letter's initial charge against false teachers, it is more likely that Timothy had to defrock some of the pastors and find replacements.[385]

If this reconstruction of the scenario for 1 Timothy is correct, it provides a logical explanation for Paul's decision on his trip from Corinth to Jerusalem to bypass Ephesus and yet arrange a meeting with the pastors of the church. Luke writes: "For Paul had decided to sail past Ephesus, lest he should spend a lot of time in Asia; for he was in a hurry to be able to be in Jerusalem for the

---

[382] Reicke, *Re-examining Paul's Letters*, 56, suggests that Paul wrote 1 Timothy *before* departing from Ephesus, leaving it with Timothy as his authorization papers. In light of his hasty departure after the riot, this scenario is unlikely. Paul's stated desire to join Timothy in Ephesus (1 Tim 3:14; 4:13) offers no clear help, as it could as easily have been written on the eve of departure as later.

[383] The final greeting is plural: ἡ χάρις μεθ᾽ ὑμῶν, "grace be with you all" (1 Tim 6:21). "Let no one despise your youth" (1 Tim 4:12) is a pointless command unless it is read aloud to the gathered church. Reicke, *Re-examining Paul's Letters*, 56–57: "Throughout 1 Timothy it is clear that the whole congregation in Ephesus and even outsiders were intended to hear the message, whereas much of the content would appear quite trivial and superfluous if Timothy were the only hearer or reader." Reicke views the letter as a written record of Paul's departing exhortation to the disciples at Ephesus (Acts 20:1). So also Kelly, *A Commentary on the Pastoral Epistles*, 42.

[384] Early fathers refer to Timothy as the first bishop of Ephesus: Eusebius, *Ecclesiastical History*, 3:4.6; *Apostolic Constitutions*, 7:46. He is, at the very least, Paul's authorized delegate, his plenipotentiary. See Johnson, *The First and Second Letters to Timothy*, 91–97.

[385] L. T. Johnson views the criteria for appointing pastors in 1 Timothy 3 in light of the charges raised against them in 1 Timothy 5: "The letter suggests that the local leadership of the Ephesian community is troubled in two ways. First, some of the leaders appear to have demonstrated questionable moral character [citing 1 Tim 5:19, 22]. ... Second, there is a competition for leadership among some whom Paul thinks unworthy and disruptive" (*The First and Second Letters to Timothy*, 235). In his later exegesis of 1 Timothy 5, Johnson suggests that the primary charge against one or more elders was making personal use of community funds that were intended for the support of the widows (286–87). Mounce, *Pastoral Epistles*, lvii–lix, lxxxi–lxxxii, 153, goes further and suggests that Timothy dismissed the elders and appointed new ones.

day of Pentecost" (Acts 20:16). Paul's fear of a delay in Ephesus makes sense to any pastor who has returned for a visit to a former congregation. In light of Paul's three-year ministry in Ephesus, it would have been difficult for him to select just some of the members to visit or to avoid becoming entangled again in local affairs.[386] At the same time, he sent word that the pastors of the church (τοὺς πρεσβυτέρους τῆς ἐκκλησίας) should meet him at Miletus (Acts 20:17). Miletus, a port city at the mouth of the Meander River, was a significant hike from Ephesus (ca. fifty miles or eighty kilometers south over the hills). This was no casual trip for the Ephesian pastors, implying that Paul may have had an urgent reason to address them.

The possibility that the church at Ephesus had been divided by doctrinal strife, some pastors removed from office, and new pastors ordained by the hand of Timothy explains the urgency. In addition, Paul's sermon to the Ephesian pastors (Acts 20:18–35) contains telltale signs of this situation. It sounds like an ordination/installation sermon (particularly Acts 20:28–35) and aligns with the subsequent letter to the Ephesians:

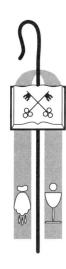

- Paul describes his own pattern of selfless ministry and lays it before them for imitation (Acts 20:18–20, 24, 31, 33–35).
- He urges them to treat Jew and Gentile alike under the Gospel (Acts 20:21).
- He prophesies his imminent imprisonment in Jerusalem (Acts 20:23).
- He refers to the Holy Spirit's work of placing them into office, as if it is a recent event: "Pay attention to yourselves and to the whole flock [ποιμνίῳ] among whom the Holy Spirit has [just] appointed [ἔθετο] you as bishops/overseers [ἐπισκόπους] to pastor/shepherd [ποιμαίνειν] the church of God, which he has obtained through his own blood" (Acts 20:28; cf. Eph 1:7; 4:7–12).
- He warns that false teachers will yet arise, even from their own midst (Acts 20:29–30).[387]
- And he blesses them and commends them to God, using vocabulary that is characteristically Ephesian (Acts 20:32; cf. Eph 1:14; 4:12; 5:26).

Not only does this sermon in Acts 20:18–35 reflect the situation of 1 Timothy, but it also explains the emphasis on the office of the ministry as a gift of the ascended Christ to the church in Eph 4:7–16. In his letter to the Ephesians, Paul encourages them to treasure their new pastors and rely upon them to reestablish unity through one Baptism and the truth of the Gospel (4:1–16).

---

[386] There are, of course, other explanations for Paul's avoidance of Ephesus. Perhaps a consequence of the riot and his rapid exit (Acts 20:1) was that he was persona non grata in the city. Charles K. Barrett suggests that he was concerned for the safety of the collection of money for Jerusalem ("Paul's Address to the Ephesian Elders," in *God's Christ and His People: Studies in Honour of Nils Alstrup Dahl* [ed. Jacob Jervell and Wayne A. Meek; Oslo: Universitetsforlaget, 1977], 108).

[387] Paul calls the false teachers "fierce wolves" (Acts 20:29); Paul writes of his ministry there: "I fought with beasts at Ephesus" (1 Cor 15:32). Rev 2:1–7 suggests there was serious heresy at Ephesus, including false apostles at work.

Paul's Trip to Jerusalem, Arrest, and Imprisonment (Acts 21:1–36)

The subsequent chronology is not entirely clear, but can be worked out with some precision. Paul's ministry in Ephesus had been cut short by the silversmiths' riot, leading him to depart for Macedonia before he was ready (Acts 20:1). Writing to the Corinthians, Paul explained that he intended to stay in Ephesus until Pentecost (1 Cor 16:8). Yet he later bypassed Ephesus in order to reach Jerusalem in time for Pentecost (Acts 20:16). There are two possible explanations: (1) his early departure from Ephesus thwarted his desire to spend Pentecost in Ephesus, meaning that he left Ephesus early in the spring and arrived in Jerusalem in late spring of the same year in which he wrote 1 Corinthians; or (2) he spent Pentecost in Ephesus one year, but in Jerusalem the next. In either case, the prominence of Pentecost in Paul's relationship to Ephesus is notable (see "Caesarea!" in "Location and Date of Writing," as well as "Purpose and Themes," below).

When Paul arrived in Jerusalem, he met with James and the presbyters of the church to describe the divine success of the Gospel among the Gentiles (Acts 21:17–20). Yet they were also aware that through his Gentile mission Paul had managed to stir up the ire of many Jews. They propose a plan to demonstrate that Paul is no threat: he is to take four men under a vow to the temple, purify himself with them, and pay the expenses of their sacrifices (Acts 21:21–26). Paul's assent to this plan demonstrates his willingness to abide by the OT Law, even while proclaiming to the Gentiles their freedom under Christ. Yet his Jewish enemies, far from being appeased, seize on the opportunity to entrap him. While he is in the temple, "Jews from Asia" (!) stir up the crowd by raising two accusations: (1) he teaches people everywhere "against the people and the Law and this place"—meaning Israel, the Torah, and the temple; and (2) "he has brought Greeks into the temple and defiled this holy place" (Acts 21:27–28). Crucial to our present concern is the basis of their charge: "for they had previously seen *Trophimus the Ephesian* in the city with him, whom they supposed Paul had brought into the temple" (Acts 21:29).

Is it insignificant that the particular Greek involved in the charge against Paul is from *Ephesus*? Could it be that word of Paul's arrest in Jerusalem quickly made its way back to Ephesus and that the church there felt the blame for the imprisonment of the apostle to the Gentiles? Paul's words to them support this likelihood: "For this reason, I, Paul, the prisoner of Christ [Jesus] for the sake of you Gentiles. … I ask [you] not to lose heart in my tribulations for your sake, which is your glory" (Eph 3:1, 13). In other words, his imprisonment is not their fault; Paul's mission to the Gentiles was mandated by Christ himself, who alone takes responsibility for Paul's suffering. Paul turns the situation around and proclaims to them that, as Christ suffered for us, so also Paul's sufferings are *for their benefit*.

The specific charge raised against Paul is that he had taken a Gentile into the portion of the temple reserved for Jewish men. Since the second temple was built in postexilic times, its precincts had been divided into concentric levels of holiness, from the innermost court of the priests, to the court of the Israelite men, to the court of the Israelite women, to the outermost court of the Gentiles. A low stone wall (Soreg) surrounded the temple, with signs mounted at each opening warning Gentiles not to violate the barrier upon pain of death. The temple itself was, therefore, a vivid, visible symbol of the divide between Jew and Gentile. Paul's erasure of this divide in Christ had inflamed his Jewish enemies and thereby caused perpetual opposition to his mission. This situation most likely influenced Paul to describe the destruction of the Law in Christ's death on the cross as the tearing down of a barrier and the erection of a new, spiritual temple (Eph 2:11–22; see the commentary on those verses).

Location and Date of Writing
Paul's Imprisonment

Paul writes to the Ephesians while a prisoner, "an ambassador in chains" (Eph 6:20; cf. Col 4:18; 2 Tim 2:9). As an apostle of Christ, he is like a diplomatic representative who, contrary to all norms of international law, has been imprisoned by those to whom he had been sent. To act against an ambassador is to act against the one who sent him. Those who have imprisoned Paul have imprisoned Christ. Creation has affronted its Creator. At the same time, although his prison is literal, Paul believes that no human power could confine him against God's will. He calls himself "the prisoner *of Christ [Jesus]* for the sake of you Gentiles" (3:1; see also 3:13) and "the prisoner *in the Lord*" (4:1). He is imprisoned for the sake of the Gospel, in accord with God's plan, and because the apostle must be conformed to the image of the Christ who sent him (Acts 9:16). He suffers in order to "fill up" the sufferings of Christ for the sake of the church (Col 1:24). He hopes by his trial to sacrifice his own freedom that the Gospel might remain free, to vindicate the Christian message publicly and promote it (Phil 1:7, 12–17). For Paul, this theological perspective on his imprisonment is paramount; he does not wallow in self-pity when he refers repeatedly to his suffering. In so doing he points to the Lord, not to himself (2 Tim 1:8).

Paul's imprisonment can, at the same time, illuminate the circumstances and purposes of the group of writings known collectively as the Prison Epistles or Captivity Letters: Ephesians, Colossians, Philemon, and Philippians, to which one might also add 2 Timothy. Within this group exists a clear division that is not always respected.[388] The first three are united, first, by the geographical proximity of their destinations in the Lycus-Meander Valley and, second, by their letter carrier. Tychicus was a native of Asia Minor who accompanied Paul to Jerusalem as a representative of the Asian churches in delivering aid to the

---

[388] While the traditional view is that all five letters were written from Paul's Roman imprisonment, Bo Reicke places Ephesians, Colossians, Philemon, and 2 Timothy in Caesarea, but Philippians in Rome. J. A. T. Robinson places all five in Caesarea, with Philippians the earliest of the five. See Reicke, *Re-examining Paul's Letters*, 131–40; Robinson, *Redating the New Testament*, 57–61.

mother church (Acts 20:4). He is then named as Paul's representative carrying the letters to the Ephesians (Eph 6:21) and the Colossians (Col 4:7). For him this was a journey home. Tychicus was accompanied by Onesimus (Col 4:9), the runaway slave whom Paul was returning to his master, Philemon. The letters to the Colossians and Philemon are also united by the figures of Archippus (Col 4:17; Philemon 2) and Epaphras (Col 1:7; 4:12; Philemon 23), suggesting that the letter to Philemon was delivered at the same time. Paul later writes to Timothy that he has sent Tychicus to Ephesus (2 Tim 4:12), presumably a reference to his carrying these three letters.

Philippians, by contrast, has little in common with these three letters. The people mentioned are different, except for Timothy, who is present with Paul (Phil 1:1; 2:19). No letter carrier is named, though it is probably Epaphroditus, who has been the Philippians' messenger to Paul in prison and, having recovered from a grave illness, is returning to them (Phil 2:25–30; 4:18). Paul refers to the imminent possibility of his execution (Phil 1:23; 2:17; 3:14), but also to the chance of his release (Phil 1:19, 25; 2:24). This may imply that he is in Rome, where his fate would ultimately be decided; in any captivity prior to that point, he could have appealed to Caesar, as he did in Caesarea (Acts 25:11–12). Paul describes the soldiers guarding him as members of "the Praetorian guard [τῷ πραιτωρίῳ]" (Phil 1:13), an elite group appointed to protect the emperor and the capital city. Some scholars have argued that this term could refer to soldiers outside Rome; as governor Felix commanded that Paul be detained "in the praetorium of Herod [ἐν τῷ πραιτωρίῳ τοῦ Ἡρῴδου]" (Acts 23:35), it is not impossible that its soldiers were known as a "praetorian guard."[389] But greetings given by "those from Caesar's household [οἱ ἐκ τῆς Καίσαρος οἰκίας]" (Phil 4:22) more strongly suggest Rome as the origin of Paul's letter to the Philippians. Philippi was a Roman colony (Acts 16:12), to whose residents such Roman references might have been quite meaningful.

Rome?

But what of Ephesians and its companions? There are strong arguments in favor of a Roman origin also for the four remaining Captivity Letters.[390] The *subscriptio* to Ephesians in major manuscripts from the fourth century onward (B[1] P 0278 1739 1881) indicates that it was written ἀπὸ Ῥώμης, "from Rome."[391] Paul's relative freedom under house arrest in Rome would have allowed him to write such letters, as he was able to receive visitors and proclaim the Gospel (Acts 28:30–31). At the same time, he was occasionally in chains (Act 28:20),

---

[389] Cf. Robinson, *Redating the New Testament*, 60. Reicke, *Re-examining Paul's Letters*, 136–40, disagrees, arguing that it must mean Rome.

[390] The preceding paragraph discusses the Roman provenance of Philippians. The four other Captivity Letters are Ephesians, Colossians, Philemon, and 2 Timothy.

[391] This was the universal tradition in the fourth century. E.g., Chrysostom: "He wrote the Epistle from Rome, and, as he himself informs us, in bonds" ("The Argument" in *Homilies on Ephesians* [*NPNF*[1] 13:49]). Yet earlier manuscripts are silent on the letter's place of origin.

which aligns with his words to the Ephesians (6:20). Paul expects to be released soon and to visit Colossae (Philemon 22). Luke is with him (Col 4:14; Philemon 24), which aligns with the record of Acts (Acts 27–28 is a "we" section, indicating that the author, Luke, was with Paul). Onesimus, the runaway slave from Colossae, may have found Rome an easy place to blend into the crowds of freed slaves—though this argument easily runs in reverse, and Rome may have been the *last* place he would have gone.

Ephesus?

Indeed, it is the lowly slave Onesimus who has spurred the greatest doubts about the Roman captivity theory. For, though he may have stolen from his owner (Philemon 18), would he have had the resources to fund a trip to faraway Rome? The nearby big city of Ephesus seems a more likely alternative (though one wonders how he hoped to disappear in a city so close to home). An Onesimus is later named bishop of Ephesus[392] (though, even if it is the same person, this surely has no bearing on where he fled *before* he returned to his master). The letter to the Philippians implies a series of journeys back and forth (Phil 2:19–30) that are likewise more easily imagined from a nearby city.[393] Some scholars have, therefore, suggested that Paul wrote some or all of the Captivity Letters from an Ephesian prison.[394] In Ephesus, a watchtower on Mount Coressos is referred to as Paul's prison, though this is considered a late tradition.[395] The Old Latin "Marcionite Prologues" to the Pauline epistles say that Paul wrote the letter to the Colossians from prison in Ephesus (though they assert he wrote Ephesians and Philemon from Rome).[396]

The NT does not explicitly refer to Paul being imprisoned in Ephesus, though this silence does not exclude its possibility. Paul speaks of being in prison "many more times [περισσοτέρως]" than the false apostles (2 Cor 11:23;

---

[392] Ignatius, *To the Ephesians*, 1:3.

[393] The number of journeys implied by Philippians and the time required has, however, been overemphasized. There may have been no more than one trip in each direction before Paul wrote his letter. A trip from Rome to Philippi need not have taken more than a week. See Reicke, *Re-examining Paul's Letters*, 138. In fact, a presumably brief imprisonment in Ephesus is *more* problematic for this timetable than his lengthy stay in Rome.

[394] The first thorough defense of the Ephesian imprisonment was George Simpson Duncan, *St. Paul's Ephesian Ministry: A Reconstruction with Special Reference to the Ephesian Origin of the Imprisonment Epistles* (New York: Scribner, 1929), who notes that it was first proposed by H. Lisco in 1900. Helmut Koester, "Ephesos in Early Christian Literature," in Koester, *Ephesos: Metropolis of Asia*, 122, concludes in favor of the Ephesian imprisonment.

[395] Trebilco, *The Early Christians in Ephesus from Paul to Ignatius*, 85.

[396] See Guthrie, *New Testament Introduction*, 490, 493. Franzmann, *The Word of the Lord Grows*, 146, incorrectly cites the "Monarchian Prologues." Dahl, "The Origin of the Earliest Prologues to the Pauline Letters," in *Studies in Ephesians*, 179–209, contends that these prologues were not actually Marcionite in origin or use. In light of their commendation of Tychicus as the letter carrier (Eph 6:21; Col 4:7–9; cf. 2 Tim 4:12) and common circumstances, surely Ephesians, Colossians, and Philemon had a common origin—which casts doubt on the reliability of the prologues' testimony.

cf. Rom 16:7; 2 Cor 6:5)—writing from Ephesus at a time when only Philippi had been mentioned hitherto in Acts and his Caesarean and Roman imprisonments still awaited him. Clement of Rome refers to seven imprisonments of Paul (*1 Clement*, 5:6). Paul wrote of a strong "tribulation" in Asia, to the point that he virtually despaired of life itself and felt under a death sentence (2 Cor 1:8–9). Prisca and Aquila, Paul's co-workers in Ephesus, "risked their necks" for Paul's life (Rom 16:3–4). In Ephesus the Jews were particularly troublesome,[397] and the Gentiles rose up in riot (Acts 19:23–40). Certainly Paul experienced great strife in Ephesus, writing that he "fought with wild beasts" (1 Cor 15:32).[398] He may well have been imprisoned in Ephesus—but concrete evidence that he was incarcerated there long enough to have written at least three letters is entirely absent. On one obvious occasion—the silversmiths' riot (Acts 19)—the text states explicitly that the city officials settled the matter, Paul was not imprisoned, and he left town immediately afterward (Acts 20:1). Furthermore, the account of Acts 19 does not place Luke or Mark in Ephesus with Paul, though they are with Paul when writing these letters (Col 4:10, 14; Philemon 24). For these reasons, the theory of an Ephesian origin for the Captivity Letters must be dismissed as conjecture.[399]

Caesarea!

What remains to be considered is the possibility that Paul wrote some or all of the Captivity Letters during his two-year imprisonment in Caesarea (Acts 23:33–26:32).[400] Whether or not Caesarea is a sensible destination for the runaway slave Onesimus to hide has been argued in both directions. Certainly it was a cheaper and more accessible destination than Rome, as it could be reached over land, and was closer.[401] He might have viewed a trip eastward (from Colossae to Caesarea) as running *away* from Roman authority toward a more remote location. And one cannot dismiss the possibility that he already

---

[397] Acts 19:8–9, 33; 20:19; 21:27; cf. 1 Cor 16:9.

[398] If Paul had been literally thrown to beasts in Ephesus he would have been imprisoned first. But a literal reading of the expression is surely excluded by the fact that Paul was a Roman citizen (thus protected from such a fate) and that he likely would not have survived to write about it!

[399] Guthrie, *New Testament Introduction*, 489–95, has a thorough discussion and rejects the Ephesian hypothesis. So also Reicke, *Re-examining Paul's Letters*, 3–4, 132–33, 136–37; Robinson, *Redating the New Testament*, 58–59; and Trebilco, *The Early Christians in Ephesus from Paul to Ignatius*, 83–87. Trebilco, 86, catches Duncan in a circular argument when that original proponent of the Ephesian origin writes (*St. Paul's Ephesian Ministry*, 141): "Yet there must have been one or more imprisonments if the Epistles are to be assigned to this period"!

[400] Here we are reliant on the persuasive argumentation and reconstruction of Reicke, "Caesarea, Rome, and the Captivity Epistles," in *Re-examining Paul's Letters*, 131–40; the essay was first published in 1970. Robinson, *Redating the New Testament*, 57–67, follows substantially the same line, though he places Philippians in Caesarea as well. See also Lewis Johnson, "The Pauline Letters from Caesarea," *Expository Times* 68 (1956–1957): 24–26.

[401] Reicke, *Re-examining Paul's Letters*, 135.

knew something of Christianity and sought out either Paul or the Christians near Jerusalem.

Most of the arguments in favor of Rome are equally applicable to Caesarea. The conditions of his arrest there were apparently not onerous: he was given some liberty (ἄνεσιν) and access to his friends (Acts 24:23) and was frequently trotted out to discuss theology with his captors (e.g., Acts 24:24–27; 25:23–27). (See the photo of the "audience hall" [Acts 25:23] at the end of the introduction.) At the same time, he was occasionally chained (Acts 21:33; 26:29), which accords with his claim in Ephesians (6:20). Luke, who was with Paul when he was writing at least two of his letters (Col 4:14; Philemon 24; cf. 2 Tim 4:11), was with Paul in Caesarea (Acts 21–26 is also a "we" section).

But there are additional data in favor of Caesarea. The request for lodging in Colossae after his possible release (Philemon 22) makes sense if he is still planning to head from Caesarea to Rome and Spain (Rom 15:24, 28). Epaphras, a Colossian (Col 4:12), is under arrest with Paul (Philemon 23), as is Aristarchus (Col 4:10)—more likely the case after the trouble in Jerusalem than in Rome, to which only Paul had appealed. Tychicus, the letter carrier (Eph 6:21; Col 4:7–9; 2 Tim 4:12), is probably in Jerusalem with Paul, but is not mentioned later on the trip to Rome.[402] Bo Reicke adds the supposition that, if Tychicus was a native of Ephesus like his companion Trophimus (Acts 20:4; 21:29), and since Paul later tells Timothy that he has sent Tychicus to Ephesus (2 Tim 4:12), it is most likely that Ephesus was the *last* stop on his route in delivering the three letters to the Meander Valley (Colossians, Philemon, Ephesians). These details imply that Tychicus journeyed from the east (Caesarea), not the west (Rome), delivering to Colossae and Laodicea copies of the three letters before going home to Ephesus (with at least the letter to the Ephesians).[403] Reicke further postu-

---

[402] Tychicus is mentioned in one breath with Trophimus as "the Asians" traveling with Paul on the way to Jerusalem (Acts 20:4); Trophimus, at least, is later said to be in Jerusalem (Acts 21:29). Conceivably both men remained with Paul throughout (or for portions of) his Caesarean imprisonment. But it is unlikely that the large number of companions named with Paul in Ephesians, Colossians, and Philemon were all able to travel with him to Rome contends Reicke, *Re-examining Paul's Letters*, 134. Perhaps only Timothy (Phil 1:1) and Luke (2 Tim 4:11) did so. Trophimus may have started the journey with them, but was let off ill at Miletus (2 Tim 4:20; cf. Acts 27:7). Reicke, who has Paul writing 2 Timothy from Caesarea, seems to overlook the fact that Trophimus was with Paul in Jerusalem and then *later* was left in Miletus—implying that the trip to Rome has intervened. Robinson, *Redating the New Testament*, 76–77, postulates that when Paul wrote "I left Trophimus in Miletus" (2 Tim 4:20), he was speaking "like a general reporting on the movements of his commanders in the field," not necessarily asserting that he had been with Trophimus at the time. Thus, Robinson believes Trophimus might have gone to Ephesus with Tychicus and then fallen ill on his return journey to Caesarea.

[403] Reicke, *Re-examining Paul's Letters*, 80, 89, 129, 132. This assumes that the letters to Colossae and Laodicea were delivered as follows: the letter to Philemon to Philemon in Colossae; Colossians to the church in Colossae; and a copy of Ephesians to the church in Laodicea. For the view that "the letter from Laodicea" that Paul encourages the Colossians to read (Col 4:16) is Ephesians, see "Evidence from the Fathers" in "Addressees" above.

lates that Paul's words to Philemon—"an old man *and now also* [νυνὶ δὲ καί] a prisoner" (Philemon 9)—imply that his imprisonment is *recent*.[404]

Reicke's observations on the *content* of Ephesians present the most compelling reasons for locating its writing in Caesarea. First is the charge on which Paul was arrested.[405] As noted in the survey of Acts,[406] Paul's arrest was precipitated by *"Jews from Asia"* (Acts 21:27; 24:19), that is, from the region of Ephesus, who had pursued him to Jerusalem probably hoping to persuade the chief Jewish authorities that Paul had to be eradicated. Their fabricated claim was that Paul had "brought Greeks into the temple and defiled this holy place. For they had previously seen *Trophimus the Ephesian* in the city with him, whom they supposed Paul had brought into the temple" (Acts 21:28–29). The letter to the Ephesians appears to address these charges quite directly. Paul argues that Jews and Gentiles are united in both sin and grace, having died, risen, and ascended with Christ (Eph 2:1–10); they are united with him through one Baptism (4:5). The Gentiles who were once "far off" (forbidden to draw near to the Holy of Holies) "have become near" by the blood of Christ (2:11–13). In his body, put to death on the cross, "the dividing wall of partition, the hostility, … [and] the Law" were nullified, and the two peoples were made one (2:14–16). Both together now have access to God, having been built up into a new, Spiritual temple (2:18–22). Paul continues by defending his mission to the Gentiles, saying that Christ himself mandated it (3:1–12) and concluding that the Ephesians ought not lose heart over his imprisonment for them (3:13). These concentrated allusions imply strongly that Paul has only recently been arrested and is writing to the Ephesians to explain his situation from God's perspective.

Second, Reicke calls attention to the political situation at this time in Caesarea (as described by Josephus):

> Greeks (according to Josephus, they were Syrians) and Jews threw stones at one another. Each party denied the other the right of citizenship (*isopoliteia*). The street battles spread even to Jerusalem after a new high priest by the name of Ishmael ben Phabi had come to power (in A.D. 59). The two parties in Caesarea appealed to the emperor; and, as one would expect, Burrus and Nero (in A.D. 61) declared the Greeks to be lawful citizens in Caesarea (Josephus, *Ant. XX.* 173–84). Similar riots in the year 66 in Caesarea ignited the Jewish War (Josephus, *Bell.* I. 284–92).[407]

This local fight over citizenship perhaps suggested to Paul another metaphor to address the Jew/Gentile divide. He writes to the Ephesians:

---

[404] Reicke, *Re-examining Paul's Letters*, 133. Robinson, *Redating the New Testament*, 79, avers: "This is surely to read a great deal into one word ['now' in Philemon 9]."

[405] Reicke, *Re-examining Paul's Letters*, 81–82, 135.

[406] See "Paul's Trip to Jerusalem, Arrest, and Imprisonment (Acts 21:1–36)" in "The City of Ephesus and Paul's Relationship to It" above.

[407] Reicke, *Re-examining Paul's Letters*, 136 (cf. 82–83).

¹²You [Gentiles] were at that time separated from Christ, alienated from the commonwealth [πολιτείας] of Israel and strangers to the covenants of the promise. … ¹⁹So, then, you are no longer strangers and sojourners, but you are fellow citizens [συμπολῖται] with the saints and members of God's household. (2:12, 19)

Again, the language of Ephesians suggests a Caesarean provenance. The privilege of citizenship was also of particular interest to the Ephesians, where the Jews had long ago been given the right to practice their religion,[408] and the local Christians may have felt disadvantaged.

A third connection between Ephesians and the time period immediately following Paul's arrest in Caesarea lies in the feast of *Pentecost*. While Paul's arrest took place when he was at the temple to aid four brothers in completing a vow (Acts 21:23–27), the timing of his visit to Jerusalem was primarily determined by his desire to celebrate Pentecost (Acts 20:16; cf. 1 Cor 16:8). This may be an example of Paul's proud "Hebrew of Hebrews" heritage (Phil 3:5), his intent to be a Jew to the Jews in order to win the Jews (1 Cor 9:20). He may have observed Pentecost in the traditional Jewish way, while understanding that it pointed to Christ. Or, as Paul understood the Passover to be fulfilled in Christ, never to be celebrated again in the old way, but superseded by the Lord's Supper (1 Cor 5:7; 11:24–25), he may have gone to Jerusalem to observe Pentecost as a renewed *Christian* feast, a remembrance of Christ giving the Spirit (Acts 2), as it would come to be celebrated universally in the Christian church.[409] Either way, the letter to the Ephesians bears the impact of Pentecost in a series of three subtle, but quite remarkable, ways.

First, evidence from rabbinic sources, apocryphal literature, and Qumran suggests that Jews as early as the first to second centuries AD made a thematic connection between Pentecost and the giving of the Law at Mount Sinai.[410] This thematic connection was also evident in the Jewish lectionary, in which Exodus 19–20 was the reading from the Torah on the Feast of Pentecost in the second year of the triennial cycle, which was used for a time in Palestinian synagogues.[411] The Ten Commandments (Ex 20:1–17), contained in that reading,

---

[408] See "Judaism" in "The City of Ephesus and Paul's Relationship to It" above.

[409] See Kirby, *Ephesians: Baptism and Pentecost*, 73–82, who argues that both Easter (*Pascha*) and Pentecost were observed as *Christian* festivals already in apostolic times.

[410] Kirby, *Ephesians: Baptism and Pentecost*, 64–69, 97–100, 145–46; see *Jubilees*, 1:5; 6:11, 17, 19. Kirby, 67–69, also cites evidence from rabbinic sources and Qumran for this thematic connection.

[411] See Kirby, *Ephesians: Baptism and Pentecost*, 90–94, who discusses lectionary reconstructions based on rabbinic literature. For the use in Palestine of a triennial cycle of readings from the Torah, see Talmud, *Megillah*, 29b. Although the rabbinic sources on which these lectionary reconstructions are based probably postdate the NT in most, if not all, cases, Kirby cites scholars who argue that the lessons appointed for festivals may date back at least as far as 200 BC. The triennial cycle was eventually replaced by a one-year lectionary, in which Exodus 19 was one of the Torah readings (97).

give structure to Paul's preaching of the Law in Eph 4:25–29, and the Fourth Commandment (Ex 20:12) is quoted explicitly in Eph 6:2. Psalm 68 was one of the psalms appointed for Pentecost in the Jewish one-year lectionary. The rabbis interpreted the psalm as referring to the ascent of Moses upon Mount Sinai to receive the Torah as a gift to men.[412] Psalm 68 features prominently in Eph 4:7–16, where Paul interprets it Christologically, as Christ, the new Moses, ascends on high to give gifts to men through the work of the Holy Spirit. Christ's ascension and Pentecost follow naturally upon one another in Paul's argument (Eph 1:20–23; 2:6; 4:7–16). Furthermore, in Eph 1:20–22 Paul applies Psalm 110 to Christ's ascension, just as Peter does on the day of Pentecost (Acts 2:34–35).

Second, extending the prominent image of *marriage* as the primary way to describe God's relationship with Israel in the OT, the rabbis identified the Law-giving at Mount Sinai as the wedding day of God and Israel.[413] Thus, Pentecost, with its thematic connection to the giving of the Law on Sinai, was observed as their "wedding anniversary."[414] Paul, of course, would have been deeply familiar with this OT marriage image, but its prominence in the recent Pentecost celebration may have given him an additional impetus to write his most thoroughgoing reflection on marriage as an image of Christ's relationship with the church (5:21–33).

Third, the role of the Holy Spirit is particularly prominent in Ephesians, more so than in any Pauline writing outside 1 Corinthians. This theme, too, might have been prompted in part by his recent celebration of Pentecost from a Christian perspective. And could it be that Paul had the accusation against the apostles on Pentecost in mind when he wrote: "Do not get drunk with wine, … but be filled up in the Spirit" (Eph 5:18; cf. Acts 2:13–18)?

The above arguments are sufficiently persuasive for us to proceed on the assumption that Paul wrote to the Ephesians from imprisonment in Caesarea, shortly after his arrest in Jerusalem. This provenance gives the richest color to the interpretation of Paul's letter. The date assigned to this time of imprisonment will vary, depending on how one aligns the Gallio inscription (AD 52) with Paul's time in Corinth (see Acts 18:12) and how one determines the precise dates of his subsequent journeys.[415]

---

[412] Kirby, *Ephesians: Baptism and Pentecost*, 93, 97–99; see also Lincoln, *Ephesians*, 243.

[413] Kirby, *Ephesians: Baptism and Pentecost*, 99–100, 148–49.

[414] The intertestamental writing *Jubilees* identified Pentecost as the date on which *all* God's covenants with Israel were enacted (see *Jubilees*, 6:10, 11, 19; 14:20; 15:1–24; 16:13; 44:4–8) and the date on which the Sinaitic covenant was to be annually renewed (*Jubilees*, 6:11, 17). See Kirby, *Ephesians: Baptism and Pentecost*, 64–66.

[415] On the Gallio (Delphi) inscription, see C. E. B. Cranfield, *A Critical and Exegetical Commentary on the Epistle to the Romans* (2 vols.; Edinburgh: T&T Clark, 1975), 1:12–14. Cranfield believes Paul probably appeared before Gallio in AD 51, but concedes "that any date between mid-50 and mid-54 is theoretically possible on the basis of the Delphi inscription" (1:13). This date marks the end of Paul's Corinthian ministry and his first visit to Ephesus at the end of his second journey. By Cranfield's early dating of the Gallio inscription (so also,

At the same time, if the reader is not convinced by the present argument and prefers to abide by the early tradition of a Roman origin for the writing of the Captivity Letters (ca. AD 59–61), no point of substance in the present commentary is affected. The memories of Paul's arrest in Jerusalem would have remained vivid for him as he recounted it again and again to his captors, and it could still have influenced his writing to the Ephesians more than two years later in Rome. The important point is not to lose sight of this connection.

Relationship to Colossians

The letters to the Ephesians and to the Colossians bear a genetic relationship that goes beyond their common origin in Paul's Caesarean imprisonment and their simultaneous delivery by the letter carrier Tychicus. If not identical twins, they are at least fraternal, bearing a striking resemblance to each other that sets them apart even from their siblings in the Pauline family. Among the NT writings, the only comparable cases are 2 Peter with Jude, and the Synoptic Gospels. The bare statistics were considered above:[416] (1) It is thought that a fourth of the *words* in Ephesians are found in Colossians, while a third of the words in the shorter letter Colossians are found in its longer twin.[417] (2) Between a third and half of the *verses* of Ephesians are parallel to Colossians.[418] Critics have examined the manner in which the parallels occur and have contended that no single author would make use of his own writings this way. If so, it is unimaginable that the creative and independent mind of Paul would stoop to borrowing so directly from a lesser author. While numerous permutations have been proposed, the most common critical hypothesis is that Paul first wrote Colossians, and then a later author reassembled its contents to produce Ephesians.[419] Since we have already concluded in favor of the Pauline authorship of Ephesians,[420] and since the authorship of Colossians lies outside this commentary's purview, this brief treatment will be confined to describing the relationship between the two letters and proposing how and why Paul might indeed have written both

---

e.g., Lockwood, *1 Corinthians*, 14–15), Paul would have been imprisoned in Caesarea in AD 57, giving the same date for Ephesians. So concludes Robinson, *Redating the New Testament*, 35, 51. By contrast, Reicke, *Re-examining Paul's Letters*, 36, 83, 133, places the Gallio hearing at the *beginning* of Paul's Corinthian ministry and thus dates Paul's arrest to AD 59—but this is not the natural reading of Acts 18:11–18.

[416] See "The Literary Relationship between Ephesians and Other Pauline Epistles" in "Arguments against Pauline Authorship" in "Authorship" above.

[417] Guthrie, *New Testament Introduction*, 501. Mitton, *Ephesians*, 57, provides the statistics: 34 percent of the 1,570 words in Colossians reappear in Ephesians; 26.5 percent of the 2,411 words in Ephesians recur in Colossians. Best, *Ephesians*, 28, also notes that Colossians and Ephesians share some twenty-one vocables not found in the rest of the NT.

[418] Brown, *An Introduction to the New Testament*, 627.

[419] For a survey of critical opinions, see, e.g., Best, "Who Used Whom? The Relationship of Ephesians and Colossians," as well as Best, *Ephesians*, 20–25, 36–40. Best's own conclusion is that they were written by independent authors in a "Pauline school" who had discussed the thought they had inherited. He is not convinced that there is any literary dependence (aside from the commendation of Tychicus).

[420] See "Authorship" above.

letters as he did. While the present commentary does not extensively explore the Colossian parallels to every passage in Ephesians, the curious reader will be well served by the marginal references in his Nestle-Aland Greek NT, directing him to the earliest and most reliable commentary provided by Paul himself in his twin letter.

The bare vocabulary statistics demonstrate no more than that Colossians and Ephesians deal extensively with the same subject matter. This simple observation has been summarized by Martin Franzmann: "If the Letter to the Colossians is the Letter of Christ the Head of the Church, the Letter to the Ephesians is the Letter of the Church, the Body of Christ."[421] But what is most striking is the number of passages in which entire *phrases* are word-for-word identical—or, more perplexingly, *nearly* identical. The most extensive parallel is found in the commendation of Tychicus as the letter carrier:

Colossians 4:7–8	Ephesians 6:21–22
[7]τὰ κατ᾽ ἐμέ	[21]ἵνα δὲ εἰδῆτε καὶ ὑμεῖς τὰ κατ᾽ ἐμέ, τί πράσσω,
πάντα γνωρίσει ὑμῖν Τύχικος ὁ ἀγαπητὸς ἀδελφὸς καὶ πιστὸς διάκονος καὶ σύνδουλος ἐν κυρίῳ,	πάντα γνωρίσει ὑμῖν Τύχικος ὁ ἀγαπητὸς ἀδελφὸς καὶ πιστὸς διάκονος ἐν κυρίῳ,
[8]ὃν ἔπεμψα πρὸς ὑμᾶς εἰς αὐτὸ τοῦτο, ἵνα γνῶτε τὰ περὶ ἡμῶν καὶ παρακαλέσῃ τὰς καρδίας ὑμῶν.	[22]ὃν ἔπεμψα πρὸς ὑμᾶς εἰς αὐτὸ τοῦτο, ἵνα γνῶτε τὰ περὶ ἡμῶν καὶ παρακαλέσῃ τὰς καρδίας ὑμῶν.
[7]My circumstances, everything he will make known to you, Tychicus, the beloved brother and faithful minister and fellow slave in the Lord,	[21]And so that you, too, may know my circumstances, how I am getting along, everything he will make known to you, Tychicus, the beloved brother and faithful minister in the Lord,
[8]whom I have sent to you for this very purpose, that you may know our circumstances and [that] he may comfort your hearts.	[22]whom I have sent to you for this very purpose, that you may know our circumstances and [that] he may comfort your hearts.

Apart from minor differences (underlined), more than thirty words in a row are identical. There is a similar parallel between the two letters' opening verses (Col 1:1–2; Eph 1:1–2), though Paul's salutations are typically formulaic.[422]

---

[421] Franzmann, *The Word of the Lord Grows*, 132. Schnackenburg, *Ephesians*, 31: "In its theological concern we have a shift of emphasis from Christology [in Colossians] to Ecclesiology [in Ephesians]."

[422] Best, "Who Used Whom? The Relationship of Ephesians and Colossians," 76: "Parallels therefore drawn from traditional material must be ignored in deciding priority and dependence between the two letters."

Other extensive verbal parallels include the following (notable divergences being underlined):

Colossians	Ephesians
ἐν ᾧ ἔχομεν τὴν ἀπολύτρωσιν, τὴν ἄφεσιν τῶν ἁμαρτιῶν in whom we have redemption, the forgiveness of <u>sins</u> (1:14)	ἐν ᾧ ἔχομεν τὴν ἀπολύτρωσιν <u>διὰ τοῦ αἵματος αὐτοῦ</u>, τὴν ἄφεσιν τῶν <u>παραπτωμάτων</u> in whom we have redemption <u>through his blood</u>, the forgiveness of <u>trespasses</u> (1:7)
<u>εἴτε</u> τὰ ἐπὶ τῆς γῆς <u>εἴτε</u> τὰ ἐν τοῖς οὐρανοῖς <u>whether</u> the things on earth <u>or</u> the things in heaven (1:20)	τὰ ἐπὶ τοῖς οὐρανοῖς <u>καὶ</u> τὰ ἐπὶ τῆς γῆς <u>ἐν αὐτῷ</u> the things in heaven <u>and</u> the things on earth <u>in him</u> (1:10)
καὶ αὐτός <u>ἐστιν</u> ἡ κεφαλὴ <u>τοῦ σώματος</u> τῆς ἐκκλησίας and he himself <u>is</u> the head <u>of the body</u>, the church (1:18)	καὶ αὐτὸν <u>ἔδωκεν</u> κεφαλὴν <u>ὑπὲρ πάντα τῇ</u> ἐκκλησίᾳ and he <u>appointed</u> him as head <u>over all things for</u> the church (1:22)
καὶ ὑμᾶς νεκροὺς ὄντας [ἐν] τοῖς παραπτώμασιν καὶ <u>τῇ ἀκροβυστίᾳ τῆς σαρκὸς ὑμῶν</u>, συνεζωοποίησεν ὑμᾶς <u>σὺν αὐτῷ</u> and you—when you were dead [in] trespasses and <u>the uncircumcision of your flesh</u>, he [God] made you alive together <u>with him</u> (2:13)	καὶ ὑμᾶς ὄντας νεκροὺς τοῖς παραπτώμασιν καὶ <u>ταῖς ἁμαρτίαις ὑμῶν</u>, ... καὶ ὄντας ἡμᾶς νεκροὺς τοῖς παραπτώμασιν συνεζωοποίησεν <u>τῷ Χριστῷ</u> and you—when you were dead in <u>your</u> trespasses and <u>sins</u>, ... even us, when we were dead in [our] trespasses he [God] made alive together with <u>Christ</u> (2:1, 5)
ἐγενόμην ἐγὼ Παῦλος διάκονος I, Paul, became a minister (1:23)	ἐγὼ Παῦλος ... τὴν οἰκονομίαν <u>τῆς χάριτος</u> τοῦ θεοῦ τῆς δοθείσης μοι εἰς ὑμᾶς I, Paul, ... the stewardship <u>of the grace</u> of God that was given to me for you (3:1–2)
ἐγενόμην ἐγὼ διάκονος κατὰ τὴν οἰκονομίαν τοῦ θεοῦ τὴν δοθεῖσάν μοι εἰς ὑμᾶς I became a minister according to the stewardship of God that was given to me for you (1:25)	ἐγενήθην διάκονος κατὰ τὴν <u>δωρεὰν τῆς χάριτος</u> τοῦ θεοῦ τῆς δοθείσης μοι I was made a minister according to the <u>gift of the grace</u> of God that was given to me (3:7)

Colossians	Ephesians
τὸ μυστήριον τὸ ἀποκεκρυμμένον ἀπὸ τῶν αἰώνων the mystery that was hidden from the ages (1:26)	ἡ <u>οἰκονομία</u> τοῦ μυστηρίου τοῦ ἀποκεκρυμμένου ἀπὸ τῶν αἰώνων <u>the administration</u> of the mystery that was hidden from the ages (3:9)
ἐξ οὗ πᾶν τὸ σῶμα διὰ τῶν ἁφῶν <u>καὶ συνδέσμων</u> ἐπιχορηγούμενον καὶ συμβιβαζόμενον αὔξει τὴν αὔξησιν <u>τοῦ θεοῦ</u> from whom the whole body, through the ligaments <u>and bonds</u> <u>being</u> supplied and knit together <u>grows</u> with a growth <u>from God</u> (2:19)	ἐξ οὗ πᾶν τὸ σῶμα <u>συναρμολογούμενον</u> καὶ συμβιβαζόμενον διὰ <u>πάσης</u> ἁφῆς τῆς ἐπιχορηγίας <u>κατ᾿ ἐνέργειαν ἐν μέτρῳ ἑνὸς ἑκάστου μέρους</u> τὴν αὔξησιν <u>τοῦ σώματος ποιεῖται</u> from whom the whole body, <u>being jointed together</u> and knit together through <u>every</u> ligament supplied, <u>in accord with [his] activity in apportioning each single part,</u> <u>makes</u> growth <u>of the body</u> (4:16)
ψαλμοῖς ὕμνοις ᾠδαῖς πνευματικαῖς <u>ἐν [τῇ] χάριτι</u> ᾄδοντες <u>ἐν</u> ταῖς καρδίαις ὑμῶν τῷ <u>θεῷ</u> in psalms, hymns, songs of the Spirit <u>in grace</u>, singing <u>in</u> your hearts to <u>God</u> (3:16)	ψαλμοῖς <u>καὶ</u> ὕμνοις <u>καὶ</u> ᾠδαῖς πνευματικαῖς, ᾄδοντες <u>καὶ ψάλλοντες</u> <u>τῇ</u> καρδίᾳ ὑμῶν τῷ <u>κυρίῳ</u> in psalms <u>and</u> hymns <u>and</u> songs of the Spirit, singing <u>and psalming</u> <u>with</u> your heart to the <u>Lord</u> (5:19)
τὰ τέκνα, ὑπακούετε τοῖς γονεῦσιν <u>κατὰ πάντα</u>, τοῦτο γὰρ <u>εὐάρεστόν</u> ἐστιν ἐν κυρίῳ children, heed [your] parents <u>in all things</u>, for this is <u>well pleasing in the Lord</u> (3:20)	τὰ τέκνα, ὑπακούετε τοῖς γονεῦσιν <u>ὑμῶν</u> [<u>ἐν κυρίῳ</u>]· τοῦτο γάρ ἐστιν <u>δίκαιον</u> children, heed <u>your</u> parents [<u>in the Lord</u>], for this is <u>righteous</u> (6:1)

What is both puzzling and informative about these representative parallels is the word-for-word similarities combined with minor differences in both grammar and vocabulary. Note, for example, the exchange of the synonyms ἁμαρτιῶν, "sins" (Col 1:14), and παραπτωμάτων, "trespasses" (Eph 1:7), in a statement that is otherwise identical. And why does one citation of the Fourth Commandment call obedience to parents εὐάρεστόν ἐν κυρίῳ, "well pleasing in the Lord" (Col 3:20), while the other says obedience ἐν κυρίῳ, "in the Lord," is δίκαιον, "righteous" (Eph 6:1)? Note not only the different adjective but also that the phrase "in the Lord" modifies a different part of each sentence! The pattern does not give the appearance of one author "cutting and pasting" texts from another, nor even of a single author recycling his earlier writing mechanically.

The puzzle is deepened if one examines the *distribution* of parallel texts between the two epistles. In the chart below, which follows the order of Ephesians, note *where* the parallels in Colossians occur:[423]

Colossians	Ephesians	Colossians	Ephesians
1:14	1:7	2:19	4:15–16
1:20	1:10	3:5	4:19
1:3–4	1:15–17	3:8–10	4:22–25
1:27	1:18	3:8; 4:6	4:29
3:1	1:20	3:8	4:31
1:16	1:21	3:12–13	4:32
1:18–19	1:22–23	3:5	5:3
1:21	2:1, 12	3:8	5:4
2:13	2:5	3:5	5:5
3:1	2:6	3:6	5:6
1:20, 22	2:13–16	4:5	5:15
2:14	2:15	3:16–17	5:19–20
2:20	2:16	3:18	5:21–22
1:24	3:1, 13	3:19	5:25
1:25	3:2	3:20	6:1
1:26	3:3–5, 9	3:21	6:4
1:23, 25, 29	3:7	3:22–25	6:5–8
1:27–28	3:8–9	4:1	6:9
1:10	4:1	4:2–4	6:18–20
3:12–15	4:2–4	4:7–8	6:21–22

Two observations are pertinent. First, while the order of material in the two letters is *broadly* similar, the parallels between the two letters are nevertheless quite jumbled up. Note, for example, that Eph 1:18–23 (which treats one topic in a logical order) appears to draw on passages from Colossians *randomly*: 1:27; 3:1; 1:16–19. No author (whether Paul or not) who is simply cutting and pasting from his source would do this. Second, there are numerous places where the parallels *cluster*; these clusters are double-outlined in the chart above. In these places, Paul treats the same topics in roughly the same order in the two letters—though even here the material is often rearranged (particularly in Eph 4:22–5:6).

Finally, it is important to step back and examine the big picture, noting the larger chunks of material that are held in common and those that are unique to

---

[423] The chart was adapted from Abbot, *The Epistles to the Ephesians and to the Colossians*, xxiii.

each.[424] These chunks coalesce into three groups. First, as expected, there is a long series of common content:

- salutation, thanksgiving, intercessory prayer (Col 1:1–14; Eph 1:1–2, 15–23)
- death, resurrection, and ascension with Christ (Col 2:11–13; 2:20–3:4; Eph 2:1–10)
- reconciliation of the Gentiles, who once were alienated from God (Col 1:21–23; 2:14–15; Eph 2:11–22)
- the mystery of Paul's suffering according to the mandate of Christ for the sake of the Gentiles (Col 1:24–29; Eph 3:1–13)
- warnings against a return to the old pagan way of life, on the basis of the Decalogue and baptismal rebirth (Col 3:5–11; Eph 4:17–5:7)
- encouragement to maintain the bond of peace and to practice true worship (Col 3:12–17; Eph 4:1–16; 5:15–20)
- a "household code" describing subordination to one another in Christ in three relationships (Col 3:18–4:1; Eph 5:21–6:9)
- encouragement to prayer (Col 4:2–4; Eph 6:18–20)
- the commendation of Tychicus and the concluding blessing (Col 4:7–9, 18; Eph 6:21–24)

Second, there is significant material that is unique to Colossians:

- the Christ hymn (Col 1:15–20)
- rejection of ascetic-Jewish philosophical false teaching (Col 2:1–23)
- a significant list of greetings and instructions about Paul's co-workers (Col 4:10–17)

Third, there is an even longer list of major material that is unique to Ephesians:

- the *Berakah* prayer (1:3–14)
- intercessory prayer and doxology (3:14–21)
- light/darkness/fellowship imagery and the baptismal hymn (5:8–14)
- an extended treatment of Christ's marriage to the church (5:22–32)
- the armor of God (6:10–17)

If Paul is the author of both Colossians and Ephesians, how can these data be explained? This important question is best answered by working through the evidence in reverse order. First, the large amount of *common* material in a common order makes sense when one recognizes that Ephesus and Colossae were not very far apart in Asia Minor. Their congregations likely faced similar challenges from Greek philosophy, Diaspora Judaism, and pagan religion. The *unique* material simply reminds us that the two church situations were not identical. The particular (ascetic-Jewish) false teaching treated in Colossians 2 may not have troubled Ephesus. The long list of greetings in Colossians may be explained by the fact that Paul had much less personal contact with that church than he had with the one in Ephesus, and so he was keen to nurture the relationship by naming the co-workers they had in common. If Paul wrote Ephesians after Colossians, it is admittedly difficult to understand why he would omit the

---

[424] Lincoln, *Ephesians*, xlix, has a well-constructed chart of similarities and differences.

great Christ hymn (Col 1:15–20) in Ephesians; it may be that the hymn was particularly favored in Colossae or was just the right tool to address the false teaching there. But the unique material in Ephesians is more extensive than the unique material in Colossians. So rather than postulating reasons why he might have *omitted* the Ephesian material in writing Colossians *later*, it is easier to accept that Paul has *expanded* his *earlier* Colossian material in writing Ephesians. Thus, for example, the extended treatment of marriage as typological of Christ's relationship with the church (Eph 5:22–32) looks like the result of further reflection on the brief treatment of marriage in Col 3:18–19. And the armor of God allegory (Eph 6:10–17) slots neatly between Col 4:1 and 4:2. It is much more difficult to explain why he would omit the armor of God in Colossians if that epistle were written later.

Thus, a bird's-eye view of the two letters favors the hypothesis that Colossians was written first.[425] The likelihood that Ephesians is a later expansion of the shorter letter to the Colossians may be substantiated by the minor differences in the two commendations of Tychicus (Col 4:7–9; Eph 6:21–22). The first five Greek words in Eph 6:21, ἵνα δὲ εἰδῆτε καὶ ὑμεῖς, "and so that *you, too*, may know," are the most significant departure from the Colossian parallel. By writing that, Paul may have been (consciously or not) indicating that this was his *second* letter to churches in that part of the world (see the first textual note on Eph 6:21). This order (Colossians, then Ephesians) may also find support in the presence of Timothy with Paul in the writing of Colossians (1:1), but his absence from the salutation of Ephesians (1:1). Between the writing of the two letters, Timothy may have been sent to Troas (2 Tim 4:13).[426] On the other hand, if "the letter from Laodicea" (referred to in Col 4:16) is Ephesians,[427] this identification *might* suggest that Colossians was written later; but it is equally conceivable that Paul could refer to a letter he was intending shortly to write.

The pattern of distribution of parallel material is puzzling only if one imagines a modern writer working at his desk with the earlier letter lying open next to a blank sheet of paper—even more so if he is using cut-and-paste on a word processor! Certainly the nearly random rearrangement of words from Colossians into Ephesians (or vice versa),[428] drawing one phrase from here and another

---

[425] Best, "Who Used Whom? The Relationship of Ephesians and Colossians," 74, calls the priority of Colossians "the accepted position," and it is worked out most exhaustively by Mitton, *Ephesians*. Lincoln, *Ephesians*, l–li, calls it "the far more obvious hypothesis." However, one must note that this consensus among critical scholars usually follows upon the judgment that Colossians is Pauline, but Ephesians is not.

[426] As postulated by Reicke, *Re-examining Paul's Letters*, 80. Certainly the reverse order is more difficult to explain on the basis of the NT evidence.

[427] See "Evidence from the Fathers" in "Addressees" above.

[428] At the level of word-for-word detail, the evidence on which letter came first is fairly evenly split, if one assumes that one letter is a *literary* source for the other. Best, "Who Used Whom? The Relationship of Ephesians and Colossians," 92, concludes:

> We see that in almost every case it is impossible to say with any certainty that A/Eph [the author of Ephesians] used Colossians or that A/Col [the author of Colossians] used

from there, makes no sense in such a scenario.[429] If Paul desired to recycle his older letter—and he had the freedom to use his own work as he wished—he *could* have copied entire pericopes word for word, personalizing and adapting as necessary for the new audience. But this envisioning of the process is an anachronism derived from an age in which paper is cheap and memories are poor. Ancient peoples certainly used cheap writing materials like wax tablets, broken pottery, old leather, and re-scraped papyrus to take notes. But since writing was normally considered to be a servant of speech, it was natural to prepare a composition mentally, as if it were to be delivered orally, before committing it to papyrus.[430] Paul would have worked through the stages of his schoolboy rhetorical training[431] until he knew precisely what he wished to say; only then would he have brought in a scribe to receive the dictation of his epistle and commit it to writing. Once this process was complete for the epistle to the Colossians, Paul did not need to open the document on his desk in order to compose a similar letter to the Ephesians.[432] The outline, the arguments, the biblical texts and exegesis, the proofs and refutations, the images and illustrations were already in his head.[433] The pattern of evidence in the relationship between Colossians and Ephesians points precisely to this manner of composition. The similarities and differences look like the similarities and differences between two speeches given by an experienced public speaker at related venues. The wording comes from Paul's memory and contains divergences of his making and of his volition. He may even have chosen different vocabulary or phrasing without intending to make a strong contrast.

The best explanation of the similarities and differences between these twin epistles, therefore, is the following scenario. Having received a delegation from

---

Ephesians. In many instances the similarity exists simply because both were indebted to tradition. There are no passages where it is possible to come down firmly and say with certainty that either author used the other.

[429] Best, *Ephesians*, 21:

But this is not the way authors use documents. Normally when one author draws on a document it is to borrow its ideas. Authors normally do not search the documents of other writers to find suitable words with which to express their own ideas. They may however remember phrases and words in the other document and use them again, combining them in new ways. The random nature of the way AE [the author of Ephesians] is supposed to have drawn on references from Colossians, and vice versa, suggests neither had a copy of the other's writing in front of him as he wrote but may have had its words in his mind.

[430] See "Orality and the Interpretation of the Epistles: A Brief Introduction" above.

[431] See "Structure and Rhetoric" below.

[432] Guthrie, *New Testament Introduction*, 515, argues: "It is clearly more reasonable to suppose that Paul did not consult his own epistle than that an admirer of his, who had possessed a copy of Paul's Colossian epistle and who set out to produce a résumé of his master's doctrine, would have discarded the immeasurable advantage of consulting it."

[433] Best, "Who Used Whom? The Relationship of Ephesians and Colossians," 92, believes that memory is the best explanation, even if there are two authors: "If one author is the user of the other probably he did not have the letter of the other in front of him as he wrote but carried its wording in his mind and used it with slight variations."

Colossae, likely headed by Pastor Epaphras (Col 1:7; 4:12), Paul responds to a series of problems in that church with the letter to the Colossians. While this writing was relatively fresh in his memory, perhaps within a few weeks, he responds to similar news from Ephesus with the letter to the Ephesians.[434] The need to send the runaway slave Onesimus back to his master Philemon in Colossae provided the opportunity to send the three letters together in the hand of Tychicus.

Purpose and Themes

The textual variant "in Ephesus" (1:1) lies before the interpreter as a fork in the road. The majority of commentators conclude against the originality of this address and choose the path to the left. They see the letter as a circular aimed at a number of churches in Asia Minor and therefore interpret it as a general letter characterized by a rich ecclesiology and Christology. Goodspeed's fanciful theory about a postapostolic reader of Acts gathering together the letters of Paul and producing Ephesians as a cover letter[435] may not have many serious adherents, but it represents the prevailing view of Ephesians as a compendium of Pauline thought, which is the view even of most conservative commentators such as Martin Franzmann, Donald Guthrie, and F. F. Bruce.[436]

But is it just a general letter? Rudolf Schnackenburg avers: "Most Commentaries pay too little attention to the letter's pragmatic dimension. Almost all proceed from the idea that it has no concrete background; but this would be unique in the whole of the NT literature."[437] Many hypotheses have been put

---

[434] So, e.g., Carson, Moo, and Morris, *An Introduction to the New Testament*, 308; Deterding, *Colossians*, 13. Even Best, who denies Pauline authorship, admits that common authorship of the two letters makes good sense: "It is also possible that the two letters had a common author who simply repeated in the second more or less what he had written in the first; this would necessarily imply that the letters were written about the same time and that their common author had a good memory" (*Ephesians*, 613–14). Schnackenburg, *Ephesians*, 32, agrees: "It is certain that the author of Eph. knew Col. It is not so certain whether he had it before him while writing and could refer to it as a written document. In spite of [Eph] 6,21 f. it is enough to assume that he had it 'in his head' and was so familiar with it that words and phrases from Col. constantly flow from his pen." So also Schlier, who affirms Pauline authorship:

> If one is not burdened by the obsession of a *literary* dependence of the two letters upon one another, one then recognizes that the intimate connection of the two letters—each of which is in itself complete, unique, and original—can be explained most simply and naturally by focusing on something completely different: that Paul wrote Ephesians not long after he had written Colossians, and in any case at a time when Colossians "was still fresh in his mind" (in the words of E. F. Scott), and his thoughts were still dwelling on the congregations in eastern Asia Minor, and he had the intention of sending Tychicus there. (*Epheser*, 24–25, quoting Ernest Findlay Scott, *The Literature of the New Testament* [New York: Columbia University Press, 1932], 181)

[435] Goodspeed, *The Key to Ephesians*, xiv–xvi.

[436] Franzmann, *The Word of the Lord Grows*, 130–32; Guthrie, *New Testament Introduction*, 535–36; Bruce, *The Epistles to the Colossians, to Philemon, and to the Ephesians*, 229–33, 240–46.

[437] Schnackenburg, *Ephesians*, 23, n. 10. See also Lincoln, *Ephesians*, xl, who contends that Ephesians, though homiletical, is a real letter addressed to specific concerns among the

forward.[438] Heinrich Schlier sees the letter as a refutation of a growing Gnostic movement.[439] Nils Dahl has developed a complex liturgical theory, viewing the letter as an address to newly baptized Gentiles.[440] J. C. Kirby sees the letter as a reworked homily for a baptismal renewal ceremony on Pentecost.[441] Ernst Käsemann believes it was written to further the cause of early Catholicism in the postapostolic era.[442] But all these theories falter on a complete lack of evidence within the historical record of the NT.

The present introduction, contending for the originality of the address "in Ephesus"[443] and therefore walking the path to the right of the fork, has sketched the historical background to Ephesians on the basis of the record of Acts and Paul's other letters. Drawn together, those data paint a very rich picture of the problems in the Ephesian church and in Paul's life and help us to discern the verbal tools with which he responded.[444]

False Teaching and Paganism

The possibility of false teaching threatening the Ephesian church from the *inside* is rarely investigated, chiefly because Ephesians does not specifically mention any false teachers. But there are plenty of clues. The record of Acts tells us that the Ephesian church was troubled by faulty theology at its very founding, as Apollos misunderstood both Baptism and the Holy Spirit (Acts 18:24–26; 19:1–3; see "Baptism and the Spirit," below in "Purpose and Themes"). Paul's sermon to the Ephesian pastors (Acts 20:18–35), delivered some months after he was prematurely driven from the city (Acts 20:1), contains both explicit and implicit references to false teaching. "I know that after my departure fierce wolves will come in among you, not sparing the flock, and from among you yourselves will arise men speaking distorted things, to draw away the disciples after them" (Acts 20:29–30). Was this merely a prophetic

---

churches of Asia Minor. Even Romans, once treated as Paul's "dogmatics," is now related more closely to the situation of the Roman church and Paul's proposed visit there on his way to Spain. See, for example, the essays in Karl P. Donfried, ed., *The Romans Debate* (rev. ed.; Edinburgh: T&T Clark, 1991).

[438] See Best, *Ephesians*, 63–75, for a range of proposals.

[439] Schlier, *Epheser*, 19 and passim. See "Gnosticism" in "Arguments against Pauline Authorship" and "Gnosticism" in "Evaluation of the Case," both in "Authorship" above.

[440] Nils Alstrup Dahl, "Dopet i Efesierbrevet," *Svensk Teologisk Kvartalskrift* 21 (1945): 85–103; N. A. Dahl, "Adresse und Proömium des Epheserbriefes," *Theologische Zeitschrift* 7 (1951): 241–64. Dahl himself later admitted ("The Concept of Baptism in Ephesians," in *Studies in Ephesians*, 415): "Against the suggestion that I myself presented many years ago [1945, p. 99; 1951, p. 261], it has been correctly objected that in early Christianity, as well as later, it was completely possible that when readers or hearers were reminded of their baptism, it need not have been a recent event but may have also happened long ago."

[441] Kirby, *Ephesians: Baptism and Pentecost*.

[442] Käsemann, "Ephesians and Acts."

[443] See "The Textual Variant 'in Ephesus' in Ephesians 1:1" in "Addressees" above.

[444] See "Authorship," "The City of Ephesus and Paul's Relationship to It," "Location and Date of Writing," and "Relationship to Colossians" above.

warning of a distant, post-Pauline era?[445] His subsequent admonition to "keep alert" and his reference to his own vigilant three-year ministry among them (Acts 20:31) suggest, on the contrary, that the threat was already at hand. Paul implies he is aware of specific men who will spring upon the flock as soon as he is gone. His decision to meet with the Ephesian pastors, despite his hurry to reach Jerusalem for Pentecost (Acts 20:16–17), likewise suggests that there was an immediate concern. The lurking wolves may well be the false teachers whom Timothy had opposed and removed from office before ordaining new presbyters in accord with Paul's instructions (1 Timothy 1–3). If Paul's letter to the Ephesians was written short weeks later from imprisonment in Caesarea, we might view it as the counterpart of his sermon to the pastors. Writing to the whole church in Ephesus, he reiterates what he first taught their pastors (Acts 20:18–35). After encouraging the church to view their new pastors as gifts of the ascended Christ (Eph 4:7–12), Paul warns the Ephesians that they need to grow in the knowledge of Christ, that they should "no longer be infants, so as to be tossed to and fro by waves and carried about by every wind of doctrine, in the trickery of men, in craftiness in accordance with deceitful scheming which leads into error" (4:14). Thus, one purpose of Ephesians is to inculcate a love of God's truth in Christ (4:15, 21, 25; 6:14) and to value the pastors who teach it to his people.

Yet, like all the churches of the ancient world, the church in Ephesus was equally threatened by the philosophical and religious environment in which it was located. The twin letter to the Colossians is more explicit in describing the kind of syncretistic, ascetic, Jewish-Gnostic religious philosophy that was prevalent, what Paul calls the διδασκαλίας τῶν ἀνθρώπων, "teachings of men" (Col 2:22). That similar deceptive thinking threatened the Ephesian church is clear from Paul's first letter to Timothy, who was representing him in Ephesus.[446] Bo Reicke sums up the evidence from 1 Timothy:

> Evidently the heresy was a sort of Judaism, known partially from Galatians, but here reinforced by special claims that were based on genealogies ([1 Tim] 1:4). This Jewish pretentiousness (cf. 2 Cor. 11:22) led to legalism ([1 Tim] 1:7; cf. Titus 3:9), asceticism ([1 Tim] 4:3; cf. Col. 2:21), and materialism ([1 Tim] 6:5; cf. Phil. 3:19). The concluding rejection of a "falsely so-called knowledge" ([1 Tim] 6:20) corresponds with Paul's words against the Corinthian overemphasis on wisdom and knowledge (1 Cor. 1:18–2:16). This "knowledge" was only a preliminary stage of the later philosophy referred to as gnosticism.[447]

---

[445] The letter to the Ephesians in Rev 2:1–7, presumably written decades after Paul's, speaks of the Ephesians' rejection of false apostles and the works of the Nicolaitans. Ignatius, *To the Ephesians*, 7:1–2; 9:1, alludes to a Docetic heresy threatening the Ephesians.

[446] In the chronology we have adopted above, 1 Timothy was written *before* Ephesians, shortly after Paul left Ephesus (Acts 20:1). Yet if 1 Timothy was written a few years *after* Ephesians, its description of the religious and philosophical environment in Ephesus would remain relevant.

[447] Reicke, *Re-examining Paul's Letters*, 58.

Purpose and Themes

The dichotomy between false and true "knowledge" (1 Tim 2:4; 6:20; also 2 Tim 2:25; 3:7; Titus 1:1) resonates well with the contents of Ephesians (1:8–9, 17–18; 3:1–12, 17–19; 4:13).[448]

What Paul's letter to the Ephesians sharpens to a fine point, however, is the danger posed to Christians by the pagan religion of their former lives, symbolized graphically in Ephesus by the temple and cult of Artemis Ephesia.[449] To those Christians who had been rescued from their pagan past by their baptismal death and resurrection in Christ, their former "life" was a kind of walking death to which they dared never return (Eph 2:1–10). The promise of acceptance, sexual pleasure, power, and worldly success was a perpetual enticement as they watched their friends and neighbors participating in the old ways. But Paul warns them fiercely that they cannot return to that old worship or have fellowship with the works of darkness (4:17–24; 5:3–14). He encourages them to immerse themselves in the true worship of Christ inspired by the Spirit (5:15–20). They were living in a battle with foes more powerful than flesh and blood (6:12). Yet the constant message of Ephesians is that Jesus Christ has risen and ascended far above any earthly or heavenly powers (1:20–23; 3:10). Since he has defeated all their spiritual enemies, Christians can stand firm in battle, clothed in the armor and weapons of the Victorious One (6:10–17).

Jews and Greeks in the Body of Christ

Paul's opening prayer (1:3–14) serves as a prologue to the epistle, briefly touching on the themes and language that will be developed later. It is therefore significant that he introduces there a subtle distinction between "us" and "you":

> [12]that <u>we</u> should be to the praise of his glory, <u>[we] who first hoped</u> in Christ; [13]in whom <u>also you</u>, having heard the Word of truth, the Gospel of your salvation, … having also believed, <u>you</u> were sealed with the promised Holy Spirit. (1:12–13)

It is possible that the distinction is merely between longstanding Christians like Paul and recent converts like the Ephesians. But subsequent evidence in the epistle suggests that Paul has in mind a contrast between *Jewish* Christians and *Gentile* converts.[450] Paul subsequently describes "you" as people who formerly were not only dead in sin, but who also lived under the dominion of the prince of this world (2:1–2). When he proceeds to describe the former situation of "we/us all," he speaks only of conduct "in the passions of our flesh" and being "by

---

[448] Ephesians uses γνωρίζω, "to make known" (Eph 1:9; 3:3, 5, 10; 6:19, 21), more often than any other NT book; it has six of the twenty-four NT occurrences (three of which are in Colossians).

[449] See "The Temple of Artemis Ephesia" and "The Cult of Artemis Ephesia" in "The City of Ephesus and Paul's Relationship to It" above.

[450] Schnackenburg, *Ephesians*, 49, cites the long list of interpreters who understand "[we] who first hoped" (1:12) as Jewish Christians: Chrysostom, Ambrosiaster, Abbott, Beare, Meinertz, Schlier, Scott, Barth, Bultmann, Lyonnet, and Mitton. Schnackenburg himself prefers to read it as "all Christians" (64); so also Dahl, "Gentiles, Christians, and Israelites in the Epistle to the Ephesians," in *Studies in Ephesians*, 445.

nature children of wrath like the rest" (2:3). This contrast would be consistent with a distinction between Jewish ("we") and Gentile ("you") believers, as Paul would scarcely have accused faithful OT believers of being under the devil's dominion before they acknowledged that Jesus of Nazareth was the promised Messiah, though he would admit that they were sinful by nature. Only in the following pericope does Paul fully show his hand:

> [11]Therefore, remember that at one time you Gentiles in the flesh, who are called Uncircumcision by what is called Circumcision (made in the flesh by hands), [12]that you were at that time separated from Christ, alienated from the commonwealth of Israel. (2:11–12)

As this unit develops (2:11–22), it becomes clear that Paul is deeply concerned with the relationship between God's chosen people, Israel, and the rest (οἱ λοιποί) of the world (Eph 2:3)—a subject rarely noticed outside Galatians and Romans. At the heart of the unit, Paul declares that Christ has destroyed the hostility and bridged the divide between the two peoples by uniting them in his one body on the cross (Eph 2:14–16).

Why is the opposition between Jew and Gentile a concern of this letter? The answers lies either in the situation of the Ephesians or in Paul's own—or in both. On the one hand, the story of Paul's mission in Ephesus discloses sufficient reasons for the concern. Luke reports more than once that Paul's message went to both Jews and Greeks at Ephesus and that he won believers from both groups (Acts 19:10, 17; 20:21). Yet, as usual, it was also true that many Jews rejected the Gospel (Acts 19:9). As they watched Paul's success, they became increasingly hostile toward his mission—and the Jews were not an insignificant force in the area.[451] During the silversmiths' riot in the theater, prompted by the impact that the Christian message was having on the cult of Artemis Ephesia, the crowd turned against Alexander as he attempted to speak for the Jews (Acts 19:33–34). Thus, the Jews who did not accept Christianity may have seen the upstart religion as a threat to their own religious freedom, established by the Roman authorities. The extent of their hostility can be gauged by the facts that the Jews in Greece (probably prompted by the Ephesians) immediately afterward plotted against Paul's life (Acts 20:3) and that some of the "Jews from Asia" pursued him all the way to Jerusalem to denounce him before the Sanhedrin and were instrumental in getting him arrested in the temple (Acts 21:27; 24:18–20).

How might this hostility have affected the church at Ephesus? Acts is clear that *some* Jews entered into the Christian church. But Paul's letter addresses the Ephesian congregation as if it were entirely or mostly Gentile (1:12–13; 2:1–2, 11–19; 3:1). It refers to the Ephesians' recent conversion, Baptism, and catechesis (1:13, 18; 2:5–6; 4:4, 20) and warns them against returning to a pagan

---

[451] MacDonald, *Colossians and Ephesians*, 9: "Given the presence of Jewish elements in the false teaching described in [Col] 2:16–23 it is important to note the evidence for a significant Jewish minority in the cities of the Lycus Valley."

life they seem to know personally (4:17–19; 5:3–8). One can only hypothesize about the situation. Was the predominantly Gentile church at Ephesus under threat from *unconverted* Jews, who might have urged the authorities to deny the Christians such religious freedom as Jews enjoyed on the grounds that Christians were not true heirs of the OT faith? Were Jews *within* the Christian church devalued or despised by the Gentile majority because of the actions of their unconverted brothers in the flesh?[452] Or is the reverse possible, that the Jews *within* the church were puffed up by their status as "[we] who first hoped in Christ" (1:12), so that they needed to be reminded that they, too, were "children of wrath like the rest" (2:3)? In this exercise we are limited by the information available in Ephesians; only because Paul appeals to the true unity of Jews and Gentiles in Christ (e.g., 2:11–22; 4:1–6) might we deduce that there was a conflict.

What is more demonstrable, however, is that *Paul's own predicament* was related to the Jew/Gentile divide. The Jews from Asia who pursued him to Jerusalem claimed that he was teaching κατὰ τοῦ λαοῦ καὶ τοῦ νόμου καὶ τοῦ τόπου τούτου, "against the people [the Jews] and the Torah and this place [the temple]" (Acts 21:28). His arrest was on the charge of violating the temple's "dividing wall" (cf. Eph 2:14) that kept Gentiles distant from the place of sacrifice and the Holy of Holies (Acts 21:28). The Greek whom they assumed he had taken into the temple was "Trophimus the Ephesian" (Acts 21:29). Thus, as we have proposed,[453] the Ephesian Christians may have concluded with trepidation that they were responsible for the arrest of Christ's apostle.

Paul's letter responds to this fear with a double message. First, he argues that the divide between Jew and Gentile has been erased in Christ. Jesus carried both peoples in his own body on the cross, killing the hostility between them by reconciling them both to God (2:14–16) and drawing them both into God's presence, thus removing the distance that once kept the Gentiles farther away from God than the Jews (2:13, 17–18). In Christ they have together been made into a new people of God (2:19)—indeed, they are the true Israel.[454] They have

---

[452] Käsemann, "Ephesians and Acts," 291, postulates that this is a sign of the letter's late, postapostolic provenance: "The letter betrays its historical setting precisely here. What Paul mentioned hypothetically in Rom. 11:17 ff. has happened here: Jewish Christianity is pushed aside and despised by the steadily growing Gentile Christianity." Yet such conditions may not have arisen only in the postapostolic era. Local circumstances could have created this situation within Paul's lifetime. MacDonald, *Colossians and Ephesians*, 19: "It is certainly within the realm of possibility that Eph 2:11–22 spoke in general to the realities of a community comprised of a Gentile majority and a dwindling Jewish minority."

[453] See "Paul's Trip to Jerusalem, Arrest, and Imprisonment (Acts 21:1–36)" in "The City of Ephesus and Paul's Relationship to It" above.

[454] Barth, *Ephesians*, 1:66, remarks: "Ephesians, more than any other NT epistle, will press the point that Gentiles receive no salvation other than the one they share with Israel and receive through the Messiah. It is the salvation first promised and given to this people alone: Israel." Reicke, *Re-examining Paul's Letters*, 13–15, 21–25, 37–38, argues that Paul's encounter with rising Jewish Zealotism (which culminated in the rebellion against Rome in AD 66–73) was a factor in his addressing the status of Gentile Christians.

been built into a new temple (2:20–22) and incorporated as members of Christ's own body (1:23; 3:6; 4:4, 12, 16–17; 5:23, 30). They are *one church* (4:4–6). This is the great mystery that has been revealed to Paul.[455] The emphasis on ecclesiology in Ephesians is a corollary of its emphatic denial of any such distinction in the body of Christ.

Second, Paul's own mandate, given directly by Christ speaking to him from heaven (3:1–12), compels him to proclaim the Gospel to the Gentiles and bring them into the kingdom. There can be no division between Jew and Gentile if Christ himself wills Paul's mission. And so the Ephesian Christians should not lose heart over Paul's imprisonment, which is not to their shame but to their glory (3:13). The letter to the Ephesians is therefore a significant word of consolation to a troubled people.

Baptism and the Spirit

Paul's response to the threat of Gentiles backsliding into their old pagan life was to assert the superiority of the Christ who has ascended far above every power or name that is named. His reply to the thorny problem of Jews and Gentiles within the one body of Christ is more diverse, consisting of a series of tightly ordered rhetorical "proofs."[456] Yet the proofs are interwoven by a golden thread, a direct or indirect appeal to one great unifying act of God: Holy Baptism. Baptism most likely suggested itself because of the baptismal misunderstanding that lay at the Ephesian church's founding (Acts 18:24–19:7). Because one group had received a false baptism, the sacrament of unity may have become a cause of division.[457] Because Apollos had misinterpreted the Baptism that John practiced, to the point that he did not even teach the person and work of the Holy Spirit (Acts 18:24–26; 19:1–3), Paul went to great lengths in his epistle to detail and exalt the Spirit's work.[458] He also may have concluded that he needed to emphasize the essential unity between John's Baptism—particularly of Christ himself—and the Baptism conducted in the Christian church subsequent to Christ's mandate (Mt 28:19). In his prologue (Eph 1:3–14) Paul introduces a series of allusions to Christ's Baptism and our own, implying that what Christ received all Christians also receive:

---

[455] Schlier, *Epheser*, 20–22, explains that the revelation that the church consists of Jews *and* Gentiles together is a theme that has moved from the background of other Pauline epistles into the foreground of Ephesians. It is the mystery that has been revealed. "He now does not merely pray for God's wisdom and knowledge for them ([Eph] 1:17; cf. 3:16ff.; 4:13), but he himself brings it to them in his letter. … This letter is thus not 'Kerygma' in the narrow sense of 1 Cor 1:18ff., which lies as the necessary foundation of wisdom, but it *is* wisdom, the wisdom of the mystery" (21–22).

[456] See "Structure and Rhetoric" below.

[457] See "Conflict over Baptism and the Spirit (Acts 18:24–19:7)" in "The City of Ephesus and Paul's Relationship to It" above.

[458] On a percentage basis, the twelve uses in Ephesians of πνεῦμα, "Spirit/spirit," to refer to the Holy Spirit stand behind only Galatians (sixteen) and 1 Corinthians (twenty-six).

- "in him [Christ] he [the Father] chose us for himself" (Eph 1:4; cf. Lk 9:35)
- "that we should be holy and without blemish" (Eph 1:4; cf. 5:27)
- "to be adopted as his [the Father's] sons through Jesus Christ" (Eph 1:5)
- "according to the good pleasure of his will" (Eph 1:5; cf. Mt 3:16–17)
- "the forgiveness of trespasses" (Eph 1:7; cf. Mk 1:4)
- "which he poured out upon us" (Eph 1:8)
- "you were sealed with the promised Holy Spirit" (Eph 1:13)
- "the deposit of our inheritance" (Eph 1:14)[459]

The present-day reader may find such references to Baptism by way of allusion to Christ's Baptism to be unconvincing. Few modern commentaries on Ephesians have paid much attention to its baptismal flavor.[460] There is a small but significant body of critical literature hypothesizing that Ephesians is a reworked baptismal rite or homily.[461] Though there is no reason to accept these theories literally (as the only such text we possess is the letter by Paul), their persistence indicates that the letter's baptismal language is compellingly obvious to many readers. If not a liturgical rite reworked into a letter, it is at least a letter deeply influenced by the baptismal rite (as well as the eucharistic liturgy).[462] Andrew Lincoln expresses the opposition's voice: "The single mention of the term 'baptism' (4:5) in a context devoted not to baptism but to unity, and a few metaphors, behind which a baptismal reference may lie, make it unlikely that baptism itself was a major concern in the writing of the letter."[463] Yet ancient writers were much more likely to assume and recognize baptismal allusions in

---

[459] These allusions to Christ's Baptism are explored in more detail in the textual notes and the commentary on 1:3–14 and in Winger, " 'One Baptism' and the Purpose of Ephesians." See also Dahl, "Das Proömium des Epheserbriefes," 327, and "The Concept of Baptism in Ephesians," 424–26, both in *Studies in Ephesians*. 1 Peter's *Berakah* prayer also contains clear references to Baptism (1 Pet 1:3–4).

[460] Schlier, *Epheser*, is an exception. So also Patzia, *Ephesians, Colossians, Philemon*. Nils Dahl, if his commentary in the Meyers Kritisch-exegetischer Kommentar über das Neue Testament series (Göttingen: Vandenhoeck & Ruprecht) had been completed, would have been another.

[461] E.g., Kirby, *Ephesians: Baptism and Pentecost*; Nils Alstrup Dahl, "Dopet i Efesierbrevet," *Svensk Teologisk Kvartalskrift* 21 (1945): 85–103; N. A. Dahl, "Adresse und Proömium des Epheserbriefes," *Theologische Zeitschrift* 7 (August 1951): 241–64; Coutts, "Ephesians I.3–14 and I Peter I.3–12"; Gnilka, *Epheserbrief*, 33; R. R. Williams, "The Pauline Catechesis," in Cross, *Studies in Ephesians*, 89–96. See Schnackenburg, *Ephesians*, 22, and Arnold, *Power and Magic*, 207, n. 32, for further references.

[462] Schnackenburg, *Ephesians*, 23:

> We cannot deny the influence of the liturgy, but along with other kerygmatic, catechetical and exhortatory traditions which enrich the language of Eph., but which cannot be seen in isolation as its constitutive material. The epistolary pattern is not an assumed cloak but a literary form deliberately chosen by the author because it was probably in keeping with the objective or aim of his writing.

[463] Lincoln, *Ephesians*, lxxix. Cf. Arnold, *Power and Magic*, 135. Lincoln's own diminished opinion of Baptism may be the reason for his skepticism: "But, although the letter contains some strong baptismal motifs, its content is not simply to be reduced to an exposition of the significance of this rite. Its subject is much broader—Christian existence as a whole" (xl). Is not the entire Christian life lived from one's Baptism?

the NT.[464] The explicit mention of Baptism in the midst of Paul's culminating argument for Christian unity (4:1–6) is not an exception, but the key to unlock the rich metaphorical allusions that fill the rest of the letter.[465] Baptism is[466]

- adoption as a son (Eph 1:5; cf. Gal 3:26–27; 4:5);
- an eternal inheritance (Eph 1:11, 14, 18; 3:6);
- the seal of Spirit (Eph 1:13; 4:30; cf. 2 Cor 1:21–22);
- being made God's child (Eph 4:14; 5:1, 8; cf. Jn 3:5);
- enlightenment (Eph 1:18; 5:8–14; cf. Acts 9:18);
- death and resurrection (Eph 2:5; 5:14; cf. Rom 6:1–4; Col 2:11–13);
- sanctifying by washing (Eph 5:26; cf. Titus 3:5–7; Heb 10:22);
- stripping off the old man, putting on the new man (Eph 4:21–24; cf. Gal 3:27); and
- being clothed with Christ (Eph 6:10–17).

From the impact of these repeated baptismal references one might distill the letter's major theme: *all those who have been joined to Christ by Baptism into his death and resurrection have not only been reconciled to God the Father but have also been united with one another in his body, the church.*

If this theme sounds familiar, it is because we have heard it before!

For in Christ Jesus you are all sons of God through faith. For as many of you as were baptized into Christ have been clothed with Christ. There is neither Jew nor Greek, there is neither slave nor free, there is not male and female; for you are all one in Christ Jesus. (Gal 3:26–28)

For in one Spirit we were all baptized into one body—whether Jews or Greeks, whether slaves or free—and we all were given to drink of one Spirit. (1 Cor 12:13)

The letter to the Ephesians might be viewed as a "midrash"—an exegetical expansion—on these earlier brief apostolic acclamations. Baptism, Spirit, unity, Christology, and ecclesiology all coalesce here. These are not separate themes,

---

[464] E.g., Cyprian, *Epistles*, 63:8 (CSEL 3/2:706): "As often as water alone is mentioned in the Holy Scriptures, Baptism is meant." See also Tertullian's tractate *On Baptism*. Such allusions are explored in detail by Jean Daniélou, *The Bible and the Liturgy* (Notre Dame, Ind.: University of Notre Dame Press, 1956). See also Oscar Cullmann, *Early Christian Worship* (trans. A. Stewart Todd and James B. Torrance; Chicago: Regnery, 1953).

[465] Deterding, *Colossians*, 161, draws a similar conclusion about Colossians: "Baptism plays a far more significant and extensive role in the message of this letter than the single occurrence of the vocable βαπτισμός ('Baptism,' [Col] 2:12) might suggest."

[466] Frequently the baptismal allusion can be demonstrated from parallel passages in Paul, some of which are noted in the bulleted items that follow in the text. For further discussion of these allusions, see Kirby, *Ephesians: Baptism and Pentecost*, 150–61; Dahl, "The Concept of Baptism in Ephesians," in *Studies in Ephesians*; and Schnackenburg, " 'Er hat uns mitauferweckt': Zur Tauflehre des Epheserbriefes." Detailed explication of each allusion may be found in the present commentary's textual notes on the relevant verses. Compare this list of allusions with the excursus "Baptism in the Message of Colossians" in Deterding, *Colossians*, 161–64.

but the varying bright facets of the baptismal jewel.[467] It is all about God's work in Christ for the sake of his children, whom he has washed, cleansed, forgiven, and reconciled through the seal of the promised Holy Spirit. Baptism is our personal Pentecost.[468]

Subsidiary Characteristics: Ecclesiology, Christology, Love, and Marriage

Most of the letter's remaining distinctive characteristics can be easily related to the above themes, and we need only touch upon them briefly. The emphasis on the universal church has been misused to suggest that the letter belongs to an era of "incipient Catholicism," when the church as a transparochial organization was supposedly emphasized at the expense of diversity, freedom, and local autonomy.[469] Yet this analysis misses the mark in more than one way. The noun ἐκκλησία, "church," occurs nine times in Ephesians (1:22; 3:10, 21; and six times in 5:23–32), in every instance referring to the universal church (see the commentary on 1:15–23). Aside from the very brief epistle 3 John, Ephesians has a greater statistical concentration of church vocabulary than any other NT book. But one must not confuse this universal church with a Catholic institution on this earth. Although Paul describes the pastoral ministry as a gift of God to the church on earth (4:7–16), nowhere does he occupy himself with structural concerns or institutional discipline. The church is universal because Christ is lifted up above all things and encompasses all things in himself (1:10, 20–23). Since all Christians are baptized into him, the church as his body shares in his existence spanning earth and heaven. If the metaphor of the divine marriage, which was rooted in the OT theology of God's marriage with Israel, was brought to Paul's mind by his recent observance of Pentecost,[470] he nonetheless took possession of the ball that was passed to him and dribbled it far beyond his former teammates. That six of the nine uses of the term ἐκκλησία, "church," occur in his description of the marriage between Christ and his bride (Eph 5:23–32) ought to remind us that ecclesiology is never separated from

---

[467] Dahl, "The Concept of Baptism in Ephesians," in *Studies in Ephesians*, 416:

> It has been customary in dogmatics to treat baptism in a special section as a part of the teaching on the mediation of grace or on the sacraments. Ephesians contains a few texts that can be used in such a presentation, but it never views baptism for its own sake in isolation from salvation in Christ, the gospel, faith, incorporation into the church and the gifts of the Holy Spirit.

[468] Thus, one needs no fantastically concocted theories about a baptismal liturgy enacted on Pentecost (Kirby, Dahl) to explain the letter's contents. If Baptism is understood as the "cleansing" (5:26) that makes us "holy and without blemish" (1:4), then Barth's reference to sanctification (God's making us holy) is apropos: "The whole of Ephesians may be understood as a treatise on the ground, the means, the extension, the purpose of sanctification" (*Ephesians*, 1:66–67).

[469] See "Incipient Catholicism" in "Arguments against Pauline Authorship" and "Incipient Catholicism" in "Evaluation of the Case," both in "Authorship" above.

[470] See the discussion of Pentecost in "Caesarea!" in "Location and Date of Writing" above.

Christology. The church is a body because she subsists in Christ's body, into which she was baptized and in which she finds her holy life. The church can only be spoken of as exalted because she is united with Christ at the right hand of God (Eph 1:20; 2:6).

The traditional contrast of Colossians with Ephesians as a shift from Christology to ecclesiology[471] ought therefore to be accepted only with severe caveats. Martin Franzmann's chiastic rephrasing of the contrast is subtly brilliant: "If the Letter to the Colossians is the Letter of Christ the Head of the Church, the Letter to the Ephesians is the Letter of the Church, the Body of Christ."[472] The church can only be the focus of attention because she is Christ's body. She is his body only because he has died for her to purchase her as his own with the price of his blood. It was an act of sacrificial love with which any human marital devotion only pales in comparison. But the comparison is never far away, as the marital metaphor suffuses the letter. The phrase ἐν ἀγάπῃ, "in love," occurs a remarkable six times in Ephesians (1:4; 3:17; 4:2, 15, 16; 5:2).[473] Love and marriage go together like … well, you know. Human love, even as a sacrificial act motivated by the love of Christ, is only a secondary facet of Paul's proclamation. Primarily the letter declares the wonders of God's love for his human bride in Christ. We are to walk "in love" because that love has first been shown to us by Christ's atoning act (Eph 5:1–2). Paul's message is in utter harmony with John's: "[10]In this is love, not that we have loved God, but that he loved us and sent his Son as the propitiation for our sins. [11]Beloved, if God loved us in this way, we also are indebted to love one another" (1 Jn 4:10–11).

Structure and Rhetoric
Epistolary Outline

Paul's letters on the whole (aside from their unusual length!) conform to the standard structure of a Jewish or Hellenistic letter of the day. From thousands of ancient examples and on the basis of contemporary letter-writing handbooks,[474] William Doty summarizes the pattern:

Introduction (prescript or salutation)
> including: sender, addressee, greetings, and often additional greetings or wish for good health

Text or Body, introduced with characteristic introductory formulae

---

[471] E.g., Schnackenburg, *Ephesians*, 31: "In its theological concern we have a shift of emphasis from Christology [in Colossians] to Ecclesiology [in Ephesians]."

[472] Franzmann, *The Word of the Lord Grows*, 132.

[473] The only other NT occurrences are in 1 Cor 4:21; 16:14; 2 Cor 6:6; Col 2:2; 1 Thess 5:13; 1 Tim 4:12; Jude 21. Its sixfold repetition in Ephesians marks its significance, strikingly so in contrast to its single appearance in Colossians (Col 2:2).

[474] The most significant ancient handbooks were two books attributed to Demetrius of Phaleron, *Epistolary Types* [τύποι ἐπιστολικοί], and *On Style* [περὶ ἑρμηνείας]; and Proclus (i.e., Libanius), *Epistolary Styles* [ἐπιστολιμαῖοι χαρακτῆρες]. See Klauck, *Ancient Letters and the New Testament*, 183–206.

Conclusion
>   including: greetings, wishes, especially for persons other than the
>   addressee; final greetings or prayer sentence; and sometimes dating[475]

The *introduction* of Ephesians is easily matched up to this model:

Sender: [1]Paul, apostle of Christ Jesus through the will of God,

Addressee: to the saints and faithful ones in Christ Jesus who are in Ephesus:

Greetings: [2]Grace to you and peace from God our Father and the Lord Jesus Christ. (1:1–2)

In addition to a wish for good health, classical letters often included in their introduction a *thanksgiving* to the gods for the recipient's prosperity, health, accomplishments, or good fortune, as well as intercessions that they might continue. By referring to the recipient's good qualities and deeds, the writer hoped to capture his goodwill for the request that usually followed (see "Rhetorical Outline," below in "Structure and Rhetoric"). In Paul's letters one finds a corresponding thanksgiving and prayer—though to the true God in the name of Jesus. Ephesians contains a typical thanksgiving prayer (1:15–23); but, in accord with Paul's usual tweaking of the model, he focuses more on the saving deeds of God than on the accomplishments of his addressees. While he indeed gives thanks for their "faith in the Lord Jesus and love toward all the saints" (1:15), he praises more extensively God's exaltation of Christ on their behalf and prays that they might come to benefit from it (1:16–23). In addition—and somewhat perplexingly—Paul inserts a lengthier prayer of thanksgiving that rehearses the eternal (indeed, prehistorical) plan of God for the reconciliation of all things and the election of his children in Christ (1:3–14). The prayer, which responds to the revelation of God's mysterious plan to unite all things in Christ (1:9–10), follows the model of a Jewish *Berakah* prayer. Such Jewish prayers begin with the acclamation "blessed is the LORD" or "blessed are you, O LORD," which Paul modifies to address the Triune God (1:3). While 1:3–14 is the most complete *Berakah* prayer in the epistles, it is not unique, as both 2 Corinthians (1:3–11) and 1 Peter (1:3–9) form their thanksgiving prayers in this traditional mold. What is unusual about Ephesians is the inclusion of *both* the *Berakah* prayer (1:3–14) and the more usual thanksgiving (1:15–23).[476]

The *conclusions* of Paul's letters are more varied than his salutations, drawing variously upon at least twelve possible elements (see the commentary on 6:18–24). While **greetings** are perhaps conspicuous by their absence from

---

[475] Doty, *Letters in Primitive Christianity*, 14. See also the more detailed discussions in Aune, *The New Testament in Its Literary Environment*, 163–69, 183–91; Stowers, *Letter Writing in Greco-Roman Antiquity*, 20 and passim; and Klauck, *Ancient Letters and the New Testament*, 17–42.

[476] Some, such as Kirby, *Ephesians: Baptism and Pentecost*, have suggested that the entire first three chapters of Ephesians are an extended thanksgiving, on the analogy of 1 Thess 1:2–3:13. This analysis assumes that the doxology in Eph 3:14–21 is the conclusion to the thanksgiving. Yet it is hard to see that the extended Gospel proclamation of 2:1–22 and Paul's disclosure of his apostolic mission in 3:1–13 could be part of the thanksgiving.

Ephesians, a careful examination of their appearance in Paul's letters reveals that Paul greets more people by name in churches with which he does *not* have a close personal relationship (e.g., Romans), while he greets few or none in churches where he had an intense ministry (e.g., 1 Corinthians, Galatians, 1 and 2 Thessalonians). The function of the concluding greetings is the inverse of what many interpreters suppose: Paul greets a few people by name in order to *establish* a relationship with a church, but refrains from singling out people in churches where he was known to all, as was surely the case in Ephesus. A second notable absence from the conclusion to Ephesians is any reference to an upcoming visit or **travel plans** ("apostolic parousia"). If Paul wrote Ephesians shortly after his arrest in Jerusalem,[477] such plans might have been impossible for him to propose.[478] A few minor divergences from form in the conclusion of one of his letters is really quite unremarkable. What remains are these standard elements:

Prayer Request: "With every prayer and petition be praying at every opportune time in the Spirit" (6:18–20).

Commendation of the Letter Carrier: "Tychicus, the beloved brother and faithful minister in the Lord, will make everything known to you" (6:21–22).

Peace Greeting: "Peace be to the brothers and love with faith from God the Father and the Lord Jesus Christ" (6:23).

Grace Greeting and Communion Fellowship: "Grace be with all those who love our Lord Jesus Christ in incorruptibility" (6:24).

Traditional epistolary outlines normally insert between the carefully analyzed salutation and conclusion the word "body" (see Doty, quoted above). Since the interpreter is most concerned about the *body* of the letter, it is ironic that it has often received the least amount of structural analysis.[479] The reason, of course, is that epistolary analysis concerns itself only with the *formal* elements of a letter, those introductory and concluding words that are unique to a text delivered to a far-distant audience. The *content* of letters (as found in the body) was not dependent on the epistolary packaging. Certainly the ancient epistolary handbooks provide some analogues for Paul's letters that might help us to understand what he was doing: official letters (from someone in authority to the public), public letters (from an individual who wished to persuade the body

---

[477] See "Paul's Trip to Jerusalem, Arrest, and Imprisonment (Acts 21:1–36)" in "The City of Ephesus and Paul's Relationship to It" above.

[478] However, Paul's expressed desire to visit Philemon (Philemon 22) stands against this explanation. Since all other evidence points to Ephesians, Colossians, and Philemon having been written and delivered at the same time (see "Paul's Imprisonment" in "Location and Date of Writing"), it is difficult to offer an explanation of Philemon 22, except that Paul might have been using the promise (or threat) of a visit as a rhetorical device in his persuasive letter to the slave owner.

[479] See Winger, "Orality as the Key to Understanding Apostolic Proclamation in the Epistles," 249–56.

politic), and discursive letters (concerning philosophical issues).[480] Paul's letters share many characteristics with these, as he bore the authority of Christ himself and wrote to the churches under his care to command, teach, and encourage them. Yet the Christian context is sufficiently different that no single secular category of ancient letter is of much help in analyzing the body of Paul's letters.

The most common standard analysis of the body of the Pauline letter is a division into two halves: doctrinal and ethical; kerygmatic and didactic; the Pauline "indicative" followed by the Pauline "imperative."[481] In Romans this divide has been located between chapters 11 and 12, in the transition from the teaching on justification by faith alone to the exhortation on how to live. The doxology at the conclusion of Romans 11 has been taken as a marker that Paul has concluded the first task and is ready for the second. In Ephesians the division is supposedly even more stark; most commentators offer an outline something like this:

1:1–2	Salutation
1:3–14	*Berakah* Prayer
1:15–23	Thanksgiving
2:1–3:21 *3:14–21*	**Body 1 (Doctrine)—*Kerygma*** *Doxology*
4:1–6:17	**Body 2 (Paraenesis)—*Didache***
6:18–24	Epistolary Conclusion

Yet there are a number of serious problems with this simplistic division of the body (see the first textual note on 4:1 and the commentary on 4:1–16 for more detail):

1. The placement of doxologies in Paul's letters is much more complex than this. Only in the cases of Romans and Ephesians do they conceivably mark a turning point in the major argument of the letter. A more careful analysis suggests that the doxologies are responses to a great mystery that has been contemplated in the immediately preceding pericope, rather than markers of a letter's midpoint or another major division. Thus, Eph 3:14–21 is a response to 3:1–13, Paul's contemplation of the

---

[480] On the handbooks and the types of letters they identify, see Doty, *Letters in Primitive Christianity*; 8–11; Aune, *The New Testament in Its Literary Environment*, 161; and Stowers, *Letter Writing in Greco-Roman Antiquity*, 32–35.

[481] Brown, *An Introduction to the New Testament*, 621. Cf. Aune, *The New Testament in Its Literary Environment*, 199, who leans decidedly toward the ethical: "Most of Paul's letters, apart from the opening and closing epistolary formulas, consist of three elements. The first is conciliatory; he compliments the addressees for their past performance [the thanksgiving]. The middle section contains advice. The final section contains paraenesis." This analysis is difficult to reconcile with Paul's own claims about his epistolary purpose: "we preach Christ crucified" (1 Cor 1:23), and "we beseech you on behalf of Christ, be reconciled to God" (2 Cor 5:20).

mystery of the Gospel being taken to the Gentiles, rather than a conclusion to the letter's supposed first half (see the commentary on 3:14–21).

2. The expression παρακαλῶ οὖν ὑμᾶς, "so I encourage you" (4:1), has also been interpreted as marking the transition into a letter's "ethical half." Yet a careful analysis of the verb παρακαλέω, "encourage; exhort; comfort," in Paul's letters and in expressions similar to Eph 4:1 shows that they do not, as a rule, appear more frequently in a supposed "ethical" half or act as infallible markers of the same. Nor is it accurate to associate the word group παρακαλέω/παράκλησις exclusively with the Law, with exhortation to *act* (rather than consolation of those who *trust*). See Eph 6:22, where παρακαλέω is translated as "to comfort."

3. Aside from 4:1–3, the opening three verses that encourage the Ephesians to maintain the unity of the Spirit, the first pericope in chapter 4 (4:1–16) is not particularly paraenetic. In fact, the most explicit creedal, doctrinal statement in the entire letter sits at the heart of this pericope (4:4–6), immediately *after* the supposed divide between doctrinal and ethical halves.

4. It is a gross caricature of the relationship between Law and Gospel to suggest that Paul could complete his proclamation of the Gospel in a doctrinal section and then proceed to focus exclusively on how to live. This entails a distortion of Christianity itself, as if salvation in Christ were merely a pretext for sorting out Christian behavior in this world. It flies in the face of the evidence, for there is just as much pure Gospel proclamation in the letter's second half as in its first (e.g., 4:4–13; 5:1–2, 14, 25–32; 6:10–17). Furthermore, it involves a confusion concerning what Lutherans classically call the three functions of the Law.[482] The third function— that the Law informs Christians of God's will and guides their actions in the way that pleases him—can never be separated from the Gospel proclamation that alone has the power to create such obedience. And whenever the Law is preached with the goal of guiding behavior, it will always also convict the Christian of his sinful failings, for *lex semper accusat* ("the law always accuses"). This second function of the Law[483] always accompanies the third function. Indeed, the second half of Ephesians contains as much stark, condemnatory language (the second function of the Law; e.g., 4:17–24; 5:3–14) as it does apparently hortatory words (the third function; e.g., 4:25–32; 5:22–25; 6:1–9). When the human preacher proclaims the Law, he may intend certain results but cannot control them. The condemning and guiding functions happen at once as the Holy Spirit, who alone knows the heart and is the true "user" of the Law, sees fit.[484]

---

[482] Classic Lutheran definitions of the three functions of the Law are provided in the Formula of Concord: "The law has been given to men for three reasons: (1) to maintain external discipline against unruly and disobedient men, (2) to lead men to a knowledge of their sin, (3) after they are reborn, and although the flesh still inheres in them, to give them on that account a definite rule according to which they should pattern and regulate their entire life" (FC Ep 6:1).

[483] Lutherans consider the second function of the Law to be its "chief" (SA 3:2.4) and "proper" (FC SD 5:17) one.

[484] A clear presentation of this point is found in Roger J. Humann, "Four Theses and Some Auxiliary Statements on Preaching to the Christian," *Lutheran Theological Review* 1.2 (Spring/ Summer 1989): 51–60.

Ironically, it was Markus Barth, the son of Karl Barth (who famously condemned the Lutheran Law-Gospel theological sequence, proposing instead "Gospel-Law"), who most scathingly critiqued this outline of Ephesians:

> Indeed the juxtaposition of preaching and teaching (*kerygma* and *didache*), of indicative and imperative, may have had its day. Their undeniable usefulness as hermeneutical tools may be exhausted. ... The sequence, God (or Christ) did *this* for you—now you have to do *that* for him, is a ridiculous caricature of the relationship between God's grace and the good works for which man is created, according to Eph 2:5–10.[485]

Rhetorical Outline

Epistolary analysis is an avenue of enquiry that has reached a dead end.[486] A more promising route is suggested by the oral theory with which this introduction began.[487] The real "form" to which the epistles belong is "sermon," "liturgical proclamation."[488] They are "epistles" only because their oral delivery is interrupted by distance and time.[489] As oral proclamation, they are best interpreted according to the rubrics of ancient rhetoric, as we know it from the handbooks of Aristotle, Quintilian, and Cicero.[490] Whether or not Paul had read

---

[485] Barth, *Ephesians*, 1:54–55. Barth, nevertheless, does not reevaluate the division at the end of chapter 3, but merely reexamines the label "ethical."

[486] Epistolary theory on the basis of ancient epistolary handbooks is not fruitless, but does not help to analyze the *body* of the letter. Epistolary and rhetorical analyses are not alternatives, but complementary techniques. See Classen, "St Paul's Epistles and Ancient Greek and Roman Rhetoric," 288–91; Reed, "Using Ancient Rhetorical Categories to Interpret Paul's Letters: A Question of Genre."

[487] See "Orality and the Interpretation of the Epistles: A Brief Introduction" above.

[488] Schlier, *Epheser*, 34: "Our entire letter is, in fact, as 'Lection' a part of the λόγος τοῦ Χριστοῦ ['Word of Christ'] (Col 3:16) in the liturgy [*Kultus*]." See also Best, *Ephesians*, 61–62, who compares Ephesians with Hebrews, James, and Jude as homilies to which epistolary openings and conclusions have been added.

[489] Lincoln, *Ephesians*, xxxix, summarizes a view that agrees with our own earlier proposal:

> [Hartwig] Thyen (*Der Stil der jüdisch-hellenistischen Homilie* [Göttingen: Vandenhoeck & Ruprecht, 1955], 63, 119–20) proposed that the body of the letters of Paul, with their teaching and paraenesis, reflected the manner in which Paul preached to his congregations and may therefore have been influenced by the synagogue homily. The body of Ephesians seems even more like the written equivalent of the oral presentation the writer would have delivered to a congregation at its assembly for worship. It is the written equivalent of a sermon or homily. ... Certainly its liturgical forms would have enabled the reading of the letter to fit appropriately into a liturgical setting.

[490] See Kennedy, *New Testament Interpretation through Rhetorical Criticism*; Mack, *Rhetoric and the New Testament*; Davis, *Oral Biblical Criticism*, 64–97; Harvey, *Listening to the Text*, 22–33; Winger, "Orality as the Key to Understanding Apostolic Proclamation in the Epistles," 255–67. Porter, "The Theoretical Justification for Application of Rhetorical Categories to Pauline Epistolary Literature," is more negative toward rhetorical analysis of the epistles, as is Klauck, *Ancient Letters and the New Testament*, 206–9, 224–25, and Mark P. Surburg, "Ancient Rhetorical Criticism, Galatians, and Paul at Twenty-five Years," *Concordia Journal* 30 (2004): 13–39. But even if some ancient authors distinguished letter writing from oratory, Paul's lengthy epistles have far more in common with speeches than with other ancient letters.

one of those particular authors, it is nearly certain that such a highly educated man learned by schooling and/or absorbed by reading the basic methods of rhetoric: the art of constructing a persuasive argument for oral delivery in various circumstances.[491] Such rhetorical training was routine in Western society until the early part of the twentieth century (and was extensively employed by Melanchthon in his exegetical work[492]), but is now unfamiliar to most people. In modern society the term "rhetoric" has taken on a decidedly negative connotation (e.g., "just a bunch of rhetoric"), referring to flowery language intended to disguise a lack of substance. This criticism was appropriate at certain times and places also for ancient rhetoric, particularly as practiced in the Second Sophistic era. In places like Corinth it degenerated to the point of being an oratorical rival to the Olympic Games, a spectacle for the crowds designed to win praise and profit—hence Paul's careful rejection of "manipulative words of wisdom" (1 Cor 2:4).[493] At the same time, Paul committed himself to preaching true knowledge and wisdom, so long as it centered on the power of the cross (1 Cor 1:5, 18–25). He was not opposed to the rhetoric of careful argumentation based on sound evidence that characterized rhetoric in its classical form. Rhetoric was about persuasion by *proof.*[494]

Understanding the design and argumentation of the Pauline epistles can be greatly aided by examining rhetorical methods. George Kennedy notes: "Rhetoric as taught in the schools consisted of five parts which recapitulate five stages in the act of composing a speech."[495] These stages were (1) invention, (2) arrangement, (3) style, (4) memory, and (5) delivery.[496] The first two

---

[491] Kennedy, *New Testament Interpretation through Rhetorical Criticism*, 9–10, admits that proof is lacking, but contends Paul is the NT author most likely to have been schooled in rhetoric. See also Classen, "St Paul's Epistles and Ancient Greek and Roman Rhetoric," 269.

[492] Melanchthon wrote three rhetorical handbooks and three works on dialectic. His application of rhetoric to the NT is most easily seen by the English reader in his *Commentary on Romans* (trans. Fred Kramer; 2d ed.; St. Louis: Concordia, 2010). Classen, "St Paul's Epistles and Ancient Greek and Roman Rhetoric," 279, concludes: "It seems fair to say that no one contributed more to the development of rhetorical criticism than Melanchthon."

[493] See Mack, *Rhetoric and the New Testament*, 28–29; Winger, "Rhetoric and Media in the Judgement of St Paul"; Anthony Thiselton, *The First Epistle to the Corinthians* (Grand Rapids: Eerdmans, 2000).

[494] Kennedy, *New Testament Interpretation through Rhetorical Criticism*, 13: "Rhetoric is defined by Aristotle ([*The Art of Rhetoric* (mid fourth century BC)] 1.2.1355b) as the faculty of discovering in each case the available means of persuasion, and by Quintilian ([*Institutio oratoria* (ca. AD 92–95)] 2.15.38) as *scientia bene dicendi*, the knowledge of how to speak well." In *The Art of Rhetoric*, Aristotle would distinguish between philosophical dialectic, which was about proof in the area of natural and rational order (φύσις), and rhetoric, which was about persuading with respect to issues of social moment (νόμος). See Mack, *Rhetoric and the New Testament*, 36–37. In a sense, NT rhetoric is closer to the latter, as it seeks to inculcate not simply ideas about God, but life with God. See also Chaïm Perelman and L. Olbrechts-Tyteca, *The New Rhetoric: A Treatise on Argumentation* (trans. John Wilkinson and Purcell Weaver; Notre Dame, Ind.: University of Notre Dame Press, 1969).

[495] Kennedy, *New Testament Interpretation through Rhetorical Criticism*, 13.

[496] The Greek and Latin terms for these are (1) εὕρεσις, *inventio*; (2) τάξις, *dispositio*; (3) λέξις, *elocutio*; (4) μνήμη, *memoria*; and (5) ὑπόκρισις, *actio* or *pronuntiatio*.

are particularly helpful for understanding the structure and argumentation of a letter like Ephesians.

At the stage of *invention* the orator needed to identify his thesis (the point that he wished to prove) and set out the lines of evidence he would use. "External proofs" consist of material the author uses but does not invent: quotations of Scripture, evidence of miracles, and naming of witnesses are common in the NT. In Ephesians Paul cites or alludes to OT Scripture (1:22; 4:8, 25–31; 5:31; 6:2–3, 10–17). He quotes what is presumably a liturgical hymn (5:14) and creed (4:4–6) that the Ephesians might have known. He cites the resurrection and ascension of Christ as powerful acts of God that prove what he will do for the Ephesian Christians (e.g., 1:20–23; 2:1–10) and appeals to his miraculous encounter with Christ (3:1–12).

"Internal" or "artistic proofs," by contrast, are the first stage of the author's creativity. Aristotle identified three basic kinds:[497]

- *Ethos* (ἦθος) is the attempt to establish the character of the speaker as trustworthy or authoritative. Paul appeals to nothing in himself (being quite self-deprecating about his public-speaking abilities [1 Cor 1:12–15; 2:1–5; cf. 2 Cor 10:10]), but asserts his apostolic credentials and appeals to the call and mandate of Christ (Eph 1:1; 3:1–13; 4:1; 6:20).
- *Pathos* (πάθος) is the attempt to engage the audience, appeal to their emotions or intelligence. While Paul will not stoop to manipulation (1 Cor 2:1, 4), he does lift up the hearts of his hearers by giving thanks to God for the good work he is doing in and through them. Thus, he can give thanks for their faith in God and love toward all the saints (1:15) in an opening appeal that might be called a *benevolentiae captatio*, "capturing of goodwill" (1:15–23).
- *Logos* (λόγος) refers to logical argumentation, including inductive reasoning (citing examples from which a conclusion is drawn) and deductive reasoning (applying a logical syllogism to a specific situation). The first three and a half chapters of Ephesians contain the most intense sequence of such "proofs" (1:18–23; 2:1–10; 2:11–22; 3:1–13; 4:1–16).

The final decision the orator needed to make at the stage of *invention* was the "species" of rhetoric. Classical Greco-Roman rhetorical handbooks concentrated on three species,[498] each of which corresponded to a specific social context:

- "Judicial"[499] rhetoric belonged to the law court. It was the form of argumentation by which the prosecution and defense lawyers asked the jury, judge, or public to make a decision about what happened in the *past* in order to declare the accused guilty or innocent.

---

[497] See chapters 1 and 2 of Aristotle's *The Art of Rhetoric*.

[498] E.g., Aristotle, *The Art of Rhetoric*, 1:3.1358a–b. While Aristotle and others use the term γένος, *genus*, which might be translated as "genre" or "kind," most modern authors refer to these as "species."

[499] The Greek and Latin terms are γένος δικανικός, *genus iudiciale*.

- "Deliberative"[500] rhetoric belonged to the realm of politics, being the form of public speaking by which someone tried to persuade the parliament or crowd to take a specific course of action in the *future* (go to war, adopt a law, etc.).
- "Epideictic"[501] rhetoric belonged to the public square, to ceremony. It was the form of speech by which an orator sought to praise or blame a person, event, or concept in the *present*, appealing to the crowd to hold or reaffirm a point of view.[502]

While the contexts identified here were the classical examples of each species, such rhetoric was not confined to those specific places alone. It is also a mistake to assume that an entire speech or writing must be confined to one species.[503] Lengthy discourses like Paul's letters might move from one species to another as different topics arose. Galatians includes judicial rhetoric, calling on the hearers to render judgment against the Judaizers. Romans 6 addresses the deliberative question "shall we continue in sin so that grace may abound?" (Rom 6:1). And 1 Corinthians 13 is epideictic rhetoric in praise of love.

It is tempting to identify Ephesians with one of the three classical species of rhetoric. Epideictic rhetoric—the attempt to persuade an audience to hold a specific point of view—is most compatible with Christian preaching.[504] The surfeit of praise in the first three chapters of Ephesians suggests this category.[505] Andrew Lincoln argues that the letter combines two species: epideictic in chapters 1–3, followed by deliberative in chapters 4–6:

> The congratulatory and the paraenetic, the reminder of the readers' calling and the appeal to live out that calling, combine the epideictic and the deliberative rhetorical genres. …
>
> Though some of the paraenesis in Ephesians is a reminder of common values (cf., e.g., 4:20, 21) and calls for a preservation of what is already the case

---

[500] The Greek and Latin terms are γένος συμβουλευτικόν, *genus deliberativum*.

[501] The Greek and Latin terms are γένος ἐπιδεικτικόν, *genus demonstrativum*. The verb ἐπιδείκνυμι, *epideiknumi*, means "to demonstrate."

[502] Some scholars dispute the application of these three rhetorical species to epistles, since the ancient epistolary handbooks tended to distinguish the goals of letter writing from the goals of oratory. Erasmus' *De conscribendis epistolis* added a fourth species, the *genus familiare*, to accommodate letters (Klauck, *Ancient Letters and the New Testament*, 210). Classen, "St Paul's Epistles and Ancient Greek and Roman Rhetoric," 286, contends: "It is not surprising that the categories of rhetoric fail us with respect to the structure of this epistle [Galatians], because it is an epistle, and they were not made nor meant to fit such kinds of composition." Demetrius, *Epistolary Types*, identifies twenty-one different types of letters. But to set these in opposition to the three species of rhetoric is to confuse categories. Each type of letter might have made use of the three species as needed. See Stowers, *Letter Writing in Greco-Roman Antiquity*, 51–57.

[503] Aune, *The New Testament in Its Literary Environment*, 203: "Attempts to classify one or another of Paul's letters as *either* judicial *or* deliberative *or* epideictic (or one of their sub-types) run the risk of imposing external categories on Paul and thereby obscuring the real purpose and structure of his letters."

[504] Kennedy, *New Testament Interpretation through Rhetorical Criticism*, 73–74.

[505] Brown, *An Introduction to the New Testament*, 631, notes that the rhetoric of Ephesians has been called epideictic, "a letter using praise as a basis for an appeal." See also Stowers, *Letter Writing in Greco-Roman Antiquity*, 80–81; Lincoln, *Ephesians*, xli–xlii.

(cf. 4:3; 6:10–17, which returns to the epideictic genre …), for the most part the writer is seeking an adjustment in the readers' behaviour so that, where necessary, it will become more distinctly Christian, that is, more in line with what he deems to be appropriate for those who belong to the Church.[506]

Yet Lincoln's analysis raises a number of concerns. First, while attempting to apply rhetorical insights to the letter, Lincoln has not really progressed beyond the traditional two-part epistolary outline; he has simply replaced the terms "doctrinal" and "ethical" with "epideictic" and "deliberative."[507] Renaming does not increase understanding. Second, one wonders whether a proclivity to understand Christianity ultimately as a pattern of behavior (the Gospel as a path to the obedience of the Law) rather than a way of redemption has irredeemably biased his interpretation.[508] Third, this tendency to identify the goal of the oration chiefly with changed behavior (rather than repentance and faith in Christ) may be an inherent danger when the epistles are pressed into the mold of secular rhetorical species. Neither epideictic nor deliberative is entirely satisfactory. Even "epistolary rhetoric" (as described by Demetrius) is an unsuitable model, as it centers on the *petitio*—the request for a favor that prompted the letter's writing and took the place of the proofs in the other rhetorical species.[509] Though the classical art of rhetoric surely had great influence on Paul, as an apostolic writer he was nevertheless operating in an entirely new realm. *We ought, therefore, to speak of the proclamation of salvation by the grace of God through faith in Jesus Christ as an entirely different species of rhetoric: Christian rhetoric.*[510]

---

[506] Lincoln, *Ephesians*, xli–xlii.

[507] Lincoln's epistolary and rhetorical outlines, *Ephesians*, xliii–xliv, are essentially identical.

[508] Aune, *The New Testament in Its Literary Environment*, 199, also suffers from this presupposition:

> With few exceptions, early Christian letters were either written with a basically deliberative purpose, or included major deliberative elements. The two basic forms of deliberative rhetoric, persuasion and dissuasion, included not only advice but also most of the features associated with moral and religious exhortation: encouragement, admonition, comfort, warning, and rebuke.

Best, *Ephesians*, 74–75, likewise identifies the main purpose of Ephesians with the third function of the Law:

> AE [the Author of Ephesians] writes to ensure the corporate maturity of believers and does so by driving home the nature of the body they joined when they left the pagan world, and the type of behaviour which would produce true growth in their communities; since they are Gentiles he has necessarily to touch on the Jewish–Gentile question. …
>
> Now as Christians they have entered a new group and it is important that they should realise its nature and the conduct required of them in it.

Where in this is the delivery of Christ and all his blessings?

[509] See Walter J. Ong, *Rhetoric, Romance, and Technology: Studies in the Interaction of Expression and Culture* (Ithaca, N.Y.: Cornell University Press, 1971), 3, 54, 73–74.

[510] Melanchthon assigns Galatians to an invented *genus didacticum* ("didactic species"); see Classen, "St Paul's Epistles and Ancient Greek and Roman Rhetoric," 272–73, citing student notes from Melanchthon's 1520 and 1521 lectures on Galatians in *Texte aus der Anfangszeit Melanchthons* (ed. Ernst Bizer; Neukirchen-Vluyn: Neukirchener Verlag des

Christian rhetoric is unique because it intends to "prove" a thesis that is of a different nature than was at stake in other rhetorical situations of the day. Yet the methods taught in the second stage of producing an oration, *arrangement* (τάξις, *dispositio*), were easily adaptable to the new goals. The rhetorical handbooks broke down the arrangement of an oration into four quite natural parts, as Klauck explains:

(1) προοίμιον, *exordium*, exordium or opening speech

(2) διήγησις, *narratio*, narrative or statement of the case

(3) πίστις, *argumentatio*, argument or proof

(4) ἐπίλογος, *peroratio*, peroration or effective conclusion[511]

Within these four parts, the precise elements would differ according to the species of rhetoric, and the terminology varied from one handbook to another. But the following description of judicial rhetoric provides a rather complete model:

> A judicial speech usually begins with a *proem* or *exordium* which seeks to obtain the attention of the audience and goodwill or sympathy toward the speaker. It then proceeds to a *narration* of the facts, or background information, and states the *proposition* which the speaker wishes to prove, often with a *partition* of it into separate headings. The speaker then presents his arguments in the *proof*, followed by a *refutation* of opposing views; here he may incorporate what was called a *digression*, often a relevant examination of motivations or attendant circumstances. Finally comes an *epilogue* or *peroration*, which summarizes the argument and seeks to arouse the emotions of the audience to take action or make judgment.[512]

Ephesians, though not judicial rhetoric in the strict sense, follows this pattern more closely than it does any of the other species.

Introductory Sections (*Exordium* and *Narratio*)

The introductory sections of Ephesians appear in its first chapter. It is difficult to apply distinctive rhetorical terms to each of its three pericopes, as Paul was not working rigidly with the forms. The opening sentence (1:1–2) serves as the letter's *salutatio*, "salutation, address"; its structure is determined by epistolary norms (see "Epistolary Outline," above in "Structure and Rhetoric"). The next pericope is, in liturgical terms, a *Berakah* prayer (1:3–14), a prayer of praise modeled on Jewish patterns in which Paul responds to the remarkable and mysterious acts of God in prehistory and in the saving work of Jesus. Adapted for Christian usage, the *Berakah* prayer was particularly connected

---

Erziehungsvereins, 1966), 34. George Kennedy notes that while NT writers often work with classical methods of proof on the basis of historical evidence or logical proof, sometimes they simply *proclaim*: "Most modern critics, however, recognize that there is a distinctive rhetoric of religion. It can be found in many cultures, East and West, and at the heart of it lies authoritative proclamation, not rational persuasion. ... This phenomenon is often known as 'sacred language'" (*New Testament Interpretation through Rhetorical Criticism*, 6).

[511] Klauck, *Ancient Letters and the New Testament*, 218.

[512] Kennedy, *New Testament Interpretation through Rhetorical Criticism*, 23–24.

with the celebration of the Lord's Supper in the central act of the church: the Divine Service. It is highly significant that Paul's rhetoric begins with the praise of God before any praise of the recipients (a traditional *exordium* focused solely on the latter). Yet the *Berakah* does carry out three important rhetorical tasks. First, it functions as a *narratio*—not in this case setting out the story of the human actors in a trial, but the acts of the Triune God in planning and executing his plan for the world's salvation in Christ. Nothing in the letter makes sense if one does not first understand the οἰκονομία, "plan," of God.[513] Second, while Ephesians does not appear to have a formal *propositio* (thesis statement) along the lines of Rom 1:16–17, this comes close:

> [9]He has made known to us the mystery of his will, according to his good pleasure which he declared in him, [10]to administer the fulfilling of the opportune moments, that all things might be brought together in Christ, the things in heaven and the things on earth in him. (Eph 1:9–10)

If this is the thesis—that all things are united in Christ—it only makes sense once its unfolding at the cross and in Baptism is explained, particularly in chapter 2. The *Berakah* (1:3–14), third, serves also as a *proem* (προοίμιον), a prologue which briefly introduces the various themes of the letter.

We have already noted that Ephesians is unusual in having both a *Berakah* prayer (1:3–14) and a thanksgiving (1:15–23). This is also unusual from a rhetorical perspective, giving the letter a double introduction. Yet Paul makes efficient use of his second prayer. For clarity's sake, we have labeled this second introduction (1:15–23) an *exordium* (a rhetorical term that is nearly synonymous with *proem*). Here Paul not only fulfills the epistolary function of giving thanks for his addressees (1:16) but also performs the rhetorical act of *benevolentiae captatio*, capturing their goodwill. He does this by praising their "faith in the Lord Jesus and love toward all the saints" (1:15) and by showing his deep love and concern by praying for them (1:16–19).[514] Subsequently Paul departs from convention by suspending the praise of his addressees in order to offer even greater praise to the God who has made them what they are in Christ (1:20–23). By appealing to the resurrection and ascension of Christ above all spiritual powers for the sake of his body, the church, Paul also appeals to evidence that will support his subsequent argument concerning the unity of Jew

---

[513] This commentary translates οἰκονομία as "administer" in 1:10; "stewardship" in 3:2; and "administration" in 3:9.

[514] Lincoln's comments on the epideictic rhetoric in chapters 1–3 are especially relevant to the *exordium*:

> The ornamentative thanksgiving and prayer of Eph 1–3 is an effective rhetorical strategy. It is one thing for a writer to argue a case with his readers, which may or may not be persuasive, but it is another thing to give thanks and pray for them. This sets up a different relationship in which the readers are affirmed, in which their sympathies are gained, and in which a common relationship to God and to Christ and common values grounded in this relationship are consolidated. (*Ephesians*, xlii)

and Gentile in Christ. Thus, the *exordium* (1:15–23) prepares for and overlaps with the letter's proofs.

Argumentation (πίστις, *Argumentatio*)

The main argument is usually subdivided into two parts, positive and negative: proofs (*probatio, confirmatio*) and refutations (*refutatio, confutatio*).

Proofs

If the thesis of Ephesians is that all people (Jew and Gentile alike) are united with one another through their common Baptism into the death of Christ, their unity in his one body, then the next four pericopes of the letter can be viewed as offering a series of discrete proofs of the same:

- **2:1–10:** Jew and Gentile are united by their common sinfulness (2:1–3) and also by their common reception of the grace of God in Christ (2:4–9). If they have joined Christ in Baptism, then they have also traveled with him through death to life at the right hand of God in heaven. Consequently, their new life is a common walk in God's ways (2:10).
- **2:11–22:** Here Paul reflects on the temple divisions that kept Gentiles farther away from the Holy Place than Jews. This was one visible example of the Law's divisive power. The death of Christ destroyed the Law's power to divide and also satisfied the punitive justice of God on behalf of all people. Because Christ united Jews and Gentiles in his one body, both were reconciled to God and to one another.
- **3:1–13:** Formally this section is a *digression*, as Paul interrupts his movement toward further prayer (3:1, 14). Yet it is a planned digression that contributes a further proof: Jew and Gentile are surely one in Christ because Christ himself revealed the nature of their salvation by grace and sent Paul to proclaim it. The flow of proofs is temporarily interrupted by Paul's doxological response to this great mystery (**3:14–21**).
- **4:1–16:** The final proof caps the series with an explicit appeal to Baptism in the midst of a creedal quotation—an external, evidential proof (4:1–6). Paul then refers to Scripture (quoting Ps 68:19 [ET 68:18]), arguing that it was fulfilled in the ascension of Christ and his distribution of gifts to the church in the office of the ministry (Eph 4:7–12) in order that the body might be built into an organic unity (4:13–16). Here the positive proofs close.

Refutations

The term περιπατέω, "to walk," appearing in 4:1, 17, has been understood as a sign that the supposed paraenetic, didactic, ethical half of the epistle (4:1–6:9) has begun. Yet the description of various "walks" began as early as 2:2, 10. "Walking" is an OT metaphor for one's entire life with (or without) God, faith and deeds, life as gift and life as conduct. Rhetorically considered, Paul is introducing here not a new concept but a contrast. If the "walk" the Ephesians were given by grace through faith in Christ is characterized by resurrected life, enjoying all the benefits of being seated at the right hand of God (2:1–10), then any movement back toward the old "walk" is a return to death. It is utterly unthinkable. In **4:17–5:2** Paul examines the old life on the basis of death and resurrection in Baptism and the Ten Commandments and appeals to the Gentile Ephesians not to return to the darkness and futility of their pagan past. In **5:3–14**, perhaps having in mind the outwardly magnificent worship of Artemis Ephesia, Paul characterizes their old pagan worship life as dark and evil, fellowship with demons. In a sort of chiastic contrast Paul responds with an exhortation to the even more magnificent worship of the true God (**5:15–6:9**). He begins with the formal, liturgical worship of the gathered congregation (**5:15–20**), but continues with a renewed examination of the Christian's life under the Ten Commandments (**5:21–6:9**). Here he discloses how, in contrast to the futility of the old pagan life, the Christian's everyday life in obedience to God's order is itself the worship of God. Even more remarkably, the Gospel itself is proclaimed by God's order when seen through Christian eyes. Husbands demonstrate Christ to their wives, who are the image of the church (5:21–33). Parents and masters act as the Lord himself in caring for their children and slaves (6:1–9). Thus, Paul's refutations of the abhorrent notion that the baptized could return to their old pagan life are crowned by a positive depiction of the glorious Christian existence on this earth.

Conclusion (ἐπίλογος, *Peroratio*)

The concluding section of a speech or letter consists of two parts: the effective "summing up" and the formal conclusion. In outlining Ephesians, which is a speech nested within the formal conventions of a letter, we shall restrict the term *peroratio* or "epilogue" to the first part of the conclusion (**6:10–17**). In judicial rhetoric the *peroratio* is the lawyer's grand speech at the end of the trial, summing up his argument in the hope of persuading the jury or judge to convict or acquit the accused. In general, the primary functions of this concluding section "are to recapitulate the points the speaker has made and to arouse the emotions of the audience toward action."[515] In calling the Ephesians to take up, stand firm in, and rejoice in the armor of God (6:10–17), Paul acts like a general exhorting and comforting his troops at the decisive moment of a great, victorious battle.[516] This is not the time to introduce new evidence or arguments. As the *proem* (1:3–14) anticipated the letter's contents, so the *peroratio* (6:10–17) sums up the letter—not in a mechanical way, but as a rousing rally cry, a final great message of Gospel. Like Moses exhorting the Israelites trapped with their backs to the Red Sea, "Do not fear, stand and see the salvation of YHWH, which he will work for you today" (Ex 14:13), and like Joshua comforting the people Israel before entering the promised land, "Be strong and courageous" (Josh 1:6–9, 18), so Paul points the Ephesians back to the victory Christ has won for them on the cross and has placed on them with the armor-like robe of Baptism. The impact of his repeated OT references in the *peroratio* would not have been lost on them: Jews and Gentiles together are heirs of the saving deeds and promises of God to his people Israel.

The letter's formal conclusion (**6:18–24**) follows epistolary conventions (see "Epistolary Outline," above in "Structure and Rhetoric").

---

[515] Kennedy, *New Testament Interpretation through Rhetorical Criticism*, 48.

[516] Best, *Ephesians*, 63: "Indeed the exhortation of 6.10–18 comes much closer to the peroration of a speech than anything normally found in a letter."

161

Rhetorical Outline

1:1–2	**Epistolary Salutation**
1:3–14	***Proem* (Prologue):** *Berakah* prayer, functioning as a *narratio* and including a *propositio* (1:9–10) • Baptismal images 1: election, predestination, "in Christ," sonship, inheritance, sealing
1:15–23	***Exordium*:** *Hodayah* prayer, including epistolary thanksgiving (1:15–16), *benevolentiae captatio* (1:15–18), and further *narratio* (1:19–23)
2:1–4:16	**Proofs:**

	2:1–10	"Made Alive Together in Christ" • Baptismal images 2: death, resurrection, ascension with Christ; salvation by grace; new creation
	2:11–22	"Reconciled in One Body through the Cross" • Baptismal images 3: Gentile/far off versus Israel/near; strangers versus citizens; old temple versus new spiritual temple
	3:1–13	"The Mystery of Paul's Apostolic Mandate: The Gospel of Christ for the Gentiles" (digression)
	3:14–21	"Intercession and Doxology: The Revelation of the Mystery Is for Their Strengthening and to God's Glory"
	4:1–16	"Creedal Unity in the Spirit: One Lord, One Faith, One Baptism" • Baptismal catechesis; the office of the ministry as a unifying gift of Christ

4:17–6:9	**Refutations:**

	4:17–5:2	"The Baptismal Walk: Clothed in Christ" • Baptismal images 4: death to the old sinful life and rising to life with Christ; putting off the old Adam and putting on Christ; repenting in accord with the Decalogue; forgiving one another
	5:3–14	"Once You Were Darkness, but Now You Are Light in the Lord" • Baptismal images 5: rejecting false worship and fellowship with darkness; Baptism as enlightenment
	5:15–21	"The Liturgy of the Spirit-Filled Baptized" • False worship is replaced by true worship

	5:21–6:9	"The Gospel in God's Order: The Bridegroom and the Bride" (5:21–33)
		"Order 'in the Lord': Parents/Children, Masters/Slaves" (6:1–9)
		• Baptismal images 6: Baptism reorders our relationships one to another in the likeness of our relationship to Christ
		a. Husband/wife (5:22–33)
		b. Parents/children (6:1–4)
		c. Masters/slaves (6:5–9)
6:10–17	*Peroratio* (**Epilogue**): "The Armor of God: Baptismally Enclosed in Christ"	
	• Baptismal images 7: the baptismal robe is a suit of armor which clothes the Christian with the victorious Christ	
6:18–24	**Epistolary Conclusion:** "Fellowship in Prayer, Commendation, and Blessing"	
	a. Prayer for Paul (6:18–20)	
	b. Commendation of the letter bearer (6:21–22)	
	c. Final greetings and blessing (6:23–24)	

The "audience hall" (Acts 25:23) at Herod's palace and praetorium at Caesarea Maritima where the imprisoned Paul was interviewed by Agrippa and Festus.

Photo: © 2015 Thomas M. Winger.

Ephesians 1:1–23

Introduction

Ephesians 1:1–2
Epistolary Salutation

Translation

1 [1]Paul, apostle of Christ Jesus through the will of God,
   to the saints and faithful ones in Christ Jesus who are in Ephesus:
      [2]Grace to you and peace
         from God our Father
         and the Lord Jesus Christ.

Textual Notes

1:1 Παῦλος ἀπόστολος—"Apostle" means "one who is sent." In pre-Christian usage the noun ἀπόστολος usually refers to a naval expedition (the ships or their commander).[1] Only in two rare occurrences (Herodotus, *Histories*, 1:21; 5:38) does it refer to an authorized person dispatched for a specific purpose: "ambassador, delegate, or messenger." In diplomatic or administrative contexts, the normal vocabulary would be ἄγγελος, κῆρυξ, or πρεσβευτής,[2] though verbal forms of ἀποστέλλω such as ὁ ἀπεσταλμένος ("the sent one") were also used. Christians thus took up a rare meaning of the noun ἀπόστολος as their *terminus technicus*, probably following Christ himself (if he was speaking Greek in Lk 6:13). To a Jewish audience it would have resonated with the rabbinic institution of the שָׁלִיחַ or שָׁלוּחַ, "sent one": "the one sent by a man is as the man himself."[3] The Sanhedrin designated שְׁלוּחִים to carry their regulatory decrees to the Diaspora; they were usually set apart for the task by the laying on of hands. Their going forth in pairs parallels the sending of the seventy[-two] (Lk 10:1) and Saul and Barnabas (Acts

---

[1] LSJM, s.v ἀπόστολος; Karl Heinrich Rengstorf, "ἀπόστολος," *TDNT* 1:407. See also C. G. Kruse, "Apostle," in *Dictionary of Jesus and the Gospels* (ed. Joel B. Green, Scot McKnight, and I. Howard Marshall; Downers Grove, Ill.: InterVarsity, 1992), 27.

[2] Cf. Paul's use of the verb πρεσβεύω in 2 Cor 5:20 and Eph 6:20.

[3] Mishnah, *Berakoth*, 5:5; *Mekilta*, 12:4 (5a); 12:6 (7a); Talmud, *Kiddushin*, 41a; *Ḥagigah*, 10b; *Nazir*, 12b; *Baba Meẓiʿa*, 96a; *Menahoth*, 93b. Such a delegate could carry out legal transactions as significant as betrothal and divorce. ἀπόστολος appears as a translation of שָׁלוּחַ in the Alexandrian LXX text of 3 Kgdms 14:6 (MT/ET 1 Ki 14:6), where שָׁלוּחַ refers to a prophet sent from God with a message. Yet ἀπόστολος remained a rare term even among Hellenistic Jews.

The validity of using rabbinic materials to interpret the NT has been taken for granted since the late Middle Ages. In the latter half of the twentieth century, voluminous "form-critical" work by Jacob Neusner, in particular, has cast doubt on this process, suggesting that many rabbinic writings represent the thinking of post–AD 70 Pharisaism. Certainly the Mishnah was compiled ca. AD 180–220, at a time when the destruction of Jerusalem and the dispersal of its scholars were compelling them to put the oral tradition into writing. Yet the contents of the Mishnah (in contrast to the rest of the later Talmud) describe a Judaism with an intact temple ritual, thus depicting the same religious scene that obtained in the NT era. For the present author, therefore, rabbinic parallels retain their relevance. The new series edited by David Instone-Brewer, *Traditions of the Rabbis from the Era of the New Testament* (Grand Rapids: Eerdmans, 2004–), examines the dating of each section of the Mishnah in turn.

13:2–3).[4] Some rabbis identified four great prophets as God's שְׁלוּחִים: Moses, Elijah, Elisha, and Ezekiel, for they did what only God could do (raising the dead, bringing rain, etc.).[5] The NT recognizes Christ as the pinnacle of this tradition, the Great Prophet (Jn 6:14; 7:40), "the Apostle and High Priest of our confession" (Heb 3:1), God's ultimate Ambassador (Jn 17:18; 20:21), who carries his Father's authority (Mt 28:18) and does what only God can do (Mt 9:8).

By appealing to this office, Paul connects himself through Christ to God the Father. All of Paul's letters except Philippians, 1 and 2 Thessalonians, and Philemon begin with an assertion of his apostleship. The precise six-word phrase ἀπόστολος Χριστοῦ Ἰησοῦ διὰ θελήματος θεοῦ is found also in 1 Cor 1:1; 2 Cor 1:1; Col 1:1; and 2 Tim 1:1. Paul writes not independently, but as an authorized representative of Christ himself, commissioned and sent by him (Jn 20:21; Acts 26:15–18), to speak on his behalf (Lk 10:16) as his ambassador (2 Cor 5:20). By designating himself "apostle," Paul also includes himself in what his letter will teach about that office: the apostles are the foundation of the church (Eph 2:20), recipients of divine revelation through the Holy Spirit (3:5), and gifts to the church from the ascended Christ (4:11). "The apostles preached the Gospel to us from the Lord Jesus Christ; Jesus Christ was sent out from God. Christ therefore is from God, and the apostles are from Christ. Therefore both originated in good order from the will of God."[6]

Χριστοῦ Ἰησοῦ—While solid early and diverse manuscript evidence supports this reading, the majority of manuscripts invert the order of "Christ Jesus" to read "Jesus Christ." Both forms are used frequently in the NT. It is often thought that "Christ Jesus" is the more primitive word order, reflecting the understanding of "Christ" as a title meaning "the Messiah, Anointed One" rather than as a second name. Certainly "Christ" should be understood as a title, but the alternation with Ἰησοῦ Χριστοῦ in 1:2 suggests the word order may be merely a matter of stylistic variation. By qualifying "apostle" with "of Christ Jesus,"[7] Paul stresses the immediate character of his call from the Lord and appeals to the source of authority for what he writes.

διὰ θελήματος θεοῦ—"Through the will of God": the divine origin of Paul's call to the office of apostle is asserted in precisely these words also in the opening of 1 and 2 Corinthians, Colossians, and 2 Timothy. They summarize the lengthier description of Gal 1:1: "not from men nor through men, but through Jesus Christ and God the Father,

---

[4] Eastern Orthodoxy traditionally refers to the "Seventy Apostles," going so far as to name later figures such as Timothy as one of their number.

[5] See J. Duncan M. Derrett, *Law in the New Testament* (London: Darton, Longman & Todd, 1970), 52–55; also Rengstorf, "ἀπόστολος," *TDNT* 1:414–20.

[6] *1 Clement*, 42:1–2.

[7] It is possible that the phrase could be translated as "the apostle of Christ Jesus," as if Paul is distinctive among the apostles or distinguished from the original twelve. Many church fathers refer to Paul in this manner as "the apostle" par excellence. Since "Christ Jesus" is definite, "apostle," even without the article, may be interpreted likewise. See Wallace, *Greek Grammar*, 250: "The general rule (discussed earlier in this chapter [pp. 239–40]) is that *both* the head noun and the genitive noun either have the article or lack the article (known as Apollonius' Canon). … The corollary to this rule (Apollonius' Corollary) … is that *when both nouns are anarthrous, both will usually have the same semantic force*."

who raised him from the dead." No man chooses to be an apostle, nor does the apostle pursue his own scheme. Rather, he acts and speaks always as God directs. This is the first of many references to the will, plan, and choice of God in Ephesians.[8]

τοῖς ἁγίοις τοῖς οὖσιν ἐν Ἐφέσῳ καὶ πιστοῖς ἐν Χριστῷ Ἰησοῦ—Paul's description of the addressees is difficult grammatically, particularly if read in a linear fashion. In this discussion we assume the presence of the contested words ἐν Ἐφέσῳ, "in Ephesus."[9] The articular participle τοῖς οὖσιν, "the ones being/those who are," appears to hang a twofold modification onto τοῖς ἁγίοις, "to the saints," as if one should translate "to the saints who are (1) in Ephesus and (2) faithful in Christ Jesus." One might visualize this as follows:

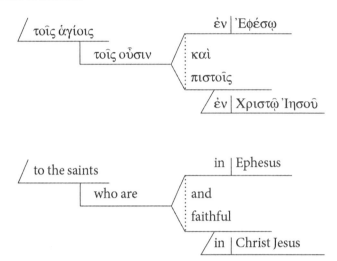

The diagram exposes a flaw in this analysis: the two prepositional phrases with ἐν, "in Ephesus" and "in Christ Jesus," are not parallel; rather it is πιστοῖς, "faithful (ones)," that stands in grammatical parallelism to "in Ephesus." A more logical analysis would place ἁγίοις, "saints," and πιστοῖς, "faithful (ones)," into parallel as follows:[10]

---

[8] The noun θέλημα, referring to the "will" of God or the Lord, occurs in 1:1, 5, 9, 11; 5:17; 6:6 (and in reference to the "will" of the flesh in 2:3). These six Ephesian instances of θέλημα referring to the divine "will" are more than in any other NT book except John (eleven instances, eight of which refer to the will of God or Christ).

[9] See "The Textual Variant 'in Ephesus' in Ephesians 1:1" in "Addressees" in the introduction. If these two words are omitted, as in some manuscripts, the reading becomes grammatically well-nigh impossible, according to BDF, § 413 (3): "The ptcp. ὤν can only be used when there are other adjuncts to the predicate: A[cts] 28:17 τοὺς ὄντας τῶν Ἰουδαίων πρώτους ... ; otherwise it must be omitted ... ; therefore E[ph] 1:1 τοῖς ἁγίοις οὖσιν καὶ πιστοῖς (𝔓[46]; D adds ἐν Ἐφέσῳ which satisfies the rule) is impossible (ὁ ὤν 'the existing one or thing' is different § 474(5c))."

[10] This second diagram follows Randy A. Leedy, as provided in BibleWorks 8.

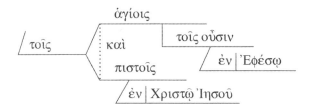

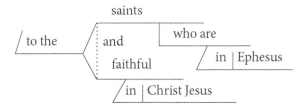

This analysis, nevertheless, continues to assume a parallelism between the two prepositional phrases with ἐν, "in," associating each phrase with just one adjective, as if one should translate "to the (1) saints who are in Ephesus and (2) [to the] faithful in Christ Jesus." This might be misinterpreted as if number 1 and number 2 were two different groups being addressed. Furthermore, it fails to explain the presence of the articular participle τοῖς οὖσιν, "the ones being/those who are," in just one half of the pair (only in number 1).

The solution may be found by comparing this verse to the following Pauline parallels:

τοῖς ἐν Κολοσσαῖς ἁγίοις καὶ πιστοῖς ἀδελφοῖς ἐν Χριστῷ

to the in-Colossae saints and faithful brothers in Christ (Col 1:2)

πᾶσιν τοῖς ἁγίοις ἐν Χριστῷ Ἰησοῦ τοῖς οὖσιν ἐν Φιλίπποις

to all the saints in Christ Jesus who are in Philippi (Phil 1:1)

πᾶσιν τοῖς οὖσιν ἐν Ῥώμῃ ἀγαπητοῖς θεοῦ, κλητοῖς ἁγίοις

to all those who are in Rome who are beloved of God, called as saints (Rom 1:7)

τῇ ἐκκλησίᾳ τοῦ θεοῦ τῇ οὔσῃ ἐν Κορίνθῳ σὺν τοῖς ἁγίοις πᾶσιν τοῖς οὖσιν ἐν ὅλῃ τῇ Ἀχαΐᾳ

to the church of God which is in Corinth, with all the saints who are in the whole of Achaia (2 Cor 1:1)

From this varied Pauline usage, two conclusions can be drawn: (1) Paul often uses participial phrases like τοῖς οὖσιν ἐν, "to those who are in," to indicate the *location* of the church;[11] and (2) he tends to mix together the *geographical* and the *spiritual* location of his addressees, heaping up adjectives and adjectival phrases without clear

---

[11] This is one of the chief reasons to retain the words "in Ephesus" in the text, despite their omission in some early manuscripts. See "The Textual Variant 'in Ephesus' in Ephesians 1:1" in "Addressees" in the introduction. Ignatius addresses his epistles with the same formula: e.g.,

differentiation. Thus, it is likely that in Eph 1:1 "saints/holy (ones)" and "faithful (ones)" are parallel descriptions of the Ephesian Christians and that *both prepositional phrases with "in" modify the whole unit* (as in Col 1:2). Thus, these "saints and faithful ones" are "in Christ" spiritually and "in Ephesus" physically. Their earthly location is described (parenthetically) with the participial phrase τοῖς οὖσιν ἐν Ἐφέσῳ, "those who are in Ephesus." A slight modification of the diagram puts this phrase into its proper location:

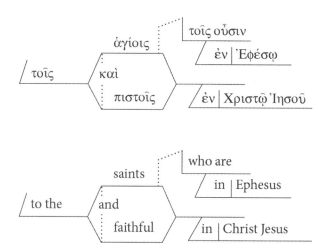

Thus, we might interpret Paul's meaning as this: "to the saints (the ones who are in Ephesus) and faithful ones in Christ Jesus." The phrase "in Christ Jesus" is therefore to be attached to *both* substantival adjectives, "saints/holy (ones)" and "faithful (ones)." This means, furthermore, that we ought *not* translate πιστοῖς ἐν Χριστῷ Ἰησοῦ as "those *who believe in* Christ Jesus," but rather as "faithful ones [faith-full ones] *who are in* Christ Jesus."[12] The terms "saints" and "faithful ones" are not to be separated,[13]

τῇ ἐκκλησίᾳ ... τῇ οὔσῃ ἐν Ἐφέσῳ, "to the church ... which is in Ephesus" (*To the Ephesians*, Preface).

[12] The personal object of πιστεύω, "to believe," is commonly expressed by the simple dative or εἰς with the accusative. BDAG, s.v. πιστεύω, 2 a ε, argues that the use of ἐν to indicate the object of πιστεύω ("*believe in* someone") is "questionable in our lit[erature]" (though documented in the LXX, e.g., Ps 77:22 [MT/ET 78:22]); see also Moule, *Idiom Book*, 80–81. This supports our judgment that ἐν Χριστῷ Ἰησοῦ, "in Christ Jesus" (Eph 1:1), is not the grammatical object of πιστοῖς, "faithful ones/believers," but their spiritual location: "saints and faithful ones/believers, [who are] in Christ" (see the fifth textual note on 1:3). The interpretation "saints in Christ" is supported by parallels: πᾶσιν τοῖς ἁγίοις ἐν Χριστῷ Ἰησοῦ τοῖς οὖσιν ἐν Φιλίπποις, "to all the saints in Christ Jesus who are in Philippi" (Phil 1:1); ἀσπάσασθε πάντα ἅγιον ἐν Χριστῷ Ἰησοῦ, "greet every saint in Christ Jesus" (Phil 4:21). Likewise, the interpretation of Eph 1:1 as "faithful people who are in Christ" (rather than "people who believe in Christ") is supported by Col 1:2: τοῖς ἐν Κολοσσαῖς ἁγίοις καὶ πιστοῖς ἀδελφοῖς ἐν Χριστῷ, "to the in-Colossae saints and faithful brothers in Christ." See also the fifth textual note on Eph 1:15.

[13] Kirby, *Ephesians: Baptism and Pentecost*, 170, refers them to two different groups: "the saints" being Jewish Christians, and "the faithful ones" being Gentile Christians. This is far-fetched and contradicts the letter's central message of their unity in Christ.

but describe all Christians in the Ephesian church according to two key characteristics: holiness and faith. Likewise, the phrases "in Ephesus" and "in Christ" are, ironically, more parallel than one might have expected: both describe the Christians' location (see the textual note on "in Christ" in 1:3).

"The saints" (τοῖς ἁγίοις) are "the holy ones." Only 2 Cor 1:1; Phil 1:1; and Col 1:2 share the use of this title in the address (cf. Rom 1:7; 1 Cor 1:2). It is a particularly suitable way to open Ephesians, which proceeds to use the term ἅγιος more frequently (for its size) than any other NT book.[14] ἅγιος refers to the holiness given by the Holy Spirit in Holy Baptism (1 Cor 6:11; Eph 5:26) and located "in Christ Jesus" (see the commentary on Eph 1:3). This usage is rooted in the OT, which regularly calls the people Israel together into a "holy assembly";[15] the LXX regularly calls them ἅγιοι, "saints," in the context of worship.[16] Paul's introductory application of the term to *Gentile* Ephesians anticipates the epistle's argument that Jew and Gentile are one in Christ (cf. 2:19). As in the OT God alone makes his people holy,[17] so also in the NT it is God alone who sanctifies through Christ, who is our sanctification.[18] The language is primarily cultic, not ethical, marking status before God, not people (see the fourth textual note on 1:4). Because this holiness is located in Christ, it may be hidden in the life of believers; but it remains a reality of their new identity to which Paul may continually direct them. For a further discussion of "saints," see the third textual note on 2:19.

By adding the words καὶ πιστοῖς, Paul indicates that this baptismal holiness is never disconnected from faith,[19] which continuously trusts in the Christ into whom the Christian has been baptized. When translating πιστός as "faithful" (as above)— one might say "faith-full"—it is this "saving faith" that is intended, not "faithfulness" in the sense of being obedient, trustworthy, or reliable.[20] Thus, Christ as the object of faith, while not the best grammatical solution to the syntax of this passage,[21] is certainly included in its meaning.

The difficult *textual problem* affecting the addressees has been discussed fully in the introduction.[22] The earliest manuscript witness, 𝔓[46], has the grammatically difficult reading τοῖς ἁγίοις οὖσιν καὶ πιστοῖς, "to the saints being and/also faithful," omitting the location of the addressees, ἐν Ἐφέσῳ, "in Ephesus." These words are also omitted

---

[14] In Ephesians ἅγιος, employed either as a substantive, "saint," or an adjective, "holy," appears fifteen times (1:1, 4, 13, 15, 18; 2:19, 21; 3:5, 8, 18; 4:12, 30; 5:3, 27; 6:18).

[15] E.g., Ex 12:16; Leviticus 23; Numbers 28–29.

[16] E.g., Lev 19:2; 20:7, 26; Num 16:3; Ps 33:10 (MT 34:10; ET 34:9); Is 4:3; Dan 7:18–27; Tobit 8:15.

[17] Ex 31:13; Lev 20:8; 21:8, 23; 22:9, 16, 32; Ezek 20:12.

[18] E.g., Jn 17:17; 1 Cor 1:2, 30; 6:11; 1 Thess 4:3; 5:23. See also Kleinig, "Sharing in God's Holiness." Schlier, *Epheser*, 33: "It is a cultic, sacramental, and pneumatic [Spiritual] holiness, which belongs to the Christian as a baptized member of the holy people and of the holy festal gathering of the new Israel."

[19] Mt 28:19–20; Mk 16:16; Acts 8:12; 16:31–34; 18:8; 19:4; Col 1:22–23.

[20] See Lincoln, *Ephesians*, 6, who cites 2 Cor 6:15; Gal 3:9; 1 Tim 4:10, 12; 5:16; 6:2; Titus 1:6.

[21] See the fourth textual note on Eph 1:1.

[22] See "The Textual Variant 'in Ephesus' in Ephesians 1:1" in "Addressees" in the introduction.

by the uncorrected manuscripts of ℵ and B, but are included by correctors and most later manuscripts. By traditional criteria, the "oldest and best" reading would favor the omission of the addressees. However, even on so-called "external evidence," the manuscript witness is so evenly split as to be indecisive. The omission in some early manuscripts does not necessarily cast doubt on the original addressees of the epistle and is capable of a variety of explanations. Most likely these words were omitted for liturgical use; later manuscripts may have omitted the addressees under the influence of lectionary practice.[23] This commentary proceeds on the assumption that the letter was indeed originally written "to the saints who are in Ephesus."

1:2 χάρις ὑμῖν καὶ εἰρήνη—Ten of Paul's thirteen letters greet the saints with these exact words: "grace to you and peace." The three pastoral epistles differ only slightly. The greeting has become a fixed formula in the Christian epistle. Probably Paul himself established the pattern. 1 and 2 Peter and Revelation adopt it exactly.[24]

"Grace" (χάρις) is a pious wordplay on the common greeting χαῖρε, χαίρετε, or χαίρειν, "joyful greetings."[25] Perhaps Paul developed this greeting in reflection upon Gabriel's words to Mary as they had been reported to his colleague Luke: χαῖρε, κεχαριτωμένη, "greetings, O recipient of grace" (Lk 1:28; cf. Eph 1:6). In the LXX χάρις most often translates חֵן, the undeserved "grace, favor" shown by God (e.g., Gen 6:8; Zech 12:10) to which his people appealed (e.g., Gen 18:3; Ex 33:12–17).[26] The cognate verb חָנַן, "to be gracious," denotes the undeserved favor shown by a superior (particularly God) to an inferior (Ex 33:19; Num 6:25; Ps 4:2 [ET 4:1]; Is 30:18) and is closely related to the noun חֶסֶד, "loving-kindness" (Ex 34:6–7). While this verb and noun are commonly translated with ἐλεέω, "to show mercy," and ἔλεος, "mercy," in the LXX, χάρις begins to predominate in Jewish usage by the NT era, which may explain Paul's preference for the term. χάρις, "grace," and ἔλεος, "mercy," are very closely related ideas.[27] Like חֶסֶד, "loving-kindness" (Ps 89:29 [ET 89:28]; Is 54:8–10), χάρις describes God's love and mercy shown to his people, particularly in accordance with

---

[23] See "Generalization/Lectionary Theory" in "Addressees" in the introduction.

[24] Peter adds the optative verb πληθυνθείη, "may ... be multiplied," in his two epistles (1 Pet 1:2; 2 Pet 1:2), as does Jude (Jude 2). Jude, however, goes his own way with "mercy, peace, and love": ἔλεος ὑμῖν καὶ εἰρήνη καὶ ἀγάπη πληθυνθείη. See Giese, *2 Peter and Jude*, 240–42, for a discussion of this unique greeting.

[25] 1 Macc 10:18, 25 and passim in the Apocrypha; Lk 1:28; Acts 15:23; 23:26; James 1:1. In Is 48:22 and 57:21, χαίρειν translates שָׁלוֹם. Etymologically, χάρις is related to χαίρω as that which creates "joy" (e.g., Acts 11:23). The infinitive χαίρειν is best explained as the relic of an oral delivery formula: "John tells [λέγει] Mary to rejoice [χαίρειν]" (to cite a hypothetical example). Cf. 2 Jn 10–11. See Klauck, *Ancient Letters and the New Testament*, 18.

[26] While the secular Greek meaning of χάρις as "gracefulness, charm" is sometimes found in the LXX (e.g., Deut 24:1), the evidence does not support the sweeping conclusion of *TDNT*: "χάρις is never a theological word in the LXX" (Walther Zimmerli and Hans Conzelmann, "χαίρω κτλ.," *TDNT* 9:389).

[27] See Zimmerli and Conzelmann, "χαίρω κτλ.," *TDNT* 9:376–99; Lincoln, *Ephesians*, 102–3. In the later Greek translation of Symmachus, χάρις begins to take over from ἔλεος in translating חֶסֶד.

his covenant promises.[28] To apply God's grace to the Gentiles is to incorporate them into the true Israel.

"Peace" (εἰρήνη) reflects the traditional Hebrew greeting שָׁלוֹם, meaning wellness in body and soul (e.g., Ex 18:7; 1 Sam 25:5–6). Such peace was also intimately connected with God's covenant promises.[29] "Peace to you be multiplied" is an established Semitic greeting at the beginning of letters.[30] In the NT εἰρήνη ὑμῖν, "peace to you," is the resurrected Lord's greeting (Lk 24:36; Jn 20:19, 21, 26). In this letter Paul brings Christ's reconciling peace (Eph 2:14–16) to bear on a church that is suffering division. "Grace to you and peace" has the rhythm and dignity of a liturgical greeting, suitable to a congregation assembled for worship.[31] As liturgical language is often compact, no verb is provided in the original text; the verb one supplies should not imply that it is just a wish or even a prayer. When an apostle, the Lord's authorized representative, gives the Lord's grace and peace, one can be confident that his words do what they say (Lk 10:5–6, 16), delivering the gifts to which faith clings. This is the nature of a divine blessing (Num 6:24–26). Through his apostle, Christ himself preaches peace to the nations (Eph 2:17).

ἀπὸ θεοῦ πατρὸς ἡμῶν καὶ κυρίου Ἰησοῦ Χριστοῦ—It is important to define precisely the source of the grace and peace, for "the giver determines the contents and value of the gift."[32] Although "God" could be attached to both "our Father" and "Jesus Christ" ("God, that is, our Father and … Jesus Christ"), it is more likely that "God" qualifies "Father," and "Lord" qualifies "Jesus Christ" in parallel, which is in accord with common NT usage (see the textual note on 4:5). Nonetheless, the single preposition ἀπό, "from," unites the two Persons as one source of blessing. Calling God *our Father* (rather than Christ's Father) is an implicit plea for unity within a potentially divided family (cf. 4:6). κύριος, "Lord," has two implications. First, it should be understood in accord with LXX usage, where it is the common translation of the divine name יהוה, "YHWH," normally glossed in rabbinic Judaism as אֲדֹנָי, "the Lord." Thus, calling Jesus κύριος, "Lord" (e.g., Rom 10:9; 1 Cor 12:3), is asserting his divinity by identifying him with YHWH, the God of the OT (see the textual note on Eph 4:5). Second, as

---

[28] "חֶסֶד always contains an element of spontaneous freedom in the demonstration of goodness or in kindly conduct, and it cannot be reduced to what is owed or to a duty. On the other hand, the polemic [of the debate] constantly ignores something that is plain in the texts, namely, that the nature of חֶסֶד is conduct in relation, and in demonstration of this relation [i.e., covenant promise]" (Zimmerli and Conzelmann, "χαίρω κτλ.," *TDNT* 9:382).

[29] See the "covenant of peace" (Num 25:12; Is 54:10; Ezek 34:25; 37:26; Sirach 45:24) to be established by the Suffering Servant (Isaiah), the new Shepherd David (Ezekiel). See Lessing, *Isaiah 40–55*, 643; and Hummel, *Ezekiel 21–48*, 1003–7, 1092–96. In Num 25:12 this covenant is connected with the mediating work of the Aaronic priesthood, whose privilege it was to pronounce the peace (Num 6:24–26).

[30] E.g., Dan 3:31 (ET 4:1). This Semitic greeting is translated into Greek as εἰρήνη ὑμῖν πληθυνθείη in Dan 4:37c (LXX); 4:1 (θ; MT 3:31); 6:26 (θ; ET 6:25). Cf. 1 Pet 1:2; 2 Pet 1:2; Jude 2.

[31] As Barth, *Ephesians*, 1:71, suggests. Also Schlier, *Epheser*, 34: "It has probably been patterned after the blessing in the Divine Service." Parallel blessings occur at the end of most epistles; after the reading of the epistle, the liturgy would continue.

[32] Barth, *Ephesians*, 1:71. Cf. Jn 14:27: "my peace I give to you; not as the world gives do I give to you."

Ambrosiaster comments: "He calls Christ Lord because he redeems us, offering himself on our behalf."[33] Luther interprets "Lord" similarly in explaining the Second Article in the Small Catechism: Christ became our Lord when he purchased us out of slavery with the price of his blood (SC 2:4).

Commentary

Structure and Rhetoric: The Epistolary Salutation

"Structure and Rhetoric" in the introduction unpacked the traditional Hellenistic letter form, the various genres available in the handbooks of the day, and the way in which Paul adapted the form to the needs of an apostolic writer. It was suggested there that a rhetorical analysis of the content of the epistle is more productive than a formal analysis of the address and conclusion. Here we consider the *theological* function of the address.

The salutation or epistolary address—which comes on the inside of the scroll, not the outside!—is more than just delivery instructions. It opens a dialogue between the author and the addressee on the basis of a conventional fiction that through the letter they are present to each other personally.[34] We may analyze the epistolary address and the rest of the letter's components in order to discern Paul's genre of letter writing, his Christian epistolary rhetoric, but categorizing it is not the same as understanding it. The function of the address is bound up, first, with Paul's apostolic and pastoral office (see "Divine Apostleship" below). Paul writes as an extension of his preaching.[35] The letter proclaims Law and Gospel to the saints in the same way Paul would if he were there. It is a *Hirtenbrief*, "pastoral letter."[36] This is not a catholic epistle, with a general audience; nor is it anonymous. With its first word, "Paul," the letter names a real man and invites the reader to bring all that he knows about Paul to bear on the text. This Paul has a relationship with these people that goes back to his second and third missionary journeys and to the nearly three-year pastorate he exercised in Ephesus. This places Paul into a relationship with the Ephesian church unlike any other (with the possible exception of the church in Corinth).[37]

This relationship perhaps explains why Paul names no coauthor, while he does in all other epistles save Romans and the Pastorals. Romans is unique in the corpus as a lengthy apology for what Paul calls "my Gospel" (Rom 2:16;

---

[33] Ambrosiaster, *Ephesians*, 1:2 (ACCS 8:108).

[34] See Klauck, *Ancient Letters and the New Testament*, 189–93. Turpilius described letters as "the only means of making absent people present" (Frag. 215 Rychlewska, in Jerome, Letter 8:1 [quoted in Klauck, 191]). Cicero defines a letter as "the communion of friends in absence" (*Philippics*, 2:4.7 [quoted in Klauck, 192]). And Libanius explains: "One will speak in it as though one were in the company of the absent person" (*Epistolary Styles*, 2 [quoted in Klauck, 193]).

[35] See "Orality and the Interpretation of the Epistles: A Brief Introduction" in the introduction.

[36] Schlier, *Epheser*, 29.

[37] See "Paul and Ephesus in Acts" in "The City of Ephesus and Paul's Relationship to It" in the introduction.

16:25), a circumstance of writing that precludes sharing authorship with another (despite the fact that Timothy was with him at the time, Rom 16:21). Some have suggested that Ephesians lacks a coauthor because it is a similarly individual, theological monument—but such a view makes the most sense when the epistle is viewed as a circular letter. By contending that the letter was indeed written to Ephesus, this commentary eschews such an impersonal interpretation of its purpose.[38] The Pastorals are partly personal letters, issuing from Paul's fatherly relationship with Timothy and Titus, which cannot be shared. Ephesians might be said to carry that relationship to an ecclesiastical level. No other man can share the pastoral fatherhood that characterizes Paul's relationship with the Ephesian church. Colossians, twin to Ephesians in its origin and content, names Timothy as coauthor (Col 1:1), but Paul did not have the same lengthy pastoral relationship with Colossae.[39]

When Paul begins the letter with the familiar pastoral greeting "grace to you and peace" (Eph 1:2), he has stepped into the pulpit among them. Luther memorably explains this phrase as embracing the entire Christian Gospel:

> Grace and peace—these two words embrace the whole of Christianity. Grace forgives sin, and peace stills the conscience. The two devils who plague us are sin and conscience, the power of the Law and the sting of sin (1 Cor. 15:56). But Christ has conquered these two monsters and trodden them underfoot, both in this age and in the age to come. The world does not know this; therefore it cannot teach anything sure about how to overcome sin, conscience, and death. Only Christians have this kind of teaching and are equipped and armed with it, so that they can overcome sin, despair, and eternal death. It is a teaching that is given only by God; it does not proceed from free will, nor was it invented by human reason or wisdom.

> These two words, "grace" and "peace," contain a summary of all of Christianity. Grace contains the forgiveness of sins, a joyful peace, and a quiet conscience.

---

[38] See "Addressees" in the introduction. Nor would we suggest that Romans is impersonal or disconnected from the circumstances of the Roman church; but Paul cannot be said to have had a personal pastoral relationship with the saints in Rome before writing his epistle.

[39] One might also postulate that Timothy was with Paul when he wrote Colossians, but absent when he wrote Ephesians. "According to 2 Timothy, Paul at some earlier point had sent Timothy to work in Troas (2 Tim. 4:13), and it is quite possible that Ephesians was composed somewhat later than Colossians, when Timothy was no longer with Paul in Caesarea" (Reicke, *Re-examining Paul's Letters*, 80). When Tychicus is commended as letter carrier (Eph 6:21–22; Col 4:7–8), Timothy is not mentioned. This view, plausible as it is, requires one to accept the writing sequence of Colossians first and then Ephesians (which is possible) and implies that Timothy's role as coauthor of Colossians consisted in little more than his presence with Paul during its writing—something that could have been conveyed well enough in the closing greetings rather than in the opening verse, Col 1:1. Colossians and Ephesians are so similar that it is difficult to conceive of Timothy contributing materially to one but not the other. Yet if Timothy was with Paul when he wrote Ephesians, it is hard to imagine Paul leaving him completely unmentioned in this epistle, since Timothy had worked in Ephesus as Paul's delegate (1 Tim 1:3).

> But peace is impossible unless sin has first been forgiven, for the Law accuses and terrifies the conscience on account of sin.[40]

As the same words appear at the beginning of the Service of the Sacrament in many early Eastern rites, we are reminded also of the Paul who surely presided over the Lord's Supper among the Ephesians countless times.[41] The language of this greeting is repeated at the close of the epistle (6:23–24) according to Paul's custom, forming a liturgical *inclusio* around the writing. Where the epistolary close appears in its most developed form (e.g., 1 Cor 16:19–24),[42] it evokes the language of the Preface dialogue and the practices of dismissing the catechumens before the Supper and exchanging the kiss of peace among the communicants at the beginning of the sacramental rite,[43] suggesting that the epistle was being read in the context of the Divine Service.[44] Paul tailors his writing to this liturgical context (see also the *Berakah* prayer in 1:3–14). Through his words, though

---

[40] Luther, *Lectures on Galatians* (1535), AE 26:26.

[41] Although only one NT text speaks explicitly of Paul breaking bread, in a context that does not clearly identify it as a sacramental act (Acts 27:35), and although Paul avers that he did not perform many Baptisms (1 Cor 1:13–17), he does assert that he baptized (1 Cor 1:14), and there is every reason to imagine that he also presided at the Lord's Supper where there were properly baptized and catechized people to receive it. The Paul who delivered to the Corinthians the tradition of the Lord's Supper (1 Cor 11:23) surely did more than teach the words. This commentary perceives allusions to the Lord's Supper in 1:7; 4:4; 5:3–20, 29–31; 6:18–24 and a eucharistic quality to the prayers in 1:3–14; 3:14–21.

[42] See Robinson, "Traces of a Liturgical Sequence in 1 Cor. 16:20–24," and Winger, "Orality as the Key to Understanding Apostolic Proclamation in the Epistles," 212–17.

[43] Apart from direct biblical texts like the Lord's Prayer and the Words of Institution, the Preface dialogue is the oldest recorded portion of the Christian liturgy, found in Hippolytus' *Apostolic Tradition*, 4 (ca. AD 215). There is no way of knowing how early the practice of dismissing the catechumens before the Sacrament was established (it is frequently attested in such fourth-century fathers as Ambrose and Augustine). But the earliest complete description of the liturgy, from the mid second century AD, includes a strong statement of closed Communion: "This food we call Eucharist, of which no one is allowed to partake except one who believes that the things we teach are true, and has received the washing for forgiveness of sins and for rebirth, and who lives as Christ handed down to us" (Justin Martyr, *First Apology*, 66 [trans. Edward Rochie Hardy, LCC 1:286]). This is fully consistent with Paul's words, pronouncing a curse on those who do not love the Lord (1 Cor 16:22) and inviting those who do (Eph 6:24; see the commentary on this verse), a fellowship sealed by the "holy kiss" (Rom 16:16; 1 Cor 16:20; 2 Cor 13:12; 1 Thess 5:26; cf. 1 Pet 5:14: "the kiss of love"). Hippolytus, *Apostolic Tradition*, 19, records that the catechumens have prayers on their own at the end of their catechesis and are then dismissed (i.e., before the prayer of the church and the Lord's Supper). Following an account of their Baptism he writes: "Henceforth they will pray with the rest of the people, for they do not pray with the faithful before obtaining all this [i.e., Baptism]" (*Apostolic Tradition*, 21:25 [quoted in Cabié, *The Eucharist*, 69, n. 1]). Tertullian, *Prescription against Heretics*, 41, finds fault with the heretics for allowing the unbaptized to participate in the general prayer. See Cabié, *The Eucharist*, 69–70.

[44] Evidence for reading the epistles in the Divine Service is given in "The Mandate to Proclaim Scripture" and "The Liturgical Context of the New Testament Epistles," both in "Orality and the Interpretation of the Epistles: A Brief Introduction" in the introduction. See also Gibbs, *Matthew 1:1–11:1*, 5–12, which discusses the use of Matthew's Gospel in public worship.

absent in body, he takes his place in front of the gathered congregation and blesses the saints.[45]

This Pastor Paul suffers anxiety over the flock from which his travels and sufferings have separated him. He has "heard" of their faith in the Lord (1:15), which brings joy to his heart, and he daily gives thanks for them and intercedes for them in his prayers (1:16). Yet the letter evidences some concern over disunity in the Ephesian church (e.g., 4:1–3), which must have burdened his heart. Into this situation he speaks the Lord's blessed gift of "grace ... and peace" (1:2).

The identity of the author not only personalizes the letter but also lends it authority (see "Authorship" in the introduction). No one else can speak to the Ephesians Christians as Paul does. Yet this Paul is also an "apostle" (1:1)—which does not merely identify which "Paul" it is but also draws in the divine authority that stands behind the human author. Because he is an apostle of Christ, who comes from the Father, his words are the very Word of God. While Paul's name stands first in the address, names for God appear five times.[46] There is no parallel to this in Hellenistic epistolary forms; the Gospel has transformed such forms. This letter is not just from Paul, but from God. It is written not just to people, but to "saints" (1:1), those made holy by God and kept faithful in Christ Jesus.[47] Paul writes not just a wish for joy (χαίρειν, as in Acts 23:26), but conveys the gracious goodness of God as a gift. He speaks not just information, but Spirit-filled, transformative, divinely powerful Gospel words.

Divine Apostleship

Christianity ever suffers the derogatory charge of being derivative, that its chief teachings and institutions are borrowed from this or that pagan or secular source. What is secondary or inauthentic can more easily be dismissed. As we noted in "Authorship" in the introduction, theories that label Ephesians "Deutero-Pauline" are intended to distance the reader from the text's authority, thereby evading its supposedly "catholicizing tendencies."[48] Such theories

---

[45] "The blessing with grace and peace is always imparted to the saints by an authorized man, here by an 'apostle.' Like Aaron's Blessing (Num 6:24–26), it is not just a good wish or a kind offer of God or a man; rather it is God's deed" (Barth, *Ephesians*, 1:73). The Aaronic benediction (Num 6:24–26) could only be uttered by a priest ("Aaron and his sons," Num 6:23), to whom the Lord had given such authority to bless ("thus you will bless the people," Num 6:23). So also the Pauline speaking of peace is connected to his apostolic office.

[46] The five in Eph 1:1–2 are "Christ Jesus ... God ... Christ Jesus ... God our Father ... the Lord Jesus Christ."

[47] Schlier, *Epheser*, 34, says:

Those to whom the messenger of God and Christ writes are just a few inhabitants of some small Phrygian towns in the Lycus Valley, who can be found in this or that house church. And it is to them that it is said, they are "holy"! This they are "in Christ Jesus." They are indeed not only in Laodicea or Hierapolis or wherever, but their dwelling place and abode is now, since God has opened up this "dimension," also Christ Jesus.

[48] See the two sections titled "Incipient Catholicism," the first in "Arguments against Pauline Authorship" and the second in "Evaluation of the Case," both in "Authorship" in the introduction.

fly in the face of the testimony of the early fathers who decried pagan influence on the church and rejected the immorality inherent in identity theft and plagiarism.[49] The term "apostle" gives evidence of this wholly different mind-set among early Christians. For though ἀπόστολος had a recognizable meaning in Greek literature prior to the NT,[50] Christian usage was almost completely different. Whether our Lord, speaking Greek, chose the term, or the Evangelists chose it to translate his Aramaic/Hebrew original, it appears to have been chosen because it did not carry great secular freight and could be invested with unambiguous Christian meaning. In this process, form met function, for its meaning points to the divine origin of the Christian message, as the apostles were sent by God, not men.

As a noun derived from the verb ἀποστέλλω, "to send," ἀπόστολος, "apostle," designates one who has been "sent." While this activity is never absent, it would seem that the physical aspect of being sent to a distant location on behalf of someone else is secondary to the authorization implied by the act of sending. There is some evidence in the NT of a general use of ἀπόστολος ("apostle") for an emissary of a person or group on a temporary mission (2 Cor 8:23; Phil 2:25; possibly Jn 13:16). But the overwhelming number of the eighty NT occurrences imply divine sending. Paul's colleagues, inasmuch as they, too, carried on a divine mission (θεοῦ γάρ ἐσμεν συνεργοί, "for *we* are God's co-workers," 1 Cor 3:9), might be included among the ἀπόστολοι, "apostles" (Acts 14:4, 14; 1 Thess 2:6–7). The seventy[-two] sent out by the Lord (Lk 10:1) are not called ἀπόστολοι, "apostles," but they might well have been, inasmuch as Christ "sent them" (ἀπέστειλεν αὐτούς) to carry out a mission on his behalf and with his authority. While this mission has parallels in Jewish rabbinic sources (see the first textual note on 1:1) and OT background (2 Chr 17:7–9), Christ clearly did something new.

The apostles in the narrow sense of the term, embracing only the Twelve and Paul, derive their meaning, worth, and authority from the new messianic act of Jesus' own "being sent" from the Father. Just as Jesus is a prophetic spokesman from God of an entirely different order from the occasional prophets who had gone before (Heb 1:1–2), so Jesus is God's Apostle (Heb 3:1) in a unique and superlative sense. Not only does he speak for God, but he is also God himself and God's incarnate message (Jn 1:1, 14). He possesses "all authority" from God (Mt 28:18). Jesus testifies of heavenly things because he has come down from heaven (Jn 3:11–13). When Jesus chooses the Twelve, sending them as the Father sent him (Jn 20:21), the divine uniqueness of this apostleship appears. Unlike ordinary ambassadors, the apostles do not speak for a Lord who is absent, but who is present and who continues to work through them. As the apostles preach, teach, and baptize, Christ is with us always, to the close of the

---

[49] See particularly the recent study by Terry Wilder, *Pseudonymity, the New Testament, and Deception.*

[50] See the first textual note on 1:1.

age (Mt 28:19–20). When Paul appeals to the Corinthians, God is making his appeal through his apostle (2 Cor 5:20). Jesus' promise to the seventy[-two]—"he who hears you hears me" (Lk 10:16)—is particularly true of the apostles. Like Jesus, who speaks with his own authority (Mt 7:29; Lk 4:36), Paul speaks and expects to be obeyed (1 Cor 5:3–5).

When "apostle" is used in this narrow sense, the number is usually twelve. They are the NT counterpart of the twelve patriarchs with their twelve tribes, the figureheads of a new Israel (Mt 19:28); their names are written on the foundation walls of the heavenly Jerusalem (Rev 21:14). When Judas defected from the original number, the post-Easter church gathered to seek the Lord's gift of another to take his place and restore the number of the Twelve (Acts 1:15–26). From that account we learn the criteria for inclusion: "It is necessary [δεῖ], therefore, that of the men who have accompanied us during all the time that the Lord Jesus went in and out among us, beginning from the Baptism of John until the day when he [Jesus] was taken up from us—one of these men [must] become with us a witness [μάρτυρα] to his resurrection" (Acts 1:21–22). These words stress a legal aspect of apostleship that is often overlooked: it is not simply that an apostle must have been an eyewitness to the Lord's words, deeds, and particularly his resurrection, but that he must also be a "witness" (μάρτυρα), that is, he must "bear testimony" (μαρτυρέω) to his resurrection. In the NT, unlike loose contemporary Christian usage, "witness" language refers quite precisely to this legal testimony that only the apostles (supported by a small group of additional eyewitnesses) could officially give. Peter and John's final act when visiting the new mission in Samaria, for example, after granting the Holy Spirit to the newly baptized, was to give their testimony (διαμαρτυράμενοι) and speak the Word of the Lord (Acts 8:25), most likely a reference to the apostolic duty to deliver the legal, eyewitness account in support of the Gospel message. The same John opens his first epistle by affirming that the testimony continues where and when the written word of the apostles is proclaimed: "we testify [μαρτυροῦμεν] and we announce [ἀπαγγέλλομεν] to you" (1 Jn 1:2; both verbs are present tense).[51]

The foundational role of the apostles in Christ's mission is a central theme in the writings of Paul (who uses ἀπόστολος, "apostle," thirty-four times) and of Luke his companion (ἀπόστολος, "apostle," appears six times in Luke and twenty-eight times in Acts). Twice Paul places the apostles first in the list of Christ's gifts to the church (1 Cor 12:28; Eph 4:11), and in our epistle he places them with the prophets at the church's foundation (Eph 2:20; cf. 1 Cor 3:10). Their central role in Ephesians explains the present lengthy exposition. On the one hand, there is nothing unusual in Paul calling himself an "apostle" in the address of his epistle, as he does in nine of his thirteen letters. As an apostle carrying out his role as Christ's mouthpiece for the church of all time through his writings, Paul first lays down the authority by which he writes what he writes.

---

[51] See Winger, "From Apostolic Witness to Christian Confession: I John 4:1–6."

Nonetheless, there are particular reasons why he might wish to stress his office in this particular letter.

The chain of revelation from God the Father through the Son to his church through the mouth of the prophets and apostles is a major theme of Ephesians, particularly as it stands behind the revelation of the mystery of the inclusion of the Gentiles in the kingdom of God (Ephesians 3). The role of the pastoral office in maintaining the unity of the body of Christ in the Spirit begins with the apostolic message (Ephesians 4). Paul writes to the Ephesians like a father intervening in a dispute between his children, firmly but lovingly drawing them back together. Paul's role as apostle to the Gentiles is also the reason for his imprisonment (Eph 3:1). Could it be that the Ephesians felt pangs of guilt when they heard of his suffering? For not only was Paul persecuted by the Jews for his mission to Gentiles like the Ephesians, but this hostility also resulted in his arrest by the Romans after Jews *from Asia* stirred up a riot by the rumor that he had taken Trophimus—an uncircumcised *Ephesian*—into the temple's Court of the Jews (Acts 21:27–29).[52] In his Captivity Letters, Paul gently dismisses the suggestion that the Gentiles (or the Ephesians in particular) were responsible for his suffering; he suffered as an apostle of Christ (Eph 1:1), in conformity to Christ (Col 1:24), and at God's good pleasure (Eph 4:1).[53]

Paul's apostleship had been tested, indeed disputed, on more than one occasion. It seems that his enemies delighted in his unimpressive personal impact (2 Cor 10:10; 11:5–6). He seems even to have suffered personal, ongoing *Angst* and self-doubt as a result of his one-time persecution of the church, calling himself "the least of the apostles" (1 Cor 15:9; cf. Eph 3:8). He did not fulfill the apostolic requirements (Acts 1:21–22) in one obvious way, in that he had not been a disciple of Christ during his earthly ministry. In addition, he may have wondered how there might be room for a thirteenth apostle.[54] Nonetheless, Paul was able to rely on his direct call from Christ, an event that Luke recounts three times, perhaps in defense of Paul (Acts 9; 22:3–21; 26:9–20). On this basis the apostle defends himself to the Galatians (1:11–17), arguing that his apostleship is from God, not from men, and that he did not need to seek the approval of the earlier apostles (Gal 1:19; 2:6). It is therefore with great faith—not in himself, but in the Lord who would choose such a humble instrument—that Paul opens Ephesians with "Paul, apostle of Christ Jesus" (1:1).

---

[52] See "Paul's Trip to Jerusalem, Arrest, and Imprisonment (Acts 21:1–36)" in "The City of Ephesus and Paul's Relationship to It" in the introduction.

[53] See "Paul's Imprisonment" in "Location and Date of Writing" in the introduction.

[54] Some have argued that Paul should have replaced Judas as the twelfth apostle, though Peter was convinced that the Holy Spirit guided their choice of Matthias (Acts 1:15–26).

Proem: *Berakah* Prayer: Election and Unity in Christ

Translation

1 ³Blessed be the God and <u>Father</u> of our Lord <u>Jesus Christ</u>,
   who has blessed us with every blessing of the <u>Spirit</u> in the heavenly places <u>in Christ</u>,

(margin: Father)

⁴inasmuch as it was <u>in him</u> that he chose us for himself before the foundation of the world
   that we should be holy and without blemish before him,
      since in love ⁵he had predestined us to be adopted as his sons through Jesus Christ,
         according to the good pleasure of his will,
            ⁶*to the praise of his gracious glory*,
               which he has graciously shown us <u>in the Beloved</u>;

⁷<u>in whom</u> we have redemption through his blood,
   the forgiveness of trespasses,
      according to the richness of his grace, ⁸which he poured out upon us,
         as with all wisdom and understanding ⁹he has made known to us the mystery of his will,
            according to his good pleasure which he declared <u>in him</u>,
               ¹⁰to administer the fulfilling of the opportune moments,
                  that all things might be brought together <u>in Christ</u>,
                     the things in heaven and the things on earth <u>in him</u>;

(margin: Son)

¹¹<u>in whom</u> also we have been appointed—
   since we had been predestined according to the purpose of the One
      who accomplishes all things according to the plan of his will—
         ¹²that we should be *to the praise of his glory*,
            [we] who first hoped <u>in Christ</u>;

¹³<u>in whom</u> also you,
   having heard the Word of truth, the Gospel of your salvation,
      <u>in whom</u>, having also believed, you were sealed with the promised Holy Spirit,
         ¹⁴who is the deposit of our inheritance,
            for the redemption of [his] special possession,
               to the praise of his glory.

(margin: Holy Spirit)

Textual Notes

1:3 εὐλογητός—This is the common LXX equivalent of the Hebrew בָּרוּךְ, "blessed," which begins a traditional Jewish style of prayer known as a בְּרָכָה, *Berakah*. Such prayers usually begin בָּרוּךְ יהוה, "blessed is/be YHWH."[1] See the commentary. While

---

[1] For prayers with בָּרוּךְ, "blessed," see Gen 9:26; 14:20; 24:27; Ex 18:10; Ruth 4:14; 1 Sam 25:32, 39; 2 Sam 18:28; 22:47; 1 Ki 1:48; 5:21 (ET 5:7); 8:15, 56; 10:9; 1 Chr 16:36; 29:10;

no verb is provided by Paul, Koine and NT Greek usage suggest that verbal adjectives like εὐλογητός describe a state of affairs ("blessed *is*"), rather than a wish or necessity ("blessed *be*").[2] In the language of praise, however, which magnifies God by proclaiming who he is and what he has done and calls upon others to join in the act, this may be a distinction without a difference. "We best bring out its religious significance along the lines of Luther that God is praised in Himself but that we pray here that He may be praised among us."[3] In the NT εὐλογητός is used exclusively of God.[4] μακάριος is usually used for the "blessed" state given by God to people (used, e.g., in psalms and beatitudes).

ὁ θεὸς καὶ πατὴρ τοῦ κυρίου ἡμῶν Ἰησοῦ Χριστοῦ—This form of address, "the God and Father of our Lord Jesus Christ," is common enough in NT prayers that we can assume it had become a fixed liturgical expression.[5] With the addition of "our Lord Jesus Christ," this *Berakah* prayer confesses something beyond its Jewish roots. It is common NT practice to pray to the Father through Jesus Christ as Mediator,[6] as Jesus himself taught us to pray, "Our Father" (Mt 6:9; cf. Lk 11:2). Grammatically, both "God" and "Father" are modified by "of our Lord Jesus Christ." Paul can both confess Jesus' divinity (see the second textual note on 1:2) and speak of the Father as Jesus' God (1:17). Christ himself, as true man, addressed or described the Father as "my God."[7] If we are "in Christ," then he is our God and Father also.

ὁ εὐλογήσας ἡμᾶς ἐν πάσῃ εὐλογίᾳ πνευματικῇ—In accord with Jewish precedent, a participial phrase introduces the saving action of God that is the specific reason for praising him in this *Berakah* prayer. The subject of the participle εὐλογήσας, "who has blessed," is God the Father. He remains the doer of almost all the verbs (whether active or passive) throughout the long sentence that forms this prologue (1:3–14). God's action forms the substance of the Gospel; it is God's action alone that is praised. The threefold repetition thus far in this verse of words beginning with εὐλογ- (εὐλογητὸς ... εὐλογήσας ... εὐλογίᾳ, "blessed ... has blessed ... blessing") is characteristic of

---

2 Chr 2:11 (ET 2:12); 6:4; 9:8; Ezra 7:27; Psalms (sixteen times); Ezek 3:12; Zech 11:5 (see also Neh 9:5; Job 1:21; Dan 2:20; 3:28). In the LXX, see Tobit 8:5–6, 15–17; 11:14–15, 17; 13:1–18; Judith 13:18; 1 Esdras 4:40, 60; 8:25; 3 Macc 7:23; Song of Three 29–68. In the NT, see Lk 1:68; 2 Cor 1:3; 1 Pet 1:3.

[2] See Barth, *Ephesians*, 1:77; Schnackenburg, *Ephesians*, 50; BDF, § 128 (5); Hermann Beyer, "εὐλογητός," *TDNT* 2:764. Rom 1:25 includes the verb in the indicative (cf. 1 Pet 4:11). See also the doxology to the Lord's Prayer (Mt 6:13 [variant reading]); *Didache*, 9:4; 10:5; *1 Clement*, 58:2. Many Jewish prayers preserved in Greek begin εὐλογητὸς εἶ πάτερ, "blessed *are* you, Father." On the other hand, in a similar construction in LXX 3 Kgdms 10:9 (MT/ET 1 Ki 10:9) and Job 1:21 we find an optative (γένοιτο and εἴη, respectively) translating the Hebrew jussive יְהִי, "may/let it be."

[3] Beyer, "εὐλογητός," *TDNT* 2:764, referring to Luther's explanation of the Lord's Prayer in the Small Catechism.

[4] Mk 14:61; Lk 1:68; Rom 1:25; 2 Cor 1:3; 11:31; Eph 1:3; 1 Pet 1:3. In Rom 9:5 εὐλογητός applies either to θεός, "God," or Χριστός, "Christ," who is identified as "God." With the possible exception of Mk 14:61, all these expressions with εὐλογητός are in language of praise.

[5] Rom 15:6; 2 Cor 1:3; 11:31; Eph 1:3; 1 Pet 1:3; cf. Eph 1:17; Rev 1:6.

[6] Rom 1:8; 7:25; 16:27; Jude 25.

[7] Mt 27:46; Mk 15:34; Jn 20:17.

183

liturgical (prayer) language and reflects the root's multifaceted meaning. Etymologically the verb בָּרַךְ may have referred to the bending of the "knee" (בֶּרֶךְ) involved in paying homage and receiving a blessing; thus, its twofold meaning in the OT comprises "bless" when applied to God's bestowal of gifts on people and "praise" when applied to their response to God.[8] In the present verse, God is praised for giving gifts that are described as πνευματικός. Is this "pertaining to man's spirit" (as opposed to his physical needs), contrasting heavenly with earthly blessings?[9] Or does it identify the divine person through whom the Father gives his gifts and who gives them his (capital S) Spiritual character: blessings "of/through the [Holy] Spirit"?[10] If it is the latter, then the prayer opens with a distinctly Trinitarian flavor. This past (aorist) moment of blessing through the Spirit embraces both the atoning work of Christ and the moment when the Spirit sealed the benefits of that work upon us (1:13): Holy Baptism.[11] This blessing is total, whole, complete (πάσῃ, "every")—neither partial nor in parts. So it is with the Gospel.

ἐν τοῖς ἐπουρανίοις—The adjective ἐπουράνιος, "heavenly" (pertaining to οὐρανός, "heaven"), may refer to the celestial realm as an astronomical phenomenon consisting of stars and planets (1 Cor 15:40). More often in biblical literature it refers to "heaven" as the dwelling place of God and his hosts (Phil 2:10),[12] and also, surprisingly, the location of the enemy hosts arrayed against him (Eph 3:10; 6:12). It may also refer by way of metonymy to the (non-local) exercise of God's dominion and the spiritual matters associated with him (Jn 3:12; 1 Cor 15:48–49; Heb 3:1; etc.). Its opposite is τὰ ἐπίγεια, "earthly things."[13] Similarly, Paul contrasts the heavenly realm with the present, evil world: "the Lord will rescue me from every evil work and will save [me] for his *heavenly* kingdom [σώσει εἰς τὴν βασιλείαν αὐτοῦ τὴν *ἐπουράνιον*]" (2 Tim 4:18).[14]

---

[8] The two meanings are evident in Gen 14:19–20: "blessed [בָּרוּךְ; LXX: εὐλογημένος] be Abram by God Most High, Possessor of heaven and earth; and blessed/praised [בָּרוּךְ; LXX: εὐλογητός] be God Most High, who has delivered your enemies into your hand!" See Mitchell, *The Meaning of* BRK *"To Bless" in the Old Testament*, 8–16, 116, 165–79.

[9] This contrast is common in Paul's writings (Rom 15:27; 1 Cor 3:1; 9:11; 15:44, 46). Though this is a common traditional interpretation of this verse, Paul himself does not explicitly make that contrast here.

[10] Stoeckhardt, *Ephesians*, 37: "blessings which are of the nature of God's Spirit." Barth, *Ephesians*, 1:101: "that decision, action, and revelation of God which has culminated and been 'sealed' when the 'Holy Spirit' was given to both Gentiles and Jews." Cf. Gal 3:14. Schlier, *Epheser*, 38, translates: "mit allem, was Segen des Geistes heißt," "with all that is called a blessing of the Spirit." Most instances of πνευματικός can possibly refer to the Holy Spirit (e.g., Rom 1:11; 1 Pet 2:5).

[11] It is hardly coincidental that Peter's *Berakah* prayer at the beginning of his first epistle also roots spiritual blessedness in Baptism: "Blessed be the God and Father of our Lord Jesus Christ, who according to his great mercy caused us to be born anew to a living hope through the resurrection of Jesus Christ from the dead, to an inheritance that is imperishable and undefiled and unfading, kept in heaven for you" (1 Pet 1:3–4).

[12] Cf. LXX Ps 67:15 (MT 68:15; ET 68:14); 2 Macc 3:39; 3 Macc 6:28; 7:6.

[13] Jn 3:12; 1 Cor 15:40; Phil 2:10; 3:19; cf. 2 Cor 5:1; James 3:15; Ignatius, *To the Ephesians*, 13:2; Ignatius, *To the Trallians*, 9:1; Polycarp, *To the Philippians*, 2:1.

[14] Cf. the Second Petition of the Lord's Prayer: "Thy kingdom [reign] come, on earth as it is in heaven" (Mt 6:10; Lk 11:2).

The exact phrase ἐν τοῖς ἐπουρανίοις, literally, "in the heavenlies," occurs five times in Ephesians (1:3, 20; 2:6; 3:10; 6:12) and nowhere else in the Greek Bible.[15] This plural form may be masculine or neuter and so may refer to heavenly persons, matters, or places. "Heavenly persons" is unlikely here. Being blessed "in heavenly matters" suits the present context. However, elsewhere in Ephesians, "heavenly places" is clearly intended.[16] The plural may reflect the Hebrew dual form הַשָּׁמַיִם, "the [two] heavens," in which case one could translate the phrase simply as "in heaven." But the worldview of Ephesians suggests it refers to heaven as multilayered (Eph 4:10), a diverse playing field for both good and evil spirits (6:12; cf. 2:2).

The use of the phrase here, in the first verse of the letter's *proem*, or prologue (1:3–14),[17] sets out a key feature of the letter's agenda: to demonstrate the triumphant superiority of Christ over all hostile spiritual forces and the ultimate blessings granted to the elect children of God in him (1:20; 4:10). The distinctive message of Ephesians is that reception of these heavenly blessings is not delayed until the believer passes from earth into heaven, but they are already possessed now through incorporation into Christ (2:6). The saint thus lives in two realms simultaneously (cf. Col 3:1–4). Luther suggests these blessings allude to the bestowal on the bride of the keys that open the storehouse of God's heavenly goods. It is because the church is made one flesh with Christ through the spiritual marriage inaugurated in Holy Baptism that all the blessings of heaven are hers (cf. Eph 5:21–33).[18]

ἐν Χριστῷ—These precise words, "in Christ," occur some seventy-six times in the NT, with nine in Ephesians.[19] The prepositional phrase with the definite article, ἐν τῷ Χριστῷ, appears six more times in the NT, four of which are in Ephesians (1:10, 12, 20; 3:11). Including pronominal variations ("in him," "in whom," etc.), the phrase occurs more often in Ephesians than in any other NT book.[20] It is commonly understood

---

[15] See Andrew T. Lincoln, "Re-examination of 'The Heavenlies' in Ephesians," *New Testament Studies* 19 (1973): 468–83; and M. Jeff Brannon, *The Heavenlies in Ephesians: A Lexical, Exegetical, and Conceptual Analysis* (London: T&T Clark, 2011). The uniqueness of the phrase is tempered by the fact that the apparently synonymous phrases ἐν τῷ οὐρανῷ, "in the heaven," and ἐν τοῖς οὐρανοῖς, "in the heavens," occur seventy-three times in the Greek Bible. In Ephesians there appears to be no distinction between the compound adjective ἐπουράνιος, "heavenly," and the simple noun οὐρανός, "heaven" (1:10; 3:15; 4:10; 6:9). This lexical conclusion is bolstered by Heb 9:23, where both τῶν ἐν τοῖς οὐρανοῖς and τὰ ἐπουράνια are usually translated as "the heavenly things."

[16] See Eph 1:20; 2:6 with reference to the ascension and session in heaven. Eph 3:10 and 6:12 are ambiguous. Of nineteen NT occurrences of the adjective ἐπουράνιος, five are in Ephesians (1:3, 20; 2:6; 3:10; 6:12). This is illustrative of Ephesians' particular concern for eternal matters, spiritual battles, and knowledge of higher things. Only Hebrews has a higher frequency (six times), where it features in the typological comparison of the heavenly and earthly tabernacles (Heb 8:5; 9:23).

[17] See "Rhetorical Outline" in "Structure and Rhetoric" in the introduction.

[18] Luther, "Second Wedding Sermon on Ephesians 5:22–33," StL 12:2027, § 19.

[19] Eph 1:1, 3; 2:6, 7, 10, 13; 3:6, 21; 4:32.

[20] Allan, "The 'In Christ' Formula in Ephesians," 54, calculates that some form of the phrase occurs thirty-four times in Ephesians. This can be compared to Deissmann's count of one hundred sixty-four in the entire corpus of undisputed Pauline letters (i.e., excluding Colossians, Ephesians, and the Pastorals; Adolf Deissmann, *The Religion of Jesus and the Faith of Paul*

185

instrumentally, "by means of Christ," or mystically, referring to the believer's incorporation into Christ and his body, the church, and thereby the participation in his gifts of life and salvation.[21] Although the latter is to be preferred in Ephesians (see especially 2:6, 16), these are not mutually exclusive interpretations. It is through the action of the progenitor that "incorporation" (the creation of a family or body) occurs.

> The background of the concept comes from the Hebrew idea of corporate personality or solidarity according to which the head of a family or tribe is the representative of all his members. For Paul, Adam and Christ are the representative figures of old and new humanity (1 Cor 15:22; Rom 5:12–21).[22]

We are "in Christ" because he is the firstfruits, the firstborn of the new creation, the elder brother, the new Adam.[23] Thus, "the body of Christ" motif, so prevalent in Ephesians,[24] is a logical consequence of being "in Christ." Key texts suggest the phrase also carries a *baptismal* flavor. One who has been baptized "into" Christ is now "in Christ."[25] "For in Christ Jesus you are all sons of God through faith. For as many of you as were baptized into Christ have been clothed with Christ" (Gal 3:26–27). (This Galatian text encapsulates the theme of Ephesians; see "Purpose and Themes" in the introduction.) The baptized are wrapped in Christ as in a garment.[26] All those who share this common Baptism are one.[27] "In Christ" is a theme that dominates Eph 1:3–14, as it is repeated

---

[trans. William E. Wilson; London: Hodder & Stoughton, 1923], 171). Considering the size of the documents, it therefore occurs twice as often in Ephesians as in the Pauline corpus as a whole. Allan argues that Ephesians has departed from the Pauline emphasis on the mystical union (see the next footnote) by emphasizing the instrumental sense: " 'In Christ' is no longer for this Writer the formula of incorporation into Christ, but has become the formula of God's activity through Christ" (59). But as Lincoln, *Ephesians*, 22, rightly objects: "It is particularly hard to avoid the more intensive incorporative connotation in 2:6 where believers are said to have been raised and seated in the heavenly realms together with Christ 'in Christ Jesus.' "

[21] See Moule, *Idiom Book*, 80. By "mystical" we do not mean "mysticism," "for that close communion-with-Christ mediated by the Spirit and experienced in faith is clearly different from a mystical experience as witnessed to elsewhere, especially from a fusion with the Godhead, a blessed participation in the union, a deification" (Schnackenburg, *Ephesians*, 321). Luther, the Lutheran Confessions, and early Lutheran dogmaticians affirmed the *unio mystica*, the indwelling of Christ and indeed the entire Holy Trinity, as a consequence of justification (see, e.g., FC SD 3:54, 65; Elert, *The Structure of Lutheranism*, 154–76; Pieper, *Christian Dogmatics*, 2:409–10). What is to be avoided is the notion that union with Christ can be achieved "through our own preparations, thoughts, and works without the external word of the Gospel" (AC 5:4) or that justification is a result of Christ's inner transformation of the Christian achieved by his indwelling (Osiandrianism; see FC Ep and SD 3). Note that, with the exception of Eph 3:17, Paul speaks of the believer being "in Christ," rather than Christ being in the believer.

[22] Arnold, *Power and Magic*, 136. See also Allan, "The 'In Christ' Formula in Ephesians," 55.

[23] Rom 8:29; Col 1:18; Heb 1:6; Rev 1:5.

[24] Eph 1:23; 2:16; 3:6; 4:4, 12, 16; 5:23, 30.

[25] Rom 6:3, 11; 8:1; 16:7; 1 Cor 15:22; 2 Cor 5:17; Gal 3:26; 1 Pet 5:14.

[26] Gal 3:27; see also Rom 13:14; Eph 4:24; Col 2:9–12. Schlier, *Epheser*, 48, asserts that "ἐν Χριστῷ is naturally to be understood just as 'locally' as ἐν τοῖς ἐπουρανίοις ['in the heavenly places']."

[27] Rom 12:5; Gal 3:28; Eph 3:6; 4:4–6.

in numerous variations: ἐν αὐτῷ, "in him" (1:4, 9, 10); ἐν ᾧ, "in whom" (1:7, 11, 13a, 13b); ἐν τῷ ἠγαπημένῳ, "in the Beloved" (1:6); and ἐν τῷ Χριστῷ, "in (the) Christ" (1:10, 12).

1:4 καθώς—Here this conjunction indicates not a comparison ("just as"), but a cause or explanation: "inasmuch as, because."[28] The rest of the prayer is an elucidation of the manner in which God has blessed us in Christ, which is the reason for us blessing him (1:3a).

ἐξελέξατο ἡμᾶς ἐν αὐτῷ—The verb ἐκλέγομαι, "choose," is related to the adjective ἐκλεκτός, "elect, chosen." The middle voice (reflexive) is significant: "he chose us for himself."[29] In the OT, Israel was God's chosen people.[30] Jesus Christ is called God's "Chosen One" as all Israel rolled into one, particularly at his transfiguration: "And a voice came from the cloud, saying, 'This is my Son, the Chosen One [ὁ ἐκλελεγμένος]'" (Lk 9:35).[31] The Father's declaration is then taken up as a taunt by the crowds at Christ's crucifixion: "He saved others; let him save himself, if he is the Christ of God, the Chosen One [ὁ ἐκλεκτός]" (Lk 23:35). The voice of God at the transfiguration recalls Christ's Baptism:

οὗτός ἐστιν ὁ υἱός μου ὁ ἀγαπητός, ἐν ᾧ εὐδόκησα.

This is my Son, the Beloved, in whom I am well-pleased. (Mt 3:17; see also Mk 1:11; Lk 3:22)

Also in the parallel accounts of the transfiguration, Christ is called "the Beloved" (Mt 17:5; Mk 9:7), a name that Paul will take up shortly (Eph 1:6). Taken together, these facts suggest that Paul intended an allusion to Christ's Baptism in this opening section.[32] Christ, the Chosen One, chooses disciples for himself; they do not choose him (Jn 15:16). "Chosen" is a key NT designation for Christians.[33] It is in Baptism that the Christian—whether male or female—is chosen by God to be his "beloved son" (see the second textual note on 1:5). The baptismal image of putting on a new robe is specifically combined with God's election or choosing in Col 3:12, where the saints are also given Christ's designation as beloved: "be *clothed* then, as God's *chosen* ones [ἐνδύσασθε οὖν, ὡς ἐκλεκτοὶ τοῦ θεοῦ], *holy* and *beloved* [ἅγιοι καὶ ἠγαπημένοι], with compassion, kindness, …" What is said of Christ at his Baptism, transfiguration,

---

[28] BDF, § 453 (2); BDAG, s.v. καθώς, 3; cf. 1 Cor 1:6; Phil 1:7; 2 Thess 1:3.

[29] Even so-called "deponent" verbs usually retain an element of the original meaning of the middle. See Wallace, *Greek Grammar*, 421: "God chose us *for* himself, *by* himself, or for his own interests" (cf. 428).

[30] E.g., Ex 19:5; Deut 4:37; 14:2; 1 Chr 16:13; Ps 105:6; Is 65:9, 15, 22.

[31] See also Mt 12:18 (quoting Is 42:1); Jn 1:34 (textual variant); 1 Pet 2:4, 6.

[32] See Winger, "'One Baptism' and the Purpose of Ephesians"; Coutts, "Ephesians I.3–14 and I Peter I.3–12," 124–25.

[33] E.g., Mt 22:14; 24:22, 24, 31; Rom 8:33; 16:13; Col 3:12; Titus 1:1; 1 Pet 1:1–2; 2:9; Rev 17:14. See also Jn 6:70; 13:18; Acts 1:2, 24; 9:15; 10:41; Rom 11:5; 1 Thess 1:4; 2 Thess 2:13; James 2:5; 1 Pet 5:13.

and crucifixion is said of those who are baptized into him. When God chose Christ, he also chose all of those who are "in him."[34]

Nevertheless, as the modifying prepositional phrase πρὸ καταβολῆς κόσμου, "before the foundation of the world" (see the next textual note), suggests, there is more than Baptism in mind. This "choosing" occurred not only in history at the moment of Baptism, but also before history in the eternity of God's will. For Gentiles who had been raised in the belief that their fate was controlled by gods and hostile spiritual forces, by enemies wielding magic, and by astrological signs, the message that they were chosen by a loving Father would have been immensely liberating.[35] Paul's classic words on the subject in Rom 8:29–30 emphasize that God's foreknowledge (οὓς προέγνω, "whom he foreknew") involved more than a passive preview of the future.[36] God actively "predestined" (προώρισεν, Rom 8:29) those whom he foreknew (a related participle, προορίσας, "he had predestined," occurs in Eph 1:5). This predestination led to their call (ἐκάλεσεν), justification (ἐδικαίωσεν), and ultimate glorification (ἐδόξασεν, Rom 8:30). Peter likewise calls his hearers "chosen … according to God the Father's foreknowledge/predestination [ἐκλεκτοῖς … κατὰ πρόγνωσιν θεοῦ πατρός]" (1 Pet 1:1–2).[37] All of this occurs "in him" (ἐν αὐτῷ, Eph 1:4), in Christ, that is, because of the work of Christ (*propter Christum*) and by means of one's incorporation into Christ (*per Christum*).[38] With these two prepositional phrases—"before the foundation of the world" and "in him"—Paul thus stresses two aspects of election: God's eternal plan (see the next textual note) and the concrete, historical working out of the plan in Christ, whose merit is applied to the saint in Holy Baptism (see the fifth textual note on 1:3). This baptismal application stands at the center of Paul's prayer for the Ephesians. Baptism into Christ is the moment when God's eternal choosing is made manifest, emerging from his hidden will to become the certain object of saving faith.[39]

---

[34] "God … who chose the Lord Jesus Christ and us through him to be a people for his special possession" (*1 Clement*, 64:1).

[35] See Arnold, *Power and Magic*, 128–29. On statues of the goddess Artemis Ephesia, her neck was ringed with the signs of the zodiac. See "The Cult of Artemis Ephesia" in "The City of Ephesus and Paul's Relationship to It" in the introduction.

[36] See the lengthy discussion of the nature of God's foreknowledge in FC SD 11, "Of God's Eternal Foreknowledge [Predestination] and Election."

[37] See also 1 Cor 1:26–28; 2 Thess 2:13. Stoeckhardt, *Ephesians*, 38–53, 84–99, discusses election at length with reference to Eph 1:3–14.

[38] "In him" (1:4) distinguishes Paul's teaching on predestination from the Jewish idea, which is otherwise similar (Schnackenburg, *Ephesians*, 52).

Those who have taught an election *intuitu fidei*, "in view of faith" (as if God chose those whom he foreknew would believe), interpret ἐν αὐτῷ as qualifying ἡμᾶς *adjectivally*: "he chose us, who were in him." If this were the case, the prepositional phrase ἐν αὐτῷ would probably be preceded by an article: ἐξελέξατο ἡμᾶς τοὺς ἐν αὐτῷ. The grammar, however, suggests ἐν αὐτῷ be understood *adverbially*, as modifying the verb ἐξελέξατο: "in him [Christ] he chose us." Faith in Christ as the receiving instrument of these blessings is not a precondition of predestination, but its consequence, as worked out by the calling of the Word.

[39] "The blessing, however, with which God (in Baptism) blessed us, opened up to us this eternal election and surrounds us with it" (Schlier, *Epheser*, 50–51).

πρὸ καταβολῆς κόσμου—"The foundation of the world" is a NT way of referring to creation (Heb 4:3), resting upon OT language.[40] It is frequently connected to predestination. The Son was predestined to be the Messiah from before the foundation of the world (1 Pet 1:20; cf. Heb 9:26). God's plan remained hidden from that time until the appearance of Christ (Mt 13:35). The saints who enter heaven are those whose names were recorded in the book of life before the foundation of the world (Mt 25:34; Jn 17:24; Rev 13:8; 17:8).

εἶναι ἡμᾶς ἁγίους καὶ ἀμώμους—The exact phrase ἁγίους καὶ ἀμώμους, with masculine plural adjectives, "holy and without blemish," occurs elsewhere only in Col 1:22, where Christ presents (παραστῆσαι) Christians as "holy and without blemish." But feminine singular forms of the adjective (ἁγία καὶ ἄμωμος) are applied to the church as the spotless bride of Christ by virtue of Holy Baptism in Eph 5:27, where Christ presents (παραστήσῃ) her as "holy and without blemish." Thus, a baptismal reference may be intended in 1:4 also. Indeed, the label "holy/saints" (ἅγιοι) can be applied to Christians because they have been made holy in Baptism.[41] The language is cultic, echoing the temple, where priests were required to be unblemished, and they consecrated sacrificed beasts without blemish to make people holy.[42] In the NT ἄμωμος, "without blemish," is an essential description of Christ as the perfect sacrifice for our sins (Heb 9:14; 1 Pet 1:19). Hence, "he chose us ... that we should be holy and without blemish" (Eph 1:4) is not primarily a call to holy behavior (an ethical imperative), but a declaration of God's gift of a holy (justified) status through Christ that enables us to stand in his presence, now and on the Last Day.[43]

κατενώπιον αὐτοῦ—In the NT and early Christian literature, the preposition κατενώπιον, "before [someone]," is used only of God.[44] It implies the authority of judgment and points to the glorious face of God, before which only those who are holy and without blemish may stand. A holy God consumes anything in his presence that is unholy. The work of the Gospel is to prepare God's people to stand before him in a position of privilege and intimacy. As Zechariah prophesied in the Benedictus, God's Gospel promise is "that we, being delivered from the hand of our enemies, might serve him without fear, in holiness and righteousness *before him* [ἐνώπιον αὐτοῦ] all our days"

---

[40] 2 Sam 22:16; Job 38:4; Pss 18:19 (ET 18:15); 24:1–2; 82:5; Prov 8:29; Is 24:18; 40:21; 51:13; Amos 9:6.

[41] Cf. 1 Cor 6:11: "but you have been washed, but you have been made holy, but you have been justified in the name of the Lord Jesus Christ and in the Spirit of our God" (ἀλλὰ ἀπελούσασθε, ἀλλὰ ἡγιάσθητε, ἀλλὰ ἐδικαιώθητε ἐν τῷ ὀνόματι τοῦ κυρίου Ἰησοῦ Χριστοῦ καὶ ἐν τῷ πνεύματι τοῦ θεοῦ ἡμῶν).

[42] "Without blemish" (ἄμωμος) is a key term for a sacrifice: LXX Ex 29:1; 29:38; Lev 1:3, 10; Num 6:14; 19:2; etc. See also the regulations for priests in Leviticus 21; they may not have a μῶμος "blemish" (LXX Lev 21:17).

[43] "Without blemish" (ἄμωμος) is used of present holiness in Eph 5:27; Phil 2:15; and of Christ's eschatological presentation of the redeemed to God in Col 1:22; Jude 24; Rev 14:5. The distinction between the two, however, is not always clear.

[44] BDAG, s.v. κατενώπιον. In the LXX κατενώπιον is sometimes used of Israel's enemies not being able to stand before God's people. More apropos is LXX Lev 4:17, where it is used of holiness rituals before the presence of YHWH.

(Lk 1:74–75). Holy Baptism, as the application of that Gospel, fulfills and explodes the holiness rituals of the old covenant that needed to be repeated continually in order to prepare God's priests and people to stand before him.

ἐν ἀγάπῃ—Does "in love" modify what precedes or what follows? That is, do we stand "before him in love," or does the phrase mean "in love he [God] had predestined us"?

1. If it modifies what precedes, it would seem an extraneous modifier. "In him [Christ]" already modifies the verb "he chose us"; and "holy and without blemish" modifies "that we should be … before him." A further question would be the external entailments of "love": does it refer to standing in God's love or to exercising our own love toward God? The former is more likely, in that the emphasis is on being accepted by God, thus experiencing his love rather than his wrath. If it referred to our life of love, it would be a significant shift from a context in which God is always doing the verbs.

2. If the phrase modifies what follows, the grammar would be slightly unusual, with the prepositional phrase preceding the participle προορίσας, literally, "having predestined" (1:5). However, there is a pattern in 1:3–14 of prepositional phrases beginning clauses.[45] In 1:13 a prepositional phrase twice precedes an aorist participle, as here; the prepositional phrase in 1:8b may also modify the participle that follows in 1:9. Our translation of 1:4–5 follows this pattern. God's predestination is neither arbitrary nor vindictive, but proceeds from his overwhelming love[46] and is accomplished "in the Beloved" (1:6). "Love" thus forms an *inclusio* or frame around 1:4c–6.

1:5 προορίσας ἡμᾶς—"*Since* he had predestined us" renders the causal participle. See the textual note on ἐξελέξατο ἡμᾶς (1:4). Because this is an aorist participle, it should be understood as an action that preceded the act of choosing (1:4).[47] God's choice (both in eternity and in the act of Baptism) arises from his plan. προορίζω is used in the NT exclusively of God's plan of salvation.[48]

---

[45] As noted, e.g., by Dahl, "Das Proömium des Epheserbriefes," in *Studies in Ephesians*, 322. See also Col 1:11b–12a.

[46] Schlier and Schnackenburg, constrained by the text, express well the characteristically Lutheran emphasis on God's love as the motivation behind election. "It is—if one might speak for a moment about some erroneous interpretations of election—not a choosing whose motive is simply the sovereignty of God, and therefore consists in the *gemina praedestinatio* [double predestination], but it is a sovereign choosing of love, a choosing of sovereign love. … Our eternal election in Christ is a definition of love that precedes everything else" (Schlier, *Epheser*, 52–53). "He [the author] clearly shows God's election as a predestination freely given in love (modal [i.e., 'in love' is the mode or manner of predestination]). This manner of describing our predestination … always refers to God's positive, salvific act. This of itself prohibits the conclusion that there is also a divine decree concerning the non-elect of humanity by which they have been predestined, without any guilt of their own, to destruction and damnation (Determinism)" (Schnackenburg, *Ephesians*, 54).

[47] This is not necessarily the case. As the aorist participle here *follows* the main verb, it could be taken as adverbial: "he chose us *by* predesting us." See Wallace, *Greek Grammar*, 624–25, 628–30. But the parallels in Rom 8:29–30 (see above) suggest we make a temporal and lexical distinction between predesting and choosing.

[48] Acts 4:28; Rom 8:29–30; 1 Cor 2:7; Eph 1:5, 11.

εἰς υἱοθεσίαν—The noun υἱοθεσία is a legal technical term for "adoption as a son." In Roman law adoption brought a person into a new family, chiefly to ensure the continuation of the line, though there were also clear benefits to the adoptee.[49] Although neither the OT nor Second Temple Judaism used the term "adoption," Paul's use of the term owes much to OT precedents. He applied it to Israel's adoption (Rom 9:4), for God had called Israel his son.[50] In his Sarah/Hagar allegory, Paul asserts that the Son of God has made us sons by way of adoption, redeeming us from slavery (Gal 4:5; cf. Rom 8:14–17). Galatians 4 describes a conclusion that may be drawn from Baptism (Gal 3:26–29). Sonship is a result of new birth to a new Father. Again we see that by virtue of Baptism, what can be said of Christ is said of the Christian: Son, sons. Only because we are sons may we call God "Father" (Eph 1:3). Thus, sonship, though it describes a relationship to the Father, also relates Christians to Christ, *the* Son. One can only be a son of God through Christ; if one will not be such a son, one has no part of Christ and no blessing from the Father. Sonship includes an allusion to ancient Near Eastern and Greco-Roman inheritance customs, which generally allowed only sons to inherit.[51] All Christians, whether male or female, are theologically "sons": "if a son, then an heir" (Gal 4:7). The inclusivity of sonship is asserted explicitly in those places where Christians are called τέκνα θεοῦ, "children of God."[52]

διὰ Ἰησοῦ Χριστοῦ—Though this portion of the *Berakah* prayer is directed to the Father, glorifying his eternal work for our salvation, it continuously invokes the redeeming work of Jesus Christ. He is God's Son by nature, we by adoption. Because of his work and through our incorporation into him, our relationship with God has been restored so that with Christ we may dare to call him "our Father": "For in Christ Jesus you are all sons of God through faith. … And because you are sons, God has sent the Spirit of his Son into our hearts, crying, 'Abba! Father!'" (Gal 3:26; 4:6).[53]

εἰς αὐτόν—The referent of the pronoun "him" is probably the Father; thus, the prepositional phrase "for him" qualifies the adoption: to be sons *for* the heavenly Father. The translation above renders this by "adopted as *his* sons." As the Spirit's work leads to the Son, not to himself (Jn 16:14), so the Son's work leads to the Father. This is the

---

[49] See W. W. Buckland, *A Text-Book of Roman Law from Augustus to Justinian* (3d ed.; Cambridge: Cambridge University Press, 1963), 121–28; Francis Lyall, "Roman Law in the Writings of Paul—Adoption," *Journal of Biblical Literature* 88 (1969): 458–66. Lyall summarizes:

> The adoptee is taken out of his previous state and is placed in a new relationship with his new *paterfamilias*. All his old debts are canceled, and in effect he starts a new life. From that time the *paterfamilias* owns all the property and acquisitions of the adoptee, controls his personal relationships, and has rights of discipline. On the other hand he is involved in liability by the actions of the adoptee and owes reciprocal duties of support and maintenance. (466)

[50] E.g., Ex 4:22; Is 1:2; Hos 11:1. However, the LXX never uses this exact term υἱοθεσία.

[51] The provision for Israel in Num 27:1–11 that in the absence of sons, the daughters should inherit their father's portion, was remarkably countercultural in its egalitarianism.

[52] Jn 1:12–13; Rom 8:16–17; Phil 2:15; 1 Jn 3:1, 2.

[53] Cf. Jn 1:12–13; Rom 8:14–15; 1 Pet 2:5.

Trinitarian pattern. Christ makes us not his sons, but the Father's, even as he is Son in relation to the Father. (See the commentary.)

κατὰ τὴν εὐδοκίαν τοῦ θελήματος αὐτοῦ—Once again the work of salvation accomplished by Christ is referenced back to the Father, "according to the good pleasure of his will." εὐδοκία ("good pleasure, favor") does not appear in secular Greek literature, but only in the LXX and the NT, and is especially frequent in Paul. It adds warmth, joy, personal pleasure, and perhaps even divine freedom to θέλημα, God's "will" or "plan."[54] With this phrase Paul's prayer calls for submission to the Father's will, as Christ first prayed, "Your will be done" (Mt 26:42), and also as the Christian learns to pray (Mt 6:10). In the context of Paul's *Berakah* prayer, the fact that all things happen according to God's good pleasure enhances his glory (Eph 1:6). In εὐδοκία, "good pleasure," one again hears echoes of Christ's Baptism, when the Father declared:

οὗτός ἐστιν ὁ υἱός μου ὁ ἀγαπητός, ἐν ᾧ εὐδόκησα.

This is my Son, the Beloved, in whom I am well-pleased. (Mt 3:17; see also Mk 1:11; Lk 3:22)

These words are repeated at his transfiguration (Mt 17:5; see also Mk 9:7). (See the second textual note on Eph 1:4, with ἐξελέξατο.) As the Father is pleased with the Son and because of the Son's work, the Father is also pleased with Christians.[55] θέλημα here is naturally taken not in the objective sense of "what is willed," but in the subjective sense of "the will that acts." Similar thoughts occur in 1:9, "he has made known to us the mystery of his will [τοῦ θελήματος αὐτοῦ], according to his good pleasure [κατὰ τὴν εὐδοκίαν αὐτοῦ]." And again in 1:11 we have κατὰ τὴν βουλὴν τοῦ θελήματος αὐτοῦ "according to the plan of his will." Such repetition is typical of liturgical prayer; yet it is not vain repetition—it emphasizes the priority of God's plan of salvation, of his grace. This emphasis in the prologue of the letter (1:3–14) is a clue to the letter's purpose.

1:6 εἰς ἔπαινον δόξης—Here the liturgical character of the *Berakah* prayer takes over again. "Praise" and "glory" are characteristic of doxological conclusions. The *Berakah* prayer in 1 Peter closes with a remarkably similar statement, that our faith should lead εἰς ἔπαινον καὶ δόξαν καὶ τιμὴν ἐν ἀποκαλύψει Ἰησοῦ Χριστοῦ, "to the praise and glory and honor [of Christ] at the revelation of Jesus Christ" (1 Pet 1:7). The eschatological flavor of these statements—that the presentation of a holy people to God on the Last Day will be the ultimate act of praise—is heard again in the opening thanksgiving of Philippians: εἰς δόξαν καὶ ἔπαινον θεοῦ, "to the glory and praise of God" (Phil 1:11; cf. LXX 1 Chr 16:27; Phil 2:11).

This phrase (with slight variations) occurs twice more in this section, εἰς ἔπαινον (τῆς) δόξης αὐτοῦ, "to the praise of his glory," 1:12, 14, the last of which is also eschatological. The phrase appears to be a formulaic close to each of three sections in the prayer: 1:3–6; 1:7–12; and 1:13–14.[56] It marks out a Trinitarian pattern: what is said

---

[54] Barth, *Ephesians*, 1:81: "Not a grim Lord watching over the execution of his predetermined plan, but a smiling Father is praised. He enjoys imparting his riches to many children."

[55] Lk 2:14; 12:32; 1 Cor 1:21; Phil 2:13.

[56] See Coutts, "Ephesians I.3–14 and 1 Peter I.3–12," 116.

respectively of Father, Son, and Holy Spirit in each section always redounds to the praise and glory of the Father (see the commentary as well as the textual notes on 1:17; 3:20–21). Thus, one should not try to connect this prepositional phrase too closely to any one particular verb that precedes; it is a refrain that responds to what precedes as a unit.[57]

Profound parallels in the eucharistic prayers of an early Christian liturgical document suggest that Paul's prayer may also echo and evoke the way he would pray at the Lord's Supper. For the *Didache* includes similar refrains three times in each of its two prayers: σοὶ ἡ δόξα εἰς τοὺς αἰῶνας, "to you be the glory into the ages" (*Didache* 9:2, 3; 10:2, 4); ὅτι σοῦ ἐστιν ἡ δόξα καὶ ἡ δύναμις διὰ Ἰησοῦ Χριστοῦ εἰς τοὺς αἰῶνας, "for yours is the glory and the power through Jesus Christ into the ages" (*Didache* 9:4); ὅτι σοῦ ἐστιν ἡ δύναμις καὶ ἡ δόξα εἰς τοὺς αἰῶνας, "for yours is the power and the glory into the ages" (*Didache* 10:5).

The heaping up of genitives into luxurious chains is characteristic of the language of Ephesians, and particularly of this opening section. Many critics have claimed it to be un-Pauline. However, the formalized liturgical character of this opening prayer easily accounts for the unusual style.

What is the relationship between the two genitives δόξης, "of glory," and χάριτος, "of grace" (see also the next textual note)? One or the other could be understood adjectivally, as is common in Semitic Greek (reflecting the Hebrew/Aramaic construct state). Is then God's grace characterized by glory ("his glorious grace"), or is his glory characterized by grace ("his gracious glory")? Either is grammatically possible; but seeing "glory" as the primary noun would be more consistent with the subsequent two occurrences of the phrase (1:12, 14). The "glory" of God in the OT often refers to his presence on earth. But God's coming may be either to judge and destroy his enemies or to save his people. The addition of "grace" leads us to understand "glory" in the latter sense. The "gracious glory" of God, his presence on earth to save, is located precisely in Jesus Christ.

τῆς χάριτος αὐτοῦ ἧς ἐχαρίτωσεν ἡμᾶς—The liturgical redundancy of the original is difficult to reproduce in English: "of his *grace* [or '*gracious* glory'; see the previous textual note] which[58] he *graced* upon us." χάρις, "grace," is, of course, a weighty NT word (see the first textual note on 1:2). It is a key term in Ephesians, occurring twelve times in its 155 verses.[59] Most significant is its occurrence in 2:8, where salvation "by grace" is defined as θεοῦ τὸ δῶρον, "the gift of God," "not from yourselves" (2:8), and "not from works" (2:9). From such passages arises the classical Lutheran definition of grace as a favorable attitude in God; but χάρις can also refer to the gifts of God that

---

[57] Schlier, *Epheser*, 56: "Our existence as saints and believers, which is the blessed existence as elect [*das gesegnete Erwähltsein*], praises in its very self the grace which is responsible for it."

[58] The relative pronoun ἧς, which should be accusative (ἥν) according to its function in the subordinate clause, is genitive by attraction to its antecedent (χάριτος), a characteristic of liturgical style. The same is true of ἧς at the start of 1:8.

[59] Only 2 Thessalonians, Titus, Philemon, and 1 Peter have a higher frequency on a percentage basis.

proceed from his favorable attitude.[60] In this verse χάρις would seem to be a quality in God, inasmuch as it is combined with his "glory" and can be praised (see the preceding textual note). This χάρις is the source of God's Gospel actions toward us, expressed by the following related verb χαριτόω, "bestow favor" or "show favor,"[61] here translated as "he has graciously shown." The only other NT occurrence of the verb is κεχαριτωμένη, used of Mary as "one shown favor [by God]" (Lk 1:28). Mary has been shown favor by God's choosing to put Christ in her; in Eph 1:6 we are shown favor because we are in Christ. God's "grace" is often said to be ours "in Christ."[62]

ἐν τῷ ἠγαπημένῳ—"The Beloved" again recalls the Baptism of Christ, where the Father declared: οὗτός ἐστιν ὁ υἱός μου ὁ ἀγαπητός, "this is my Son, the Beloved" (Mt 3:17; see also Mk 1:11; Lk 3:22). The grammatical form is different—a perfect passive participle here (ἠγαπημένῳ) instead of an adjective (ἀγαπητός)—but the root and the meaning are the same.[63] A textual variant inserts the words υἱῷ αὐτοῦ after ἠγαπημένῳ, resulting in "his Beloved Son" (D* F G 629 it vg^cl sy^h** sa; Ambst). This variant is probably not original; it appears that a scribe has simply added the two words by memory. But this slip suggests that the allusion to Christ's Baptism was obvious to him.

"Beloved" is frequently used of Israel in the OT[64] and is applied to Christians on innumerable occasions in the NT.[65] Thus, like "chosen one," it is a term of endearment for Israel, taken up and applied to Christ as Israel rolled into one,[66] and then to Christians as the new Israel. Put another way, as Christians are "in Christ," they experience the very love that God has shown his Son from all eternity.[67] Col 3:12 illustrates the combination of "beloved" and "chosen" as applied to Christians: "be clothed then, as God's chosen ones [ἐκλεκτοὶ τοῦ θεοῦ], holy and beloved [ἠγαπημένοι], with

---

[60] χάρις is frequently combined with a passive form of δίδωμι: *grace given* to me" (e.g., 3:2, 7, 8; 4:7; cf. 4:29).

[61] The Vulgate and some church fathers (particularly Chrysostom, *Homilies on Ephesians*, 1:1.6 [*NPNF*[1] 13:52–53]) understood χαριτόω as a causative verb form, which could be read in the way of the Roman doctrine of *gratia infusa*, "fill with grace." While verbs ending in -όω can have a causative meaning, the three occurrences of χαριτόω in the LXX and the NT (Sirach 18:17; Lk 1:28; Eph 1:6) give no support in context for a translation that implies grace is a substance.

[62] Rom 3:24; 1 Cor 1:4; Eph 2:7; 2 Tim 1:9; 2:1.

[63] Schlier, *Epheser*, 57, suggests that the verbal aspect is stronger in this participial form; i.e., it emphasizes God's continuous and intimate loving of his Son.

[64] E.g., LXX Deut 33:12 (of Benjamin); Pss 59:7 (MT 60:7; ET 60:5); 107:7 (MT 108:7; ET 108:6); Is 5:1, 7; Jer 11:15; 12:7; Hos 3:1; Baruch 3:37; also Song of Songs; cf. Hos 11:1. The LXX translates Jeshurun (a pet name for Israel) as "the beloved" in Deut 32:15; 33:5, 26; Is 44:2. The city of Jerusalem is called "beloved" in Rev 20:9 and Sirach 24:11. Cf. Rom 9:25, where Paul adds "beloved" to his reading of Hos 2:25 (ET 2:23).

[65] E.g., Rom 1:7; 1 Cor 4:14; 10:14; Eph 5:1.

[66] Schlier, *Epheser*, 57, n. 1, gives considerable evidence that "the Beloved" was used as a messianic title.

[67] Cf. Schlier, *Epheser*, 57, who refers us to Rom 8:39, that nothing "will be able to separate us from the love of God that is in Christ Jesus, our Lord"; and Jn 17:23.

compassion, kindness, …" 1 Thess 1:4 is similar: "knowing, brothers beloved of God [ἀδελφοὶ ἠγαπημένοι ὑπὸ (τοῦ) θεοῦ], that he has chosen you [τὴν ἐκλογὴν ὑμῶν]."[68]

1:7 ἐν ᾧ—The obvious antecedent of ᾧ, "whom," is τῷ ἠγαπημένῳ, "the Beloved" (1:6), which in turn refers back to the initial ἐν Χριστῷ, "in Christ," at the end of 1:3 (see the fifth textual note there). Three times ἐν ᾧ, "in whom," begins a section or subsection of this prayer (1:7, 11, 13). Here it begins the prayer's Christological center (1:7–12). The meaning is this: "because we are 'in Christ' through Holy Baptism, we have …" The Spirit's gifts are never disconnected from Christ, to whom the Spirit always points. For a fuller discussion of the structure of 1:3–14, see the commentary.

ἔχομεν—"We have" now introduces the blessing of the Spirit ("redemption") that is chief among his "every blessing" (1:3). The present tense indicative is deliberately chosen to emphasize the continued possession of this gift, the continuing relevance of Christ as the source of the gift, and its importance for the subject "we." It is not simply a disconnected action in the distant past.

τὴν ἀπολύτρωσιν διὰ τοῦ αἵματος αὐτοῦ—The noun ἀπολύτρωσις, "redemption," introduces the imagery of slavery or captivity, from which a person is rescued by the payment of a ransom. The NT speaks of "redemption" (ἀπολύτρωσις or λύτρωσις) in two ways: (1) as a past action on our behalf producing a present state of freedom[69] and (2) as a future action that will take place on the Last Day.[70] It even applies the term ἀπολύτρωσις to Christ himself, who is our redemption (1 Cor 1:30). The present tense verb ἔχομεν, "we have," indicates that Paul has the first use in mind: redemption as a present state resulting from a past action accomplished in Christ. It is, of course, a proleptic redemption; the forgiveness of sins is a substantial down payment (1:14) of the fullness that will finally be experienced at the resurrection of the dead (4:30). "His [Christ's] blood" is the price that was paid for that redemption.[71] Blood as the purchase price of redemption evokes the sacrifices of the OT temple, where once a year the high priest took the blood of a sacrifice into the Most Holy Place in order to secure redemption (Ex 30:10; Heb 9:12). In the case of Christ's high priesthood, the redemption is eternal; his blood only needed to be sacrificed once (Heb 9:26). Col 1:20 connects blood to reconciliation; Heb 9:14 and Heb 13:12 connect Christ's blood to sanctification; 1 Jn 1:7 and Rev 7:14 to cleansing; Heb 12:24 and 1 Pet 1:2 to sprinkling—all of these are cultic images drawn from the temple. They reflect the divine teaching that it is blood that makes atonement (Lev 17:11). Rom 5:9 speaks of justification by his blood. In Eph 2:13 Christ's blood brings the Gentiles near to God. In the Gospels Christ promised that he would give his life (by the shedding of his blood) as a λύτρον, "ransom," for many (Mt 20:28; Mk 10:45). The blood of Christ is one of the richest scriptural images of salvation. As blood is virtually synonymous with the covenant in the OT (Ex 24:8), so Christ takes up "blood of the covenant/testament" language at the Last Supper, in

---

68 Cf. 2 Thess 2:13; Jude 1; also Rom 11:28 (Israel as chosen and beloved).

69 Lk 1:68; Rom 3:24; Col 1:14; Heb 9:15.

70 Lk 21:28; Rom 8:23; Eph 1:14; 4:30.

71 Acts 20:28; Heb 9:14–15; 1 Pet 1:18–19; Rev 5:9.

order that the church might continually be forgiven, cleansed, purified, and sanctified in the NT Sacrament of the Altar.[72] For Christ's blood is truly life-giving (Jn 6:53–54). If we continuously "have" (ἔχομεν, Eph 1:7) Christ's blood, we continuously have redemption.[73]

τὴν ἄφεσιν τῶν παραπτωμάτων—As Paul moves from thoughts of eternal predestination and God's plan for history to "the forgiveness of trespasses" as their goal, so also Melanchthon concludes that the final purpose of history is "the forgiveness of sins" (Ap 4:51). The forgiveness of sin is specifically connected to the blood of Christ in Heb 9:22 and 1 Jn 1:7, in addition to the (other) cultic references in the preceding textual note. In the NT it is in the Lord's Supper that Christ's blood is most concretely given εἰς ἄφεσιν ἁμαρτιῶν, "for the forgiveness of sins" (Mt 26:28).[74] For by receiving Christ's blood with the mouth in faith, the sinner is forgiven. The Christian who is intimately familiar with the Lord's Words could not help but think of the Sacrament when hearing Eph 1:7. At the same time, Paul may imply a further allusion to John's Baptism, which was "for the forgiveness of sins" (Mk 1:4; Lk 3:3). The term παράπτωμα, "transgression, trespass," is virtually synonymous with παράβασις, "transgression," and even with the more common ἁμαρτία, "sin," with which it is combined in Eph 2:1 (see the third textual note there). Louw-Nida suggests that παράπτωμα may focus more upon the "false step," or "unpremeditated violation of God's will and law"[75]—but this distinction need not be pressed here. In Col 1:14 Paul uses ἁμαρτία in exact parallel: ἐν ᾧ ἔχομεν τὴν ἀπολύτρωσιν, τὴν ἄφεσιν τῶν ἁμαρτιῶν, "in whom we have redemption, the forgiveness *of sins*."[76]

κατὰ τὸ πλοῦτος τῆς χάριτος αὐτοῦ—The noun πλοῦτος may be used literally of "an abundant wealth of earthly possessions" or figuratively of a rich abundance of anything. The genitive τῆς χάριτος, "of grace," is epexegetical/descriptive, indicating what kind of richness it is. πλοῦτος, "richness, wealth," occurs particularly frequently in Ephesians and Colossians.[77] The phrase "the richness of his grace" occurs only here and in Eph 2:7. In Eph 3:8 Paul speaks of τὸ ἀνεξιχνίαστον πλοῦτος τοῦ Χριστοῦ, "the unfathomable richness of Christ"; in 1:18 of ὁ πλοῦτος τῆς δόξης τῆς κληρονομίας αὐτοῦ, "the richness of his glorious inheritance"; and in 3:16 of τὸ πλοῦτος τῆς δόξης αὐτοῦ, "the richness of his glory." Liturgical language is characterized by such gran-

---

[72] Mt 26:28; Mk 14:24; Lk 22:20.

[73] The variant reading ἔσχομεν (second aorist), "we had," by moving the verb into a past tense, focuses solely on Calvary and misses the reference to the ongoing possession of redemption through the present-day sacramental reception of Christ's blood.

[74] Most interestingly, the phrase "for the forgiveness of sins" is used in the NT of all the means of grace: Baptism (Mk 1:4; Lk 3:3), the Lord's Supper (Mt 26:28), and preaching (Lk 24:47; cf. Acts 13:38; 26:18).

[75] Louw-Nida, § 88.297, including n. 21.

[76] In the NT τὴν ἄφεσιν τῶν παραπτωμάτων occurs only here in Eph 1:7. Various forms of ἄφεσις ἁμαρτιῶν occur eleven times.

[77] τὸ πλοῦτος (neuter) occurs four times in Ephesians (1:7; 2:7; 3:8, 16), twice in Colossians (1:27; 2:2); and elsewhere in the NT only in 2 Cor 8:2 and Phil 4:19. The masculine form ὁ πλοῦτος also appears in Eph 1:18.

diloquent phrases. But one must also presume that the superabundant richness of God's gifts is something Paul wishes to stress. Neither sin itself nor anything in man can place a limit on God's forgiveness (we may not say, "Only so much and no more"). God's forgiveness is as immeasurable as the gracious God himself, who is "rich [πλούσιος] in mercy" (2:4). On χάρις, "grace," see the first textual note on 1:2 and the first and second textual notes on 1:6.

1:8 ἧς ἐπερίσσευσεν εἰς ἡμᾶς—The verb περισσεύω, "pour out," evokes the image of a pitcher being filled to overflowing, as if held in the midst of a thundering waterfall. The size of the receiving vessel does not give the measure of the gift, but rather the generosity of the giver, who gives in abundance. This verb is the opposite of ὑστερέω, "to lack" (1 Cor 1:7). Here the giver is God, and his graciousness far surpasses our need, so that we are not lacking in any way. "Lavished upon us" (RSV) captures this admirably, but "poured out" captures the presumed baptismal allusion in the text. Grammatically, the gift being poured out is χάριτος αὐτοῦ, "his grace" (1:7), which is the antecedent of the relative pronoun ἧς, "which."[78] It is not necessary, however, to understand grace thereby as a substance (*gratia infusa*). It is a figure of speech similar to pouring out love upon someone (cf. Rom 5:5). The image is intended to express the overwhelming graciousness of God, who has revealed to us the Gospel of salvation in Jesus Christ.

ἐν πάσῃ σοφίᾳ καὶ φρονήσει—In accordance with the pattern of this section, this prepositional phrase should be understood as modifying the participial phrase that follows (rather than the pouring out that precedes). It is "with all wisdom and understanding" that God "has made known to us the mystery of his will" (1:9). σοφία, "wisdom," and φρόνησις, "understanding," occur together in the NT only here, but are a common pairing in other Greek literature, where they are contrasted with mere seeing.[79] In the LXX they are God's own attributes[80] and also his gift to people (cf. Eph 1:18; James 1:5).[81] Here they modify "making known"—suggesting that there can be knowledge that is without wisdom or understanding (1 Cor 8:1–3). σοφία ("wisdom") as practical knowledge suggests the application of the knowledge of God's plan to oneself and one's condition. "Wisdom" is also associated particularly with Christ;[82] Christ promises it to the apostles (Lk 21:15), and Peter writes that it was a special gift to Paul (2 Pet 3:15). φρόνησις is the "understanding" of God possessed by the righteous (Lk 1:17). The two terms are similar enough to be labeled a hendiadys.[83]

---

[78] The relative pronoun ἧς, which should be accusative (ἥν) according to its function in the subordinate clause, is genitive by attraction to its antecedent (χάριτος), a characteristic of liturgical style. See the same phenomenon with ἧς in the second textual note on 1:6.

[79] BDAG, s.v. φρόνησις, 2.

[80] Jer 10:12; Sirach 1:4.

[81] See one or both of these words or their cognates in reference to Solomon (LXX 3 Kgdms 3:12 [MT/ET 1 Ki 3:12]; 5:9 [MT 1 Ki 5:9; ET 1 Ki 4:29]; cf. LXX 3 Kgdms 2:35 [MT/ET 1 Ki 2:35]; Wis Sol 7:7) and to the four youths in Babylon (LXX Dan 1:17; see also Dan 2:23).

[82] Proverbs 8; Mt 11:19; 13:54; Lk 2:40, 52; 1 Cor 1:24, 30; Col 1:28; 2:3.

[83] Schlier, *Epheser*, 59. In Proverbs they are clearly synonymous (LXX Prov 1:2; 3:13, 19; 7:4; 8:1; 10:23; 16:16). 4 Macc 1:18 makes φρόνησις a subspecies of σοφία.

Does the attachment of this phrase to the verb that follows (1:9) imply that *God's* wisdom is the source of the "making known" or that man's wisdom is the result of God's revelation? It may be that Paul simply intends to emphasize the fullness of the "making known," which proceeds from and produces "all wisdom and understanding": wise teacher, wise students. Once again the lavishness of the gift is extolled.

1:9–10 These two verses might be considered the *propositio*, or thesis statement of the *proem* (1:3–14), presenting the theme of Ephesians.[84] Yet, as it is in the language of prayer, it does not have the rhetorical force of a true thesis (such as Rom 1:16–17) and is difficult to isolate from the language that precedes it. Perhaps we could say that it gives *a* theme of Ephesians.

1:9 γνωρίσας ἡμῖν τὸ μυστήριον τοῦ θελήματος αὐτοῦ—One-quarter of the NT occurrences of γνωρίζω, "to make known," are in Ephesians (six of twenty-five), with three more in Colossians. These occurrences can be classed into two contexts: (1) the revelation of Christ that God gave through the Holy Spirit to the apostles and prophets (3:3, 5)[85] and (2) the ongoing revelation that occurs in the church through apostolic preaching (3:10; 6:19).[86] μυστήριον, "mystery," is likewise a characteristic term, occurring six times in Ephesians and four times in Colossians (out of twenty-eight NT occurrences).[87] Although "mystery" has various referents in the NT,[88] at the heart of them all is the Gospel of Jesus Christ itself—or rather, himself (Col 2:2–3). Col 1:27, in fact, defines the mystery as "Christ in you" (ὅ ἐστιν Χριστὸς ἐν ὑμῖν)—the oneness with Christ established by Holy Baptism and sustained by hearing his Word and receiving his sacramental body and blood, the corollary of being "in Christ" (1:3, etc.).

Although the Law had been revealed in many ways over the ages, God's gracious, forgiving nature could only be known through the revelation of his Word. Prior to the advent of Christ, the Gospel was revealed only partially. Its fullness in Christ, especially

---

[84] See "Rhetorical Outline" in "Structure and Rhetoric" in the introduction.

[85] Although Paul traces this revelation directly to Christ (Gal 1:12), the "making known" (γνωρίζω) to the apostles was not always immediate, but occurred through preaching, teaching, and Holy Scripture. For Christ taught the apostles (Jn 15:15; 17:26) through the Scriptures (Lk 24:44–46), and Paul learned from the Scriptures (Rom 16:26; perhaps Gal 1:17–18; 2:1), as did Peter (2 Pet 1:19–21). Paul also uses the language of oral tradition (1 Cor 11:23; 15:3), which surely informs our reading of Gal 1:12. And Peter learned from Paul (Gal 2:14; 2 Pet 3:15–16). In addition, the pervasive appeal to the OT in the apostolic writings is evidence that they were an instrument of revelation to the apostles.

[86] Cf. Col 1:25–27; 2 Pet 1:16. Indeed, Paul's act of writing is described with the same verb, γνωρίζω, "make known" (1 Cor 12:3; 15:1; Gal 1:11), indicating that it is a continuation of his preaching and teaching.

[87] Eph 1:9; 3:3, 4, 9; 5:32; 6:19; Col 1:26, 27; 2:2; 4:3.

[88] Caird, *The Language and Imagery of the Bible*, 54–55, clarifies the confusion over "mystery" that is present in so much literature on Ephesians:

> Among the arguments put forward to prove that Paul could not have written Ephesians there is one which states that *mysterion* has a meaning in Ephesians different from that which it has in Colossians. In fact the sense of the word is identical in both letters: it means "a secret"; and it is only the referent, the nature or content of the secret, that is different. Yet there is no reason why one writer should not have detected in the person of Christ two different, though related, secrets.

as it would be worked out on the cross and from the grave, was hidden in God's mind as part of his eternal plan (τοῦ θελήματος αὐτοῦ, "of his will," 1:9). But now the mystery has been unveiled. Hence, even though the human mind may never fully grasp the complexity of the divine plan, Paul's emphasis in his use of μυστήριον is not on the *persistence* of "mystery" in the faith, but on the *revelation* of what was formerly hidden. In 3:1–13 Paul defines the "mystery," first, as the Gospel of Christ that was revealed to him as Christ's apostle, and, second, as the revelation that by this Gospel the Gentiles (together with faithful Jews)[89] have been incorporated into the body of Christ (3:6).

This revelation of mystery has nothing to do with pagan mystery religions, nor is it borrowed from contemporary Jewish apocalyptic movements like Qumran. Rather, it follows naturally upon the general apocalyptic view of the OT, that God's prophets are commissioned to reveal the heavenly truths of the coming age.[90] μυστήριον, "mystery," came into Latin ecclesiastical language as *sacramentum*. Though the Sacraments may legitimately be called "mysteries" in that they are part of the continuing revelation of the Gospel of Christ, it would be anachronistic to restrict μυστήριον in Ephesians specifically to them.[91] See further the first and second textual notes on 5:32.

κατὰ τὴν εὐδοκίαν αὐτοῦ—See the fifth textual note on 1:5.

ἣν προέθετο ἐν αὐτῷ—The relative pronoun ἥν, "which," refers back to εὐδοκίαν, "good pleasure," not θελήματος, "will." Because εὐδοκία, "good pleasure," can itself refer to the plan God is pleased to carry out, the distinction is not great; but it suggests a different historical referent for this phrase. The meaning of προτίθημι is either "to set forth a plan [beforehand]" (Rom 1:13) or "to set forth [publicly]" (Rom 3:25). In the present context the former meaning is indeed possible: God "planned" his εὐδοκία, "good pleasure," in prehistory. But the connection of εὐδοκία, "good pleasure," with ἐν αὐτῷ, "in him," suggests the latter meaning.

When did God "set forth publicly" his "good pleasure" in Christ? At Christ's Baptism, when he spoke from heaven: ἐν ᾧ [or σοὶ] εὐδόκησα, "in whom [or you] I am well-pleased" (Mt 3:17; Mk 1:11; Lk 3:22). This crucial event, which occurs at the beginning of all four Gospels, does not simply mark the moment when God's eternal plan is set in motion. The baptismal starting point colors the entire Gospel; Jesus' Baptism leads inexorably to his death, which he describes as a baptism (Mk 10:38–39;

---

[89] It is therefore unnecessary to define the referent of ἡμῖν, "to us" (1:9), more precisely (to us Christians or to us Jews or to us apostles, etc.). Schlier, *Epheser*, 60: "Those holy apostles and prophets [3:2ff.] are receivers of the σοφία καὶ φρόνησις ['wisdom and understanding'] in the sense that it has been imparted to them in the manner of an immediate revelation that is foundational for the church, whereas the members of the church only receive it in connection with them and upon them as a foundation, as 2:20 and 4:7ff. provide."

[90] In the LXX the specific term μυστήριον occurs only in Daniel (translating רָז) and the Apocryphal writings; most interesting is Dan 2:16–47, where the "mystery" revealed is the advent of the kingdom of God within the chronology of world kingdoms (see "The *Berakah* Prayer" in the commentary). See also Grothe, "The Mysteries and the Ministry"; Scharlemann, "The Secret of God's Plan"; Deterding, *Colossians*, 73–75; thorough, but less helpful, is Markus N. A. Bockmuehl, *Revelation and Mystery in Ancient Judaism and Pauline Christianity* (Tübingen: Mohr, 1990).

[91] See particularly Barth, *Ephesians*, 1:123–27.

Lk 12:50). So also for the Christian, Baptism into Christ is Baptism into his death (Rom 6:3–4; Col 2:12), which leads to resurrection with Christ (Eph 2:5; Col 2:13). And this is a major theme of Paul's argumentation in Ephesians. Paul takes up what is said here of Christ and applies it to every Christian by virtue of his Baptism into Christ: i.e., as God was well-pleased with Christ, so he is well-pleased with Christians (cf. Lk 2:14). Through Baptism God reveals to the Christian his gracious attitude, which previously had been hidden in the mystery of his eternal plan.

1:10 εἰς οἰκονομίαν—This phrase, literally, "for administration," is rendered in the translation above as "to administer." οἰκονομία is another characteristic word in Ephesians. Of its nine NT occurrences, three are in Ephesians (1:10; 3:2, 9), and one is in Colossians (1:25). It can be notoriously difficult to translate, but most often it relates to the work of a steward in managing a large household or estate (cf. Lk 16:2–4). Paul often uses it of his office as an apostle.[92] Here God is the Steward, and the reference is to his administration of his cosmic household according to his plan. Thus, it is one more member of the large complex of words Paul uses in this section to refer to God's eternal will, plan, and purpose.[93] Barth suggests plausibly that Paul has Christ in mind as the Arch-steward of God's plan, sent by the Father to manage the times of fulfillment, distributing the goods of God's household.[94] The preposition εἰς would then introduce the purpose of God's declaration of his favor in Christ: that his plan might be carefully administered in order to fulfill it at the right time.

τοῦ πληρώματος τῶν καιρῶν—Our translation takes the two genitives as objective: πλήρωμα, "fulfillment, fulfilling," is the direct object of the verb underlying οἰκονομία, "to administer"; and καιρός is the direct object of the verb underlying πλήρωμα, "to fulfill," thus, "to administer the fulfilling of the opportune moments." This precise phrase (τοῦ πληρώματος τῶν καιρῶν) occurs only here in the NT. Similar expressions such as πεπλήρωται ὁ καιρός, "the time is fulfilled,"[95] indicate that the coming of Christ is the great moment at the culmination of God's plan for the salvation of mankind. Paul has located the incarnation of Christ at τὸ πλήρωμα τοῦ χρόνου, "the fullness of time" (Gal 4:4). That parallel, incidentally, cautions one against making too fine a distinction between καιρός (Eph 1:10) and χρόνος (Gal 4:4). Classically, however, the unique

---

[92] 1 Cor 9:17; Eph 3:2; Col 1:25; cf. οἰκονόμος, "steward, manager," in Lk 12:41–48; 1 Cor 4:1–2; Titus 1:7.

[93] Interestingly, Ignatius, *To the Ephesians*, 18:2, uses οἰκονομία in the same sense: "For our God, Jesus Christ, was conceived by Mary according to the *plan* of God [κατ᾽ οἰκονομίαν θεοῦ], from the seed of David and of the Holy Spirit: who was born and was baptized in order that by his suffering [or submission] he might cleanse the water" (Ignatius, *To the Ephesians*, 20:1). This creedal declaration makes particular reference to Christ's Baptism, as we suggest that Paul does in Ephesians 1. See "Baptism and the Spirit" in "Purpose and Themes" in the introduction.

[94] Barth, *Ephesians*, 1:88. It was not uncommon in the ancient world for a son to be appointed steward of his father's household. If Christ is indeed the Steward, this may not be the only place where he is viewed as such. The parable of the Steward of Unrighteousness (Lk 16:1–9) may be read Christologically, the Steward representing Christ in his work of canceling man's debts with the divine Master.

[95] Mk 1:15; cf. Lk 1:20; 2:6; Jn 7:8.

emphasis of καιρός is that the moment is opportune, crucial, or precisely right. Hence God's stewardship of history, especially the history of Israel, entailed his acting at each precise moment that his plan required, culminating in the incarnation and ministry of Christ. The time of Christ is an era that surpasses all previous eras.[96]

ἀνακεφαλαιώσασθαι τὰ πάντα ἐν τῷ Χριστῷ—In its only other NT occurrence, ἀνακεφαλαιόω, "to sum up,"[97] is used literally of a brief summary of the Law (Rom 13:9). Here the meaning is less literal but still refers to the bringing together of disparate items into one place. Thus, the ESV's "to unite all things in him" is not inaccurate; likewise the KJV's "that … he might gather together in one." The careful οἰκονομία, "administration," of God's orderly plan has in view this further goal: that Christ should be the location where all things come together. In Christ, τὰ πάντα, "all things" (Eph 1:10),[98] are reconciled: God to people, heaven to earth, and people one to another (2 Cor 5:19). All that was created through him (Col 1:16) is redeemed through him (Col 1:20). Paul will unfold these ideas later in the epistle as they are relevant to the unity of the church (e.g., Eph 2:16), which is the place where this reconciliation is proclaimed and effected. Indeed, Paul's choice of this unusual word, which has κεφαλή, "head," at its root, may hint at his later location of this unity in the sole headship of Christ (see κεφαλή, "head," in 1:22; 4:15; 5:23).[99]

τὰ ἐπὶ τοῖς οὐρανοῖς καὶ τὰ ἐπὶ τῆς γῆς ἐν αὐτῷ—"The things in heaven and the things on earth in him" parallels and expands upon the preceding phrase, τὰ πάντα ἐν τῷ Χριστῷ, "all things in Christ." The unity of heavenly and earthly things certainly refers to God's reconciliation with mankind. It probably also includes the spiritual forces of the heavenly places of which pagan Gentiles were so afraid, for both Ephesians and Colossians emphasize Christ's superiority and victory over spiritual forces.[100] It may also refer to the restoration of all creation through Christ's work (Rom 8:19–23). Thus, it confesses the universality of Christ's atonement. In the present context, however, in a prayer that may well have been based on the presider's prayers at the Lord's Supper,[101] it describes the worship of the NT church: heaven and earth, angels and saints, are joined

---

[96] It would be wrong to move the fulfillment into the future: "to be put into effect when the times will have reached their fulfillment." Such a translation stands in contradiction to the consistent NT witness we have noted, that the καιρός is now (cf. 1 Cor 10:11; 2 Cor 6:2).

[97] The meaning "renew, restore, recapitulate," found particularly in Irenaeus, should not be imported into the NT (as the Vulgate does).

[98] Stoeckhardt's interpretation of τὰ πάντα as "the entirety of the children of God," the elect, the *una sancta* (*Ephesians*, 67), is untenable, since τὰ πάντα is neuter ("all *things*") and is defined more universally by the subsequent phrase.

[99] Barth, *Ephesians*, 1:91; Schnackenburg, *Ephesians*, 60. Lexicographers may argue that the verb ἀνακεφαλαιόω is derived from the noun κεφάλαιον, "sum, completion," not κεφαλή, "head" (Heinrich Schlier, "ἀνακεφαλαιόομαι," *TDNT* 3:682), but surely κεφάλαιον itself is derived from κεφαλή, and Paul is likely to have understood it that way.

[100] Eph 1:21; 2:2; 3:10; 6:12; Col 1:13, 16; 2:10, 15.

[101] Note the words of the Preface: "Therefore with angels and archangels and with all the company of heaven we laud and magnify Your glorious name …" (e.g., *LSB Altar Book*, 145). See further "Liturgical Context" in "Authorship" in the introduction.

together in giving doxology to God through Christ, because where Christ is present, there is God's glory. (See also the textual notes on 3:20–21.)

1:11 ἐν ᾧ—See the fifth textual note on 1:3 with ἐν Χριστῷ and the first textual notes on 1:7 and 1:13 with ἐν ᾧ.

καὶ ἐκληρώθημεν—The verb κληρόω commonly referred to the casting of lots through which public officials were chosen (in Greek democracy) or through which the gods declared their choice to people (in Greek religion). The true God also used such methods.[102] But there is no implication of randomness; God is in control of the lots to declare his will. In this context, κληρόω need not be taken literally; it simply refers to God's choice or appointment of man. That this appointment is not arbitrary is indicated by ἐν ᾧ, "in whom," referring to Christ (see the preceding textual note). In a sense, Christ himself is the "lot" that has been cast down by God; for us Christ is a lot that always reads "yes" (2 Cor 1:20). The verb appears to be supplemented grammatically by the infinitive clause at the beginning of the next verse: "[11]we have been appointed … [12]that we should be to the praise of his glory." The participial phrase in the middle, beginning with προορισθέντες, "since we had been predestined" (1:11b; see the next textual note), is then parenthetical with a causal force, as punctuated in the translation.

The verb κληρόω has further connotations when viewed against certain OT background themes. It is reminiscent of God's *election* of Israel as his chosen people, his "special possession" (περιποίησις, Eph 1:14), even his *heirs*, as κλῆρος can refer to an inherited share.[103] Thus, it hints at the church as the new Israel and implies the allotment of a place in God's kingdom as the Christian's inheritance.[104] Such an allotment also implies the corollary—that God has claimed us as his portion.[105] In the OT, the one tribe of Israel that did not receive an allotment of land was Levi, whose members were spread among the people. Their allotment was the place given them in the worship of God's temple. The Levites were allotted a place in the choir that they might sing God's praise.[106] Perhaps in the context of the present *Berakah* prayer Paul had this kind of allotment in mind for Christians, who are "appointed … to the praise of his glory" (Eph

---

[102] E.g., Urim and Thummim (e.g., Num 27:21; LXX 1 Kgdms 14:41–42 [MT/ET 1 Sam 14:41–42]); also the choice of an apostle by casting lots (Acts 1:26).

[103] Acts 26:18; Col 1:12; cf. Mt 25:34. In the OT the language for "lot" and "inheritance" merges when applied to Israel as God's "possession." See סְגֻלָּה, "special/treasured possession," translated in the LXX by περιούσιος (cf. περιούσιος also in LXX Ex 23:22; Titus 2:14; περιποίησις in Eph 1:14), in Ex 19:5; Deut 7:6; 14:2; 26:18 and by περιποίησις in Mal 3:17. See also terms for "inheritance" and/or "lot, portion" in, e.g., Deut 9:26; 32:9; Ps 74:2, and περιποιέω in LXX Is 43:21.

[104] κληρονομία, "inheritance" (Eph 1:14), is cognate to κληρόω, "appoint," and κλῆρος, "lot." Some commentators and translations (e.g., ESV), following BDAG, s.v. κληρόω, 2, translate ἐκληρώθημεν (Eph 1:11) as "we have obtained an inheritance" (which is perhaps an over-translation); this translation precludes reading εἰς τὸ εἶναι ἡμᾶς as a supplementary completion to the verb (see the first textual note on 1:12).

[105] Bruce, *The Epistles to the Colossians, to Philemon, and to the Ephesians*, 263, referring to Deut 32:8–9.

[106] See particularly the use of κλῆρος, "lot," for the places given to the sons of Aaron and the Levites in the temple choir in LXX 1 Chr 24:5, 7, 31; 25:8, 9 (cf. 1 Chr 26:13, 14).

1:11–12).[107] The precise referent of "we" will be considered in the third textual note on 1:12, but the OT flavor of ἐκληρώθημεν already hints that "we" are *Jewish* Christians.

Here καί means "also." But is it "*also we* have been appointed" or "we have *also been appointed*"? That is, does it qualify the subject of the verb or modify the action of the verb? If it modifies the verb, then one struggles to understand how this differs from what has already been said of "us" in earlier verses. If it qualifies the subject, it implies that a comparison is being made with Christ, who had first been appointed to be the location of reconciliation between heaven and earth (1:10): as he (Christ) was appointed, also we (Jewish Christians) have been appointed.

προορισθέντες κατὰ πρόθεσιν—While ἐκληρώθημεν, "we have been appointed" (1:11), refers to the public revelation of God's choice (as in Baptism; see ἐξελέξατο, "he chose," in 1:4), the aorist participle προορισθέντες refers to the prior choice God had already made before creation itself: "since we had been predestined." (On προορίζω, "to predestine," see the textual notes on 1:4, 5.) πρόθεσιν follows the verb προορισθέντες with fine poetic sound. πρόθεσις is a noun derived from the verb προτίθημι, which has just been used in 1:9. There the verb ("he declared," 1:9) referred to the revelation of God's plan; here the noun ("purpose," 1:11) refers to the plan itself that was set down in prehistory.[108] πρόθεσις, "purpose," is virtually synonymous with βουλή, "plan" (1:11), as that "plan" that arises from God's θέλημα, "will" (1:5, 9, 11). The fact that Paul uses so many words from this semantic field indicates that God's eternal plan is a significant theme in Ephesians.

τοῦ τὰ πάντα ἐνεργοῦντος κατὰ τὴν βουλὴν τοῦ θελήματος αὐτοῦ—"All things" (τὰ πάντα) is perhaps the most significant thing Paul wishes to add here. The logic is this: if God is at work in *all things* to accomplish his plan—a fact that is inherent in the very definition of "God"—then surely his children can trust that their own salvation is in his hands. Inasmuch as ἐνεργέω with a direct object can mean "to accomplish, produce, effect" something (with an emphasis on results as much as effort), this sentence of Paul's verges on determinism: all things are accomplished by God. When viewed in the way of the Law, this is indeed a terrifying thought. But by appending "according to the plan of his will" in Christ, Paul speaks it as Gospel, as reassurance and comfort (cf. 1:20).

1:12 εἰς τὸ εἶναι ἡμᾶς—This clause is probably the continuation of the main verb ἐκληρώθημεν (1:11), indicating purpose: "[11]we have been appointed ... [12]that we should be ..." (cf. Rom 7:4). As Israel's very existence in the world was praise to God,[109] so also the Christian church has been appointed *to be* his glory. The RSV changes this Gospel promise into Law by translating εἶναι as "to live": "we ... have been destined and appointed *to live* for the praise of his glory." Paul's point is not that we praise God by our right conduct or merely in our actions, but more fundamentally that our very existence as God's redeemed gives praise to the God who redeemed us; it is a testimony to

---

[107] Thanks to John Kleinig for this insight, which came too late to be incorporated more thoroughly into this chapter.

[108] Similar is the usage of πρόθεσις for God's eternal plan or "purpose" in Rom 8:28; 9:11; Eph 3:11; 2 Tim 1:9.

[109] Deut 26:19; Is 43:21; 62:7; Jer 13:11.

the world and a snub to the devil, who thought we were his. Ambrosiaster comments: "Just as it is the glory of a doctor if he cures many, so it is to the praise of God's glory when many are won for the faith."[110] For the specific referent of "we," see the third textual note on 1:12.

εἰς ἔπαινον δόξης αὐτοῦ—See the first textual note on 1:6, where a similar phrase occurs. This prepositional phrase marks the end of the second, Christological section of the prayer (1:7–12). The genitive δόξης αὐτοῦ, "of his glory," is objective, indicating what is praised. The referent of αὐτοῦ, "his," is the Father,[111] to whom Christ's redeeming work brings glory, e.g., "and every tongue confess that Jesus Christ is Lord, to the glory of God the Father" (Phil 2:11).[112]

τοὺς προηλπικότας ἐν τῷ Χριστῷ—Although προελπίζω is a hapax legomenon, its meaning is straightforward: "to hope beforehand." The subject of the participle is also clear: ἡμᾶς, "us," at the beginning of the verse.[113] But two difficult questions of referent arise: (1) Who is hoping? That is, what is the referent of the participle's subject, ἡμᾶς, "us"? (2) Before whom (or what[114]) did "we" hope? That is, what is the referent of προ-, "before, earlier"? In the context of the letter thus far, one would assume "we" refers to Paul and those Christians who came to faith in Christ before the Ephesians (to whom he refers with ὑμεῖς, "you," in 1:13). But there is sufficient evidence in the rest of the letter to suggest that the distinction might be between Jewish and Gentile Christians in general.[115] This distinction is crucial for the interpretation of the epistle as a whole, which appears to address a division between Jewish and Gentile Christians

---

[110] Ambrosiaster, *Ephesians*, 1:14 (ACCS 8:119).

[111] In Eph 1:17 "glory" is uniquely descriptive of the Father: ὁ πατὴρ τῆς δόξης, "the Father of glory"; cf. 2 Pet 1:17.

[112] Cf. Rom 16:27; Eph 3:21; 1 Pet 4:11; Jude 25; Rev 1:6.

[113] The personal pronoun ἡμᾶς is accusative, "us," because that is the normal way to express the subject of an infinitive in Greek: εἰς τὸ εἶναι ἡμᾶς, "for *us* to be …" In English translation it works better as a subordinate clause with the nominative: "that *we* should be …" The subsequent participle προηλπικότας, then, is also in the accusative to agree with the pronoun: ἡμᾶς … τοὺς προηλπικότας, "us/we … who first hoped."

[114] BDAG, s.v. προελπίζω, suggests that the preposition προ- in the compound verb may "be understood syntagmatically: hope is prior to realization"—meaning that it is synonymous with the simple verb ἐλπίζω itself. But such a redundancy is less likely than the other options.

[115] In 2:12 Paul speaks of the Gentiles before they heard the Gospel as "having no hope." And in 4:4 "hope" is provided in their call to faith (cf. Col 1:23, 27). That those who "first hoped" (Eph 1:12) are the Jews is a traditional interpretation going back as far as Tertullian:

> Who can have previously hoped, which means hoped in Christ before his coming, except those Jews to whom since the beginning Christ was previously announced? He then that was previously announced was also previously hoped in. And so the apostle refers to himself and his own, which means the Jews, in such form as to make a distinction when he turns to the gentiles: *In whom ye also …* (*Against Marcion*, 5:17.4 [trans. Evans])

Dahl, "Gentiles, Christians, and Israelites in the Epistle to the Ephesians," in *Studies in Ephesians*, 445, represents those commentators who deny that "we" ever means "we Jews" in Ephesians, insisting that "first person plural forms include all Christians, Gentiles and Jews"—though he admits that, in places, the letter addresses the separation between Jews and Gentiles. Certainly he is right that, for the author, the distinction between Jew and Gentile can only be expressed in the past tense in light of the unifying work of Christ (2:14–16).

(see "Jews and Greeks in the Body of Christ" in "Purpose and Themes" in the introduction). That Jewish Christians hoped "before" could refer either to the fact that the Gospel first went to the Jews (Rom 1:16), who therefore hoped before the Gentiles, or that Israel had set its hope on the Messiah even before he had come (Rom 4:18; Gal 3:16). It is unlikely that the "we" is simply all Christians, who hope in Christ "before" he returns,[116] since Paul makes a contrast with "you" in the very next verse (see the next textual note). While ἐν τῷ Χριστῷ is certainly evocative of all that "in Christ" means in this section (see the fifth textual note on 1:3), in this instance it is also a natural way to supply an object for the verb "first hoped" (cf. 1 Cor 15:19: ἐν Χριστῷ ἠλπικότες ἐσμέν, "we have hoped in Christ").

1:13 ἐν ᾧ καὶ ὑμεῖς—Here begins the third section of the Trinitarian prayer, which focuses on the Holy Spirit (see the commentary). The antecedent of "in whom," however, is still Christ, mentioned at the end of the previous verse (1:12); he has been the referent of "in whom" throughout the prayer (see the fifth textual note on 1:3 and the first textual note on 1:4). "In Christ" continues to have a baptismal flavor, which is particularly evident when we come to the main verb of this section, ἐσφραγίσθητε, "you were sealed" (see the fifth textual note on 1:13). καὶ ὑμεῖς, "also *you*," stands in contrast to "*we* ... who first hoped" in the previous verse (1:12). The referent of "you" is clearly the Ephesians to whom Paul writes, but in what capacity? Most likely: "you *Gentiles* in Ephesus, who became Christians through hearing the Gospel." Jew and Gentile are united through the same Gospel of Christ.

ἀκούσαντες τὸν λόγον τῆς ἀληθείας—The aorist participle ἀκούσαντες, "having heard," refers back to that concrete, missionary moment when Paul (and then Apollos) first proclaimed the Gospel in Ephesus (Acts 18:19–26). When Paul later puts this into a conditional expression, "if indeed you have heard" (3:2; 4:21), it is simply a rhetorical device intended to draw a strong positive response from the Ephesians: "indeed we have heard!" As 1:13 demonstrates, Paul is in no doubt as to whether or not they have heard the Gospel![117] λόγος, commonly translated as "word," here does not mean "individual word" (vocable), but "message." τῆς ἀληθείας, "of truth," should be understood as an adjectival genitive: the message characterized by truth. This begins with Christ himself, the λόγος, "Word," who reveals God's truth in his speaking (4:21).[118] The genuine preacher of God continues this speaking only when he conforms his message to the truth of Christ.[119] So is it also for every Christian, for falsehood characterizes the

---

[116] This is the interpretation of, e.g., Schnackenburg, *Ephesians*, 64, who takes the perfect participle as present in emphasis. Such a participle could be translated as "who have hoped and are now still hoping."

[117] Contra numerous commentators who believe on the basis of 3:2 and 4:21 that the author of Ephesians disavows any direct knowledge of his addressees. See "Authorship" and "Paul and Ephesus in Acts" in "The City of Ephesus and Paul's Relationship to It" in the introduction, as well as the first textual notes on 3:2 and 4:21.

[118] Cf. Jn 1:14; 14:16; 17:17; James 1:18.

[119] 2 Cor 4:2; 6:7; 2 Tim 2:15.

old, Gentile way of life that was laid aside in Baptism (4:15, 25).[120] Col 1:5 parallels this verse closely.

τὸ εὐαγγέλιον τῆς σωτηρίας ὑμῶν—The genitive has two aspects: "the Gospel message whose *content* is the salvation accomplished for you" and "the Gospel message that *brings* you salvation." This exact phrase is not paralleled elsewhere in the NT. Rom 1:16 comes closest: "for I am not ashamed of the Gospel; for it is God's power for salvation for everyone who believes, to the Jew first and also to the Greek." There Paul combines the same three terms we have here: εὐαγγέλιον, "Gospel"; σωτηρία, "salvation"; and πιστεύω, "believe."[121] In doing so, Paul makes precisely the same point here as he made in Romans 1: the Gentiles who heard the Gospel message and believed it received salvation, just as the Jewish Christians who first believed.

ἐν ᾧ καὶ πιστεύσαντες—"In whom, having also believed" reminds us that hearing in biblical terms is never neutral. Hearing involves either rejection of or belief in the message (cf. the parable of the Sower: Matthew 13; Mark 4; Luke 8). Here Paul makes it explicit that the Ephesians' hearing of the Gospel was indeed fruitful, resulting in faith.[122] The corollary is emphasized in Rom 10:14: there can be no believing unless there is a preacher to hear. The antecedent of ἐν ᾧ might be "the Gospel" (cf. Mk 1:15); but as it has elsewhere referred to Christ, we have maintained the translation "in whom" rather than "in which." Furthermore, it is unlikely that the object of faith would be expressed with the preposition ἐν.[123] The phrase ought still to be understood as the mystical, sacramental location in which the act of sealing took place. In other words, it means not "you-who-also-believed-in-him [or 'it'] were sealed," but "*in him* you were sealed, after you also had believed."

ἐσφραγίσθητε τῷ πνεύματι τῆς ἐπαγγελίας τῷ ἁγίῳ—The aorist verb ἐσφραγίσθητε, "you were sealed," refers to a specific action that followed upon the proclamation of the Gospel and people believing it: Holy Baptism (see "The Seal of the Spirit" in the commentary). The agent of this sealing was God the Father (cf. Jn 6:27; 2 Cor 1:21–22; Eph 4:30); thus, "were sealed" is a divine passive. The instrument or means, expressed in the dative, was, literally, "*the Holy Spirit* of the promise."[124] Like

---

[120] Cf. Mt 28:19–20, where Christ mandates that those who are baptized should be taught to hold fast to the fullness of his teaching.

[121] Cf. 1 Cor 1:18; 15:1–2. A similar combination is in 2 Thess 2:13–14, adding also ἀλήθεια, "truth"; in 1 Tim 2:4 "to be saved" and "to come to the knowledge of the truth" are equated.

[122] Hearing and believing is the pattern of mission reported in Acts 4:4; 13:48; 15:7; 18:8.

[123] See the fourth textual note on 1:1, including the footnote on the personal object of πιστεύω, "to believe." BDAG, s.v. πιστεύω, 2 a ε, states, "π[ιστεύω] ἐν τινι *believe in someone* ... is questionable in our lit[erature]: ... in Eph 1:13 both occurrences of ἐν ᾧ are prob[ably] to be construed w[ith] ἐσφραγίσθητε (='in connection with whom you have been sealed' [cp. 4:30])." See also Moule, *Idiom Book*, 80–81, who argues that πιστεύω does not normally take an object with ἐν. See also the fifth textual note on 1:15.

[124] The Spirit is the instrument of the Father's work. This is not to deny the personhood of the Holy Spirit. But the language is analogical. The Holy Spirit takes the role of the oil of anointing, the wax of sealing, or the fire of branding. He may be the signet ring (pressed into clay or wax) or the firebrand (searing wood or flesh), but the image bestowed is not his own, but the Son's. See further "The Seal of the Spirit (1:13; 4:30)" below. A dative of personal agent is rare in the NT (BDF, § 191; Wallace, *Greek Grammar*, 163–66). In the LXX and the NT,

the parallel τήν ἐπαγγελίαν τοῦ πνεύματος, "the promise of the Spirit" (Acts 2:33; Gal 3:14), this phrase means "the promised Holy Spirit." The Spirit was first promised in the OT, which connected his coming with the time of the Messiah.[125] The initial fulfillment of this promise was twofold: (1) his pouring out upon Christ at his Baptism (Mt 3:16 and parallels); (2) his pouring out upon Christians at Pentecost (Acts 2:4, 16–18). Christ, who had received this promised Spirit from the Father, reiterated the promise with reference to the imminent outpouring of the Spirit at Pentecost.[126] The giving of the Spirit in fulfillment of God's promise, however, is by no means exhausted in these two events, but rather initiated. Through faith (Gal 3:14) and Holy Baptism,[127] all Christians receive the same promised Holy Spirit. Hearing the Gospel, believing it, and being baptized is a pattern of mission amply illustrated in Acts.[128] But in the present context we are reminded most explicitly of Paul's diagnostic question to the Ephesian Christians at the beginning of his long pastorate there: "Did you receive the Holy Spirit when you believed [πιστεύσαντες]? … Into what then were you baptized?" (Acts 19:2–3). The subsequent account demonstrates that Paul believes the gift of the Holy Spirit is inextricably bound to those who believe and are baptized (see "Paul and Ephesus in Acts" in "The City of Ephesus and Paul's Relationship to It" in the introduction).

1:14 ὅ ἐστιν ἀρραβὼν τῆς κληρονομίας ἡμῶν—There are two possible antecedents for the neuter relative pronoun ὅ, "which" or "who":

1. The "sealing" implied by the verb ἐσφραγίσθητε (1:13). Although the Greek noun σφραγίς, "seal," is feminine, the neuter relative pronoun could refer in a general way to the action of the verb.

2. The Holy Spirit. This is the more obvious antecedent, in that πνεῦμα is a neuter singular noun standing readily at hand in the previous phrase. Although the Spirit is neuter in Greek, good English usage requires referring to this person of the Holy

---

the instrument of sealing is normally expressed with a dative: 3 Kgdms 20:8 (MT/ET 1 Ki 21:8); Esth 8:8, 10; Manasseh 3 (= Odes 12:3); Dan 6:18 (ET 6:17); Bel 14; Rev 5:1.

[125] E.g., Is 42:1; 44:3; Ezek 11:19; 36:25–27; 39:29; Joel 3:1–2 (ET 2:28–29). Käsemann, "Ephesians and Acts," 295, observes: "2:12; 3:3; 6:2 show that in Ephesians ἐπαγγελία always means the promise made to Israel." Thus, the Gentiles, by incorporation into Christ's body, receive what was first promised to Israel. This is not to deny that the Holy Spirit was present and at work in the OT era; see the commentary on Is 63:10–11 in Lessing, *Isaiah 56–66*, 369–75.

[126] Lk 24:49; Acts 2:4–5, 33; also Jn 15:26; 16:7.

[127] Acts 2:38; 8:14–17; 9:17–18; 19:5–6; 1 Cor 12:13. Ambrosiaster, *Ephesians*, 1:14: "The Gentiles have as a sign of their redemption and future inheritance the Holy Spirit, given at baptism" (ACCS 8:119).

[128] E.g., Acts 2:37–38, 41; 8:12–13, 35–38; 10:44–48; 16:14–15, 32–33; 18:8. The Roman Catholic exegete Heinrich Schlier, whose marvelous commentary views Ephesians as a thoroughly baptismal writing, argues unconvincingly that Baptism is included in πιστεύσαντες, "having believed." He proceeds to identify ἐσφραγίσθητε, "you were sealed," with a subsequent act of laying on hands (*Epheser*, 70). That this exegesis misses the mark is conclusively demonstrated by Lampe, *The Seal of the Spirit*. Dinkler, "Die Taufterminologie in 2 Kor. i 21 f.," 185, writes that σφραγίζω, "to seal," is "der *gesamte* Akt der Taufe und nicht etwa *ein* Motiv innerhalb desselben" ("the *entire* act of Baptism and not simply *one* theme within it").

Trinity as "he" or "who," not "it" or "which."[129] That this also became the practice of the early church is evident in the manuscript tradition, as the majority of later manuscripts substitute the masculine pronoun ὅς for the neuter ὅ.

The noun ἀρραβών is a Semitic loanword, transliterating the Hebrew עֵרָבוֹן, something given as a "pledge." In Gen 38:17–20 the עֵרָבוֹן is an item of value given by the debtor as security and returned to him when the debt is paid. Paul would appear to be alluding to a slightly different practice: a "payment of part of a purchase price in advance, *first installment, deposit, down payment, pledge* … , which secures a legal claim to the article in question, or makes a contract valid."[130] The Holy Spirit himself is placed into the one baptized as this first payment, God's guarantee that he will make the final payment.[131] This promised "payment" is a κληρονομία, "inheritance." Inheritance flows from sonship and so is richly baptismal—for those who have been made sons of God through rebirth in Holy Baptism are made heirs of God's wealth.[132]

It is thus no surprise that inheritance is a key theme of Ephesians.[133] In the NT, Christ as the Son of God is the primary heir;[134] those who are baptized into Christ are sons by adoption (1:5) and through him receive all the benefits of his sonship, inheriting what he inherited: "if children, then heirs, heirs of God and fellow heirs with Christ" (Rom 8:17). When the content of the inheritance is concretely defined by the NT, it is "the kingdom,"[135] "eternal life,"[136] or "salvation."[137] In Baptism the mortal body is marked by and filled with the Holy Spirit as a guarantee that this very body will be raised from the dead to live forever in God's kingdom. This eschatological interpretation of inheritance is confirmed by the parallel in Eph 4:30: "and do not grieve the Holy Spirit of God, in whom you were sealed [ἐσφραγίσθητε] for the day of redemption [ἡμέραν

---

[129] In NT Greek the noun πνεῦμα is always accompanied by neuter pronouns, as the grammar requires. The terms παράκλητος, "comforter, advocate," used regularly of the Spirit in John's Gospel, is masculine and takes masculine pronouns. Occasionally the masculine pronoun ἐκεῖνος, "that one, he," is used of the Holy Spirit when the antecedent may be either πνεῦμα or παράκλητος (Jn 14:26; 15:26; 16:13–14)—passages traditionally used to support the personhood of the Spirit, but which are grammatically somewhat ambiguous. 1 Jn 5:7–8 uses a masculine participle for the Spirit, the water, and the blood, personifying all three. See Wallace, *Greek Grammar*, 331–32.

[130] BDAG, s.v. ἀρραβών.

[131] The seal of the Spirit is called a "deposit" also in 2 Cor 1:22. See Dinkler, "Die Taufterminologie in 2 Kor. i 21 f.," 183–91. The "final payment" guaranteed by the deposit of the Spirit is the resurrection of the body in 2 Cor 5:1–5. Likewise, when the Spirit is called "the firstfruits" (τὴν ἀπαρχὴν τοῦ πνεύματος), the full harvest which follows is the resurrection, "the redemption of our body" (τὴν ἀπολύτρωσιν τοῦ σώματος ἡμῶν," Rom 8:23).

[132] Rom 8:16–17; Gal 3:29; 4:7. If sons, then κληρονόμοι, "heirs." Baptism in Titus 3:5 results in the baptized being heirs of eternal life in Titus 3:7.

[133] Of the fourteen NT occurrences of κληρονομία, three are in Ephesians (1:14, 18; 5:5), and one is in Paul's speech to the Ephesian pastors (Acts 20:32).

[134] Cf. the parable of the Wicked Tenants, who seek to kill the heir—a Christological parable (Mt 21:33–46; Mk 12:1–12; Lk 20:9–19). See also Heb 1:2–4.

[135] Mt 25:34; 1 Cor 6:9–11; 15:50; Gal 5:21; Eph 5:5; James 2:5.

[136] Mt 19:29; Mk 10:17 and parallels; Titus 3:7.

[137] Heb 1:14. Here, as often in the NT, "salvation" is not a past action, but a future gift.

ἀπολυτρώσεως].” This “day” is surely the Day of the Lord, Christ’s parousia, until which day the inheritance is preserved imperishably in heaven.[138] In the second textual note on 1:11, we examined the OT background of κληρόω, “to allot a share.” Each tribe of Israel was given an allotment of land as its inheritance in the promised land (Josh 13:6–19:48; cf. Ezek 45:1; 48:29); the Christian’s future inheritance might rightly be seen as that allotment’s true fulfillment—an inheritance in the greater promised land.[139]

εἰς ἀπολύτρωσιν τῆς περιποιήσεως—Here ἀπολύτρωσις has a double sense. There is certainly an echo of the theological meaning of “redemption” as salvation in Christ (1:7). But in the present verse it refers more specifically to the metaphor of deposit. In a commercial transaction, when one wishes to collect the goods that were promised when the deposit was first paid, one produces the receipt and redeems them. The merchant is legally bound to give the goods in exchange for that receipt. Here Paul pictures the Spirit deposited within us as such a pledge given by God.

The next noun, περιποίησις, means “possession.” The deposit and redemption image may be understood as the Christian laying claim to eternal life as his “possession,” due to him because of Christ’s work.[140] But context suggests περιποίησις should be understood according to its frequent scriptural application to God’s *people* as his “special possession.”[141] Inasmuch as God is the one who made the deposit, he is also the one who will redeem the goods to be his very own. On the Last Day Christ will return to claim the people for whom he has paid with the price of his blood (Acts 20:28) and take them to the Father as his special possession, bringing them fully into the inheritance awaiting them. The Holy Spirit is a sure and certain pledge of this inheritance because life is the Spirit’s peculiar gift.[142]

εἰς ἔπαινον τῆς δόξης αὐτοῦ—With this refrain, the end of the third section (1:13–14) of this Trinitarian prayer is marked. The insertion of the definite article τῆς (in distinction from the previous two anarthrous occurrences of εἰς ἔπαινον δόξης in 1:6, 12) does not change the meaning, but is an oral/aural technique that, by changing the rhythm, draws the prayer to a close. As in 1:6 and 1:12 the referent of αὐτοῦ, “his,” must be the Father: “to the praise of his [the Father’s] glory.”

Although no manuscripts of Ephesians contain “amen” at the end of 1:14, it is not unreasonable to presume that the congregation would have voiced its amen at this point in the reading of Ephesians in the Divine Service. The Ephesians would have recognized

---

[138] 1 Pet 1:4; see also Heb 9:15.

[139] Early baptismal rites (such as that recorded by Hippolytus, *Apostolic Tradition*, 21:28) often included the gift of milk and honey to the candidate, alluding to the blessings of the promised land (Ex 3:8 and passim).

[140] Such an interpretation would be supported by 1 Thess 5:9; 2 Thess 2:14; cf. 1 Pet 1:4.

[141] In 1 Pet 2:9 Christians are called God’s περιποίησις, “treasured possession,” alluding to סְגֻלָּה in, e.g., Ex 19:5; Deut 7:6; 14:2; Mal 3:17. Though all the world is God’s, we are his most treasured possession. See also *1 Clement*, 64:1, quoted in a footnote in the second textual note on 1:4; see also the footnote that discusses סְגֻלָּה in the second textual note on 1:11.

[142] The Nicene Creed’s teaching that the Spirit is “the Lord and giver of life” is based on scriptural teaching: see Rom 8:11; also Gen 2:7; Job 33:4; Jn 6:63; Rom 8:2; 2 Cor 3:6; Gal 6:8; Rev 2:7; 22:17.

the prayer character of the section and would have heard the doxological conclusion as the cue to respond with their amen (cf. 1 Cor 14:16; 2 Cor 1:20; Rev 5:14). At times the author himself writes the expected amen into his manuscript.[143] At times the manuscript tradition is confused—indicating that the amen was expected and naturally vocalized by the congregation, even if it was not originally written in the text.[144] For the OT background, see the fourth textual note on 3:21.

Commentary

Structure and Rhetoric

Eph 1:3–14 is one long sentence in Greek (204 words in the NA[27] text!), by some reckonings the longest in the entire NT. This feature is maintained in the above translation by punctuating it as one sentence. In this way we preserve the sensibilities of people in ancient times with their love for rhetoric, rather than breaking the pericope up into the short sentences favored in modern (particularly American) English. At the same time the reader is helped by the indenting that gives direction to the text and breaks it up into sense lines. The ancient lector would have taken the time to rehearse his reading of the text, mentally noting the structure that is made visible above. In addition to its length, the sentence is marked by an extraordinary complexity of heaped-up prepositional phrases, genitive chains, synonyms, and circumstantial participles. What explanation might we offer for its unusual length and complexity? As noted in the introduction,[145] Ephesus was a place where sophisticated rhetoric was treasured. Yet a more significant explanation lies in the liturgical context we have proposed for the reading of the NT epistles.[146] In this grand prelude, Paul's private prayer takes on the flavor of corporate worship.[147] He falls back into the language of liturgical presidency to which he was so accustomed after nearly three years of pastoral ministry among the Ephesian churches.[148] The modern reader can best experience this *majesté liturgique*[149] by reading the grand sentence aloud, with the careful dignity of public prayer.

---

[143] E.g., Rom 1:25; 9:5; 11:36; Gal 1:5; 6:18; Eph 3:21; Phil 4:20; 1 Tim 1:17; 6:16; 2 Tim 4:18; Heb 13:21; 1 Pet 4:11; Rev 7:12.

[144] E.g., Rom 15:33 and at the end of virtually every epistle, including Rom 16:27; 1 Cor 16:24; Phil 4:23; Col 4:18; 2 Tim 4:22; Titus 3:15; Heb 13:25. See the last textual note on Eph 6:24.

[145] See "Contextual/Rhetorical Factors" in "Authorship" in the introduction.

[146] See "The Liturgical Context of the New Testament Epistles" in "Orality and the Interpretation of the Epistles: A Brief Introduction" and "Liturgical Context" in "Authorship" in the introduction.

[147] "Repetition and redundance are of the essence of liturgy" (Lincoln, *Ephesians*, 12).

[148] See "Paul and Ephesus in Acts" in "The City of Ephesus and Paul's Relationship to It" in the introduction.

[149] "Liturgical majesty" is from Charles Masson, *L'Épitre de Saint Paul aux Éphésiens* (Neuchâtel: Delachaux & Niestlé, 1953), 149, quoted in Lincoln, *Ephesians*, 11.

The *Berakah* Prayer (1:3–14)

In most of his epistles, Paul follows the traditional Hellenistic epistolary tradition of giving thanks immediately after his address. In writing to the Galatians, Paul famously abandoned any thanksgiving in the heat of his distress over their apostasy. Titus, likewise, has no thanksgiving, but gets down to business quickly. In 1 Timothy—somewhat in parallel to Ephesians—the thanksgiving (1 Tim 1:12–17) is deferred until after the introductory *narratio*. In Ephesians the thanksgiving (1:15–23) is delayed while, similar to 2 Corinthians,[150] Paul breaks into doxology to the Triune God using a familiar pattern of prayer known as the *Berakah* (see the first textual note on 1:3).[151]

The Berakah *Prayer: Background and Parallels*

The Jewish character of this pattern is strong, with more than forty examples in the OT alone, and more in the Apocrypha, the NT, and the synagogue liturgy. Most early OT examples are brief, spontaneous prayers uttered by the faithful when they experience an extraordinarily gracious (usually salvific) act of God. Thus, when Jethro hears of Israel's miraculous escape from Egypt, he exclaims:

> Blessed be YHWH [בָּרוּךְ יְהוָה; LXX: εὐλογητὸς κύριος], who saved you from the hand of Egypt and from the hand of Pharaoh and who saved the people from under the hand of Egypt. Now I know that YHWH is greater than all the gods, because in this matter they [the Egyptians] acted arrogantly against them [the Israelites]. (Ex 18:10–11)

Two features of these prayers are most notable: (1) they bear the characteristic of true praise in that they (a) speak of God in the third person and (b) proclaim his mighty, saving deeds; and (2) petitions, often thought to be at the heart of prayer, are notably absent.[152] In this respect, the *Berakah* prayer differs from the typical thanksgiving at the beginning of a letter: it focuses more on the work of God than on the situation of the recipients.[153] In other OT examples, such prayers arise when God has granted such blessings as a revelation of heavenly mysteries (Dan 2:19–20; see below), the death of David's enemy Nabal (1 Sam 25:39), Solomon as David's successor (1 Ki 1:48), the gift of a wife for Isaac (Gen 24:27), or a redeemer for Naomi and Ruth (Ruth 4:14).[154] The

---

[150] 2 Corinthians has a pseudo-thanksgiving (2 Cor 1:11) after a *Berakah* prayer that shifts smoothly into prose.

[151] On the *Berakah* prayer in general, see Kirby, *Ephesians: Baptism and Pentecost*, 84–89; Dahl, "Benediction and Congratulation," in *Studies in Ephesians*, 279–314; and Dahl, "Das Proömium des Epheserbriefes," in *Studies in Ephesians*, 315–34.

[152] "The characteristic notes of Jewish prayer are praise and thanksgiving to God for his mercies vouchsafed to Israel, primarily for creation and for his choice of her as his own people; actual intercessions and petitions are placed in a very subordinate position" (Kirby, *Ephesians: Baptism and Pentecost*, 84).

[153] Dahl, "Das Proömium des Epheserbriefes," in *Studies in Ephesians*, 317. Nonetheless, as Dahl notes, God is praised for what he does for the recipients.

[154] See Schlier, *Epheser*, 41–42; Kirby, *Ephesians: Baptism and Pentecost*, 85.

increasing popularity of this style of praying is evidenced by the inclusion of five *Berakoth* in the final chapters of Tobit.[155]

In a second OT trajectory, the *Berakah* pattern became characteristic of public prayer in worship. Solomon's great prayer at the dedication of the temple begins with praise of God for fulfilling his promises to David and recalls God's saving deeds, beginning with the exodus (1 Ki 8:14–21). The two characteristics of private *Berakoth* are developed in the direction of a prayer that praises and thanks God for his saving deeds toward Israel (or all mankind) and the addition of intercessions cautiously appended to the praise. On the basis of God's historic promises and acts, the liturgist dares to beg for God's future blessing. Some seventeen examples of *Berakoth* in the Psalms give evidence of the genre's dominance in temple worship (Psalms 104–106 are prime examples). Notably, each of the five "books" of the Psalter concludes with a *Berakah*.[156]

The prayers of the synagogue developed the pattern one step further by (1) changing the address from third person to second, "blessed are you,"[157] and (2) creating virtually set texts for daily prayer. Three times a day[158] the pious Jew would be expected to pray *Berakoth* consisting of the creedal *Shema‘* (Deut 6:4) with its surrounding prayers and the so-called "Eighteen Benedictions."[159] An abbreviated version of the same prayers formed the beginning of the synagogue service on the Sabbath. The *Shemoneh ‘Esreh*, "Eighteen" Benedictions, also known as the *Amidah*, "Standing" Prayer, or *Tefillah*, "The Prayer," were characterized in each of their eighteen sections by the clause "blessed are you, O Lord," followed by a declaration of his saving work or high character. The first *Berakah* is illustrative of the pattern:

---

[155] Tobit 8:5–6, 15–17; 11:14–15, 17; 13:1–18.

[156] Pss 41:14 (ET 41:13); 72:19; 89:53 (ET 89:52); 106:48; and Psalm 150 as the conclusion of the whole Psalter. Claus Westermann proposes a dubious evolutionary development of the *Berakah* form from the historical books (private experience of God's saving deeds) through to the Psalter (corporate worship of Israel) in *The Praise of God in the Psalms* (trans. Keith R. Crim; London: Epworth, 1965), 81–90.

[157] This is apparently a change that took place in the two centuries before Christ, as both the synagogue and Qumran illustrate the second person address. A notable exception are the third-person *Berakoth* of the *Beth Midrash* (house of study, separate from the synagogue, probably post AD 70), which were used before and after the reading and exposition of Scripture, e.g., "blessed be the name of the Holy One, who has chosen Israel and given to us the Torah" (Kirby, *Ephesians: Baptism and Pentecost*, 94–95).

[158] The Mishnah tractate *Berakoth* describes in magnificent detail the ways in which a Jewish man would fulfill the obligation in the face of daily challenges to his discipline. In addition it suggests a variety of further occasions when one might utter a *Berakah*, such as before and after meals, when visiting holy sites, in the face of natural wonders, and when blessing a new house or vessels. In addition, it is said that one is to bless God for evil as much as for good (Mishnah, *Berakoth*, 9:5; cf. Job 1:21; 2:10).

[159] See Instone-Brewer, *TRENT*, 1:95–117. Though there is considerable development of the prayer texts in later times, leading to distinct Babylonian and Palestinian versions, Instone-Brewer dates the origin of these prayers prior to the destruction of the temple (AD 70). Benediction 14 explicitly calls down the blessing of God upon the temple.

> Blessed are you, Lord, our God and God of our fathers; God of Abraham, God of Isaac, and God of Jacob; The great God, powerful and revered; Exalted God, creator of heaven and earth; Our shield, and shield of our fathers; Our refuge in all generations. Blessed are you, Lord, shield of Abraham.[160]

The influence of these patterns on Christian prayer, particularly in the eucharistic liturgy, may be seen from a *Berakah* recorded for use in blessing a cup of wine at a family meal:

> Blessed art thou, O Lord our God, King of the universe, who feedest the whole world with thy goodness, with grace, with lovingkindness and tender mercy; thou givest food to all flesh, for thy lovingkindness endureth for ever. Through thy goodness food has never failed us; may it not fail us for ever and ever for thy great name's sake. … We bless thee, O Lord our God, because thou didst give as an heritage unto our fathers a desirable good and ample land, and because thou didst bring us forth, O Lord our God, from the land of Egypt, and didst deliver us from the house of bondage; as well as for thy covenant which thou hast sealed in our flesh, thy law which thou hast taught us, thy statutes which thou hast made known to us, the life, grace and lovingkindness which thou hast vouchsafed to us, and for the food wherewith thou dost constantly feed us on every day, in every season, at every hour. For all this, O Lord our God, we bless thee; blessed be thy name by the mouth of all living continually and for ever.[161]

The influence of such language on Ephesians 1 is evident not only in the opening address, which Paul has made Trinitarian, but also in the references to God's historic, saving deeds; its reference to circumcision as being "sealed"; and the "making known" of the mysteries of divine life and grace. One begins also to understand the florid, repetitive style of such prayers, which has ever perplexed interpreters of Eph 1:3–14. In light of such forebearers, it is completely understandable.

St. Paul would certainly concur with the Mishnah's directives to bless the Lord wherever and whenever the occasion suggested it,[162] as he writes: "giving thanks always for all things in the name of our Lord Jesus Christ to [our] God and Father" (Eph 5:20). Yet, the evidence suggests that the highly stylized and carefully constructed form of *Berakah* found in Eph 1:3–14 has more in common with these Jewish prayers of public worship than with private prayers. In fact, there is a remarkable coherence between this prayer and the brief prayers recorded in connection with the liturgy of the Lord's Supper in the *Didache*—a text which might perhaps date to the lifetime of the apostles:[163]

---

[160] Quoted in Instone-Brewer, *TRENT*, 1:97–98, where it is laid out in poetic lines.

[161] Quoted in Kirby, *Ephesians: Baptism and Pentecost*, 89.

[162] See the footnote above on the Mishnah tractate *Berakoth*.

[163] *Didache*, 9:1–2; see also *Didache*, 9:3–4 and 10:2–6.

¹περὶ δὲ τῆς εὐχαριστίας, οὕτως εὐχαριστήσατε· ²πρῶτον περὶ τοῦ ποτηρίου· Εὐχαριστοῦμέν σοι, πάτερ ἡμῶν, ὑπὲρ τῆς ἁγίας ἀμπέλου Δαυεὶδ τοῦ παιδός σου, ἧς ἐγνώρισας ἡμῖν διὰ Ἰησοῦ τοῦ παιδός σου· σοὶ ἡ δόξα εἰς τοὺς αἰῶνας.	¹Now concerning the Eucharist, thus give thanks: ²first concerning the cup: "We give thanks to you, our Father, for the holy Vine of David, your Servant, which you made known to us through Jesus, your Servant. To you be the glory into the ages."

Note (1) the address to the Father, giving thanks for the Son (cf. Eph 1:3–14); (2) language of revelation (ἐγνώρισας, "you made known"; see γνωρίζω also in Eph 1:9); and (3) the concluding doxology, which is repeated three times in each prayer, with some variation the final time (*Didache* 9:2, 3, 4 and 10:2, 4, 5), which parallels the refrain in Ephesians 1, "to the praise of his (gracious) glory" (1:6, 12, 14).

The prayers in these two chapters of the *Didache* use εὐχαριστέω, "to give thanks," in place of εὐλογέω, "to bless," which more literally translates the Hebraic language of the *Berakah*. This fluidity of vocabulary—the interchangeability of εὐχαριστέω and εὐλογέω—parallels Christian practice evident in NT accounts of the Lord's Supper. The parallel Synoptic accounts of the Words of Institution say "when he had *blessed*" or "when he had *given thanks*."[164] Paul speaks of "the cup of blessing [over] which we bless [τὸ ποτήριον τῆς εὐλογίας ὃ εὐλογοῦμεν]" (1 Cor 10:16), presumably referring to a *Berakah*-style prayer such as that recorded in the *Didache*,[165] but uses εὐχαριστήσας, "having given thanks," in the Words of Institution (1 Cor 11:24). Thus, it appears that Paul has composed a prayer fully consistent with Jewish patterns[166] and also evocative of the manner in which the presider would pray in the liturgy of the Lord's Supper.[167]

---

[164] Note the alternation of these two verbs in Mt 26:26–27 and Mk 14:22–23, indicating their equivalence. In both passages, the first verb, used with the bread, is εὐλογήσας (Mt 26:26; Mk 14:22), and the second verb, used with the cup, is εὐχαριστήσας (Mt 26:27; Mk 14:23). Likewise, Matthew uses εὐλογέω when Jesus feeds the five thousand (Mt 14:19) and εὐχαριστέω when he feeds the four thousand (Mt 15:36).

[165] By contending that the expression "the cup of blessing" is a technical term from the Passover liturgy referring to the *Berakah* prayer that accompanied its distribution, we do not mean to imply that the pastor's recitation of the Words of Institution is not a "blessing." When the pastor speaks Christ's words in the context of the Lord's Supper, Christ himself continues to exercise his power so that the bread and the wine become his body and blood, which are given to those who commune (FC SD 7:75–76). This blessing or consecration is explained by Luther with a quotation from Augustine, *Tractates on John*, 80:3: "Let the Word come to the element and it is made a Sacrament" (quoted in LC 5:10 [my translation]; cf. LC 4:18).

[166] This way of putting it avoids the pitfalls to either side of assuming, on the one hand, that everything in the NT is borrowed from somewhere else (parallelomania) or, on the other, that Paul owes nothing to his context. Markus Barth comments: "Perhaps very small units were taken up from various traditions (including poems) by the biblical authors and cemented together into larger hymnodic structures. The latter compositions would then inevitably sound like larger earlier poems, but they would still be original works" (*Ephesians*, 1:100).

[167] So also concludes Dahl, "Das Proömium des Epheserbriefes," in *Studies in Ephesians*, 326–27, who adds that such a eulogy would also be used in a baptismal rite (e.g., *Apostolic Constitutions*, 7:43). Further fruitful comparisons might be made with the early eucharistic

(One might also note, not completely incidentally, the influence of the *Berakah* pattern on the briefer Christian collect pattern: address, rationale [appeal to the saving deeds and gracious nature of God], petition, result/goal, doxology.)

In form, this *Berakah* is quite similar to the other two *Berakoth* that begin epistles in the NT,[168] yet distinct in content and far more developed. The *Berakah* at the beginning of 2 Corinthians (starting with 1:3) begins in characteristic fashion, responding to the comfort God grants in the midst of suffering as the cause for the praise; but it quickly shifts into prose and has no clear closing structure. Peter's *Berakah* (1 Pet 1:3–9) likewise moves swiftly into prose, but in content blends the thanksgiving for divine sustenance in the midst of suffering with praise for eternal gifts kept in heaven for us until the Last Day. The most thoroughly traditional *Berakah* in the NT is the Benedictus, the prayer of Zechariah in response to the revelation that he will have a son to inaugurate the messianic age (Lk 1:67–79). Remarkably, one of the few prayers recorded from Jesus' own lips bears the same marks of a *Berakah* in response to revelation from God (Mt 11:25–26). Ephesians 1 has revelatory elements both cosmic and messianic. *The great gift of God which appears to be the cause of Paul's prayer of praise is the revelation of the mystery that has been granted to him as Christ's apostle, particularly the message that in Christ the division between Jew and Gentile has been removed, creating true unity among all mankind, to be appropriated by Baptism into Christ.*

Here we venture to offer one final forerunner of Paul's prayer, which contains stunning parallels to the theme, contents, and vocabulary of Ephesians 1. Daniel had been granted the ability to interpret King Nebuchadnezzar's dream, a divine gift which spared his life and that of his Judean companions. To this great wonder he responded in praise:

> Then the mystery was revealed to Daniel in a vision of the night. Then Daniel blessed [LXX: εὐλόγησε] the God of heaven. Daniel responded and said:
> "Blessed [LXX: εὐλογημένον] be the name of God from eternity
>   to eternity,
>   to whom wisdom [LXX: σοφία] and might belong.
> He changes times [LXX: καιρούς] and seasons;
>   he removes kings and raises up kings;
>   he gives wisdom to the wise [LXX: σοφοῖς σοφίαν]
>   and knowledge to those who know understanding;
>   he reveals deep things and hidden things;
>   he knows what is in the darkness,
>   and the light dwells with him.

---

prayer of Hippolytus, *Apostolic Tradition*, 4:4–13 (ca. AD 215), which is, admittedly, far more fully developed than the brief examples in the *Didache*. Kirby, *Ephesians: Baptism and Pentecost*, 137–38, notes: "There is no direct copying of Ephesians by Hippolytus here, but the two prayers belong to the same general field of ideas. ... Ephesians marks a stage in the transition from the Jewish berakah form to the eucharistic form that we find in Hippolytus."

[168] The use of a Berakah prayer in a letter is found also in 2 Chr 2:10–11 (ET 2:11–12); Josephus, *Antiquities*, 8:53; and perhaps 2 Macc 1:17.

215

> To you, O God of my fathers, I give thanks and praise,
>> for you have given me wisdom and might [LXX: σοφίαν καὶ
>> φρόνησιν],
>> and now you have made known to me [Theodotion: ἐγνώρισάς
>> μοι] what we asked from you,
>> for you have made known to us [Theodotion: ἐγνώρισάς μοι,
>> 'made known to *me*'] the king's matter." (Dan 2:19–23)

The clear parallel to Paul's prophetic ministry is the revelation of the mystery hinted at in his *Berakah* (Eph 1:9) and fleshed out when Paul describes his divinely vouchsafed insight into God's plan for the salvation of the Gentiles (3:1–6). In light of his imprisonment for proclaiming that mystery,[169] his desire to comfort the Ephesians over his suffering for it, and his need to promote the bond of peace between Jew and Gentile in Ephesus, the opening prayer makes perfect sense.

The Berakah *Prayer: Structure*

Countless attempts have been made to determine the structure of the prayer, most of which can be dismissed as forced or speculative.[170] Nevertheless, some structural features are noteworthy. Schnackenburg notes a rhythm consisting in the combination of καθώς ("inasmuch as," 1:4) and κατά ("according to," 1:5, 7, 9, 11), which reflects on the preceding thought, and infinitives (1:4, 10, 12) with or without εἰς (literally, "for"), which form purpose clauses. The result is "a definite movement of thought,"[171] though his resulting six-part outline makes too much of it. Lincoln is persuaded that the three aorist participles (1:3b, 5, 9) divide the prayer into three parts, with the *Berakah* formula (1:3a) as a prelude:[172]

1:3a	εὐλογητὸς ὁ θεός … ,	"blessed be the God …"
I. 1:3b–4	ὁ εὐλόγησας … ,	"who has blessed …"
II. 1:5–8	προορίσας … ,	"since he had predestined …"
III. 1:9–12	γνωρίσας … ,	"he has made known …"
IV. 1:13–14		additional ἐν ᾧ, "in whom," statement addressing recipients

It is significant to note the subordinating structure brought about by this string of circumstantial participles (1:3b, 5, 9), which is more characteristic of Hellenistic than Hebraic style (which would be more paratactic). But to take these three participles as division markers results in a significantly imbalanced outline. The

---

[169] See "Paul's Trip to Jerusalem, Arrest, and Imprisonment (Acts 21:1–36)" in "The City of Ephesus and Paul's Relationship to It" in the introduction.

[170] See Lincoln, *Ephesians*, 12–15. Thomson, *Chiasmus in the Pauline Letters*, 46–83, argues for a chiastic structure that embraces only 1:3–10. The most intriguing aspect of his argument is his identification (69) of "in whom we have redemption through his blood, the forgiveness of trespasses" (1:7) as the center, and therefore the central thought, of the pericope.

[171] Schnackenburg, *Ephesians*, 46–47.

[172] Lincoln, *Ephesians*, 15–16. The following analysis is adapted from Lincoln.

parts are neither equal in size nor parallel in meaning; nor does this pay sufficient regard to the numerous finite verbs in between, to which the participles are sometimes subordinate.

The most thought-provoking analysis, by John Coutts, compares this *Berakah* with 1 Peter's, noting baptismal language and a Trinitarian structure that the two hold in common.[173] While his radical reconstruction of Paul's words into a supposed *Urtyp* from a baptismal rite is fanciful (requiring him to omit 76 of the 202 words!),[174] the features he discerns are not. Most significant is the threefold repetition (with minor variations) of the refrain εἰς ἔπαινον δόξης αὐτοῦ, "to the praise of his (gracious) glory" (1:6, 12, 14). When coupled with the Trinitarian language of the opening verse (1:3), this suggests a Trinitarian outline to the prayer. The content fits: 1:4–6 speaks of the Father's act of predestination; 1:7–12 expounds the Son's work of redemption in expansive language that echoes the Second Article of the Apostles' and Nicene Creeds; and 1:13–14 speaks of the Spirit's work through hearing and sealing in the Word and Baptism. Other Trinitarian features include the following:

- the threefold use of εὐλογέω cognates ("blessed/blessing") in 1:3
- the threefold repetition (with minor variations) of "according to the good pleasure of his will" (1:5; also 1:9, 11)
- three uses of ἐν ᾧ, "in whom," to begin a section or subsection of the prayer (1:7, 11, 13)

Throughout, the imprint of the oft-repeated phrase "in Christ/him/whom/the Beloved"[175] stamps a Christological image on every aspect of salvation. These features, highlighted by the layout of the translation above, are even more obvious in the Greek:

---

[173] Coutts, "Ephesians I.3–14 and I Peter 1.3–12." Thomson, *Chiasmus in the Pauline Letters*, 48–50, gives further examples of hymnic analyses.

[174] Coutts, "Ephesians I.3–14 and I Peter 1.3–12," 124, proposes:

> If we are right in thinking that in Eph. i. 3–14 there are the remains of a liturgical formula, we shall clearly go on to enquire, with what occasion in the life of the Church it was connected. The passage itself, and the subject-matter of the Epistle as a whole, suggest a connexion with baptism, and possibly with baptism at Easter. … It was a pastoral letter … written … perhaps at Easter, but at any rate on an occasion when converts were to be baptized, reminding them and those who had been previously baptized of the privileges and obligations of the new life upon which they will have entered when the Epistle is actually read.

> One might note that R. Perdelwitz, H. Preisker, and F. L. Cross once made the same suggestion about 1 Peter. See Richard Perdelwitz, *Die Mysterienreligion und das Problem des I. Petrusbriefes: Ein literarischer und religionsgeschichtlicher Versuch* (Giessen: Töpelmann, 1911); Herbert Preisker, "Anhang zum ersten Petrusbrief," in Hans Windisch, *Die katholischen Briefe* (3d ed. edited by Herbert Preisker; Tübingen: Mohr [Siebeck], 1951), 156–62; and F. L. Cross, *I. Peter: A Paschal Liturgy* (London: Mowbray, 1954).

[175] Eph 1:3, 4, 6, 7, 9, 10 (twice), 11, 12, 13 (twice).

Trinitarian	[3]εὐλογητὸς ὁ θεὸς καὶ πατὴρ τοῦ κυρίου ἡμῶν Ἰησοῦ Χριστοῦ,
	ὁ **εὐλογήσας** ἡμᾶς ἐν πάσῃ **εὐλογίᾳ** πνευματικῇ ἐν τοῖς ἐπουρανίοις ἐν Χριστῷ.
Father	[4]καθὼς ἐξελέξατο ἡμᾶς ἐν αὐτῷ πρὸ καταβολῆς κόσμου
	εἶναι ἡμᾶς ἁγίους καὶ ἀμώμους κατενώπιον αὐτοῦ,
	ἐν ἀγάπῃ [5]προορίσας ἡμᾶς εἰς υἱοθεσίαν διὰ Ἰησοῦ Χριστοῦ εἰς αὐτόν,
	κατὰ τὴν εὐδοκίαν τοῦ θελήματος αὐτοῦ,
	[6]εἰς ἔπαινον δόξης τῆς χάριτος αὐτοῦ
	ἧς ἐχαρίτωσεν ἡμᾶς ἐν τῷ ἠγαπημένῳ.
Son	[7]ἐν ᾧ ἔχομεν τὴν ἀπολύτρωσιν διὰ τοῦ αἵματος αὐτοῦ,
	τὴν ἄφεσιν τῶν παραπτωμάτων,
	κατὰ τὸ πλοῦτος τῆς χάριτος αὐτοῦ [8]ἧς ἐπερίσσευσεν εἰς ἡμᾶς,
	ἐν πάσῃ σοφίᾳ καὶ φρονήσει [9]γνωρίσας ἡμῖν τὸ μυστήριον τοῦ θελήματος αὐτοῦ,
	κατὰ τὴν εὐδοκίαν αὐτοῦ ἣν προέθετο ἐν αὐτῷ
	[10]εἰς οἰκονομίαν τοῦ πληρώματος τῶν καιρῶν,
	ἀνακεφαλαιώσασθαι τὰ πάντα ἐν τῷ Χριστῷ,
	τὰ ἐπὶ τοῖς οὐρανοῖς καὶ τὰ ἐπὶ τῆς γῆς ἐν αὐτῷ.
	[11]ἐν ᾧ καὶ ἐκληρώθημεν
	προορισθέντες κατὰ πρόθεσιν
	τοῦ τὰ πάντα ἐνεργοῦντος **κατὰ τὴν βουλὴν τοῦ θελήματος αὐτοῦ**
	[12]εἰς τὸ εἶναι ἡμᾶς **εἰς ἔπαινον δόξης αὐτοῦ**
	τοὺς προηλπικότας ἐν τῷ Χριστῷ.
Spirit	[13]ἐν ᾧ καὶ ὑμεῖς
	ἀκούσαντες τὸν λόγον τῆς ἀληθείας, τὸ εὐαγγέλιον τῆς σωτηρίας ὑμῶν,
	ἐν ᾧ καὶ πιστεύσαντες
	ἐσφραγίσθητε τῷ πνεύματι τῆς ἐπαγγελίας τῷ ἁγίῳ,
	[14]ὅ ἐστιν ἀρραβὼν τῆς κληρονομίας ἡμῶν,
	εἰς ἀπολύτρωσιν τῆς περιποιήσεως,
	εἰς ἔπαινον τῆς δόξης αὐτοῦ.

The threefold repetition of the refrain "to the praise of his (gracious) glory" (1:6, 12, 14) is, of course, not merely a division marker. It cries out the ultimate goal of the mystery revealed to Paul: "that we should be to the praise of his glory" (1:12). Not only does the very existence of a redeemed people bring praise to God's name as the Redeemer (see the first textual note on 1:12), but also those very people who once could not please God or worship him rightly are now transformed by their union with Christ into "praise singers." Thus, the "Christianizing" of the Jewish *Berakah* does not consist merely in expanding the address to include the three persons of the Trinity. It is transformed by the person and work of Christ, in whom and through whom the praise now occurs. As true praise occurs only in the presence of God himself, the OT identifies praise as the proper work of the angels and all the company of heaven who stand in the beatific vision. It could not have properly occurred on earth—except on those rare occasions when the Son of God manifested himself as the Angel of YHWH. But, as John Kleinig argues, the incarnation broke open the heavenly realm:

> With the coming of Christ, doxology began to be performed by humans on earth together with the angels in heaven. In fact, in Eph 1:3–12, Paul declared that Christ had joined the human choir with the angelic choir through his resurrection and ascension. Together they form one assembly before God and sing one song of praise. Both Jew and Gentile joined together with the angels in the praise of his glory (Eph 1:6, 12, 14). So, as Paul notes in Eph 3:21, doxology to God is now performed "in the church and in Christ Jesus." The performance of that doxology by the saints shows that they have access to the glory of the Father, in and through Jesus.[176]

The church thus replaces the Levitical choirs of the old temple, as, led by Christ himself, she continually praises God in the Spirit, "in psalms and hymns and songs of the Spirit, singing and psalming with [her] heart to the Lord, giving thanks always for all things in the name of our Lord Jesus Christ to [her] God and Father" (5:20). As Christ is raised up to the heavenly places, above the angels, with the church as his body (1:20–23), the church is where he is. Thus, in her earthly worship, the church can claim to "laud and magnify [God's] glorious name" together "with angels and archangels and with all the company of heaven" (Proper Preface)[177]—experiencing already now a foretaste of her promised eternal inheritance in the new creation.

The *Berakah* Prayer (1:3–14) as Prologue

In addition to its rich liturgical function, the opening prayer has a significant rhetorical role. In the introduction we labeled it the *proem*, a rhetorical unit that might also be called a prologue.[178] Within the "rules" of argumentation taught

---

[176] Kleinig, "The Mystery of Doxology," 135. See also John Kleinig, "What's the Use of Praising God," *Lutheran Theological Journal* 38 (2004): 81–82.

[177] E.g., *LSB Altar Book*, 145.

[178] See "Rhetorical Outline" in "Structure and Rhetoric" in the introduction.

in classical rhetoric, the *proem* was the introduction to the matter, including a *narratio* of the history thus far and perhaps a thesis statement.[179] It preceded the detailed unfolding of the argument in the proofs and refutation. More simply put, one might view the *proem* as a summary or table of contents of the material to be dealt with in the rest of the letter.[180] This common technique occurs in other NT writings: famously in the Johannine Prologue (John 1),[181] but arguably also in Matthew 1; 1 Corinthians 1; Galatians 1; Hebrews 1; 1 John 1—to some degree in almost every NT writing. Paul Deterding speaks of the first pericope of Colossians (1:3–20) as an overture, which "introduces musical themes that will be taken up later in the work"[182]—a lovely image.

The chief theme introduced in the Ephesian prologue is, of course, "in Christ."[183] The textual notes have argued that this phrase and its equivalents, which occur more frequently in Ephesians than in any other NT book, should not be interpreted merely instrumentally. The phrase is the dominant feature of Paul's Christianizing of the *Berakah* pattern. In the unique context of Ephesians, however, *it also lays out Paul's chief argument that all Christians find their true spiritual unity in their common, baptismal incorporation into Christ.* They are "in him" because they have been baptized into him. Eleven occurrences within the twelve verses of the prologue point toward some nineteen further verbal parallels in the body of the epistle.[184] The theme is best illustrated by the central words of chapter 2:

> [13]But now <u>in Christ Jesus</u> you who at one time were far off have become near by the blood of Christ. [14]For he himself is our peace, who has made both one, and has broken down the dividing wall of partition, the hostility, <u>in his flesh,</u>

---

[179] The usual *benevolentiae captatio*, the attempt to capture the goodwill of the audience, is delayed in Ephesians until the thanksgiving (1:15–23). It is not clear that one passage could be isolated as a thesis, as, e.g., Rom 1:16–17. Perhaps Eph 1:9–10 comes closest.

[180] Cf. Barth, *Ephesians*, 1:55, 97; Nils A. Dahl, "Adresse und Proömium des Epheserbriefes," *Theologische Zeitschrift* 7 (1951): 241–64, the second part of which (250–64) was reprinted as "Das Proömium des Epheserbriefes" in *Studies in Ephesians*, 315–34; Christian Maurer, "Der Hymnus von Epheser 1 als Schlüssel zum ganzen Briefe," *Evangelische Theologie* 11 (1951–1952): 151–72; and Peter T. O'Brien, "Ephesians I: An Unusual Introduction to a New Testament Letter," *New Testament Studies* 25 (1979): 504–16. This view, often adopted in the commentaries, cannot, however be pressed too far. This is poetry, not prose. Best, *Ephesians*, 111–12, points out significant features of the *Berakah* that are *not* developed further in the letter, such as God's choice or election of believers. Less persuasive is his argument that some elements of the letter do not feature in the prologue, which asks it to carry a weight it cannot bear.

[181] "One might almost say that it exercises the function of the Johannine Prologue in our letter" (Schlier, *Epheser*, 38).

[182] Deterding, *Colossians*, 26. The Greek term προοίμιον, *prooimion*, was used both for a prose introduction and for a musical overture, literally meaning "before the song" (προ-οἶμος).

[183] See "in Christ," "in him," "in whom," or "in the Beloved" in 1:3, 4, 6, 7, 9, 10 (twice), 11, 12, 13 (twice).

[184] Eph 1:20; 2:6, 7, 10, 13, 14, 15, 16 (twice), 21, 22; 3:6, 11, 12 (twice), 21; 4:21 (twice), 32. Note the preponderance of the expression in the foundational arguments of the "proofs" in 2:1–4:16.

[15]by nullifying the Law of commandments in decrees, that <u>in him</u> he might create the two into one new man, making peace, [16]and might reconcile both <u>in one body</u> to God through the cross, by killing the hostility <u>in him</u>. (2:13–16)

Further verbal and thematic parallels between the prologue and the body of the epistle include the following:

Theme, Language	Prologue	Body of the Epistle
grace	1:2, 6, 7	2:5–8; 3:2, 7–8; 4:7
heavenly places/matters	1:3, 10	1:20; 2:6; 3:10; 4:10; 6:12
holy and without blemish	1:4	5:27
will, plan, purpose	1:5, 9, 11	3:9, 11; 5:17; 6:6
inheritance, sonship	1:5, 14	1:18; 5:5
blood of Christ	1:7	2:13
richness of grace/glory	1:7	2:7; 3:8, 16
mystery	1:9	3:3, 4, 9; 5:32; 6:19
stewardship	1:10	3:2, 9
uniting in him	1:10	2:13–16
Jew/Gentile relations	1:13–14	2:1–4, 11–22
seal [of the Spirit]	1:13	4:30
the Spirit	1:13–14	2:18, 22; 3:5, 16; 4:3–4, 30; 5:18; 6:17–18

In addition we might note the vocabulary of completeness with the repetition of various forms of πᾶς to refer to "all, every, all things" that are effected and affected by Christ's cosmic redemption:

Theme, Language	Prologue	Body of the Epistle
πᾶς, "all, every"	1:3, 8	1:15, 21 (twice), 23; 2:3, 21; 3:8–9, 15, 18–21; 4:2, 10, 13–14, 16 (twice), 19, 29, 31 (twice); 5:3, 5, 9, 14, 24; 6:16, 18 (four times!), 24
πάντα, "all things"	1:10, 11	1:22 (twice), 23; 3:9; 4:6 (four times), 10, 15; 5:13, 20; 6:16, 21

The context of the occurrences is not identical, but the purely statistical story backs up the initial impression: πᾶς forms 2.147 percent of the total words in Ephesians (52 out of 2,422 words), placing it second in the NT behind its twin,

Colossians.[185] Clearly, *Paul is overwhelmed by the fullness of God's majesty, his grace, and the completeness of the reconciliation of heaven, earth, and all mankind achieved in Christ Jesus.*

Baptism in the Prologue (1:3–14)

Allusions are tricky things. There is always a danger that the unspoken connection between two texts or events is made in the mind of the reader, but would take the author completely by surprise if suggested to him. Firm textual constraints must apply to any claim that an author intended an allusion. In the textual notes we have argued that Paul had the Baptism of our Lord in mind when he put together the *Berakah* prayer.[186] The constraint at work was a series of verbal similarities between the language of the prologue, the transfiguration, and the Baptism of our Lord. Working by way of allusion rather than direct reference is characteristic of liturgical language, and indeed of NT thought in general,[187] where Baptism is more often referred to indirectly than named directly: as washing (Acts 22:16; Titus 3:5); stripping (Col 3:9) and clothing (Gal 3:27; Col 3:10) with white robes (Rev 7:9–14); rebirth (Jn 3:5); adoption (Gal 3:26); election (1 Pet 2:9); death and resurrection (Rom 6:3–4; Col 2:11–13; 3:9–10); rescue from drowning (1 Pet 3:20–21); a new creation (2 Cor 5:17); a circumcision without hands (Col 2:11); sealing (2 Cor 1:22; Eph 1:14; 4:30); living water, which comes from Christ (Jn 4:10–14; 7:37–39; 19:34); cleansing and sanctifying (1 Cor 6:9–13; Eph 5:26); and a crossing into a new land (1 Cor 10:1–2)—need we add "etc."?[188] Edmund Schlink rejoices in this diversity:

---

[185] Nor is this fact particularly un-Pauline. If the NT books are arranged according to the statistical frequency of πᾶς, ten of the top twelve are Pauline epistles. Only Galatians and Philemon score particularly low. See further the discussion in "Vocabulary" in "Authorship" in the introduction.

[186] At the very least, Baptism itself is evoked by such language as "holy and without blemish" (1:4; cf. 5:26–27); "adopted as his sons" (1:5); "forgiveness of trespasses" (1:7); "poured out upon us" (1:8); "sealed with the promised Holy Spirit" (1:13); and "deposit of our inheritance" (1:14). See "Baptism and the Spirit" in "Purpose and Themes" in the introduction; cf. Dahl, "Das Proömium des Epheserbriefes," in *Studies in Ephesians*, 327. Cyril of Jerusalem, *Catechetical Lectures*, 18:35, concludes his address to the baptismal candidates by quoting Eph 1:3; 1:7; 2:4–6; and 1:17–18 (*NPNF*[2] 7:142–43).

[187] The opinion of the fathers was that an allusion to Baptism was virtually presumed: "As often as water alone is mentioned in the Holy Scriptures, Baptism is meant" (Cyprian, *Epistles*, 63:8 [CSEL 3/2:706]). See also Tertullian's tractate *On Baptism*. Such allusions are explored in detail by Jean Daniélou, *The Bible and the Liturgy*. See also Oscar Cullmann, *Early Christian Worship* (trans. A. Stewart Todd and James B. Torrance; Chicago: Regnery, 1953).

[188] "How great is Baptism: it is the redemption of prisoners, the remission of sins, the death of guilt, the rebirth of the soul, the garment of light, the holy and ineradicable seal (*sphragis*), the vehicle to carry us to heaven, the delights of Paradise, the pledge of the kingdom, the grace of adoption" (Cyril of Jerusalem, *Procatechesis*, 16 [PG 33:360–61]; trans. Daniélou, *The Bible and the Liturgy*, 55).

There is an exuberance about the New Testament baptismal material, a character of restlessness, since the event spoken of signifies so profound and revolutionary an inroad into the life of a person that *one* word cannot grasp it. …

One and the same divine deed is given expression through a multiplicity of Biblical terms which are not simply interchangeable, even though each concept bears witness to the whole.[189]

There is no way of knowing what may have brought to Paul's mind the event of Christ's Baptism, except to note that it held a far greater prominence in historic Christianity than it often does today. Whereas Lutheran dogmatic works tend to begin with Christ's words in Mt 28:16–20 as the mandate of Holy Baptism for the church—which is entirely in order, as only Christ can institute a Sacrament—nonetheless, the prominence of art depicting the Baptism of Christ in baptisteries and on fonts in ancient and medieval Christendom suggests that the minds of earlier Christians reached back farther to this fundamental event. Ignatius, perhaps the earliest commentator on Paul's letter to the Ephesians, seems to allude to its *Berakah* when attributing a foundational character to Christ's own Baptism:

For our God, Jesus the Christ, was conceived by Mary according to the plan [κατ᾿ οἰκονομίαν; cf. οἰκονομία in Eph 1:10] of God, from the seed of David and from the Holy Spirit, who was born and was baptized in order that by submitting [τῷ πάθει, perhaps "suffering" instead of "submitting"] he might purify the water. (Ignatius, *To the Ephesians*, 18:2)

His suggestion is that Christ's entry into the water of the Jordan gave baptismal water its transformative, sacramental power. This idea, given prominence by Tertullian's treatise *On Baptism*, can be misunderstood to suggest that water thereafter has in its nature a saving power—a position rejected in the Small Catechism by Luther, who argues that the Word of God comes to the water to give it this quality. Yet Ignatius need not be understood so literally, and together with Tertullian he illustrates the early view that Christ's own Baptism is fundamental and central to the Baptism of all Christians into him.

If one argues that Christ was baptized "to fulfill all righteousness" (Mt 3:15) merely in the sense of his active obedience to the will of God,[190] then his

---

[189] Edmund Schlink, *The Doctrine of Baptism* (trans. Herbert J. A. Bouman; St. Louis: Concordia, 1972), 33–34.

[190] See R. C. H. Lenski, *The Interpretation of St. Matthew's Gospel* (Minneapolis: Augsburg, 1943), 126–27. Lenski argues that the fulfillment of righteousness refers not to an obligation of the Law as such, but to the offices given to John and Jesus. By being baptized, Jesus enters into his mediatory office and signals his willingness to identify with the sinners being baptized. But Lenski expressly rejects Luther's view that in Christ's Baptism our sins are removed on the grounds that it would imply a double removal of sins (in Baptism and also on the cross). Luther's view is best illustrated by this brief excerpt from his "Second Sermon at the Baptism of Bernhard von Anhalt, Matthew 3:13–17" (April 2, 1540):

But Christ says, "Let it be so now; for thus it is fitting for us to fulfil all righteousness" [Matt. 3:15]; as much as to say: The purpose of my baptism is to wash away and drown

223

Baptism belongs in the same category as his childhood obedience to his parents and his paying the temple tax. If, on the other hand, the fulfillment of righteousness is understood in the sense of his atoning work (passive obedience), then his Baptism should be proclaimed in the same breath as his death on the cross and his resurrection.[191] He is baptized as the one who is *already* "bearing the sins of the world" (Jn 1:29); and so, since Christ has our sins on his back when he is baptized, we are in effect baptized with him for the removal of our sins. He is not baptized to take away his own sins, but ours (for our sins have become his, and his cleansing becomes ours). In a sense, he died and rose again already in that moment, as his passion was a fulfillment of his Baptism (see "baptism" and "baptized" in Mk 10:38–39; Lk 12:50).[192] Thus, the Christian's Baptism into Christ's death and resurrection parallels Christ's own Baptism (Rom 6:3–4; Col 2:11–13). Its full meaning comes only at the cross.

In his sermon preached on Epiphany 1546, short weeks before his death, Martin Luther answered the question of what Christ's Baptism means "to me" in this way:

14. Here you may perhaps respond: "Yes, I surely believe that the baptism of our dear Lord Jesus Christ, who is the Son of God, is adorned and honoured in such a way that the divine Majesty himself is the highest preacher, the Holy Spirit the greatest student and listener, in addition the hosts of God's dear angels are there. But how does that help me? Of what use is it to me? Christ is God's Son, begotten of the Father from eternity, conceived of the Holy Spirit, without sin, born a true man of the Virgin Mary; for this reason

---

the sins of all the world, that through it all righteousness and salvation may be accomplished. Therefore baptism was instituted by God primarily for Christ's sake and then afterwards also for the sake of all men. For first he must sanctify baptism through his own body and thereby take away the sin, in order that afterwards those who believe in him may have the forgiveness of sins. Therefore baptism is not a useless, empty thing, as the sectarians blasphemously say, but in it all righteousness is fulfilled. (AE 51:318; WA 49:126)

[191] See Luther's "First Sermon at the Baptism of Bernhard von Anhalt, Matthew 3:1–12" (April 1, 1540):

And whosoever believes that his sin and the sin of the world is laid on our dear Lord, who was baptised and nailed to the cross for it, and shed His precious blood in order that He, the only sin-bearer, should thus cleanse us from sin, and make us holy and blessed, that man receives forgiveness of sins, and eternal life; and Christ's baptism, cross and blood become his own. (*Day by Day We Magnify Thee*, 144; WA 49:121)

[192] J. A. T. Robinson, following the work of Oscar Cullmann, sums up the propitiatory view of Christ's Baptism:

The essential meaning of Jesus' baptism is precisely that he was "numbered with the transgressors" and "bare the sins of many" (Isa. 53.12). He entered upon it "to fulfil all righteousness" (πληρῶσαι πᾶσαν δικαιοσύνην [Mt 3:15]). That is to say, "Jesus will effect a general forgiveness" (Cullmann), or, in the words again of Isa. 42.1, "he will bring forth judgment for the nations." Cullmann also comments on Luke 3.21 ("Now when *all* the people [ἅπαντα τὸν λαόν] were baptized, Jesus also was baptized"): "He is distinguished from the mass of other baptized people, who are baptized for their own sins, as the One called to the office of the Servant of God who suffers *for all others*." ("The One Baptism," 162, quoting Oscar Cullmann, *Baptism in the New Testament* [trans. J. K. S. Reid; London: SCM, 1950], 18–19)

it took place in such a wondrous fashion. But I am a poor sinner, conceived and born in sin. For this reason such splendid things will certainly not happen at my baptism, will they?"

15. But you should in no way think or say, that, because you are a sinner, you would want to despise your baptism or hold it in contempt, as if it were not as splendid as Christ's baptism, or that you would not want to accept Christ's baptism for yourself. No! You should not act this way; that would not be good. You should not separate your baptism from Christ's baptism. Rather, you must by means of your baptism enter into the baptism of Christ, so that Christ's baptism *is* your baptism, and your baptism Christ's baptism, and in the end there is only one baptism.

16. For baptism is the sort of bath in which our sins are washed away; just as we sing in the Nicene Creed: "I confess one single baptism for the forgiveness of sins."[193] Also St Paul says, "We are all baptized into the death of Christ" (Rom 6:4); and "As many of you as are baptized have put on Christ" (Gal 3:27). And if baptism did not bring this also to us, namely the forgiveness of sins, then baptism would be for us of no use, and would be no better than any other bath. Therefore, we must know and believe that Christ was baptized for our sake, and thus say: "His baptism is mine, and my baptism is his baptism; for he is the Lamb of God, who carries [*trägt*] the sin of the world." And inasmuch as he is now baptized, there he is baptized in our person and for our sake, we who are of the world and full of sin—which sin he has taken upon himself, and through this his baptism he has been washed clean of it. For St John says, "Behold, that is God's Lamb, who carries the sin of the world" (John 1:29). Thus John calls his baptism a baptism for repentance, through which the sinner who repents and is baptized attains to and receives the forgiveness of sins.[194]

---

[193] In German, the Nicene Creed reads: "Ich bekenne eine einige Taufe zur Vergebung der Sünden."

[194] Martin Luther, "Sermon on the Festival of Christ's Epiphany: On the Baptism of Christ" (1546); my translation from StL 12:1135–36, as first printed in Winger, " 'One Baptism' and the Purpose of Ephesians," 268–69. Luther speaks in line with patristic interpretation such as that found in the baptismal rite of the *Didascalia Apostolorum* (early third century):

> … the bishop, through whom the Lord gave you the Holy Spirit, and through whom you have learned the word and have known God, and through whom you have been known of God, and through whom you were sealed, and through whom you became sons of the light, and through whom the Lord in baptism, by the imposition of the hand of the bishop, bore witness to each one of you and uttered His holy voice, saying: *Thou art my son: I this day have begotten thee* [Ps 2:7]. (*Didascalia Apostolorum*, 9 [trans. Connolly, *Didascalia Apostolorum*, 93; quoted in Whitaker, *Documents of the Baptismal Liturgy*, 12])

Likewise, Cyril of Jerusalem's *Mystagogical Catecheses*, 3:1:

> Having been *baptized into Christ* and having *put on Christ* [Gal. 3.27], ye have been made conformable to the Son of God; for God, having *predestinated us to the adoption of sons* [Eph. 1.5], made us *share the fashion of Christ's glorious body* [Phil. 3.21]. Being made therefore *partakers of Christ* [Heb. 3.14], ye are properly called Christs, and of you God said *Touch not my Christs* [i.e., anointed ones: Ps. 105.15]. Now ye were made Christs by receiving the emblem of the Holy Ghost; and all things were done upon you in representational fashion, because ye take the part of Christ. He also

St. Paul, therefore, by alluding to Christ's Baptism in a *Berakah* which praises God for all his cosmic saving works, sets down a presupposition for the argument he will make in the body of the epistle. It serves one of his major themes: the unity of Jew and Greek (all people) in Christ. Not only is Holy Baptism a Sacrament of which all Christians have partaken, but it also serves as a uniting act even more deeply in that every Christian who has ever been baptized has participated in the *same* act of Baptism and thereby has been joined to the one Christ in one body in his one death and resurrection. We were all together sealed in his sealing (Eph 1:13) so that we can be called little christs ("anointed ones").[195] If Jews and Gentiles are united in Christ's one body on the cross (2:16), this has been made possible because both have first been united with Christ in his Baptism. Thus, when Paul expands the thought further in chapter 4, he is able to state unequivocally that there is but "one Baptism" (4:5), on the basis of which all divisions between members of the body of Christ are broken down and replaced by a spiritual unity, the bond of peace (4:1–4), in one faith (4:5), under one Father (4:6).[196]

Predestination and Baptism

Ephesians 1 has historically served as a crucial proof text for the biblical teaching on predestination. It features prominently in the Formula of Concord,

---

bathed himself in the river Jordan. (Quoted in Whitaker, *Documents of the Baptismal Liturgy*, 29–30)

[195] Lampe, *The Seal of the Spirit*, 6, arguing against the view that "sealing" refers to confirmation, writes:

In these texts, explicitly in 2 Cor. i. 21–2, and less obviously in Eph. i. 13, iv. 30, St. Paul is not referring to any material unction or other rite of Confirmation, but is reminding his readers that by their incorporation into the Body of Christ, effected through Baptism into Him, they have become partakers in the effects of His own Baptism at the hands of John; they have been made sharers in the Messianic character, "anointed" by God with the Spirit which stamps them for the day of redemption. …

The descent of the Spirit upon Jesus at His Baptism "was a descent upon us because of His bearing our body; and it happened … for our sanctification, that we might share his anointing." "Every baptism administered according to Christ's ordinance," says Wirgman, "is linked to our Lord's Baptism in Jordan." As Cullmann, Flemington, and others have lately demonstrated, Christian Baptism is the application to each believer of the Baptism of Christ as it was consummated and fulfilled in His death and resurrection.

The first quotation is from Athanasius, *Orations against the Arians*, 1:47 (PG 26:108C); the second is from A. Theodore Wirgman, *The Doctrine of Confirmation Considered in Relation to Holy Baptism as a Sacramental Ordinance of the Catholic Church* (London: Longmans, 1897), 52. Re Cullmann and Flemington, Lampe lists these works in his bibliography (*The Seal of the Spirit*, 324–25): Oscar Cullmann, "La Signification du Baptême dans le Nouveau Testament," *Revue de théologie et de philosophie* 30 (1942): 121–34; Oscar Cullmann, *Die Tauflehre des Neuen Testaments: erwachsenen- und Kindertaufe* (Zürich: Zwingli, 1948); W. F. Flemington, *The New Testament Doctrine of Baptism* (London: SPCK, 1948).

[196] See the textual notes on 4:1–6; "Purpose and Themes" in the introduction; and Winger, " 'One Baptism' and the Purpose of Ephesians."

Article 11, "Of God's Eternal Foreknowledge [Predestination] and Election," particularly in its rejection of the Calvinist double predestination:

> The *eternal election of God*, however, *vel praedestinatio* (or *predestination*), that is, *God's ordination to salvation*, does not extend at once over the godly and the wicked, but only over the children of God, who were elected and ordained to eternal life before the foundation of the world was laid, as Paul says, Eph. 1, 4. 5: *He hath chosen us in Him, having predestinated us unto the adoption of children by Jesus Christ.* (FC SD 11:5 [*Triglotta*, 1065])

The Formula argues, with solid exegetical substance faithful to the vocabulary of Ephesians 1, that "predestination" is not to be equated with "foreknowledge," as if God merely foresees who will be saved (as he foresees who will not), but that he actively appoints (ἐκλέγομαι, "choose," Eph 1:4; προορίζω, "predestine," Eph 1:5, 11) some to his kingdom.

The Formula's purpose is, first, to reject the notion that God is somehow responsible for evil, such as the evil deeds of the damned, as if God had caused their evil life by predestining them for eternal damnation. There is not a hint of that notion in Ephesians 1, which speaks only to God's elect children. The Formula therefore rejects any use of predestination that might induce despair among those who believe they have not been chosen and any use that might condone licentiousness ("I can do whatever I want") among those who believe they have been chosen. God's eternal election cannot be separated from the means by which he brings it about in this life; conversely, the life of the believer should not contradict the fact of his election. God's Word is not intended to produce impenitence or despair, but is intended to assure us of salvation (FC SD 11:12).

The Formula emphasizes that God's eternal decree is not carried out like some sort of military muster ("you, you, not you"). Instead it emphasizes the role of the merits of Christ and the Spirit's work in Word and Sacrament (FC SD 11:15–18). In line with this Lutheran emphasis, the textual notes have argued for a subtle exegetical distinction between the aorist indicative main verb ἐξελέξατο, "he chose" (1:4), and the aorist participle προορίσας, literally, "having predestined" (1:5). While aorist participles may be used in coordination with a main verb to indicate means or manner ("he chose us by predestining us"), more often they express a precondition or preceding action: "having predestined us, he [then] chose us." Paul qualifies the act of predestination with the phrase ἐν ἀγάπῃ, "in love" (1:4)—thus rejecting any arbitrariness or callousness in God's motivation. But the act of choosing is fleshed out more fully with "that we should be holy and without blemish [ἁγίους καὶ ἀμώμους, 1:4]"—language later applied to the washing of Holy Baptism (5:26–27). Though Paul locates both the acts of predestining and choosing "before the foundation of the world" (1:4–5), choosing comprehends also the fulfillment of that predestination in the Spirit's work of calling, enlightening, and sanctifying through

Word and Sacrament,[197] particularly the act of Baptism in which Christ himself was declared to be God's "Chosen One" (see the second textual note on 1:4).

When the Christian doubts God's love or his own salvation, Paul directs him not inward to his own strength or merits, nor toward the inscrutable mysteries of the hidden God, but rather to the concrete, historical act of his own Baptism. In the hearing of God's Word (1:13) and Baptism, God's eternal decree is revealed to the Christian. Following Paul, Luther points the Christian to the acts of God *in history*:

> And it is true that God wanted to counteract this curiosity at the very beginning; for this is how He set forth His will and counsel: "I will reveal My foreknowledge and predestination to you in an extraordinary manner, but not by this way of reason and carnal wisdom, as you imagine. This is how I will do so: From an unrevealed God I will become a revealed God. Nevertheless, I will remain the same God. I will be made flesh, or send My Son. He shall die for your sins and shall rise again from the dead. And in this way I will fulfill your desire, in order that you may be able to know whether you are predestined or not. Behold, this is My Son; listen to Him (cf. Matt. 17:5). Look at Him as He lies in the manger and on the lap of His mother, as He hangs on the cross. Observe what He does and what He says. There you will surely take hold of Me." For "He who sees Me," says Christ, "also sees the Father Himself" (cf. John 14:9). If you listen to Him, are baptized in His name, and love His Word, then you are surely predestined and are certain of your salvation. But if you revile or despise the Word, then you are damned; for he who does not believe is condemned (Mark 16:16).[198]

The Seal of the Spirit (1:13; 4:30)

The verb σφραγίζω, "to seal," is used metaphorically in Ephesians (1:13; 4:30). To understand the metaphor, one must first investigate the literal meanings of the term and then ask which of these kinds of "sealing" Paul might be evoking:

1. "Sealing" that is primarily intended to secure or fasten, as in the sealing of Jesus' tomb (Mt 27:66) or the closing of the abyss to contain Satan (Rev 20:3).
2. The application of a wax seal at the bottom of a legal document that serves as attestation of its origin and authority (Jn 3:33); such a seal may also be placed on the outside of a scroll, certifying that it has not been unrolled and thus tampered with, but kept secret (e.g., Rev 5:1–5; 10:4; 22:10).

---

[197] Even Markus Barth, son of the great Calvinist dogmatician, picks up on Paul's message:

> Election cannot be identified with an event of the remote past or with a timeless divine will. Rather, in Eph 1:4 ff. the election which precedes the time and space of the created world is coupled with deeds effected by God and experienced by men in time and history. God elects not only before the creation of the world but He is and remains the electing God when his grace is poured out, when sins are forgiven, when revelation opens the eyes of man's mind, and when the seal of the Spirit quickens the dead and assembles those dispersed. … In sum, election is an event which is still being fulfilled. (*Ephesians*, 1:106)

[198] Luther, *Lectures on Genesis* (1542), AE 5:44–45.

3. Placing a mark on something or someone as a mark of *ownership* (examples below).[199]

The first kind of sealing seems a highly unlikely allusion for the metaphorical use in Ephesians, as there is no reference to closing or opening. In the second and third kinds, the seal or mark is created by an engraved, reverse-image original, which is pressed into hot wax, stamped into the surface with a hammer, or heated and applied as a brand. The wax or surface of the object then bears the image from the original. The implications of sealing with the Spirit would then include the restoration of the image of God that was lost through the fall into sin[200]—an idea made explicit in Eph 4:24, in close proximity to the second occurrence of the sealing metaphor (4:30). The fact that *people* are the object of sealing in Eph 1:13 (and 4:30) suggests that Paul has the third kind of sealing in mind—although the three are by no means mutually exclusive.[201] Geoffrey Lampe, who has written the finest study of the metaphor of sealing,[202] explains the cultural background of the third kind:

> This really consists in the application to religious ideas of the practices of branding cattle with the owner's name, the branding or tattooing of slaves, and the tattooing by which soldiers were signed as the emperor's men and easily recognized if they deserted the service. The latter custom is post-Pauline, but it illustrates the type of practice upon which his metaphor of "sealing" is ultimately based. …
>
> From this picture of the soldier or member of a guild "stamped" with the emperor's mark upon his hand, brow, or neck, it is no great distance to the idea of the "sealing" of a religious devotee with the sign or emblem of the god whom he serves. This seal may be a physical mark, or it may be some inward token by which he is assured of his status in relation to the god, and

---

[199] For ancient practices of sealing and biblical references to it in the OT and NT, see Mitchell, *The Song of Songs*, 1175–80, 1211–15 (commenting on the "seal" in Song 8:6).

[200] Gen 1:26–27; Wis Sol 2:23–24; Rom 8:29; 1 Cor 15:49; Col 3:10.

[201] Schlier, *Epheser*, 70, confines himself to cases where sealing is applied to persons. Lampe, *The Seal of the Spirit*, 7–8, notes that once one moves into the early church fathers, "there are few of the many meanings of σφραγίς, σφραγίζειν, *signaculum*, *signare* ['a seal' or 'to seal'], which are not adopted by Christian writers to serve as baptismal metaphors, and in many cases the metaphorical application combines more than one of the literal senses of the term."

[202] Lampe, *The Seal of the Spirit*. Lampe's purpose in writing was to challenge the High-Church Anglican notion of his day that "Baptism in the Spirit" and "the seal of the Spirit," when occurring in the NT, are not identical with "water Baptism," but refer to a subsequent action which is then identified with confirmation as a sacramental act. The implication of this notion is that Baptism with water initiates, but does not give the Spirit, who comes later through a separate rite. Lampe demonstrates quite convincingly that this interpretation is false. "Baptism in the Spirit," "the seal of the Spirit," and "water Baptism" are one and the same act. Unfortunately later Christian baptismal rites identified "the seal of the Spirit" with a postbaptismal anointing with oil, rather than with the pouring of the sacramental water itself. "Confirmation" properly speaking (the laying on of hands by the bishop in imitation of Acts 8:17), as well as the subsequent sign of the cross on the forehead, was also later referred to as a "seal." See Cabié, "Christian Initiation." Mischief is done when these rituals are pulled apart from the washing of water and the Word.

enabled to hope that in some future "gathering in" of the god's people he will be recognized and admitted among the chosen.

The conception of the believer as bound, like a soldier or a servant, in loyalty, service, and devotion to his god is a striking feature of the pagan mysteries. … Among Christians the idea of religious vocation as a *militia* is even stronger, and we shall find that it plays an important role in the history of Baptism and of the conception of the "seal" by which a convert is enrolled, and, as it were, "signed on" under the standard of Christ.[203]

God's marking of those who are his own recurs frequently in Scripture. In order to protect Cain from retribution for the murder of Abel, God set a mark (אוֹת; LXX: σημεῖον) upon him (Gen 4:15)—which is rightly understood as a sign of ownership and protection. In messianic times, it is prophesied that the true Israelite "will write on his hand 'belonging to YHWH [לַיהוָה]' " (Is 44:5). In Ezek 9:4–6 the man with the writing instrument is told to go through the city of Jerusalem and mark those who are still faithful to YHWH with a תָּו on their foreheads; those who are thus marked will be preserved from the coming slaughter.[204] This תָּו is the last letter of the Hebrew alphabet, which in the old Hebrew script was written in the shape of a cross, often a *chi cross* (X)![205] This is the OT background to the marks of identification given in John's Revelation. The 144,000—the new Israel—are sealed on the forehead (Rev 7:2–4, with the noun σφραγίς, "a seal," and the verb σφραγίζω, "to seal"), marking them as God's people. The locusts who then come forth from the abyss to destroy the world are only allowed to touch "those people who do not have the seal of God [τὴν σφραγῖδα τοῦ θεοῦ] upon their foreheads" (Rev 9:4).[206] Sealing thus comprises

---

[203] Lampe, *The Seal of the Spirit*, 9, 12. He adds: "It is therefore not surprising to discover that the practice of tattooing or otherwise setting a mark upon the body as a sign of consecration to a deity was common in many of the cults of pagan antiquity." Such a pagan practice may be behind the prohibition in Lev 19:28 against Israelites making cuttings in their flesh. The prohibition suggests caution in understanding 1 Ki 20:41 as referring to a mark on the forehead identifying a true prophet, but it is possible.

[204] Similar motifs occur in apocryphal descriptions of the end times, in which the righteous are preserved from destruction because they have God's mark upon them, while the wicked are marked for destruction (Ps Sol 15:6–10; *4 Ezra*, 6:5). In *Jubilees*, 15:26, circumcision is the mark that protects God's people from slaughter on the Day of Judgment.

[205] See the shapes of the letter *taw* in extrabiblical Hebrew and Moabite in John C. L. Gibson, *Textbook of Syrian Semitic Inscriptions*, vol. 1: *Hebrew and Moabite Inscriptions* (Oxford: Oxford University Press, 1971), 117–18, and the shapes of the letter *taw* in Phoenician inscriptions in John C. L. Gibson, *Textbook of Syrian Semitic Inscriptions*, vol. 3: *Phoenician Inscriptions* (Oxford: Oxford University Press, 1982), 180. In addition to X the paleo-Hebrew letter *taw* was sometimes written in these forms: ✗ T †. See further Christopher Mitchell, "(How) Should Lutherans Read the Old Testament? A Test Case: The Saving Cross in Ezekiel 9," in *The Restoration of Creation in Christ: Essays in Honor of Dean O. Wenthe* (St. Louis: Concordia, 2014), 37–52.

[206] The mark of the beast must be understood in contrast to God's mark. The antichrist imitates Christ thoroughly. He marks those who are his own with his name, which is merely a number, 666 (Rev 13:16–17; 14:9, 11; 16:2; 19:20; 20:4). This is no more to be taken as a literal, visible branding than God's seal. Both are quite real marks of ownership but are visible only to the one who is the master of those thus marked.

both election or choosing as God's own[207] and the protection from harm that it pledges. In OT and Apocalyptic examples, the significance of sealing is particularly *eschatological*: that is, the seal is a mark that preserves a person from final judgment or destruction.

Circumcision itself may be viewed in this way. It was a mark in the flesh, a sign (אוֹת) of the covenant (Gen 17:11), that identified the Israelite as belonging to YHWH—and yet it was hidden (in normal circumstances), for the mark was meant more for God's eyes than for people's. Circumcision is viewed by the NT as a "type" of Baptism. The lines of typology include the following:

* Both are divinely mandated actions that incorporate the individual into the people of God and give him the blessings of the covenant.

* Circumcision is done to the procreative organ (as a continual reminder that the Messiah will come from the seed of Israel); Baptism is new birth (for the Messiah has now been born).

* Circumcision involves the shedding of blood; Baptism is into the death of Christ, who shed his blood for us. Circumcision is cutting off the flesh; Baptism is putting off the sinful flesh, the old man.

Paul makes this typological connection explicit in Col 2:11–12:

> In him you were also circumcised with a circumcision not done with [human] hands in the putting off of the fleshly body in the circumcision of Christ, since you were buried with him in Baptism, in which you were also raised to life with [him] through faith in the working of the God who raised him from the dead.

Once this theological connection is established, one can easily identify the sealing referred to in Eph 1:13. For Paul has called circumcision the "seal" of the old covenant, writing that Abraham "received the sign [σημεῖον] of circumcision as a seal [σφραγῖδα] of the righteousness which he had by faith" (Rom 4:11).[208] Therefore, the seal of the NT is that which corresponds to circumcision: *Holy Baptism.*[209] "Having heard the Word of truth, the Gospel of your salvation, ...

It is possible to describe the mark on the forehead more clearly. For if John's Revelation is consciously alluding to Ezekiel, the mark may again be understood as cross-shaped (see the previous footnote). The marking of the candidate for Baptism with the sign of the cross upon the forehead and upon the breast is an ancient liturgical practice that probably goes back to the apostles themselves. Christians would easily recognize it in John's vision. The Christian who daily makes the sign of the cross in remembrance of that baptismal occasion is thus tracing out a pattern that has been invisibly set upon him. One must be careful, however, not to interpret "the seal of the Spirit" merely as the liturgical act of signing. The seal is the Baptism; the sign of the cross is merely a remembrance thereof.

[207] "But God's firm foundation stands, having this seal: 'the Lord knows those who are his'" (ἔχων τὴν σφραγῖδα ταύτην· ἔγνω κύριος τοὺς ὄντας αὐτοῦ, 2 Tim 2:19).

[208] *Barnabas,* 9:6, and later rabbinic texts also refer to circumcision as a seal.

[209] The identification is made explicit in the Apostolic Fathers: *2 Clement,* 7:6; 8:6 (cf. *2 Clement,* 6:9); *Shepherd of Hermas, Similitudes,* 8:6.3; 9:16.3–7; 9:17.4. See Schnackenburg, "'Er hat uns mitauferweckt': Zur Tauflehre des Epheserbriefes," 174–77; Dinkler, "Die Taufterminologie in 2 Kor. i 21 f.," 183–91. For further exegetical support of this identification of sealing with Baptism and some classic Lutheran advocates of it, see Mitchell, *The Song of Songs,* 1211–15 (commenting on "place me like a seal" in Song 8:6).

having also believed, you were sealed with the promised Holy Spirit" (Eph 1:13) means "having heard the Gospel and believed, you were baptized."[210] To separate sealing from Baptism results either in severing the Holy Spirit from Baptism or in fractioning the Gospel. "There cannot be a baptism for some aspects of membership of Christ (such as regeneration or remission of sins) and another for the other aspect of the same experience (reception of the indwelling Spirit) by which we are sealed."[211]

Now, just as Ephesians 1 implies a connection between the Baptism of our Lord and the Baptism of all Christians, so also the NT draws a connection between Christ's sealing and the Christian's. Jesus is called "the one whom God the Father has sealed [τοῦτον … ὁ πατὴρ ἐσφράγισεν ὁ θεός]" (Jn 6:27). In the Apocalypse, his identifying name "King of kings and Lord of lords" is written upon his garment and upon his thigh (Rev 19:16). Inasmuch as Christ was baptized, he was sealed with the Spirit, given the name above all names, and marked as God's Chosen One. All this becomes the Christian's when he is baptized into Christ by the same Spirit. Paul draws out the implications of this connection in 2 Cor 1:21–22:

> And the One who establishes us together with you into Christ and has anointed [χρίσας] us is God, who has also sealed us [σφραγισάμενος] and given us the deposit [ἀρραβῶνα] of the Spirit in our hearts.

As Jesus was anointed with the Spirit at his Baptism to be the Christ ("the Anointed One"), so also the one who is baptized into him is anointed with the same Spirit to be a Christian ("anointed one"). This Baptism is God's mark of ownership upon those whom he has chosen for eternal redemption.

> You pruned my dying branches
> That could produce no wine;
> By grafting me in Jesus,
> Made me a living vine.
> In Your baptismal flood
> You drowned cruel death, that tyrant,

---

[210] Eph 1:12–13 has laid down the pattern: hearing the Gospel, believing, sealing with the Spirit. A baptismal interpretation of the seal receives further confirmation from discovering the same pattern described in Acts, in which hearing the Gospel is followed by faith and then Baptism: Acts 2:37–38, 41; 8:12, 35–38; 10:44–48; 16:14–15, 32–33; 18:8. Even Paul himself heard the voice of the Lord and then was baptized (Acts 9:4–6, 18; 22:7–10, 16). See also Dinkler, "Die Taufterminologie in 2 Kor. i 21 f.," 185.

As these examples refer to new missions, this pattern is natural. The fact that adults hear the Gospel and believe before they are baptized in no way militates against the church's ongoing practice of infant Baptism. Acts itself reports the Baptism of entire households (Acts 10:1–2, 48; 11:14; 16:15, 31–34; 18:8). In fact, the pattern may not be so different, for even infants may have faith on the basis of the Gospel proclaimed and confessed in the liturgy before Baptism. See David P. Scaer, *Baptism* (Confessional Lutheran Dogmatics 11; St. Louis: Luther Academy, 1999), 152–56.

[211] Lampe, *The Seal of the Spirit*, 62. The same criticism is applicable to anyone who would accept that John's Baptism gave the forgiveness of sins, but deny that it gave the Holy Spirit or incorporation into the body of Christ. The Spirit's Gospel gifts are not divisible in this way.

And made my spirit vibrant
Through Jesus and His blood.

You give us Your anointing
Through God's most holy Word.
You've made us priests and prophets
And kings with Christ our Lord.
You are the holy oil,
The oil of consecration
That makes us Christ's possession
And marks us with His seal.[212]

---

[212] Paul Gerhardt, "Zeuch ein zu deinen Toren," stanzas 3–4; trans. John W. Kleinig, "Paul Gerhardt as a Teacher of Lutheran Spirituality, Pt 1," *Lutheran Theological Review* 20 (Academic Year 2007–2008): 46.

Exordium: *Hodayah* Prayer: Thanksgiving

Translation

1 ¹⁵For this reason, I myself—

having heard of your faith [which is yours] in the Lord Jesus and [your] love toward all the saints—

¹⁶I do not cease giving thanks for you, making remembrance [of you] at the time of my prayers,

¹⁷that the God of our Lord <u>Jesus Christ</u>, the <u>Father</u> of glory, might give to you

the <u>Spirit</u> of wisdom and revelation in the knowledge of him,

¹⁸[and give] enlightened eyes of [your] heart,

so that you might know

what is the hope of his calling,

what is the richness of his glorious inheritance among the saints, ¹⁹and

what is the surpassing greatness of his power for us who believe,

according to the working of his mighty strength,

²⁰which he worked in Christ Jesus

by raising him from the dead,

and by seating [him] at his right hand in the heavenly places,

²¹far above every ruler and authority and power and lordship,

and every name that is named,

not only in this age but also in the one to come,

²²and "he subordinated all things under his feet,"

and he appointed him as head over all things for the church,

²³which is his body, the fullness of the one who fills all things in all.

Textual Notes

1:15 διὰ τοῦτο—The meaning of this common phrase ("for this reason, therefore") is not in doubt, but its referent is unclear. Normally it appeals to a cause that has just been mentioned (Eph 5:17; 6:13; Col 1:9). It could be a specific reference to the Ephesians having heard the Word and been baptized (Eph 1:13), which would lead naturally into his thanksgiving for their continued faith and love. Or it may be a more general marker of rhetorical progression: just as God is to be praised for the cosmic, saving deeds he has accomplished for us in Christ (the *Berakah* prayer, 1:3–14), so also he is thanked for preserving the Ephesians in this faith.[1]

κἀγώ—This is a contraction of καὶ ἐγώ. There are two possible interpretations: (1) καί may modify εὐχαριστῶν (1:16): "I do not cease giving thanks *also*." Thus, his act

---

[1] Often such logical conjunctions lose their full force and serve merely to introduce a new section (e.g., 2:11; 3:1, 14).

of thanksgiving is appended to the preceding act of praise (1:3–14). (2) καί may modify ἐγώ, "*also/even* I do not cease giving thanks." This implies that Paul sees the *Berakah* prayer (1:3–14) as a churchly act of thanksgiving, to which he appends his personal, but apostolic prayer (cf. Rom 16:4). The κἀγώ would probably also be emphatic, "I myself" (cf. 1 Thess 3:5). Since the καί is elided with the pronoun ἐγώ, it is unlikely that it modifies the verb εὐχαριστῶν; hence, it is natural to follow the second interpretation (cf. καὶ ἡμεῖς, "also we," in Col 1:9; 1 Thess 2:13).

ἀκούσας—The aorist participle ἀκούσας is adverbial, expressing the cause or occasion ("since I have heard") for Paul's giving thanks (1:16).[2] The introduction noted that this verse (together with 3:2; 4:21) has been interpreted to mean that the writer has no personal knowledge of his addressees (he merely "heard" about them) and that this interpretation has been used either in support of the circular letter theory or in denial of Pauline authorship.[3] Yet, it need not be interpreted differently than similar statements in other letters, where an emissary has brought Paul up-to-date news about a group of Christians from whom he has been separated for some time.[4] Perhaps it was the same Epaphras, the pastor who had brought news from Colossae (Col 1:7–8), who also brought news about Ephesus; perhaps it was someone in his retinue. The point is not that Paul has *only* heard of the Ephesians' faith and love, but that since he left them he has worried over them as a father worries over his children and is gladdened by current news of their persistence in the faith. The slow, long-distance conversation thus begun continues not only through the letter but also through the additional oral news brought back to Ephesus by the letter carrier, Tychicus (Eph 6:21–22).

τὴν καθ᾽ ὑμᾶς πίστιν—This use of the preposition κατά is a circumlocution for the possessive, "your own faith"—though a hint of distributive force may remain, "the faith that is found in each and every one of you."[5] Paul allows for no distinction or division among the Ephesians on the basis of big or little faith. Giving thanks for his addressees' faith is a prominent feature of his epistles.[6]

ἐν τῷ κυρίῳ Ἰησοῦ—"In the Lord Jesus": see the fifth textual note on 1:3 for a discussion of "in Christ." Faith in Christ Jesus was introduced in 1:1, where the Ephesians were defined as "faithful [ones who are] in Christ Jesus." Here in English, the translation "your faith in Christ" implies Christ as the object of saving faith, which is never to be excluded from the Christian Gospel. However, that may not be the precise meaning

---

[2]   A temporal meaning indicating a mere sequence of events, "after I heard" (Wallace, *Greek Grammar*, 627), does not seem strong enough. At the same time, it is clear that Paul would have given thanks continually (1:16) even if he had not heard of the Ephesians' continued faith. The news simply confirms and strengthens his thanksgiving prayer.

[3]   See "Arguments against Pauline Authorship" in "Authorship" in the introduction.

[4]   1 Cor 1:11; Phil 1:27; Col 1:4, 7–8; 1 Thess 3:5–10; 2 Thess 3:11; Philemon 5.

[5]   See BDF § 224 (1). BDAG, s.v. κατά, 7 b, suggests it may represent "a possessive pron[oun], but with limiting force," as in Rom 1:15 ("my eagerness"). Thus, "it was *your* faith I heard about, not someone else's."

[6]   Rom 1:8; 1 Thess 1:3; 2 Thess 1:3; 2 Tim 1:3, 5; Philemon 4–5.

of the grammar in this verse. The object of πιστεύω, "to believe," is not normally expressed with ἐν.[7]

Thus, the meaning here might be "the faith that is yours as you are in the Lord Jesus" rather than "your believing in the Lord Jesus"; it expresses Christ as the location of the believers, rather than the object of their faith.[8] When Christ is the object of the verbal idea implicit in πίστις, "faith" ("believing in Christ"), it is usually expressed by an objective genitive,[9] by πρός plus the accusative (1 Thess 1:8), or by εἰς plus the accusative (Col 2:5). Other passages with ἐν Χριστῷ, "in Christ," after πίστις, "faith," are ambiguous: Gal 3:26 (witness RSV/ESV [locative] versus KJV [objective]); Col 1:4;[10] 1 Tim 3:13 (where πίστις is most likely *fides quae creditur*, "the faith which is believed"); 2 Tim 3:15. Lincoln suggests that ἐν Χριστῷ, "in Christ," expresses "the realm in which faith operates."[11] In one parallel case, Paul removes the ambiguity with another preposition: "having heard of your love and faith, which you have toward [πρός] the Lord Jesus and for [εἰς] all the saints" (Philemon 5). Paul's use of ἐν in Eph 1:15 might be explained as a way of asserting that not only is the believer's faith *directed* toward Jesus from the outside but also that the believer is *in* Christ. "Faith in the Lord Jesus" and "love toward all the saints" (see the next textual note) are not entirely parallel thoughts.

καὶ τὴν ἀγάπην[12] τὴν εἰς πάντας τοὺς ἁγίους—"Faith" (πίστιν in the fourth textual note on 1:15) and "love" (τὴν ἀγάπην) are a frequent NT coupling that often appears in Paul's thanksgivings.[13] "Hope" (ἐλπίς) is added in Col 1:4–5 and 1 Thess 1:3, and pops up in Eph 1:18, making the triad (1 Cor 13:13) complete in Eph 1:15–18, though not obvious. "Grace," "peace," "faith," and "love"—the chief gifts of God in Christ— form an *inclusio* around the letter (1:2, 15; 6:23–24).

---

[7] See the fourth textual note on 1:1 and the fourth textual note on 1:13.

[8] Cf. Mt 8:10. Schnackenburg, *Ephesians*, 72, and Schlier, *Epheser*, 76, prefer this view. See also Deterding, *Colossians*, 23–25. Barth, *Ephesians*, 1:146, takes it a step further, interpreting πίστις as "faithfulness" that is rooted in the Lord Jesus, but that collapsing of faith and love seems contrary to the context.

[9] Sometimes it is clearly objective, as with πίστις θεοῦ, "faith in God" (Mk 11:22; similarly Col 2:12). The phrase πίστις Ἰησοῦ (Rom 3:22, 26; Gal 2:16; 3:22) has famously been disputed as either subjective, "Jesus' faithfulness," or objective, "faith in Jesus" (the traditional view). For discussions, see the excursus "πίστις Ἰησοῦ Χριστοῦ, 'Faith of/[in] Jesus Christ,' " in Middendorf, *Romans 1–8*, 304–12, and "Faith in/of Christ" in Das, *Galatians*, 250–53, as well as "By the Hearing of Faith (3:2, 5)" in Das, 289–93, and pages 369–71, commenting on Gal 3:22.

[10] Deterding, *Colossians*, 28, translates this parallel passage "having heard of your faith [which is yours, as you are] in Christ Jesus."

[11] Lincoln, *Ephesians*, 55.

[12] Many early manuscripts omit τὴν ἀγάπην, "(the) love," resulting in "faith in the Lord Jesus and toward all the saints." That omission is easily explained by the repetition of τήν. This might have caused the scribe's eye to jump from its first occurrence (τὴν ἀγάπην) to its second (τὴν εἰς), i.e., haplography caused by homoeoarcton. The correctors of ℵ and D have undoubtedly got it right by including τὴν ἀγάπην (NA[27] text).

[13] Col 1:4; 1 Thess 1:3; 3:6; Philemon 5; cf. Rev 2:19.

Here "*all* the saints" (πάντας τοὺς ἁγίους) emphasizes (1) Christian concern for every last, lowly member of Christ's body (the Ephesian church is called "saints" in 1:1) and (2) the trans-parochial character of the catholic church.[14] (It is unlikely that Paul means simply "love" to one another, i.e., within the Ephesian congregations.) This trans-parochial love is evident in the Ephesians' likely participation in the collection for the saints in Jerusalem (1 Cor 16:1–9); their greetings sent with Paul's letter from Ephesus to Corinth (1 Cor 16:19); and the travels of Trophimus, the Ephesian, and Tychicus, the Asian, who supported Paul in his mission. Perhaps "love toward *all* the saints" reminds them that their own actions belie any division in the church on the grounds of race.

Rev 2:4 indicates that the "love" for which the Ephesians were once renowned had later waned, and in Rev 2:5 the Lord calls them to repentance. Love, which flows from faith (1 Tim 1:5),[15] must ever be nourished by the Gospel for it to flourish. Love for one another follows upon God's love for us in Christ (1 Jn 4:10, 19), and together with faith is a gift of the Holy Spirit (Gal 5:22). Thus, when Paul praises these qualities in the saints, he is praising God's work. On the baptismal flavor of "saints," see the fourth textual note on 1:1.

1:16 οὐ παύομαι εὐχαριστῶν ὑπὲρ ὑμῶν—The participle εὐχαριστῶν is complementary, completing the thought of οὐ παύομαι: "I do not cease giving thanks."[16] On the surface, "I do not cease" should not be taken literally, as if Paul does nothing other than give thanks. It is hyperbole, expressing the ongoing, regular, intensive nature of his prayer. This is rooted in Christ's mandate, as he urged unceasing prayer in the parable of the Persistent Widow (Lk 18:1–8) and in Gethsemane (Lk 21:36). Paul frequently repeated this mandate and observed it himself.[17] Yet at a deeper level, as all prayer is directed by the Holy Spirit, who continually moves faith into conversation with God (Rom 8:26–27), and as Paul (like all Christians) is "in Christ," who stands in continual intercession for us before the Father's throne (Rom 8:34; Heb 7:25), Paul might say that he does continually give thanks. As in the *Berakah* pattern (Eph 1:3–14), giving thanks/praise to God (1:15–16) precedes petitions for the saints (1:17–19).

μνείαν ποιούμενος—Literally "making remembrance," this is more than "remembering" as a mere mental recollection. Paul speaks the addressees' names and circumstances before the Lord to "remind" him of his gifts and promises to them. The addition of the pronoun ὑμῶν, "of you," would complete the thought; but though it is supplied by later manuscripts, it was most likely absent from the original text. Like εὐχαριστῶν (in the preceding textual note), the participle ποιούμενος is complementary, completing the thought of οὐ παύομαι: "I do not cease … making remembrance."

---

[14] At the same time the phrase is restrictive, for it confines love to the body of Christ (cf. Gal 6:10).

[15] "For this is the sum of things, this is virtue, this is the mystery, that there should be faith in Christ Jesus. This faith also encourages one to love all the saints, all who have faith in Christ and have been sanctified through him. Thus one who is faithful in Christ loves the saints" (Victorinus, *Ephesians*, 1:1.15 [ACCS 8:120]).

[16] Wallace, *Greek Grammar*, 646.

[17] Rom 1:9–10; 12:12; Eph 6:18; Phil 1:4; Col 1:3; 4:2; 1 Thess 5:17; 2 Thess 1:11.

Thus, "giving thanks" and "making remembrance" are parallel verbs describing the same act of prayer according to its two aspects.

ἐπὶ τῶν προσευχῶν μου—The construction with ἐπί plus the genitive means "*at the time of* my prayers." Raised as a Jew, Paul would have been accustomed to prayer three times a day: morning, noon, and afternoon/evening.[18] These times were intended to coincide with the sacrifices being offered at the temple.[19] When it is reported that the God-fearer Cornelius "prayed constantly," the account subsequently mentions prayer at the ninth hour.[20] Acts testifies that the apostles maintained these hours of prayer—the third, sixth, and ninth hours (counting from sunrise)—going to the temple when possible.[21] Early Christians connected these hours with a remembrance of Christ's time on the cross.[22] So it is likely that Paul is referring to his maintenance of the three normal hours of prayer, at which times he made specific mention of all the churches and saints under his care—both his apostolic duty and his joy.[23] Paul's depiction of his fellow minister at Colossae, Epaphras, is parallel: πάντοτε ἀγωνιζόμενος ὑπὲρ ὑμῶν ἐν ταῖς προσευχαῖς, "always struggling for your sake in the/his prayers" (Col 4:12).

1:17 ἵνα ... δώῃ ὑμῖν—The combination ἵνα plus the subjunctive[24] gives the object of the verb "making remembrance," thus unfolding the content of his prayer's petitions: "that he might give to you ..."

ὁ θεὸς τοῦ κυρίου ἡμῶν Ἰησοῦ Χριστοῦ—See the second textual note on 1:3. Like the *Berakah* prayer (1:3), Paul's regular prayers are addressed to the Father in a Trinitarian fashion (cf. 3:14; 5:20; 6:18). The qualification "the God *of our Lord Jesus Christ*" is not merely an identification of the true God but forms the basis of the appeal. Paul prays that God the Father would give, for the sake of his Son, the Holy Spirit with all his gifts.

ὁ πατὴρ τῆς δόξης—"The Father of glory" is an expression unique in the Bible.[25] δόξα, "glory," is a quality frequently attributed to God the Father in the NT and shared

---

18 Ps 55:18 (ET 55:17); Dan 6:11, 14 (ET 6:10, 13); 9:21; Judith 12:5–7; 13:3. More extensive prayer, seven times a day plus midnight, is noted in Ps 119:62, 164, which influenced later pious Christian and monastic practice.

19 Ex 29:38–39; Ps 141:2; Dan 9:21; and Judith 9:1. Josephus, *Antiquities*, 14:65, reports that the "evening" sacrifice normally happened at the ninth hour (midafternoon), earlier than had originally been intended. In 1 Macc 12:11, the author of another letter connects the time of remembrance to the hours of sacrifice and prayer.

20 Acts 10:2–3, 30.

21 Acts 2:15; 3:1; 10:9.

22 Mt 27:45–46; Mk 15:25. See, e.g., Cyprian, *The Lord's Prayer*, 24, and Hippolytus, *Apostolic Tradition*, 41.

23 Rom 1:9–10; Phil 1:3–4; Col 1:3; Philemon 4; 1 Thess 1:2; 2 Tim 1:3; cf. 1 Cor 1:4; 2 Thess 1:3; 2:13.

24 Though δώῃ might possibly be confused with the optative δῴη, it is to be taken as the second aorist subjunctive of δίδωμι, "give." See BDAG, s.v. δίδωμι; BDF § 95 (2). The variant reading in manuscript B is δῷ (as in Eph 3:16), the more normal form of the subjunctive.

25 Though we have "the God of glory" in Ps 29:3 (LXX 28:3) and Acts 7:2; "the King of glory" in Ps 24:7 (LXX 23:7); "the glory of the Father" in Rom 6:4; and Jesus as "the Lord of glory" in 1 Cor 2:8.

with his Son,[26] particularly through the declaration given at his transfiguration (2 Pet 1:17; cf. Jn 12:28), and through his passion, resurrection, and ascension (Jn 7:39; 12:23). God's glory is active, able to raise Christ from the dead and give life to the baptized (Rom 6:4; 8:17). It is, of course, acclaimed of God in doxologies.[27] But it is not merely a quality of God; he is the source, the giver of glory.[28] In secular Greek, δόξα relates to δοκέω, "to think," thus expressing a person's "fame" or "honor." When the LXX linked δόξα with כָּבוֹד, YHWH's "glory" (e.g., Ex 40:34–35; Ps 19:2 [ET 19:1; LXX 18:2]; Ezek 1:28), and with הוֹד, his "splendor" (e.g., Num 27:20; Is 30:30), the qualities of other-worldly brightness, beauty, and radiance were added (e.g., Is 4:5; 60:1); thus, it can bring light to men (Eph 1:18; 2 Cor 4:6; Rev 21:23). As a quality of the naked God, it is a consuming holiness (Ex 33:18–23); in Christ God's glory is made approachable (Jn 1:14, 18; 2 Cor 3:18). Thus, δόξα in the NT should be associated with God's gracious, incarnational "glory" (כָּבוֹד) dwelling among his people, as in the tabernacle and temple, which later rabbinic thought called his שְׁכִינָה, *shekinah* ("dwelling"). See also the textual notes on Eph 1:6; 3:20–21.

πνεῦμα—Paul prays not that the Ephesians would be given "a spirit" (a human quality), but "the Spirit" (cf. Eph 3:5; 1 Cor 12:8). The gift of the Spirit himself is not quantifiable, as if one can have only a bit and then a little more; he is a Person. Thus, there is no conflict between the Ephesians' having already received the Spirit in Baptism (1:13) and Paul's prayer that the Father would continue to give the Spirit to them. The petition is in accord with our Lord's promise to send the Holy Spirit to guide us in his truth (Jn 16:12–15).

σοφίας καὶ ἀποκαλύψεως ἐν ἐπιγνώσει αὐτοῦ—The prayer for the Spirit is given specificity by the two genitives (σοφίας, "of wisdom," and ἀποκαλύψεως, "of revelation") and the prepositional phrase (ἐν ἐπιγνώσει αὐτοῦ, "in the knowledge of him") that modify the noun πνεῦμα, "Spirit." These genitives of product[29] explain what Paul desires the Father to provide through the giving of his Spirit: "wisdom" and "revelation." Continuing the theme of the *Berakah* (1:3–14), Paul prays that the Ephesians would more fully understand the contents of the divine mystery (cf. Col 2:2). The language bears the redundancy of liturgical prayer: all three terms—"wisdom," "revelation," and "knowledge"—refer to the same revelation.[30]

The three terms are combined only here in the whole Greek Bible. All have a distinctly spiritual flavor, as they are almost uniquely associated with the knowledge of

---

[26] Mt 16:27 (‖ Mk 8:38; Lk 9:26); Jn 1:14; 8:54; 17:5, 24; Phil 2:11.

[27] Lk 2:14; Eph 3:20–21; Phil 4:20; Rev 1:6; passim.

[28] "Father" as source: "Father of mercies" (2 Cor 1:3); "Father of lights" (James 1:17); "Father of spirits" (Heb 12:9). Chrysostom: "*The Father of glory* means 'the one who has given you these most extraordinary gifts.' Through his subordinate effects his glory is revealed" (*Homilies on Ephesians*, 3:1.15–19 [ACCS 8:120]).

[29] See Wallace, *Greek Grammar*, 106; cf. "the God of hope" (Rom 15:13) and "the God of peace" (Rom 15:33).

[30] Since the Father provides these gifts, the antecedent of αὐτοῦ, "the knowledge of *him*," may be God the Father; but 4:13 speaks of τῆς ἐπιγνώσεως τοῦ υἱοῦ τοῦ θεοῦ, "the knowledge of *the Son* of God," so the antecedent may be left ambiguous here.

divine matters granted first to Paul (along with the other apostles) as the recipient of insight into the heavenly mystery (1 Cor 2:6–16; Eph 3:1–13), and then through the apostolic Word to all those who have been reborn.[31] They are major themes of Ephesians: "wisdom" (1:8, 17; 3:10; see also 5:15), "revelation" (1:17; 3:3; see also 3:5), and "knowledge" (1:17; 4:13; see also 1:9, 18; 3:3, 5, 10, 19). Paganism is ignorance (4:18); false religious philosophies give false knowledge (Gnosticism). Faith and love lead to complete knowledge of the true God (3:17–19); but true knowledge is to be known *by* God (1 Cor 8:3; Gal 4:9). Paul can pray confidently for this understanding because it has already been disclosed in Christ (Eph 1:7–8).

The triad of the Spirit's gifts evokes Is 11:2: "and the Spirit of YHWH shall rest upon him, the *Spirit of wisdom* and *understanding* [πνεῦμα σοφίας καὶ συνέσεως], the Spirit of counsel and might, the *Spirit of knowledge* [γνώσεως] and the fear of YHWH."[32] These are the gifts bestowed on the Messiah at his Baptism and consequently on all those baptized into him (1 Cor 12:13).

1:18 πεφωτισμένους τοὺς ὀφθαλμοὺς τῆς καρδίας [ὑμῶν]—Syntactically, the perfect accusative participle πεφωτισμένους, "enlightened," should be understood as an adjectival modifier of τοὺς ὀφθαλμούς, "the eyes," which are the direct object of δώῃ, "give" (1:17). Hence, Paul's prayer is "that God would give to you … eyes that have been [and remain] enlightened."[33] In the OT God is said to enlighten the eyes through his Word (Ps 19:9 [ET Ps 19:8; LXX 18:9]).[34] The precise expression "eyes of the heart" is unique in the Bible, though thoroughly Hebraic in conception, for in the OT "heart" is roughly equivalent to "mind" in Greek thought. The phrase appears to be shorthand for "heart, eyes, and ears," a triad that appears frequently, rooted in Is 6:10.[35] Note the parallelism of "heart" and "eyes" in Ps 19:9 (ET Ps 19:8): "the precepts of YHWH are right and make the heart rejoice; the commandment of YHWH is pure and enlightens the eyes." The reference is to the human faculties that perceive (or do not perceive) the workings of God. Blindness is a frequent image for the ignorance of pagan (Gentile) existence apart from God.[36]

---

[31] E.g., Col 1:10; 3:10; 1 Tim 2:4; 2 Tim 2:25; 3:7; Titus 1:1.

[32] Cf. Wis Sol 7:7.

[33] For similar constructions, see the first textual note on 2:1 and the first textual note on 2:5. Barth, *Ephesians*, 1:149, however, suggests that the participle πεφωτισμένους is circumstantial, which could be translated as "since your eyes have been enlightened"; likewise Lincoln, *Ephesians*, 47; Schlier, *Epheser*, 79. Though this would strengthen the reference to the past action of Baptism, such an accusative absolute is nearly undocumented in the NT (possibly Acts 26:3; 2 Cor 3:14). See BDF § 424; Wallace, *Greek Grammar*, 631.

[34] In the LXX φωτίζω, "to enlighten," takes the object ὀφθαλμούς, "eyes," in Ezra 9:8; Ps 12:4 (MT 13:4; ET 13:3); 18:9 (MT 19:9; ET 19:8); Sirach 34:17; Baruch 1:12.

[35] Cf. Mt 13:14–16; Jn 12:39–41; Acts 28:25–27. See also *4 Ezra*, 14:25; 1 Cor 2:9; 2 Pet 2:14. Influenced by Paul we have "eyes of the heart" in *1 Clement*, 36:2; 59:3. "Enlighten your heart" is found in a priestly blessing in the covenant-renewal service at Qumran (1QS 2:3).

[36] Similar are the mixed metaphors ἐσκοτωμένοι τῇ διανοίᾳ, "darkened in their understanding" (Eph 4:18), and "their foolish hearts were darkened" (Rom 1:21). See also Is 9:1 (ET 9:2); Mt 6:23; 8:12; Rom 2:19; Col 1:13; 1 Thess 5:5; 1 Pet 2:9; passim.

The antithesis of darkness and light is a widespread OT metaphor for the opposition between the realm of evil and the kingdom of God.[37] God is light (1 Jn 1:5), and outside his kingdom there is only darkness (Mt 8:12); the spiritual forces arrayed against God's kingdom occupy the darkness (Eph 6:12). Light shines into our hearts (2 Cor 4:6) and eyes (Acts 26:18) through the Gospel, which the Lord sent Paul to preach. The parallel in Col 1:12–13 speaks of light as an "inheritance," a rebirth/sonship term that hints at Baptism.[38] The transition from pagan darkness to enlightened life is described in Eph 5:11–14, which includes a presumed baptismal hymn (so also 1 Pet 2:9 in a baptismal context). "Those who have once been enlightened" (Heb 6:4; cf. Heb 10:32) was understood by the early fathers as a reference to the baptized. See "Enlightened Eyes of Your Heart (1:18)" in the commentary below for an explanation of the baptismal allusion. Even in pagan religions, "enlightenment" was used to describe initiation.[39]

εἰς τὸ εἰδέναι ὑμᾶς—The articular infinitive with its subject in the accusative (ὑμᾶς), governed by the preposition εἰς, indicates purpose: "so that you might know." It delineates the goal of giving the Spirit (1:17) and his enlightenment (1:18a). Without these primary gifts (the Spirit and his enlightenment), there is no possibility of spiritual knowledge. The Lord needed to open the disciples' minds to understand that everything was prophesied in Scripture (Lk 24:45–47). The purpose clause is followed by three things that the addressees are to know deeply, each introduced by τίς or τί (the next three textual notes).

τίς ἐστιν ἡ ἐλπὶς τῆς κλήσεως αὐτοῦ—"Hope" is the third member of the triad whose first two members were in 1:15 ("faith" and "love"). The concept of hope was introduced in 1:12 ("[we] who first hoped in Christ"), where it was a virtual synonym for saving faith. It will be contrasted with the hopelessness of the Gentile Ephesians' former life in 2:12 (cf. 1 Thess 4:13). The phrase here ("the hope of his calling") is repeated virtually verbatim in Eph 4:4, "the one hope of your calling," where it is connected with "one body and one Spirit, … one Lord, one faith, one Baptism." Paul Deterding's excellent commentary on hope[40] connects the Gentile lack of hope with the cyclical view of time that provided no hope for escape. The scriptural viewpoint sees history as progressing toward a salvific goal.[41] Hope is confidence about this future (Rom 8:24–25;

---

[37] 2 Sam 22:29; Job 29:3; Pss 18:29 (ET 18:28); 27:1; 112:4; 119:105; 139:12; Is 5:20, 30; 9:1 (ET 9:2); 42:6, 16; 47:5; 49:6; 51:4; 59:9; 60:1–2; Dan 2:22; Micah 7:8.

[38] Thus, Deterding, *Colossians*, 37–38.

[39] Arnold, *Power and Magic*, 76:

> It is of special significance, however, to note that the word "enlightened" (φωτίζω) was used in the Mystery Religions in a technical sense for the rite of initiation. Scott suggests that it was originally connected with some culminating moment when the initiate suddenly emerged from an unlit chamber into the shrine in a blaze of light. This "illumination" supposedly represented the new condition of his soul. (Citing E. F. Scott, *The Epistles of Paul to the Colossians, to Philemon and to the Ephesians* [London: Harper, 1930], 154)

[40] Deterding, *Colossians*, 31–33, commenting on Col 1:4–5.

[41] On this point, see also Oscar Cullmann, *Christ and Time: The Primitive Christian Conception of Time and History* (trans. Floyd V. Filson; rev. ed.; London: SCM, 1962), 51–80.

Titus 1:2) and thus holds much in common with faith in God (1 Pet 1:21).[42] In contrast even to contemporary usage, where "hope" is little more than optimism, the biblical concept of "hope" is rooted in the utterly reliable promises of God. God's calling through his Word in Holy Baptism (cf. Eph 1:3–14) becomes the basis of Christian confidence (Rom 5:5; 15:4). As in Col 1:5, "hope" may be understood as the object of faith/hope—the thing hoped for—rather than the subjective act of hoping. Paul prays that the Ephesians would understand what is in store for them in the heavenly realm (Eph 1:3; 1 Pet 1:3–4), to be unveiled at the second coming of our Lord Jesus Christ (Titus 2:13), who is our hope (Col 1:27). God's "calling" is not merely an invitation, but an active, creative Word that brings about what it says (see the third textual note on 4:1).[43]

τίς ὁ πλοῦτος τῆς δόξης τῆς κληρονομίας αὐτοῦ ἐν τοῖς ἁγίοις—This is the second item of knowledge introduced by the purpose clause discussed in the second textual note on 1:18. The heaping up of genitives with hyperbolic vocabulary of "richness" has been considered un-Pauline,[44] but is better explained as characteristic of liturgical language (e.g., Rom 11:33). Still recovering from the *Berakah* (Eph 1:3–14), Paul is overwhelmed by the majesty of the revelation of God's mystery. God holds nothing back from his saints; his riches suffice for both Jew and Gentile (Rom 9:23–24; 11:12). The masculine form ὁ πλοῦτος, "the richness," occurs fourteen times in the NT, but only here in Ephesians and never in Colossians. Its neuter synonym, τὸ πλοῦτος, is quite distinctive of Ephesians and Colossians, which together have six of its eight NT occurrences (see the fifth textual note on 1:7). It denotes an abundance, an inexhaustible supply, a richness of something. The noun δόξης ("glory") is best understood as an adjectival genitive modifying κληρονομίας ("inheritance"), thus not "an abundance of glory," but "a glorious inheritance."[45] "Inheritance" refers to the eternal divine goods promised by the heavenly Father to his new children in the rebirth of Baptism; thus, the genitive αὐτοῦ, "his," indicates the source of the inheritance, that it comes from him. Paul prays that the Ephesians would have the eyes to see and understand the glorious inheritance precisely because it is hidden and received only proleptically in this life through the Spirit; it remains the eschatological object of faith (see the first textual note on 1:14). On "saints," see the fourth textual note on 1:1.[46]

This petition is paralleled in Paul's speech to the Ephesian pastors (Acts 20:32) and coheres remarkably with the words of Paul's mandate from Christ (Acts 26:18).

---

[42] "But faith differs from hope because faith receives in the present the forgiveness of sins and reconciliation, or God's acceptance of us, on account of Christ. But hope is directed toward future good and future deliverance" (Ap 4:312 [Kolb-Wengert, 165]).

[43] Rom 4:17; 8:30; 9:11–12; 1 Cor 1:9; Gal 1:15. "The call of God is the actualization in history of his electing purpose" (Lincoln, *Ephesians*, 59). See the commentary on 1:3–14.

[44] See "Style" in "Authorship" in the introduction.

[45] Wallace, *Greek Grammar*, 90, suggests "glorious riches." The meaning of these lengthy genitive chains cannot easily be pinned down and perhaps ought not be.

[46] Though "saints/holy ones" certainly includes the heavenly host—and in view of the heavenly quality of the inheritance (1:3; 2:6), it may even emphasize it—the view that it refers exclusively to the angels (Schnackenburg, *Ephesians*, 75; Schlier, *Epheser*, 84; Best, *Ephesians*, 168) is unlikely, given Paul's common use of the term for Christians, and places too much emphasis on Qumran parallels (Lincoln, *Ephesians*, 60).

1:19 καὶ τί τὸ ὑπερβάλλον μέγεθος τῆς δυνάμεως αὐτοῦ—This is the third and final item of knowledge introduced by the purpose clause discussed in the second textual note on 1:18. The hyperbolic language continues with "the surpassing greatness of his power," a unique biblical expression. ὑπερβάλλω, "to surpass," is uniquely Pauline in the NT and is always connected with Christ's work.[47] μέγεθος, "greatness," though common in the LXX, is a NT hapax legomenon. Together, the two terms emphasize the superiority of God's power over that of the demons (1:21). δύναμις is the most common term for power, referring to "capacity, ability," the potential to act. While in pagan religious usage, such "power" can be an impersonal force, the subsequent reference to faith ("who believe") and the three active synonyms in the second half of the verse make it clear that God's power is *personal*.

εἰς ἡμᾶς τοὺς πιστεύοντας—In contrast to 1:12–13 and 2:1–5, 11–14, no distinction between Jew and Gentile is implied by the first person plural pronoun, here "us." Structurally "us who believe" is parallel to "among the saints" (1:18), being identical in referent and nearly so in meaning. As in 1:1, "(those) who believe" and "saints" refer to all the baptized. Faith is the instrument by which God's power becomes theirs, by which they are protected from their spiritual foes.

κατὰ τὴν ἐνέργειαν τοῦ κράτους τῆς ἰσχύος αὐτοῦ—With the preposition κατά, "according to," Paul anchors the three petitions of 1:18–19 (each beginning with τίς or τί, "what") in the power of God.[48] Another string of liturgical redundancies extends the rejoicing in its greatness. Paul uses four nearly synonymous terms for "power" in this single verse: τῆς δυνάμεως αὐτοῦ … τὴν ἐνέργειαν τοῦ κράτους τῆς ἰσχύος, "his *power* … the *working* of his *mighty strength*." By highlighting these mighty divine qualities, Paul emphasizes Christ's ability to triumph over all demonic foes (1:21).[49] This gives grounds for confidence that the petitions will be fulfilled and forms a transition into the final section of the prayer, which is creedal and doxological (1:20–23). The terms are characteristic of Paul and of Ephesians in particular. ἐνέργεια is "working, operation" (1:19; 3:7; 4:16; three of eight times in Paul), here referring specifically to God's powerful act of bringing resurrection to Christ and to the baptized (Eph 1:20; Col 2:12). κράτος, "might," and ἰσχύς, "strength," are virtual synonyms for each other[50] and for δύναμις, "power." The two are combined again in 6:10 as the place of refuge for the Christian in spiritual battle. They are characteristic of doxology.[51] What Paul

---

[47] 2 Cor 3:10; 9:14; Eph 1:19; 2:7; 3:19.

[48] Stoeckhardt, *Ephesians*, 105, connects κατά more narrowly with πιστεύοντας, "who believe," so as to clarify that the act of believing is brought about by God's power, not man's own. Without disputing this dogmatic truth, we would contend that κατά connects more generally to the whole preceding context, as the parallel in Col 1:11 suggests.

[49] See Arnold, *Power and Magic*, 70–85.

[50] This combining of nouns to form a genitive of quality is a common enough Hellenistic-Jewish redundancy: Is 40:26 (LXX); Dan 4:30 (LXX and θ; MT 4:27). The terms κράτος and ἰσχύς are frequently combined in the LXX so as to suggest their synonymy. See also Deut 8:17; Job 12:16; Prov 27:24.

[51] See κράτος in 1 Tim 6:16; 1 Pet 4:11; 5:11; Jude 25; Rev 1:6; 5:13; and ἰσχύς in Rev 5:12; 7:12; cf. Eph 3:20.

describes is the Creator God, who is not just *omnipotens* in the way of a static attribute (δύναμις, potential "power"), but is always at work (ἐνέργεια, "working," active power) through his Spirit[52] in his creation to carry out his purpose, particularly for the rescue of his elect in Christ (Lk 1:51). It is instructive to note that Paul can write this while remaining a prisoner![53]

1:20 ἣν ἐνήργησεν ἐν τῷ Χριστῷ—The pronoun ἣν refers back to ἐνέργειαν in 1:19, "the working … which he worked"—a cognate accusative characteristic of Hebrew. Thus, the sentence continues from the previous verse and should not be broken (as in NA[27]). A minor textual variant substitutes the perfect tense ἐνήργηκεν for the aorist ἐνήργησεν, with little change in meaning.[54] "In Christ" carries the full freight described in the fifth textual note on 1:3. It emphasizes that, for the saint, God's power is not destructive or terrifying, but put in service of his grace for the sake of the Gospel. The power that was first shown in Christ is available to all of us who believe. God's power was demonstrated through four actions (all subordinate to the main verb ἐνήργησεν) which "he worked" on Christ's behalf:

- raising him (ἐγείρας, 1:20) from the dead
- seating him (καθίσας, 1:20) at his right hand
- subordinating (ὑπέταξεν, 1:22) all things to him
- appointing (ἔδωκεν, 1:22) him as head of the church

The final two are really explications of the second. These four constitute Christ's exaltation/glorification (Acts 2:33; 5:31; see the third textual note on Eph 1:17) and bear the marks of early creedal affirmations.

ἐγείρας αὐτὸν ἐκ νεκρῶν— The aorist participles ἐγείρας, "raising," and καθίσας, "seating" (see the next textual note), should not be taken as temporally prior to the main verb ἐνήργησεν (i.e., "*after* raising and *after* seating he worked"), but as giving the verbal means or manner for accomplishing its action: "he worked … *by* raising … and *by* seating."[55] Raising Christ was a demonstration of God's power (Rom 1:4), an act of vindication (proving that Christ was righteous), and an act of acceptance (declaring his sacrifice to be sufficient).[56]

καὶ καθίσας ἐν δεξιᾷ αὐτοῦ—There is a double symbolism at work in this reference to Christ's ascension. "Sitting down" implies the cessation of work, the completion and success of his mission.[57] "At the right hand" implies all that is symbolized by the seat to the right of a monarch. That seat is reserved for the heir to the throne or the prime

---

[52] Cf. Is 11:2. As Käsemann comments: "Spirit and power are for Paul interchangeable terms (Rom 15:13, 19; 1 Cor 2:4; 5:3–4; Gal 3:5; 1 Thess 1:5)" (Ernst Käsemann, *Leib und Leib Christi: Eine Untersuchung zur paulinischen Begrifflichkeit* [Tübingen: Mohr, 1933], 125, quoted in Arnold, *Power and Magic*, 76).

[53] See "Caesarea!" in "Location and Date of Writing" in the introduction.

[54] The perfect tense is preferred by Lincoln, *Ephesians*, 47.

[55] See Voelz, *Fundamental Greek Grammar*, 260; Wallace, *Greek Grammar*, 624, 628–30; BDF § 339 (1).

[56] Acts 17:31; Rom 4:24–25; 1 Cor 15:14; 1 Tim 3:16.

[57] Heb 1:3; 10:12; Rev 3:21.

minister, who shares fully in the monarch's power as a plenipotentiary. Contrary to some modern notions that power comes from the people, in the ancient Near East, where the king himself was understood to rule on behalf of the local god, he was pictured as sitting at the god's right hand.[58] Pagan notions aside, the same image is present in the original context of Psalm 110, which looms large in the background of these verses. This psalm of David appears to picture King David ruling at God's right hand, achieving mighty victories by God's power working through him. But its opening line includes a grammatical inconsistency that would have caused any OT reader to stumble: "utterance of YHWH to *my lord*" (Ps 110:1). Though a suppliant to the king might have referred to David as "my lord," how could David have referred to himself this way? This apparently unresolvable puzzle is only solved in the Messiah, the one who truly sits at God's right hand. Jesus declared that David spoke of him; if King David could be said to sit at God's right hand, it was only a typological foreshadowing of Christ's rightful place.[59]

God's right hand is a place of favor[60] and represents his power that triumphs over our enemies.[61] Though the right hand is symbolically a location, it is not a place where Christ is confined, but rather the opposite: it indicates the restoration of his divine glory with authority over all things and all places (see 1:21–23 and the commentary). God's power was most fully displayed when he took hold of the Suffering Servant, raised him from the dead, and restored him to the place of honor that he had willingly set aside during his state of humiliation, when he had taken on the form of a slave.[62] Paul presses this one step farther and declares that Christ's resurrection and ascension (his exaltation) is shared with all those who have been baptized into him.[63] See Eph 2:6.

ἐν τοῖς ἐπουρανίοις—See the fourth textual note on 1:3 for this distinctive Ephesian phrase, "in the heavenlies." Although no noun is expressed, in the present context the adjective ἐπουράνιος certainly refers to "heavenly places" as the location of Christ's ascension. This does not preclude the significance of the action: if Christ is seated at the right hand of God in the heavenly *places*, then it symbolizes his power in heavenly *matters* (cf. Col 3:1). More precisely, it expresses the triumph of Christ over the hostile spiritual forces that oppose God's people, as described in the next verse.[64]

1:21 ὑπεράνω πάσης ἀρχῆς καὶ ἐξουσίας καὶ δυνάμεως καὶ κυριότητος—The preposition ὑπεράνω (a compound of ὑπέρ, "beyond," and ἄνω, "up") occurs only twice more in the NT: in the same context of Christ's ascension (Eph 4:10) and with reference to the cherubim "above" the ark (Heb 9:5). In nonliteral usages in the LXX, it

---

[58] The next step is the deification of the ruler himself, as with the Roman emperors. Cf. Ps 82:1, 6–7; Ezek 28:2.

[59] Christ applies Psalm 110 to himself in Mt 22:44; Mk 12:36; Lk 20:42. It is quoted or alluded to some seventeen times in the NT (e.g., Acts 2:34; Heb 8:1), more than any other OT text, and it ranks among the major messianic psalms.

[60] Ps 80:18 (ET 80:17); Jer 22:24; Rom 8:34.

[61] Ex 15:6; Pss 20:7 (ET 20:6); 44:4 (ET 44:3); 48:11 (ET 48:10); 110:1; Is 41:10; passim.

[62] Mt 26:64; Phil 2:5–11.

[63] Rom 8:11; 1 Cor 6:14; 15:20; 2 Cor 4:14; 13:4; Col 2:12.

[64] Schnackenburg, *Ephesians*, 76–77: "It is meant to show the superiority of the divine power over that which is dark and debilitating in our earthly existence."

implies high rank, majesty, or power.[65] That Christ is *"far* above" all other spiritual forces implies a distinction in kind, not just degree, between his spiritual power and theirs.[66] The fourfold list of lesser powers that follows, "every ruler and authority and power and lordship," is parallel, but not identical, to other NT lists:

- οὔτε ἄγγελοι οὔτε ἀρχαί, "neither angels nor rulers" (Rom 8:38)
- πᾶσαν ἀρχὴν καὶ πᾶσαν ἐξουσίαν καὶ δύναμιν, "every ruler and every authority and power" (1 Cor 15:24)
- ταῖς ἀρχαῖς καὶ ταῖς ἐξουσίαις ἐν τοῖς ἐπουρανίοις, "to the rulers and authorities in the heavenly places" (Eph 3:10)
- πρὸς τὰς ἀρχάς, πρὸς τὰς ἐξουσίας, πρὸς τοὺς κοσμοκράτορας τοῦ σκότους τούτου, πρὸς τὰ πνευματικὰ τῆς πονηρίας ἐν τοῖς ἐπουρανίοις, "against the rulers, against the authorities, against the world powers of this darkness, against the spiritual forces of evil in the heavenly places" (Eph 6:12)
- εἴτε θρόνοι εἴτε κυριότητες εἴτε ἀρχαὶ εἴτε ἐξουσίαι, "whether thrones or lordships or rulers or authorities" (Col 1:16)
- ἡ κεφαλὴ πάσης ἀρχῆς καὶ ἐξουσίας, "the Head of every ruler and authority" (Col 2:10)
- τὰς ἀρχὰς καὶ τὰς ἐξουσίας, "rulers and authorities" (Col 2:15)
- ὑποταγέντων αὐτῷ ἀγγέλων καὶ ἐξουσιῶν καὶ δυνάμεων, "with angels and authorities and powers being subjected to him" (1 Pet 3:22)

The noun ἀρχή, "ruler," derived from "beginning," has the sense of "premier" or leadership. ἐξουσία, "authority," derives from the verb ἔξεστιν, "it is permitted," thus emphasizing the *right* to do something rather than the power. δύναμις, "(potential) power, ability," often connected with miracles in the NT, thus can refer to spiritual power. κυριότης, "lordship," is the ruling power of a κύριος, "lord." While these might be taken as earthly authorities,[67] the use of the term "angels" in Rom 8:38; 1 Pet 3:22, the biblical usage of δύναμις,[68] and the similar lists later in Ephesians (3:10; 6:12) support the traditional interpretation that they are spiritual forces (both good and evil).

---

[65] E.g., Deut 26:19; 28:1; Ps 8:2 (ET 8:1); Is 2:2; Ezek 10:19.

[66] In Heb 8:1 and 10:12 Christ is at the right hand of God in heaven; in Heb 4:14 he passes through the heavens to God; in Heb 7:26 he is ὑψηλότερος, "exalted above," the heavens. If levels of heavens are occupied by angels of different ranks, Christ is not merely placed at the highest rank (as if he were the highest created creature), but ὑπεράνω, "far above" (Eph 1:21), the whole lot. The magical papyri describe the abode of the spiritual powers as ὁ ἄνω κόσμος, "the world above"; see Arnold, *Power and Magic*, 78.

[67] See Lk 12:11 (τὰς συναγωγὰς καὶ τὰς ἀρχὰς καὶ τὰς ἐξουσίας, "the synagogues and the rulers and the authorities"); Lk 20:20 (τῇ ἀρχῇ καὶ τῇ ἐξουσίᾳ τοῦ ἡγεμόνος, "the rule and authority of the governor"); Rom 13:1–3 (ἐξουσία, "authority"); Titus 3:1 (ἀρχαῖς ἐξουσίαις, "rulers [and] authorities"); perhaps κυριότης, "lordship," in 2 Pet 2:10; Jude 8. Deterding, *Colossians*, 124–31, is more positive toward the inclusion of earthly institutions such as government and family.

[68] In the LXX δύναμις, "power," is often used in translating the phrase "YHWH of hosts" (e.g., Zeph 2:9; Zech 7:4) and can refer to the powers of heaven, both good and evil (e.g., 2 Ki 17:16; 4 Macc 5:13; see also θ Dan 8:10). Cf. Mt 24:29 (and parallels); likewise in early patristic literature (e.g., Ignatius, *To the Ephesians*, 13:1).

Intertestamental (apocalyptic) and rabbinic Jewish literature developed elaborate hierarchies of angelic beings using many of the above terms.[69] The *Testament of Solomon*, containing such a hierarchy, may have originated in Ephesus.[70] A gold amulet has been discovered at Ephesus listing the cosmic powers of twenty-six supposed angels.[71] Nonetheless, the diversity (and shifting order) of NT vocabulary defies any attempt to identify each term with a specific rank of angels. In the context of this verse and the later lists in Ephesians, the four terms are best taken as comprehensive references to all the spiritual forces, particularly the evil ones (2:2; 6:12), who are subject to the exalted Christ's power and authority. Christ's superiority over even the good angels—significant in Colossians, which disputes a philosophic cult that offers them worship (Col 2:18)—is naturally included, but less significant in the context of Ephesians.[72] As far as spiritual forces are concerned, the Christian need not worship them, appease them, nor fear them.

καὶ παντὸς ὀνόματος ὀνομαζομένου—"And every name that is named" superficially means little more than *et cetera*, implying that the list is not intended to exhaust the ranks of spiritual beings, whether angels or demons.[73] The reader/hearer need not fear that this or that spiritual foe remains undefeated. However, the idea of "naming a name" likely also refers to the *invocation* of a god or spiritual being.[74] The possession and invocation of its name was thought to give one control of it—though the name of the true God cannot be mastered.[75] The ancient world knew of six magical names

---

[69] Enoch is shown a vision of the seven levels of heaven. He describes what he saw in the seventh heaven: "And I saw there a very great light, and fiery troops of great archangels, incorporeal forces, and dominions, orders and governments, cherubim and seraphim, thrones and many-eyed ones, nine regiments, the Ioanit stations of light, and I became afraid" (*2 Enoch*, 20 [*APOT*, 2:441]). These heavenly forces are arranged by rank on ten steps (though the specific order is not given). Enoch's fear is allayed by seeing God himself in the tenth heaven—thus *far above* these lesser creatures. See also *1 Enoch*, 61:10; *Testament of Levi*, 3:8; *Testament of Solomon*, 34, 114; *Apocalypse of Elijah*, 1:10 ("thrones"). Note that there is no attempt in these texts to give a coherent or consistent ranking of the names. The diagram reproduced in Scharlemann, "Secret," 340, is misleading if it suggests that specific ranks of angels can be slotted into each of the seven heavens.

[70] See Arnold, *Ephesians*, 38. Schwindt, *Das Weltbild des Epheserbriefes*, 301, asserts that the *Testament of Solomon* reflects the magical Jewish folk religion of Asia Minor.

[71] This amulet is lodged at the Fitzwilliam Museum, Cambridge. See Arnold, *Ephesians*, 36.

[72] Christ's superiority to the good angels is taught by Psalm 8, quoted in Eph 1:22 and exegeted at length in Hebrews 1 and 2.

[73] Scharlemann, "Secret," 341: "The use of many names suggests, however, that the subject is not adequately described by any one name. We are basically dealing with a single phenomenon, but it is diffused and confronts us in various manifestations."

[74] For the expression ὀνομάζω ὄνομα, "to name a name," see LXX Lev 24:16; Josh 23:7; Is 26:13; Jer 20:9; Amos 6:10; Sirach 23:10 (variant reading); Acts 19:13; 2 Tim 2:19. For ἐπικαλέω ὄνομα, "to call upon a name," see LXX Gen 4:26; 12:8 (and passim); 1 Ki 18:24–26; Ps 115:4 (MT/ET 116:13); Joel 3:5 (ET 2:32); 1 Cor 1:2.

[75] Christ names the demons in order to vanquish them (Mk 5:9). The disciples cast out demons in Jesus' name because he had given them the authority to do so (Mt 10:1; Lk 10:17). But saying "Lord, Lord" does not give automatic entry into the kingdom (Mt 7:21; 25:11–12). Even if Moses was perhaps seeking this sort of secret knowledge and control when he asked for God's name, the true God does not have a name that can be used to control him; he calls himself according to his promises and essence (Ex 3:13–15). Thus, יהוה (YHWH) is not a

247

known as the Ephesian Grammata, associated with the power of Artemis Ephesia.[76] An ancient magical text reads: "I conjure you by the 'great names.' … You, these holy names (ὀνόματα) and these powers (δυνάμεις), confirm and carry out this perfect enchantment."[77] The foolish sons of Sceva wrongly thought they could manipulate Jesus' power by using his name to cast out demons (Acts 19:13–17); it is noteworthy that this event happened in Ephesus.[78] Ironically, their failure to wield Jesus' name led powerfully to true praise of his name and adherence to the Gospel Paul had preached. The subsequent burning of magic books (Acts 19:19) provides informative background to Paul's claims about Jesus' superiority over all evil spiritual forces in these verses. The divine name given to Christ is above every other name (Phil 2:9; Heb 1:4). Appeal to his name brings salvation (Acts 2:21; Rom 10:13).

οὐ μόνον ἐν τῷ αἰῶνι τούτῳ ἀλλὰ καὶ ἐν τῷ μέλλοντι—"This [present] age" is identified with ongoing earthly concerns, rejection of Christ, and the persistence of wickedness in this world (Eph 2:2).[79] "The age to come"[80] is the time inaugurated by the resurrection of the dead at the second coming of Christ (see "the coming ages" in Eph 2:7). The reign of Christ over his enemies is complete, now and eternally; we need not wait for some cosmic battle to be waged in the final days. Nor is there a divide between victory won in the earthly and heavenly realms, as if Christ's victory in the spiritual realm had no effect on our present lives in this world—indeed his triumph on the cross was a very down-to-earth event! For those baptized into Christ the victory has had an even more direct impact, for on them the age to come has proleptically (in part, as a foretaste) already dawned (1 Cor 10:11; Heb 6:5). These complementary perspectives of "futurist" and "realized" eschatology are present throughout Paul's thought and must not be set at odds with each other.

1:22 καὶ πάντα ὑπέταξεν—The verb ὑποτάσσω, "subordinate," has a military flavor, referring to the assignment of one's proper place in the τάγμα, "division, order" (see the first textual note on 5:21 in the pericope consisting of 5:21–33). Paul states this explicitly in a parallel context: ἕκαστος δὲ ἐν τῷ ἰδίῳ τάγματι, "but each one in his own [place in the] order" (1 Cor 15:23). God has established Christ's place at the head of the order, the Captain of the heavenly hosts, by placing everything under him; beneath him are appropriate places for all people and things, which not only have a lower rank, but are also subject to him. Paul compares Christ to Adam (1 Cor 15:21–22); as Adam exercised headship over creation by naming the creatures brought to him, so Christ reigns

---

name as the gods have names. Calling on his name does not manipulate him against his will, but appeals to his promises.

[76] See "The Cult of Artemis Ephesia" in "The City of Ephesus and Paul's Relationship to It" in the introduction.

[77] *PGM* 101:52, quoted in Arnold, *Ephesians*, 114.

[78] Arnold, *Power and Magic*, 30: "Luke does not describe any other location with so many accounts of the demonic in Acts. … If Ephesus and its environs were reputed as a center for 'demonic' activity, Luke's purpose of demonstrating the superior power of the gospel would be well established by this account."

[79] Lk 16:8; 20:34; Rom 12:2; 1 Cor 1:20; 2:6, 8; 3:18; 2 Cor 4:4.

[80] Mt 12:32; Mk 10:30; Lk 18:30; Heb 6:5; cf. "the close of the age" in Mt 24:3; 28:20.

over the new creation by giving his name to all those re-created (cf. Phil 3:21) through Baptism.

The quotation marks in the translation draw attention to Ps 8:7 (ET 8:6), another messianic psalm, which glorifies man as the crown of creation and the Son of Man as the psalm's perfect fulfillment. In 1 Cor 15:20–28 Paul quotes the same verse to demonstrate that Christ is raised from the dead first, and then at his second coming, having destroyed "every rule and authority and power," he will destroy death, raise all those who are "in Christ," and deliver them to the Father's kingdom, where Christ himself is subject to God. What is remarkable in this parallel is that what is described as completed on the Last Day in 1 Corinthians 15 is pictured in Eph 1:20–23 as an action begun already at Christ's ascension (cf. Heb 2:5–9; 1 Pet 3:22). This is a perfect illustration of the prolepsis noted in the third textual note on 1:21.

ὑπὸ τοὺς πόδας αὐτοῦ—The interpretation of subjection just given fits with the context of the sentence in Psalm 8. In other OT contexts, "under one's feet" and similar expressions imply crushing enemies,[81] or at least placing them in a position of abject servitude where they can do no harm (Ps 47:4 [ET 47:3]). Thus, Paul may be applying this psalm text not only to the subordination of these evil spiritual forces (Eph 1:21) but also to their defeat by Christ for sake of the church (1:22b).

καὶ αὐτὸν ἔδωκεν κεφαλήν—The verb δίδωμι, "give," with a double accusative (αὐτὸν ... κεφαλήν, "him as head") can have the sense of "appoint" to an office, while maintaining the sense of the officer as a gift (cf. Acts 13:20; Eph 4:11). "Head" has been interpreted as "source" (as in the headwaters of a river), a figurative meaning attested in Herodotus, Philo, and some Jewish pseudepigraphic literature, but not in the LXX.[82] The evidence for this meaning tends to be exaggerated by those who are offended by Paul's teaching on women in the church and marriage (see the textual note on 5:23). The more common figurative meaning in the centuries leading up to the NT, frequently attested in the LXX[83] (as well as in Philo, Josephus, and Plutarch), is one with "high status, superior rank," who is "governor, leader," a function that is consonant with Greek medical theory of the time.[84] This is surely the meaning in the NT when applied to the Father's relationship to Christ, Christ's relationship to the church, man's relationship to woman, and the husband's relationship to his wife (1 Cor 11:3; Eph 5:23–24). It is part of Christ's exaltation, the restoration of his full divine glory, that the Father grants

---

[81] Gen 3:15; Josh 10:24; 2 Sam 22:39; 1 Ki 5:17 (ET 5:3); Ps 18:40 (ET 18:39); Lam 3:34; Mal 3:21 (ET 4:3); Rom 16:20.

[82] For a succinct overview of the debate, see Joseph Fitzmyer, "Κεφαλή in 1 Corinthians 11:3," in *To Advance the Gospel: New Testament Studies* (2d ed.; Grand Rapids: Eerdmans, 1998), 341–48.

[83] LXX Deut 28:13; Judg 11:11; 2 Kgdms 22:44 (MT/ET 2 Sam 22:44); Ps 17:44 (MT 18:44; ET 18:43); Is 7:8–9; Jer 38:7 (MT/ET 31:7). The Hebrew term רֹאשׁ, "head," is frequently used with this sense in the OT, but often is translated in the LXX with ἀρχή, "rule," or ἄρχων, "ruler."

[84] In anatomical/physiological matters, it would be more in accord with *Greek* theory (from Plato to Hippocrates to Galen) to say that the head directs the body. *Hebrew* thought (with Aristotle and the Stoics) would attribute this role to the heart—yet the preceding passages from the LXX demonstrate that "head" did have the symbolic meaning of "governor, leader" in the OT. See Barth, *Ephesians*, 1:186–92.

him headship over all things, such that the church need fear no other power (cf. Col 2:10). The immediately preceding context suggests, therefore, that by calling Christ the "head" Paul has in view his supreme rank and the subordination of all things to him. Yet the term suggests a further organic application (4:15–16), as found elsewhere in Paul: the church is Christ's body.[85]

ὑπὲρ πάντα τῇ ἐκκλησίᾳ—The dative might be interpreted as an indirect object: "he gave him as head over all things *to* the church."[86] This is unobjectionable so long as it does not limit πάντα, "all things," to the realm of the church—this would be contrary to the cosmic referent of πάντα, "all things," in the original context of Ps 8:7 (ET 8:6), which Paul quotes in the first half of the verse. If πάντα has the same cosmic referent in both halves of the verse—Christ is appointed head over "all things" in creation—then τῇ ἐκκλησίᾳ could be taken as a dative of advantage, "*for the benefit of* the church" (cf. RSV). As the Fatherhood of God (4:6) applies to all creation and yet particularly to Christians, Christ's headship is over all things and *especially for* the church. Eph 1:22 thus draws together the thoughts of Col 1:18 and 2:10.

1:23 ἥτις ἐστὶν τὸ σῶμα αὐτοῦ—Christ's headship over all creation, including spiritual forces both good and evil, prompts reference to the counterpart: the church as "his body." In distinction from other Pauline uses, where the body image is used to make sense of *diverse* roles within the church (Rom 12:3–8; 1 Cor 12:12–31), here Paul emphasizes *unity* within the body (cf. Eph 4:4: "one body"; 4:15–16: "knit together"). There is already a hint of the marriage analogy (5:23–33), in which the husband as head is united to his wife through the sexual act that makes them "one flesh" (5:31) and loves her as his own body (5:28, 33). So also Christ and the church are united, as inseparable in life as a head from its body. The church is not entirely other than Christ, but is one with him. This union is brought about through Baptism (1 Cor 12:13; Eph 4:4–6); but perhaps Paul also has in mind the sacramental union brought about through the oral participation in Christ's body and blood in the eucharistic feast (1 Cor 10:16–17).

τὸ πλήρωμα τοῦ τὰ πάντα ἐν πᾶσιν πληρουμένου—The alliteration of words beginning with π and the paronomasia (play on words) of the cognates πλήρωμα and πληρόω (repeated in 3:19) illustrate the oral character of the prayer (1:15–23), its careful construction, and its public, liturgical dignity. The antecedent of the noun πλήρωμα, "fullness," is possibly αὐτόν, "him," in 1:22, yielding the theologically satisfying statement that Christ is the fullness of God (cf. Col 1:19; 2:9); but that pronoun is rather distant from the noun. The closer and more natural antecedent is τὸ σῶμα αὐτοῦ, "his body": thus, the church is Christ's πλήρωμα, "fullness" (cf. Eph 3:19; Col 2:10).

The sense of πλήρωμα can be either active or passive, that which "fills up/completes" (most common in the NT, e.g., 1 Cor 10:26) or that which "is filled." The active meaning is difficult here, both physiologically and theologically: the body does not "fill" the head (though it may make it complete), and in what sense would the church fill up Christ?[87] Wary of the notion that the divine Christ can be incomplete, most inter-

---

[85] Eph 1:23; 2:16; 3:6; 4:4, 12, 16; 5:23, 30; also Rom 12:4–5; 1 Cor 12:12–31; Col 1:18, 24.

[86] E.g., Lincoln, *Ephesians*, 66; ESV.

[87] Chrysostom: "The fullness of the head is the body and that of the body is the head. ... Then the head is fulfilled, then the body becomes perfect, when we are all combined and gathered

preters apply the passive meaning to the noun in this verse. Physiologically it scarcely makes more sense (does the head "fill up" the body?),[88] but theologically the passive, "the church is filled by Christ," is satisfying and in accord with Pauline theology.[89]

It is difficult to choose between the active and passive interpretations of πλήρωμα. The biblical God defies attempts to isolate him from his creation as a purely transcendent being, unaffected by his creation. At the same time, Paul avoids philosophic (e.g., Stoic) panentheistic systems that collapse the distinction between God and the universe. Paul does not call the cosmos Christ's body, but the church. If this body makes Christ complete (active sense), it is by way of the marriage analogy of chapter 5. Like a husband who feels incomplete without his "better half"—rooted in the reality of their one-flesh relationship—God is incomplete without his people (and his people are incomplete without him). God permits his church to fulfill astonishing roles in the order of salvation,[90] such as Paul's completing "what is lacking in Christ's afflictions" in his bodily suffering "for the sake of his body, which is the church" (Col 1:24).

Yet there are compelling contextual reasons to favor the passive sense. First, the syntax of the participle πληρουμένου favors the meaning, "the one who fills up,"[91] rather than "the one who is filled up."[92] Second, later occurrences of the vocabulary in Ephesians support the passive interpretation: "that you [Ephesians] might be filled up" (3:19); "that he [Christ] might fill all things" (4:10); and "be filled up in the Spirit" (5:18). If the parallels in Ephesians, Colossians, and the OT are determinative, the scales are tilted toward the passive meaning of πλήρωμα. At a cosmic level, as true God, Christ fills all things and is able to extend this fullness to others.[93] Likewise, the church, like the tabernacle/temple of old, is empty unless Christ comes to fill it with his presence

into one" (*Homilies on Ephesians*, 3:1.20–23 [ACCS 8:126]). This active interpretation is common among the fathers and found also in the marginal gloss of Luther's 1546 Bible (WA DB 7:195).

[88] Yet Barth, *Ephesians*, 1:190, argues on the basis of medical theory contemporary to Paul, that "by its power the head is omnipresent in the whole body; its relation to the body is as a 'dynamic presence.'" Certainly Paul teaches that Christ dwells in the Christian and the church (Eph 3:17), but this does not appear to be the way he thinks of the Head and the body.

[89] Thus, Theodoret: "This body he has filled with all gifts. *He lives in it and goes about in it*, as the voice of prophecy says. … He lives in those who fear him and who put hope in his mercy" (*Ephesians*, 1:23 [ACCS 8:126]). Origen speaks of Christ as the soul that indwells the body, the church (*Ephesians*, on Eph 1:22b–23 [ACCS 8:125–26]). Lincoln, *Ephesians*, 73–76, is thorough and persuasive in arguing for the passive meaning.

[90] Schnackenburg, *Ephesians*, 344: "Christ 'needs' the Church to reach the world with his message and power to bless, and he 'uses' her according to her presence in the world."

[91] The participle πληρουμένου would thus be parsed as middle voice, with the phrase τὰ πάντα ἐν πᾶσιν as its direct object. The middle of πληρόω is otherwise unattested in the NT, but this analysis accords well with the meaning of the active voice in 4:10. See BDF, § 316 (1).

[92] This translation takes πληρουμένου as passive voice, as do Barth, *Ephesians*, 1:159; Best, *Ephesians*, 185; and Moule, *Idiom Book*, 25. This interpretation is grammatically unlikely in that it requires a rather unusual adverbial use of τὰ πάντα ἐν πᾶσιν, "filled up totally in all respects." It is further complicated by the question again of who fills up Christ: the church or God the Father?

[93] Here Paul applies to Christ the same divine attribute he gives the Father in 4:6, rooted in OT thought (Is 6:3; Jer 23:24; Ps 72:19; Wis Sol 1:7). In fact, in Christ dwells all the fullness of God (Col 1:19; 2:9).

and his gifts.[94] J. B. Lightfoot put it this way: "All the Divine graces which reside in Him are imparted to her; His 'fulness' is communicated to her: and thus she may be said to be His pleroma ['fullness'] (i. 23)."[95]

Commentary

Structure and Rhetoric

Following hard upon the longest sentence in the NT (1:3–14; 204 Greek words), Paul manages the second longest (169 words)! The same grandiloquence of expression and liturgical redundancy characterize this sequel to the opening prayer. Indeed, some have questioned why Paul should include both a *Berakah* prayer (1:3–14) and a formal thanksgiving (1:15–23) at the head of one letter, an apparent redundancy not matched in any other NT letter. This question will occupy a portion of the commentary below.

Though 1:15–23 is formally labeled "thanksgiving," perhaps by way of synecdoche ("giving thanks," 1:16), it is clear that more than one aspect of Christian prayer is at work. As in most letters, thanksgiving leads into intercession for the letter's recipients, after which Paul returns to the language of praise that had dominated the *Berakah*:

1:15–16a	**Thanksgiving** for faith and love
1:16b–19	**Supplication** to the Triune God
	for knowledge and enlightenment
	with the threefold object of hope, inheritance, and power
1:20–23	**Praise** of the exalted Christ

- God raised him from the dead
- God seated him at his right hand
- God subordinated all things under him
- God appointed him as head over all things for the church

Though some have argued that the *Berakah* prayer continues right through to the end of chapter 3,[96] the doxology in 3:20–21 is best viewed as the conclusion to chapter 3 only. The letter's thanksgiving proper draws to a distinct close in 1:23 before Paul moves into the first rhetorical proof of the letter's body.[97]

---

[94] Cf. Ex 33:9–10; 40:34–35; Num 14:14; 1 Ki 8:10–11; Is 6:1–4; Ezek 43:5; Hag 2:7; Jn 1:14. Barth concludes forcefully:

> *Plērōma* may therefore be considered a synonym of the name, the glory, the Spirit, or the *shekina* of God. Not an unmoved essence, a static nature, a dormant attribute or quality, but the gift of God's self in revelation, salvation, self-presentation is then meant. In this case the notion that God or Christ may be filled by the church is absurd. (*Ephesians*, 1:205)

[95] J. B. Lightfoot, *Saint Paul's Epistles to the Colossians and to Philemon* (5th ed.; Cambridge: Cambridge University Press, 1880), 263.

[96] Notably Kirby, *Ephesians: Baptism and Pentecost*, 126–38.

[97] See the rhetorical outline at the end of "Rhetorical Outline" in "Structure and Rhetoric" in the introduction.

The Ephesian Thanksgiving (1:15–23) Compared to the Colossian Thanksgiving (1:3–20)

At a superficial level it seems that Colossians lacks an equivalent to the Ephesian *Berakah* (Eph 1:3–14), contenting itself with a thanksgiving alone (Col 1:3–20). The opening Colossian thanksgiving certainly bears a striking resemblance to its Ephesian fraternal twin:

Ephesians 1:15–23	Colossians 1:3–20
for this reason, even I (1:15)	for this reason, even we (1:9)
having heard of your faith in the Lord Jesus and [your] love toward all the saints (1:15)	having heard of your faith in the Christ Jesus and the love you have toward all the saints (1:4)
I do not cease giving thanks for you, making remembrance at the time of my prayers (1:16)	we give thanks to God … always concerning you when praying (1:3)
that God … might give to you the Spirit of wisdom and revelation in the knowledge of him (1:17)	that you might be filled with the knowledge of his will in all wisdom and understanding of the Spirit (1:9)
so that you might know what is the hope of his calling (1:18)	the hope stored up for you in heaven (1:5)
what is the richness of his glorious inheritance among the saints (1:18)	to share in the inheritance of the saints in light (1:12)
according to the working of his mighty strength (1:19)	according to his glorious might (1:11)
far above every ruler and authority and power and lordship … not only in this age but also in the one to come (1:21)	in him all things were created, in heaven and on earth, seen and unseen things, whether thrones or lordships or rulers or authorities (1:16)
he appointed him as head over all things for the church, which is his body (1:22–23)	he is the head of the body, the church (1:18)
the fullness of the one who fills all things in all (1:23)	for in him he was pleased for all the fullness to dwell (1:19)

Yet significant portions of the Ephesian *Berakah* prayer's content are woven into the vastly extended thanksgiving section in Colossians:

Ephesians 1:3–14	Colossians 1:3–20
the God and Father of our Lord Jesus Christ (1:3)	God, the Father of our Lord Jesus Christ (1:3)
in whom we have redemption through his blood, the forgiveness of trespasses (1:7)	in whom we have redemption, the forgiveness of sins (1:14) making peace through the blood of his cross (1:20)
that all things might be brought together in Christ, the things in heaven and the things on earth (1:10)	in him all things were created, in heaven and on earth (1:16) all things in him hold together (1:17) through him to reconcile all things to him, … whether the things in heaven or the things on earth (1:20)
who is the deposit of our inheritance (1:14)	to share in the inheritance of the saints in light (1:12)

These are not minor parallels, but touch upon the central themes of both letters.

Thus, Colossians and Ephesians accomplish the same purpose, but go about it in formally different ways. Ephesians, with its elegant *Berakah* (1:3–14), has a more churchly and liturgical aura, though the great Christ hymn (Col 1:15–20) lends Colossians a worshipful character of its own. The complex relationship of these sections of the two letters resists any simple source analysis; it cannot be easily demonstrated that one is developed into the other (either by Paul or some supposed imitator). On the contrary, the very complexity of the relationship is best explained as a single, brilliant author (Paul) reworking his own thoughts in two close, but distinct, writings.[98]

A close comparison of the content also raises questions about the traditional distinction between the two letters, memorably phrased by Martin Franzmann: "If the Letter to the Colossians is the Letter of Christ the Head of the Church, the Letter to the Ephesians is the Letter of the Church, the Body of Christ."[99] While some commentators have argued that the thanksgiving in Ephesians (1:15–23) builds up to 1:23 as its climax (the church as the body of Christ),[100] the content of the thanksgiving is overwhelmingly Christocentric. The church bears no more weight here than in Colossians. The Christ hymn in

---

[98] See "Relationship to Colossians" in the introduction.

[99] Franzmann, *The Word of the Lord Grows*, 132.

[100] Lincoln, *Ephesians*, 67, quite inexplicably states:

The writer has elaborated on the supremacy God has given to Christ in relation to the cosmos in vv 20–22a [of Ephesians 1], but now all these statements about his lordship over the cosmos are subordinated to a statement about God's purpose for Christ in regard to the Church. Syntactically, the weight of this clause falls on τῇ ἐκκλησίᾳ at the end [of Eph 1:22], and the emphasis on the Church continues in the two descriptive clauses which follow [in Eph 1:23].

Colossians (1:15–20), admittedly more extensive than the creedal conclusion in Eph 1:20–22, gives no more weight to Christ than the central section of the Ephesian *Berakah* (1:4–12). While the body of Ephesians includes ecclesiological sections (4:1–16; 5:21–33) that are absent from Colossians, these sections remain focused on Christ, as does the Ephesian thanksgiving, in which the exaltation of Christ is the major theological theme.

We may speculate on the problems facing the recipients of these letters, noting the Colossian emphasis on "philosophy and empty deceit" (Col 2:8) over against the Ephesian concern for unity of Jewish and Gentile Christians. Yet they share a concern about the power wielded against the church by hostile spiritual forces. The answer Paul gives is similar: baptized into Christ (Col 2:11–13; Eph 4:5), who has triumphed over all spiritual powers that might threaten us (Col 1:16; Eph 1:21–22), we are now reconciled to one another and to God through his body on the cross (Col 1:22; Eph 2:14–16). Christ and his work are the central message of both letters.

The Thanksgiving (1:15–23): Formal Features

The inclusion of a formal thanksgiving shortly after the salutation is a common feature of the prescript in Hellenistic and Roman letters.[101] In a pagan context where the good graces of the gods could not be presumed upon, whose patronage needed continual grooming, the writer "gives thanks to the gods" as a matter of course. The common expression "making continual mention of you before the gods" strikes any reader of Paul as familiar. Often the gods are thanked for saving the writer or addressee from some recent calamity. An Egyptian sailor writes to his father:

> Apion to Epimachus his father and lord many greetings. Before all things I pray that thou art in health, and that thou dost prosper and fare well continually together with my sister and her daughter and my brother. I thank the lord Serapis that, when I was in peril in the sea, he saved me immediately. When I came to Miseni I received as viaticum (journey money) from the Caesar three pieces of gold. And it is well with me. I beseech thee, therefore, my lord father, …[102]

The same sailor (with a new name) in a subsequent letter refers to his ongoing intercession for his family's well-being and the great joy he felt when he received good news:

> Antonius Maximus to Sabina his sister many greetings.
>
> Before all things I pray that thou art in health, for I myself also am in health. Making mention of thee before the gods here I received a little letter from Antoninus our fellow-citizen. And when I knew that thou farest well, I rejoiced greatly.[103]

---

[101] Doty, *Letters in Primitive Christianity*, 31–37.

[102] Letter from an Egyptian soldier in the Roman navy, second century AD, quoted in Deissmann, *Light from the Ancient East*, 180.

[103] Quoted in Deissmann, *Light from the Ancient East*, 184.

Similar news of the Ephesians' persistence in faith and love brought equal relief and joy to Paul's heart (1:15), for the joy is greater when news comes of those we love than of complete strangers.

The extensive work done in the twentieth century on Hellenistic letter-writing conventions means that few students of Paul are unaware that his letters generally conform to such patterns.[104] Paul includes a formulaic thanksgiving in all his letters except Galatians—where the absence of a thanksgiving drives home his anger at their apostasy—and Titus, which simply gets down to business quickly. 2 Corinthians has only a pseudo-thanksgiving (2 Cor 1:11) after a *Berakah* prayer that shifts smoothly into prose. In 1 Timothy, Paul gives thanks, but not entirely in the normal pattern (1 Tim 1:12). By contrast, 1 Thessalonians returns to thanksgiving so frequently (1 Thess 1:2; 2:13; 3:9) that its first three chapters have been viewed as an extended thanksgiving section; the letter's rhetorical purpose may, in fact, be to give thanks.[105] This diversity demonstrates the flexibility of the pattern rather than disproving the rule. Paul is not bound by a formula, but masterfully and effortlessly adapts it to his needs. It is interesting to note that no other NT writer begins an epistle with a formal thanksgiving (not Hebrews, James, Peter, John, or Jude). Perhaps this betrays a difference in their schooling, with Paul most likely to have had a proper Hellenistic rhetorical training—or at least to have been influenced by the Hellenistic rhetorical environment.

The thanksgiving in Ephesians bears most of the formal characteristics of Paul's habit.[106] It is comprised of the following:

- a principal verb of thanksgiving: εὐχαριστῶν, "giving thanks" (1:16)
- a temporal expression giving the frequency of thanksgiving: οὐ παύομαι, "I do not cease" (1:16)
- a pronominal object phrase: ὑπὲρ ὑμῶν, "for you" (1:16)
- a participial clause giving the cause for thanksgiving: ἀκούσας τὴν καθ᾽ ὑμᾶς πίστιν, "having heard of your faith" (1:15)
- a participial clause giving the time of the thanksgiving: μνείαν ποιούμενος ἐπὶ τῶν προσευχῶν μου, "making remembrance at the time of my prayers" (1:16)
- a final clause giving the content of intercessory prayer: ἵνα ὁ θεὸς ... δώῃ, "that God might give ..." (1:17)

The parallels in Paul's other letters are so extensive that they scarcely bear citing. Philemon offers the most compressed example. In precise wording, Ephesians is most like Colossians (see above). The lack of specific grounds for the Ephesian

---

[104] See Aune, *The New Testament in Its Literary Environment*, 163–69, 183–91; Stowers, *Letter Writing in Greco-Roman Antiquity*, 17–26; and Klauck, *Ancient Letters and the New Testament*, 17–42.

[105] See Robert Jewett, *The Thessalonian Correspondence: Pauline Rhetoric and Millenarian Piety* (Philadelphia: Fortress, 1986).

[106] See Paul Schubert, *Form and Function of the Pauline Thanksgivings* (Berlin: Töpelmann, 1939), 34–39; Lincoln, *Ephesians*, 48.

thanksgiving has been taken as evidence that the letter is addressed to a general audience;[107] yet its general character is paralleled often enough to dispel this notion. Faith and love are sufficient grounds for thanksgiving in Romans (1:8),[108] Colossians (1:3–4), 1 Thessalonians (1:2–3), 2 Thessalonians (1:3–4), and Philemon (4–5), and are the basis of further thanks in 1 Thessalonians (3:6, 9) and 2 Timothy (1:3, 5, 13).

The Thanksgiving (1:15–23): Purpose

So much for formalities. The thanksgiving is not written simply to satisfy the dictates of a rhetorical handbook.[109] The main purpose of the thanksgiving, following upon the salutation, was to exercise the personal relationship that was strained by absence. Jerome states this clearly in a letter to Florentius: "Wishing to do the best I can, as I cannot come in person I send you a letter instead; and thus, though absent in the body, I come to you in love and in spirit."[110] Paul repeatedly expresses the same sentiment, as he does, for example, in Colossians:

> This I say in order that no one should deceive you with persuasive speech. For if indeed I am absent in the flesh [τῇ σαρκὶ ἄπειμι], nevertheless in spirit [or "by the Spirit"] I am with you [τῷ πνεύματι σὺν ὑμῖν εἰμι], rejoicing and seeing the proper order and steadfastness of your faith in Christ. (Col 2:4–5)[111]

As in Eph 1:15 ("having heard of your faith … and love"), news of their steadfastness in faith has brought him joy, making him feel that he is restored to their presence again. Yet, the translation ambiguity (in Eph 1:17 and Col 2:5, "spirit" or "Spirit"?) hints at something deeper in this apostolic and churchly relationship. By the power of the Spirit through the written Word, Paul is indeed with them, as he continues to be with the church today through the reading of his

---

[107] E.g., Lincoln, *Ephesians*, 49.

[108] Rom 1:8 speaks of "faith," but not "love."

[109] Some scholars are reluctant even to apply rhetorical categories to ancient epistles: e.g., Porter, "The Theoretical Justification for Application of Rhetorical Categories to Pauline Epistolary Literature"; Klauck, *Ancient Letters and the New Testament*, 206–9, 224–25; and Mark P. Surburg, "Ancient Rhetorical Criticism, Galatians, and Paul at Twenty-five Years," *Concordia Journal* 30 (2004): 13–39. See "Structure and Rhetoric" in the introduction. The rhetorical handbooks of Aristotle, Quintilian, and Cicero do not specifically treat epistolary style, but letters, as transcribed oratory, were assumed to fall under their domain. Demetrius of Phaleron specifically focused on epistolary rhetoric in a first-century BC handbook. Though some scholars dispute the suggestion that Paul had a formal Greek education, to the present author it seems most likely that he did and that he studied at least one of these handbooks. The handbooks emphasized imitation of classic letters rather than comprehensive rules. Formal adherence to structure was expected only of the beginner. See Stowers, *Letter Writing in Greco-Roman Antiquity*, 32–35.

[110] Jerome, Letter 5 (*NPNF*[2] 6:7; quoted in Stowers, *Letter Writing in Greco-Roman Antiquity*, 69).

[111] Paul frequently points to his letter writing as a substitute for his personal presence: 1 Cor 5:3–5; 2 Cor 10:11; 13:10; Phil 1:27; 2:12; 1 Thess 2:17; 2 Thess 3:14; cf. 2 Jn 12; 3 Jn 13–14. See Winger, "Orality as the Key to Understanding Apostolic Proclamation in the Epistles," 292–304.

letters.[112] Not only is Paul rejoiced by news of their faith and love, but his letter also causes them to be strengthened and to increase in faith and love, thus increasing the reason for the thanksgiving (1:15).

This perhaps explains why Paul does not always give thanks for an act of salvation—though this would certainly be in order, as he does in the *Berakah* (1:3–14) and in the concluding portion of the thanksgiving (1:20–23). But as an act that strengthens and rejoices in his pastoral relationship to the Ephesians, he calls attention to their "faith" in Christ and their "love" (1:15) for the fellow saints engendered through the Word he proclaimed and that is now being proclaimed, even in his absence. By giving thanks for their faith and love, he subtly directs their thanks to God; if it is a matter of thanks, then it is not of their own doing (2:8). It is no mere coincidence that the same word χάρις is used in Greek for both grace (e.g., Eph 1:2, 6, 7; 2:5, 8) and thanks (e.g., Rom 7:25; 2 Tim 1:3), and that its root χάρ- stands behind the vocabulary of thanksgiving (εὐχαριστέω, "give thanks," 1:16; 5:20; εὐχαριστία, "thanksgiving," 5:4). Furthermore, as a wise pastor writing to a church of his long service, Paul avoids any flattery that might divide the congregation, as might happen if he were to give thanks for one person's work but not another's. "Faith" and "love" (1:15) are gifts common to all, and gifts that, as they increase, will heal all.

The Thanksgiving (1:15–23): Liturgical Features

The presence of both a *Berakah* prayer (1:3–14) and an epistolary thanksgiving (1:15–23) in Ephesians has prompted this extended contemplation of the thanksgiving's function. As the *Berakah* is deeply Jewish in origin and liturgical in context, the thought arises that the thanksgiving may also have elements that are theological/liturgical in nature and, while superficially Hellenistic, Jewish in origin. For, in parallel to the *Berakah* pattern of prayer that begins "blessed be YHWH," there was a common Jewish pattern of prayer known as the *Hodayah* that begins "we give thanks."[113] One of the earliest discoveries at Qumran was the scroll *Hodayoth* (1QH) that contained a virtual service book of thanksgiving prayers or hymns. An analysis of these and other synagogue

---

[112] The presence tense of the verbs in μαρτυροῦμεν καὶ ἀπαγγέλλομεν ὑμῖν, "we testify and we announce to you" (1 Jn 1:2), indicates that, for John, his apostolic testimony and preaching continues whenever and wherever his letter is read.

[113] *Hodayah* derives from the Hiphil of יָדָה, whose sense comprehends the meanings "confess, praise, give thanks," often translated in the LXX with ἐξομολογέω. It is a near synonym of הָלַל, "praise," and בֵּרֵךְ, "bless." In liturgical contexts these terms intertwine in meaning and usage. God is blessed, praised, and thanked equally in the act of declaring back to him what he has done for us. See, e.g., both the Hiphil of יָדָה and הָלַל as synonyms meaning "praise" in 1 Chr 16:4; 23:30; 25:3; Ezra 3:11; Neh 12:24; Pss 35:18; 44:9 (ET 44:8); 106:1; 109:30. See also both the Hiphil of יָדָה, "praise," and בֵּרֵךְ, "bless," as synonyms in Pss 100:4; 145:10, and the combination of both הָלַל, "praise," and בָּרוּךְ, "blessed," in 1 Chr 16:36; Pss 106:48; 135:21.

prayers suggests that the two patterns of blessing and thanksgiving were virtually interchangeable.[114]

This interchange was at work in early Christianity, in whose liturgy a shift began to occur from a preference for blessing prayers to a preference for thanksgiving prayers. The distinction, however, may be overwrought. For in the transition to Greek, the language of *Berakah* was almost indiscriminately translated with both εὐλογέω and εὐχαριστέω. To bless/praise God was to thank him; to thank him was to praise him. Thus, if Paul's *Berakah* may be modeled not only on Jewish synagogue prayers but also on Paul's own liturgical practice while presiding at the Lord's Supper among his Ephesian flock, the language of his thanksgivings may be influenced by the same context. Not only in the *Berakah* (1:3–14) but also in the *Hodayah* (1:15–23), there may be echoes of the presider's prayer in the early Christian eucharistic (thanksgiving) liturgy.[115] Paul prays as an apostle of Christ, who carries out Christ's intercessory office here on earth. But he also prays as a parish pastor, who never forsakes his flock, though absent in body.

Interchangeable does not, however, mean identical. The presence of both forms of prayer in Ephesians is neither completely redundant nor as unusual as it might seem. Colossians, in fact, could be said to have a double thanksgiving (Col 1:3–4, 9–12; see εὐχαριστέω in Col 1:3, 12). 1 Thessalonians has three thanksgivings (1 Thess 1:2–3; 2:13; 3:9). Both *Berakah* and *Hodayah* are included (in reverse order) in the letter that opens 2 Maccabees (1:11, 17). And Daniel's great *Berakah* prayer moves easily from blessing into thanksgiving (Dan 2:20, 23). Blessing and thanksgiving are complementary aspects of Christian prayer. In Ephesians the two prayers have a related but distinct content. F. F. Bruce notes: "Whereas the *eulogia* [blessing] praises God for blessings received by the writer and his fellow-Christians, the thanksgiving is concerned rather with the work of God in the lives of those addressed."[116] The distinction is not between God's work and man's work, but between God's *cosmic* work and his *personal* work. By turning his prayer to the saints' faith and love, Paul focuses the prayer and draws in his listeners.

Supplication (1:16b–19)

The thanksgiving section (1:15–23), which began with thanksgiving in the narrow sense of the term (1:15–16a), moves seamlessly into supplication for

---

[114] James M. Robinson, "The Historicality of Biblical Language," in *The Old Testament and Christian Faith* (ed. Bernhard W. Anderson; New York: Harper & Row, 1963), 124–58; James M. Robinson, "Die Hodajot-Formel in Gebet und Hymnus des Frühchristentums," in *Apophoreta: Festschrift für Ernst Haenchen zu seinem siebzigsten Geburtstag am 10. Dezember 1964* (ed. Walther Eltester and Franz H. Kettler; Berlin: Töpelmann, 1964), 194–234.

[115] The Words of Institution use the vocabulary of both "blessing" (*Berakah*, εὐλογέω) and "giving thanks" (*Hodayah*, εὐχαριστέω). See the discussion in "The *Berakah* Prayer: Background and Parallels" in the commentary on 1:3–14.

[116] Bruce, *The Epistles to the Colossians, to Philemon, and to the Ephesians*, 268.

the addressees (1:16b–19; technically a report of Paul's ongoing supplication). In this he again follows the pattern of the *Berakah* prayer, in which praise of God and appeal to his saving acts always precedes and forms the basis of the petitions that are cautiously appended. Throwing caution to the wind, however, Paul confidently proposes a series of petitions (1:17–19a) that are rooted in his confession of the Lord's power and grace (1:19b–23). Imitating the Trinitarian address of the *Berakah* (1:3), Paul appeals to God the glorious Father through the name of our Lord Jesus to give the Holy Spirit with all his gifts (1:17a). This Trinitarian prayer, echoing Isaiah 11, is exuberant in its repetitiveness, appealing to the Spirit for "wisdom and revelation in the knowledge of him" (1:17).[117] Thus, he prays that the great revelation of the "mystery" (1:9) that was extolled in the *Berakah* might be taken up by the Ephesians and suffuse their minds and souls.

Paul takes no joy in pious ignorance, nor does he view the Christian faith as a mystery so deep that it cannot be fathomed. While God remains unplumbable in his depth, the Christian forsakes idle speculation and clings to what God has revealed of himself. Knowledge of God is a potent weapon against spirits like the ancient serpent who would question whether we can truly know God's will (Gen 3:1). Though Paul's letter to the Ephesians makes no comparable reference to the deceitful philosophies that were threatening to mislead the Colossians (Col 2:8–23), the same cultural context reigned in their part of Asia Minor. Paul not only prays for the gift of knowledge, but he later insists that they have already been so equipped (Eph 4:20).

Such knowledge was begun in them with the opening of their eyes in Holy Baptism (1:18a; see "Enlightened Eyes of Your Heart" below). The Trinitarian address is balanced by a threefold petition, that they might understand the following more fully:

- τίς: what is the hope of his (God's) calling (1:18b)
- τίς: what is the richness of his glorious inheritance among the saints (1:18c)
- τί: what is the surpassing greatness of his power for us who believe (1:19a)

Three petitions, neatly made parallel by the repetition of τίς, "what" (once feminine, once masculine, and once neuter), progress from the gift to the power that guarantees it. The present-oriented gifts of "faith" and "love" (1:15) are complemented by their perpetual partner, a "hope" (1:18) that looks to the goal set before those whom God has called. And the hope will not be disappointed because it is backed up by the glorious might of the world's Creator.

Astonishingly, though, Paul appeals not to God's irresistible power as demonstrated in dividing the seas and raising the mountains, but to God's actions in Christ. God's power was revealed when he raised Christ from the dead and seated him at his right hand in the heavenly places (1:20). Only this power can give true comfort that he will do the same for me. The Christian's hope of an

---

[117] See the fifth textual note on 1:17.

eternal inheritance is guaranteed by Christ's trailblazing journey through death into life and on high. Paul will later tease out the connection between Christ's actions and our own (2:5–10); for the moment he contents himself to confess that this power is at work "for us who believe" (1:19).

Praise (1:20–23)

The transition from the supplications (1:16–19) to the concluding lines of praise (1:20–23) is therefore entirely natural. The petitions are not groundless, but are guaranteed in Christ. First Paul appeals to the ancient promises of God that were fulfilled in Christ: the enthronement psalms that promised Christ's rescue from his enemies and ascension to God's right hand (Psalms 8 and 110). Then through a lengthy creedal affirmation of Christ's high office, Paul demonstrates how Christ's exaltation leads to great benefit for the church, which, as his body, participates in all that enlivens and enriches the Head.

Commentators have postulated and searched in vain for a hymnic source that Paul might be quoting in this beautifully crafted doxological conclusion. It is poetic in structure, with parallelism of grammar (two participles parallel to two main verbs) and thought (raised, ascended, superordinated, appointed), though not so tightly crafted as the Christ hymn of Col 1:15–20. On the one hand, we need look no farther than Paul's own thought and writings. He has developed the same ideas from reflection on Psalm 110 in 1 Cor 15:24–28 and Phil 2:5–11. Yet similar thoughts in other NT authors (Hebrews 1–2; 1 Pet 3:18–22) suggest that these creedal statements and sequences were already entering the common Christian storehouse in apostolic days. This was the way Paul taught Christ (Eph 4:20–21). This was the way Peter preached (e.g., Acts 10:34–43). This was the way early Christians confessed Christ, they who gathered up *testimonia* (collections of OT messianic passages) and began to formulate things like the Old Roman Creed (forebearer of the Apostles' Creed).

Rhetorical Factors

As the epistle was a substitute for the author's presence, good letter writing conveyed the impression that he was present with his audience when an orator "performed" the letter at the receiving end. *Mutatis mutandis*, when Paul's letters were read in the midst of the gathered congregation by his authorized representative (in the case of Ephesians, by Tychicus) or a subsequent lector, an oratorical event ensued which approached the act of preaching in the liturgy.[118] Typical Hellenistic rhetoric suggested that in the epistolary prescript the author endeavor to achieve what an orator sought from his audience in his proem or exordium: to "capture their goodwill" and make them favorably disposed to the speaker (*benevolentiae captatio*). This set the stage for the request that typically prompted the letter. A good example is found in the speech of the Jewish

---

[118] See Winger, "Orality as the Key to Understanding Apostolic Proclamation in the Epistles," 200–217.

authorities seeking to condemn Paul before Felix, which began with words of fawning flattery (Acts 24:2–4).

Hellenistic rhetoric approached this task by noting and appealing to good qualities within the audience, "buttering them up." Paul's thanksgiving captures the saints' goodwill in a slightly different manner. He typically has more to say about *God's* work than that of the addressees, about *God's* qualities than theirs. The gifts of the Spirit and the office and work of Christ (1:17–23) occupy far more territory in the Ephesian thanksgiving than the opening appeal to the Ephesians' faith and love (1:15–16). Even there, while Paul drew them into his joy over their persistence in these virtues, it was clear that these, too, were gifts of God. God acted first with his monergistic actions that filled the *Berakah*, which confessed that God chose us (1:4), predestined us in his love (1:5), and bestowed grace upon us in the Beloved One (1:6). Faith in this loving God has come through hearing the Word of truth, the Gospel that brings salvation and creates belief in him, and baptismal sealing by the action of the Holy Spirit (1:13). All this colors the report that the Ephesians have persisted in faith and love (1:15)—they have remained in the gifts that were given. Thus, when Paul gives thanks for these gifts, he truly praises the Giver; not the one who believes, but the One who is trusted; not the ones who love, but the One who is love. As they love one another, they are abiding in his love (Jn 15:9).

In a typical Hellenistic oration, the *narratio* ("narration" or statement of the case) follows the *benevolentiae captatio* ("capturing of goodwill"), closely followed by the *propositio* ("proposition" or thesis statement). The *narratio* sets down the background story that is necessary for the audience to understand the ensuing argument and draw the right conclusion. The *propositio* sums up the purpose of the speech. Gal 1:11–2:21 is the best NT example of a *narratio*, as Paul sets down the story of his conversion and encounters with the Jerusalem apostles, in defense of his apostleship. A clear *propositio* appears in Rom 1:16–17. In most of his letters, however, Paul seamlessly blends these functions into his epistolary thanksgiving and the prayers that accompany it. Not all species of rhetoric have the same need for a well-developed *narratio*. Christian rhetoric has its own needs and conventions. We have noted how the function of the *narratio* has been taken up by the *Berakah* (Eph 1:3–14), as it laid down the cosmic and redemptive narration that undergirds Paul's appeal for unity in Christ. The thanksgiving (1:15–23) continues this function and, to a lesser extent, continues to act as a prologue or table of contents for the rest of the epistle. A clear example is 1 Cor 1:4–9, in which Paul touches on "speech," "knowledge," "gift," and "the revealing of our Lord Jesus Christ"—a veritable outline of the epistle—and lays down the proposition that the Corinthians are not lacking in any way with regard to the Lord's gift (singular!).

In Ephesians, likewise, we may be confident that the thanksgiving introduces points that are vital to Paul's later arguments. Astonishingly, nearly every major term in the thanksgiving is repeated or expanded in the body of the letter:

Theme, Language	Thanksgiving	Body of the Epistle
praying at all times	1:16	6:18
Spirit of wisdom	1:17	3:10
Spirit of revelation	1:17	3:5
knowledge of him	1:17	4:13 (cf. 4:23)
enlightened eyes of the heart (baptismal)	1:18	4:5, 18; 5:6–14
heart	1:18	3:17; 5:19; 6:5, 22
hope of his (God's) calling	1:18	2:12; 4:1, 4
inheritance among the saints	1:18	2:19, 21; 5:5, 27
power	1:19	3:7, 16, 20
at work, working	1:19, 20	2:2; 3:7, 20; 4:16
strength of his might	1:19	3:16; 6:10
resurrection from the dead	1:20	2:6; 5:14
ascension to God's right hand	1:20	2:6; 4:10
heavenly places	1:20	2:6; 3:10; 6:12
rule and authority and power and lordship	1:21	2:2; 3:10; 6:12
this age	1:21	2:2
the age to come	1:21	2:7; 3:21
subordinated	1:22	5:21, 24
head for the church	1:22	4:15; 5:23
the church, which is his body	1:22–23	2:16; 4:4, 12, 16; 5:23, 28, 30
fullness, fill	1:23	3:19; 4:10, 13; 5:18

Scan this list, and you have a bird's eye view of the Ephesian landscape, whose contours seem to converge on the twin peaks of knowledge of Christ and his exaltation over all spiritual powers. The church, which arrives in 1:23 as the beneficiary of these gifts, forms a bridge into the application Paul begins to make in chapter 2.

Enlightened Eyes of Your Heart (1:18)

A most remarkable image accompanies the first petition of Paul's prayer. It hints at the origin of a Christian's spiritual knowledge and introduces a theme that will play quietly throughout the epistle. Paul prays that God would give

263

them "enlightened eyes of the heart" (1:18). While the imagery of enlightening the heart and opening the eyes is found in Jewish literature (see the first textual note on 1:18), the combination of the two, including the odd expression "eyes of the heart," seems to be invented by Paul. There is good reason why he might have done so.

Two parallel NT stories elucidate these words. First, a man blind from birth meets the One who is the light of the world (Jn 9:1–5). Jesus anoints his eyes with spittle and sends him to wash in the Pool of Siloam (Jn 9:6–7). Water restores his sight. The Pharisees are scandalized by the miracle, since they view the man as a sinner unworthy of God's mercy. They refuse to believe in the Son of God. Thus, though they have physical eyes, they are blind to the most important spiritual realities (Jn 9:39–41). At the same time, the man who was physically blind is given sight into heavenly things (Jn 9:35–38).[119] Second, this irony is worked out again in the life of St. Paul, the Pharisee. While physically sighted, he persecutes the Lord by pursuing his disciples. When the Lord calls him to repentance and faith in the Messiah, he strikes him with physical blindness (Acts 9:8). The restoration of his sight through Ananias coincides with his Baptism (Acts 9:17–18). As a Pharisee he was struck blind so that as a disciple of Christ he might see. This intense, personal experience, in which the effects of Baptism were given a physical manifestation, surely explains Paul's unique expression "enlightened eyes of the heart."

Most likely under Paul's influence, "enlightened" or "illuminated" became a common early patristic term for the newly baptized.

> This washing [Baptism] is called illumination [φωτισμός], since those who learn these things are illumined [φωτιζομένων] within. The illuminand [φωτιζόμενος] is also washed in the name of Jesus Christ, who was crucified under Pontius Pilate, and in the name of the Holy Spirit, who through the prophets foretold everything about Jesus.[120]

---

[119] Early prebaptismal catechesis often drew a connection between John 9—read as a Sunday Gospel in Lent—and the candidates' upcoming Baptism at the Easter Vigil. See Cabié, "Christian Initiation," 28.

[120] Justin Martyr, *First Apology*, 61:12 (trans. Edward Rochie Hardy, LCC 1:283; see also PG 6:421). Cf. Justin Martyr, *First Apology*, 65:1; Justin Martyr, *Dialogue with Trypho*, 39:2; 122:1–2, 6; 123:2. Baptism is explicitly called enlightenment in Clement of Alexandria, *The Instructor*, 1:6; Cyril of Jerusalem, *Procatechesis*, 1; *Acts of Thomas*, 132; *Apostolic Constitutions*, 8:8; Gregory of Nazianzus, *Theological Orations*, 40:3–4; *Sibylline Oracles*, 1:411–12; 8:325, 360. John Chrysostom speaks of Baptism:

> When you come to the sacred initiation, the eyes of the flesh see water; the eyes of faith behold the Spirit. Those eyes see the body being baptized; these see the old man being buried. The eyes of the flesh see the flesh being washed; the eyes of the spirit see the soul being cleansed. The eyes of the body see the body emerging from the water; the eyes of faith see the new man come forth brightly shining from that sacred purification. (*Baptismal Instructions*, 11:12 [trans. Paul W. Harkins, ACW 31:164; quoted in Whitaker, *Documents of the Baptismal Liturgy*, 35–36])

These words are reminiscent of Luther's baptismal hymn: "Das Aug allein das Wasser siht, Wie Menschen Wasser giessen, Der Glaub im Geist die krafft versteht Des Blutes Jhesu

Paul's prayer, therefore, is that those who have been enlightened in their understanding through Baptism might continue to grow in that knowledge of God by his Spirit.[121]

Christ's Victorious Ascension to God's Right Hand (1:20–23)

At the time of the Reformation, Christ's session at the right hand became an exegetical bone of contention between the pit-bull fanatics and the bulldog Luther. In brief, Zwingli and Oecolampadius had adduced two main scriptural arguments against the real presence of Christ's body and blood in the Sacrament: first, that the ascension caused Christ's human body to be locally confined at God's right hand in heaven (Eph 1:20);[122] and second, that, in any case, "the flesh is of no avail" (Jn 6:63). The exegesis of these two passages formed a substantial portion of Luther's *That These Words of Christ, "This Is My Body," Etc., Still Stand Firm against the Fanatics* (1527).[123] In dealing with the second passage, Luther responded that Christ was speaking of *our* flesh, not his; if *Christ's* flesh were of no avail, then neither the incarnation nor the atonement could be of any value to us. But it is Luther's argument against the first assertion that concerns us here.

Two questions were at issue: (1) Is God's right hand a place? (2) Is the human nature of Christ locally confined to it? In response to the first, Luther runs rampant through the OT, demonstrating the absurdity of glossing "God's right hand" with a locality. He concludes (as does the third textual note on 1:20) that "the right hand," though referring figuratively to a place, represents a power that is, ironically, active everywhere.[124] The right hand can no more be taken in a literally circumscribed sense than the other anthropomorphic descriptions of God's power and presence in the OT.[125] In fact, Luther contends, if God's right hand is an OT image for his almighty power and if God's mighty power can be shown to be at work in all places, then the right hand of God to which

---

Christi" (WA 35:470). "The eye sees nothing but the water, As men pour water, [But] in the Spirit faith comprehends the power Of the blood of Jesus Christ" (cf. *LSB* 406:7).

[121] Schlier, *Epheser*, 79–80, explains that the perfect tense participle πεφωτισμένους, "enlightened" (Eph 1:18), "points to the duration [*Dauer*] and, if we are correct to see a recollection of a baptismal expression in it, to the persistence [*Fortdauer*] and unceasing renewal and deepening of the enlightenment."

[122] E.g., Zwingli: "This word 'until' [i.e. until Christ's return, Ps. 110:1] binds him to the right hand of God until the predetermined day, so that we may easily understand that he will never be anywhere else than at the right hand of God until the judgment is completed" (*Reply to Billican, Corpus Reformatorum*, 91:907, quoted in AE 37:73, n. 121).

[123] AE 37:3–150.

[124] "The Scriptures teach us, however, that the right hand of God is not a specific place in which a body must or may be, such as on a golden throne, but is the almighty power of God, which at one and the same time can be nowhere and yet must be everywhere" (AE 37:57).

[125] "Come and tell me now, where are his head, arm, breast, body, if with his feet he fills the earth and with his legs he fills heaven?" (AE 37:59).

Christ is appointed is also everywhere. The power and person of God cannot be separated:

> It has been shown convincingly enough by now that the right hand of God is not a particular place where Christ's body is seated, as the fanatics dream, but is the power of God himself. For God's right hand of course cannot be a creature but must be something above and apart from all creatures, for there is no one and nothing other than God himself who is in all things everywhere. Therefore this also must be true, that God's right hand is in all things everywhere, as we have heard. … They, however—the fanatics—lose the point and fail to maintain their position when they say it is a particular place, supporting their carnal ideas from Augustine.

> … Christ's body is at the right hand of God; that is granted. The right hand of God, however, is everywhere, as you must grant from our previous demonstration. Therefore it surely is present also in the bread and wine at table. Now where the right hand of God is, there Christ's body and blood must be, for the right hand of God is not divisible into many parts but a single, simple entity. So too, the article of the Creed does not say that Christ is at one part, such as a little finger or fingernail of the right hand of God, but it says without qualification, "at the right hand of God," that wherever and whatever God's right hand is in reality and in name, there is Christ, the Son of man.

> This is also the intention of Christ wherever he confesses in the gospel that all things have been delivered to him by the Father [Luke 10:22] and all things put under his feet, Psalm 8[:6 (MT 8:7)]. That is, he is at the right hand of God, which means nothing else than that even as a man he is over all things, has all things under him, and rules over all. Therefore he must also be near at hand, in and about all things, and have all things in his hands. For nothing is delivered to him or put under his feet according to his divinity, since he himself made all things at the beginning and preserves them. But to sit at God's right hand is the same as to rule and have power over all things. If he is to have power and rule, surely he must also be present there in his essence through the right hand of God which is everywhere.[126]

In the final paragraph, Luther introduces the communication of attributes (the conferral of divine attributes upon the human nature of Christ), important to grasp for a correct understanding of these verses of Ephesians. If Paul were talking only of the *divine* nature of Christ being seated at the right hand of God, he could not say that all spiritual powers were made subject to Christ at his ascension and session—for as true God, he already held all things under his authority.[127] In fact, such divine powers had already been communicated to Christ's *human* nature, as he proclaims in the Gospels (Mt 28:18; Jn 3:35).

---

[126] Luther, *That These Words of Christ, "This Is My Body," Etc., Still Stand Firm against the Fanatics* (1527), AE 37:63–64.

[127] "First, it is a clear rule shared by the entire ancient, orthodox church that whatever Christ received in time according to the testimony of Holy Scripture he received not according to the divine nature (according to which he had all things from eternity), but that the person received it in time *ratione et respectu humanae naturae* (that is, according to the assumed human nature)" (FC SD 8:57; Kolb-Wengert, 626).

The demons were already subject to his name (Lk 10:17–20). During Christ's "state of humiliation," when he took on "the form of a slave" (Phil 2:7), Christ merely refrained from the full, visible exercise of these divine powers. Thus, when talking about Christ's exaltation to the right hand of God, Paul must be speaking of something different from the mere communication of divine attributes to the human nature of Christ: the transformation of Christ from his slave-like state to his state of glorious exaltation, of which Paul sings so beautifully in the *Carmen Christi*, "Hymn of Christ" (Phil 2:5–11). The Formula of Concord, thus, does not speak of receiving power that had not previously been his, but of the full and unrestricted exercise of powers that he had once laid aside voluntarily. The exaltation entails not a change in his nature as man or God but change in the state of his mission:

> [26]Hence also the human nature, after the resurrection from the dead, has its exaltation above all creatures in heaven and on earth; which is nothing else than that He entirely laid aside the form of a servant, and yet did not lay aside His human nature, but retains it to eternity, and is put in the full possession and use of the divine majesty according to His assumed human nature. However, this majesty He had immediately at His conception, even in His mother's womb, but, as the apostle testifies [Phil. 2, 7], laid it aside; and, as Dr. Luther explains [AE 15:293–94], He kept it concealed in the state of His humiliation, and did not employ it always, but only when He wished.

> [27]But now He does, since He has ascended, not merely as any other saint, to heaven, but, as the apostle testifies [Eph. 4, 10], above all heavens, and also truly fills all things, and being everywhere present, not only as God, but also as man [has dominion and] rules from sea to sea and to the ends of the earth. … [28]Yet this occurred not in an earthly way, but, as Dr. Luther explains [AE 37:55–59, 63–64], according to the manner of the right hand of God, which is no fixed place in heaven, as the Sacramentarians assert without any ground in the Holy Scriptures, but nothing else than the almighty power of God, which fills heaven and earth, in [possession of] which Christ is installed according to His humanity, *realiter*, that is, in deed and truth, *sine confusione et exaequatione naturarum*, that is, without confusion and equalizing of the two natures in their essence and essential properties. (FC SD 8:26–28 [*Triglotta*, 1023, 1025])

To exalt Christ in the substance of his *divine* nature would be nonsense (God cannot become greater than he already is). But as Paul will later conclude (2:6), the remarkable glorification of Christ according to his *human* nature gives true comfort to us who share that nature.[128]

As Paul moves on to confess, the exaltation of Christ is not proclaimed as an event that occurred exclusively for his own benefit, but also "for the sake of

---

[128] "For it would hardy be remarkable to say that God sits by God if fellowship in power is a corollary of their identity of nature as Father and Son. But that the human nature assumed from us should partake of the same honor as the one who assumed him, so that no difference in worship is apparent, so that the invisible Godhead is worshiped through the visible human nature—this exceeds all wonder!" (Theodoret, *Ephesians*, 1:20 [ACCS 8:123]).

the church" (τῇ ἐκκλησίᾳ in 1:22 is a dative of benefit/advantage). Although Christ had triumphed over demons in his earthly ministry, this, too, was proleptic; the devil's kingdom was being conquered in part. As a result of his death and resurrection, however, Christ fully trounced the enemy. The mopping up of Satan's forces may continue throughout the age of the church, but in principle they are already defeated. This is the nature of the so-called "realized eschatology" governing Paul's language in Ephesians 1. These "lower parts" to which Christ descended (4:9) are still inhabited by "the ruler of the authority of the air" (2:2), but Christ's ascension[129] above the heavens, above all spiritual forces, as a past historical action for the benefit of his people (1:20–23; 4:8), means that already now we benefit from his great victory. Christ brings forward the benefits of the full-blown, without-remainder dominion over Satan's forces that characterizes his coming in majesty on the Last Day (Dan 7:14; Rev 12:10).

As "pagans," the Gentiles who apparently predominated in the Ephesian church would have been keenly interested in this cosmic dimension of Christ's work. As Paul reminded them, in their previous lives they had been obligated to placate and serve these demonic forces through the elaborate systems available in the local temples. The same could not have been said of Jews, who, though at times misled into a pharisaical, synergistic interpretation of their relationship with God, would never have seen themselves as subject to the power of demons or idols—certainly not since the terrors of the pre-Maccabean period had led them to a renewed devotion to the true God alone. Thus, Christ's trouncing of the powers that had subjected the Gentiles put them on equal footing with the Jews. Eph 1:20–23 leads naturally into chapter 2.

Perhaps the Ephesians were also plagued by the syncretistic false teachers that appear to have affected Colossae, who pressed them to hedge their bets by fulfilling both the Jewish ceremonial regulations and appeasing the old spiritual powers.[130] Whether these false teachers played on fear of persecution from secular powers, demonic forces, or influential Jews, Paul's answer in Christ would have brought great relief. For the distinction between earthly and spiritual powers is not as clear in biblical and ancient thought as it might seem to us. Earthly rulers were thought to rule on behalf of their respective gods (see the third textual note on 1:20 regarding "right hand"). Jesus reminds Pilate that his power is given from on high (Jn 19:11); Paul teaches the same of the Roman authorities (Rom 13:1–2). The book of Daniel draws back the veil so that we might see the spiritual battle taking place simultaneously with the clash of earthly empires; Persia, Greece, and Israel have divinely appointed angelic guardians or demonic allies (Dan 10:13, 20–21; 12:1). Similarly, in Revelation the letters to the angels of the seven churches do not clearly differentiate the spiritual

---

[129] The large number (twelve) of ascension hymns in *TLH* (1941), compared to just five in *LSB* (2006), illustrates the greater liturgical role this festival once had among Lutherans. Even today *Christi Himmelfahrt* (Ascension) is a national holiday in Germany.

[130] Col 2:8–23; see Deterding, *Colossians*, 124–31; Lincoln, *Ephesians*, 63.

guardian from the human flock (e.g., τῷ ἀγγέλῳ τῆς ἐν Ἐφέσῳ ἐκκλησίας, "to the angel of the church in Ephesus," Rev 2:1). Judas is directed by Satan (Lk 22:3; Jn 13:2), as are Paul's enemies (2 Cor 11:15). The Roman authorities that Paul exhorts us to obey (Romans 13) are driven in their evil actions by corresponding spiritual forces (Revelation 13). This is the thought-world occupied by the Ephesians. If any hostile earthly forces persecute or threaten the Christian church, Paul would have us not lose sight of the real enemy that stands behind the flesh and blood (Eph 6:12).

For Paul, then, the triumph of Christ means that these evil spiritual forces no longer rule over the Christian. But Paul is hardly a modern secularist who simply denies the influence of the supernatural on the natural. The Christian remains under spiritual influence; there has simply been a change of lordship.[131] Christ is now our Head. His name is the greater power that his baptized brothers and sisters may wield in spiritual battle against the enemies he has defeated on their behalf. His name puts them to flight, strikes terror into their hearts. Thus, Luther can refer quite favorably to a Christian ritual that may strike modern Westerners as impossibly archaic: "the custom learned in childhood of making the sign of the cross when something dreadful or frightening is seen or heard, and saying, 'LORD God, save me!' or, 'Help, dear Lord Christ!' and the like" (LC 1:74 [Kolb-Wengert, 396]). Luther likely had the words of Ephesians in mind when he crafted his great hymn, appointed in the Lutheran Church to accompany the Gospel text of Christ's temptation (Mt 4:1–11; Lent 1). Since Christ overcame the devil for us, we need have no fear:

> Though devils all the world should fill,
> All eager to devour us,
> We tremble not, we fear no ill;
> They shall not overpow'r us.
> This world's prince may still
> Scowl fierce as he will,
> He can harm us none.
> He's judged; the deed is done;
> One little word can fell him. (*LSB* 656:3)

Christ, the Head—The Church, His Body (1:22–23)

The final accolade given to Christ in this creedal/doxological conclusion to the thanksgiving is his appointment as Head over all things, with particular benefit accruing to the church. In line with Pauline thought elsewhere,[132] the church is called "his body" (1:22–23). The image is unpacked later in Ephesians, as part of the appeal to unity in Christ (4:4, 15–16) and more extensively in the

---

[131] Best, *Ephesians*, 56, comments: "For Gentiles the stars laid out what would happen; magic was used to affect their own lives and the lives of others; natural disasters, famine, plague, flood were the result, not of natural causes, but of supernatural; fate was dominant. When they became Christians the supernatural did not cease to control them but it emanated from God."

[132] 1 Cor 12:12–31; Rom 12:3–8; Col 1:18, 24; 2:19; 3:15.

great marriage allegory (5:21–33). It is inherent in the image that the church is envisioned in its universal aspect, as in every occurrence of the word ἐκκλησία in Ephesians (1:22; 3:10, 21; 5:23–32 [six times]). While the local congregation can equally be called Christ's body, this is not a sort of ecclesial polygamy, as if Christ had many brides! It is the same church in every instance. Indeed, dominance of the "body" image in Ephesians is likely the chief reason why the letter shows little interest in the local congregation.[133]

Because the church is the body *of Christ*, one should not assume there is a change of subject when Paul shifts the weight from Christology to the church at the end of the thanksgiving. For the analogy would be broken if one were to consider the church apart from her Head. But what is the point of the body analogy? Where Paul has previously developed it, the emphasis has fallen on the legitimate role and equal importance of every part of the Christian community (Romans 12; 1 Corinthians 12).[134] The body analogy or allegory was used to explain *diversity* within the church in recognition of the fact that each member is different from the next, with unique gifts and responsibilities. Within that scheme, the head played no major role. In Romans 12 and 1 Corinthians 12, Christ is not declared to be the Head, but the place in which the church as body subsists. In one instance, the head is referred to like any other body part (1 Cor 12:21). Thus, while baptismal incorporation (meaning "embodiment") "in Christ," including unity (1 Cor 12:12–13), is the premise of the analogy, it is diversity that concerns Paul in those other passages.

In Ephesians the analogy is in service of a somewhat different task. Nowhere is diversity of roles mentioned. On the contrary, it is the *oneness* of the body, its organic *unity* that is stressed (Eph 4:4). Not the diversity of body parts, but their bond to one another through joints and ligaments is stressed (4:16). In the great marriage allegory, likewise, the church as body is "one flesh" with Christ, united to her Bridegroom (5:31–32). The Head views his bride not as something other than himself, but as his own body (5:29–30). The role given to the head in Ephesians and Colossians, therefore, takes the allegory one step beyond its previous occurrences. The Head (Christ) gives direction to the body, leads it, indeed gives life to it (4:15–16). The body is therefore viewed as a unit

---

[133] Thus, the dominance of the universal church in Ephesians is merely thematic and should not be viewed as un-Pauline, as some critics assert. Reference to the universal church is not so unusual in other letters of Paul (e.g., 1 Cor 10:32; 12:28; 15:9; Col 1:18, 24). Note also the coupling of local with universal, particularly with the phrase "the church of God," in Acts 20:17, 28 (Paul's speech); Rom 16:5; 1 Cor 1:2; 11:18, 22; 2 Cor 1:1. Among the remaining NT occurrences of ἐκκλησία, "church," more often than not the referent is a grouping of churches in a larger geographical unit, or "diocese," spanning a whole city or territory, rather than a local congregation, strictly speaking. See "Ecclesiology" in "Evaluation of the Case" in "Authorship" in the introduction; also Jeffrey J. Kloha, "The Trans-Congregational Church in the New Testament," *Concordia Journal* 34 (2008): 172–90.

[134] The shift in emphasis from Romans/1 Corinthians to Colossians/Ephesians is investigated by James D. G. Dunn, " 'The Body of Christ' in Paul," in *Worship, Theology and Ministry in the Early Church: Essays in Honor of Ralph P. Martin* (ed. Michael J. Wilkins and Terence Paige; Sheffield: JSOT, 1992), 146–62.

in relation to its head, rather than as a collection of diverse parts. This is how it comes into service of one of Paul's major concerns in Ephesians: the unity of all people, particularly Jew and Gentile, within the church. As such, it forms a bridge from the letter's prologue (1:3–23) into the first argument about ecclesial unity in the next chapter (2:1–10).

The occurrence of similar analogies in secular Greek literature has raised the question, first, of whether Paul has borrowed from these sources, and therefore, second, whether they can be helpful in understanding Paul's meaning. Political rhetoric of the day had compared the city or state to a body in order to explain its complex function and to appeal for unity under the leadership of a figure identified with the head (or stomach!). Plato, for example, writes in his *Republic*: "And this unity of feeling we admitted to be the greatest good, as was implied in our own comparison of a well-ordered State to the relation of the body and the members, when affected by pleasure or pain."[135] The same Plato describes the entire cosmos as a body, created as a perfect sphere without need of eyes or legs, or any members that would be needed for interaction, as there is nothing outside itself.[136] Into this perfect body the Creator infused a spirit, or soul, a higher element to guide and direct it. As Heinrich Schlier notes,[137] in these Platonic schemes there is no place for a head, only for a ψυχή, "spirit" or "soul." This is quite different from Paul's depiction of Christ's role as Head—and the Holy Spirit is more than simply the ecclesial body's "soul." While he speaks of the Spirit of Christ indwelling us (e.g., Rom 8:9) and of all in the body drinking of one Spirit (1 Cor 12:13), the Spirit remains a person distinct from the body. Indeed, it is the virtual pantheism of the Hellenistic philosophical systems that distinguishes them from Paul's body analogy. This blurring of Creator and creation is explicit in Stoicism, as illustrated by Seneca: *Omne hoc, quod vides, quo divina atque humana conclusa sunt, unum est: membra sumus corporis magni*, "all that you behold, that which comprises both god and man, is one: we are members of one great body."[138]

These ideas were known and perpetuated among Hellenized Jews, as in Philo: "The *head* of all things is the eternal Logos of the eternal God, under which, as if it were his feet or other limbs, is placed the whole world, over

---

[135] Plato, *Republic*, 5:464 (trans. Benjamin Jowett, *The Works of Plato* [4 vols. in 1; New York: Tudor, ca. 1936], 2:197). See further examples in Lincoln, *Ephesians*, 68; Barth, *Ephesians*, 1:194.

[136] Plato, *Timaeus*, 30b–35a.

[137] Schlier, *Epheser*, 91.

[138] Seneca, *Ad Lucilium Epistulae Morales*, 95:52. Cf. Seneca, *De Clementia*, 1:5.1: "For if … you [Nero] are the soul of the state and the state your body [corpus], you see, I think, how requisite is mercy: for you are merciful to yourself when you are seemingly merciful to another. And so even reprobate citizens should have mercy as being the weak members [membris] of the body" (quoted in Sampley, *"And the Two Shall Become One Flesh,"* 65).

which He passes and firmly stands."[139] The Orphic Fragments attribute this role to Zeus: "Zeus is the first. Zeus the thunderer, is the last. Zeus is the *head*. Zeus is the middle, and by Zeus all things were fabricated. … Fire and water, earth and ether, night and day. … All these things are united in the vast body of Zeus."[140] Later Gnosticism developed these ideas, including the notion of the "Primal Man" or Aion, one huge body in which the deity is the head and the world its body. Rudolf Bultmann pioneered the theory that these ideas present in Colossians and Ephesians were borrowed from Gnosticism and therefore point to a very late date for their composition (certainly not by Paul).[141] More recent scholarship has tended to reject this explanation (thoroughly explored by Markus Barth),[142] proving that the developed concept is too impossibly late (third century) to have influenced a NT document; the relationship is more likely to have been the reverse. But there is sufficient evidence to suggest that Paul knew the image from Greek thought. Perhaps like seizing on the unknown god as a means to proclaim the true God in opposition to Athenian idolatry (Acts 17:23), or declaring Jesus to be Lord in opposition to the similar claims of the Roman emperor (Rom 10:9; 1 Cor 12:3), Paul was polemical in declaring Christ to be the Head. Not Zeus, no other deity, but Jesus of Nazareth is the Head of the cosmos. At the same time, Paul modifies the image by declaring not the universe but the church to be his body, thus personalizing it and making it more intimate.

At first blush, there seems to be little help from the OT. Although "head" is routinely used as an image for leadership (see the third textual note on 1:22) and on one occasion God is said to be at Judah's head,[143] there is no instance in which the people of Israel are called a body. People, tribe, or family are more

---

[139] Philo, *Questions and Answers on Exodus*, 2:117 (trans. Ralph Marcus, LCL; emphasis added). It is disputed to what extent a later Christian hand may have edited this passage, which continues:

> Now it is not because Christ is Lord that He passes and sits over the world, for His seat is with His Father and God, but because for its perfect fullness the world is in need of the care and superintendence of the best ordered dispensation, and for its own complete piety, of the Divine Logos, just as living creatures (need) a head, without which it is impossible to live.

[140] Emphasis added; cited in Isaac Preston Cory, *Ancient Fragments* (2d ed.; London: William Pickering, 1832), 290; omitted from the 1876 edition because the editor considered them neoplatonic forgeries.

[141] Rudolf Bultmann, "Die Bedeutung der neuerschlossenen mandäischen und manichäischen Quellen für das Verständnis des Johannesevangeliums," *Zeitschrift für die neutestamentliche Wissenschaft* 24 (1925): 100–46; Bultmann, *Theology of the New Testament* (trans. Kendrick Grobel; 2 vols.; New York: Harper, 1951–1955), 1:178–79 (cited in Barth, *Ephesians*, 1:194, n. 252).

[142] Barth, *Ephesians*, 1:183–210.

[143] 2 Chr 13:12: "behold, God is with us at/as (our) head" (בְרֹאשׁ, LXX: ἐν ἀρχῇ). Other OT images of God's (and the Messiah's) leadership over Israel might be cited, particularly the pervasive depiction of God as Shepherd. In one memorable prophetic passage, Ezekiel is told to illustrate the reunification of Israel (north) and Judah (south) into one people of God by writing their names onto two sticks and joining them (Ezek 37:15–25)—akin to the union

natural images. "Children" issuing from one body comes close, as in "the sons of Israel" or the "seed" of Abraham (e.g., Gen 15:5); they were, so to speak, enclosed in Abraham's loins (Heb 7:9–10). The same might be said of Adam at a more cosmic level; Eve is drawn from Adam's body, so that all mankind stems from him. Again it is Paul who draws the explicit conclusion that when Adam sinned, all sinned "in" him (Rom 5:12; 1 Cor 15:22). The creation of a new body in Christ is therefore a natural solution to the problem which entered the world through Adam. The similarity of content in 1 Cor 15:20–28 and Eph 1:20–23 suggests that Christ as the new Adam may be a significant part of what Paul had in mind when he called the church *Christ's* body.

A comparison with Jewish anthropology might call into question Paul's choice of the head as that which directs or gives life to the body. For the Hebrews it was the heart that was the seat of reasoning and the will, with the kidneys and bowels being the source of strong emotions. While the OT speaks of the thoughts of man, these are not located in the head.

This puzzle raises the question of medical knowledge at the time of Paul.[144] In the Greek world, Aristotle and the Stoics stood close to the Jews in ascribing a leading physiological role to the heart. But, following on from Platonic theories,[145] Greek physicians from Hippocrates (ca. 460–380 BC) to Galen (AD 130–200) worked with a remarkably modern understanding of the way the head directs the body's muscles through a network of nerves. The eye, ears, tongue, hands, and feet—those members that carry out actions with moral implications—are directed by the "brain" (ἐγκέφαλος, literally, "that which is within the head") according to its knowledge. The brain exerts its authority over the members by sending "dispatches" and interpreting their replies. Within this view of the body, only the brain has a causative role. For Hippocrates the brain is the source of thought and awareness, ruling and judging all other parts.[146] Galen even postulates that the brain is the source of the other parts, the spinal marrow acting like the sap of a tree trunk, bringing life to its members.[147] Here we find the beginnings of an explanation for Paul's ideas in Eph 4:15–16, that the head gives growth and life to the body. Clearly Paul was willing to move beyond Jewish physiological thinking and allow more mainstream Greek

---

of Jew and Gentile that Paul proclaims in Christ. God adds in messianic tones: "My servant David shall be King over them [עֲלֵיהֶם], and they will all have one Shepherd" (Ezek 37:24).

[144] Thoroughly discussed in Barth, *Ephesians*, 1:186–92.

[145] Plato, *Timaeus*, 44d–e, 69–70, 73d–e.

[146] Barth, *Ephesians*, 1:187–88, draws on Hippocrates' treatise on epilepsy, *De morbo sacro*, "On the Sacred Disease."

[147] Barth, *Ephesians*, 1:187–88, draws on Galen's treatises *De constitutione artis medicae*, "On the Art of Medicine," and *De usu partium corporis humani*, "On the Usefulness of the Parts of the Human Body."

medical thought to color his description of the head and body. Perhaps Luke the physician (Col 4:14) provided Paul with such knowledge.[148]

Ultimately, none of these secular sources are entirely satisfactory in explaining what the image means for Paul or in unfolding its full meaning. On the one hand, one must discern why Paul declines to identify the cosmos with Christ's body and focuses instead on the church. There may be a missiological motivation. The church stands over against the rest of creation. "The church is the mode of the head's appearance in the cosmos."[149] "The church is the self-manifestation of the crucified and risen Jesus Christ to all powers, all things, all men."[150] Unlike Plato's image of a cosmic body that has no interaction with anything outside itself, Christ's body is in the world and confesses him to it. The church and the world have been compared to concentric circles in which the church, the inner circle, is ever widening and laying claim to the rest of creation. Because Christ is the Head of all things, the church may view the world around it as a gift, not an enemy.

In light of such significant divergences from philosophical and medical ideas contemporary with Paul, the body image may simply have arisen out of his own ponderings on the incarnation and the atonement. In Romans 5 Paul considers the need for the Christ to reverse Adam's curse by taking on the same flesh in which sin was first conceived. In opposition to Gnostic ideas that would devalue the physical body of Christ (as well as the Christian's own body), Irenaeus famously contended that Christ, "on account of His great love, became what we are, so that He might bring us to be what He Himself is."[151] Irenaeus connects this act explicitly with Christ's human flesh:

> When he became incarnate and was made man, he summed up in himself [*in seipso recapitulavit*; cf. ἀνακεφαλαιόω, "bring together," in Eph 1:10] the long line of men and furnished us, in a brief, comprehensive manner, with salvation; so that what we had lost in Adam—namely, to be according to the image and likeness of God—that we might recover in Christ Jesus.[152]

The great unity of all mankind is achieved, Paul concludes, by the crucifixion of the body that includes us all:

> For he himself is our peace, who has made both one and has destroyed the dividing wall of partition, the hostility, in his flesh, … that in him he might create the two into one new man, making peace, and might reconcile both in one body to God through the cross. (Eph 2:14–16)

---

[148] Barth, *Ephesians*, 1:191, cautions, however, that Paul omits significant aspects of medical language, for he speaks of "head" not "brain" and makes no reference to nerves.

[149] Schlier, *Epheser*, 94.

[150] Barth, *Ephesians*, 1:199.

[151] Irenaeus, *Against Heresies*, 5, Preface (trans. Jurgens, *The Faith of the Early Fathers*, vol. 1, § 248).

[152] Irenaeus, *Against Heresies*, 3:18.1 (adapted from *ANF* 1:446).

As all mankind went forth from Adam, so they were brought together into the flesh of the Second Adam, so that as his body made peace with God, all who are in him might also be reconciled to God. The church as the body of Christ thus evokes the very acts of the incarnation and atonement.

Yet the universal aspect of the atonement (which pertains to all mankind and may be spurned) still differs from the particular image of the church as Christ's body (comprising only those baptized into Christ). The unique intimacy of the latter is illustrated by the marriage analogy of Ephesians 5. The church is Christ's body in the same way that husband and wife are one flesh. In the OT God frequently spoke of Israel as his bride, particularly in the negative context of accusing her of adultery by chasing after other gods.[153] The identification of Christ as the Bridegroom and the church as his bride is a stunning development of this theme, equating Jesus with YHWH himself. Christ himself made the equation, and thus it became a major messianic image in the NT.[154] Paul's depiction of Christ as the Head and the church as his body within the context of a marriage analogy (5:23) grew directly from these roots. Christ's sacrifice of his life on the cross (2:15) is precisely what a husband is to do for his wife (5:25). The ultimate celebration of this sacrificial victory is repeatedly described as a wedding feast (Mt 22:1–14; Rev 19:7, 9).

In the present age, the church is given a proleptic share in the joys of the marriage feast in the Sacrament of the Altar. A. E. J. Rawlinson has argued that the key to the body of Christ image is precisely the convergence of the sacramental body and the mystical body in the Lord's Supper.[155] The meaning of κοινωνία is that something held in "common" creates a "communion" or "community": "the bread which we break, is it not a *communion* of the body of Christ?" (1 Cor 10:16). Perhaps, in the end, it was meditation on the real presence that first suggested to Paul that he might speak of the church as Christ's body. This is the place where Christ and his bride become one flesh, as his flesh enters and enlivens our flesh, transforming us from what we were into what he is. It is the continuation of the gift that was first given in Holy Baptism:

> For just as the body is one and has many members, and all members of the body, even though they are many, are one body, thus also Christ. For by one Spirit we all were baptized into one body, whether Jews or Greeks, whether slaves or free, and all were given to drink of one Spirit. (1 Cor 12:12–13; cf. Gal 3:26–29)

---

[153] E.g., Is 54:1, 5–6; Is 61:10; 62:4–5; Jer 2:2–3, 32; Ezekiel 16; 23; Hos 1:2; 2:16–22 (ET 2:14–20); 3:1.

[154] Mt 9:15 (and parallels Mk 2:19–20; Lk 5:34–35); 25:1–13; cf. Jn 3:29; 2 Cor 11:2; Rev 21:2, 9; 22:17. But there is no evidence that Judaism had portrayed the coming Messiah as a Bridegroom. See Gibbs, *Matthew 1:1–11:1*, 478–79.

[155] Alfred Edward John Rawlinson, "Corpus Christi," in *Mysterium Christi: Christologische Studien britischer und deutscher Theologen* (ed. G. K. A. Bell and Adolf Deissmann; London: Longmans, 1930), 225–44.

The eucharistic and baptismal language converges at the "one body." In fact, in light of the sacramental reality Paul confesses, it becomes difficult to speak of the "body" of Christ as just an "image"—as if it were merely figurative language. Though Christ's physical body remains a distinct reality to which our bodies are conformed but with which they are never completely identical (Phil 3:21), sacramentally speaking the church is not just *like* a body.[156] She *is* his body, drawing her life from him, never separated from her Head, led by him, united in him, saved by him, and reconciled in his body to the Father. As Luther memorably wrote to Pastor Bugenhagen: "We are Christs—with and without the apostrophe (*Christi sumus in nominativo et genitivo*)."[157]

---

[156] Schlier's equation, "σῶμα + κεφαλή = Χριστός" (*Epheser*, 91), that is, "body + head = Christ," is controversial among the commentators, but can be properly understood in light of Paul's sacramental teaching.

[157] July 5, 1537, quoted in the editor's introduction, AE 22:x. Cf. Luther, *The Freedom of a Christian* (1520): "Hence, as our heavenly Father has in Christ freely come to our aid, we also ought freely to help our neighbor through our body and its works, and each one should become as it were a Christ to the other that we may be Christs to one another and Christ may be the same in all, that is, that we may be truly Christians" (AE 31:367–68).

Ephesians 2:1–4:16

Proofs

Made Alive Together in Christ

Translation

2 ¹And *you*—when you were dead in your trespasses and sins

    ²in which you once <u>walked</u> according to the age of this world,

        according to the ruler of the authority of the air,

        the spirit of the one now working in the sons of disobedience,

            ³among whom also *we* all once conducted ourselves in the passions of our flesh,

            doing the desires of the flesh and of the thoughts,

                and we were by nature children of wrath like the rest—

                    ⁴but *God*, being rich in mercy, because of his great love with which he loved us,

                        ⁵even *us*, when we were dead in [our] trespasses,

                           [God] made alive together <u>with Christ</u>

                               —by grace you have been saved!—

                               ⁶and he raised [us] together and seated [us] together in the heavenly places <u>in Christ Jesus</u>,

                        ⁷in order that in the coming ages he might show the surpassing richness of his grace in kindness upon us <u>in Christ Jesus</u>.

                    ⁸For by grace you have been saved through faith;

                and this is not from yourselves; it is the gift of God,

            ⁹not from works, lest anyone should boast.

    ¹⁰For we are what he has made, created <u>in Christ Jesus</u> for good works which God prepared beforehand, that in them we should <u>walk</u>.

Textual Notes

2:1 καὶ ὑμᾶς ὄντας—The conjunction καί, "and," connects this pericope to the preceding: the same, powerful God who raised and exalted Christ (1:20–23) has raised and exalted "also you" (as καὶ ὑμᾶς could be translated). As καὶ ὑμεῖς, "also you" (1:13), distinguished new Gentile Christians in Ephesus from Jewish Christians who had first hoped in Christ (1:12), so here the referent of "you" is the Ephesian Christians of a Gentile background. Eph 2:2 makes this identification clear and more certain than in 1:12–13: although the devil tempts all to sin, only Gentiles could accurately be accused of having followed evil spirits (idolatry). The identification is made explicit in 2:11 by "you Gentiles in the flesh" (cf. 4:17). The older, Jewish portion of the church (with Paul) is introduced as "we" in 2:3, a group who may not have been enslaved by demons, but who nonetheless followed their sinful desires and were equally under God's wrath.

Syntactically ὑμᾶς ("you [Gentiles]") is a suspended accusative:[1] Paul introduces and elaborates on the *object* of the main verb first (2:1–2); then he digresses onto a

---

[1] Cf. Col 1:21–22; 2:13; 1 Pet 3:21. Since the subject, ὁ θεός, "God" (2:4), is prefaced by the (postpositive) conjunction δέ, "but," one might argue instead that we have anacoluthon (broken

second object, "we [Jews]" (2:3); finally he introduces the *subject*, "God" (2:4), after which he reintroduces the two objects combined into "us" (2:5a). The main verbs themselves do not appear until 2:5b–6. From 2:4 onward, "us" and "you" are inclusive of Jews and Gentiles in Christ.[2] In light of the particle ποτε, "once" (2:2), the participle ὄντας must be temporal: "*when* you were …"

νεκρούς—"Dead in trespasses" is repeated in 2:5 and paralleled in Col 2:13. The theme reappears in the hymn of Eph 5:14, where spiritual death is compared to sleep and Baptism to awakening through the light of Christ. The nonliteral use of "death" for spiritual inactivity or incapacity is found in Christ's words about unbelieving Israelites (Mt 8:22 ‖ Lk 9:60). In the parable, the prodigal son is called "dead" because he was lost to his father and living a dissolute life (Lk 15:24, 32). Those who are spiritually dead are marked out by their lack of God-pleasing works;[3] thus, the lives of the Gentiles are characterized by their sins.[4] Because this is not "death" in the usual sense of the term, some interpreters soften it, suggesting that man is severely weakened by sin, but not completely incapable of reaching out to God (semi-Pelagianism). But Paul's avoidance of simile (he does not say "*as* dead") and his evocation of the (literal) death and resurrection of Christ suggest otherwise; and he hammers home his meaning with the phrases "not from yourselves" and "not from works" (2:8–9), as well as "what he has made" and "created [by God *ex nihilo*]" (2:10).

Spiritual death means that man is completely unable to make a move toward God. Such death is not figurative, but "nonliteral" only in the sense that it is different from the kind of death we normally ponder (of the body); it is actually a more profound and real kind of death, being "alienated from the life of God" (4:18), embracing or leading to physical death as its inevitable consequence. In this state, man's only hope is that rebirth which brings to life a new man. The baptismal reference is made explicit in the parallel: "… being buried with him in Baptism, in which you were also raised with him through faith in the working of the God who raised him from the dead, and you—when you were dead in trespasses and the uncircumcision of your flesh—he made you alive together with him" (Col 2:12–13; cf. Rom 6:1–4).[5] The effective power of Baptism is

---

grammar): after the clauses that provide the direct objects of the main verbs in 2:1–3, Paul breaks off and "reboots" the sentence: "but God …" (2:4). The grammar is slightly messy and defies simple diagramming. Whether analyzing the sentence this way or as in the text above, one should understand 2:1–3 as containing the direct objects of the main verbs in 2:5.

[2] Dahl, "Gentiles, Christians, and Israelites in the Epistle to the Ephesians," in *Studies in Ephesians*, 445, denies that "we" ever means "we Jews" in Ephesians, insisting that "first person plural forms include all Christians, Gentiles and Jews." Yet in the present pericope (2:1–10) things are more complicated than that!

[3] Heb 6:1; 9:14; James 2:17, 26; Rev 3:1; cf. 1 Jn 3:14.

[4] Death is also the work brought about by God's Law, as it kills self-righteousness and rebellion, preparing the way for the Gospel to bring life or punishing eternally those who refuse the Gospel: Mt 10:28; Rom 6:23; 7:10–11; 8:10; 2 Cor 3:6; Gal 2:19; Eph 2:16.

[5] The idea that through a ritual washing a heathen convert passed from death to life was likely current in Judaism already before Paul. The School of Hillel interpreted proselyte baptism as a ritual cleansing necessary because the pagan had been in contact with corpses, that is to say,

the Word of Christ, by which those who hear and believe have "passed from death to life" (Jn 5:24–25; cf. Eph 1:13).

τοῖς παραπτώμασιν καὶ ταῖς ἁμαρτίαις ὑμῶν—The dative is probably of respect, dead "with respect to" sin (not dead in the body), but it could be instrumental, killed "by" sin, or locative as the realm "in which" unbelievers are dead men walking ("walked," 2:2).[6] παράπτωμα, "trespass," evokes the image of making a false step so as to lose one's footing; it derives from παρά + πίπτω, "to fall to the side." In secular Greek παράπτωμα can be a mere "blunder" or "error in judgment." In the LXX it occurs only in the Prophets and the Writings; it is used once for a שְׁגִיאָה, "sin of ignorance" (Ps 19:13 [LXX Ps 18:13; ET Ps 19:12]). But it is also used for פֶּשַׁע, "rebellion" against God (e.g., Ezek 14:11; 18:22), and for מַעַל, a "faithless, treacherous act" against him (Ezek 14:13; 15:8; 18:24; 20:27); this is stronger than a misstep—more like falling off a cliff! In the NT it refers chiefly to an offense against God.[7] It is a characteristic way for Paul (who employs sixteen of its nineteen NT occurrences) to describe sin as a violation of God's commandment, beginning with Adam (Rom 5:15) and continuing in the "stumblings" of every person's "walk" (cf. Eph 2:2, 5).

In contrast, the second term here, ἁμαρτία, "sin," is more general and occurs often in the liturgical sections of the Pentateuch (especially Leviticus with its treatment of the "sin offering") and throughout the OT and NT. It stresses the moral character of sin as a lack of God's holiness and describes acts that violate his standards. In line with the secular meaning of "failure to reach a goal," Paul says that "all have sinned [ἥμαρτον] and lack the glory of God" (Rom 3:23)—so sin involves not missing a target slightly, but coming nowhere near it.

The distinction between these two near synonyms should not be overdrawn.[8] Paul places them together for emphasis, rhythm, and comprehensiveness.

2:2 ἐν αἷς ποτε περιεπατήσατε—The enclitic particle ποτέ, "once, formerly," alludes to the change in life and lordship brought on by these Christians' baptismal

---

the spiritually dead. Commenting on the necessity for such a convert to be baptized before participating in the Passover, the School of Hillel judges: "He who separates himself from the uncircumcision is like one who separates himself from the grave" (Mishnah, *Eduyyoth*, 5:2, quoted in Daube, *The New Testament and Rabbinic Judaism*, 108). Whether the Jewish practice of proselyte baptism predates Paul is, however, debated. Scot McKnight, "Proselytism and Godfearers," *DNTB*, 845, offers a cautious yes. Craig S. Keener, *A Commentary on the Gospel of Matthew* (Grand Rapids: Eerdmans, 1999), 120–21, is more confident. Jonathan D. Lawrence, "Washing, Ritual," *EDEJ*, 1331–32, is also positive. Everett Ferguson, *Baptism in the Early Church: History, Theology, and Liturgy in the First Five Centuries* (Grand Rapids: Eerdmans, 2009), 76–82, is more reluctant to conclude that proselyte baptism predated and influenced Christian Baptism.

[6] These somewhat ambiguous datives parallel the enigmatic passage in 1 Pet 3:18: θανατωθεὶς μὲν σαρκὶ ζωοποιηθεὶς δὲ πνεύματι. There the first dative is clearly of respect; the second may be respect or means/instrument: "put to death *in* the flesh, but made alive *in* the spirit [or *by* the Spirit]." See Wallace, *Greek Grammar*, 166, who suggests a dative of means for the latter.

[7] BDAG, s.v. παράπτωμα, b.

[8] The nouns παράπτωμα, "trespass," and ἁμαρτία, "sin," are used together in the Greek OT only in LXX Ezek 3:20; 18:24; θ Dan 4:27; and in the NT only in Rom 5:20; Eph 2:1. In each case they are interchangeable (cf. Eph 1:7; Col 1:14; Rom 5:12–21).

incorporation into Christ (cf. 1 Cor 6:11; Eph 5:8; see also the commentary on 2:11–22). περιπατέω, "to walk" (2:2, 10; 4:1, 17; 5:2, 8, 15), might evoke the rabbinic notion of הֲלָכָה, *halakah*, how to walk in the way of the Lord. Unfortunately, the rabbis tended to focus on the ethical component of behavior in the interpretation of God's commandments. Paul's use of the verb is closer to the actual OT language of הָלַךְ, "to walk," a metaphor for the believer's lifelong relationship with God (see the commentary on 4:17–5:2, titled "The Baptismal Walk: Clothed in Christ"). One's path is set by the spiritual force (good or evil) that controls one's life; thus, "walking" leads either to life or death (Deut 30:15–16). The pagan walks "in darkness" (Is 9:1 [ET 9:2]), "in the counsel of the wicked" (Ps 1:1). God's stubborn people "walked away" from him (Jer 5:23), "walked in their own counsels" (Jer 7:24), each "in the stubbornness of his evil heart" (Jer 11:8). Gentile Christians "once walked" in "fornication" and "idolatry" (Col 3:5–7), in "futility" (i.e., idolatry, Eph 4:17).

But the child of God walks in his Word,[9] walks in his way (1 Ki 3:14; Jer 7:23), walks "with God" (Gen 5:24; 6:9), and so is deemed blameless (Gen 17:1). This is the life of faith (Rom 4:12; 2 Cor 5:7), of new life (Rom 6:4), of the Spirit (Rom 8:4; Gal 5:16, 25), of those who flee immorality and live in Christ (Rom 13:13–14), who walk according to God's calling (Eph 4:1), in Christ's love (5:2), in the path of light (5:8), and wisely (5:15). To "walk in him [Christ]" is to be "rooted and built up in him and established in the faith" (Col 2:6–7). To walk is thus to believe and trust and so to follow. Christianity is called "the Way" because it involves walking in the path forged by Christ; it is following him along the road to life.[10]

Paul reminds the Ephesian Gentiles that their lives were once walked under the control of evil spiritual forces, a path leading only to death (cf. Eph 4:17). The image of "dead" (2:1, 5) men walking conjures the frightening specter of a zombie-like existence.

κατὰ τὸν αἰῶνα τοῦ κόσμου τούτου—This κατά phrase and the following one each define the power formerly controlling the Gentiles' walk (cf. Rom 8:4; Col 2:8). "The age of this world" is the only period in which God permits these hostile forces any length of leash. Paul can call the devil "the god of this age" (2 Cor 4:4). "This world" is synecdoche for "this evil world," viewed not as God's good creation but as a realm in rebellion against him. See the third textual note on 1:21. Though αἰών had been used as a proper name for a "god of eternity" in Alexandria already in 200 BC, it seems unlikely that Paul would suddenly make such a reference when elsewhere in Ephesians the term has a purely temporal meaning, "age."[11]

κατὰ τὸν ἄρχοντα τῆς ἐξουσίας τοῦ ἀέρος—The "air" as a lower level of the heavens (cf. 3:10; 6:12) is the realm in which spiritual forces, both good and evil, do battle, in parallel to and influencing events on earth, which the air touches.[12] "Ruler" and "authority" are the same vocabulary terms Paul applied to the spirits in 1:21 (see the

---

[9] In passages such as Pss 1:1–2; 119:1, 44, תּוֹרָה, "Torah," does not mean "Law" but "teaching," including both Law and the Gospel.

[10] E.g., Mt 7:14; 8:22; 16:24; Jn 10:27; Acts 9:2; 18:25; cf. Ex 13:21; Neh 9:19.

[11] See Hermann Sasse, "αἰών," *TDNT* 1:198, 207; Schlier, *Epheser*, 102; Best, *Ephesians*, 203–4.

[12] See the extensive references in Best, *Ephesians*, 204.

first textual note on that verse), though here ἐξουσία, "authority," appears not to designate a rank of spirit but the realm where authority is exercised (as in Lk 4:6; Col 1:13). Here the singular number of τὸν ἄρχοντα, "the ruler," suggests that the devil is in mind, as the prince of evil spirits.[13] He is a personal opponent of the baptized in the spiritual battle (Eph 4:27; 6:11, 16). Paul's mandate from the Lord is to preach the Gentiles out of Satan's authority and into the kingdom of God (Acts 26:18).

τοῦ πνεύματος τοῦ νῦν ἐνεργοῦντος ἐν τοῖς υἱοῖς τῆς ἀπειθείας—If, as is likely, τοῦ πνεύματος is in simple apposition to τὸν ἄρχοντα, i.e., "the ruler" *is* "the spirit," then the accusative case (τό πνεῦμα) would be expected for "the spirit." The genitive here (τοῦ πνεύματος) may be caused by attraction to the two preceding genitives.[14] The devil is portrayed as an anti-Christ and anti-Spirit. As Christ is the energizing force at work in believers, to give them life (1:19–20), and as the Spirit indwells the sons of God (Rom 8:14–15; Gal 4:6; Eph 5:18), so the devil indwells and directs the disobedient sons.[15] Christians must be aware that the devil is "now" (νῦν) at work, fighting against them, so long as this present age endures. "The sons of disobedience" (cf. 5:6) is a Hebraism[16] used to describe people (males and females) who are characterized in their very nature by rebellion against God and his Law (Rom 2:8), his Gospel and his Son (1 Pet 2:8; 4:17). Disobedience entails unbelief (Jn 3:36; Heb 3:18–19).[17] But there is yet hope that such people may repent and receive mercy (Rom 11:30–32).

2:3 ἐν οἷς καὶ ἡμεῖς πάντες—The masculine plural pronoun οἷς, "whom," refers to the preceding "sons of disobedience," with whom "we" are associated by following our sinful desires. καὶ ἡμεῖς, "also we," introduces Paul and his fellow (Jewish) Christians, in contrast to "you [Gentiles]" (see the first textual note on 2:1). πάντες, "all," may imply, however, that the Gentiles shared this addiction to fleshly passions (1 Thess 4:5; 1 Pet 4:3) and forbids us to separate widely the sins of Gentiles from the sins of Jews. Paul's point is not to distinguish the two groups but to include both under the Law's condemnation. As in Romans 1–3 (like Amos 1–2), he demonstrates the equal status of Gentile and Jew before God beginning with their inability to please him, indeed their

---

[13] The devil is "the ruler of this world" (Jn 12:31; 14:30; 16:11). In apocalyptic literature, he inhabits the air: "the devil is the evil spirit of the lower places" (*2 Enoch*, 31:4 [*APOT*, 2:450]); "Beliar's spirit of the air [τὸ ἀέριον πνεῦμα]" (*Testament of Benjamin*, 3:4 [*ANF* 8:36]; cf. 2 Cor 6:15); "I threw him out from the height with his angels, and he was flying in the air continuously above the bottomless [abyss]" (*2 Enoch*, 29:4–5 [*APOT*, 2:447]).

[14] If the genitive is not just by attraction but is intended, it cannot be a genitive of apposition, for "the ruler ... of the spirit" is not the same kind of construction as "the land of Israel"; Wallace, *Greek Grammar*, 94–100, argues that a genitive of apposition never involves two personal nouns. Lincoln, *Ephesians*, 96, proposes a subjective genitive. In that view τὸν ἄρχοντα ... τοῦ πνεύματος, "the ruler ... of the spirit," means "the one who rules the spirit," thus interpreting "spirit" as the human spirit of the disobedient. This is not entirely contradictory to our interpretation. Less likely is the suggestion that τοῦ πνεύματος is in simple apposition to τοῦ ἀέρος: "the spirit" *is* "the air" (advocated by Schlier, *Epheser*, 104).

[15] Jn 8:44; 13:2; Acts 13:10; 1 Cor 2:12; 2 Tim 2:26.

[16] BDF, § 165.

[17] Luther translates with "den Kindern des unglaubens" (WA DB 7:195), "the children of unbelief."

rebellion against him. Jew and Gentile are first united by their sinfulness (Rom 3:9, 22–23) before they can be united in the grace of Christ (Eph 2:5–8; see also Romans 4–5).

ἀνεστράφημέν ποτε—The aorist passive form ἀνεστράφημεν, with an active meaning, is from ἀναστρέφω, "to conduct oneself," an infrequent[18] near synonym of περιπατέω, "to walk" (2:2). It may lean more toward actions in the moral sphere, as the rest of this verse suggests. Paul later uses the cognate noun ἀναστροφή to refer to the Ephesians' former "way of life," their old man, that was stripped off at their Baptism (4:22).

ἐν ταῖς ἐπιθυμίαις τῆς σαρκὸς ἡμῶν—The preposition ἐν, "in," introduces the controlling power in the Jewish Ephesians' walk apart from Christ. The noun ἐπιθυμία can be a morally neutral "craving" (1 Thess 2:17; Rev 18:14) or a "desire" for noble things (Lk 22:15; Phil 1:23), but overwhelmingly in the NT it refers to a "passion" for something forbidden, a base "desire"[19] that needs to be overcome by a higher, spiritual force (1 Pet 1:14–15). The genitive τῆς σαρκός, "of the flesh," confirms this; "flesh" here refers not to the body as a morally neutral component of man's makeup (as in 2:11; 6:5, 12), but to that corrupt nature which presses him toward sin (Rom 7:5, 14, 18). The genitive is subjective, "the flesh that has passions," not objective, "passions for flesh." "Flesh" thus refers to body and soul together, insofar as they are unregenerate.[20] "Passions of the flesh"[21] does not necessarily refer to sexual sins—though that is often the implication of ἐπιθυμία, "passion" (Col 3:5)—but is equivalent to "covetousness" (Rom 7:8; Ninth/Tenth Commandments), which is the launching pad for all sin (James 1:14–15).

The flesh of Christ, by contrast, is the medium for redeeming and rehabilitating our sinful flesh (Eph 2:14; 5:29–31); to be baptismally clothed with his flesh smothers the passions of our flesh (Rom 13:14; Gal 5:24). By appealing to a universal, sinful human failing—fleshly passions—Paul draws Jews under the same lawful condemnation as Gentiles and prepares them for the same solution in Christ.

ποιοῦντες τὰ θελήματα τῆς σαρκὸς καὶ τῶν διανοιῶν—This restatement of the controlling power at work in men before their incorporation into Christ confirms our interpretation of the preceding words. The participle ποιοῦντες, "doing," expresses the manner of conduct, supplementing the main verb ἀνεστράφημεν, "we conducted

---

[18] The word with this meaning occurs also in 2 Cor 1:12; 1 Tim 3:15; Heb 10:33; 13:18; 1 Pet 1:17; 2 Pet 2:18.

[19] Particularly in Stoic thinking, ἐπιθυμία was a lower instinct of the flesh that needed to be controlled or eliminated by reason. The NT accords reason (which is equally fallen) no such ability; only the Holy Spirit can overcome ἐπιθυμία.

[20] Luther: "Paul calls everything 'flesh' that is born of the flesh—the whole man, with body and soul, mind and senses—because everything about him longs for the flesh. ... Paul calls heresy and hatred 'works of the flesh' [Gal 5:19–21]. And in Romans 8[:3] he says that 'the law is weakened by the flesh'; yet this is said not of unchastity, but of all sins, and above all of unbelief, which is the most spiritual of all vices" ("Preface to Romans" [1522/1546], AE 35:371–72).

[21] The phrase "passion(s) of the flesh" occurs also in Gal 5:16; 2 Pet 2:18; 1 Jn 2:16; cf. Rom 13:14.

ourselves." "Flesh" (σαρκός in the preceding textual note) is no worse (asceticism) or better (hedonism) than διάνοια, "mind/thought"; both share the same "passions" (ἐπιθυμίαις) or "desires" (θελήματα) that are contrary to the mind of Christ. The genitives are again subjective: "flesh" and "mind/thoughts" drive the "desires." The plural of διάνοια occurs only here in the NT and should probably be translated as "thoughts" (cf. 2 Macc 2:2; Sirach 3:24);[22] it is comprehensive in attributing evil to all our thoughts. Again Paul attributes to Jews a sinful faculty that is characteristic of Gentiles (who are "darkened in their mind/understanding," Eph 4:18; cf. Col 1:21). θέλημα in Ephesians (and the rest of the NT) normally refers to God's "plan and will" (see the third textual note on 1:1 and the fifth textual note on 1:5). Its application to the will of the flesh is rare (Jn 1:13; 1 Cor 7:37; cf. Lk 23:25), but clear in meaning in the context here.

καὶ ἤμεθα τέκνα φύσει ὀργῆς—"Children of wrath" stands in parallel to "the sons of disobedience" (2:2), though the genitive is subtly different. Rather than expressing an inherited characteristic ("disobedience"), ὀργῆς, "of wrath," describes what is coming to the "children." They are "destined to receive [God's] wrath."[23] The noun φύσις, "nature," refers to what something is in its natural condition, for humans in this age from conception and birth. Only here in the NT does the context suggest that φύσις refers to the "sinful nature" inherited from Adam; thus, φύσει, "by nature," expresses the doctrine of original sin, or "sin of origin."[24] The metaphor of "children" is thereby pressed farther to explain that each generation is like the previous one because they share the same Adamic flesh, a common spiritual DNA. This early part of Ephesians continues to share the thought-world of Rom 5:12–21. If it might perhaps be objected that *Gentiles* are sinful because of their environment, Paul, by pointing to their fleshly inheritance, allows *Jews* no room to escape: they are conceived and born sinful because their parents were.[25] The only remedy is the creation of a new, godly nature (2 Pet 1:4), brought about by a new birth.

ὡς καὶ οἱ λοιποί—The expression οἱ λοιποί, "the rest," is common enough for "other people," but occasionally, as here, has the connotation of "the unbelieving masses" (Lk 18:11; 1 Thess 4:13; 5:6). With this phrase Paul levels the playing field for Jews and Gentiles, who stand equally under God's condemnation (apart from Christ). This prepares for uniting them with one great "us" (2:5) as the object of God's saving power.

---

[22] Contra BDAG, s.v. διάνοια, 5.

[23] See Ezek 20:21; Sirach 47:20; Baruch 4:25; Rom 1:18; Col 3:6; cf. Jn 17:12; 2 Thess 2:3; 2 Pet 2:14.

[24] "We speak of 'nature' in two ways. When we are speaking strictly of nature itself we mean the nature in which humanity was originally created—after God's own image and without fault. The other way we speak of nature refers to that fallen sin nature, in which we are self-deceived and subject to the flesh as the penalty for our condemnation" (Augustine, *On Nature and Grace*, 81, ACCS 8:130).

[25] By contrast, the Stoics taught that living by nature was true living. Some Jewish writers had asserted that only Gentiles are by nature under God's judgment (Wis Sol 13:1–14:31), while the giving of the Torah preserved Jews from the degeneration of their nature (Josephus, *Antiquities*, 4:193). Cf. Helmut Köster, "φύσις κτλ.," *TDNT* 9:274–75.

2:4 ὁ δὲ θεὸς πλούσιος ὢν ἐν ἐλέει—To sinners oppressed by the power of the devil and his forces, including the flesh and its desires, "but God!" sounds forth like a trumpet call in battle. This nominative (ὁ θεός) is the long-awaited subject of the complex, inverted sentence that began with its first direct object in 2:1 (see the first textual note on 2:1 and "Structure and Rhetoric" in the commentary). The noun ἔλεος, "mercy," is a kindness or concern expressed for someone in need; with God it is a defining characteristic and is related to his covenant promises. In the LXX ἔλεος commonly translates חֶסֶד, "loving-kindness, faithful graciousness." This is the covenant faithfulness expressed in God's very name: he is "YHWH, YHWH, a God merciful and gracious [חַנּוּן; LXX: ἐλεήμων, 'merciful'], slow to anger, and abounding in steadfast love [רַב־חֶסֶד; LXX: πολυέλεος, 'very merciful'] and faithfulness" (Ex 34:6).[26] The characterization of God as "rich [πλούσιος] in mercy" brings the same gracious answer to mankind's predicament that Paul previously offered in Romans: "for God locked all [Jew and Gentile, Rom 11:25, 30–31] into disobedience that he might have mercy [ἐλεήσῃ] upon all" (Rom 11:32). As there is nothing in us deserving new life (Eph 2:8b), God's mercy is its only cause (cf. Titus 3:5; 1 Pet 1:3, both referring to God's action in Baptism). The application of his mercy to Jews overturns their rebellion (Hos 1:7), and its application to Gentiles incorporates them into the people of God (1 Pet 2:10). The richness of God's mercy ensures that it overflows beyond the overwhelming tide of mankind's sinfulness and coincides with the Ephesian theme of God's abundance (see the fifth textual note on 1:7 and the fourth textual note on 1:18).

διὰ τὴν πολλὴν ἀγάπην αὐτοῦ ἣν ἠγάπησεν ἡμᾶς—As God in "mercy" is "rich," so his "love" (ἀγάπην) is "great" (πολλήν). Cf. 1 Pet 1:3 (τὸ πολὺ αὐτοῦ ἔλεος, "his great mercy"). As love alone caused God to elect and redeem Israel (Deut 7:7–8), so love was the sole motivating cause of electing his children in Christ (Eph 1:4c–5) to be like his Son, the Beloved (1:6). Here the prepositional phrase with διά, "because," gives the cause for the action of the main verbs in 2:5–6, beginning with συνεζωοποίησεν, "he made alive together with." The combination of the verb ἀγαπάω ("to love") with its cognate noun ἀγάπη ("love") in the accusative adds emphasis by giving a place for the qualifying adjective πολύς ("great"): "he loved with a great love."[27]

The uniqueness of *"agape* love" has (in the opinion of the present writer) been much overdrawn. The English word "love" is not so terribly inadequate. The freight of ἀγάπη is found not in Greek lexicons but in its NT contextual usage.[28] It is a quality in God neither motivated by the loveableness of its object ("dead" men! 2:1, 5), nor

---

[26] See also Num 14:18; Neh 9:17; Pss 86:15; 103:8; 145:8; Joel 2:13; Jonah 4:2.

[27] BDF, § 153. This is a Semitism not entirely without Greek pedigree. Cf. Mt 2:10; Jn 17:26. Its apparent foreignness, however, may account for the substitution of ἠλέησεν in 𝔓⁴⁶ b d; Ambst, which (together with the omission of αὐτοῦ) results in "God ... *had mercy* on us because of his great love." The use of a cognate *dative* (e.g., ἐπιθυμίᾳ ἐπεθύμησα, Lk 22:15), by contrast, is distinctly Semitic, representing the Hebrew infinitive absolute (Moule, *Idiom Book*, 177–78).

[28] Cf. Donald Carson's discussion of the overwrought distinction between ἀγαπάω and φιλέω in much interpretation of John 21, "Simon, do you *love* me?" in *Exegetical Fallacies* (2d ed.; Grand Rapids: Baker, 1996), 51–53.

evidencing a mere weakness or pity in him. Love is of God's very essence (1 Jn 4:16), ever leading him to love those whom he created with his hands and the breath of his mouth. God's love was manifested in Christ, God taking on the form of the ones he made: "Love caused Your incarnation; Love brought You down to me" (Paul Gerhardt, *LSB* 334:4). No better definition could be given than Paul's second combination of the verb and the noun (ἀγαπάω and ἀγάπη): "walk in *love*, just as also Christ *loved* us and gave himself up for us as an offering and sacrifice to God with a pleasing fragrance" (5:2). This is the self-sacrificial love of the heavenly Bridegroom for his bride, the church (5:25, 28, 33), the love of the Father for his Son, conveyed by the Son to us (Jn 15:9).

2:5 καὶ ὄντας ἡμᾶς νεκροὺς τοῖς παραπτώμασιν—In the progressively inclusive movement of this pericope, Paul has referred to Gentile Christians as καὶ ὑμᾶς, "and *you*" (2:1), to Jewish Christians as καὶ ἡμεῖς πάντες, "also *we* all" (2:3), and now draws the groups together with καὶ ... ἡμᾶς, "even *us*" (2:5). This inclusive pronoun, encompassing the previous two direct objects, remains the direct object of the saving verbs through to the end of 2:6.[29] On the interpretation of "dead in trespasses," see the first textual note on 2:1, which has the identical phrase (νεκροὺς τοῖς παραπτώμασιν). The omission here of καὶ ταῖς ἁμαρτίαις, "and sins" (2:1), is not significant and is likely an abbreviation for rhetorical purposes. The participle is temporal and emphasizes our complete passivity in salvation: "*when* we were [still] dead," God made us alive.

συνεζωοποίησεν τῷ Χριστῷ—Here Paul introduces the first of three compound verbs beginning συν-, "together, with": συνεζωοποίησεν, "he made alive together with"; συνήγειρεν, "he raised together with"; and συνεκάθισεν, "he seated together with." Taken together with 2:19, 21, 22; 3:6; 4:3, 16; 5:7, 11, this is the densest concentration of such compounds in the NT. The prepositional prefix συν-, "together, with," points to τῷ Χριστῷ: God acts upon us "with Christ."[30] Yet there remains more than just a hint of "with one another"[31]—if God included all of us in Christ, then he also united us *with one another* (1 Cor 15:22).[32] This thought is not yet made explicit, but the foundation is laid for Paul's later arguments (Eph 3:6). These shared acts of salvation form part of Paul's appeal to unity. Most important is to be with Christ, but we are not there alone.

The baptismal[33] referent of συνεζωοποίησεν, "he made alive together with," is made explicit in the Colossian parallel (Col 2:13):

---

[29] It is possible to take καὶ ὑμᾶς ... καὶ ... ἡμᾶς, "and you ... even us" (2:1, 5), as a compound object, "both you [Gentiles] and us [Jews]," but the interruption of the syntax caused by the introduction of the subject with ὁ δὲ θεός, "but God," in 2:4, makes this improbable.

[30] This is explicit in Col 2:13, where the prefix σύν, "with," from the compound verb is repeated before "him [Christ]": συνεζωοποίησεν ὑμᾶς <u>σὺν αὐτῷ</u>, "he made you alive together with him"; cf. Rom 6:8; 8:17; 2 Cor 4:14; Col 3:4; 1 Thess 4:14; 5:10.

[31] Cf. 1 Cor 5:11; 2 Cor 7:3; Phil 2:25.

[32] The textual variant that inserts ἐν, "in," before τῷ Χριστῷ (𝔓⁴⁶ B 33 ar (g) vg^cl; MVict Ambst Chr) would make this meaning more obvious: "God made you alive together with [one another] in Christ." But this is likely just the accidental repetition of the final letters of συνεζωοποίησεν or a harmonization with ἐν Χριστῷ Ἰησοῦ in 2:6.

[33] "[The σύν-] means the 'with one another' [*Miteinander*] of Jews and Greeks, who according to 2:15–16 were made in the crucified body of Christ into one new man. What happened

In him you were also circumcised with a circumcision not done with [human] hands in the putting off of the fleshly body in the circumcision of Christ, since you were buried with him [συνταφέντες] in Baptism, in which you were also raised to life with [συνηγέρθητε] [him] through faith in the working of the God who raised him from the dead; and you, when you were dead in trespasses and the uncircumcision of your flesh, *he made you alive together with* [συνεζωοποίησεν] him, having forgiven us all [our] trespasses. (Col 2:11–13)

The triply compound verb συζωοποιέω (σύν + ζωός + ποιέω), "make alive *together with*," occurs only in these two passages (Eph 2:5; Col 2:13) and in later Christian literature dependent on them. The simpler compound form ζωοποιέω (ζωός + ποιέω), when it has the meaning "to make alive" (as opposed to preserving life, Judg 21:14), is the distinctive work of God[34] and his Spirit, "the Lord and giver of life" (Nicene Creed: τὸ κύριον καὶ ζωοποιόν, literally, "the Lord and the one who makes alive").[35] This "making alive," which takes place spiritually now in anticipation of the resurrection of the flesh on the Last Day, should not be understood as merely figurative or as any less real. In overcoming spiritual death (cf. Eph 2:1), it is the greater resurrection (Jn 5:24; Rev 2:11; 20:6).

χάριτί ἐστε σεσωσμένοι—See the first textual note on 2:8, where Paul unfolds the meaning of this key clause, "by grace you have been saved." If our analysis of the chiastic structure of the pericope is correct (see "Structure and Rhetoric" in the commentary), this forms the exact midpoint, an emphatic position. Set apart by dashes in the NA[27] text and in our translation, the phrase appears to be a doxological interjection (not a parenthesis) spurred by the remarkable proclamation that God has raised us from the dead with Christ. (As such it *might* be a preexisting liturgical acclamation quoted by Paul, especially since it abruptly shifts the person from "us" to "you.") What could be more "by grace" than resurrection from the dead? And who could be more in need of rescue than those under control of the devil, the world, and the sinful flesh? From all this you have been saved, Paul cries!

The textual variant that inserts οὗ before χάριτι makes the grace *Christ's*: "Christ, by *whose* grace you have been saved." Without this relative pronoun, one assumes it is the grace of God the Father, the one "rich in mercy" (2:4). The inclusion of so many versions and fathers in the list of witnesses attesting οὗ (D* F G ar b vg[cl] sy[p]; MVict Ambst Aug) suggests that an interpretative expansion has crept back into the Greek text. While the omission of the pronoun (NA[27] text) makes the most sense in context, there can be no theological objection to thinking of Christ's grace.

2:6 καὶ συνήγειρεν—Aside from commonplace uses like "wake from sleep" and "lift up," in the NT the simple verb ἐγείρω most frequently means "to raise from the dead."[36]

---

potentially there on the cross has actually occurred now through Baptism" (Schlier, *Epheser*, 109).

[34] See ζωοποιέω in LXX 4 Kgdms 5:7 (MT/ET 2 Ki 5:7); Neh 9:6; Ps 70:20 (MT/ET 71:20); and in Jn 5:21; Rom 4:17; 8:11; 1 Cor 15:22, 36, 45.

[35] See Jn 6:63; Rom 8:11; 2 Cor 3:6; 1 Pet 3:18.

[36] E.g., 1 Corinthians 15 passim; Eph 1:20; 5:14.

The compound form συνήγειρεν, "he raised together with," could, therefore, be a virtual synonym of συνεζωοποίησεν, "he made alive together with" (2:5), thus referring to resurrection from the dead (as in Col 2:12). On the other hand, the sequence of verbs and the clause that follows suggests "lift up" to heaven (ascension), as is implied in Col 3:1: "if then you have been *raised with* [συνηγέρθητε] Christ, seek the things that are above, where Christ is, seated at the right hand of God." The two uses in Colossians (2:12; 3:1) in such close proximity suggest that for Paul συνεγείρω includes both ideas: "God *raised* and *lifted* us *up* together with and in Christ." συνεγείρω, "to raise up with," is thus subtly distinguished from the initial act of making alive.[37]

καὶ συνεκάθισεν—The rare compound verb συγκαθίζω can simply mean "to sit down together" (intransitive), like Peter and company around the fire (Lk 22:55; 1 Esdras 9:6) or for a meal (Jer 16:8). The causative sense "to *make* sit together" appears only here in the Greek Bible. But the concept is expressed elsewhere with the simple verb καθίζω: "the one who conquers—I will cause him to sit with me [καθίσαι μετ᾽ ἐμοῦ] on my throne, as I also conquered and sat down [ἐκάθισα] with [μετά] my Father on his throne" (Rev 3:21). Sitting together with Christ (on his throne) is connected with victory over death; it is an act of glorification. As Paul applies to Christians what happened to Christ, he (deliberately?) omits the most focused expression of Christ's divine authority: "at his [the Father's] right hand" (said of Christ in Eph 1:20). While Christ promises to his apostles that they will sit on twelve thrones and judge Israel (Mt 19:28), there is no suggestion here that all of us are seated with Christ in order to participate actively in his acts of governing the cosmos or the church. Those who "reign with him [βασιλεύσουσιν μετ᾽ αὐτοῦ]" (Rev 20:6b) do so by sharing in the spoils of his triumph; they reign not over the cosmos but over death, for "over these the second death has no authority" (Rev 20:6a).

ἐν τοῖς ἐπουρανίοις ἐν Χριστῷ Ἰησοῦ—See the fourth textual note on 1:3 (and the fourth textual note on 1:20) for the distinctive Ephesian phrase "in the heavenlies." The exaltation granted to the resurrected Christ is shared with all those who are baptized into him. The assertion that believers are already located in heaven is quite stunning but finds its meaning in the saints' incorporation into Christ. While "in the heavenly places" is a *location*, it is not a place where Christ is confined as if to exclude him from the earth; the location symbolizes the full extent of his exalted, heavenly *power*, which transcends the universe. See "Christ's Victorious Ascension to God's Right Hand (1:20–23)" in the commentary on 1:15–23.

So also the Christian now is not transferred to heaven as if removed from earth (physically), but granted a proleptic share in heavenly blessings (1:3).[38] These do not belong to believers by nature, but are theirs insofar as they remain "in Christ" (see the

---

[37] Thus, for example, the Apostles' Creed first confesses Christ's descent into hell and then his resurrection from the dead (ἀναστάντα ἐκ τῶν νεκρῶν) on the third day, whereas Peter writes: "he was made alive by the Spirit [ζωοποιηθεὶς δὲ πνεύματι], in which he went and proclaimed to the spirits in prison" (1 Pet 3:18–19). The full sequence is this: made alive, descended to hell, rose from the dead.

[38] Cf. Phil 3:20: "our citizenship is in heaven"; Heb 12:23: "enrolled in heaven."

fifth textual note on 1:3). "With Christ" or "in Christ" is expressed four times in the Gospel part of this unit (2:4–10). Because of our incorporation into Christ through Baptism, where he goes, we go.[39] And when he comes again in victory, his victory will be ours (cf. 2 Tim 4:18), as Paul's next clause shows (Eph 2:7). The present section of Ephesians expresses the paradoxical nature of Christian existence in both spatial and temporal terms: just as the baptized live simultaneously in the present *age* and the age to come, so they live simultaneously in this *world* and in the one above.

2:7 ἵνα ἐνδείξηται ἐν τοῖς αἰῶσιν τοῖς ἐπερχομένοις—The verb ἐνδείκνυμι, "to show," can have a juridical sense, "to prove, give evidence."[40] The future, eschatological consummation of these proleptic gifts of life will testify to the Lord's grace—vindicating God and his promises. But the demonstration is chiefly for our benefit. Although Paul has expressed our salvation in the perfect tense (σεσῳσμένοι, "have been saved," 2:5, 8; a completed event with ongoing consequences), there is always more. The fullness of salvation is yet to come in the age inaugurated by Christ's reappearance on the Last Day. Although "the coming ages" (plural) is a unique expression in the NT, the phrase should not be distinguished from similar singular phrases that mean "the age to come" (e.g., Mk 10:30; Lk 18:30; Heb 6:5; see the third textual note on 1:21).[41] This is not a reference to hostile spiritual forces ("Aeons") or hostile earthly forces in subsequent eras of earthly history.[42] Future "ages" (plural) are commonly expressed in doxological eternity formulae (e.g., Rom 1:25: "forever"); the word is a sort of plural of majesty, emphasizing the ongoing succession of time in eternity. It is in that heavenly era that all hidden things will be revealed (Col 3:3–4), faith giving way to sight as the saints gather around the glorious, visible presence of Christ on the throne of the Almighty.

τὸ ὑπερβάλλον πλοῦτος τῆς χάριτος αὐτοῦ—See the fifth textual note on 1:7 and the fourth textual note on 1:18.

ἐν χρηστότητι ἐφ᾽ ἡμᾶς—In the LXX χρηστότης, "kindness," sometimes translates טוֹב, the "goodness" of God, particularly in working salvation (e.g., LXX Pss 24:7 [MT/ET 25:7]; 30:20 [MT 31:20; ET 31:19]). Frequently in the NT it is a reflected quality in God's children, worked by the Holy Spirit.[43] But here it is God's saving goodness, voiced in succession to "mercy" (Eph 2:4) and "grace" (2:5, 7) in overwhelming proclamation of God's generosity toward his fallen creatures (cf. Titus 3:4–5, where it is placed in parallel to φιλανθρωπία, "love for man").

---

[39] See "Die Taufe als Weg zum Leben und himmlischen Wohnen mit Christus" in Schnackenburg, " 'Er hat uns mitauferweckt': Zur Tauflehre des Epheserbriefes," 167–74.

[40] Rom 2:15; 9:17, 22; 2 Cor 8:24; 1 Tim 1:16. See Barth, *Ephesians*, 1:238–42.

[41] Hermann Sasse, "αἰών," *TDNT* 1:206–7; Lincoln, *Ephesians*, 110.

[42] Contra Schlier, *Epheser*, 112–13; Barth, *Ephesians*, 1:223: "God will prove ... his grace ... to the Ciceros and Neros of tomorrow." To these forces God demonstrates his wrath, not his grace. In any case, this would require εἰς or a simple dative, not ἐν (ἐν τοῖς αἰῶσιν); cf. Eph 3:9–10; Col 1:26.

[43] 2 Cor 6:6; Gal 5:22; Col 3:12.

ἐν Χριστῷ Ἰησοῦ—See the fifth textual note on 1:3. This is the third repetition of "with Christ" or "in Christ" (2:5, 6, 7) in the second part of this pericope, and the Greek here (as in 2:6) is repeated verbatim in 2:10 ("in Christ Jesus").

2:8 τῇ γὰρ χάριτί ἐστε σεσῳσμένοι—The definite article τῇ, which seems to distinguish this statement from its earlier anarthrous occurrence (2:5), may simply be included because of the postpositive conjunction γάρ, "for" (which cannot stand first in the sentence). With or without an expressed article, χάρις, "grace," is a definite noun. The article τῇ is also resumptive: *the* grace previously mentioned and described in 2:4–7, "by *this* grace you have been saved."[44] On χάρις, see the first textual note on 1:2 and the second textual note on 1:6. Its position at the beginning of this new sentence is emphatic. The dative χάριτι, "*by* grace," is of means or instrument, stressing God's gracious, favorable attitude toward us in Christ as the efficient cause of salvation.

The participle σεσῳσμένοι, "having been saved," is perfect tense, denoting a past action with present consequences. The use of a past tense verb meaning "saved" is unusual for Paul. He typically distinguishes "justification" (δικαιόω, δικαιοσύνη) as a present act through the means of grace from "salvation" (σῴζω, σωτηρία) as a *future* deliverance from God's wrath on the Day of Judgment.[45] But sometimes he expresses the great mystery that salvation has *already* occurred for us, even if we do not yet see it, for "in hope we *were* saved" (ἐσώθημεν, aorist tense, Rom 8:24).[46] It is brought forward as a present and ongoing reality: "behold, *now* is the favorable time; behold, *now* is the day of salvation" (2 Cor 6:2).[47] This is the perspective expressed in the current verse, emphasized by the perfect passive participle σεσῳσμένοι: "you are already now in the state of having been saved." It is a state akin to (and including) the Ephesians' present resurrection and ascension (2:5–6): it is experienced now proleptically and in part, with the fullness to be confirmed without remainder at the coming of our Lord Jesus Christ. Paul's emphasis on the *present* reality of salvation may be explained by the Ephesian context of battle with hostile spiritual forces (cf. 6:10–17): as *Christ* has already risen above them in triumph (1:20–23), so also he has raised *us* above them in triumph (2:5–8); therefore we need not fear them, even in this present life.[48]

---

[44] Zerwick, *Biblical Greek*, § 176, may be overinterpreting the difference:

As we have said, the absence of the article draws attention to the nature or quality as distinct from the individual. ... Note for example how great a difference of meaning there is between χάρις with the article and the same noun without the article in Eph 2,8 and 5. In verse 8 ... the apostle understands by ἡ χάρις the entire work of redemption, that concrete historical fact, which inasmuch as it is due to the mercy and liberality of God is called χάρις; while in verse 5 ... attention is called to the manner of our redemption as being salvation by divine grace and not by our works.

[45] Rom 3:24; 5:9; 10:9–10, 13; 13:11; Phil 2:12; 1 Thess 5:9; cf. Joel 3:5 (ET 2:32); Mt 10:22; Heb 9:28; 1 Pet 1:5.

[46] Cf. Rom 11:11; 2 Tim 1:9; Titus 2:11; 3:5.

[47] Cf. Lk 4:21; 19:9; Acts 2:47; 1 Cor 1:18; 15:2; 2 Cor 2:15.

[48] Arnold, *Power and Magic*, 147: "Salvation is thus described as deliverance from the power and influence of the cosmic 'powers.'"

διὰ πίστεως—There is nothing in context to suggest that "through faith" might be the "faithfulness" of Christ;[49] it is *fides qua creditur*, subjective faith. The preposition διά subtly distinguishes the role of the Christian's faith from God's grace. While grace is the efficient cause, faith is merely the receiving instrument of the gift of salvation. Although Paul can vary his use of prepositions,[50] it is important to maintain this distinction: "*by* grace" (2:5, 8), "*through* faith" (2:8). The two are inseparable; man's faith (not works) is the necessary correlative of God's grace: διὰ τοῦτο ἐκ πίστεως, ἵνα κατὰ χάριν, "for this reason it is from faith, that it might be by grace" (Rom 4:16). The threefold definition of justification given in the Augsburg Confession provides normative language rooted in Ephesians 2 and Romans 3–5:

> Likewise, they [Lutherans] teach that men are not able to be justified before God by their own strengths, merits, or works, but are justified freely [*gratis*, "by grace"], on account of Christ [*propter Christum*], through faith [*per fidem*], when they believe that they are received into grace and their sins are forgiven on account of Christ, who made satisfaction for our sins by his death. (AC 4 [my translation])

Like "grace," "faith" is the very opposite of works (Rom 4:4–5). "Faith justifies and saves, not on the ground that it is a work in itself worthy, but only because it receives the promised mercy" (Ap 4:56 [*Triglotta*, 137]). Faith excludes the works of man, but embraces the works of God. Baptism does not stand in opposition to faith, but is the powerful working of God by which he gives new life as a gift to be received through faith (Col 2:12).[51] In this sense we may also understand the words of our Lord to the woman whose sins he had just forgiven, "your faith *has saved* you" (σέσωκεν, perfect tense, Lk 7:50); by faith she is already in a saved condition, but the Lord has done the saving.

καὶ τοῦτο οὐκ ἐξ ὑμῶν—"And this is not from yourselves": some have referred the neuter pronoun τοῦτο, "this," to faith. Chrysostom, for example: "Even faith, he says, is not from us. For if the Lord had not come, if he had not called us, how should we have been able to believe? *For how*, he says, *shall they believe if they have not heard?* [Rom 10:14.] So even the act of faith is not self-initiated. It is, he says, *the gift of God*"

---

49 Contra Barth, *Ephesians*, 1:224–25, who admittedly also includes the faith of the saints. Eph 1:13, 15; 3:17; 6:23 clearly refer to subjective faith. Eph 3:12 could possibly refer to Christ's faithfulness, but it is unlikely. Eph 4:5 and 4:13 probably mean objective faith, *fides quae creditur*, the body of Christian doctrine, "the faith." Eph 6:16 is ambiguous as to whether the faith is subjective or objective.

50 In Paul, justification is most often ἐκ πίστεως, literally, "*from* faith" (e.g., Rom 5:1). Gal 3:26, which always looms in the background of Ephesians, has διὰ τῆς πίστεως, "*through* faith." But διὰ πίστεως ("through faith") is synonymous with ἐκ πίστεως ("from faith") in Gal 2:16 and Rom 3:25–26, 30, although the latter occurrences might be divided into our faith and Christ's faithfulness. In Eph 3:12, 17 we have διὰ τῆς πίστεως, "*through* faith." Once Paul places ἐπὶ τῇ πίστει, "on the basis of faith," in parallel to διὰ πίστεως, "through faith" (Phil 3:9). We also have κατὰ (τὴν) πίστιν, "according to faith" (Mt 9:29; Heb 11:7), and ἐπὶ τῇ πίστει, "on the basis of faith" (Acts 3:16).

51 See Luther, LC 4:35, quoted in the first textual note on 2:9.

[Eph 2:8].[52] Doubtless correct theologically, this is grammatically unlikely since πίστις is feminine. The neuter τοῦτο must refer to the immediately preceding clause, "for by grace you have been saved through faith" (2:8a); faith, of course, is included.[53] This way of salvation does not proceed from any cause, act, or worthiness in man, who is the object of salvation. After all, what does a "dead" man (2:1, 5) have to contribute to his own rescue or resuscitation?

θεοῦ τὸ δῶρον—For emphasis θεοῦ is placed first: literally, "*of God* is the gift." (In contrast, in the preceding clause ὑμῶν, "yourselves," was placed last.) The connection of "grace" with the language of "gift" (here δῶρον)[54] is a frequent and intimate pairing in the NT. For example, in Rom 3:24, "being justified freely [δωρεάν, 'by way of gift'] by means of his grace [τῇ αὐτοῦ χάριτι] through the redemption that is in Christ Jesus" is set in a pericope in which "faith" is hammered home eight times (Rom 3:21–31). The present pericope is encapsulated well in the theme verse of Romans 5: "for if by the trespass of the one man all died, how much more did the grace of God and the gift in/by the grace [ἡ δωρεὰ ἐν χάριτι] of the one man Jesus Christ overflow to the many" (Rom 5:15).

2:9   οὐκ ἐξ ἔργων—With "not from works," Paul restates and explains what he means by οὐκ ἐξ ὑμῶν, "not from yourselves" (2:8). He unequivocally opposes grace and works: "if by grace, no longer from works, since grace would then no longer be grace" (Rom 11:6).[55] Some proponents of the so-called New Perspective on Paul have interpreted ἔργων νόμου, "works of the Law" (e.g., Gal 2:16), restrictively as only those ceremonial requirements that distinguished Jews from Gentiles (Sabbath, circumcision, etc.) and by which Jews pridefully exalted themselves (Rom 2:17) and Judaizers oppressed the consciences of Gentiles (Gal 2:14; Col 2:11, 16–17).[56] Whether ἔργων νόμου refers only to these distinguishing marks is highly debatable.[57] In the absence of νόμος, "Law," in our present verse, it would certainly be inappropriate to restrict Paul's meaning here. In fact, the present verse presents a major obstacle to the view that Paul is opposed only to works of the Law that set apart Jews from Gentiles. We might

---

[52] Chrysostom, *Homilies on Ephesians*, 2:8, ACCS 8:134. Schlier, *Epheser*, 115, n. 1, cites in addition Theodoret, Augustine, Prosper, Beza, Estius, Bengel, Westcott, and Staab.

[53] Cf. Phil 1:28. BDF, § 290 (5), suggests that καὶ τοῦτο is adverbial: "and at that."

[54] While δῶρον, "gift," is common in the Synoptic Gospels (e.g., Mt 2:11; Lk 21:1) and Hebrews (e.g., Heb 5:1; 11:4), remarkably, this is its only occurrence in Paul's writings. However, cognates appear in similar Pauline contexts, such as δωρεάν, "freely" (e.g., Rom 3:24), which is an adverbial accusative of δωρεά, "gift" (Rom 5:15, 17; 2 Cor 9:15; Eph 3:7; 4:7), as well as δώρημα, "gift" (Rom 5:16), and δίδωμι, "to give" (e.g., 1 Cor 1:4; Eph 4:7); see also χάρισμα, "gracious gift" (e.g., Rom 5:15–16).

[55] Cf. Rom 3:27; 9:16; 10:3; Phil 3:9; 2 Tim 1:9.

[56] This view is most closely associated with James D. G. Dunn. The reader unfamiliar with the New Perspective is best served by Stephen Westerholm, *Perspectives Old and New on Paul: The "Lutheran" Paul and His Critics* (Grand Rapids: Eerdmans, 2004).

[57] For a scholarly critique upholding the traditional Lutheran view that Paul teaches salvation by grace alone apart from *any* kind of human works (not just ceremonial Jewish identity markers), see " 'Works of the Law' " in Das, *Galatians*, 245–49, and the rest of his commentary on Gal 2:16 on pages 241–57.

paraphrase with "not from any sort of works"—though, of course, the works God does are not excluded (cf. 2:10)![58]

ἵνα μή τις καυχήσηται—Just as "works" are excluded from salvation if they are "of men" but included if they are "of God" (see the previous textual note), so also the moral quality of καυχάομαι, "to boast, take pride in," depends on "in whom" one boasts. To boast "in God" (Rom 5:11), "in the hope of the glory of God" (Rom 5:2), "in Christ Jesus" (Phil 3:3), and "in the cross" (Gal 6:14) is to place confidence where it belongs. To boast "in sufferings" (Rom 5:3) or "in my weaknesses" (2 Cor 12:9) is an ironical way of boasting in Christ instead of one's own strength. For to boast in oneself or one's works, "in men" (1 Cor 3:21), "in your flesh" (Gal 6:13), or simply "to boast" (1 Cor 1:29) is contrary to the passive way of salvation; it is the opposite of "grace" (Eph 2:5, 7–8) and "gift" (Rom 4:2–4), and must be excluded (Rom 3:27). "What do you have that you did not receive? But if you received it, why do you boast as if you did not receive it?" (1 Cor 4:7). Because of the significant role of honor/shame in Greco-Roman culture, boasting pops up frequently in Paul's verbal interaction with that culture. But he redirects its focus: "let the one who boasts, boast in the Lord" (1 Cor 1:31). God excludes all contributing human works from salvation so that our trust would be placed in the only One who is completely reliable and worthy of glory.

2:10 αὐτοῦ γάρ ἐσμεν ποίημα—Here Paul inverts the categorical statement "not from works" (2:9) as if to say, "well, not from *our* works." He stresses the contrast by placing the pronoun αὐτοῦ, "his [God's]," in emphatic first position. In the LXX ποίημα may refer to a "deed" done by men (Ecclesiastes passim), either good (1 Sam 19:4) or bad (Ezra 9:13). But more frequently it is used of God's "deeds" of judgment and redemption (LXX Pss 63:10 [MT 64:10; ET 64:9]; 91:5 [MT 92:5; ET 92:4]; 142:5 [MT/ET 143:5]). God stands over against creation as the potter to the clay (ποίημα, "the thing made," Is 29:16).[59] His working makes us into something new. The noun ποίημα is derived from the verb ποιέω, "to do, make," which is certainly used of God's creation in the LXX (even *ex nihilo*, e.g., Gen 1:1, 7, 16); but ποιέω sometimes distinguishes itself from κτίζω, "to create," by an emphasis on working with a material (cf. LXX Gen 1:26–27 with ποιέω and the forming of Adam from the earth in Gen 2:7). God takes us fallen creatures and remakes us, restoring his image in us. Since nouns ending with -μα normally refer to the *result* of an action, the noun ποίημα ("what is made") is what comes from doing ποιέω ("make"). Thus, the use of the noun in Eph 2:10 is appropriate to highlight the completion of God's gracious, saving, re-creating work upon us.

---

[58] Luther notes:

> However, it is often objected, "If Baptism is itself a work, and you say that works are of no use for salvation, what becomes of faith?" To this you may answer: Yes, it is true that our works are of no use for salvation. Baptism, however, is not our work but God's (for, as was said, you must distinguish Christ's Baptism quite clearly from a bath-keeper's baptism). God's works, however, are salutary and necessary for salvation, and they do not exclude but rather demand faith, for without faith they could not be grasped. …
>
> Thus you see plainly that Baptism is not a work which we do but is a treasure which God gives us and faith grasps. (LC 4:35, 37)

[59] In secular Greek ποίημα can refer to a "poem" or work of fiction.

This is reemphasized by the subsequent *aorist* participle κτισθέντες, "created" (see the next textual note), referring back to Baptism as a causal action that took place prior to the main verb ἐσμεν, "we are." We are what we are because God made us so.[60]

κτισθέντες ἐν Χριστῷ Ἰησοῦ—With "created" (κτισθέντες), the language of new creation is now made explicit. What was dead is made alive, just as God took clay and created a man, breathing life into it (Gen 2:7). In Holy Baptism the old man is put to death and a new man is created (cf. Eph 4:22–24). This is the fourth instance of "with/in Christ" in the pericope. As all mankind were present in Adam's creation (and fall), so the new creation embraces and benefits all those who are "in Christ" (2 Cor 5:17; Gal 6:15).

ἐπὶ ἔργοις ἀγαθοῖς—The traditional translation "*for* good works" needs scrutiny. The preposition ἐπί plus the dative normally introduces the basis of an action, the opposite of the translation "for": e.g., "live *on* bread" (Mt 4:4); "*by* faith in his name" (Acts 3:16); "righteousness of God *on the basis of* faith" (Phil 3:9); "my flesh will dwell *on the basis of* hope" (Acts 2:26). Authorization "upon the name of" is related (Mt 18:5; Acts 4:18; etc.). Purpose, goal, or result can be expressed with ἐπί plus the accusative (e.g., Mt 3:7; Lk 4:43), but the expected preposition is πρός or εἰς, as in εἰς πᾶν ἔργον ἀγαθὸν ἡτοιμασμένον, "prepared *for* every good work" (2 Tim 2:21; see also πρός in Titus 3:1). If the more common meaning of ἐπί plus the dative were to be maintained here without contradicting everything Paul has just said about the role of works, it has been suggested that Paul has *Christ's* works in mind: "created in Christ Jesus *on the basis of* [Christ's] good works."[61] The contrast is then with *our* works ("not from works," 2:9). Unfortunately, there is no hint in the context that Christ's works are in mind, nor is his work of salvation ever called a "good work" in the NT (Phil 1:6 being a possible exception).[62]

It is more likely that Paul means to draw a contrast with the evil works in which we walked prior to Christ (2:1–3). BDAG cites three other instances of ἐπί plus the dative with the meaning "for [result, purpose]" (Gal 5:13; 1 Thess 4:7; 2 Tim 2:14);[63] though debatable, they confirm the possibility of this meaning. Wis of Sol 2:23 is persuasive,[64] and extrabiblical evidence is extensive.[65]

---

[60] This is not to exclude God's continual, powerful working in us, preserving us and leading us to the day of our redemption (2 Cor 4:12, 16; Phil 1:6; Eph 1:19; 3:20; 1 Thess 2:13).

[61] E.g., Jon S. Bruss, "Ephesians 2:10 and Sanctification," *Logia* 2.4 (Reformation/October 1993): 59.

[62] With a different adjective for "good," the singular καλὸν ἔργον and plural ἔργα καλά are frequent phrases that refer to Christ's "good work(s)" or the Christian's "good work(s)" in the Gospels, the Pastoral Epistles, and 1 Pet 2:12 (a total of fifteen instances in the NT). The wording ἔργα ἀγαθα ("good works") occurs only here and in Acts 9:36 and 1 Tim 2:10, undoubtedly with the same meaning and referent. The singular ἔργον ἀγαθόν ("good work") has the same meaning in 2 Cor 9:8; Col 1:10; 2 Thess 2:17. The dative plural here in Eph 2:10 strengthens the parallel to the contrasting dative plural "trespasses and sins" in 2:1.

[63] BDAG, s.v. ἐπί, 16.

[64] ὁ θεὸς ἔκτισεν τὸν ἄνθρωπον ἐπ᾽ ἀφθαρσίᾳ, "God created man *for* incorruption."

[65] Moule, *Idiom Book*, 50, connects this meaning with "movement ending in a definite spot" (e.g., Jn 4:6). BDF, § 235 (4), appeals to classical usage, as does Zerwick, *Biblical Greek*, § 129, who also cites Josephus.

If, then, we accept the traditional translation, "*for* good works," Paul's point is nevertheless *not* to identify good works as the ultimate goal of salvation by grace. In the present context his purpose is to put good works in their proper place: it is not "*from* works" (2:9) but "*for* works" (2:10).[66] Good works are not the *purpose* of salvation, but they are its *result*. The new creation worked in Christ restores the original positive function of the Law by providing a God-pleasing way for the Christian to live. The order of things is best expressed by Luther: "[First] that I may be His own and live under Him in His kingdom and [second] serve Him in everlasting righteousness, innocence, and blessedness."[67]

οἷς προητοίμασεν ὁ θεὸς, ἵνα ἐν αὐτοῖς περιπατήσωμεν—The case of οἷς, "which," is dative by attraction to its dative antecedent, ἔργοις ἀγαθοῖς ("good works"). Strictly speaking the relative pronoun should be accusative (οὕς) as the direct object of the verb προητοίμασεν: "which [works] God prepared beforehand." The compound verb προετοιμάζω, "to prepare beforehand," is rare in the NT (only here and in Rom 9:23), though the simple verb ἑτοιμάζω is common and refers frequently to the work of God in preparing eternal gifts for his children.[68] Our relationship with God is so unequivocally based on his monergism that the very good works we do are prepared by him beforehand (which coheres with the predestination language of Eph 1:4–5, 11–12). *He places us into them.* Even here we can lay no claim. This is chiefly because they are works of Christ in and through us; as we are in him, we do the good works that he does. Our good works are Christ's good works (Phil 1:6; 2:13).

That "in them we should walk" forms an *inclusio* with the opening lines of the pericope (2:1–2, with περιεπατήσατε, "you walked," in 2:2). This is how we are transformed: from dead men walking in trespasses and sins (2:1, 5) into living, newly created children of God who walk in good works. If in Baptism we have put off the old man "with his works" and "put on the new" (Col 3:9–10; cf. Eph 4:22–24), then with the new man we have received new works. This passage is thoroughly abused if it is used to *coerce* Christians into doing "good works," for the power to do them lies not in us (Rom 7:18–25; 2 Cor 3:5), and works striven for may cease to be good (Mt 25:37–40). Rather, Paul wishes us to rejoice that God is pleased to do good works in us, and he directs all praise for those works to God.

Commentary

Structure and Rhetoric

Paul's rhetorical creativity and theological energy is not exhausted by the two grand sentences that filled chapter 1. He continues with one of the most beautiful, elegant, and Gospel-rich passages in the NT. As the chiastic structure demonstrates (see below), 2:1–10 forms a neatly defined, well-balanced

---

[66] "Werke sind nicht das Woher, aber das Wozu der christlichen Existenz," "works are not the whence but the whither of Christian existence" (Schlier, *Epheser*, 117).

[67] SC 2:4 (*LSB* 323).

[68] Mt 20:23; 22:4; 25:34; Jn 14:2–3; 1 Cor 2:9; Heb 11:16.

unit. Within it, however, lie three clear sentences: 2:1–7; 2:8–9; and 2:10. The first sentence falls into two parts: our dead condition in sin (2:1–3) and God's saving work in Christ (2:4–7). The next two sentences, as indicated by the conjunction γάρ, "for, since," beginning each (2:8, 10), are explanatory of two key points made in the first sentence: saved by grace, not works (2:8–9), and transferred from walking in sins to walking in God-given good works (2:10).

The first, lengthy sentence can be quite confusing if its grammatical structure is missed. It begins with an accusative, "you" (2:1), which is not readily identified as a direct object until the main verbs are reached in 2:5–6. In between, the description of "you" (2:1a) as formerly "dead in your trespasses and sins" (2:1b) leads Paul into a lengthy digression on the nature of this spiritual death, as found among both Gentiles (2:1–2) and Jews (2:3). But these subordinate clauses do not cause any severe anacoluthon (disruption of the sentence's grammar), as the sentence resumes in 2:4 with the introduction of its grammatical subject, "God." If we were to rearrange things into a "normal" subject-verb-object order, the sentence would look like this:

Subject:	⁴ᵃGod
Verbs:	⁵ᵇmade alive together, ⁶raised together, and seated together
Objects:	¹⁻²you [Gentiles] who were dead in your trespasses and sins, ³all of us [Jews], who once conducted ourselves according to passions, ⁵ᵃus [Jews and Gentiles] who were dead in our trespasses.

This prompts the question of why Paul should choose such a convoluted sentence structure, when, from the perspective of modern English writing style at least, he might have done it much more simply. The answer lies in the broader structure that encompasses all ten verses. First, there is a basic flow of plight-solution-result that is made possible by putting the direct object first:

2:1–3 Dead in trespasses and sins
  ↓
2:4–9 Resurrection with Christ by the grace of God
  ↓
2:10 New life walking in works prepared by God

But an even stronger pattern is at work, indeed the strongest pattern in Semitic literature (and not unknown among the Greeks): the extended chiasm. The pattern is marked out by the *inclusio* (bracketing) of περιπατέω, "to walk," in 2:2 and 2:10. But beyond this framing, often noted by commentators, there is a highly sophisticated balance of content between the two parts of the pericope. The chiasm is marked out in the following paraphrase, with key terms underlined:

> A   You Gentiles were dead <u>in sins,</u> <u>walking</u> according to the age of this world,
> > B   following the evil spirit who is at <u>work</u> in the disobedient sons,
> > > C   among whom also we [Jews] were, following the passions of the <u>flesh and thoughts</u>;
> > > > D   thus, we [Jews], too, <u>by nature</u> deserved God's <u>wrath</u> like the rest of mankind;
> > > > > E   but God, <u>rich</u> in mercy, because of his great love with which he loved us,
> > > > > [A] even us, who were dead <u>in sins,</u>[69]
> > > > > > F   [God] made alive <u>together</u> with <u>Christ,</u>
> > > > > > > G   —by grace you have been saved!—
> > > > > > F'   and God raised us and seated us <u>together</u> in heaven in <u>Christ,</u>
> > > > > E'   that he might show the <u>richness</u> of his grace in Christ.
> > > > D'   For <u>by grace</u> you have been <u>saved</u> through faith;
> > > C'   this is not from <u>yourselves,</u> but God's gift,
> > B'   not from your <u>works,</u> lest anyone should boast.
> A'   God has re-created us in Christ to <u>walk</u> <u>in good works.</u>

What is the significance of the chiasm? First, there is an in-out movement by which the depths of man's plight are introduced step-by-step and then undone step-by-step by God's actions. For each failure, lack, or rebellious act on man's part there is a corresponding act of redemption or gift on God's part. The old walk in trespasses and sins is replaced by walking in good works. Slavery to the devil is replaced by a new creation in Christ. Desires of the sinful flesh are replaced by God's gift from outside ourselves. Our sinful nature's work is replaced by the grace of God. Wrath gives way to salvation.

Second, the chiasm highlights the unit's key theme. A chiastic structure normally functions quite differently from ordinary prose, replacing an inexorable forward movement with a spiral toward the center. The chief thing is found not at the end but in the middle. Thus, the pericope does not aim toward the good works of 2:10 as its goal, but focuses on the grace of God in its center. The chiastic structure explains the location of Paul's great interjection, "by grace you have been saved!" (2:5), which interrupts the pericope's three main verbs.[70] Clustered in the middle are the great saving actions of God that are rooted in his grace. The ancient lector was trained to find these structures in his preparation and to highlight them in his reading; the ancient listener was attuned to the emphasis placed on the center of the chiasm.[71]

---

[69] One should be suspicious of a chiastic arrangement that works out too neatly, and this one does not! This line recapitulates part of 2:1, but does not fall in quite the expected place. Paul's lengthy sentence requires him to restate the object of the verb.

[70] The three main verbs (and their objects) are "made us alive together with" in 2:5, preceding the interjection, and "raised [us] together" and "seated [us] together" in 2:6, following the interjection.

[71] See "Chiasm and *Inclusio*" in "Orality and the Interpretation of the Epistles: A Brief Introduction" in the introduction.

The chiasm highlights the pericope's division into two parts (2:1–3 and 2:4–10), which, in theological terms, correspond to the distinction between Law and Gospel. The first three verses are dominated by language of the Law. Paul reveals the forces at work to control the sinner, the unholy triumvirate of sin, death, and the devil or "the devil, the world, and our sinful nature."[72] The sinner under their control is barreling downhill toward the gaping maw of hell (Is 5:14), where Satan claims his own and God's wrath is vented. In the second part of the pericope (2:4–10), the distinctive language of the Gospel dominates: "grace" (2:5, 7, 8), "gift" (2:8), "in/with Christ" (2:5, 6, 7, 10), "faith" (2:8), re-creation ("created," 2:10), and "what he [God] has made" (2:10). Wrath is averted by rescue. It is a movement from old life to new life, brought about by the transformative power of God's paschal actions in Christ.

This pericope has been called the most succinct presentation of Paul's theology (despite the fact that it uses σῴζω, "save" [2:5, 8], to described our present condition rather than Paul's more usual verb δικαιόω, "justify"; see the first textual note on 2:8). The letter to the Ephesians has been seen as a compendium of Pauline theology; one early theorist even suggested that it was written by a student of Paul to introduce a collected edition of his epistles![73] If Ephesians were a circular letter, a catholic epistle, it would make perfect sense that Paul would begin the body of the letter with such a general statement of his Gospel.[74] Yet the circular theory does little justice to the place of this pericope in the letter as a whole, nor to the question of why Paul wrote these words to the *Ephesians* (1:1).

In the ancient practice of rhetoric, the art of persuasion, the body of a discourse began with a series of "proofs" that put forth an argument in favor of the speaker's thesis. At the end of this series, the speaker would deal with the presumed objections of the opposition, which he would proceed to refute. The introduction[75] has proposed that 2:1–4:16 consists of a series of "proofs" for the thesis that Jews and Gentiles are united baptismally in Christ, followed by "refutations" of the notion that Gentiles might still live like the unbaptized or be joined again to their false worship (4:17–6:9). Commentators divide into camps and argue fiercely whether "you" (2:1) and "we" (2:3) indicate that the Jew/Gentile question is already in view at this point in the epistle, but they are generally agreed that this is the case by 2:11. The epistle's pericopes, however, cannot be so atomized and isolated from one another. Certainly Paul does not make the distinction between Gentile and Jew explicit in 2:1–10 (though our textual notes have contended that this is implied by "you" Gentiles in 2:1 and "we" Jews in 2:3). Yet Paul is already busy assembling a coherent argument that will reach its crowning glory in the great unity hymn of 4:4–6. His first proof consists in the nature of the Gospel itself. If it is true that we all are united in

---

[72] SC 3:11 (*LSB* 324).

[73] See "Theories about 'in Ephesus' " in "Addressees" in the introduction.

[74] See "my Gospel" in Rom 2:16; 16:25; 2 Tim 2:8.

[75] See "Rhetorical Outline" in "Structure and Rhetoric" in the introduction.

sin and that we all are united by God in Christ, if we are united in death and in resurrection, then the foundation has been laid for his later conclusion that we are united also with one another. Explicitly stated or not, the thesis depends on the truth of the Gospel expressed here. This unit presents the most general proof, but also the most profound. Its very generality and foundational character explains why it has become such a beloved summary of the Christian faith, even where the original Ephesian context fades from view.[76]

Death and Life with Christ

The movement of the pericope is from death to life. The thought is prompted by consideration of Christ's exaltation (1:20–22). Christ, who was put to death for our transgressions, was vindicated by God, restored to his rightful place of honor, lifted up to the right hand of God. Because Paul had already declared that the Father "has blessed us with every blessing of the Spirit in the heavenly places in Christ" (1:3), he draws the conclusion that we who are "in Christ" have also died and risen to new life. But this deduction is qualified by the persistence of the present age, in which we have the pledge and seal, but not the acquisition of the eternal inheritance (1:13–14). During this age the eternal resurrection of the body has been fully experienced only by Christ, the firstfruits (1 Cor 15:20, 23). Until the fulfillment at the dawn of the coming age, those who are "in Christ" experience the resurrection only proleptically; they have eternal life (Jn 5:24), but it is not yet visible to the eyes or fully realized in our bodies.

The same logic underlies Paul's repeated statement that we were "dead in trespasses (and sins)" (2:1, 5). It arises not from an analysis of the human condition, as if humans were manifestly dead,[77] but is derived from the analogy of Christ. If we were to look at outward appearances, we would find the full spectrum of human morality: the selfless saint, the philanthropist, the upright and generous person, the man on the Clapham omnibus, the perpetrator of "victimless crimes," the cheat, the swindler, the child abuser, the mass murderer. But Paul allows for no spectrum. And this is more than a demand for utter perfection. It is not simply that "whoever keeps the whole Law but fails in one point has become guilty of all of it" (James 2:10). The sinner apart from Christ does not just fall short quantitatively ("nearly good enough") but also qualitatively ("completely different"). What matters is that everyone lacks that divine life (with its divine holiness and perfection), which is found in Christ. Only in him and in conformity to him can these gifts be given. So Paul looks at the Christian

---

[76] In early postapostolic days, Paul's words appear already to have become a beloved summary of the Gospel, as Polycarp writes to the Philippians: "knowing that by grace you have been saved, not from works, but by the will of God through Jesus Christ [εἰδότες, ὅτι χάριτί ἐστε σεσωσμένοι, οὐκ ἐξ ἔργων, ἀλλὰ θελήματι θεοῦ διὰ Ἰησοῦ Χριστοῦ]" (*To the Philippians*, 1:3).

[77] Nor does Paul here deduce our deadness in sin from our incorporation into Adam—a logic quite prominent in Romans 5, for example, but not yet appearing in Ephesians (see 4:22–24).

who is now alive in Christ and concludes that he must have been dead without Christ.[78]

This logic explains why the image of death in Christ appears with such frustrating inconsistency in Paul. There are at least three perspectives on death and life in Paul's writings. First, in our present pericope, he argues that Gentile Christians were "dead in trespasses and sins" (2:1, 5) before the action of God in Christ brought them life. Effectively, Jewish Christians were in the same coffin (they, too, were "dead in trespasses," 2:5), even if they had not been enslaved by the demonic forces at work in pagan idolatry. Paul makes no distinction between faithful and unfaithful Jew, orthodox or liberal.[79] All share the same sinful flesh whose desires are diametrically opposed to God's Law (2:3). Thus, Paul draws together all people (2:3b, 5) under the blanket judgment that they were dead before being incorporated into Christ—and if they were still alive in the flesh, their deadness must have been "in trespasses." But then, second, we confront Paul's argument in Romans 6 and Col 2:12, where he teaches that we are put to death and buried with Christ by Baptism into him. This seems to imply that the object of Baptism was alive beforehand, albeit living an ungodly kind of anti-life that needed to be snuffed out through the drowning action of the sacramental flood. Third and finally, reflecting on baptismal theology (Romans 6), Paul recognizes the ongoing work of God's Law, which continues day by day to put to death the old man (Rom 7:9–11), or rather, it is sin working through the Law that brings such death (Rom 7:13).

We might despair of bringing any consistency to Paul's imagery. Are people dead in sins from the moment of their conception? Or are they put to death by Baptism, in which they are buried with Christ? Or are they put to death each day as God's Law does its work on them? We may speak an appropriate yes to each question without contradicting Paul. For within a few short verses in Colossians Paul can say that you were "buried with him [Christ] in Baptism" (Col 2:12), that "you were dead in trespasses and the uncircumcision of your flesh" (2:13), that "you died with Christ to the elemental principles of the cosmos" (2:20), and that you are to "put to death the earthly parts" (Col 3:5).

Yet this language is not truly inconsistent. On the one hand, Paul confesses that the appearance of life that is found among those born naturally in this world disguises a lack of true, eternal, spiritual life. All people are, in this way, dead without Christ. But Holy Baptism, by uniting the sinner to Christ in everything he underwent, brings a real act of execution to the old man with all his desires. In other words, we were dead with respect to following God, but also needing to

---

[78] "It [the statement that the Ephesians were 'dead' (2:1, 5)] is equivalent to the confession of many a psalmist and the pronouncement of the Prodigal Son's father: as it is being proclaimed only after the salvation of the dead and lost man, it must be called [not a *post-mortem* but] a *post-resurrectionem*. Only in the light of the reality of God's resuscitating power can the reality of man's former death be recognized" (Barth, *Ephesians*, 1:233).

[79] Stoeckhardt, *Ephesians*, 121, for example, says that Paul is not speaking here of the pious Israelite of the OT, but he misses the point.

be slain by virtue of our active hostility against him.[80] And the ongoing work of the Law, which returns us to our Baptism by daily drowning the old man, simply illustrates the "in between" character of the age in which we exist. As our resurrection with Christ and ascension to heaven is proleptic, anticipating our once-for-all exaltation with the resurrection of the dead on the Last Day, so the act of death with Christ is proleptic, bringing forward repeatedly the death of the flesh that comes once and for all at the end of our earthly lives. It is, therefore, foolish to stipulate whether this death to sin happens through hearing the Word, through believing it, through Holy Baptism, or through a repentant return to that event. It has happened, and it goes on happening so long as we are in this age.

The same factors apply to the gift of new life confessed in Eph 2:5–6: God "made [us] alive together with Christ … and he raised [us] together and seated [us] together in the heavenly places in Christ Jesus." It is entirely contrary to Paul's argument to reduce this act of resurrection to a single, future event, which is only put in the aorist tense[81] as a sort of prophetic future, which is sure and certain but as yet has no reality.[82] Paul's point is that we are so truly united to Christ in Baptism that we also truly experience what he has experienced. We have risen and ascended.

Some have suggested that this language goes beyond the Paul of Romans, who saw in Baptism our death with Christ (Rom 6:3) but reserved resurrection for an eschatological fulfillment (Rom 6:4–5). Yet Rom 6:11 clearly sees the Christian as already "alive to God in Christ Jesus."[83] In this same section of Romans, Paul moves on to the more outrageous claim that "those whom he justified he also glorified" (Rom 8:30).[84] It is no wonder that Paul's strong proleptic statements were sometimes misunderstood as if to say that the resurrection

---

[80] The Formula of Concord illustrates this with its astonishing refutation of any spiritual life in natural man, followed by its swift affirmation of his vitality in opposing God:

Namely, that in spiritual and divine things the intellect, heart, and will of the unregenerate man are utterly unable, by their own natural powers, to understand, believe, accept, think, will, begin, effect, do, work, or concur in working anything, but they are entirely dead to what is good, and corrupt, so that in man's nature since the Fall, before regeneration, there is not the least spark of spiritual power remaining, nor present, by which, of himself, he can prepare himself for God's grace, or accept the offered grace, nor be capable of it for and of himself, or apply or accommodate himself thereto, or by his own powers be able of himself, as of himself, to aid, do, work, or concur in working anything towards his conversion, either wholly, or half, or in any, even the least or most inconsiderable part; but that he is the servant [and slave] of sin, John 8, 34, and a captive of the devil, by whom he is moved, Eph. 2, 2; 2 Tim. 2, 26. Hence the natural free will according to its perverted disposition and nature is strong and active only with respect to what is displeasing and contrary to God. (FC SD 2:7 [*Triglotta*, 883]; cf. FC SD 2:11, 61; 3:19–20)

[81] The three main Greek verbs in 2:5–6 are aorist tense, which usually refers to a past completed action.

[82] E.g., "in the light of God's foreknowledge, Paul is speaking of what is to come as though it had already been done" (Jerome, *Ephesians*, 1:2.1, ACCS 8:132).

[83] See Lincoln, *Ephesians*, 105–6, for a defense of Paul's "now-not yet" theology in Romans 6.

[84] Bruce, *The Epistles to the Colossians, to Philemon, and to the Ephesians*, 287, says that the force of the aorist tense of the verbs in Rom 8:30 expresses "a purpose which is so sure of

of the dead had already happened, that the resurrection does not matter, or that there is nothing left to be fulfilled (1 Cor 4:8; 2 Tim 2:18). What they misunderstood, but Paul recognized, was that the reality of our new existence in Christ remains hidden in this age: "for you have died, and your life has been hidden with Christ in God; but when Christ is manifested, who is our life, then also you will be manifested with him in glory" (Col 3:3–4).

Clearly, Paul's claims about present Christian existence are not based on observable phenomena in the Christian life, but on observing the Christ in whom the Christian lives. Like Romans 6–8, this section of Ephesians applies to the Christian each creedal statement about Christ that has first been confessed in Eph 1:20–21: resurrection, ascension, glorification, and triumph over all the spiritual hosts of darkness. We cannot know what incipient-Gnostic ideas might have challenged the Ephesian Christians, though it is a safe bet that their context was little different from that of Colossae, where syncretistic false teachers offered an alternate path of access to higher, heavenly matters through denial of the flesh and appeal to spiritual agents (Col 2:8–23). Paul's trump card is that in Christ the Christian has already been raised far above such things. His imperative to the Colossians to "seek the things that are above" is based on the indicative "since you have been raised with Christ" (Col 3:1).[85]

But there is more going on than apologetics. Paul would claim for us our place with Christ in heaven even if no opponent had suggested otherwise. It is the marvelous, divine answer to our sorry state of death, the action of "but God" (2:4) brought to bear on those who by definition could do nothing to help themselves. This is the nature of grace, which cannot be a response to anything in the one who receives or else it ceases to be grace. But salvation's cause lay not just in an attitude of God; once God became man, it lay also in his new nature, as brought on by the incarnation itself. Our place is claimed for us in heaven, not merely because we have been incorporated baptismally into Christ, but because he first incorporated (enfleshed) himself with us by being born of the Virgin. What is said of Christ (1:20–21) is now said of us (2:5–6) precisely because we share his flesh (Heb 2:14–15, in a similar context). And what Christ experienced was only possible for him because he took on our flesh. Theodoret writes:

> If Christ the Lord did not share our human nature, he would have been falsely called our firstfruits. If so his bodily nature was not raised from the dead and did not receive its seat at the right hand in heaven. And if none of this occurred how can it be said that God has raised us and seated us with Christ, that is, if we have nothing by nature that belongs to him?[86]

Not all of Christ's exaltation, however, is shared with every Christian. The line between Creator and creation remains unblurred. It is probably significant that Paul omits "at his [God's] right hand" (1:20) when he applies Christ's

---

fulfilment that it can be spoken of as having already taken place" (prophetic future), but this, too, is surely not strong enough for the reality Paul describes.

85   Lincoln, *Ephesians*, 106.

86   Theodoret, *Eranistes*, 1, ACCS 8:132.

journey to all Christians (2:6). For this phrase describes not a literal place where we might exist with Christ, but an office of divine authority that is given to Christ alone.[87] It is only with such a safeguard in place that we might speak of the *theosis* or "divinization" of the Christian,[88] such as in the previously cited words of Irenaeus, that Christ, "on account of His great love, became what we are, so that He might bring us to be what He Himself is."[89]

To become what he is is to receive divine life and godly gifts, but not to become God. Neither is our share in his ascension to be understood as the bestowal on *our* human nature of his divine omnipotence, omnipresence, and so on, as confessed of Christ in the *genus maiestaticum*.[90] To be seated in the heavenly places with Christ (2:6) means neither to be transferred bodily from one dwelling place to another nor to be given the sort of illocal omnipresence that the glorified Christ enjoys. But, as "at his [God's] right hand" (1:20) indicates an authority, not a literal location, so the ascension of all Christians with Christ indicates not a preemptive exodus from this world but a spiritual exaltation, the conferral of divine honor on God's children. Ultimately, what is so astonishing in this section of Ephesians is not the differences between the exaltation of Christ and Christian, but their remarkable likeness!

Baptismal Unity with One Another and Exaltation with Christ

Whether or not it be accepted that Paul already has in mind the division between Jew and Gentile that becomes explicit in the following section (2:11–22), a clear twofold argument for the unity of all in Christ is at work in this pericope. When Paul refers to his Gentile Christian audience's former life under the dominion of Satan's forces, he is not thereby intending to distinguish them from their Jewish Christian brothers and sisters. Nor, when he asserts of himself and his fellow Jewish Christians that "we all once conducted ourselves in the passions of our flesh … like the rest" (2:3) does he mean to imply that Gentile Christians were somehow free from this fleshly disease. The purpose is not to separate but to unite all people, whether Jew or Greek, under the single, crushing condemnation of God's Law.

Thus, we find in 2:1–3 an epitome of the method Paul developed at length in the opening chapters of Romans (1:18–3:31). For if the Gospel is "the power of God for salvation to everyone who believes, to the Jew first and also to the Greek" (Rom 1:16), it must first be demonstrated that both parties were equally in need of that great power. Rom 1:18–32 exposes the hopeless state of

---

[87] See "Christ's Victorious Ascension to God's Right Hand (1:20–23)" in the commentary on 1:15–23.

[88] See the excursus "Theosis and 2 Peter 1:4" in Giese, *2 Peter and Jude*, 62–68.

[89] Irenaeus, *Against Heresies*, 5, Preface (trans. Jurgens, *The Faith of the Early Fathers*, vol. 1, § 248).

[90] This refers to the communication of attributes of the divine and human natures in Christ whereby the attributes of his divine nature (i.e., "majesty," hence *maiestaticum*) are communicated to his human nature; see FC SD 8, "The Person of Christ," 48–96.

all Gentiles on the basis of God's condemnation written on their conscience. Rom 2:17–29 proves that the Jew, who has the written Law of God, is no more capable of keeping it than the supposedly lawless Gentile. With a series of sweeping summary statements, Paul hammers home his conclusions: "All who have sinned without the Law without the Law will also perish; and all who sinned under the Law through the Law will be condemned" (Rom 2:12). "What then? Are we [Jews] better off? Not at all! For we have already charged that all, both Jews and Greeks, are under sin" (Rom 3:9). "For there is no distinction, for all have sinned and lack the glory of God" (Rom 3:23). This is what Paul means by his brief summary of the object of God's saving deeds: "even *us*, when we were dead in [our] trespasses" (Eph 2:5). This "us" comprehends both the Gentiles, who likewise once were "dead in trespasses and sins" (2:1) and "walked" according to the ruler of this age (2:2; cf. Gal 4:8), and the Jews, who likewise did the will "of the flesh" and its "thoughts" (Eph 2:3; cf. Titus 3:3).

Following the principle of Rom 11:32, "for God locked all into disobedience, that he might have mercy upon all," Paul moves directly from wrath to grace. The actions of God are described in Eph 2:5–6 with a series of verbs prefixed with the preposition σύν, "together, with," that forms the densest concentration of such compounds in the NT: συνεζωοποίησεν, "he made alive together with"; συνήγειρεν, "he raised together with"; and συνεκάθισεν, "he seated together with." As discussed in the textual notes, there is sufficient evidence to believe that Paul intends "with" to include Jew and Gentile, or at least all Christians, in the orbit of these saving verbs. Thus, in parallel to the act of locking all together into disobedience (Rom 11:32), God joins all people together in having mercy on them.

Yet it is important to stress that horizontal unity (with one another) is a *consequence* of salvation, but not its ultimate *goal*. More significant to Paul is the union with Christ and reconciliation to God that lay at the heart of the Ephesian prologue (1:3–14). Echoing its language, Paul repeats "with Christ" or "in Christ" four times in the Gospel part of the present pericope (2:4–10). In doing so, he ties together 1:20–21[91] and 2:1–10. The exaltation of Christ is our exaltation. We are "caught up in what happened to Christ."[92] It is, in the inimitable words of a German, "ein In-Christus-mit-Christus-in-die-Himmel-versetzt-worden-Sein."[93] All that once characterized our lives has been given up in exchange for what belongs to Christ.

---

[91] See also "in Christ" (or "in him/whom/the Beloved") in 1:1, 3, 4, 6, 7, 9, 10, 11, 12, 13.

[92] Best, *Ephesians*, 199.

[93] "A having-been-transferred-in-Christ-with-Christ-into-heaven-kind-of-existence" (Schlier, *Epheser*, 110–11).

Here Paul advances beyond any consequences he has elsewhere drawn from our incorporation into Christ.[94] For not only have we died and risen with him so that we experience new life already in this age, but we have also already ascended and been seated in the heavenly places. Though it is hidden from our fleshly eyes, the eyes of our hearts (1:18) have been opened to see such a magnificent present glorification. Commenting on Psalm 110, the same OT passage Paul previously quoted in Eph 1:22, Luther writes:

> But although David personally had the physical advantage which we do not have, namely, that Christ was to be born of his body, we have just as much reason to be glad and to boast of the honor and glory which we share with David and the holy fathers of the Jewish nation. For in Christ a part of our flesh and blood, that is, our human nature, sits in heaven above at the right hand of God. He wants to be our Lord just as much as the Lord of David and the other fathers. It is an unspeakably great glory and honor for mankind to have been raised so high by Him, not merely to heaven among the holy angels and archangels, who are certainly great and excellent princes and lords, but to the level of direct equality with God Himself. How could the High Majesty become humbler than by honoring this sorry flesh and blood and exalting it through His divine honor and authority? He descends to the level of our nature and becomes a member of the human race! It is an honor which no angel in heaven shares.[95]

As St. Stephen looked to heaven in his martyrdom, saw the Son of Man standing at the right hand of God, and was given courage to face his death (Acts 7:56–60), so also we look to heaven in faith and see our Brother, our flesh and blood, on the throne and see with confidence our own present and future. Like John, granted a vision of the saints surrounding the Lamb and God's throne (Rev 7:9–17), we are equipped by the sight of our own ascension with Christ to face a hostile world and all spiritual opposition. It is a stunning consequence of the incarnation that man and God can never again be separated. Christopher Wordsworth sang:

> Thou hast raised our human nature
>> On the clouds to God's right hand;
> There we sit in heavenly places,
>> There with Thee in glory stand.
> Jesus reigns, adored by angels;
>> Man with God is on the throne.
> Mighty Lord, in Thine ascension
>> We by faith behold our own.[96]

---

[94] "The statement that God has both raised up believers with Christ and seated them with him in the heavenly realms spells out the implications of the relationship of incorporation in Christ in their most developed form in the Pauline corpus" (Lincoln, *Ephesians*, 105).

[95] Luther, "Lecture on Psalm 110" (1535), AE 13:243.

[96] Christopher Wordsworth, "See the Conqueror Mounts in Triumph" (1862), *TLH* 218:5; cf. *LSB* 494:5.

For Paul this glorification of humanity happened in principle when Christ became man, suffered, died, rose, and ascended in human flesh. But its application to individual humans took place through an act of appropriation, a work that brought union with Christ. The language of death and resurrection in this pericope makes sufficiently clear a reference to Holy Baptism as the action of God that brought it about.[97] While Baptism is named only once in Ephesians (4:5), it is the subject of continual allusion through the creative language of early Christianity.[98] That death and resurrection with Christ occurs through Baptism is made explicit in Rom 6:1–4 and Col 2:11–13. Extensive parallels of language with Titus 3:4–7 suggest that the same "washing of regeneration and renewal of the Holy Spirit" by which God "saved us" (Titus 3:5) is in mind here.[99] Only theologians who stubbornly deny the power of Baptism to accomplish this great work would try to drive a wedge between "conversion" and "initiation" so as to suggest that this text is speaking of one but not the other.[100]

No early Christian immersed in Paul's thought-world would have separated these two acts or missed the allusion to Baptism in this pericope. Our modern need to make everything explicit reflects both our polemical past and our lamentable loss of the poetic. When patristic writers refer to this passage— alluding to the allusion—one set of oblique references replaces another, but the baptismal code becomes all the more obvious. Hermas, for example, draws together baptismal images from across the NT, unites them with his own triad of Ephesians-like "with" verbs,[101] and develops it all into his own image of the church as a building that arises out of Baptism:

> "So these also who had fallen asleep received the seal of the Son of God and 'entered into the kingdom of God' [Jn 3:5]. For before," said he, " a man bears the name of the Son of God, he is dead. But when he receives the seal he puts away mortality and receives life. The seal, then, is the water. They go down then into the water dead, and come up alive. This seal, then, was preached to them also, and they made use of it 'to enter into the kingdom of God.' " … "Through them [the apostles], therefore, they were made alive [ἐζωοποιήθησαν], and received the knowledge of the name of the Son of God. For this cause they also came up with [συνανέβησαν] them and were joined

---

[97] Schlier, *Epheser*, 101: "The event that divides the 'once' and the 'now' of world time and mankind's situation is the cross and resurrection of Jesus Christ (Rom 5:9; 2 Cor 6:2; etc.). But the event that divides the life of the individual into two eras is Baptism, which places one into the new era and world in Christ (cf. Rom 6:1ff.; 6:15ff.; 1 Cor 6:11; Titus 3:3–7)."

[98] See "Baptism and the Spirit" in "Purpose and Themes" in the introduction.

[99] Ephesian parallels in Titus 3:4–7 include "kindness," "not from works," "according to his mercy," "he saved us," "richly," and "justified by grace."

[100] Lincoln, *Ephesians*, 89–91, quite sensibly accepts the baptismal connection, while rejecting theories that a baptismal hymn or rite stands behind the present text.

[101] These three verbs prefixed with the preposition σύν, "with, together," can be compared to Paul's triad; see the second textual note on 2:5.

[συνηρμόσθησαν] into the building of the tower, and were used together with them for the building [συνῳκοδομήθησαν]."[102]

In this Christian church, where that vivifying Gospel is proclaimed and applied with the water, Christians enter into paradise with Christ.[103]

---

[102] *Shepherd of Hermas, Similitudes,* 9:16.3–4, 7 (trans. Kirsopp Lake, LCL).

[103] "Those who are regenerated through divine baptism are placed in paradise—that is, in the church" (Origen, *Select Notes on Genesis,* 2:13, quoted in Bruce, *The Epistles to the Colossians, to Philemon, and to the Ephesians,* 287, who cites Schlier, *Epheser,* 111).

Reconciled in One Body through the Cross

Translation

2 ¹¹Therefore, remember that at one time you Gentiles in the flesh,
>who are called "Uncircumcision" by what is called "Circumcision" (made in the flesh by hands),
>>¹²that you were at that time separated from Christ,
>>>alienated from the commonwealth of Israel
>>>>and strangers to the covenants of the promise,
>>>>>having no hope and godless in the world.
>>>>>>¹³But now in Christ Jesus you who at one time were far off
>>>>>>have become near by the blood of Christ.
>>>>>>>¹⁴For he himself is our peace, who has made both one,
>>>>>>>and has destroyed the dividing wall of partition, the hostility,
>>>>>>>in his flesh,
>>>>>>>>¹⁵by nullifying the Law of commandments in decrees,
>>>>>>>>that in him he might create the two into one new man, making peace,
>>>>>>>¹⁶and might reconcile both in one body to God through the cross,
>>>>>>>by killing the hostility in him.
>>>>>>¹⁷And when he came he preached peace to you who were far off
>>>>>>and peace to those who were near;
>>>>>¹⁸for through <u>him</u> we both have access in one <u>Spirit</u> to the <u>Father</u>.
>>>>¹⁹So, then, you are no longer strangers and sojourners,
>>>>but you are fellow citizens with the saints and members of God's household,
>>>²⁰having been built up upon the foundation of the apostles and prophets,
>>>the cornerstone being Christ Jesus himself,
>>²¹in whom the whole building, being joined together, grows into a holy temple
>>in the <u>Lord</u>,
>²²in whom also you are built up together into a dwelling place of <u>God</u> in the <u>Spirit</u>.

Textual Notes

2:11 διὸ μνημονεύετε—The conjunction διό, "therefore," ties this pericope to the previous one (see "Structure and Rhetoric" in the commentary). It draws a more particular conclusion from the preceding general Gospel presentation (2:1–10). μνημονεύετε, "remember" (imperative of μνημονεύω), asks the Ephesians to recall their previous pagan existence, with repentance and gratitude for God's action in rescuing them from it, and to focus on their present incorporation into the kingdom of God.[1] But it also

---

[1] "Eph 2:11–12 is the only biblical text admonishing saved and sanctified people to remember their pernicious past" (Barth, *Ephesians*, 1:256). But that is not the chief goal, for "in an anamnesis of this kind it is not a question of remembering human things but of recalling

directs them back to Paul's oral teaching among them.[2] Their alienation from the covenants and separation from Christ is not something they had understood until Paul revealed it to them. Paul does not introduce new teaching in a letter, but confirms and explains what he has previously done in person (Gal 1:8; 2 Thess 2:2).[3] He is part of a chain of authoritative teaching extending back to Christ himself; he expects his faithful catechumens to hold fast the teachings that he received and handed down.[4] Such language likely indicates the use of Jewish techniques of memorization and oral traditionalism.[5]

ὅτι ποτὲ ὑμεῖς τὰ ἔθνη ἐν σαρκί—The adverb ποτέ, "formerly, at one time," introduces the same contrast of "then and now," "old, dead existence versus new life in Christ," as in 2:2 (see the textual notes on 2:2; 4:17; 5:8; and the commentary below). If there was any doubt that ὑμᾶς, "you," referred to *Gentile* Christians in 2:1, Paul makes the reference explicit here. ὑμεῖς, "you," are τὰ ἔθνη, "Gentiles."[6] This does not necessarily mean that all members of the Ephesian church were ἔθνη, but Paul addresses those who were surely in the majority. Although ἔθνος can simply refer to a "nation" or "people," from the NT Jewish perspective, it typically refers to "other nations," that is, "Gentiles." In the LXX it translates גּוֹיִם, "nations," which is often used in contrast to הָעָם, "the people," Israel. The "Gentiles" are the unique object of Paul's ministry, as given by the Lord's mandate[7] and affirmed by Paul repeatedly in Ephesians (ἔθνη, 3:1, 6, 8).

The qualification ἐν σαρκί, "in the flesh," has a double meaning. On the one hand, it alludes to the Gentile Ephesians' lack of the distinctive fleshly mark of God's

---

God's deed in the perspective of faith" (Schnackenburg, *Ephesians*, 108). "Remember" can also mean to focus attention on a current state of affairs (Gal 2:10; Col 4:18; 2 Tim 2:8); in other words, Paul does not ask the Gentile Ephesians to dwell on the past but to keep in mind how different their circumstances are now.

[2] For Paul's ministry of almost three years in Ephesus, see "Paul and Ephesus in Acts" in "The City of Ephesus and Paul's Relationship to It" in the introduction.

[3] In his letters Paul regularly points the churches back to the teachings he gave in person: 1 Cor 4:17; 15:1–2; Eph 4:20–21; Phil 3:18; 1 Thess 3:4; 4:1–2, 9, 11; 5:1–2; 2 Thess 2:5, 15 (cf. Rom 15:15; Col 1:5–6). See Winger, "Orality as the Key to Understanding Apostolic Proclamation in the Epistles," 258–60.

[4] See, e.g., 1 Cor 11:2; 15:1–3; and the extensive references in Winger, "Orality as the Key to Understanding Apostolic Proclamation in the Epistles," 221.

[5] Classically presented by Birger Gerhardsson, *Memory and Manuscript: Oral Tradition and Written Transmission in Rabbinic Judaism and Early Christianity* (Uppsala: Boktryckeri Aktiebolag, 1961). See also Winger, "Orality as the Key to Understanding Apostolic Proclamation in the Epistles," 217–21.

[6] At the same time it is intriguing that in this pericope Paul no longer uses "we" to identify Jewish Christians (as he did in 1:12; 2:3) as a group distinct from the Gentiles. Instead, he uses "we" only for the entire body of Christ, united by his atoning ("at-one-ing") work on the cross (2:16, 18). When referring to Israel as a group from which the Gentiles were distinct, he uses only third person expressions (2:12, 14, 15, 17, 19). See Dahl, "Gentiles, Christians, and Israelites in the Epistle to the Ephesians," in *Studies in Ephesians*, 445; Dahl argues that distinctions between Jew and Gentile are expressed only in the past tense in Ephesians.

[7] Acts 9:15; 26:17–18; Rom 1:5; 11:13; Gal 1:16; 2:7; 1 Tim 2:7.

covenant people: circumcision. Their flesh itself shows that they were pagans.[8] On the other hand, Paul hints with these words, "Gentiles *in the flesh*," that "Gentile" is no longer the primary point of reference for these Ephesian Christians. "In the flesh" does not define them any longer, but rather "in Christ" (2:13, etc.). Nor can a mark in the flesh (circumcision) any longer lay claim to God's blessings (Gal 6:15; Phil 3:3). Paul elsewhere applies the same criterion to Jews, who are not true Jews simply "in the flesh" (by the mark of circumcision), but by faith (Rom 2:28–29). Since Paul does not say that the Ephesians are *no longer* "in the flesh," it is unlikely that he is using the phrase as a reference to the rebellious, sinful life (as he does in Rom 8:8). The flesh itself is not by definition incapable of the spiritual life—for Christ himself worked our salvation in the flesh (1 Tim 3:16)—but is transformed by Baptism into a dwelling place for Christ's Spirit (Gal 2:20).

οἱ λεγόμενοι ἀκροβυστία—The articular participle οἱ λεγόμενοι should not be translated as "so-called," as if it expressed something that is not true. "Uncircumcision" and (in the next textual note) "Circumcision" are legitimate names for the two groups into which the OT and Judaism divided humanity. Naming, for Jews, was not a mere label hung on something, but reflected its reality. Yet, "who are called" indicates Paul's reluctance to use a term that in his former life he might have hurled in abuse, as Jews and Judaizers continued to do (Acts 11:3). ἀκροβυστία literally means "foreskin."[9] Only propriety prevents us from using this suitably rude term in our translation. One notes also that Paul in all other places uses the term in a non-abusive manner simply as a reference to those who have not been circumcised.[10]

ὑπὸ τῆς λεγομένης περιτομῆς ἐν σαρκὶ χειροποιήτου—The articular noun ἡ περιτομή, "the Circumcision," can likewise refer in a quite neutral manner to Jews as distinct from Gentiles,[11] and far be it from Paul to criticize circumcision itself as a divinely mandated mark of the covenant. But τῆς λεγομένης, "what is called," implies that Paul has something else in mind. It has become not a term of abuse, but of pride: the Jews referred to themselves as "the Circumcision" to elevate themselves above the uncircumcised.[12] Their prideful use of the term is ironic in light of the OT prophets' frequent call to repentance as a circumcision of the heart, an alignment of thoughts

---

[8] Thus, Paul has the mixed-race Timothy circumcised (Acts 16:3) so that his very flesh would show that he was by confession not of the Gentiles but of God's covenant people. The Judaizers have a different motive when they force circumcision upon purely Gentile Christians (Gal 6:12).

[9] Only found in biblical and ecclesiastical Greek, ἀκροβυστία is probably a euphemism for (and a wordplay on) the usual Greek anatomical term ἀκροποσθία, "tip of the foreskin." Etymologically (and thus popularly) ἀκροβυστία was once thought to come from ἄκρος and βύω, thus "top of the stopper"; but -βυστία is more likely related to a Semitic root such as בֹּשֶׁת, "shame" (LSJM, s.v. ἀκροβυστία, II 2), thus "top of the shameful parts." See BDAG, s.v. ἀκροβυστία, 1; Karl Ludwig Schmidt, "ἀκροβυστία," *TDNT* 1:225–26; BDF, § 120 (4); Moulton and Howard, *Accidence and Word-Formation*, 277.

[10] Rom 2:25–27; 3:30; 4:9–12; 1 Cor 7:18–19; Gal 2:7; 5:6; 6:15; Col 2:13; 3:11.

[11] E.g., "believers from among the circumcision" (Acts 10:45); see also the passages with "uncircumcision" cited in the previous footnote, as well as Rom 15:8; Gal 2:8–9; Col 4:11.

[12] Acts 11:2–3; Gal 2:12; Titus 1:10; cf. Gal 6:13; Phil 3:5.

and deeds with the outward mark of God's covenantal ownership.[13] For cutting off the flesh symbolized a repentant death to sin—and as a bloodletting (cf. Ex 4:24–26) confessed the need for the sort of atoning sacrifice that was ultimately fulfilled in Christ (Col 2:11–13). In line with such OT thought is Paul's belief that true circumcision as a mark of God's covenant graciousness is not found in the flesh but in the faith of the heart (Rom 2:28–29; Phil 3:3; Col 2:11). Thus, he qualifies the old "circumcision" with ἐν σαρκί, "in the flesh," and χειροποιήτου, "made by hands." With these terms Paul levels Jews and Gentiles with respect to their fleshly powers. Insofar as the Jews put their trust in the works of their own hands, they are no better than pagan idolaters.[14] Infinitely superior is the circumcision of the heart, of which fleshly circumcision was only ever a mark and a prophecy, the circumcision "made without hands" (Col 2:11) by union with Christ's death in Holy Baptism (Col 2:12). "Made with hands" (Eph 2:11) recalls Christ's dismissal of the Jerusalem temple (Mk 14:58), whose sacrifices were made obsolete by his coming, to be replaced by his body, a spiritual temple into which the saints are built up.[15] By this thought the "temple" in Eph 2:20–22 forms a subtle *inclusio* with 2:11.

2:12 ὅτι ἦτε τῷ καιρῷ ἐκείνῳ—The noun καιρός denotes a particular moment in time. Thus, "at that time" is equivalent to ποτέ, "at one time" (2:11), a reference to the Gentile Ephesians' existence before they were baptized into Christ.

χωρὶς Χριστοῦ—It is interesting to compare Paul's approach here with 2:1–3. There he characterized their former pagan life as all sin and demons. Here he is more concerned with what they were lacking, but what was available to Israelites through the covenant. "You were … separated from Christ"[16] certainly refers to their life before Baptism into him. But in light of what follows, it may also refer to their separation from Israel, to whom belonged the promises of the coming Messiah (Rom 9:4), from whom came the Christ according to the flesh (Rom 9:5), among whom the preincarnate Christ was present and acted (e.g., 1 Cor 10:4), and whose faithful members put their trust in him (Lk 2:38).

ἀπηλλοτριωμένοι—This participle is in the predicate position, used like an adjective: "you were … *alienated*."[17] ἀπαλλοτριόω, "to estrange, alienate," occurs only three times in the NT (Eph 2:12; 4:18; Col 1:21). Col 1:21 is a precise, though abbreviated parallel to this verse. Eph 4:18 refers to the existence of Gentiles who are "alienated from the life of God." The term evokes the common experience of an ἀλλότριος, "foreigner"—a synonym of ξένος, "stranger" (2:12, 19), and πάροικος, "sojourner"

---

[13] The call to "circumcise the foreskin of your heart" (Deut 10:16) entailed repentance for thoughts and deeds that contradicted the covenantal mark. See also Lev 26:41; Deut 30:6; Jer 4:4; 9:24–25 (ET 9:25–26); Ezek 44:7, 9; Acts 7:51; Rom 2:28–29; cf. *Jubilees* 1:23.

[14] The adjective χειροποίητος, "handmade," is a term of derision for idols in LXX Lev 26:1, 30; Is 2:18; 10:11; 16:12; 19:1; 21:9; 31:7; 46:6; Dan 5:4, 23; 6:28; Judith 8:18; Wis Sol 14:8.

[15] Cf. Acts 7:48; 17:24; 2 Cor 5:1; 1 Pet 2:5; Heb 9:11, 24.

[16] Thus taking χωρὶς Χριστοῦ as a predicate. Stoeckhardt, *Ephesians*, 144, and others (Schlier, *Epheser*, 120, n. 1) take the phrase adverbially: "at that time [when you were] *without Christ*, you were alienated …"

[17] Burton, *Moods and Tenses*, § 432 b.

(2:19). ἀπηλλοτριωμένοι does not imply that the Gentiles had been part of Israel and then were "alienated" (passive transitive), but that they stood in the condition of being "alienated" foreigners (intransitive). The OT's view of foreigners is twofold. On the one hand, the alien or sojourner in Israel was to be treated with care as an object of God's love and a potential member of his people,[18] for the Israelites themselves were aliens in Canaan (Gen 23:4), Egypt (Ex 22:20 [ET 22:21]; 23:9), Babylon, and eventually throughout the Diaspora. On the other hand, as idolaters, Gentile sojourners were alienated from the true God (cf. Ezek 14:4–7). So long as they remained uncircumcised, foreigners could not participate in the holy things of Israel.[19] This left the foreigner separated from the blessings of God that were to be found among his chosen people—which is Paul's meaning here.

τῆς πολιτείας τοῦ Ἰσραήλ—The genitive τῆς πολιτείας is one of separation:[20] "alienated *from* the commonwealth of Israel." πολιτεία can be translated as "citizenship," a privilege to which Paul appealed in the Roman Empire (Acts 22:28; cf. 3 Macc 3:21, 23). In Maccabees πολιτεία frequently means "the Jewish way of life" or "customs," which the Jews fought to protect.[21] The word can also be translated as "state" or "body of citizens," traditionally "commonwealth" (cf. 2 Macc 13:14). These three aspects of meaning really form one whole and clarify that it is not from the land of Israel, as such, that Gentiles were excluded, or even from Israel as a political unit, but from the privileges and way of life of God's chosen people[22] under his covenant.

While Paul was imprisoned in Caesarea, furious street battles broke out over the question of who were the rightful citizens of the city. The Jews claimed this right (over against the Syrians) because Herod had founded the city and eventually pressed their right with a process in Rome. These Jew/Gentile battles over citizenship[23] may lie in the background of Paul's language in this pericope. His response is to point the Ephesians away from such earthly claims to their higher, common citizenship in God's house (Eph 2:19–22; cf. Phil 3:20; Heb 12:23).

καὶ ξένοι τῶν διαθηκῶν τῆς ἐπαγγελίας—The phrase ξένοι τῶν διαθηκῶν has a genitive of separation,[24] literally, "strangers (separated) *from* the promise." ξένος, "stranger" or "estranged" (which occurs also in 2:19), is used in parallel to

---

[18] Ex 20:10; Lev 19:10; Deut 10:18–19; 1 Ki 8:41–43; Is 14:1; 56:3; Jer 7:6; 22:3; Ezek 47:22–23.

[19] Ex 12:43; Lev 22:25; Jer 51:51; Ezek 44:9.

[20] BDF, § 180 (1).

[21] 2 Macc 4:11; 8:17; 4 Macc 3:20; 8:7; 17:9.

[22] Schnackenburg, *Ephesians*, 109, suggests that Paul means "the Congregation of Israel" as a worshiping assembly but for obvious reasons could use neither ἐκκλησία ("church") nor συναγωγή ("synagogue").

[23] See "Caesarea!" in "Location and Date of Writing" in the introduction; see also Reicke, *Re-examining Paul's Letters*, 82–83, 135–36; Josephus, *Antiquities*, 20:173–84. These events eventually precipitated the great war in AD 66 that led to the Roman destruction of Jerusalem in AD 70. Reicke dates Paul's Caesarean imprisonment to AD 59–60, but it could have begun as early as AD 57.

[24] BDF, § 182 (3).

ἀπηλλοτριωμένοι, "alienated" (2:12), and πάροικος, "sojourner" (2:19). Though διαθήκη takes on the distinctively Greek meaning "last will and testament" in the NT (Mt 26:28 and parallels; Gal 3:15; Heb 9:16–17), it is also the common LXX translation for בְּרִית, "covenant." The choice of this Greek term (rather than συνθήκη, "bilateral agreement") highlights the unilateral initiative of God in making disposition of his goods as he chooses. A διαθήκη is God's "decree," "declaration of purpose."[25] Its content is τῆς ἐπαγγελίας, "the promise"; the covenant is defined by the Gospel, not the Law. This explains Paul's use of "covenants" (plural)[26] here, for God repeatedly declared his single unalterable "promise" (ἐπαγγελίας is singular here) in the form of a "covenant" (בְּרִית; LXX: διαθήκη) reiterated to Abraham (e.g., Gen 15:18; 17:2–21), Isaac and Jacob (Lev 26:42), Moses (e.g., Ex 24:7–8; 34:10, 27), and David (2 Sam 23:5; Ps 89:4 [ET Ps 89:3]).[27] These perpetual declarations of the promise were the glorious treasure of the people Israel (Rom 9:4).[28]

In the intertestamental *Book of Jubilees*[29] every major giving or renewing of God's covenant is said to take place on the Feast of Weeks (Pentecost): the covenant with Noah (*Jubilees*, 6:10), the covenant with Abraham (*Jubilees*, 14:20; 15:1–24), the birth of Isaac (*Jubilees*, 16:13), YHWH's appearance to Jacob before he left for Egypt (*Jubilees*, 44:4–8), and most significantly the Sinai covenant (*Jubilees*, 6:11, 19). Thus, the annual celebration of Pentecost was understood by (at least some) Jews as a celebration and renewal of the covenant (*Jubilees*, 6:11, 17).[30] As Paul writes Ephesians, his celebration of Pentecost in Jerusalem is fresh in his mind (Acts 20:16), particularly if we are correct in accepting his immediately subsequent Caesarean imprisonment as the place and time of its writing.[31] This celebration provides a sensible explanation for τῶν διαθηκῶν τῆς ἐπαγγελίας, "the covenants of the promise."

ἐλπίδα μὴ ἔχοντες—On "hope," see the third textual note on 1:18. Ancient Greek culture was not characterized by hope, and where it offered any, such hope was false in Paul's eyes.[32] "Having no hope" is a corollary of being "godless" (2:12) because God is "the God of hope" (Rom 15:13). The Gentile Ephesians may have put their hope in many things, but Christ is the one true hope that does not disappoint (Rom 5:5; Eph 4:4;

---

[25] See BDAG, s.v. διαθήκη, 2.

[26] This is not simply a plural standing for the singular. See BDF, § 141 (8).

[27] The promise declared to Adam (Gen 3:15) and the covenant with Noah (Gen 6:18; 9:9–17) would not seem to be in mind, as they were not specifically given to Israel.

[28] In the NT διαθήκη is used in the plural only here in Eph 2:12 as well as in Rom 9:4 and Gal 4:24 (where it has the sense of old and new covenants). But in the LXX the plural of διαθήκη has the sense of repeated promises to the fathers in 2 Macc 8:15; Wis Sol 18:22; Sirach 44:12, 18.

[29] In his older classic work, R. H. Charles (*The Apocrypha and Pseudepigrapha of the Old Testament in English*, 2:6) dated *Jubilees* between 109 and 105 BC. The more recent introduction by O. S. Wintermute (in Charlesworth, *The Old Testament Pseudepigrapha*, 2:43–44) dates it somewhat earlier in light of Qumran parallels, suggesting 161–140 BC.

[30] See Kirby, *Ephesians: Baptism and Pentecost*, 64–66.

[31] See "Caesarea!" in "Location and Date of Writing" in the introduction.

[32] Deterding, *Colossians*, 31–33.

Col 1:27). The characterization of Gentiles as people without hope is particularly poignant in the face of death (1 Thess 4:13; cf. Wis Sol 3:18). God's people, by contrast, have hope even in the face of weariness and tragedy (Is 57:10; Ezra 10:2).

καὶ ἄθεοι ἐν τῷ κόσμῳ—The *alpha*-privative noun ἄ-θεοι should not be translated literalistically as "a-theists" (those who deny the existence of God or gods), since the pagan background of the Gentile Ephesians was polytheistic. Christians, ironically, were later called "atheists" for rejecting the panoply of Greco-Roman gods[33] and their public rituals in favor of the one true God.[34] Two scenes from the *Martyrdom of Polycarp* illustrate the ironic, dual meaning of the term. First is an arena scene, where the crowd shouts concerning the Christians, αἶρε τοὺς ἀθέους, "away with the atheists" (*Martyrdom of Polycarp*, 3:2). Then after his own arrest, Polycarp is asked to deny his God by repeating the pagan taunt:

> "Swear by the genius of Caesar, repent, say: 'Away with the Atheists' "; but Polycarp, with a stern countenance looked on all the crowd of lawless heathen in the arena, and waving his hand at them, he groaned and looked up to heaven and said: "Away with the Atheists."[35]

Polycarp's words inform the meaning of ἄθεοι in the present context: the Gentiles formerly were "without the true God"—that is, failing to acknowledge him and lacking his gifts (1 Thess 4:5).[36] What they worshiped as gods were not (Acts 19:26; Gal 4:8). They were not part of his chosen people, who were separated from the world (Ex 19:5; 1 Ki 8:53). Instead, they were ἐν τῷ κόσμῳ, "in the world" (Eph 2:12), which echoes 2:2 and implies an existence outside the kingdom of God, under the power of demons. The world is subject to God's judgment.[37] "In the world" parallels "in the flesh" (2:11) as a chief characteristic of the Gentile Ephesians' former existence. The effect of these phrases is undone in the latter half of the chiastic pericope with "in the Lord" and "in the Spirit" (2:21–22).

2:13 νυνὶ δὲ ἐν Χριστῷ Ἰησοῦ—"But now" (νυνὶ δέ) contrasts the present situation of Gentile Christians with the "then" of their pagan life before Christ (2:11–12; cf. 2:2). It is an interjection as emphatic as "but God" (ὁ δὲ θεός, 2:4). ἐν Χριστῷ Ἰησοῦ, "in Christ Jesus," stands in contrast to χωρὶς Χριστοῦ, literally, "without Christ" (2:12). Paul thus begins to overturn point by point their old state of existence, a change of location and lordship brought about by Baptism into death and resurrection of Christ (cf. 2:16). If they are in Christ, they are truly "near" (2:13) to God. Thus, it is not that they

---

[33] Socrates, too, had once been accused of atheism for rejecting the polytheistic practices of his day.

[34] "Hence are we called atheists. And we confess that we are atheists, so far as gods of this sort are concerned, but not with respect to the most true God" (Justin Martyr, *First Apology*, 6:1 [*ANF* 1:164]; cf. 13:1). The same charge had been laid against Jews (Josephus, *Against Apion*, 2:148).

[35] *Martyrdom of Polycarp*, 9:2 (trans. Kirsopp Lake, LCL).

[36] Contra Schnackenburg, *Ephesians*, 111, this cannot be viewed as a neutral state, that they simply did not have God. Paul's critique in Rom 1:20–21 is pertinent: they had plenty of evidence for the existence of the Creator but rejected him in favor of idolatry.

[37] Acts 17:31; Rom 3:6; 1 Cor 6:2; 11:32; cf. Jn 12:31; 16:11.

have moved to Israel but that Christ has drawn near to them.[38] On "in Christ," see the fifth textual note on 1:3.

ὑμεῖς οἵ ποτε ὄντες μακρὰν ἐγενήθητε ἐγγύς—The contrast of μακράν, "far off," with ἐγγύς, "near," refers in a general sense to the dispersion of Gentiles throughout the world at a distance from Israel, God's people, who were in possession of the holy things of God (see also the second textual note on 2:17). In the OT, the Gentiles are often called רָחוֹק, "far off,"[39] in contrast to God's people who are קָרוֹב, "near."[40] To make a "proselyte" (προσήλυτος, from προσέρχομαι [aorist προσῆλθον], "to come toward") is to draw a person near to God. Paul thus adapts the language of conversion to Judaism for Baptism into the new Israel (2:19). In light of the allusion to the divisions in the temple in 2:14–15, however, it is likely that Paul has something more specific in mind: at Herod's temple "far off" describes the so-called Court of the Gentiles.[41] Standing outside the Soreg (barrier wall), the Gentiles were kept farther away from the Holy of Holies and the priestly court and would have been barely able to snatch a glimpse of the sacrificial altar through the gateways. Standing in the temple on Pentecost,[42] Peter preaches that in Christ this apartness is overcome: "For the promise is for you and for your children and for all who are *far off*, all whom the Lord our God calls to himself" (Acts 2:39).[43] And those who heard and believed the promise were baptized into

---

[38] Cf. Gospel statements that in Christ the kingdom of God has "drawn near" (ἤγγικεν, from ἐγγίζω), e.g., Mt 3:2; 4:17; 10:7 (cf. Lk 17:21).

[39] Deut 28:49; 29:21 (ET 29:22); 1 Ki 8:41 ‖ 2 Chr 6:32; Is 5:26; 33:13; 49:1, 12; 57:19; 66:19; Micah 4:3; Zech 6:15.

[40] Lev 10:3; Ps 148:14. Cf. Dan 9:7, which refers both to Israelites who are still "near," such as the inhabitants of Jerusalem, and to those who are "far away," such as those banished in exile in foreign lands.

[41] The term "the Court of the Gentiles" is not found in the Bible, nor in ancient Jewish literature, where the normal term for that court is "mountain of the house" according to Alfred Edersheim, *The Temple: Its Ministry and Services as They Were at the Time of Jesus Christ* (London: Religious Tract Society, 1874), 22, n. 3. Though offering no reference for the phrase, Lee I. Levine, "Temple, Jerusalem," *EDEJ*, 1284, writes: "The entire Temple Mount, exclusive of the Temple precincts, functioned as the *agora* or forum of Jerusalem; the vast courtyard area outside the Temple precincts was called the Court of the Gentiles, for only here were they permitted to enter."

[42] The text of Acts 2 does not specifically say that Peter's sermon took place in the temple. But the size of the multitude (Acts 2:6, 41) and the extensive list of the Diaspora Jews and God-fearers who were gathered to hear him (Acts 2:5–11) suggest that the apostles had left the small confines of the house (Acts 2:2). The immediately subsequent narrative of Acts places the apostolic community in the temple (Acts 2:46; 3:1–10). There, Peter preaches his next sermon (Acts 3:11–26); after the apostles' angelic release from prison, Peter, along with the other apostles, again goes to the temple to preach (Acts 5:17–25). The apostles were in the temple every day proclaiming Jesus as the Christ (Acts 5:41–42).

[43] Although "far off" here refers mainly to Jews of the dispersion, they are "far off" because they are in the lands of Gentiles and like them have been separated from the blessings found in Israel. These words echo a significant number of OT passages which refer to God's messianic ingathering of the dispersion to worship him together (Is 43:6; 57:19; 60:4; Jer 31:10; Dan 9:7; and some of the passages noted above). This blurring of Jews and Gentiles in far-off places hints already at the unity of God's people throughout the world in his true Israel. See Schlier, *Epheser*, 121. James A. Meek, *The Gentile Mission in Old Testament Citations in Acts: Text, Hermeneutic, and Purpose* (London: T&T Clark, 2008), 93–113, argues strongly

it (Acts 2:41). It is to the people "far off" that Paul is sent (Acts 22:21). In the second half of the chiastic structure, those both far and near receive peace (Eph 2:17). See further the next textual note.

ἐν τῷ αἵματι τοῦ Χριστοῦ—See the third textual note on 1:7. With the allusion to the temple (see the preceding textual note), "the blood of Christ" gains even more sacrificial import. The blood of the daily sacrifices in the temple was for the sins of all God's people, but its sprinkling was directly available only to those Jewish men who could stand close to the altar. The requirement that Gentile converts be circumcised, shedding their blood, was also a significant obstacle to their drawing near to God. But Christ's blood, shed once for all on the cross (Col 1:20), is sprinkled equally on all Christians through the cleansing water of Holy Baptism, which unites them with his death on the cross (Eph 2:16).[44] The aorist verb in the preceding textual note, ἐγενήθητε, "you have become," points to such a pivotal past event. But they also remain "near" to God through their ongoing, eucharistic participation in that sacrificial blood through the cup of blessing (1 Cor 10:16). The liturgical context of this pericope is important. The Gentiles who were once far off from the *worship* of the inner parts of the temple are now drawn near to join with the Jews in one new "temple" (Eph 2:21), receiving God's gifts and praising him (cf. 3:20–21; 5:18–20).

2:14 αὐτὸς γὰρ ἐστιν ἡ εἰρήνη ἡμῶν—By definition and by its position in the sentence, αὐτός is emphatic: "for *he himself* is our peace." ἡ εἰρήνη, "peace," stands in contrast to τὴν ἔχθραν, "the hostility, enmity" (2:14, 16). It is repeated at the end of 2:15 to form a frame around these central verses of the pericope. On "peace," see the first textual note on 1:2. There, in the letter's salutation, "peace" emphasized the general state of well-being that comes from God. In the rest of Ephesians, "peace" is particularly connected to "reconciliation"—unity between men and God, and with one another (2:17; 4:3; 6:23), the first one leading to the second. As such, "peace" is "nearly synonymous w[ith] messianic salvation."[45] The Messiah was promised to be our peace (Is 9:5–6 [ET 9:6–7]; 53:5; Micah 5:4 [ET 5:5]), and the age of his coming was to be characterized by Jews and Gentiles coming together peacefully in God's house.[46] Peace was announced by the angels as the gift the Messiah would bring (Lk 2:14; cf. Rom 5:1). Furthermore, it is the content of Christ's preaching (Eph 2:17) and formed the basis of Paul's ministry of reconciliation (cf. 2 Cor 5:18–19). To say that Christ is "our peace"

---

that when Peter cites Joel in Acts 2:16–21, both Joel and Peter are suggesting the inclusion of the Gentiles in God's plan of salvation. Meek writes about Peter's use of Joel: "This early anticipation of the Gentile mission sets the stage for its more explicit treatment in Acts 13 and 15" (113).

[44] Note the connection of the OT rituals of blood sprinkling with the baptismal washing of water in Heb 9:19–22; 10:19–22, permitting all Christians to "draw near" (Heb 10:22). Already Isaiah prophesied that the Suffering Servant would sprinkle his shed blood on Gentiles as well as on Israelites: "Thus, he will sprinkle many nations" (Is 52:15).

[45] BDAG, s.v. εἰρήνη, 2 b.

[46] Is 2:2–4; 56:6–8; 57:19; 66:12; Micah 4:1–4; Zech 8:20–23.

(Eph 2:14; cf. "the peace of Christ," Col 3:15) is to confess his divinity, as God is "the God of peace"—one of Paul's favorite expressions.[47]

ὁ ποιήσας τὰ ἀμφότερα ἕν—It is clear from the parallel in 2:16 ("that he might reconcile both [τοὺς ἀμφοτέρους] in one body to God") that "both" here (τὰ ἀμφότερα) does not mean God and men, but refers to a division within mankind. These are "you who were far off" and "those who were near" (2:17). By their reconciliation to God in the one body of a common Savior, Gentiles and Jews are made "one" (εἷς, Gal 3:28).[48] This is the most personal application of the cosmic work of Christ, who on the cross brought together in himself all things in heaven and on earth (Eph 1:10; Col 1:20).

καὶ τὸ μεσότοιχον τοῦ φραγμοῦ λύσας—The participle λύσας completes a syntactical unit that began with the participle ὁ ποιήσας earlier in 2:14: Christ is the one "who has made … and has destroyed."[49] The NT hapax legomenon μεσότοιχον means "middle [μεσό-] wall [τοιχον]," as would divide a house into two or more rooms. φραγμός is a "fence, partition" (Mt 21:33; Mk 12:1; Lk 14:23). τοῦ φραγμοῦ is a genitive of apposition, the second noun (φραγμοῦ) defining the first (μεσότοιχον) more precisely: "the dividing wall that acts as a partition."[50] What does Paul have in mind? At least four possibilities have been proposed:

1. In light of Paul's recent emphasis on the evil spiritual forces arrayed against us and destroyed by Christ (1:20–22), "the dividing wall" could be "the air" (2:2) as the realm these spirits occupy. Many Greek religious systems conceived of the air as a liminal space touching both the heavens (God's realm) and the earth (man's realm), a battleground between good and evil. Gnostic myths spoke of a redeemer penetrating the divide to lead us up to God. Jewish Gnostic writings spoke of a river or ocean (sometimes with a wall next to it), separating heaven from earth, which could be a metaphor for the Law.[51] However, Paul's language ("dividing wall of partition") invites a more literal referent (see option 4). Moreover, what Paul has said is that Christ triumphed over and subordinated these forces, not that he destroyed their realm—though newfound access to God is certainly a Pauline idea. A further problem with this interpretation is

---

[47] Rom 15:33; 16:20; 1 Cor 14:33; 2 Cor 13:11; Phil 4:9; 1 Thess 5:23; cf. Phil 4:7; 2 Thess 3:16; Heb 13:20.

[48] Tertullian, *Against Marcion*, 5:17.15: "… *that he might reconcile both to God*—the God whom both nations had offended—both the Jewish and the gentile people *in one body*, as he expresses it, *when in it he had slain the enmity by the cross*" (trans. Evans).

[49] On this as an example of the Granville Sharp Rule, see Wallace, *Greek Grammar*, 275.

[50] BDF, § 167. Turner, *Syntax*, 214–15, calls it *genitivus materiae* and *epexegeticus*, thus the dividing wall "consists of" a fence.

[51] Schlier, *Epheser*, 124–33, promotes this theory primarily because τὰ ἀμφότερα, "both," is neuter, not masculine: "Christ is the one who makes both realms one" (124). But the neuter can be used for groups of people (see other neuter words in Gal 3:28; Col 3:11), and in context τὰ ἀμφότερα here probably refers back to the abstract "Uncircumcision" and "Circumcision" (Eph 2:11). Paul uses masculine forms in 2:15 (τοὺς δύο, "the two") and 2:16 (τοὺς ἀμφοτέρους, "both").

that it assumes that the two parties of the reconciliation are God and men,[52] whereas 2:17 shows that the division Paul primarily has in mind is between two classes of men.[53]

2. Paul might have had in mind the great curtain that hung between the Holy Place and the Holy of Holies in the temple sanctuary (Ex 26:31–33). At Christ's death on the cross, this partition was literally torn in two (Mt 27:51; Mk 15:38), symbolizing the new access to the atoning, most-holy things of God that Christ's death achieved (Rom 5:2; Heb 6:19; 9:1–12; 10:19–22). This explanation is subject to the same objection that it refers to a division between God and men (rather than between two classes of men), but it has the advantage of alluding to a quite literal division—except that it is strange to refer to a curtain as a "dividing wall."

3. The dividing wall may be interpreted as the Law itself (Eph 2:15; cf. Acts 10:28)[54] and/or the man-made "fence around the Torah" by the traditions of the elders (cf. Mt 15:2; Mk 7:8).[55] The Law and its traditions had the effect of separating Jews and Gentiles. Jews held Gentiles in contempt as filthy "dogs" for their diet, sexual habits, and idolatry.[56] In return, anti-Judaism, which may well be called ἔχθρα, "hostility" (Eph 2:14), arose where Jewish traditions marked the Jews off from the people around them.[57] The Soreg (option 4) is simply one example of such traditions.

4. The most compelling literal referent of τὸ μεσότοιχον τοῦ φραγμοῦ is suggested by the account of Paul's arrest, which likely took place shortly before he penned the letter to the Ephesians in Caesarean captivity.[58] "They [the hostile (!) Jewish authorities] had previously seen Trophimus the Ephesian [!] in the city with him [Paul], whom they supposed that Paul had taken into the temple" (Acts 21:29). Paul had, of course, entered the temple to celebrate Pentecost, and his desire to participate in this celebration had been the reason for his haste in returning to Jerusalem (Acts 20:16). Putting one and one together, the Jews calculated that Paul had violated the prohibition against taking non-Jews inside the courts of the temple proper. Whether or not Paul would actually have violated this precept on the basis of his understanding of the Gospel is unclear, but it is unlikely in view of his claim to blameless Hebrew credentials and the directive given

---

[52] This is the interpretation of Chrysostom, who sees "the hostility in the [human, sinful] flesh," separating man from God, as that which Christ destroyed (*Homilies on Ephesians*, 5:2.13–15). Cf. Is 59:2.

[53] This is a view Chrysostom referenced but dismissed (*Homilies on Ephesians*, 5:2.13–15); Ambrosiaster's commentary adopts it (*Ephesians*, 2:14.1).

[54] "Our Lawgiver … fenced us round [περιέφραξεν, from περιφράγω, related to φραγμός, "fence"] with impregnable ramparts and walls of iron, that we might not mingle at all with any of the other nations, but remain pure in body and soul" (*Letter of Aristeas*, 139 [*APOT*, 107–8]).

[55] Mishnah, *Aboth*, 1:1, says: "Moses received the Law from Sinai and committed it to Joshua, and Joshua to the elders, and the elders to the Prophets; and the Prophets committed it to the men of the Great Synagogue. They said three things: Be deliberate in judgement, raise up many disciples, and make a fence around the Law" (Danby, *The Mishnah*, 446).

[56] See *DBI*, s.v. "Gentile," 325; cf. Str-B, 1:359–63; 3:588–91.

[57] Martin Scharlemann, "Secret," 414, notes that Caesar exempted Jews from military service because they would not work on the Sabbath or eat ordinary rations. Such special privileges were bound to raise hostility.

[58] See "Caesarea!" in "Location and Date of Writing" in the introduction.

him previously by James to prove publicly that he observed the Law (Acts 21:24). He claims before Festus to be innocent of any crime "deserving of death [ἄξιον θανάτου]" (Acts 25:11; see also Acts 25:25).[59] The Bible itself knows of no divisions in the grounds of the temple except regarding the Holy Place and the Holy of Holies. In fact, Solomon had expressly invited foreigners to pray at the temple (1 Ki 8:41–43), and Isaiah prophesied that foreigners would be full participants in temple worship (Is 56:3–8; "in my house and *within my walls*," Is 56:5).[60] But the temple as rebuilt by Herod had clear divisions between the Court of the Priests, the Court of the Israelites, and the Court of the Women.[61] Gentiles were prohibited from entering the temple proper, but could watch through the gateway from outside on the Temple Mount.[62] Both Josephus and the Mishnah speak of a low wall or fence some 3 cubits (4.5 feet; 1.5 meters) high that surrounded the temple, 10 cubits (15 feet; 5 meters) away from its outer steps. Known as the Soreg, this fence had openings opposite the gates into the temple, with guards posted and warning signs in Greek and Latin forbidding Gentiles to enter on pain of death.[63] In 1871 an archaeological excavation undertaken by Charles Simon Clermont-Ganneau discovered a stone inscription, echoing the warning recorded by Josephus, that must have hung at one of the entry points on the Soreg:[64]

---

[59] On the other hand, Paul may simply mean according to *Roman* law (cf. Acts 23:29; 26:31; 28:18). Yet, in Acts 25:10 he claims to have done nothing against the Jews.

[60] See Lessing, *Isaiah 56–66*, 60–69.

[61] Lee I. Levine, "Temple, Jerusalem," *EDEJ*, 1287, notes that the Court of the Women was not strictly for women alone, but for all who were not proceeding further in to offer sacrifices. A separation between women and men even in this court may have been introduced only in the mid first century AD.

[62] Mishnah, *Kelim*, 1:6–9, describes ten degrees of holiness: the land of Israel, walled cities, the area within the wall of Jerusalem, the Temple Mount, the Rampart (a ten-cubit area surrounding the temple itself, inside the Soreg), the Court of the Women, the Court of the Israelites, the Court of the Priests, the area between the Ulam (entry porch) and the altar, the *Hekal* (sanctuary), and the Holy of Holies (yes, this makes eleven!). Of the area inside the Soreg: "The Rampart is still more holy, for no gentiles and none that have contracted uncleanness from a corpse may enter therein" (Danby, *The Mishnah*, 605). There is an ongoing Jewish dispute whether Jews today can enter the Temple Mount, lest they accidentally wander into an area forbidden them, for these divisions did not only affect Gentiles.

[63] Josephus, *Wars*, 5:193–94; Josephus, *Antiquities*, 15:417. The historical origins of the fence are unknown, but it was in place at the time of the Greek conquest (early second century BC), when Greek oppressors broke thirteen gaps in the fence in order to enter the temple. The Hasmoneans repaired the breeches with low fences, that Jews would ever remember the sacrilege and be vigilant. See Mishnah, *Middoth*, 2:3. The death sentence is discussed in Mishnah, *Sanhedrin*, 9:6.

[64] See Deissmann, *Light from the Ancient East*, 80; the translation is his. The tablet now resides in the Archaeological Museum in Istanbul. A second example, discovered in the 1930s, is in the Rockefeller Museum, Jerusalem.

μηθένα ἀλλογενῆ εἰς πο- ρεύεσθαι ἐντὸς τοῦ πε- ρὶ τὸ ἱερὸν τρυφάκτου καὶ περιβόλου. ὃς δ᾽ ἂν λη- φθῇ, ἑαυτῶι αἴτιος ἔσ- ται διὰ τὸ ἐξακολου- θεῖν θάνατον.	Let no foreigner enter within the screen and enclosure surrounding the sanctuary. Whosoever is taken so doing will be the cause that death over- taketh him.

Soreg inscription.

Photo: © 2000 Tamar Hayardeni.

This fence with its dire warning may well have been what Paul had in mind.[65]

In context, a combination of the third and fourth interpretations is most likely. This best suits the historical situation in which Paul wrote the letter, having been arrested on the charge of violating the temple division between Jews and Gentiles. Their reconciliation is the central thought of this pericope. This interpretation also makes good sense of the concluding reference to a new, "holy temple" (2:21). The temple barrier that divided and caused hatred had not yet been literally destroyed (though God would bring that about in AD 70),[66] but it had, like the Law itself, been bereft of all force through the

---

[65] Some have objected that this sign uses a different term for the wall than Paul: τρύφακτος. Josephus, *Wars*, 5:193, uses the alternate spelling of the sign's term, δρύφακτος. Yet Josephus uses vocabulary in line with Paul's when discussing the greater wall surrounding the Court of the Women (which also separated the temple proper from the Court of the Gentiles), saying that it was τείχει περιπεφραγμένον, "fenced around with a wall" (*Wars*, 5:195–96). He also refers to the wall between the two main parts of Solomon's temple as τὸν μέσον τοῖχον, "the middle/dividing wall" (*Antiquities*, 8:71). See Reicke, *Re-examining Paul's Letters*, 81, 135–36.

[66] In support of our interpretation, we note that λύω, the verb in Eph 2:14, or its compound καταλύω is frequently used in the NT for "breaking" or "tearing down" the temple (Mt 24:2; 26:61; Jn 2:19; Acts 6:14) and the Law (Mt 5:17, 19; Jn 7:23; Gal 2:18).

cross of Christ, in whose body (the new temple) there are no divisions. Although distant Gentiles might not ordinarily be expected to catch such a reference to the layout of the Jerusalem temple, the details of Paul's arrest would have been conveyed to them, particularly in light of the role of Trophimus the Ephesian (Acts 21:29).[67] But Paul's message is that the Ephesians need not fear that they are responsible for his imprisonment; by his cross Christ has destroyed all charges (Col 2:14), and indeed captivity itself (Eph 4:8). Reference to the temple's inner curtain is not entirely excluded, however, for it is because the divide between God and men had been destroyed in Christ and his cross that all things could be united one with another (2:16).

τὴν ἔχθραν ἐν τῇ σαρκὶ αὐτοῦ—"Hostility" characterized the Jewish authorities who sought Paul's death, as also those who sought our Lord's. As noted above, it characterized the relationship between Jews and Gentiles in the world. But the word ἔχθρα also evokes the "enmity" between Satan and the seed of Eve (LXX Gen 3:15), which was destroyed when Christ crushed Satan's head in triumph on the tree.[68] And ἔχθρα characterizes the relationship between the fleshly mind and God (Rom 8:7; cf. Gal 5:20). When all such ἔχθρα and their Satanic author are destroyed, man's relationship with God is restored; hostility is replaced with peace, toward both God and one another. ἐν τῇ σαρκὶ αὐτοῦ, "in his flesh" (2:14), parallels ἐν ἑνὶ σώματι, "in one body" (2:16), and refers to Christ's crucifixion.

Syntactically τὴν ἔχθραν ἐν τῇ σαρκὶ αὐτοῦ is difficult. τὴν ἔχθραν appears to be the direct object of the preceding verb, the participle λύσας, and it stands in apposition to τὸ μεσότοιχον. Thus, Christ "has destroyed the dividing wall of partition," which is "hostility." But some interpreters take τὴν ἔχθραν in apposition to τὸν νόμον, "the Law," as a direct object of the verb that follows, the participle καταργήσας, "by nullifying" (see the second textual note on 2:15); thus, "the Law" is "the hostility." Likewise, ἐν τῇ σαρκὶ αὐτοῦ, "in his flesh," may modify either participle (preceding or following). We have attached both phrases ("the hostility, in his flesh") to the preceding participle ("has destroyed"), since it is easier to conceive of "the hostility" as "the dividing wall" than as "the Law." But since these two statements run in parallel, the difference between the interpretations is not great.[69]

---

[67] Since the Ephesians are experiencing anxiety over Paul's afflictions for their sake (3:13), news of Paul's imprisonment must have previously reached them, perhaps through the same person who brought Paul news of their faith and love (1:15). Paul writes this letter in part to allay their fears over his arrest. See "Caesarea!" in "Location and Date of Writing" and "Jews and Greeks in the Body of Christ" in "Purpose and Themes," both in the introduction, and the textual notes on 3:1, 13.

[68] Thus, Schlier, *Epheser*, 130, connects "hostility" to the attacks of evil spiritual forces on the kingdom of God.

[69] "In his flesh" should be taken as an adverbial modifier of one or the other of the participles as the location of the *action* not the location of the *hostility*. "The hostility in his flesh" is possible (see the third textual note on 2:16), but less likely. Yet, it makes little sense to separate "the hostility" from "in his flesh" by taking "hostility" with the preceding clause and "flesh" with the following (RSV). ESV takes both phrases with the preceding, as in our translation. Lincoln, *Ephesians*, 124, argues that if this were intended, the phrases should have preceded λύσας, and he prefers to take them with the participle that follows, καταργήσας.

2:15 τὸν νόμον τῶν ἐντολῶν ἐν δόγμασιν—This rather heavy-handed threefold description emphasizes the oppressive power of the entire Law, which lays demands upon us and increases hostility, not least between Jew and Gentile. It leaves no room to limit Christ's nullifying work to the traditions of men or only to the ceremonial components of the Law. νόμος reflects תּוֹרָה, *Torah*, which is traditionally but rather inaccurately glossed persistently as "Law." תּוֹרָה derives from the Hiphil of יָרָה, "to instruct, teach," and thus means "instruction." As the Word of God, *Torah* can be either Law or Gospel teaching or both together. It is for this reason that Paul adds the qualifying (epexegetical) genitive and prepositional phrase[70] ("of commandments in decrees"), which serve to narrow the meaning to doctrinal "Law." The feminine noun ἐντολή is an individual word of instruction that carries the authority of someone in high position. While it could be a mandate/commission[71] or a promise,[72] the entire covenant (Mt 22:36; cf. ἐντέλλομαι in Heb 9:20), or any individual component of it (Heb 9:19), in the plural it most often refers to specific "commandments" within the Law (cf. Eph 6:2),[73] thus, "the Law consisting of commandments." Likewise, δόγμα might simply be a teaching or belief, but in the NT it is either a "decree" from an imperial figure (Lk 2:1; Acts 17:7) or the apostles (Acts 16:4) or a requirement of the Law (Col 2:14).

καταργήσας—This participle, though aorist, should be taken as simultaneous with the preceding two (articular) participles (ὁ ποιήσας, "who has made," and λύσας, "[who] has destroyed"), indicating means: "by nullifying."[74] The translation of καταργέω is bound up with the theological problem of Christ's relationship to the Law. It can mean either to "abolish, destroy" (1 Cor 6:13; 15:26) or to "nullify, invalidate, make powerless" (Rom 3:3). With reference to the Law, the latter is more consistent with Paul's theology and our Lord's (cf. Mt 5:19; Rom 3:31).[75] The law, for example, that binds a woman to a man in marriage is not "destroyed" by the husband's death, but "nullified"—it no longer has a hold on her (Rom 7:2). What Paul means here, then, is that by Christ's cross we are released from the Law's power to condemn and kill (Rom 7:6; 8:1).

---

[70] Some Greek fathers take ἐν δόγμασιν as instrumental: the Law is nullified "by [Christ's] decrees." Not only does this run the risk of seeing Christ as a new Moses (Lawgiver), but it would also seem to contradict "in his flesh" (2:14). The omission of ἐν δόγμασιν in 𝔓[46] vg[ms] is surely by accident or because it appeared redundant.

[71] Jn 10:18; 11:57; 12:49; Col 4:10; cf. ἐντέλλομαι in Acts 1:2; 13:47.

[72] Jn 12:50; Rev 14:12; cf. ἐντέλλομαι in Mt 28:20 (Jesus' teaching is scarcely to be characterized as doctrinal Law alone). John seems least likely to use ἐντολή as "commandment" (e.g., of the Decalogue). It is possible to interpret ἐντολή (or ἐντέλλομαι) plus ἵνα in John as a purpose clause: "I have given you this new kind of covenant teaching in order that you might love one another" (Jn 13:34; also Jn 15:12, 17; cf. 1 Jn 2:7–8; 3:23; 4:21; 2 Jn 5–6). See Jonathan F. Grothe, " 'Abide in My Love' (John 15:9)," *Lutheran Theological Review* 6.2 (Spring/Summer 1994): 11–14.

[73] E.g., Mt 5:19; 22:38–40; Mk 10:19; cf. Lk 23:56; Rom 7:8–13; 13:9.

[74] Wallace, *Greek Grammar*, 630; Voelz, *Fundamental Greek Grammar*, 260; BDF, § 339 (1). Cf. Eph 1:20; 5:26.

[75] Some critics have posited that Eph 2:15 is incompatible with Rom 3:31 and therefore un-Pauline. A most thorough explanation is given by Jonathan Grothe, "Romans 3:31 and Ephesians 2:15," in *The Justification of the Ungodly*, 229–32.

ἵνα τοὺς δύο κτίσῃ ἐν αὐτῷ εἰς ἕνα καινὸν ἄνθρωπον—The ultimate purpose of Christ's work may be to reconcile men to God (2:16), but in this particular context Paul emphasizes a subsidiary purpose: to be reconciled to one another. κτίζω, "to create," in combination with καινὸν ἄνθρωπον, "new man," alludes to fallen Adam as the origin of sin and Christ as the Second Adam. Rom 5:12–21 again lurks in the background (see the fifth textual note and the commentary on 2:3). As the first Adam's fall consigned all mankind to sin, as all were in him when he sinned, so Christ brings freedom to all men (Jew and Gentile) by including all "in him,"[76] that is, in his body on the cross.[77] Through Baptism into his death, all people are reborn, made new, restored to the image of God (Rom 6:6; Eph 4:22–24; Col 3:9). Yet we must reckon with the phrase "*one* new man" (Eph 2:15): it is not simply that everyone is made new, but that all are enclosed in *the one new Man*, Jesus Christ.[78] Though the church is the body of Christ (1:23), Paul is not merely saying that Jew and Gentile are united in one church. They are united in Christ himself. "If anyone is in Christ, [there is a] new creation!" (2 Cor 5:17; cf. Gal 6:15). "You are all *one man* [εἷς is masculine!] in Christ Jesus" (Gal 3:28).

ποιῶν εἰρήνην—See the first (re "peace") and the second (re "has made") textual notes on 2:14. If Christ has made peace, then those who are in him can have or make peace with one another (James 3:18).

2:16 καὶ ἀποκαταλλάξῃ τοὺς ἀμφοτέρους ἐν ἑνὶ σώματι τῷ θεῷ—The aorist subjunctive ἀποκαταλλάξῃ, "that he might reconcile," is the second verb of the purpose clause that began with ἵνα (2:15b): creating one new man (2:15b) and reconciling both Jews and Gentiles to God (2:16) are the two reasons why Christ nullified the Law. The triply compound form ἀποκαταλλάσσω, "to reconcile," is found only here and in the Colossian parallel (Col 1:20, 22), where Paul speaks of the cosmic reconciliation of all things that is the presupposition of this text. The reconciliation of Jews and Gentiles to one another can happen only if both have first been reconciled to God. This, too, is a thought Paul first expressed in Romans 5 (Rom 5:10, 11, with the cognates καταλλάσσω, "reconcile," and καταλλαγή, "reconciliation"). ἐν ἑνὶ σώματι, "in one body," points forward to the phrase "through the cross" (see the next textual note) and backward to "in him" (see the third textual note on 2:15). Paul will not have us lose sight of the crucifixion as the central event through which this reconciliation or "atonement"[79] is achieved. It happens through putting to death the two old, hostile

---

[76] Since ἐν αὐτῷ, "in him," refers back to Christ, the subject of the verb, it has a reflexive meaning, "in him*self*." Perhaps this should more properly be expressed by ἐν ἑαυτῷ (the variant reading). But the reflexive use of the simple pronoun αὐτός is common in the NT, particularly when governed by a preposition (BDF, § 283; see also the third textual note on 2:16). Paul is fond of saying ἐν αὐτῷ, "in him"! See the fifth textual note on 1:3.

[77] "He became a Jew when he was circumcised. Then, being cursed, he became a Greek outside the law and one more excellent than either Greek or Jew" (Chrysostom, *Homilies on Ephesians*, 5:2.15 [ACCS 8:140]).

[78] The textual variant κοινόν (𝔓⁴⁶ F G), by changing just one vowel of καινόν, turns "new man" into "common man." Though probably not the original text, it is a significant early interpretation of Paul's meaning.

[79] The word "atonement," or "at-one-ment," was coined in the early sixteenth century (according to the *OED*). In his translation of 2 Cor 5:18–20, Tyndale (1526) translated καταλλαγή

parties and replacing them with a newly created man who is not only in the image of Christ, but is in Christ. Thus, "in one body" does not refer here to the church,[80] even though one might speak of the apostolic ministry in the church as an ongoing act of reconciliation (2 Cor 5:18–20). It refers, rather, to the historical, concrete, fleshly body of Christ that was crucified—there is no reason to read the phrase here differently than the similar phrase ἐν τῷ σώματι τῆς σαρκὸς αὐτοῦ, "in the body of his flesh," in Col 1:22—though certainly that one-time, past historical action forms the basis of every subsequent, subjective act of reconciliation through the means of grace in the church.[81] Through Holy Baptism each of us has consequently died with Christ to the Law and risen with him that we might belong to God (Rom 7:4, drawing a conclusion from Romans 6). But if reconciliation in Christ's crucified body had not first happened, reconciliation through the Gospel would be impossible.

διὰ τοῦ σταυροῦ—Though the vocabulary of justification (δικαι-) is nearly absent from Ephesians and Colossians, "the cross" is still central. Appearing on the heels of "by grace you have been saved through faith" (2:8), the cross forms the theological backbone of the epistle and the basis of everything that follows. The unity of the entire argument depends on it. It is intriguing that references to the cross and crucifying (σταυρόω) are absent from Romans but concentrated somewhat in the Prison Epistles;[82] perhaps as Paul's own suffering increased, he was drawn to the cross of Christ.

ἀποκτείνας τὴν ἔχθραν ἐν αὐτῷ—The aorist participle ἀποκτείνας, like the preceding one (καταργήσας, 2:15), is not temporal ("*after* killing") but indicates means: "*by* killing." "Killing the hostility," though accomplished through a literal death (of Christ), is another figure for rendering the Law incapable of arousing hostility. ἐν αὐτῷ could refer either to the cross ("by it") or to Christ ("in him[self]").[83] Although the former is syntactically more likely, as "the cross" is the nearer antecedent, Paul's consistent usage of ἐν αὐτῷ in Ephesians to mean "in him [Christ]" is persuasive, as is the parallelism in the two statements of purpose:

---

in 2 Cor 5:18–19 as "atonement" and καταλλάσσω in 2 Cor 5:20 as "be atone [at one]" (see *Matthew's Bible: A Facsimile of the 1537 Edition* [Peabody, Mass.: Hendrickson, 2009]).

[80] Contra Lincoln, *Ephesians*, 144; Best, *Ephesians*, 265; and the majority of commentators. The church as Christ's body is a major theme in Ephesians (also 1:23; 3:6; 4:4, 12, 16; 5:23, 30), but this letter does not always promote ecclesiology over Christology or soteriology (as Lincoln, 144, admits).

[81] Schlier, *Epheser*, 135: "The ἓν σῶμα ['one body'] in the apostle's thinking in this context is without a doubt the body of Christ on the cross. … But one must not overlook the fact that in the body of Christ on the cross, which/who took both Jews and Gentiles upon itself/himself and reconciled God, the church is present there virtually and potentially."

[82] 1 Corinthians (six times); 2 Cor 13:4; Galatians (six times); Eph 2:16; Phil 2:8; 3:18; Col 1:20; 2:14.

[83] By way of clarification, the variant in F G *pc* latt reads ἑαυτῷ, "in himself." The use of a simple pronoun (αὐτῷ) where a reflexive pronoun (ἑαυτῷ) is required by the syntax is not unusual in Koine Greek. See the third textual note on 2:15. The same ambiguity of referent occurs with ἐν αὐτῷ in Col 2:15.

2:15	that he might create	the two	in him	into one new man	making peace
2:16	that he might reconcile	both	in him	in one body	by killing the hostility

This parallelism also pictures the force of Paul's argument, that horizontal reconciliation is accomplished through the vertical. "In him" is the location of the act of killing; but in a profound sense it is also the location of the hostility. Those who object to the idea that hostility was found "in him"[84] fail to reckon with this identification. Because God made Christ to be sin (2 Cor 5:21), by the death of Christ God killed sin and the hostility that goes with it.

2:17 καὶ ἐλθὼν εὐηγγελίσατο—"Peace to you" is the characteristic message of the resurrected Christ (Lk 24:36; Jn 20:19–20, 26). Like Aaron and his sons, who were to proclaim peace to the people in the benediction (Num 6:24–26)[85] after performing the sacrifices that achieved it, Christ declares what his work has accomplished. Thus, it also becomes the apostle Paul's characteristic greeting (1:2), as through his apostles and ministers Christ continues to preach peace. But there are good reasons to believe that Paul has in mind also the pre-passion phase of Christ's earthly ministry. εὐαγγελίζομαι, "to preach good news" (the verb might come from Is 52:7), is an apt and accurate summary of Christ's ministry.[86] Paul is not simply saying that Christ preached a message of peace that was applicable both to those "who were far off" and to those "who were near" (2:17), but he is referring also to the historical circumstances of Christ's ministry, in which he preached not only in Galilee and Judea, but also in Samaria (Lk 9:52; Jn 4:1–42), Tyre and Sidon (Mt 15:21–28), the Decapolis (Mt 4:25; Mk 7:31), and Caesarea Philippi (Mt 16:13)—territories populated by Samaritans and Gentiles. In fact, Galilee itself was known as "Galilee of the Gentiles" (MT/LXX Is 8:23 [ET 9:1], quoted in Mt 4:15), as it was the meeting point of multilingual and multiethnic peoples. Thus, from the very start Christ saw his ministry as a gathering in of people of all kinds, though beginning with the elect people of old (Mt 15:24). His mandate to the apostles was to continue as he had done (Mt 28:19–20).

εἰρήνην ὑμῖν τοῖς μακρὰν καὶ εἰρήνην τοῖς ἐγγύς—Similar is 2:13 (see the second textual note there), but here Paul comes closer to an actual quotation of MT Is 57:19, "peace, peace, to the far away and to the near," either paraphrasing it himself or quoting a version other than the LXX.[87] Eph 2:13–18 is a typical example of the midrash

---

[84] E.g., Best, *Ephesians*, 266.

[85] The use of the Aaronic Benediction at the end of the Divine Service is an addition to the Roman rite made by Luther, and until recently it was uniquely Lutheran. Luther suggested that it was what our Lord spoke to bless the apostles just before his ascension (*Formula Missae* [1523], AE 53:30).

[86] As a précis of Jesus' ministry, "preach good news" (εὐαγγελίζομαι) is characteristic particularly of Luke's Gospel (Lk 4:18, 43; 7:22; 8:1; 16:16; 20:1). Luke's Gospel is Paul's Gospel.

[87] LXX Is 57:19 reads: εἰρήνην ἐπ' εἰρήνην τοῖς μακρὰν καὶ τοῖς ἐγγὺς οὖσιν· καὶ εἶπεν κύριος ἰάσομαι αὐτούς, "peace upon peace to those far off and to those being near, and the

technique of biblical interpretation, as Paul draws together a number of passages featuring the key word "peace" to interpret Is 57:19 and apply it to Christ. Isaiah's passage, which in its original context may have referred to *Israelites* both near and far (that is, at home and in the dispersion—scattered "far off" because of their sins and brought near through God's forgiveness), is now, not inappropriately, applied to the *Gentiles*. Paul may be following existing rabbinic exegesis of the passage in doing so.[88] The implication is that the Gentiles, too, may become God's people, but need to be gathered into the true Israel through a divine act of reconciliation. The Messiah came to preach peace (Acts 10:36; cf. Lk 2:14), to accomplish it on his cross (Eph 2:14–17), and, alluding to the proclaimer's "beautiful feet" (Is 52:7), to armor the Christian's feet with "the Gospel of peace" (Eph 6:15). See further "peace" in the first textual note on 2:14. As in Rom 5:1–2, justification leads to peace with God, and peace leads to access to his grace.

2:18 ὅτι δι᾿ αὐτοῦ ἔχομεν τὴν προσαγωγὴν οἱ ἀμφότεροι ἐν ἑνὶ πνεύματι πρὸς τὸν πατέρα—We hold these words together to highlight their Trinitarian message. Paul has made his way from the lesser to the greater, from reconciliation between Jew and Gentile to the ground and reason (ὅτι, "because") of their reconciliation, namely, their reconciliation with Almighty God. The relationship of the three divine persons in the economy of salvation is scarcely expressed better in the NT. The role of the Son ("through him") is to lead mankind to "the Father," in and by the Holy "Spirit." These words receive a more extensive exposition in 4:1–6, where again we have "one Spirit" (4:4), emphasizing the theme of Christian unity and the location where it comes about: in the "one body and one Spirit" into which we are all baptized (cf. 1 Cor 12:13). The "reverse creedal" pattern of Eph 4:4–6 is explained and reflected also in this verse: the Spirit leads us to Christ, who leads us to the Father.

As in 2:14, 16, "both" (οἱ ἀμφότεροι) refers back to the two groups (Jews and Gentiles) who find their unity with each other in the one body of Christ, who through the working of the one Spirit brings access to the (one) Father. In the present context, τὴν προσαγωγήν, "access," may allude to the division of "far off" and "near" (2:17)— those previously blessed with access to God through the temple and those denied it by their location and race (see the third textual note on 2:14). In Christ the divisions present in the earthly temple no longer apply, replaced by worship in the Spirit (Jn 4:23). As prophesied,[89] both groups now have equal, unfettered access to God; they are equally consecrated and holy that they may be near to him, to offer sacrifices and receive his blessings (cf. 2 Chr 29:31). Like Israel of old, which was "a kingdom of priests" (Ex 19:6), all Christians are privileged to be holy people who live in the house of God and are near and dear to him. Through Christ and in the Spirit we can offer the Father

---

Lord said, 'I shall heal them.' " Lincoln, *Ephesians*, 148, plausibly argues that Paul's wording emphasizes a vertical reconciliation of each group to God, while the LXX and MT could be read as also including the horizontal.

[88] Barth, *Ephesians*, 1:276–77; Lincoln, *Ephesians*, 147; Kirby, *Ephesians: Baptism and Pentecost*, 157–58.

[89] E.g., Is 2:2–4; 56:6–8; 66:20–21; Micah 4:1–4; Zech 8:20–23.

true worship.[90] In addition to such ritual/liturgical access to God, "a status factor is implied."[91] Like favored subjects approaching a king's throne or children with intimate access to a prestigious father, we have the privilege of approaching the Father to have our petitions answered and to receive his gifts.[92]

2:19 ἄρα οὖν—"So, then": Paul draws out the implications of Christ's work (2:13–18), which undid the predicament of the Gentiles (2:11–12), and leads into his description of the new people of God (2:19–22).

οὐκέτι ἐστὲ ξένοι καὶ πάροικοι—The two synonyms here, ξένοι, "strangers," and πάροικοι, "sojourners, resident aliens," are parallel to the synonyms ξένοι, "strangers," and ἀπηλλοτριωμένοι, "alienated," in 2:12 (see the third and fifth textual notes there). Though the Gentiles might from a fleshly perspective still be ξένοι, "foreigners," to Israel, in Christ such distinctions no longer carry weight. Like Ruth, their status changed when they were shown undeserved mercy (Ruth 2:10). As "strangers and sojourners" (Eph 2:19) in relation to Israel, the Gentiles were formerly like beggars, relying on the (spiritual) hospitality of their hosts under the common code of the Middle East (2 Sam 12:4; Job 31:32; 3 Jn 5), but now they have the twin privileges of citizenship and family (Eph 2:19b). In this experience, the Gentiles were not so different from Israel. Even they experienced alienation through their many exiles, which made them sojourners in foreign lands (Gen 23:4; Ex 2:22; Acts 7:6), teaching them not to be conformed to this world. In fact, even the promised land was not theirs; it belonged to the Lord, their bene- factor, upon whose hospitality they continued to rely; they were sojourners in the Lord's land (Lev 25:23; 1 Chr 29:15). Thus, the common experience of sojourning teaches all mankind to rely on mercy (Ps 39:13 [ET 39:12]). Ironically, our redemption was accomplished through the alienation of the Messiah from his own people, by his trad- ing places with the people he came to save.[93] Those who are baptized into Christ share in this alienation from the present, evil world (Heb 11:13; 1 Pet 1:17; 2:11) but receive eternal hospitality in their final, eschatological home (Mt 22:1–14; 25:1–13; Rev 19:9).

ἀλλὰ ἐστὲ συμπολῖται τῶν ἁγίων—The noun συμπολῖται, "fellow citizens," con- trasts with the Ephesian Gentiles' earlier status as ἀπηλλοτριωμένοι τῆς πολιτείας τοῦ Ἰσραήλ, "alienated from the commonwealth/citizenship of Israel" (2:12). It is another significant occurrence of a compound word created with σύν, "with," emphasizing the unity of all peoples in Christ (cf. the compounds in 2:5, 6, 21, 22; 3:6; 4:3, 16; 5:7, 11). The Gentiles are not to seek safety and privilege in any kingdom of this world, but to rejoice in their heavenly citizenship (Phil 3:20; Heb 12:23). τῶν ἁγίων must surely be understood as "*all* the saints," the all-inclusive group of the baptized that incorporates

---

[90] See Rom 5:2 and Eph 3:12, the only other biblical uses of προσαγωγή, "access." Cf. προσάγω, "to grant access, to bring," in 1 Pet 3:18 (which introduces a baptismal statement); προσέρχομαι, "to draw near, approach," in Heb 4:16; and εἴσοδος, "entrance," in Heb 10:19. The most frequent use of προσάγω in the LXX is in sacrificial/cultic contexts for "drawing near" to God with a sacrifice (forty-three times in Leviticus; twenty-three times in Numbers). See Winger, "The Priesthood of All the Baptized," 1–68.

[91] BDAG, s.v. προσαγωγή.

[92] Cf. Gen 48:9; Jn 14:9; Rom 8:14–15; Gal 4:6.

[93] E.g., Ps 69:9 (ET 69:8); Is 53:3; Jn 1:11; 5:43.

Christians of both Jewish and Gentile background, on earth and in heaven (cf. the Apostles' Creed: *sanctorum communionem*, "the communion of saints," which is also a "communion in holy things"). This is their new citizenship. They form, as many early fathers put it, "a third race,"[94] which is not a completely new thing but the fulfillment of what Israel was truly meant to be, "the Israel of God" (Gal 6:16; cf. Rom 9:6).[95]

The lack of a word like "all" in the Greek text, however, has led some readers to wonder whether τῶν ἁγίων, "the holy ones," refers to a group distinct from the Gentile Ephesian Christians. The suggestion that it might refer exclusively to OT believers/saints or Jewish Christians can be quickly dismissed, as the term "holy ones/saints" is not used this way in the NT.[96] The support for an all-inclusive referent ("all believers/Christians") is strong, since, as elsewhere in his epistles (e.g., Rom 1:7; 1 Cor 1:2), Paul consistently uses ἅγιοι in Ephesians as a designation for Christians in general ("saints"),[97] among whom the "holy" apostles are a subgroup (Eph 3:5). Furthermore, there is indeed precedent for this terminology in the OT and apocryphal literature, as the people of God are said to be ἅγιος, "holy,"[98] and are often called ἅγιοι, "holy ones/saints."[99]

On the other hand, it is true that (οἱ) ἅγιοι, "(the) holy ones," in the Septuagint often refers to the host of God in heaven, particularly the angels.[100] This usage is also found in the Qumran literature.[101] Paul himself may use ἅγιοι to refer to the angels (1 Thess 3:13; 2 Thess 1:10; cf. 2 Thess 1:7). The citizenship (συμπολῖται, "fellow citizens") to which Paul refers in Eph 2:19 is elsewhere called a heavenly citizenship (Phil 3:20); Paul has just previously asserted that the baptized have been lifted up with Christ to the heavenly places (Eph 2:6). Such data have led some interpreters to suggest that συμπολῖται

[94] Cf. *Preaching of Peter*, quoted in Clement of Alexandria, *Stromata*, 6:5.41.6: "we who worship God in a new way, as the third race [τρίτῳ γένει], are Christians"; *Epistle to Diognetus*, 1: "this new race [καινὸν τοῦτο γένος]" (quoted in Bruce, *The Epistles to the Colossians, to Philemon, and to the Ephesians*, 296, n. 110). This may be Paul's meaning in 1 Cor 10:32: "give no offense to Jews and to Greeks and to the church of God."

[95] The Talmud expresses this thought concerning so-called proselyte baptism: "When he has undergone baptism and come up [*ṭabhal we'ala*], he is like an Israelite in all respects" (*Yebamoth*, 47b, quoted in Daube, *The New Testament and Rabbinic Judaism*, 111).

[96] See Lincoln, *Ephesians*, 150–51; Best, *Ephesians*, 277–78.

[97] Eph 1:1, 15; 3:8, 18; 4:12; 5:3; 6:18; cf. 1:4 and 5:27, in which the church is called "holy." Eph 1:18 is less clear and could mean "among the holy ones [of heaven]."

[98] LXX Ex 19:6; 22:30 (ET 22:31); Lev 11:44–45; 19:2; 20:7, 26; 21:6; etc. Ps Sol 17:32 prophesies that in the messianic age "all will be holy" (cf. Num 16:3; Is 4:3).

[99] LXX Num 16:5; Pss 15:3 (MT/ET 16:3); 21:4 (MT 22:4; ET 22:3); 33:10 (MT 34:10; ET 34:9); 82:4 (MT 83:4; ET 83:3); Is 41:16; Dan 7:18, 21, 22, 25; 8:24–25; Tobit 12:15 (second occurrence); Pss Sol 11:1; 17:43; cf. Wis Sol 5:5; 18:5 (ὁσίων), 9. Some texts (such as LXX Ps 109:3 [MT/ET 110:3]; Sirach 42:17) are ambiguous (heavenly or earthly holy ones).

[100] E.g., LXX Job 5:1; 15:15; Pss 67:36 (MT 68:36; ET 68:35); 88:6–8 (MT 89:6–8; ET 89:5–7); Zech 14:5; Tobit 8:15; 11:14; 3 Macc 2:2, 21; Sirach 45:2. By placing ἅγιοι, "holy ones," before "apostles and prophets" among the company of heaven (Rev 18:20), Revelation may be implying a reference to angels; so suggests Otto Procksch, "ἅγιος," *TDNT* 1:109.

[101] E.g., 1QS 11:7, 8; 1QH 3:21–23; 6:10–14; 1QM 12:1, 2, cited by Lincoln, *Ephesians*, 151. See also references in Barth, *Ephesians*, 1:269, n. 71, and the discussion in Hofius, "Gemeinschaft mit den Engeln im Gottesdienst der Kirche," 182–86.

τῶν ἁγίων should be translated or interpreted as "fellow citizens [of heaven] with all the holy ones [the angels]."[102] This interpretation is, on the whole, unobjectionable, as it implies incorporation into the spiritual temple and dwelling place of God that transcends earth into the heavenly realm. It is consistent with the proleptic soteriology of 2:1–10 and the claim of the *Berakah* prayer (1:3–14) that the baptized have been incorporated into the heavenly choir to God's eternal praise. It follows naturally from the claim that in Christ the divide between men and God has been broken down (2:14–16). Nonetheless, as Lincoln cautions, "the consistency of meaning for ἅγιοι in its other appearances in Ephesians must give one pause before proposing a different reference in 2:19."[103] Thus, we are probably on more solid ground to maintain "[all] the saints [OT believers and NT Christians]" as the primary referent of τῶν ἁγίων, while acknowledging that we are also united with all the host of heaven (saints and angels), as the Proper Preface in the Divine Service declares before we sing the angelic song of Isaiah 6 (the Sanctus): "therefore with angels and archangels and with all the company of heaven we laud and magnify Your glorious name."[104]

καὶ οἰκεῖοι τοῦ θεοῦ—The adjective οἰκεῖοι is used as a substantive, "(people) belonging to a household," usually family members (see οἰκεῖος in, e.g., LXX Lev 18:6, 12, 13, 17; 21:2; 1 Tim 5:8). It stands in verbal contrast to πάροικοι, "sojourners" (earlier in 2:19), who are παρά, "alongside," the household, but not in it. In this sense, brothers and sisters in Christ, who share a heavenly Father, form a household of faith (Gal 6:10 has οἰκεῖοι, as here; 1 Tim 3:15 and Heb 3:6 have οἶκος). This is a dear and intimate relationship into which these former strangers are incorporated.

However, the following verses suggest another aspect to the image. The LXX almost always avoided the common Greek word for a "temple," τὸ ἱερόν, when referring to the temple of the true God in Jerusalem, probably because of pagan associations (just as it preferred the adjective ἅγιος to ἱερός for "holy"). The Jerusalem temple is called ναός or ναὸς ἅγιος, or more frequently, οἶκος, "house," often qualified by ἅγιος, "holy," τοῦ θεοῦ, "of God," or κυρίου, "of the Lord."[105] This allows for the play on words involved in Nathan's conversation with David about his plans to build a temple for God. Through the prophet God declares to David, in effect, "You need not make me a *house*, but I shall build you a *house*" (2 Sam 7:1–14)—meaning the messianic lineage

[102] Schlier, *Epheser*, 140–41, opts for this interpretation, though he includes believers in heaven as well as the angels.

[103] Lincoln, *Ephesians*, 151.

[104] E.g., *LSB Altar Book*, 145. See Hofius, "Gemeinschaft mit den Engeln im Gottesdienst der Kirche." Hofius concludes his article by quoting the sixth stanza of Luther's Christmas hymn "Gelobet seist du Jesu Christ": "Er ist auf Erden kommen arm, / daß er unser sich erbarm / und in dem Himmel mache reich / und seinen lieben Engeln gleich. Kyrieleis." "He has come to earth in poor estate / that he might have mercy upon us / and in heaven make us rich / and like his dear angels. Lord, have mercy" (cf. *LSB* 382:6). Cf. these words of Jesus concerning the resurrected saints in the coming age: *ἰσάγγελοι* γάρ εἰσιν, "for they are *like angels*," Lk 20:36.

[105] Gottlob Schrenk, "ἱερόν," *TDNT* 3:233.

leading to Christ and the family of faith he would bring into existence.[106] Thus, as "members of God's household" (Eph 2:19) and as the body of Christ, Christians themselves would constitute the new temple in which God would dwell.[107]

2:20 ἐποικοδομηθέντες ἐπὶ τῷ θεμελίῳ τῶν ἀποστόλων καὶ προφητῶν—The verb ἐποικοδομέω, "to build up upon [something already built]," is commonly used in the NT to describe the incorporation of saints into Christ's church and their strengthening in the faith.[108] The aorist passive participle ἐποικοδομηθέντες is causal, grounding the Gentile Ephesians' status as fellow citizens (2:19) in the action of God: it is a divine passive, "built up (by God)," for God builds his church (Mt 16:18; 1 Cor 3:7). But what is the role of "the apostles and prophets"? The genitives in τῶν ἀποστόλων καὶ προφητῶν could be understood as subjective, so that the θεμέλιος, "foundation," is something laid *by* the apostles and prophets (e.g., NEB, TEV). This would allow the foundation itself to be Christ, as in Paul's analogy in 1 Cor 3:9–14.[109] But more likely the genitive is appositional: the apostles and prophets *are* the foundation.

Critics often drive a wedge between these two passages, arguing that the authentic Paul taught that Christ alone was the foundation (1 Cor 3:9–14) and would not have spoken of the apostles (including himself) in the same category (Eph 2:20).[110] The Ephesian high view of the apostles is said to be a mark of incipient Catholicism and a sign that the age of the living apostles is long past.[111] But that Paul refers to himself as a "master builder" in laying the foundation (1 Cor 3:10) is equally stunning (cf. Heb 11:10, where God is the builder). One might as easily object that Christ's identification of himself as the temple (e.g., Jn 2:19–22) conflicts with Paul and Peter speaking of Christians as temple stones (1 Cor 3:12; 1 Pet 2:5). Writers can and do vary their metaphors. In the present context (2:20–22), Paul makes a strong theological point by including both Christ and the church (Head and body) in the new temple building. He adapts the analogy in such a way that Christ is the cornerstone (or capstone), not the entire foundation, with the apostles and prophets completing it, and all Christians built upon it. This adaptation is not completely unknown in Paul's other writings. For example, he refers to the inner circle of apostles as "pillars" (Gal 2:9), though with the qualification οἱ δοκοῦντες, "reputed to be." It is hardly out of character for Paul to emphasize the divine origin and authority of his office (e.g., 2 Corinthians 10–12; Galatians 1–2), as he does at the beginning

---

[106] The noun בַּיִת, literally, "house," occurs in 2 Sam 7:1, 2, 5–7, 11, 13, 16, 18, 19, 25–27, 29. This is the most frequent term in the OT for a "temple," as well as a common word for a family "household."

[107] Eph 2:20–22; 2 Cor 6:16–18; 1 Pet 2:1–10; cf. 1 Cor 6:19. See Scharlemann, "Secret," 415–16.

[108] Also 1 Cor 3:9–14; Col 2:7; Jude 20; cf. Acts 9:31; 20:32; Eph 4:12.

[109] The textual variant in 1 Pet 2:5 that substitutes ἐποικοδομεῖσθε, "you are being built up *upon*," for the simple form of the verb, οἰκοδομεῖσθε, "you are being built up," likewise has the living stones (Christians) built upon the Living Stone (Christ).

[110] This is part of the critical argument that Ephesians must have been written later and by another author, not Paul. See "Arguments against Pauline Authorship" in "Authorship" in the introduction.

[111] See "Incipient Catholicism" in "Arguments against Pauline Authorship" and "Incipient Catholicism" in "Evaluation of the Case," both in "Authorship" in the introduction.

of most of his epistles with the self-identification "Paul, apostle of Christ Jesus" (as in Eph 1:1). In context, this is precisely what he is about to do (Eph 3:1–10). It is, therefore, not at all un-Pauline for him to call the apostles the foundation of the church and to include himself at that level.

Ultimately Paul's expression is rooted in our Lord's own words to Peter: "You are Peter [Πέτρος, *Petros*, 'rock'], and on this rock [πέτρα, *petra*] I will build my church" (Mt 16:18). In the official Lutheran response to Roman claims that this established the papal office (primacy of Peter), Melanchthon averred that Christ was not addressing Peter in his person but in his apostolic office:

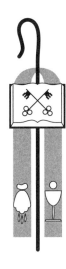

> Therefore it is necessary that in these passages Peter is the representative of the entire assembly of the apostles, and for this reason they do not accord to Peter any prerogative, or superiority, or lordship.

> However, as to the declaration: *Upon this rock I will build My Church* [Mt 16:18], certainly the Church has not been built upon the authority of man, but upon the ministry of the confession [Latin: *super ministerium illius professionis*; German: *auf das Amt, welches das Bekenntnis führt*] which Peter made, in which he proclaims that Jesus is the Christ, the Son of God. He [Christ] accordingly addresses him as a minister [Latin: *tamquam ministrum*; German: *als einen Diener solches Amts*]: *Upon this rock, i.e.*, upon this ministry [Latin: *ministerium*; German: *Predigt und Predigtamt*]. (Treatise, 24–25 [*Triglotta*, 511])

Thus, the apostles laid the foundation by their preaching, which was by direct mandate of Christ. They themselves are foundational—not in their person, but in their office, set in place to make the unchangeable proclamation of the Gospel (Col 1:23), whether in person or by letter (2 Thess 2:15). Their apostolic writings in the NT continue to be the church's foundation. In John's Revelation, the new Jerusalem has twelve foundations marked with the names of the twelve apostles (Rev 21:14).

An added complication is determining the precise referent of "prophets" (Eph 2:20).[112] Considering Paul's respect for the OT and his constant use of its prophecies to proclaim Christ, it is tempting to form an OT/NT parallel between prophets and apostles.[113] The prophets proclaimed the Gospel of Christ before the apostles took

---

[112] Some would apply the Granville Sharp Rule to suggest that the two nouns joined by one article must refer to the same thing, i.e., "the apostle-prophets." Although the apostles did have prophetic functions (Rev 1:3; 10:11; 22:6–10), Eph 4:11 and similar verses clearly indicate that "the prophets" refers to a distinct office, which Paul groups together with the apostles for his present purpose. Furthermore, Wallace, *Greek Grammar*, 285, argues that the Granville Sharp Rule does not usually apply to plural nouns and that there are no clear NT examples in which two groups indicated by plural nouns are made identical by a common article.

[113] Tertullian, *Against Marcion*, 5:17.16, says:

> The heretic [Marcion] has taken away "and prophets" [Eph 2:20], forgetting that the Lord has set in the church prophets as well as apostles: for he was afraid lest the building up of ourselves in Christ should stand upon the foundation of the older prophets, though the apostle himself ceases not in every place to quote those prophets for our edification. For from whom did he learn to call Christ the *chief corner stone*, unless it were from the indication given in the psalm, *The stone which the builders rejected, the same is become the head of the corner* [Ps 118:22]? (Trans. Evans)

up the message (Rom 1:1–3). Yet Paul's order is the other way round, "apostles and prophets"—as it will be also in 3:5 and 4:11 (cf. Rev 18:20). Eph 3:5 is particularly informative, as Paul had the opportunity with the phrase "in other generations" to speak of OT prophets, but chose instead to speak of "his holy apostles and *prophets* in the Spirit," to whom "*now* it has been revealed." In 4:11 the prophets rank *after* the apostles as gifts of the risen and ascended Christ. The prophets are subordinate to the apostles, who deliver the eyewitness testimony of Christ to the church by preaching and teaching in the office he gave them.[114] Thus, it is probable that "prophets" refers to the NT manifestation of the phenomenon of the Spirit's direct inspiration, by which the Word of God was proclaimed to specific needs of the early church.[115] Paul was intimately connected to the prophets in Antioch, by and from whom he was chosen for his first mission (Acts 13:1); Agabus prophesied Paul's imprisonment shortly before his writing of this letter (Acts 21:10–14). Like the apostles, these prophets belong to the foundation of the Christian church. Yet there is no hint here that the present-day church should seek the voice of the prophets anywhere but in Holy Scripture.[116]

ὄντος ἀκρογωνιαίου αὐτοῦ Χριστοῦ Ἰησοῦ—This clause forms a genitive absolute construction, necessitated by the change in subject of the verbs from "you [Gentiles]" in 2:19–20a to "Christ Jesus" in 2:20b. αὐτοῦ refers with emphasis to Christ "himself" (though it could refer back to the foundation, "*its* cornerstone"). ἀκρογωνιαῖος is an adjective used here as a substantive (λίθος, "stone," is implied here and supplied in 1 Pet 2:6); it combines ἄκρος, "high/extreme," and γωνία, "corner." As the term is used only once outside the Bible and in only one context inside (LXX Is 28:16, alluded to in Eph 2:20 and quoted in 1 Pet 2:6), it is difficult to know which meaning is appropriate:

Other ancient commentators sharing this interpretation include Origen, Chrysostom, Theodoret, Ambrosiaster, and Jerome. Likewise, Aquinas, Calvin, Stoeckhardt, *Ephesians*, 153. Karl Heinrich Rengstorf, "ἀπόστολος," *TDNT* 1:441, including n. 212, is one of the few modern scholars to maintain a reference to OT prophets.

[114] Hermann Sasse, "Jesus Christ Is Lord: The Church's Original Confession," in *We Confess Jesus Christ* (trans. Norman Nagel; St. Louis: Concordia, 1984), 16–17:

In Christendom the office of prophet is an office within the church, certainly subordinate to the apostolate. [He cites Eph. 2:20.] …

The recognition that the revelation in Christ is not something inconclusive or relative stands and falls with the primacy of the apostolate over prophecy. Wherever prophecy asserts its independence and power, it is a threat to the finality of the revelation that happened once in history, of which the apostolic office bears witness. Christ's church is an apostolic, not a prophetic church.

[115] Examples include John the Baptist (Lk 1:76; see also Mt 14:5; 21:26); Agabus and others from Antioch (Acts 11:27–28; 13:1–3; 21:10); Judas and Silas (Acts 15:32); prophecy in the Divine Service at Corinth (1 Cor 11:4–5; 14:29, 32, 37); prophecy after Baptism in Ephesus (Acts 19:6); and Philip's daughters (Acts 21:8–9). Cf. προφητεία, "prophecy," as a current gift in apostolic times (Rom 12:6; 1 Cor 12:10; 13:2, 8; 14:22; 1 Thess 5:20; Rev 19:10). Prophets are still a factor in *Didache*, 10:7; 11:7–12; 13:1; 15:2. See the massive data in Gerhard Friedrich, "προφήτης κτλ.," *TDNT* 6:828–61.

[116] In postapostolic literature, supposed ongoing prophetic activity is a feature only of heretical groups. See Barth, *Ephesians*, 1:317. The very early *Didache* is already quite concerned with criteria for distinguishing true prophets from false, in line with our Lord's warnings (Mt 24:11, 24; cf. 1 Jn 4:1; Rev 16:13).

(1) "capstone" as the final stone put in place to complete the top of the temple[117] or (2) "cornerstone" as lying at the extreme corner of the building's ground-level foundation.[118] The term ἀκρογωνιαῖος derives from LXX Is 28:16, where the subsequent phrase εἰς τὰ θεμέλια αὐτῆς, "for its [Zion's] foundations," suggests that it is a "cornerstone." The apparently synonymous κεφαλὴ γωνίας, "head of the corner" (LXX Ps 117:22 [MT/ET 118:22]), is more ambiguous.[119] Certainly, if the apostles and prophets are the foundation and Christians are the living stones (1 Pet 2:5), it might make sense to view Christ as the final stone that caps and perfects the building. It would fit the Ephesian emphasis on Christ's exaltation and headship (1:20–23; 4:8–16).

Yet, in the present verse (2:20), where there is no mention of the living stones, the ἀκρογωνιαῖος is spoken of in the same breath as the "foundation" (2:20a), suggesting that "cornerstone" is the more likely translation.[120] Paul draws the term from Is 28:16, where the stone is clearly in the foundation; Paul would expect us to recall the entire OT passage to which he alludes. A cornerstone is more fundamental to the construction of the building than a capstone.[121] It must be perfectly squared, as it is set in place first and gives direction to every other stone.

---

[117] *Testament of Solomon*, 22:7–23:4. Joachim Jeremias, "ἀκρογωνιαῖος," *TDNT* 1:792, the most influential proponent of this translation, suggests it is the stone set over the main gate. In Symmachus' translation of 4 Kgdms 25:17 (2 Ki 25:17), it is the capital of a column.

[118] This traditional view, somewhat out of favor today, has been most ably defended by R. J. McKelvey, "Christ the Cornerstone," *New Testament Studies* 8 (1962): 352–59; R. J. McKelvey, *The New Temple: The Church in the New Testament* (Oxford: Oxford University Press, 1969).

[119] "Head of the corner" (κεφαλὴ γωνίας) in LXX Ps 117:22 (MT/ET 118:22) is quoted in Mt 21:42; Mk 12:10; Lk 20:17; Acts 4:11; 1 Pet 2:7. This phrase, as interpreted by Christ in Mk 12:10 and parallels, probably conjures a different image than Is 28:16. If a stone has been rejected by the builders during the course of construction, it cannot end up as the cornerstone (which must be laid first), but may at the last moment emerge as the final stone to bring the building to completion. Jesus says two things about this stone: one can stumble over it on the ground, and it can fall down upon someone from above (Lk 20:17–18). If these are not to be interpreted as two *different* images, one might imagine a stone lying on the ground that is later raised to the top of the building—which confirms the view that Ps 118:22 is referring to a capstone. See Joachim Jeremias, "λίθος," *TDNT* 4:274–75. Complicating matters further, in Ps 117:22 (MT/ET 118:22), Symmachus uses ἀκρογωνιαῖος rather than κεφαλὴ γωνίας, as in the LXX.

[120] In 1 Pet 2:6–8 the apostle strings together a series of OT passages in which the Messiah is called a "stone," including λίθον ἀκρογωνιαῖον, "a cornerstone [or capstone]" (1 Pet 2:6, quoting Is 28:16); κεφαλὴ γωνίας, "head of the corner" (1 Pet 2:7, quoting LXX Ps 117:22 [MT/ET 118:22]); and λίθος προσκόμματος, "a stone of stumbling" (1 Pet 2:8, quoting Is 8:14). Joachim Jeremias, "κεφαλὴ γωνίας," *TDNT* 1:793, suggests that, taken together, 1 Pet 2:7 and 1 Pet 2:8 describe a stone which is at ground level: "The κεφαλὴ γωνίας ['head of the corner'] is not so much the final stone but a sharp stone at the corner of the building against which men stumble and fall. This interpretation is suggested by the quotation from Is. 8:14 which immediately follows (1 Pt. 2:8)." However, in collating these OT passages connected by the word "stone" (1 Pet 2:6–8), Peter is not necessarily implying that the metaphor in each case is identical. Nor need the figures be read in strict sequence, as if the stone is *first* made "head of the corner" and *then* serves as "a stone of stumbling." They may be compatible but diverse images for the same messianic figure.

[121] A "capstone" has no structural function. A "keystone" holds an arch together, but not the entire building. Vaulted or domed ceilings in which a keystone's removal would cause the collapse

There is no conflict between the apostles and prophets as the "foundation" and Christ as the "cornerstone," since these human messengers proclaim only what Christ has given them to say. The movement of 2:20–22 suggests Christ and the apostles coming first, with the saints continually being added as the temple is built up. At the same time, the realized component of Ephesian eschatology does not preclude viewing the temple as (proleptically) already complete, with Christ already set at its pinnacle ("head," 1:22; 4:15; 5:23).

It may be that we should not press the details of these analogies too far, as they vary even within Paul's writings (see the textual note on "foundation" in 2:20), and the two OT passages (Is 28:16; Ps 118:22 [LXX 117:22]) so frequently conflated in the NT may have originally painted slightly different pictures. The point is that Christians do not constitute the new temple to the exclusion of Christ; on the contrary, the building depends entirely on him.[122] The ancient Latin hymn sings:

> Christ is made the sure foundation,
>> Christ, our head and cornerstone,
> Chosen of the Lord and precious,
>> Binding all the Church in one;
> Holy Zion's help forever
>> And our confidence alone.[123]

---

of the whole building were unknown in Paul's day. At the same time, there is no clear evidence that a "cornerstone" played a specific role in Greek construction techniques (witness the absence of a technical term for it). Likewise, while the OT narrates the laying of a building's foundation (e.g., Josh 6:26; 1 Ki 5:31; 6:37 [ET 1 Ki 5:17; 6:37]), it does not expressly describe the structural role of a cornerstone. It has been suggested that the final stone in a pyramid might well satisfy the picture, but what does that have to do with the construction of the Jerusalem temple?

[122] Though the term ἀκρογωνιαῖος is not used, Zerubbabel lays both the foundation of the new temple and the final stone, הָאֶבֶן הָרֹאשָׁה, literally, "the stone, the top," or "the top/head stone," which the LXX frustratingly translates as τὸν λίθον τῆς κληρονομίας, "the stone of inheritance" (Zech 4:7). Like Christ, Zerubbabel is the builder from first to last. Jerome, *Ephesians*, on Eph 2:20 (PL 30:829), combines the two images: Christ "is the foundation and the top because in him the church is founded and completed" (quoted in Barth, *Ephesians*, 1:318, n. 266). Likewise, Chrysostom: "See how he joins himself to us. Sometimes it is as if holding together and unifying the whole body from above. Sometimes it is as if joining the edifice from below, as if supporting the building with underpinnings and being its root" (*Homilies on Ephesians*, 6:2.17–22, ACCS 8:143).

[123] *LSB* 909:1; adapted from the translation by John Mason Neale. The original eighth-century text has no reference to "head":

> Angularis fundamentum
>> lapis Christus missus est,
> Qui compage parietis
>> in utroque nectitur,
> Quem Sion sancta suscepit,
>> in quo credens permanet. (Dreves-Blume, 51:110)

The first two lines could be translated literally as "as the cornerstone, the foundation Christ was sent [or 'was laid'; see Vulgate Is 28:16]" (*HS98 Handbook*, 133). *HS98 Handbook* includes a version of Neale's original translation, which also does not include "head."

2:21 ἐν ᾧ πᾶσα οἰκοδομὴ συναρμολογουμένη—"In whom" carries all the freight of baptismal incorporation into Christ that it has borne through this letter (see the fifth textual note on 1:3), with the added component here of being built into a living temple in Christ, who himself is the new temple (Jn 2:19–21). πᾶσα οἰκοδομή, even in the absence of the definite article, means not "*every* building" (local congregations) but "the *whole* building" (the universal church).[124] Paul introduces the new temple with the generic term οἰκοδομή, "building," perhaps as a transition from the Greek cognate οἰκεῖοι, "members of the household" (2:19), certainly with a view toward the language of "building up" (συνοικοδομεῖσθε, 2:22). Thus, it is not a static term; like Herod's massive project in Jerusalem (cf. Mk 13:1), which must have been a constant beehive of activity, the new temple is ever under construction. Unlike Herod's temple, which was destined for destruction (Mk 13:2), the new temple is not declining but increasing. οἰκοδομή, "building," is a key term in Ephesians 4 (4:12, 16, 29). The church is built up by the work of the pastoral office (4:11–12; cf. 1 Cor 3:9; 2 Cor 10:8) and the exchange of godly words among Christians (Eph 4:29; cf. 1 Cor 14:12). It is a living edifice (Eph 4:16)—the body image controls the temple figure—as the verb in the next clause implies (αὔξει, "grows").

The rare compound verb συναρμολογέω, "to join together so as to form a coherent entity,"[125] continues the long string of compounds of συν-, "with, together," in this epistle.[126] The cognate noun ἁρμός refers to the "joint" between stones, which in classical times was carefully created by smoothing the two surfaces, drilling holes, and fitting bronze dowels, to be cemented in place with molten lead. In the same way, each new member is given place in the church with such care and precision that the building has not only beauty but also the strength to support further growth.[127] But ἁρμός can also refer to an anatomical "joint" (cf. Heb 4:12); the verb συναρμολογέω thus fits the organic language of the body of Christ (cf. Eph 4:16). The English cognate "harmony" is not inappropriate (cf. 5:19). The living temple image wonderfully combines the unity with one another and with Christ that is the central theme of this pericope. In the new temple of Christ there are no divisions.

αὔξει εἰς ναὸν ἅγιον ἐν κυρίῳ—From the foundation of the apostles and prophets, with Christ the cornerstone (2:20), the church ever "grows" (αὔξει: present tense of αὔξω, an early variant of αὐξάνω).[128] ναὸς ἅγιος, "holy temple," is a common OT

---

[124] BDAG, s.v. πᾶς, 4 a; Turner, *Syntax*, 199–200; Moule, *Idiom Book*, 94–95; BDF, § 275 (4): "Hebraizing." Cf., e.g., Mt 28:18; Acts 2:36; Rom 3:20; Col 1:15.

[125] BDAG, s.v. συναρμολογέω.

[126] Compounds of συν- appear in 2:5, 6, 19, 21, 22; 3:6; 4:3, 16; 5:7, 11.

[127] The force of the participle συναρμολογουμένη is difficult to pin down. It seems to identify a necessary precondition for the action of the main verb, αὔξει (in the next textual note): "*since* it is properly joined together, it grows."

[128] In earlier Greek, the active voice of αὐξάνω was used only transitively, as in "to grow vegetables." The intransitive meaning was expressed by the passive of αὐξάνω ("the vegetables were grown") or by the simple form αὔξω ("the vegetables grew"). By NT times, both αὐξάνω and αὔξω could be used in the active voice with an intransitive meaning ("the vegetables grew")—but the sense of passive transitive ("were grown *by someone*") is still there. Thus, that the church αὔξει, "grows," implies a divine passive: "is grown *by God*." In the only

expression for the Jerusalem temple,[129] indicating that the Christian church is a new temple (cf. 1 Cor 3:16–17). The phrase ἐν κυρίῳ, "in the Lord," modifies "temple," expressing the transformation of an old institution (cf. Eph 4:1, 17; 6:1; Col 3:18), just as Christ spoke of his body as a new temple "not made with hands" (Mk 14:58; contrast Eph 2:11). Unlike much contemporary misuse, the NT does not equate αὔξω with numerical increase, but with organic "growth."[130] The growth of the new temple is not a feature that is counted but a vital characteristic of its life in comparison to the static, crumbling temple of old. The growth of the whole is never separate from the growth of its members in knowledge of the Lord and in his Spirit.[131] But primarily what grows is the kingdom of God (Lk 13:19), Christ himself (Jn 3:30), the Word of the Lord (Acts 6:7; 12:24; 19:20), the Gospel (Col 1:6), righteousness (2 Cor 9:10), and faith (2 Cor 10:15). The apostolic Word plants and waters, but God gives the growth (1 Cor 3:6–7; Col 2:19). It is the natural (and necessary) development of a living body that is connected to a life-giving Head (Eph 4:15).

2:22 ἐν ᾧ καὶ ὑμεῖς συνοικοδομεῖσθε εἰς κατοικητήριον τοῦ θεοῦ ἐν πνεύματι— This verse stands in nearly perfect parallel to the previous verse. It takes that general statement about the church and applies it directly to "you Gentiles" (2:11). Like 2:18, this verse is Trinitarian, forming a veritable doxology at the close of this pericope: "in whom [in Christ[132]] also you are built up together into a dwelling place of God [the Father] in/by the [Holy] Spirit."

The verb συνοικοδομεῖσθε, "you are being built up *together*," is another compound of συν-, "with, together."[133] With its root -οικο- the verb forms a group with

---

other NT occurrence of the simple form αὔξω, Paul makes the divine agent explicit: αὔξει τὴν αὔξησιν τοῦ θεοῦ, "grows with a growth that is from God" (Col 2:19). The longer form αὐξάνω, which in later Greek almost completely replaced αὔξω, occurs twenty-one times in the NT.

[129] LXX Pss 5:8 (ET 5:7); 27:2 (MT/ET 28:2); 78:1 (MT/ET 79:1); 137:2 (MT/ET 138:2); Sirach 49:12; Jonah 2:5, 8 (ET 2:4, 7). See also ναὸς ἅγιος, "holy temple," in reference to God's heavenly temple in LXX Pss 10:4 (MT/ET 11:4); 17:7 (MT 18:7; ET 18:6); Hab 2:20. See the textual note on οἰκεῖοι in Eph 2:19.

[130] Even in Mk 4:8 (with αὐξάνω), the growth of grain produced by sowing the Word, "thirtyfold and sixtyfold and a hundredfold," does not suggest that each kernel is an individual Christian that one would count. In Acts 6:7 the Word "grew" (αὐξάνω), while the number of disciples "multiplied" (πληθύνω). The latter is presented as one of the great miracles of the apostolic age. αὐξάνω in Acts 7:17 refers to the numerical increase of Israel in Egypt, but this is not to be identified simplistically with the kingdom of God (non-Israelites were included in the "mixed multitude" that participated in the exodus [Ex 12:38], and many of the Israelites disbelieved, as Exodus and Stephen [Acts 7] demonstrate). Nonetheless, as the church Paul has in mind is the universal church, not just the visible church on earth, it does ever grow even numerically, since her sainted members are never lost. Even the addition of one new stone in the temple is growth.

[131] Lk 1:80; 2:40; Col 1:10; 1 Pet 2:2.

[132] It is possible that the antecedent of ᾧ is ναόν (2:21), so ἐν ᾧ would mean "in which [the temple]," or κυρίῳ (2:21), so "in whom [the Lord]," but it is better to read ἐν ᾧ in 2:22 as parallel to ἐν ᾧ in 2:21, and so as referring back to Χριστοῦ Ἰησοῦ, "Christ Jesus" (2:20), thus giving a consistent referent to the expression.

[133] See the third textual note on 2:19 and the second paragraph of the first textual note on 2:21.

other key terms in this context: οἰκεῖοι (2:19; cf. also πάροικοι), ἐποικοδομέω (2:20), οἰκοδομή (2:21), and κατοικητήριον (2:22); thus, God's "house/building" is the central theme of 2:19–22. In the only other biblical occurrence of συνοικοδομέω, the verb refers to "building" the second temple (1 Esdras 5:65 [ET 5:68]), though what is συν- there is the cooperative act of people building "together." Here the prefix συν- refers to the joint incorporation of Jews and Gentiles "together" as living stones into the walls of this great and final temple.

The verbal-noun formation κατοικητήριον indicates a place where something happens.[134] The temple is not just God's residence but also the place he inhabits, where he does his thing. The meaning of the old temple was always that God had made a dwelling among his people,[135] as the twelve tribes were arrayed all around the tabernacle in the wilderness (Numbers 2) and the temple was built in the heart of Israel, Jerusalem, where God caused his name to dwell (1 Chr 23:25; Ezra 6:12). The new temple, likewise, is the place where God dwells, as by the Spirit of Christ, God lives within his people (1 Cor 3:16; 6:19; 2 Cor 6:16) and among them with his Word and Sacraments (Mt 18:20; 28:19–20; 1 Cor 10:16). Christ himself thus fulfills the purpose of the temple (Ezek 37:26–28; Jn 1:14; Rev 21:3). As they are one body by their Baptism into one Spirit (1 Cor 12:13; Eph 4:4), so they are one building ἐν πνεύματι, "in the Spirit" (Eph 2:22), by his work and through his indwelling, not ἐν σαρκί, "in the flesh" (2:11), by reason of any fleshly tie. The transformation of the Gentiles is thus complete.

Commentary
Structure and Rhetoric

The letter to the Ephesians has some of the tightest pericopal divisions in the NT. Only in three places (4:32/5:2; 5:20/5:21; 6:17/6:20) is there the slightest doubt where one unit ends and the next begins. Rarely do the editors of modern editions disagree with the ancient *kephalaia*—the "chapter" divisions noted in the inner margins of the Nestle-Aland Greek NT. We note keenly, therefore, that there is no ancient division between the two pericopes of chapter 2; in the great manuscripts they form one *kephalaion*. This is not to suggest that our division is inappropriate. Eph 2:1–10 and 2:11–22 have distinct structures of their own, chiastic markers that signal the beginning and end of each extended thought. However, there is an important overall convergence of language, thought, and subject matter that binds these two pericopes closely together:

---

[134] It is derived from the verb κατοικέω, "to inhabit, dwell." See also BDAG, s.v. κατοικητήριον; BDF, § 109 (9).

[135] Ex 29:45–46; Lev 26:11; 1 Ki 6:13; 8:13; Ps Sol 7:6. κατοικητήριον, "dwelling place," is used of the temple in LXX Ex 15:17; Ps 75:3 (MT 76:3; ET 76:2). Heaven is God's κατοικητήριον in LXX 3 Kgdms 8:39, 43, 49 (MT/ET 1 Ki 8:39, 43, 49); 2 Chr 30:27; 3 Macc 2:15; Ps 32:14 (MT/ET 33:14).

- Eph 2:1–2 and 2:11 are bound by the same time reference, ποτέ, "once/at one time," reminding the readers/hearers of their past life.[136]
- "You (Gentiles)"[137] (2:1–2; and 2:11–13, 19, 22) are contrasted with "we [Jewish Christians]" (2:3 and 2:14, 16, 18).
- Eph 2:3 with "the flesh" parallels 2:11 with "in the flesh."
- The interjections "but God" (ὁ δὲ θεός, 2:4) and "but now in Christ Jesus" (νυνὶ δὲ ἐν Χριστῷ Ἰησοῦ, 2:13) serve the same function.
- Both units conclude with a similar result: "we are what he has made" (2:10) and "the whole building … a holy temple in the Lord" (2:21).

While parallel to each other, the two pericopes also advance Paul's argument in a logical progression. First he establishes our common salvation in Christ (2:1–10); then he more specifically draws out its implications for the unity of all people (Gentile and Jew) within Christ's one body (2:11–22). It is in this sense that we should read διό, "therefore" (2:11), which connects the two pericopes—or, one might say, the larger pericope's two parts.

The present unit, like the previous one, can be analyzed in more than one way. Three schemes are evident. The primary scheme is a temporal division between "then" and "now."[138] As much as there is a comparison between Gentiles and Jews, there is also a contrast between the Gentiles' former life and their new life in Christ. The temporal markers ποτέ, "at one time, then" (2:11), and τῷ καιρῷ ἐκείνῳ, "at that time" (2:12), stand over against νυνὶ δέ, "but *now*" (2:13). The subsequent contrasts mark not only the two peoples ("Uncircumcision" versus "Circumcision," 2:11) but also the two stages of the Gentiles' lives:

"then" (2:11–12)	**"now" (2:13)**
"in the flesh" (2:11)	"in the Lord," "in the Spirit" (2:21–22)
"separated from Christ" (2:12)	"built up upon … Christ" (2:20)
"alienated from … Israel" (2:12)	"fellow citizens with the saints" (2:19)
"strangers," "sojourners" (2:12, 19)	"members of God's household" (2:19)
"godless" (2:12)	"access … to the Father" (2:18)
"far off" (2:13, 17)	"near" (2:13, 17)
"hostility" (2:14, 16)	"peace" (2:14–17)
"dividing wall of partition" (2:14)	"joined together," "holy temple" (2:21)

---

[136] Thomson, *Chiasmus in the Pauline Letters*, 112: "In 2.1–10 there is an implicit ποτέ … νῦν ['then … now'] contrast drawn. In fact, the ποτέ ['then'] of 2.2 is never specifically balanced by νῦν ['now']. It may, however, have served as the trigger for the more fully developed *schema* of 2.11–22."

[137] Eph 2:11 reads ὑμεῖς τὰ ἔθνη, "you *Gentiles*," leaving no doubt that the other "you" references are to Gentiles. See also ὑμῶν τῶν ἐθνῶν, "you *Gentiles*," in 3:1.

[138] Cf. Rom 11:30; Eph 2:2–3; 5:8; Col 1:21–22; 3:7–8; 1 Pet 2:10.

Like the new life and heavenly blessings that were brought by their baptismal incorporation into Christ (2:5–8), this great transformation was worked upon them in that sacramental moment.

In addition to this individual change in status, the reconciliation Christ achieved on the cross brought about an ironic reversal in the fortunes of the two peoples (though in the present context Paul has nothing to say about the tragedy of Jewish rejection of the Messiah). Speaking only to the Gentiles in the Ephesian church, Paul's then-now scheme echoes his great conclusion to Romans 9–11: "for just as you [Gentiles] *formerly* [ποτέ] were disobedient to God, but *now* [νῦν] have received mercy by their [the Jews'] disobedience, thus also they now [νῦν] have been disobedient with respect to the mercy shown to you in order that also they might now [νῦν] be shown mercy" (Rom 11:30–31). Or as Peter puts it, quoting prophecy: "[you] who *once* [ποτέ] were 'not a people' but *now* [νῦν] are God's people, who 'were not shown mercy' but *now* [νῦν] have been shown mercy" (1 Pet 2:10, quoting Hos 1:6, 9; 2:25 [ET 2:23]).[139] Thus, the temporal scheme of baptismal transformation corresponds to the change in status of the Gentiles as a whole.

Second, this pericope falls into three sections that form a clear progression of thought:

2:11–12	The Gentile Christians' former status, alienated from God and his people
2:13–18	The reconciling work of Christ on the cross
2:19–22	The resulting new temple, Jews and Gentiles built on Christ

The central section (2:13–18) consists of a Christological-Soteriological pivot that brings about the transformation from "then" to "now." By the cross of Christ, Gospel peace overcomes the hostility of the Law. In the final emphasis on the new, living temple (2:19–22), Paul shows how Christ's work overcomes the alienation from God and his people that was symbolized so graphically by the divisions in the temple and, more broadly, by the distinctive provisions of the Torah.

Finally, these major polarities (then-now, pagan-baptized, Gentiles-Israel) so dominate Paul's thinking that the entire structure takes on a grand chiastic pattern.[140] Whether thematic or verbal, significant parallels and contrasts

---

[139] Wolfgang Nauck, "Eph 2,19–22—ein Tauflied?" *Evangelische Theologie* 13 (1953): 362–71, connects these verses with 1 Pet 2:4–10, suggesting that a baptismal hymn lies behind both. Whether or not this supposition is true, he has discerned a significant common theme.

[140] Our chiastic structure is inspired by Kirby, *Ephesians: Baptism and Pentecost*, 156–57, and Kenneth E. Bailey, *Poet and Peasant: A Literary-Cultural Approach to the Parables in Luke* (Grand Rapids: Eerdmans, 1976), 63. It is also in harmony with Thomson, *Chiasmus in the Pauline Letters*, 84–115, who notes (87) that five major scholars had independently produced chiastic analyses of the passage previous to his own. Objections from Lincoln, *Ephesians*, 126, and Best, *Ephesians*, 236, are based on too rigid a conception of what a chiasm must look like. Ephesians 2 is prose, not poetry, and involves parallels and antitheses of both words and ideas. Paul arranges his thoughts in chiasm not to show how clever he is, but because it is a natural way to express the subject of reversal. Lincoln falsely poses the "then-now" schema

emerge as Paul walks from past to present, from problem to solution, from condition to result.

A   [11]Therefore, remember that at one time you Gentiles <u>in the flesh,</u>

    B   called Uncircumcision by what is called Circumcision (made <u>in the flesh, by hands</u>),

        C   [12]that you were at that time <u>separated from Christ,</u>

            D   <u>alienated</u> from the <u>commonwealth</u> of Israel

                E   and <u>strangers</u> to the covenants of the promise,

                    F   having no hope and <u>godless</u> in the world.

                        G   [13]But now <u>in Christ Jesus</u> you who at one time were <u>far off</u> have become <u>near</u> by the blood of Christ.

                            H   [14]For he himself is our <u>peace</u>, who has made both <u>one</u>, and has destroyed the dividing wall of partition, the <u>hostility</u>, <u>in his flesh</u>,

                                I   [15]by nullifying the Law of commandments in decrees,

                                that <u>in him</u> he might create the two into one new man, making <u>peace</u>,

                          H'   [16]and might <u>reconcile</u> both <u>in one body</u> to God through the cross, by killing the <u>hostility</u> <u>in him</u>.

                        G'   [17]And when he came he preached <u>peace</u> to you who were <u>far off</u> and <u>peace</u> to those who were <u>near</u>;

                    F'   [18]for <u>through him</u> we both have access in one Spirit to the <u>Father</u>.

                E'   [19]So, then, you are no longer <u>strangers</u> and <u>sojourners</u>,

            D'   but you are <u>fellow citizens</u> with the saints and members of God's household,

        C'   [20]having been built up upon the foundation of the apostles and prophets, the cornerstone being <u>Christ Jesus himself</u>,

    B'   [21]<u>in whom</u> the whole building, being joined together, grows into <u>a holy temple</u>, <u>in the Lord</u>,

A'   [22]<u>in whom</u> also you are built up together into a dwelling place of God <u>in the Spirit</u>.

As in 2:1–10, such a chiastic structure draws our attention not so much to the end as to the middle (2:15). There we find the central Gospel thought that Christ has triumphed over the Law with its power to create hostility, condemnation, and division. By removing that hostile power, Christ brought peace to all mankind through the cross.[141] Indeed, the fourfold repetition of "peace" at the heart of the

---

and the chiasm as incompatible alternatives (Thomson, 91). Best admits to significant parallels and antitheses between the first and third sections, which is the real point.

[141] Lincoln, who dismisses the chiasm, nevertheless notes: "The judgment that in Ephesians Christology has been swallowed up by ecclesiology surely misses the emphasis of this passage, where it is Christ's reconciling death on the cross on which the very existence of the Church depends" (*Ephesians*, 161).

pericope (together with its antithesis, "hostility") marks this as its theme, a significant precondition for the unity that is the letter's major goal. "Peace" is the golden thread that runs through the tapestry of Isaiah,[142] whose major messianic prophecies undergird Paul's argument. This is a sort of midrash on Is 9:5 (ET 9:6); 28:16; 52:7; and 57:19, according to the rabbinic principle that diverse passages tied together by one word may be used to interpret one another.[143]

The chiastic structure places similar weight on the entire central section of the chiasm (2:13–18), which forms a sort of "Second Article"[144] confession of the work of Christ on the cross. Many scholars have tried to identify behind it a preexisting hymn which the author has worked into his writing.[145] That notion, partly tied to a rejection of Pauline authorship and therefore an inclination to view the work as secondary,[146] also arises because of the shift from second person plural address (2:11–13) to first person plural (2:14–18) and then back again (2:19–22): "you … we … you." Yet this feature is better explained in accordance with Paul's argument. He addresses the Gentiles first according to their former existence. He then appeals to the work of Christ, which is for all of us Christians (Jewish and Gentile alike). Finally, he turns back to address the Gentiles in drawing out the implications of this confession. It is the alternation of "Christ" and "for you" that characterizes creedal statements and their explanation. The central role of Christ is again emphasized by the repetition of "in Christ Jesus," "in his flesh," "in him," "in one body," "through him," "in whom," and "in the Lord" (noted, where possible, in the above chiasm with dotted underlining). Paul never tires of this affirmation.

---

[142] שָׁלוֹם, "peace," occurs twenty-nine times in Isaiah, in frequency trailing only Jeremiah (thirty-one times). Its first occurrence is in the thematic statement that the Messiah will be the "Prince of Peace" (Is 9:5–6 [ET 9:6–7]). Peace in Isaiah cannot be achieved by men, but is a gift of God through his Messenger (Is 52:7), brought about through that Messenger's suffering (Is 53:5).

[143] Hillel's second rule: *Gezerah Shawah* (equivalence of expressions). This is not to suggest that Paul was rigidly following an arbitrary rabbinic technique, but that he discerned a commonality of theme in these prophetic passages that Isaiah himself may have intended by his choice of vocabulary. Within the book of Isaiah, these passages interpret one another. Paul's flexibility is evident from his inclusion of Is 28:16, which does not include the vocabulary of "peace," but is chosen as a prophecy of the new, spiritual temple.

[144] I.e., the Second Article of the Apostles' or Nicene Creed.

[145] See, e.g., Ernest Best, "The Use of Credal and Liturgical Material in Ephesians," 60–63, in Best, *Essays on Ephesians*, and the list of studies on p. 63, n. 30. Attempts to connect this hymn with the Christ hymn of Col 1:15–20 falter on the recognition that there are significant parallels only in its final verse. It might be better to say that Paul has expanded Col 1:20 into the more substantial creedal affirmation of Eph 2:14–18. In addition, Col 1:21–23 bears more resemblance to this section of Ephesians than do the earlier verses of the Colossian Christ hymn.

[146] Most critics note an excess of unusual vocabulary in these verses. Best, *Ephesians*, 249, does the math and calculates that there is no greater percentage of hapax legomena here than in Ephesians as a whole.

Rhetorically considered, we have reached the second major proof for Paul's contention that we are baptismally united in Christ.[147] Andrew Lincoln identifies this section as part of the *narratio*, that is, the background story which is preliminary to Paul's chief argument.[148] For Lincoln, the so-called hortatory section of the letter (chapters 4–6) is the main point. The narration of the Gospel is designed merely to produce thankfulness in the Ephesians in order to work the ethical change that Paul ultimately desires. Our introduction ("Structure and Rhetoric") has treated this perspective on epistolary outlining in more detail. But suffice it to say here that Lincoln's analysis seriously skews the relationship between Law and Gospel. The Gospel of Christ is not simply a story intended to motivate a change in behavior. As Barth comments: "The sequence, God (or Christ) did *this* for you—now have you to do *that* for him, is a ridiculous caricature of the relationship between God's grace and the good works for which man is created, according to Eph 2:5–10."[149] Far from merely recounting a story, Paul in this pericope draws significant implications out of the fact of Christ's death on the cross: that he embodied both races in his flesh and thereby united them to each other and to God; that his death drew the sting out of the Law; that it nullified the Law's ability to divide Jew from Gentile; and that it created a new Israel and a new, living temple. With these points proved, Paul can proceed toward his goal of confessing "one body and one Spirit … one Lord, one faith, one Baptism, one God and Father of all" (4:4–6).

Gentiles and Jews United in One Body through the Cross

In the *Berakah* prayer (1:3–14), which served as a prologue introducing the themes of the entire letter, Paul expressed the eternal plan and purpose of God for the restoration of the cosmos to himself and praised him for it. "In Christ" God would draw together all things (ἀνακεφαλαιώσασθαι τὰ πάντα), whether in heavenly places or on earth (1:10). This grand plan of administration (οἰκονομία, 1:10) would involve overcoming the hostile spiritual forces opposed to God and his hosts (1:21) and uniting those who first put their hope in Christ with those who later heard the Word, believed, and were sealed by the Spirit (1:12–13). Thus, already in the prologue we saw how Paul connected cosmic battles with human conflict and universal reconciliation with the unity of all people. The effect of his argument is to say, "How can there be any divisions within the Christian church, the body of Christ, when God has reconciled all things to himself?" On this basis, Paul addresses the division between Gentiles and Jews in the present pericope, beginning with a description of what had separated them from one another and from God.

Paul's motivation for dissecting in such detail the depravity of the Gentiles' prebaptismal life can be misunderstood. It would be a mistake to view it as

---

[147] See "Proofs" in "Structure and Rhetoric" in the introduction.

[148] Lincoln, *Ephesians*, 131–32.

[149] Barth, *Ephesians*, 1:55.

a morbid fascination with evil, a kind of *Schadenfreude* that takes delight in debauchery. This is not a quasi-Pentecostal testimonial that seems proud of an exaggerated former godlessness, that seems to give more glory to the saved than to the Savior. Rather, Paul points the Gentiles back to their life before Christ to give greater praise to God for their rescue.[150] Nor is there the slightest emphasis on morality as such. Entirely absent is any reference to fornication, prostitution, homosexuality, abortion, murder, theft, drunkenness—characteristics of the pagan lifestyle that Paul does not hesitate to condemn elsewhere.[151] Paul is entirely concerned with what they did not have and what they did not do in relation to God: they were lacking the good gifts of God and the right worship of him that were available all along to the people of Israel.

In describing their previous status in 2:11–12, Paul begins with the opposition and division the Gentiles suffered by their lack of circumcision. His use of "who are called" (οἱ λεγόμενοι, 2:11) might imply name-calling as an act of prejudice. Paul's later repetition of the term "hostility" (ἔχθρα, 2:14, 16) certainly suggests the kind of anti-Jewish sentiments that were often voiced in the ancient world, and the anti-Gentile attitudes found among strict Jews, who referred to Gentiles as "filthy dogs."[152] But the question at hand is what sort of Jew/Gentile divide might specifically have affected the Ephesian church. In a general sense we must recognize the problems reported in Acts 15, as to whether Gentiles must be circumcised and observe the ritual laws that marked Israel as God's chosen people. Judaizers were at work in the early Christian church, particularly in Asia Minor (cf. Galatians). This was the burning issue in the apostolic age.

Can we deduce from Ephesians that Judaizers were active in that particular church? The distinctive polemical language of Galatians is lacking, but we cannot rule out the possibility. The reference to Judaizing in Col 2:16 indicates that it was a live issue in the area near Ephesus, but Paul does not repeat the concern in the present epistle. The narrative of the Ephesian church's founding makes clear that it consisted of both Jews and Greeks (Acts 19:17; 20:10, 21), and the tensions that came with such a mix would inevitably have been felt. Jewish Christians ("[we] who first hoped," 1:12) may have played their

---

[150] True praise is rooted in and created by the saving deeds of God. Breaking down the barrier between God and men enables praise:

> [Doxology] acknowledges and announces that the eternal glory of God has been made manifest to the saints here on earth in time and space. Its epiphany divides human history into two aeons. The performance of doxology by humans in their worship here on earth announces that the iron curtain between heaven and earth, the gulf between time and eternity, has been breached and is bridged by the risen Lord Jesus. Those who sing this doxology show that they have access to God's heavenly glory already now here on earth. Wherever it is sung the new age has begun. (Kleinig, "The Mystery of Doxology," 141)

[151] E.g., Rom 1:18–32; 1 Cor 5:9–13; 6:9–11; Gal 5:19–21; Eph 5:3–5; Col 3:5–9; 1 Tim 1:9–10; cf. Rev 22:15.

[152] See option 3 in the third textual note on 2:14.

priority as a trump card; the Gentiles, who appear from the letter's language to have been in the majority, may have asserted their dominance and boasted that they were now supporting their Jewish forebearers (Rom 11:18).

In the context of this pericope, however, we note that there is no particular reference to hostility *within* the Christian church at Ephesus (though it may have existed). Paul's language focuses more on hostility between the two peoples as a whole.[153] Certain features of the text suggest allusions to two historical events. First, the claim that the Gentiles were "godless" (ἄθεοι, 2:12) recalls the charge of the rioting silversmiths against Paul, that he "has persuaded and turned away a considerable number of people, saying that those [things] made with hands are not gods" (Acts 19:26). Paul's persuasive speech had hit them in the pocketbooks, as the trade in silver statues of Artemis and her temple was seriously flagging. Thus, it was in Ephesus that Paul raised considerable ire among Gentiles. At the same time, the success of his message brought hostility from the non-Christian Jews in the area (Acts 19:9), who later plotted against his life (Acts 20:3).

Second, Paul's references to his imprisonment (Eph 3:1; 4:1; 6:20) and the Ephesians' anxiety about it (3:13), as well as the "dividing wall of … hostility" (2:14) in the present pericope, call to mind the circumstances of his arrest in Jerusalem, in which the hostility of the Jews against Paul's message—particularly his "relaxing" of the provisions of the Law—featured prominently. The charge against him was that he was teaching against the Jewish people, their Law, and their temple (Acts 21:28), and that he had violated the prohibition against Gentiles entering the inner courts of the temple—Trophimus, an Ephesian, was the alleged trespasser (Acts 21:29). If Ephesians was written shortly afterward from Paul's Caesarean imprisonment, as we have suggested,[154] it is not surprising that these Jewish hostilities should feature largely in the letter. These two historical factors suggest that the letter is directed not to the question "why do Jewish Christians look down on us Gentile Christians?" but rather "how can Christians and Jews possibly be reconciled?" and "how is it that Jew/Gentile hostilities do not divide the Christian church?"

As in Romans 9, Paul does not permit the Gentiles to reject or ignore the blessings God placed among his chosen people Israel. The Gentiles were indeed disadvantaged by their distance from Israel—in comparison with this divide, the petty name-calling and prejudice on both sides paled. They were once

---

[153] Critics who deny Pauline authorship and place the letter late in the first century have difficulty accounting for its emphasis on the problem of Jewish-Gentile relations. By that time, in their evolutionary scheme, either the problem had been solved or the number of Jews in the church had become so small as to make it a non-issue. For example, Best opines: "The dispute in the early church about the admission of Gentile Christians as full and equal members with Jewish Christians had lost its virulence by the time of Ephesians" (*Ephesians*, 235). The presence of the topic, however, is a significant indicator of the letter's early provenance and authenticity.

[154] See "Caesarea!" in "Location and Date of Writing" in the introduction.

"separated from Christ, alienated from the commonwealth of Israel and strangers to the covenants of the promise, having no hope and godless in the world" (2:12). Now, there was plenty of hopelessness to be found in their lives even without comparing them to Israel. Martin Scharlemann highlights two aspects of contemporary Greek culture that left them without hope: First, the glory days of their civilization were in the past. Second, like most ancient peoples, they held a cyclical view of history, that history simply repeats itself, leaving no hope of any significant future improvement to one's lot. The Bible's linear view of history moving toward an eschatological rescue and its teaching about the resurrection of the dead were alien and revolutionary ideas.[155] The chorus near the conclusion of *Oedipus Rex* opines that the best thing that could happen to a man is never to be born and that the second best is to be born and then die straight away.[156] But even if these cultural factors were not in play, Paul would still confront the Gentiles with the false, deceptive nature of their hope. They were without the Messiah, without the promise, without God—this Paul characterizes as "having no hope" (2:12).

The solution Paul offers is not the old way, by which Gentiles could draw near to God through submission to the provisions of the OT Torah. Although the language of proselytism (a "proselyte" is one who "draws near") is echoed in this pericope, its day had passed, to be replaced by a new thing in Christ. The Gentiles were no longer to be drawn near to God by adopting the Law of Moses, by becoming Israelites in life as well as in faith. In fact, as Paul argues in Romans 7, to a certain extent the Law itself was always part of the problem. This is partly why Paul again stresses "in Christ," the location of a new kind of Israel and a new kind of temple worship. Christ accomplishes what the Law could not. In Christ, God the Father has reached out to those who were far off, like the father who glimpses his prodigal son "while he was yet far off" and has compassion on him; setting aside his cultural norms, he runs to meet him (Lk 15:20).

At the same time, it can be said that the Law created the division in the first place. We have highlighted the Soreg (see the third textual note on 2:14)—the dividing wall existing in the temple since at least the Hasmonean period that kept Gentiles out of the inner courts. The Soreg had no divine mandate; there is no reference to it in the canonical Scriptures of the OT, nor in the commonly received apocryphal writings. It appears to have arisen out of the same motives that gave rise to the Pharisees and their figurative "fence around the Torah"[157] constructed from man-made traditions designed to prevent the transgression of God's commandments. It was part of an attempt to achieve and mandate a

---

[155] Scharlemann, "Secret," 413.

[156] Sophocles, *Oedipus Rex*, 1:1187–1222 (trans. F. Storr, LCL), as summarized by Scharlemann, "Secret," 413.

[157] See option 3 in the third textual note on 2:14.

national holiness and obedience to God that would forestall any future exiles and perhaps usher in the age of the Messiah.

So, then, is Paul, like our Lord, railing against such traditions of men (Mk 7:8)? Does he imply that the division between Jew and Gentile is an artificial, man-made construct that is contrary to the original intention of God's Law? Though to a certain extent this is true, Paul's words go far beyond this. The Soreg not only serves as a physical manifestation and symbol of the divisive traditions of men, but it also represents the very Law of God as given to Israel, in which the distinctive status of Israel over against the nations was ensconced. Paul draws this parallel expressly in the center of the pericope as he places "the dividing wall of partition, the hostility" into parallel with "the Law of commandments in decrees" (2:14–15). The Soreg is a metaphor for the whole Law, which divided sinful men from one another *and sinful men from God*. This latter claim forms a crucial step in Paul's argument. For if his concern were only with man-made rules designed to separate Judaism ever more from the Gentile world around it, Paul could not speak of the need for both parties to be reconciled to God (2:16). On the other hand, if all mankind's failure to observe the Law separated everyone from God (as Paul proved in 2:1–3), this primary barrier needed to be overcome before the barrier separating man from man could be destroyed.

Thus, it is less than crucial whether or not Paul is actually alluding to the Soreg in Eph 2:14. Markus Barth wisely points us to the conclusions we can draw simply from the explicit assertions Paul makes:

> The context identifies the "wall" [Eph 2:14] in four ways: it is the fact of separation between Israel and the nations; it has to do with the law and its statutes and interpretations; it is experienced in the enmity between Jews and Gentiles; it also consists of the enmity of both Jews and Gentiles against God.[158]

Nonetheless, Barth does not entirely do justice to Paul's words in the heart of the pericope (2:15–16) when he asserts: "Christ has abrogated the divisive function of the law—and therefore not God's holy law itself."[159] Certainly the verb καταργέω (2:15) can and should be translated as "nullify" rather than "abolish." The Law is not gone. Those who have been baptized cannot simply choose to sin all the more (Rom 6:2, 15). However, what has been nullified in Christ is not merely the Law's ability to divide people from one another. It would be unfair to Paul's thought to import the later dogmatic distinctions between the ceremonial, ritual, and moral functions of the Law, as if Christ had annulled only the first two.[160] Christ destroyed the power of the whole Law to punish and condemn, to

---

[158] Barth, *Ephesians*, 1:286.

[159] Barth, *Ephesians*, 1:291.

[160] E.g., Ambrosiaster: "The law that he abolished was that which had been given to the Jews concerning circumcision and new moons and food and sacrifices and the sabbath. He ordered it to cease because it was a burden. In this way he made peace" (*Ephesians*, 2:15, ACCS 8:139).

separate us from God.[161] Through him we have died to the Law (Rom 7:4). He discharged us from its custody (Rom 7:6); he redeemed us from its curse (Gal 3:13). He did this not by destroying the Torah, certainly, but by fulfilling and upholding it (Mt 5:17; Rom 3:31).

Critical scholars often draw the conclusion from this pericope that a post-Pauline writer has drawn these conclusions from the destruction of the temple in AD 70. If this were the case (and assuming the author was not trying to maintain a fiction of writing pre-70), it is hard to imagine why the author would not have directly cited that categorical act. How else could it be interpreted but as the judgment of God against Israel for rejecting the promised Messiah and therefore continuing the provisions of the old covenant after the new had come? What greater argument would there be for the reconciliation of Jew and Gentile than the physical destruction of the temple courts that kept them apart? Yet, even in the pre-70 lifetime of the historic St. Paul, the destruction of the temple was as sure and certain as if it had already happened, for our Lord had foretold it (Mk 13:2; 14:58 and parallels; cf. Jn 2:19–22). It was perhaps an abiding hope of Gentile Christians, who, like Trophimus the Ephesian (Acts 20:4; 21:29), may have stared across the deeply symbolic divide in Jerusalem. It was the necessary final act, akin to tearing down the Berlin Wall (which was a physical manifestation of the philosophical Iron Curtain that separated atheistic Communism from the West).

The destruction of the temple also reminds us of the difference between the old way of proselytism (the mission God had given Israel[162]) and the reconciliation achieved by Christ in the Christian church. It is not simply that in Christ the Gentiles are finally incorporated en masse into the nation of Israel. But, Paul argues, Christ died that "he might create the two into one new man" (2:15)—not incorporating one group into the other, but creating a *new* man. He died that he "might reconcile both in one body to God through the cross" (2:16)—not as if only the Gentiles needed reconciliation, but to reconcile *both* to God. When Christ came, "he preached peace to you who were far off and peace to those who were near" (2:17)—not peace only to those who were far off, but peace to *both*.

If a contemporary analogy might be helpful, consider the ecumenical movement. Is the unity of all Christians best achieved when some Lutherans seek union with some Anglicans and some Presbyterians join up with Methodists, while other Anglicans head toward Rome and other Lutherans and Presbyterians remain separate? Unity is not achieved while everyone runs off in different directions. The old joke is that the union of two churches results in three. The classical path of ecumenism, by contrast, is creedal: draw closer to God through

---

[161] "Oh, what love of humanity! He gave us a law that we might keep it, but when we failed to keep it and deserved punishment he dissolved the law" (Chrysostom, *Homilies on Ephesians*, 5:2.13–15, ACCS 8:139).

[162] See "Mission in the Old Testament" in Lessing, *Jonah*, 151–69.

a common confession of the scriptural truth, and you will by definition draw closer to one another. So, too, Paul argues here that Jews and Gentiles are brought into peace with one another by being reconciled to God. Those "far off" and those "near" (2:13, 17) both need to be drawn to God. Eph 2:1–3, in parallel to Romans 1–3, consigned both near and far to judgment as a universal call to repentance[163] in order that God might have mercy on both (Rom 11:32). With respect to the reconciliation of the two peoples, it is an argument from the greater to the lesser: if we have both been reconciled to God, then what can divide us from one another?

The result is not the enlargement of the old Israel (according to the flesh), but the creation of a new Israel (in the Spirit).[164] Certainly, the faithful remnant of Israel (including Paul himself!) marks a continuity between the two entities. But in the present address to Gentiles, Paul shows no interest in the question of what happens to the unbelieving majority of Israel according to the flesh (i.e., those outside Christ).[165] This is not to suggest that God's promises to Israel of old are null and void. Her advantages were many (Rom 3:1–2; 9:4–5). It was from those great privileges and gifts that the Gentiles were formerly estranged. But there is a subtle shift in Paul's argument here that greatly parallels Romans 9–11. Once the Gentiles were estranged from Israel (in the flesh); now they are incorporated into Israel (in the Spirit). In a sense, it is the very shift from flesh to Spirit that facilitates the incorporation of the Gentiles into "the Israel of God" (Gal 6:16). The temple itself becomes the obvious vehicle for illustrating this shift. The OT prophecies that spoke of all nations streaming to Mount Zion to worship the true God[166] were understood literally by most Jews (and by modern-day Jewish and Christian Zionists). But in line with our Lord's prophecies concerning the destruction of that earthly temple, Paul sees the fulfillment in a new and greater temple. On the one hand, it is simply the physical

---

[163] Paul states to King Agrippa that he called to repentance people in Damascus, Jerusalem, and all Judea, as well as the Gentiles. The Jews tried to kill him for both acts: saying that Jews needed to repent and taking the message of the Messiah to Gentiles (Acts 26:19–21). John the Baptizer, likewise, called Israel to repentance.

[164] Lincoln, *Ephesians*, 163:

> The Gentiles' former disadvantages have been reversed, not by their being incorporated into Israel, even into a renewed Israel of Jewish Christians, but by their being made members of a new community which transcends the categories of Jew and Gentile, an entity which is a new creation, not simply a merging of the former groupings. ... There is no escaping the conclusion that Eph 2 depicts the Church in terms of a new third entity, one which transcends the old ethnic and religious identities of Jew and Gentile.

Lincoln suggests that this is a divergence from Romans 9–11; yet there, too, Paul speaks of a new and distinct people, "Israel" (Rom 9:6) and "all Israel" (Rom 11:26), not only of a grafting of Gentiles onto the faithful remnant of Israel (Rom 11:17–24).

[165] Thus, unlike Romans, the letter to the Ephesians does not address Jewish-Gentile relations in both directions, but is almost exclusively concerned with the Ephesian Christians as Gentiles. This continues to characterize the later parts of the letter, in which Paul admonishes them not to return to their old, Gentile life (4:17–6:9).

[166] See the first textual note on 2:14 and the OT passages cited in a footnote there.

body of Jesus Christ himself, which was torn down in death and rebuilt in resurrection (Jn 2:19–21). But as Paul has asserted that the church herself is the body of Christ (Eph 1:23), so, too, he sees the new temple as a construction of Christ's members.

The Greek term οἰκοδομή, rendered as "building" (2:21), has, as does its English translation, both a passive and an active sense: the (built) temple itself and the act of building it. Perhaps like the original Twelve (Mk 13:1), Paul had watched in awe the ongoing construction of the magnificent new Herodian temple complex.[167] The temple site must have been continually abuzz with activity. In addition to the contemplation of Christ's own living body, this construction site may have influenced the living and active language Paul uses for the new temple. Like Peter (1 Pet 2:4–8), Paul envisions a temple of living stones, who breathe with the Spirit's breath. It is an architectural counterpart to Peter's "royal priesthood" (1 Pet 2:9), whose members offer living, spiritual sacrifices (Rom 12:1; 1 Pet 2:5).[168] Both the new temple and the priesthood of the baptized proclaim a new and open access to the presence of God.[169] Unlike the residents of Qumran, who saw their community as a sort of new temple because they believed the Jerusalem temple was occupied by an illegitimate priesthood,[170] neither Paul nor our Lord questions the legitimacy of the temple under the terms of the old covenant. Yet it is obsolete because Christ has come and the old has passed away (2 Cor 5:17). So also Israel of the flesh is replaced by Israel of the Spirit, a church incorporating children of Abraham who believe as he believed in the Messiah to come.

The new temple image captivated the minds of early postapostolic writers, bringing a simple answer to the divisive Jew-Gentile problem that plagued them for so long. Indeed, it is not the diversity of stones in the temple image that interested them, but the unity of its construction. Hermas, whose vision includes the longest extended metaphor of the church as temple, writes:

> And when the shepherd saw that the tower was beautifully built, he was very joyful; for the tower was so built that when I saw it, I envied its building, for

---

[167] The Jews in Jn 2:20 exclaim that the temple had been under construction for forty-six years.

[168] Priests in the ancient world were not so much defined by what they did but by their closeness to the deity and their perpetual privilege of access to the gods. In other nations, only a privileged minority had this priestly status, but Israel was called to be "a kingdom of priests and a holy nation" (Ex 19:6). The NT teaching of a priesthood of all the baptized is in this sense a continuation of the old, but with the incorporation of the Gentiles into this general priesthood. At the same time, with the rending of the sanctuary veil (Mt 27:51), the destruction of the Jerusalem temple in AD 70, and the rendering obsolete of the Aaronic priesthood, another level of division between God and men was broken down. See Winger, "The Priesthood of All the Baptized."

[169] As in Exodus 29 the sons of Aaron were first washed before they were permitted to enter the Holy Place of the tabernacle, so Holy Baptism gives access to the holy things of God, opening up to us the most holy place. See Eph 5:26 and 1 Cor 6:11, in which Baptism is described in language derived from the OT liturgical actions through which God brought about cleansing and consecration.

[170] E.g., 1QS 5:5–6; 8:4–15; 9:3–8; 11:7–8.

it was so built, as if it were all one stone, without a single joint in it, and the stone appeared as if it had been hewn out of a rock, for it seemed to me to be a single stone.[171]

With this image Hermas confesses that the church finds her unity in the Rock, Jesus Christ himself. Like other fathers (cited in the last textual note on 2:20), Hermas cannot envision Christ as located only in the cornerstone or only at the capstone. He is the entire building, into whom the baptized are incorporated. Ignatius, writing to the same Ephesians, confesses like Paul the central role of the cross in creating this unity with a vivid architectural image:

> You are as stones of the temple of the Father, made ready for the building of God our Father, carried up to the heights by the engine of Jesus Christ, [which] is the cross, and using as a rope the Holy Spirit.[172]

He sees the cross standing high and proud above the new temple, like a massive crane, lifting up each new member and placing him into the appropriate place in the building. He thus sees the work of the cross not merely as a one-time historical act of reconciliation, but as an ongoing process, as through Baptism all Christians are given to participate in his death and resurrection, lifted up like Christ into the heights of God's kingdom. It is through that bestowal of the Triune name, confesses Barnabas, that we receive our place in the temple:

> Now give heed, in order that the temple of the Lord may be built gloriously. Learn in what way. When we received the remission of sins, and put our hope on the Name, we became new, being created again from the beginning; wherefore God truly dwells in us, in the habitation [κατοικητήριον, as in Eph 2:22] which we are.[173]

---

[171] *The Shepherd of Hermas, Similitudes*, 9:9.7 (trans. Kirsopp Lake, LCL).

[172] Ignatius, *To the Ephesians*, 9:1 (trans. Kirsopp Lake, LCL).

[173] *Barnabas*, 16:8 (trans. Kirsopp Lake, LCL).

The Mystery of Paul's Apostolic Mandate: The Gospel of Christ for the Gentiles

Translation

3 ¹For this reason, I, Paul, the prisoner of Christ [Jesus] for the sake of you Gentiles—
²if indeed you have heard of the stewardship of the grace of God that was given to me for you,
³that in accord with revelation the mystery was made known to me, as I previously wrote in brief,
⁴in accordance with which, when you read it, you are able to understand my insight into the mystery of Christ,
⁵which in other generations was not made known to the sons of men
as now it has been revealed to his holy apostles and prophets in the <u>Spirit</u>,
⁶that the Gentiles are fellow heirs and fellow members of the body and fellow partakers of the promise in <u>Christ Jesus</u> through the Gospel,
⁷of which I was made a minister according to the gift of the grace of <u>God</u> that was given to me in accord with the working of his power.
⁸To me, quite the least of all the saints, this grace was given:
to proclaim to the Gentiles the unfathomable riches of Christ,
⁹and to enlighten [all men] as to what is the administration of the mystery that was hidden for ages in the God who created all things,
¹⁰in order that the multifaceted wisdom of God might now be made known to the rulers and authorities in the heavenly places through the church,
¹¹in accord with the eternal purpose which he carried out in Christ Jesus, our Lord,
¹²in whom we have boldness and access in confidence through faith in him.
¹³Therefore I ask [you] not to lose heart in my tribulations for your sake, which is your glory.

Textual Notes

3:1 τούτου χάριν—The accusative of χάρις used as a preposition following a genitive noun (or pronoun) can indicate either purpose or cause, but here it is surely the latter: "for this reason."[1] τούτου, "this," refers to an immediately preceding antecedent, probably the entire preceding chapter or pericope (2:1–22 or 2:11–22). But what precisely is the cause, and what is its result? The antecedent and meaning are not clear until the broken sentence, which is interrupted by 3:2–13, reaches its completion in 3:14: "*for this reason* I bend my knees to the Father …" Thus, the meaning is that because of the great act of reconciliation Christ effected between Gentile, Jew, and God (2:11–22),

---

[1] BDAG, s.v. χάριν, a–b. The phrase is used only three times in the NT: in Eph 3:1, 14 it refers back to a cause; in Titus 1:5 it points forward to a purpose.

Paul is moved to intercessory and doxological prayer (3:14–21). In between, Paul pursues a most significant digression (3:2–13).

ἐγὼ Παῦλος ὁ δέσμιος τοῦ Χριστοῦ ['Ιησοῦ]—This is the first of three references in the letter to Paul's imprisonment (3:1; 4:1; 6:20). The pronoun ἐγώ is probably not emphatic, but simply serves to introduce the predicate Παῦλος ὁ δέσμιος "I, Paul, the prisoner."[2] ὁ δέσμιος, "the prisoner," is definite because it stands in apposition to a proper noun, Παῦλος. Yet there is also a sense that Paul is *the* prisoner [par excellence]," as he may be called "*the* apostle of Christ Jesus" (1:1).[3] He virtually holds an office of prisoner. Paul's suffering is not only Christlike but also continues the sufferings of Christ himself: "now I rejoice in my sufferings for your sake, and I take my turn in filling up what is lacking in the sufferings of Christ in my flesh for the sake of his body, which is the church" (Col 1:24; cf. Acts 5:41).[4] These explanatory words from Colossians introduce the text parallel to our pericope, in which Paul explains the nature of his apostolic calling (Col 1:24–29). To suffer is part of the commission given him by Christ (Acts 9:16)—thus, he is Christ's prisoner, not Caesar's.[5] He is bound to do what Christ has given him to do (thus, he is δοῦλος Χριστοῦ, "Christ's slave," Rom 1:1; Gal 1:10; Phil 1:1). His imprisonment advances the proclamation of the Gospel (Phil 1:12–17). His suffering is almost vicarious, as it brings Gospel blessings to his flock (2 Cor 1:6; 4:12). This is the astonishing extent to which the apostolic office is representative of Christ. Paul frequently reminds his readers/listeners of his suffering for the sake of Christ and the Gospel[6] as a mark of the genuineness of his office and message, to entreat their prayers for him—and to encourage them in their own suffering. For though Paul in his office is the supreme example of such Christlike suffering, he is not completely unique. It is a role carried on by others who take up the apostolic ministry (2 Tim 1:8), just as the cross is the mark of all who follow Christ.[7]

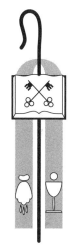

The omission of 'Ιησοῦ in the first hand of ℵ and D, together with F G (365) *pc* sa[mss]; MVict, is balanced by its inclusion in the earliest text, 𝔓[46], the first correctors of ℵ and D, as well as A and B and a host of significant early and late manuscripts. The omission is surely the more difficult (and therefore more likely to be original) reading; it is easier to understand scribes adding the name than taking it away (perhaps harmonizing it to Philemon 1, 9). Yet the overwhelming manuscript evidence in favor of its inclusion led the NA[27] editors to include it in brackets, indicating the decision is uncertain.

---

2   Turner, *Syntax*, 37.

3   Since "Christ Jesus" is definite, "apostle," even without the article, may be interpreted likewise. See Wallace, *Greek Grammar*, 250: "The general rule (discussed earlier in this chapter [pp. 239–40]) is that *both* the head noun and the genitive noun either have the article or lack the article (known as Apollonius' Canon). … The corollary to this rule (Apollonius' Corollary) … is that *when both nouns are anarthrous, both will usually have the same semantic force*."

4   On this translation of ἀνταναπληρόω, see BDAG, s.v. ἀνταναπληρόω.

5   Cf. Christ's response to Pilate (Jn 19:10–11) and Paul's appeal to Rome, by which he made himself a prisoner (Acts 25:10–12; 26:32).

6   Phil 1:7; Col 1:24; 4:3, 18; 2 Tim 1:8; 2:9; Philemon 1, 9–10, 13.

7   Mt 16:24; Mk 8:34; Lk 9:23; Rom 5:3; 8:17–18; 2 Cor 1:6–7.

ὑπὲρ ὑμῶν τῶν ἐθνῶν—For "you Gentiles," see the second textual note on 2:11. ὑπὲρ ὑμῶν combines the senses of "because of you" and "for your benefit." Paul later uses the same preposition to indicate Christ's sacrificial death "for us" (5:2; see also 5:25). The prepositional phrase recalls Paul's arrest, which was on the charge that he had violated the boundary marker in the temple that prohibited Gentiles from entering the inner courts; "Trophimus the Ephesian" was specifically cited (Acts 21:28–29).[8] But it also alludes to Paul's intention to defend "my Gospel" (2 Tim 2:8–9), with his specific mandate to preach it to the Gentiles (Acts 26:16–18).[9] His arrest would enable him to carry this legal defense and Gospel proclamation all the way to Rome,[10] and (assuming his acquittal and release) from there to proceed in his mission to the Gentile lands to the west, as far as Spain (Rom 15:24, 28). It is the mention of "you Gentiles" (Eph 3:1) that spurs Paul's excursus into the uniqueness of his apostolic mandate that occupies this pericope. The sentence is interrupted (anacoluthon), to resume in 3:14.

Two manuscript variants attempt to amend the lack of a verb in this anacoluthic sentence. The manuscripts D 104* *pc* provide πρεσβεύω, *I am acting as an ambassador* for you Gentiles." This captures the spirit of the preposition ὑπέρ and is borrowed from Eph 6:20. The second, κεκαύχημαι, "I have boasted," in 2464 *pc* (cf. 2 Cor 7:14) borrows from Paul's tendency to boast in his sufferings (Rom 5:3; 2 Cor 11:30; 12:5, 9). These attempts are unnecessary once one realizes that the verb κάμπτω, "I bend," arrives in 3:14.

3:2 εἴ γε ἠκούσατε τὴν οἰκονομίαν—"If indeed" does not imply uncertainty on Paul's part as to whether they have heard what he is about to repeat. εἴ can mean "since,"[11] and εἴ γε "inasmuch as,"[12] indicating something that the writer assumes to be true.[13] The identical expression in 4:21, "*if indeed* [εἴ γε] you heard about him [Christ] and were taught in him," could be rendered as "*since* ... ," for it surely refers to a confident statement of reality, not something about which Paul was uncertain. ἠκούσατε, "you have heard" (3:2), refers not to secondhand reports, but to Paul's personal preaching and catechesis among the Ephesian Gentiles. The participle ἀκούσαντες, "having heard," in 1:13 likewise refers to an event Paul knows is true. These expressions are rhetorical devices that encourage the readers/listeners to recall and ponder their past experience. (For analysis

---

8   See "Paul's Trip to Jerusalem, Arrest, and Imprisonment (Acts 21:1–36)" in "The City of Ephesus and Paul's Relationship to It" in the introduction.

9   Though he emphasizes to the Ephesians that his imprisonment is for the Gentiles, it is not exclusively so. Just as he was sent to preach first to the Jews and then to the Gentiles (Acts 9:15; Rom 1:16), so his imprisonment is also for "the hope of Israel" (Acts 28:20).

10 Acts 19:21; 23:11; 26:32; 27:24; 28:30–31.

11 See BDAG, s.v. εἰ, 3. If-clauses in the indicative can introduce a condition thought of as real (BDAG, s.v. εἰ, 1). Consider the devil's temptation of Christ: εἰ υἱὸς εἶ τοῦ θεοῦ, "*if* you are the Son of God, tell these stones to become loaves of bread" (Mt 4:3). Neither Satan nor Jesus doubted his divine sonship. The εἰ clause expresses rhetorically the presupposition for the devil's temptation: "*since* you are God's Son, as we both well know, ..."

12 BDAG, s.v. εἰ, 6 b.

13 BDF, § 454 (2): "Εἴγε is used similarly [to εἴπερ], but implies a more definite assumption." Moule, *Idiom Book*, 164: "It depends upon the context whether or not such a strengthened *if* implies doubt or confident assumption."

of the alternative view, that the particle εἰ, "if," indicates the writer did *not* know his audience, see "Internal Evidence" in "Addressees" in the introduction.) ἀκούω normally takes the genitive for the person whose words are heard and the accusative for the content of the message, as here (ἠκούσατε τὴν οἰκονομίαν).[14] "Hearing" in the NT, under influence of the Hebrew שָׁמַע, normally implies understanding. Thus, what they learned from Paul is his οἰκονομία, a key term in Ephesians that has been translated as "stewardship" (see the first textual note on 1:10, where, however, εἰς οἰκονομίαν was translated as "to administer"). Here it refers to the authority given to Paul over the οἶκος, "household,"[15] of God, the church, in his office as apostle (3:7–9). The term is suggested by God's stewardship of all creation (1:10, where the same noun, οἰκονομία, was translated as "administer") and the immediately preceding reference to the church as God's temple or house (2:19–22). In the Colossian parallel, the phrase is τὴν οἰκονομίαν τοῦ θεοῦ, "the stewardship from [i.e., representing] God" (Col 1:25), translated not inappropriately by the RSV as "the divine office." A steward has the full authority of the master of the household to administer its goods for the well-being of its members. Thus, it serves as a frequent NT image for the apostolic and pastoral office.[16]

τῆς χάριτος τοῦ θεοῦ τῆς δοθείσης μοι εἰς ὑμᾶς—The genitive τῆς χάριτος is objective: "stewardship of grace" means Paul administers grace. If this phrase were viewed in isolation, one might interpret "grace" as the quality of God by which he chooses to save people freely, monergistically, through faith, apart from any works they might contribute (2:5–9). If one did not look closely at the Greek grammar, one might assume that "stewardship" is what "was given" to Paul by God. However, the genitive adjectival participle τῆς δοθείσης actually modifies the genitive τῆς χάριτος (not the accusative τὴν οἰκονομίαν).[17] It is therefore "grace" that "was given" to Paul.[18] This suggests that "the grace of God that was given to me for you"—the grace of which Paul has "stewardship"—is the apostolic office itself. This referent of "grace" occurs twice more in the pericope, in each case unmistakably a reference to Paul's apostolic call (3:7, 8). Naturally, there is an intimate connection between the "grace" given to Paul to

---

[14] BDF, § 173 (1). See also the first textual note on 4:21.

[15] While the lexical connection is lost in English, οἰκονομία, "stewardship," has the same root, οἰκο-, as οἶκος, "house, household; temple." While Paul does not use οἶκος in Ephesians, he has just described the church as the new temple in 2:19–22 using the related term οἰκοδομή, "building" (see the first textual note on 2:21), and he has called Christians οἰκεῖοι, "[people] belonging to a household" (see the fourth textual note on 2:19). Writing to Timothy in the same Ephesian church, Paul compares a pastor's presiding over his own household (οἶκος) to caring for the church (1 Tim 3:4–5).

[16] 1 Cor 9:17; Col 1:25; cf. οἰκονόμος, "steward," in Lk 12:41–48; 1 Cor 4:1–2; Titus 1:7.

[17] If the antecedent is τὴν οἰκονομίαν, the participle might have become genitive by attraction to the nearer noun, χάριτος. This interpretation finds support in Col 1:25 (where τὴν δοθεῖσαν is accusative), but is inconsistent with Eph 3:7–8.

[18] χάρις, "grace," is frequently connected to δίδωμι, "to give," in the NT, either in the sense of "showing favor" or "granting a supernatural gift," particularly in reference to Paul's apostolic office: Acts 7:10; Rom 12:3, 6; 15:15; 1 Cor 1:4; 3:10; 2 Cor 8:1; Gal 2:9; Eph 3:7–8; 4:7, 29; 2 Tim 1:9; James 4:6; 1 Pet 5:5; cf. Jn 1:17: χάρις with ἐγένετο; 1 Tim 4:14: χάρισμα with δίδωμι. χάρις, "grace," is also connected with Paul's apostolic calling in Rom 1:5; 1 Cor 15:10; Gal 1:15. This is not identical to what the Roman church means by *gratia infusa*, which entails salvation by gradual transformation of the sinner into a saint who merits God's grace.

preach the Gospel and the "grace" which lies at the Gospel's heart, likewise between οἰκονομία, "stewardship," and χάρις, "the office that was given." But the chief subject of this pericope is the unique mandate of Paul's apostolic office. With the string of terms ὁ δέσμιος, "the prisoner" (3:1); τὴν οἰκονομίαν, "the stewardship"; and τῆς χάριτος τοῦ θεοῦ τῆς δοθείσης μοι, "the grace of God that was given to me" (3:2), Paul draws attention away from the person "I, Paul" (3:1) toward the Christ who is at work through him as a mere instrument. Paul expects a hearing because of the office, not the man.

3:3 [ὅτι] κατὰ ἀποκάλυψιν ἐγνωρίσθη μοι τὸ μυστήριον—A "mystery" (μυστήριον) is something hidden in the mind of God (see the first textual note on 1:9). As in 1:9, the "mystery" has now been disclosed. In the immediate context here, Paul defines the mystery first as the Gospel of Christ that was revealed to him as an apostle and second as the revelation that by this Gospel the Gentiles (together with faithful Jews) are incorporated into the body of Christ (3:6). This mystery was made known to him κατὰ ἀποκάλυψιν, "in accord with revelation."[19] The obvious reference is to Paul's encounter with the risen and ascended Lord on the road to Damascus, recounted three times in Acts (Acts 9:1–19; 22:4–21; 26:12–18). On the third telling, before Agrippa, Paul highlighted the Lord's mandate to him to bring the Gospel specifically to the Gentiles (Acts 26:15–18; cf. Gal 1:16). But in accordance with the meaning of κατά, "in accord with," and in light of Paul's fourteen-year retreat before embarking on his first missionary journey (Gal 1:17; 2:1), it is likely he would also include his study of Holy Scripture under "revelation" (Rom 16:25–26). Those prophetic Scriptures feature prominently in Paul's written defense of the Gentile mission (Romans 4; 9–11; Galatians 3–4; etc.). Finally, Paul also speaks of further revelation from God that directed his actions (Gal 2:2 = Acts 11:27–30?), whether through a vision (2 Cor 12:1–5) or by prophetic utterance (Acts 13:1–3; 21:10–14). Through these events Paul was given certain knowledge (ἐγνωρίσθη μοι, "it was made known to me," Eph 3:3) of God's intention for the Gentiles. For γνωρίζω, "to make known," see the first textual note on 1:9. ἐγνωρίσθη recurs in 3:5, and the aorist subjunctive γνωρισθῇ is in 3:10.

The omission of ὅτι, "that," is supported by significant early manuscripts and is the more difficult (and on these grounds likelier) reading. The omission requires a full stop at the end of 3:2 and a new sentence in 3:3. However, it might equally be argued that the omission is an attempt to smooth the grammar, since with its inclusion the verb ἠκούσατε, "you have heard," has two unequal objects, one a noun in accusative (τὴν οἰκονομίαν, "the stewardship," 3:2), and the other a subordinate clause beginning with ὅτι (3:3). The brackets in NA[27] indicate the difficulty of the decision, but the meaning is scarcely affected either way.

καθὼς προέγραψα ἐν ὀλίγῳ—If προέγραψα be understood as a true aorist, what Paul "*previously* wrote in brief" might be Galatians, which addressed the salvation of the Gentiles apart from the works of the Law, spoke of the revelation of Paul's mission (Gal 1:12, 16), and was directed broadly to the Ephesian part of the world. If this is too remote a possibility (considering that Galatians was written nearly a decade previously

---

[19] The preposition κατά plus the accusative does not simply indicate instrument, "*by* revelation," but marks the norm that is at the same time the reason (BDAG, s.v. κατά, B 5 a δ).

and is scarcely "brief"), there may be a lost correspondence in mind. Colossians is unlikely, as it was sent to Asia Minor at the same time as Ephesians (Col 4:7; Eph 6:21).[20] Those who believe Romans 16 was originally intended for Ephesus point to Rom 16:25–27, but this theory has no evidence to support it. If the act of revelation alone is in mind, 2 Cor 12:1–4 might be a candidate, but could Paul be sure the Ephesians had read it? Most likely προέγραψα is an epistolary aorist, referring to Paul's present act of writing as something that is in the past from the perspective of the future recipients.[21] Thus, the revelation of the mystery he has "just written in brief" is likely Eph 1:9–10 and/or 2:11–22.

3:4 πρὸς ὃ δύνασθε ἀναγινώσκοντες νοῆσαι—The expression πρὸς ὅ is unusual and difficult. Many translations simply reduce it to "which." However, it expresses a logical relationship, "in accordance with which," such as "they acted in accordance with what [word] Darius sent" (LXX Ezra 6:13).[22] Thus, if ὅ, "which," refers back to what Paul has briefly written, the meaning of πρὸς ὅ is that their ability "to understand" (νοῆσαι) would correspond precisely to it. In other words, "if you grasp what I have written when you read it, you will be able to understand …" The participle ἀναγινώσκοντες ("when you read it"), as its etymology indicates (from ἀνα-γινώσκω), connects knowledge with the reading experience (cf. 2 Cor 1:13). Like the Hebrew יָדַע, "to know intimately," the Greek verb implies a personal involvement with the text: "to know exactly, recognize."[23] Ancient readers normally read aloud, even when alone (e.g., Acts 8:30), as the vocalization of the text involved all the senses (including hearing) in the experience.[24] In the LXX ἀναγινώσκω regularly translates קָרָא, "to call out" or "read aloud."[25] In the present verse, therefore, ἀναγινώσκω does not simply refer to private reading of Paul's letter by the Ephesian Christians—if that were possible given the physical and economic limitations involved in reproducing and distributing scrolls or codices—but to public reading. The NT refers to the role of ὁ ἀναγινώσκων, "the lector" (Mt 24:15; Mk 13:14; Rev 1:3). Paul expects that his letters will be read aloud in the Divine Service of the gathered congregation (Col 4:16; 1 Thess 5:27) and mandates young pastor Timothy to devote himself to this practice in his ministry of the Word (1 Tim 4:13).[26] It is to this practice that Paul alludes in this verse, asking the Ephesian Christians to give heed to the reading of the letter and gain understanding into the mystery.

---

[20] See "Location and Date of Writing" and "Relationship to Colossians" in the introduction.

[21] See, e.g., the epistolary aorist ἔγραψα, "I wrote/am writing," in 1 Cor 5:11; Gal 6:11; Philemon 19, 21; δι᾽ ὀλίγων ἔγραψα, "I wrote/am writing briefly," in 1 Pet 5:12; διὰ βραχέων ἐπέστειλα, "I sent/am sending briefly," in Heb 13:22; BDF, § 334; Burton, *Moods and Tenses*, § 44; Turner, *Syntax*, 73; Moule, *Idiom Book*, 12; Wallace, *Greek Grammar*, 562–63.

[22] See BDAG, s.v. πρός, 3 d δ. Cf. "act rightly in accordance with [πρός] the truth of the Gospel" (Gal 2:14); "act according to [πρός] his will" (Lk 12:47); "to receive good or evil according to [πρός] what he has done" (2 Cor 5:10).

[23] See Rudolph Bultmann, "ἀναγινώσκω, ἀνάγνωσις," *TDNT* 1:343.

[24] See "Orality and the Interpretation of the Epistles: A Brief Introduction" in the introduction.

[25] See *HALOT*, s.v. I קָרָא, Qal, B.

[26] On the public reading of Scripture in the Bible, see Winger, "Orality as the Key to Understanding Apostolic Proclamation in the Epistles," particularly pages 200–12.

τὴν σύνεσίν μου ἐν τῷ μυστηρίῳ τοῦ Χριστοῦ—The combination of the infinitive in the preceding textual note and the noun here, νοῆσαι τὴν σύνεσίν μου, in effect "to understand my understanding," suggests that through the medium of the written and proclaimed Word, the Ephesians' minds will be conformed to Paul's. Paul has been the recipient of a remarkable σύνεσις, "insight, understanding," like the prophet Daniel of old (Dan 10:1), whom Paul perhaps imitated in his *Berakah* prayer (Eph 1:3–14; see Dan 2:19–23); prayer and praise flow from revelation. This insight into the mystery is not for Paul's own benefit—as it relates to the Gentile mission, this would be absurd—but is to be shared with his flock. Just as Paul gained it by "revelation" (3:3), such σύνεσις, "insight, understanding," of divine things is always a gift of God (2 Tim 2:7). As such, it is the object of prayer; God is asked to grant what we cannot gain by our own strength.[27] Knowledge of God is a quality of Jesus himself (σύνεσις, Lk 2:47) and is gained by incorporation and growth in him (Eph 3:17–19; 4:13, 15). In the present verse Paul can promise it through the Ephesians' reading of his Word because he is confident that his apostolic Word is from God. The content or object of the σύνεσις, "insight, understanding," is given by ἐν plus the dative:[28] ἐν τῷ μυστηρίῳ τοῦ Χριστοῦ, "into the mystery of Christ." This is the central theme of this section (3:1–13). Although the genitive τοῦ Χριστοῦ might be understood as subjective ("the mystery revealed *by* Christ"), it is more likely epexegetical: "the mystery that *concerns* Christ." It might even be taken as a genitive of apposition, "the mystery that *is* Christ."[29] For there is no conflict between the definition Paul gives in 3:6—that the mystery is the incorporation of the Gentiles into the body of Christ through the Gospel—and the mystery's definition in Col 1:27, "Christ in you."[30] The mission to the Gentiles, to which Paul also refers in the Colossian parallel, does not in any way exhaust what Paul means by "the mystery of Christ" (Eph 3:4).[31]

---

[27] See σύνεσις in Col 1:9; 2:2; cf. Eph 1:17. In the LXX, see σύνεσις in Ex 31:3, 6; 35:31. Also Ignatius, *To Polycarp*, 1:3; *Shepherd of Hermas, Mandates*, 4:2.2.

[28] BDAG, s.v. σύνεσις, 2; cf. 2 Tim 2:7.

[29] This hedging about the nuance of the genitive is not a failure to make up one's mind, but a recognition that it is usually inadequate and misleading to restrict a genitive to one such grammatical category. Zerwick urges us to consider

the fundamental force of the genitive, namely the indication of the appurtenance of one notion to another. The exact nature of that appurtenance, of the relation between the notions, depends upon context and subject matter, so that of itself the use of the genitive may have as many varieties as there are ways in which two notions may be associated. Hence to the question, with regard to the expression "gospel of Christ" and many others, whether the genitive is subjective or objective or one of origin or the like, we must answer: it is not any of these alone, but is a "general" genitive, a genitive used in general, indicating simply the appurtenance of "gospel" to "Christ" etc. (*Biblical Greek*, § 39)

[30] This supposedly conflicting definition in Col 1:27 is sometimes used to question the Pauline authorship of Ephesians. See "The Literary Relationship between Ephesians and Other Pauline Epistles" in "Evaluation of the Case" in "Authorship" in the introduction.

[31] Lincoln, *Ephesians*, 176, puts it this way: "The insight for others with which the apostle is credited is insight into the mystery of Christ (cf. Col 4:3; also [Col] 1:27), the mystery of which the content is Christ. The particular aspect of what God has done in Christ which is in view becomes clear in v 6 [of Ephesians 3]." Best, *Ephesians*, 304: "The uniting of Jew and

3:5 ὃ ἑτέραις γενεαῖς οὐκ ἐγνωρίσθη τοῖς υἱοῖς τῶν ἀνθρώπων—The dative ἑτέραις γενεαῖς, "in other generations," indicates "time when."[32] γενεά can refer to "a generation of people" or "the age in which that generation lives" (Col 1:26 expressly includes both notions). Thus, the mystery was not "made known"[33] "at the time of other generations." The subsequent dative phrase gives the verb's indirect object: τοῖς υἱοῖς τῶν ἀνθρώπων, "to the sons of men." "Sons of men" is a Hebraism which denotes all people, males and females.[34] But the *connotation* of the expression is twofold. First, as "sons of men" they have the characteristics only of their human parents, and thus only natural abilities (see the textual notes on 2:2, 3); apart from revelation they could have no deeper knowledge of divine matters. The OT uses the expression when contrasting human beings with God.[35] Second, together with γενεά, "generation," it pictures the succession of people who either clung to the promise of the coming Messiah generation after generation or, in the case of the Gentiles, were born and died without hope of the promise ("having no hope," Eph 2:12).

ὡς νῦν ἀπεκαλύφθη—Like "but now" in 2:13 (cf. also 2:4), ὡς νῦν, "as now," refers to a decisive change, a turning point in history, marking the transition from "then" to "now."[36] The revelation was not gradual, but a dramatic intervention into the normal course of history. ἀπεκαλύφθη, "it has been revealed," is a divine passive, referring to an act by God. ἀποκαλύπτω refers to the removal of a κάλυμμα, "veil, covering." Thus, it is the revelation of something that was present all along, but hidden: "the mystery which was hidden [τὸ ἀποκεκρυμμένον] for ages and for generations [ἀπὸ τῶν αἰώνων καὶ ἀπὸ τῶν γενεῶν], but now has been manifested [ἐφανερώθη] to his [God's] saints" (Col 1:26). Paul subsequently explains that the location where this mystery was hidden was "in ... God" (Eph 3:9), that is, it was part of his plan all along (1:9–10). In Jewish "apocalyptic" literature, so popular in the intertestamental and NT eras and represented in the NT by John's Revelation, the veil hides spiritual realities behind the scenes, including battles, judgments, and victories. The revelatory writing pulls back the veil briefly, but discloses what is happening only in symbolism and allegory, as human beings are unable to grasp fully the divine mysteries. Paul's expression, as the context makes clear, goes beyond these contemporary extrabiblical parallels. νῦν ἀπεκαλύφθη, "now it has been revealed," means full disclosure that leads to knowledge and understanding. Although

---

Gentile can be described as the mystery of Christ because it is through him that it is attained, for both Jew and Gentile are now in the one body of Christ."

[32] It is unusual Greek, however, to use a simple dative for a period of time rather than a single point in time. A period of time would normally be expressed with the preposition ἐν plus the dative. See BDF, § 200 (4); Turner, *Syntax*, 243.

[33] For γνωρίζω, "to make known," see the first textual note on 1:9. ἐγνωρίσθη also appeared in 3:3, and the subjunctive γνωρισθῇ is in 3:10.

[34] "Sons of men" is frequent in the OT (forty-four times in LXX, of which twenty-six are in Psalms), but appears only one other time in the NT (Mk 3:28).

[35] E.g., Gen 11:5; 1 Sam 26:19; Ps 146:3 (LXX 145:3); 1 Esdras 4:37.

[36] See the first textual note on 2:13 and the chart contrasting "then" with "now" in "Structure and Rhetoric" in the commentary on 2:11–22.

the verb is aorist, the emphasis is on the present result of the disclosure. Combined with νῦν, "now," the verb functions more like a perfect tense,[37] "it *has been* revealed."

τοῖς ἁγίοις ἀποστόλοις αὐτοῦ καὶ προφήταις ἐν πνεύματι—This revelation has been granted "to his holy apostles and prophets." The preceding particle νῦν, "now," indicates that Paul does not have in mind OT prophets but contemporaries of the apostles, who with them received the Word of God and laid the church's foundation (see the first textual note on 2:20).

Does this phrase refer to a group separate from Paul or inclusive of him? On the one hand, as Paul has already referred to the revelation granted him personally (3:3), this may indeed be a reference to the twelve original apostles who were first mandated by the Lord to take the Gospel to all nations (Mt 28:19–20; Lk 24:47; Acts 1:8). Peter received a revelation concerning the Gentiles just as explicit as Paul's (Acts 10:9–16, 34–35). Paul can refer to Christ's Easter appearances "to all the apostles" (1 Cor 15:7) without including himself (1 Cor 15:8).

On the other hand, νῦν, "now," indicates that the revelation of the mystery was not simply a past-time event, but is a continuous disclosure in Paul's generation. It comprises not only Christ's appearance to Paul from heaven on the Damascus road, but perhaps also to events like the Jerusalem apostles' Spirit-led discernment that Paul's mission to the Gentiles was from the Lord (Gal 2:9). Thus, in this pericope Paul moves from the narrow to the broad, from his unique mandate to the Gentiles (3:1–4) to the fact that all the apostles and prophets (including himself) received the same revelation and commission (3:5). Yet, it may be that the reference to the apostles and prophets (3:5) should be regarded as parenthetical, as Paul subsequently returns to his unique mandate (3:7–9).

Critics have contended that Paul would not include himself in a category of "apostles" called "holy," as if this were a term of awe appropriate only for a sainted generation,[38] but they may be unduly influenced by later Christian use of the term "saint." If Paul can refer to all baptized Christians in Ephesus as "saints" (1:1), surely he would not be ashamed to apply the term to himself. In Col 1:26 Paul omits the apostles and prophets as media of the revelation and declares that the mystery "was manifested to his [God's] saints [holy people]," as in Eph 1:9 it was "made known to us."[39] (The

---

[37] See the aorists that function as perfect tenses in Rom 5:11; 11:30, 31; Eph 2:13.

[38] As an example of such criticism, Schnackenburg refers to "the singular expression 'the *holy* apostles' (which Paul himself would certainly never have used)" (*Ephesians*, 133). Lincoln, *Ephesians*, 179, cites the language of Ignatius, *To the Magnesians*, 3:1, referring to "the holy presbyters" of a prior generation. Lincoln also argues that the authentic Paul would not have shared credit for the revelation with the other apostles—which is effectively an argument in a circle, as this is the only passage where this sharing is explicitly discussed. Lincoln prefers to have Paul in conflict with the Gospels and Acts rather than to reconcile them.

[39] There is no reason to see a conflict between Eph 3:5 and Col 1:26 (as does Lincoln, *Ephesians*, 178), for the mystery was revealed to the apostles and prophets so that they might manifest it to all the saints. The distinction of verbs between the two passages (ἀπεκαλύφθη, "has been revealed," in Eph 3:5 and ἐφανερώθη, "was manifested," in Col 1:26) is probably quite deliberate. Best, *Ephesians*, 307, quite astonishingly contradicts his own reasons for viewing Ephesians as pseudepigraphical when he quite correctly writes: "A revelation restricted to the apostles [Eph 3:5] and not to all believers [Col 1:26] does not indicate a later stage in church

omission of ἀποστόλοις in Eph 3:5 in B b; Ambst is probably an assimilation to the Colossian parallel, Col 1:26.) To call the apostles and prophets "holy" is not to elevate their personal status or qualities, but to attach them to the holy God who set them apart for himself (cf. Rom 1:1).[40] In that they are set aside for a unique office, they are, indeed, distinct from "the saints" in general. That Paul is one of these apostles is the claim he makes emphatically at the beginning of every letter, as he has done in this one (Eph 1:1).

As the two nouns are joined by only one article (τοῖς ... ἀποστόλοις ... καὶ προφήταις), it is best to treat "apostles and prophets" as a unit, though not a single office.[41] The adjective ἁγίοις, "holy," and the pronoun αὐτοῦ, "his," apply to both equally, as does the final phrase ἐν πνεύματι, "in the Spirit." It is not as if the apostles alone are "holy and his" and only the prophets are "in the Spirit." Though the Spirit is closely connected with prophecy,[42] so, too, the apostles are baptized with and directed and empowered by the Holy Spirit.[43] Likewise, the prophets can be called "holy."[44] ἐν πνεύματι, "in the Spirit," is best understood as modifying the verb ἀπεκαλύφθη, "it has been revealed": it does not describe *which* apostles and prophets are in mind (adjectival), but *how* the act of revelation took place (adverbial).[45] He is "the Spirit ... of revelation" (1:17). This is not to say, of course, that the Spirit is the exclusive possession of these foundational officeholders; "in the Spirit" is the location of all the baptized, giving access to God the Father (2:18, 22; 5:18; 6:18). Thus, we might paraphrase: "now revealed in the Spirit to the holy apostles and holy prophets, all of whom are his."

3:6 εἶναι τὰ ἔθνη συγκληρονόμα καὶ σύσσωμα καὶ συμμέτοχα—The infinitive εἶναι, "to be," with its subject in the accusative τὰ ἔθνη, "the Gentiles," stands in epexegetical apposition to τὸ μυστήριον, "the mystery" (back in 3:3). In other words, this clause now offers a definition of "the mystery," returning to the subject after the somewhat parenthetical comment on revelation to the apostles and prophets (3:3–5). Thus, "the mystery" is "that the Gentiles are ..."

---

development; the revelation to a limited group was part of the tradition from the beginning (cf Mt 28.16–20, etc.); it is the revelation to all believers which is the new element."

[40] Commenting on "holy," Schlier, *Epheser*, 150, writes: "The apostles and prophets are thereby designated as those who have been selected and consecrated for God's service. Through this predication they are honored as the foundation of the church (2:20), and as the first of the gifts of the ascended Christ."

[41] The Granville Sharp Rule, which asserts that two personal, singular, non-proper nouns joined by καί after just one definite article refer to the same person, does not apply to plural nouns. But plural noun pairs joined by καί after the article *do* form a closely related group. See Wallace, *Greek Grammar*, 277–90, especially 285–86. See also the first textual note on 2:20 and the second textual note on 4:11.

[42] Acts 2:17–18; 11:27–28; 13:1–2; 19:6; 21:10–11; 1 Pet 1:12; 2 Pet 1:21; Rev 19:10.

[43] Acts 1:5, 8; 2:1–47 (Pentecost); 16:6; 19:21; 1 Cor 2:4, 13.

[44] Lk 1:70; Acts 3:21; 2 Pet 3:2; though these are all references to "holy" prophets of the OT. It is therefore possible that (because of the word order) "his holy" applies only to "apostles," while maintaining that "in the Spirit" applies to both "apostles" and "prophets," but because of the single article, this is unlikely.

[45] ἐν πνεύματι, "in the Spirit," is adverbial in Eph 5:18; 6:18. For the phrase as descriptive of revelation, see Rev 1:10: "I was in the Spirit on the Lord's day"; also Rev 4:2; 17:3; 21:10.

The threefold definition that follows, formed with compound substantival adjectives[46] created from the preposition σύν, "together with," continues the theme of joint blessings shared by Gentiles and Jews in Christ, which permeates Ephesians more than any other NT book (especially 2:5, 6, 19, 21, 22; 3:6; 4:3, 16; 5:7, 11). The verbal rhythm is difficult to reproduce in English, though our translation attempts it with "fellow."

- συγκληρονόμα, "fellow heirs" (like the others, an adjective used as a substantive) recalls the prologue's promise that an "inheritance" is reserved for us with Christ until the Last Day, guaranteed now by the seal of the Spirit (1:13–14; see the last textual note on 1:13 and the first textual note on 1:14). "Heirs" also implies the present reality of a new birth that makes both Jews and Gentiles sons of God through Holy Baptism. The true heirs of God's eternal kingdom are no longer defined by the flesh, but by the Spirit. The subsequent modifier (τῆς ἐπαγγελίας, "of the promise") clarifies this, recalling Paul's argument in Gal 3:26–29 that the true offspring and heirs of Abraham are not those born of his flesh, but those who believe the promise as he did.[47]

- σύσσωμα—the plural of σύσσωμος, a NT hapax legomenon unknown outside Christian writers influenced by this text (i.e., Paul made it up)—is an adjective literally meaning "co-bodied, con-corporate" or, as a substantive here, "fellow members of a body." It is an acute summary of the central verse of the previous pericope that located the union of Gentiles and Jews in the one "body" of Christ crucified (2:16).

- συμμέτοχα, "fellow partakers," is an adjective coined from the rare classical verb συμμετέχω, "to share in the possession of something." The double prepositions in the compound (σύν and μετά, both meaning "with") emphasize that multiple parties hold something in common, here expressed by the genitive τῆς ἐπαγγελίας, "of the promise." Though συμμέτοχος occurs only here and in 5:7 (where Paul warns the Ephesians against being "fellow partakers" with "the sons of disobedience" in 5:6), the measure of the word is best gained from Paul's use of the cognate compound verb μετέχω, "to share, participate in." This verb in 1 Cor 10:17, 21, 30 has a particularly strong eucharistic flavor, referring to the body and blood of Christ as the common thing shared by the faithful, who are drawn into fellowship with one another by their communion in the common gifts.[48] Thus, ironically, while Jew and Gentile are not joined together by their own flesh (like Israel of old), they are joined by the flesh of Christ.

τῆς ἐπαγγελίας ἐν Χριστῷ Ἰησοῦ διὰ τοῦ εὐαγγελίου—The new status described by the three συν- adjectives is further modified by these three terms or phrases: "of the promise," "in Christ Jesus," and "through the Gospel." The genitive τῆς ἐπαγγελίας, "of the promise," seems to modify at least the first and third adjective: "fellow heirs …

---

[46] These three adjectives are neuter plural, in agreement with τὰ ἔθνη, "the Gentiles."

[47] Cf. Heb 11:9, where Isaac and Jacob (who indeed shared his flesh) are commended as "fellow heirs" (συγκληρονόμοι) for sharing his faith in the promise. Likewise, husband and wife, though joined in the flesh, are more significantly identified as "fellow heirs [συγκληρονόμοι] of the grace of life" (1 Pet 3:7). In Rom 8:17 it is Christ himself with whom we are "fellow heirs" (συγκληρονόμοι). He is the common location that binds together all Christians.

[48] 1 Cor 10:21 parallels the communion-exclusion contrast of Eph 3:6 and 5:7. Heb 2:14 (with μετέχω) points to the incarnate flesh and blood of Christ as that nature which binds God to his children.

of the promise" and "fellow partakers of the promise." It indicates what is shared, what the Jews and Gentiles hold in common.[49] This affirmation reflects again the reversal of the Gentiles' former status ("strangers to the covenants of the promise," 2:12). This co-participation finds its concrete location ἐν Χριστῷ Ἰησοῦ, "in Christ Jesus" (Paul's favorite phrase in Ephesians; see the fifth textual note on 1:3). If they are "in him," they are "with one another." διὰ τοῦ εὐαγγελίου, "through the Gospel," is likely an adverbial modifier of the infinitive εἶναι, "to be"; in other words, the Gentiles' new state of being comes about "through the Gospel."[50]

3:7 οὗ ἐγενήθην διάκονος—The passive verb ἐγενήθην could be intransitive, "I became," but is more likely a true passive, "I was made [by God]." The Vulgate rendering of διάκονος as "minister" was standard throughout the Middle Ages. Since the nineteenth and early twentieth centuries, it has become popular to gloss διάκονος as "servant" and διακονία as "service" (see the first and third textual notes on 4:12). This shift cannot be considered apart from the European Protestant movement to resurrect what was believed to be "the historic diaconate" (male and female) concerned with church-sponsored social work.[51] The meaning of the term was sought in the glory days of the diaconate (third century until the early Middle Ages) when deacons and deaconesses were concerned with alleviating physical distress, before the male diaconal office was reduced to a minor liturgical role and the female absorbed into monastic orders. Particularly influential was the 1923 dissertation of Wilhelm Brandt.[52] Recently his work has been comprehensively overturned by John Collins, who writes: "Care, concern, and love—those elements of meaning introduced into the interpretation of this word and its cognates by Wilhelm Brandt—are just not part of their field of meaning."[53] Collins' research demonstrates that the essential component of meaning of the διακον-word group is the authorization of a subordinate to carry out a specific act.[54] Thus, it does not refer to any and every act of humble, selfless service (particularly not self-chosen works),[55] but to official responsibilities of an agent carried out on behalf of a

---

[49] BDF, § 182 (1), includes τῆς ἐπαγγελίας as an example of a "genitive with adjectives" and notes that that use of the genitive is particularly common with the idea of "taking part in."

[50] Cf. 1 Cor 4:15; 2 Thess 2:14; 2 Tim 1:10, where the same phrase functions adverbially.

[51] Later the Roman Church would also be affected. Vatican II (1962–1965) adopted the notion of a permanent diaconate, whereas since the early Middle Ages a Roman deacon was always in transition to the priesthood (somewhat like a Lutheran vicar).

[52] Published as Wilhelm Brandt, *Dienst und Dienen im Neuen Testament* (ed. Otto Schmitz; Neutestamentliche Forschungen, 2d series, vol. 5; Gütersloh: Bertelsmann, 1931).

[53] Collins, *Diakonia: Re-interpreting the Ancient Sources*, 254. See also Collins, *Deacons and the Church: Making Connections between Old and New*; Donfried, "Ministry: Rethinking the Term *Diakonia*."

[54] The latest edition of Bauer's lexicon (BDAG) incorporates Collins' ideas into its twofold definition of διάκονος: (1) "one who serves as an intermediary in a transaction, *agent, intermediary, courier*," and (2) "one who gets someth[ing] done, at the behest of a superior, *assistant*."

[55] The point of Jesus' words to the disciples about greatness through becoming a διάκονος is not that they perform acts of charity, but that instead of exalting themselves and their own desires, they subordinate themselves to the will of the one who sends them (Mt 20:26; Mk 9:35; 10:43; cf. Lk 22:26).

commissioning superior.[56] Furthermore, διάκονος does not refer to one specific office (e.g., "deacon"), but to any office whose bearer is an authorized representative of another (which is what "office" means).[57] It has some of the connotations of the English prefix "vice-," which can be attached to any number of offices.

The specific content of the office of "minister" is determined by context and the external entailments of the term διάκονος. Thus, Paul the apostle can also be a διάκονος because he—like others in the office of the ministry—is a representative of Christ,[58] or of God,[59] from whom he has received a commission with specific reference to the Gentiles (διακονία, "ministry," Acts 21:19; Rom 11:13). Christ himself is a minister of God in that he carries out his mission according to the Father's plan and sending.[60] The διάκονοι who stand alongside the ἐπίσκοποι ("bishops") in Phil 1:1 are therefore probably not "deacons" in the later sense, but "ministers" who stand in a subordinate relationship to the "bishops."[61] The translational move from "minister" (KJV) to "servant" (RSV/ESV) runs counter to this research.[62]

The relative pronoun οὗ, "of which" or "of whom," could refer back either to "the Gospel" or to "Christ Jesus" (3:6). Either makes good sense, the former being the closer and more likely antecedent. The genitive in "minister of the Gospel" would not necessarily imply that the Gospel is Paul's master, but that his ministry is defined

---

[56] The etymology of διάκονος is probably related to διώκω, "to run," as the διάκονος was originally a go-between. See Rom 15:25, where Paul is διακονῶν, "delivering" the collection from the wider church to Jerusalem. A minister of God delivers something from God.

[57] Thus, it may be anachronistic to call Phoebe a "deaconess," though that is possibly an office she held. But the point of Rom 16:1 is that Phoebe is a "representative" of the church at Cenchreae when she visits Rome.

[58] 2 Cor 11:23; Col 1:7; 1 Tim 4:6. Note the language of the Apology concerning the pastoral office: "The Sacraments are efficacious even though dispensed by wicked ministers, because the ministers [*ministri*] act in the place of Christ [*vice Christi*], and do not represent their own persons, according to Luke 10, 16" (Ap 7:47 [*Triglotta*, 243]). This is what it means to be a minister: to represent the person above, whose authority one bears.

[59] 2 Cor 6:4; 1 Thess 3:2 (variant reading); "as the Lord gave" (1 Cor 3:5); "in the Lord" (Eph 6:21; Col 4:7). Even a political ruler can be "a minister of God" (Rom 13:4) because his authority comes from above (Jn 19:11). This political usage of the term "minister" is familiar to those in countries with a British parliamentary system. Government "ministers" represent not the people but the queen ("from above"), who herself rules as an agent of God.

[60] Mt 20:28; Mk 10:45; Lk 22:27; Jn 12:26; Rom 15:8; cf. Jn 5:23, 36–37; 17:21; 20:21; passim.

[61] This may also be the sense of διάκονοι ("ministers") in 1 Tim 3:8, 12, which stands subordinate to the discussion about ἐπίσκοπος ("bishop") in 1 Tim 3:1–7. In sixteenth-century Germany, the term *Diakon* was used in this sense. For the first few centuries of Lutheranism, called and ordained ministers who performed the full duties of Word and Sacrament within the pastoral office, but were subordinate to a *Hauptpfarrer*, "senior pastor," in a large parish were called "deacons." Thus, *Diakon* was equivalent to "assistant pastor" today. Norman Nagel suggests that, from the evidence of the NT and the apostolic fathers, this was the common meaning of the term διάκονος in the early church, before its pastoral elements were stripped out in making it an office of charity. In these early days, the pastoral office included responsibility for the care of the Christian poor. See Norman Nagel, "The Twelve and the Seven in Acts 6 and the Needy," *Concordia Journal* 31 (2005): 113–26; and Albert Collver, "Deacons: Office of Service or Office of the Word?" *Logia* 16.2 (Eastertide 2007): 31–35.

[62] Compare the translations of διάκονος in KJV and RSV/ESV in Mt 20:26; Mk 10:43; Rom 13:4; 15:8; 1 Cor 3:5 (but not 3:6!); 6:4; 2 Cor 11:15, 23; 1 Tim 4:6 (in which RSV has "minister," but ESV "servant").

by the Gospel, is concerned with the Gospel. The Gospel is what he administers as a διάκονος.[63]

κατὰ τὴν δωρεὰν τῆς χάριτος τοῦ θεοῦ τῆς δοθείσης μοι—See the second textual note on 3:2. Paul again stresses the divine origin of his office and mission. The redundancy involved in two words for gift (δωρεάν, "gift," and δοθείσης, "was given") and one for "grace" (χάριτος) is typical of Ephesians' high, liturgical language. The textual variants attest to some confusion over the subject of τῆς δοθείσης: what is it "that was given"? As the NA[27] text stands (with τῆς δοθείσης in the genitive case), the subject of the participle must be the genitive χάριτος, "grace … was given," and this is the more likely reading. The Majority text reads the accusative τὴν δοθεῖσαν, whose antecedent is the accusative τὴν δωρεάν, so "the gift … was given." It may be a distinction without a difference, since the epexegetical genitive in τὴν δωρεὰν τῆς χάριτος means "grace" *is* the "gift" anyway, but the accusative variant is evidence that the scribes might have been confused over the notion that "grace" is something (a substance) that could be given.[64] In 3:8 the grammar allows no escape (" to me … this grace was given").

κατὰ τὴν ἐνέργειαν τῆς δυνάμεως αὐτοῦ—This second κατά phrase in succession, "in accord with the working of his power," appears to modify τῆς δοθείσης ("that was given"), the act of God's giving the office to Paul; God gave the office with power. But as the Colossian parallel (Col 1:29) makes clear, divine power characterizes not merely the bestowal of the office but also its execution. All the work that Paul invests in carrying out its tasks is, in reality, the work of God, who operates in and through him: "striving in accord with his energy that he powerfully works within me" (Col 1:29). δύναμις, "power," was therefore a characteristic of the Gospel Paul preached,[65] though he himself remained weak to show that the power was of God (2 Cor 4:7; 12:9). Through that Gospel this same power, rooted in the resurrection of Christ, is available to all who believe and are baptized.[66] In light of the modern-day Western theology of glory, however, it is important to note that this is the power to create wisdom and understanding of Christ, the power unto life and salvation, not earthly success.[67]

3:8 ἐμοὶ τῷ ἐλαχιστοτέρῳ πάντων ἁγίων—The superlative of ἐλαχύς, "small, short, little," is ἐλάχιστος ("smallest, littlest"), which is also used as the superlative of μικρός, "small [in stature, age, importance, etc.]." *Paulus* in Latin means "little," so Paul may have intended a play on words! Here we have ἐλαχιστότερος, in which a comparative

---

[63] Cf. Paul's declarations that he is a minister (διάκονος) of the Gospel (Col 1:23); of his [Christ's] body, the church (Col 1:24–25); "of the new testament" (2 Cor 3:6); "of righteousness (2 Cor 11:15); and "of God in the matter of the Gospel" (1 Thess 3:2 [variant reading]). These parallels suggest that "minister" of Christ's body, the church (Col 1:24–25), need not be understood to mean that Paul preaches as a representative of the church, as this would contradict his oft-repeated fundamental understanding of his office as from Christ.

[64] "Grace belongs to the giver, not to the recipient" (Victorinus, *Ephesians*, 1:3.7–8, ACCS 8:148). The Roman notion of *gratia infusa* is to be rejected because it contradicts what the NT teaches about the Gospel (e.g., Eph 2:5–9), not because "grace" is never "given" in the NT. See the second textual note on 3:2 and the second textual note on 3:8.

[65] Rom 1:16; 1 Thess 1:5; cf. Rom 15:19; 1 Cor 2:4; 2 Cor 12:12.

[66] Eph 1:19; cf. Eph 3:16, 20; 4:16; Col 2:12.

[67] Rom 1:16; 15:13; 1 Cor 1:18, 24; 6:14; 15:43.

ending (-τερος) is added to the superlative (ἐλάχιστος), making either a crude super-superlative, "more littlest," or a literary flourish, "quite the least."[68] Certainly Paul uses the adjective to distinguish himself from the rest of the apostles because he had formerly persecuted the church.[69] But here he compares himself to "all the saints," suggesting he may have more in mind. John the Baptizer was called lower than the "least" in the kingdom of God (μικρότερος, a comparative used as a superlative, Mt 11:11). At the Last Judgment, the referent of "these *least* brothers of mine" (τῶν ἐλαχίστων, super-lative, Mt 25:40) may, in fact, be the apostles and preachers, whose reception and care was equated with believing their message (cf. Mt 10:40–42).[70] The messengers of the kingdom are not the greatest, but the least, the servants (Mt 20:26; Mk 10:43). Ignatius, likewise, referring to the church of Syria, says: "I am not worthy to be called their mem-ber, being the *least* of them [ἔσχατος, superlative]."[71]

Thus, Paul puts his office into perspective: with respect to the Christ he represents, it is glorious; with respect to the saints, he is merely a servant. Paul's ranking of himself at the bottom of the heap of saints surely informs his reference to the apostles and proph-ets as "holy" (3:5). Whether Paul is "least" in comparison to the other apostles or in his office over against the saints he serves, Paul is careful to distinguish the office from the man. It is not because he deserved it that he was given this commission, nor does it bring any glory to him. In this respect, the grace given for the office corresponds to the grace given for salvation: it places all responsibility on the God who works monergistically.

ἐδόθη ἡ χάρις αὕτη—For "grace … given," see the second textual notes on 3:2 and 3:7. Now Paul's emphasis will shift from the giving of the office to its purpose, from revelation to proclamation (see the next textual note).

τοῖς ἔθνεσιν εὐαγγελίσασθαι τὸ ἀνεξιχνίαστον πλοῦτος τοῦ Χριστοῦ—The infinitive εὐαγγελίσασθαι introduces the purpose of the revelation of the mystery given to Paul (3:3–5): "to proclaim it as Good News to the Gentiles." The verb εὐαγγελίζομαι, "to preach Good News," is concentrated in the writings of Luke, Paul's disciple (twenty-five times in Luke and Acts), and Paul himself (twenty-one times of fifty-four total in the NT), confirming that Paul took the commission seriously. He has previously writ-ten that, when Christ came, "he preached [εὐηγγελίσατο] peace to you who were far off and peace to those who were near" (2:17)—thus, Paul is continuing the ministry of Christ. τὸ πλοῦτος τοῦ Χριστοῦ, "the riches of Christ," is characteristic Ephesian

---

[68] BDF, §§ 60 (2); 61 (2); Turner, *Syntax*, 31. Cf. μειζοτέραν in 3 Jn 4 (μείζων, the comparative of μέγας, with an additional comparative ending, literally, "more greater"). Wallace, *Greek Grammar*, 302, notes how this statement in Eph 3:8 makes 1 Cor 15:9 even more extreme, just as 1 Tim 1:15 presses further with "chief of sinners." While Lincoln, *Ephesians*, 183, considers such exaggeration a mark of pseudepigraphy, Wallace rightly argues the opposite: postapostolic writings tend to put the apostles on a pedestal, not highlight their failings. This may have been the motive for the omission of ἁγίων from Eph 3:8 in 𝔓[46], which brings the text back into harmony with 1 Cor 15:9 (unless its omission were simply by homoioteleuton). Paul himself is willing to expose the full extent of his shame in order to glorify God's grace.

[69] 1 Cor 15:8–10; Eph 3:8; see also Acts 7:58; 8:1, 3; 9:1–2; Gal 1:13, 23; Phil 3:6; 1 Tim 1:15.

[70] See Gibbs, *Matthew 1:1–11:1*, 57–59; and David E. Garland, *Reading Matthew* (Macon, Ga.: Smyth & Helwys, 2001), 247–49.

[71] Ignatius, *To the Trallians*, 13:1.

language that emphasizes the overflowing generosity of God's giving and is connected with grace, inheritance, glory, and always Christ (see the last textual note on 1:7; cf. 1:18; 2:7; 3:16). The adjective ἀνεξιχνίαστον, an *alpha*-privative (ἀ-) which negates ἐξιχνιάζω, "to search out," means "inscrutable" (God's ways are ἀνεξιχνίαστοι in Rom 11:33)[72] or "unfathomable," like an inky black sea whose depth cannot be sounded. Though this means that man may not discover the riches of Christ on his own strength, apart from revelation, it also implies that the mystery is revealed only to the extent that the human mind can comprehend it. But no human can fully understand or take control of it (1 Cor 13:12). What is "unfathomable" is the generosity God has shown in Christ toward creatures who in no wise deserve it and the unplumbable depths of the gifts God through Christ unfolds to us as time passes.

3:9 καὶ φωτίσαι [πάντας]—Paul used the verb φωτίζω, "to enlighten," in his prayer for the Ephesians that they would more fully know the richness of God's grace (see the first textual note on 1:18). Paul was likely reflecting on the movement from blindness to sightedness that he experienced at his Baptism.[73] Here the verb echoes the language of Paul's mandate from Christ: "to open their [the Jewish people's and the Gentiles'] eyes, so that they might turn from darkness to light and from the authority/realm of Satan to God, that they might receive forgiveness of sins and an allotment among those who are sanctified by faith in me" (Acts 26:18). As Paul has been called, has baptized, and has seen the light, so he is to preach, baptize, and enlighten others. The shift from darkness to light is particularly appropriate to the conversion of pagan Gentiles.[74]

The substantivized adjective πάντας, "all men," is omitted from the first hand of Sinaiticus, from Alexandrinus, and from a few minuscules and patristic texts. The overwhelming strength of manuscripts supports its inclusion. It may have been excluded by a scribe who thought "all" contradicted Paul's mission to "Gentiles" (3:8). If it is not original, it may have been added by a scribe who wished to provide a direct object for the verb φωτίσαι, "to enlighten," drawing on Jn 1:9. In any case, there is no conflict between "Gentiles" and "all," for the Gentiles join with the Jews to make the body of Christ complete. Without the direct object, it would be better to translate with "to bring to light what is the administration ..."

τίς ἡ οἰκονομία τοῦ μυστηρίου τοῦ ἀποκεκρυμμένου ἀπὸ τῶν αἰώνων ἐν τῷ θεῷ τῷ τὰ πάντα κτίσαντι—Within the context of 3:1–13, it is sensible to understand οἰκονομία as the "stewardship" or "administration" of the mystery (τοῦ μυστηρίου) that the preaching office carries out (as with οἰκονομία in 3:2). However, in the present verse, it would be peculiar if the message proclaimed were restricted to the particularities of Paul's office. Thus, we should probably refer οἰκονομία to God's "administration"

---

[72] Likewise, God's actions are ἀνεξιχνίαστα in LXX Job 5:9; 9:10; 34:24.

[73] See "Enlightened Eyes of Your Heart (1:18)" in the commentary on 1:15–23.

[74] Rom 1:21; Eph 4:18; cf. Is 9:1 (ET 9:2); Mt 6:23; 8:11–12; Rom 2:19; Col 1:13; 1 Thess 5:5; 1 Pet 2:9; passim.

of the entire mystery (see the textual notes on 1:10).[75] On "mystery," see the textual notes on it in 1:9 and 3:4.

For the first time in Ephesians, Paul notes explicitly that the "mystery" had been ἀποκεκρυμμένου, "hidden" (perfect participle of ἀποκρύπτω). Though characteristic of intertestamental apocalyptic (= "revelatory") literature, this verb is not used in the sense of "mysteries hidden in God" in the canonical OT or the standard apocryphal (= "hidden") writings—though the simple form κρύπτω appears occasionally.[76] For it is only when the mystery has been revealed that anyone is aware something was hidden. The mystery was not simply unseen and inaccessible; the divine passive "hidden" implies God deliberately kept it secret, as NT texts expressly state.[77] This "hiding" implies both the security of its being in God's care, and the divine wisdom that withholds its disclosure until the strategic moment.

"From the ages" (ἀπὸ τῶν αἰώνων) emphasizes the full extent of the mystery that has never before been made known,[78] as well as the eternally distant origin of God's plan for the election of his children and the reconciliation of the cosmos to himself (1:4–5, 9–10). As an expression of "then," it also repeats the "then-now" temporal comparison that has repeatedly featured in Ephesians (2:1–4, 11–13; 3:5), with the "now" coming in 3:10.[79] This evidences a simple "two age" view of history (1:21; 2:2, 7); with the coming of Christ, the new age is already upon us (1 Cor 10:11; Heb 6:5). The description of God as τῷ τὰ πάντα κτίσαντι, "(the one) who created all things,"[80] emphasizes the eternal origin of the plan, but, more important, links redemption with creation. The God of creation will set right what has gone wrong. The new creation (2:10, 15; 4:24) is not an abandonment of the old, but its perfection.

---

[75] RSV renders οἰκονομία in 3:2 as "stewardship" but as "plan" in 3:9, though "plan" is too static a translation for God's active administration of the work of salvation. Using the same verb (φωτίζω) as here in Eph 3:9, Paul declares to Timothy that "our Savior Christ Jesus [himself!] … brought life and immortality to light [φωτίσαντος] through the Gospel" (2 Tim 1:10).

[76] LXX Prov 25:2; 2 Macc 12:41.

[77] Mt 11:25; Lk 10:21; cf. Lk 18:34; 19:42; Col 2:3.

[78] Cf. Col 1:26; "since the foundation of the world" (Mt 13:35); "for long ages" (Rom 16:25); "before the ages" (1 Cor 2:7); "at the end of times" (1 Pet 1:20). The phrase in Eph 3:9 should not be understood as "hidden *from* the *Ages*," as if the Aeons were hostile spiritual forces; see the first textual note on 2:7 as well as the textual notes on 2:2.

[79] See "once/then" (ποτέ) and/or "now" (νῦν) in 2:2, 3, 11, 13; 3:5, 10; 5:8, 29 (cf. 2:4; 4:17). See also the table contrasting "then" with "now" in "Structure and Rhetoric" in the commentary on 2:11–22; the table in "Structure and Rhetoric" as well as the section entitled "Darkness Has No Fellowship with Light" in the commentary on 5:3–14; and the table of antitheses in "Structure and Rhetoric" in the commentary on 5:15–21a.

[80] The concentration of doxological phrases like "Creator of all things" in intertestamental literature is curious, but suggests it was familiar language in Paul's day: Judith 13:18; 2 Macc 1:24; 7:23; 3 Macc 2:3; 4 Macc 11:5; Wis Sol 1:14; Sirach 18:1; 24:8. The acclamation is repeated in Acts 14:15; Rev 4:11 (cf. Acts 4:24; 14:15; 17:24; Rom 4:17; Rev 10:6; 14:7), and early patristic writings: *Didache*, 10:3; *1 Clement*, 60:1; *Shepherd of Hermas, Mandates*, 1:1; *Shepherd of Hermas, Similitudes*, 5.5.2. All things were created through Christ (Jn 1:3; Col 1:16; Heb 1:2), a NT confession that influenced the textual variant in the current verse that inserts διὰ Ἰησοῦ Χριστοῦ, "through Jesus Christ."

The textual variant that omits ἐν from the phrase ἐν τῷ θεῷ ("in the God") is particularly interesting. With this omission, Marcion argued that the mystery was hidden "*from* the [inferior] god who created all things," thus distinguishing the Demiurge (who created the material world; called "God" in the OT) from the God of the NT.[81] However, this need not be the only way to understand the text that results from the omission of ἐν; it would be better to translate the resulting simple dative as an unusual dative of personal agent: "hidden *by* the God who created all things."[82] If the inclusion of the preposition ἐν is original to Paul—as it surely is on the basis of overwhelming manuscript evidence—the phrase "hidden *in* the God who created all things" may have been formulated precisely to exclude the sort of matter-spirit divide that characterized Greek and early Gnostic thinking as reflected in Marcion.[83] The mystery of cosmic salvation in the Messiah was hidden all along in the Creator of the universe; the God of the OT is the very same as the God of the NT.

3:10 ἵνα γνωρισθῇ νῦν ταῖς ἀρχαῖς καὶ ταῖς ἐξουσίαις ἐν τοῖς ἐπουρανίοις—The phrase "the rulers and authorities" is a summary of the fourfold description of spiritual forces Paul listed in 1:21. Though good angels would be included, the primary reference there was to the hostile forces whom Christ overcame for the sake of the church (cf. 6:12). In the preceding verse (1:20), Paul had proclaimed that Christ was seated ἐν τοῖς ἐπουρανίοις, "in the heavenly places," far above these forces that were now subordinated under his feet (see the textual notes on 1:3 and 1:20). In the cosmology of these texts, "the heavenlies" does not refer simply to "heaven," i.e., the domain of God with his angelic hosts and the repose of the blessed dead. Rather, this is a multilayered spiritual realm, governed by the God who is over all, but occupied in its lower levels by good and evil forces doing battle in parallel to the war under way between God's forces and devil's on this earth.[84] Because of the triumph of Christ and his exaltation to the right hand of God, there is no doubt that God's forces have won the victory.

This victory is "now" (νῦν, 3:10) being "made known,"[85] though until the second coming, skirmishes will continue (6:10–17). This revelation takes place through apostolic proclamation, which not only announces salvation to the Gentiles but also makes the victory known to the combatants in the spiritual realm. Primarily this is a fear-inspiring announcement to the forces of evil that their rout has been accomplished (cf. 1 Pet 3:19–22), even though these spiritual forces continue to attack as if they could win (Eph 6:12). But as some commentators and most patristic writers emphasize,[86] apostolic

---

[81] Tertullian, *Against Marcion*, 5:18.

[82] BDF, § 191. The only clear examples of a dative of agency in the NT involve perfect passive verbs (as here: ἀποκεκρυμμένου), in accord with classical usage (Lk 23:15; James 3:7). See Wallace, *Greek Grammar*, 163–66; Smyth, *Greek Grammar*, §§ 1488–94.

[83] See Schlier, *Epheser*, 155.

[84] Job 1:6; Dan 10:13, 21; 2 Macc 5:2.

[85] For γνωρίζω, "to make known," see the first textual note on 1:9. The aorist passive γνωρισθῇ here is subjunctive; the indicative ἐγνωρίσθη appeared in 3:3, 5.

[86] See, e.g., Bruce, *The Epistles to the Colossians, to Philemon, and to the Ephesians*, 321; Chrysostom, *Homilies on Ephesians*, 7:3.9–10 (NPNF¹ 13:80).

preaching also brings comfort to the hosts of God's good spiritual creatures (angels), who are rallied in their fight by the knowledge that the victory has been won. This is a knowledge for which they had longed (1 Pet 1:12).

διὰ τῆς ἐκκλησίας—This phrase, "through the church," occurs only here in the NT. Should the phrase be understood as giving the personal agent of the passive verb γνωρισθῇ, "might be made known," as if Paul meant to say "the church will make known [= proclaim] to the evil forces"? In a context that has univocally stressed the apostolic ministry, it would be strange if Paul suddenly substituted proclamation *by* the church for his own preaching (recognizing, of course, that Paul and the apostles are part of that very church). Elsewhere in Ephesians the church is the recipient, not the dispenser, of divine gifts (4:7–12; 5:23–32). Therefore "through [διά] the church" is better understood in the instrumental sense. As Paul's preaching delivers the Gentiles into God's hands, their very existence as a growing, living, and united church[87] serves as testimony to the evil spiritual forces that their authority over this earth and this age is at an end (cf. 2:2) and to the good angels that their side has won the battle. Through his chosen instruments, Christ is reclaiming the territory that is rightfully his (contra the devil's claims that he could deliver it to Christ, Mt 4:9; Lk 4:6). The visible unity of Gentiles and Jews through one Baptism in this church (cf. Jn 17:21), which with Christ has been raised into the heavenly places (Eph 2:6), signals the failure of the devil's plan to divide.[88]

ἡ πολυποίκιλος σοφία τοῦ θεοῦ—The σοφία, "wisdom," of God was introduced in 1:8 (see the second textual note there) as the attribute of God which governed his making known the mystery (1:9), and in 1:17 as a corresponding virtue to be prayed for and nourished in the children of God. Christ promised "wisdom" to the apostles (Lk 21:15), and Peter writes that it was a special gift to Paul (2 Pet 3:15).[89] "Wisdom"

---

[87] Wallace, *Greek Grammar*, 433–34, helpfully clarifies the grammar: "διά + genitive. Here, the agent named is intermediate, not ultimate. Though common, this usage is not as frequent as ὑπό + genitive for ultimate agency," though he disagrees with our exegesis of 3:10: "The implication seems to be that God's wisdom should be displayed by what the church collectively does, rather than via its mere existence (which would be expressed by ἐν ἐκκλησίᾳ)." The distinction between ultimate agent (ὑπό) and intermediate agent (διά, as in Eph 3:10) is most clear in Mt 1:22: "spoken by [ὑπό] the Lord through [διά] the prophet."

[88] "By her very existence as a new humanity, in which the major division of the first-century world has been overcome, the Church reveals God's secret in action and heralds to the hostile heavenly powers the overcoming of cosmic divisions with their defeat" (Lincoln, *Ephesians*, 187). Best, *Ephesians*, 325, likewise. Schlier, *Epheser*, 157, maintains that the proclamation takes place through "das gesamte Dasein und Leben der Kirche [the utter 'there-ness' and life of the church]." Dahl, "The Concept of Baptism in Ephesians," in *Studies in Ephesians*, 431, summarizes his own earlier (1965) essay (which was reprinted as "Das Geheimnis der Kirche nach Epheser 3,8–10" in *Studies in Ephesians*, 349–63):

> The thought is that this cosmic proclamation takes place when the powers that rule in a divided world receive knowledge that Christ has conquered division and created peace and reconciliation, namely when they see that Gentiles and Jews have been united in one body through baptism.

[89] Paul, however, is careful to distinguish Spirit-given wisdom from the false wisdom of this world (1 Cor 1:17–2:13; 3:19; 2 Cor 1:12). His wisdom is not his own, but God's (cf. Dan 2:30). See Winger, "Rhetoric and Media in the Judgement of St Paul."

personified (i.e., the Son of God) sent the apostles and prophets (Lk 11:49). Paul connects wisdom with understanding the inscrutable depths of God's ways in Rom 11:33, which is very near in vocabulary to these verses (3:8–10). It is somewhat perplexing here that "wisdom" should be made known to God's spiritual enemies (see the preceding textual note). The implication is surely not that the foes could "become wise unto salvation" (1 Pet 2:2), but that they would see and understand in terror the strategic plan of God that would lead to their downfall. For the good angels, this revelation would lead to their praise of God.

"Wisdom" is connected intimately with the "mystery" (1 Cor 2:7). The compound adjective πολυποίκιλος, "many sided, multifaceted" (like a gem), is a NT hapax legomenon, though the simple adjective ποικίλος, "diverse, various," is relatively common (ten times). The exuberant embellishment of the common adjective is typical of Ephesians, and it is more appropriate to designate God's wisdom as "multifaceted" (cf. Wis Sol 7:22) than "varied."

3:11 κατὰ πρόθεσιν τῶν αἰώνων—This κατά phrase ("in accord with ...") indicates a standard or norm for the preceding action (see the first textual note on 3:3 and the second and third textual notes on 3:7). As elsewhere in Ephesians, the logical connection created by the prepositional phrase is somewhat loose. It would appear to modify the verb γνωρισθῇ (3:10): the act of being "made known" took place "in accord with" the purpose of God (i.e., it was no "leak"). πρόθεσις, "plan, purpose," first appeared in 1:11 as part of a large complex of words describing God's eternal design for the reconciliation of a fallen creation (see the third textual note on 1:11). The genitive τῶν αἰώνων, "of the ages," is probably qualitative, "*eternal* purpose, purpose *from ages ago*" (cf. 3:21), although it could be objective ("purpose for administering the ages"). Paul emphasizes that all things remain under the guiding hand of God, who worked out our salvation—and his plan for its revelation—before the creation of the world, kept it hidden for his own wise reasons (3:5, 9), and then unfolded the plan without let or hindrance.

ἣν ἐποίησεν ἐν τῷ Χριστῷ Ἰησοῦ τῷ κυρίῳ ἡμῶν—Here the verb ποιέω means to "carry out, execute" the plan, not simply to "make, prepare" it.[90] The continual insertion of Paul's favorite preposition phrase, "in Christ," is not merely formulaic (see the fifth textual note on 1:3), and the threefold name here gives it special gravity ("Christ," "Jesus," "Lord"). The execution of God's eternal purpose might be misunderstood (as predestination so often is) as a coldly calculated mechanism, as if God accomplished salvation like programming a computer. Or one might misunderstand Paul's stewardship (3:2) or the church's instrumentality (3:10) as excluding the personal, ongoing involvement of Christ, as if he were "retired" in heaven. On the contrary, Paul argues, all things were and are accomplished in and by "Christ Jesus, our Lord." God acted personally. His eternal purposes were not accomplished simply because he planned them, but because he took on human flesh to carry them out (note the use of ποιέω in LXX

---

[90] The verb ποιέω has the same nuance, "carry out, execute," in Eph 2:3; 3:20. Cf. ποιέω in LXX Is 44:28 (Cyrus executes God's will); Jn 6:38 (Christ has come to earth to execute the Father's will).

1 Kgdms 2:35 [MT/ET 1 Sam 2:35]). In this way God's actions "in the heavenlies" (Eph 3:10) are brought home to mankind, which dwells below.

3:12 ἐν ᾧ ἔχομεν τὴν παρρησίαν καὶ προσαγωγήν—The clause ἐν ᾧ ἔχομεν, "in whom we have," first appeared in the prologue, where it was completed by "redemption through his blood, the forgiveness of trespasses" (1:7; cf. Col 1:14). It introduces the blessings that are ours through baptismal incorporation into Christ, the privileges of being God's sons. In Eph 2:18 Paul wrote in words so similar to the present verse: "through him [δι᾽ αὐτοῦ] we both have access [προσαγωγήν] in one Spirit to the Father." Such verbal parallelism in three pericopes (1:3–14; 2:11–22; 3:1–13) illustrates how Paul approaches the same topic (Jewish and Gentile reconciliation in Christ) from different angles, but with the same goal in mind.

The noun προσαγωγή implies cultic/liturgical "access" to the holy things of God, as well as the intimate status of one who has the ear of the king or a prestigious patriarch/father (see the textual note on 2:18; προσαγωγή is used elsewhere only in Rom 5:2). Joined to it by a single article (τήν), the more common term παρρησία, "boldness," forms a hendiadys with προσαγωγή: "bold access" or "access with boldness." When used of public speaking, "boldness" connotes an attitude that does not allow the audience to intimidate the speaker, even if the audience is hostile; it is used in Classical Greek contexts for the democratic right to free speech.[91] In speaking to God (in prayer) or having access to him, the connotation is subtly different, as it is the quality of God himself that inspires the παρρησία, "boldness," in God's child. The Christian approaches God on the basis of his promises (1 Jn 5:14), in the faith (1 Tim 3:13), in hope (2 Cor 3:12; Phil 1:20; Heb 3:6), in Christ (Philemon 8), by his blood (Heb 10:19), and in his love (1 Jn 4:17). What binds these varied causes together, however, is Paul's chief point in this verse, "in him [Christ]": because he has created access and we are joined to him, we can approach God with "boldness." Our confidence is rooted in the incarnation, for we know that Christ shares our humanity and has experienced every trouble that plagues us (Heb 4:15–16). It does not express an arrogance, self-confidence, or swagger, but a quiet confidence that God will not turn us away.

ἐν πεποιθήσει διὰ τῆς πίστεως αὐτοῦ—The noun πεποίθησις is formed from the perfect tense stem of πείθω, "to persuade." Thus, it means "the quality of having been persuaded; trust, confidence." Confidence placed in men is foolhardy (πεποίθησις, LXX 4 Kgdms 18:19 [2 Ki 18:19]), but in God it is well-founded (πεποίθαμεν, LXX 4 Kgdms 18:22 [2 Ki 18:22]). Paul rests the confidence with which he conducts his apostolic office not on his own qualities (Phil 3:4–8), but on Christ (2 Cor 3:4–6), who gives him boldness (2 Cor 3:12). The phrase ἐν πεποιθήσει, "in confidence," modifies the preceding noun προσαγωγήν, "access," and complements its other modifier, παρρησία "boldness," leading to the language of "faith" (τῆς πίστεως) as the ground of confidence. Access to God is a frightening thought if one considers what might happen to a sinner in the presence of a holy God. But the modifiers emphasize that the access Paul has in mind is good news. διὰ πίστεως, "through faith," first appeared as

---

[91] LSJM, s.v. παρρησία. See παρρησία in contexts of public speaking of the Gospel in, e.g., Jn 7:26; Acts 4:29; 28:31; Eph 6:19.

the receiving instrument for salvation by grace, where it was clearly the Christian's faith that was in mind (see the second textual note on 2:8). The addition of the genitive αὐτοῦ, "of him" (referring to Christ, 3:12), might possibly mean that τῆς πίστεως refers to the faithfulness which Christ showed (αὐτοῦ as a subjective genitive: "his [Christ's] faithfulness")[92] as the ground of the Christian's confidence and as that which creates access to the Father. But this usage is undocumented elsewhere in Ephesians, and it is better to maintain the objective genitive meaning here: "faith *in him*" (cf. Eph 3:17; Col 2:12). As in Rom 5:1–2, Paul is saying here that justification by faith (*fides qua creditur*) leads to access to God. That is to say, "through trusting in Christ," the Christian has a sure and certain foundation to be confident of open access to God the Father. This prepares the way for the prayer to which Paul returns in 3:14.

3:13 διὸ αἰτοῦμαι μὴ ἐγκακεῖν—Literally translated, the clause is quite ambiguous: "I ask not to lose heart." αἰτοῦμαι, "I ask," has no expressed direct object, and ἐγκακεῖν, "to lose heart," has no expressed subject. Thus, three translations are possible: (1) "I ask [God] that [I] would not lose heart" (see the RSV footnote); (2) "I ask [God] that [you] would not lose heart"; (3) "I ask [you] not to lose heart" (see the RSV text). The first would be an uncharacteristic way for Paul to approach his own suffering, as he normally boasts or rejoices in it.[93] Paul does not pray for himself, but for the Ephesians, and asks them to pray for him (6:18–20). The second requires a change from "God" to "you" halfway through the clause with no indication in the text. In the absence of any explicit nouns or pronouns, the third translation is the most likely. ἐγκακέω (composed of ἐν, "in," + κακός, "bad") can mean "to lose enthusiasm, be discouraged" (Lk 18:1; Gal 6:9) or "to be afraid in the face of a great difficulty." The latter meaning is more suitable to the context of Paul's imprisonment and possible execution. Such fear is set aside by knowledge that the ministry is God's, as Paul has demonstrated throughout the pericope (cf. 2 Cor 4:1). αἰτοῦμαι (middle of αἰτέω)[94] denotes the sort of "asking" that includes a claim to an answer:[95] Paul *expects* them not to lose heart, even in the face of his suffering. The conjunction διό, "therefore," indicates that this verse sums up the pericope: Paul's call for the Ephesians not to lose heart comes on the basis of what

---

[92] E.g., Barth, *Ephesians*, 1:347, including n. 111, who understands διὰ τῆς πίστεως αὐτοῦ as "through his [Christ's] faithfulness," citing Rom 3:22; Gal 2:16; 3:22; and Phil 3:9 as other places where (in his opinion!) Paul uses a subjective genitive. Referring back to Eph 2:18 ("through him we both have access"), he argues that Christ himself (not faith in Christ) is the instrument of access to the Father. But surely this is a misunderstanding of the relationship between faith and its object; *faith* in Christ grants access precisely because *Christ* grants access. See the discussion of the subjective and objective interpretations of "faith in/of Christ" in the fifth textual note on 1:15 and the second textual note on 2:8.

[93] See Best, *Ephesians*, 330–31. Barth, *Ephesians*, 1:348, notes that the subsequent prayer in 3:14–19 is entirely for the Ephesians; thus, it would be strange if 3:13 were a prayer for Paul's own peace of mind.

[94] The active and middle forms of αἰτέω do not differ significantly in meaning; "asking" normally implies the middle, "for one's benefit." The middle voice is common in prayers; BDF, § 316 (2).

[95] BDAG, s.v. αἰτέω.

he has just explained about the divine origin of his office and mandate to preach to the Gentiles and represent Christ (3:1–12). All is in God's hands.

ἐν ταῖς θλίψεσίν μου ὑπὲρ ὑμῶν—This phrase gives the context or cause of the Ephesians' potential discouragement ("lose heart"). ἐν can express cause: "*because of* my tribulations,"[96] but more likely it gives the context or circumstances: "I ask you not to be disappointed *in connection with* my tribulations."[97] "Tribulations" (the plural of θλῖψις) are foretold by Christ as the consequence of following him.[98] They result from the hostile opposition of the evil foe, who steps up his attacks as the Last Day approaches (6:10–17),[99] and they focus particularly on the preachers of the Gospel.[100] Christians can endure tribulations knowing that they result in endurance (Rom 5:3; 12:12; Rev 1:9), even joy (2 Cor 8:2; 1 Thess 1:6) and glory (2 Cor 4:17), and because the love of Christ shelters us (Rom 8:35) and God comforts us (2 Cor 1:4). Paul endures, even boasts in his sufferings (see the last textual note on 2:9) because of the knowledge that these tribulations draw him closer to Christ and are a necessary part of his office as Christ's representative to the church and the world.

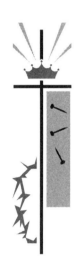

Like Christ, who fulfilled Isaiah's prophecies,[101] Paul is a *suffering* servant. The Colossian parallel expands and clarifies the way in which Paul's experiences and Christ's are related: "now I rejoice in my sufferings for your sake [ἐν τοῖς παθήμασιν ὑπὲρ ὑμῶν], and I take my turn in filling up what is lacking in the sufferings of Christ [τῶν θλίψεων τοῦ Χριστοῦ] in my flesh for the sake of his body, which is the church" (Col 1:24). In these two passages, Paul sets out a logical progression from Christ's tribulations to the apostle's sufferings to the Gentiles' glory. For the Ephesians, the temptation to "lose heart" (Eph 3:13) arises from a natural fear of losing their father in the faith, and perhaps also from a belief that his sufferings are their fault—because he preached to the Gentiles, and specifically because of Trophimus the Ephesian (Acts 21:28–29).[102] Paul's repetition of ὑπὲρ ὑμῶν, "for your sake" (3:1, 13), frames the pericope and draws it to a close. In his argument he has shown them that he does not suffer *because* of them but *for* them, and because the *Lord* called him to it.

ἥτις ἐστὶν δόξα ὑμῶν—The feminine singular relative pronoun ἥτις, "which," has no antecedent in grammatical agreement. It likely refers back to the feminine plural θλίψεσιν, "tribulations," but is made singular by attraction to the following feminine singular noun δόξα, "glory."[103] As the Gentile Ephesians are not the cause of Paul's suf-

---

[96] Wallace, *Greek Grammar*, 372; BDF, § 219 (2). Cf. Mt 6:7; Gal 1:24.

[97] See BDAG, s.v. ἐγκακέω, 2.

[98] See the singular in Mt 13:21; Jn 16:33; cf. Acts 11:19; 14:22; 2 Thess 1:4, 6.

[99] Mt 24:9, 21, 29 (and parallels); Rev 2:9–10; 7:14.

[100] Acts 20:23; 2 Cor 1:8; 6:4; 7:4; Phil 1:17; Col 1:24; 1 Thess 3:3, 7.

[101] See especially Isaiah's four Suffering Servant Songs: Is 42:1–9; 49:1–13; 50:4–11; and 52:13–53:12.

[102] See "Paul's Trip to Jerusalem, Arrest, and Imprisonment (Acts 21:1–36)" in "The City of Ephesus and Paul's Relationship to It" in the introduction, as well as the second and third textual notes on 3:1.

[103] In Greek a pronoun may be made to agree with the predicate noun that follows, as here and in, e.g., Acts 16:12. See BDF, § 132 (1).

fering but the beneficiaries of it (ὑπὲρ ὑμῶν, "for your sake," 3:1, 13), Paul calls their attention to the benefits they receive. Christ's passion was his glorification (Jn 12:16, 23; 13:31) and brings glory to those who die with him in Baptism without their being literally crucified with him. Thus, we share his glory eternally in body and soul (2 Cor 3:18), even though our participation in his suffering is sacramental and partial, for comprehensive suffering belongs to Christ's unique office (Heb 2:10).

Paul frequently states that the road to glory is only through suffering (Rom 8:17–18; 2 Cor 4:17), for which labor pains are a vivid analogy.[104] But Paul's reference here to his suffering is more like Christ's than the Christian's. Paul's suffering, which is not entirely shared by the Gentiles, is nevertheless for their benefit and leads to their glory (cf. 2 Tim 2:10).[105] He suffers for the sake of Gospel, the revelation of the mystery which leads us to "glory" (cf. 1 Cor 2:7). δόξα is the definitive quality of God (see the first textual note on 1:6). His "glory" is his presence, focused in the OT on the tabernacle/temple, and in the NT on Christ himself; but it is only fully revealed in heaven. Thus, the bestowal of glory on Christians is an eschatological hope, "the richness of his glorious inheritance among the saints" (1:18), to be fulfilled on the Last Day.[106]

Commentary

Structure and Rhetoric

Revelation leads to prayer. God speaks his gracious gifts, arousing in his children the impulse to thank and praise. We have observed this pattern in the great *Berakah* prayer of 1:3–14, in which contemplation of the eternal plan and promises of God evoked in Paul an elaborate and finely crafted prayer of blessing on the pattern of OT prophetic and apocalyptic literature (particularly Daniel). In the two pericopes of chapter 2, Paul unfolded his understanding of the mystery that involves salvation by grace through faith and the reconciliation of Gentiles with Jews, and both with God, through their common incorporation into the body of Christ. Together they constitute a new people of God and a spiritual temple. Contemplation of such things again moves Paul to doxological prayer. He begins: "For this reason, I, Paul, the prisoner of Christ Jesus for the sake of you Gentiles" (3:1)—and then breaks off his thought. The obvious continuation appears in 3:14, where the opening phrase is repeated and a main verb is provided: "for this reason I bend my knees to the Father … ," which leads to intercession for the Ephesians and a grand doxology to God (3:14–21). It is to that *prayerful* conclusion that Paul is heading, but it is the "digression" of 3:2–13 that calls for a word of explanation.

---

[104] Mt 24:8; Jn 16:21; 1 Thess 5:3; cf. *2 Clement*, 2:2.

[105] "How is it 'for them?' How is it 'their glory?' It is because God so loved them, as to give even the Son for them, and to afflict His servants for them: for it was in order that they might attain so many blessings, that Paul was in prison" (Chrysostom, *Homilies on Ephesians*, 7:3.13 [*NPNF*[1] 13:81]).

[106] In Colossians, when "glory" is applied to Christians, it is eschatological: "Christ in you, the *hope* of glory" (Col 1:27); "when Christ is manifested, who is your life, then also you *will be* manifested with him in glory" (Col 3:4).

A Digression?

To what extent are these verses a true "digression," that is, a departure from the subject at hand in order to discuss a related, but ultimately secondary, matter? Prayer can be seen to characterize the first three chapters of Ephesians, but whether it is *the* dominating feature may be disputed (see the commentary on 1:15–23). Of all of Paul's letters, we have noted that Ephesians is the only instance where we find both a report of intercession in the thanksgiving section (1:16–19) and an extensive, liturgical *Berakah* prayer (1:3–14; cf. 2 Cor 1:3–4). Together with the prayer that will be resumed in Eph 3:14, these pericopes do, indeed, constitute exceptionally rich prayer content. It has even been suggested that the entire first three chapters constitute one long *Berakah* prayer (or an extended thanksgiving section).[107] On the other hand, chapter 2 is in no way prayer, and from a rhetorical perspective appears to be the meatiest chunk of *probatio*, "proofs," in the letter.[108] Likewise, the concluding verses of the first chapter (1:20–23), though arising from prayer, already introduce significant teaching about Christ and the church that will undergird the ensuing argument. In light of these observations, the proposition that the present pericope (3:2–13) is a digression from the general flow loses strength. In fact, rather than characterizing the entire first three chapters as one long prayer, it would be better to note the repeated pattern of revelation-teaching-prayer-doxology.

Obviously, the present pericope is a *grammatical* digression, inasmuch as its first verse (3:1) ends in anacoluthon—a grammatical interruption of a sentence that consequently lacks a verb (which does not appear until the resumption in 3:14, "I bend"). But in terms of its *content* it is not a digression in the classical sense of an argument that is relevant but out of logical order, or unnecessary to the case being made.[109] The interruption of the sentence in 3:1 strikes modern eyes as unpolished, especially in an era of computerized word processing that allows any sloppiness to be cleaned up rapidly. But this is not sloppiness. On the one hand, it is natural to imagine that, in the oral environment of the first century, Paul's amanuensis (scribe) might have followed Paul's dictation so closely that the sentence was already begun before Paul decided to hold back his prayer while he discussed another subject. It is wholly in line with the "stream of consciousness" modus operandi of Paul's giant and creative intellect to imagine him suspending one thought while generating a new one, and then returning to the first without missing a beat. On the other hand, the letter elsewhere betrays none of the passionate haste of a letter like Galatians. Its pericopes are grand, sober, and designed with immense precision. It is worthwhile considering the possibility that, first, the content of this pericope is a vital part of Paul's argument, and therefore planned, and that, second, the introduction

---

[107] See Kirby, *Ephesians: Baptism and Pentecost*, 126–38.

[108] See further "Proofs" in "Structure and Rhetoric" in the introduction.

[109] For "digression," see Quintilian, *Institutio oratoria*, 4:3.1, 14; Lincoln, *Ephesians*, 171.

of Paul the prisoner (3:1) as the subject of prayer is a vital preface to the subsequent words of this pericope.

Connections

When one views its contents closely, this pericope displays striking connections with the material that has gone before in at least five ways. It appears, first, to be an expansion of 1:9–10, in which the vocabulary of "making known," "mystery," and "stewardship/administration" were introduced. Second, "fellow heirs ... of the promise" (3:6) follows up on the language of "inheritance" and "promise" in 1:13–14. Third, the threefold compounds with συν-, "together with; fellow," in 3:6 (συγκληρονόμα καὶ σύσσωμα καὶ συμμέτοχα, "fellow heirs and fellow members of the body and fellow partakers") repeat and sum up the argument and vocabulary of chapter 2 (particularly 2:5, 6, 19, 21, 22). Fourth, the manifestation of God's wisdom to hostile spiritual forces through the church (3:10) builds upon Christ's defeat of the former and headship of the latter (1:20–23). Finally, the dominance of the χάρις, "grace," of God in this pericope (3:2, 7, 8) ties it together with the *Berakah* (1:3–14) and the first pericope of chapter 2 (2:1–10), where grace was the key to understanding God's relationship with mankind. These close ties with the foregoing drive home the fact that this pericope stands in tight continuity with what precedes, rather than being a digression from it.

Ethos

In some respects the opening words of this pericope, "for this reason, I, Paul," sound out of place at this point in the letter. They echo the first words of his thanksgiving (1:15), which is the more typical place for Paul to discuss his personal circumstances and pray for his addressees.[110] But Paul's normal way does not constrain what he may do in other circumstances. Within the unfolding of his argument in Ephesians, these words about his office and calling hold third place. First, he delves into the prehistory of God's eternal plan (1:3–14). Second, he locates the accomplishment of the plan in Christ's earthly ministry, cross, and exaltation (1:15–2:22). Third, he turns to his role as the one blessed with the disclosure of the mystery of Christ and the mandate to proclaim it to the Gentiles. It makes perfect sense that his office and calling enter play here.

These matters, furthermore, are intimately connected with the prayer he will subsequently offer (3:14–21). For as he enters into his intercession for the Ephesian Gentiles, the facts of his appointment as their herald are entirely relevant. In this pericope he sets down who he is, how he relates to them, and why he should be praying for them. In rhetorical terms it works to establish *ethos*—the character and credibility of the speaker (Paul), which gives the audience reasons why they should believe what he says. Thus, we might locate the three classical types of "internal proofs" in the first chapters of Ephesians: *pathos*, capturing

---

[110] See Rom 1:11–15; 2 Cor 1:8–14; Phil 1:12–26; Col 1:24–29; 1 Thess 1:4–2:12; 2 Tim 1:15–18.

the audience's goodwill (1:15–23); *logos*, logical argumentation (2:1–22); and *ethos*, the character of the speaker (3:1–13).[111]

Internal Structure

When we come to examining the internal structure of this pericope, we find it somewhat less patterned than the chiastic and Trinitarian pericopes that have come before. However, a number of features suggest that Paul did put careful thought into its design. First, while τούτου χάριν, "for this reason" (3:1a, 14), marks the pericope's borders as an "external *inclusio*," the phrase ὑπὲρ ὑμῶν, "for your sake" (3:1b, 13), frames it as an "internal *inclusio*."[112] Thus, in one sense 3:1 is not part of the pericope properly speaking, as 3:2–13 is parenthetically inserted after the broken sentence (3:1) that is resumed in 3:14 (see "A Digression?" above). At the same time, the phrase ὑπὲρ ὑμῶν, "for your sake" (3:1b, 13), is programmatic for the content of the pericope. The two phrases that form the external and internal *inclusios*, therefore, not only define the unit but also identify its theme. In brief, Paul demonstrates in the pericope how it is that he came to be a prisoner "for your sake" and how the Ephesians should respond to this fact.

Second, while the unit is not otherwise chiastically structured, it does have a clear center, consisting of the declaration in 3:5–6 that the mystery, which for ages past was hidden, has now been revealed to Paul and the other apostles, and that its contents in Christ include the reconciliation of Gentiles and Jews through the Gospel. These two central verses are remarkably poetic, containing *parallelismus membrorum* ("which was not made known to the sons of men" ‖ "as now it has been revealed to his holy apostles and prophets") and alliteration by the aforementioned three συν- compounds ("fellow heirs and fellow members of the body and fellow partakers").[113]

Third, there are two main sentences in the unit, which correspond to the two chief points in Paul's argument (revelation and proclamation). The punctuation in NA[27], which places a full stop at the end of 3:7, is undoubtedly correct. These two sentences are framed by the anacoluthic half sentence in 3:1 and the summary sentence of 3:13, such that the pericope looks like this:

3:1   Introduction of Paul as the prisoner of Christ "for the sake of you" Gentiles

3:2–7   The *revelation* of the mystery to Paul and the other apostles that the Gentiles are included in the body of Christ (Paul's *office*)

---

[111] For an explanation of these terms and their applicability to Ephesians, see "Structure and Rhetoric" in the introduction.

[112] An "external *inclusio*" is a unit marked by the repetition of words before its start and after its end, words that are *not* part of the unit itself; an "internal *inclusio*" is a unit marked by repeated words at the beginning and end that *are* part of the unit itself.

[113] These qualities led Markus Barth, *Ephesians*, 1:331, to postulate that 3:5–6 is a quotation from a preexisting source. This hypothesis is unwarranted, but confirms the impression that Paul has crafted the verses carefully.

Pivot   *"The grace of God that was given to me"* (3:7b, 8a)

3:8–12   The *proclamation* of that Gospel revelation to the Gentiles and in testimony against their spiritual enemies (Paul's *mandate*)

3:13   Conclusion: do not lose heart over Paul's imprisonment, which is "for your sake"

As we shall discuss further below, the entire pericope is concerned with the twofold matter of the mystery and Paul's office as an apostle. But within the pericope there is a neat division of the subject into two parts: the revelation of the mystery to Paul as the apostle uniquely concerned with the salvation of the Gentiles (yet without excluding the other apostles), and the mandate to proclaim the mystery. Revelation leads to proclamation. The office does not exist for its own sake, but for its functions.

This revelation schema is central to Paul's understanding of his office and mandate and so recurs frequently in his writings,[114] though nowhere with the fullness it assumes in Ephesians 3. The maturity of thought found in this pericope is evident from a simple comparison with the corresponding unit of Colossians (1:24–29)—words which Paul may have written short weeks before and which developed in his mind in the meantime.[115] That unit was immediately preceded by a parallel claim, οὗ ἐγενόμην ἐγὼ Παῦλος διάκονος, "of which [Gospel] I, Paul, was made a minister" (Col 1:23c). What the two units hold in common is the following progression:[116]

Col 1:23c	Introduction of Paul	Eph 3:1
Col 1:24	Suffering of Apostle	Eph 3:1, 13
Col 1:25	Office of Apostle	Eph 3:2
Col 1:26	Revelation of Hidden Mystery	Eph 3:4, 5, 9
Col 1:27	Content of Mystery	Eph 3:6
Col 1:28	Proclamation of Content	Eph 3:8, 9

Where Ephesians goes farther than Colossians is in (1) developing the role of Paul, the apostles, and the prophets as the recipients of the revelation for the sake of the church; (2) defining the mystery as not only the inclusion of the Gentiles in Christ but also their reconciliation to the Jews in that one body; and (3) identifying the very existence of the church as a testimony against the hostile spiritual forces. Overall, such a comparison reveals an even stronger emphasis in Ephesians on the apostolic office as the means by which God manifests his salvation to the world.

---

[114] Rom 16:25–27; 1 Cor 2:7–10; 2 Tim 1:9–10; Titus 1:2–3.

[115] See "Relationship to Colossians" in the introduction.

[116] The table is taken from Lincoln, *Ephesians*, 169, where he also displays the relevant words of the Greek text in parallel.

Paul's Apostolic Office and Call to the Gentiles

"The Prisoner of Christ Jesus" (3:1, 13)

For the first time in the epistle, its character as a Prison Letter comes to the fore. From Paul's perspective, what occasioned his writing was his personal circumstances as a suffering apostle and his concern for the impact this news was having on the Ephesians.[117] It is likely that Paul's enemies made great hay of his confinement, suggesting that it proved the unreliability of his message. Paul is therefore deeply concerned that his imprisonment might lead to the Ephesians' falling away from the Gospel (cf. 2 Tim 1:15). Thus, the first task he approaches in this pericope is to provide a defense and explanation of his suffering. If indeed it is also true, as we have suggested, that the Ephesians felt a twofold personal responsibility for Paul's imprisonment,[118] Paul was further compelled to provide an alternate perspective. He was certainly in prison, first, because of Jewish hostility over his Law-free Gospel, his proclamation of salvation by grace through faith to Gentiles such as the Ephesians. It was true, second, that the visit of Trophimus the Ephesian to the city of Jerusalem gave Paul's hostile Jewish foes an excuse to seek his death (Acts 21:28–29).

But these were not the ultimate reasons for the confinement of one who called himself "the prisoner *of Christ Jesus*" (3:1). This multifaceted genitive (τοῦ Χριστοῦ) implies not only that he is in prison because the Lord wills it but also that ultimately he is not bound by chains but by Christ. In Greco-Roman culture there was no honor in slavery (though in Eastern religions it was more common to think of oneself as the deity's slave, as also in the OT).[119] But Paul unabashedly calls himself δοῦλος Χριστοῦ, "Christ's *slave*,"[120] even when not physically restrained. When that bond leads him into shackles, Paul views them as a badge of honor, as an outward symbol of his relationship to Christ, so that he can rejoice to be "an ambassador in chains" (6:20).

When in jail in Philippi, Paul and Silas testified to their reinterpretation of such suffering by singing hymns and praying out loud (Acts 16:25). The other prisoners were listening to them, presumably marveling at the reaction imprisonment had produced in these ambassadors of Christ. When an earthquake knocked down the walls, the jailer was surprised to find Paul and Silas still there—for it was not the walls that held these prisoners of Christ. The jailer's subsequent faith and Baptism (Acts 16:30–33) illustrate the kind of glory that Paul's suffering can bring to others (Eph 3:13). To the same Philippians Paul

---

[117] For the Prison Letters and Paul's personal circumstances, see "Paul's Imprisonment" and "Caesarea!" in "Location and Date of Writing" in the introduction.

[118] See "Paul's Trip to Jerusalem, Arrest, and Imprisonment (Acts 21:1–36)" in "The City of Ephesus and Paul's Relationship to It" in the introduction, as well as the second and third textual notes on 3:1.

[119] See Karl Heinrich Rengstorf, "δοῦλος," *TDNT* 2:261–80.

[120] Rom 1:1; Gal 1:10; Phil 1:1; cf. 1 Cor 7:22; Eph 6:6; Col 4:12; 2 Tim 2:24; Titus 1:1; James 1:1; 1 Pet 2:16; 2 Pet 1:1; Jude 1; Rev 1:1; 2:20; 7:3; passim.

would later write that his Roman imprisonment was serving "for the advancement of the Gospel," that his imprisonment had become widely known as "in Christ," and that the brothers were thereby emboldened to speak the Word without fear (Phil 1:12–14). This is not an occasional thought in Paul's writings, but a persistent interpretation of his ministry. To the Corinthians he reflects deeply on his (and his apostolic colleagues') ongoing sufferings and offers three complementary interpretations:

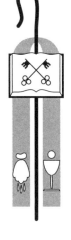

- "We have this treasure in earthen vessels, that the extraordinary power might be [shown to be] from God and not from us" (2 Cor 4:7).
- "We are always being given over to death because of Jesus, that also the life of Jesus might be manifested in our mortal flesh" (2 Cor 4:11).
- "So death is at work in us, but life in you" (2 Cor 4:12).

Thus, first, Paul's suffering demonstrates that the power of his message lies not in his own personal abilities or success, but in the God whose Word it is. Second, as an agent of Christ, Paul not only speaks Christ's words but also displays Christ's death and life in his own body. And third, as Christ's victory over death brought life to others, so the suffering of his agents would bring life to those they serve.

These thoughts crystalize in the succinct and profound Colossian parallel that stands in the background of our text: "now I rejoice in my sufferings for your sake, and I take my turn in filling up what is lacking in the sufferings of Christ in my flesh for the sake of his body, which is the church" (Col 1:24). Clearly this text should not be interpreted as suggesting that the sufferings of Christ were incomplete from the perspective of accomplishing our salvation; Christ himself declared from the cross: τετέλεσται, "it has been brought to completion" (Jn 19:30). Yet that accomplishment (objective justification) needed to be proclaimed to the world and appropriated in faith (subjective justification).[121] The apostolic agents of that proclamation were not only promised that they would speak for Christ and be received as Christ but also warned that they would be rejected as he was first rejected (Lk 10:16).[122] This is in the

---

[121] "Objective justification" refers to the objective fact that Christ suffered for the sins of the whole world and earned forgiveness and eternal life for all mankind. "Subjective justification" refers to the need for each individual to appropriate these gifts earned by Christ through (personal, subjective) faith. See AC 3 and 4 and Ap 3 and 4. This distinction must not be confused with the interpretations of the genitive τῆς πίστεως αὐτοῦ, literally, "the faith of him [Christ]" (3:12), discussed above. The *subjective* genitive (Christ's faithfulness) corresponds to *objective* justification; the *objective* genitive (our faith in Christ) corresponds to *subjective* justification!

[122] Preaching on this text, Luther puts words into God's mouth:

"Hear, O world, devil, emperor, tyrant! ... What shall I say but that thou hast imprisoned and bound, not Paul, but me?" ...

Note, when Paul says he suffers for the Ephesians, he means that his suffering is for their profit, to teach them they have nothing to fear in suffering. They, not he, are the subjects of concern in this matter. His pains are not merely those of Paul—upon whom not so much depends—but of an apostle or preacher of the Church of Christ. When the latter name [Christ] is associated with the suffering, when it is not John or Peter who

nature of being Christ's ambassador (Eph 6:20). Paul's message and life could not be separated. His suffering was a veritable picture of the Gospel itself. His apostleship was made most clear in his suffering for the Gospel.

"The Stewardship of the Grace of God That Was Given to Me for You" (3:2)

With this in mind, the Ephesians should not fear that Paul's suffering is their fault.[123] Using a somewhat ambiguous prepositional phrase, capable of being read their way or his way, Paul begins to turn around their order of thinking. He is not a prisoner *because of* you Gentiles" but "*for the sake of* [ὑπέρ] you Gentiles" (3:1; cf. 3:13). To help them understand his suffering, Paul directs them back to his teaching among them about the nature of his office as apostle (3:2).

Commentators have expressed surprise that the author of Ephesians would include the nature of the apostolic office in the basic catechetical material that would have been delivered to these Gentile converts. Yet there are at least two sound cultural and theological reasons why this must have been so. For, first, ancient rhetoric teaches that the speaker must establish his credibility (*ethos*) in order to persuade his hearers to believe his message.[124] Rhetorical techniques aside, the climate of the ancient world, whose highways and byways were frequented by philosophers and scoundrels hoping to parlay a novel message into bed and breakfast, meant that Paul would have to establish his own honorable origins and intentions in each new community he reached if he wished his message to take deep root. But, second, the office of preacher could not be separated from the message itself. Christ instituted not just the Gospel and Sacraments but also the office to deliver them to the nations (Mt 28:16–20; Lk 24:46–49; Jn 20:19–23). Particularly in the case of the apostles (in distinction from others in the office of the ministry), their eyewitness testimony to the bodily resurrection of Christ was a unique and crucial component in the spread of the Gospel.[125] The medium and the message stand together.[126]

---

is cast into prison—that God might tolerate—but a minister of the Church, then the deed is a too gross jesting with the majesty of God; it is tempting him too far. ("Sermon for the Sixteenth Sunday after Trinity, Ephesians 3:13–21," printed in 1525, Lenker, 8:263–64; StL 12:872–73, §§ 11, 13)

[123] See "Paul's Trip to Jerusalem, Arrest, and Imprisonment (Acts 21:1–36)" in "The City of Ephesus and Paul's Relationship to It" in the introduction, as well as the second and third textual notes on 3:1.

[124] See "Ethos" above in "A Digression?" in this pericope.

[125] Lk 24:48; Acts 1:8; 8:25; 1 Jn 1:1–4. See Winger, "From Apostolic Witness to Christian Confession: I John 4:1–6."

[126] Luther, "Sermon for the Sixteenth Sunday after Trinity, Ephesians 3:13–21," printed in 1525:

Up to this time [Eph 3:13] Paul has been extolling the office of the ministry, which proclaims the Gospel of the New Testament. In lofty and impressive terms he introduces its purpose, power and wisdom—in a word, the great benefits the office effects, since God thereby bestows upon us abundantly all manner of wisdom, strength and blessings, all which things, in heaven or earth, are of his dispensing. (Lenker, 8:259; StL 12:868, § 1)

In the context of Ephesians 3 and the message that the Gentiles are coheirs of the promise in Christ, it is crucial for Paul to demonstrate that he has not invented the idea. By deferring to the One who sent him, Paul makes his message more sure and certain. He does not speak or act on his own, but is Christ's servant for the Ephesians. This perspective on his ministry is best encapsulated by the characteristic Ephesian word οἰκονομία, "stewardship" or "household administration" (3:2; also 1:10; 3:9). The steward holds the authority of his master in administering the goods of the household—this is one side of the equation. The faithful steward does only what he is told. The one responsible for his actions, however, is always the master himself—this is the other side of the equation. As Paul is bound to Christ as his slave, Christ binds himself to Paul as long as Paul acts and speaks according to his mandate. Writing less than a generation later to the same Ephesians, Ignatius explains clearly what such stewardship means:

> For everyone whom the master of the house sends for his own stewardship [εἰς ἰδίαν οἰκονομίαν]—we must receive him as him who sent him. Therefore it is necessary that we regard the bishop as the Lord himself.[127]

Thus, when Paul proclaims that the Gentiles are fellow members of the body of Christ (3:6; cf. 2:19), it is not one man's opinion, but the binding promise of the God who sent him. Through a personal encounter with the resurrected Christ—a *sine qua non* for anyone claiming to be an apostle—the Gospel and its significance for the Gentiles was revealed to Paul (3:3). It was an essential component of his apostolic office that this stewardship of the Gospel was given to Paul specifically for the Gentiles (3:2).

"The Mystery of Christ" (3:3–7)

Perhaps with a touch of irony we note that the most perplexing feature of this pericope—even of Ephesians as a whole—is the precise nature of the "mystery" (1:9; 3:3, 4, 9; 5:32; 6:19). Paul claims at the outset to have been given a unique insight into the "mystery" of Christ (3:4), after which he gives a pretty clear explanation of what he means by the term (3:5–6). He sees history, at least up to his day, as divided into two parts. In former ages, the content of the mystery had been hidden (3:5, 9), was not disclosed to any of "the sons of men" (3:5)—a Hebraism meaning that no human being, no one outside of God's heavenly hosts, understood it. But now, in the new age inaugurated by the coming of Jesus Christ in the flesh, the content of the mystery has been disclosed by revelation to Paul (3:3) and to the "holy apostles and prophets" (3:5).

Two vital questions arise from this explanation: (1) what is the content of the mystery that has been disclosed? and (2) what is so new about the message? The answers to the two questions are intertwined.

Critics seeking to drive a wedge between Colossians and Ephesians, or between Ephesians and the supposedly "genuine Pauline letters," have alleged

---

[127] Ignatius, *To the Ephesians*, 6:1.

that the definition of the "mystery" varies between these writings. We have noted, of course, that it is not the definition of the mystery that varies, but its referent—what is *the* mystery, not what is *a* mystery.[128] But this does not solve the problem. The dilemma is sometimes put this way: Col 1:27 defines the mystery as Christ himself; Eph 3:5–6 defines it as the incorporation of the Gentiles into the body of Christ. Yet a closer look reveals that these two passage are not in such stark disagreement. First, Col 1:26b–27 reads in full: "but now [the mystery] has been manifested to his [God's] saints, to whom God desired to make known what is the richness of the glory of *this mystery* among the Gentiles, *which is Christ in you* [plural], the hope of glory." Seen in context, this text's agreement with Ephesians 3 in content and vocabulary is more obvious, and it would be strange to imagine Paul (or some writer pretending to be Paul) using the same words with an entirely different meaning or referent. Clearly in Colossians the "mystery" is not simply "Christ," but includes the truth that "Christ" is "in you Gentiles." Since the indwelling of Christ is the corollary and counterpart of incorporation into his body, the church, Col 1:27 confesses that the mystery includes bringing the Gentiles to Christ, as taught by Eph 3:5–6. Second, Ephesians 3 does not simply identify the "mystery" with the incorporation of heathen peoples who previously were separated from Israel; Paul speaks here of "the mystery of Christ" (3:4), as later in Ephesians he will identify the "mystery" with the Gospel (6:19) and refer it to Christ and the church (5:32).

The commonality in all these passages, of course, is Christ himself. There are not multiple mysteries, into which novices in the faith are progressively initiated, as in the Qumran or Mithras.[129] There is *one* "mystery," which is Christ. How this relates to the incorporation of the Gentiles is eloquently and emphatically explained by Markus Barth:

> The one mystery is the mystery of Christ the pre-existent, the revealer, the savior, the regent of church and world, the one to unite Jews and Gentiles, and the high priest leading the church to the Father. The inclusion of the Gentiles into God's people is not a further mystery added to the mystery of Jesus Christ. Neither is the equation of the mystery with "Christ among you [Gentiles]" (Col 1:27) a different interpretation of the Christ mystery. Rather to speak of the savior Messiah who includes the Gentiles in his body is to speak of the one revealed secret of God. Revelation, salvation, and unification in Christ are not only an indivisible whole. In Christ they are identified.[130]

---

[128] See "The Literary Relationship between Ephesians and Other Pauline Epistles" in "Evaluation of the Case" in "Authorship" in the introduction.

[129] In the various apocalyptic traditions of the day, multiple mysteries were revealed to insiders, but left hidden from those not yet worthy. Paul's approach to the mystery is quite the opposite. Through him the mystery is made known to all. Schnackenburg, *Ephesians*, 138, writes: "The main difference to Apocalyptic is that the eschatological revelation concentrates on *Christ* (*the* Secret per se) and is *already* fulfilled: It is not only made known to the receivers of revelation in secret but is at the same time revealed through them as a self-fulfilling event."

[130] Barth, *Ephesians*, 1:331.

The mysterious jewel that is Christ is both an unbroken whole and yet brilliant in its multifaceted beauty. For this reason Paul prays repeatedly in both Colossians and Ephesians that his flock would be strengthened in their understanding, "toward knowing the mystery of God—Christ—in whom all the treasures of wisdom and knowledge are hidden" (Col 2:2–3). Thus, there is one Christ, but many treasures in him.

This perspective helps us to understand what appears on the surface to be a wholly inadequate reading of the OT by Paul, and a flat contradiction of what he writes elsewhere. Is it true to assert that God did not reveal to the OT prophets that the Gentiles were to be incorporated into his kingdom, as Eph 3:5–6 defines the revelation? Certainly we cannot put it so boldly. From Abraham to Zechariah, God promised to the patriarchs and through the prophets that Israel would be a source of blessing to all nations, that the Gentiles would stream to the temple to worship the true God, that ultimately God would redeem those he chose from every part of the earth.[131] Paul himself appeals to such texts in Romans 4; Romans 9–11; and Galatians 3–4 in defense of the Law-free Gospel for the Gentiles.[132] Closer to home, Paul has pressed texts from Isaiah to demonstrate that both Gentiles and Jews are recipients of God's peace (Eph 2:13–17). How can he now claim that the OT prophets were *not* privy to this revelation?

A number of correct, but not entirely satisfactory, answers are available to us: (1) The OT revelation was partial and incomplete. The prophets knew *that* the Gentiles would be brought into the kingdom, but did not understand *how*. (2) The OT made provision for the incorporation of Gentiles into Israel by becoming Israelites, through circumcision and obeying the distinctive provisions of the Torah. What is new about the mystery of Christ is therefore that Gentiles and Jews would now enter the kingdom on an equal footing.[133] (3) The content of the mystery, therefore, is that Israel according to the flesh would no longer be the point of entry into God's kingdom, but that there would be a new Israel, a new temple, a new sacrifice, a new people of God.

Whether these answers satisfy may depend on how one understands the word "hidden" (3:9). If partial disclosure is compatible with Paul's words— if "not made known" (3:5) means "not fully known" or "disclosed through the prophets as an instrument without their understanding their own prophecy" (cf. 1 Pet 1:10–12)—then this threefold solution may suffice. But Paul's words, read

---

[131] See, for example, Gen 12:1–3; 18:18; Is 2:2–4; 11:10; 49:6; 60:3; Jer 3:17; Jonah 4:1–11; Zech 9:9–10. Such texts are read as predicting the Gospel going to the Gentiles by, e.g., Lk 2:32; Gal 3:7–8, 29.

[132] The NT claims specifically that the OT promised Gentile inclusion: e.g., Acts 15:13–18; Rom 1:2–6; 9:23–26; Gal 3:8; 1 Pet 1:10–12.

[133] "That God would bless the Gentiles, then, was not a new revelation. What then was the new revelation, the mystery hitherto concealed? It was this: that God's blessing of the Gentiles would involve the obliteration of the old line of demarcation which separated them from Jews and the incorporation of Gentile believers together with Jewish believers, without any discrimination, in the new, comprehensive community of God's chosen people" (Bruce, *The Epistles to the Colossians, to Philemon, and to the Ephesians*, 314).

naturally, suggest a more thoroughgoing rupture between the kind of revelation that the OT prophets received and that which was given to him and the other apostles.[134] The answer suggested above, which arose out of a comparison of Colossians and Ephesians, is that *the revelation of the mystery is Jesus Christ himself*. Thus, it is not simply information, but the appearance of the person.[135]

The problem with the threefold answer above is that there is no specific role for Christ; at any time, God could have revealed that Gentiles were welcome into the kingdom on the basis of faith apart from the works of the Law. But this would not have been the new testament/covenant. This would not be the Gospel that Paul preached. A mystery that is merely disclosed *by* Christ is not the same as a mystery that *is* Christ. What is truly revolutionary is that this God-man Jesus Christ took the curse of the Law upon himself and killed it on the cross, thus making the two peoples one with each other and with God. This may have been prophesied in part, but it had not happened before. It was wholly new. And together with the revelation of Christ himself to Paul and the apostles, the consequences of that action were unfolded so that Paul understood what it meant for all the peoples of the world. The Messiah was hidden in the OT in such a way that only Christ himself could open the apostles' eyes to find him there (Lk 24:45–47; cf. Jn 5:39; 2 Cor 3:14–16).

Because the revelation of the mystery comes through the very person of Jesus Christ, Paul is not troubled by the question of precisely when a certain piece of information was made known or to which apostle. There is no contradiction between his statements that "the mystery was made known to me" (3:3) and that "now it has been revealed to his [God's/Christ's] holy apostles and prophets in the Spirit" (3:5). Both Paul and the other apostles encountered Jesus Christ himself and were called by him—the very definition of an apostle. All of them were the mouthpiece of the Holy Spirit—the very definition of a prophet. Even the news that the Gospel of Christ would transcend the boundaries of Jew and Gentile was revealed repeatedly to all Christ's apostles. Christ's words to the Twelve echo Paul's assertion that he had received a revelation not made known to the prophets of old (Mt 13:17; Lk 10:24). Christ's departing mandate to the apostles must surely be understood as directing them to take a message of faith and Baptism to the Gentiles—not simply the old Torah to

---

[134] "There is both continuity and discontinuity between the testaments; our passage stresses the discontinuity" (Best, *Ephesians*, 306).

[135] Markus Barth is heading in this direction when he writes:

For him [the author of Ephesians] Isa 57:19 predicted the approach of the nations! But an event prophesied is for him not the same as an act of revelation. Revelation includes word and deed, announcement and performance, promise and actual salvation. Equally knowledge of revelation is, as already stated, not just intellectual perception, but includes acknowledgment and corresponding action. Such revelation and knowledge may have been foreseen by elect men of Israel, but they had not yet occurred. (*Ephesians*, 1:334, n. 45)

a larger audience, but Christ's new Torah[136] of forgiveness of sins through his name (Mt 28:19–20; Lk 24:47; Acts 1:8). To Peter the revelation was given that he should not fear fellowship with the Gentile Cornelius and that all food was now clean (Acts 10). And the Jerusalem apostles, together with the presbyters, were inspired by the Holy Spirit to accept the legitimacy of Paul's Gentile mission (Acts 15:22–29). Thus, the entire NT confirms that there is no contradiction between the assertions of Eph 3:3 and 3:5. Paul and the other apostles stand in complete harmony.[137] Nevertheless, Paul singles out his own receipt of revelation because of his unique role. In accord with the words of his mandate from Christ (Acts 26:16–18), and in harmony with his agreement with the Jerusalem apostles (Gal 2:9), Paul had the primacy in the mission to the Gentiles and rightly mentions himself first (Eph 3:3) as the recipient of the revelation.

"To Proclaim the Unfathomable Riches of Christ" (3:8–12)

In the first half of the pericope (3:1–7), Paul has unpacked the brevity of the corresponding text in Colossians: "the mystery which was hidden for ages and generations, but now has been manifested to his [God's] saints" (Col 1:26). Paul has clarified the role that the officeholders of the first generation played in receiving this revelation. In the second major sentence (3:8–12), Paul follows through on the latter part of the Colossian text, explaining how the mystery is "manifested to his saints." On the one hand, as an office of stewardship, the apostolic role is mediatorial: Paul and his apostolic brethren are commissioned faithfully to deliver the gifts given by God for the sake of his people. This is a divine office and worthy of utmost respect. On the other hand, the respect is not due because of who Paul is. He, "quite the least of all the saints" (3:8), the former persecutor of Christ, was not chosen because of his personal credentials! But that is precisely the kind of mediator Christ chooses—not to glorify Paul's abusive past, but to diminish the preacher and exalt the One preached (cf. Jn 1:26–27; 3:30). Thus, not only is the office a "grace … given" (3:2, 7) to Paul—hence entirely undeserved—but also the task of preaching the Gospel to the Gentiles is a "grace … given" (3:8).

---

[136] The noun ἐντολή and the verb ἐντέλλομαι are prominent vocabulary in the Pentateuch for God's giving of the Torah. ἐντολή, often translated as "commandment, precept," refers to an instruction given by someone in authority. In the Pentateuch it is used for individual mandates within the Torah (e.g., Ex 24:12; cf. Eph 2:15; 6:2). As the Torah contains provisions of both commandment and promise, so also ἐντολή includes both Law and Gospel (e.g., Ex 12:17; LXX Ps 118:66 [MT/ET 119:66]; 1 Jn 3:23). The cognate verb ἐντέλλομαι, "to mandate, give authoritative instruction," is its counterpart. When that verb appears in Christ's parting words to the apostles (διδάσκοντες αὐτοὺς τηρεῖν πάντα ὅσα ἐνετειλάμην ὑμῖν, "teaching them to hold fast all such things as I have *mandated* you, Mt 28:20), it implies that he is giving a new Torah (cf. Deut 4:2; Jn 13:34; 1 Tim 6:14; 1 Jn 2:7–8). See Winger, "The Office of the Holy Ministry according to the New Testament Mandate of Christ," 41, 45.

[137] "He teaches that there is a perfect harmony—a complete unity and identity—between the revelations given to him and those given to the apostles. His purpose is to avoid discord and any appearance of having received by revelation something that was not given to the apostles by the living Christ" (Victorinus, *Ephesians*, 1:3.5, ACCS 8:146–47).

The two halves of this pericope, far from exalting the apostles and prophets above all the saints, place the two groups into complete parallel. The mystery revealed to the apostles is not for them alone to possess, but for them to proclaim to all people, indeed, to the whole of creation. This is the distinguishing mark of the Christian mystery, that it is to be made known. All Christians—and even the spiritual forces of good and evil (angels and demons)—receive knowledge of the mystery through the apostolic office (whether through the apostles' preaching in person or by their written word, as proclaimed by ministers following in their office). But the knowledge and the salvation obtained is the same.

In fact, through hearing the apostolic Word, every Christian participates in the personal experience of Jesus Christ that was a criterion for appointment to the apostolic office. And through that union with Christ, every Christian gains access to the throne of God in such a personal way that Paul can make no greater claim, even if he has been raised to a vision of the third heaven (2 Cor 12:2). For in Christ all the baptized have already been raised and exalted to sit with God in the heavenly places (Eph 2:6). And given that honor, they have boldness of access in faith to the very ear of God in every need (2:18; 3:12). Paul's extraordinary claim is fully in line with Jesus' own exhortation that we should address the exalted God as "our Father" (Mt 6:9). For, as Luther explains:

> With these words God tenderly invites us to believe that He is our true Father and that we are His true children, so that with all boldness and confidence we may ask Him as dear children ask their dear father.[138]

---

[138] SC 3:2 (*LSB* 323).

Intercession and Doxology: The Revelation of the Mystery Is for Their Strengthening and to God's Glory

Translation

3 ¹⁴For this reason I bend my knees to the <u>Father,</u>
   ¹⁵from whom every family in <u>heaven</u> and on <u>earth</u> is named,
      ¹⁶<u>that</u> he might grant you according to the riches of his glory
         to be strengthened with power through his <u>Spirit</u> for the inner man,
            ¹⁷that <u>Christ</u> would dwell in your hearts through faith,
               so <u>that</u> you, being rooted and founded in love, ¹⁸might be fully enabled
                  to comprehend with all the saints
                     what is [its] <u>breadth</u> and <u>length</u> and <u>height</u> and <u>depth,</u>
                        ¹⁹and to know the love of Christ that surpasses knowledge,
                           so <u>that</u> you might be filled up to all the fullness of God.
²⁰Now to the One who is powerfully able to accomplish more than all things, quite
beyond anything we might ask or imagine,
   in accord with the power that is working in us,
      ²¹to him be the glory in the church and in Christ Jesus for all generations
      into the age of ages. Amen.

Textual Notes

3:14 τούτου χάριν κάμπτω τὰ γόνατά μου—The sentence begun in 3:1 resumes. For
the meaning and referent of τούτου χάριν, "for this reason," see the first textual note
on 3:1. Although at that point the reason for Paul's doxological prayer was the reconciliation of Jew and Gentile to each other and to God, as explained in chapter 2, the
intervening verses (3:2–13) continue the theme and can be considered part of the present cause of Paul's prayer. κάμπτω, "to bend, bow," a body part, usually the head or the
knee, is normally understood in biblical literature as an act of submission, respect, worship, or prayer. "To bend the knee" might be interpreted as prostration, though this is
often made explicit by the phrases "face to the ground" or "upon his face" (e.g., LXX
2 Chr 20:18; Mt 26:39). More commonly the idiom just denotes kneeling.[1] Bending
the knee displays one's loyalty and confession to God or an idol (LXX 3 Kgdms 19:18
[MT/ET 1 Ki 19:18]; 1 Chr 29:20; Rom 11:4). To bend the knee before the true God is
to acknowledge his sovereignty over the one who bends the knee, akin to the symbolic

---

[1] Best, *Ephesians*, 1:336, notes that in 1 Ki 8:54; 1 Esdras 8:70; and 3 Macc 2:1 the possibility
of prostration with the face to the ground is excluded because the hands are raised to heaven
in a gesture of prayer. Thus, bending the knees means kneeling.

actions of homage in a feudal system or the posture of a slave before his master.[2] Such worshipful acknowledgement is at best an act of faith (Ps 95:6), but the majesty of God will compel all creation to bend the knee on the Last Day (Is 45:23; Rom 14:11; Phil 2:10). Kneeling by Israelites can be a sign of humble entreaty before men (2 Ki 1:13) or of prayer before the true God (1 Ki 8:54; 2 Chr 6:13; Ezra 9:5; Dan 6:11 [ET Dan 6:10]; cf. 1 Ki 18:42). Whereas Jews traditionally stood to pray, like a subject who has been granted audience with a king on his throne,[3] kneeling for prayer was common enough, displaying an attitude of grief, repentance, agony, despair, unworthiness, intensity, or profound awe.[4] Thus, if we exclude the attitude of repentance or grief as inappropriate to this context, Paul's act of bending his knees may be interpreted as either worship or intercession—or both.[5] The continuance of the sentence with ἵνα δῷ, "that he might grant" (3:16), indicates it is an intercession, while the doxology (3:20–21) suggests Paul prays on his knees out of humble awe before the majesty of God unveiled by the revelation of the mystery.

πρὸς τὸν πατέρα—The preposition πρός means "toward," indicating the orientation of Paul's bending the knee and the direction in which his prayer is sent. It is often used with verbs of entreaty or prayer.[6] As in 1:3, 17 (see the textual notes on those verses), Christian prayer is normally *to* the Father, *through* the Son, *in* the Spirit (cf. 5:20; 6:18). Jesus taught his disciples to pray, "Our Father" (Mt 6:9; cf. Lk 11:2). The access Christ has opened up is "to the Father" (Eph 2:18; cf. 3:12). The well-attested, but secondary textual variant that inserts "of our Lord Jesus Christ" (א[2] D F G Ψ 0278. 1881 𝔐 lat sy) likely crept in by memory from 1:3 and disrupts the play on words that follows.[7]

---

[2] Karl Heinrich Rengstorf, "δοῦλος," *TDNT* 2:265, notes that there was no place for kneeling in Greek religion, as it was seen as the posture of a slave—a repulsive idea to those who treasured freedom as the highest philosophical good.

[3] 1 Sam 1:26; 1 Ki 8:14, 22; Mt 6:5; Mk 11:25; Lk 18:11, 13; Azariah 2. Catacomb drawings consistently depict a figure standing with hands extended in prayer (*orantes*), indicating that this was the common early Christian posture of prayer, at least in the public liturgy.

[4] 1 Esdras 8:70–71; 3 Macc 2:1; Lk 22:41; Acts 7:60; 9:40; 20:36; 21:5; cf. Mt 17:14; Mk 1:40; 10:17. Although many of these references, including those cited in the text above, use different vocabulary (e.g., κλίνω ἐπὶ τὰ γόνατά, LXX Ezra 9:5; or τίθημι τὰ γόνατα, Lk 22:41; or γονυπετέω, Mt 17:14), it is not possible to distinguish intercession from worship on the basis of terminology alone. τίθημι τὰ γόνατα is a Latinism (*genua ponere*); BDF, § 5 (3) (b).

[5] In Theodotion Dan 6:11 (ET 6:10), κάμπτω translates the Peal of בְּרַךְ, *berak*, "kneel," which may derive from בֶּרֶךְ, *berek*, the "knee" that is bent. Some have posited a connection between "knee" and בֵּרַךְ, *berak,* "to bless." But there is disagreement as to whether the two verbs with the same triliteral root ברך are related. See Mitchell, *The Meaning of* BRK *"To Bless" in the Old Testament*, 8–16. Thus, it is possible that with "I bend my knees" Paul is indicating the resumption of the *Berakah* ("blessing") prayer (1:3–14) or at least using prayer vocabulary from the same Jewish context.

[6] LXX 1 Kgdms 12:19 (MT/ET 1 Sam 12:19); 3 Kgdms 8:54 (MT/ET 1 Ki 8:54); Neh 2:4; 2 Macc 2:10; Acts 8:24; Rom 10:1; 15:30; 2 Cor 13:7; Phil 4:6. See BDAG, s.v. πρός, 3 a ζ.

[7] Following the Majority text requires Luther (1546), for example, to repeat the name of the Father in 3:15: "der der rechte Vater ist über alles was da Kinder heisset, im Himel und auff Erden" (WA DB 7:199), "who is the true Father over all that is called 'children' in heaven and on earth."

3:15 ἐξ οὗ πᾶσα πατριὰ ἐν οὐρανοῖς καὶ ἐπὶ γῆς ὀνομάζεται—The word πατριά, "family," is derived etymologically from πατήρ, "father," for it refers to a group of people descended from a common ancestor. The play on words in Greek cannot be reproduced in English.[8] But there is more than a pun at work—Paul is not simply saying that πατριά comes from πατήρ, but that families derive their identity from their father. The descendants of David are ever known by his family name (Lk 2:4) in order to confess the ongoing character of God's promises through that line. The promised Messiah would be a Son of David, a fact emphasized in the NT by the presence of two genealogies (Mt 1:1–17; Lk 3:23–38). Jesus is called "the Son of David" thirteen more times in the Gospels. The promise to David was also that his son would be God's Son (2 Sam 7:14), an all-pervasive title for Jesus in the NT. Just as a man inherits his physical characteristics from his father, so Jesus is what his father is: as "Son of David," he is fully human; as "Son of God," he is truly divine.

In Hebrew/OT thinking, which is carried through into the NT, naming (here ὀνομάζω, "to name") does not refer just to hanging a label on something; the name indicates the reality, and to give a name indicates mastery over something or taking it under one's protection (see the second textual note on 1:21).[9] In the present context, however, ἐξ οὗ, "*from* whom [is named]," means even more than ὑφ' οὗ, "*by* whom"; God gives his children not just a name but *his* name. When Jesus, the Son of God, teaches his brothers and sisters to call upon God as their Father, he teaches that we are truly children of God; it is not just a metaphor. We have received from him the Triune name into which the sacramental water placed us (Mt 28:19), and through that name a new identity. Families come into being through birth. The Christian's new birth (in analogy to biological birth[10]) comes through water and the Spirit; that which is born of the Spirit is spirit (Jn 3:5–6). We are what our new Parent is.

The preceding explanation assumes that Paul addresses God as the Father of all Christians in Jesus Christ, that is, as the Father of his "*whole* family" (Eph 3:15 KJV) in heaven and on earth (without necessarily implying that πᾶσα should be translated

---

[8] The hymn "Our Father, by whose name All *fatherhood* is known Who dost in love proclaim Each family Thine own" (*LSB* 863:1; F. Bland Tucker; © The Church Pension Fund; used by permission; emphasis added) approximates the pun but subtly changes the meaning. The English word "family" derives from the Latin *familia*, "household," which included biological and adopted family members, as well as slaves and servants. πατριά never means "fatherhood" in the LXX or NT, and that meaning is unattested in LSJM for Classical Greek. The translation "fatherhood" (Bruce, *The Epistles to the Colossians, to Philemon, and to the Ephesians*, 325; cf. "all that is called father" in Tyndale, Coverdale, the Great Bible, probably following the Vulgate: *paternitas*) is thus unsupportable. Cf. Gottlob Schrenk, "πατριά," *TDNT* 5:1016–19. This text in the Vulgate led to much philosophizing in the Middle Ages over the analogical relationship between divine and human fatherhood.

[9] See לְ קָרָא, "to name/call," in Gen 1:5, 8, 10; 2:19–20; Ps 147:4; Is 40:26. Compare the appointment and naming of Christ's apostles, which includes the giving of authority: Mt 10:1–4; Mk 3:14–19; Lk 6:13–16; cf. Mt 16:18–19 (Barth, *Ephesians*, 1:383).

[10] Biological birth is signaled by the gush of water from the womb. The Holy Spirit is the giver of life (2 Cor 3:6).

391

as "whole"). But if, as is likely, πᾶσα πατριά is rightly translated as "*every* family,"[11] then God's Fatherhood should also be understood with respect to his *creative* act (cf. Deut 32:6; Mal 2:10; Eph 3:9). As Maker of heaven and earth, God is the Father of all things, of every family in heaven and on earth. This creedal perspective is clearly in Paul's mind a few verses later when he writes of "one God and Father of all [things/ men], who is over all and through all and in all" (4:6).

It is probably best not to exclude either interpretation; creation and redemption cannot be so easily separated. Through Christ, God created all things (Jn 1:3; Col 1:16); and through Christ, the descendent of Abraham, every family on earth was blessed (Gen 12:3; Acts 3:25). The universal character of that promise to Abraham well suits the present context of Ephesians, in which Paul draws Gentile and Jew together under one Gospel. God is our Father by creation and redemption, and such an acknowledgement gives greater confidence in all aspects of prayer. The pun suggests the thought that God is the Father of all people; but it is only those who are "in Christ" who have the privilege, like Paul, of addressing him as their Father, confident that he will hear their prayers and be gracious to them.

A similar dual reference must apply to "every family *in heaven*." While it surely refers to the sainted children of God who stand before his heavenly throne, it also comprehends the spiritual forces of the heavenly places, both good and evil (cf. "heavenly places" in 1:20; 3:10; 6:12; "the air" in 2:2). This is not to imply that angelic beings are grouped into "families" (as in some apocalyptic and rabbinic speculation[12]), but simply to say that they, too, were created by God the Father and owe their existence to him (cf. Heb 12:9). Evil spirits, too, are subject to the God who made them and still has power over them (cf. Eph 1:21). On the Last Day, the good angels will worship willingly (Mt 25:31; Rev 7:11) and the demons will be forced to their knees before the majesty of God (Phil 2:10).

3:16 ἵνα δῷ ὑμῖν κατὰ τὸ πλοῦτος τῆς δόξης αὐτοῦ—The subordinate clause introduced by ἵνα with δῷ (aorist subjunctive of δίδωμι, "give") provides the object of the unexpressed verb of prayer, i.e., the content of the petition implied by Paul's bending the knees (3:14): "[I pray] that he might grant you …" The prepositional phrase that follows with κατά, "according to," expresses the quality in God to which Paul appeals, the standard against which the gift is measured.[13] The measure of the Lord's generosity is found not in the strength of the petition, the merit of the petitioner, or the greatness

---

[11] Moule, *Idiom Book*, 94–95, adduces evidence that either translation, "the whole family" or "every family" is possible, though in the absence of a definite article the latter would be considered better Greek.

[12] Some Jewish rabbinic writings called the world of angels "the upper family" and Israel "the lower family." See Str-B, 1:744c; 3:594b.

[13] Schlier, *Epheser*, 168, expresses it eloquently: "It [δόξα, 'glory'] is the source and norm of his gift and his giving. … That for which the apostle prays for his Gentile Christians arises from and corresponds to [*entspringt und entspricht*] the 'brilliant might [*Machtglanz*]' of God, a little bit of might and light from his fullness."

of the need, but in the glorious riches of the Giver.[14] God gives more than we could ever ask (3:20). Paul returns to the elevated language of public, liturgical prayer that characterized the first chapter. The eloquent phrase, τὸ πλοῦτος τῆς δόξης αὐτοῦ, "the riches of his glory" (genitive of contents) or "his glorious riches" (qualitative genitive), echoes the use of πλοῦτος, "riches" (1:7, 18; 2:7; 3:8), and δόξα, "glory" (1:6, 12, 14, 17, 18), in those previous prayers and is a common way for Paul to express God's generosity.[15] See the fifth textual note on 1:7 and the fourth textual note on 1:18.

δυνάμει κραταιωθῆναι—In answer to the possibility that the Ephesians would "lose heart" over Paul's afflictions (ἐγκακεῖν, 3:13), Paul prays that they would κραταιωθῆναι, "be strengthened" (by God; a divine passive). κραταιόω, "strengthen," is rare in the NT, being used in Luke of a child's growth (John the Baptist, Lk 1:80; Jesus, Lk 2:40), and by Paul with the sense of spiritual strength (1 Cor 16:13). It is used seventeen times in LXX Psalms, frequently with regard to God strengthening someone.[16] Paul's use of the verb in prayer may be influenced by these worship texts. The related noun κράτος, "strength," features prominently in Paul's petitions elsewhere in Ephesians (1:19; 6:10) and substitutes for the verb in the opening prayer of Colossians: ἐν πάσῃ δυνάμει δυναμούμενοι κατὰ τὸ κράτος τῆς δόξης αὐτοῦ, "with all power being empowered according to the strength of his glory" (Col 1:11). In both Eph 3:16 and Col 1:11, the somewhat redundant use of δυνάμει as an instrumental dative (here "strengthened by means of [God's] power") is likely a Semitism; its appearance in both prayer passages (cf. also Eph 1:19; 3:7, 20) suggests that this language is formulaic: this is how Paul prays.

διὰ τοῦ πνεύματος αὐτοῦ—The role of the Spirit is strongly emphasized in Ephesians.[17] Those who have been baptized ("sealed" with the Spirit, 1:13; 4:30) are ever thereafter animated by his indwelling with his life and gifts. Because he is a person, not a substance, Paul can pray that those who already have the Spirit may continue to receive him (1:17). The Spirit functions in prayer as the medium, the connecting link, the umbilical cord by which life courses between Father and children (2:18, 22; 3:5; 6:18). Because the same Spirit dwells in all Christians (5:18), he is also the source of their unity with one another through "the bond of peace" (4:3–4). The Spirit's role is never to direct attention to himself (Jn 16:13–15). He is to strengthen the Ephesians by enabling Christ's love to be more deeply rooted in them (Eph 3:17). The role of the

---

[14] In the LXX, interestingly, the coupling of πλοῦτος, "riches," and δόξα, "glory," describes the wealth and glory of a king: first, God himself (1 Chr 29:12; Ps 111:3 [MT/ET 112:3]; Prov 8:18), and then those kings whom he blesses (3 Kgdms 3:13 [MT/ET 1 Ki 3:13]; 2 Chr 1:12; 17:5; 18:1; 32:27; Esth 1:4).

[15] Rom 9:23; Phil 4:19; Col 1:27. Note the same coupling of terms in David's *Berakah* prayer (1 Chr 29:12). This is liturgical language. Cf. "riches" and "glory" in the doxology of Rev 5:12.

[16] E.g., LXX Pss 79:18 (MT 80:18; ET 80:17); 102:11 (MT/ET 103:11); 104:4, 24 (MT/ET 105:4, 24); 116:2 (MT/ET 117:2).

[17] If statistics matter, the fourteen occurrences of πνεῦμα (not distinguishing "spirit" from "Spirit") in Ephesians, out of its total of 2,422 words (about 0.58 percent), place the book third in the Bible on a percentage basis behind Galatians and 1 Corinthians.

"Spirit" in this verse (3:16), coupled with "Christ" in the next (3:17), lends a Trinitarian pattern to the prayer, which began "to the Father" (3:14) and returns to "God" (3:19).

εἰς τὸν ἔσω ἄνθρωπον—The preposition εἰς, "into," might simply be interchangeable with ἐν, "in," as indicating the location of the strengthening;[18] but taken in its natural meaning, it gives the orientation of God's gift of strength, which is directed "toward" the inner man, "for" his benefit. The expression ὁ ἔσω ἄνθρωπος, "the inner man," occurs only three times in the Bible, all in Paul's writings. In Rom 7:22 it is the component of Paul's makeup that delights in the Law of God. In 2 Cor 4:16 it is that part of man that is being renewed, as opposed to the "outer man," which is wasting away. These passages suggest a spiritual rather than a psychological interpretation of the phrase. "The inner man" is not the mind or spirit in contrast to the flesh, or the higher functions that control the baser instincts.[19] "The inner man" is the saint, the whole person viewed by God through the lens of Christ, but hidden from mortal eyes.[20] We retain "man" in translation (rather than "person" or "being") to highlight the implied comparison to "the old man" (4:22), Adam. In Rom 5:12–21 (to which Ephesians has alluded extensively), Christ was portrayed as the New Adam who undid the damage done to creation by the first Adam. The language of "inner man" and the inner battle being waged in the Christian in Romans 7 implies an identity between the New Adam (Christ) and the Christian's inner man. Christ comes to dwell in a person through Holy Baptism, an act of new birth by which "the new man" is created (4:24), who is identical with Christ himself (2:15); this is so difficult to comprehend that dogmaticians call it the *unio mystica*, "mystical union" (cf. "the mystery of Christ" in 3:4).

3:17 κατοικῆσαι τὸν Χριστὸν διὰ τῆς πίστεως ἐν ταῖς καρδίαις ὑμῶν—This second infinitive, κατοικῆσαι, like κραταιωθῆναι in 3:16, is dependent on ἵνα δῷ ὑμῖν, "that he might grant you …" Thus, the petition is twofold: "to be strengthened" and "for Christ to dwell in your hearts through faith." The second infinitive clause interprets the first, explaining that the indwelling of Christ is the means through which one is strengthened. τὸν Χριστόν is accusative as the subject of the infinitive κατοικῆσαι. The cognate noun κατοικητήριον ("a *dwelling place* of God in the Spirit," 2:22) was central to the closing argument of chapter 2 (2:19–22), where Paul taught that Gentiles and Jews together were being built up into a new kind of temple in which God himself would dwell by his Spirit. Thus, the current verse implies the equation of Christ with God and places his work in parallel to the Spirit's. The prepositional phrases here (διὰ … ἐν, "through …

---

[18] BDF, § 205; Turner, *Syntax*, 255–56. Cf. the interesting discussion in Zerwick, *Biblical Greek*, § 110, who begs that we take seriously the distinctive use of εἰς. He is briefly taken by the notion of goal, "to produce the inner man," before rejecting it in view of Rom 7:22; 2 Cor 4:16.

[19] Here we suggest that Paul is keeping his distance from the Platonic idea of an "inner man" (e.g., Plato, *Republic*, 9:589a), found also in Philo. Nor is he dependent on Gnostic ideas of a divine spark within humanity (see Lincoln, *Ephesians*, 205). There is no part of man that is particularly predisposed to God's message (contra Lincoln, *Ephesians*, 206). The whole man needs to be reborn.

[20] Schlier, *Epheser*, 169: "The inner, new, hidden man, who is not simply a part of us, but we ourselves as baptized people, who are permeated and carried along by the Spirit."

in") suggest that indwelling is not a static concept, as if Christ comes to dwell within the Christian as a one-off act, hangs his shingle and draws the curtains. Rather, just as Paul can say that we have the Spirit and yet we pray for his coming to us, so Christ can dwell within us and yet we can pray that he continue to dwell.[21] We live because Christ lives in us; if he does not continue to live in us, we die (Rom 8:10; Gal 2:20). The emphasis here, therefore, is not on the fact of indwelling, but on the activities of faith (3:17a) and love (3:17b) that accompany it. By praying that Christ might "dwell in your hearts through faith," Paul is pleading that faith might be strengthened and continue to cling to the Christ who is its object.

As the two infinitive clauses (3:16b, 17a) are parallel to each other, the prepositional phrase "through faith" (3:17b) is parallel to "through his Spirit" (3:16a), pointing to the divine person who plants, germinates, and nurtures faith in Christ (Eph 2:8; see also Gal 5:22).[22] So also "in your hearts" (3:17a) is parallel to "for the inner man" (3:16b). This parallelism is more apparent from a literal translation of the two clauses that are the object of Paul's prayer:

| 3:16b | κραταιωθῆναι, "to be strengthened" | διὰ τοῦ πνεύματος αὐτοῦ, "through his Spirit" | εἰς τὸν ἔσω ἄνθρωπον, "for the inner man" |
| 3:17a | κατοικῆσαι τὸν Χριστόν, "Christ to dwell" | διὰ τῆς πίστεως, "through faith" | ἐν ταῖς καρδίαις ὑμῶν, "in your hearts" |

The heart is the seat of thinking and will, not emotion (see the first textual note on 1:18). Thus, if Christ dwells in our hearts, he moves us to trust in the things of God. The heart is therefore a natural accompaniment to "through faith." As with the things of faith, the presence of Christ in our hearts ("the inner man") is hidden from human eyes, which might not always see how Christlike we are.[23]

ἐν ἀγάπῃ ἐρριζωμένοι καὶ τεθεμελιωμένοι—The prepositional phrase ἐν ἀγάπῃ, "in love," almost certainly modifies the two participles that follow it, rather than the preceding infinitive κατοικῆσαι, "to dwell." In Ephesians (particularly in 1:3–14) Paul has frequently "front loaded" clauses with prepositional phrases in advance of the verb, even with this very expression ἐν ἀγάπῃ, "in love" (1:4).[24] The participles ἐρριζωμένοι, "rooted," and τεθεμελιωμένοι, "founded," require "in/on something" (cf. Col 1:23;

---

[21] The indwelling of the Spirit and the indwelling of Christ run parallel in Paul's writings: 1 Cor 15:45; 2 Cor 1:22; 3:17; Rom 8:9–11; Gal 4:6; Phil 1:19; cf. 1 Pet 1:11.

[22] Cf. Acts 6:5; 11:24; 1 Cor 12:9; 2 Cor 4:13; Gal 3:2, 5, 14; 5:5; 2 Thess 2:13.

[23] Luther preaches on this text:

It is possible for me to be truly in the kingdom of grace and at the same time outwardly weak enough to be regarded of men as a knave. My faith is not apparent to men, but God sees it and I am myself sensible of it. You meantime erroneously judge me by my outward conduct, thus bringing judgment upon yourself. We are aware of, and also lament, our weakness and imperfection. Hence we cry and groan, and pray to God to grant us strength and power. ("Sermon for the Sixteenth Sunday after Trinity, Ephesians 3:13–21," printed in 1525, Lenker, 8:274; StL 12:882, § 35)

[24] Eph 4:16 and 5:2 violate this pattern; 4:2 is ambiguous.

2:7). A secondary question is whether the two participles modify the pronoun that precedes (ὑμῖν, "you," Eph 3:16) or the verb that follows (ἐξισχύσητε, 3:18); in other words, does the rooting in love explain how Christ dwells in the Ephesians (3:16) or how they are enabled to comprehend (3:18)? Since the participles are *nominative* plural, it is grammatically natural to connect them with the verb that follows (ἵνα ἐξισχύσητε, "so that *you* [plural] might be fully enabled," 3:18), rather than with the preceding dative plural pronoun ὑμῖν, "(to) *you*" (3:16). But since the referent is the same ("you"), the distinction is of minimal significance and the participles may just as easily be taken independently.[25] To express the connection of the participial clause with the verb that follows, our translation places the words "so that you" (which actually reflect the beginning of 3:18: ἵνα …) *before* the words "being rooted and founded in love."

The two participles form a mixed metaphor. ἐρριζωμένοι, "rooted" (perfect passive of ῥιζόω), is organic, recalling the Parable of the Sower (Mt 13:6, 21 and parallels). τεθεμελιωμένοι, "given a foundation" (perfect passive of θεμελιόω), continues the construction image from 2:19–22.[26] A similar combination of organic and architectural metaphors occurs in Col 2:7, where it is ἐν αὐτῷ, "in him [Christ]," that Paul's addressees are "rooted" (ἐρριζωμένοι) and "built up" (ἐποικοδομούμενοι), and it is τῇ πίστει, "in the faith," that they are established. The Christ-centered and Word-centered nature of these parallels suggests that the "love" in which they are rooted is Christ's love for them, not their love for him or one another. Only his love can provide a sure foundation for their lives. God's love has been the focus of the monergistic salvation Paul has previously proclaimed (1:4–5; 2:4), and "the love of Christ that surpasses knowledge" (3:19) must surely be Christ's love for us. Although the Christian life is consequently characterized by love for one another (4:2, 15–16), the root and source is always God's love for us in Christ (5:2, 25; 6:23; cf. Rom 5:5, 8). It is unclear whether Paul is praying that *they might be* "rooted" and "established" in love, or whether these participles should be taken as established facts that give a reason for the action of the main verb: "*because you are* rooted and founded in love, [I pray] that you would be fully enabled to comprehend …" The latter seems preferable.[27]

3:18 ἵνα ἐξισχύσητε καταλαβέσθαι—Rather than standing in parallel to the previous ἵνα clause (3:16a), as if it introduced a *parallel* petition, this clause should be understood as *subordinate* to the preceding two clauses and the ἵνα clause that they modify (3:16–17a). In other words, Paul prays that they might be strengthened (3:16) and that Christ would dwell actively in them (3:17) with this consequent goal: that they might

---

[25] BDF, § 468 (2); Turner, *Syntax*, 230; Moule, *Idiom Book*, 31. Stoeckhardt, *Ephesians*, 170, discerns a more sinister consequence of connecting the phrase with the preceding: it might suggest that Christ's indwelling is *dependent* on a prior act of being rooted in love. This would indeed be troubling if the love were man's love; but if it is God's love in Christ, worked on the cross, the theological concern evaporates.

[26] See the first textual note on 2:20 for the identity of the θεμέλιος, "foundation" (the apostles and prophets, with Christ as the cornerstone). Mt 7:25 identifies the rock on which a wise man is "founded" (passive of θεμελιόω) as Christ's Word. Col 1:23 likewise refers to the Christians as "founded" (τεθεμελιωμένοι, as here in Eph 3:17) on the Gospel Paul preached.

[27] See Wallace, *Greek Grammar*, 631; Best, *Ephesians*, 342.

be *further* "enabled to comprehend …" The compound verb ἐξισχύω is a NT hapax legomenon, an intensive form of ἰσχύω, "to be able, capable." καταλαβέσθαι (aorist middle infinitive of καταλαμβάνω) means literally "attain, seize, catch up with" (Rom 9:30; 1 Cor 9:24; Phil 3:12–13), which leads to the figurative meaning "grasp, comprehend" (Acts 4:13; 10:34; cf. Jn 1:5). Paul varies his vocabulary, but continues to hammer home the need to understand the things of God and his role as recipient of the revelation that is to be made known (3:3–5).

σὺν πᾶσιν τοῖς ἁγίοις—"With all the saints" reminds the Ephesians of their Baptism, in which holiness and enlightenment was given to them (1:18), and places them into the context of the universal church. Baptism is not simply the rebirth of the individual but also the common bond among all the saints (1:18; 4:4–6). There is no secret knowledge in Christ's body, nor is knowledge of God to be sought in the mystical experiences of the isolated saint, but each member is to be taught and strengthened until all grow together into the full knowledge of the new man (4:13–16, 20–24). Thus, Paul calls the Ephesians to unity on the basis of common gifts.

τί τὸ πλάτος καὶ μῆκος καὶ ὕψος καὶ βάθος—The noun πλάτος means "breadth," the extent from side to side (x-axis); μῆκος is "length," presumably a measurement straight ahead and behind (z-axis); ὕψος is "height," the extent of distance upward, with βάθος, "depth," the distance beneath the surface (y-axis). In modern (and ancient Greek) terms this is a three-dimensional, spatial perspective; no reference to a "fourth dimension" (time) should be sought. Four terms are used either in imitation of the four points of the compass and four corners of the earth or because "height" and "depth" are necessary to include the realms of good and evil spirits (which would appear to be the meaning of "height" and "depth" in Rom 8:38–39; ὕψος, "height, highest place," is the location of Christ's heavenly ascent in Eph 4:8). Thus, the four terms embrace the heavens and the earth and all the powers therein.[28]

The key question is the predicate noun to which these four terms refer. One expects a genitive, such as "the length and breadth and height *of it* [the heavenly city]" (Rev 21:16)[29] or "the depth of the riches and wisdom and knowledge *of God*" (Rom 11:33). We might suppose that Paul has the *mystery* in mind, whose riches in Christ were declared to have unplumbable depth ("unfathomable," Eph 3:8–9), or God's *wisdom*, which he called "multifaceted" (3:10). OT parallels cite the vast dimensions of the universe as an analogy to the unsearchable depths of God's knowledge and wisdom

---

[28] Arnold, *Power and Magic*, 91–92, finds the same four terms in magical papyri as expressions of supernatural power. Cf. BDAG, s.v. βάθος, 1. If these parallels are relevant, the application of the four terms to the love of Christ would emphasize that it is greater than any magical forces that the Ephesians might have feared.

[29] The appearance of three of the four terms in Revelation in describing the heavenly Jerusalem, an image of the church, does not mean that Paul had the church in mind in our present passage (contra Stoeckhardt, *Ephesians*, 173). This would be a confusion of meaning and referent. The application of dimensional terms to two different objects that can be measured does not equate the objects in any way.

(Job 11:5–9; Sirach 1:3).[30] Clinton Arnold contends that God's *power* is in view, which stands parallel to his love in this prayer (cf. Eph 3:16–17, 20–21).[31]

In the immediate context, however, the quality Paul has in mind may be discovered by tracing the fourth term, βάθος, "depth." In the Parable of the Sower, the soil that lacks "depth" does not allow the seed to develop a sufficient "root" (ῥίζαν), so that the plants sprang up quickly but withered under the heat of the sun (Mt 13:5–6). In Eph 3:17 Paul has prayed that the Ephesians might be well "rooted … in *love*." In 3:19 he will pray that they "know the *love* of Christ that surpasses knowledge"—a clause that stands in grammatical parallelism to the present one. Christ's love surpasses knowledge because of its great extent, as described by the four nouns in the current verse. The love of Christ was described with similar terms in Rom 8:35–39. Thus, we convey Paul's meaning by inserting "its," meaning "what is the breadth and length and height and depth *of Christ's love*."

Some ancient commentators saw a cruciform image, the four dimensions representing the four arms of the cross on which Christ's love was acted out.[32] While homiletically useful and theologically on the mark, as a literal interpretation of Paul's words, it does not do justice to the terms "breadth" and "length," which can hardly be a reference to the left and right extensions of the cross; nor can "depth" be usefully interpreted as the part of the cross that is anchored in the earth.[33] If Paul had the cross directly in mind, "height" and "breadth" would have been sufficient and more obvious.

3:19 γνῶναί τε τὴν ὑπερβάλλουσαν τῆς γνώσεως ἀγάπην τοῦ Χριστοῦ—The infinitive γνῶναι, "to know," stands in parallel to καταλαβέσθαι, "to comprehend" (see the first textual note on 3:18). The postpositive conjunction τε, "and," suggests a close connection between the two clauses. The two infinitives are subordinate to ἵνα ἐξισχύσητε, "so that you might be fully enabled" (see the first textual note on 3:18), and together with that clause form the second petition of Paul's prayer (the first was 3:16–17a). After the dramatic, fourfold expression, "what is the breadth and length and height and depth" (3:18), Paul breaks off his thought and starts again with this clause, in which he proceeds

---

[30] Cf. Deut 30:11–14; Job 28:12–14, 21–24; Ps 139:8–10; Is 7:11; 40:12–14; Amos 9:2–3; Rev 5:13; cf. *4 Ezra*, 4; *1 Enoch*, 60:11; 93:12–14; *2 Apocalypse of Baruch*, 54:1–4; 59:4–11. Dahl, "Cosmic Dimensions and Religious Knowledge (Eph 3:18)," in *Studies in Ephesians*, 365–88, contends on the basis of such background texts that the author of Eph 3:18 must be referring to revealed knowledge of the immeasurable dimensions of the universe (380). The point in the present context is that knowledge of the love of Christ surpasses even this (381). Yet such a contrast is not in any way explicit in the text of 3:18–19. Why would Paul pray that the Ephesians receive knowledge of the dimensions of the universe?

[31] Arnold, *Power and Magic*, 93–96. "The four dimensions therefore function in the prayer as a dynamic, rhetorical expression for the vastness of the power of God" (95). Arnold's tempting suggestion falters on the lack of an expressed genitive (e.g., "of his power") in the verse.

[32] See Augustine, *On Christian Doctrine*, 2:41; Irenaeus, *Against Heresies*, 5:17.14 (cited in the commentary below); Gregory of Nyssa, *On the Three Days*; Jerome, *Ephesians*, 2:3.16. See Schlier, *Epheser*, 173–74.

[33] Luther ("Sermon for the Sixteenth Sunday after Trinity, Ephesians 3:13–21," printed in 1525, Lenker, 8:278; StL 12:886–87, § 45) acknowledges and rejects this patristic interpretation. He applies the fourfold immeasurability to the kingdom of Christ: wherever I am, I still find Christ.

to define the object of such knowledge as "the love of Christ." It thus stands in place of a possible genitive construction at the end of 3:18 (see the preceding textual note). By way of climactic parallelism,[34] it repeats and expands upon the previous clause. With the transition from καταλαβέσθαι, "comprehend" (3:18), to γνῶναι, "know," Paul moves from intellectual apprehension to the deeper, experiential knowledge that is implied by γινώσκω (and יָדַע).[35]

It is impossible to say that "the love of Christ" can merely be grasped with the mind. Even though "knowledge" of God and his mystery in Christ has been Paul's goal throughout the epistle, in the depths of its mysteriousness it remains beyond human comprehension (cf. Phil 4:7, where "the peace of God" "surpasses all understanding"). This oxymoron, to know what is unknowable, is an essential facet of the Christian faith. We know what God reveals, and yet we cannot know in full because God remains partly hidden.[36] This is not a limitation on revelation (as if the true God cannot make himself fully known), but a warning not to seek God outside what he chooses to reveal (cf. Is 55:8–9). Thus, Paul calls this mysterious love ὑπερβάλλουσαν, "surpassing, extraordinary"—a feminine participle of the verb with whose neuter participle he had earlier used to describe the greatness of God's power at work in those who believe (ὑπερβάλλον, 1:19) and the richness of his grace (ὑπερβάλλον, 2:7).[37] The love that caused Christ's incarnation and his sacrificial death on the cross surpasses human comprehension (cf. Jn 15:13; Rom 5:8). That τὴν ἀγάπην τοῦ Χριστοῦ, "the love of Christ," should be taken as having a subjective genitive ("Christ's love for us") is clear from two facts: first, the description of this love as beyond human comprehension; and second, Paul's later statements about God's love for us in Christ (5:2, 25; 6:23).[38]

ἵνα πληρωθῆτε εἰς πᾶν τὸ πλήρωμα τοῦ θεοῦ—This ἵνα clause stands subordinate to the previous two ἵνα clauses and the clauses that modify them (3:16–19a); it gives the final goal of Paul's prayer. The language of πληρόω, "to fill up," and τὸ πλήρωμα, "the fullness," was the subject of much debate in 1:23, where it was unclear whether the church is that which fills up Christ or Christ is the one who fills up the church (see the second textual notes). Here, since "you [Ephesians]" are the subject of the passive

---

[34] See Lincoln, *Ephesians*, 212. Schlier, *Epheser*, 174: "eine Steigerung," "an escalation."

[35] This is the first occurrence of γινώσκω, "to know," in Ephesians, which has previously used γνωρίζω, "to make known" (1:9; 3:3, 5, 10); οἶδα, "to know" (1:18); νοέω, "to understand" (3:4); and καταλαμβάνω, "to comprehend" (3:18). The recurrence of γινώσκω, "to know," in 5:5; 6:22 has the same sense of deep, personal understanding and experience.

[36] Although knowledge of God's love in Christ is limited, Paul does not *contrast* knowledge and love, as he does in 1 Cor 8:1–3 or 1 Cor 13:2, 9–13, where human knowledge is a source of arrogance that excludes brotherly love. Here in Eph 3:19 Paul speaks of divinely granted knowledge of the love that God shows in Christ. Just as to be loved by Christ has primacy over loving him (2 Cor 5:14; Eph 5:2; cf. 1 Jn 4:10), so it is more important to be known by God than to have knowledge (Gal 4:9; cf. 1 Cor 8:3).

[37] These three occurrences in Ephesians constitute the majority of the occurrences of the verb ὑπερβάλλω, "to surpass," in the NT (the two others are in 2 Cor 3:10; 9:14, where it refers respectively to God's glory and grace). It is characteristic of the letter's exuberant liturgical language.

[38] Cf. Rom 8:35, 37–39; 2 Cor 5:14; Gal 2:20; 2 Thess 2:16.

verb πληρωθῆτε, "might be filled up," it is clearly Christians who are filled up, not God. Thus, the genitive τὸ πλήρωμα τοῦ θεοῦ, "the fullness of God," must be the fullness that God provides.[39] Not only in 1:23 and 3:19 but also later in Ephesians, it is Christ who fills all things (4:10) and his Spirit who fills the saints (5:18). By the indwelling of Christ and his Spirit through faith and in God's love (3:16–17), all the saints are brought to the completion God has in mind for them. Because Christ possesses "all the fullness of the deity" (Col 2:9) and "you are brought to fullness in him" (Col 2:10), to be brought to "the fullness of God" (Eph 3:19) is both an astonishing act of virtual "deification" and a humbling message that such fullness is never ours by nature or right; God's fullness is ours only through connection to the person of Christ.[40] Paul has asked not that God would give the Ephesians possession of the fullness of his glory, but that he would give "according to the riches of his glory" (3:16). Like in so much of Paul's previous prayer language, he asks for the ongoing gift of what is already theirs: they are filled with God's fullness (1:23), but continue to be filled by him.

In light of this discussion, the textual variant that replaces πληρωθῆτε εἰς (second person plural) with πληρωθῇ (third person singular) is understandable. Rather than the Ephesians being filled up, the variant makes the fullness of God itself the subject of the verb: "so that it [the fullness of God] might be filled up." Though the manuscript evidence for the variant is weighty (𝔓[46] B 0278. 33. 1175 *pc* sa), the support for the NA[27] text is equally strong, more numerous, and more geographically diverse. The scribe who introduced the change may have hesitated at the thought that the church could achieve a perfection equal to God's (misunderstanding it as "the fullness that God has" rather than "the fullness that God gives").

3:20 τῷ δὲ δυναμένῳ ὑπὲρ πάντα ποιῆσαι ὑπερεκπερισσοῦ ὧν αἰτούμεθα ἢ νοοῦμεν—The language of Paul's doxologies is somewhat formulaic (see the commentary). The opening words τῷ δὲ δυναμένῳ, "now to the One who is powerfully able," occur in Rom 16:25 and Jude 24 (also *Martyrdom of Polycarp*, 20:2). Likewise, the combination of δύναμαι with the infinitive of ποιέω is a common idiom, "to be

---

[39] It is certainly not "the fullness God demands," considering that in context it is Christ and his love for the Ephesians that fills them—contra Wallace, *Greek Grammar*, 375, who comments that the content of πληρόω (3:19) is God's fullness, "probably a reference to his moral attributes"! This is theological axe-grinding in the guise of a Greek grammar. Luther interprets it as we have:

> "Filled unto all the fullness of God" means, if we follow the Hebrew [i.e., Semiticism], filled with everything God's bounty supplies, full of God, adorned with his grace and the gifts of his Spirit—the Spirit who gives us steadfastness, illuminates us with his light, lives within us his life, saves us with his salvation, and with his love enkindles love in us; in short, it means having God himself and all his blessings dwelling in us in fullness and being effective to make us wholly divine—not so that we possess merely something of God, but all his fullness. ("Sermon for the Sixteenth Sunday after Trinity, Ephesians 3:13–21," printed in 1525, Lenker, 8:279–80; StL 12:888, § 48)

[40] Lincoln, *Ephesians*, 215, loses his balance on this tightrope when he questions "whether there is any difference in kind between the fullness of deity that dwelt in Christ and that which is available to believers." This is to divorce our reception of God's fullness from Christ, as if we can possess it on our own.

able to do," and is used frequently in the Gospels to describe Christ's divine power.[41] With the addition of πάντα, "all things," it is an obvious way to describe the omnipotence of God.[42] The Lord's mighty capability, his δύναμις ("power," the noun cognate to the verb δύναμαι here), has been frequently extolled in Ephesians (1:19; 3:7) as that which far exceeds any other spiritual δύναμις (1:21) and as the source of the Christian's strength (1:19; 3:16, 20; cf. δύναμαι in 6:11, 13, 16).

The five words following δυναμένῳ are syntactically complex[43] and redundant, though the meaning is clear enough. Paul uses two forms of comparison to describe the overwhelming power of God: (1) he is able ὑπὲρ πάντα ποιῆσαι, "to do beyond all things," "to accomplish more than all things"; and (2) this is ὑπερεκπερισσοῦ ὧν αἰτούμεθα ἢ νοοῦμεν, "quite beyond what things we ask or imagine."[44] The adverb[45] ὑπερεκπερισσοῦ, "quite beyond all measure," is described by BDAG as the "highest form of comparison imaginable." This comparison reminds us again that the measure of God's giving is not our asking, but his strength and generosity (cf. 3:16). He is a king who treats us not as subjects, but as kin (cf. 1 Esdras 4:42). The use of αἰτούμεθα, "we ask," refers back to Paul's petitions (Eph 3:16–19). The addition of ἢ νοοῦμεν, "or we think, imagine" (from νοέω), suggests, first, prayers of the mind that never reach vocal expression, and, second, petitions we fail to offer but that God grants nonetheless (Rom 8:26).

κατὰ τὴν δύναμιν τὴν ἐνεργουμένην ἐν ἡμῖν—On the noun δύναμις, "power," see the previous textual note. κατά introduces the standard "in accord with" which God acts: his power. But in the context of the present prayer it is qualified by reference to "us" (ἐν ἡμῖν). God's power at work in the universe is irrelevant if it offers no answer to the needs of his children. This prepositional phrase greatly parallels 1:19, where the "power" at work in us was rooted in the power God "worked" in Christ "by raising him from the dead" (1:20). The same thought is surely in mind here: this power is God's continual sustenance of our life in Christ (cf. 2 Cor 4:12). ἐνεργέω, "to be at work effectively in someone," is used more frequently in Ephesians (four times: 1:11, 20; 2:2; 3:20) than any other book of the Greek Bible, highlighting the divine power that Paul praises and offers to his children in the faith.[46] It is very close to a *terminus technicus* for God's spiritual work within. The form

---

[41] See, e.g., Mt 9:28; Jn 3:2; 5:19, 30; 9:33; 11:37; 15:5.

[42] BDAG, s.v. δύναμαι, c. Cf. *Shepherd of Hermas, Mandates*, 12:6.3.

[43] See Moule, *Idiom Book*, 42.

[44] The first phrase, ὑπὲρ πάντα ποιῆσαι, may be used absolutely: "who is able to do more than all things." Or it may stand in parallel to the next phrase, providing a compound object for the subsequent verbs: "to do more than all things … we might ask or imagine." In the second phrase, the antecedent of the relative pronoun ὧν, "which," is missing (elided). Normal grammar would expect ὑπερεκπερισσοῦ to be followed by a genitive (of comparison) plural noun ("[beyond] *the things*") followed by an accusative relative pronoun as the object of the verb ("*which* we ask"). In this compressed clause, the two (presumably τούτων ἅ) have been merged into a single genitive pronoun (ὧν).

[45] Used as an improper preposition; see Moule, *Idiom Book*, 86. Cf. 1 Thess 3:10; 5:13.

[46] Cf. 1 Cor 12:6, 11; Gal 3:5; 5:6; Phil 2:13; Col 1:29; 1 Thess 2:13.

ἐνεργουμένην could be middle or passive;[47] the former is commonly used in the NT for impersonal subjects (like faith or death); the latter would imply a divine agent. The meaning is the same in any case, as the "power" is God's.

3:21 αὐτῷ ἡ δόξα—The pronoun αὐτῷ, "to him," repeats the indirect object of the doxology, in parallel to τῷ … δυναμένῳ, "to the One who is powerfully able" (3:20), which has become distant by the lengthy interlude. As in most doxologies and doxological prayers in the NT, no verb is present. Although there is a strong argument for supplying the indicative "is" (see the first textual note on 1:3), the language of doxology implies a twofold message: God *has* glory (indicative), and we are exhorted to *give* him glory (optative/subjunctive). Thus, it is appropriate to translate both "his *is* the glory" and "to him *be* the glory." The latter is not a mere wish (on which grounds grammarians and commentators often dismiss it), but standard liturgical language for the ascription of praise. It is equivalent to a Hebrew jussive.[48] On δόξα, "glory," see the first textual note on 1:6 and the third textual note on 1:17. In the present context, the appropriate meaning is "radiance, splendor" rather than "[incarnate] presence."

ἐν τῇ ἐκκλησίᾳ καὶ ἐν Χριστῷ Ἰησοῦ—The two prepositional phrases are parallel but use ἐν in slightly different senses. "In the church" identifies the location of the praise, but this may be too simple. The church herself gives glory to God because her very existence as a people redeemed from the world and from the power of the enemy testifies to God's power and grace (1:6, 12, 14; 3:10).[49] The church gives God "glory" by sharing in it and displaying it (3:13; 5:27). The unique presence of the words "in the church" lends this doxology a distinctiveness among NT doxologies and demonstrates how they can be shaped by the subject at hand.

Throughout Ephesians "in Christ Jesus" (and similar "in" phrases) expresses the baptismal locatedness of Christians who have been clothed with Christ (see the fifth textual note on 1:3). In this doxology the phrase identifies the means by which Christians are able to give God pleasing worship in a twofold fashion. First, they approach God clothed in the righteousness of Christ, and therefore they are welcome in his sight and protected from his wrath. Second, the phrase identifies the person and name of Christ as the one through whom the praise is given: to the Father through the Son (and in the Spirit).

Textual variants, primarily in later manuscripts, omit καί (cf. KJV) or reverse the order of "church" and "Christ."[50] This is evidence of discomfort over the coordination of the church and Christ, and the evident priority given to the former. But it is questionable whether Paul always placed the emphasis on the first item in a list. In 4:4–6 we find this order: church, Spirit, Lord, Father—an ascending order of priority perhaps based on the Christian's experience of God (see the textual notes there). Here it appears that

---

[47] See Moule, *Idiom Book*, 26.

[48] See, e.g., יְהִי כְבוֹד יְהוָה לְעוֹלָם, "may the glory of YHWH be forever!" (Ps 104:31), or יְהִי שֵׁם יְהוָה מְבֹרָךְ, "may the name of YHWH be blessed" (Ps 113:2; Job 1:21).

[49] Cf. Jn 17:10; Phil 1:11; 2 Thess 1:12.

[50] For evidence that goes beyond the summary in NA[27], see Barth, *Ephesians*, 1:375–76.

Paul mentions the church first as the location where the praise is experienced, followed by Christ as its basis and means, akin to prayer that concludes in the holy name of Jesus.

εἰς πάσας τὰς γενεὰς τοῦ αἰῶνος τῶν αἰώνων—This particular combination of words is unique among biblical doxologies, but combines features found elsewhere.[51] The mystery that was hid for "generations" and "ages" (Eph 3:5, 9, 11; Col 1:26) is now revealed in such a way that "for all generations," leading into the "age" which crowns all "ages," God will be praised for the revelation of the mystery and its accomplishment. Praise arises not simply from the contemplation of God's eternal attributes, but in thanks and awe for his saving work. The genitive phrase τοῦ αἰῶνος τῶν αἰώνων, "of the age of ages," has, first, a qualitative genitive (a Semitism[52]) describing τὰς γενεάς, "the generations," as eternal. It contains, second, a genitive that is a superlative ("the greatest age"), but also qualitative ("the age that lasts for ages"). Paul's basic view of history divides time around the Christ point into two ages. This is primarily a reference to Christ's second coming ("not only in this age but also in the one to come," 1:21; cf. 2:2),[53] even though the messianic age is proleptically initiated at his first coming (1 Cor 10:11; cf. Heb 6:5). The singular τοῦ αἰῶνος, "the age," in the present verse is best understood as a reference to "the one to come." But this basic two-age eschatology does not preclude a looser use of "ages" (plural) to indicate successive periods of time stretching from before creation into the infinity of God (2:7; 3:9). Although in the LXX εἰς τὸν αἰῶνα is sometimes just a translation of the Hebrew idiom לְעוֹלָם, meaning "forever,"[54] it is inadequate to understand similar phrases in NT doxologies in this minimalistic way without taking into account the significance of the new "age" inaugurated by Christ.[55]

ἀμήν—This transliterates אָמֵן, "amen," an affirmation derived from the verb אָמַן, "to be trustworthy, faithful, true." אָמֵן is a solemn formula by which the hearer accepts

---

[51] This is the only NT doxology that includes γενεά, "generation." But that noun is found in *1 Clement*, 61:3 (εἰς γενεὰν γενεῶν), and *Martyrdom of Polycarp*, 21:1 (ἀπὸ γενεᾶς εἰς γενεάν). The language is Septuagintal (Pss 105:31 [MT/ET 106:31]; 144:13 [MT/ET 145:13]; Tobit 1:4; 13:12–13; 14:5; cf. Ex 40:15; Dan 6:27 [ET 6:26]; passim). The combination of the singular and the plural in τοῦ αἰῶνος τῶν αἰώνων, "into the age of ages," reflects LXX Dan 3:90 (= Song of the Three 68); 7:18. Elsewhere in Paul we have εἰς τοὺς αἰῶνας (Rom 1:25; 9:5; 11:36; 16:27; 2 Cor 11:31) or εἰς τοὺς αἰῶνας τῶν αἰώνων (Gal 1:5; Phil 4:20; 1 Tim 1:17; 2 Tim 4:18), the latter also occurring frequently in the doxologies of Revelation.

[52] Moule, *Idiom Book*, 175, 185. A noun in the Hebrew construct state (akin to the Greek genitive) is often used adjectivally.

[53] See the third textual note on 1:21.

[54] See, e.g., Gen 3:22; 6:3; Ex 32:13.

[55] In the Latin rite of the Western liturgy these words were regularly rendered as *per omnia saecula saeculorum* (based on similar phrases in the Vulgate) when they occurred in the doxological termination of collects. The phrase came into English as "world without end," in which "world" held the archaic meaning of "age" (documented from the thirteenth century; Old English "w(e)orold," from a Germanic root meaning "age," related to "old"; see *OED*, s.v. "world," especially I 6 b). As "world" lost this meaning, it was feared that the phrase might be misunderstood as implying the eternality of the earth, of fallen creation. Modern hymnals adopted the insipid translation "forever and ever," which, quite unfortunately, lost the reference to the messianic "age." See Philip H. Pfatteicher, *Commentary on the Lutheran Book of Worship* (Minneapolis: Augsburg Fortress, 1990), 130–31.

the validity of a curse or blessing (e.g., Deuteronomy 27 [twelve times]; Jer 11:5) or an order or announcement (1 Ki 1:36; Jer 28:6); it is usually translated in the LXX as γένοιτο, "let it be so."[56] It is also common at the end of liturgical doxologies, where the LXX tends to transliterate it as ἀμήν. The double אָמֵן וְאָמֵן, "amen and amen," in Pss 41:14 (ET 41:13); 72:19; 89:53 (ET 89:52) signifies that each of those verses concludes a liturgical book of the Psalter. The LXX sometimes gives the transliteration ἀμήν at the end of a liturgical doxology.[57] Transliteration is a sign that a word has become an integral part of the liturgy (e.g., alleluia, hosanna, Sabaoth).[58] "Amen" is the response and affirmation of the people when the liturgical leader concludes a *Berakah* prayer.[59] The explicit statements that the people responded with the "amen" suggest that even in doxologies it should be understood as a response and not simply as a conclusion. The stylized "eternity formula" (see the preceding textual note) gives fair warning that the doxology has drawn to a close and that the amen may now be voiced. Thus, in the present verse Paul is inserting himself into the liturgy of the congregations of Ephesus, voicing to his own doxology the "amen" that he expects the people will cry out when it is read.[60] For the NT evidence, see the last textual note on 1:14.

Commentary

Structure and Rhetoric

The comments on the progression of the letter that applied to 3:1 apply also here, as Paul takes up again the movement toward prayer that he began, but temporarily set aside (3:2–13). The impetus for his prayer is the thanksgiving inspired by Christ's reconciling work on the cross (2:11–22) and the awe which arises in response to the revelation of the mystery that was central to Paul's office as apostle (3:2–13). Revelation leads to prayer. Two further thoughts might have prompted his prayer: first, the figure that arose at the conclusion of chapter 2, that Gentiles and Jews are built up together into a holy temple on the foundation of the apostles and prophets, with Christ himself the cornerstone (2:19–22); second, the conclusion that in Christ Jesus we have "boldness and access in confidence" to God, our Father (3:12). In context, then, this is not private prayer; but Paul, the apostle, leads the public prayer of God's people, the

---

[56] *HALOT*, s.v. אָמֵן, 2.

[57] 3 Macc 7:23; 4 Macc 18:24; Odes 12:15; 14:28, 35.

[58] The statistics are informative. אָמֵן, "amen," is relatively rare in the Hebrew OT (thirty times). In the LXX, אָמֵן is almost always translated as γένοιτο, "let it be so," once with ἀληθῶς, "truly" (Jer 35:6), while only occasionally transliterated as ἀμήν (twice). In the later intertestamental portions of the LXX, the transliteration ἀμήν occurs with significantly higher frequency (eight times). ἀμήν is surprisingly frequent in the NT (one hundred twenty-nine times). This suggests a historical movement in which "amen" became a much more popular religious and liturgical expression.

[59] 1 Chr 16:36; Ps 106:48; "amen, amen," Neh 8:6; 1 Esdras 9:46–47; cf. "amen, amen" also in Num 5:22 as the spoken response to the utterance of the priest.

[60] See Winger, "Orality as the Key to Understanding Apostolic Proclamation in the Epistles," 212–17.

figurative temple, who have been granted the right to bring their petitions into the presence of their heavenly Father.

The prayer (3:14–21) parallels and repeats much of the "prayer report" in the thanksgiving (1:15–23), which, though Paul's personal prayer, was a pastoral act for his flock. Now, enlightened and encouraged by the intervening words, the congregation is drawn into Paul's prayer as a united, liturgical community. Certainly Paul prays *for* them (ἵνα δῷ ὑμῖν, "that he might grant you [plural]," 3:16); but they are invited to make the prayer their own, just as they would do by adding their "amen" to a public prayer. In the public reading of the letter in the liturgy, they might well have voiced that "amen" (3:21). One might suppose that this is an unusual place for Paul to turn to prayer, as he normally prays only in the exordium or thanksgiving section near the beginning of his epistles. Yet Paul's letter format is as flexible as the mind that governs it and the needs to which he puts it. He turns to prayer because the subject matter calls for it, even in the middle of a letter (cf. 1 Thess 3:11–13). The question of the doxology's function in the overall structure of the epistle will be taken up below (in "Doxology").

The prayer divides neatly into two sentences, comprising *intercession* (3:14–19) and *doxology* (3:20–21). It would be misleading to label these two parts as "prayer" and "worship," as if Christian prayer were exhausted by intercession alone. The catechetical mnemonic that identifies the parts of prayer as adoration, confession, thanksgiving, and supplication (ACTS)—not necessarily in that order—is apropos. As we discuss the characteristics of the doxology below, we shall note the difficulty of separating neatly the genre of doxology from the *Berakah* prayer in the OT.

The first sentence (3:14–19) is a long and complicated one that bears the same marks of liturgical prayer that characterized the *Berakah* ("blessed … ," 1:3–14): complex subordination of clauses (one purpose clause leading to another, modified by multiple infinitives), extravagant vocabulary extolling the richness of God's glory, the heaping up of genitives, a profusion of prepositional phrases that modify the verbs, and the loose grammatical connection of phrases and clauses. It divides into two parts:

- **Address (3:14–15):** "I bend my knees to the Father …"
- **Petitions (3:16–19):** "that …"

The latter part consists of three petitions, each introduced by ἵνα, "(in order) that." The first ἵνα clause serves as the object of the presumed verb of prayer, "(this is what I pray), that …" It appears that the second and third ἵνα clauses are not coordinate but subordinate to it; that is, they express not parallel objects of prayer, but purpose clauses, each petition leading to the next as its consequence and goal:

405

- 1. "<u>that</u> he might grant you … to be strengthened … for the inner man, that Christ would dwell …" (3:16–17a)
  → 2. "so <u>that</u> you … might be fully enabled to comprehend … and to know the love of Christ …" (3:18–19a)[61]
    → 3. "so <u>that</u> you might be filled up to all the fullness of God" (3:19b)

The first two petitions contain three parts each. In the first petition, the ἵνα clause is modified by two infinitives (though the second is difficult to reproduce as an infinitive in English and the parallelism is obscured by the use of "that" in our translation):

1. "that he might grant you according to the riches of his glory" (3:16a)
  - "<u>to be strengthened</u> with power through his Spirit for the inner man" (3:16b)
  - "for Christ <u>to dwell</u> in your hearts through faith" (3:17a)

(These clauses contain further parallelism between their prepositional phrases; see the first textual note on 3:17). The intervening clause, "being rooted and founded in love" (3:17b), breaks the neat structure, but is an essential component of the message Paul wants to convey and either modifies the subject of the next verb ("*you* might be fully enabled," 3:18) or stands independently. In the second petition, the ἵνα clause is likewise modified by two infinitives, the second building on the first in climactic parallelism:

2. "so that you might be fully enabled" (3:18a)
  - "<u>to comprehend</u> with all the saints what is the breadth and length and height and depth" (3:18b)
    - "and <u>to know</u> the love of Christ that surpasses knowledge" (3:19a)

The final petition is briefer and simpler:

3. "so that you might be filled up to all the fullness of God" (3:19b)

It is possible to discern a movement in the three petitions from faith to understanding to the fullness of love.[62] But, as the petitions are more concerned with what God does than what we do, it might be better to see the three petitions as prayers:

1. to be strengthened by the Spirit and the indwelling of Christ
2. to know Christ's love for them
3. to be filled up by God

The first (and main) petition also contains a Trinitarian skeleton, as it is addressed to the *Father* (3:14), for strengthening through the *Spirit* (3:16), that *Christ* might dwell in their hearts through faith (3:17).

---

[61] The first ellipsis represents the words "being rooted and founded in love" (3:17b).

[62] "Since he has taught that three things tend toward maturity in Christ—faith, understanding and love—he here brings them all into a brief compass. He is now praying that God will bestow all these gifts upon the Ephesians" (Victorinus, *Ephesians*, 1:3.18–19, ACCS 8:154).

The prayer as a whole bears a remarkable similarity to the later collect structure that predominates in liturgical prayer from the early Middle Ages to the present day:

- **Address:** "I bend my knees to the Father" (3:14)
- **Rationale:** "from whom every family in heaven and on earth is named" (3:15)
- **Petition:** "that he might grant you … to be strengthened with power through his Spirit for the inner man, for Christ to dwell in your hearts through faith" (3:16–17a)
- **Result:** "so that you might be fully enabled to comprehend … and to know the love of Christ … , so that you might be filled up to all the fullness of God" (3:18–19)
- **Doxology:** "To the One who is powerfully able … , to him be the glory in the church and in Christ Jesus for all generations into the age of ages. Amen" (3:20–21)

It is, of course, most likely that such NT prayers taught the church how to pray and are, therefore, the very model of the collect pattern.

(For the structure of the doxology, see "Doxology" below.)

As much as we might desire to find a function for this pericope in the rhetorical techniques of the secular ancient world, this may not be possible. As we have argued that the epistle does not fall neatly into two parts (chapters 1–3 and chapters 4–6; see "Structure and Rhetoric" in the introduction and the commentary on 4:1–16), this prayer and doxology cannot be considered the conclusion of the first part, though it may mark the conclusion to the main discussion of the "mystery" (3:3, 4, 9).[63] We are faced here with the uniqueness of Christian rhetoric, in which logical argumentation frequently must make way for faith and worship. Here Paul is not seeking to persuade the Ephesians of anything, but to fill them with God's gifts and draw them into his worship. Nonetheless, the prayer does not digress from the goal of unity that pervades the letter. Common intercession and doxology is the ultimate expression of the unity in one body in Christ that Paul has proclaimed.

Prayer (3:14–21)

Paul's prayer (3:14–21) is a response to revelation (3:2–13). It is cued by the vocabulary of "temple" and "access" at the end of the preceding pericope (2:18–22; see "Structure and Rhetoric" in this pericope). But as Paul's defense of his apostleship arose partly from fears prompted by his imprisonment (3:1, 13), so his prayer is not simply spurred by cold facts of structure or vocabulary. He prays out of pastoral concern for his flock. He seeks the gifts of God that will protect them from losing heart over his sufferings for them (3:13). He directs them to the work of Christ's Spirit within them, that is, to the Gospel itself. Their trust is not to be placed in Paul, certainly not in his person. Their

---

[63] Lincoln, *Ephesians*, 200, sees the doxology functioning as "the *transitus* between the *narratio* of 2:11–22 and the *exhortatio* of 4:1–6:9, and as functioning as a new *exordium*." Although there are noteworthy parallels to the *exordium* of 1:15–23, one wonders how the doxology could conceivably have been seen as an *exordium* (introduction, preface) to the rest of the letter.

faith is not to be shaken by his imprisonment,[64] because the message he proclaims is not about him. While Paul may be separated from them, Christ still dwells within them through faith. The world may hate them, demons may attack them, Jewish foes may persecute them, but the love of Christ far surpasses all such things. Nothing will divert them from the goal to which they are heading: the fullness God has in store for them now and eternally.[65] These are the broad contours of the prayer. This is how Paul the apostle prays for his flock.

The Posture of Kneeling (3:14)

That Paul can say, "I bend my knees to the Father" (3:14), and expect that his reference to prayer is obvious, invites some consideration. In his own historical context, Luther was understandably concerned about the relationship between external actions and the faith-life of the heart. Preaching on this text, he challenges a legalistic attachment to bodily postures and gestures if they are not accompanied by the inner movement of the soul. Such a warning against mindless ritualism is often necessary. Yet, he continues, faith does not leave the body unmoved. "When the Spirit of prayer is enkindled and burns within the heart, the body will responsively assume the proper attitude; involuntarily, eyes and hands will be upraised and knees bended."[66] Certainly the outward posture without the attitude of the heart is hypocritical and worse than worthless—even dangerous, as it leads confidence away from Christ. But where faith embraces both body and spirit, either one can move the other. The humble attitude conducive to prayer not only leads *to* the posture of kneeling, but can also be engendered *by* it, as Augustine writes:

> For those who pray do things with their bodily limbs—kneeling down, stretching out their hands, even prostrating themselves on the ground, and other visible gestures—that befit the posture of suppliants. Howbeit, their invisible will and the intention of their hearts is known to God, nor does He need these pieces of outward evidence for the human mind to be opened up to Him. But these gestures cause man to rouse himself to pray and sigh more humbly and fervently. And since these movements of the body cannot come about apart from a preceding movement of the soul, I do not know how the latter, interior and invisible as it is, is increased by these visible and external acts: and yet the affection of the heart grows through the doing of these things, preceding them to bring them about.[67]

---

[64] See "Paul's Trip to Jerusalem, Arrest, and Imprisonment (Acts 21:1–36)" in "The City of Ephesus and Paul's Relationship to It" in the introduction.

[65] "The fullness of God" (3:19) that he desires for them is only completely attained in the life of the age to come and so remains the continual object of prayer in this age. See Luther, "Sermon for the Sixteenth Sunday after Trinity, Ephesians 3:13–21," printed in 1525, Lenker, 8:280; StL 12:888–89, §§ 49–50.

[66] Luther, "Sermon for the Sixteenth Sunday after Trinity, Ephesians 3:13–21," printed in 1525, Lenker, 8:268; StL 12:877, § 22.

[67] Augustine, *On Care for the Dead*, 7 (PL 40:597; trans. John R. Stephenson [unpublished]).

Markus Barth has proffered the opinion that kneeling for prayer was origi-nally a pagan custom, a posture Paul adopts not because it is natural for him as a Jew but because it would have been familiar to the Ephesian Gentiles.[68] This would be passing strange if one considers Paul's view of pagan worship in such texts as 1 Corinthians 8, where he warns against partaking of meat sacrificed to idols (even if it is agreed that they do not exist) because it might cause the weaker brethren to stumble, and 1 Corinthians 10, where he rejects participation in pagan worship in the strongest of terms. Barth's opinion is based on a simple misreading of the OT text quoted by Paul in Romans: "But I will leave in Israel seven thousand, all the knees that have not bent to Baal, and every mouth that has not kissed him" (1 Ki 19:18, quoted in Rom 11:4). The implication of these words is not that "bending the knee" was a posture used only in the worship of idols, but that to "bend the knee" to anyone, any god, is to acknowledge its sov-ereignty. It is not the posture but the object of worship that is pagan. To suggest that a faithful worshiper of YHWH might have bent the knee in acknowledge-ment of the true God's reign over all the earth is not to deny the evidence that Jews regularly stood for prayer (see the first textual note on 3:14). But where biblical texts provide examples of faithful Israelites who did kneel for prayer,[69] we must recognize in this posture a sense of utter awe, worship, submission, or perhaps repentance, fear, or abject humiliation.[70] In the present text it is clearly the former that are at work in Paul's heart.

While the Bible offers no commentary on the significance of the posture, its continuation in early Christian piety is instructive. Tertullian (like Paul) is able to refer to prayer simply as "our kneelings."[71] Eusebius reports that the knees of James, half-brother of our Lord, were calloused like a camel's (cf. Gen 24:11) from his continual prayer.[72] He speaks of such kneeling as "our custom," in a text where an army prepares for battle.[73] These texts indicate that kneeling for prayer was common in the first four centuries leading up to the time when Eusebius wrote. But one might also deduce that kneeling for prayer was considered par-ticularly pious and appropriate to situations of grave, mortal need (like battle).

---

[68] Barth, *Ephesians*, 1:377–78.

[69] See 1 Ki 8:54; 2 Chr 6:13; Ezra 9:5; Ps 95:6; Dan 6:11 (ET Dan 6:10); cf. 1 Ki 18:42; Is 45:23.

[70] "We do well to lower our bodies lest we create an impression of elevation or an appearance of pride" (Victorinus, *Ephesians*, 1:3.14, ACCS 8:152).

[71] Tertullian, *To Scapula*, 4, ca. AD 217 (*ANF* 3:107).

[72] Eusebius, *Ecclesiastical History*, 2:23.6 (*NPNF*[2] 1:125): "And he was in the habit of enter-ing alone into the temple, and was frequently found upon his knees begging forgiveness for the people, so that his knees became hard like those of a camel, in consequence of his con-stantly bending them in his worship of God, and asking forgiveness for the people."

[73] Eusebius, *Ecclesiastical History*, 5:5.1 (*NPNF*[2] 1:219–20): "But the soldiers of the so-called Melitene legion, through the faith which has given strength from that time to the present, when they were drawn up before the enemy, kneeled on the ground, as is our custom in prayer."

By the third and fourth centuries patristic texts show that a debate was under way about precisely when it was appropriate to stand for prayer and when to kneel. Origen writes with great clarity:

> Of all the innumerable dispositions of the body that, accompanied by outstretching of the hands and upraising of the eyes, standing is preferred—inasmuch as one thereby wears in the body also the image of the devotional characteristics that become the soul. I say that these things ought to be observed by preference except in any special circumstances, for in special circumstances, by reason of some serious foot disease one may upon occasion quite properly pray sitting, or by reason of fevers or similar illnesses, lying, and indeed owing to circumstances, if, let us say, we are on a voyage or if our business does not permit us to retire to pay our debt of prayer, we may pray without any outward sign of doing so.
>
> Moreover, one must know that kneeling is necessary when he is about to arraign his personal sins against God with supplication for their healing and forgiveness, because it is a symbol of submission and subjection. For Paul says: For this cause I bow my knees unto the Father from whom is all fatherhood named in heaven and on earth [Eph 3:14–15]. It may be termed spiritual kneeling, because of the submission and self-humiliation of every being to God in the name of Jesus, that the apostle appears to indicate in the words: that in the name of Jesus every knee should bow in heaven and on earth and under the earth [Phil 2:10].[74]

These debates stand behind the famous decision of the Nicene Council (canon 20),[75] which decreed that on Sundays and during the fifty days from Easter to Pentecost, kneeling for prayer was forbidden—or put positively, prayer was to be rendered from a standing position. It appears that certain people were making a show of their kneeling for prayer even when in the Divine Service. The council's decision confirms the view that in the first centuries standing for prayer was considered most appropriate for the public liturgy, while kneeling was reserved for private prayer and as an expression of the exceptional attitudes discussed above.[76] To kneel is the posture of humble supplication; to stand is an expression of joy and a celebration of the resurrection.[77]

---

[74] Origen, *On Prayer*, 20, ca. AD 230 (trans. William A. Curtis; Christian Classics Ethereal Library; http://www.ccel.org/ccel/origen/prayer.xxi.html).

[75] "Forasmuch as there are certain persons who kneel on the Lord's Day and in the days of Pentecost, therefore, to the intent that all things may be uniformly observed everywhere (in every parish), it seems good to the holy Synod that prayer be made to God standing" (*NPNF*[2] 14:42).

[76] This classic view is expressed by Warren's standard work: "The recognized attitude for prayer, liturgically speaking, was standing, but kneeling was early introduced for penitential and perhaps ordinary ferial seasons, and was frequently, though not necessarily, adopted in private prayer" (F. E. Warren, *The Liturgy and Ritual of the Ante-Nicene Church* [London: SPCK, 1897], 145).

[77] "Which period of fifty days [Easter] we celebrate after the Lord's resurrection, as representing not toil, but rest and gladness. For this reason we do not fast in them; and in praying we stand upright, which is an emblem of resurrection" (Augustine, Letter 55, *To Januarius*, 28 [*NPNF*[1] 1:312–13]).

Consideration of kneeling to receive the Sacrament of the Altar brings an additional dimension to our understanding. Kneeling was the universal posture in the early and medieval church, so far as one can determine on the basis of written accounts and artistic representation. While this surely indicated the appropriate penitential attitude on the part of the communicant, it also arose from a deep conviction that God was truly present. Just as a supplicant before a monarch would kneel in humble homage, so the communicant knelt to acknowledge that he was in the presence of the heavenly King. Even in the High Middle Ages, when the oral communion of the faithful tragically dwindled, the congregants still dropped to their knees when the sacring bell was rung, indicating the moment in the (silent) canon of the mass when the priest spoke the Words of Institution and the real presence was effected. They often rushed forward to kneel at the rood screen and peep through holes made for the purpose in order to see the priest elevate the body of Christ.[78]

The Lutheran Reformation, which emphasized the actual reception (communion) of Christ's body and blood in the Sacrament and confessed the real presence of the same upon the altar and in the mouth, logically maintained the practice of kneeling to receive the Sacrament.[79] The Reformation in England was more confused, owing to the infiltration of Calvinist theology. The first comprehensive English-language adaptation of the liturgy after the death of the conservative Henry VIII, *The Book of Common Prayer* (1549), retained a clear confession of the real presence and, correspondingly, the posture of kneeling to receive the Sacrament. Three short years later, Archbishop Thomas Cranmer issued a radical revision of *The Book of Common Prayer* (1552)—significantly influenced by Martin Bucer's criticism of the first edition—in which he reworked the eucharistic prayers and distribution formulae to remove any reference to a real presence of Christ's body and blood in the bread and wine. While the earlier distribution rubric spoke of the priest giving "the Sacramente of the body of Christe" (1549), the revised edition directed the minister to give out "the bread" and instructed the communicants to receive it "in their handes kneling" (1552).[80]

Parliament approved the new volume in September 1552, not without resistance from even more radical Protestants such as the Duke of Northumberland. At his behest, John Knox preached a sermon to the king and privy council in

---

[78] See Eamon Duffy, *The Stripping of the Altars: Traditional Religion in England, c. 1400–c. 1580* (New Haven: Yale University Press, 1992), 95–102. It was not uncommon for the laity to run from church to church to witness the real presence over and over. See also Frank C. Senn, *Christian Liturgy: Catholic and Evangelical* (Minneapolis: Fortress, 1997), 225.

[79] This practice is unanimously witnessed by Lutheran art from the sixteenth century, such as the famous altarpiece from Torslunde, Denmark (1561), which depicts a Lutheran congregation in the Divine Service with communicants on their knees. See Joseph Leo Koerner, *The Reformation of the Image* (Chicago: University of Chicago Press, 2004), 314–15. Further depictions of Lutherans kneeling for the Sacrament abound in this volume.

[80] *The First and Second Prayer Books of Edward VI* (London: Prayer Book Society, 1999), 225, 389.

which he attacked the practice of kneeling for the Sacrament. Although Cranmer objected to their interference in this liturgical matter, the privy council was persuaded to intervene.[81] Unfortunately, the book was already printed, with its rubric prescribing kneeling. The only solution was to print a new, explanatory rubric on a separate piece of paper and tip it into the book at the appropriate place. Printed in black ink (rather than the usual red ink appropriate to rubrics), the instruction came to be known ominously as the "Black Rubric":

> Although no ordre can be so perfectlye deuised, but it may be of some, eyther for theyr ignoraunce and infirmitie, or els of malice and obstinacie, miscon- strued, depraued, and interpreted in a wrong part : And yet because brotherly charitie willeth, that so much as conueniently may be, offences shoulde be taken awaye : therefore we willing to doe the same. Whereas it is ordeyned in the booke of common prayer, in the administracion of the Lord's Supper, that the Communicants knelyng shoulde receyue the holye Communion : whiche thynge beyng well mente, for a sygnificacion of the humble and gratefull acknowledgyng of the benefites of Chryst, geuen unto the woor- thye receyuer, and to auoyde the prophanacion and dysordre, which about the holy Communion myght els ensue : Leste yet the same kneelyng myght be thought or taken otherwyse, we dooe declare that it is not ment thereby, that any adoracion is doone, or oughte to bee doone, eyther unto the Sacramentall bread or wyne there bodily receyued, or unto anye reall and essencial pres- ence there beeyng of Christ's naturall fleshe and bloude. For as concernynge the Sacramentall bread and wyne, they remayne styll in theyr verye naturall substaunces, and therefore may not be adored, for that were Idolatrye to be abhorred of all faythfull christians. And as concernynge the naturall body and blood of our sauiour Christ, they are in heauen and not here. For it is agaynst the trueth of Christes true natural bodye, to be in moe places then in one, at one tyme.[82]

The rubric expresses a Calvinist understanding of the Lord's Supper, the presence of Christ's body being restricted to heaven; consequently, kneeling *cannot* imply adoration of a truly present Jesus. The rubric's protestations testify ironically to the universal interpretation of the act of kneeling: it *was* under- stood as a confession of the real presence. Thus, when the Lutheran confession rejects the local confinement of Christ's body in heaven (FC SD 7:119) and con- demns the adoration of the bread and wine itself, it correspondingly affirms the validity of adoring the truly present body and blood of Christ in the Sacrament:

---

[81] See A. G. Dickens, *The English Reformation* (2d ed.; London: Batsford, 1989), 276–78; Diarmaid MacCulloch, *Thomas Cranmer: A Life* (New Haven: Yale University Press, 1996), 525–30. MacCulloch, 528, contends that this was a *political* defeat for Cranmer, who lost control of his own production, but not a *theological* defeat; the rubric expressed quite clearly Cranmer's own eucharistic theology.

[82] *The First and Second Prayer Books of Edward VI*, 392–93. The Black Rubric was omitted in the third (1559) edition of the prayer book, reflecting Queen Elizabeth's Lutheran leanings concerning the Sacrament. It was restored, with minor variations, in the fourth (1662) edi- tion and remains in *The Book of Common Prayer* to this day.

> Likewise, [we reject and condemn as false] when it is taught that the elements or the visible species or forms of the consecrated bread and wine must be adored. However, no one, unless he be an Arian heretic, can and will deny that Christ Himself, true God and man, who is truly and essentially present in the Supper, should be adored in spirit and in truth in the true use of the same, as also in all other places, especially where His congregation is assembled. (FC SD 7:126 [*Triglotta*, 1015])

The Lutheran communicant drops to his knees because he believes he is facing the holy God.[83] This historical digression into the Reformation dispute over kneeling for the Sacrament, therefore, adds a significant dimension to our understanding of Paul's words "I bend my knees to the Father" (3:14). For he utters his prayer not just to a distant God in heaven above but also to a God who is with him and before him, into whose presence Christ has granted access by the Holy Spirit (2:18; 3:12).

Trinitarian Praying (3:14–17)

Paul's prayer expresses a Trinitarian theology far richer than many critics would admit is possible, and gives a distinctive role to each divine person that warns against a systematic flattening of the Godhead. Like most NT prayers, the petitions are directed "to the Father" (3:14), as Jesus himself taught us to pray. The textual variant that adds "of our Lord Jesus Christ" was rejected for its weaker attestation and because it appears to be a harmonization to 1:3 (see the second textual note on 3:14). But that harmonization is instructive, for it demonstrates that the scribe recognized the Trinitarian pattern of the prayer: petitions to the Father are heard because the Son has brought us access, "through Jesus Christ, our Lord." Nonetheless, in the present context, Paul is not restricting God's Fatherhood to internal Trinitarian relations, but relating it to all creation, and particularly to the families in heaven and on earth who derive their name from him (3:15). Hidden in this superficial pun[84] is the truth that we may be confident of God's mercy just as children can trust that their loving Father will hear their needs and care for them (cf. Luther's explanation of the introduction to the Lord's Prayer, quoted at the end of the commentary on 3:1–13). Far from being just a cute double entendre, Paul's wordplay anchors the petition in our relationship with God. It gives the rationale for the prayer, the reason we may have confidence of being heard.

Paul's first petition calls for God the Father to strengthen the Ephesians by his Spirit (3:16) with a might limited by nothing short of the full riches of God's glory. It is easy to infer a problem from this petition, to suggest that the

---

[83] In the mid twentieth century, the Roman Catholic Church widely adopted the practice of standing to receive Communion—either to express an attitude of joy rather than penitence or merely for the practical expedient of speeding up the distribution. Some Lutheran churches have borrowed the same practice. In neither case is the posture of standing to be understood as a denial of the real presence, though one fears that something of the reverential attitude before the holy God has been lost.

[84] See the textual note on 3:15.

Ephesians were somehow weak and in need of Paul's prayer. Certainly we might point to their anxiety over his imprisonment, which might have entailed a loss of confidence in the truth and power of the Gospel itself.[85] Paul does not want them to "lose heart" (3:13). In the face of these challenges, he prays for their strengthening. But there is no reason to limit the petition to a perceived need. Strengthening through the Spirit is a universal pastoral prayer for a universal Christian need. The Spirit is the giver of life and the Christian's constant source of strength. Paul does not descend into moralizing, exhorting the Ephesians to find strength in themselves, but through prayer he points to a strength that comes from above and becomes their own internal strength through God's inworking.

He prays also for the indwelling of Christ (3:17), the third person of the Holy Trinity to appear in the opening words of the prayer. As noted above (in the first textual note on 3:17), Paul's writings tend to blur the distinction between Christ and the Spirit when he speaks of God's indwelling (cf. 2 Cor 3:17). Christ dwells in us by his Spirit (Rom 8:9–10); Christ sends the Spirit to dwell in our hearts (2 Cor 1:22); our bodies are the temple of the Holy Spirit (1 Cor 3:16; 6:19); he is the Spirit of Christ (Gal 4:6). We have put on Christ in Holy Baptism (Gal 3:27); the Spirit baptized us into that one body, and we all have come to drink of the one Spirit (1 Cor 12:13). The two cannot be separated because the Spirit speaks only of Christ (Jn 16:13–15). Thus, Paul in the present prayer can place into parallel a prayer for the Spirit's strengthening (Eph 3:16) with a petition that the Lord Jesus would continue to dwell in us through faith (3:17). "Through faith" (3:17) and the strengthening of the Spirit by the Word[86] rescue us from a "mystical" interpretation of Christ's indwelling.[87] Paul does not suggest that his Christian hearers could achieve a unity with Christ by meditation or works of their own doing; as it is the object of prayer, it is a gift of God. If it is "through faith," it is by his Word, the object of faith.

"Through faith" (3:17) is also a necessary precondition and interpretation of the prayer for understanding "the love of Christ" that follows (3:17b–19). Even as the text stands, many commentators, mostly patristic, have interpreted the "love" in which we are rooted and founded as the love Christians show for one another. From here it is a very short step to basing the indwelling of Christ

---

[85] See "Paul's Trip to Jerusalem, Arrest, and Imprisonment (Acts 21:1–36)" in "The City of Ephesus and Paul's Relationship to It" in the introduction.

[86] This prayer for strengthening by the Spirit comes immediately after Paul's explication of the Gospel that he was sent to proclaim to the Gentiles (3:7–12). His exhortation that the Ephesians not lose heart (3:13) is predicated on this Gospel Word that delivered Christ to them.

[87] Schnackenburg, *Ephesians*, 321:

> Today we avoid the expression "mysticism" almost completely; and rightly so, for that close communion-with-Christ mediated by the Spirit and experienced in faith is clearly different from a mystical experience as witnessed to elsewhere, especially from a fusion with the Godhead, a blessed participation in the union, a deification. The in-dwelling of Christ in Christians is thought of rather as an effective presence of the heavenly Lord, who through his Spirit stimulates the inner life of Christians and desires to bind them ever more closely to himself.

on man's activity of showing love.[88] But "through faith" rescues us from this perilous interpretation. The indwelling of Christ through faith is the cause of love for one another, but certainly not its consequence. The Reformation debate over whether one is justified *sola fide*, "by faith alone," or whether the faith that justifies must be *fides caritate formata*, "faith formed by love," hinged precisely on this question.[89]

The Cruciform Love of Christ (3:18–19)

The knotty relationship of faith and love is best cut through by the keen discernment that in this passage Paul has in mind Christ's love for us, not our love for him. The understanding of the immeasurable greatness of this love is what Paul begs God would give his children in Ephesus. There is no need to pit this understanding of 3:18–19 (that it is Christ's love which is unfathomable) against the unfathomable "mystery" (3:3–4, 9) of the previous pericope or against the inscrutable wisdom and essence of God himself. These are parts of the same mysterious whole. It is beyond man's ken how the immeasurable God could take up residence in human flesh, how he could reveal the mysteries of salvation to a man who once persecuted the church (3:3–9), how his promises to Israel could be kept while admitting the Gentiles into the kingdom apart from the works of the Law. And most important, it is beyond our comprehension how God could die on a cross: "Can any words adequately describe this mystery, that God is born as a man? That God dies for the human race, the master for his servants, the Creator for his creation, the righteous for the unrighteous?"[90]

Thus, although it may not be correct to interpret the fourfold dimensional description of the love of Christ as an allegory of his cross (see the third textual

---

[88] Having run an allegorical interpretation of the four arms of the cross (extrapolated from the four measures "breadth and length and height and depth" in 3:18), Augustine concludes very much in the way of the Law:

> And by this sign of the cross all Christian action is symbolized, viz., to do good works in Christ, to cling with constancy to Him, to hope for heaven, and not to desecrate the sacraments. And purified by this Christian action, we shall be able to know even "the love of Christ which passeth knowledge," who is equal to the Father, by whom all things were made, "that we may be filled with all the fullness of God" [Eph 3:19]. (*On Christian Doctrine*, 2:41 [*NPNF*[1] 2:555])

[89] Luther, *Lectures on Galatians* (1535), on Gal 2:16, AE 26:130; WA 40/1:229:

> Therefore faith justifies because it takes hold of and possesses this treasure, the present Christ. But how He is present—this is beyond our thought; for there is darkness, as I have said. Where the confidence of the heart is present, therefore, there Christ is present, in that very cloud and faith. This is the formal righteousness on account of which a man is justified; it is not on account of love, as the sophists say. In short, just as the sophists say that love forms and trains faith, so we say that it is Christ who forms and trains faith or who is the form of faith. Therefore the Christ who is grasped by faith and who lives in the heart is the true Christian righteousness, on account of which God counts us righteous and grants us eternal life. Here there is no work of the Law, no love; but there is an entirely different kind of righteousness, a new world above and beyond the Law. For Christ or faith is neither the Law nor the work of the Law.

[90] Ambrosiaster, *Ephesians*, 3:19.1, ACCS 8:156.

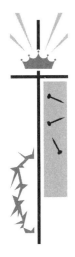

note on 3:18), that is certainly the place where Christ pointedly displayed his incomprehensible love. Irenaeus is perhaps guilty of overinterpreting the image—particularly in relating the two arms of Christ to the incorporation of both Jew and Gentile—but his exegesis is remarkably faithful to the message of chapters 2 and 3 of Ephesians:

> This word, then, what was hidden from us, did the dispensation of the tree make manifest, as I have already remarked. For as we lost it by means of a tree [Gen 3:6], by means of a tree again was it made manifest to all, showing the height, the length, the breadth, the depth [cf. Eph 3:18] in itself; and, as a certain man among our predecessors observed, "Through the extension of the hands of a divine person, gathering together the two peoples to one God." For these were two hands, because there were two peoples scattered to the ends of the earth; but there was one head in the middle, as there is but one God, who is above all, and through all, and in us all [Eph 4:6].[91]

This is not an allegory that Paul intended, but it is certainly an allegory Paul could have made, being entirely consonant with his claim that in the one body of Christ on the cross, both peoples were reconciled to each other and to God (2:14–16). The same may be said for interpretations that metaphorically extend the arms of the cross into the highest heavens and across every dimension of the universe in order to highlight the all-embracing significance of Christ's death and the thoroughly inclusive nature of his love.[92]

Doxology (3:20–21)

The term "doxology" derives from the basic vocabulary of this form of praise: the confession that δόξα, *doxa*, "glory, splendor, radiance," belongs to God and ought to be acclaimed as his. In Scripture we find at least three basic patterns of doxology.

The structure that underlies the present passage is this:

1. the object of praise (God) in the dative case
2. a noun such as δόξα, "glory"; τιμή, "honor"; or δύναμις, "power"
3. an eternity formula
4. "amen"

---

[91] Irenaeus, *Against Heresies*, 5:17.4 (*ANF* 1:545–56); cf. *Against Heresies*, 4:19.2; see also Irenaeus, *Proof of the Apostolic Preaching*, 34.

[92] Gregory of Nyssa, *On the Three Days*, ACCS 8:155–56:

> The divine mind of the apostle did not imagine this fourfold figure of the cross to no purpose. He knew that this figure, which is divided into four segments from the common center, represents the power and providence of the one displayed upon it. This dimensionality runs through all things. For this reason he calls each of four projections by its own name. By the height he means what is above, by the depth the underworld, by the length and breadth the intermediate domain which is under the control of his all-governing power. Hence the worship of the cross is viewed in relation to the fourfold figure of the cross. The heavenly order is symbolically paying its devotion to the Lord in the upper part, the cosmic order in the middle part and even the infernal order in the lower part.

In brief, such a doxology might look like this:

τῷ θεῷ ἡ δόξα εἰς τοὺς αἰῶνας, ἀμήν.

To God [be] the glory into the ages. Amen.

The simplest NT example of a doxology that follows this pattern is this:

τῷ δὲ θεῷ καὶ πατρὶ ἡμῶν ἡ δόξα εἰς τοὺς αἰῶνας τῶν αἰώνων, ἀμήν.

Now to our God and Father [be] the glory into the ages of the ages. Amen. (Phil 4:20)

As a framework, this simple sentence can be elaborated in any number of ways in order to fit the context and express the particular reason why God is praised. In Eph 3:20–21 there is, first, an elaborate insertion at the beginning that describes the qualities and works of God that connect with the context of prayer and the emphasis on God's power that characterizes the letter (3:20). Second, the ascription of praise in 3:21 is qualified by the insertion of two Ephesian themes, "in the church" and "in Christ Jesus." No verb is present, and it is debated whether the indicative ("is") or optative ("be") of εἰμί should be provided (see the first textual note on 3:21). This verbless pattern of doxology is rare in the Greek OT, but becomes more common in intertestamental literature (and in the NT).[93]

More frequently in the LXX, doxology appears with a verb of exhortation such as φέρω, "bear, ascribe," or δίδωμι, "give." For example, "ascribe to the LORD [ἐνέγκατε τῷ κυρίῳ], O sons of God, ... ascribe to the LORD glory and honor [δόξαν καὶ τιμήν]" (LXX Ps 28:1 [MT/ET 29:1]). This is most appropriate to the context of temple worship, in which it appears on the lips of the Levitical choirs exhorting the people to praise God.[94] This pattern is alluded to in most parts of the NT and appears frequently in Revelation.[95]

Finally, there is a related pattern of doxology that is an abbreviated form of *Berakah* ("blessed ...") prayer. Scattered throughout the OT, this brief acclamation tends to appear when the holy name of God causes the speaker or hearer to pause, or when a great blessing or disaster stirs up a person to call upon the Lord. It may be as simple as בָּרוּךְ יהוה (LXX: εὐλογητὸς κύριος, "blessed [be] the Lord," Ps 28:6 [LXX 27:6]).[96] More relevant to Ephesians, however, are the frequent examples that include the eternity formula, such as the following:

εὐλογητὸς κύριος εἰς τὸν αἰῶνα. γένοιτο γένοιτο.

Blessed [be] the Lord into the age. Amen. Amen. (LXX Ps 88:53 [MT 89:53; ET 89:52])

---

[93] See 1 Chr 29:11–13 (which forms the basis of the doxology added to the Lord's Prayer in the early church; see the variant reading appended to Mt 6:13); 1 Esdras 4:59; 4 Macc 18:24; Manasseh 15; cf. *Didache*, 9:2.

[94] E.g., 1 Chr 16:28–29; Pss 29:1–2 (LXX 28:1–2); 66:2 (LXX 65:2); 68:35 (ET 68:34; LXX 67:35); 96:7–8 (LXX 95:7–8).

[95] Lk 17:18; Jn 9:24; Acts 12:23; Rom 4:20; Rev 4:9; 11:13; 14:7; 16:9; 19:7.

[96] Cf. Gen 9:26; Ps 31:22 (ET 31:21; LXX 30:22); the formula occurs thirty times in the LXX; cf. Lk 1:68.

This type of *Berakah* doxology appears at the close of each of the first four books of the Psalter.[97]

The apostle Paul uses all three of the above patterns in his writings. He does not invent his own worship, but receives and joins in the way his people were given to glorify God. His piety leads him to acclaim God's glory, might, and wisdom in response to the same stimuli that would evoke awe and doxological interjection in any of the faithful.

Aside from the prompting of faith itself (!), what *rhetorical* function might these doxologies have played in the movement of Paul's epistles? The pursuit of this vital question will inform the role the present doxology (3:20–21) plays in the structure of Ephesians. The following is a summary of the various doxological interjections found in Paul's writings:

Rom 1:25	παρὰ τὸν κτίσαντα, ὅς ἐστιν εὐλογητὸς εἰς τοὺς αἰῶνας, ἀμήν. "rather than the Creator, who is blessed into the ages. Amen."	The pious response to the abhorrent thought of idolatry. Paul continues his thought afterward.
Rom 9:5	ὁ Χριστὸς ... ὁ ὢν ἐπὶ πάντων θεὸς εὐλογητὸς εἰς τοὺς αἰῶνας, ἀμήν. "Christ ... , who is God over all, be blessed into the ages. Amen."	A pious response to the gifts of God and the name of Christ. Paul's thought then continues unabated.
Rom 11:36	ὅτι ἐξ αὐτοῦ καὶ δι' αὐτοῦ καὶ εἰς αὐτὸν τὰ πάντα· αὐτῷ ἡ δόξα εἰς τοὺς αἰῶνας, ἀμήν. "For from him and through him and to him are all things; to him be the glory into the ages. Amen."	Conclusion to the Jew-Gentile discussion (Romans 9–11). Response to God's mysterious ways.
Rom 16:25–27	τῷ δὲ δυναμένῳ ... μόνῳ σοφῷ θεῷ, διὰ Ἰησοῦ Χριστοῦ, ᾧ ἡ δόξα εἰς τοὺς αἰῶνας, ἀμήν. "Now to the One who is able ... , to the only wise God, through Jesus Christ, to whom be the glory into the ages. Amen."	Lengthy doxological conclusion to the epistle. Its location shifts in the manuscripts to the end of chapter 14, 15, or 16.

[97] Pss 41:14 (ET 41:13; LXX 40:14); 72:18–19 (LXX 71:18–19); 89:53 (ET 89:52; LXX 88:53); 106:48 (LXX 105:48).

2 Cor 1:3	εὐλογητὸς ὁ θεὸς καὶ πατὴρ τοῦ κυρίου ἡμῶν Ἰησοῦ Χριστοῦ, ... "Blessed be the God and Father of our Lord Jesus Christ, ..."	Beginning of a *Berakah* prayer; parallel to Eph 1:3.
2 Cor 11:31	ὁ θεὸς καὶ πατὴρ τοῦ κυρίου Ἰησοῦ οἶδεν, ὁ ὢν εὐλογητὸς εἰς τοὺς αἰῶνας, ὅτι οὐ ψεύδομαι. "The God and Father of the Lord Jesus knows—who is blessed into the ages—that I do not lie."	Prompted by the holy name and used to strengthen an oath formula.
Gal 1:4–5	κατὰ τὸ θέλημα τοῦ θεοῦ καὶ πατρὸς ἡμῶν, ᾧ ἡ δόξα εἰς τοὺς αἰῶνας τῶν αἰώνων, ἀμήν. "according to the will of our God and Father, to whom be the glory into the ages of the ages. Amen."	At the conclusion of the epistolary exordium. A response to the name of God and the mystery of the Gospel.
Phil 4:20	τῷ δὲ θεῷ καὶ πατρὶ ἡμῶν ἡ δόξα εἰς τοὺς αἰῶνας τῶν αἰώνων, ἀμήν. "Now to our God and Father be the glory into the ages of the ages. Amen."	Conclusion of prayer (Phil 4:19) and close of the epistle.
1 Tim 1:17	τῷ δὲ βασιλεῖ τῶν αἰώνων, ἀφθάρτῳ ἀοράτῳ μόνῳ θεῷ, τιμὴ καὶ δόξα εἰς τοὺς αἰῶνας τῶν αἰώνων, ἀμήν. "And to the King of ages, immortal, invisible, the only God, be honor and glory into the ages of the ages. Amen."	At the conclusion of the epistolary exordium (thanksgiving). Response to the extraordinary grace given to Paul, the sinner.
1 Tim 6:16	ᾧ τιμὴ καὶ κράτος αἰώνιον, ἀμήν. "to whom be honor and eternal might. Amen."	Conclusion of a hymn and the letter.
2 Tim 4:18	ᾧ ἡ δόξα εἰς τοὺς αἰῶνας τῶν αἰώνων, ἀμήν. "to whom be the glory into the ages of the ages. Amen."	Response to the Lord's rescue of Paul. Conclusion of the epistle.

419

From these examples we can summarize Paul's use of doxologies:

1. "Blessed" (εὐλογητός) formulae (brief *Berakah* prayers) occur in response to the holy name of God or in horror against great evil. Afterwards Paul returns to what he was saying (Rom 1:25; 9:5; 2 Cor 11:31).

2. Full *Berakah* ("blessed …") prayers occur in the opening section of two epistles (2 Cor 1:3; Eph 1:3).

3. Brief doxologies occur in response to the revelation and contemplation of a great mystery or a great rescue (Rom 11:36; Gal 1:4–5; 1 Tim 1:17; 2 Tim 4:18).

4. Doxologies occur at the end of prayers, particularly in the thanksgiving section near the beginning of epistles (Gal 1:4–5; Phil 4:20; 1 Tim 1:17).

5. Doxologies may conclude a section of a letter (Rom 11:36) or the letter as a whole (Rom 16:25–27; Phil 4:20; 1 Tim 6:16; 2 Tim 4:18).[98]

Which of these features is relevant to Eph 3:20–21? There are elements of the third through fifth. The doxology is a natural way to end the prayer that began in 3:14. In this respect it forms a counterpart to the *Berakah* wording ("blessed …") that began the great opening prayer (1:3–14). More significant, however, is the relationship of doxologies to the revelation of a great mystery or divine rescue, both of which characterize the three preceding pericopes of Ephesians (2:1–10; 2:11–22; 3:1–13). The doxology, therefore, serves the same function as the brief or fuller *Berakah* pattern of prayer, uttered in response to great acts of God. Paul himself expresses this relationship with the words "for this reason" (3:1, 14).

This examination, however, has uncovered little evidence to support the widespread belief that the doxology marks a major break in the letter, a division of the letter into supposed "doctrinal" and "ethical" halves. Certainly it marks the close of a unit, as Rom 11:36 marks the close of Romans 9–11. That parallel is instructive, however, for the contention that Romans can be neatly divided into doctrinal (1:18–11:36) and ethical (12:1–15:33) halves is likewise open to profound objection. Rhetorical analysis suggests there are at least four major sections in Romans.[99] The doxology at the end of chapter 11 is a response to the great mystery into which Paul has delved and is the conclusion to chapters 9–11, but it does not mark the close of the first "half" of the letter. Although Rom 8:38–39 is not structurally a doxology, it provides an equivalent doxological conclusion to the preceding section (probably Romans 5–8), and Rom 15:33 provides a benedictory close to the succeeding one (Romans 12–15). Thus, while the doxological prayer in Eph 3:14–21 provides a satisfying conclusion

---

[98] We have confined our examination to Paul's writings. But the remaining doxologies in the NT do not contradict our findings: Heb 13:21; 1 Pet 4:11; 5:11; 2 Pet 3:18; Jude 24–25; Rev 1:6; 5:13–14; 7:12; 19:1–4. Cf. *1 Clement*, 20:12; 38:4; 58:2; *Martyrdom of Polycarp*, 20:2.

[99] Robert Jewett, "Following the Argument of Romans." Jewett divides the body of Romans into four proofs (Rom 1:18–4:25; 5:1–8:39; 9:1–11:36; 12:1–15:13) and argues (p. 269) that the formal argumentation does not cease at the end of chapter 11, but continues into the next section. Cf. Martin Franzmann, *Romans* (St. Louis: Concordia, 1968), who likewise divides the body into four parts.

to the discussion of the great mystery of the Gentile inclusion in Christ, there is no evidence to suggest that the letter has reached a rhetorical midpoint.[100] In fact, the "proofs" applying to the problem of Gentile-Jewish unity would appear to continue until the end of chapter 4 (see the rhetorical outline at the conclusion of "Structure and Rhetoric" in the introduction).

It should be no surprise that doxology is such a prominent feature of Ephesians, more so than any other Pauline letter, given its liturgical flavor and heavenly, mysterious themes. Essential to the meaning of δόξα, *doxa*, is "brilliance," the bright, shining "glory" of God. This is true of the Greek term not by etymology (δόξα comes from δοκέω, "to think"; doxology might thus express one's "opinion" of God), but because it is rooted in the OT usage of כָּבוֹד, "glory."[101] As brightness, δόξα is not something that Christians can render to God from their own resources. It is God's own δόξα, reflected back to him by those who stand in his presence.[102] This, first, resolves the conundrum of which verb to supply in the verbless doxologies: δόξα both "is" God's and may "be" given to God because it is his own glory reflected back to him by the hosts that surround him. In the OT, doxology is the *proprium* of the heavenly hosts, chiefly the angels, who dwell eternally in the presence of God (Is 6:3).[103] Heaven is therefore the proper place for doxology—or better put, the place for doxology is where God dwells and where he reveals himself. The prophets Isaiah (in the temple) and Ezekiel (in exile) were given a glimpse of that heavenly host and the doxology of the angels (Is 6:1–5; Ezek 1:1–28). On earth God revealed himself in part, but always hid his glory lest it consume those who could not bear his holiness (Ex 16:10; 24:15; 33:18–23). The temple was the appropriate place for the choirs to sing their doxology because God had caused his name to dwell there; yet he still veiled himself, appearing behind a cloud of smoke that protected his people from his consuming holiness by hiding himself from their sight, even from the high priest in the Holy of Holies (Lev 16:2, 13).

---

[100] Indeed, the division into "doctrinal" and "ethical" halves is not a rhetorical distinction at all, but the application of theological categories that are highly dependent on the bias of the interpreter. It is worth recalling the caution voiced by Markus Barth that was quoted in our introduction (in "Epistolary Outline" in "Structure and Rhetoric"):

> Indeed the juxtaposition of preaching and teaching (*kerygma* and *didache*), of indicative and imperative, may have had its day. Their undeniable usefulness as hermeneutical tools may be exhausted. … The sequence, God (or Christ) did *this* for you—now you do *that* for him, is a ridiculous caricature of the relationship between God's grace and the good works for which man is created, according to Eph 2:5–10. (*Ephesians*, 1:54–55)

[101] BDAG, s.v. δόξα, 1: "the condition of being bright or shining, *brightness, splendor, radiance* (a distinctive aspect of Hb. כָּבוֹד)."

[102] See John Kleinig, "The Mystery of Doxology," 131, who quotes Brunner, that doxology is "nothing but a reflection of God's glory" (Peter Brunner, *Worship in the Name of Jesus* [trans. M. H. Bertram; St. Louis: Concordia, 1968], 210). This section is heavily dependent on Kleinig.

[103] "Sons of God," often translated as "heavenly beings" (Job 1:6; 2:1; 38:7; Ps 29:1 [LXX 28:1]).

But the OT looked to a future when the Lord would appear in all his glory. God told Moses that the whole earth would be filled with his glory (Num 14:21). The psalmists prayed for the day when the Lord's glory would cover the earth like the transit of the sun.[104] These prophecies coalesced particularly in Isaiah, who foretold the day when all Jerusalem would be the Lord's temple and all nations would stream there to see the Lord revealed in his glory.[105] John Kleinig comments on the transition that took place between the Testaments:

> As soon as we come to the New Testament, we notice a shift in the location of doxology and in those who performed it. It is still axiomatic that doxology could only be performed where the Lord was present in his glory. …

> [But] with the incarnation of God's Son, the place for doxology changes. God's glory is now revealed in the face of Christ (2 Cor 4:6; cf. John 17:5).[106]

Thus, at the birth of Christ, the angels come to earth to sing their glory before him (Lk 2:14). This Child is the place where God's glory now tabernacles with his people (Jn 1:14); Christ's body is the Lord's temple (Jn 2:21; 12:41). In his earthly ministry, Christ was glorified by all who heard his teaching and saw his miracles (e.g., Lk 4:15; 5:25; 7:16; 18:43). Seeing the glory of God in Christ, we are transformed into God's likeness, reflecting his glory (Jn 17:22; 2 Cor 3:18; 2 Thess 2:14). It is Christ who gives us access to the full glory of God and who enables our doxology (Rom 5:2; 1 Pet 5:10). The doxologies of the NT therefore connect the glorification of the Father on earth with his Son, Jesus Christ, as in Eph 3:20–21 (cf. Phil 4:19–20; Jude 25).

Paul began his prayer with the claim that he had dropped to his knees "to the Father" (Eph 3:14)—implying not just vague acknowledgement that God is out there somewhere, but that Paul was in his very presence. This confidence was possible for Paul only because he believed Christ had opened access to God through his atoning work (2:18; 3:12). The context of Paul's prayer is thus the liturgical presence of God, as his people gather around the Christ who promised to be in the midst of those who call on his name (Mt 18:20). Where Christ is present, the glory of the Lord shines and is shone back to God in doxology by those who sing his praises. This is the fundamental explanation of why Paul's letters are filled with doxology to God. Giving glory to God is the goal that has been achieved by Christ's work (1:6, 12, 14; see the commentary on 1:3–14). Because Christ has ascended to heaven and yet continues to be with his church on earth through his Word and Sacraments, by the continual work of the Holy Spirit, heaven and earth are united in the praise of God (1:10).

The ever-present "amen" that faith adds to the Trinitarian praise of God is likewise made possible only through the indwelling of Christ in our hearts.

---

[104] Pss 57:6, 12 (ET 57:5, 11); 72:19; 85:10 (ET 85:9); 86:9; 96:3; 97:6; 108:6 (ET 108:5); 138:4–5.

[105] Is 4:5 (cf. 2:2–4); 6:3; 24:23; 35:2; 40:5; 59:19; 60:1–2, 13; 62:2; 66:11, 18–23.

[106] Kleinig, "The Mystery of Doxology," 134.

Apart from Christ, there can be neither faith in God nor love for him. Apart from Christ, we cower in fear before God's judgment. But through the reconciliation the Son achieved with his Father, we can be confident of receiving good things from him. "For whatever promises of God [there are], in him [Christ] is the 'yes.' Therefore it is also through him that [we utter] our 'amen' to God's glory" (2 Cor 1:20). Luther's explanation of the amen says it best:

> This means that I should be certain that these petitions are pleasing to our Father in heaven, and are heard by Him; for He Himself has commanded us to pray in this way and has promised to hear us. Amen, amen means "yes, yes, it shall be so."[107]

---

[107] SC 3:21 (*LSB* 325).

Creedal Unity in the Spirit: One Lord, One Faith, One Baptism

Translation

4 ¹So I encourage you—I, the prisoner in the Lord—
to walk in a manner appropriate to the calling by which you were called,
²with all humility and meekness, with patience,
bearing with one another <u>in love</u>,
³being eager to hold fast the unity of the Spirit in the bond of peace:

⁴<u>one</u> body and <u>one</u> <u>Spirit</u>
—just as you were also called in the <u>one</u> hope of your calling—
⁵<u>one</u> <u>Lord</u>, <u>one</u> faith, <u>one</u> Baptism,
⁶<u>one</u> God and <u>Father</u> of all, who is over all and through all and in all.

⁷Now, to each one of us grace was given in accord with the measure of the gift of Christ.
⁸Therefore it says:
"When he ascended to the highest place he took captivity captive,
he gave gifts to men."
⁹Now, what does "he ascended" mean, if not that he also descended into the lower parts, the earth? ¹⁰The one who himself descended is also the one who ascended far above all the heavens, that he might fill all things.
¹¹And he himself gave the apostles and the prophets and the evangelists and pastors and teachers,
¹²for bringing the saints to completion, for the work of the ministry, for building up the body of Christ,
¹³until we all should attain to the unity of the faith and of the knowledge of the Son of God, to the complete man, to the measure of the maturity of the fullness of Christ,
¹⁴that we might no longer be infants, so as to be tossed to and fro by waves and carried about by every wind of doctrine, in the trickery of men, in craftiness in accordance with deceitful scheming which leads into error,
¹⁵but, being truthful <u>in love</u>, that we might grow up in all things into him, who is the Head, Christ,
¹⁶from whom the whole body, being jointed together and knit together through every ligament supplied, in accord with [his] activity in apportioning each single part, grows bodily toward the building up of itself <u>in love</u>.

Textual Notes

4:1 παρακαλῶ οὖν ὑμᾶς—The commentary on 3:14–21 and 4:1–16 discusses in detail (and rejects) the assertion that Ephesians is neatly divided at this point into doctrinal (chapters 1–3) and ethical (chapters 4–6) halves. Certainly the clause παρακαλῶ οὖν ὑμᾶς cannot alone bear the weight of this crass division, even if it be translated as "therefore, I exhort you." It would need to be demonstrated that exhortation language dominated the second half of the book; as παρακαλέω occurs only once more in Ephesians (in 6:22, with the sense of "comfort, encourage"), this is clearly not the case. Nor does the vocabulary consistently demonstrate such a division in other Pauline epistles.[1] Neither does οὖν, "therefore, so," itself indicate a major division, as similar inferential particles and phrases (οὖν, διό, διὰ τοῦτο, τούτου χάριν) appear at the beginning of nearly every pericope.[2]

BDAG identifies five distinct meanings of παρακαλέω in the NT: (1) "call to one's side" (literal); (2) "urge, exhort"; (3) "request, implore, entreat"; (4) "comfort, encourage"; (5) "invite in, conciliate, be friendly to." The first and last are not relevant to our passage. In the OT canonical books of the LXX, meaning 4 predominates overwhelmingly. παρακαλέω is the comfort offered to mourners, and, more significantly, God's gracious consolation shown to his people in their suffering and distress. The latter is particularly frequent in Psalms (where παρακαλέω occurs twelve times) and Isaiah (twenty-eight times) and is prominent in messianic prophecies concerning God's future comforting of his people.[3] The verb is exceptionally common in the Maccabean literature (thirty-five times), where the second meaning predominates, as the Jews are exhorted to stand firm in the true faith against their Hellenistic oppressors—though the sense of God's comfort remains.[4]

In the NT it is often difficult to discern which of meanings 2–4 is appropriate to a given passage. Exegetes of the Pauline epistles are often heavily influenced by Hellenistic epistolary traditions, in which παρακαλῶ may mark a letter of "entreaty" (a request for a favor) or serve as a semi-technical term for philosophic moral exhortation.[5] This pushes them toward meaning 2. But it is wiser to look to OT and NT usage within the Christian faith than to interpret Paul according to the moral philosophers. Biblical usage of the cognate noun παράκλησις is enlightening. It often comes very close to meaning "preaching" (1 Cor 14:3; 1 Tim 4:13), as in the expression λόγος παρακλήσεως, "word of encouragement," that describes a sermon based on Scripture in the synagogue (Acts 13:15). The same phrase (but articular) is applied to the entire

---

[1] The terminology παρακαλέω, "exhort," and παράκλησις, "exhortation," is not confined to the latter half of Paul's other epistles, but (with the exception of Romans) the terms are found scattered throughout. The exact expression παρακαλῶ οὖν ὑμᾶς occurs also in Rom 12:1 and 1 Cor 4:16—quite different locations within each epistle's structure. The same is true for similar expressions: παρακαλῶ δὲ ὑμᾶς (Rom 15:30; 16:17; 1 Cor 1:10; 16:15); παρακαλοῦμεν δὲ ὑμᾶς (1 Thess 4:10; 5:14); διὸ παρακαλῶ ὑμᾶς (2 Cor 2:8); παρακαλῶ οὖν (1 Tim 2:1); παρακαλῶ (Phil 4:2; Philemon 10); and παρακαλοῦμεν (2 Cor 6:1). See Grothe, *The Justification of the Ungodly*, 615.

[2] See, e.g., διὰ τοῦτο in 1:15; διό in 2:11; and τούτου χάριν in 3:1.

[3] E.g., LXX Gen 24:67; Ex 15:13; Deut 3:28; 2 Kgdms 12:24 (MT/ET 2 Sam 12:24); Job 2:11; Pss 22:4 (MT/ET 23:4); 118:76 (MT/ET 119:76); Is 22:4; 40:1–2, 11; 49:13; 51:3; 61:2; 66:13; Lam 1:2; Zech 10:2; cf. Sirach 17:24.

[4] E.g., "and he exhorted/encouraged his men not to fear the attack of the Gentiles, but to keep in mind the former times when help had come to them from heaven, and now to look for the victory which the Almighty would give them" (2 Macc 15:8). Cf. 2 Macc 6:12; 9:26.

[5] See Stowers, *Letter Writing*, 24.

letter to the Hebrews (Heb 13:22; cf. Acts 15:31; 1 Macc 10:24).[6] παράκλησις is the "comfort" of the Holy Spirit (Acts 9:31), whose name is παράκλητος, "Comforter" or "Preacher" (Jn 14:16, 26; 15:26; 16:7). παράκλησις is God's gift in the messianic age (Lk 2:25), is rooted in the Scriptures, and leads to hope and unity (Rom 15:4–5). Paul shares the OT idea that παράκλησις as "comfort" is one of God's chief gifts, found ultimately in Christ (2 Cor 1:3–7; 2 Thess 2:16).

The verb παρακαλέω, likewise, can simply refer to the act of "preaching" (Lk 3:18; Acts 2:40; 15:32), the content of the message influencing the term used for the act. How one understands the Christian message will therefore influence one's interpretation of this fact: translations that more often render the verb as "exhort, urge, appeal" (rather than "comfort") often stem from Calvinist circles in which Karl Barth's sequence "Gospel-Law" has triumphed, but the Lutheran view that Christian preaching is Gospel preaching, that the Law is a pedagogue in service of the Gospel (Gal 3:24–25), finds more support in St. Paul. As an apostle whom Christ himself appointed and equipped for office, Paul first received God's "comfort" that he might give it to God's people.[7] This pattern is clearest in 2 Corinthians, which is dominated by παρακαλέω and παράκλησις vocabulary. Its opening *Berakah* ("blessed …") sets out the theology:

> Blessed be the God and Father of our Lord Jesus Christ, the Father of mercies and God of all *comfort* [παρακλήσεως], who *comforts* [παρακαλῶν] us in all our tribulation, so that we might be able *to comfort* [παρακαλεῖν] those who are in any tribulation, through the *comfort* [παρακλήσεως] with which we ourselves *are comforted* [παρακαλούμεθα] by God. (2 Cor 1:3–4)

Paul identifies this comfort and reconciliation from God as the central message of his ambassadorial, apostolic office (2 Cor 5:20–21).[8]

In Eph 4:1–3 παρακαλέω with its supplementary infinitives and participles should not, then, be understood in the Hellenistic sense of exhortation to change one's behavior through the application of philosophical principles. In Christian terms, παρακαλέω does not indicate a wholesale shift from Gospel to Law. Paul's οὖν, "therefore, so," roots his words of encouragement in the Gospel he has so thoroughly proclaimed in chapters 1–3—not as if the Christians' action is generated in response to "motivation" (in the popular sense), but rather by showing the gracious effects that the Gospel itself works.[9] For this reason, the translation "encourage" better captures the "comfort" Paul

---

[6] See Winger, "Orality as the Key to Understanding Apostolic Proclamation in the Epistles," 264–66.

[7] 2 Cor 1:3–7; 7:6–7, 13; 1 Thess 3:2, 7; 4:18; 1 Tim 5:1; 6:2; 2 Tim 4:2; Titus 1:9; 2:6, 15. In each case the verb παρακαλέω or the noun παράκλησις can be translated as "comfort," whereas in some of these verses English translations commonly render them as "exhort/ exhortation."

[8] See the analysis of the παρακαλῶ οὖν ὑμᾶς formula in Grothe, *The Justification of the Ungodly*, 615–16.

[9] See Grothe, *The Justification of the Ungodly*, 617. In popular usage, "Gospel motivation" may mean to exhort Christians to produce their own response to the Gospel message. But the Latin verbal root of "motivation," *movere,* is transitive; thus "Gospel motivation" should mean that the Gospel itself moves the Christian through its own power.

offers with this verb, rather than the Law-oriented translation "exhort."[10] The related question of whether περιπατῆσαι, "to walk," refers exclusively to behavior or includes faith and a life under the beneficence of God must also be taken into account (see the third textual note on 4:1).

ἐγὼ ὁ δέσμιος ἐν κυρίῳ—See the second textual note and the commentary on 3:1. The pronoun ἐγώ is probably not emphatic but simply serves to introduce its predicate ὁ δέσμιος, "I, the prisoner."[11] The noun δέσμιος, *desmios,* "prisoner," is introduced again (as in 3:1), here with a view to a play on words with τῷ συνδέσμῳ τῆς εἰρήνης, "the *bond [syn-desmos]* of peace" (4:3).[12] As Paul is bound both literally and figuratively (in prison and to the Lord, as his bondservant), so the Ephesians (all the baptized) are bound to one another in the Spirit by the common Gospel. Paul's imprisonment[13] thus serves his message: we are not free to choose which consequences of the Gospel we would like for our lives. Paul unfolds what has been given to the baptized and encourages them to see how the Lord by his Spirit has overcome all divisions between them and set them on a new and common path. Like "in Christ" (see the fifth textual note on 1:3), and "of Christ" (3:1), the phrase "in the Lord" (4:1) marks the new, Gospel perspective that has come to bear on Paul's suffering and all aspects of this life (cf. Eph 2:21; 6:1; Col 3:18).

ἀξίως περιπατῆσαι τῆς κλήσεως ἧς ἐκλήθητε—"To walk" (הָלַךְ; LXX: περιπατέω) is an OT image for the life of faith lived under the guiding wisdom of God's Word (see the first textual note on 2:2 and the commentary on 2:10). This verb (4:1, 17; 5:2, 8, 15) frames this (4:1–16) and the following two pericopes (4:17–5:2; 5:3–14), which contrast the result brought by the Gospel with the old, pagan life. It should not be translated as "behave" or "lead a life" (RSV), glosses that shift the balance from faith to works. There are both Law and Gospel components to the image. To walk in God's Word (cf., e.g., Gen 12:4; Josh 22:5; Ps 119:1; Is 2:3) is both to trust him and to examine one's deeds in light of his normative revelation.

---

[10] Heinrich Schlier's sober reassessment of the term in Paul's writing has mostly been ignored by later commentaries:

> παρακαλεῖν is quite inadequately rendered as "exhort [*ermahnen*]." This is much more characteristic of παρακαλεῖν: (1) that it has within it the meaning of urgent and caring encouragement [*Zuspruch*] to the brothers, which embraces request or admonition, or comfort, and seen more deeply can embrace all of these in one, an imploring request [*beschwörenden Anspruch*]. ... (2) that this encouragement and request, as the appeal of fatherly, apostolic love, is on principle to be distinguished from the demand of the Law. ... (3) that it is an appeal [*Anweisung*] from the mercy of Christ. ... (*Epheser,* 178–79; the ellipses stand in place of lengthy scriptural references that support his interpretation)

[11] Turner, *Syntax,* 37.

[12] "Again he uses the metaphor of bonding. We have left it behind, and now it comes running back to us. Beautiful was Paul's bond; beautiful too is this [bond of peace among Christians], and the former arises from the latter" (Chrysostom, *Homilies on Ephesians,* 9:4.1–3, ACCS 8:159).

[13] See "Paul's Trip to Jerusalem, Arrest, and Imprisonment (Acts 21:1–36)" in "The City of Ephesus and Paul's Relationship to It" in the introduction.

The adverb ἀξίως is derived from the adjective ἄξιος, often translated as "worthy," which implies great value or merit. Yet the adjective can also mean "correspondingly fitting or appropriate" (BDAG, 2), and it is that meaning which applies to the adverb here. Paul does not mean to imply that the Ephesians' walk can merit or equal the worth of God's calling; rather, he encourages them to walk "in accord with, in a manner appropriate to" their calling.[14] As ἀξίως is an adverb modifying the verb περιπατῆσαι, "walk," and at the same time is completed by the genitive of comparison τῆς κλήσεως, "of the calling," good grammar in English translation is difficult to achieve: literally, "to walk suitably of," or more idiomatically, "to walk in a manner appropriate to your calling."

The adverb recurs in a remarkable parallel, influenced by the distinctive Philippian theme of "citizenship": "only be a citizen [πολιτεύεσθε] *appropriate to* [ἀξίως] the Gospel of Christ, that, whether I come and see you or remain away, I hear about you that you stand in the one Spirit, with one mind striving together for the faith of the Gospel" (Phil 1:27; cf. 1 Thess 2:12). The Colossian parallel to Eph 4:1 includes Paul's prayer that the Colossians would περιπατῆσαι ἀξίως τοῦ κυρίου, "walk in a manner appropriate to the Lord," which includes "bearing fruit in every good work and growing in the knowledge of God" (Col 1:10), faith and works together. As prayer (not exhortation) Paul's words imply that these things are not within man's capacity, but are God's gifts.

The redundant phrase here, τῆς κλήσεως ἧς ἐκλήθητε, "the calling by which you were called," is a Hebraism (verb with cognate accusative noun, but the noun κλήσεως has been made genitive by the comparison using ἀξίως). The passive verb ἐκλήθητε is divine: God is the one who calls (1:18). The NT knows of only two callings: the call to the apostolic office[15] and the call to faith in Christ,[16] which Paul connects to Baptism (1:18; 4:4–5). Luther's idea of vocation (that God calls everyone to God-pleasing jobs and roles in life) is consistent with NT thought, but is never expressed with the vocabulary of καλέω, "call." The Christian's calling is not normally a call to *do* something, but to *be* someone.[17] Thus, Paul encourages the Ephesians to walk in accord with who they are now. God has called each one of them equally, without regard to their merit or

---

[14] BDF, § 337 (1), is surely wrong when it analyzes περιπατῆσαι as an ingressive aorist, as if the Ephesians had not previously been walking in accord with their calling. The aorist should rather be regarded as marking "uncolored" action, with no particular emphasis on beginning or continuing.

[15] Mt 4:21; Lk 6:13; Rom 1:1; 1 Cor 1:1; and passim; (Gal 1:15).

[16] Mt 9:13; Rom 8:30; 9:24; 1 Cor 1:9; 7:17–22; (Gal 1:15); 1 Thess 2:12; 2 Thess 2:14; 1 Tim 6:12; Heb 11:8; 1 Pet 2:9; 5:10; Rev 13:10.

[17] "It is a call to be justified (Rom. 8:30), a call into His kingdom (I Thess. 2:12), a call to be God's people (Rom. 9:25), to be His children (I Jn. 3:1), to be in fellowship with Christ (I Cor. 1:9) and God (Jam. 2:23), to be saved out of this world (II Thess. 2:13–14; I Pet. 2:9), a call to eternal life (I Tim. 6:12; Heb. 9:15; I Pet. 5:10), to the marriage supper of the Lamb (Mt. 22:1–14; Rev. 19:9), and to receive God's blessing (I Pet. 3:9); it is a call to repentance (Lk. 5:32) and to faith (Heb. 11:8; Rev. 13:10). Indeed, what all these aspects of God's call have in common is their emphasis on God's work and God's giving, rather than on man's work. It is difficult to find any passage in the New Testament in which the Christian is 'called' to do anything. The Christian calling is primarily a gift not an obligation" (Commission on Theology and Church Relations of Lutheran Church–Canada, *Pastor and People Together in Christ's Church* [2008], 10).

worthiness, race or origin, social status or wealth. This leads to a humble acknowledgement of their unity in the one Spirit, whose calling Paul is about to elaborate.

4:2 μετὰ πάσης ταπεινοφροσύνης καὶ πραΰτητος—The noun ταπεινοφροσύνη, "humility, modesty," is part of a large word group in the NT that describes the "lowliness of mind" appropriate to one who receives salvation as a pure gift. Its opposite is ὑψηλὰ φρονεῖν, "to think high things [of oneself]" (Rom 11:20; 12:16). It is often noted that humility (as "servility") was despised among Greeks, but valued by Jews.[18] However, the humility of which Paul speaks is not a precondition, a quality to be produced in those seeking God's favor; rather, it is the only appropriate evaluation of oneself in the face of God's gracious, saving deeds that are received apart from human works. Therefore ταπεινοφροσύνη, "humility," marked Paul's composure during his ministry among the Ephesians (Acts 20:19). He describes it as a self-deprecating attitude that places a greater value on others than oneself and so is vital for Christian concord (Phil 2:3).[19] Like all such godly qualities, it must be a gift of God and, ironically, can lead to arrogance if it is pursued on one's own strength, as in the self-abasing, ascetic false religion that plagued the Colossians (thus, ESV renders ταπεινοφροσύνη in Col 2:18, 23 as "asceticism"). As divine clothing, "humility" is a gift of Holy Baptism (ταπεινοφροσύνη, Col 3:12); thus, it is a quality of Christ himself (ταπείνωσις, "humility," LXX Is 53:8; ταπεινός, "humble," Mt 11:29; ἐταπείνωσεν ἑαυτόν, "humbled himself," Phil 2:8) that is placed over the arrogance of the old man (1 Pet 5:5). The humble are readied for the exaltation brought by Christ (ταπεινοί, Lk 1:52; 2 Cor 7:6; ταπεινόω, Mt 23:12; 2 Cor 11:7).

The next noun, πραΰτης, "gentleness, considerateness, meekness," is a near synonym (cf. Mt 11:29) and may have been chosen by Paul here for its alliterative value (each of its consonants was in ταπεινοφροσύνης). Together with faithfulness, it characterized the Christlike figure of Moses (Sirach 45:4) and those poor subjects whom the messianic king defends (LXX Ps 44:5 [MT 45:5; ET 45:4]). As "meek" characterizes Christ (πραΰς, Mt 11:29), so "meekness" typifies Paul's ministry as a representative of Christ (πραΰτης, 1 Cor 4:21; 2 Cor 10:1) and the ministry of the Lord's servant (2 Tim 2:25). It is a gift of the Spirit to (and fruit of the Spirit in) the baptized (πραΰτης, Gal 5:23; 6:1; Col 3:12). The common thread in both "humility" and "meekness" is the Spirit-wrought gift of Christlike humility. Like the unity of the Spirit, these God-given attitudes[20] are not so much sought out as clung to.

μετὰ μακροθυμίας—The noun μακροθυμία denotes a quality of "patience," whether endurance in suffering (Col 1:11, with μακροθυμία parallel to ὑπομονή; James 5:10, μακροθυμία ‖ κακοπάθεια) or forbearance of the weaknesses of other people. It,

---

18 Walter Grundmann, "ταπεινός," *TDNT* 8:2–4, 11; Epictetus, 3:24.56.

19 Words from the root ταπειν- dominate *1 Clement* (twenty-nine times), in which bishop Clement appeals for humility in his attempt to restore concord in the Roman church that had fallen into strife between pastors and people.

20 "Gentleness and humility and meekness [ἐπιείκεια καὶ ταπεινοφροσύνη καὶ πραΰτης] are with those who are blessed by God" (*1 Clement*, 30:8 [trans. Kirsopp Lake, LCL]).

too, is a quality of God himself, particularly his patience with sinful humanity,[21] and is his gift to his broken people (LXX Is 57:15; Gal 5:22). It marks Paul's apostolic ministry (2 Cor 6:6; 2 Tim 3:10) and is to characterize Timothy's pastoral work (2 Tim 4:2). In fact, Paul saw Christ's "complete patience" (τὴν ἅπασαν μακροθυμίαν) toward him, the great sinner, as the perfect ὑποτύπωσις, "pattern," to which all believers are being conformed (1 Tim 1:16). The three terms in Eph 4:2, ταπεινοφροσύνη and πραΰτης (in the preceding textual note) and μακροθυμία (here), stand with "heart(s) of compassion" (σπλάγχνα οἰκτιρμοῦ) and "kindness" (χρηστότητα) in the Colossian parallel, where they are framed in baptismal language, as qualities that are "put on" (Col 3:12; cf. Gal 3:27). Then the same phrase follows in Col 3:13 as here in Eph 4:2, "bearing with one another" (see the next textual note), after which Paul encourages the Colossians to forgive one another as God has first forgiven them. Thus, μακροθυμία, "patience," is a divine quality which does not condemn sinful weakness in others, but endures it patiently in the hope of forgiving reconciliation. It is not simply human optimism or Stoicism in the face of matters one cannot change, but an aspect of faith in God which commits all things into his hands (Heb 6:12, μακροθυμία ‖ πίστις).

ἀνεχόμενοι ἀλλήλων ἐν ἀγάπῃ—The participle ἀνεχόμενοι (middle deponent of ἀνέχω) is the verbal equivalent of μακροθυμία, meaning "to endure, bear with, put up with" (plus an objective genitive ἀλλήλων, "one another"). The verb ἀνέχω, too, is used to convey a quality of Christ (Mt 17:17) and his apostles (1 Cor 4:12). In the face of suffering, it stands with "endurance" (ὑπομονή) and "faith" (πίστις) as an admirable quality in the Thessalonian Christians (2 Thess 1:4). This equivalent usage suggests the present clause stands in semantic parallel to the preceding prepositional phrase, "with patience," and offers further explanation of it. This is probably the strongest reason to take the phrase ἐν ἀγάπῃ, "in love," with this clause (rather than the next), for without it the participle ἀνεχόμενοι adds little to the preceding noun μακροθυμία, "patience."[22] "In love" (ἐν ἀγάπῃ) is a major feature of Ephesians (also 1:4; 3:17; 4:15–16; 5:2; cf. Col 2:2; 3:14). Love is the source and manner of the patience Christians show to one another; like forgiveness (Eph 4:32; Col 3:13), this love proceeds from Christ's love for us (Eph 5:2, 25).

Some interpreters argue that the participles ἀνεχόμενοι (4:2) and σπουδάζοντες (4:3) have imperatival force,[23] in effect, "Bear with one another! Be zealous!" Since they are in the nominative case (and thus appear to lack agreement with ὑμᾶς, "you"), the participles are interpreted as independent verbs equivalent to imperatives.[24] Proponents

---

[21] LXX Jer 15:15; Rom 2:4; 9:22; 1 Pet 3:20; 2 Pet 3:15.

[22] Cf. 1 Cor 13:4: ἡ ἀγάπη μακροθυμεῖ, "love is patient."

[23] E.g., Lincoln, *Ephesians*, 235; Best, *Ephesians*, 364. Barth, *Ephesians*, 2:427–28, argues that the verb παρακαλέω (4:1), which he translates as "I beseech," requires the participles to be understood imperatively.

[24] See the discussion in Turner, *Grammatical Insights*, 165–68. The grammars give qualified and nuanced support for interpreting a series of participles as imperatives when there is no main verb on which they might depend: BDF, § 468 (2); Moule, *Idiom Book*, 31, 105, 179; Turner, *Syntax*, 343. See the first textual note on 5:21 in the pericope consisting of 5:21–33. Wallace, *Greek Grammar*, 652, argues that the participles are in the nominative because of

of this interpretation also claim support from rabbinic examples,[25] but ultimately it seems to derive from a theological bias that wants to find moral exhortation in this passage. But where there is an obvious main verb on which the participles can be dependent, there is no sound reason to interpret them as independent imperatives. It is therefore better to interpret them as dependent on the infinitive περιπατῆσαι, "to walk" (4:1). They describe the manner in which the walk takes place. Paul's language is descriptive, not prescriptive. He encourages the Ephesians to walk in the very manner that the Gospel engenders in them.

4:3 σπουδάζοντες τηρεῖν τὴν ἑνότητα τοῦ πνεύματος—The verb σπουδάζω literally means "to hurry," but most commonly in the NT it has the figurative meaning of "being zealous, eager, or conscientious" to do something. When the Jerusalem apostles encouraged Paul to remember the poor, his report suggests he was already "eager" to do so (ἐσπούδασα, Gal 2:10). When attached to entry into God's rest, such eagerness must describe attitude more than effort,[26] else the Gospel would be nullified (σπουδάσωμεν, Heb 4:11; cf. σπουδάσατε, 2 Pet 1:10). Thus, it describes a joyful inner compulsion (1 Thess 2:17, from the heart) that responds naturally to the external Word.

The verb τηρέω, "to keep," describes not the attainment of a possession but the careful guarding of what one already has. One guards or keeps (τηρέω) good wine (Jn 2:10), Christ's Word (Jn 8:51–52; 14:23–24), God's Word (Jn 8:55; 17:6; 1 Jn 2:5; Rev 1:3; 22:7, 9), precious ointment (Jn 12:7), one's precious betrothed (1 Cor 7:37), and the faith (2 Tim 4:7). Our inheritance is "kept" for us in heaven (1 Pet 1:4), Jesus has "kept" his disciples safe (Jn 17:11–12, 15), and Paul prays God would "preserve" us till Christ's return (1 Thess 5:23; cf. 1 Jn 5:18; Jude 1). With respect to the gifts of God, which do not need our protection, the translations "treasure" or "hold fast" commend themselves for τηρέω. Although it may be translated as "observe, fulfill" when the object is God's Law (Mt 19:17; James 2:10), this translation should not be imposed on Gospel contexts.[27] Thus, the true unity of the Spirit is not a *goal* toward which the Ephesians aim, but a *gift* given for them to treasure, and the source of harmony with one another.

---

constructio ad sensum, "construction according to sense rather than according to strict grammar 'rules.'" Cf. Turner, *Syntax*, 230. Despite denying that the participles should be analyzed as independent imperatives, Wallace interprets them imperativally because he believes that is the sense of παρακαλῶ ... ὑμᾶς ... περιπατῆσαι, "I encourage you ... to walk" (4:1), which he makes equivalent to (ὑμεῖς) περιπατήσατε, "(you) walk!"

[25] Some have argued that the rabbis couched their injunctions with Hebrew/Aramaic participles to avoid trespassing on the divine prerogative of commanding. See the first textual note on 5:21 in the pericope consisting of 5:21–33.

[26] Contra Lincoln, *Ephesians*, 237, who translates the participle as "making every effort."

[27] In Mt 28:20, when Jesus mandates his apostles with respect to the nations with the words διδάσκοντες αὐτοὺς τηρεῖν πάντα ὅσα ἐνετειλάμην ὑμῖν, his ministry is restricted unnecessarily to the realm of the Law if they are translated as "teaching them *to obey* everything I have commanded you." Christ has come to deliver the gifts of God to his people, and his authorized representatives are sent to distribute them, "teaching them [all nations] *to treasure/hold fast* everything I have committed to you" (cf. Jn 14:15, 21; 15:10; 1 Tim 6:14; 1 Jn 2:3; 3:22, 24; 5:3; Rev 12:17; 14:12). See Winger, "The Office of the Holy Ministry according to the New Testament Mandate of Christ." For the range of possible meanings of ἐντέλλομαι, "to mandate, instruct authoritatively," and ἐντολή, "mandate, authoritative instruction" (traditionally

The treasure which has been placed into their care is ἑνότης, "oneness, unity," a noun that in the NT only occurs here and in 4:13 (τὴν ἑνότητα τῆς πίστεως, "the unity of the faith").[28] Oneness is thematic for Ephesians and will be treated intensively in the next three verses (4:4–6). The noun is prominent in the writings of Ignatius, particularly in his letter to the Ephesians.[29] As Paul will subsequently appeal to the role of the office of the ministry in maintaining Christian unity (4:7–16), so Ignatius stresses the unifying role of the bishop as representing the headship of Christ.[30] Similar to Paul, Ignatius appeals to faith and love as the beginning and end of divine unity.[31] As Paul locates the unity sacramentally in Holy Baptism (4:5), Ignatius finds it where the bishop, presbyters, and people are gathered around the Sacrament of the Altar.[32] These parallels tie the two letters closely together, confirming the destination of Paul's letter to the Ephesians[33] and reinforcing unity as the letter's theme.

The genitive τοῦ πνεύματος indicates both subject and contents: the unity is given by "the Spirit" and consists in the shared possession of "the Spirit."[34] The subsequent reference to the Spirit together with the other two persons of the Trinity (4:4–6) establishes the fact that this is the Holy Spirit, not a unity of human spirit. The one Spirit has accomplished this unity in Holy Baptism (1 Cor 12:13).

ἐν τῷ συνδέσμῳ τῆς εἰρήνης—The noun σύνδεσμος, "uniting bond," forms a wordplay with the noun ὁ δέσμιος, "the prisoner, bound one" (see the second textual note on 4:1). This noun is concentrated in Ephesians and Colossians,[35] where it describes a bond that is organic (ligaments in the body of Christ, Col 2:19) and consists of love (Col 3:14). In secular Greek σύνδεσμος is used metaphorically for what binds together the citizens of a state or city (e.g., law, customs, or loyalty),[36] or the chief virtue that unites all other virtues.[37]

"The bond of peace" (with an epexegetical genitive, "the bond" that consists of "peace") is a unique expression in biblical literature.[38] Ironically, "peace" normally results from *loosing* bonds, e.g., the release from prison that follows the end of a war

---

translated as "to command" and "commandment"), see the first textual note on 2:15 and " 'The Mystery of Christ' (3:3–7)" in the commentary on 3:1–13.

[28] It also appears in a variant reading in Col 3:14, σύνδεσμος τῆς ἑνότητος, "bond of unity" (D* F G it vg^mss; Ambst), a reading clearly dependent on Eph 4:3.

[29] Ignatius, *To the Ephesians*, 4:2; 5:1; 14:1; *To the Philadelphians*, 2:2; 3:2; 5:2; 9:1; *To the Smyrnaeans* 12:2; *To Polycarp*, 8:3.

[30] Ignatius, *To the Ephesians*, 4:1; 5:1.

[31] Ignatius, *To the Ephesians*, 14:1.

[32] See Ignatius, *To the Ephesians*, 20:2.

[33] See "Addressees" in the introduction.

[34] Wallace, *Greek Grammar*, 104–5, calls it a "genitive of production," i.e., "the unity produced by the Spirit."

[35] σύνδεσμος, "uniting bond," appears four times in the NT: in Acts 8:23 and in Eph 4:3; Col 2:19; 3:14.

[36] LSJM, s.v. σύνδεσμος, I 2.

[37] Barth, *Ephesians*, 2:429, cites the Pythagoreans.

[38] Cf. the "covenant of peace" in the Gospel promises of Is 54:10; Ezek 34:25; 37:26.

(3 Macc 6:27) or the declaration of the prisoner's innocence (Acts 16:36). But Christian freedom, while involving release from slavery to sin, death, and the devil,[39] entails becoming a bondservant of Christ and one another.[40] See the textual notes on 3:1 and 4:1 and the commentary on 3:1–13. Like so many other gifts of God that Paul highlights in this letter, the common possession of "peace" achieved by Christ on the cross can be appealed to as that which unites Gentiles and Jews together in the one body (2:13–18). It is part of the baptismal armor in which God clothes his soldiers (6:15). Thus, like unity, the peace that binds together is the peace that is given, not the peace the Ephesians might strive to achieve. Peace is especially connected with the work of the Holy Spirit, whose mind is "life and peace" (Rom 8:6; cf. Gal 5:22).

4:4–6   These three verses stand apart from their surroundings as poetry in the midst of prose; see "Structure and Rhetoric" in the commentary.

4:4   ἓν σῶμα καὶ ἓν πνεῦμα—We immediately stumble over the lack of verb in this opening line. This suggests the form of a hymnic refrain or acclamation, whether invented for the purpose by Paul or (more likely) quoted from a portion of the liturgy that would be familiar to the Ephesians. To get at its meaning in the form of a proposition, we might preface it with an indicative verb, "there is ... ," for "one body" is not a task or goal to be achieved, but an established reality in Christ.[41]

"One body and one Spirit" should be treated as a unit, as the one body is brought into being by the common possession and work of the one Holy Spirit. As man himself is composed of body and spirit, so the church is a living organism in which the body of Christ is quickened by the Spirit of Christ;[42] if one were to be severed from the other, the church would die.[43] This is a highly compressed version of 1 Cor 12:13, "for in one Spirit we all were baptized into one body [ἓν σῶμα], whether Jews or Greeks, whether slaves or free, and we all were given to drink of one Spirit [ἓν πνεῦμα]." That passage

---

[39]   Ps 146:7; Is 61:1; Lk 4:18; Eph 4:8.

[40]   Rom 13:8; 1 Cor 9:19; Gal 5:13; cf. Mk 10:43; 1 Pet 2:16.

[41]   With reference to the parallel text "we are one body in Christ" (Rom 12:5), C. E. B. Cranfield writes: "The words ἐν Χριστῷ here in v. 5 indicate that the unity of those whom Paul is addressing, unlike the unity of the various communities which ancient authors liken to a body, is a matter neither of nature nor of human contriving but of the grace of God. Whatever other unity the Christians in Rome may have had, the unity to which Paul is appealing is the unity which they have by virtue of what God has done for them in Christ" (*A Critical and Exegetical Commentary on the Epistle to the Romans* [2 vols.; Edinburgh: T&T Clark, 1975], 2:618). Unity in Christ is thus the *presupposition* of Paul's argument, not its goal. Cf. Grothe, *The Justification of the Ungodly*, 656–57.

[42]   See Rom 8:9; Gal 4:6; 1 Pet 1:11; "Christ, the Head—The Church, His Body (1:22–23)" in the commentary on 1:15–23; and "Trinitarian Praying (3:14–17)" in the commentary on 3:14–21.

[43]   The church consists of Christ, the Head, and believers, his body (1:22–23; 4:12, 15–16; 5:21–24, 30). Although the church as body is distinguished from the Head, it is clear that the image is meant to unite, not separate, the two. We are one with Christ; we are "in him." So also the Spirit of Christ is distinguishable from the church, but the church does not exist without him. Thus, AC 7 defines the church not merely as believers, but as believers gathered around the means of grace being given out, in which the Holy Spirit is active to create faith. The Spirit is fundamental to any definition of the church.

arose in a similar context of a congregation divided (more deeply than Ephesus), before whose eyes Paul held up the image of Christ's body as the source of unity (cf. Rom 12:4–5). In both 1 Corinthians 12 and Ephesians, a baptismal focus is explicit;[44] but "one body" can equally evoke the uniting gift of the Lord's Supper, in which the common reception of the Lord's sacramental body unites the mystical body of the church (1 Cor 10:17; 11:23–29).[45] It is in the nature of the Sacraments to make the Gospel concrete in a way that touches both soul and body.

Previously in Ephesians, one "body" has been an image for the unity of all Christians in the church under her "head," Jesus Christ (1:22–23), who united both Jew and Gentile in his "one body," crucified on the tree (2:16). The body metaphor will intensify in the next two chapters (4:12, 16; 5:23, 28, 30). "One Spirit," likewise, has featured earlier in Ephesians as a uniting element in the church (2:18), just as Paul appealed also to the Corinthians that the Spirit and his gifts should not divide but unite (1 Cor 6:17; 12:9, 13; cf. Phil 1:27).

καθὼς καὶ ἐκλήθητε ἐν μιᾷ ἐλπίδι τῆς κλήσεως ὑμῶν—If 4:4–6 is a hymnic refrain, this clause, which breaks the rhythm, appears to be a Pauline exposition of the first line (see the preceding textual note). Yet, it is not an unwelcome insertion. The inclusion of μιᾷ ἐλπίδι, "one hope," brings the repetitions of "one" in the hymn to seven, the number of divine completeness. Paul repeats the verb καλέω, "to call," with its cognate noun κλῆσις, "calling," as they appeared at the end of 4:1 (see the last textual note there). This repetition cannot be insignificant. The divine passive ἐκλήθητε, "you were called," hammers home the divine origin of the Christian church and her every member; they are what they are because God has called them to it (cf. 1:4, the primacy of God's eternal election). Not only have they all been called by the same Spirit and into the same body (cf. Col 3:15), but also the eschatological goal ("hope," Eph 4:4) of their calling is identical. Thus, their unity is not static, but involves walking together on a common pilgrimage. There is not one path and one eternal reward for the Jew and another for the Gentile (cf. Rom 9:24), but they are called ἐν μιᾷ ἐλπίδι, "in *one* hope" (Eph 4:4)—which is to say, called to the same hope, the same eternal bliss. Like "one faith" (4:5), this "one hope" is not the act of hoping (subjective), but the substance in which Christians unanimously put their hope (objective). See the third textual note on 1:18, "the hope [ἐλπίς] of his calling."

4:5 εἷς κύριος, μία πίστις, ἓν βάπτισμα—*Eph 4:5 is perhaps the central line of the entire epistle.* This lovely poetic line plays on the diverse genders of the three nouns in "one *Lord*, one *faith*, one *Baptism*": masculine, feminine, and neuter, which results in the declination of the numeral as εἷς ... μία ... ἕν. In light of the reverse Trinitarian structure of this three-line creedal hymn (see the commentary), κύριος, "Lord," should be understood as the second person of the Trinity, Jesus Christ. Whereas ὁ θεός, "God,"

---

[44] So also in Col 3:15, where "the peace of Christ" and "one body" flow from the baptismal language of "putting on" (3:10–12; cf. Gal 3:27; Eph 4:24; Col 2:12).

[45] Cf. Ignatius, *To the Philadelphians*, 4:1, where we find μιᾷ εὐχαριστίᾳ, "*one Eucharist*"; μία σάρξ, "*one flesh* of our Lord Jesus Christ"; and ἓν ποτήριον, "*one cup* for union with his blood."

is a common NT designation for the Father, in Pauline usage, at least, ὁ κύριος, "the Lord," usually refers to the Son.[46] This identification is made explicit in a text quite parallel to this: "but for us there is one God [εἷς θεός], the Father, from whom are all things and we for him, and one Lord [εἷς κύριος], Jesus Christ, through whom are all things and we through him" (1 Cor 8:6).

The Holy Spirit who called us moves us to acclaim Jesus as "the Lord"—which is to say, Adonai, YHWH, the only true God of the Old and New Testaments.[47] "No one is able to say, 'Jesus is the Lord,' except by the Holy Spirit" (οὐδεὶς δύναται εἰπεῖν· Κύριος Ἰησοῦς, εἰ μὴ ἐν πνεύματι ἁγίῳ, 1 Cor 12:3).[48] This confession was particularly poignant in the face of Roman imperial claims that Caesar was a divine κύριος; in refusing to make that confession, martyrs would shed their blood shortly after the apostolic era.[49] Only Jesus is truly Lord, despite claims to the contrary from earthly or spiritual powers (Eph 1:21).

The referent of πίστις, "faith," could be either subjective or objective faith, *fides quae creditur* ("the faith by which it is believed") or *fides qua creditur* ("the faith which is believed"). Since the other elements in this section are objective gifts that are received and held in common, it is probable that Paul means the latter here: not our act of believing,[50] but "the faith," the body of teaching concerning the work of Father, Son, and Holy Spirit for our salvation.[51] This is surely also its meaning short verses later,

---

46 Eph 1:2, 3, 17; 5:20; 6:23; cf. Rom 1:7; 15:6; 1 Cor 1:3; 8:6; 2 Cor 1:2, 3; 11:31; Gal 1:3; Phil 1:2; 2:11; Col 1:3; 3:17; 1 Thess 1:1, 3; 3:11, 13; 2 Thess 1:1, 2; 2:16; 1 Tim 1:2; 2 Tim 1:2; Philemon 3; 1 Pet 1:3.

47 This equation is well-known, but in brief: since at least the third century BC (just prior to the production of the LXX), pious Jews refrained from pronouncing the divine name written in the OT with the Tetragrammaton, יהוה (whose original vowels are unknown, but are commonly reconstructed as יַהְוֶה, "Yahweh," on the basis of proper names derived from God's name and Greek transcriptions; see BDB s.v. יהוה, sub הָיָה). This unfortunate custom was meant to protect God's name from defamation and therefore protect Israel from punishment. The Masoretic superimposition of the vowels of the noun אֲדֹנָי upon the consonants יהוה warned the reader to say *Adonai*, "the Lord" (although *BHS*, our present critical edition of the Hebrew Bible, based on codex L, often uses the vowels of the Aramaic שְׁמָא, "the name"). Thus, it is reasonable to assume that κύριος in the NT often means YHWH. See BDB, s.v. יהוה, sub הָיָה; Joüon, § 16 f (1); D. N. Freedman, "יהוה," *TDOT* 5:501; Otto Eissfeldt, "אָדוֹן," *TDOT* 1:72.

48 Cf. Rom 10:9; Phil 2:11.

49 In Acts 25:26 Festus calls Emperor Nero κύριος, though this in itself does not imply a claim to deity. Pliny the Younger, governor of Bithynia, wrote to Emperor Trajan that he had forced Christians to offer sacrifices to the emperor's image in order to demonstrate that they had given up the faith; those who refused to do so were executed (*Epistles*, 10:96–97; ca. AD 112). The most famous early martyr explicitly to reject the words "Caesar is Lord" was Polycarp († ca. AD 155).

50 Even if all Christians believe the same thing and place their trust in the same Christ, this common act of believing would not naturally be called "one faith." The oneness lies in *what* they are believing about the one in whom they believe. Contra Bruce, *The Epistles to the Colossians, to Philemon, and to the Ephesians*, 336, n. 16, who doubts that πίστις ever has the objective meaning in the NT aside from Jude 3, 20 (see also the next footnote).

51 The judgment as to whether πίστις be subjective or objective in a given NT passage is most challenging. BDAG, s.v. πίστις, 3, tentatively offers the following as objective: Rom 1:5; 12:6; Gal 1:23; 3:23–25; 1 Tim 1:19; 4:1, 6; 6:10, 21; 2 Tim 2:18; 4:7; Jude 3, 20. The earlier examples put to lie the frequent critical contention that the objective meaning of πίστις

"until we all should attain to the unity of *the faith* [εἰς τὴν ἑνότητα τῆς πίστεως] and of the knowledge of the Son of God" (4:13). Encapsulated in creedal statements of which this text itself is a prototype, "the faith" was intimately connected in the early church with Baptism, at which point the Creed was delivered catechetically and recited back by the baptizand.

The phrase ἓν βάπτισμα, "one Baptism," introduces the Sacrament by name for the first and only time in the letter. It is hardly fair to assert that Baptism is therefore of minor significance to the writer.[52] Baptism as a unifying factor is prominent in Paul (e.g., 1 Cor 12:13; Gal 3:26–28). The previous allusions to Baptism that have been amassing for three chapters in Ephesians now reach the surface and explode in this grand hymn.[53]

4:6 εἷς θεὸς καὶ πατὴρ πάντων, ὁ ἐπὶ πάντων καὶ διὰ πάντων καὶ ἐν πᾶσιν—In light of common NT usage, in which "God" means "Father" when placed in contrast to (Jesus) "the Lord" (see the textual note on 4:5), εἷς θεὸς καὶ πατὴρ describes not two divine persons, but one: "one God and Father" is God the Father.[54] For the various referents of God's Fatherhood, see the textual notes on 3:14–15. In a creedal framework, God is "Father" first with reference to his Son, Jesus Christ, within the Holy Trinity (1:3). He is, second, Father to all Christians who are born into his heavenly family through Holy Baptism (1:5),[55] which is analogous to Israel's belief that God was uniquely their Father.[56] But, third, by making all things, the one God is Father to all creation (Eph 3:9, 15). The fourfold, emphatic repetition of πᾶς, "all," in this verse suggests the third referent of God's Fatherhood is primarily in view here.

"Father of all" (πατὴρ πάντων) has a genitive of relationship, indicating that God holds the office of Father with respect to "all." Whether πάντων is masculine ("all men/people") or neuter ("all things") is not of decisive importance,[57] since "fatherhood" is mainly relevant to people who are capable of acknowledging it. But in view of the use of the neuter (τὰ) πάντα, "all things," elsewhere in Ephesians,[58] the neuter is more likely here. This is supported by 1 Cor 8:6:

---

is a mark of postapostolic, early Catholicism. BDAG's location of Eph 4:5 under 2 d α, "true piety, genuine devotion," is baffling. Parallel passages in Colossians (1:23; 2:7) surely also use πίστις in the objective sense (see also 1 Tim 3:9; 6:12).

[52] As Lincoln, *Ephesians*, lxxix, claims.

[53] See "Baptism and the Spirit" in "Purpose and Themes" in the introduction and the extended note on "The Seal of the Spirit (1:13; 4:30)" in the commentary on 1:3–14. Besides Eph 4:5, the noun βάπτισμα, "Baptism," occurs only once more in all Paul's writings (Rom 6:4); and he uses the verb βαπτίζω, "to baptize," only twice (Rom 6:3; Gal 3:27) outside 1 Corinthians (1:13–17; 10:2; 12:13; 15:29)—but this scarcely means that Baptism holds an insignificant place in his theology!

[54] The καί is perhaps epexegetical: "God, that is to say, the Father." See BDF, § 442 (9).

[55] See also Jn 1:12–13; 3:3–8; Gal 3:26–28; 4:6; 1 Pet 1:3.

[56] See "one Father," Mal 2:10; Mt 23:9; Jn 8:41; "our Father," Is 63:16; cf. Is 64:7 (ET 64:8).

[57] In Col 3:11 the neuter πάντα, "all things," stands in parallel to ἐν πᾶσιν, which could be neuter ("all things") or masculine ("all people"). In context, since it follows a list of people, the latter is more likely. A similar ambiguity is found in 1 Cor 15:28.

[58] Eph 1:10–11, 22–23; 3:9, 20; 4:10, 15; cf. Rom 11:36; 1 Cor 15:28; Col 1:16.

But for us [ἡμῖν] there is one God, the Father,
    from whom are all things [τὰ πάντα] and we for him,
and one Lord, Jesus Christ,
    through whom are all things [τὰ πάντα] and we through him.

This text from 1 Corinthians, however, displays the same tension between God's Fatherhood over all things and his Fatherhood of his baptized children. It resolves the tension with the dative of benefit, ἡμῖν, "for us," which implies God's Fatherhood over all creation is a fact that is of ultimate benefit only to those who acknowledge it by faith (Mt 7:11; Lk 11:13; 1 Jn 3:1). Thus, while Eph 4:6 may refer to the Fatherhood of God over all creation, it is only those who have been brought to the Father by the Spirit through the Son who are able to make this confession. This is the gift given in Baptism with the delivery of the creedal faith and its confession by the one baptized: to be born again to a new Father and acknowledge him as such.

Thus, the dual referent of "all" may be expressed by a paraphrase: "one God and Father of *all us Christian children*, the Creator-God who, after all, is over *all things* and through all things and in all things." ἐπὶ πάντων, "over all," implies God's transcendence, but also his authority (cf. Rom 9:5). διὰ πάντων καὶ ἐν πᾶσιν, "through all and in all," correspondingly asserts both his immanence and his extension throughout creation.[59] God dwells uniquely in Christians, but in the present context this would not appear to be the emphasis.[60] The threefold assertion of God's omnipresence ("over ... through ... in"), when coupled with his Fatherhood, confesses not a mere fact, but the all-embracing realm in which he exercises his fatherly care and preserving power.

The textual variant that, after ἐν πᾶσιν, appends the pronoun ἡμῖν (D F G Ψ 0278. [1739ᶜ] 𝔐 lat sy; Ir) makes πᾶσιν masculine, "in all *of us people*." Strictly speaking this applies only to the third instance of πᾶς, which is dative plural (ἐν πᾶσιν; cf. Ambrosiaster's interpretation in the previous footnote). This may be an attempt to avoid the impression of pantheism (collapsing God into creation).[61] But if the addition is meant to apply to all three prepositional phrases (*ad sensum*), it would shift the entire

---

[59] Schlier, *Epheser*, 189, who interprets the πᾶς expressions as masculine (referring to Christians), suggests that διὰ πάντων, "through all," refers to Christians as the instruments of God's work (cf. 1 Cor 12:4–11). The difficulty with this view is that there is no appropriate verb like ἐνεργέω, "to work" (cf. Gal 2:8; 5:6; Eph 3:20); "God ... *is* ... through all" does not suggest instrumentality. The expression διὰ πάντων appears nowhere else in a creedal statement about God, though its application to wisdom in Wis Sol 7:23–24 supports the interpretation that it refers to God's omnipresence (cf. διὰ πάντων in Acts 9:32).

[60] Ambrosiaster recognizes the indwelling of God as a gift unique to believers, but is forced thereby to interpret the fatherhood of God in two different senses within the verse:

> God the Father owes his existence to no one. Hence he is declared to be *over all* and *through all*. He is *through all* in the sense that all things come from him. Necessarily he will be *over all* the things that come from him. And God is *in all*, that is, dwelling in all the faithful. For he is in us by our confession, because we confess him, and he has given us his own Spirit, through which without doubt he is dwelling in us. He is not in the same sense dwelling in unbelievers who deny that he is the Father of Christ. (*Ephesians*, 4:5.1–2, ACCS 8:161)

[61] Cf. Diogenes of Apollonia (fifth century BC), who uses a similar threefold attribution when describing the air as his god ("it appears ... to reach over everything, to permeate everything

437

referent of God's Fatherhood from "all things" to "all Christians," i.e., "Father of *all of us* [Christians], who is over *all of us* and through *all of us* and in *all of us*" (cf. 1 Cor 8:6).

4:7 ἐνὶ δὲ ἑκάστῳ ἡμῶν ἐδόθη ἡ χάρις—The expression "grace was given" dominated the first pericope of chapter 3, in which it referred to the office of apostle and the mandate to preach the Gospel to the Gentiles, given to Paul by Christ (3:2, 7, 8). Although χάρις, "grace," is fundamentally an attitude or quality in God by which he is disposed to act kindly toward his people, it can be used (by way of metonymy) to refer to the free gifts themselves that proceed from his grace—thus, Paul's office can be a grace that was given. By nature the two are intimately connected: Paul's office is not a gift completely separate from God's graciousness in Christ by which he monergistically saves sinners through faith apart from their works (see the second textual note on 3:2). The office that is given is a medium or instrument for the saving grace of God to act on his people. So here Paul can proceed to say "to each of us grace was given."[62] Although in 1 Corinthians 12 Paul used the body of Christ image to draw into unity the various gifts of the Spirit at work in the members of Christ, there is no indication in the present text that diversity is in mind.[63] (Not until 4:16 is there any reference to individual parts.) The emphasis is entirely on unity. It would therefore be quite out of character if Paul meant, "to each one of us a *different* grace is given," as most commentators interpret the passage. Paul's point is precisely the opposite: the body of Christ is one because all her members hold in common the very same gifts of God ("one Lord, one faith, one Baptism, one God and Father," 4:5–6).[64] In the ensuing verses Paul will appeal to further gifts of the ascended Lord that are likewise held in common, specifically the men in the office of the ministry given to the church.

κατὰ τὸ μέτρον τῆς δωρεᾶς τοῦ Χριστοῦ—Thus, "the measure of the gift of Christ" should not be interpreted as "a different-sized gift given by Christ to each Christian"—which would contradict and undo the unity that Paul hitherto has so carefully described.[65] Such an interpretation of μέτρον risks dividing Christ's body by inflating the self-estimation of those who receive more. In the NT such a quantifying

---

and to be in everything"); quoted in Schnackenburg, *Ephesians*, 167. Marcus Aurelius, the Stoic (*Meditations*, 4:23), speaks similarly of nature, quoted in Lincoln, *Ephesians*, 240.

[62] Schlier, *Epheser*, 191, adopts the unusual interpretation that "to each of us" means "to us apostles, prophets, etc.," by which Paul extends the grace of his office to all ministers. This restriction of Christ's giving (to some, the ministers, instead of to all) violates the context. However, Schlier wisely recognizes that these ministers are given for the benefit of the whole church: "They, too, are recipients, bearers, and mediators of the grace of Christ and so [are] themselves [a] 'gift' for the members of the church." Thus, as we shall argue, the ministers are among these gifts—not for their own benefit, but for the whole church and every member of her.

[63] The vocabulary that suggests diversity in Rom 12:5–6 (χαρίσματα ... διάφορα, "differing gifts") and 1 Cor 12:4 (διαιρέσεις ... χαρισμάτων, "diversities of gifts") is missing here.

[64] " 'The truly capital things,' he [Paul] says, 'are common to all: baptism, salvation by faith, having God as Father and partaking of the same Spirit' " (Chrysostom, *Homilies on Ephesians*, 11:4.4–7, ACCS 8:163). Chrysostom, however, also speaks of a diversity of gifts with respect to lesser matters.

[65] That interpretation normally coincides with an interpretation of 4:11–12 as the giving of spiritual gifts to individuals: e.g., to some Christ gave the gift (aptitude) of being a pastor and to

and evaluative use of "measure" is connected with the work of the Law when judgment is apportioned in accord with what people deserve.[66] In the realm of the Gospel, as Paul indicates with the qualifier, "the gift *of Christ*," the gift is given not in accord with what each person deserves but in accord with what Christ has to offer. For Christ is the "measure" of what is given to us (μέτρον, 4:13); we receive as much as *he* has merited.[67] In this sense, it is not by measure in the way that humans reckon things: "for it is not by measure that he [Christ] gives the Spirit" (Jn 3:34). In Christ, where grace is concerned, everyone gets everything, the full "measure," heaped up and overflowing, nothing held back (μέτρον, Lk 6:38; cf. Mk 4:24). A "measure" that overflows is something different from a "measurement" that is limited to the size of the vessel (Law); this kind of μέτρον is an exuberant "apportionment" that is more in line with the generous way of the Gospel.[68] Similarly, τῆς δωρεᾶς τοῦ Χριστοῦ, "the gift of Christ" (Eph 4:7), should not be understood as a different gift given to each person. The genitive may be either (1) objective or appositional, "the gift that is Christ";[69] or (2) subjective, "the gift Christ gives." But in either case, Paul's point is that Christ, not the individual, is the reference point of the gift. In every NT occurrence of the noun δωρεά, "gift," it is quite clearly a reference to the common gift of salvation itself.[70]

4:8 διὸ λέγει—"Therefore it says" is a rare NT formula for introducing a quotation (though λέγει on its own is very common). Twice it announces a quote from the OT (Eph 4:8; James 4:6), and once from an unknown liturgical text (Eph 5:14). The implied subject of λέγει, "says," is probably Scripture itself,[71] and includes the recognition that *God* speaks. See καθὼς εἶπεν ὁ θεὸς ὅτι, "just as *God* said …" (2 Cor 6:16); τῷ Μωϋσεῖ γὰρ λέγει, "for to Moses *he* [God] says …" (Rom 9:15).

---

others he gave the gift of being a teacher. Our interpretation (below) stresses the concrete gift of the apostles, prophets, etc., to the church as a whole, the same gift to all.

[66] See μέτρον, "measure," in Mt 7:2; 23:32.

[67] "It does not mean according to our own merit, for if so then no one would have received what he has received. But of his gift we have all received" (Chrysostom, *Homilies on Ephesians*, 11:4.4–7, ACCS 8:163).

[68] Grothe, *The Justification of the Ungodly*, 643.

[69] Barth, *Ephesians*, 2:429: "It is probable that the Messiah is himself the gift and that Rom 8:32 is parallel: '*He [God] who did not spare his own Son but gave him up for us all, will he not also give [us] all things?*' (RSV)." Barth's point is that if God has given Christ (Eph 4:7), we can expect his other gifts to be equally rich (Eph 4:8, 11).

[70] Jn 4:10; Acts 2:38; 8:20; 10:45; 11:17; Rom 5:15, 17; 2 Cor 9:15; Eph 3:7; 4:7; Heb 6:4. The only possible exception to this observation is Eph 3:7, in which the δωρεά might be the office of apostle given to Paul. The normal noun for an individual and distinct "gift" of the Spirit is χάρισμα. Schlier, *Epheser*, 191, n. 1, states succinctly: "ἡ δωρεά ['gift'] is almost equal to ἡ χάρις ['grace']."

[71] (ἡ) γραφὴ λέγει, "(the) Scripture says," introduces quotations in Jn 19:37; Rom 4:3; 9:17; 10:11; 11:2; Gal 4:30; 1 Tim 5:18; James 4:5. Best, *Ephesians*, 378–82, suggests that the absence of a subject in Eph 4:8; 5:14 means the author of Ephesians was not intending to quote Scripture (as he does not in 5:14), which (all too) handily dodges the problem of the variance of the citation in 4:8 from the MT and the LXX of Ps 68:19 (LXX 67:19; ET 68:18). It is better to suppose that Paul intended to cite Scripture, even if he did so according to the Targum or his own translation (see the next textual note).

ἀναβὰς εἰς ὕψος ἠχμαλώτευσεν αἰχμαλωσίαν, ἔδωκεν δόματα τοῖς ἀνθρώποις—

Paul quotes Ps 68:19 (ET 68:18; LXX 67:19) in a distinctive form whose variations from both the MT and the LXX warrant some scrutiny:

עָלִיתָ לַמָּרוֹם ׀ שָׁבִיתָ שֶּׁבִי לָקַחְתָּ מַתָּנוֹת בָּאָדָם
וְאַף סוֹרְרִים לִשְׁכֹּן ׀ יָהּ אֱלֹהִים׃

You [masculine singular] ascended to the height, you took captive captivity, <u>you received gifts among mankind</u>—

and, indeed, stubbornly rebellious men—to dwell [there as] Yah[weh] God. (MT Ps 68:19)[72]

ἀνέβης εἰς ὕψος ᾐχμαλώτευσας αἰχμαλωσίαν ἔλαβες δόματα ἐν ἀνθρώπῳ καὶ γὰρ ἀπειθοῦντες τοῦ κατασκηνῶσαι κύριος ὁ θεὸς εὐλογητός.

You ascended on high, you took captive captivity, <u>you received gifts among mankind</u>—

and indeed, when they were being rebellious—to dwell there as the blessed Lord God. (LXX Ps 67:19)[73]

---

[72] Translation problems begin with the Hebrew. The *BHS* editors suggest the final three words are corrupt and point to the Syriac as a solution. Its second line reads:

ܘܐܦ ܡܪ̈ܕܐ ܠܐ ܢܫܪܘܢ ܩܕܡ ܐܠܗܐ

And, indeed, rebellious men will not dwell before God.

Our translation, "you … to dwell *as* Yah[weh] God" (rather than "for Yah[weh] God to dwell"), follows from the fact that the verse is addressed to God in the second person masculine singular, "*you* ascended …"

[73] The second half of the verse is grammatically confused. The translation offered above assumes that the LXX is following the MT woodenly, in defiance of good Greek, and that it should be translated as close to the MT as possible.

If one were to take the LXX Greek on its own merits, the following problems would arise:

1. The participle ἀπειθοῦντες, "being rebellious" (nominative masculine plural), would need a subject in grammatical agreement, but there is none. The force of the participle is also debatable: is it concessive, "*even though* they were rebellious"; temporal, "*when* they were rebellious"; or causal, "*because* they were rebellious"? The conjunction καὶ γάρ favors the temporal force ("when") since it has an emphatic meaning: "and in fact, and indeed" (Smyth, *Greek Grammar*, §§ 2813–14).

2. The genitive articular infinitive τοῦ κατασκηνῶσαι, "to dwell," would need a subject in the accusative, but the only available subjects are nominative (either the preceding ἀπειθοῦντες, "rebellious men," or the following ὁ θεός, "God." It would not be clear, then, whether it is the "rebellious ones" who are dwelling or "God." The Rahlfs edition of the LXX (*Septuaginta* [ed. Alfred Rahlfs; Stuttgart: Deutsche Bibelgesellschaft, 1935, 1979]) punctuates the Greek so as to make the participle the subject of the infinitive ("the rebellious ones dwell") by adding a full stop afterwards; and it takes the final four words (κύριος ὁ θεὸς εὐλογητός) with the next verse. The word εὐλογητός, "blessed," at least, is apparently borrowed from the next verse.

Similar to Rahlfs, *A New English Translation of the Septuagint* (ed. Albert Pietersma and Benjamin G. Wright; Oxford: Oxford University Press, 2007) offers: "You ascended on high; you led captivity captive; you received gifts by a person, indeed, when [footnote: or *although*] they were disobedient to encamp. The Lord God be blessed; …"

ἀναβὰς εἰς ὕψος ᾐχμαλώτευσεν αἰχμαλωσίαν, ἔδωκεν δόματα τοῖς ἀνθρώποις.

Having ascended on high <u>he</u> took captive captivity, <u>he gave gifts to men</u>. (Eph 4:8)

What is the significance of the variant renderings? The shift from second person address to third person ("you" in MT and LXX to "he" in Eph 4:8) is an insignificant adaptation to the context in which Paul quotes it.[74] The real puzzle lies in Paul's apparent liberty taken by changing "*received* gifts among mankind" to "*gave* gifts to men." In its original context Psalm 68 appears to be written for a procession up Mount Zion to the site of the Jerusalem temple. Labeled a psalm of David (cf. Rom 11:9), it may well have been written for the occasion when the ark of God's presence was brought up to Jerusalem (2 Sam 6:16–19; on that occasion, after completing the sacrifices, King David blessed the people and distributed [חָלַק] gifts to them!). It would also have been well suited to the dedication of Solomon's temple (1 Ki 8:1–11). The psalm portrays God taking up residence on Mount Zion as the culminating event of the exodus, the goal of God redeeming his people from slavery. They are now home, where they can gather around their God in worship. The psalm places Mount Sinai into parallel with Mount Zion, as type to antitype (Ps 68:18 [ET 68:17]); God's presence on the wilderness mountain before his worshiping people serves as a foretaste of the Jerusalem temple (which itself is a foretaste of the church and of the coming new creation; cf. Heb 12:22 and the "high mountain" in Rev 21:10). In Ps 68:19 (ET 68:18) God is pictured as a king returning victoriously from a great victory. Like King David going up to Jerusalem, with crowds lining the road and showering gifts upon him, God ascends his holy mount amidst a procession of worshipers proclaiming his praises and bringing sacrifices. Thus, in its original context, "you took captivity captive" refers to God's thorough destruction of Israel's slavery through the exodus liberation, and "you received gifts among mankind" refers to the subsequent acts of worship at Sinai.

Because of the exodus allusions and the Sinai references, Psalm 68 was appointed in the Jewish lectionary for the celebration of Pentecost.[75] Since Israel arrived at Sinai about two months after leaving Egypt (Ex 19:1), which is close to the fifty days that separated Passover and Pentecost, the giving of the Law on Sinai became a major theme of the Pentecost liturgy, for which Exodus 19–20 was an appointed reading.[76] Rabbinic interpretation proceeded to allegorize Ps 68:19 (ET 68:18), "you ascended to the height," as a reference to *Moses* ascending Mount Sinai to receive from God the gift of the Torah.[77] Thus, "received gifts *among* mankind" came to be troped as "received gifts *for* mankind" (cf. Acts 7:38). It was a small step, then, for contemporary Targumim (Aramaic paraphrases used in the synagogue) to phrase the verse as "you ascended to

---

[74] Codex Vaticanus, in fact, begins LXX Ps 67:19 (MT 68:19; ET 68:18) with the participle ἀναβάς, as Paul does in his quotation of it.

[75] Kirby, *Ephesians: Baptism and Pentecost*, 93, 97–100, 145–46; cf. *Jubilees*, 1:5; 6:11, 17, 19. See the fifth textual note on 2:12.

[76] See "Caesarea!" in "Location and Date of Writing" in the introduction.

[77] See the references to Jewish literature in Lincoln, *Ephesians*, 243.

the *firmament, O prophet Moses*, you took captives, *you taught the words of the Law, you gave them as gifts to the sons of man*."[78]

It is clear that Paul is quoting Ps 68:19 (ET 68:18), and it seems that he has adopted the popular paraphrase available in the Targums. But why does he adopt this seemingly distorted version of the text? If indeed Psalm 68 was used in the Jewish Pentecost liturgy in apostolic times, Paul might well have heard it read or sung at the temple shortly before he was arrested (Acts 20:16; cf. 1 Cor 16:8); thus, it would have been bouncing around his mind while he was creating Ephesians in his Caesarean prison.[79] The ascension of Christ to the heavenly right hand of God is a prominent feature of Ephesians (1:20–23; 2:6). As the NT draws strong typological connections between Moses and Christ (e.g., Mt 5:1; Jn 1:17), between the exodus and Easter (Lk 9:31;[80] 1 Cor 5:7), it would be natural for Paul to see Christ's ascent on high as the fulfillment of Psalm 68. As God ascended to the temple receiving gifts from men, as Moses ascended the mountain receiving gifts from God for men, so Christ ascended into heaven receiving the spoils of his victory so that he might distribute them to men (Acts 2:33; cf. Is 53:12).[81] For Paul, this is the deeper meaning of Psalm 68; his translation, while not a literally exact rendering of the OT text, gives its true sense in light of Christ.[82] Furthermore, this text, read

---

[78] David M. Stec, trans., *The Targum of Psalms* (vol. 16 of *The Aramaic Bible*; London: T&T Clark, 2004), 131–32; italics original, marking divergences from the MT. *Midrash Tehillim*, 68:11, likewise applies this passage to Moses, who "received gifts for men" (cf. Str-B, 3:596). Barth, *Ephesians*, 2:475, adds that the Ethiopian, Sahidic, Bohairic, several Arabic, and the printed Syriac versions of Psalm 68 render לְקַחְתָּ, "you *received*" (Ps 68:19 [ET 68:18]), as "you *gave*" or "he *gave*"; Justin Martyr, *Dialogue with Trypho*, 39:4; 87:6, likewise. It is more likely that the shift from "received" to "given" represents an interpretation of the text than an underlying textual variant such as לְחַלֵּק, "to distribute" (as in 2 Sam 6:19; Is 53:12), in place of לָקַח, "to receive," though the pun is intriguing.

[79] See "Paul's Trip to Jerusalem, Arrest, and Imprisonment (Acts 21:1–36)" in "The City of Ephesus and Paul's Relationship to It" in the introduction.

[80] The Greek noun in Lk 9:31 commonly translated as "departure" is actually ἔξοδος, *exodos*.

[81] Luther, commenting on Psalm 68 shortly after experiencing the text liturgically at the feasts of Ascension (versicle) and Pentecost (introit), saw Peter first giving this interpretation to the psalm at the first Pentecost:

> The psalmist does not say: "Thou hast given mankind gifts [cf. Eph 4:8]," but "Thou hast received gifts among men." This may be construed to mean, as St. Peter says [in] Acts 2:33, that He has received such gifts from the Father to relay to men. For He has not received them only for Himself and into Himself, but they were bestowed on Him to infuse into men. This outpouring of gifts came to pass at Pentecost and repeatedly thereafter. (*Commentary on Psalm 68: About Easter, Ascension, and Pentecost* [1521], AE 13:21; cf. AE 13:ix)

[82] Jerome, noting the change, writes:

> Since in the psalm the act had not yet occurred but was promised in the future, the phrase was accordingly *he received*. But the apostle is seeing this as a promise earlier given and later fulfilled. At this time of writing Christ has already made the gift and churches have been established throughout the whole world. Accordingly he is said to have already given to humanity rather than received gifts among humanity. (*Ephesians*, 2:4.8, ACCS 8:163–64)

Thus, Jerome believes the NT writers, under the guidance of the Holy Spirit, have the right to cite an OT text according to its fulfillment in Christ. Stoeckhardt, *Ephesians*, 194, proposes that the final four words of 4:8 were never meant by Paul as a quotation from the psalm, but

typologically of Christ, provides the biblical background to the prominence throughout Ephesians of the Holy Spirit (see the third textual note on 3:16), whom Christ at his ascension promised to send upon his church (Lk 24:49; Acts 1:8; Eph 1:13). The "gifts" (plural) all proceed from the "one Spirit" (4:4).

The following textual note looks more closely at the second clause of Paul's quotation from Psalm 68.

… ἠχμαλώτευσεν αἰχμαλωσίαν—Most translations paraphrase and blunt this astonishing clause as, e.g., "he led a host of captives" (RSV). This presents the image of freed slaves or prisoners of war parading behind the victorious king, being brought joyfully home, like Israel marching out of Egypt into the promised land behind their God and King. But taken literally it is much stronger: "he captured captivity" or "he took captivity captive." This might be pictured as a king who captures the people's great enemy and leads him caged through the jeering and cheering crowds, who rejoice to see their captor declawed. More strongly yet, it states that "captivity" itself is captured, that there is no longer any captivity to threaten God's people. This is the effect of Christ's work: on the cross, in the tomb, and by his resurrection, Christ has conquered sin, death, and the devil (cf. Eph 1:21–22; Col 2:15) and then led them on parade before his people that they might see and believe that those slave masters can no longer hold any power over us.[83] True freedom exists when captivity is made captive. Note that the two translations of this clause correspond to the two traditional aspects of the "harrowing of hell" (see the next textual note). The literal translation ("he took captivity captive") lends support only to one, the capturing of the devil.

4:9 τὸ δὲ ἀνέβη τί ἐστιν, εἰ μὴ ὅτι καὶ κατέβη εἰς τὰ κατώτερα [μέρη] τῆς γῆς—Paul selects the word ἀναβάς, "when he ascended," from 4:8's quotation of Psalm 68 and makes it the object of further consideration.[84] He changes the participle ἀναβάς into a finite verb, ἀνέβη, and asks, τὸ δὲ ἀνέβη τί ἐστιν, "what is the 'he ascended'?"—in other words, "what are the implications of the statement that Christ ascended?" Answer: he must first have descended (κατέβη). The comparative form τὰ κατώτερα is from κάτω, "below." μέρη, the plural of μέρος, "part," combines with it to form "lower parts."[85]

---

are his own addition to it—but by sidestepping the textual problem, he fails to come to grips with the sophisticated ways that NT writers use the OT. Stoeckhardt also seems unwilling to accept that the psalm might have both a historical referent in the time of David and a fulfillment in Christ; he sees it as a purely rectilinear prophecy of Christ (188–92).

[83] The interpretation that the rebellious angels were those whom Christ took captive is found as early as Irenaeus, *Proof of the Apostolic Preaching*, 83.

[84] Paul practices a form of midrash known as *pesher*, a term that appears in Qumran in the phrase "this refers to" or "this is to be interpreted as." It involves the reapplication of a text word by word to a new setting and is demonstrable in Jesus' own interpretation of the OT. See Richard N. Longenecker, *Biblical Exegesis in the Apostolic Period* (2d ed.; Grand Rapids: Eerdmans, 1999), 24–30, 113–16. Paul's purpose is partly to demonstrate that the OT text is indeed speaking of Christ (Schlier, *Epheser*, 192).

[85] The well-attested omission of μέρη ($\mathfrak{P}^{46}$ D* F G it; Ir[lat] Cl[ex Thd] Ambst) is likely a harmonization to LXX Ps 62:10 (MT 63:10; ET 63:9). It is included by the NA[27] editors (but in brackets as uncertain) because of the significant early and widespread manuscript support for it.

Most church fathers[86] interpreted τὰ κατώτερα μέρη τῆς γῆς, literally, "the lower parts of the earth," as having a partitive genitive ("the parts of the earth that are lower") or a genitive of comparison ("the places that are lower than the earth").[87] They take it as a reference to Christ's death and rest in the realm of the dead (Mt 12:40; Rom 10:7)[88] or to his descent into Hades/hell as the risen and victorious Lord (1 Pet 3:19; Apostles' Creed).[89] There is solid support for this interpretation of the phrase in the OT, particularly in the closest LXX equivalent, εἰς τὰ κατώτατα τῆς γῆς, "to the lowest places of the earth," in a context which indicates death or hell (LXX Ps 62:10 [MT 63:10; ET 63:9]).[90] κάτω in the LXX regularly refers to burial "under" the earth (Gen 35:8; Eccl 3:21) and to Sheol as a place "below."[91] Although it is unpopular among modern commentators, the idea that Paul is referring to Christ's rest in the grave or descent into hell ought not be dismissed out of hand.[92]

---

[86] See Bales, "The Descent of Christ in Ephesians 4:9." Notable exceptions, fathers who interpreted it as "the lower parts, that is, the earth," include Theodore of Mopsuestia and Thomas Aquinas (Schlier, *Epheser*, 192–93, nn. 4–5). From Cajetan and Calvin onwards, this view became more common, though most old Lutherans maintained the patristic view.

[87] A partitive genitive implies a two-story (or two-part) cosmology, "heaven and earth" (e.g., Eph 1:10; 3:15; Heb 12:26; Rev 21:1), in which Sheol is the lower/lowest part of the earth. A genitive of comparison implies a three-story cosmology, in which Sheol is beneath the earth (e.g., Phil 2:10; Rev 5:3, 13; see also the OT references below). Both views are found in Scripture, even within Paul's writings. See Hermann Sasse, "γῆ," *TDNT* 1:678–80; BDF, § 167. Friedrich Büchsel, "κάτω," *TDNT* 3:641, contends that the word μέρα, "parts," implies a partitive genitive.

[88] E.g., "Christ our God, Who because He was man died according to the Scriptures, and was buried according to the same Scriptures, satisfied this law also by undergoing the form of human death in the underworld, and did not ascend aloft to heaven until He had gone down to the regions beneath the earth" (Tertullian, *On the Soul*, 55 [CCSL 2:862–63], quoted in Kelly, *Early Christian Creeds*, 380).

[89] E.g., "the *lower parts of the earth* [Eph 4:9] here means death, by a human metaphor [citing Gen 44:29]. … And why does he mention this region here? What sort of captivity is he speaking of? That of the devil. He has taken captive the tyrant, the devil and death, the curse and sin" (Chrysostom, *Homilies on Ephesians*, 11:4.9–10, ACCS 8:164). This commentary cannot deal fully with the definitions of and distinctions between Sheol, Hades, and hell—whether the "prison" to which Christ descended (1 Pet 3:19) is a place of death in which all people reside or more narrowly the place of punishment for demons and unbelievers. The distinction is not crucial to the present argument.

[90] Note, however, that LXX Ps 62:10 (MT 63:10; ET 63:9) uses the superlative, "the *lowest* parts," whereas Eph 4:9 uses the comparative, "*lower* parts." This may be a significant difference, although in Koine Greek the comparative form had largely replaced the superlative form even when expressing a superlative idea (BDF, § 60). Cf. LXX Pss 85:13 (MT/ET 86:13); 87:7 (MT 88:7; ET 88:6); 138:15 (MT/ET 139:15); Lam 3:55; Manasseh 13.

[91] LXX Deut 32:22; Sirach 51:6; Ps Sol 15:10; Tobit 4:19 (S); 13:2 (S).

[92] Bales, "The Descent of Christ in Ephesians 4:9," 94–97, also stresses the following linguistic parallels:
- ἀναβήσομαι ἐπάνω τῶν νεφελῶν, ἔσομαι ὅμοιος τῷ ὑψίστῳ. νῦν δὲ εἰς ᾅδου καταβήσῃ καὶ εἰς τὰ θεμέλια τῆς γῆς. The king of Babylon boasts, "'I will ascend above the clouds; I will be like the Most High,'" and God replies, "But now you will go down into Hades and into the foundations of the earth" (Is 14:14–15; cf. Mt 11:23).
- καὶ κατέβησαν αὐτοὶ καὶ ὅσα ἐστὶν αὐτῶν ζῶντα εἰς ᾅδου, καὶ ἐκάλυψεν αὐτοὺς ἡ γῆ, καὶ ἀπώλοντο ἐκ μέσου τῆς συναγωγῆς, "and they [Korah and sons] went down and

But there is another side to the linguistic data. κάτω can also refer to the earth itself as being "under" or "below" heaven.[93] If these OT examples are compared to the previous ones, a pattern appears whereby, when contrasted with heaven "above," "below" refers to the earth itself (cf. Jn 8:23; Acts 2:19). Since that very contrast is in view in the present verse, it seems more likely that "the lower parts of the earth" should be understood as having a genitive of apposition, "the lower parts [compared to heaven], that is, the earth." This interpretation is supported by the use of τὰ μέρη with a genitive of apposition elsewhere in the NT.[94]

Aside from the linguistic data, there are contextual and theological considerations. If the patristic interpretation were adopted, the external entailments of the descent and the ascension respectively would be different: i.e., if the descent was from earth to the underworld, then the ascent would have to mean a return to earth (cf. Rom 10:7);[95] but if the descent was from heaven to earth, then the ascent would be Christ's return to heaven.[96] This syllogism is important because the descent is not explicitly taught in Psalm 68, but is deduced by Paul from the ascent. (How would a descent into Hades be logically deduced from Christ's ascension into heaven?)

What is at stake, furthermore, is the referent of the preceding clause "he took captivity captive" (4:8). Following the interpretation that the descent was to hell, many church fathers read this as the "harrowing of hell," a journey of the risen Christ to

---

all that they had, alive into Hades; and the earth covered them, and they perished from the midst of the congregation" (Num 16:33).

• ἐὰν ἀναβῶ εἰς τὸν οὐρανόν, σὺ εἶ ἐκεῖ· ἐὰν καταβῶ εἰς τὸν ᾅδην, πάρει, David prays to God, "if I should go up into heaven, you are there; if I should go down into Hades, you are present" (LXX Ps 138:8 [MT/ET 139:8]).

Bales concludes: "In sum, assuming that both the author and the audience of Ephesians were familiar with the LXX, it is very likely that both would have readily understood the phrase κατέβη εἰς τὰ κατώτερα τῆς γῆς in Eph 4:9 as indicating (1) in a literal sense, a descent of some sort to the underworld that happens upon death; (2) metaphorically, death itself; or (3) metaphorically, some manner of serious adversity or affliction" (97).

[93] LXX Ex 20:4; Deut 4:39; 5:8; Josh 2:11; 3 Kgdms 8:23 (MT/ET 1 Ki 8:23); Is 51:6; Jer 38:35 (MT/ET 31:37). Cf. ὑποκάτω, "underneath," in LXX Gen 6:17; 7:19; Deut 28:23.

[94] See Wallace, *Greek Grammar*, 99–100, who cites LXX Is 8:23 (ET 9:1); Mt 2:22; 15:21; 16:13; Mk 8:10; Acts 2:10 for the plural τὰ μέρη with a genitive of apposition. Wallace, in fact, understands such phrases as a partitive genitive with an implied noun; thus, "the lower parts of the earth" would mean "the lower parts [of the cosmos], i.e., the earth." See also Zerwick, *Biblical Greek*, § 45. See also *Barnabas*, 10:5, for κάτω with a genitive of apposition.

[95] Stoeckhardt, *Ephesians*, 195–96, counters that the descent is from the earth to the underworld and that the ascension is from the earth to heaven. But this would not suit the point Paul is making, that Christ ascends to the place from which he had first descended.

[96] Friedrich Büchsel, "κάτω," *TDNT* 3:641, argues, to the contrary, that if Christ has ascended "far above all the heavens" (4:10), then he must have descended below the earth. Lincoln, *Ephesians*, 245, counters that one would then expect a superlative, "the low*est* parts," rather than the comparative "low*er*" in Eph 4:9. One might add that, while the translation "the places that are lower than the earth" would describe a different location than "the lower parts, that is, the earth" (4:9), "*far above* all the heavens" (4:10) does *not* describe a different location than heaven or "the heavenly places" (1:20). It merely makes a theological point about the superiority of Christ over all spiritual forces (1:21). Christ did not return to a heavenly place that is different from where he began.

trounce death and the devil and free the captive souls of OT believers, to lead them finally into heaven.[97] If "hell" is understood as the place of suffering (rather than simply death), then the latter part of this view is inconsistent with the NT's confession that the saints of old were already with God (e.g., Lk 16:22–31; 20:37) and that justification by faith was already available to Abraham (Romans 4; Galatians 3). To be fair, later medieval commentators, including Lutherans from the Reformation to modern times, understood "taking captivity captive" as only the defeat of the devil, brought to its climax by Christ's descent into hell.[98]

Christ's triumph over hostile spiritual forces is an important theme in Ephesians (1:21; 2:2–3; 6:11–12). But the "genitive of apposition" translation ("the lower parts" *are* "the earth") has the advantage of including Christ's entire earthly ministry, from incarnation to ascension (and including his descent into hell!), in the work by which "he took captivity captive." The meaning then is the capture of the devil, the defeat of death, and the release of *all* people from the devil's grip. Paul does not restrict the devil's work to the underworld;[99] and in Ephesians, it is chiefly through his resurrection and ascension that Christ triumphs over his enemies (1:20–23; 2:6). So also in 4:8 Paul stresses the ascent (not the descent) as the ultimate moment of this triumph. This interpretation has the added advantage of consistency with Christ's own words: "And no

---

[97] This captivity of the OT saints was thought to be implied by Heb 11:39: "they did not receive what was promised." Some fathers included also the notion of a second chance to believe the Gospel: e.g., "after his triumph over the devil, he descended to the heart of the world, so that he might preach to the dead, that all who desired him might be set free. It was necessary for him to ascend. He had descended to trample death underfoot by the force of his own power, then only to rise again with the former captives" (Ambrosiaster, *Ephesians*, 4:9, ACCS 8:164). The view that anyone other than the OT faithful were liberated was later declared heretical (Kelly, *Early Christian Creeds*, 381). By the time the descent into hell found its way into the Apostles' Creed, in fact, the notion of a mission to the patriarchs was itself fading into the background, and the doctrine was interpreted as symbolizing Christ's triumph over the devil and death (Kelly, 383). For a Lutheran rehabilitation, see Peter Burfeind, "The Harrowing of Hell: Filling in the Blanks," *Logia* 18.1 (Epiphany 2009): 5–14. Burfeind contends that Hades should be understood in the OT sense of Sheol as the place of death to which all people descend and that Christ's entry into Hades was indeed to proclaim release to his saints who were held captive by death.

[98] Stoeckhardt, *Ephesians*, 196, is illustrative:

By returning alive from the dead Christ had actually broken the power of death and of the prince of death. By His descent into hell thereupon, He had revealed and demonstrated His victory to the inhabitants of hell, "had destroyed the power of the devil," He had bound Satan and the spirits of hell, and at His ascension up into heaven He had triumphed gloriously over the powers of darkness and put them to open shame. Calov: "In His descent He vanquished the captivity which had made us captives, namely, the devil and the gates of hell; in His ascension He led captivity captive, as was the custom followed by a victorious general in his public triumph."

The view prevalent today, that Christ descended into hell merely to make a proclamation of his victory, is milder than traditional Lutheran interpretations of the descent as the storming of the devil's castle to take him captive.

[99] Cf. 1 Cor 8:5; Col 1:16. Elsewhere in Ephesians Paul has described the realm of the devil's activity as the air (2:2) and heavenly places (6:12); thus, it would not be immediately obvious if he were suddenly to refer to the underworld as the place where Christ captured the devil. Ephesians associates Christ's triumph over evil spiritual forces more with the ascension (1:20–23; 4:8) than with the descent.

one has ascended [ἀναβέβηκεν] into heaven except the one who descended [καταβάς] from heaven, the Son of Man" (Jn 3:13).[100] In Eph 4:9, then, κατέβη, "he descended," most probably refers to the incarnation,[101] at which time the Son of God not only took on human flesh but also hid his divine glory and took on the form of a servant.

One last interpretation deserves some thought. The intimate connection between the gifts of the ascended Christ and the Holy Spirit has led to the recent proposal that the descent is actually the descent of Christ *in the Spirit*; after his ascension to heaven, Christ descended on Pentecost when he came to his church through the person of the Holy Spirit to give his gifts (cf. 4:8, 11).[102] The advantages of this view are, first, that it maintains the temporal sequence of ascent and then descent in 4:9. Second, it resolves the peculiarity that Paul should think that the descent of Christ is logically derived from his ascension (4:9). For the descent of Christ through the Holy Spirit, though promised by Christ, is not wholly obvious and is more likely to be the object of demonstration by Paul. The giving of gifts, the gifts which Paul is about to expound (4:11–16), is (by this interpretation) connected not with Christ's ascension as such, but with his subsequent descent in the Spirit, which forms a more logical progression into the next section. This also forms a more natural parallel to the Moses midrash, as he brought the gifts from God when he "descended" from the mountain (Ex 32:15; MT: וַיֵּרֶד; LXX: κατέβη; cf. also יָרַד in Ex 19:24–25). This interpretation, furthermore, continues the allusion to Pentecost, which the psalm quotation began.

Nonetheless, there are persuasive objections to this last view, including, first, the fact that Christ speaks of *sending* the Holy Spirit, not *coming as* the Spirit. It is odd to speak of Pentecost as the descent of *Christ*. The frequent interchangeability of Christ and the Spirit in the NT (see the first textual note on 3:17) is insufficient grounds for assuming the two persons are blurred in the present passage. Second, while Christ is certainly with us always (Mt 18:20; 28:20), when the NT promises his future descent (καταβαίνω), it is connected to his return on the Last Day (1 Thess 4:16). Third, while the sequence ascent-descent might be derived from 4:9, in 4:10 the sequence is descent-ascent, culminating in "that he might fill all things."[103] Finally, 4:8 explicitly connects the giving of gifts with the ascension, not the descent. Thus, while the giving of Christ's

---

[100] Cf. Deut 30:12; Prov 30:4; Jn 3:31; 6:33, 38, 62; Rom 10:6; 1 Thess 4:16; Baruch 3:29.

[101] This is not to deny that the descent of the resurrected Christ into hell, as taught in the Apostles' Creed, is a correct and biblical teaching. But it is more properly demonstrated from 1 Pet 3:19–20 and perhaps 1 Pet 4:6. The exegetical difficulty faced in the interpretation of texts like Ps 16:10–11; Acts 2:27–31; and Rom 10:7 is whether the terms "Sheol," "Hades," and "abyss" refer to death itself or to hell as a place of punishment.

[102] See the references in Lincoln, *Ephesians*, 246; Bales, "The Descent of Christ in Ephesians 4:9," 85.

[103] Thus, the RSV translates κατέβη in 4:9 as a pluperfect, "he had … descended." The textual variant that inserts πρῶτον after κατέβη, "he descended *first*" (א² B C³ Ψ 𝔐 f mᶜ vg sy saᵐˢˢ; Eus), supports the sequence "descent-ascent." Though this variant represents the probable meaning of the text, it is to be rejected textually as an attempt to improve it.

447

gifts is certainly through the Spirit, it is probably still best to understand the descent as Christ's incarnation.[104]

4:10 ὁ καταβὰς αὐτός ἐστιν καὶ ὁ ἀναβὰς ὑπεράνω πάντων τῶν οὐρανῶν—With these words Paul inverts Jesus' statement in Jn 3:13 to make a parallel point. Jesus had emphasized his divine, heavenly origin in order to affirm his insight into heavenly matters; he spoke the truth about God because he was there. Paul now moves on to Christ's return to the right hand of God, the ascension that has featured so prominently in Ephesians (1:20–23; 2:6). Glorified by God the Father, taking up again the full exercise of his divine majesty, the ascended Christ is now in a position to fulfill his promise to shower heavenly gifts on his church through the Holy Spirit (Eph 1:3, 13; 2:7; cf. Lk 24:49; Acts 1:8). The phrase ὑπεράνω πάντων τῶν οὐρανῶν, "far above all the heavens" (Eph 4:10), implies the superiority of Christ over every spiritual force that was thought to inhabit lower levels of the spiritual realm (see the first textual note on 1:21).[105] Christ does not simply occupy the place of an angelic being or even a privileged "son of God," but is seated in the highest heights, on the throne of God. His gifts are therefore God's gifts.

ἵνα πληρώσῃ τὰ πάντα—The divine nature of Christ is affirmed even more strongly by applying to him the divine quality of omnipresence. Christ has all the fullness of God (Col 1:19; 2:9) and fills all things (Eph 1:23).[106] In addition to this *static* quality, the verb πληρόω connotes the *activity* of a creative, preserving, ruling, and energetic presence throughout creation. Christ is thereby placed into synergy with the Father (Eph 4:6; cf. Col 1:16). As the Father's indwelling is only recognized by and ultimately beneficial to his baptized children, so also Christ's filling all things has a special meaning for those in whom he dwells by faith (Eph 3:17, 19). Thus, Paul hammers home the glory and divinity of Christ in order to rejoice in the gifts Christ gives to his church, which Paul is about to elaborate. See also the second textual notes on 1:23 and 3:19.

It is not beyond the realm of possibility that Paul also has in mind the proclamation of the Gospel through all creation as the means by which Christ fills all things. This is in accord with Christ's own interpretation of his ascension—that his departure is for our benefit, that he might come to us in another way (Jn 14:28; 16:7), and that he continues to be with us always through the proclamation of his Word (Mt 18:20; 28:20). This, then, forms a sensible bridge into the next two verses, which acclaim the ministers of Christ as his gift to the church.

---

[104] Lincoln's final warning is significant: "Whichever interpretation one takes, however, the real stress in the progress of thought is on the ascent. The concept of a descent, though it inevitably attracts so much discussion in an exegesis of the passage, was only brought in by the writer to help make his point about Christ's ascent in the context of his giving of gifts" (*Ephesians*, 247). Formula of Concord, Article 9, makes the same point about the descent into hell: in light of its minor role in the NT, don't get hung up on its details!

[105] The plural οὐρανοί, "heavens," a common Jewish-Greek translation of the Hebrew dual form שָׁמַיִם, could in this instance with the modifier πάντων, "all," reflect the intertestamental idea of levels of heaven (Turner, *Syntax*, 25), though it may simply refer to "all the heavenly bodies and places."

[106] Cf. Ps 72:19; Is 6:3; Jer 23:24; Wis Sol 1:7.

4:11 καὶ αὐτὸς ἔδωκεν—For the second time (as in 4:10) the reflexive pronoun αὐτός, "himself," emphatically stresses Christ as the subject of the verbs—the very One who ascended into heaven.[107] This verse (with "he gave") introduces the specific example of the gifts Paul had in mind when he spoke of "grace given" in 4:7.[108] These men, the ministers, are therefore not to be regarded as officers created by the church at her own good pleasure, but are gifts to her, appointed and given by God himself.

τοὺς μὲν ἀποστόλους, τοὺς δὲ προφήτας, τοὺς δὲ εὐαγγελιστάς, τοὺς δὲ ποιμένας καὶ διδασκάλους—The nature of the gifts is bound up with the grammar of the definite articles and conjunctions in this list. The RSV translation represents the culmination of a slide from concrete to abstract that began as early as the Vulgate: "and his gifts were that some should be apostles, some prophets, some evangelists, some pastors and teachers" (RSV). The implication of the change of the active verb ("gave") into a noun ("gifts") and the insertion of "that some should be" is that Christ's gifts among men were certain spiritual aptitudes that the church would do well to recognize by appointing them to the roles for which they are well suited. This understanding appears already in the Vulgate translation:

> et ipse dedit quosdam quidem apostolos quosdam autem prophetas alios vero evangelistas alios autem pastores et doctores

> and he himself gave some on the one hand[109] as apostles, and some as prophets, others truly as evangelists, and others as pastors and teachers

It is not entirely clear what understanding of the grammar led to the insertion of a phrase like "some to be" into such translations. Most likely the Vulgate took the construction as equivalent to ὁ μὲν ... ὁ δέ, meaning "the one ... the other," but significant points of difference distinguish the current verse from that idiom.[110]

---

[107] Wallace, *Greek Grammar*, 349; BDF, §§ 277 (3); 288 (2). There is not only an intensive but also a demonstrative aspect: he is the person just referred to in 4:8–10.

[108] Lincoln, *Ephesians*, 249: "He gives not just grace to people, but he gives specific people to people."

[109] "Quidem" is commonly used in Latin translations of the Greek μὲν ... δέ construction.

[110] BDAG, s.v. ὁ, 1 b, cites as examples of a contrasting ὁ μὲν ... ὁ δέ (singular or plural): Acts 14:4; 17:32; 28:24; 1 Cor 7:7; Gal 4:23; Phil 1:16–17; Heb 7:5–6, 20–21. (Similar contrasts with τινές or ἄλλοι include Mt 16:14; Jn 7:12; Acts 17:18.) Significantly, BDAG notes that Eph 4:11 uses μὲν ... δέ *"without* such a [contrasting] relationship expressed." For these examples of contrasting differ from Eph 4:11 in significant respects. First, in none of these occurrences is there a predicate noun attached to each article as in Eph 4:11. Second, in every case the contrast expressed with μέν and δέ is between two parties only (whereas five nouns are here). Third, in each example the article is used in the *nominative*, as the subject of the verb and, in the second part, to indicate a change in subject (as in, e.g., Mt 26:67; 28:17; see Smyth, *Greek Grammar*, § 1112). The use of the *accusative* nouns in Eph 4:11 surely places the verse outside this usage (Lk 23:33 and 1 Cor 12:28 use the relative pronoun in the accusative before μέν and/or δέ, but those verses do not use the article). Wallace, *Greek Grammar*, 212, writes of this contrasting construction: "The article is only found in the nom. case." The accusative article without the noun is found in Classical Greek (Smyth, *Greek Grammar*, § 1108), but not the NT. The classical original of the article as a demonstrative pronoun ("this") shows through in the pattern BDAG cites. The article normally refers to a noun that has previously been mentioned, "this [previously named man]"—which again is not possible in Eph 4:11.

It is possible that the definite article τούς is a substantive representing τούς ἀνθρώπους, "men," with each successive noun in predicate position (or as a double accusative, in which case δίδωμι would mean "appoint"): "he appointed these men as apostles, and these men as prophets, etc."—but since "these men" have not previously been mentioned, this is highly unlikely. The shift from "some" to "others" in such translations is probably an attempt to render the contrast implied by μέν and δέ, though the *three* occurrences of δέ followed by a final καί surely muddies any possible contrast.[111]

The conceptual problem raised by the Vulgate translation is that the office of apostle (and possibly also the offices of prophet and evangelist) was a foundational, non-repeatable office in the church. It is nonsensical to speak of the ascended Christ giving the "spiritual gift" of being an apostle when the twelve (or thirteen) positions were already filled. The fact that Matthias and Paul were called by the ascended Christ does not contradict the datum that the apostolate was essentially a closed rank. The need for Matthias to complete the Twelve, in fact, reinforces the picture of a fixed group. Certainly, "pastors and teachers" are offices that continue to be occupied and filled throughout church history. But the impression remains that Paul is speaking of Christ's giving concrete people to the church, not simply aptitudes. This is implied by the use of the aorist verb ἔδωκεν, "he gave," with reference to the moment of his ascension.

The explanation of the construction τοὺς μὲν … τοὺς δὲ … τοὺς δὲ … τοὺς δὲ … καί must lie elsewhere, most likely in the techniques for structuring a list. Ancient Greek, not having the benefit of punctuation, was unable to aid the reader via commas and full stops to indicate that a list was drawing to a close and that he should therefore adjust his intonation and pace. In this oral environment, a variety of phrases and lexical markers was brought into play instead.[112] Many lists simply pile up nouns and use καί to

---

Nor is it likely that Eph 4:11 is referring to nouns that are wholly indefinite, particularly in the case of the apostles. See BDF, § 250; Turner, *Syntax*, 36–37; Robertson, *Grammar*, 694.

[111] It is possible for μέν to be followed by multiple contrasting phrases with δέ (e.g., Mt 13:4–8, 23; 16:14; 21:35; 25:15; 1 Cor 1:12; 15:39; Jude 8), but the conclusion of the list in Eph 4:11 with καί breaks the notion of contrast. "It is thus the context that decides how pointed is the contrast. It is not the words μέν and δέ that inherently mean opposition" (Robertson, *Grammar*, 1153).

[112] See "Lists" in "Orality and the Interpretation of the Epistles: A Brief Introduction" in the introduction; also Winger, "Orality as the Key to Understanding Apostolic Proclamation in the Epistles," 274–77. In Rom 9:4 Paul groups six nouns into two sets of three, singular-singular-plural, singular-singular-plural. In 1 Cor 3:21–23 eight nouns are grouped into two groups of threes with a concluding set of two, and the first six nouns are framed by "all things are yours," repeated before and after. In Rev 2:19 the pronoun "your" is repeated at the beginning and end of a list of five nouns. In Rom 12:6–8 Paul rhythmically divides his list of seven: four clauses with εἴτε, "whether," and then three participles.

mark the final element, as we do in English (e.g., Col 3:5).[113] Other lists conclude with a phrase like "and anything else."[114] Perhaps most relevant to the present verse is Gal 3:28:

οὐκ ἔνι Ἰουδαῖος *οὐδὲ* Ἕλλην, οὐκ ἔνι δοῦλος *οὐδὲ* ἐλεύθερος, οὐκ ἔνι ἄρσεν *καὶ* θῆλυ.

There is neither Jew *nor* Greek, there is neither slave *nor* free, there is not male *and* female.

While some interpreters have highlighted the shift to καί in the final coupling as if it placed the distinction between male and female into a different category than the others, it is most likely nothing more than an oral formula indicating the end of the list. This pattern οὐδὲ ... οὐδὲ ... καί bears a striking similarity to μὲν ... δὲ ... δὲ ... δὲ ... καί in Eph 4:11.[115] The variation here in 4:11, therefore, may simply mark the beginning, middle, and end of a list, patterned for oral interpretation:

τοὺς μὲν	ἀποστόλους		the	apostles
τοὺς δὲ	προφήτας		and the	prophets
τοὺς δὲ	εὐαγγελιστάς		and the	evangelists
τοὺς δὲ	ποιμένας		and the	pastors
καὶ	διδασκάλους		and	teachers

From this arrangement the role of the definite article now becomes clear. First, one must recall the difference in the use of the article between Greek and English. While in English nouns are sometimes definite without the article, the rule is nearly inverted in Greek: nouns are assumed to be definite, even without the article, unless something in context or a lexical marker (like τις) suggests they are indefinite. The Greek article is introduced more often for syntactical (sentence structure), lexical (to place a noun into a certain class of meaning), or demonstrative ("this") reasons than to make a noun definite.[116] In the above list the article is necessary with each of the first four nouns because the conjunctions used (μέν then δέ thrice) are postpositive and cannot stand in first

---

[113] Note that Col 3:5 has a list in which the first five nouns are anarthrous, while the final noun has an article. This suggests that the article is introduced not to make one particular noun definite, but simply to mark the end of the list by varying the structure and rhythm. This is an equal but opposite parallel to Eph 4:11, where four arthrous nouns are concluded by an anarthrous fifth.

[114] Rom 8:38–39; 13:9; Gal 5:19–21; 1 Tim 1:10; 5:10. In Eph 1:21, four terms for spiritual forces, connected by καί, are concluded with καὶ παντὸς ὀνόματος ὀνομαζομένου, "and every name that is named," followed by the adversative οὐ μόνον, "not only." Cf. the four nouns connected by καί and followed by τε in Eph 3:18–19. In Eph 5:3 and again in Eph 5:4 a list of three shifts from καί, "and," to ἤ, "or," to mark the conclusion of the short list.

[115] See also Rom 2:17–19, where the conjunctions in the list are δὲ ... καὶ [four times] ... τε.

[116] See Wallace, *Greek Grammar*, 209: "The function of the article is *not* primarily to make something definite that would otherwise be indefinite. ... There are at least ten ways in which a noun in Greek can be definite without the article."

position in the phrase (i.e., μὲν ἀποστόλους by itself is impossible). This is not true of the last conjunction, καί. Paul, therefore, signals the end of the list with a rhythmic, lexical, and syntactic shift, by dropping the definite article before the fifth noun and switching to a conjunction that does not require it. Thus, the articles should be translated in English not with a phrase like "some as," but simply as definite articles. Christ's gifts were concrete: "the apostles and the prophets, etc."

If valid, this explanation may, furthermore, discredit the common interpretation of "pastors and teachers" as hendiadys—as if, according to the Granville Sharp Rule, two nouns coupled by one article referred to one office of pastor-teacher, or "teaching pastor."[117] It makes little sense for Paul to break the pattern of distinct offices with a double reference to one office. Pastors and teachers should most likely be exegeted as distinct offices in the list.

In line with our conclusions below, that the first three terms refer to foundational offices and the last two to ongoing ones, our translation uses the English article with the first three and omits it from the last two. This shift produces smoother English, but also imitates the rhythmic flow of the original text, signaling the end of the list.

We are left, finally, with the question of what Paul means by each of the five nouns. That question will be discussed in the following textual notes.

... τοὺς μὲν ἀποστόλους, τοὺς δὲ προφήτας ...—On ἀπόστολος, "apostle," see the first textual note and the commentary on 1:1. The noun "apostles" heads the list here as the foundational NT office, endowed with Christ's authority to extend his church, speaking for him and teaching what he gave them to teach (cf. Eph 2:20; 3:5; also 1 Cor 12:28). It can be easily demonstrated that when Christ ascended he gave the apostles to the church.[118]

For the meaning and referent of the second noun, προφήτας, "prophets," see the first textual note on 2:20. The ordering of "the prophets" after "the apostles" and their place in a list of gifts from the ascended Christ to his church suggest that these are not OT prophets, but people who received direct inspiration from the Holy Spirit for the guidance of the church in the early apostolic age.[119] Coupled with "apostles" (as in 2:20; 3:5) and standing near the head of the list, "the prophets" are presented as having a foundational office, not an ongoing role in the later church.

---

[117] E.g., Barth, *Ephesians*, 2:438–39, who calls them "teaching shepherds." Wallace, *Greek Grammar*, 284, denies that the Granville Sharp Rule applies to this plural phrase, arguing that Sharp restricted his rule to singular nouns: "There are no clear examples of *nouns* being used in a plural TSKS [article-substantive-καί-substantive] construction to specify one group." Nevertheless, Wallace maintains the idea that the one article τούς puts the two nouns ποιμένας and διδασκάλους into a related group: "Eph 4:11 seems to affirm that all pastors were to be teachers, though not all teachers were to be pastors." This odd conclusion seems to be supported not by his syntactical evidence but by a survey of NT parallel passages.

[118] Mt 28:16–20; Mk 16:15–19; Lk 24:45–51; Acts 1:2–9; 26:16–18.

[119] "What prophets does Paul speak of here? It is obviously those who being full of the Spirit spoke of God after his coming, continuing to expound the divine teaching" (Victorinus, *Ephesians*, 2:4.11, ACCS 8:165). Referring to Ambrosiaster's commentary on these verses, Joel Elowsky summarizes: "The offices that disappeared were the ones associated largely with the mission work of the rapidly growing church: the apostles, prophets, and those with charismatic gifts" ("The Ministry in the Early Church," 296).

... τοὺς δὲ εὐαγγελιστάς ...—The Greek noun εὐαγγελιστής, "evangelist," is clearly related to the noun εὐαγγέλιον, "Gospel," and the verb εὐαγγελίζω, "to preach the Gospel," but one must be careful not to read modern ideas of "evangelist" into the term without textual justification (as with the term πρεσβύτερος, which bears no relationship to the modern Protestant office of "elder"). The word εὐαγγελιστής appears only three times in the NT (Eph 4:11; also Acts 21:8; 2 Tim 4:5).[120] In the second instance, Acts 21:8, it is applied to Philip "the evangelist," who had been appointed as one of the Seven (Acts 6:1–5) and lived in Caesarea with four unmarried daughters who prophesied (Acts 21:8–9). Philip's preaching and baptizing dominates Acts 8. He is prominent among the preachers who were scattered into new regions of Judea and Samaria after the martyrdom of Stephen (Acts 8:1–4; cf. Acts 11:19). Philip "proclaimed Christ [ἐκήρυσσεν ... τὸν Χριστόν]" (Acts 8:5) and "preached the Gospel [εὐηγγελίσατο]" (Acts 8:35; see also Acts 8:12, 40). He, like the apostles, was enabled to perform signs and great miracles (Acts 8:6, 13), and he baptized many (Acts 8:12), including Simon the magician (Acts 8:13) and the Ethiopian eunuch (Acts 8:38). These actions may explain why he was called "the evangelist"; but it is not clear whether the emphasis is on ministry in new locations or on the act of preaching, nor is it clear why the term is not applied to other significant preachers in the book of Acts.[121] Commentators who see "evangelist" as having an exclusively missionary role often mistakenly presume that the Gospel is a message only for unbelievers.[122] Yet if Philip is the model "evangelist," both the structure of Acts and the order of Paul's list commend the interpretation of "evangelist" as a foundational role that is also transitional between apostles and pastors.[123] This is how Eusebius explains it.[124]

---

[120] Its rarity in the NT is compounded by the term's absence from the *Didache* and the Apostolic Fathers. The first patristic occurrences are in Hippolytus, *On Christ and Antichrist*, 56, and Tertullian, *Against Praxeas*, 23, where it means "author of a Gospel."

[121] Gerhard Friedrich, "εὐαγγελιστής," *TDNT* 2:737, suggests that Timothy was called an "evangelist" (2 Tim 4:5) because he was God's servant ἐν τῷ εὐαγγελίῳ τοῦ Χριστοῦ, "in the Evangel/Gospel of Christ" (1 Thess 3:2; cf. Phil 2:22). By associating the phrase ἐν τῷ εὐαγγελίῳ with the function or office of evangelist, Friedrich is able to draw this conclusion: "The number of evangelists must have been greater than one might suppose" from the three instances of "evangelist" in the NT (Acts 21:8; Eph 4:11; 2 Tim 4:5); as possible additional evangelists, he cites the women who labored with Paul "in the Gospel" (ἐν τῷ εὐαγγελίῳ, Phil 4:3); the brother whose praise is "in the Gospel" (ἐν τῷ εὐαγγελίῳ, 2 Cor 8:18); and Epaphras, whom Paul calls his "fellow slave" and "a slave of Christ Jesus" (Col 1:7; 4:12). However, to conclude that anyone who worked "in the Gospel" is therefore an "evangelist" empties the term of distinctive meaning and contradicts its restricted usage in the NT and early church.

[122] Particularly egregious is, e.g., Bruce, *The Epistles to the Colossians, to Philemon, and to the Ephesians*, 347. Aside from its roots in Reformed theology, as expressed famously by Karl Barth, this notion owes much to C. H. Dodd's overwrought distinction between *kerygma* and *didache* (*The Apostolic Preaching and Its Developments* [London: Hodder & Stoughton, 1936], 1–2).

[123] Schnackenburg, *Ephesians*, 181.

[124] Eusebius uses the term "evangelist" of early missionaries who took the Gospel into fresh areas, e.g., *Ecclesiastical History*, 1:13.4; 3:37.2; 5:10.2. He understands these figures to have a foundational role similar to the apostles in those territories, and he includes distribution of

A certain amount of caution is prompted by the third and final use of "evangelist" in the NT. Paul tells Timothy, ἔργον ποίησον εὐαγγελιστοῦ, "do the work of an evangelist," after which he adds τὴν διακονίαν σου πληροφόρησον, "fulfill your ministry" (2 Tim 4:5). It is unclear whether "the work of an evangelist" is the same as "your ministry" or additional to it. It is possible that Paul means "preach the Gospel in new places" (as did Philip, who was "scattered," Acts 8:1–4), with the implication of continuing the foundational apostolic work. But there is nothing in the context of the Pastoral Epistles to suggest Timothy should leave his flock for such a mission. The admonition may simply mean that Timothy is to remain focused on the proclamation of the Gospel in the place where God had put him (cf. Phil 2:22; 1 Thess 3:2).[125] Likewise, in the present context of Ephesians, there is no specific reference to missions; the work of the five offices is directed toward the saints and their upbuilding (4:12). Yet, this generalized explanation of evangelist is less than satisfying in light of the specific place the term holds in Paul's list.

Though it is not often given serious consideration today, it is worth pondering a third solution: that "evangelist" is the office held by Matthew, Mark, Luke, and John, the four writers of the Gospels. This meaning is established as early as the first decade of the third century in patristic literature.[126] Is it possible that other men besides the four

---

the written Gospels in their work. It is interesting that in paragraph 1 he includes the daughters of Philip among the most notable evangelists:

1. Among those that were celebrated at that time was Quadratus, who, report says, was renowned along with the daughters of Philip for his prophetical gifts. And there were many others besides these who were known in those days, and who occupied the first place among the successors of the apostles. And they also, being illustrious disciples of such great men, built up the foundations of the churches which had been laid by the apostles in every place, and preached the Gospel more and more widely and scattered the saving seeds of the kingdom of heaven far and near throughout the whole world.

2. For indeed most of the disciples of that time, animated by the divine word with a more ardent love for philosophy, had already fulfilled the command of the Saviour, and had distributed their goods to the needy. Then starting out upon long journeys they performed the office of evangelists, being filled with the desire to preach Christ to those who had not yet heard the word of faith, and to deliver to them the divine Gospels.

3. And when they had only laid the foundations of the faith in foreign places, they appointed others as pastors, and entrusted them with the nurture of those that had recently been brought in, while they themselves went on again to other countries and nations, with the grace and the co-operation of God. For a great many wonderful works were done through them by the power of the divine Spirit, so that at the first hearing whole multitudes of men eagerly embraced the religion of the Creator of the universe. (*Ecclesiastical History*, 3:37.1–3 [*NPNF*² 1:169])

[125] See Moe, "Εὐαγγελιστής: Evangelist?" Moe cites and translates Luther's translation: " '*Thue das Werk eines evangelischen Predigers*'—'Do the work of a gospel preacher' " (5 [cf. WA DB 7:281]). Likewise Best, *Ephesians*, 390, notes that Philip is called "the evangelist" not in Acts 8, but when he is settled in Caesarea (Acts 21:8). "The NT use of the word then provides no evidence that it relates to a ministry outside the church."

[126] The term "evangelist" appears with the sense of "Gospel writer" already in Hippolytus, *On Christ and Antichrist*, 56; and Tertullian, *Against Praxeas*, 23. Chrysostom, *Homilies on Ephesians*, 11:4.11–12, says: "… 'evangelists' [Eph 4:11], who did not go about everywhere, but only preached the Gospel, as Priscilla and Aquila. … Or perhaps by 'evangelists' he means those who wrote the Gospel" (*NPNF*¹ 13:104).

were called "evangelists"? Bo Reicke has emphasized the use of oral and written testimony by the Gospel writers. Philip, a prominent leader of the Jerusalem "Hellenists" (Acts 6:1), may have been among those people who preserved the eyewitness testimony and written notes concerning the words and deeds of Jesus that were circulated in the apostolic era until they were definitively assembled into the four Gospels (cf. Lk 1:1–4). Notably, Luke was with Paul when he stayed with Philip the evangelist in Caesarea (Acts 21:8), at which time, Reicke suggests, Luke may have drawn on Philip's resources for his Gospel.[127] When Paul says "do the work of an evangelist," he may be telling Timothy to dedicate some of his time to this important "archival" work, preserving and copying the stories and words of Jesus for liturgical and proclamatory needs. In Eph 4:11, then, Paul might be referring to the work of these Gospel "archivists," including perhaps Luke and his three fellow evangelists, who probably were already at work on their Gospels.[128] If this is the meaning of εὐαγγελιστής, then this third office fits well with the first two as foundational for the NT church.

... τοὺς δὲ ποιμένας καὶ διδασκάλους—Our structural analysis of the list of terms (see the second textual note on 4:11) suggested that these two be taken as distinct offices (or aspects of the one office of the ministry), "pastors and teachers," rather than as an hendiadys representing "pastor-teachers."[129] Aside from the literal uses of ποιμήν, "shepherd," as one who tends sheep (e.g., LXX Gen 4:2; Lk 2:8), the noun has a long history of metaphorical use. In the OT it refers to the leaders of Israel as those responsible for feeding and protecting the nation, who more often than not forsake and abuse their flock (Ezekiel 34),[130] and to God as the Good Shepherd whom they imperfectly represent on earth (Psalm 23).[131] While politics and religion cannot easily be separated in Israel, the term "shepherd" is clearly not used primarily or exclusively of a spiritual curate; it is far broader. Moses applies the image to his successor, Joshua, as the leader of Israel, who is a type of Christ (Num 27:16–18; cf. Is 63:11).[132] God promises to give Israel good shepherds,[133] who likewise will reach their fulfillment in Christ, even the One he calls "my servant David," the "one Shepherd" (Ezek 34:23–24; 37:24–25).

---

[127] Reicke, *The Roots of the Synoptic Gospels*, 170.

[128] Few modern commentators accept this meaning. Henry Hamann, "Church and Ministry," 124, is an exception: "Evangelists make present and plastic their Lord Jesus through their accounts of his works and sayings, as the later written form of the Gospels indicates." The most thorough recent proponent of this interpretation is Dikran Y. Hadidian, *"Tous de euangelistas* in Eph 4,11," *CBQ* 28 (1966): 317–21.

[129] Jerome represents the common view: "For he does not say 'some shepherds, some teachers' but *some shepherds and teachers,* meaning that he who is a shepherd should at the same time be a teacher. No one in the church, even a saintly person, should take to himself the name of shepherd unless he can teach those whom he feeds" (*Ephesians*, 2:4.11–12, ACCS 8:166).

[130] Cf. LXX 2 Kgdms 24:17 (MT/ET 2 Sam 24:17); 3 Kgdms 22:17 (MT/ET 1 Ki 22:17) ‖ 2 Chr 18:16; Jer 10:21; 12:10; 23:1; 27:6 (MT/ET 50:6); Zech 10:3; 11:5, 15–17; 13:7; cf. Nah 3:18.

[131] Cf. Gen 49:24; Ps 80:2 (ET 80:1); Is 40:11; Ezek 34:12; Eccl 12:11; Sirach 18:13.

[132] See Harstad, *Joshua,* 12–13, who traces the spellings of the single Hebrew and Greek name that can refer either to Joshua or Jesus.

[133] Jer 3:15; 23:4; Micah 5:4 (ET 5:5); cf. Is 40:11.

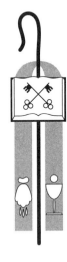

Jesus, as the Good Shepherd, thus perfects the role of Israel's leaders and takes up the staff of God himself (Jn 10:1–18; Heb 13:20; 1 Pet 2:25).[134]

In the NT only the present verse applies the noun ποιμήν, "shepherd," to men in the office of the ministry.[135] However, the cognate verb ποιμαίνω, "to shepherd," is applied to the office beginning with Christ's words to Peter (Jn 21:16). Paul himself exhorts the πρεσβυτέρους, "presbyters," of the Ephesian church (Acts 20:17) "to shepherd [ποιμαίνειν] the church of God in which the Holy Spirit has made you overseers [ἐπισκόπους]"—thus equating πρεσβύτερος, "presbyter"; ἐπίσκοπος, "overseer"; and ποιμήν, "shepherd," at least in the NT era (Acts 20:28; cf. 1 Pet 2:25; 5:1–2). This equation both explains the absence of those other terms in Eph 4:11 (since "shepherd" may stand in for them) and strengthens the contention that "teacher" is distinct from "shepherd."

It is therefore not difficult to identify τοὺς ποιμένας as representatives of Christ who care for his people at the level of the local church, that is, "pastors." As a Middle Eastern shepherd would lead from the front rather than driving the sheep from behind, calling out to the sheep who know his voice (Jn 10:3–4, 27), so pastors lead the church; but rather than diverse secular notions of leadership, the pastoral image suggests leading the flock to water, food, and safety. Their role is to speak Christ's Word[136] and give his cleansing and nourishing sacramental gifts. Paul's designation of "pastors" as gifts of the ascended Christ to the church is particularly relevant to the Ephesians if, as postulated in the introduction[137] and hinted by Acts 20, the pastors of Ephesus had only recently been placed into office.

If the word διδασκάλους, "teachers," is not simply to be identified with "pastors,"[138] its referent is more difficult to identify. It is again significant that διδάσκαλος, "teacher," is primarily a title for Jesus (passim in the Gospels, e.g., Mt 8:19); it is a Greek equivalent of the Jewish term "rabbi," "teacher/master" (Jn 1:38; 3:2; 20:16).[139] But Jesus

---

[134] Cf. Mt 9:36; 25:32; 26:31; Rev 7:17; 12:5; 19:15; Ignatius, *To the Romans*, 9:1; Ignatius, *To the Philadelphians*, 2:1.

[135] The terms ἐπίσκοπος, πρεσβύτερος, and διάκονος are far more common in the NT. While these terms vary in meaning throughout church history, sometimes having hierarchical connotations, sometimes not, Lutherans in the early days after the Reformation retained and used the terms *Bischof*, "bishop," or *Superintendent* for the first, *Priester*, "priest," for the second (etymologically derived from πρεσβύτερος, "elder," not the Latin *sacerdos*), and *Kirchendiener*, "church minister," or *Diakon*, "assistant minister," for the third. The term "pastor" (from the Latin for "shepherd"), which is dominant in Lutheran usage today, came into prominence only in the seventeenth century as the term preferred by Pietists.

[136] "For, thank God, a child seven years old knows what the Church is, namely, the holy believers and lambs who hear the voice of their Shepherd" (SA 3:12.2 [*Triglotta*, 499]).

[137] See "Paul's Sermon to the Ephesian Pastors (Acts 20:15–38; cf. 1 Timothy)" in "The City of Ephesus and Paul's Relationship to It" in the introduction. This proposal rests on the assumption that 1 Timothy can be fit into the chronology of Acts; that it was written prior to Ephesians; and that 1 Tim 1:3–7, 19b–20; 3:1–13; 4:1–6 imply that Timothy had been sent to depose false teachers and ordain new pastors for the church.

[138] Schnackenburg, *Ephesians*, 181–82, notes and references the modern trend to interpret "pastors" and "teachers" distinctly.

[139] Cf. Lk 19:39; 20:39, where even the Pharisees and scribes call Jesus διδάσκαλος, "Teacher."

informs the disciples that they are not to adopt the title "rabbi," since they have only one true Teacher (Mt 23:8). Thus, he breaks the Jewish tradition of each rabbi transmitting and building on the teaching of his predecessors and places himself into an abiding teaching office in the church. "For Jesus is the absolute διδάσκαλος. He is the One in whom Moses sees himself to be fulfilled (Jn. 5:45[–46])"[140] (cf. Deut 18:15–20).

As all pastors were agents of Christ, they were to a certain extent to be teachers.[141] Nonetheless, the apostolic church identified certain figures as "teachers" (but "not many of you," James 3:1). They are coupled with "prophets" as significant figures at the church in Antioch (Acts 13:1). Paul maintains part of the hierarchy of Eph 4:11 when he numbers "first apostles, second prophets, third teachers" (1 Cor 12:28–29)— which suggests teachers held an authoritative position together with, but subordinate to, the founding officers of "apostles" and "prophets." "Teachers" teach what the apostles and prophets have first set down, even as Paul and Barnabas themselves followed up the initial preaching of the Gospel with teaching (Acts 15:35). Their placement at the *end* of the list in Eph 4:11 is somewhat puzzling in comparison, but nevertheless maintains their subordinate ranking.

Paul himself was a preacher, apostle, and teacher (1 Tim 2:7; 2 Tim 1:11); the letter to the Ephesians, in which he expounds the revelation of the mystery[142] in order to increase wisdom and knowledge, is surely an example of Paul's teaching. The term "teacher" is common in the Apostolic Fathers, where it is sometimes applied to the authors themselves and where it is often asserted that Jesus is the only true Teacher.[143] Hermas includes among the foundation stones of the church "apostles and bishops and teachers and deacons/ministers."[144] The *Didache* likewise speaks of "the prophets and teachers" as foundational figures whose ministry is continued by "bishops and deacons/ministers."[145]

That only certain central figures were considered "teachers" is implied by the description of Polycarp as "an apostolic and prophetic teacher, bishop of the catholic church in Smyrna; for every word which he uttered from his mouth both was fulfilled

---

[140] Karl Heinrich Rengstorf, "διδάσκαλος," *TDNT* 2:156.

[141] Timothy, for example, was instructed by Paul not only to do the work of an "evangelist" (2 Tim 4:5) but also to "teach" (1 Tim 4:11; 6:2; cf. 1 Tim 4:13; 2 Tim 2:2). Apt teaching was a fundamental qualification for an ἐπίσκοπος, "overseer" (1 Tim 3:2; Titus 1:7, 9), and a πρεσβύτερος, "elder" (1 Tim 5:17). The liturgy included teaching (1 Cor 14:26), and teaching is included with the pastoral gifts (Rom 12:6–8). Pastors were to defend their flock against false "teachers" (2 Tim 4:3).

[142] See τὸ μυστήριον, "the mystery," in Eph 1:9; 3:3, 4, 9; 5:32; 6:19.

[143] *Barnabas*, 1:8; 4:9; *Diognetus*, 9:6; 11:1; Ignatius, *To the Ephesians*, 15:1; Ignatius, *To the Magnesians*, 9:1–2; *Martyrdom of Polycarp*, 12:2; 16:2; 17:3; 19:1; *Didache*, 13:2; 15:1–2; *Shepherd of Hermas, Visions*, 3:5.1; *Shepherd of Hermas, Mandates*, 4:3.1; *Shepherd of Hermas, Similitudes*, 9:15.4; 9:16.5; 9:19.2; 9:25.2.

[144] *Shepherd of Hermas, Visions*, 3:5.1; cf. *Shepherd of Hermas, Similitudes*, 9:15.4. These "apostles and teachers" have now "fallen asleep" (*Similitudes*, 9:16.5) and have passed to be with the angels (9:25.2).

[145] *Didache*, 15:1–2.

and will be fulfilled."[146] Thus, while the term is broad enough to include any teacher of the Gospel (and even false teachers, 2 Tim 4:3; 2 Pet 2:1), it may be that Paul has in mind again the foundational role of certain figures who were prominent in promulgating the apostolic doctrine received from Christ himself through the apostles and holding the churches to that norm. This appears to be a role that was carried out beyond the sphere of one local congregation, a "transparochial" theologian.[147] At the same time, the usage of the five terms in Eph 4:11 elsewhere in the NT demonstrates a certain overlap of categories; within the one divinely instituted office of the ministry, certain men held only one, but others held many, of these five offices.

4:12 πρὸς τὸν καταρτισμὸν τῶν ἁγίων, εἰς ἔργον διακονίας, εἰς οἰκοδομὴν τοῦ σώματος τοῦ Χριστοῦ—The relationship of these three prepositional phrases that articulate the purpose of Christ's gifts has attained an undue prominence since the mid twentieth century, owing to the verse's connection to the new theology of "everyone a minister."[148] Crucial to the debate is the meaning and referent of διακονία, "ministry," which will be taken up as the phrases are discussed in detail below. But questions of the term's external entailments—who is doing διακονία and to whom—are bound up with the phrases' structure. There is no doubt that πρός and εἰς introduce purpose (or perhaps result) phrases subordinate to the giving of gifts in 4:7–11; the difficult question is their relationship to one another.

The traditional understanding is represented by the KJV: "for the perfecting of the saints, for the work of the ministry, for the edifying of the body of Christ." Here the three prepositional phrases are taken as coordinate; each in parallel fashion identifies the work that the officers of 4:11 are to do; that is, the work of the ministry is done by the apostles, prophets, evangelists, pastors, and teachers.[149] The KJV is completely consistent with the Vulgate;[150] though the Vulgate in its original form lacks punctuation, the

---

[146] *Martyrdom of Polycarp*, 16:2 (translation adapted from Kirsopp Lake, LCL).

[147] Elowsky, "The Ministry in the Early Church," 297, concurs:

> The fathers speak of the ministry operating on two tracks in the first centuries of the church: the missionary track and the local church track. The apostles, prophets, and teachers remain, we learn from the *Didache*, but largely as itinerants. They go from place to place establishing and strengthening churches so that faith will be created. … Bishops and deacons, along with presbyters, carry on the work of the prophets, apostles, and teachers at the local level in the one ministry that Christ gave to his church.

[148] This popular slogan is widely known among Lutherans from Oscar Feucht's *Everyone a Minister* (St. Louis: Concordia, 1974). But it is not absent even from scholarly exegetical resources such as Barth's commentary on Ephesians: "Every one of the special ministers is a *servus servorum Dei*. He is a 'pastor' of God's flock, who understands himself as a minister to ministers" (*Ephesians*, 2:481). In recent times this novel anticlerical interpretation of Eph 4:12 has been challenged, most notably by Hamann, "The Translation of Ephesians 4:12—A Necessary Revision"; and Lincoln, *Ephesians*, 252–56; see also Gordon, " 'Equipping' Ministry in Ephesians 4?"

[149] Referring to the five officers of 4:11 as holding the same "office" (singular) of the ministry, Chrysostom proceeds to interpret 4:12: "Perceive ye the dignity of the office? Each one edifies, each one perfects, each one ministers" (Chrysostom, *Homilies on Ephesians*, 11:4.11–12 [*NPNF*[1] 13:104]).

[150] "Ad consummationem sanctorum in opus ministerii in aedificationem corporis Christi."

Latin term *ministerium* would have been understood (according to medieval ecclesiastical usage) as "the ministry" carried out by the officeholders themselves.

From the mid twentieth century onwards, however, a wholesale shift in interpretation was reflected in the new translations of that era. With the removal of the comma between the first two phrases (as, e.g., the RSV did between its first [1952] and second [1971] editions), the doers of the διακονία shifted from the apostolic officers themselves (4:11) to the "saints" (4:12). The second and third phrases were then interpreted as describing purposes subordinate to (rather than coordinate with) the first purpose. The result is either that the "saints" are equipped by the pastors to do the "ministry" themselves[151] or to do some form of general Christian "service" (διακονία being reinterpreted).[152]

From a grammatical viewpoint, the question is whether the shift in preposition from πρός to εἰς and then to εἰς again indicates a significant syntactical change or whether it is a purely stylistic variation. On the one hand, the shift might indicate that the second two prepositional phrases are subordinate to and dependent on the first, indicating two secondary goals to be achieved by the "saints" after they have first been equipped by the ministers:

to [πρός] equip the saints
 i. for [εἰς] the work of ministry/service
 ii. for [εἰς] building up the body of Christ

Yet almost no English translation actually interprets the relationship of the phrases this way.[153] Those who opt for subordination make the second phrase subordinate to the first and leave the third hanging independently ("to equip the saints for the work of ministry, to build up the body of Christ")—which makes the least sense of the actual alternation of prepositions and would require πρός … εἰς … πρός. Despite frequent assertions in the commentaries, the subordination of one purpose phrase to another by alternation of preposition cannot be demonstrated in the Greek Bible.[154] Unfortunately, not even the sort of oral structuring considered in 4:11 provides a satisfactory explanation, for the variation is precisely the opposite of what one might expect: an A-A-B pattern (πρός … πρός … εἰς) might signal the end of a list, but this A-B-B pattern (πρός … εἰς … εἰς) defies such analysis. Nor is there any comparable use of these two prepositions (πρός

---

[151] E.g., "to equip the saints for the work of ministry, for building up the body of Christ" (ESV).

[152] E.g., "for the equipping of the saints for the work of service, to the building up of the body of Christ" (NASB; similar is NIV).

[153] A possible exception is the unique translation of the Darby version (1884): "for the perfecting of the saints; with a view to *the* work of *the* ministry, with a view to the edifying of the body of Christ." See also the NLT and AAT (Beck).

[154] Lincoln, one of the few modern commentators to support the traditional translation, states: "The change of preposition cannot bear the weight of such an argument, and there are, in fact, no grammatical or linguistic grounds for making a specific link between the first and second phrases" (*Ephesians*, 253). The natural way to make the second and third statements subordinate to the first would not be through the use of additional prepositions but with simple infinitives of purpose. In fact, the supplementary sentence in 4:13 performs this very function: it describes a secondary goal of the gift of the ministry using the conjunction μέχρι, "until."

and εἰς) in an A-B-B pattern in the Greek Bible, though there are perhaps sufficient data to demonstrate that the shift in prepositions is merely a stylistic variation.[155] It is significant, however, that in Ephesians Paul frequently hangs a series of prepositional phrases on one main verb, all of which stand coordinate to one another, as in the traditional translation of this verse. See, e.g., "who has blessed us [ἐν] with every blessing of the Spirit [ἐν] in the heavenly places [ἐν] in Christ" (1:3).[156]

In the absence of a decisive *syntactical* explanation of the relationship between the three phrases, the *lexical* relationship of the nouns (their meanings) must be the deciding factor.[157] Henry Hamann brings the insight that the new translations not only assume a subordination of the purpose phrases but also subordinate the second and/or third phrase to the meaning of the noun in the first phrase, καταρτισμός, "completion." Against the modern translations, Hamann avers:

> The verbal idea contained in the noun ["completion"] is carried through into the prepositional phrase εἰς ἔργον διακονίας: to equip (literally, for the equipping of) the saints for the work of the ministry (or ministry).

> [But] a lexical study of the verb καταρτίζω and the noun καταρτισμός shows that there is no case of the noun καταρτισμός being used in the way the popular translations use it.[158]

---

[155] There are many examples in which πρός is used for speaking or sending "to" someone followed by εἰς for movement "to" or "into" a place. See LXX Gen 31:3; 32:4 (ET 32:3); 35:27; Ex 4:27; 17:14; Num 10:30; 12:4; 15:18; 34:2; Josh 9:6; 10:6; 11:2; Judg 21:8; 2 Sam 13:7; etc. In the NT, see Lk 5:4; Gal 1:17. Only in 1 Macc 10:5 is the sequence πρός ... εἰς ... εἰς used in complete parallel, which may be sufficient to suggest that in Eph 4:12 the change of preposition is simply a stylistic variation. Nonetheless, in none of these many examples are the prepositional phrases used for purpose. The closest parallel would be Rom 15:2, which gives two *coordinate* purposes with εἰς and πρός; significantly, the latter phrase is πρός οἰκοδομήν, "for building up" (compare εἰς οἰκοδομήν here in Eph 4:12). Cf. Philemon 5, in which πρός and εἰς are in parallel. The alternation of these prepositions is surely just a matter of style.

[156] As further examples, Lincoln, *Ephesians*, 253, notes Eph 1:5–6, 20–21; 2:7; 4:14. The immediately subsequent verse (4:13) is highly significant for its coordination of three εἰς phrases of goal or purpose. The next verse (4:14) also includes three parallel adverbial phrases, though the first lacks a preposition. In 6:12 four prepositional phrases with πρός are coordinated. Lincoln concludes: "It is certainly preferable, therefore, to see the three prepositional phrases here [in 4:12] as each dependent on the notion of the giving of ministers, and hard to avoid the suspicion that opting for the other view is too often motivated by a zeal to avoid clericalism and to support a 'democratic' model of the Church" (253).

[157] Hamann, "The Translation of Ephesians 4:12," writes: "The actual linguistic support for the almost universal translation of Ephesians 4:11, 12 (especially v. 12) in our day approaches zero." Voelz, *What Does This Mean?* 136–38, offers no syntactical solution, but hints that

> the **key *may* lie in relationships among meanings/thoughts**, specifically the relationship between the meaning of these verses and that of the surrounding context, both before and after: ... The thought of verses 8–10 and verse 13 is that God and Christ have given gifts to humanity, for the benefit of all, which may signify that the gifts of verse 11 (the people in the "offices") have been given to be a blessing to the church in terms of what is expressed in each prepositional phrase (i.e., these "offices" are given for the outfitting of the saints, for the work of [the] ministry, for the building up of the body of Christ [not to equip someone else to do the work]). (137)

[158] Hamann, "The Translation of Ephesians 4:12," 43.

Hamann examines all occurrences of the noun καταρτισμός in the Greek OT (it occurs only once, in Symmachus Is 38:12) and in classical literature; he determines that the action of the noun always draws to a close with the dependent noun in the genitive and is not extended by a prepositional phrase.[159] For example, one finds "the setting of a bone" or "the preparation of a hall," but never the addition of something like "to bring about this secondary purpose." He finds the same results with the related verb καταρτίζω, for which he can find only two possible and highly doubtful instances of its being completed with an εἰς phrase.[160] Hamann's brief analysis of διακονία, "ministry," tends in the same direction: it is simply not used in the NT with the general sense of "service," but, in his words, "is always restricted to some special kind of service, some special ministry."[161] Thus, in addition to the stylistic patterns in Ephesians, these observations on the normal usage of καταρτισμός and διακονία shift the burden of proof onto those who would translate them otherwise.

If there is no syntactical or lexical support for the modern retranslation of the verse, the impetus for the change must be sought elsewhere. Hamann finds the motivation in "an underlying dogmatic position": "those who for one reason or another are anti-clerical see here a convenient text to support their point of view."[162] In other words, the dogmatic position has come first, and the text has been distorted to provide justification after the fact. Hamann points to a footnote in Marcus Barth's commentary that locates the advent of the new interpretation historically: it "has been promoted since about 1940 especially by D. T. Niles and the World Council of Churches' Departments of the Laity and [of] Evangelism."[163] Barth's own preference for the anticlerical reading is philosophically, not textually, motivated. He writes:

> If a comma is put between the first two concepts, no doubt is left that the gift
> of the ministries has a double object: all the saints benefit from it, but only
> select ministers carry out the work of building the body. This interpretation has
> an aristocratic, that is, a clerical and ecclesiastical flavor; it distinguishes the

---

[159] Hamann, "The Translation of Ephesians 4:12," 43–44. His logic might be illustrated by appeal to two different possible translations in English. One can say "for the <u>preparation</u> of the saints <u>for</u> works of service"; but it is unidiomatic English to say "for the <u>perfection</u> of the saints <u>for</u> works of service." "Preparation for" is natural, but "perfection for" is nearly impossible. Hamann's argument is that καταρτισμός, "completion," follows the usage of the latter rather than the former.

[160] Hamann, "The Translation of Ephesians 4:12," 44–45. Hippolytus, *Commentary on Daniel*, 4:9.2: "He prepares the most noble for war [τοὺς γενναιοτάτους καταρτίζει εἰς πόλεμον]." This is not a complete parallel to Eph 4:12 inasmuch as it has the verb καταρτίζω, "prepare," not the noun καταρτισμός, and the prepositional completion is a simple noun (πόλεμον, "war"), not a verbal activity (it is not "prepares them to do something"). The citation of the expression in Rom 9:22 as a parallel, "objects of [his] wrath—ripe for destruction [σκεύη ὀργῆς κατηρτισμένα εἰς ἀπώλειαν]," is open to the same objections. In 2 Tim 3:17 the related verb ἐξαρτίζω is adverbially extended by a phrase beginning with πρός ("for every good work well prepared [πρὸς πᾶν ἔργον ἀγαθὸν ἐξηρτισμένος]"), but it is not a true syntactical parallel.

[161] Hamann, "The Translation of Ephesians 4:12," 45. Cf. our analysis of the term in the third textual note on 4:12, relying on the work of John Collins (cited in the first textual note on 3:7).

[162] Hamann, "The Translation of Ephesians 4:12," 45.

[163] Hamann, "The Translation of Ephesians 4:12," 45–46, citing Barth, *Ephesians*, 2:479, n. 265.

(mass of the) "saints" from the (superior class of the) officers of the church. A clergy is now distinct from the laity, to whom the privilege and burden of carrying out the prescribed construction work are exclusively assigned.[164]

Barth's exegesis derives from an underlying denial of any divinely mandated distinction between pastor and people within the Christian church.[165] He cites no textual evidence for his perspective, but dismisses the traditional view with pejorative terms like "aristocratic" and "superior class"—ideas which find no support in Paul's language of gift and suffering service.[166] Barth is patently uncomfortable with the idea that the ministers bring divine gifts to the laity, who correspondingly are passive with respect to the grace of salvation—yet that has been a major theme of Ephesians throughout and is precisely the point that Paul has just made about the ascended Lord who gives gifts to men (4:7–11). Thus, Barth's hostile dismissal of the notion that "laymen are ultimately only beneficiaries"[167] verges on denying the Gospel itself. A more positive and textually based assessment of Paul's words on the apostolic ministry will be presented in the commentary below. The three propositional phrases will now be examined individually.

… πρὸς τὸν καταρτισμὸν τῶν ἁγίων …—The preposition πρός introduces the first purpose of Christ's giving the gifts of men in the office of the ministry (4:11). The noun καταρτισμός ("completion") is a NT hapax legomenon and notoriously difficult to gloss in English. It is derived from ἄρτιος, which denotes what is "right, proper, fitting," or "complete" with respect to its purpose or function (cf. 2 Tim 3:17, where both ἄρτιος and the related verb ἐξαρτίζω, "to equip," are used). In classical usage καταρτισμός can be "restoration, reconciliation";[168] "setting, mending, healing" a bone;[169] or the

---

[164] Barth, *Ephesians*, 2:478–79.

[165] The section of Barth's commentary in which these words occur is titled "The Church without Laymen and Priests" (*Ephesians*, 2:477–84). He continues: "Indeed, the traditional distinction between clergy and laity does not belong in the church. Rather, the whole church, the community of all the saints together, is the clergy appointed by God for a ministry to and for the world" (2:479). "There is but one calling or vocation valid in the church: the call of God into his kingdom" (2:480). One wonders how such statements can stand in the exegesis of a verse immediately following Eph 4:11, in which Paul in no uncertain terms proclaimed Christ's appointment of ministers for the church. Indeed, contradicting his own exegesis, Barth had written: "Christ gives the church the officers she needs. … He appoints ministers to the church (4:8–11)" (*Ephesians*, 2:435; cf. 2:482). These illustrative comments from Barth's magisterial commentary reveal that what is at stake in the interpretation of this verse is the very rejection of Christ's gifts to the church and the substitution of what is thought to be a better way. Of course, not all modern interpreters of the verse go as far down the anticlerical path as Barth, but the danger of the trajectory must be noted.

[166] Hamann wisely observes that Barth's view does little to change the "hierarchical" relationship of clergy to laity that he decries: "I find just as much clericalism and aristocratic action involved in the second description as in the first. Only we are now thinking in democratic terms rather than in monarchical or aristocratic terms. Ministers have become bureaucrats and teachers of method, telling everybody else in the church what to do in order to fulfil their ministry" ("The Translation of Ephesians 4:12," 47).

[167] Barth, *Ephesians*, 2:479.

[168] See also Symmachus Is 38:12: ἀπὸ καταρτισμοῦ ἐξέτεμέν με.

[169] Heliodorus, *Apud Oribasium*, 49:1.1 (first/second century AD); Soranus, 1:73 (LSJM) = Soranus, 150:8 (BDAG; second century AD).

"furnishing, preparation" of a hall or garment.[170] The cognate noun κατάρτισις can be translated as "training, maturation" when used by Paul for the desired movement from weak to strong in the Christian faith (2 Cor 13:9); the noun is paralleled with παιδεία, "discipline," in classical examples.[171]

The metaphorical sense of καταρτισμός in the present verse is not documented in classical examples, but is easily derived from the related verb καταρτίζω. Significantly, the verb is used seven times in the LXX for "rebuilding" Jerusalem or its temple.[172] In Psalms it denotes God "providing" ears to hear, a path to walk on, etc.[173] In the NT, the sons of Zebedee are καταρτίζοντας, "mending," their nets (Mt 4:21; Mk 1:19). A disciple will be like his teacher when he is κατηρτισμένος, "fully provisioned [= taught]" (Lk 6:40). Vessels of wrath are "fit" only for destruction (κατηρτισμένα, Rom 9:22). Related uses of the verb include "having/seeking reconciliation" in mind or with one another (1 Cor 1:10; 2 Cor 13:11), "restoring" a sinner (Gal 6:1), "supplying" what is lacking in faith (1 Thess 3:10), and "equipping" with good to do God's will (Heb 13:21). It is also used for God "preparing" the ages (Heb 11:3). It is placed into parallel with "confirm, strengthen, and establish" (1 Pet 5:10).

This survey suggests that the semantic group (καταρτισμός, κατάρτισις, καταρτίζω) can have a very broad application indeed but that the common thread is the provision of what is necessary to bring (or return) people to their completion or goal.[174] In the immediate context, the phrase may (like the verb in Ezra[175]) evoke the gradual "completion" of the spiritual temple (cf. οἰκοδομή in 4:12c, 16; also 2:21). It implies growth toward "the complete man," the image of Christ himself (4:13). But it may also look forward to the illustration of the divine armor described in the peroration (6:10–17);[176] thus, the "full equipment of the saints" could be like a quartermaster's provision for a new soldier. So the first purpose of the ministers Christ gives to the church is to provide the saints with what they need to be complete, to outfit them with the gifts of God, rooted in Holy Baptism, by which they will be defended from the assaults of the evil one and brought to the completion God has in mind for them. By this process

---

[170] *P.Tebt.* 33:12 (112 BC); *P.Ryl.* 127:28 (first century AD).

[171] BDAG, s.v. κατάρτισις.

[172] LXX Ezra 4:12–13, 16; 5:3, 9, 11; 6:14.

[173] LXX Pss 8:3 (ET 8:2); 10:3 (MT/ET 11:3); 16:5 (MT/ET 17:5); 17:34 (MT 18:34; ET 18:33); 28:9 (MT/ET 29:9); 39:7 (MT 40:7; ET 40:6); 67:10 (MT 68:10; ET 68:9); 73:16 (MT/ET 74:16); 79:16 (MT 80:16; ET 80:15); 88:38 (MT 89:38; ET 89:37); cf. Mt 21:16; Heb 10:5.

[174] Lincoln, *Ephesians*, 253, translates this phrase in Eph 4:12 as "for bringing the saints to completion." He says: "It is the notion of making complete, which can include making complete by restoring or training, that best fits the context, where, in the next verse, different images for the Church's completion will be used" (254).

[175] LXX Ezra 4:12–13, 16; 5:3, 9, 11; 6:14.

[176] καταρτίζω sometimes appears in classical literature in a military context: e.g., "equipped in battle array" (Herodotus, *Histories*, 9:66; see LSJM, s.v. καταρτίζω, II).

the spiritual temple, the church, is itself built up stone by stone and brought to its perfection.[177]

… εἰς ἔργον διακονίας …—The second purpose of Christ's gifts of men in the office of the ministry (4:11) is "for the work of the ministry." The two action nouns imply the two verbs ἐργάζομαι, "to work," and διακονέω, "to minister," whose implied subjects, as argued above in the first textual note on 4:12, would be the ministers themselves; they are the ones who are commissioned "to do the work of ministering." The precise genitival phrase ἔργον διακονίας occurs nowhere else in the Greek Bible. Closest is 2 Tim 4:5, where the terms ἔργον and διακονία run in parallel: "do the *work* of an evangelist, fulfill your *ministry* [ἔργον ποίησον εὐαγγελιστοῦ, τὴν διακονίαν σου πληροφόρησον]." The contours of the vocabulary of διακον- were traced in the first textual note on 3:7. If a διάκονος ("minister") is a delegated representative of someone in authority who has been given authority to carry out specifically mandated tasks on behalf of his superior, then διακονία ("ministry") is the abstract noun that names the work. διακονία itself should therefore not be translated as "service," as if it referred to any and every form of generous work, including self-chosen works.[178] Instead, it refers to a public service (i.e., an official task to which a person is appointed for the sake of the public), which is usually a mediatorial or ambassadorial commission.[179] Where διακονία refers to the collection of money for famine relief in Jerusalem, the import of the term is not that the work was charitable or generous but that it was an officially designated gift sent on behalf of the churches.[180]

Because the apostles were chosen by Christ and sent by him, διακονία, "ministry," is an appropriate term for the office he gave them.[181] It is for this reason that in the majority of NT cases, διακονία is used of the apostolic office,[182] though the διακονία is also given by the Lord to other men who hold the pastoral office.[183] The specific form

---

[177] We have thus far avoided the traditional (e.g., KJV) translation, "for the *perfecting* of the saints," because modern holiness movements have inappropriately shifted the freight of that language from a perfection given by God (forensic/imputed through the means of grace) to a perfection to be achieved by men (ethical).

[178] Paul's statement "varieties of ministries, but the same Lord" (1 Cor 12:5), emphasizes not the self-chosen nature of the diverse activities, but the divine Lord who is the common point, the one represented in the διακονία, "ministry."

[179] The angels are called λειτουργικὰ πνεύματα εἰς διακονίαν ἀποστελλόμενα, "liturgical [i.e., doing God's work for the people] spirits sent forth for [their particular] ministry" (Heb 1:14). They are sent by God to carry out a mandate he gave them.

[180] Acts 11:29; 12:25; Rom 15:31; 2 Cor 8:4; 9:1, 12–13. BDAG, s.v. διακονία, 1, defines this as a "service rendered in an intermediary capacity, *mediation, assignment*" and translates ἡ διακονία … εἰς Ἱερουσαλήμ as "*my embassy in behalf of J[erusalem]*" (=my role as delivery agent [for the gift] for J. …) Rom 15:31." The thoroughly revised entry on διακονία in BDAG (the third edition of the lexicon) is heavily dependent on John Collins' work (see first textual note on 3:7).

[181] Acts 1:17, 25; 20:24; 21:19; Rom 11:13.

[182] In addition to the previous examples, see 2 Cor 5:18; 6:3; 11:8; 1 Tim 1:12; cf. 1 Cor 4:1. BDAG, s.v. διακονία, 3, provides the gloss "office."

[183] E.g., 2 Tim 4:5, 11; also "and say to Archippus, 'Look to the ministry [διακονία] that you have received in the Lord, that you fulfill it' " (Col 4:17).

of service is not conveyed by the semantic freight of the term itself, but by the external entailments—the genitives or prepositional phrases that modify the word. The Law of Moses had a "ministry of death/condemnation" (2 Cor 3:7, 9), which is contrasted with Paul's "ministry of the Spirit" (2 Cor 3:8). In general, the apostles were occupied with τῇ διακονίᾳ τοῦ λόγου, "the ministry of the Word" (Acts 6:4), that is, they were ambassadors who spoke the Word of God to the people on his behalf.[184] Where the external entailments are lacking, as in the present verse, they are best supplied from the normal use of the term elsewhere in the NT or by the immediate context. As διακονία is overwhelmingly a reference to the ministry of the Word carried out by the apostles (and their pastoral delegates), and as these various servants within the one ministry of the Word have been referenced in 4:11, immediately prior to this text in 4:12,[185] "the work of the ministry" is surely to be understood as the apostolic proclamation of God's Word with his authority to the saints.[186]

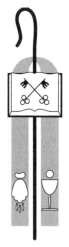

… εἰς οἰκοδομὴν τοῦ σώματος τοῦ Χριστοῦ—This third purpose of Christ's giving the men in the office of the ministry (4:11), "for building up the body of Christ," connects the current pericope with the final image of chapter 2, in which Paul had described the incorporation of the once distant Gentiles into the spiritual temple of the Christian church. Whereas they were once excluded from the inner courts of the Jerusalem temple, now they have the right of access (2:18; 3:12) and are actually built into the very structure of the temple (2:21–22; 3:17). The work of the ministry, therefore, is to continue this incorporation, to build up the body of Christ. Paul speaks of this as the purpose of the authority given him by God (εἰς οἰκοδομήν, "for building up," 2 Cor 13:10); "edification" is thus part of his pastoral work.

In the NT there are two aspects to this οἰκοδομή, "edification": (1) the incorporation of new stones, one by one, into the temple through Baptism into Christ; and (2) the movement from weak to strong, from milk to meat, from babes to mature people, from ignorant to knowledgeable within the faith. Like καταρτίζω, the cognate verb of καταρτισμός, "completion" (see the second textual note on 4:12), οἰκοδομή is used for the "construction" of the Jerusalem temple (and its maintenance)[187] and for the "buildings" (οἰκοδομαί) themselves.[188] Paul's metaphorical use of "building up" is likely

---

[184] The use of διακονία in Rom 12:7, often translated as "service," ought to be informed by the terms "prophecy" and "teaching" which surround it. It, too, is a ministry of the Word.

[185] Schnackenburg, *Ephesians*, 183: "But since in the whole section there is no discussion of activities other than preaching, guiding and teaching, we are bound to limit the διακονία to the 'ministry' of the preachers, pastors and teachers."

[186] It is therefore best translated as *the* ministry," not simply "ministry" or "ministering," for it refers to a specific office. The lack of article in the Greek text is not an impediment for two reasons: first, articles routinely disappear after prepositions (thus, it is εἰς ἔργον, not εἰς τὸ ἔργον), and second, genitive nouns attached to anarthrous nouns tend themselves to be anarthrous (and vice versa). Neither phenomenon means that the noun διακονίας is indefinite. Compare τὸ ἔργον τοῦ θεοῦ in Jn 6:29; Rom 14:20 and τὸ ἔργον τοῦ νόμου in Rom 2:15 to ἔργων νόμου in Rom 3:20, 28; Gal 2:16; 3:2, 5, 10 and ἔργον πίστεως in 2 Thess 1:11.

[187] LXX 1 Chr 26:27; 29:1; 1 Esdras 2:26; 4:51; 5:60, 70–71; 6:6, 21; Tobit 14:5; cf. 1 Macc 16:23.

[188] Mt 24:1; Mk 13:1–2.

intended to allude to the church as the temple of God.[189] The other three uses of the noun οἰκοδομή in Ephesians refer to this temple (2:21); to the church as the body of Christ that is growing (4:16); and to the "building up" of the church (4:29).

4:13 μέχρι καταντήσωμεν οἱ πάντες—With this supplementary clause Paul describes the consequent, ultimate purpose of the gift of the ministry (4:11) and its work (4:12).[190] The subjunctive[191] verb καταντήσωμεν, "we should attain," is followed by three coordinate prepositional phrases with εἰς, "to":

until we all should attain
[εἰς] to the unity of the faith and of the knowledge of the Son of God,
[εἰς] to the complete man,
[εἰς] to the measure of the maturity of the fullness of Christ

The beneficiaries of this lofty, threefold goal are designated as οἱ πάντες, "we all" (with "we" supplied as the subject of the first person plural verb καταντήσωμεν, "we should attain"), just as the recipients of Christ's gifts were first announced in 4:7 "to each one of us." "We all" draws together Jews and Gentiles, indeed the whole body of Christ as they are united by the Spirit in "one Baptism" (4:5) and built up in the faith through "the work of the ministry" (4:12). καταντάω, "to come to, arrive at," is used literally of reaching a place or figuratively of attaining a condition or goal. Not surprisingly, in all figurative uses of the verb in the NT the goal is eschatological: "promised hope" (Acts 26:7); "the end of the ages" (1 Cor 10:11); "the resurrection of the dead" (Phil 3:11).[192] This flavor may be intended in the present verse, whose goal is only partly reached in the present age, but brought to completion in the age to come. The translation "attain" (rather than "achieve") conveys the passive nature of the movement toward this goal, to which Christ through his ministry brings us.

εἰς τὴν ἑνότητα τῆς πίστεως—"The unity" repeats the significant noun ἑνότης, whose only other NT occurrence is in 4:3. However, the referent has shifted slightly: in 4:3 it is "the unity of the Spirit" that is already given and is to be treasured; in 4:13 it is "the unity of the faith" as a goal yet to be attained. In dogmatic language, in 4:3 this is *unitas* (the unity of all the baptized that is a reality established by God), while in 4:13 it is *concordia* (the harmony of confession toward which men strive by God's grace and

---

[189] Rom 14:19; 15:2; 1 Cor 3:9; 14:3, 5, 12, 26; 2 Cor 10:8; 12:19; 13:10; Eph 4:29. Like the temple and the tabernacle, whose prototype in heaven was shown to Moses to construct on earth (Ex 25:9, 40), the church on earth has as its typological counterpart the dwelling of the saints with God in heaven (2 Cor 5:1).

[190] Stoeckhardt, *Ephesians*, 202: "This is the terminus which is to be reached through the work of the preachers of the Gospel."

[191] The subjunctive is used to indicate the contingency of a future event. BDF, § 383 (2), calls it "the old prospective subjunctive" and notes that the classical use of ἄν in such clauses has mostly fallen away in the NT. Cf. Turner, *Syntax*, 111.

[192] It is also significant that the cognates ὑπάντησις and ἀπάντησις are used of an anticipated "meeting" with Christ on the Last Day (Mt 25:1, 6; 1 Thess 4:17). Pressing the evidence too far, Barth, *Ephesians*, 2:484–96, argues that the present verse means, in effect, "until we meet the Son of God on the day of his parousia." While his interpretation brings massive support for a christological reading of "the Perfect Man" (4:13), he fails to acknowledge the unity with the Son of God that is already attained sacramentally in this life.

on the basis of his Word). As μία πίστις, "one faith" (4:5), in its creedal context was understood as objective faith, so here "the unity of the faith" is surely *fides quae creditur*, "the faith that is believed" (cf. Col 1:23; 2:7). See the textual note on Eph 4:5. This unity in confession, this clinging to the common faith once delivered to the saints (Jude 3), is achieved through "the work of the ministry" as carried out by those men who are "apostles and ... *teachers*" (4:11–12).

καὶ τῆς ἐπιγνώσεως τοῦ υἱοῦ τοῦ θεοῦ—This second genitive, τῆς ἐπιγνώσεως, is also dependent on ἑνότητα: thus, it is "the *unity* [both] of the faith and *of the knowledge* of the Son of God."[193] The parallel between "faith" and "knowledge" supports the interpretation of "the faith" as objective (*fides quae creditur*; see the preceding textual note). ἐπίγνωσις, "knowledge," of God is the gift of the Holy Spirit (1:17), but it is not achieved mystically; it is given through the means of God's Word, as (according to the present context[194]) it is proclaimed and taught by Christ's ministers. The movement in and toward this full knowledge is part of the maturing of the newborn child of God (cf. Col 3:10). As the following context indicates, such unity in the faith and in knowledge combats false doctrine brought in by deceitful teachers (Eph 4:14). One aspect of Christ's gift is therefore that pastors protect their flock from such dangers.

As elsewhere in Ephesians, however, this knowledge is not mere intellectual attainment of facts, even the vital knowledge of the mystery of Christ (Eph 3:1–13; cf. Col 2:2), but "the knowledge of the Son of God [himself!]"—to know God personally (Eph 1:17), to experience his love (Eph 3:17–19), to be known by him (Gal 4:9). This is a knowledge that surpasses all others (Phil 3:8). As a personal, experiential knowing of Christ, it is achieved not only through the taught Word but also through the sacramental union with Christ brought about by such things as the "one Baptism" (Eph 4:5) and the communion in his "one body" (4:4), the communion of the body and blood of Christ (1 Cor 10:16–17; 11:23–29), the giving of which gifts is a central part of "the work of the ministry" (Eph 4:12).

εἰς ἄνδρα τέλειον—The expression ἀνήρ τέλειος, "perfect/complete man," occurs only twice more in the Greek Bible. It is the LXX translation of גִּבּוֹר תָּמִים, "sound/blameless man of valor" (2 Sam 22:26), whom the Lord treats "blamelessly," i.e., the Lord is righteous in his treatment of the righteous. In James 3:2 the τέλειος ἀνήρ is one who makes no mistakes—an unattainable status which James uses to expose hypocrisy. The ἀνήρ τέλειος, "complete/perfect man," is therefore one in whom God finds no fault. In the present context this is not presented as Law (an unattainable goal) but as Gospel, a goal to be reached through the work of the ministry. It stands in parallel to

---

[193] The phrase "of the Son of God," however, applies only to "knowledge"; the repetition of the article in τῆς ἐπιγνώσεως separates this phrase from the previous. That is to say, it is not "the faith ... of the Son of God," contra Barth, *Ephesians*, 2:489, who suggests the verse is talking about Christ's faithfulness to God and his knowledge of the church as his bride. It makes little sense to speak of our attaining to Christ's faithfulness to God.

[194] The work of "teaching and admonishing one another in all wisdom" (Col 3:16) through singing psalms, etc., as carried out by all the baptized in the Divine Service, is not in view here, given the context of the long sentence that began with the gift of ministers (Eph 4:11). The Ephesian parallel (5:19) to the Colossians text (Col 3:16) intriguingly omits that clause, perhaps evidencing our letter's greater stress on the work of the office of the ministry.

τὸν καταρτισμὸν τῶν ἁγίων, "the completion/perfection of the saints" (Eph 4:12). As the objective of teaching with the Word of God, the attainment of such completion is underway through the ministry in the church (Col 1:28), but its fullness is not obtained in this life. τέλειος, "perfect," is eschatological talk (1 Cor 13:10; cf. Phil 3:12). "The perfect/complete man" is the final fulfillment of Holy Baptism, which proleptically had stripped off the old Adam and replaced him with the new man re-created in the image of God (Eph 4:22–24)—who is Christ himself. The use of the distinctively masculine and singular term ἀνήρ, "male adult" (in contrast to the generic ἄνθρωπος), strengthens the reference to Christ, as does the explicit reference in 4:15 ("grow up … into him, who is the Head, Christ"). The terms "inner man" (3:16), "complete/perfect man" (4:13), and "new man" (4:24) should be read synonymously as the baptized Christian viewed through the lens of the Christ who clothes him. What we are to become has been already achieved in Christ (cf. 2:14, where Christ himself is our peace, and 2:15, where he is the "one new man" into whom we are placed). It is therefore not necessary to choose between the Christian and Christ as the ἀνήρ τέλειος. Christ is the "perfect man" whom the Father sees in each Christian in this life. While hidden from human eyes, this "man" is displaying what will be fully and visibly attained at the resurrection of the dead.

εἰς μέτρον ἡλικίας τοῦ πληρώματος τοῦ Χριστοῦ—This parallel phrase, "to the measure of the maturity of the fullness of Christ," further defines the preceding one, "the complete/perfect man," in relation to Christ. ἡλικία is a span of time in one's life (Mt 6:27) or a reference to bodily stature (Lk 19:3). It can therefore refer to the attainment of a legal age or "maturity" (Lk 2:52; Jn 9:21, 23), with the mental and bodily vigor that implies (cf. Heb 11:11). It is the attainment of the ἀνήρ τέλειος in the sense of "manhood." The opposite is "infants" (4:14). The noun μέτρον, "measure," first met in 4:7, again presents Christ as the measure against which the gifts and goals of God are judged. The ministry is not intended to "bring out the best in people," to help them achieve their potential, as if the measure of growth were distinctive to each, but to draw them to the fullness of Christ as their common goal. From start to finish, from Baptism into Christ to maturity in him, Christ is the pattern to which Christians are conformed. As the noun πλήρωμα, "fullness," implies,[195] this is not a lesser goal than achieving human potential but a far loftier one. By leading the baptized toward the maturity of the fullness of Christ, as Christ is filled with all the fullness of the Godhead (Col 1:19; 2:9), the ministry leads Christians toward the very likeness of God (Eph 1:23; 3:19; 4:10; cf. Col 1:9), the restoration of the image once lost in Eden (Eph 4:23–24; Col 3:10).

4:14 ἵνα μηκέτι ὦμεν νήπιοι—The conjunction ἵνα introduces another goal in what has now become a long sequence of purposes dependent (both syntactically and theologically) on Christ's gift of the ministers of the Word (4:11). But it is not a temporal

---

[195] πλήρωμα should not be taken merely as an adjectival modifier of ἡλικία, "maturity of fullness = full maturity" (e.g., Stoeckhardt, *Ephesians*, 203; Luther [WA DB 7:201]). Rather, in light of the use of πλήρωμα earlier in Ephesians (1:23; 3:19), it surely refers to the divine "fullness" that characterizes Christ and is conferred on his body, the church. It should not be understood in a simplistically physical manner (i.e., "size"), so as to imply that ἡλικία must mean "physical stature" (contra Schlier, *Epheser*, 201). Maturity is more complex than that.

sequence, as if this purpose clause could introduce something subsequent to the eschatological goal of the ministry's work (4:13). This verse introduces instead a present-day consequence of the work of the ministry in building up the church (4:12): "that we might no longer be infants." The use of the plural νήπιοι, "infants," in clear contrast to the singular ἄνδρα τέλειον, "complete/perfect man," and the singular ἡλικίας ... τοῦ Χριστοῦ, "maturity ... of Christ" (4:13), demonstrates that no sharp divide can be drawn between the church viewed corporately and the life of her members. The church (as his body) grows up into Christ as a whole and in her parts.

Here, of course, νήπιοι, "infants," is used figuratively. In the NT it is not always negative. In relation to God, it is more blessed to be "infants" than adults, as infants receive his care without claiming to merit it by strength or understanding (νήπιοι, Mt 11:25; Lk 10:21). They are the very model of faith and worship (Mt 21:16).[196] The term νήπιοι, "infants," surely alludes to the new birth of Holy Baptism (Jn 3:3–8; 1 Pet 2:2), which is the presupposition for this pericope (Eph 4:5). In the present verse, however, it is the Ephesians' relationship not to God but to false teachers that is key to the point of comparison. In this respect, with regard to "faith and ... knowledge" (4:13), it is necessary to be more than "infants." The contrast of immaturity versus maturity in the faith is commonly made in the NT with νήπιος.[197] The work of the ministry, by giving God's people growth and building them up in the body of Christ, is preparing them to stand firm against all foes (6:10–17).

κλυδωνιζόμενοι καὶ περιφερόμενοι παντὶ ἀνέμῳ τῆς διδασκαλίας—With these participles of result[198] Paul introduces an undesirable consequence of being "infants," immature in the faith (the particular sense in which infancy is negative). The imagery is a little jarring—one should not necessarily imagine babies set adrift in a boat! The metaphor has probably shifted. The verb κλυδωνίζομαι, "to be tossed here and there by waves," is used only here in the NT. The image arises naturally enough in a land by the sea,[199] but has a deeper meaning in biblical culture. In the LXX it is found only in Is 57:20, where the wicked are compared to the tossing sea. The noun κλύδων, "rough water," is the enemy of Noah's ark (4 Macc 15:31).

The disciples' experiences as fishermen on the Sea of Galilee are central to the Gospels. But Jesus' stilling of the storm with its τῷ κλύδωνι τοῦ ὕδατος, "rough water" (Lk 8:24; cf. Mt 8:24; Mk 4:37), and his walking on the water while the disciples' boat was being "beaten by waves" (Mt 14:24–25; cf. Mk 6:48; Jn 6:18–19) assumes a more-than-naturalistic explanation of the water's hostility. The sea represents the devil's opposition to Jesus' ministry; it is the traditional abode of the many-headed dragon Leviathan (Ps 74:13–14; Is 27:1), also called Rahab (Ps 89:10–11 [ET Ps 89:9–10]; Is

---

[196] Cf. the synonym βρέφος, "infant" (still in utero), in Lk 1:41, 44; and (postpartum) in Lk 18:15; 2 Tim 3:15; 1 Pet 2:2.

[197] See νήπιος, "infant," in Rom 2:20; 1 Cor 3:1; 13:11; Gal 4:3; 1 Thess 2:7; Heb 5:13. In Heb 5:14 and 1 Cor 14:20, the opposite of "infants" is τέλειος, "complete, mature" (cf. 1 Cor 2:6; Phil 3:15; Col 1:28; 4:12; James 1:4).

[198] See Wallace, *Greek Grammar*, 637–39, who notes participles of result in Eph 2:15; 5:19–21.

[199] Paul himself had already been shipwrecked three times (2 Cor 11:25) and would be again (Acts 27).

51:9), and of demons (Mk 5:13; Lk 8:33). From it the dragon conjures the beast from the sea (Rev 12:17–13:1; in Canaanite religion the god Yam, "Sea," is the personification of the primordial chaos). By treading on and defeating the sea, Jesus shows his lordship over these demonic forces, even as God trampled on the sea's waves (Job 9:8) and divided the Red Sea before his people by walking through it ahead of them (Ps 77:20 [ET 77:19]; Is 43:16). The allusion in Eph 4:14 to the stilling of the storm is strengthened by the phrase περιφερόμενοι παντὶ ἀνέμῳ, "carried about by every wind," as the personified hostility of the wind is a feature of the Gospel narratives referenced above (especially ἦν … ἐναντίος ὁ ἄνεμος, "the wind was against them," Mt 14:24).

Although the term "false" is not added, the phrase "every wind of doctrine" implies that the διδασκαλία Paul has in mind blows one way one day and the other way the next, but always against the truth. To be tossed about aimlessly is characteristic of doubters (James 1:6) and false teachers (Jude 12–13), but not of Christ's disciples. Doctrine that constantly changes cannot be true,[200] unlike the oneness of the true faith (Eph 4:4–6). There is no reference in Ephesians to a specific false doctrine Paul might have in mind, but the adjective πᾶς, "every," renders such identification unnecessary here.[201]

The implication of this verse is therefore twofold: first, that the danger presented by false doctrine is as deep as its demonic origin; but, second, that the same Christ who stilled the storm and walked on the waves will protect his people through the defensive power of his Word and enable them to share in his victory (cf. Mt 14:29; Rom 16:20, alluding to Gen 3:15).

ἐν τῇ κυβείᾳ τῶν ἀνθρώπων—The noun κυβεία (another NT hapax legomenon, like καταρτισμός in 4:12) means "craftiness, trickery" (cf. the synonym πανουργία in the next textual note). In Classical Greek it was literally "dice-playing," with the connotation of cheating (as in "loaded dice").[202] This negative connotation is confirmed and strengthened by the phrase that follows. If this is to be taken as a figurative reference to such swindlers, Paul has abandoned the nautical metaphor and introduced another.[203]

---

[200] "Do not winnow with every wind, nor follow every path" (Sirach 5:9).

[201] See "False Teaching and Paganism" in "Purpose and Themes" in the introduction for a discussion of false doctrine in Ephesus on the basis of the evidence in Acts. At an early stage there was false teaching on Baptism (Acts 18:24–19:7). See "Conflict over Baptism and the Spirit (Acts 18:24–19:7)" in "The City of Ephesus and Paul's Relationship to It" and "Baptism and the Spirit" in "Purpose and Themes," both in the introduction. In his farewell address to the Ephesian pastors, Paul referred to the certainty that false teachers would attack them (Acts 20:29–30). In Col 2:22 the phrase διδασκαλίας τῶν ἀνθρώπων, "teachings of men," refers to a syncretistic, ascetic, Jewish-Gnostic religious philosophy. Paul left Timothy in Ephesus to deal with false teachers (1 Tim 1:3–4; 6:3–5, 20).

[202] The English word "cube" derives from the related root κύβος.

[203] G. B. Caird comments tongue-in-cheek on Paul's rapidly shifting metaphors: "We may, if we are so disposed, form a mental picture of a group of children playing dice in an open boat. But the point is that the readers are offered three mutually interpretative metaphors for caprice or arbitrariness: children are easily led, a rudderless boat goes where wind and wave drive it, the roll of a dice is at the mercy of chance" (*The Language and Imagery of the Bible*, 150). Unfortunately, Caird misses the demonic and deliberate nature of the hostile forces at work against these poor children!

ἐν πανουργίᾳ πρὸς τὴν μεθοδείαν τῆς πλάνης—By its component parts πανουργία would mean "readiness to do anything." Though in the LXX it may carry the meaning "cunning" in a positive sense (e.g., Prov 1:4; 8:5), it more often bears the negative connotation of "craftiness, trickery," exclusively so in the NT.[204] It characterizes the scribes and chief priests in their attempt to entrap Jesus (Lk 20:23) and the wise of this world who try to live without God (1 Cor 3:19). Paul, as an honest preacher of God's Word, renounces πανουργία as a means to manipulate people into the church and simply speaks the truth (2 Cor 4:2). The devil, who deceived Eve with "trickery" (πανουργία, 2 Cor 11:3), has no such scruples—nor do his servants (2 Cor 11:4).

Likewise, μεθοδεία in the sense of "method" can have a neutral connotation, but here and in its only other NT occurrence (Eph 6:11; cf. 6:12 in 𝔓[46]), it must be "deceitful scheming." The demonic origin of such scheming is evident from 6:11: τὰς μεθοδείας τοῦ διαβόλου, "the devil's schemes." With typical redundancy, Paul adds the qualifier τῆς πλάνης, "of error, deception," implying "wandering from the path of truth." This, too, is a characteristic of the sort of charlatans and false teachers from whom Paul scrupulously distances himself.[205] The Christian message is simply incompatible with deceit, manipulation, trickery, and falsehood—qualities which tempted in the ancient world (as also today) because of the apparent "success" they so easily brought. But Paul will have none of it.

Finally, as if to make a complicated statement even more difficult, the use of πρός is unclear. Unless it introduces a coordinate and independent prepositional phrase (meaning "with"; cf. "and" in KJV), it must provide a further explanation of ἐν πανουργίᾳ: perhaps "tending toward" or "in accordance with."[206] The statement as a whole might then be translated as "by the sort of craftiness that tends to [or accords with] deceitful scheming which leads into error."

4:15 ἀληθεύοντες δὲ ἐν ἀγάπῃ—The verb ἀληθεύω, "be truthful, tell the truth," is found in the NT only here and in Gal 4:16 (where Paul contrasts the truth of his teaching with the deceptions of the Judaizers). In the LXX it has the obvious meaning of "telling the truth" (Gen 20:16; 42:16), but occasionally means "to do what is right."[207] The textual variant ἀλήθειαν δὲ ποιοῦντες, "and doing truth"[208] (F G, possibly derived from the Latin, *veritatem autem facientes*), is therefore not insignificant as a witness to how the text was understood. Doubtless the emphasis is on "speaking the truth," but this traditional translation does not form a clear contrast to being tossed to and fro by false doctrine (4:14); "listening to the truth" would make more sense. The verb is broader, connoting speaking, teaching, believing, and doing what is true, all of which

---

[204] BDAG, s.v. πανουργία.

[205] 1 Thess 2:3; 2 Thess 2:11; cf. 2 Pet 3:17; 1 Jn 4:6.

[206] Moule, *Idiom Book*, 53–54. Cf. πρός in Eph 3:4.

[207] In Prov 21:3, עֲשֹׂה צְדָקָה וּמִשְׁפָּט, "to do righteousness and justice," is translated by the LXX as ποιεῖν δίκαια καὶ ἀληθεύειν. Cf. Sirach 34:4, where ἀληθεύω means "to make something true."

[208] Or "acting faithfully"; cf. LXX Gen 32:11 (ET 32:10); 47:29; Josh 2:14; Judg 9:16, 19; Neh 9:33; Tobit 4:6; also Jn 3:21; 1 Jn 1:6.

forms a contrast to following the way of the false teachers (4:14). This is not simple moralism, but marks out the full contours of confessional Christianity. The "truth" is not just anything that might be true, but "the Word of truth" that brings faith (Eph 1:13; also 2 Cor 6:7), "the truth of the Gospel" (Gal 2:5, 14; Col 1:5).[209] The modifier ἐν ἀγάπῃ, "in love," likewise, stands in contrast to the two previous prepositional phrases that described the false teachers ("in trickery," "in craftiness"). "In love" qualifies not just a way of speaking, but a way of believing, confessing, and acting. The phrase has been a refrain in Ephesians (1:4; 3:17; 4:2; see also 4:16; 5:2), where more often than not it refers to God's love for us: the driving force behind our predestination (1:4) and Christ's sacrifice for us (5:2), the very soil in which we are rooted (3:17). But as such it gives us growth (4:15–16), so that God's love fills us and spills over into our words and deeds toward one another (4:2). Paul will not permit truth and love to be pulled apart, as if love for others could countenance false teaching, or faithfulness to apostolic doctrine could exclude the love of God in which it is rooted. Truth and love do not soften or dilute each other; they are not competing forces to be kept in balance or traded off; divine love is the content of the true Gospel. Where both are from God, they exist in perfect harmony.[210] Although it is possible that "in love" modifies the verb that follows (αὐξήσωμεν), as in 1:4–5; 3:17, its (antithetical) parallelism with the preceding two ἐν phrases in 4:14, perhaps chiastically, militates against that; in any case the meaning is scarcely affected.

αὐξήσωμεν εἰς αὐτὸν τὰ πάντα, ὅς ἐστιν ἡ κεφαλή, Χριστός—The subjunctive verb αὐξήσωμεν may be understood either as a continuation of the purpose clause begun in 4:14, "that we might grow," or as a hortatory subjunctive, "let us grow." In the context of this pericope, in which Paul has been speaking continuously of gift, the former is preferable. That we should grow up into Christ cannot happen by exhortation; it is not man's work, but is a gift of God through the work of the ministry (4:11–12), through the nourishing activities of his Word and Spirit.[211] αὐξάνω or αὔξω, "to grow," is consistently used in contexts that emphasize God's work in his kingdom, the gift nature of life and salvation.[212] Used intransitively,[213] it is virtually a divine passive (see the textual note on αὔξει in 2:21). Growth is a quality of the kingdom itself (Mt 13:32; Lk 13:19)

---

[209] Cf. Rom 1:18; Gal 5:7; Eph 4:21; 6:14; 2 Tim 2:15.

[210] On the inseparability of love and truth, see LXX Pss 50:8 (MT 51:8; ET 51:6); 83:12 (MT 84:12; ET 84:11); Zech 8:19; Tobit 14:7; Wis Sol 3:9; 2 Thess 2:10; 1 Pet 1:22; 1 Jn 2:5; 3:18; 2 Jn 1, 3; 3 Jn 1.

[211] This does not mean that Paul entirely excludes human effort. The Christian life is an ἀγών, "struggle" (see that noun or the cognate verb ἀγωνίζομαι in Lk 13:24; 1 Cor 9:25; Phil 1:30; Col 1:29; 2:1; 1 Tim 4:10; 6:12; 2 Tim 4:7; Heb 12:1), involving something like bodily training (1 Tim 4:8; cf. Eph 6:4; Hebrews 12). Yet it is God who *gives* the growth (1 Cor 3:6–7).

[212] E.g., "consider the lilies (of the field), how they *grow*; they neither toil nor spin" (Mt 6:28; Lk 12:27; cf. Lk 1:80; 2:40; Acts 7:17; 2 Cor 9:10; Col 1:9–10); "*grows* with a *growth* that is from God" (Col 2:19).

[213] Since αὐξήσωμεν is intransitive, τὰ πάντα is not the direct object of the verb (not "we might grow all things"), contra Schlier, *Epheser*, 205–6, but an accusative of respective, an adverbial accusative, "we might grow in every respect." See BDF, § 160.

and is brought about by the Word of God (Mk 4:8; Col 1:6; 1 Pet 2:2). In fact, the refrain in Acts is that "the Word of the Lord grew" (Acts 6:7; 12:24; 19:20).

So also in this verse, growth can only occur because we are the body of Christ. We grow (intransitive) as he grows us (transitive). The body grows up into the Head—a remarkable image, difficult to explain on the basis of medical theory (see the textual notes on 1:22–23 and "Christ, the Head—The Church, His Body" in the commentary there). But in the extraordinary body of Christ, this is true: the Head gives life and growth to the body. Only "in the Lord" does the body, the spiritual temple, live and grow (2:21). Certainly the opposite is obvious: cut off from the Head, the body withers and dies. This is the effect of the false teaching against which Paul is warning; by cutting the Ephesians off from the true Word, it cuts off their life. But "being truthful in love" (4:15) happens when they are connected to Christ, the Head, through his Word and Sacraments.

4:16 ἐξ οὗ πᾶν τὸ σῶμα συναρμολογούμενον καὶ συμβιβαζόμενον—Once again the body image in Ephesians emphasizes unity rather than diversity. This is stressed by the reiteration of compounds formed with συν-, "together with," which occur more often in Ephesians than any other NT writing (see also 2:5, 6, 19, 21, 22; 3:6; 4:3; 5:7, 11). The first of the two συν- compounds here is the rare verb συναρμολογέω, "to join together so as to form a coherent entity,"[214] which occurred in 2:21 in the construction of the spiritual temple. As so often throughout Ephesians, Paul combines and blurs the architectural and anatomical metaphors of the church. At the root of the verb is ἁρμός, which can mean a "joint" in stone; but in the present context the idea is a biological "joint" (cf. Heb 4:12). The second compound, συμβιβάζω, nearly as rare, means "to draw or knit together, unite"; in the anatomical metaphor the reference is probably to sinews and tendons (cf. Col 2:2, 19). Both participles are passive, stressing the role of Christ, the Head, in giving growth to his body.[215] Christ is both the source (ἐξ οὗ, "from whom," 4:16) and the goal (εἰς αὐτόν, "into him," 4:15) of the body's growth.

The stunning image is of a head that energizes its body, drawing its parts together by fitting the joints and providing tendons, the growth emanating from the head in defiance of any scientific pedantry.[216] It is significant that Paul returns to the role of Christ at the end of this pericope. The ministers (4:11) are simply instruments. It is not they who produce the growth, but the Christ, who gave the ministers (4:7–11) and continues to work through them (1 Cor 3:6–7).

---

[214] BDAG, s.v. συναρμολογέω.

[215] This must be stressed in contrast to the propensity to focus attention on what the body parts might be doing for themselves. Lincoln, *Ephesians*, 262, for example: "The two present participles … , taken together, underline forcefully that for the unified growth of the body its members have to be involved in a process of continual mutual adjustment." This is not what the text says. What it does say is that, under and through the work of Christ, every member of the body of Christ grows in love.

[216] Chrysostom avoids a thoroughly medical explanation by referring to the spirit: "Just as the spirit comes down from the brain, passes through the nerves and communicates with the senses, so it makes sense of the whole body. … So it is with Christ. The spirit is like a root. The souls of persons depend upon Christ as members. Each member depends on his providential distribution of gifts" (*Homilies on Ephesians*, 11:4.15–16, ACCS 8:168).

διὰ πάσης ἁφῆς τῆς ἐπιχορηγίας—The noun ἁφή (from the verb ἅπτω, "to take hold of") is a medical term for "ligament," used here metaphorically for that which binds together the various parts of the body of Christ into one (cf. Col 2:19).[217] The rare noun ἐπιχορηγία, "assistance, support" (cf. Phil 1:19), is related to the more common verb ἐπιχορηγέω, "to give what is necessary for support," used in the parallel text of Col 2:19. The genitive is either subjective, "ligament of (that gives) support," or objective, "the ligament that is supplied"—the difference is slight inasmuch as Christ provides the ligament that ties the members together.[218] The point is significant, though: the binding ligaments are not the members themselves, who remain passive in Christ's work of drawing them together in his church.[219] While the precise medical referent of ἁφή may elude us, the role it plays in Paul's metaphor is clear: "It represents whatever (i) holds the body together … , (ii) enables nourishment to pass from one part to another, [and] (iii) the whole to be controlled by the head."[220]

κατ᾽ ἐνέργειαν ἐν μέτρῳ ἑνὸς ἑκάστου μέρους—The noun ἐνέργεια means "working, operation"; it is an active, verbal noun characteristic of Ephesians.[221] In all three occurrences in this letter (1:19; 3:7; 4:16), it is combined with κατά ("according to, in accord with") to indicate the source, standard, or mode of God's mighty work. As so often in Ephesians, it is unclear whether this prepositional phrase modifies what precedes or follows; our translation assumes the latter.[222] Although the subject of the implied verbal action is not stated here, it should be assumed to be God. Thus, the translation "when each part is working properly" (RSV/ESV) misses the point entirely. It is God who is mightily at work and God who gives to each part its role and the strength to accomplish it.[223] As previously (4:7, 13), μέτρον, "measure," should not be understood as indicating a diversity of gifts, as if to stress the difference between each member,

---

[217] The precise meaning of ἁφή is difficult to determine. Is it to be distinguished from σύνδεσμος, "bond, ligament" (Eph 4:3), with which it is coupled in Col 2:19? Or are they synonyms, both of which refer to a sinewy connection holding two parts together at a joint? See Barth, *Ephesians*, 2:448–49, for the options.

[218] Barth, *Ephesians*, 2:448, sees a marital image in the noun ἐπιχορηγία, "assistance, support," which could refer to the responsibility of a husband to "provide" for his wife (cf. Eph 5:29). He understands ἐπιχορηγία as "supply" in an active sense, following Aristotle's physiological theories by which the head energizes each member through a point of contact.

[219] Andrew Lincoln, *Ephesians*, 263, suggests the ligaments are the ministers (4:11), whose role in uniting and building up the body is highlighted in this pericope. Schlier, *Epheser*, 208, and Schnackenburg, *Ephesians*, 189, likewise. Best, *Ephesians*, 411, suggests that this view goes back at least to Erasmus. This may be pressing the details of the metaphor beyond what Paul intended and finds no support in Col 2:19, but it well suits the present context.

[220] Best, *Ephesians*, 411. He suggests a combination of "ligaments, arteries and nerves."

[221] See ἐνέργεια also in Eph 1:19; 3:7; Col 2:12; cf. ἐνεργέω in Eph 1:11, 20; 2:2; 3:20; Col 1:29.

[222] If the former, it would mean, "every ligament supplied in accord with [God's] powerful working." The textual variants reveal early confusion as to how the phrase fits.

[223] "Since elsewhere in Ephesians energy (*energeia*) is always ascribed to God acting in Christ, it is probable that Eph 4:16 refers to the divine work going on in the church for her benefit, rather than to an operation performed by the church or her members" (Barth, *Ephesians*, 2:447).

but as marking the external and overwhelming standard of God's giving in Christ. The emphasis is not on the size of the gift, but on God's activity of allotment, which is graciously available to every member.[224]

τὴν αὔξησιν τοῦ σώματος ποιεῖται εἰς οἰκοδομὴν ἑαυτοῦ ἐν ἀγάπῃ—As this long and complex clause draws to a close, it is easy to lose track of the subject and main verb.[225] The basic structure is this:

ἐξ οὗ πᾶν τὸ σῶμα ... τὴν αὔξησιν τοῦ σώματος ποιεῖται

from whom [Christ] the whole body ... makes for itself the growth of the body

Although πᾶν τὸ σῶμα, "the whole body," is grammatically the subject of the main verb ποιεῖται, "makes for itself," the prepositional phrase ἐξ οὗ, "from whom," the preceding passive participles, and the reference to divine ἐνέργεια, "activity," indicate that the true actor remains Christ, the Head. The final part of the sentence ("the body *makes for itself growth*") cannot be read apart from the Christ who actually works it. The middle voice verb ποιεῖται, "makes *for itself*," with the object τὴν αὔξησιν, "the growth," should perhaps be understood as a simple intransitive, "the body grows."[226] If the context is not sufficient justification for this understanding, the parallel Colossians text makes it explicit:

τὴν κεφαλήν, ἐξ οὗ πᾶν τὸ σῶμα διὰ τῶν ἁφῶν καὶ συνδέσμων ἐπιχορηγούμενον καὶ συμβιβαζόμενον αὔξει τὴν αὔξησιν τοῦ θεοῦ

the Head, from whom the whole body, supported and knit together through ligaments and tendons, grows with a growth that is from God (Col 2:19)

The metaphor again becomes mixed as Paul reintroduces οἰκοδομή, "building up" (Eph 4:16; also 2:21; 4:12, 29), as the final goal of this sentence. This evokes the spiritual, living temple (2:21–22) and "the work of the ministry" which is for "building up" (4:12). The reflexive possessive pronoun ἑαυτοῦ, "of itself," does not imply that the body *causes* its own growth.[227] The reflexive pronoun is used because the direct object of the verbal noun οἰκοδομή, "building up," is grammatically the same as the subject of the main verb (ποιεῖται): "*the whole body* [πᾶν τὸ σῶμα]... building up of itself [not of something else]."[228] This is the goal of Christ's work through the gifts he gave at his

---

[224] See Grothe, *The Justification of the Ungodly*, 643.

[225] Schlier, *Epheser*, 208, calls the verse "recht umständlich," "quite complicated." Chrysostom, rather politely, says: "Paul has not explained himself clearly due to his desire to say everything at once" (*Homilies on Ephesians*, 11:4.15–16, ACCS 8:168).

[226] BDAG, s.v. ποιέω, 2 d: "used w[ith] a noun as a periphrasis for a simple verb of doing." Cf. 2:21, where αὔξει, "grows," is clearly intransitive.

[227] E.g., Lincoln, *Ephesians*, 264: "It now becomes clear that, however significant the writer deems their role to be in this regard, ministers do not have exclusive claims to this function. In the building up of itself the whole body is involved." In contrasting the ministers (4:11) with the other members of the body, Lincoln seems to have missed Paul's primary emphasis on Christ as the efficient cause of the growth. The ministers build up the church only as his instruments. The body is certainly involved in its own growth—as that which grows. To have such divine life worked within by Christ is not an insignificant gift!

[228] Wallace, *Greek Grammar*, 350: "The force of the reflexive is *frequently* to indicate that the subject is also the object of the action of the verb." Cf. BDF, § 283 (1): "In all authors we find

ascension: "the complete/perfect man" (4:13), the mature body of Christ, the completion and perfection of the temple "in the Lord" (2:21). Defended from false teaching (4:14), speaking, confessing, and living what is true (4:15), Christ's body in its every part will grow ever closer to Christ, and its members to one another.

Their unity and mutual relationship is finally characterized by that "love" that began with God, poured forth in Christ, and forms the good soil in which the body grows ("in love," 3:17). The body that is loved grows; the body that grows loves. "In love" (4:16) is therefore not a frivolous platitude at the end of this section, but a vigorous and intentional final word, forming a neat frame around the pericope with "in love" in 4:2, filling it up ("in love" in 4:15), and tying it to its surroundings (3:17; 5:2). It serves the same function as 1 Corinthians 13 in tying together the teachings on the body of Christ and its edification in the two surrounding chapters (Ephesians 3 and 5; 1 Corinthians 12 and 14).[229] Love and edification are indissoluble (1 Cor 8:1).

Commentary

Structure and Rhetoric

Doctrine and Ethics, Gospel and Law? (4:1–16 in the Context of the Epistle)

The consensus among most commentators is that a continental divide has been crossed in the transition from Ephesians 3 to Ephesians 4. The textual data that have prompted this analysis are twofold: the major doxology at the end of chapter 3 that appears to mark the end of a large unit and the clause παρακαλῶ οὖν ὑμᾶς (4:1), usually rendered as "therefore I *exhort* you," that seems to signal a shift from doctrinal to ethical material. Typically, Romans (allegedly with chapters 1–11 as "doctrine" and chapters 12–15 as "ethics") is cited as proof of this "standard" Pauline structure—though commentators struggle to find other letters that fit.[230] Our survey and analysis of the place of doxologies in Paul's letters has demonstrated a remarkable diversity and suggested that Eph 3:14–21 be taken as a response (and conclusion) to 3:1–13, but not to the first part of the letter as a whole, nor as a dividing point in the epistle (see the commentary on 3:14–21). With respect to the second factor, the usage of παρακαλέω in Paul

---

the reflexive used almost exclusively as the direct complement of the verb referring to the subject."

[229] Barth, *Ephesians*, 2:451.

[230] Bruce, *The Epistles to the Colossians, to Philemon, and to the Ephesians*, 333, for example, writes: "As in other Pauline letters, the doctrine expounded in the earlier part is to be worked out according to the practical guidance given in the later part, the transition from one to the other being marked by the adverb 'therefore.'" But the only example Bruce can offer from "other Pauline letters" is Rom 12:1. Schlier, *Epheser*, 177, makes the same argument, but notes specifically that only Romans has the same pattern, as does Best, *Ephesians*, 353. Barth, *Ephesians*, 2:426, adds 1 Thess 4:1, but that (like Eph 4:1!) comes immediately before a significant teaching section (1 Thess 4:13–18), at the conclusion of which παρακαλέω is clearly used with the sense of "comfort," not "exhort." Best, *Ephesians*, 353, quite rightly observes that in 1 Thessalonians most of the doctrine comes after 1 Thess 4:1, the earlier portion being personal, not doctrinal.

does not support this consensus either (see the first textual note on 4:1).[231] A less dramatic translation such as "so I *encourage* you ..." is more appropriate to the clause's role in Ephesians as the introduction to this pericope (4:1–16), but not to the second half of the letter as a whole.

Despite the exegetical consensus of others, it is apparent that an underlying dogmatic assumption has guided their conclusion, rather than a sober analysis of Paul's practice. The dissection of Paul's letters into dogmatic and ethical halves is the exegetical counterpart of a theology that restricts the work of the Gospel to conversion and gives the Law pride of place in the Christian life (so as to "disciple" the believer). Such a distortion of the right relationship between Law and Gospel is as much characteristic of various strains of modern Protestantism as it was of medieval Romanism. It is ironic that the son of the man who so famously challenged Luther's Law-Gospel framework[232] should so cogently express the dangers inherent in reversing that sequence:

> Indeed the juxtaposition of preaching and teaching (*kerygma* and *didache*), of indicative and imperative, may have had its day. Their undeniable usefulness as hermeneutical tools may be exhausted. ... The sequence, God (or Christ) did *this* for you—now you have to do *that* for him, is a ridiculous caricature of the relationship between God's grace and the good works for which man is created, according to Eph 2:5–10.[233]

Indeed, the fundamental and simplistic error is to view the relationship of Law and Gospel as a neat temporal or rhetorical sequence—whether Law-Gospel, Gospel-Law, or Law-Gospel-Law. The Law (as an expression of God's holy will that both condemns our sin and guides our behavior) and the Gospel (as a proclamation of the powerful message that forgives sins and gives new life) exist side by side in the Scriptures in continuous, dynamic interchange. Paul does not segregate them into separate sections of his letters. Nor can it be claimed that Paul uses the Law in its second function (to condemn sin) in the first half of his letters and confines the Law to its third function (guiding Christians) in the latter half.[234] The uses of the Law are the Holy Spirit's uses, despite the intentions of

---

[231] See Grothe, *The Justification of the Ungodly*, 615, n. 5.

[232] See, for example, the 1935 essay by Karl Barth, "Gospel and Law," *Community, State, and Church: Three Essays by Karl Barth* (ed. Will Herberg; trans. A. M. Hall; Garden City, N.Y.: Doubleday, 1960), 71–100. "We must first of all know about the Gospel in order to know about the Law, and not vice versa" (72). See also the thorough response by Werner Elert, *Law and Gospel* (trans. Edward H. Schroeder; Philadelphia: Fortress, 1967).

[233] Barth, *Ephesians,* 1:54–55. Unfortunately, Barth's alternative analysis, 2:426, that the first half of Ephesians is doxological (not dogmatic), does little to improve the situation. See also Winger, " 'One Baptism' and the Purpose of Ephesians," 247. Another critic of the two-part outline is P. S. Cameron, "The Structure of Ephesians," *Filologia Neotestamentaria* 3 (1990): 3–17. He claims to have discovered a "palistrophic" (chiastic) outline, with pairs of units balanced around a midpoint at 4:15–16 (the body of Christ). His vocabulary-based argument, which deliberately ignores other criteria, is founded on many of the same patterns discovered in the present commentary, but is on the whole unconvincing.

[234] For the three uses or functions of the Law, see "Epistolary Outline" in "Structure and Rhetoric" in the introduction.

human writers or preachers. In other words, the Law is the Law and will continue both to condemn and to guide as the Spirit sees fit and in accord with the spiritual condition of the reader/hearer.

A few examples from Ephesians demonstrate this. The Gospel certainly dominates the first three chapters, particularly the second. These chapters are thick with doctrinal teaching, including election in Christ (1:4–6), redemption through his blood (1:7), the baptismal seal of the Spirit (1:13–14), the ascension and triumph of Christ over hostile forces (1:20–23), salvation by grace through faith (2:1–10), the reconciliation achieved by Christ on the cross (2:11–22), and the revelation of the mystery of Christ (3:1–13). But the condemnation of sin is not absent (2:1–4, 11–12, 14–15), nor is the encouragement to knowledge (1:15–19; 3:2–12), good works (2:10), hope (1:18; 3:13), and worship (3:14–21). The same can be said of the latter three chapters.[235] The encouragement to treasure the unity of the Spirit is anchored in the strongest doctrinal, creedal declaration of the entire letter (4:1–6), followed by unfolding the manifold gifts of the ascended Christ to the church (4:7–16). Warnings against false doctrine imply condemnation of false belief (4:14), and the admonitions not to fall back into Gentile ways of belief and life condemn as much as they guide (4:17–19, 25–31; 5:3–15). Interspersed in the gaps are proclamations of pure Gospel (4:21–24; 5:1–2, 8, 14). The exhortation to worship (5:16–20) parallels the doxology (3:14–21). The exhortation to prayer (6:18–20) parallels the epistolary thanksgiving (1:15–16). The major emphasis of the so-called *Haustafel* ("table of duties," 5:21–6:9) is not a change of behavior but the way the Gospel is proclaimed by each relationship and the way the Gospel transforms the same. So also the peroration on the armor of God (6:10–17) is as much a comfort to Christians under threat in a hostile world as it is an exhortation for them to do anything.

Viewed objectively, then, it is clear that doctrine and exhortation, Law and Gospel, are present and intertwined in all parts of the letter. Indeed, those who believe that 4:1 begins Paul's exhortation are perplexed by his immediate and thoroughgoing digression into proclaiming the Gospel in 4:4–16![236]

Certainly there is a different flavor to the latter chapters of Ephesians. However, it is not the verb παρακαλέω ("exhort, encourage") which dominates,[237] but περιπατέω, "to walk." Introduced in 2:2, 10 as a way of describing the way of faith and life that changed when these Gentiles were baptized into Christ, this "walking" serves as the chief metaphor in the latter chapters when describing the Law and Gospel consequences of Baptism.

---

[235] Even Best admits: "Yet doctrine to which behaviour is the response is not missing from the final three chapters (see 4.4–16; 4.32; 5.23–32) just as it is not wholly absent from chaps. 12–15 of Romans (see [Rom] 12.3–8; 13.1–6; 14.9, 14, 17)" (*Ephesians*, 354).

[236] E.g., "the paraenetic motif of 4.2[–3] seems to disappear in 4.4–16" (Best, *Ephesians*, 354).

[237] In Ephesians παρακαλέω occurs only in 4:1 and 6:22. In the former it likely means "to encourage," and in the latter it clearly means "to comfort." Thus, its use as "to exhort" is conspicuously absent from Ephesians.

"To walk" is an OT image that should not be interpreted moralistically, merely as a type of behavior, but includes all aspects of faith, confession, and obedience to God's Word that characterize his children (see the first textual note on 2:2). In the latter parts of Ephesians, Paul's aim is both to teach the Christian walk (περιπατέω in 4:1; 5:2, 8, 15; as previously in 2:10) and to warn the Gentiles against falling back into their old, pagan system of belief and behavior (περιπατέω in 4:17; 5:15; as previously in 2:2). Behavior is addressed chiefly as it influences or reflects belief. Pagan behavior cannot be separated from idolatry. Christian lives are informed by the Law and formed by the Gospel. Chiefly, the Christian walk is about being molded into the image of Christ that was given in Baptism (4:24), to grow up into the perfect man (4:13), into the Head (4:15), learning to see Christ and his Gospel in every aspect of our lives (5:21–6:9). It demonstrates the power of the Gospel brought to bear on Christ's body by his apostolic messenger.[238]

Rhetorical Purpose and Units (4:1–16)

Rhetorically, then, this pericope can be seen to advance the argumentation of the epistle rather than change its course. This is, in fact, the point at which Paul makes his rhetorical thrust most explicit: that the Ephesians would treasure the unity that is theirs through Baptism into Christ (4:1–7). The ground has been prepared for this conclusion by the cosmic scope of the *Berakah* prayer (1:3–14), the adoration of the exalted Christ (1:15–23), the major christological "proofs"[239] of 2:1–10 and 2:11–22, together with the apologetic for Paul's apostolic ministry in 3:1–13—each of which in its own way has demonstrated the unity and equal standing of Jew and Gentile in Christ. The introduction of the carefully constructed, poetic baptismal creed (4:4–6) is the high point of this progression. But the argumentation is not finished. Paul follows up the creed (and its teaching) with reference to the means by which Christ delivers the goods: the ministerial representatives whom he gave to the church (4:11), through whom he would continue to be active in uniting and building up the church (4:12) even after visibly ascending to an unseen place of glory (4:8). The latter part of this pericope (4:7–16) therefore balances 3:1–13, forming a frame around the doxological and creedal material that intervenes. Paul's role and work as an apostolic messenger (3:1–13) does not end with him, but continues as Christ ever gives ministers as his gifts to the church (4:7–16).

These rhetorical comments assume the natural division of this pericope between 4:6 and 4:7. This is marked by the shift in person from the second and (implied) third person of the creed (4:4–6) to the first person plural ("to ... us") in the gift section (4:7–16). The grammar marks two further subdivisions, as 4:1–3 is direct "I to you" address, and 4:11–16 forms one long sentence drawing out the purposes of Christ's gifts. The pericope thus falls into four sections:

---

[238] See Grothe, *The Justification of the Ungodly*, 632–33.

[239] See "Proofs" in "Structure and Rhetoric" in the introduction.

The first unit (4:1–3) is one long sentence, not overly stylized, but neatly arranged with two prepositional phrases ("with …") and two participial clauses ("bearing … being …") modifying the infinitive ("to walk"):

> I encourage you … to walk …
>> [μετά] with all humility and meekness, [μετά] with patience,
>>> bearing with one another [ἐν] in love,
>>> being eager to hold fast the unity of the Spirit [ἐν] in the bond of peace.

Each participial clause is modified by a prepositional phrase with "in" (ἐν), introducing two of the main themes of the pericope: "love" and "unity."

The second unit (4:4–6) is, by contrast, probably the most stylized sentence in the book. It stands out as poetry in the midst of prose by its lack of a main verb; its brief, rhythmic lines; its parallelism; and its organization into three groups. It is impossible to know whether this is a preexisting creed,[240] hymn, or liturgical chant (possibly from a baptismal rite) that Paul may have incorporated because it was familiar to his addressees (like 5:14) or whether Paul simply created it for the occasion.[241]

> [4]ἓν σῶμα καὶ ἓν πνεῦμα,
>> καθὼς καὶ ἐκλήθητε ἐν μιᾷ ἐλπίδι τῆς κλήσεως ὑμῶν·
> [5]εἷς κύριος, μία πίστις, ἓν βάπτισμα,
> [6]εἷς θεὸς καὶ πατὴρ πάντων, ὁ ἐπὶ πάντων καὶ διὰ πάντων καὶ ἐν πᾶσιν.

> [4]one body and one Spirit
>> —just as you were also called in the one hope of your calling—
> [5]one Lord, one faith, one Baptism,
> [6]one God and Father of all, who is over all and through all and in all.

---

[240] The existence of Christian creeds in apostolic times should not be discounted. Though the earliest Christian Communion rites do not include a creed (a creed first appears in a Communion rite in the sixth century), baptismal rites included creeds from the very beginning. Kelly, *Early Christian Creeds*, 13–23, notes creedal fragments in the NT. See also Hermann Sasse, "Jesus Is Lord: The Church's Original Confession," in *We Confess Jesus Christ* (trans. Norman Nagel; St. Louis: Concordia, 1984), 9–35; and Best, "The Use of Credal and Liturgical Material in Ephesians."

[241] Hamann, "Church and Ministry," 122, comments: "It is quite sufficient to hold that St Paul was capable of such an arrangement. Since I am quite capable of doing that same sort of thing in writing, and a number of you present here as well, I don't see why we should suddenly run away from a writer we know something about, to one we know nothing about, in order to explain the careful construction of these verses." Though the language of 4:4–6 is traditional, it can all be located in the first half of Ephesians.

The rhythm and structure is broken by the insertion of "just as you were also called in the one hope of your calling," which, if the creed consisted of traditional material, would appear to be Paul's addition. Despite the resulting imbalance in the first line, the NA[27] editors are surely wrong not to mark it as part of the poem. The Trinitarian pattern of 4:4–6 is obvious—though reversed.[242] This reversal has been explained as experiential, as the Christian is led by the Spirit to the Son and by the Son to the Father.[243] This accords with Luther's explanation of the Creed in the two catechisms and suits the poem's escalating movement toward the Father's sovereignty over the entire cosmos. While this Spirit-Son-Father order did not carry through into the ecumenical Creeds, the emphatic repetition of the term "one" did. It is the characteristic feature of the Eastern creeds to confess "one God" and "one Lord," as represented by the Nicene Creed.[244] Can it be insignificant that Paul's presentation of this creed includes precisely *seven* occurrences of the word "one"? The divine perfection is presented as seven, three (the Trinity), and "one." Christian unity is rooted in the divine unity.

The third unit (4:7–10) is defined by the quotation from Psalm 68, around which Paul's words are hung as exegesis. There is little to commend the bracketing of 4:9–10 in many translations. Paul's exegesis of the text is not parenthetical, but stresses the exaltation of Christ which is the presupposition of his great gifts. The effect of this unit's shift into the first person plural ("to each one of *us* grace was given," 4:7) is to personalize the objective, creedal statements that precede.

In the fourth unit (4:11–16), which is one long sentence, Paul returns to the complicated concatenation of subordinate clauses and phrases that so often has featured in the letter. The governing verb is ἔδωκεν, "he gave" (4:11). The entire sentence unpacks the gifts of Christ and their consequences for the church. Though the tendency among commentators is to seek a shift from Christ's work to the ministers' work to the work of every member of Christ's body, in point of

---

[242] The NA[27] marginal reference to 1 Cor 8:6 (which is a "binitarian" creed), but not to 1 Cor 12:4–6 (which is a Trinitarian creed in the same "reverse order" [Spirit, Lord/Son, God/Father] as Eph 4:4–6), indicates the editors are reading this text as binitarian. Presumably the editors did not view 4:4 as poetic because it includes the extended subordinate clause, "just as you were called in the one hope of your calling" (4:4b). But surely the parallelism of "one body and one Spirit" (4:4a) with the rest of the creed is more significant.

[243] Williams, "Logic *versus* Experience in the Order of Credal Formulae." Williams contrasts the experiential order with the "logical" order of the historic creeds (Father, Son, Spirit), which he believes to be more suited to apologetic purposes, especially when confronting pagans. Williams also notes the peculiar location of Baptism—in the Second Article, not the Third— which we have explained as a reference to Christ's own Baptism. See "Baptism and the Spirit" in "Purpose and Themes" in the introduction; "Baptism in the Prologue" in the commentary on 1:3–14; and "Creedal, Baptismal Unity (4:4–6)" in the commentary below. See further Winger, " 'One Baptism' and the Purpose of Ephesians," 259–63.

[244] See Kelly, *Early Christian Creeds*, 195, who notes, but does not explain, this characteristic distinction between Eastern and Western creeds. While the creedal "one God, the Father" may equally derive from 1 Cor 8:6, Williams, "Logic *versus* Experience in the Order of Credal Formulae," 43–44, notes that the appearance in Eastern creeds of "one church" and "one Baptism" is most likely under the influence of the present passage.

fact Christ himself remains the actor throughout the unit. The arrangement of the five nouns in 4:11 as well as the three prepositional phrases in 4:12 is discussed at length in the textual notes. The five nouns represent the one office of the holy ministry as a gift of Christ in concrete men who carry out the office in distinct ways. The purpose of the office is unfolded in a series of phrases and clauses that follow in 4:12–16.

It is first:

[πρός] for the completion of the saints,
[εἰς] for the work of the ministry,
[εἰς] for building up the body of Christ (4:12)

With due recognition given to the distinctiveness of each phrase, the three are essentially parallel in describing the benefits conveyed to the church by the ministerial work.

The next verse portrays a threefold, proleptic and eschatological consequence—in other words, the results the ministry in the church is to effect in this life, which are only brought to completion on the Last Day. The unifying factor in this threefold goal is conformity to the image of Christ as brought by Holy Baptism:

[μέχρι] until we all should attain
    [εἰς] to the unity of the faith and of the knowledge of the Son of God,
    [εἰς] to the complete man,
    [εἰς] to the measure of the maturity of the fullness of Christ (4:13)

These three prepositional phrases (εἰς, "to …"), like those in the preceding verse, are parallel and equivalent statements of the one goal.

Paul's third statement of goal returns to the present life of the church:

[ἵνα μηκέτι ὦμεν] that we might no longer be infants,

being tossed to and fro by waves and carried about by every wind of doctrine,

[ἐν] in the trickery of men, [ἐν] in craftiness in accordance with deceitful scheming which leads into error (4:14)

In these parallel lines, Paul pictures the dangers posed by false teaching in three distinct metaphors: the immaturity of children, the danger of a boat in a storm, and the trickery of charlatans.

In contrast to those perils, Paul presents the consequence of the faithful work of Christ's ministry:

but, being truthful [ἐν] in love, that we might grow up in all things into him, who is the Head, <u>Christ</u>,
    from whom the whole body,
        being jointed together and knit together through every ligament supplied,
        in accord with [his] activity in apportioning each single part,
    grows bodily toward the building up of itself [ἐν] in love. (4:15–16)

This confusing and heavily laden conclusion to the long sentence does not constitute a shift from the logic of the preceding verses, but returns to the theme of the giving Christ (4:7–11), the Head of the church (1:22–23).

Creedal, Baptismal Unity (4:1–6)

"So I encourage you—I, the prisoner in the Lord" (4:1). In two ways Paul connects his ensuing words of encouragement with what has preceded: (1) οὖν, "so, then, therefore," marks them as a consequence or conclusion drawn from the revelation of the mystery of Jew-Gentile unity in Christ and the proclamation of the peace-making, reconciling Gospel of his cross. (2) The appeal to Paul's imprisoned status recalls again the charge on which he was arrested—officially, that he had brought a Gentile (Trophimus, an Ephesian!) into the forbidden parts of the temple; unofficially, because the Jews were furious over his proclamation of an apparently Law-free Gospel, incorporating Gentiles into the kingdom of God without circumcision.[245] But his imprisonment serves a further purpose in the present argument: he demonstrates practically the consequences of the Gospel in his own life. Rather than asserting his preeminence in the church, as he might well have done as an apostle of the ascended Christ, he willingly suffers for the sake of the other members of Christ's body. By appealing to his weakness rather than his authority, he sets a Christlike tone for the words of encouragement that follow. He does not command obedience (as indeed he could), but leads by example.[246] He embodies the qualities of humility, meekness, patience, and forbearing to which he subsequently encourages them (4:2).

We cannot know whether Paul's major concern was to address an existing division or hostility between Jew and Gentile in the Ephesian church (context at their end) or whether his own situation as a prisoner because of the Gentiles was more significant (context at his end). But what is clear is his response. In the beginning of this chapter, he draws out more explicitly the implications of the "proofs"[247] for unity in Christ that he has carefully assembled in the preceding chapters. He then develops the intimate relationship between the unity that is given by God and the harmony that Christians seek to preserve with one another.

The qualities of humility, meekness, patience, and forbearing do not make the top ten list of virtues in Greco-Roman philosophies of life. In many cases they are despised qualities, displaying weakness, servility, and contemptibility.[248] But Paul highlights them, first, precisely because they are virtues of weakness, the denial of self and individuality, qualities that strengthen harmony

---

[245] See "Paul's Trip to Jerusalem, Arrest, and Imprisonment (Acts 21:1–36)" in "The City of Ephesus and Paul's Relationship to It" in the introduction.

[246] Recall Luther's dictum: "A Christian is a perfectly free lord of all, subject to none. A Christian is a perfectly dutiful servant of all, subject to all" (*The Freedom of a Christian* [1520], AE 31:344).

[247] See "Rhetorical Purpose and Units" immediately above as well as "Proofs" in "Structure and Rhetoric" in the introduction.

[248] See the references in Barth, *Ephesians*, 2:457–58; Lincoln, *Ephesians*, 235–36.

within the body of Christ. Second, and more important, like Paul's own imprisoned suffering and weakness in conformity to Christ as his apostle, these qualities are Christlike. The body of Christ is strengthened and drawn together when its members look like the whole, when they are like Christ. In this way the opening salvo of encouragement to Christlike virtues flows naturally into the proclamation of "one Baptism" (4:5), as that which has put the image of Christ upon the Christians, and the work of the ministry (4:11–12), as that which brings growth into "the complete/perfect man" (4:13), into the fullness of Christ's likeness. This is the cord that binds the pericope together. Paul's thought does not run in the way of mere ethics,[249] but is entirely molded by the thought that "it is no longer I who live, but Christ who lives in me" (Gal 2:20; cf. Rom 13:14).

In an epistle that has so strongly emphasized the monergistic work of Christ in bringing salvation to Jew and Gentile alike, apart from works, the reconciliation Christ has achieved in his one body on the cross, it would be passing strange if Paul were now to speak of true, essential Christian unity (*unitas*) as something to be created by human works.[250] If it were not obvious from the choice of such humble human "virtues" as meekness and humility (4:2), the vocabulary of 4:3 ought to make it so: "being eager to *hold fast* [τηρεῖν] the unity of the Spirit in the bond of peace." That verb, "to hold fast, keep, treasure," is not to create, but to hold onto something of value that is given. "The unity of the Spirit" (τὴν ἑνότητα τοῦ πνεύματος) is not a reference to a human quality but to a oneness that God's Holy Spirit has created. "In the bond of peace" (ἐν τῷ συνδέσμῳ τῆς εἰρήνης) recalls the work of Christ, who "is our peace," who created peace between those near and far by uniting them in his one body on the cross (2:13–17). Paul points the Ephesians to virtues that are in accord with the unity that is already theirs, the virtues that display that unity and strengthen its external manifestations in the church and toward the world.

What is at stake is not the true unity of the church, but the Christians' continued connection to it. The unity of the church is not of human making (it is the work of Christ) or preserving (which is the Spirit's gift), nor can it be destroyed

---

[249] "It is important to realize that unity is created through understanding and appropriation of the one great reality, not by the resolution to keep peace and unity nor by a reasonable, moderate, and judicious weighing of virtues and failures in others and in ourselves. There are no moralistic directions here" (Hamann, "Church and Ministry," 122).

[250] On the distinction between *unitas* (true, essential Christian unity) and *concordia* (agreement on doctrine), see the second textual note on 4:13 and the discussion below in the commentary. Hermann Sasse alludes to this distinction in his discussion of the present passage: "As the Spirit cannot be divided, so Christ cannot be divided (1 Cor. 1:13), and so also His body can not be divided. It is thoughtlessness, to say the least, if one speaks of the divisions between earthly church organisations as divisions of the body of Christ. Paul, when speaking of the schisms at Corinth, does not speak of divisions of the body of Christ" ("Intersynodical Exegetical Theses [Jn 17:20–23; Eph 4:1–6]," 3). These theses were presented as part of the work toward uniting the two Australian Lutheran synods, which finally occurred in 1966. That merger took place through the hard work of discussions aimed at achieving doctrinal agreement. Sasse's own labors toward that goal demonstrate the value he placed on *concordia*, for disagreement on doctrine can drive people out of the body of Christ.

by human neglect or hostility.[251] The *true* unity of the church is always a perfect, holy thing, because it is of God. But there is a grave danger that Christians can fall away from that divinely given unity (*unitas*), as happens when they forsake the faith or lead others to do so through false teaching (a violation of *concordia*).[252] "No one can split the body of Christ. But what can happen is that we cease to be members of this body, that we defect from the Una Sancta by the grave sins of schism and heresy."[253] This was, of course, the issue behind Article 7 of the Augsburg Confession in 1530, which quotes Ephesians 4 in defense of its position. The Lutherans had not voluntarily departed from visible union with the Western, Roman Catholic Church; they had been excommunicated. The question that faced them was not the ecumenical one of what is the minimum agreement necessary for us to reestablish visible, organizational unity, as agreement in the Gospel and the Sacraments in AC 7 is often interpreted.[254] The question was rather the opposite: since we are now separated from the Roman Church, has the true unity of the church been broken? Are we still truly church in such a way that we still have Christ's gifts? The answer the article gives is a resounding yes! The true unity of the church is established by the true Gospel

---

[251] Here we disagree with the second half of such interpretations as those of Best, *Ephesians*, 364: "If unity needs to be preserved it must already exist. ... They did not create their unity, though they can destroy it"; and Stoeckhardt, *Ephesians*, 179: "And it is through their earnest endeavor to live a life of love, of peace, of lowliness, gentleness, long-suffering, and patience, that they will retain this unity of the Spirit. If, on the other hand, they neglect these virtues, then the unity of the Spirit will again fade away." The *true* unity of the Spirit (*unitas*) never fades away, though the external unity of the earthly church (*concordia*) may be damaged by human unfaithfulness.

[252] Dahl, "The Concept of Baptism in Ephesians," in *Studies in Ephesians*, 433, concludes: "It suffices to say that Ephesians discloses a tension between the actual situation in the church and the sacramental reality of belief. As such, it gives us a picture in which we recognize ourselves."

[253] Sasse, "Intersynodical Exegetical Theses," 3.

[254] Certainly the modifiers in the text of AC 7, "the Gospel *rightly* taught and the Holy Sacraments administered [*rightly*—Latin] *in accord with the Gospel*" (my translation), imply more than a bare minimum of agreement in doctrine. But the article is not talking about ecumenical dialogue. The ecumenical movement tends to confuse the organizational structure of the church with its essential oneness. Sasse comments:

> Man can join an earthly society, he can join also an ecclesiastical organisation, the Church as the "societas externarum et rituum" ["society of externals and rites"]. But this does not make him a member of the Church as the "societas fidei et Spiritus Sancti in cordibus" ["society of faith and of the Holy Spirit in the hearts"] which is the people of God, the body of Christ, a reality in this world, but hidden to our human eyes, hidden in, with and under the outward organisation which is never [to be equated with] the body of Christ. To this true church man is called by the Holy Spirit: "For by one Spirit we were all baptised into one body ... and all were made to drink of one Spirit" (1 Cor. 12:13). This passage illustrates the words "one body and one Spirit" Eph. 4:4. The Spirit is the Holy Spirit, the body the Body of Christ. It is noteworthy that both are connected with Baptism and the Lord's Supper, see 1 Cor. 10:16ff. and 12:13 and the "one baptism" [Eph 4:]5. ... The earthly organisation of the church is never [to be equated with] the body of Christ. The mystical body of Christ is hidden in it. It exists in, with, and under the external church, just as the sacramental body is in, with, and under the bread and wine. ("Intersynodical Exegetical Theses," 3)

and Sacraments and exists wherever they do their work; it is not established or broken by human works, though humans can sever themselves from it. Human traditions, rites, and ceremonies do not create or constitute the true unity of the church, whether or not their use is helpful, harmful, or desirable.

This confessional and historical digression is helpful not only because the Augsburg Confession (7:4) cites Eph 4:5–6 in defense of its position but also because it illustrates so well Paul's own line of argumentation in chapter 4. Though directing the Ephesians to the humble, Christlike virtues that are appropriate to the body of Christ, Paul does not at all imply that these human activities can create the true unity of the Spirit. To prove the point, he quotes a creed-like, poetic confession of the gifts of God that have indeed created the unity of the church (4:4–6). In this the Ephesians are passive; this is the one hope to which they "were called" (ἐκλήθητε, 4:1). The creed includes no verbs; it is neither exhortation ("let us make one body" or "let us preserve one body") nor wish ("may there be one body"). The only verb we might supply is indicative: "*there is* one body." What is given is given from the one God through the one Lord by the work of the one Spirit, who through one Baptism draws us into the unity of the church.[255] The sevenfold repetition of "one" not only emphasizes the importance of unity, but it also highlights its divine quality (seven is the number of divine perfection). The three "articles" of the mini creed attribute everything to the Triune Godhead.

The Trinitarian character of this creed warns against overemphasizing the ecclesiological character of Ephesians. The point of departure is not the unity of the church as such, since that is only a derived unity. What comes first is the unity of God (*unitas Dei*). The essential oneness of God is the OT creed, the *Shemaʿ* (Deut 6:4, quoted in Mk 12:29).[256] It is likewise the basis of NT creedal statements[257] and the defining characteristic of Eastern creeds that begin "I believe in one God."[258] Paul has used this sort of creedal argument before: "Or is God [the God] of Jews only? Is he not [the God] of Gentiles also? Yes, also of Gentiles, since God is one [εἷς ὁ θεός], who will justify the circumcised by faith and the uncircumcised through faith" (Rom 3:29–30). The implication is

---

[255] See "Die Taufe als Teilhabe am Heil der Kirche" in Schnackenburg, " 'Er hat uns mitauferweckt': Zur Tauflehre des Epheserbriefes," 177–83.

[256] Barth, *Ephesians*, 2:464–65, explicates the role of the oneness of God in the OT with six points. He emphasizes that God's oneness is not a static quality, but leads to his desire and action to unite all things. Philo notes how the confession of one God by the Hebrews brought a visible unity that caused the nations to take note:

> You see how invincible the multitude of the Hebrews is; and a defence to them more formidable than even their number is their unanimity and agreement; and the greatest and most powerful cause of this unanimity is the idea which they entertain of the one God, from which, as from a fountain, they derive a united and indissoluble affection for one another. (*On the Virtues*, 7 [35]; trans. Yonge, *The Works of Philo*)

[257] Rom 3:30; 1 Cor 8:4, 6; 12:12–13; Gal 3:20; 1 Tim 2:5–6; James 2:19. Jesus' claim of oneness with the Father is an essential facet (Jn 10:30; 17:21).

[258] See the discussion of 4:4–6 in "Rhetorical Purpose and Units (4:1–16)" above.

that destroying the harmony of the church is actually an offense against God himself; it is to abandon the faith.[259]

Paul's words thus cut with both Law and Gospel edges. On the one hand, he warns the Ephesians what they are giving up if they deny the oneness of Jew and Gentile in the church: it is a rejection of Christ's work, of the Spirit's bond, of the essential oneness of God himself. Such admonitions are common in the early postapostolic fathers:

> Why are there strife and passion and divisions and schisms and war among you? Or have we not one God, and one Christ, and one Spirit of grace poured out upon us? And is there not one calling in Christ? Why do we divide and tear asunder the members of Christ, and raise up strife against our own body, and reach such a pitch of madness as to forget that we are members one of another?[260]

But Paul's chief thrust is surely the Gospel. These great gifts of the Triune God are the *source* of the church's essential unity and are therefore the strength for all efforts to treasure it and maintain harmony among Christians. Because he is one, we are one.[261] Paul thus moves quickly from encouraging certain harmonious qualities to proclaiming the gracious source of such virtues in the Triune God himself.

What stands out in this brief creed are the additions that accompany the three persons of the Holy Trinity in each "article." Taking them in the "reverse Trinitarian" order of the text (Spirit, Son, Father), in the "First Article" (4:4) we note the terms that are coupled with the Holy Spirit: "one body" and "one hope" (4:4). The former may take pride of place simply as the first point of contact, the experiential entry into the Holy Trinity (see "Structure and Rhetoric" above). The church is where we begin. But Paul has in mind more than the local congregation where one first meets Christ. The "one body" is the (one holy catholic and

---

[259] Schlier, *Epheser*, 188.

[260] *1 Clement*, 46:5–7 (trans. Kirsopp Lake, LCL). Echoes of Ephesians are strong in this quotation.

[261] Abraham Calov, *Systema locorum theologicorum*, 2:290–91, comments on Eph 4:3, 6:

> If the one God is above us all, then all of us who live under the power of this one God and are children of this one Father ought to worship in response to this unity. If the one God by His benevolent care is present among us all, then it is incumbent upon us to be one with all, since He desires to embrace all with equal care and providence. If the one God is in us all and wishes to dwell in us all as in one temple, then we should all be of one heart and mind (Acts 4:32). If the one God dwells in us all, then whatever would rend our unity would by that very act seek to tear apart the one God. The apostle heaps up many arguments for unity and harmony of worship among the faithful, but he traces all the arguments back to the wonderful and glorious unity which we worship and praise in God. ... In the end he recalls our attention to the one God and Father of all, by whom we were all created and adopted as His children, who by His majesty is above all, by His providence is through all, and by His grace is spread abroad in all, so that under, through, and in Him we all move and possess true blessedness. (Quoted in Robert D. Preus, *The Theology of Post-Reformation Lutheranism* [St. Louis: Concordia, 1972], 2:69)

apostolic) church.[262] The term "body" represents a (perhaps *the*) major theme of Ephesians (see the first textual note and the commentary on 1:23; also 2:16; 3:6; 4:12, 16; 5:23, 28, 30). As the adjective "one" (4:4) makes clear, the emphasis in this letter has been on the body as a unity (rather than as an illustration of diversity, as in Rom 12:3–8 and 1 Cor 12:4–31) and on its intimate connection to Christ, the Head (Eph 1:22; 4:15; 5:23). The latter part of this pericope (4:15–16) will expound at length the way in which the Spirit infuses all parts of the ecclesial body, as the human spirit gives life, unity, and direction to the human body.[263] In this way, though it is the body of Christ, the church belongs to the article on the Spirit. Thus, "one body" is the bridge between the initial encouragement to hold fast the Spirit's unity (4:1–3) and the creedal confession of its source (4:4–6). The prominence given to "one hope," especially the excursus Paul devotes to it in 4:4, is more difficult to explain. "Hope" has been less prominent in Ephesians at a purely quantitative level (ἐλπίς elsewhere only in 1:18; 2:12). But conceptually it is highly significant as marking the transition of the Gentiles from the hopelessness of pagan life ("having no hope," 2:12) into the Christian faith. It is perhaps self-evident that "one hope" (4:4) lends an eschatological flavor to the creed, but it is important that Paul sees the one body united not only in its source but also in its destination.

Inserted into the "Second Article" (4:5) are "one faith" and "one Baptism" (4:5). In the third and fourth centuries, this passage was a battleground in the debate over whether baptisms administered in schismatic groups were legitimate, whether those who had received such baptisms were to be baptized (again or in fact) when they returned to the Catholic Church.[264] In the sixteenth century this phrase was used to condemn (quite rightly) the "Anabaptists [re-baptizers]" who rejected the legitimacy of infant Baptism. But these later appropriations of the passage have little to do with its original context.

If what Acts 18–19 tells us of the origins of the Ephesian church is at all relevant,[265] these two expressions are mutually dependent. Certainly "the faith" is what is delivered to all new Christians with their Baptism, as the true confession of God is taught, instilled, and confessed. It is the "standard of teaching" (τύπον διδαχῆς) to which they were "handed over" in their Baptism (Rom 6:17). "The faith" is represented *in nuce* by this very creed. But Ephesus was a place where a false teaching concerning Baptism was part of the church's early

---

[262] "What is this one body? They are the faithful throughout the world—in the present, in the past and in the future" (Chrysostom, *Homilies on Ephesians*, 10:4.4, ACCS 8:159).

[263] "In the body it is the living spirit that holds all members together, even when they are far apart. So it is here. The purpose for which the Spirit was given was to bring into unity all who remain separated by different ethnic and cultural divisions: young and old, rich and poor, women and men" (Chrysostom, *Homilies on Ephesians*, 9:4.1–3, ACCS 8:159).

[264] See Winger, " 'One Baptism' and the Purpose of Ephesians," 249–55.

[265] See "Paul and Ephesus in Acts" in "The City of Ephesus and Paul's Relationship to It" in the introduction.

history.[266] The expressions "one faith" and "one Baptism" would have had for the Ephesians a certain apologetic ring. They would have recalled the misunderstanding and false practice that Paul discovered when he first arrived, the controversy over John's Baptism and the possible confusion between water Baptism and Spirit Baptism (Acts 19:1–7). If there was any discord induced by the twelve early converts having received "two Baptisms," if there was any confusion resulting from the return to Ephesus of legitimate disciples of John or Pentecost-day converts, if the ongoing mundane work of catechesis and Baptism was viewed with disdain in comparison—Paul cuts through such dangerous tendencies to use the Sacrament divisively and proclaims that there is only "one Baptism" (cf. 1 Cor 10:2; 12:13). Indeed, as we have argued,[267] Paul may have in mind Christ's own Baptism, so as to say that there are not many Baptisms (of individuals), but only one Baptism into which each individual is placed as they put on the one Christ (Gal 3:26–29). As Luther preaches on the occasion of the Baptism of our Lord: "You should not separate your baptism from Christ's baptism. Rather, you must by means of your baptism enter into the baptism of Christ, so that Christ's baptism *is* your baptism, and your baptism Christ's baptism, and in the end there is only one baptism."[268]

Thus, "one faith, one Baptism" (4:5) stands in antithesis to false teaching and false belief (cf. 4:14). The creed Paul confesses resources and emboldens the Ephesian church to stand firm against any teaching or practice that would contradict the unity that is given them. Creeds exclude false teaching, but their essential purpose is to unite. The faith that is given forms an absolutely essential precondition to the gift of preachers in the latter half of this pericope (4:11), for both hearers and teachers are bound by the same baptismal confession. As Luther preaches on this text:

> Now you have the reason why the apostles Paul and Peter everywhere so faithfully enforce this virtue, the unity of the Spirit. It is the most necessary and beautiful grace that Christians possess. It holds together the Christian community, preventing factions and schisms, as before explained. So Paul here admonishes men to be careful for harmony, making every endeavor to preserve it. The term "unity of the Spirit" is used to make plain the apostle's meaning. He would thus emphasize oneness of doctrine—the one true faith. Since the Holy Spirit is present only where there is knowledge of and faith in the Gospel of Christ, "unity of the Spirit" implies a unity of faith. Above

---

[266] Acts 18:24–19:7. See "Conflict over Baptism and the Spirit (Acts 18:24–19:7)" in "The City of Ephesus and Paul's Relationship to It" in the introduction.

[267] Winger, " 'One Baptism' and the Purpose of Ephesians," 264–69, and "Baptism in the Prologue" in the commentary on 1:3–14.

[268] Martin Luther, "Sermon on the Festival of Christ's Epiphany: On the Baptism of Christ" (1546); my translation from StL 12:1135–36, as first printed in Winger, " 'One Baptism' and the Purpose of Ephesians," 268. See the commentary on 1:3–14 for a lengthier excerpt.

all things, then, the effort must be to preserve, in the Church, the doctrine of the Scriptures, pure and in its unity.[269]

Luther's careful distinction between the true unity (*unitas*) of the church that is given by God's Spirit and the harmony (*concordia*) of Christians that they strive to maintain on the basis of agreement in confessing the doctrine of Scripture accords precisely with Paul's movement from 4:4–6 to 4:7–16. Christians are one; Christ makes them one; Christ provides gifts to maintain that harmony, and all Christians are to seek it as their goal.[270]

The Gift of the Ascended Christ: The Office of the Ministry (4:7–16)

The next verse serves as a transition: "now, to each one of us grace was given in accord with the measure of the gift of Christ" (4:7). By the words "grace was given," Paul refers first to the contents of the creed, as just cited in brief (4:4–6). On this basis alone the exegetical consensus that Paul now introduces a *diversity* of gifts should be challenged. His term "grace" (χάρις, unlike χάρισμα, "[spiritual] gift," as in, e.g., Rom 12:6 and 1 Cor 12:4) is not the language of diverse gifts, but of common salvation. The grace that is given "to each one of us" (Eph 4:7) is the one faith, one Baptism, to be incorporated into the one body of Christ. Such context necessitates interpreting μέτρον not as a different "measure" or amount given to each Christian, but the same "measure," the overwhelming apportionment whose standard is not the needs or distinctiveness of the individual, but the superabundant merit and generosity of Christ himself. Paul says, in effect, "Look not to what makes you different from one another, but to what has been graciously poured out upon you to bring you into conformity with the image of Christ." But, second, as a transition, the "grace given" looks forward also to the specific gift of the men named in 4:11 as those who continue to carry out Christ's gracious work—or rather, those through whom Christ does the giving.

But before exploring those ministerial gifts, Paul sets down the exegetical basis for contending that Christ was in a position to give gifts at all. Quoting Ps 68:19 (ET 68:18), with its description of God as a conquering King being showered with tribute from his joyful subjects, Paul discerns a typological meaning. As God ascended on high to the mount where his temple would be

---

[269] Luther, "Sermon for the Seventeenth Sunday after Trinity, Ephesians 4:1–6," Lenker, 8:288–89; StL 12:896, § 17.

[270] Hermann Sasse, "Theses on the Seventh Article of the Augsburg Confession," *The Springfielder* 25.3 (Autumn 1961): 14, explains:

> The Church of Christ is essentially one, *Una sancta*. The doctrine of the Church is, therefore, always also a doctrine of the unity, the oneness of the Church. Also, the unity of the Church is at the same time a gift and a task, an indicative and an imperative. This becomes clear in the Scripture passage that underlies *Confessio Augustana*, VII, Eph. 4: "There is one body and one Spirit ... one Lord, one faith, one baptism, one God and Father ..." [4:4–6]. This is the indicative. It is bound up with the imperative "that ye walk worthily of the vocation with which ye are called ... endeavouring to keep the unity of the Spirit in the bond of peace" [4:1, 3].

built,[271] so Christ ascended to the heights of heaven. As God had victoriously led his people out of slavery to the Egyptians into the freedom of the promised land, so Christ had won his victory over the devil and destroyed captivity to sin. Tweaking the verse via Jewish exegetical tradition (which had associated it with Moses on Mount Sinai) and the Targum translation, Paul unveils the true christological meaning of the text, proclaiming that Christ not only "received gifts from men"[272] but "gave gifts to men" (see the second textual note on 4:8). In line with the epistle's emphasis on the exaltation of Christ (1:20–23; 2:6, with the resurrection and ascension being viewed as a unit), Paul here associates the distribution of the spoils of Christ's victory on the cross with his ascension to the right hand of God.[273] Perhaps because of a danger of syncretism or fear of hostile forces that troubled Christians in Asia Minor (as is particularly clear in Colossians), Paul stresses the subjugation of all spiritual forces under the feet of this victorious Christ (1:21; 2:2; 3:10; cf. 6:10–12).

The debate over the meaning of "he descended" in 4:9–10 has tended to overshadow the chief point Paul is making. Even the traditional translation, "he led [or set free] a host of captives" (4:8), seems influenced by the ancient belief that Christ's descent involved a plundering of hell and the release of OT saints. Setting aside for a moment the question of whether Christ's descent into hell is what Paul has in mind, a more vivid picture appears when the clause ἠχμαλώτευσεν αἰχμαλωσίαν is translated with full force: "he took captivity [itself] captive." Luther, who in his 1546 Bible translates the clause from Eph 4:8 as "hat das Gefengnis gefangen gefüret ['has led captivity captive'],"[274] captures the drama of the image in his preaching on the text for Ascension Day:

> How magnificently, majestically this is said. He has ascended on high and sits above in heaven, in order to imprison the prisons and chain up the stocks. The kingdom, office, and work which he has executed on high is that he has cast captivity into captivity. …
>
> Had he not ascended on high and not led captivity captive, we would have had to remain captive forever. But by his ascending on high he led the great and overpowering, deep and unyielding captivity captive before God, namely, sin to sin, death to death, hell to hell. …

---

[271] That is, Mount Zion in Jerusalem. See 2 Sam 6:16–19 and the second textual note on Eph 4:8.

[272] The image of the ascending Christ being showered with praise by his subjects is captured well in this hymn: "Up through endless ranks of angels, Cries of triumph in His ears, To His heav'nly throne ascending, Having vanquished all their fears, Christ looks down upon His faithful, Leaving them in happy tears" (Jaroslav J. Vajda, *LSB* 491:1; © 1974 Augsburg Publishing House; used by permission of Augsburg Fortress).

[273] See "Christ's Victorious Ascension to God's Right Hand (1:20–23)" in the commentary on 1:15–23.

[274] WA DB 7:201. Luther's marginal note on "das Gefengnis," "captivity," reads: "Das ist, die Sünde, Tod, und Gewissen, das sie uns nicht fahen, noch halten mögen ['that is, sin, death, and conscience, that they may not seize or hold us']." In his "Defense of the Translation of the Psalms" (1531–1533), AE 35:216, WA 38:13, Luther explains his decision to offer a very literal translation, "du … hast das gefengnis gefangen ['you … took captivity captive']," in Ps 68:19 (ET 68:18; see WA DB 10/1:312–13), the OT source for Eph 4:8.

Sin, death, devil, and hell had taken us captive; but Christ has in turn taken them captive. … He takes my captivity captive, intercepts my hangman, interdicts my sins, exterminates my death, damns my hell. …

Christ's power and might over sin are now given to those who believe in him, who know that they, too, are masters over sin, while heretofore they were its slaves. Sin will not any longer compel them to transgress against God or to despair, because Christ, ascended on high, helps them resist sin when they believe in him and call upon him. …

This captivity of sin, which, even though it is not completely dead, nevertheless cannot rule over the believers who are under Christ, continues until Judgment Day. However, on Judgment Day sin will have its head chopped off and be put to death completely. In the meantime sin is confined to prison, bound like a thief with the hangman's rope. What sin has done to us, that Christ has done to it.[275]

In our textual notes on 4:9–10 we have presented several arguments against the traditional interpretation that κατέβη εἰς τὰ κατώτερα [μέρη] τῆς γῆς means "he descended into the lower parts of the earth" (4:9) and refers to the descent into hell. The genitive is more likely appositive, "he descended into the lower parts, *that is,* the earth," referring to his incarnation and earthly ministry, which forms a better contrast to the ascension into heaven and accords well with Christ's language, particularly in the Gospel of John. This is not in any way to deny the factuality of the descent into hell event as confessed in the Apostles' Creed and Article 9 of the Formula of Concord,[276] which stands firm on the basis of 1 Pet 3:18–20. It is, in fact, with great reluctance that we diverge from what is the majority interpretation of the text in patristic times and throughout Lutheran history. One would not wish to lend any support to those who deny the existence of hell, the devil, or eternal punishment—matters well-attested throughout Scripture.

But, as with the clause "he took captivity captive," one might find that the view we have adopted offers a more comprehensive picture of Christ's victory over the devil. For Christ's assault on the devil and his destruction of the devil's power were not confined to the moment of his descent into hell, but began with his incarnation, continued through his earthly ministry, and culminated at the cross, tomb, resurrection (including the descent into hell), and ascension. Already while casting out demons, Jesus declared that he was entering the strong man's house and binding him (Mt 12:29; Mk 3:27; Lk 11:21–22). Already when the disciples were sent on their first mission, Christ declared

---

[275] Luther, "First Sermon for the Day of Christ's Ascension, Acts 1:1–11 and Psalm 68:19," Klug, 2:118–21.

[276] "We simply believe that the entire person [of Christ], God and man, after the burial descended into hell, conquered the devil, destroyed the power of hell, and took from the devil all his might. … Thus we retain the substance [sound doctrine] and [true] consolation that neither hell nor the devil can take captive or injure us and all who believe in Christ" (FC SD 9:2–3 [*Triglotta,* 1051, 1053]).

that he saw Satan fall like lightning from heaven (Lk 10:18). In the wilderness Christ defeated Satan with the Word of God (Mt 4:1–11), and on the cross, as Satan bit Christ's heel, the Victorious One crushed his head (Gen 3:15). Thus, the defeat of the devil and his forces was accomplished by the entire ministry of Christ, including the descent into hell.

The logical movement from the ascension of Christ (Eph 4:9–10) to the giving of the fivefold office of the ministry (4:11) may escape commentators whose theological instincts do not incline them to appreciate this gift. But the logic is not so obscure as it might at first seem. All four Gospels conclude with the sending of the apostles to preach the forgiveness of sins.[277] The longer ending of Mark (16:9–20) and two passages in Luke's writings (Lk 24:45–51; Acts 1:7–9) explicitly connect this mandate with the ascension.[278] It is through his apostles' teaching and baptizing in his name that Christ continues to be with his church until the close of the age (Mt 28:20). The connection of the office with baptizing and teaching also suits the present context well. The creed to which Paul has just appealed (4:4–6) can only bring harmony if it is actually taught and if the Baptism it proclaims is actually administered. Thus, first, the ministry is introduced as the means Christ puts in place to convey the gifts of grace that have just been confessed.[279] But, second, the ministry has a more distinctive role to play in furthering the *concordia* toward which Paul urges the Ephesians. It has been noted that what unites the five offices named in 4:11 is the preaching or teaching of the Word. Thus, if there is to be unity in the "one faith" (4:5), it will best be attained by careful, faithful, truthful, and loving teaching.[280] The office of the ministry comes into play as one more instrument in Paul's orchestra.

---

[277] Mt 28:16–20; Mk 16:14–20; Lk 24:45–51; Jn 20:19–23. Of course, the longer ending of Mark (16:9–20) is almost universally acknowledged to be a secondary addition to the text, but it likely includes genuine tradition about Christ.

[278] Stoeckhardt, *Ephesians*, 199–200, astutely reveals the inverse aspect of this argument, that the victorious ascension of Christ makes the ministry possible:

> Thus this conquest of the foes of Christ and this leading them in triumph make possible and feasible the bestowal of the gifts of grace and all that is connected with it, namely, the successful work of the shepherds and teachers whom the Lord has given to His Church. By conquering Satan, by fettering him when He descended into hell, and by leading him in triumph when He ascended into heaven, Christ has in advance opened and cleared a road for the teachers of the Church. … Thus is prepared an effective comfort for the ministers of the Word, since they know beforehand that the devil, who is continually at work trying to frustrate their work, is a fettered prince, a prisoner of the Lord Christ, that he cannot and dare not go farther than Christ permits.

[279] With the institution of each means of grace, our Lord also institutes the office of the ministry to administer it (Mt 16:19–20; 26:26–29 [and parallels]; 28:16–20; Mk 16:15–16; Lk 10:16; Jn 20:21–23). See Winger, "The Office of the Holy Ministry according to the New Testament Mandate of Christ."

[280] Dahl, "Interpreting Ephesians: Then and Now," in *Studies in Ephesians*, 468, correctly interprets Paul's purpose not as glorifying the status of the ministers but as highlighting their role:

> But I doubt that the interest of the author lies in either a charismatic … or an institutional … ministry. His whole emphasis revolves rather around the task, the role, the function of ministers, namely to promote unity in faith and knowledge of the Son of

It is all too easy to flatten Paul's thought patterns by pressing this passage into the mold of the body of Christ metaphors in Romans 12 and 1 Corinthians 12. Though they are not in contradiction, these passages are treating rather different concerns. The recognition of the distinctive role of each individual member, with the unique gifts the Spirit has given, forms the warp and woof of those passages, but simply is not the fabric of Ephesians. In fact, quite ironically, to insist that the distinct gift of Eph 4:7–12 (the office of the ministry's unifying role) be identical to the diverse gifts of those other passages would contradict the very diversity they proclaim. Paul must be permitted to rejoice in the gifts as he sees fit without our objecting that he has neglected some. What suits his purposes in the present passage is to mark those men who are gifts to the church from above, who bring the Lord's unity to people whose harmony is perhaps strained from within. Thus, even Paul's language resists the urge to make the bodily members help themselves.

Despite how 4:11 has often been translated, it does not refer to "spiritual gifts" in the way we typically think of them.[281] Paul does not point to the ability to be a pastor as a gift to be sought within Christians, but speaks of "pastors" as a concrete gift from Christ. This meaning is made amply clear by the first two (or three) terms in the list. "The apostles" (not the gift of apostleship) are men whom the Lord himself chose, mandated, and sent to the church, in fact, to bring churches into existence through his creative Word. They are a foundational (2:20) source of unity because they speak for Christ with unique authority; the church that falls away from apostolic teaching defines the word "apostate." Although a precise referent is difficult to determine, "prophets" and "evangelists" appear to be adduced by Paul in a similarly foundational role (see the third and fourth textual notes on 4:11). "Pastors" and "teachers" (see the fifth textual note on 4:11) are of no use unless they continue in the path of apostolic teaching; but where they are faithful, the church is built up in oneness.

Because the terms are concrete, referring to specific men whom the Lord has given, it is in a sense correct to say that Paul is not talking here about "offices." But if the opposite of "offices" is mere "functions," then the latter has moved farther away from his meaning.[282] Paul is not simply saying that "teaching" and "shepherding" need to happen (and how would one speak of "apostling" as a mere function?). The Ephesians need to know where they may find these functions with the certainty that they are there as gifts of the Lord. So Paul speaks of the men themselves. But he does not speak of "Paul" or "Peter" or "Timothy"; and in this sense, because he uses titles not names, it is indeed correct to say

---

God and thus to ward off these many winds of doctrine so that the church, united in all its limbs, can grow up to the head who is Christ (4:13–16).

[281] If we were to speak of such, it is the officers themselves who are the spiritual gifts (Schlier, *Epheser*, 195).

[282] "Functions" is used by, for example, Barth, *Ephesians*, 2:436; Best, *Ephesians*, 388–99.

that Paul speaks of the gift of *offices* for the church.[283] The movement among the five from "apostle" to "pastor" and "teacher" implies a continuation of these offices beyond the apostolic generation, "to the close of the age" (Mt 28:20). One generation of pastors is replaced by another, in such a way that Christ's church is never bereft of his gifts.[284]

The restriction of the list in Eph 4:11 to ministers of the Word also sets it apart from the somewhat parallel texts in Romans 12 and 1 Corinthians 12. Paul appeals to the teacher half of the equation that defines the church as consisting of "teachers and hearers."[285] This fact alone should lead us to expect that Eph 4:12 describes the work that the ministers do (not what "the saints" do). The complex stylistic and grammatical questions that have arisen in 4:12 in the interpretation of its three prepositional phrases are addressed in the textual notes. But it is clear that the reinterpretation that would turn "the work of the ministry" (4:12) into general "Christian service" arose in the twentieth century not from a close reading of the Greek text, but from theological presuppositions that generated an instinctive hostility to the office of the ministry. Henry Hamann's careful study begins with a reference to a typical modern example of that reinterpretation: "Christ did not appoint pastors to do the work of the church by themselves, but *to equip God's people to be servants, and to do his work for him*."[286] Markus Barth's monumental commentary has given this reinterpreta-

---

[283] "Their ministries are viewed not simply as spontaneous and haphazard functions but more as offices that are constitutive for the life of a Church on the move toward becoming what it already is as the fullness of Christ" (Lincoln, *Ephesians*, 268).

[284] Melanchthon argues not only that the church has the *right* to call ministers but also that she *must* call ministers, since Christ wills her to have them:

> For wherever the Church is, there is the authority [command] to administer the Gospel. Therefore it is necessary for the Church to retain the authority to call, elect, and ordain ministers. And this authority is a gift which in reality is given to the Church, which no human power can wrest from the Church, as Paul also testifies to the Ephesians, 4, 8, when he says: *He ascended, He gave gifts to men*. And he enumerates among the gifts specially belonging to the Church *pastors and teachers*, and adds that such are given for the ministry, *for the edifying of the body of Christ*. Hence, wherever there is a true church, the right to elect and ordain ministers necessarily exists. (Treatise, 67 [*Triglotta*, 523])

[285] C. F. W. Walther, *Die Stimme unserer Kirche in der Frage von Kirche und Amt* (2d ed.; Erlangen: Deichert, 1865), 251, said: "The congregation, which, when *properly ordered* [*gehörig geordnet*], consists of both preachers and hearers." But in his translation of that work, Mueller translated *gehörig geordnet* as "properly *organized*" (C. F. W. Walther, *Church and Ministry* [trans. J. T. Mueller; St. Louis: Concordia, 1987], 220; emphasis added). The point of the verb *ordnen* is not organization (by human right), but divine institution. Walther's definition follows Melanchthon's *Loci Communes*, taken up by Martin Chemnitz in his *Loci Theologici*, who writes under the title "Teachers and Hearers in the Church": "For since the foundation of the church is the doctrine of Christ taught by the prophets and apostles, Eph. 2:20, the doctrine concerning Christ cannot be taught and cannot be proclaimed in the church unless there are teachers, Rom. 10:14. And … there are promises of the perpetual preservation of the ministry in the church, Is. 59:21; Eph. 4:11" (*Loci Theologici*, part 3 [trans. Jacob A. O. Preus; Chemnitz's Works 8; St. Louis: Concordia, 1989, 2008], 1312).

[286] Hamann, "The Translation of Ephesians 4:12," 42, quoting Harry Wendt, *Doctrine in Diagram* (Indianapolis: Parish Leadership Seminars, 1980), 215. Hamann's italics reflect Wendt's emphasis.

tion the veneer of scholarly respectability, but it is clear that Barth himself can find no convincing linguistic support for this new reading. His extended comment "The Church without Laymen and Priests"[287] proceeds on ideological—not exegetical—grounds and evidences what must simply be called an anticlerical spirit.[288] Where exegesis is brought into play, commentators either draw unsupportable conclusions from the alternation of the prepositions πρός … εἰς … εἰς ("for … for/to … for/to") in 4:12 or import a "spiritual gifts" reading of 4:7 and 4:16 into this verse.[289]

Paul's thesis is that when Christ ascended on high, he did not abandon the church, but gave her men as teachers and preachers, who represent him, and through whom he builds up his church. Whether or not this suits a modern, egalitarian view of society is beside the point if we are to take seriously the Scriptures as God's Word of revelation and instruction. C. F. W. Walther, preaching on this text, warns against a spirit that would reject such a divine gift:

> The distinction between preachers and those who hear what they preach is quite certainly not something which is so ordered at the option of church or men. It is so instituted by the Son of God himself, and it is therefore quite clearly a violation of what God has so ordered, indeed nothing other than a rebellion in the kingdom of Jesus Christ when Christians, who have not been rightfully called and put into the holy office, presume to exercise it.[290]

Walther's harsh word "rebellion" is reminiscent of earlier thoughts prompted by the mini-creed (Eph 4:4–6). If rejection of the unity of the church is rejection of God, then rejection of Christ's ministry is likewise rejection of Christ.[291]

---

[287] Barth, *Ephesians*, 2:477–84. Only one Greek word appears in these eight pages of his interpretation.

[288] Pejorative terms abound in Barth, e.g., "this interpretation challenges both the aristocratic-clerical and the triumphalistic-ecclesiastical exposition of 4:11–12. It unmasks them as arbitrary distortions of the text" (*Ephesians*, 2:479).

[289] Lincoln, *Ephesians*, 253, who reads 4:16 as rejoicing in the diversity of roles Christ inspires within the body, nevertheless warns against trumping 4:11–12 with the later verse.

[290] C. F. W. Walther, "Dritte Predigt zur Eröffnung der Synode" (1876), on Eph 4:11–14, in *Lutherische Brosamen: Predigten und Reden* (St. Louis: Barthel, 1876), 421 (trans. Norman E. Nagel, "How 'Valid' Is It to Trust Translations?" *Concordia Journal* 17 [1991]: 382).

[291] Luther, *On the Councils and the Church* (1539), AE 41:154, identifies the office of the ministry as one of the marks of the church, citing our text:

> The church is recognized externally by the fact that it consecrates or calls ministers, or has offices that it is to administer. There must be bishops, pastors, or preachers, who publicly and privately give, administer, and use the aforementioned four things [Word, Baptism, Lord's Supper, office of the keys] or holy possessions in behalf of and in the name of the church, or rather by reason of their institution by Christ, as St. Paul states in Ephesians 4 [:8], "He received gifts among men …"—his gifts were that some should be apostles, some prophets, some evangelists, some teachers and governors, etc. The people as a whole cannot do these things, but must entrust or have them entrusted to one person. Otherwise, what would happen if everyone wanted to speak or administer, and no one wanted to give way to the other? It must be entrusted to one person, and he alone should be allowed to preach, to baptize, to absolve, and to administer the sacraments. The others should be content with this arrangement and agree to it. Wherever you see this done, be assured that God's people, the holy Christian people, are present.

This is true because the ministers he has given stand *vice Christi*, "in the place of Christ."[292] It is immensely significant that each of the five titles given in 4:11 is first and foremost an office held by Christ. He is the apostle of the Father, the Prophet, the preacher of the Gospel, the Good Shepherd, the Teacher, who continues to carry out his work through his earthly representatives.

Paul's purpose, of course, has little to do with modern-day disputes over the distinction between pastor and people. There is no hint of hierarchy or aristocracy in the worst sense of those terms. The term διακονία, "ministry" (Eph 4:12), which Paul applies to the work of Christ's ministers, does not simply mean "humble service" or "charitable work" as it is often glossed. It refers to authorized, delegated tasks to be carried out by those who have been mandated by the one in authority.[293] But ministers of Christ are not only commissioned to do what he tells them; they are also to be Christlike. If the qualities of humility, meekness, patience, and forbearing (4:2) are Christlike virtues to be inculcated in every Christian, how much more are they to characterize the official representatives of Christ in his office? As Christ came in the form of a slave (Phil 2:7), so his ministers serve in Christlike meekness (Mt 20:25–28). The essence of the term "minister" is that all the power and authority a minister wields is delegated from a higher authority, not possessed intrinsically by the minister. As gifts of Christ, the fivefold ministers proclaim not themselves, but him.[294]

Paul cites the ministers of Christ not for their own sake, but for the sake of the unity of the church.[295] First, as noted, they represent Christ himself and therefore unite the church, his body, by bringing the presence of the Head to the church. It is in this sense that Ignatius' appeal to the episcopacy as a uniting force in the church should be understood. It is not the bishop by himself, but Christ, who unites the church through him:

---

[292] Ap 7:47, quoting Lk 10:16 (*Triglotta*, 242–43); cf. Ap 7:28.

[293] The reevaluation of the term διακονία, "ministry," by John Collins (see the first textual note on 3:7), while overturning a modern misconception, was in many ways a return to the traditional understanding of the term. The classic commentator Abbot writes: "But in a connexion like this, where offices in the Church are in question, διακονία can only mean official service; and this does not belong to the saints in general" (*The Epistles to the Ephesians and to the Colossians*, 119).

[294] "Of course, ministers are to be just that, servants, *servi servorum Dei* ['servants of the servants of God']. ... We have profane counterparts of this. The head of state in British countries is known as the Prime Minister, the first servant of all the servants of the state. But the idea of 'above' and 'below' does not at all fit the actual scheme of things, either in the church or in the state" (Hamann, "The Translation of Ephesians 4:12," 47–48).

[295] Schnackenburg, *Ephesians*, 191:

They do not as a consequence stand above the Church or the rest of the faithful; rather their "office" alone can bind the members of the Church to Christ, the Head, and to one another to serve the building-up of Christ's Body. But in this sense it is an essential, constitutive component part of the Church. It is an "office of unity" which should ward off deviation and disintegration, unite the Christians through preaching and doctrine, care and exhortation, and lead them to Christ, the Head.

Therefore it is fitting that you should live in harmony with the will of the bishop, as indeed you do. For your justly famous presbytery, worthy of God, is attuned to the bishop as the strings to a harp. Therefore by your concord [ὁμονοίᾳ] and harmonious love [συμφώνῳ ἀγάπῃ] Jesus Christ is being sung. Now do each of you join in this choir, that being harmoniously in concord you may receive the [musical] key of God in unison [ἑνότητι], and sing with one voice [ἐν φωνῇ μιᾷ] through Jesus Christ to the Father, that he may both hear you and may recognise, through your good works, that you are members [μέλη] of his Son. It is therefore profitable for you to be in blameless unity [ἐν ἀμώμῳ ἑνότητι], in order that you may always commune [μετέχητε] with God.[296]

But, second, the ministers' "work of the ministry" (4:12), which is commonly defined as "the ministry of the Word" in NT phraseology,[297] is an effective activity which actually brings about the organic growth of Christ's body.

This growth is the subject of the extended purpose statements that occupy the lengthy extension of Paul's sentence in 4:12–16. The work of ministry is to effect "bringing the saints to completion" (τὸν καταρτισμὸν τῶν ἁγίων, 4:12). The meaning of this phrase is clear enough in light of NT parallels,[298] but difficult to gloss with a single English equivalent. "Perfecting of the saints" (KJV) can be rightly understood as "bringing the saints to the perfection God has in mind for them," but is language that is easily misunderstood in moralistic terms. "Equipping the saints" captures the image of the armor of God provided to defend the saints from the devil's assaults (6:10–17), but is tainted today by its connection with "everyone a minister" theology (i.e., "equipping the saints to do the work of ministry"). "Bringing the saints to completion," to the goal God has in store for them, is the most appropriate rendering.[299] The phrase's meaning is, of course, developed by the parallel phrase "for building up the body of Christ" (εἰς οἰκοδομὴν τοῦ σώματος τοῦ Χριστοῦ, 4:12).

The image evoked is the spiritual temple (2:19–22), which involved three facets: (1) the incorporation of both Jew and Gentile as living stones in the one new temple, thus emphasizing unity; (2) the foundation of the apostles and prophets, with Christ as the cornerstone, thus defining the proclamation of the Gospel of Christ as that which builds this temple; and (3) the indwelling of God by the Spirit of Christ[300] in this new temple. It is not insignificant that the image (like the body of Christ) is corporate: Paul is addressing not specifically

---

[296] Ignatius, *To the Ephesians*, 4:1–2 (trans. Kirsopp Lake, LCL); cf. *To the Ephesians*, 5:1. The echoes of Paul's wording in Ephesians are astonishing.

[297] See the textual note on εἰς ἔργον διακονίας, "for the work of the ministry," in 4:12 (the third textual note on that verse).

[298] Particularly elucidating are NT parallels with the cognate verb καταρτίζω, "rebuild, repair, reconcile, supply." See the second textual note on 4:12.

[299] "All believers are to be brought to a state of completion, and it is the ministers Christ has given who are the means to this end as they exercise their ministries of proclamation, teaching, and leadership" (Lincoln, *Ephesians*, 254).

[300] See the first textual note on 4:4.

the edification of individuals, but the building up together of the whole church. The rest of the pericope explicates this upbuilding.

The role of the ministry in bringing about unity of belief and confession is stressed in 4:13.[301] "The unity of the faith and of the knowledge of the Son of God" is achieved through proclaiming the true Gospel. But this knowledge, though it is necessary that it be true (cf. 4:15), is more than intellectual. The role of the ministry is not merely to impart facts, but to bring about—through that knowledge of the faith—the conformity of all members of the church to the image of Christ, "the perfect/complete man" (4:13).[302] There is more than a hint of baptismal language in this verse, as Baptism (confessed in 4:5) is the means by which candidates "put on Christ" (Gal 3:27). What simpler path to unity is there than for each individual to be placed into Christ so that all are found together in him? This careful combination of teaching and Baptism (rooted in Christ's mandate, Mt 28:19–20), which touches mind and spirit, body and soul, pictures vividly the contours of the Word and Sacrament ministry that Paul stresses. It is hardly a fair objection to claim that the role of the other members of Christ's body are thereby left out of the equation. For Paul's purpose is to point Christians to the great benefits they receive from this ministry. He addresses concerns over disunity not by asking them to dig deeper and work it out for themselves, but by bringing to light the gifts of Christ that can achieve it.

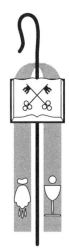

Certainly in this context every member of the body has a role to play, but Paul describes the church's role in a passive fashion.[303] The members are no longer to be infants, no longer to be led astray by every wind of false doctrine, no longer to be tricked by every charlatan that sails into town (4:14). This entails vigilance, careful adherence to the confession into which they were baptized, dedication to the Word of God that has been passed down from the apostles of Christ and taught by their pastors. In every respect they are to hold to its truth, including rejoicing in the love of Christ and radiating it to one another (4:15).[304] There can be no unity if they decline the proclamation of the truth and choose

---

[301] Lincoln, *Ephesians*, 268:

> These offices are, above all, characterized by service which unifies, which builds up, which stabilizes, and which enables growth toward Christ. Evangelists, pastors, and teachers produce unity and maturity as they proclaim, preserve, and apply the apostolic tradition. The writer is particularly concerned with the part they have to play in contributing to the unity of faith and knowledge, in providing an antidote to false teaching, and in bringing about a community that proclaims the truth in love.

[302] "He says that the church's order has been so formed as to join the human race together in the profession of unity, so that all may be in Christ, having Christ as their single head, that is, as the source of life" (Ambrosiaster, *Ephesians*, 4:12.6, ACCS 8:166).

[303] The passive nature of church in her edification is a simple counterpart of her passive role in salvation itself (2:5–8). Such a comparison makes such comments as the following appear quite synergistic: "The church is more than the passive object of ministerial activity (Dahl). Each individual has an important contribution to make if unity is to be maintained and growth to take place" (Best, *Ephesians*, 410).

[304] "None of these things are unknown to you if you possess perfect faith towards Jesus Christ, and love, which are the beginning and end of life; for the beginning is faith and the end is

falsehood (cf. 4:25; also Jn 7:18). Ultimately this is because the message proclaimed comes from Christ, and the unity it brings is from him.

Thus, Paul closes the argument with a return to the divine Giver. The body does not grow itself,[305] but receives growth from the Head that provides it with spiritual energy, ligaments that bind together, and direction for its work (4:16). Working through his ministers, Christ is the one who ultimately gives edification to his church, his own body.[306] Ecclesiology has not swallowed up Christology. It is not about us in the end, but about Christ. But as a servant himself, Christ devotes all his energy to the growth of his body. The end result is a vitality of life that shows itself not in disunity, but in love.

A Note on Luther's Translation of Ephesians 4:12

In Luther's 1522 translation of the NT, he appears to support the "everyone a minister" interpretation that is otherwise unattested until the twentieth century:

> damit die heyligen alle zusamen gefugt worden, durch gemeynen dienst, zu bessern den leyb Christi.[307]

> so that the saints might all be fit together, through common service, to improve the body of Christ.

Tyndale (1534) follows this early Luther translation: "that the saints might have all things necessary to work and minister withal, to the edifying of the body of Christ."[308] But most interestingly, Luther completely reworked the translation for the second edition of his NT published in 1527:

> das die heyligen geschickt seien zum werck des ampts, zur besserung des leibs Christi.[309]

> that the saints might be prepared for the work of the office, for the improvement of the body of Christ.

---

love, and when the two are joined together in unity it is God, and all other noble things follow after them" (Ignatius, *To the Ephesians*, 14:1 [trans. Kirsopp Lake, LCL]).

[305] Contra, e.g., Barth: "The body makes its own growth so that it builds itself up in love" (*Ephesians*, 2:447). "It is he [Christ] who gives each individual saint the right and the equipment to be, to live, and to act as a distinct person. Every saint is to make his own contribution to the mission and unity of the church" (2:450).

[306] Christ builds his church (Mt 16:18), and he does so through his ministry. As Melanchthon explains this passage: "As to the statement, 'On this rock I will build my church' (Matt. 16:18), it is certain that the church is not built on the authority of a man but on the ministry of the confession which Peter made when he declared Jesus to be the Christ, the Son of God. Therefore Christ addresses Peter as a minister and says, 'On this rock,' that is, on this ministry" (Treatise, 25).

[307] WA DB 7:200.

[308] William Tyndale, *Tyndale's New Testament* (in a modern-spelling edition and with an introduction by David Daniell; London: Yale University Press, 1989), 285.

[309] WA DB 7:200, footnote. For a chart showing the different editions of the *Lutherbibel* published in Wittenberg, see WA DB 6:XXI–XXIII. On the abbreviations and sigla used in the footnotes in WA DB 6–7, see WA DB 6:XCII–XCIV.

Luther then changed the last part of the verse again in the first edition of his NT published in 1530:

> das die heyligen geschickt seien zum werck des ampts, dadurch der leib Christi erbawet werde.[310]

> that the saints might be prepared for the work of the office, through which the body of Christ is built up.

In the second edition of 1527, Luther also added a new marginal notation:

> (geschickt) Das ist, wol gerüsst, und allenthalben versorget und zubereit, das nichts feile zum Ampt der Christenheit etc.[311]

> (prepared) That is, well equipped, and in every respect provisioned and prepared, that nothing should be lacking for the office of Christendom, etc.

The new translations and marginal note indicate a thoroughgoing change of interpretation of the text. Rather than speaking of a "common service," Luther now understands Paul to be talking about the ongoing provision of ministers for the church. Luther interprets the text as saying that one of the duties of the pastoral office is to perpetuate itself, to take some Christians and make them into pastors through proper training. Through this ongoing provision of pastors for the church, the body of Christ is built up. This shift in interpretation would be consistent with Luther's general tendency to defend the office more vigorously in the late 1520s, particularly in the face of the sneak preachers and *Schwärmer*.[312] Beginning in 1541 a slight change appears in subsequent editions of the *Lutherbibel* ("geschickt seien," "might be prepared," becomes "zugerichtet werden," "might be trained"),[313] but otherwise the preservation of the translation indicates that Luther is happy with this interpretation to the very end.

Unfortunately, later "upgrades" of the *Lutherbibel* confuse the meaning by changing the word "Ampt," "office," to "Dienst," "service." This infelicitous change thoroughly distorts the unique interpretation Luther had given (essentially that Paul was advocating seminary education!), shifting it toward the modern notion of generic service.

---

[310] WA DB 7:200–201, footnote.

[311] WA DB 7:201, margin note and footnote.

[312] See Luther, "Infiltrating and Clandestine Preachers" (1532), AE 40:379–94, though it is poorly translated in the AE and the translation often contradicts Luther's argument. See also, e.g., Lowell C. Green, "Change in Luther's Doctrine of the Ministry," *Lutheran Quarterly* 18 (1966): 173–83.

[313] WA DB 7:201. WA DB 4:388 indicates that, during group labor on revising the translation in 1540, the new phrase "zugerichtet werden" was added to Luther's draft revision in the handwriting of Georg Rörer, the group's secretary.

Ephesians 4:17–6:9

Refutations

The Baptismal Walk: Clothed in Christ

Translation

4 [17]This, then, I say and solemnly affirm in the Lord, that you are no longer to <u>walk</u> <u>just as</u> <u>also</u> the Gentiles <u>walk</u> in the futility of [their] mind,

> [18]being darkened in their understanding, alienated from the life of God
>> because of the ignorance that is in them, because of the hardening of their hearts,
>>> [19]the sort of people who, having become dead to all feeling, turned themselves over to licentiousness, for the insatiable pursuit of every kind of uncleanness.

[20]But you did not learn Christ this way!

> [21]—if indeed you heard him and were taught in him (as the truth is in Jesus),
>> [22]that you have put off with regard to [your] former way of life the old man who was being corrupted by deceitful lusts,
>> [23]and that you were being renewed in the spirit of your mind,
>> [24]and that you have put on the new man who has been created according to God's [likeness] in true righteousness and holiness.

[25]Therefore, since you have put off falsehood, "each one of you speak truth with his neighbor," for we are members of one another.

> [26]"Be angry and do not sin." "Let not the sun go down" on the cause of your anger, [27]nor give place to the devil.
> [28]Let the thief no longer steal, but rather let him labor, accomplishing good with his own hands, so that he has something to share with anyone in need.
> [29]Let no harmful word proceed from your mouths, but only what is good, for building up as is needed, that it might give grace to those who hear.
> [30]And do not grieve the Holy Spirit of God, in whom you were sealed for the day of redemption.
> [31]Let all bitterness and rage and anger and shouting and slander be taken away from you with all malice,
> [32]and be good to one another, tenderhearted, forgiving one another, <u>just as also</u> God in Christ has forgiven you.

5 [1]So then be imitators of God as beloved children, [2]and <u>walk</u> in love, <u>just as also</u> Christ loved us and gave himself up for us as an offering and sacrifice to God for a pleasing fragrance.

Textual Notes

4:17 τοῦτο οὖν λέγω καὶ μαρτύρομαι ἐν κυρίῳ—The particle οὖν ("then") draws a logical connection between the edifying gifts of 4:1–16 and the Christian walk Paul expounds in this section. Because of, as a consequence of, what Christ has given the Ephesians, they have been changed and must not return to their old futile life. The seriousness of the charge is emphasized by the emphatic formula "this I say and solemnly affirm in the Lord." The formula has no precise equivalent in the NT (though compare 1 Thess 2:12; 4:1; 2 Thess 3:4, 12). The vocabulary of μαρτυρέω, "to witness, testify," refers not simply to what one believes to be true, but to what one has personally experienced, "eyewitnessed." Such testimony in the NT is almost always connected with Christ, as witness to him and particularly to his resurrection.[1] But it can also refer to testimony that one is given to say by a sending authority. Thus, Paul speaks to the Ephesians what the Lord has given him to say; this is the language of his office. The less common verb form used here, μαρτύρομαι,[2] appears in contexts where the implication is "solemnly affirm" (cf. Acts 20:26)—which is "testifying" on the basis of the Word of God (Acts 26:22; Gal 5:3; 1 Thess 2:12) or which calls upon God as witness.[3] Paul's formula is the apostolic equivalent of Christ's own ἀμὴν ἀμὴν λέγω, "truly, truly, I say."[4] What Christ says on his own authority or from the Father's, Paul says ἐν κυρίῳ, "in the Lord." This phrase occurs in Ephesians where ordinary human institutions and actions are transformed by the incorporation of people through Baptism into Christ or his calling.[5] So, "in the Lord" elevates Paul's admonitions above the level of human exhortation and connects his words to the work of Christ (2 Cor 5:20).

μηκέτι ὑμᾶς περιπατεῖν, καθὼς καὶ τὰ ἔθνη περιπατεῖ—On περιπατέω, "to walk," see the textual notes on it in 2:2, 10.[6] The biblical metaphor of "walking" refers to the entire life of faith, confession, and obedience to God's Word and should not be reduced to the moralistic component of behavior alone. Here Paul contrasts the Gentiles' pagan "walking" with such faithful "walking." περιπατέω frames this pericope (cf. 5:2) and recurs throughout the latter chapters of Ephesians (also 4:1; 5:8, 15; see "Structure and Rhetoric" in the commentary on 4:1–16). Paul's concern is not simply that the Ephesians would obey God's Law better than the Gentiles around them. Rather, he warns them against falling back into their old ways—activities and patterns of life that would lead them away from faith in Christ and back into pagan beliefs. The temporal marker μηκέτι, "no longer," repeats the two-part division of their lives into "then" and "now" (cf. 2:1–4, 11–13).[7] Paul now speaks of "the Gentiles" as a group separate and distinct from the Ephesians, for the Gentile Christians must no longer define themselves according to "the flesh" (Eph 2:11; cf. 1 Cor 10:32).

---

[1] See, e.g., μαρτυρέω in Jn 1:15, 32; 3:11, 26, 28; 4:39; 8:13–14; 18:37; 19:35; μάρτυς in Lk 24:48; Acts 1:8; and διαμαρτύρομαι in Acts 8:25; 23:11. See Winger, "From Apostolic Witness to Christian Confession."

[2] μαρτύρομαι appears only five times in the NT versus seventy-six times for μαρτυρέω.

[3] I.e., swearing by the holy things of God, which no unclean man can touch, thus, asking God to strike him down if he speaks not the truth. See, e.g., Josephus, *Antiquities*, 10:104; Josephus, *Wars*, 2:401; 6:127.

[4] Note the combination of that phrase with the verb μαρτυρέω in Jn 3:11; 13:21.

[5] See ἐν κυρίῳ also in Eph 2:21; 4:1; 5:8; 6:1, 10, 21. Paul, the only NT writer (outside of Rev 14:13) to use the phrase, does so forty-seven times.

[6] Neuter plural subjects (here τὰ ἔθνη) normally take a singular verb (περιπατεῖ): "the Gentiles walk." See Wallace, *Greek Grammar*, 399–400.

[7] For the transition from "then" to "now," see "once/then" (ποτέ) and/or "now" (νῦν) in 2:2, 3, 11, 13; 3:5, 10; 5:8, 29 (cf. 2:4; 4:17). See also the table contrasting "then" with "now" in "Structure and Rhetoric" in the commentary on 2:11–22; the table in "Structure and Rhetoric" as well as the section entitled "Darkness Has No Fellowship with Light" in the commentary on 5:3–14; and the table of antitheses in "Structure and Rhetoric" in the commentary on 5:15–21a.

ἐν ματαιότητι τοῦ νοὸς αὐτῶν—The danger of backsliding is hinted at by the noun ματαιότης, which, like the adjective μάταιος, refers to what is "empty, futile, powerless, or transitory." ματαιότης is the LXX translation for הֶבֶל, "vanity, worthlessness," in Ecclesiastes (thirty-eight times), and ἐπὶ ματαίῳ (using the adjective μάταιος) is the LXX rendering of the Second Commandment's prohibition against taking the Lord's name לַשָּׁוְא, "in vain, as a useless thing" (Ex 20:7; Deut 5:11). There is a tight connection, a virtual interchangeability, between ματαιότης, "futility," and idolatry or divination in the OT (e.g., Is 44:9–20, which uses the adjective μάταιος in Is 44:9).[8] In key places in the NT, the word group refers to the practice of idolatry as "vain, worthless," inasmuch as the idols have no ability to help those who call upon them.[9] It describes the state of fallen creation apart from redemption in Christ, with the vain efforts of people to save themselves, the religion of the law.[10] Thus, it is a succinct summary of all that was wrong with the Ephesians' former Gentile life. These verses (4:17–19) encapsulate Paul's condemnation of the Gentiles in Romans 1:

> Although they knew God, they did not glorify or thank him as God, but they became futile [ἐματαιώθησαν] in their thoughts, and their senseless hearts were darkened [ἐσκοτίσθη]. Claiming to be wise, they became fools and exchanged the glory of the incorruptible God for the likeness of the image of corruptible man and birds and beasts and reptiles. (Rom 1:21–23)

Paul begins his description of Gentile depravity here in Eph 4:17 with their νοῦς, "mind," because it is the source of their evil behavior, both in its unbelief (idolatry) and as the prime mover of bodily activities. The fallen human mind's inclination to such things can be overcome only by its re-creation in Holy Baptism (4:23).

4:18 ἐσκοτωμένοι τῇ διανοίᾳ ὄντες—The two perfect passive participles ἐσκοτωμένοι and ἀπηλλοτριωμένοι (see the next textual note) form a periphrastic construction with ὄντες,[11] which in turn is a participle of manner dependent on περιπατεῖ (4:17)—that is to say, these participles describe the *way* in which the Gentiles "walk." The rare verb σκοτόω, "to darken, make blind," appears in the NT only in the passive, "to be/become darkened" (Rev 9:2; 16:10 are the only other instances). Here it has the figurative sense of not knowing the things of God, as implied by the modifier τῇ διανοίᾳ, "in (their)

---

[8] See μάταιος in LXX 3 Kgdms 16:13, 26; 17:15 (MT/ET 1 Ki 16:13, 26; 17:15); 2 Chr 11:15; Ps 23:4 (MT/ET 24:4); Is 2:20; 44:9; Jer 2:5; 8:19; 10:3, 15; 28:18 (MT/ET 51:18); Lam 2:14; Ezek 8:10; 13:6–9; 21:34 (ET 21:29); 22:28; Hos 5:11 (6:8; 12:2); Amos 2:4; Jonah 2:9 (ET 2:8); 3 Macc 6:11; Wis Sol 15:8; Sirach 34:5. See also ματαιότης in Pss 30:7 (MT 31:7; ET 31:6); 39:5 (MT 40:5; ET 40:4).

[9] Acts 14:15 (cf. 1 Thess 1:9–10); Rom 1:21–23; 1 Pet 1:18.

[10] Rom 8:20; 1 Cor 3:20; 15:17; Titus 3:9; James 1:26; 2 Pet 2:18.

[11] The participle ἐσκοτωμένοι is masculine because it refers to people (*constructio ad sensum*), even though the noun it modifies is neuter (τὰ ἔθνη, "the Gentiles," 4:17); BDF, § 134 (2). The addition of ὄντες creates a periphrasis. The periphrastic construction of εἰμί with a perfect passive participle is a normal substitute for the perfect passive indicative. In the present instance we have effectively a *double* periphrasis, with the helper verb εἰμί also in participial form, ὄντες. Sometimes, as here, the perfect passive participle functions more as an adjective than a verb, stressing the present result of the past action. This is apparently "to express still more forcibly the persistence of the new state of things" (BDF, § 352). Cf. Col 1:21. In other words: the Gentiles are not "getting darker" but are already completely "darkened."

understanding." The synonym σκοτίζω has the same figurative connotation (Rom 1:21; 11:10). Light is of God, darkness of the devil. "Being darkened" describes the Gentile Ephesian Christians' former pagan existence. By contrast, enlightenment is a baptismal image (1:18; 5:8, 14). See the first textual note on 1:18 and "Enlightened Eyes of Your Heart (1:18)" in the commentary on 1:15–23. Apart from such sacramental enlightenment, the διανοία, "understanding," is trapped by the lusts of the flesh (Eph 2:3; Col 1:21).

ἀπηλλοτριωμένοι τῆς ζωῆς τοῦ θεοῦ διὰ τὴν ἄγνοιαν τὴν οὖσαν ἐν αὐτοῖς— Language that described the Gentile Ephesians' life before Christ in chapter 2 is repeated in this warning against falling back into old ways. The verb ἀπαλλοτριόω, "to estrange, alienate," described the Gentiles' separation from the benefits of citizenship in the people Israel (2:12). Its only other NT occurrence is in the Colossian parallel (Col 1:21). Here Paul draws a starker contrast: unbelieving Gentiles are not merely separated from Israel, they are alienated from τῆς ζωῆς τοῦ θεοῦ, "the life of God," the life he has and provides. Such estrangement cannot be adequately explained via sociology or psychology; it is not just a feeling. It is a spiritually lifeless state, whose consequences will be illustrated in the next few clauses as hardness of heart, callousness, utter insensibility. The Gentiles are "dead men walking" (cf. 2:1–2). If they do not have God's life, they really have nothing at all. As so often in Ephesians, knowledge of God is key. The Gentiles are alienated by ἄγνοια, "ignorance" (Acts 17:30; 1 Pet 1:14)—not simply a lack of knowledge but a refusal to acknowledge God. This is sheer foolishness (LXX Pss 13:1 [MT/ET 14:1]; 93:11 [MT/ET 94:11]; Wis Sol 13:1). But the baptized know God and are known by him. See the textual notes on Eph 1:9, 17; 3:3, 5, 19; 4:13.

διὰ τὴν πώρωσιν τῆς καρδίας αὐτῶν—Paul lays the blame for the Gentiles' alienation not at God's feet but at the Gentiles' very own. It is because of the πώρωσις, "dullness, insensibility," of "their heart(s)."[12] Literally the noun πώρωσις means "hardening," but in NT literature it is used only in the figurative sense of inability to understand or respond to God and his Word (Mk 3:5; Rom 11:25). The verb from which the noun is derived, πωρόω, "to harden," has the same figurative sense in the NT, usually being applied to the heart or mind.[13] The "heart" is the seat of the will and of thought and is often interchangeable with διανοία, "mind," in the LXX.[14] The hardened heart is unable to function properly as the Law's instrument to convict of sin,[15] and so the slide into degradation continues. Sometimes those who reject God and his earthly witnesses receive a further hardening of the heart from God as punishment and confirmation of his righteous judgment against them (e.g., Pharaoh, Ex 4:21; Sihon, Deut 2:30; Jewish crowds, Jn 12:40), but this is an unusual act designed to further his own glory and the redemption of his people (Ex 14:4, 8, 13, 17). The Gentiles Paul has in mind here have

---

[12] καρδία is a distributive singular (Semitism), referring to the "heart" belonging to each individual within a group (Turner, *Syntax*, 23), but English idiom calls for the plural "hearts."

[13] Mk 6:52; 8:17; Jn 12:40; Rom 11:7; 2 Cor 3:14.

[14] E.g., LXX Gen 8:21; 17:17; 24:45; 27:41; Ex 28:3; cf. Heb 8:10; 10:16, both quoting LXX Jer 31:33.

[15] Deut 32:46; Pss 37:31; 40:9 (ET 40:8); Is 51:7; Rom 2:15.

hardened their own hearts (cf. Prov 28:14; Rom 2:5). This verse forms a contrast to the enlightenment of the heart brought by Baptism (Eph 1:18).

4:19 οἵτινες ἀπηλγηκότες—This verse continues the description of the Gentiles in their pagan walk (4:17) and is semantically parallel to 4:18. The pronoun ὅστις is used to describe a class of people who have the same status or quality. Its antecedent is τὰ ἔθνη, "the Gentiles" (4:17), who are now branded as "the sort of people who ..." The actions now described confirm the state of their hardened heart and darkened mind. ἀπηλγηκότες is the perfect active participle of ἀπαλγέω, a NT hapax legomenon meaning "to become callous, dead to feeling" (ἀπό, "away from," + ἀλγέω, "to feel pain").[16] Dead flesh feels nothing. There is no "moral sensitivity" to restrain such people's headlong plunge into depravity.

ἑαυτοὺς παρέδωκαν τῇ ἀσελγείᾳ—The active verb παρέδωκαν again places full responsibility for their sorry plight on the Gentiles themselves, who "handed themselves over." παραδίδωμι, which is most often used in the NT for the self-offering of Christ for our salvation (5:2, 25), can also mean "to hand over into prison" (Mt 4:12; 18:34) or "to betray into judgment" (e.g., Mt 10:4, 17, 21). It introduces an ironic parody into the lives of rebellious Gentiles, who are only able to hand themselves over into self-serving debauchery. If this is what they choose, God gives them enough of it to choke on (Rom 1:24–28). They are not delivered from debauchery but rather "handed over" into it, as if into prison or slavery. The translation "licentiousness" for ἀσέλγεια is somewhat antiquated, but conveys the sense of "violating all bounds of what is socially acceptable."[17] The unbelieving Gentiles have made themselves into their own licensing agent, giving themselves permission to do whatever they want. The term's pagan and sexual connotations are best expressed by the viciously ironic tirade in Wisdom 13–15 against the foolishness of idolatry,[18] which draws out its lawless consequences for the lives of pagans:

> [23]For whether they kill children in their initiations, or celebrate secret mysteries, or hold frenzied revels with strange customs, [24]they no longer keep either their lives or their marriages pure, but they either treacherously kill one another, or grieve one another by adultery, [25]and all is a raging riot of blood and murder, theft and deceit, corruption, faithlessness, tumult, perjury, [26]confusion over what is good, forgetfulness of favors, pollution of souls, sex perversion, disorder in marriage,[19] adultery, and debauchery [ἀσέλγεια]. [27]For

---

[16] The alternative meaning suggested by BDAG, s.v. ἀπαλγέω, 2, "be despondent," does not suit the context as well. The variant reading ἀπηλπικότες, from ἀπελπίζω, "having despaired" (cf. 2:12: "having no hope"), is a simple scribal error occasioned by this unusual verb. The participle ἀπηλγηκότες is both temporal and causal: "since they had become dead to all feeling, they turned themselves over ..." (4:18–19).

[17] See BDAG, s.v. ἀσέλγεια. The term appears frequently in NT vice lists: Mk 7:22; Rom 13:13; 2 Cor 12:21; Gal 5:19; 1 Pet 4:3.

[18] E.g., "again, one preparing to sail and about to voyage over raging waves calls upon a piece of wood more fragile than the ship which carries him" (Wis Sol 14:1 RSV).

[19] γάμων ἀταξία, literally, "disorder of marriages." Paul draws a strong contrast to such disorder when he puts in place the proper order of marriage in Eph 5:21–22 (ὑποτασσόμενοι, 5:21).

the worship of idols not to be named is the beginning and cause and end of every evil. (Wis Sol 14:23–27 RSV)

Such an extended list suggests that Paul may simply be using commonplace virtue and vice lists in such sections of his epistles as this pericope and the next. Yet the underlying structure of the Ten Commandments is also discernible; these are Jewish lists. As the reference to vain idolatry suggests the First Commandment (Ex 20:3–6; Deut 5:7–10), so the subsequent rejection of uncleanness ties in to the Sixth (Ex 20:14; Deut 5:18).

εἰς ἐργασίαν ἀκαθαρσίας πάσης ἐν πλεονεξίᾳ—The abstract noun ἐργασία, related to ἔργον, "work, deed," and ἐργάζομαι, "to work," means "engagement in some activity or behavior with sustained interest, *practice, pursuit*."[20] There is no such thing as moral neutrality. Gentiles apart from Christ are actively pursuing ἀκαθαρσία, "uncleanness." The connection of ἀκαθαρσία with the term πορνεία ("sexual immorality") in the NT suggests the primary referent of "uncleanness" in a Gentile context is sexual sin, though it encompasses more than that.[21] The main context of the terminology of "clean" and "unclean" in the OT is cultic and liturgical. Nothing unclean can come near the holiness of God in his temple (e.g., Lev 22:3).[22]

In the NT the categories of clean and holy, unclean and unholy, tend to collapse respectively into each other. Thus, Baptism both cleanses and makes holy (Eph 5:26; also 1 Cor 6:11; Titus 3:5). Unclean deeds are therefore also unholy, and the opposite of ἀκαθαρσία, "uncleanness," is ἁγιασμός, "holiness" (Rom 6:19; 1 Thess 4:7). The feverish pursuit of what is unclean and unholy characterizes pagan Gentile lives (Rom 1:24; 2 Cor 12:21) and arises from the sinful nature (Gal 5:19). The Gentiles are running away from the God who is holy. Uncleanness is incompatible with sainthood (Eph 5:3). Paul completes the picture in 4:19 with an adjectival phrase that further describes their "pursuit of every kind of uncleanness": ἐν πλεονεξίᾳ, "with greediness, insatiableness, lust." πλεονεξία is another regular feature of NT vice lists[23] and serves as an enabler for other forms of evil (cf. James 1:15). The Gentiles are driven by lust for what is filthy and ungodly. πλεονεξία is a near synonym of ἐπιθυμία, "desire, lust, passion" (Eph 2:3; 4:22; also, e.g., Mk 4:19), and may suggest the coveting that is prohibited by the Ninth and Tenth Commandments (Ex 20:17; Deut 5:21).

[20] BDAG, s.v. ἐργασία, 1.

[21] See the triad ἀκαθαρσία, "uncleanness"; πορνεία, "sexual immorality"; and ἀσέλγεια, "licentiousness," in 2 Cor 12:21; Gal 5:19; the triad πορνεία, "sexual immorality"; ἀκαθαρσία, "uncleanness"; and πλεονεξία, "insatiableness," in Eph 5:3; and the vices (four among others) πορνεία, "sexual immorality"; ἀκαθαρσία, "uncleanness"; ἐπιθυμία, "desire, lust"; and πλεονεξία, "insatiableness," in Col 3:5. Sexual immorality may be considered the primary kind of uncleanness for two reasons: the body is meant to be the temple of the Holy Spirit (1 Cor 6:15–20), and sexuality was a means to union with false gods through the use of temple prostitutes. See the textual notes on Eph 5:3, 5.

[22] For "cleansing," see, e.g., Lev 14:7; 15:28; 16:19, 30 (on the Day of Atonement). For "sanctifying/making holy" see, e.g., Ex 29:21; Lev 11:44–45. See also the first textual note on Eph 5:26 and Kleinig, *Leviticus*, 1–13.

[23] Mk 7:22; Rom 1:29; Eph 5:3; Col 3:5; 2 Pet 2:14.

4:20 ὑμεῖς δὲ οὐχ οὕτως ἐμάθετε τὸν Χριστόν—The emphatic "but you" expresses the then-now contrast that has severed the Gentiles from their pagan past (see the similar constructions in 2:4, 13).[24] The accusative direct object (τὸν Χριστόν) of the verb μανθάνω, "to learn," indicates the content of the teaching or the person with whom one becomes acquainted. It is more than just learning "*about* Christ" (as if referring to mere information); Paul states: "You did not *learn Christ* this way!"[25] Christ himself, not simply a message about Christ, is the object of apostolic preaching.[26]

Throughout the Greek Scriptures, μανθάνω is used most frequently of "learning" God's Word.[27] The consequence of this "learning" is the fear of God (μανθάνω in LXX Deut 4:10; 17:19; 31:12–13) and the avoidance of idolatry (LXX Deut 18:9). It is thus to know God in his person and works, to be placed into proper relationship with him. The verb's cognate noun μαθητής, "disciple," is a significant NT term marking "the one who learns." Disciples of Christ are made by teaching and baptizing, leading people into the Word and gifts of Christ (Mt 28:19–20). To learn Christ is to become Christlike, particularly in bearing the cross (Mt 11:29; Lk 14:27).[28] It involves renunciation of the world. Thus, Paul points the Ephesians back to their catechesis, in which they came to know Christ and the Gospel, and to their Baptism, in which they were placed into Christ and made Christlike. Falling back into Gentile ways and beliefs is thoroughly incompatible with being Christ's disciple (this is the argument of Romans 6).

4:21 εἴ γε αὐτὸν ἠκούσατε καὶ ἐν αὐτῷ ἐδιδάχθητε—The conditional phrase εἴ γε, "if indeed," does not imply uncertainty on Paul's part, but indicates something he assumes to be true.[29] See the first textual note on 3:2 (as well as the second textual note on 1:13 and the third textual note on 1:15). Paul can have no doubt that these baptized Ephesian Christians were catechized (cf. Rom 16:17, written to Christians not of his acquaintance). He likely is using a rhetorical device to remind them of what he himself had taught during his Ephesian ministry (cf. Phil 4:9)—like a parent who cries, "Haven't I ever told you … ?" NT usage of the verb ἀκούω, "hear," generally follows the classical rule: it takes the genitive for the person whose words are heard (e.g., 1 Tim

---

[24] See "once/then" (ποτέ) and/or "now" (νῦν) in 2:2, 3, 11, 13; 3:5, 10; 5:8, 29 (cf. 2:4; 4:17). See also the table contrasting "then" with "now" in "Structure and Rhetoric" in the commentary on 2:11–22; the table in "Structure and Rhetoric" as well as the section entitled "Darkness Has No Fellowship with Light" in the commentary on 5:3–14; and the table of antitheses in "Structure and Rhetoric" in the commentary on 5:15–21a.

[25] "The phrase 'to learn a person' is found nowhere else in the Greek Bible, and so far it has not been traced in any pre-biblical Greek document" (Barth, *Ephesians*, 2:529).

[26] Acts 5:42; 8:5, 35; 9:20; 17:3, 18; 19:13; 1 Cor 1:23; 15:12; 2 Cor 1:19; 4:5; 11:4; Gal 1:16; Phil 1:15; Col 1:28.

[27] E.g., LXX Deut 5:1; Ps 118:7, 71, 73 (MT/ET 119:7, 71, 73); Rom 16:17; Col 1:6–7; 2 Tim 3:14–15.

[28] Cf. Phil 4:9, in which the Philippians are encouraged to conformity to what they have learned in Paul.

[29] BDF, § 454 (2): "Εἴγε is used similarly [to εἴπερ], but implies a more definite assumption." Moule, *Idiom Book*, 164: "It depends upon the context whether or not such a strengthened *if* implies doubt or confident assumption."

4:16) and the accusative for the content of the message (e.g., Eph 1:13; 3:2; 2 Tim 2:2).[30] This would suggest that the accusative (αὐτόν) here in εἴ γε αὐτὸν ἠκούσατε means "if indeed you heard [the message about] him." But (as remarked in the textual note on 4:20), this message is more than simply information about Christ. One wonders if it is possible that here, too, Paul has violated the grammatical "rule" and intends αὐτὸν ἠκούσατε to mark Christ not as the content of the message, but as the speaker: "you heard him [Christ]."

Likewise, the clause ἐν αὐτῷ ἐδιδάχθητε gives Christ himself a central role in the act of teaching.[31] ἐν αὐτῷ could indicate the personal agent of the passive verb ("you were taught *by him*"), but that is not the usual construction.[32] It is better to take ἐν αὐτῷ in the sacramental, mystical sense that the phrase has elsewhere in Ephesians (see "in Christ" in the fifth textual note on 1:3; cf. ἐν πνεύματι, 5:18). The Ephesians were not simply taught *about* Christ, but "taught *in* him" as they were baptized into him, received him, and were therefore "in him" as Paul continued to teach them (cf. Col 2:6–7).[33]

καθώς ἐστιν ἀλήθεια ἐν τῷ Ἰησοῦ—Here the conjunction καθώς, "as," does not indicate a simple comparison (as in 4:17), nor does it merely give the grounds for the preceding statement, "inasmuch as, since" (as in 1:4; 4:32), but combines elements of both. The truth in Jesus was the norm in accord with which the Ephesians were taught. This clause is a parenthetical interruption, standing between ἐδιδάχθητε, "you were taught" (earlier in 4:21), and the infinitives that complete its thought in 4:22–24 (ἀποθέσθαι … ἀνανεοῦσθαι … ἐνδύσασθαι).

The noun ἀλήθεια, which lacks the definite article, should not be understood as indefinite: "*a* truth" or "[some sort of] truth." The article may be missing simply because the noun stands in predicate position after the verb ἐστιν, "there is"—such nouns can nevertheless be definite. The translation "there is truth" would be too vague

---

[30] Smyth, *Greek Grammar*, §§ 1361–66; BDF, § 173 (1); Zerwick, *Biblical Greek*, § 69. This appears to be the only NT example of "person [accusative]" as the content of a message heard (ἀκούω). Other examples use ἀκούω with περί (Lk 7:3; 9:9; 16:2) or a simple genitive (Rom 10:14a). In other expressions, the classical rules break down: "The NT wavers between genitive and accusative in phrases meaning 'to hear a sound,' while in classical it is ἀκούειν φωνῆς, βοῆς etc." (BDF, § 173 [2]; cf. Wallace, *Greek Grammar*, 133).

[31] "It is Christ himself who teaches us about himself!" (Ambrosiaster, *Ephesians*, 4:21, ACCS 8:171). Christ himself was present in Paul's teaching, as he promised to be with the church forever through his ministers' teaching and baptizing (Mt 28:19–20). As Christ's ambassadors (2 Cor 5:20; Eph 6:20), their words are his words (Lk 10:16; 2 Cor 13:3).

[32] One expects ὑπό plus the genitive for the ultimate agent of a passive verb (i.e., the person who would be the subject of the active verb) and διά plus the genitive for the intermediate agent (e.g., "spoken *by* the Lord *through* the prophet," Mt 1:22). A simple dative can be used for inanimate objects that are instruments or means of an action. On rare occasions a dative can refer to a personal agent (see Lk 23:15, which BDF, § 191, considers to be perhaps the only genuine example in the NT). It is often claimed that ἐν plus the dative can indicate a personal agent (a variant reading in Lk 23:15), though in most cases the phrase indicates means/instrument or perhaps sphere (e.g., ἐν πνεύματι, Mk 1:8; 1 Cor 12:3). See Wallace, *Greek Grammar*, 162–66, 373–74. See also the textual note on ἐν πνεύματι in Eph 5:18.

[33] "Thus the ἐν αὐτῷ does not really mean that [subject matter] in which one is instructed, but him in whom the Christians (already) stand when they are instructed. What is in mind, then, is the instruction which follows after Baptism, in which indeed the ἐν Χριστῷ εἶναι ['to be in Christ'] is realized (cf. 1:13b)" (Schlier, *Epheser*, 216).

an assertion; in context it is clear that Paul means "*the* truth is in Jesus."[34] Jesus himself is God's truth,[35] and the Hebrew affirmation of truth, "amen,"[36] was his characteristic formula (e.g., Mt 5:18; Jn 1:51; cf. 2 Cor 1:20). "Truth" is virtually synonymous with the Gospel in Paul's writings.[37] The Ephesians, "having heard the Word of truth, the Gospel of your salvation" and "having also believed," "were sealed [baptized] with the promised Holy Spirit" (1:13). Truth occupies a prominent place in Ephesians as a quality of the baptized (4:15, 24, 25; 5:9; 6:14). In the present verse it marks a strong contrast to the thoughts and deeds of pagan Gentiles (4:17–19, 22).

The name "Jesus" appears by itself (without "Christ" or "Lord") only here in Ephesians. The shift from "Christ" in 4:20 to "Jesus" in this verse may not be polemical, but certainly entails the confession that the man Jesus is the Messiah/Christ.[38]

4:22 ἀποθέσθαι ὑμᾶς—The aorist middle infinitive ἀποθέσθαι, from ἀποτίθημι, "to take off, lay aside," is dependent on the prior verb ἐδιδάχθητε, "you were taught" (4:21). Most translations understand the action of the infinitive as future with respect to both the act of teaching and the perspective of the present writer, Paul. In other words, they take it imperatively: "you were taught that you *should* put aside the old man," indicating an action that may have begun, but must still happen. The RSV takes this to the extreme by placing a full stop at the end of 4:21 and translating the infinitive as an imperative: "put off your old nature."[39] The baptismal flavor of the language (see below), however, suggests the action of putting off has already happened. Thus, the infinitive is better interpreted as "you were taught *to have put off*" or "you were taught *that you have put off* the old man"—likely referring back to the event of Baptism (Col 2:12).[40]

---

[34] Thus, it matters little whether ἀλήθεια, "truth," is taken as the subject or predicate completion of the verb ἐστιν: "the truth is in Jesus" or "there is Truth [with a capital T!] in Jesus." See BDF, § 258; Turner, *Syntax*, 176–87. Moule, *Idiom Book*, 112, says: "It is hard to avoid the impression that usage [of the article] is arbitrary," and tentatively capitalizes "Truth" in this verse. Lincoln, *Ephesians*, 281, lists a significant number of passages in which ἀλήθεια is anarthrous in Paul. Gal 5:7 with its textual variant illustrates the confusion evident even to Greek-speaking scribes. Lincoln concludes that we should simply take ἀλήθεια as the subject of the clause and translate it as if it had the article.

[35] Jn 1:17; 14:6; 18:37; Rom 15:8.

[36] See the fourth textual note on Eph 3:21.

[37] See "the truth of the Gospel" (Gal 2:5, 14; Col 1:5); also Rom 1:18; Gal 5:7; Col 1:6; 2 Thess 2:10–13; 2 Tim 2:15; Titus 1:1.

[38] Acts 2:36; 5:42; 9:22; 17:3; 18:5, 28; 1 Jn 5:1. Lincoln, *Ephesians*, 281–82, thoroughly investigates Pauline usage and suggests that the use of "Jesus" alone is merely stylistic variation. Schlier, *Epheser*, 217, presents the unlikely theory that it is anti-gnostic polemic. Yet Paul is not identifying an "earthly Jesus" with a "heavenly Christ," but the Messiah promised in the OT with Jesus of Nazareth.

[39] Perhaps the RSV would appeal to the so-called "imperatival infinitive," common in Classical Greek (e.g., Homer), but this is extremely rare in the NT (Wallace, *Greek Grammar*, 608, and BDF, § 389, cite Rom 12:15 [twice] and Phil 3:16 as the only NT examples) and unnecessary in the present context. In Eph 5:33 Paul uses ἵνα plus the subjunctive as what appears to be a substitute for the imperatival infinitive: ἵνα φοβῆται, literally, "that she should fear."

[40] Moule, *Idiom Book*, 139, is helpful, saying that the infinitive "seems to represent the contents of the teaching referred to, and to be 'epexegetic' … rather than final." But the question remains, what is the content of the teaching? Wallace, *Greek Grammar*, 603–5, subsumes this

The aorist tense of the infinitive represents the aorist tense of the original postbaptismal catechetical statement.[41]

Christians can be exhorted to put away the *works* of their former life[42] precisely because they have already put off the old man to whom the works belong. This is the movement of Col 3:8–10, where Christians can lay aside such sinful works because they "have already put off" (ἀπεκδυσάμενοι) the old man and "have already put on" (ἐνδυσάμενοι) the new man.[43] ἀποτίθημι, "put off," has a distinct baptismal flavor that connects with the image of putting to death (Romans 6) or stripping off the old Adam before being clothed with Christ (Gal 3:27). See ἐνδύω, "put on," in Eph 4:24. In early baptismal rites, this was acted out symbolically by removing one's everyday clothes before being baptized naked (see "The Baptismal Walk within the Body of Christ" in the commentary).[44]

---

use of διδάσκω under indirect discourse, noting: "The general principle for these infinitives is that *the infinitive of indirect discourse retains the **tense** of the direct discourse and usually represents either an **imperative** or **indicative**"* (604; emphasis original). He admits that either translation is possible in this verse. See his further discussion on p. 605. One's understanding of the context will be decisive. Best, *Ephesians*, 431, opting for the imperative over the indicative on the grounds that the author "is quite clearly not just giving information," misunderstands the work of the Gospel. Stoeckhardt, *Ephesians*, 214, cites Hofmann, Wohlenberg, Ewald, and Lueken as supporting the position we have taken, though he himself rejects it. The only English translation to take the infinitives (and the subsequent participle ἀποθέμενοι in 4:25) as indicatives is the Darby Bible (1871/1884/1890):

> [21]if ye have heard him and been instructed in him according as *the* truth is in Jesus; [22]*namely* your having put off … the old man … ; [23]and being renewed in the spirit of your mind; [24]and *your* having put on the new man. … [25]Wherefore, having put off falsehood, speak truth every one with his neighbour. (italics original)

[41] Burton, *Moods and Tenses*, § 114, is often quoted in opposition to this view: "There is apparently no instance in the New Testament of the Aorist Infinitive in indirect discourse representing the Aorist Indicative of the direct form." However, Wallace, *Greek Grammar*, 605, quotes research into the some 150 NT examples that demonstrates they all involve a main verb of command or exhortation. Thus, it is context, not grammar, that has led to the preponderance of imperatival interpretations. In the present verse, the verb διδάσκω as easily allows indicative as imperative completions—i.e., one can be taught that something *is* true, or one can be taught to *do* something.

[42] Col 3:8; Heb 12:1; James 1:21. The participle ἀποθέμενοι in Eph 4:25 and 1 Pet 2:1 is best understood as "now that *you have* put away" in its baptismal context. See the first textual note on Eph 4:25.

[43] Those commentators who take the infinitives in Eph 4:22–24 imperatively are puzzled by the different perspective of Colossians, usually explaining Col 3:8–10 as an indicative-imperative paradox: "be what you are!" Bruce, *The Epistles to the Colossians, to Philemon, and to the Ephesians*, 358, notes perceptively that if Ephesians is imperatival, it is most appropriate to the context of an actual Baptism.

[44] Relevant to this whole cluster of verses (4:22–24) are the liturgical/catechetical comments of Chrysostom, *Baptismal Instructions*, 2:24–25:

> Next after this, in the full darkness of the night, he [the priest] strips off your robe and, as if he were going to lead you into heaven itself by the ritual, he causes your whole body to be anointed with that olive oil of the spirit, so that all your limbs may be fortified and unconquered by the darts which the adversary aims at you.
>
> After this anointing the priest makes you go down into the sacred waters, burying the old man and at the same time raising up the new, who is renewed in the image of his Creator. It is at this moment that, through the words and the hand of the priest, the Holy

κατὰ τὴν προτέραν ἀναστροφὴν τὸν παλαιὸν ἄνθρωπον—The noun ἀναστροφή, "way of life," derives from the verb ἀναστρέφω, "conduct oneself," which Paul used in 2:3 to describe the Gentiles' former life before Christ. The word group spans the same breadth as περιπατέω, "to walk" (e.g., 4:17; 5:2), indicating both beliefs and behavior. προτέραν, "former," confirms that Paul is referring to a change that has happened in their past (rather than to a potential future change). The preposition κατά is often used rather loosely in Ephesians; here it ("with regard to") indicates a close connection between the old man and the former way of life, such that both are put off together.[45]

The expression παλαιὸς ἄνθρωπος, "old man," occurs only twice more in the NT (Rom 6:6; Col 3:9). In both cases it refers to what was put off and put to death in Holy Baptism. We have translated the direct object τὸν παλαιὸν ἄνθρωπον as "the old man" (rather than, e.g., "the old nature" [see RSV]) because of its connection with Paul's theology of the old Adam and the new Adam, Jesus Christ (Rom 5:12–21; 1 Cor 15:21–22, 45–49).[46] With this phrase Paul introduces an allusion to Genesis that continues with the language of new creation in the image of God (Eph 4:24; cf. Gen 1:26–27).

τὸν φθειρόμενον κατὰ τὰς ἐπιθυμίας τῆς ἀπάτης—The old man was not worth hanging onto, inasmuch as he was φθειρόμενον (present passive participle of φθείρω), "being ruined, corrupted." This is not primarily a reference to the physical deterioration that certainly results from sin, but to the moral rot (1 Cor 15:33) that leads to eternal destruction (Gal 6:8; 2 Pet 2:12). The present tense suggests this was an ongoing slide away from God, deeper and deeper into the sort of depravity Paul has just described (Eph 4:17–19). Passive forms of φθείρω describe the evil earth on the cusp of destruction by the flood (LXX Gen 6:11; see also φθορά in Rom 8:21) and apostate Israel as ripe for judgment (LXX Hos 9:9); and the active voice is used for defiling a virgin (4 Macc 18:8; cf. Rev 19:2). The connection[47] of φθειρόμενον, "being corrupted," with τὰς ἐπιθυμίας τῆς ἀπάτης, "desires of deceit," which has an adjectival genitive, "deceitful desires/lusts," suggests an allusion to Eden, where the serpent corrupted Eve and thereby Adam through deceit playing on desire (2 Cor 11:3; 1 Tim 2:14). This language strengthens the "old Adam" imagery (see the preceding textual note).

4:23 ἀνανεοῦσθαι δὲ τῷ πνεύματι τοῦ νοὸς ὑμῶν—The infinitive ἀνανεοῦσθαι is, like those in 4:22, 24, dependent on ἐδιδάχθητε (4:21) and should be translated as an

---

Spirit descends upon you. Instead of the man who descended into the water, a different man comes forth, one who has wiped away all the filth of his sins, who has put off the old garment of sin and has put on the royal robe. (Trans. Paul W. Harkins, *ACW* 31:52)

[45] Zerwick, *Biblical Greek*, § 130, suggests that "perhaps (?) the otherwise obscure text ... may be rendered: 'put off the old man of former ways,' " understanding the κατά phrase as equivalent to a possessive pronoun: "the old man that belongs to former ways" (cf. τὴν καθ᾽ ὑμᾶς πίστιν, "your faith," Eph 1:15).

[46] "What he calls 'the old man' is well known to us; namely, the whole nature of man as descended from Adam after his fall in paradise, being blinded by the devil, depraved in soul, not keeping God before his eyes nor trusting him, yes, utterly regardless of God and the judgment day" (Luther, "Sermon for the Nineteenth Sunday after Trinity, Ephesians 4:22–28," October 22, 1536, Lenker, 8:306; StL 12:913, § 7).

[47] They are connected by the preposition κατά. BDAG, s.v. κατά, B 5 a δ, suggests translating the preposition here as (being corrupted) "because of, as a result of" (the deceitful desires).

event that has already begun (rather than as an imperative).[48] Its present tense reflects the tense of the original catechetical instruction,[49] though it may also imply a continuous action: "you were taught … that you *were being* renewed." ἀνανεόω, "to renew," is a NT hapax legomenon,[50] though it should probably not be sharply distinguished from ἀνακαινόω (2 Cor 4:16; Col 3:10) and ἀνακαινίζω (Heb 6:6), "renew," and ἀνακαίνωσις, "renewal" (Rom 12:2; Titus 3:5), especially as the new man is called τὸν καινὸν ἄνθρωπον, "the *new* man" (Eph 4:24).[51] On the one hand, this renewal took place definitively in Holy Baptism (ἀνακαίνωσις, Titus 3:5). It is to this one-time transformation that Paul refers here. His language is echoed by Hermas (who employs two verbs for "renew," ἀνακαινόω and ἀνανεόω, as synonyms) in reference to a single great moment of repentance:

> I thanked the Lord for all these things, that he had mercy on all who call upon his name, and sent the angel of repentance to us who have sinned against him, and *renewed* our spirit [ἀνεκαίνισεν ἡμῶν τὸ πνεῦμα], even when we were already corrupted [κατεφθαρμένων], and *renewed* [ἀνενέωσε] our life, when we had no hope of living.[52]

---

[48] 𝔓⁴⁶ and a significant number of other early manuscripts turn ἀνανεοῦσθαι here in 4:23 and the following infinitive ἐνδύσασθαι in 4:24 into imperatives (ἀνανεοῦσθε and ἐνδύσασθε), likely an attempt to resolve the difficult syntax. Does this indicate a genuine insight into the grammar, or is it merely a natural propensity toward the Law?

[49] The present tense of ἀνανεοῦσθαι probably reflects the original wording of the teaching (4:21) to which Paul is referring (i.e., he had once said, "You *are* being renewed"). In English usage we normally shift the tense of such indirect discourse, so here, in conjunction with the aorist main verb in 4:21 (ἐδιδάχθητε), we translate as follows: "you *were* taught … that you *were* being renewed." This originally present-tense action stands in parallel and in contrast to the present tense of the participle φθειρόμενον, "the old man who was *being corrupted*" (4:22). "You were being renewed" (ἀνανεοῦσθαι) most likely refers to Baptism itself, though the process of catechesis leading into it might be included. The conjunction δέ that follows the infinitive ties together the two infinitive clauses of 4:22–23 ("that you have put off … *and* that you were being renewed"). The initial καί of 4:24 then introduces the logically subsequent step that stands over against them both: "*and* that you have put on the new man."

[50] ἀνανεόω occurs ten times in the LXX, seven of which are in 1 Maccabees with the sense of "renew a friendship or alliance." Only in Job 33:24 is it used of renewing a person.

[51] The traditional distinction between νέος (quantitatively new) and καινός (qualitatively new) is sometimes blurred by simple stylistic variation. The compound form ἀνα + νεόω, "renew again," might imply the restoration of a former state (i.e., Adam before the fall), but is probably just an intensification of the root verb.

[52] *Shepherd of Hermas, Similitudes*, 9:14.3 (trans. Kirsopp Lake, LCL, adapted; Lake's translation has "restored" in place of the second "renewed"; emphasis added). Throughout his writings, Hermas ponders the question of whether grave postbaptismal sin (e.g., murder, adultery, and apostasy) might be forgiven. It is revealed to him that one great repentance is permitted, but no more. The issue came to a head with the mass apostasies precipitated by the Decian persecution (AD 249–251), moving toward resolution when Cyprian opted for their forgiveness being remissible in principle (though not always so easily in practice). See Luther's analysis in SA 3:3.43. The difficult language of Heb 6:4–6, which denies that it is possible "to renew unto repentance" (ἀνακαινίζειν εἰς μετάνοιαν) "those who have once and for all been enlightened [= baptized]" (τοὺς ἅπαξ φωτισθέντας) if they fall away, may also be using "renew" in the sense of Baptism. Hence, apostates cannot deal with their rebellion by simply asking to be baptized again.

On the other hand, Baptism has lifelong consequences, such that Paul can call Christians to the ongoing τῇ ἀνακαινώσει τοῦ νοός, "renewal of the mind" (Rom 12:2), which goes on each day through a repentant return to the gift of Baptism (2 Cor 4:16; Col 3:10; see also Lam 5:21). The νοῦς, "mind," which was the starting point of Gentile corruption (Eph 4:17), is also the starting point of baptismal re-creation. Man's πνεῦμα ("in the spirit," 4:23) is thereby brought into harmony with God's Spirit.[53]

4:24 καὶ ἐνδύσασθαι τὸν καινὸν ἄνθρωπον—This third infinitive (ἐνδύσασθαι) is, like the preceding two (in 4:22–23), dependent on ἐδιδάχθητε (4:21) and should be translated as an event that has already happened (rather than as an imperative): "you were taught … that you *have been* clothed." This past-tense interpretation of the infinitive is supported by the use of an aorist participle in the Colossian parallel: "since you *have* put on [ἐνδυσάμενοι] the new man" (Col 3:10). ἐνδύω, "to put on clothing" (normally middle voice), has, of course, a common literal meaning. But even this is often freighted in the Bible, as clothes identify the person and his office.[54] The key is again[55] given by Galatians: ὅσοι γὰρ εἰς Χριστὸν ἐβαπτίσθητε, Χριστὸν ἐνεδύσασθε, "for as many of you as have been baptized into Christ have put on Christ" (Gal 3:27; cf. Rom 13:14).[56] Just as the first Adam was clothed with the skin of animals, which both showed the deadly consequences of his sin and covered up his sin (Gen 3:21), so the Christian is clothed with Christ, sacrificed because of him and for him. This Christological garment indicates not only the righteousness that covers our sinfulness before the Father's eyes but also the oneness with Christ that has so often been stressed in this letter. Being clothed with Christ is also defensive against the assaults of the devil and is the background to the armor-of-God image; only because Christ has first been put upon the baptized can Paul exhort them to take up the armor that has been given them (Eph 6:10–17; see also Rom 13:12; 1 Thess 5:8). The fact that Christians have been clothed with Christ can then serve as the basis for admonitions not to return to the past life when their flesh ruled them (Rom 13:14; Col 3:10, 12). Such admonitions continue in this life until the Last Day, when the resurrection completes the death of the old Adam and clothes the Christian with immortality (1 Cor 15:53–54).

---

[53] "The double expression 'spirit of your minds' could pleonastically mean the human spirit according to the style of Eph.; but since pneuma ['spirit'] is nowhere else in Eph. used this way, what must be meant is the Christian mind guided by the divine Spirit (cf. 3.16; 4.3; 5.18; 6.18)" (Schnackenburg, *Ephesians*, 200).

[54] E.g., the prophet Elijah (2 Ki 1:8) and his successor John the Baptist (Mk 1:6); the King/king of the Jews (Mt 27:28–29; Acts 12:21); the Gerasene demoniac (Lk 8:27); the restored son (Lk 15:22); the Son of Man (Rev 1:13); angels in white linen (Rev 15:6).

[55] See also the first textual note on 4:22 and "Stripping and Clothing (4:20–24)" in the commentary, as well as "Baptism and the Spirit" in "Purpose and Themes" in the introduction.

[56] The infinitive ἐνδύσασθαι in Eph 4:24 and the imperative ἐνεδύσασθε in Gal 3:27 are in the middle voice. The middle need not always be taken *reflexively* ("clothe *oneself*"), as if to stress the independence and self-sufficiency of the actor. In general, the middle stresses the recipient of the action more than its cause (agent) and so leans toward the passive (note that in Gal 3:27 the middle ἐνεδύσασθε, "you put on," is parallel to the passive ἐβαπτίσθητε, "you were baptized"). These middles could also be understood as *permissive*: "let yourselves be clothed with Christ." See BDF, § 317; Wallace, *Greek Grammar*, 425–27; and ἐνδύσασθε in the first textual note on 6:11.

In the present context Paul is making the first step: reminding the Ephesians of the decisive baptismal moment when Christ was put upon them. τὸν καινὸν ἄνθρωπον, "the new man," is therefore Christ himself, and consequently the Christian considered as one clothed with Christ. It is equivalent to "the inner man" (3:16) and "the complete man" (4:13).[57] Here the use of καινός (rather than νέος) is significant: it is a completely "new *kind*" of man, not simply the old one renovated. By reconciling all people (both Jew and Gentile) to one another within himself, and reconciling them all to God in his body on the cross, Christ himself has created this "one new man" (2:15).

τὸν κατὰ θεὸν κτισθέντα ἐν δικαιοσύνῃ καὶ ὁσιότητι τῆς ἀληθείας—Echoes of Eden continue to reverberate with the verb κτίζω, "create." The prepositional phrase κατὰ θεόν, literally, "in accord with God," indicates similarity to God[58] and recalls man's original creation in God's image (Gen 1:26–27; 9:6; cf. Sirach 17:3). The Colossian parallel, κατ᾽ εἰκόνα τοῦ κτίσαντος αὐτόν, "according to the image of the one who created him" (Col 3:10), makes this allusion explicit by using the term εἰκών, "image," from LXX Gen 1:26–27; 9:6. Paul's ambassadorial office leads him to make this remarkable announcement: "If anyone is in Christ, *new creation!* Old things have passed away; behold, new things have come about" (2 Cor 5:17; cf. Gal 6:15). Here Paul is proclaiming to the Ephesians what God has done for them in Christ. There can be no call to ethical improvement that does not recognize God's creative work; he even prepares the good works in which we simply walk (Eph 2:10 with κτίζω, "create"; also in 2:15).

In this verse the key Pauline term δικαιοσύνη, "righteousness," appears for the first time in Ephesians (also 5:9; 6:14; see also δίκαιος in 6:1). This is the saving judgment of God by which he declares the baptized to be not guilty of violating his justice on the basis of Christ's substitutionary work. As Adam and Eve were once endowed with "righteousness,"[59] not being guilty of any transgression of God's will, so Christians are re-created with this status by Baptism into Christ's righteousness. Likewise, ὁσιότης, "holiness," is not to be understood here primarily as the inner moral quality by which people seek after the things of God.[60] It is the gift of God that enables unclean and unholy people to be washed and sanctified (cf. 5:26) so that they are able to stand in the presence of a holy God. The essence of Eden was man's ability to walk with God; Baptism re-creates paradise by restoring that relationship, granting the baptized the

---

[57] "There is but one garment of salvation, namely, Christ. Hence the 'new man' created in God's likeness is none other than Christ. One who has put on Christ has thus put on the new person [*sic*; 'man'!] created in God's likeness" (Gregory of Nyssa, *Against Eunomius*, 3:1.52, ACCS 8:174).

[58] BDAG, s.v. κατά, B 5 b α. Cf. Moule, *Idiom Book*, 59; Turner, *Syntax*, 268.

[59] The *Apocalypse of Moses*, 20:1–3, describes the fall of Adam as a loss of the "righteousness" and "glory" with which he had originally been "clothed" by God.

[60] The definition given by BDAG, s.v. ὁσιότης, is unsuitable to the present context: "state of proper attitude toward God as exhibited in action, *devoutness, piety, holiness*." This definition serves well in negative contexts, such as Moses' words to Israel that it is οὐχὶ διὰ τὴν δικαιοσύνην σου οὐδὲ διὰ τὴν ὁσιότητα τῆς καρδίας σου, "not because of your righteousness nor because of the *holiness* of your heart that you are going in to possess their land" (Deut 9:5).

holy image of God that allows them to stand before him without being consumed. This is cultic language rooted in the priestly rituals of the temple. This condition of being able to come into God's presence, "holy and without blemish before him" (1:4), is granted through Christ's own work, sanctifying his bride by the washing of water and the Word (5:26–27). The complementary terms δικαιοσύνη, "righteousness," and ὁσιότης, "holiness,"[61] thus combine two major biblical images for salvation: judicial and cultic (liturgical, sacramental). As these are primary characteristics of God,[62] they are appropriately chosen to describe the image of God, which is granted to the baptized.

The genitive τῆς ἀληθείας, "of truth," likely modifies both nouns, "true righteousness and holiness," and stands in contrast to τῆς ἀπάτης, "of deceit," which modified the lusts of the old man (4:22). But "true" is not simply a rejection of hypocrisy; it is a declaration that this righteousness and holiness come from Christ, in whom is the truth (4:21).[63] These "passive" (gifted) qualities are not entirely without consequence for the Ephesians' behavior, but Paul begins with the divine source and foundation. "Active" righteousness and holiness, the thoughts, words, and deeds that are in conformity with God's Word, flow forth from the passive qualities (cf. 1 Thess 2:10; Titus 1:8).

4:25 διὸ ἀποθέμενοι τὸ ψεῦδος λαλεῖτε ἀλήθειαν ἕκαστος μετὰ τοῦ πλησίον αὐτοῦ—In 4:20–24 Paul has described the dramatic change that has come over the Ephesians through their Baptism into Christ, the work God wrought by stripping off their old Adam and clothing them with the new Man. διό, "therefore," now draws out the implications of this change for how they walk.[64] Put another way, Paul moves from the image of God (regained in Baptism) as a *passive* state of righteousness (4:20–24) to the image of God as *active* righteousness (4:25–5:2). One who has been re-created to *be* like God will necessarily *act* like God. Paul depicts this consequent active righteousness in language drawn from the Ten Commandments (see the commentary), which can be seen therefore as the image of God in action. In this progression of thought, the participle ἀποθέμενοι should not be interpreted as an imperative: "*put off* falsehood, and

---

[61] These two terms form a couplet in LXX Deut 9:5; Odes 9:75; Wis Sol 9:3; Lk 1:75. In the Benedictus (Lk 1:75), the couplet describes the status given by God that enables the saved to stand before him and worship him without fear. This is not ethical but cultic holiness.

[62] See δίκαιος, "righteous," and ὅσιος, "holy," in LXX Deut 32:4; Ps 144:17 (MT/ET 145:17); Rev 16:5.

[63] Chrysostom, *Homilies on Ephesians*, 13:4.24, explains "of truth" to mean that the righteousness and holiness God conferred on OT Israel was a type or prefiguration ("figure") of the full gifts now received through Baptism:

How is this? For man is created henceforth, not of water, nor of earth, but "in righteousness and holiness of truth." What is this? He straightway created him, he means, to be a son: for this takes place from Baptism. This it is which is the reality, "in righteousness and holiness of truth." There was of old a righteousness, there was likewise a holiness with the Jews. Yet was that righteousness not in truth, but in figure. For the being clean in body was a type of purity, not the truth of purity; was a type of righteousness, not the truth of righteousness. (*NPNF*[1] 13:114)

[64] The appearance here of διό, "therefore," reinforces the interpretation that the previous infinitives in 4:22–24 have indicative force (see the first textual note on 4:22). Conclusions are not drawn from imperatives, but from facts. See Wallace, *Greek Grammar*, 605, n. 55.

then speak truth."[65] Rather, as an *aorist* participle, it refers back to that foundational act that has changed them into people who by their new nature would now only speak truth: "therefore, *since you have put off* falsehood [in your Baptism], speak truth."[66] This subtle grammatical point changes the entire flavor of the section. Paul roots their change in behavior not in their own effort, but in the change that God has first worked. If they have received Christ, who is the truth (4:21; cf. 1:13), how can they continue to speak what is false? "Do not speak falsehood to one another, *since you have put off* [ἀπεκδυσάμενοι] the old man with his deeds" (Col 3:9).

The meaning of τὸ ψεῦδος, "falsehood," is, on the one hand, the sin against the Eighth Commandment (Ex 20:16; Deut 5:20), "lying" in such a way that it hurts the neighbor. But this is not merely ethical; it is connected to false belief (sin against the First Commandment [Ex 20:3; Deut 5:7]), the greatest sin (2 Thess 2:11).[67] False speaking/teaching and lying arise from false belief; in contrast, the Ephesians are to be completely truthful (Eph 4:15). Falsehood is the way of the devil (Jn 8:44; 2 Thess 2:9) and idolatry (Rom 1:25; Rev 22:15). Truth is a major characteristic of the post-baptismal life.[68]

With two minor exceptions,[69] the next clause (λαλεῖτε ἀλήθειαν ἕκαστος μετὰ τοῦ πλησίον αὐτοῦ) is a direct quotation of LXX Zech 8:16. Paul's wisdom is drawn from God's Word. In Zechariah, "his neighbor" is a fellow Israelite. Here, in view of the words that follow, Paul means one's fellow Christian. This is not to deny our Lord's redefinition of what it means to be a neighbor (Lk 10:29–37), but merely to focus on the present context.

---

[65] This translation is grammatically possible. The aorist tense of the participle ἀποθέμενοι makes its timeframe "past" only in relation to the main verb. As the main verb here, λαλεῖτε, "speak," is an imperative, its timeframe is future; the aorist participle could then also be in future time, so long as it is still prior to the act of speaking. Cf. πορευθέντες οὖν μαθητεύσατε, "after you have gone, then, make disciples" (Mt 28:19), which is not entirely inaccurately translated as "go, then, make disciples." Our objection to the imperatival translation of ἀποθέμενοι is on contextual, not grammatical, grounds. (It must also be observed that if ἀποθέμενοι is *interpreted* imperatively, this does not make it an example of the imperatival *use* of the participle; its force is established by the imperative verb that follows, λαλεῖτε. Cf. BDF, § 468 [2].)

[66] Wallace, *Greek Grammar*, 605, allows for the possibility of this translation, though he is noncommittal.

[67] Luther's emphasis on false belief as the chief sin is a stunning rejection of moralism: "We pray in this petition that God would guard and keep us so that the devil, the world, and our sinful nature may not deceive us or mislead us into false belief, despair, and other great shame and vice" (SC 3:18, explanation of the Sixth Petition of the Lord's Prayer [*LSB* 324]).

[68] Eph 4:15, 24, 25; 5:9; 6:14; cf. Rev 14:5; *Didache*, 3:5.

[69] Paul changes the preposition πρός, "to," to μετά, "with," requiring the articular noun τὸν πλησίον (accusative) to become τοῦ πλησίον (genitive). πλησίον is the neuter form of the adjective πλησίος, "near," used as an adverb or improper preposition, "nearby." Here it is substantivized by the addition of an article (thus serving as a noun, "the near one, neighbor"). When serving as a noun, it is indeclinable (the ending does not change). See BDAG, s.v. πλησίον; cf. BDF, § 266.

The present tense imperative λαλεῖτε, like the imperatives that follow in the rest of this pericope, is a policy command.[70]

ὅτι ἐσμὲν ἀλλήλων μέλη—"For we are members of one another," a reference to the body of Christ metaphor,[71] might be seen as a guiding thought for all the admonitions Paul gives in these verses (4:25–32). There is little concern for ethical behavior in the world (as legitimate as that subject might be). Rather, because of their common Baptism into one body, Paul is concerned about how the members of the church treat one another (cf. Rom 12:5; 1 Cor 12:25). There is unity not only with Christ, the head, but also with one another, the parts that are bound together by joints and ligaments (4:16). Speaking falsehood, particularly false teaching, is a poison that spreads through and harms the whole body.[72]

4:26 ὀργίζεσθε καὶ μὴ ἁμαρτάνετε—Paul draws two more OT passages into what now looks like a midrash (extended interpretation of key biblical texts). The first half of this verse is a direct quotation from LXX Ps 4:5 (ET 4:4). The second half (see the next textual note) draws key words from Deut 24:15. The two texts are connected not by "anger" (which is absent from Deut 24:15), but by the theme of judgment and reconciliation before nightfall.

Psalm 4 is a sort of bedtime devotion. Ps 4:5 (ET 4:4) continues with a call to repentance, "meditate in your hearts on your beds, and be silent," and the psalm concludes with reliance on God's forgiveness: "in peace altogether I will lie down and sleep; for you alone, O YHWH, cause me to dwell securely" (Ps 4:9 [ET 4:8]). It is thought that psalm quotations in the NT are often references to the entire content of the psalm. If so and if Psalm 4 were as familiar to early Christians as it has been to those using it in Compline (the night office) for nearly two millennia,[73] then this brief reference may be establishing Psalm 4 as the basis for the entire section: consider your behavior toward your fellow members of Christ's body in such a way that you are prepared to be reconciled before nightfall and to beg the Lord for forgiveness each night.

The connection of anger and not sinning in this verse has led to the proposition that there can be "righteous anger" (as when God is angry with his sinful people), as if Paul were saying, "Be angry in such a way that you do not sin."[74] Yet the Scriptures

---

[70] It is characteristic of Paul to use present tense imperatives for policy commands and prohibitions (Voelz, *Fundamental Greek Grammar*, 202). Thus, it is "speak truth" (Eph 4:25), not "keep speaking," and "do not sin" (Eph 4:26) rather than "stop sinning."

[71] See 1:23; 2:16; 3:6; 4:4, 12, 16; 5:23, 30; cf. 5:28.

[72] "It would be extremely perverse, since we belong intimately to one another, to say things that are not true. For this is not the way the body functions. The eyes, for example, when they see cliffs and steep caverns, instantly report them to the feet so that they may turn aside and protect the whole body from harm" (Theodoret, *Ephesians*, 4:25, ACCS 8:176).

[73] Benedict prescribes Psalm 4 for Compline in his early sixth-century "Rule," which he claims was a revision of existing monastic practice. See also the further description of Compline in the next textual note.

[74] Wallace, *Greek Grammar*, 492, who leans in the direction of δικαία ὀργή, "righteous anger," implies that it means "be angry with what causes sin so that you do not sin." See also Barth, *Ephesians*, 2:513.

rarely portray human anger as righteous; in James 1:20 it is contrary to God's righteousness.[75] Christ discerns that anger is the inner violation of the Fifth Commandment (Mt 5:22; cf. Ex 20:13; Deut 5:17). Furthermore, this would not appear to be the meaning of the original psalm and does not suit the context of Ephesians 4. The original text (Ps 4:5 [ET 4:4]) has the verb רָגַז, "to tremble (with anger, fear, or agitation)," which may imply an exhortation to take seriously the wrath of God. The LXX translates רָגַז with ὀργίζομαι (Paul quotes its ὀργίζεσθε) here and again in Ps 98:1 (MT/ET 99:1), which encourages fear before the enthroned Almighty.[76] It is worth considering the possibility that Paul intends "tremble" in accord with the text's original meaning; that is, fear the wrath of God in such a way that you deal with the cause of sin and anger in the church community. The more common interpretation, which takes ὀργίζομαι in its normal NT sense of "anger," analyzes ὀργίζεσθε as an implied conditional: "*if* or *when* you are angry, do not let it lead to sin." This is open to some objection on syntactical grounds,[77] but forms a logical bridge into the call to reconciliation in the second half of the verse.

The following patristic interpretations take up the conditional analysis in a theologically sensitive manner:

> It is better not to be angry at all. But if one ever does fall into anger he should at least not be carried away by it toward something worse.[78]

> He is allowing to us as vulnerable humans that in the face of some undeserved event we may be moved to some level of annoyance, as if a light breeze were disturbing the serenity of the mind. But on no account are we to be carried into swelling rapids by the impulse of rage.[79]

So also Luther:

---

[75] ὀργή is a regular feature of vice lists (Eph 4:31!; Col 3:8; 1 Tim 2:8; James 1:19; cf. ὀργίλος Titus 1:7), as is θυμός, "fury" (2 Cor 12:20; Gal 5:20; Eph 4:31; Col 3:8). Aside from LXX Pss 4:5 (ET 4:4); 98:1 (MT/ET 99:1), all the other LXX uses of ὀργίζω in the imperative mood are negated by μή preceding: "do *not* be angry" (LXX Gen 45:24; Ex 32:22; Judg 6:39; Is 64:8 [ET 64:9]). Cf. *Didache*, 3:2. For similar warnings about human anger see Eccl 7:9 and also Prov 15:1, 18; 22:24; 29:8, 11; Sirach 1:22; 27:30.

[76] ὀργίζω translates רָגַז also in LXX Gen 45:25; Ex 15:14; 2 Ki 19:28; Prov 29:9.

[77] BDF, § 387 (1, 2), calls the imperative ὀργίζεσθε concessive and translates it conditionally. But Wallace, *Greek Grammar*, 489–92, raises a series of objections. The normal pattern for concessive imperatives in the NT (over twenty times) is imperative + καί + future indicative, "If X, then Y will happen" (489), rather than two imperatives bound by καί, as in this verse. If it followed this pattern, 4:26 would mean, "if you are angry, you will not sin," which is "obviously ludicrous" (491). Furthermore, in all other NT cases, the conditional imperative still implies a desired command, "if you are angry—and I want you to be," which is again difficult. Wallace's note, while grammatically helpful, does not take into account the fact that Paul is quoting an OT text. To disprove the possibility of the conditional translation, one would need to examine the usage of the underlying Hebrew imperatives. Cf., e.g., Eccl 11:9, where an imperative seems to grant God's wholesale permission (cf. "imperative of permission," Joüon, § 114 n) for natural human behavior ("*walk* in the ways of your heart and in [after] the sights of your eyes"), but this permission is then conditioned by a warning ("God will bring you into judgment"). Hebrew imperatives can "express all the shades of will" (Joüon, § 114 m (C), e.g., "must," "may," "will," "can," "might") and so a conditional meaning, "when" or "if," should not be ruled out.

[78] Chrysostom, *Homilies on Ephesians*, 14:4.25–27, ACCS 8:176.

[79] Jerome, *Ephesians*, 2:4.26, ACCS 8:176–77.

Paul admonishes the Christians as new creatures to guard against this vice of wrath, adducing the fourth verse of the fourth Psalm: "Stand in awe and sin not." The repetition of this passage sounds, in Paul's rendering, as if permission to be angry were given; he says: "Be ye angry, and sin not." But Paul is taking into consideration the way of the world. Men are tempted and moved to anger. ... This life of ours is so constituted that such conditions must be. ...

But right here, says the apostle, you should beware and not sin; not give rein, nor yield to the impulse and promptings of wrath. ... Beware of doing what your wrath would have you do.[80]

ὁ ἥλιος μὴ ἐπιδυέτω ἐπὶ [τῷ] παροργισμῷ ὑμῶν—In its original context, Deut 24:15 lays down the duty to pay a worker his wage on the day he works for it and "not let the sun go down upon him" or "upon it [the day]" (LXX: οὐκ ἐπιδύσεται ὁ ἥλιος ἐπ᾽ αὐτῷ). Otherwise, the verse continues, he may "cry against you to YHWH, and you be guilty of sin." Paul draws this text into his contemplation of Ps 4:5 (ET 4:4; see the preceding textual note) on the basis of the common theme of sunset and sin (linking verses with common themes was a typical method of Jewish exegesis). On the one hand, this admonition is simply commonsense, was encouraged by contemporary writers,[81] and has been the recipe for many a successful marriage! But in the context of the body of Christ, and in a passage leading up to "forgiving one another, just as also God in Christ has forgiven you" (4:32), there is a heightened Christian meaning: the daily return to Baptism through repentance and forgiveness. This was enacted in the aforementioned daily office of Compline,[82] which began with an act of mutual confession and forgiveness (quite distinct from sacramental absolution) to reconcile the members of the community.[83]

The NT hapax legomenon παροργισμός is not just "anger" but "the state of being provoked into an angry mood." The communal, interpersonal nature of the condition is illustrated by use of the verb παροργίζω to describe a father's tendency to provoke his children to anger (Eph 6:4). In the LXX the noun and the verb primarily refer to provoking God to anger[84]—a reminder that sin is never just between people. The emphasis of the compound noun (παρ-οργισμός) is not simply that the sinful anger itself be dealt with by sundown, but the *cause* of the anger, the provocation. This is achieved by reconciliation, both with the fellow member(s) and with God.[85]

---

[80] Luther, "Sermon for the Nineteenth Sunday after Trinity, Ephesians 4:22–28," October 22, 1536, Lenker, 8:312–13; StL 12:919–20, §§ 23–24.

[81] Plutarch, *Moralia*, 488c: "We should next pattern ourselves after the Pythagoreans, who, though related not at all by birth, yet sharing a common discipline, if ever they were led by anger into recrimination, never let the sun go down before they joined right hands, embraced each other, and were reconciled" (quoted in Lincoln, *Ephesians*, 302; cf. BDAG, s.v. ἐπιδύω). See also the Qumran *Community Rule*, 1QS 5:26–6:1; and the *Damascus Document*, CD 7:2–3; 9:6–8.

[82] See the analysis of Psalm 4 in the first textual note on 4:26.

[83] See *LSB* 254.

[84] E.g., Deut 4:25; 1 Ki 15:30; Jer 21:5.

[85] Polycarp, *To the Philippians*, 12:1, clearly on the basis of Eph 4:26, quotes the same two OT passages (Ps 4:5 [ET 4:4] and Deut 24:15) as Paul has quoted, immediately after calling for

4:27 μηδὲ δίδοτε τόπον τῷ διαβόλῳ—The conjunction μηδέ, "nor, and not," suggests that this clause is connected tightly to the preceding. It is not an additional admonition, but the completion of the previous thought. If the cause of anger (which leads to sin) is not dealt with, then the devil is given more room to maneuver.[86] He uses anger to snare people and lead them into other sins (Eph 4:31; 1 Pet 5:8),[87] while forgiveness in the community thwarts his efforts (2 Cor 2:10–11). The expression δίδωμι τόπον means "to give an opportunity, chance."[88] The fight against the devil and his forces is a prominent theme in Ephesians, which speaks of Christ's triumph over and subordination of all spiritual forces (1:21–22; 2:2; 3:10), and calls the baptized to stand firm against them during their frantic final assaults in these last days (6:11–12). While the name or title "Satan" (σατάν, a transliteration of the Hebrew שָׂטָן, or σατανᾶς, from the Aramaic סָטָנָא) means "adversary, enemy, accuser," the noun here, διάβολος, "devil," literally means "slanderer." διάβολος ("devil") is used in the LXX as the normal translation of שָׂטָן, "Satan" (chiefly in Job), which suggests there is no great distinction between the terms. The fact that Paul uses διάβολος only in Ephesians and the Pastorals should therefore not be overinterpreted.[89] In a context which has spoken of putting off the old man (Adam) and being re-created in the image of God by taking on the new man (Christ), the reference to the devil is an appropriate further reminder of Eden. Paul's meaning is "let not Eden be played out again in your life." Or "be with Christ in the wilderness as he defeated the devil, rather than with Adam who succumbed to him in Eden."

4:28 ὁ κλέπτων μηκέτι κλεπτέτω, μᾶλλον δὲ κοπιάτω ἐργαζόμενος ταῖς [ἰδίαις] χερσὶν τὸ ἀγαθόν, ἵνα ἔχῃ μεταδιδόναι τῷ χρείαν ἔχοντι—The rhythmic pattern of prohibition-exhortation that marks 4:25–32 is most succinct in this and the following

---

reconciliation within the body of Christ (*To the Philippians*, 11:4). Here Polycarp appears to refer to Ephesians as Scripture, one of the earliest such attributions to Paul's letters (see also 2 Pet 3:16). See Paul Hartog, "Polycarp, Ephesians, and 'Scripture,'" *Westminster Theological Journal* 70 (2008): 255–75.

[86] Although we disagree with Wallace's interpretation of ὀργίζεσθε as "righteous anger" (see the first textual note on 4:26), his remaining analysis is insightful: "Verse 27, in this reconstruction, would thus mean that one should not give a place to the devil *by doing nothing about the sin in the midst of the believing community*. Entirely opposite of the 'introspective conscience' view, this text seems to be a shorthand expression for church discipline" (*Greek Grammar*, 492).

[87] The *Testament of Dan*, 4:7–5:2, immediately before quoting Zech 8:16, associates anger and lying with the rule of the devil. See also *Shepherd of Hermas, Mandates*, 5:1.3: "For the Lord dwells in long-suffering [μακροθυμίᾳ] and the devil dwells in ill temper [ὀξυχολίᾳ]" (trans. Kirsopp Lake, LCL).

[88] Wis Sol 12:10, 20; Sirach 4:5; 19:17; 38:12; Lk 14:9; Rom 12:19. Cf. τόπον ἔχω, "to have opportunity" (Rom 15:23); τόπον οὐχ εὗρεν, "he found/had no chance" (Heb 12:17). It is intriguing that in Rom 12:19 Paul warns against human revenge, admonishing rather to δότε τόπον τῇ ὀργῇ, "give way to the wrath [of God]." Human anger gives room for the devil; turning anger over to God leaves the devil no space to work. It may be that τόπος, "place," has a slightly more literal meaning with respect to the church as the temple of God and the body of Christ. Within these structures, the devil should have no place; their sacred space should not be violated.

[89] This has been used to argue against Pauline authorship of these writings. However, Paul uses σατανᾶς infrequently (ten times), and both terms appear in the Pastorals.

verse. The adverb μηκέτι, "no longer," reminds again of the two-part division of the Gentile Ephesians' lives into "then" and "now" with which this pericope began (4:17; cf. 2:1–4, 11–13).[90] As they were once defined as "Gentiles" but are no longer, being baptized, so the one who once defined himself as "thief" is no longer. Thus, ὁ κλέπτων, while technically a present participle, "thieving person," does not imply that he is *now* thieving, but that he was once defined as one who thieved.[91] Paul does not necessarily suggest that someone among the Christians at Ephesus is still thieving and should stop,[92] but rather that anyone who once lived that way should stay away from his old life, which was destructive of community, and give his attention to what supports and strengthens it. The concern is not with the principle of personal property or the right to wealth, but with the welfare of one's Christian brothers and sisters (Gal 6:10). κλέπτω, "to steal," is a violation of the Seventh Commandment (Ex 20:15; Deut 5:19), to which Paul's only other uses of the verb refer (Rom 2:21; 13:9; cf. Mt 19:18).[93] Thieves are outside the kingdom (1 Cor 6:10) and metaphorical enemies of it (Jn 10:1–10), as Judas also is derided as a thief (Jn 12:6).

By contrast, the activity of κοπιάω, "to labor," is often a positive activity in Scripture[94]—though not in itself, nor as it benefits the worker,[95] but as it serves the neighbor (as the purpose clause here expressly indicates: ἵνα ἔχῃ, "so that he has ..."). While Jesus promises rest to those who labor (Mt 11:28) and highlights the gifts of God that come without our labor (Mt 6:28–29; Jn 4:38), Paul calls pastors to labor in the

---

[90] See "once/then" (ποτέ) and/or "now" (νῦν) in 2:2, 3, 11, 13; 3:5, 10; 5:8, 29 (cf. 2:4; 4:17). See also the table contrasting "then" with "now" in "Structure and Rhetoric" in the commentary on 2:11–22; the table in "Structure and Rhetoric" as well as the section entitled "Darkness Has No Fellowship with Light" in the commentary on 5:3–14; and the table of antitheses in "Structure and Rhetoric" in the commentary on 5:15–21a.

[91] BDF, § 339 (3), explains the present participle as representing the imperfect tense, referring to an action before the main verb, i.e., "who stole up to now" (cf. Jn 9:25). Moule, *Idiom Book*, 101, 206, adds significant examples. Cf. Turner, *Syntax*, 81. In Eph 4:28, however, the participle is not used circumstantially (is not subordinate to a main verb). Schlier, *Epheser*, 225, n. 6, calls it "timeless." It should therefore be taken as equivalent to the noun ὁ κλέπτης, "thief" (Lincoln, *Ephesians*, 303), though it retains a habitual sense (Zerwick, *Biblical Greek*, § 274).

[92] Likewise, Peter does not imply that the people to whom he was writing were murderers and thieves (1 Pet 4:15). The article on ὁ κλέπτων implies a class of people, not an individual, and is equivalent to πᾶς, "everyone who" (BDF, § 275 [6]; Turner, *Syntax*, 151). The prohibition and command do not refer to a specific case (contra Wallace, *Greek Grammar*, 722), but are policy commands. Certainly if anyone in Ephesus was stealing, Paul's words would convict him of that sin and direct him to turn away from that sinful behavior toward doing good.

[93] Luther's explanation of the Seventh Commandment reminds us that thievery includes not only the physical act of taking goods from someone else, but also dishonest or unfair business practices that "get them in any dishonest way" (SC 1:14 [*LSB* 321]). Cf. LC 1:223–50.

[94] The Decalogue presumes it (Ex 20:9); God attaches conditional, earthly blessings to it (Prov 28:19; Sirach 7:15), though it is robbed of its joy by the fall (Gen 3:16–19).

[95] The NT warns against the accumulation of personal wealth for one's own sake (Mt 6:19; Lk 12:16–21; 1 Cor 7:30–31; 1 Tim 6:17–18). Other positive evaluations of labor such as to support oneself so as not to be dependent on charity (2 Thess 3:10) or artistic creations to the praise of God are not excluded, but do not fit the present context of the edification of the Christian community. Support of one's family would surely be included in "share with anyone in need" (Eph 4:28).

Word[96] and all Christians to work hard to strengthen the Christian community (Rom 16:6). Paul asks the former thief to do no more than he himself has done (1 Cor 4:12; 15:10; 2 Thess 3:6–12). While care for those who are in need is a feature of any community, it was particularly incumbent on Israel; the implication is that the church is the new Israel. Within the body of Christ, each member works for the good of all the others (Gal 6:10), but particularly for those that are weakest.[97] The verb μεταδίδωμι, "to share" (cf. Rom 12:8), connects this verse with the preaching of John the Baptizer to the community of Israel (Lk 3:11).

The multiple textual variants on ταῖς [ἰδίαις] χερσὶν τὸ ἀγαθόν try in various ways to smooth out two presumed problems with the text: (1) ἰδίαις, "one's very own," which may have been deleted as redundant (who else's hands would they be?) and unclassical (though cf. 1 Cor 4:12), or through homoioteleuton (with ταῖς); and (2) ταῖς χερσίν, "the hands," may have been omitted because of skepticism that τὸ ἀγαθόν, "moral good," might come from manual labor (though cf. 1 Tim 6:18, which connects doing good with charity).

4:29 πᾶς λόγος σαπρὸς ἐκ τοῦ στόματος ὑμῶν μὴ ἐκπορευέσθω, ἀλλὰ εἴ τις ἀγαθὸς πρὸς οἰκοδομὴν τῆς χρείας—The adjective σαπρός can have the sense of "spoilt, rotten," like fish at a market that have gone bad or olives riddled with worms. In its NT occurrences it refers to live fish that are unsuitable for eating (of the wrong kind, Mt 13:48) and to a tree that is unable to produce good fruit (Mt 7:17–18; 12:33; Lk 6:43). Thus, it refers to the nature of things. A λόγος σαπρός is therefore not simply a useless word or speaking, but one that is by nature foul, because it proceeds from a heart that is bad (Mt 12:34; 15:11, 18). Thus, Paul refers back to the kind of talk that characterized the Ephesians' lives before Baptism, before they were changed (for examples, see Eph 5:3–4; Col 3:8). Such talk is "harmful, bad, evil, unwholesome"[98] and tears down the body of Christ with all the might that words possess. As in the fruit tree metaphor (Mt 7:17–18),[99] the opposite here is ἀγαθός, "wholesome, beneficial," as well as "morally good" (cf. 5:9).[100] Good words are like the good works that God creates and places the Christian into (2:10), since they proceed naturally from the renewed nature. It must not be ignored that "good" is primarily an attribute of God[101] and therefore is the Christian's insofar as he has been clothed with Christ. That gracious words proceed

---

[96] Acts 20:35; 1 Thess 5:12; 1 Tim 5:17; 2 Tim 2:6.

[97] Note, for example, the sharing of goods in the early Jerusalem church (Acts 2:44–45; 4:32) and the collection for the saints in Jerusalem to alleviate suffering caused by famine (Acts 11:28–30; 24:17; Rom 15:25–31; 1 Cor 16:1–3; 2 Cor 8:1–6; Gal 2:10). Cf. *Didache*, 4:8.

[98] See BDAG, s.v. σαπρός, 2. The parallel in Col 3:8 is αἰσχρολογία, which can mean "obscene, filthy talk," but in connection with βλασφημία, "slander, blasphemy," it could mean "scurrilous talk" (BDAG, s.v. αἰσχρολογία). What is αἰσχρός, "shameful," is associated with darkness (Eph 5:12).

[99] In Mt 12:33; Lk 6:43, the opposite of σαπρός is καλός.

[100] The counterpart in Col 4:6, "your word … seasoned with salt," may imply not just tasty, appealing words, but the preserving quality of salt in contrast to the rottenness of evil talk.

[101] "For he [YHWH] is good" (1 Chr 16:34; 2 Chr 5:13; 7:3; Pss 118:29; 135:3); "the good YHWH" (2 Chr 30:18); God alone is good (Mk 10:18); "the Word of YHWH" is "good" (2 Ki 20:19 ∥ Is 39:8; cf. 1 Ki 8:56).

from one's mouth is therefore to be Christlike (Lk 4:22). The purpose that is added, πρὸς οἰκοδομήν, "for building up" (Eph 4:29), recalls the work of the ministry (see the third textual note on 4:12) and the metaphors of the spiritual temple (2:21–22) and the body of Christ (4:16). Here Paul stresses the role that every member of the body plays through the transformed speech that flows from their mouths (cf. Rom 14:19; 1 Cor 14:3–5). These are words of mutual forgiveness (4:32) and Spirit-directed worship (psalms and hymns and thanksgiving, 5:18–20). The genitive modifier τῆς χρείας, "of the need," is probably not objective ("for building up the need"), since it is not "the need" itself that is built up, but what the need relates to. It is adjectival, "for the building up that is needed" or "in accord with the need." The parallel repetition of ἀγαθός, "good," and χρεία, "need," in 4:28 and 4:29 suggests Paul is raising just two examples of how the good of the body may be promoted and its needs fulfilled.

The memorable, poetic expression πᾶς λόγος σαπρὸς ἐκ τοῦ στόματος ὑμῶν μὴ ἐκπορευέσθω, "let no harmful word proceed from your mouths," includes a number of Semitisms. Though στόματος, "mouth," is singular, it is modified by the plural pronoun ὑμῶν, "your," and emphasizes the communal nature of the speech and is therefore translated as a plural.[102] πᾶς ... μή, literally, "*every* harmful word ... let *not*," is a way of expressing a negative pronoun ("none") that is almost unique to Biblical Greek.[103] "To proceed from the mouth" is Septuagintal,[104] which influences NT speech[105] and culminates in the magnificent image of a sword proceeding from Christ's mouth (Rev 1:16; 19:15, 21).

ἵνα δῷ χάριν τοῖς ἀκούουσιν—The implied subject of δῷ is λόγος ἀγαθός, "that it [the good word] might give grace." This is the fifth time in Ephesians that χάρις, "grace," has been connected with δίδωμι, "give." In the prior cases it referred to the office of apostle given to Paul (3:2, 7, 8) and the creedal gifts and ministry given to the church (4:7; cf. 4:4–6 and 4:8–12). Thus, it was a gift of God that proceeded from his gracious disposition. But a reference to the gracious attitude of God by which he forgives sinners is never excluded, inasmuch as the purpose of the apostolic ministry is to be an instrument of God's grace. Here, similarly, if Christians speak "good words," God works his "grace" through them, particularly if their words are characterized by the forgiveness that they were first shown in Christ (χαριζόμενοι ἑαυτοῖς, καθὼς καὶ

---

[102] "Contrary to normal Greek and Latin practice, the NT sometimes follows the Aram[aic] and Heb[rew] preference for a distributive sing[ular]," e.g., "mouth" here (Turner, *Syntax*, 23; cf. p. 25).

[103] Turner, *Syntax*, 196. As a rule the negative particle precedes what is negated ("not ... every"), but this rule is occasionally broken, as here (Turner, *Syntax*, 287). Cf. πᾶς ... οὐκ in Eph 5:5.

[104] See BDF, § 217 (3). With ἐκπορεύομαι: LXX Num 32:24; Deut 8:3; 23:24 (ET 23:23); Prov 3:16; Job 41:11, 13 (ET 41:19, 21); Sirach 38:12. With ἐξέρχομαι: LXX Num 30:3 (ET 30:2); Judg 11:36; 1 Kgdms 1:23; 2:3 (MT/ET 1 Sam 1:23; 2:3); Job 37:2; Is 45:23; 48:3; 55:11; Jer 51:17 (MT/ET 44:17); Lam 3:38; Judith 5:5; Sirach 24:3.

[105] With ἐκπορεύομαι: Mt 4:4; 15:11, 18; Lk 4:22; Rev 9:17–18; 11:5. With ἐξέρχομαι: Mt 15:18; James 3:10.

ὁ θεὸς ἐν Χριστῷ ἐχαρίσατο ὑμῖν, "forgiving one another, just as also God in Christ has forgiven you," 4:32; the verb χαρίζομαι, "forgive," has χάρις, "grace," at its root).[106]

4:30 καὶ μὴ λυπεῖτε τὸ πνεῦμα τὸ ἅγιον τοῦ θεοῦ, ἐν ᾧ ἐσφραγίσθητε εἰς ἡμέραν ἀπολυτρώσεως—The rest of this unit (4:25–32) is characterized by asyndeton, the abrupt succession of statements without conjunctions. This suggests the conjunction καί at the beginning of this verse connects it closely to the preceding one (4:29), rather than introducing a completely new thought. Paul may mean that it is sinful words in particular ("harmful word," 4:29) that "grieve the Holy Spirit" (though one should not exclude the other sins he has listed), as the Spirit works primarily through the ("good," 4:29) Word (cf. 6:17).

The latter half of this verse is a virtual repetition of 1:13–14 (see the textual notes there). Paul refers back to the Ephesians' Baptism as the moment when they were "sealed" (ἐσφραγίσθητε, as in 1:13) with the Holy Spirit, who was given to them as a down payment and guarantee (ἀρραβών, 1:14) of the Spirit's full work on the Last Day,[107] including the final destruction of the old Adam, the resurrection of the dead (Rom 8:23), and the life everlasting.

Accordingly, the first half of the sentence would imply an action that denies or rejects the baptismal gift and work of the Spirit. λυπέω, "to cause grief" to the Spirit, or perhaps "to offend, insult,"[108] is therefore not simply to do things that make him sad.[109] Nor does Paul cite the Spirit only as the authority standing behind his words (1 Thess 4:8). To act as if one is not baptized, to return to the sort of life that was lived as a pagan Gentile, is to insult the Holy Spirit and question his work, to treat Baptism and faith as nothings.[110] Israel, likewise, "rebelled" against the God who redeemed them

---

[106] "Eph 4:29 may suggest a demonstration of human favor ... , but a ref[erence] to the means by which divine grace is mediated is not to be ruled out" (BDAG, s.v. χάρις, 3 a). After speaking of "building up," the former meaning would be redundant; the latter meaning adds something new. Luther includes "the mutual conversation and consolation of brethren" among the means of grace (SA 3:4). The NT shows little interest in speech that is merely "pleasing," in the classical sense of the expression δίδωμι χάριν.

[107] The expression in 4:30, ἡμέρα ἀπολυτρώσεως, "day of redemption," is unique to this passage in the NT, but is surely equivalent to "the day of the Lord" (e.g., 1 Cor 1:8; 5:5; 2 Cor 1:14; 1 Thess 5:2; 2 Thess 2:2), "the day of wrath" (Rom 2:5), "the day of Christ" (Phil 1:10; 2:16), and "the day" (Rom 2:16; 13:12).

[108] See BDAG, s.v. λυπέω, 1.

[109] However, the choice of the verb λυπέω, "to cause grief," dependent as it is on Is 63:10 (where the LXX uses παροξύνω), may stand in antithesis to the Spirit's fundamental characteristic of "joy" (Ps 51:14 [ET 51:12]; Rom 14:17; 15:13; Gal 5:22; 1 Thess 1:6). See Schlier, *Epheser*, 227: "All Christian existence is thus entering into a joyful being [*ein Sein der Freude*], in which the Spirit of joy places us since our Baptism." The major discussion of grieving the Spirit in *Shepherd of Hermas, Mandates*, 10, revolves around the "mournful man" who rejects the joy of the Spirit. Hermas presents human grief and the Holy Spirit as thoroughly incompatible. The siblings of grief are doubt and anger. These three not only grieve the Spirit, but "crush him out [ἐκτρίβει αὐτό]" (*Shepherd of Hermas, Mandates*, 10:2.2).

[110] Bruce, *The Epistles to the Colossians, to Philemon, and to the Ephesians*, 363, and Schnackenburg, *Ephesians*, 210, quote what is supposedly an unrecorded saying of our Lord from Pseudo-Cyprian, *De Aleatoribus* (*On Gamblers*), 3: "Do not grieve the Holy Spirit who is in you, and do not extinguish the light which has been lit in you" (as quoted by Bruce).

and "grieved his Holy Spirit" when they turned away from their salvation (Is 63:10; cf. Acts 7:51).[111] There is also a communal aspect, inasmuch as the sins just mentioned are against a fellow Christian, in whom the Spirit resides, and therefore involve denying the Spirit's work and presence in that person (cf. 1 Cor 3:16; 6:19).[112] One who tears down is fighting against the Spirit who builds up.

Thus, there is a connection to the much-debated blasphemy against the Holy Spirit (Mt 12:31–32; Mk 3:28–30; Lk 12:10).[113] Jesus laid this charge against the Pharisees because they attributed his holy work to the devil, thus rejecting the testimony of the Holy Spirit to Christ and denying his work.[114] To engage in the evil deeds and words against which Paul warns in these verses does not offend the Spirit in the way that foul language offends sensitive ears; the Spirit is grieved because these deeds and words ultimately imply a rejection of him.[115]

4:31 πᾶσα πικρία καὶ θυμὸς καὶ ὀργὴ καὶ κραυγὴ καὶ βλασφημία ἀρθήτω ἀφ᾽ ὑμῶν σὺν πάσῃ κακίᾳ—This verse is a summary statement of the kinds of sinful words and deeds that belong to the old Adam and were put off in Baptism. Anger is the common thread, and the verse may be viewed as an exposition of 4:26. Following the established rhythm, this admonition is followed by a positive encouragement to the deeds that are in accord with the new man (4:32). The verse is framed by πᾶς, "all" (the first and second-last Greek words); the final phrase σὺν πάσῃ κακίᾳ, "with all malice," does not

---

Enlightening is a baptismal image; see "Enlightened Eyes of Your Heart (1:18)" in the commentary on 1:15–23.

[111] See the second textual note and the commentary on Is 63:10 in Lessing, *Isaiah 56–66*, 346–47, 369–72. If Paul draws his language from Is 63:10, he follows the MT (the Piel of עָצַב, "to hurt someone's feelings") rather than the LXX (παροξύνω, "to anger, provoke"). The LXX uses λυπέω with πνεῦμα only in 2 Kgdms 13:21 (MT/ET 2 Sam 13:21), where King David "did not grieve the spirit of Amnon his son." Cf. Tobit 4:3, where Codex Sinaiticus uses πνεῦμα with λυπέω when Tobit commands his son Tobias about the son's mother (Tobit's wife), "Do not grieve her spirit."

[112] The sin of Ananias and Sapphira in withholding promised goods from the church in Jerusalem was a sin against the Holy Spirit, who dwells in their brothers and sisters (Acts 5:3).

[113] See Gibbs, *Matthew 11:2–20:34*, 639–45, who argues that it is what one professes about Jesus that constitutes blasphemy against the Spirit (or not): "The evidence of their [the Pharisees'] spiritual condition is their words—*their words about Jesus in 12:24.* ... An evil man speaks evil things about Jesus (12:35b), as these Pharisees have done. He blasphemes the Spirit. He speaks worthless words" (643). "It is a complete mistake, then, to suppose that blasphemy against the Spirit is anything more or anything less than ongoing rejection of Jesus" (645).

[114] Jesus calls this sin unforgivable not because such a person cannot repent, turn to the Spirit, and ask for forgiveness, but because it entails a rejection of the Holy Spirit himself. A person who continues to reject the Spirit has no recourse to repentance and forgiveness because he repudiates the means by which forgiveness comes. Martin Chemnitz, *Ministry, Word, and Sacraments: An Enchiridion* (trans. Luther Poellot; St. Louis: Concordia, 1981), 108, writes:

In short, since the Holy Spirit works repentance, faith, and renewal through the ministry of the Word, if someone, then, despises, abuses, blasphemes, and persecutes the Word of God, or impudently hinders and destroys the work of the Holy Spirit, who wants to arouse repentance, faith, and new obedience in us, he sins against the ministry and work of the Holy Spirit.

[115] "The God proclaimed in Ephesians is not an unmoved mover" (Barth, *Ephesians*, 2:548). God suffers with his people (Is 63:9). See the commentary on Is 63:9 in Lessing, *Isaiah 56–66*, 367–68.

stress this term in particular,[116] but simply marks the close of the list with rhythmic variation.[117] The final phrase with πᾶς also has the sense of "etc.," indicating that the list is not exhaustive.[118] The verb ἀρθήτω (third singular aorist passive imperative of αἴρω) means "let [something] be taken away." On the one hand, the passive construction simply allows Paul to focus on the sins that need to be removed. But there may be a hint of a divine passive, that as the old man was put off by the work of Christ (4:22, 25), so the old man's deeds cannot be put off without the action of God's Spirit.[119]

- πικρία, "bitterness," which with its cognates can refer literally to bitter foods (e.g., LXX Ex 12:8), is a resentful attitude of the heart that arises from the belief one has been treated wrongly (e.g., LXX Job 7:11; cf. LXX Gen 27:34). This leads to anger and ill words (Rom 3:14; Heb 12:15), and so it appropriately heads the list.

- θυμός is "passionate anger, wrath, rage." It is illustrative that Esau's "bitter cry" (πικρός, LXX Gen 27:34) leads to θυμός and ὀργή against his brother, Jacob (LXX Gen 27:44–45). θυμός also describes the silversmiths' rage against Paul in Ephesus (Acts 19:28).[120] It is a regular feature of Pauline vice lists (2 Cor 12:20; Gal 5:20; Col 3:8).[121]

- ὀργή is difficult to distinguish from the preceding θυμός, with which it often appears as a couplet in the LXX.[122] It simply means "anger, wrath" and in the present context is an entirely negative emotion that should not characterize relations between Christians (cf. 1 Tim 2:8). ὀργή also features in vice lists (Col 3:8) and is contrasted with God's righteousness (James 1:19–20). See also ὀργίζομαι in the first textual note on Eph 4:26.

- κραυγή is a "loud outcry, clamor" that in the present context might be "(angry) shouting" (cf. Acts 23:9). Christ, who "will not cry out," forms a strong contrast (οὐδὲ κραυγάσει, Mt 12:19, quoting Is 42:2).

---

[116] Note the medial position of κακία, "malice," in the list of five vices in Col 3:8.

[117] Similarly, in 4:11 the conjunction switches to καί for the final office, καὶ διδασκάλους, "and teachers," to signal that it is the last in the list. See the second textual note on 4:11.

[118] See the final "etc." phrase with πᾶς, "all, every," in 1:21: καὶ παντὸς ὀνόματος ὀνομαζομένου, "and every name that is named."

[119] Lincoln, *Ephesians*, 308, calls the use of the passive verb "a stylistic variation," while Barth, *Ephesians*, 2:522, argues for a divine passive, adducing the first three petitions of the Lord's Prayer (Mt 6:9–10) as parallels. See also active forms of αἴρω with Christ as subject for the divine removal of sin (Jn 1:29; Col 2:14; 1 Jn 3:5). God's forgiveness is explicit in the next verse (Eph 4:32).

[120] See "Conflict with the Cult of Artemis Ephesia (Acts 19:21–41)" in "The City of Ephesus and Paul's Relationship to It" in the introduction.

[121] In the LXX and in Revelation, θυμός most often is God's "wrath" against sin, a meaning inappropriate to this context; it may be helpful to reserve the translation "wrath" for God's righteous anger, which pays back sin. The next term in 4:31, ὀργή, "anger," has the same double usage, as here it refers to that of man, whereas it refers to God's anger in 2:3; 5:6.

[122] ὀργή and θυμός (in either order) are coupled in a hundred verses of the LXX and six times in the NT (Rom 2:8; Eph 4:31; Col 3:8; Rev 14:10; 16:19; 19:15). If there is a distinction between the words and if the ordering of the nouns here (θυμὸς καὶ ὀργή) is significant, the Stoics' definitions may be helpful: "… the former [θυμός] denoting an initial explosion of rage and the latter [ὀργή] a more settled feeling of gnawing hostility" (Lincoln, *Ephesians*, 308).

- βλασφημία is "speech that denigrates or defames,"[123] of which blasphemy against God (e.g., Mt 12:31; 26:65; Jn 10:33; Rev 13:6) is a subset that does not suit the present context.[124] Here it is "slander" against fellow members of the body, perhaps even "cursing."[125] This is another regular feature of vice lists (Mk 7:22; Col 3:8; 1 Tim 6:4) and may be connected with the Eighth Commandment (Mt 15:19, alluding to, e.g., Ex 20:16; Deut 5:20).

- κακία is the state of "wickedness, depravity,"[126] but in context must refer to an attitude or disposition toward others: "malice, ill-will, malignity,"[127] the desire to do harm. It also appears in vice lists (Rom 1:29; Col 3:8; 1 Pet 2:1) and is a characteristic of the old life (1 Cor 5:8; Titus 3:3) to which Christians ought not return (1 Pet 2:16).

The presence of these terms in standard vice lists, together with the repeated catchall πᾶς, "all," suggests Paul's individual choices should not be scrutinized too closely, but should be regarded as exemplary of the kind of behavior that is inappropriate for the baptized. There is discernible, nonetheless, a certain progression "from anger's inner center (πικρία) through its initial eruption (θυμός) and steady festering (ὀργή) to its external expression (κραυγή) and damaging of others (βλασφημία)."[128]

4:32 γίνεσθε [δὲ] εἰς ἀλλήλους …—If the conjunction δέ is part of the original text,[129] this verse is bound to the previous one as the positive encouragement that counterbalances its prohibition (4:31), following the rhythm of the section. In any case, it forms a strong summary of the positive encouragement Paul wishes to convey, for the edification of the body ("one another"). There may be a progression in this verse akin to that in the previous verse: here, from goodness to compassion to forgiveness.

---

[123] BDAG, s.v. βλασφημία.

[124] It is possible, as Barth, *Ephesians*, 2:522, suggests, that slander against a fellow Christian is to be connected with blasphemy against God because the former bears God's name.

[125] Barth, *Ephesians*, 2:521.

[126] LXX Gen 6:5; Acts 8:22; 1 Cor 14:20; James 1:21.

[127] BDAG, s.v. κακία, 2.

[128] Lincoln, *Ephesians*, 309, drawing on Schlier, *Epheser*, 228; Barth, *Ephesians*, 2:521; and Schnackenburg, *Ephesians*, 211. Cf. *Shepherd of Hermas, Mandates*, 5:2.4; Chrysostom, *Homilies on Ephesians*, 15:4.31. "He clearly wants to advance from a gentle simmer to a mighty explosion" (Schnackenburg, *Ephesians*, 211).

[129] The square brackets in NA²⁷ betray the difficulty of the decision. The strong witnesses 𝔓⁴⁶ and B omit the conjunction δέ, while a broad mix of early and late manuscripts include it (including 𝔓⁴⁹ ℵ A D² 33 and 𝔐). Its accidental omission might be explained by homoioteleuton, the ΘΕ at the end of γίνεσθε being broadly similar to ΔΕ. If it was omitted intentionally, the adversative meaning "but" may have been thought out of place. The substitution of οὖν (D* F G 1175 b) is likely caused by the copyist's eye jumping to 5:1. It seems that early scribes were more likely to *omit* small units than to *add* them, especially when the words were not crucial to the meaning of the text. See James R. Royse, "Scribal Tendencies in the Transmission of the Text of the New Testament," in *The Text of the New Testament in Contemporary Research: Essays on the Status Quaestionis* (ed. Bart D. Ehrman and Michael W. Holmes; 2d ed.; Leiden: Brill, 2013), 461–78; and the more extensive study by Royse, *Scribal Habits in Early Greek New Testament Papyri*, "The Scribe of 𝔓⁴⁶," 199–358.

χρηστοί—While it can mean "easy" or "fine," in this context χρηστός means "morally good and benevolent";[130] unless this is understood, "kind" is too weak of a translation. God is χρηστός, "good" (Lk 6:35; Rom 2:4; 1 Pet 2:3), and his χρηστότης, "goodness," is his saving benevolence, equivalent to "grace" (Eph 2:7; Titus 3:4).[131] It is not impossible that Paul implies wordplay on χρηστός, *chrēstos*, "good," and Χριστός, *Christos*, "Christ," inasmuch as both η and ι were pronounced "ee" at the time.[132] Thus, it is a Christlike virtue.[133] χρηστότης is a gift of the Spirit (Gal 5:22; Col 3:12) and characterized Paul's ministry under the Spirit (2 Cor 6:6).

εὔσπλαγχνοι—The σπλάγχνα are the inner parts of the body, particularly the gut, which in the ancient world represented the seat of emotions, chiefly love.[134] With the prefix εὖ, "well, good," the adjective εὔσπλαγχνος means "tenderhearted, compassionate." This rare compound form appears in the NT only in the virtue lists here and in 1 Pet 3:8. Elsewhere it is a quality of God,[135] and it is encouraged as a unifying virtue among Christians (1 Pet 3:8). The simple noun σπλάγχνον (always plural: "heart; compassion, affection") is likewise a basic quality of God (Lk 1:78) and of Christ (Phil 1:8), and is found in his ministers (2 Cor 6:12; 7:15).[136] The simple form's place in NT virtue lists (Phil 2:1; Col 3:12) suggests it is nearly synonymous with εὔσπλαγχνος. The verb σπλαγχνίζομαι, "to have compassion," is used in the NT almost exclusively of Christ.[137]

χαριζόμενοι ἑαυτοῖς, καθὼς καὶ ὁ θεὸς ἐν Χριστῷ ἐχαρίσατο ὑμῖν—"Grace" vocabulary has featured strongly in Ephesians, including χάρις[138] and χαριτόω (1:6). The verb χαρίζομαι can mean "to give freely, graciously," that is, "to show grace to someone" (Rom 8:32; 1 Cor 2:12), from which arises the meaning appropriate to this verse: "to forgive."[139] The participle χαριζόμενοι, "forgiving," is parallel to the two preceding adjectives (χρηστοί and εὔσπλαγχνοι) and is probably dependent on γίνεσθε ("be … forgiving"). ἑαυτοῖς is technically reflexive, but must here have a reciprocal

---

[130] BDAG, s.v. χρηστός, 3. In the LXX χρηστός regularly translates טוֹב, "good," while χρηστότης translates both טוֹב, "good," and טוּב, "goodness."

[131] Cf. χρηστότης in LXX Ps 24:7 (MT/ET 25:7); Rom 2:4; 11:22.

[132] The same wordplay may be at work in Phil 1:21: "to live is Christ [Χριστός] and to die is gain [κέρδος]" may imply the pun "to live is good [χρηστός] and to die is better" (although there is no manuscript evidence to cast doubt on Χριστός as the original reading). See also 1 Pet 2:3, in which Χριστός appears as a variant reading for χρηστός.

[133] Justin, *First Apology*, 4:5, makes a wordplay between Χριστιανοί, "Christians," and τὸ χρηστόν, "goodness." And Paul may be making the same point as Luther, who wrote to Pastor Bugenhagen: "We are Christs—with and without the apostrophe [*Christi sumus in nominativo et genitivo*]" (July 5, 1537, quoted in the editor's introduction, AE 22:x; see also AE 31:367–68).

[134] BDAG, s.v. σπλάγχνον. KJV sometimes renders σπλάγχνα as "bowels," e.g., in Phil 1:8; 2:1; Philemon 7, 12, 20.

[135] Odes 12:7 (the Prayer of Manasseh); *1 Clement*, 14:3; 29:1.

[136] Cf. εὔσπλαγχνος as a quality of διάκονοι, "ministers, deacons," in Polycarp, *To the Philippians*, 5:2, and of πρεσβύτεροι, "presbyters, elders," in *To the Philippians*, 6:1.

[137] Mt 9:36; 14:14; 15:32; 20:34; Mk 1:41; 6:34; 8:2; 9:22; Lk 7:13. In two parables, the figure who "has compassion" represents Christ (Lk 10:33) or the Father (Lk 15:20).

[138] See the textual notes on 1:2, 6, and its significant occurrences in 2:5, 8.

[139] Cf. Lk 7:21, 42, 43; 2 Cor 2:7, 10; 12:13; Col 2:13; 3:13.

meaning, "one another," not "yourselves."[140] καθώς, "just as," does not simply imply comparison, but gives the grounds or cause, "inasmuch as, since" (cf. 1:4; 5:2, 25, 29).[141] Although the Ephesians are called to imitation of God (5:1), what precedes is this appeal to God's enabling action. The mutual forgiveness that heals the Christian community begins first with God's forgiveness (2 Cor 2:5–11).[142] This logic is reflected in Luther's explanation of the Fifth Petition of the Lord's Prayer, in which he guards against the idea that God forgives us *because* we forgive one another. The order must rather be reversed.[143]

This is the true meaning of the "Gospel motivation" Paul uses here: not that we move ourselves on the basis of gratitude, but that God moves us by first forgiving, first loving (cf. Jn 13:34; 1 Jn 4:10, 19). Baptism into Christ conforms us to this pattern; to be Christlike is to forgive. The expression ὁ θεὸς ἐν Χριστῷ, "God in Christ," has been taken as a proof of Christ's divinity (cf. 2 Cor 5:19). Without denying the latter (!), it is more likely that "God" is the Father, and that "in Christ" should be taken as both instrumental and mystical/sacramental as the means and location of that forgiveness (see the fifth textual note on 1:3). Clearly "God" and "Christ" are distinct persons of the Trinity in 5:2.[144]

5:1 γίνεσθε οὖν μιμηταὶ τοῦ θεοῦ—For the reasons why 5:1–2 is included with this pericope, see "Structure and Rhetoric" in the commentary. Paul regularly encourages his flock to be μιμηταί, "imitators," of him.[145] His goal, however, is not to reproduce little Pauls, but little Christs (1 Cor 11:1; 1 Thess 1:6). What is to be imitated is suffering and humility (1 Cor 4:11–13; 1 Thess 1:6; 2:14; 1 Pet 2:21), as well as faith and patience (Heb 6:12; cf. Heb 13:7; 3 Jn 11). Here what is to be imitated is defined by

---

[140] Lincoln, *Ephesians*, 309, calls ἑαυτοῖς a "stylistic variation" after εἰς ἀλλήλους, "to one another," in the first phrase of the verse. The reciprocal use of ἑαυτῶν is normal in the NT; see Turner, *Syntax*, 43; BDF, § 287. Cf. Eph 5:19; Col 3:13, 16; 1 Pet 4:8, 10.

[141] BDF, § 453 (2); BDAG, s.v. καθώς, 3; cf. 1 Cor 1:6; Phil 1:7; 2 Thess 1:3.

[142] When Paul appeals to the Corinthians to forgive the penitent public sinner in their midst (2 Cor 2:7), he reminds them that his own forgiveness has already been granted, indeed that his forgiveness is nothing more or less than the very forgiveness given by Christ in heaven (2 Cor 2:10). He emphasizes this with a twofold use of the perfect middle deponent verb κεχάρισμαι, "I have forgiven" (2 Cor 2:10). Thus, the Corinthians are simply following Christ (and Paul) when they extend this forgiveness to the sinner among them.

[143] Luther has the proper order: "We pray in this petition that our Father in heaven would not look at our sins, or deny our prayer because of them. … So we too will sincerely forgive and gladly do good to those who sin against us" (SC 3:16 [*LSB* 324]). In the Large Catechism, Luther calls mutual forgiveness a consolation, a confirmation of the Gospel: "But there is here attached a necessary, yet consolatory addition: *As we forgive*. He has promised that we shall be sure that everything is forgiven and pardoned, yet in the manner that we also forgive our neighbor" (LC 3:93 [*Triglotta*, 725]). Logically, this implies a warning in reverse: "If, therefore, you do not forgive, then do not think that God forgives you" (LC 3:95 [*Triglotta*, 725]).

[144] Ephesians abounds in Trinitarian language and structures, which are indicated by double underlining in this commentary's translation. See 1:3, 17; 2:18, 21–22; 3:5–7, 14–17; 4:3–6; 5:19–20. The distinction between God the Father and Jesus Christ, his Son, is also regularly made in Ephesians: 1:2; 1:20–23; 2:4–10; 2:16; 3:10–12; 4:32; 5:1–2, 5; 6:23.

[145] See μιμητής or μιμέομαι in 1 Cor 4:16; 11:1; 1 Thess 1:6; 2 Thess 3:7, 9; cf. Phil 4:9; 1 Thess 2:14.

the preceding and following verses: forgiving one another (Eph 4:32) and loving one another (5:2). The two are, of course, complementary, as love is defined according to Christ's sacrificial self-offering.

Superficially there is an inherent absurdity in an admonition to imitate God: man cannot imitate God in his essence, nor equal his saving deeds, and man's original sin involved the desire to be like God.[146] So it is important to note the mode of imitation Paul highlights (forgiveness and love) and the power to do so (God's actions in Christ to forgive and love us first). Furthermore, the imitation of God is defined according to Christ's work, who, as the God-man, bridges the gap between humanity and the transcendent God.[147] The language of μίμησις, "imitation," was common in philosophical schools in the Greco-Roman world to define the relationship between a teacher and his disciples.[148] Learning was not merely the accumulation of facts, but being pressed into the pattern of the mentor (Lk 6:40).[149] In this life such imitation of Christ is only partial.

---

[146] The strict language of imitation of God occurs nowhere else in Scripture, but appears frequently in the Apostolic Fathers (likely dependent on this passage): Ignatius, *To the Ephesians*, 1:1; Ignatius, *To the Trallians*, 1:2; *Diognetus*, 10:4–6. Imitation of Christ or "the Lord" appears in Ignatius, *To the Ephesians*, 10:3; Ignatius, *To the Philadelphians*, 7:2. Ignatius speaks of Christ as God when he wishes "to be an imitator of the passion of my God" (*To the Romans*, 6:3). Imitation of Christ's suffering and patience recurs in Polycarp, *To the Philippians*, 8:2; *Martyrdom of Polycarp*, 1:2; 17:3. It is instructive that only rarely do the fathers speak of imitating men (*1 Clement*, 17:1; Ignatius, *To the Smyrnaeans*, 12:1; *Martyrdom of Polycarp*, 19:1); and Ignatius writes, "if he [God] should imitate us in our actions we are lost" (*To the Magnesians*, 10:1 [trans. Kirsopp Lake, LCL]).

[147] This may explain why the language of imitation is nonexistent in the OT (aside from human imitation, 4 Macc 9:23; 13:9). "To whom will you liken me and make me equal and compare me so that we might be alike?" (Is 46:5), which is followed by a rejection of idolatry (Is 46:6–7), which is the illicit imitation of God. Images of God are prohibited (the second part of the First Commandment [Ex 20:4–6; Deut 5:8–10]) until God himself provides the perfect one in Christ. Artwork depicting Christ is a natural consequence of the incarnation, and because Christ has shown us the Father, Christian art begins to depict the Father as well. The OT language of "following God" is not equivalent to imitation, inasmuch as it means to believe in him and keep his Word (do what he says, not what he does, contra Lincoln, *Ephesians*, 311). Perhaps the closest idea is "you shall be holy, for I, YHWH your God, am holy" (Lev 19:2)—which, though calling for imitation, would have the force of condemnation apart from the holiness that God gives as a gift ("I am YHWH, who sanctifies you/him/them," e.g., Lev 20:8; 21:15, 23; 22:9, 16, 32) and recalls the holiness that was part of the original image of God. Lincoln, *Ephesians*, 311, however, cites numerous examples of imitating God in Hellenistic Jewish writers (e.g., Philo), which suggests a kinship not to the OT but to Greco-Roman thought.

[148] Lincoln, *Ephesians*, 310, cites Seneca, *Epistles*, 6:5–6; 11:9–10; 95:72; Pseudo-Isocrates, *Demonicus*, 11:36; *Testament of Benjamin*, 3:1; 4:1; Pliny, *Epistles*, 8:13. See also Best, *Ephesians*, 466, and W. Michaelis, "μιμέομαι, μιμητής, συμμιμητής," *TDNT* 4:659–63.

[149] See the extensive list Paul gives to his junior pastor Timothy: "But you have followed my teaching [διδασκαλίᾳ], my conduct [ἀγωγῇ], my purpose [προθέσει], my faith [πίστει], my patience [μακροθυμίᾳ], my love [ἀγάπῃ], my steadfastness [ὑπομονῇ], my persecutions [διωγμοῖς], my sufferings [παθήμασιν]" (2 Tim 3:10–11). With the verb μιμέομαι Paul urges imitation of his labor (2 Thess 3:7–9), and John the imitation of good (3 Jn 11). A Christian can even become a τύπος, "pattern," for another Christian (1 Thess 1:7). This is especially incumbent upon a minister, who is a τύπος for his flock (1 Tim 4:12; Titus 2:7–8; 1 Pet 5:1–3; cf. 2 Tim 1:13). Even the Gospel itself can be spoken of as a τύπος, "pattern," into which Christians are "handed over" (Rom 6:17).

The fullness of imitation that God has in store for Christians is only attained through the resurrection of the dead ("who will change our lowly body to be like [σύμμορφον] his glorious body," Phil 3:21; cf. Rom 8:29).

ὡς τέκνα ἀγαπητά—Paul's call to the Corinthians to imitate him is rooted in his spiritual fatherhood (1 Cor 4:14–16). By calling them to faith through the Gospel and administering their new birth in Holy Baptism, Paul became their father in Christ, and so he speaks to them as his "children."[150] They then share his spiritual DNA. So also imitation of God derives from his Fatherhood (Eph 4:6) and the relationship that implies for his children (Eph 5:8) who have Christ as their brother (Eph 1:5; also Rom 8:29). The image of God was placed upon us when we were clothed with Christ (Eph 4:24), who is the very likeness of the Father (2 Cor 4:4; Col 1:15; Heb 1:3). As Christ is "the Beloved" (Eph 1:6), so in him we are God's "beloved children" (5:1). Thus, ἀγαπητά means neither "loveable" nor "loving," but "beloved" (divine passive).[151] As children look like their father, so we love because we have been loved (Mt 5:44–45; 1 Jn 3:2; 4:7). We are to be merciful because God the Father has been merciful to us; thus, if we forgive one another, we are like him (Lk 6:35–36).

5:2 καὶ περιπατεῖτε ἐν ἀγάπῃ, καθὼς καὶ ὁ Χριστὸς ἠγάπησεν ἡμᾶς—The verb περιπατέω, "to walk," and the phrase καθὼς καί, "just as also," form an *inclusio* around this pericope (see also the second textual note on 4:17). What began with a warning against returning to the old, corrupt Gentile walk now closes with a beautiful portrayal of the new walk in Christ. The phrase ἐν ἀγάπῃ, "in love," occurs here for a remarkable sixth time in Ephesians (previously 1:4; 3:17; 4:2, 15, 16).[152] In these occurrences there is a fairly even balance of referent between "being rooted in God's love for us" and "showing love to one another." Here the former idea is likely in light of ἀγαπητά, "beloved" (divine passive), at the end of the previous verse.

This then influences our interpretation of καθώς. While the idea of imitation in 5:1 might suggest it is a simple comparison (i.e., "conduct yourselves with love in imitation of the love God showed for us in Christ"; cf. 1 Jn 2:6), the context suggests a more Gospel-oriented and powerful logic. As in Eph 4:32, καθώς implies both the norm and the cause of the action. Thus, it means "walk in love, inasmuch as—because, on the basis of the fact that—God loved us."[153] "Walk in love" means to carry out one's life under the umbrella of God's love. But it implies also that one's own actions are brought into conformity with that love. "Let everything of yours happen in love" (1 Cor 16:14; cf. Rom 14:15). Once again the Johannine emphasis on the priority of God's love is apropos: "we love because he first loved us" (1 Jn 4:19). The specific reference

---

[150] See 2 Cor 12:14; Gal 4:19; 1 Thess 2:7, 11; cf. Philemon 10; 3 Jn 4.

[151] Cf. ἀγαπητοῖς θεοῦ, "beloved of God," Rom 1:7; cf. also Rom 11:28.

[152] The only other NT occurrences of ἐν ἀγάπῃ, "in love," are in 1 Cor 4:21; 16:14; 2 Cor 6:6; Col 2:2; 1 Thess 5:13; 1 Tim 4:12; Jude 21. Its sixfold repetition in Ephesians (1:4; 3:17; 4:2, 15, 16; 5:2) marks its significance, strikingly so in contrast to its single appearance in Colossians (Col 2:2).

[153] καθώς, "just as," and ἀγαπάω, "to love," are connected in the same way in Jn 13:34; 15:9, 12; 17:23; Eph 5:25; 1 Jn 3:23; cf. Lk 6:36. It is worth considering whether there is a causal connection, and not just imitation, in those passages also.

to Christ's love prepares the way for the upcoming marriage analogy (Eph 5:21–33), in which it is Christ's love for his bride, the church, that leads him to sacrifice himself for her (5:25).

καὶ παρέδωκεν ἑαυτὸν ὑπὲρ ἡμῶν προσφορὰν καὶ θυσίαν τῷ θεῷ εἰς ὀσμὴν εὐωδίας—The verb παραδίδωμι, "to hand over, deliver," is standard NT terminology for the betrayal of Christ and his self-sacrifice.[154] This loving and gracious act stands in stark contrast to the hedonistic, self-serving way in which the Gentiles once "delivered" themselves into licentiousness (4:19; cf. Rom 1:24–28). Paul stresses Christ's deliberate act by using the active voice verb (παρέδωκεν) with a reflexive pronoun (ἑαυτόν): "he delivered himself." He repeats these two words (in reverse order) in 5:25 in a striking parallel to the present text: "just as also Christ loved the church and gave himself up [ἑαυτὸν παρέδωκεν] for her" (cf. Gal 2:20). The language of sacrifice introduces imagery in character with the letter's liturgical tone and content (Eph 1:3–14; 5:19–20), temple imagery (2:19–22), sacrificial terminology (1:4; 5:27), and emphasis on holiness (e.g., 4:24; 5:3; 5:26). ὑπὲρ ἡμῶν, "for us" (5:2), is substitutionary language that embraces both senses of the preposition: "for our benefit" and "in our place" (cf. 3:1, 13).[155]

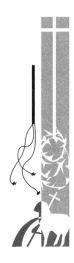

The noun προσφορά denotes an "offering" and is derived from φέρω, "to carry, lift up," prefixed with πρός, "forward (to the altar)."[156] It is a general term not connected with any one particular kind of sacrifice in the LXX.[157] Perhaps it is used so that the effects of Christ's sacrifice are not limited to any one kind (e.g., only the burnt, peace, sin, or guilt offering). Besides Eph 5:2, it refers to Christ's "offering" also in Heb 10:10, 14. The noun θυσία, "sacrifice," which forms a natural pairing with προσφορά, "offering" (as in LXX Ps 39:7 [MT 40:7; ET 40:6]; Heb 10:5, 8), is a much more common[158] and general term for "sacrifice" (Heb 5:1), which may emphasize that a living victim has been put to death. Christ is the once-and-for-all θυσία (Heb 7:27; 9:26; 10:12). Together the terms cover all kinds of unbloody and bloody sacrifices prescribed in the OT.

In the NT the noun ὀσμή, "odor, smell," can be used of a fragrant perfume (Jn 12:3) or a foul stench, also metaphorically, an "aroma" either of death or of Christ and life (2 Cor 2:14, 16). In the LXX ὀσμή most often refers to the "smell" of a burnt offering. In this regard it is frequently paired with the noun εὐωδία (εὖ, "good," + ὄζω, "to emit a smell"), "aroma, fragrance." The adjectival genitive phrase ὀσμὴ εὐωδίας means that a sacrifice

---

[154] Mt 17:22; 20:18–19; 26:2, 15–16, 21–25, 45–48; 27:2–4, 18, 26 and parallels; Rom 4:25; 8:32; cf. Gal 1:4.

[155] Cf. Rom 5:8; 8:32; 2 Cor 5:14–15, 21; Gal 2:20; 3:13; 1 Thess 5:10; 1 Tim 2:6; Titus 2:14; Heb 2:9; 1 Jn 3:16.

[156] In the LXX the verb προσφέρω, "to carry forward/to," usually refers to bringing a sacrifice for/to the altar. Of its one hundred sixty-one appearances in the LXX, one hundred nine are in the Torah, sixty-nine of which are in Leviticus (e.g., LXX Lev 1:2, 3, 5, 13–15).

[157] The noun προσφορά does not appear in the Pentateuch. Nine of its fifteen instances in the LXX are in Sirach as a general term. In the NT it can have a generic meaning as a temple offering (Acts 21:26; 24:17; Rom 15:16; Heb 10:5, 8).

[158] The noun θυσία, "sacrifice," appears three hundred eighty-six times in the LXX and twenty-eight times in the NT.

emits "a pleasing aroma"[159] and that God graciously accepts the sacrifice.[160] Sacrifices can be abominable to God and are only creditable if they are in accord with his will. The implication is that God's justice is satisfied by the sacrifice, in this case, of Christ himself.[161]

Commentary
Structure and Rhetoric
The Unit (4:17–5:2)

The inclusion of the first two verses of chapter 5 in the present pericope is neither arbitrary nor insignificant. The present chapter divisions date back no earlier than the thirteenth century (usually attributed to Archbishop Stephen Langton) and are no indication of how Paul or early Greek readers understood the text. More significant are the *kephalaia*, the chapter divisions from the great fourth-century manuscripts. The inner margins of NA[27] record the divisions from Codex Alexandrinus,[162] which places a chapter division after 5:2, as we have. The conjunction οὖν, "therefore, so then" (5:1), may be the source of confusion. Often it begins sections, but nearly as often it draws the preceding section to a close.[163] γίνεσθε οὖν, "so then be" (5:1) looks, however, like a repetition of γίνεσθε δέ, "and be" (4:32), and so is likely a continuation of the preceding rather than an introduction to something new. So also 5:2 strongly parallels 4:32. Perhaps the most compelling argument for including 5:1–2 with what precedes is the repetition of two key pieces of vocabulary: both περιπατέω, "to walk," from 4:17 and παραδίδωμι, "to hand over," from 4:19 recur in 5:2, forming an *inclusio* that frames and balances the unit (4:17–5:2). The *inclusio*

---

[159] The exact Greek phrase ὀσμὴ εὐωδίας, "a pleasing aroma," occurs forty-nine times in the LXX, first in Gen 8:21, and mostly in Leviticus (eighteen times; e.g., Lev 1:9, 13, 17) and Numbers (twenty times; e.g., Num 15:3, 5, 7, 10, 13, 14, 24).

[160] John Kleinig comments on the Hebrew formula in Leviticus (רֵיחַ־נִיחֹחַ, e.g., Lev 6:8, 14 [ET 6:15, 21]) so translated by the LXX (ὀσμὴ εὐωδίας):

Human beings do not determine which gifts are acceptable to the Lord, nor can they decide by themselves if he is indeed pleased with them. The Lord himself does that for them. … *His Word not only prescribes which offering is to be presented, and how, but it also announces what he himself promises to accomplish through it.*

Because the Lord himself ordained that these offerings are the "gift" that produces an "aroma" that is pleasing to him, the people … were assured that … *the Lord did accept them and was in fact pleased with those who brought them.* (*Leviticus*, 42; see also pp. 43, 57–58)

[161] In the NT ὀσμὴ εὐωδίας, "a pleasing aroma," appears elsewhere only in Phil 4:18, where it refers to gifts sent by the Philippians to Paul. Besides Eph 5:2 and Phil 4:18, the only other NT instance of εὐωδία is in 2 Cor 2:15, where ὀσμή has occurred in the previous verse: as they spread "the aroma [ὀσμή] of the knowledge of him everywhere" (2 Cor 2:14), Paul and his fellow preachers are "Christ's pleasing aroma [Χριστοῦ εὐωδία] to God" (2 Cor 2:15). To those who reject the message they are "an odor [ὀσμή] of death [leading] to death," while to those who believe they are "a fragrance [ὀσμή] of life [leading] to life" (2 Cor 2:16).

[162] See Metzger and Ehrman, *The Text of the New Testament*, 34.

[163] BDAG, s.v. οὖν. See also Schnackenburg, *Ephesians*, 204; Barth, *Ephesians*, 2:555. One might argue that the distinction is artificial or impossible, inasmuch as "therefore" introduces conclusions that have been drawn from what precedes and so is conjunctive rather than disjunctive.

is further highlighted by the repetition of καθὼς καί, "just as also" (4:17, 32; 5:2), which marks the contrast between the old walk as pagans and the new walk as children of God.

The exegetical consequences of this decision also affect the meaning of the exhortation "be imitators of God" (5:1). If this verse (5:1) were the introduction to a new section, then one would seek to flesh out this imitation of God in 5:2–5; though these verses begin with the self-sacrifice of Christ (5:2), they are heavily flavored by the moral requirements of the Law, particularly concerning the sexuality befitting saints (5:3–5). If imitation of God works in the way of DNA passed down from father to child (see the second textual note on 5:1), it is important to focus on the primary characteristics of the divine Father who wishes to relate to us in the way of love and forgiveness. Thus, one does not become Godlike simply by attempting to obey his Law (though Christian children are indeed obligated to heed their Father's will). We truly display his image when God's gracious love toward us enables the Godlike life described in the preceding verse: "forgiving one another, just as also God in Christ has forgiven you" (4:32). From this flows the dual meaning of "walk in love" (5:2): because he has loved us through the sacrifice of Christ for us (5:2), we can begin to love one another (4:25–32).

The Rhetoric: Refutation

Rhetorically this section begins Paul's *refutatio*, his refutation of hypothetical or real objections to or misunderstandings of what he has written thus far.[164] If Jew and Gentile have been united with each other and with God in Christ, if Holy Baptism gave them a new identity which is no longer rooted in their fleshly identity, what does this mean for their lives? Paul does not simply respond with a series of behavioral guidelines, nor does he ask the Ephesians to transform themselves or encourage them toward lofty goals. He asks them to consider their Baptism and what it has done to them.[165] The question is akin to the rhetorical questions "What shall we say then? Shall we continue in sin in order that grace may abound?" (Rom 6:1). If the pressing question for Jewish Christians was whether they were permitted or required to continue observing the distinctive ceremonial provisions of the Torah, for Gentiles the equivalent question was whether they could continue to live as Gentiles, simply with the understanding that they were forgiven. This underlay the issue of eating meat sacrificed to idols, perhaps even attending meals in pagan temples (1 Cor 10:14–33), as well as visiting prostitutes (1 Cor 6:9–20)—two prominent features of Gentile life. The pericope begins, therefore, with a strong appeal to the First and Sixth Commandments (Ex 20:3, 14; Deut 5:7, 18).

---

[164] See further "Refutations" in "Structure and Rhetoric" in the introduction.

[165] Dahl, "The Concept of Baptism in Ephesians," in *Studies in Ephesians*, 428: "It is hardly an exaggeration to say that the whole passage of Eph 4:17–6:17 is traditional early Christian baptismal paraenesis that has been freely reworked." From this perspective, the subsequent references to the Decalogue (4:25–32; 6:2–3) are entirely expected.

Paul's response is a decisive rejection of the idea that Gentile Christians might return to such characteristic features of their old life. Paul has already divided their lives into "then" and "now" (2:1–4, 11–13).[166] Now he presses the matter further so as to describe their utterly decisive break with the past. His language approaches the "two ways" pattern, found already in the OT, repeated by Christ, and developed extensively in the Apostolic Fathers.[167] The old life is introduced with the language of Rom 1:21–24; its salient feature is idolatry. The old life was not simply a collection of bad habits, but a "futility of the mind" (Eph 4:17) that was oriented away from God and resulted in a hardened heart that was unable to feel God's condemnation or desire his ways. In the introduction to the Colossian parallel (Col 3:5–14), Paul draws a contrast between a life oriented to this world and a life oriented to the one above (Col 3:1–2); he paints the radicality of the change the Colossians have undergone as death to sin and life with Christ (Col 3:3–4). Death and life, (sinful) earth and heaven, hold nothing in common. The Christian is on a path that heads in a completely different direction than his old walk.

The Structure: Decalogical and Christological

These radical antitheses characterize the structure of this section. It falls overall into four distinct parts, with the first and last balancing each other to contrast the two walks. In between is, first, the language of catechetical and baptismal transformation that unfolds the action that God has undertaken to change the Gentiles into something new. It is the Gospel indicative that precedes any prohibition or encouragement spoken to Christians. What follows, second, is a series of warnings against falling back into that old life. These warnings are to be understood not primarily as evidence of sinful behavior that was happening among the Ephesians—though this was likely the case—but as a description of the old life that has been put off.

> 4:17–19   **The old walk:** the foul heart (4:17–18) and deeds (4:18–19) of Gentiles
>> 4:20–24   The catechetical (4:20–21) and baptismal transformation: the old man has been put off (4:22) and Christ put on (4:23–24)
>> 4:25–32   The warning against old ways and encouragement to Christlike ways
> 5:1–2   **The new walk:** imitation of God's forgiveness and love in Christ

---

[166] For the transition from "then" to "now," see "once/then" (ποτέ) and/or "now" (νῦν) in 2:2, 3, 11, 13; 3:5, 10; 5:8, 29 (cf. 2:4; 4:17). See also the table contrasting "then" with "now" in "Structure and Rhetoric" in the commentary on 2:11–22; the table in "Structure and Rhetoric" as well as the section entitled "Darkness Has No Fellowship with Light" in the commentary on 5:3–14; and the table of antitheses in "Structure and Rhetoric" in the commentary on 5:15–21a.

[167] See, e.g., Deut 11:26–28; 30:15–20; Psalm 1; Proverbs 1–9; Jer 21:8; Mt 7:13–14; *Didache*, 1–5; *Barnabas*, 18–20; *Shepherd of Hermas, Mandates*, 6:1; Ignatius, *To the Magnesians*, 5; *2 Clement*, 4.

Within each subsection there is a distinct rhythm. In the first two Paul moves from the heart and mind to words and deeds. It is not the words and deeds that make the man unclean, but the unclean man that makes foul words and deeds. Hence Paul describes the corruption of the heart, oriented to idols, that tended to every kind of unclean deed (4:17–19). Likewise, the transformation accomplished in Baptism was not simply a matter of changing words and deeds, as if the man could be reformed from the outside in. Rather, the old man was first put off and the new man put on. Renewal took place in the washing of Holy Baptism, in the giving of godly righteousness and holiness (4:20–24). Only on this basis can Paul look for righteous and holy deeds and words to follow.[168]

The next section (4:25–32) provides examples of the transformation with a triplet rhythm of prohibition, encouragement, and reason:

	Prohibition	Encouragement	Reason
4:25	having put off falsehood	speak truth with one another	for we are members of one another
4:26–27	if you are angry, do not sin	do not let the sun go down on your anger	[or] you may give place to the devil
4:28	let the thief no longer steal	let him labor with his hands	so he might help anyone in need
4:29	let no harmful word proceed from your mouths	but speak what is good for edification	to give grace to those who hear
4:30	and do not grieve the Holy Spirit	———	in whom you were sealed
4:31–32	let all bitterness, rage, etc., be taken away	and be good to one another, forgiving one another	God in Christ has forgiven you

Within this section it is also possible to discern a series of references to the *Decalogue*: the Eighth Commandment (4:25, 29, 31), the Fifth (4:26–27), the Seventh (4:28), the Second (4:29), and ultimately the First (4:30).[169] The particular examples Paul cites seem influenced by, or at least parallel to, OT summaries of the Law (Lev 19:11; Jer 7:9). Paul's use of the commandments with a twofold rhythm of prohibition and exhortation is similar to Luther's explanation of the Decalogue: "We should fear and love God so that we *do not* ... , but [that *we should*] ..."[170]

---

[168] "Tell me what good it is to weed a garden if we do not plant good seed. ... Sow good habits and dispositions. To be free from a bad habit does not mean we have formed a good one. We need to take the further step of forming good habits and dispositions to replace what we have left behind" (Chrysostom, *Homilies on Ephesians*, 16:4.32, ACCS 8:180).

[169] Compare Ex 20:16; Deut 5:20 for the Eighth Commandment; Ex 20:13; Deut 5:17 for the Fifth; Ex 20:15; Deut 5:19 for the Seventh; Ex 20:7; Deut 5:11 for the Second; and Ex 20:3; Deut 5:7 for the First.

[170] SC 1:1–20 (*LSB* 321–22).

Nonetheless, while the *prohibitions* of the behavior that was characteristic of the old Adam and Gentile ways are drawn almost straight from the Ten Commandments, the *encouragements* that follow are not. Some of Paul's catalogs of virtues might seem to have been lifted straight from the Stoics, inasmuch as they appeal to natural law (cf. Ps 19:2 [ET 19:1]; Rom 1:19–20). But in this pericope there is an added dimension: the virtues are Christlike qualities that are bestowed in Baptism and work for the upbuilding of the body of Christ. This is the function of *the third element* in each proposition, to root the new action in God's work in Christ and the need of the fellow Christian. The virtues of natural law may to a certain extent be exercised by a hermit, but the Gospel naturally leads to Christian community. The baptized are moved into actions that build up their brothers and sisters: speaking the truth, reconciling, supporting one another's needs, voicing the Gospel, and loving and forgiving one another. The Law on its best day may exhort us to sustain and protect our neighbor, his property, and reputation (the Fourth–Tenth Commandments; cf., e.g., Lev 19:18, 34), but the Gospel turns us into people who build up one another with grace and forgiveness.

The above suggests a strong explanation for Paul's conclusion of the section with love (Eph 5:2). Love is the summary and fulfillment of the Law (Deut 6:5; Lev 19:18; Mt 22:37–40; Rom 13:8–10). But the love that the Law demands is enabled, transformed, and perfected only by Christ, who is God's love incarnate.[171]

The Baptismal Walk within the Body of Christ

Although it is facile and misleading to pigeonhole the entire second half of Ephesians as "exhortation" (see the commentary on 3:14–21 and 4:1–16), in this and the following pericope the proclamation of the Law in all its fullness assumes a prominent and necessary place. But the purposes of Ephesians are not abandoned while its author pursues a general course of moral exhortation. It is important to note how this succinct exhortation differs from Paul's extended discussions in other letters. As Schnackenburg perceptively notes: "In Eph. we find no guidelines for our relationship with the state and its representatives such as are found in Rom. 13.1–7; 1 Pet. 2.13–17; Tit. 3.1. Further, there are no exhortations to Christian 'good conduct' in the civic society as are emphasized in 1 Pet. and the Pastorals."[172] Paul's concern is not to elucidate every obligation placed on every Christian by the Law with respect to his role in society or the world. Instead, he focuses on those sins that disturb the church's harmony and on the Christlike virtues that edify it. He identifies the distinctive marks of the old Gentile lives that the Ephesians have left behind. Baptism has marked out a dividing line between their present Christian life and their former pagan life,

---

[171] Schlier, *Epheser*, 223, suggests that 4:25–5:2 presents admonitions that stand under the point of view of ἀγάπη, "love," while 5:3–14 chiefly has "the pure/light Christian life before the eyes."

[172] Schnackenburg, *Ephesians*, 193.

and with the force of the Law, he drives in a wedge and breaks wide open the divide. More appropriate than "Exhortation" would be the heading "Catechesis."

Having Put Aside Idolatry (4:17–19)

Paul begins with a veiled, but unmistakable rejection of idolatry and the sexual decadence that accompanied it in the ancient world. He depicts it in the harshest of terms—such that some have questioned whether he is being at all fair to the Gentiles.[173] But Paul's purpose would not be served by observing that many Gentiles live outwardly decent and even generous lives, nor would that be true in the proper sense of those terms under the strict requirements of God's Law. Paul cannot judge the Gentiles by human standards, but brings to bear the unwavering demands of the First Commandment (Ex 20:3–6; Deut 5:7–10).[174] What really matters is their idolatry, the faith and orientation of their hearts. What Paul is offering is not by sociological standards an objective and fair assessment of Greco-Roman society with its virtues and vices; but he is getting to the crux of the matter by identifying the fatal flaw that will inevitably bring down its house built of cards. He diagnoses the inner cancer that, while it may not yet have blackened every limb, will doggedly drag down each vital system in the body until the corpus fails.[175]

Writing to Christians who through Baptism had been reborn and healed of that cancer, Paul warns them in the harshest terms against returning to the destructive habits that brought on the disease in the first place. This, again, is chiefly a matter of faith and its object: idolatry or Christ. No outward righteousness will be of any value unless this is first sorted out. Paul calls Christians not to a gradual disentanglement from the world, a slow purging of its failings,[176] but to a radical rejection of its sinful, idolatrous ways. He calls them out of darkness and into the light (5:8–14). He calls them to battle (6:10–17).

The vices against which Paul so virulently warns[177] are not simply the way of the world, but are exemplified by those in the grip of idols. While sexual immorality is singled out in Scripture because of the sacredness of the human

---

[173] Best, *Ephesians*, 425.

[174] The language parallels God's words for the Israelites wholeheartedly to avoid "walking" (וַהֲלַךְ) in the way of the Egyptians among whom they formerly lived; and in the promised land they must not "walk" as did the Gentiles who once inhabited the promised land and still surrounded them (Lev 18:3–4; 20:23; Deut 6:14; 8:19; 29:17 [ET 29:18]).

[175] "At first their sickness was lawlessness. Then it became indulgence. Having slipped then into a lawless way of life, they gradually came to suffer from lack of remorse. Finally they ventured out toward every sin without fear, living the life of corruption beyond indulgence. This is what he [Paul] means by *becoming greedy to practice every kind of uncleanness* [Eph 4:19]" (Theodoret, *Ephesians*, 4:19, ACCS 8:171).

[176] "Half-way houses between impurity and saintliness are as much out of question as between idolatry and worship of Yahweh" (Barth, *Ephesians*, 2:504).

[177] "Paul is so persistent in his admonitions that he actually seems to be overdoing it. He proceeds as if the Christians were either too dull to comprehend or so inattentive and forgetful that they must be reminded and driven" (Luther, "Sermon for the Nineteenth Sunday after Trinity, Ephesians 4:22–28," October 22, 1536, Lenker, 8:305; StL 12:911–12, § 3).

body as the temple of the Holy Spirit (1 Cor 3:16; 6:19; see also "members of Christ," 1 Cor 6:15; cf. Eph 3:6; 5:30), what may have driven Paul to place licentiousness (Eph 4:19) and fornication (5:3) at the head of the queue is the reality of temple prostitution in the ancient world:

> In the OT prostitution, fornication, and related behavior are prohibited not primarily on moral grounds but rather because of their association with pagan sanctuaries and fertility rites. … The Artemis temple of Ephesus and other shrines of Paul's time were famous because of the opportunities they offered to those who identified sex and religion. In the eyes of a Jewish writer such as Paul, impurity and fornication are always expressive of a religious attitude; they are never judged as "only" carnal excesses or moral turpitude.[178]

The theological underpinnings of the unholy marriage of idolatry and prostitution is the quest for union with the deity.[179] In a devilish parody of the true mystical union, rooted in the incarnation of Christ and enacted by the Communion of his very body and blood, temple prostitution offered bodily union with the godhead through the flesh of the idol's priestesses and "virgins."[180]

---

[178] Barth, *Ephesians*, 2:503. Tertullian, *Apology*, 15, writes:

> But if I add—it is what all know and will admit as readily to be the fact—that in the temples adulteries are arranged, that at the altars pimping is practised, that often in the houses of the temple-keepers and priests, under the sacrificial fillets, and the sacred hats, and the purple robes, amid the fumes of incense, deeds of licentiousness are done, I am not sure but your gods have more reason to complain of you than of Christians. (*ANF* 3:30)

Strabo, *Geography*, 8:6.20, wrote about ancient Corinth:

> And the temple of Aphrodite [in Corinth] was so rich that it owned more than a thousand temple slaves, courtesans [ἑταῖραι], whom both men and women had dedicated to the goddess. And therefore it was also on account of these women that the city was crowded with people and grew rich. (Trans. Horace Leonard Jones, LCL)

Though Strabo visited the city in 29 BC, he was recording its ancient history from before it was refounded by the Romans in 44 BC; it is uncertain to what extent these practices continued in NT times.

The practice of cultic prostitution in the NT world or in Ephesus itself is disputed by, e.g., Baugh, "Cult Prostitution in New Testament Ephesus: A Reappraisal." But see "The Cult of Artemis Ephesia" in "The City of Ephesus and Paul's Relationship to It" in the introduction; see also the textual notes on 5:3, 5.

[179] The OT interweaves the language of prostitution (literal and spiritual) with that of idolatry; see, e.g., Ex 34:13–16; Lev 17:7; 19:29; 20:5–6; Deut 23:18–19 (ET 23:17–18); Ezekiel 16 and 23; Hosea 1–3. In ancient Near Eastern religions, cultic sexual activity was thought to bring the worshipers into the realm of their fertility gods and to initiate the gods' own sexual activity, which in turn resulted in fecundity for the worshipers. Therefore verdant trees and gardens were select locations for fertility rites (e.g., Deut 12:2; 1 Ki 14:23; 2 Ki 17:10; Is 1:29–30; 57:5; 65:3; Jer 3:6; Ezek 6:13; 20:28).

[180] A fertility goddess was envisioned as a perpetual virgin even though she bore many children through her seasonal unions with the fertility god. Thus, in the Ugaritic epic of the fertility god Baal and his consort Anat, she is regularly accorded the title Virgin Anat (see, e.g., Michael David Coogan, ed. and trans., *Stories from Ancient Canaan* [Philadelphia: Westminster, 1978], 91, 93). (This Canaanite epic, written in about the thirteenth century BC, illustrates well the religious environment of idolatry that Israel encountered in the promised land.) The cult prostitutes in the service of the "virgin" goddess could likewise be considered "virgins."

For this compelling reason Paul could not view a Christian's occasional resort to the services of a prostitute as a sin of weakness, against which the exhortations of the Law might simply strive. These are not sins that are to be slowly rooted out, but acts of rebellion against God that are thoroughly incompatible with the baptized walk. There is a reason that the water touches the body, sanctifying the flesh as the Word penetrates to the soul. In later centuries (and perhaps already in Paul's day), the primary role of the baptismal sponsor was to help the candidate for Baptism disentangle himself from this old life before Baptism impressed upon him the new. The sponsor, or "witness," was to testify that the candidate was no longer eating meals at the local temple that offered fellowship with false gods or visiting the sacred prostitutes.[181] Catechumens were taught to put off these things.

Certainly Paul is no perfectionist. His language rapidly progresses from idolatry and licentiousness to the seemingly innocuous sins of lying, stealing, and anger. The Law not only warns against the old life but also exposes the old Adam's continuing influence (so long as we are in this world) and his nasty ability to divert us from the good that God would have us do.[182] So the old man is both put off (past tense, indicative; accomplished in Baptism) and to be put off (imperative, for future behavior).[183]

Stripping and Clothing (4:20–24)

The great danger is to run too quickly to the latter (imperative), while neglecting the former (indicative), as happens when 4:22–25a is read imperativally. There is no constructive power in imperatives; they give direction, but not strength. The imperatives will come (4:25b–32a), but first Paul sets down

---

[181] The three-year catechumenate is first described by Hippolytus, *Apostolic Tradition*, 15–20, who notes the role of sponsors in the questioning of candidates. Hippolytus lists prohibited occupations (e.g., prostitutes, gladiators, magicians, and pagan priests), as well as demanding evidence of good works during the period of catechumenate. Justin Martyr, *First Apology*, 61, gives a general precondition for Baptism: "as many as are persuaded and believe that what we teach and say is true, and undertake to be able to live accordingly" (*ANF* 1:183). Tertullian, *On Repentance*, 6, states quite strongly: "We are not washed in order that we may cease sinning, but because we have ceased, since in heart we have been bathed already" (*ANF* 3:662; italics removed). Tertullian, *On Baptism*, 18, implies that the sponsor's role is to testify that the candidate does not have "an evil disposition" (trans. Evans). Egeria the pilgrim (ca. AD 400) records questions that the Jerusalem bishop would ask of candidates at their registration, summarizing: "He asks about all the serious human vices" (*Travel Diary*, 45, quoted in *The Oxford History of Christian Worship* [ed. Geoffrey Wainwright and Karen Westerfield Tucker; New York: Oxford University Press, 2006], 87). See Jack P. Lewis, "Baptismal Practices of the Second and Third Century Church," *Restoration Quarterly* 26 (1983): 1–17; Michel Dujarier, *A History of the Catechumenate: The First Six Centuries* (trans. Edward J. Haasl; New York: Sadlier, 1979); Cabié, "Christian Initiation," 20–34.

[182] "Here again is an admonition for Christians to follow up their faith by good works and a new life, for though they have forgiveness of sins through baptism, the old Adam still adheres to their flesh and makes himself felt in tendencies and desires to vices physical and mental" (Luther, "Sermon for the Nineteenth Sunday after Trinity, Ephesians 4:22–28," October 22, 1536, Lenker, 8:304; StL 12:910, § 1).

[183] See the first textual note on 4:22; see also "Stripping and Clothing (4:20–24)" and "The Indicative and the Imperative (4:25–5:2)" below.

what God has done about that rotten scoundrel. The old man has been described in such despicable terms that it is clear he cannot be reformed, but must be put to death and replaced by something completely new. God strips him off and replaces him with a new man—the metaphor of stripping off and reclothing is a pervasive biblical image for this process.[184]

The symbolic association of sin with a garment begins with God's clothing Adam and Eve with the skin of dead animals to cover the exposure of their nakedness that was a consequence of their disobedience (Gen 3:21). The bloody garments certainly foretell the sacrifice of Christ that will cover them, but first they picture the foulness of their sinful condition. Uncleanness is consistently associated with filthy garments in the ritual of the temple and the imagery of the prophets.[185] Shame and dishonor are frequently described as clothing.[186] If not always expressed, stripping off is implied by the more frequent image of "putting on" (see below on 4:24). The ritual component of the earliest baptismal rites whereby the candidate removed his clothes before entering into the water naked is attested as early as the second century.[187] It is not necessary to postulate that Paul based his language on a ritual of disrobing that was already occurring. Paul can allude to Baptism with phrases like drinking of the Spirit (1 Cor 12:13; cf. Jn 4:14) without implying that candidates actually drank the water with which they were baptized. But the precedent of Jewish baptismal rites (proselyte and Qumran) suggests the earliest Christian Baptisms would have followed the same procedure; all early Christian art depicts candidates naked.[188]

From a practical standpoint, it is likely that early Baptisms involved some kind of stripping, as they usually took place in streams or baptismal pools.[189]

---

[184] On the metaphor of stripping and clothing in ancient classical and biblical literature, see Dahl, "Kleidungsmetaphern: Der alte und der neue Mensch," in *Studies in Ephesians*, 389–411.

[185] "All of our righteous deeds are like a filthy garment" (Is 64:5 [ET 64:6]; cf. Jude 23). Jacob instructed his household to change their garments when they put away their idols (Gen 35:2). All the people of Israel were instructed to wash their garments as part of their consecration before standing in the presence of God (Ex 19:10–11). Stripping off dirty garments is implied by the ritual of ordination for the high priest (Ex 29:4) and his ritual on the Day of Atonement (Lev 16:4). Joshua the high priest was stripped of his filthy garments, which represented his iniquities (Zech 3:3–4). Garments that had come into contact with unclean things had to be washed (Lev 15:5).

[186] Job 8:22; Pss 35:26; 109:29; 132:18; 1 Macc 1:28; cf. Rev 3:18.

[187] See Dahl, "Kleidungsmetaphern: Der alte und der neue Mensch," in *Studies in Ephesians*, 401–3. Hippolytus, *Apostolic Tradition*, 21:3, 11, requires baptismal candidates to remove their clothes and describes them as naked in the water. Women must additionally unbind their hair and remove all jewelry (21:5). The *Gospel of Thomas*, 37, cryptically refers to disrobing in order to see Jesus. The *Gospel of Philip*, 107, says that we disrobe in order to be clothed with Christ. By the fourth century, testimony to this ritual practice is widespread: e.g., Cyril of Jerusalem, *Mystagogical Catecheses*, 2:2; Chrysostom, *Baptismal Instructions*, 2:24.

[188] See Wayne A. Meeks, *The First Urban Christians: The Social World of the Apostle Paul* (New Haven: Yale University Press, 1983), 150. Early Christian art, such as the fifth- and sixth-century baptisteries at Ravenna, Italy, often depicts Christ himself as naked at his Baptism.

[189] "Baptise … in running water [ὕδατι ζῶντι]; but if thou hast no running water, baptise in other water, and if thou canst not in cold, then in warm. But if thou hast neither, pour water three times on the head" (*Didache*, 7:1–3 [trans. Kirsopp Lake, LCL]). For examples of large

The later symbolism that was attached to this ritual act is theologically rich and develops Paul's own thoughts about the effects of Baptism.[190] It is a removal of the filth of sin and an identification with the death of Christ, who was himself stripped that he might die in the shame of nakedness (Mt 27:31, 35; Jn 19:23–24).[191] Nonetheless, Paul speaks even more radically than of disrobing. His language of stripping off the old man, removing an entire person, is unprecedented in the OT or ancient literature[192] and points to the radicality of the new message he was proclaiming. The man cannot be made new simply by removing vices, but must be put to death, "crucified" (Rom 6:6; Gal 2:20; 5:24)—must be completely undone.[193]

The metaphor that contrasts to stripping off is naturally the putting on of clothes. There is, on the one hand, a certain amount of cultural weight attached to the metaphor of clothing: uniforms indicate one's office; the ritual act of tearing one's clothes (or uniform) can signify that an offense against God and the office he has given has taken place (e.g., 1 Sam 15:27; Mt 26:65; Acts 14:14).[194] Going naked (Is 20:2–4) or in sackcloth and ashes was a deep expression of

---

octagonal baptismal pools set into the ground, with steps leading down in and back out, see, e.g., Renate Pillinger, "The Significance of Early Christian Monuments for the Study of Liturgy: The Example of Baptism," *Studia Liturgica* 25 (1995): 32–50.

[190] "Although his body continues he nonetheless undergoes a change to new life engendered by living baptism. What he was has been 'put off.' His old life is renewed by the holy water and the copious mercy of the anointing. He becomes new rather than old, whole rather than corrupt, fresh rather than enfeebled, an infant rather than an old man, eternal rather than ephemeral" (Origen, on Psalm 91:12–13, ACCS 8:172–73). "And so, dearly beloved, we transform you from the *old man into the new* [cf. Eph. 4.22]. … Moreover, the very sacrament of baptism which you are to receive expresses the form of this hope. For in it is celebrated a kind of death and resurrection. *The old man is put off and the new man put on* [cf. Eph. 4.22, 24]. A sinner goes into the waters and comes out justified" (*Gelasian Sacramentary*, 35, quoted in Whitaker, *Documents of the Baptismal Liturgy*, 176).

[191] "As soon therefore as ye entered in, ye put off your garment; and this was an image of *putting off the old man with his deeds* [Col. 3.9]. Having stripped yourselves, ye were naked; in this also imitating Christ, who hung naked on the Cross, and in his nakedness *spoiled principalities and powers and openly triumphed over them* [Col. 2.15]" (Cyril of Jerusalem, *Mystagogical Catecheses*, 2:2, quoted in Whitaker, *Documents of the Baptismal Liturgy*, 29). With theological irony, what is removed from Christ is the mocking royal robes; sin is not removed from him before death, but placed upon him. In imitation of Christ, Polycarp carefully removes and folds up his clothes in preparation for his martyrdom, that he, too, might face the mortal fulfillment of his Baptism naked (*Martyrdom of Polycarp*, 13:2). Further symbolism attached to the baptismal nakedness is documented in Cabié, "Christian Initiation," 42–43.

[192] Putting off vices, as found frequently in the NT (e.g., 1 Pet 2:1), is a common image in secular Greek writings (Lincoln, *Ephesians*, 284). See also the classical references in C. F. D. Moule, "'The New Life' in Colossians 3:1–17," *Review and Expositor* 70 (1973): 489; and Dahl, "Kleidungsmetaphern: Der alte und der neue Mensch," in *Studies in Ephesians*, 392–94.

[193] Contra Best, *Ephesians*, 433, who writes: "It is the vices which make the old person old and the virtues which make the new new. The putting off of the old and the putting on of the new must then be a gradual process which takes place by a renewal." This is precisely the opposite of what Paul is saying!

[194] Rending one's clothing can also indicate grief, particularly at death. It is interesting that the high priest was forbidden to tear his robes (Lev 10:6; 21:10), probably because the garments themselves represented God's holiness. Priests were forbidden to come into contact with dead

impending judgment, self-denial, grief, and repentance (Gen 37:34; Job 1:20; Jonah 3:5–8; and passim). Changing into beautiful garments represented the movement from sorrow into joy (Is 52:1–2; Baruch 5:1–2). Transfer of clothes (1 Ki 19:19) or armor (1 Sam 17:38) conveyed with it the original owner's power and spirit. Thus, clothing gives identity. But clothing has more than a cultural reverberation in Scripture. It is a persistent metaphor for holiness and righteousness (Is 59:17; 61:10; Job 29:14).

The ordination of Aaron and his sons as priests to make them holy so that they might stand in God's presence began by washing them with water, placing the priestly garments over them, and anointing them with oil (Ex 29:4–9; cf. Sirach 45:8–13). The ritual was repeated when Aaron came into the tabernacle on the Day of Atonement (Lev 16:4) and any time the priest ministered in the Holy Place (Lev 6:3 [ET 6:10]; Ezek 44:17). The Levites, likewise, were ritually cleansed, washed, and reclothed for their service (Num 8:21; cf. 1 Chr 15:27). The holiness of the clothing was emphasized by the requirement to remove the priestly garments before leaving the Holy Place (so that they remain there) and then to put on again everyday garments (Lev 6:4 [ET 6:11]; 16:23–24; Ezek 42:14)—because the garments themselves carry God's holiness (Ezek 44:19).

The priestliness of all Israel (Ex 19:6) was symbolized in parallel by the Israelites washing their clothes before appearing before God (Ex 19:10–11). In other words, the new, clean clothing represented the divinely given holiness (Ex 28:4; Lev 16:4), the covering of their iniquity that was necessary before they could stand in the presence of a holy God (Zech 3:3–5). It protected them from destruction (Ex 28:43; cf. Ex 19:12, 22). This is the meaning of the "priesthood of all believers," of Israel's being a priestly nation (Ex 19:6). In other lands only certain people (priests) were holy and able to enter the god's sanctuary and stand before him; but Israel was consecrated as a whole, clothed with God's righteousness, and brought into his presence.[195]

On this basis, the OT speaks of salvation and righteousness themselves as holy clothing that is placed upon God's people.[196] The image is brought into the NT in broad-ranging parables, such as the wedding garment that brought admission to the banquet (Mt 22:1–14) and the festal robe placed on the once-prodigal son (Lk 15:22). In John's vision of heaven, the saints are clothed in white robes, which, in a further metaphor that defies human experience, have become *white* by being washed in the *blood* of the Lamb (Rev 7:13–14; see Is

bodies (outside their immediate families) or participate in the rituals attending to death, some of which had pagan associations. See Kleinig, *Leviticus*, 225, 232, 451–54.

[195] Cf. Winger, "The Priesthood of All the Baptized," 1–68.

[196] In two passages, "the saints" are identified as God's "priests," a metaphor that is extended by the language of priestly garments: "clothed with salvation" (2 Chr 6:41); "clothed with righteousness" or "salvation" (Ps 132:9, 16). Righteousness and justice clothe Job like a robe and turban, which are priestly garments (Job 29:14). Is 61:10 combines the priestly metaphor ("garments of salvation," "robe of righteousness") with the festal garments of a bridegroom and bride.

1:18).[197] The fact that they are of "linen" emphasizes the saints' holy, priestly character (Rev 19:7–8, 14).[198] Even Paul's language of clothing the mortal with immortality may imply the same eternal priestly robe (1 Cor 15:53–54; cf. 2 Cor 5:1–4). These NT examples share an eschatological context; they speak of clothing that is given with the resurrection of the dead.

Indeed, it is in Christ's own death and resurrection that this image reaches its pinnacle. Christ's body, which was stripped before being nailed to the cross (Mt 27:31, 35; Jn 19:23–24), was reverently reclothed in linen to be lain in the tomb (Mt 27:59–60; Mk 15:46). In his resurrection he divested himself of this temporary clothing (Lk 24:12; Jn 20:5–7), and, though he hid his glory for a time (Lk 24:16; Jn 20:14), he would subsequently appear in gloriously bright vesture (Rev 1:13–16; cf. Acts 9:3), as had once been briefly revealed at his transfiguration (Mt 17:2; Mk 9:2–3; Lk 9:29). Thus, the Christian's future reclothing is prefigured by the glorious investiture of the great High Priest, Jesus Christ.

But as eschatology works in the NT, there is always a foretaste of the feast to come. The language of salvation and righteousness in the armor of God passages is deeply rooted in this OT imagery (Eph 6:14, 17; 1 Thess 5:8) and speaks of an armor that has already been granted to saints to protect them in their present battle. Here we arrive again at what is surely the crucial text to unlock the metaphor's meaning: "for as many of you as have been baptized into Christ have put on [been clothed with] Christ" (Gal 3:27).[199] The OT passages noted above give ample justification for speaking of a "priesthood of all the baptized." As the high priest Aaron was washed and then clothed, so also in Baptism are all Christians given this consecration, this cleansing that enables them to stand before the holy God. Baptism unites the temporal and eternal aspects of eschatology. That is to say, a robe of righteousness is placed on the baptized that remains unseen in this life except to God's eyes, but which will become manifest to all when bodily death and the resurrection of the dead put away the old Adam once and for all and give a body that fully reflects the glory of God.

---

[197] Likewise, in *Shepherd of Hermas, Similitudes*, 9:13.1–5, all those in the allegorical tower which is the church are clothed with the name of the Son of God.

[198] See "linen" as a material of the tabernacle itself in, e.g., Exodus 26 and 35–36; of priestly vestments in, e.g., Exodus 28 and 39; Lev 6:3 (ET 6:10); and of the vesture of the preincarnate Christ in Ezek 9:2–3, 11; 10:2, 6–7; Dan 10:5; 12:6–7.

[199] Roosien, "Putting on Christ: Metaphor and Martyrdom in John Chrysostom's *Baptismal Instructions*," 57, identifies Gal 3:27 as the central text in Chrysostom's *Baptismal Instructions*, citing the following as a summary:

We put off the old garment, which has been made filthy with the abundance of our sins; we put on the new one, which is free from every stain. What am I saying? We put on Christ Himself. *For all you*, says St. Paul, *who have been baptized into Christ, have put on Christ* [Gal 3:27]. (Chrysostom, *Baptismal Instructions*, 2:11 [trans. Paul W. Harkins, *ACW* 31:47])

It is to this baptismal clothing that Paul appeals in Eph 4:24,[200] hidden from human eyes, but not from God's. The early church's ritual placement of a white robe over the newly baptized (which surely was worn for only a limited period of time after the event) was merely symbolic of the reality that had occurred. The baptized was clothed not merely with a garment, not even just with righteousness as a quality, but with Christ himself.[201] Thus, Paul can say of his Baptism, "I have been crucified with Christ; it is no longer I who live, but Christ who lives in me; and [the life] that I now live in the flesh I live by faith in the Son of God, who loved me and gave himself up for me" (Gal 2:19b–20 [ET 2:20]).

The Indicative and the Imperative (4:25–5:2)

This is the reality Paul must firmly establish (4:20–24) before he can proceed to the warnings and encouragements that are a logical consequence of Baptism (4:25–32). There is a "once-and-for-all-ness" to Baptism. But as long as Christians are in this world, the old Adam who was renounced there clings on, harangues, and drives the Christian back to his Baptism, to a daily act of renunciation and renewal. It is for this reason that Paul can both speak of renewal as a past act (Eph 4:23) and paradoxically state that the "new man" is "being renewed" (Col 3:10). Thus, the indicative "you have put off ... the old man ... you have put off falsehood" (Eph 4:22, 25) can and must also be directed to the Christian as an imperative: "Let us then put off the works of darkness, and let us put on the armor of light. ... But put on the Lord Jesus Christ, and make no provision for the flesh" (Rom 13:12–14).[202] And to the Colossians, likewise, Paul can rephrase it as an imperative, yet without losing the indicative that stands behind it: "Therefore, as [i.e., because you are] elect ones of God, holy and beloved, put on [ἐνδύσασθε] compassion, kindness, ..." (Col 3:12). This paradox reflects the reality of life in this state between Baptism and its fulfillment

---

[200] "Hear him who bows his head before thee: may he come to the fount of baptism that being renewed by water and the Holy Ghost he may strip off the *old man and put on the new, who is created after thee* [Eph. 4.24]: may he receive a pure and spotless robe and be counted worthy to worship thee our Lord" (*Stowe Missal*, quoted in Whitaker, *Documents of the Baptismal Liturgy*, 217).

[201] "For thou shalt no more mourn, now that thou hast put off the old man; but thou shalt keep holyday, clothed in the garment of salvation, even Jesus Christ" (Cyril of Jerusalem, *Mystagogical Catecheses*, 1:10, quoted in Whitaker, *Documents of the Baptismal Liturgy*, 28).

[202] "Paul exhorts them not to return to their past vices and sins. He wants them to behave as new persons. What good is it to be called new if our evil deeds prove us to be still gripped by our old nature?" (Ambrosiaster, *Ephesians*, 4:28, ACCS 8:178). Likewise Chrysostom, *Baptismal Instructions*, 9:29:

> After baptism we are going to strip for the combat against him [the wicked demon]; he will be our opponent in the boxing bout and the fight. Let us learn, during this time of training, the grips he uses, the source of his wickedness, and how he can easily hurt us. Then, when the contest comes, we will not be caught unaware nor be frightened, as we would be if we were to see new wrestling tricks; because we have practiced among ourselves and have learned all his artifices, we will confidently join grips with him in the combat. (Trans. Paul W. Harkins, *ACW* 31:141)

on the Last Day, sometimes expressed as *simul justus et peccator*.[203] The old man and the devil who directs him are to be continuously driven into retreat by the Christian who takes his Baptism seriously.[204]

Finally, though, we must recognize that Paul's concern in this passage lies not only or even chiefly with the individual Christian. The Gospel is diminished if it leads the Christian to care only for himself. As Ephesians has stressed the unity of all people in Christ through the reconciliation of Jew and Gentile and the persistent metaphor of the one body,[205] so Paul's Law preaching and Gospel encouragement seek the good of the Christian community as well as the individual. While Paul has begun with the root sin of idolatry (Eph 4:17–19; underlying the First Table of the Law [Ex 20:1–11; Deut 5:6–15]), he continues (under the Second Table of the Law [Ex 20:12–17; Deut 5:16–21]) with the sins that harm the Christian "neighbor" (Eph 4:25–31). Anger (Eph 4:26) is an offense against the brother (Mt 5:22). Stealing, cheating, or idleness rob the thief of the opportunity to help those who have nothing (Eph 4:28). Bitterness and harmful talk not only lead to shouting and slander that divide and disrupt the church but also leave no space for the words of grace that build up (4:29–31). It is, ultimately, a passage about the work of Law and Gospel within the church to effect reconciliation, an extended commentary on Christ's own words (Mt 18:15–20). Mutual forgiveness and love are to be the work of the Christian community, as it is both made possible by Christ's work and inspired by his example (Eph 4:32–5:2). The contours of imitation (5:1) thus described exclude a moralistic imitation of God (as merely a guide to behavior) and place the Gospel at the center of the pericope.

---

[203] Luther uses the phrase *simul justus et peccator* while commenting on Gal 3:6 in his 1535 *Lectures on Galatians*: "Thus a Christian man is *righteous and a sinner at the same time,* holy and profane, an enemy of God and a child of God" (AE 26:232; emphasis added; for the Latin phrase, see WA 40/1:368.26). See also Winger, "*Simul justus et peccator*: Did Luther and the Confessions Get Paul Right?"

[204] Luther, "Sermon for the Nineteenth Sunday after Trinity, Ephesians 4:22–28," October 22, 1536, Lenker, 8:305; StL 12:912, § 3:

> It will not do to think and say: Well, it is sufficient to have the doctrine, and if we have the Spirit and faith, then fruits and good works will follow of their own accord. For although the Spirit truly is present and, as Christ says, willing and effective in those that believe, on the other hand the flesh is weak and sluggish. Besides, the devil is not idle, but seeks to seduce our weak nature by temptations and allurements.

[205] See 1:23; 2:16; 3:6; 4:4, 12, 16; also 5:23, 30; cf. 5:28.

Once You Were Darkness, but Now You Are Light in the Lord

Translation

5 ³But let not sexual immorality and all uncleanness or lust even be named among you,
as is fitting for saints,
⁴nor shamefulness and foolish talk or coarse joking, which are not fitting,
but rather thanksgiving.
⁵For know this with certainty: no sexually immoral or unclean or lustful person
(that is, an idolater) has an inheritance in the kingdom of Christ and God.
⁶Let no one deceive you with empty words; for on account of these things the wrath
of God is coming upon the sons of disobedience.
⁷Therefore do not be fellow partakers with them.
⁸For once you were darkness, but now you are light in the Lord;
walk as children of light
⁹(for the fruit of the light is in all goodness and righteousness and truth),
¹⁰testing what is pleasing to the Lord,
¹¹and do not be in communion with the fruitless works of darkness,
but rather expose them.
¹²For the things done in secret by them are shameful even to utter,
¹³but all things exposed by the light are made visible,
¹⁴for everything made visible is light. Therefore it says:
"Get up, O sleeper,
and arise from the dead,
and Christ will shine upon you."

Textual Notes

5:3 πορνεία δὲ καὶ ἀκαθαρσία πᾶσα ἢ πλεονεξία μηδὲ ὀνομαζέσθω ἐν ὑμῖν—
On the surface the first two verses of this unit seem to address not sexual immorality
as an act, but sinful speech about it. The conjunction δέ, "but," may express a contrast
between such filthy talk and the words of forgiveness that went before (4:32). Certainly
5:3–4 might be viewed as an expansion on the treatment of Christian speech in 4:29,
just as this pericope as a whole takes up many themes of the preceding one (4:17–5:2).
There may also be a contrast intended between proclaiming divine love (5:1–2) and
talking about human immorality (5:3–5). "Let [these things] not be named among you"
may simply be a prohibition of such filthy talk (cf. 5:12), inasmuch as the Law prohibits evil words and thoughts as well as deeds (Mt 5:22, 28).

But Paul has in mind more than just talk. The clause μηδὲ ὀνομαζέσθω ἐν ὑμῖν,
"let [these things] not [even] be named among you," could be a hyperbolic way of saying "don't *do* them." Yet, the verb ὀνομάζω implies something even deeper. "Naming"

in ancient cultures, particularly among the Hebrews, was not a mere reference to something, but got at the reality of what was named (see the second textual note on 1:21). To name a god was to invoke it and call on its power.[1] Paul may, therefore, have in mind a two-step progression: (1) naming filthy deeds leads to doing them; the feminine abstract nouns in 5:3 that refer to actions become masculine singular substantives in 5:5 referring to the doers of the actions; and (2) doing them places one under their power, just as invoking false gods is submitting to demons (1 Cor 10:20–21).

Thus, πορνεία, "sexual immorality" (5:3), cannot be merely named without falling under its spell (and becoming a πόρνος, "sexually immoral person," 5:5). For, first, it involves one's own body, which is also the dwelling place of the Holy Spirit (1 Cor 6:18–19). And, second, sexual immorality was intimately connected with the ritual practices of ancient paganism.[2] Paul's concern for the Ephesians is that one leads to the other. Even their very words can drag the Ephesians back into their old pagan lives. πορνεία occurs here for the only time in Ephesians (cf. Col 3:5). The translation "fornication" is misleading if it implies just one form of sexual transgression (sex between unmarried people, as opposed to adultery). Here πορνεία refers to any sexual practice that is illicit, that falls outside God's mandated order of celibacy outside marriage and of fidelity within marriage (the lifelong union of one man and one woman). In the context of pagan worship and particularly in Ephesus (with its temple of Artemis and other fertility goddesses), prostitution or orgies may be foremost in Paul's mind.[3] Prostitution is specifically mentioned in the major parallel text of 1 Cor 6:9–20, and the repeated warnings against πορνεία in the two Corinthian epistles[4] may be connected to the Corinthians' tendency to adopt or participate in the practices of the local pagan temples. This may also be the implication of πορνεία ("sexual immorality") in the judgment of the Apostolic Council, warning Gentile Christians away from the characteristic practices of their old lives (Acts 15:20).

Closely related to πορνεία is ἀκαθαρσία, "uncleanness" (the two terms are adjacent in 2 Cor 12:21; Gal 5:19; Col 3:5), which describes a state that renders one unable

---

[1] Thus, the invocation or naming of false gods is prohibited: Ex 23:13; Deut 18:20; Josh 23:7; Hos 2:19 (ET 2:17); Zech 13:2.

[2] See "The Cult of Artemis Ephesia" in "The City of Ephesus and Paul's Relationship to It" in the introduction, as well as "Having Put Aside Idolatry (4:17–19)" in the commentary on 4:17–5:2; the second textual note on 5:5; and the commentary on the present pericope.

[3] Some scholars have denied that ritual prostitution was a feature of the worship of Artemis Ephesia: e.g., Oster, "The Ephesian Artemis as an Opponent of Early Christianity"; and Baugh, "Cult Prostitution in New Testament Ephesus: A Reappraisal"; Baugh, "A Foreign World: Ephesus in the First Century," 23–26. However, see the discussions cited in the preceding footnote. As argued in "The Cult of Artemis Ephesia" in "The City of Ephesus and Paul's Relationship to It" in the introduction, in the absence of clear evidence to the contrary, one should assume that the common practices of goddess worship in Asia Minor applied to Ephesus. Even Baugh admits: "Nor was Ephesian paganism necessarily as innocent as the inscriptions portray" ("A Foreign World," 26). One must also recall that there were more than fifty other deities worshiped in Ephesus, with diverse cults. "The Ephesians did worship fertility goddesses (Demeter, Gem, and Meter)," Baugh concedes ("A Foreign World," 26).

[4] 1 Cor 5:1; 6:13, 18; 7:2; 2 Cor 12:21; cf. πόρνος, "sexually immoral person," in 1 Cor 5:9–11; 6:9; πορνεύω, "to commit sexual immorality," in 1 Cor 10:8.

to stand in the presence of God (see the third textual note on 4:19). It is cultic imagery drawn from the OT (e.g., Leviticus 11–15) and stands in utter contrast to the holiness that is given in Holy Baptism (1 Cor 6:11). The third term, πλεονεξία, is a greedy desire that might be translated as "covetousness, desire" but in the present sexual context should probably be rendered as "lust."[5] The Tenth Commandment prohibits "coveting" (LXX: ἐπιθυμέω) the neighbor's wife (Ex 20:17; Deut 5:21). The three terms (which appear together also in Col 3:5) work together to describe an insatiable desire to misuse one's body in ways that are contrary to God's holy will and that are bound up with idolatry (cf. Eph 5:5).[6] Whether or not the person who commits them consciously intends thereby to worship a false god, they constitute false worship of self and the devil.

καθὼς πρέπει ἁγίοις—The adverb καθώς, "just as, even as," appeared frequently in the preceding pericope to indicate a norm or pattern to which the Ephesians were conformed, giving impetus to their new way of life (4:17, 21, 32; 5:2). Here Paul asks them to consider what it means to be ἅγιοι, "saints, holy people." If they have been made holy by God in Baptism (cf. 5:26),[7] how can they return to the uncleanness of their pagan past? The verb πρέπω points to what is "fitting, suitable, appropriate" for them. This language has some affinity with the Stoics, who defined conduct that was in accord with nature as "fitting" and what was contrary to nature as "unfitting."[8] Paul, too, is concerned that behavior should flow from being, but he has moved beyond the requirements of natural law[9] (to which the Stoics appealed) to the consequences of being a baptized child of God.[10] Because the Ephesians are holy people, they cannot participate in unholy things. Their call was not to immorality or uncleanness, but "in [ἐν] holiness" (1 Thess 4:3–7); the significance of that preposition ἐν is that holiness must be seen as the baptismal source and location of their being, before holy deeds can be addressed as a goal (see "in [ἐν] Christ," Eph 1:3). This appeal to their holy character sets up the fellowship/communion language that dominates the rest of the pericope.

---

[5] The cognate verb πλεονεκτέω (literally, "be greedy") is used in a similar context of sexual immorality (1 Thess 4:6). Origen establishes the sexual nature of the three terms in Eph 5:3: "*Fornication* in the strict sense is consorting with prostitutes. *Impurity* is the generic name, in the maelstrom of our bodily existence, not only for adultery and pederasty but also all the other inventions of sexual licentiousness in all their many and diverse practices. *Greed* can be taken either straightforwardly or, as I have established [with regard to 1 Thess 4:4–6], in the sense of *adultery*" (*Ephesians*, ACCS 8:183).

[6] πορνεία, ἀκαθαρσία, πλεονεξία, and their cognates are regular companions in NT vice lists and proclamation of the Law and are often connected to idolatry (as in Eph 5:5): Mk 7:21–22; 1 Cor 5:10–11; 6:9–10; 2 Cor 12:21; Gal 5:19–20; Rev 17:4; 22:15.

[7] For Baptism in Ephesians, see especially 1:13; 4:4–6; 5:26. See "Baptism and the Spirit" in "Purpose and Themes" in the introduction; "Baptism in the Prologue" in the commentary on 1:3–14; "Enlightened Eyes of Your Heart (1:18)" in the commentary on 1:15–23; and "Creedal, Baptismal Unity" in the commentary on 4:1–16.

[8] F. F. Bruce, *New Testament History* (London: Thomas Nelson, 1969), 47; Heinrich Schlier, "ἀνήκει," *TDNT* 1:360; Heinrich Schlier, "καθήκω," *TDNT* 3:437–40.

[9] Cf. Ps 19:2 (ET 19:1); Rom 1:19–20.

[10] Other NT uses of πρέπω appeal not to natural law but to sound doctrine, godliness, righteousness, and the way of salvation (Mt 3:15; 1 Cor 11:13; 1 Tim 2:10; Titus 2:1; Heb 2:10; 7:26).

5:4 καὶ αἰσχρότης καὶ μωρολογία ἢ εὐτραπελία, ἃ οὐκ ἀνῆκεν—The threefold description of immoral sexual activity that should not even be "named" (5:3) is now paralleled by a threefold description of improper sexual talk. This fact alone demonstrates that the prohibition against "naming" sexual vice (5:3) does not preclude warning against it with words (5:4)! What is forbidden here is engaging in immorality through words. Paul provides three examples, each of which is a NT hapax legomenon. αἰσχρότης derives from the adjective αἰσχρός (Eph 5:12; also 1 Cor 11:6; 14:35; Titus 1:11), "ugly, base, deformed," and refers to behavior that flouts moral standards: "shamefulness, obscenity." The abstract term here, αἰσχρότης, is equivalent to αἰσχρολογία, "shameful talk," in Col 3:8, which is the culmination of the progression of anger found in the parallel verse (Eph 4:31 ‖ Col 3:8). μωρολογία, "foolish talk," seems out of place according to the weak English sense of "foolishness." But in biblical language, foolishness is associated with denial of God and idolatry,[11] while wisdom is not worldly smarts but divine knowledge about faith and life.[12] In classical literature εὐτραπελία usually had a positive sense, "wittiness" (εὖ + τρέπω, literally, "to turn [a phrase] well"), though sometimes it meant "buffoonery."[13] But it is unlikely in this context that Paul is uttering a blanket prohibition against humor among Christians. Thus, it probably means "coarse joking, [sexual] innuendo." The verb ἀνήκω identifies what is "proper, fitting, appropriate" (cf. Col 3:18; Philemon 8) and is a synonym of πρέπω in the parallel clause (Eph 5:3b).[14] The Christian's mouth was not made to utter such sounds. The problem with coarse joking is that they diminish the seriousness of sexuality and the significance of the human body as the temple of the Holy Spirit and a member of Christ (Eph 5:30).

ἀλλὰ μᾶλλον εὐχαριστία—Just as each prohibition in 4:25–31 was paralleled by an encouragement to behavior that was pleasing to God and edified the community,[15] so here Paul redirects the Ephesians' hearts and mouths to appropriate words. The term for "thanksgiving," εὐχαριστία (which may be a pun on the antonym εὐτραπελία, "coarse joking"), is so profound that it singlehandedly counterbalances and indeed outweighs the six terms in 5:3–4 that Paul has used to describe the old pagan sinful way (cf. Rom 1:21). While its meaning is "thanksgiving,"[16] it refers to more than a simple

---

[11] Deut 32:6; 2 Sam 24:10; Pss 14:1; 53:2 (ET 53:1); Is 32:6; Jer 10:14; Mt 25:2–8; Rom 1:22–23; 1 Cor 2:14; 3:19. See also the abundant "fool" vocabulary in Proverbs, versus the wisdom and knowledge rooted in the fear of (faith in) God (e.g., Prov 1:7; 9:10).

[12] See "wisdom" in Eph 1:8, 17; 3:10.

[13] Aristotle, *Nicomachean Ethics*, 2:7.1108a.23–24, calls εὐτραπελία the middle term between the extremes of buffoonery and boorishness, though elsewhere he admits it tends to innuendo (*Nicomachean Ethics*, 4:8.1128a.23–24; *Rhetoric*, 2:12.1389b.11). See BDAG, s.v. εὐτραπελία; Lincoln, *Ephesians*, 323.

[14] The imperfect form ἀνῆκεν may be used (instead of the present) to imply that this sort of filthy talk *ought* not happen, but in fact does (BDF, § 358 [2]), or simply that the fulfillment of the obligation remains uncertain (Turner, *Syntax*, 90).

[15] See the summary chart in "The Structure: Decalogical and Christological" in the commentary on 4:17–5:2.

[16] Origen and Jerome in their commentaries on this passage suggest we should instead read a newly coined term εὐχαριτία, "graciousness, the mark of fine training," but that emendation

verbal acknowledgment of a fellow Christian's love or God's good gifts (e.g., 1 Thess 5:18; 1 Tim 4:3–4). By the second century AD, "the Eucharist" would come to be the dominant technical term for the Lord's Supper or the Divine Service focused on it.[17] While it is unlikely that Paul explicitly means to say "celebrate the Lord's Supper," there is at least a hint that true worship is a more appropriate use of the tongue. The appearance here of the word εὐχαριστία foreshadows Paul's exposition of the deeper liturgical meaning of giving thanks in 5:18–20. Instead of soiling their holy mouths with "shamefulness and foolish talk or coarse joking" (5:4), the Ephesians are to occupy themselves with "psalms and hymns and songs of the Spirit" (5:19), "giving thanks" (εὐχαριστοῦντες, from εὐχαριστέω, the cognate verb of εὐχαριστία) continually in Jesus' name to the Father (5:20). εὐχαριστία means worship, both in the liturgy and in daily life.[18]

5:5 τοῦτο γὰρ ἴστε γινώσκοντες—The second person plural verb ἴστε (from οἶδα) is either indicative or imperative, meaning either "you know" (as in Heb 12:17) or "know!" (as in James 1:19).[19] In this verse the imperative is more likely. The participle γινώσκοντες, "knowing," is redundant and is likely a Semitism related to the Hebrew infinitive absolute, which adds emphasis: "know this with certainty."[20] It adds gravity to Paul's ensuing warning, paralleling his solemn testimony in 4:17.

ὅτι πᾶς πόρνος ἢ ἀκάθαρτος ἢ πλεονέκτης, ὅ ἐστιν εἰδωλολάτρης—The three abstract terms in 5:3 ("sexual immorality," etc.) are replaced by the three equivalent masculine singular substantives, meaning "the [any, every][21] person who is sexually immoral," etc. What is new is the gloss, "that is, an idolater." Many interpreters take that noun as a parenthetical explanation of the third term in the list only: *covetousness is idolatry*. The meaning would be that the insatiable desire for things God has not given is a rejection of God and turns material goods into an idol (cf. Mt 6:24; Lk 16:13).[22]

---

should not be taken seriously. See Odo Casel, "Εὐχαριστία—εὐχαριτία," *Biblische Zeitschrift* 18 (1929): 84–85.

[17] As early as *Didache*, 9:1, εὐχαριστία appears as a technical term for the Lord's Supper or at least for the prayers associated with it. See also Ignatius, *To the Ephesians*, 13:1; Ignatius, *To the Philadelphians*, 4:1; Ignatius, *To the Smyrnaeans*, 7:1; 8:1. Justin Martyr, *First Apology*, 66:1, claims: "And this food is called among us Εὐχαριστία [the Eucharist]" (*ANF* 1:185). Origen, *Against Celsus*, 8:57.20, likewise: "… the bread which we call the Eucharist" (*ANF* 4:661).

[18] Cf. εὐχαριστία in 1 Cor 14:16; Phil 4:6; Col 2:7; 4:2; 1 Tim 2:1; Rev 4:9; 7:12 and εὐχαριστέω in Col 3:17.

[19] The variant ἐστέ, "be" (D^c K L *al*), the imperative of εἰμί, is an attempt to deal with the rare form ἴστε and its unusual Semitic construction.

[20] BDF, § 422; Turner, *Syntax*, 85. See γινώσκων οἶδεν in LXX 1 Kgdms 20:3 (MT/ET 1 Sam 20:3), translating יָדֹעַ יָדַע.

[21] The construction πᾶς … οὐκ ἔχει, literally, "*every* person … does *not* have," is a Semitism properly translated as "*no* person … *has*." Cf. πᾶς … μή in the first textual note on 4:29.

[22] Luther, for example, preaches:

> The writer of the epistle passes unusually severe sentence upon the covetous man, for he calls him an idolater, or a worshiper of a false God. … All other sinners turn to use what they have and make it subservient to their lusts. Fornicators and the unclean make their bodies serve their pleasure. … The unhappy idolater alone is servant to

However, the context suggests a different interpretation. If πλεονεξία (5:3) is understood in context as "sexual lust" (a subcategory of "covetousness"), and πλεονέκτης (5:5) likewise as a "lustful person," then in each verse we have a trio of terms referring to unclean sexual practices. It is therefore likely that Paul is labeling the entire sequence of "sexual immorality … uncleanness … lust" (5:3) as idolatry and the "sexually immoral or unclean or lustful person" (5:5) as "an idolater."[23] This makes explicit the implied reason for his harsh words against sexual sin: the intimate connection between sexual immorality and the worship of false gods.[24] Implicit in the warning is the OT idea that God's people are his bride (see Eph 5:21–33), such that any departure from true worship toward idolatry is itself a kind of adultery.[25]

Thus, Paul's concern is not with moral codes as such, but with the danger to faith inherent in falling back into the pagan lifestyle. Sexual immorality leads to the worship of false gods—and vice versa. Certainly this warning should not be restricted only to the ancient practices of paganism. The present-day addiction to sexual gratification illustrates its perpetual tendency to become an idol.[26]

οὐκ ἔχει κληρονομίαν ἐν τῇ βασιλείᾳ τοῦ Χριστοῦ καὶ θεοῦ—The connection of immorality with idolatry explains why these sins seem to be singled out as particularly grievous. Like the sin against the Holy Spirit (see the textual note on 4:30), idolatry is a sin that excludes a person from the kingdom of God by its very nature: God does not forgive those who reject him completely. Thus, Paul is not speaking of sins that in

his possessions; his sin is to save, guard and preserve property. He dare not make use of it either for himself or for others, but worships it as his god. … Because he places his confidence, his trust, in his money rather than in the living God, whose promises concerning ample support are abundant, his real God is his money, and to call him an idolater is entirely just. ("Sermon for the Third Sunday in Lent, Ephesians 5:1–9," Lenker, 7:157–58; StL 12:457–58, § 17)

[23] The fact that the relative pronoun in the clause ὅ ἐστιν, "*which* is," is neuter suggests the parenthetical clause modifies the entire list. See Moule, *Idiom Book*, 130. If the pronoun referred only to the one preceding substantive, it would more likely be masculine (cf. the masculine ὅς, "who," in the variant reading). The Colossian parallel (Col 3:5) is not particularly helpful, inasmuch as it follows four abstract feminine nouns with a feminine relative pronoun.

[24] Cf. Num 25:1–9; Wis Sol 14:12, 24; Gal 5:19–20; 1 Cor 5:10–11; 6:9–10; 1 Pet 4:3; Rev 2:14, 20; 22:15. God solemnly warns the Israelites against allowing their sons or daughters to become cultic prostitutes and prohibits their earnings from being contributed to his temple (Deut 23:18–19 [ET 23:17–18]). The terms for male (קָדֵשׁ) and female (קְדֵשָׁה) cultic prostitutes (Gen 38:21–22; Deut 23:18 [ET 23:17]; 1 Ki 14:24; 2 Ki 23:7; Hos 4:13–14) are related to the word for "holy" (קָדוֹשׁ), indicating that "sacral" prostitution is an integral part of the worship of the false god; through it the worshiper and the prostitute unite with the deity and partake of its character. In place of that vocabulary for cult prostitutes (Deut 23:18 [ET 23:17]) the next verse (Deut 23:19 [ET 23:18]) substitutes the more common term for a "female prostitute," זוֹנָה, and for a male prostitute it uses "dog" (כֶּלֶב), which reappears in the list of those excluded from the new Jerusalem (Rev 22:15; see also Phil 3:2), including "the sexually immoral" and "idolaters" (Rev 22:15).

[25] Hence the OT often uses the vocabulary of "whoring [זָנָה] after other gods" (Ex 34:15–16; Deut 31:16; Judg 2:17; 8:33; 1 Chr 5:25). See also the significance of Hosea marrying a prostitute (Hos 1:2; 3:1).

[26] Mitchell, *The Song of Songs*, 63: "Sexual sin is, in its essence, idolatry or false worship, because it is a false allegiance, an unholy union (1 Cor 6:16; 7:4), a joining of beings in a relationship forbidden by God."

later dogmatic terminology would be called "venial"—sins of weakness for which the Christian remains ever penitent. He is speaking of "mortal sins," gross sins that by their very nature entail the denial of God's sovereignty and grace, the kind of sin that cannot coexist with saving faith.[27] For this reason Paul warns most severely that anyone who becomes defined in his very being as a sexually immoral person has excluded himself from God's kingdom. The noun κληρονομία, "inheritance," is baptismal and eschatological language (1:14, 18; see also υἱοθεσία, "adoption as sons," 1:5). It refers to God's eternal gifts to those who have become his children. Paul warns the Ephesians that returning to their old Gentile ways entails walking away from these family rights bequeathed by the Father through his Son. They cannot have it both ways.

The language of exclusion from God's "kingdom" is frequent in Paul and elsewhere in the NT.[28] This is the only place in the NT where the phrase "the kingdom *of Christ*" is used in place of the usual "the kingdom of God."[29] Since Christ calls it "my kingdom" (Lk 22:30),[30] since Christ has received the kingdom (Eph 1:22; cf. Lk 19:12; Act 3:21), since Christ will deliver the kingdom to the Father (1 Cor 15:24), and since Christ is true God (e.g., Rom 9:5; Col 1:15–20; 2:9; Titus 2:13), there is no contradiction. Yet the full phrase τοῦ Χριστοῦ καὶ θεοῦ invites the question whether it is "the kingdom of Christ and of God [the Father]" or "the kingdom of the one who is both Christ and God." The former would be consistent with Paul's distinction between Christ and God elsewhere in Ephesians.[31] The latter, the explicit identification of Christ with God, is not unheard of in Paul (Rom 9:5; Titus 2:13) or elsewhere in the NT[32] and is supported by the use of a single article (τοῦ) with the phrase (the Granville Sharp Rule).[33] It is likely

---

[27] On the distinction between venial and mortal sin among Lutherans, see Ap 4:48, 64, 115, 144; SA 3:3.44; Philip Melanchthon, *Loci Communes, 1543* (trans. J. A. O. Preus; St. Louis: Concordia, 1992), 126–30; Pieper, *Christian Dogmatics*, 1:568–69.

[28] Mt 25:34–46; 1 Cor 6:9–10; 15:50; Gal 5:19–21; cf. "outside" in Lk 13:25; 1 Cor 5:13; Rev 22:15; "will never enter," Rev 21:27.

[29] Hence the omission of the words Χριστοῦ καί, "Christ and," in 𝔓[46].

[30] Cf. Col 1:13; 2 Tim 4:1, 18; 2 Pet 1:11; Rev 11:15.

[31] Eph 1:1–3, 17; 2:10; 3:19; 4:32; 5:2, 20; 6:6, 23.

[32] Jn 1:1; 20:28; Heb 1:8; 1 Jn 5:20; 2 Pet 1:1 (cf. 2 Pet 1:11; 2:20; 3:18). Possibly 2 Thess 1:12; 1 Tim 5:21; 2 Tim 4:1.

[33] Zerwick, *Biblical Greek*, § 185, cautiously endorses this interpretation: "Sometimes the use of but one article with more than one noun seems even to suppose and express the divinity of Christ. ... One must however say that such examples 'seem to suggest' the divinity of Christ, and not that they are proofs of it, since the unity of article would be sufficiently accounted for by any conjunction, in the writer's mind, of the notions expressed." Turner, *Grammatical Insights*, 16, steps forth more confidently: "We must also seriously consider the possibility of departing from all our English versions by translating Eph. 5⁵, 'in the kingdom of Christ who is God.'" Wallace, *Greek Grammar*, 276, by contrast, claims that the Granville Sharp Rule does not apply here because he takes "Christ" as a proper noun. So also Murray J. Harris, *Jesus as God: The New Testament Use of* Theos *in Reference to Jesus* (Grand Rapids: Baker, 1992), 262. Yet Wallace, *Greek Grammar*, 272, has defined a proper noun as one which cannot be pluralized (thus excluding θεός as a proper noun). Though χριστός in the plural never occurs in the NT, it occurs four times in the LXX (1 Chr 16:22; Ps 104:15 [MT/ET 105:15]; Hab 3:13; 2 Macc 1:10). The NT use of related words in the plural (ψευδόχριστοι, Mt 24:24; Mk 13:22; ἀντίχριστοι, 1 Jn 2:18) also suggests it was sometimes conceived of as an office/title. Its application to Jesus is transitional from title to name; see BDAG, s.v. χριστός. The

that the scribes who modified the phrase in various manuscripts did so because they understood it as an identification of Christ with God. The fourth-century Christological debates were often played out in the *scriptoria* as Arian, semi-Arian, and orthodox (anti-Arian) scribes played around with the text to support their position.

5:6 μηδεὶς ὑμᾶς ἀπατάτω κενοῖς λόγοις—The verb ἀπατάω, "deceive, mislead," continues the parallels between this pericope and the preceding one. In 4:22 the old man—which as a description of the sinful nature includes a reference to the fallen Adam—uses "deceit" (ἀπάτη, the cognate noun) to play on desire and lead the Christian back down the road to corruption. The allusion to Satan's deception of Adam and Eve is unmistakable (cf. 2 Cor 11:3; 1 Tim 2:14). Now, however, the warning is not against an internal but an external threat. Whereas false teachers use deceitful methods to mislead immature Christians into false belief (Eph 4:14; cf. Rom 16:17–18; Col 2:4, 8), the threat here is probably from pagan friends and acquaintances in contemporary Ephesus who would tempt Christians to return to the fleshly pleasures of their old way of life. It is, of course, also possible that there were libertine elements within the church.

The enticement comes through "words" (Eph 5:6), perhaps the claim that there is no conflict between the old life and the new, that the Christian can live with one foot in each world, that deeds of the flesh can have no impact on the spiritual life, or that grace will overwhelm these failings (cf. Rom 6:1, 15). It is the temptation to identify with the culture and try to fit in. But Paul calls these enticements κενοὶ λόγοι, *"empty* words"—not powerless words, but words without any basis in fact or truth (cf. κενοφωνία, "empty talk, chatter," 1 Tim 6:20; 2 Tim 2:16). He will shortly admonish the Ephesians to have no fellowship with people who utter such dangerous nonsense (Eph 5:7, 11).

διὰ ταῦτα γὰρ ἔρχεται ἡ ὀργὴ τοῦ θεοῦ ἐπὶ τοὺς υἱοὺς τῆς ἀπειθείας—Labeling these tempting contemporaries as "the sons of disobedience" who face divine "wrath" puts distance between them and the Ephesian Christians. For they themselves were formerly among "the sons of disobedience" (2:2), the "children of wrath" (2:3), but are no longer so. This Semitic genitive of quality ("sons of disobedience" = "disobedient people") identifies the people with their sin, whereas the baptized are heirs of an entirely different character in Christ. Those who live in sexual immorality are certainly condemned by their behavior; but the wrath of God comes upon them ultimately because of their idolatry (εἰδωλολάτρης, 5:5), that is, because of their rejection of the Son of God (Jn 3:36). This vivid warning to beware the coming judgment puts to lie the suggestion that Ephesians has an entirely realized eschatology (i.e., that there is nothing more to be hoped for than what the church on earth already experiences of God's kingdom). Although Paul can write that we are already in a saved condition by grace through faith (2:5–8), Ephesians does not lose sight of the need for ultimate deliverance from

---

presence of the article with "Christ" in Eph 5:5, τοῦ Χριστοῦ, suggests "the Christ" is a title; BDF, § 260 (1). The phrase "the kingdom of God" is always either ἡ βασιλεία τοῦ θεοῦ or βασιλεία θεοῦ, but never ἡ βασιλεία θεοῦ; this suggests that in the present verse the article τοῦ goes with both χριστοῦ and θεοῦ.

the wrath to come (cf. 1:14; 4:30), which is available only through the name of Jesus (Rom 5:9; 1 Thess 1:10; 5:9).[34]

5:7 μὴ οὖν γίνεσθε συμμέτοχοι αὐτῶν—The substantival adjective συμμέτοχος, "fellow partaker," appears only twice in the NT, both times in Ephesians. In 3:6 the positive statement was made that through the mystery revealed to Paul the Gentiles joined the Jewish Christians to be "fellow heirs and fellow members of the body and *fellow partakers* of the promise in Christ Jesus through the Gospel." This union with one another in Christ has been achieved through incorporation into his death on the cross by entering into his one body through death and resurrection with him in Holy Baptism (2:5–6, 16; 4:5). Union with one another in the church is brought about by holding something in common: Christ himself.[35] This reality is utterly contradicted if the Gentile Ephesians return to the practices of their pagan life, as if they could partake of both. The meaning of συμμέτοχοι αὐτῶν in 5:7 is that by joining with the pagans[36] in their evil deeds they actually forsake their godly fellowship to become part of a different communion. They become "fellow partakers" with pagans in the works of darkness.[37]

The logic is laid bare in 1 Corinthians. The Corinthians are to have nothing to do with the sexually immoral or idolater in their midst, certainly not to "eat with" such a one (1 Cor 5:9–11). To be joined with a (cultic?) prostitute is to become one flesh with her and to join the Holy Spirit and the members of Christ's body to her (1 Cor 6:15–20). To eat at festal meals in the temple of an idol (1 Cor 8:1–10) is to be in communion with the demon that stands behind the idol (1 Cor 10:14–21). The language is liturgical and sacramental. As through Baptism they have been made members of Christ's body, through his Supper they have entered into the κοινωνία, "fellowship, communion," of

---

[34] The present tense of ἔρχεται, "is coming," should be understood as a near future. It probably does not refer to present acts of God's judgment against sin in this age (Rom 1:18–32; 13:4–5; 1 Thess 2:16), but to the Last Day (Mt 3:7; Lk 3:7; Rom 2:5; Col 3:6; 1 Thess 1:10; 5:9). The temptation to join back in with pagans arises precisely because it does not appear that God is punishing them in the present day.

[35] Paul emphasizes this unity in Christ by using words that are compounds of συν-, "together, with; fellow." Such compounds appear in 2:5, 6, 19, 21, 22; 3:6; 4:3, 16; 5:7, 11 and are a distinctive feature of Ephesians.

[36] Whether the genitive pronoun αὐτῶν is masculine (referring to the pagans themselves) or neuter (referring to their works) is difficult to determine. Underlying the substantivized adjective συμμέτοχοι, "fellow partakers," is the verb μετέχω, which normally takes the genitive for the thing which is shared (BDAG, s.v. μετέχω, 1). So BDF, § 182 (1), takes αὐτῶν as neuter. The preposition σύν in the compound συμμέτοχοι might suggest that the people with whom one shares would be placed in the dative case (cf. 2:5). Unfortunately, there is not enough data on the compound form συμμέτοχος to decide with certainty. The nearest antecedent for αὐτῶν is "the sons of disobedience," so BDAG, s.v. συμμέτοχος, takes the pronoun as masculine, the people with whom one shares. The masculine interpretation has caused concern when Paul's words are interpreted as forbidding any kind of interaction with non-Christians. However, if the context is correctly understood, that Paul is forbidding participation *with them in their immoral deeds*, then the choice between the masculine and neuter options becomes irrelevant.

[37] Moule is probably wrong when he writes: "In Eph iii. 6 [3:6] συμμέτοχος occurs in the sense of *co-participant*, but in v. 7 [5:7] it scarcely seems to mean more than *participant*" (*Idiom Book*, 61, n. 3). He misses the parallel with the godly fellowship and ignores the horizontal fellowship with pagans that is created when one partakes of their sins.

Christ's body and blood (1 Cor 10:16). This happens by "*partaking*" (μετέχω) of the one bread (1 Cor 10:17), just as the Israelites of old were "communicants" (κοινωνοί) with YHWH by eating of what had been sacrificed in the temple (1 Cor 10:18). Therefore, to eat at the table of demons is to be κοινωνοί, "communicants," with them (1 Cor 10:20). It is impossible to "drink" of the cup of the Lord and of the cup of demons and to "partake" (μετέχω) of the Table of the Lord and of the table of demons at the same time (1 Cor 10:21).

This sacramental logic explains what Paul is saying in Eph 5:3–14. Because the Ephesians have been united to Christ and to one another in his body through Baptism and the Lord's Supper,[38] it is impossible for them to continue to participate in the pagan works of darkness that he is describing and proscribing (cf. 2 Cor 6:14–7:1). The sacramental allusions and references to their immoral works clarify precisely what sort of separation from pagan Gentiles Paul has in mind: it is to stand apart from their immoral works and to have nothing to do with their worship of false gods.

There is no implication here that the Ephesians should entirely separate themselves from the life of the world around them (à la Qumran). Cf. 1 Cor 5:9–11.

5:8 ἦτε γάρ ποτε σκότος, νῦν δὲ φῶς ἐν κυρίῳ—This verse explains what Paul has been getting at in the preceding verses: the kind of immorality he has just described was an integral part of the Gentile Ephesians' former life, but has been put behind them by the change they have undergone in Baptism. The contrast of ποτε … νῦν, "once/ then … now," has featured frequently in Ephesians.[39] Various metaphors have been used to explain the stark change: death to life (2:1–5), aliens to citizens, far to near (2:11–13), ignorance to knowledge (4:17). Paul had described the Gentiles as "darkened in their understanding" (4:18), but the Ephesian Christians have the eyes of their hearts "enlightened" (1:18). Now the transition is stated in the most succinct and unequivocal words: "once you were darkness, but now you are light in the Lord" (5:8). Though this, too, is metaphorical, the categorical language has been strengthened significantly. They were not simply *in* the dark; they *were* darkness.

The implications of the second half will be drawn out in the next few verses, but it, too, has radical implications: now they are not simply *in* the light, but they *are* light, endowed with its qualities. This is the key theme of this pericope: though the verb φωτίζω, "enlighten," has appeared previously (1:18; 3:9), the noun φῶς, "light," appears only in this pericope and a remarkable five times (5:8 [twice], 9, 13, 14). By their rebirth as sons of God (1:5), Christians have taken on the image of God (4:24), who is the light; they have been drawn into communion with God through their incorporation into Christ—from which Paul will draw the conclusion that they can no longer have

---

[38] This commentary perceives allusions to the Lord's Supper in 1:7; 4:4; 5:3–20, 29–31; and 6:18–24, and a eucharistic quality to the prayers in 1:3–14 and 3:14–21.

[39] See "once/then" (ποτέ) and/or "now" (νῦν) in 2:2, 3, 11, 13; 3:5, 10; 5:8, 29 (cf. 2:4; 4:17). See also the table contrasting "then" with "now" in "Structure and Rhetoric" in the commentary on 2:11–22; the table in "Structure and Rhetoric" as well as the section entitled "Darkness Has No Fellowship with Light" in the commentary on this pericope (5:3–14); and the table of antitheses in "Structure and Rhetoric" in the commentary on 5:15–21a.

fellowship with evil.[40] The contrast of darkness and light is a standard biblical image, and there are compelling reasons to see enlightenment as a reference to Holy Baptism.[41] Disentanglement from the evil works of darkness cannot be a slow and gradual process, because they have been dramatically and decisively changed. Darkness and light cannot coexist; there is no Christian twilight.

The phrase ἐν κυρίῳ, "in the Lord," adds two components. First, it qualifies the metaphor to indicate in what sense they are "light" (just as "in the Lord" and "in the Spirit" [2:21–22] indicate that the new temple is not made of literal stone). Second, the phrase, as it is so often used in Ephesians,[42] marks the transformation of ordinary earthly institutions into vehicles of the Gospel. Light "in the Lord" is not ordinary light, but indicates the work of God's Word, just as Paul's imprisonment (4:1) and parenthood (6:1) "in the Lord" serve new functions.

ὡς τέκνα φωτὸς περιπατεῖτε—The metaphor of "walking" (περιπατέω)[43] in biblical usage includes the entire life of faith, confession, and obedience to God's Word and should not be reduced moralistically to the component of behavior alone.[44] The verb περιπατέω is a prominent feature of the latter chapters of Ephesians (4:1, 17; 5:2, 8, 15). Because they have been "enlightened" (1:18) in Holy Baptism, the Ephesians can longer believe or act as they did before. They are τέκνα φωτός, "children of the light." This Semitic genitive of quality is the counterpart to the genitive in "sons of disobedience" in 5:6.[45] Because the light of Christ shone upon them in the moment of their new birth (5:14), they themselves are characterized by light. The NT connects this image intimately with both Christ and the Word of God. Christ himself is the light that came into the world to enlighten everyone (Jn 1:9; 8:12; 9:5) so that they might become "sons of light" (Jn 12:36; 1 Thess 5:5).[46] The same Word that worked with the water by the Spirit (Jn 3:3–8) continues throughout their lives to guide them along God's path (Ps 119:105; cf. Prov 4:18). Thus, to be "light" is to be Christlike and to be led by his Word.

---

[40] The interpretation (e.g., MacDonald, *Colossians and Ephesians*, 314) that Christians are light because they shine the Word of God on the world in a missionary sense (Is 42:6; 49:6; 60:3; Mt 5:14–16; Rom 2:19) is not consistent with this particular context (Best, *Ephesians*, 488).

[41] See the first textual note on 1:18 and "Enlightened Eyes of Your Heart (1:18)" in the commentary on 1:15–23.

[42] Eph 2:21; 4:1, 17; 5:8; 6:1. See also the discussion of "in Christ" in the fifth textual note on 1:3.

[43] The verb περιπατέω, "to walk," occurs in Eph 2:2, 10; 4:1, 17; 5:2, 8, 15. See particularly the first textual note on 2:2 and the third textual note on 4:1, as well as "The Baptismal Walk within the Body of Christ" in the commentary on 4:17–5:2.

[44] See "Doctrine and Ethics, Gospel and Law? (4:1–16 in the Context of the Epistle)" in "Structure and Rhetoric" in the commentary on 4:1–16.

[45] Cf. "the sons of this world" versus "the sons of light" (Lk 16:8). The Qumran literature is replete with this antithesis; see "War of the Sons of Light against the Sons of Darkness" (the *War Scroll*, 1QM; for the antithesis, see, e.g., 1QM 1:1–16; 1QS 3:18–25; passim). There is, however, no reason to assume a dependence of Ephesians on Qumran (or Gnosticism); the parallels simply indicate the common OT roots of the imagery.

[46] The light-darkness contrast features prominently in John's writings (Jn 1:4–9; 3:19–21; 8:12; 9:5; 11:9–10; 12:35–36, 46; 1 Jn 1:5, 7; 2:8–10) and often enough also in Paul's (Rom 2:19; 13:12–13; 1 Cor 4:5; 2 Cor 4:4, 6; 6:14; Phil 2:15; Col 1:12–13; 1 Thess 5:5; 2 Tim 1:10).

5:9 ὁ γὰρ καρπὸς τοῦ φωτὸς ἐν πάσῃ ἀγαθωσύνῃ καὶ δικαιοσύνῃ καὶ ἀληθείᾳ—
The appearance of the term καρπός, "fruit," for the first and only time in Ephesians
parallels its use in Gal 5:19–23, in which the same contrast is drawn between the works
of the old life ("the flesh") and the "fruit" of the Spirit in the baptized.[47] The metaphor of
fruit implies an organic process by which a living organism produces what is in accord
with its nature. Light produces fruit;[48] darkness is fruitless (τοῖς ἔργοις τοῖς ἀκάρποις,
"the *un*fruitful works," 5:11). The image is rooted in Christ's words about a good tree
producing good fruit (Mt 7:15–20; 12:33), the parable of the Sower (Mt 13:23 and parallels), and himself as the vine that generates fruit in any branch grafted into him (Jn
15:1–8; cf. Rom 11:17–24). Even childbirth can be described as bearing fruit (Deut
7:13; 28:4, 11; Ps 127:3; Lk 1:42). It is a massive NT metaphor that defies a superficial, moralistic interpretation of the Christian faith. Paul thus sidesteps exhortation (an
appeal to the will) and simply describes what is, in fact, the case in newborn children
of God. Because they are light they will do what light does.

In contrast to the works of darkness described in 5:3–5, the children of light work
"goodness and righteousness and truth" (5:9). All three are qualities of God that are conferred upon those "in the Lord" (5:8) because they have been united with Christ.[49] This
fact lifts the language above moral exhortation. Though there is some OT precedent for
the trio[50] and its individual components appear elsewhere in the NT,[51] this combination
is unique to Ephesians, summing up language that has appeared earlier in the letter.

The first, ἀγαθωσύνη, "goodness," recalls the "good works" that God created and
placed us into (2:10), the "good" that can be done for others in the body of Christ with
one's hands (4:28; cf. 6:8), and the "good" words that edify those who hear (4:29).[52]
The second, δικαιοσύνη, "righteousness," can refer to the passive righteousness that is
the gift of God in Holy Baptism by which one is declared innocent of sin on the basis
of Christ's own righteousness (cf. 4:24; 6:14); it can also refer to the active righteousness which entails the obedience to God's Law that results from the transformation God
has wrought (cf. 6:1). As a fruit, the latter is probably meant in this verse. The third,
ἀλήθεια, "truth," was a significant theme of chapter 4 (4:21, 24–25; see also 4:15), with
its condemnation of false teaching and unwholesome words. The "truth" is originally
a quality of Jesus himself (4:21) and his Gospel (1:13), from which comes the fruit of

---

[47] The textual variant in 5:9 that replaces φωτός with πνεύματος, "fruit of the *Spirit*" ($\mathfrak{P}^{46}$ D² Ψ
$\mathfrak{M}$ sy^h), despite its early and widespread attestation, is likely the result of a scribe's memory
jumping to Gal 5:22.

[48] The genitive in καρπὸς τοῦ φωτός is one "of production" (Wallace, *Greek Grammar*, 104–5).

[49] "Christ himself is rightly called goodness, righteousness and truth" (Jerome, *Ephesians*, 3:5.9,
ACCS 8:187).

[50] See the similar expressions in 2 Chr 31:20; Micah 6:8; Tobit 12:8 (S). Cf. Deut 32:4; 1 Ki 3:6;
2 Ki 20:3 ‖ Is 38:3; Pss 37:3; 40:11 (ET 40:10); Prov 2:9, 20; 11:23; 12:17; 14:22; Is 3:10;
11:5; 59:14; Jer 4:2; Zech 8:19.

[51] E.g., Phil 1:11; Heb 12:11; James 3:18; cf. Rom 6:22; Col 1:10.

[52] Further NT parallels: "good fruit" comes from a good tree (Mt 7:17–18), and "goodness" is
a fruit of the Spirit (Gal 5:22). It is intriguing that the noun ἀγαθωσύνη, "goodness," has not
been found outside biblical literature.

truth in the believer. The similar combination of the terms "righteousness and holiness" and "truth" as descriptions of the new man (4:24–25) suggests that Paul views the three qualities here as fruits that have been plumped up by the water of Holy Baptism. Later, Paul will say that Christ's "truth" and "righteousness" clothe and defend the one baptized into him (6:14). The meaning of the preposition ἐν, "the fruit … is *in* …" (5:9), is perhaps that these three terms do not so much constitute the fruits as describe them: the fruits will be good, righteous, and true (cf. LXX Job 22:21).

The NA[27] editors have enclosed this verse in dashes to mark it as a parenthetical insertion. This is not because its contents are less than vital to the flow of the pericope, but simply because the verse interrupts the grammar of the sentence that began in 5:8, "walk [περιπατεῖτε] … ," and continues in 5:10 with a supplementary participle, "testing [δοκιμάζοντες] …"

5:10 δοκιμάζοντες τί ἐστιν εὐάρεστον τῷ κυρίῳ—The participle δοκιμάζοντες is dependent on the imperative περιπατεῖτε, "walk" (5:8), acting as a supplementary participle that describes the manner of walking. δοκιμάζω is insipidly translated here as "try to learn/discern" (RSV/ESV), but it refers to a process of critical examination to determine the genuineness of something, thus "put to the test, examine, prove." The children of light shine a light into the dark corners of pagan life to see what scuttles out (cf. 5:11: "expose them"). The connection of light with God's Word implies an objective process of examination by comparing worldly deeds against the Word's standards.[53] In doing this the Christian participates in the wise judgment of God himself against this world's unrighteousness (1 Cor 3:13; 2 Cor 10:18; 1 Thess 2:4). Because these evil deeds are a temptation even to Christians, the baptized must also examine themselves (1 Cor 11:28; 2 Cor 13:5; Gal 6:4; cf. 2 Cor 2:9). The goal is not to find out what is useful, practical, harmless, satisfying, entertaining, or culturally relevant, but to find out what is in accord with God's will, what is εὐάρεστον τῷ κυρίῳ, "pleasing to the Lord" (Eph 5:10; cf. Rom 14:18; 2 Cor 5:9; Col 3:20). This terminology contains a hint of sacrificial language, of the fragrant odor that pleases God (cf. Eph 5:2; Phil 4:18). The implication is that one's entire life is lived as a sacrifice to God, an act of worship. This stands in parallel to εὐχαριστία, "thanksgiving," as the summation of worship (Eph 5:4). As in Romans 12, the sacrifice of self is total but unbloody:

> I encourage you, then, brothers, through the mercies of God, to present your bodies as a living sacrifice, holy, pleasing [εὐάρεστον] to God, your thoughtful worship [λατρείαν]. And do not be conformed to this age, but be transformed by the renewal of your mind, that you would test [δοκιμάζειν] what is the will of God, what is good and pleasing [εὐάρεστον] and perfect. (Rom 12:1–2)

5:11 καὶ μὴ συγκοινωνεῖτε τοῖς ἔργοις τοῖς ἀκάρποις τοῦ σκότους—This verse expands on 5:7. The verb μετέχω, "to share with, participate in" (underlying συμμέτοχοι, "fellow partakers"), is replaced by συγκοινωνέω, "to have communion/fellowship with." This is the last of the many compounds of συν- ("with, together; fellow")

---

[53] Cf. Lk 12:56; Rom 2:18; 12:2; 1 Thess 5:21; 1 Tim 3:10; 2 Tim 2:15; 1 Jn 4:1.

Paul has strung together to express the church's sacramental unity in Christ.[54] The verb συγκοινωνέω is used only three times in the NT: for participating in sin (here and Rev 18:4) or sharing in Christian suffering (Phil 4:14). The cognate noun συγκοινωνός, "participant, partner," is used to express the communion between Christians created by a common reception of the Gospel of Christ.[55]

The sacramental allusions in this pericope are strengthened by this vocabulary, though that assertion bears some explanation. Paul is not saying directly, "Do not participate in the Lord's Supper in churches that do not share the true confession." The sacramental vocabulary, however, suggests that he is portraying a sort of "anti-communion" that stands in contrast to the true fellowship Christians have through the meal of Christ's body and blood.[56] "The fruitless works of darkness" (5:11) contrast with "the fruit of the light" (5:9) at every level. While the "fruit" of "goodness and righteousness and truth" (5:9) is the natural result of one born of the Spirit, and creditable only to his divine work, these evil "fruitless works" (5:11) are entirely credited to the evil nature of "the sons of disobedience" (5:6).[57] Darkness has "works," but no "fruit."[58] ἄκαρπος, "fruitless," is closely associated with false teaching (Jude 12) and worldliness (Mk 4:19). If the Ephesians return to these old deeds, they are not merely performing mechanical acts that have no spiritual consequences; rather, evil deeds place them into communion with pagans (cf. Rev 18:4–6), indeed, with "demons" (1 Cor 10:20–21; 1 Tim 4:1; Rev 9:20; 18:2).

Just as a baptized person's sexual relations with a prostitute join Christ himself to her and profane the temple of the Holy Spirit (1 Cor 6:15–20), so participating in the works of darkness draws Christ himself and the Holy Spirit into those evil deeds. As there can be no Christian twilight where darkness and light coexist, so the Christian cannot live simultaneously in the dark works of paganism and in the holy light of God. "The works of darkness" are part of the old Adam's life that was put off in Holy Baptism (Eph 4:22, 25) and must be continually shunned (Rom 13:12). This admonition therefore constitutes a warning against fraternizing with the enemy: "what communion/fellowship [κοινωνία] does light have with darkness?" (2 Cor 6:14).

In sacramental terms, when the body and blood of Christ are placed into the Christian's mouth, a communion is created between him and his fellow Christians via the gifts of Christ that are received and held in common. The resulting mystical body of Christ is profaned and drawn into sin when one member engages in ungodly works. The translation "do not be in communion with" (Eph 5:11) conveys in English the

---

[54] Compounds of συν- appear also in 2:5, 6, 19, 21, 22; 3:6; 4:3, 16; 5:7.

[55] Rom 11:17; 1 Cor 9:23; Phil 1:7; Rev 1:9.

[56] This commentary perceives allusions to the Lord's Supper in 1:7; 4:4; 5:3–20, 29–31; and 6:18–24, and a eucharistic quality to the prayers in 1:3–14 and 3:14–21.

[57] "Paul uses the term *fruits* in the case of the Spirit, *works* in the case of the sin nature" (Jerome, *Ephesians*, 3:5.11, ACCS 8:188). The word "works" tends to have a negative connotation in Paul. "Works" are the results of one's own efforts, while "fruits" are produced by God in the baptized by making their nature fruitful.

[58] Schlier, *Epheser*, 238.

theological parallel that Paul implies, while suggesting also that there are implications for church fellowship and questions of joint Communion.

μᾶλλον δὲ καὶ ἐλέγχετε—The verb ἐλέγχω, "to bring to light, expose," draws on the metaphor of light. Because Christians "are light" (5:8; "enlightened," 1:18), they have the ability to shine into the darkness to disclose the evil that lurks there. Central to the light/darkness metaphor is the fact that light always triumphs over darkness; darkness has no ability to extinguish light (cf. Jn 1:5). Nothing can remain hidden in the dark (Is 29:15; Dan 2:22). The connection of light with the Word of God (Ps 119:105; cf. Is 9:7 [ET 9:8]) implies an objective standard for this process, the "real life" application of the image. The process of δοκιμάζοντες, "testing," to see what is pleasing to the Lord (Eph 5:10) takes place by comparing the words and deeds of the world around us with the teachings of Holy Scripture. ἐλέγχω (5:11) not only means to show these deeds for what they are (Jn 3:20; Eph 5:13) but also implies "reproving" or "convicting" the perpetrators on the basis of God's Law.[59] Thus, the Christian is enabled to flee evil and at the same time to serve as God's instrument in unveiling his eschatological judgment and calling the world to repentance.[60]

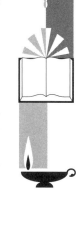

5:12 τὰ γὰρ κρυφῇ γινόμενα ὑπ᾽ αὐτῶν αἰσχρόν ἐστιν καὶ λέγειν—Paul reiterates his warning with different vocabulary. κρυφῇ, "in secret," a NT hapax legomenon, is an adverb related to the verb κρύπτω, "to hide." "In secret" (ἐν τῷ κρυφαίῳ) can be a positive attribute of deeds that are done for the eyes of God alone (Mt 6:18), and the verb κρύπτω is frequently used in Scripture for God's hidden plans and thoughts that are only revealed at the proper time (e.g., Mt 11:25; 13:35; Col 3:3). But in the present context, "in secret" draws out the implications of darkness: that it is used by "the sons of disobedience" (Eph 5:6)[61] to hide deeds that are known to be evil (Jn 3:20). It is particularly the realm of sexual sin.[62] In the modern world the vast majority of violent crimes also take place in the wee hours of darkness. Street lamps and security lights are the best defense. In ancient times, in the absence of such artificial daylight, the connection of nighttime darkness with evil was even more intense (e.g., Is 65:4; Prov 7:6–27; 9:17). Paul then rephrases the language of Eph 5:3–4 to state that it is αἰσχρός, "shameful" (5:12), even to speak of these deeds, as speaking draws one into doing. See the textual notes on 5:3–4 as well as "Darkness Has No Fellowship with Light" in the commentary.

---

[59] See ἐλέγχω with the sense "reprove, rebuke, convict" in, e.g., LXX Lev 19:17; Sirach 19:15; Mt 18:15; Lk 3:19; Jn 8:46; 16:8; 1 Cor 14:24; 1 Tim 5:20; 2 Tim 4:2; Titus 1:9, 13; 2:15; Heb 12:5; James 2:9; Jude 15; Rev 3:19.

[60] This "convicting" is, admittedly, not the primary connotation of ἐλέγχω in the present verse, in which the deeds, not the people, are the object (as Lincoln, *Ephesians*, 329–30, objects). But the doers of the deeds are named in 5:6 and 5:12. The fact that the world may scoff at the rebuke (Prov 9:7; 15:12) does not mean that the rebuke was illegitimate or in vain. Pagans are convicted by God's judgment, whether or not they accept it.

[61] The referent of ὑπ᾽ αὐτῶν, "by them," is not immediately obvious, as the preceding verse refers only to "fruitless works of darkness" (5:11). Presumably αὐτῶν refers to the people doing these works, who have been referred to explicitly as "the sons of disobedience" in 5:6. See BDF, § 282 (2), which calls this loose use of the pronoun *constructio ad sensum*.

[62] Schlier, *Epheser*, 239, thinks Paul again has the orgies of pagan religion in mind, as we have previously suggested with reference to 5:3.

5:13 τὰ δὲ πάντα ἐλεγχόμενα ὑπὸ τοῦ φωτὸς φανεροῦται—It is in the very nature of light to expose and illuminate.[63] The light both uncovers what happens in darkness and condemns it as sinful (cf. 5:11). In this context φανερόω ("make visible," 5:13, 14[64]) is a near synonym of ἐλέγχω ("expose," 5:11, 13). Hence φανερόω means "to reveal, disclose, expose" something publicly so that all people can see its true nature. For this reason it is rather unimportant whether the phrase ὑπὸ τοῦ φωτός, "by the light," modifies the verb before it (ἐλεγχόμενα, "exposed by the light") or the verb after it (φανεροῦται, "are made visible by the light"). But it is possible that the shift in verb reflects a shift in subject matter from "exposing" (ἐλέγχω) evil deeds to "making manifest" (φανερόω) what is light (cf. ἐλέγχω then φανερόω in Jn 3:20–21). This verse thus forms a transition from condemnation to illumination, from Law to Gospel.

Perhaps φανερόω ("make visible") is also chosen to add a communal dimension to the pericope. Each Christian's avoidance of the pagan works of darkness and dedication to the fruit of light serves as a testimony to fellow Christians, the strong helping the weak by revealing the dangers lurking in the shadows of their old lives and by modeling the new life. It is in the very nature of light to reveal (Lk 8:17; Jn 3:20–21; 1 Cor 4:5) and in the nature of God's Word to bring things to light, the Law exposing sin (1 Cor 14:24–25) and the Gospel revealing Christ (Rom 3:21; 2 Tim 1:10).

5:14 πᾶν γὰρ τὸ φανερούμενον φῶς ἐστιν—These concluding words are enigmatic. Previously (5:10–13) Paul has said that the light of God's Word shines into dark places and reveals what evil is in the darkness—that is, it makes them illuminated or light (adjective), so that what was concealed there becomes "visible" (5:13). In the present verse (5:14), "everything made visible is *light*" might be understood as saying nothing more, for in English the adjective "light" and the noun "light" are indistinguishable. But the Greek word for "light" here is φῶς—not an adjective, but a noun. If we take this fact seriously, then Paul is saying that whatever is enlightened by the light of God[65] becomes what it is: "light" (noun). We thereby reach the end of a progression: *light exposes, light convicts, light converts*.

Certainly Paul is not suggesting that the Word of God works irresistibly, always and unfailingly changing evil into good. The devil's evil, after all, is exposed and convicted without his being converted. But by recalling this quality of divine light, that

---

[63] Barth, *Ephesians*, 2:572, suggests the new element introduced by Paul in his argument at this point is that "only" light is able to carry out this function. In Semitic languages and Hebraizing Greek, he argues, the word "only" is often omitted in statements of exclusivity, where in modern Western languages it is needed. One thinks of Luther's insertion of "alone" in Rom 3:28 (WA DB 7:38–39).

[64] Here in 5:13 the present middle/passive form φανεροῦται is taken as passive, "is made visible." As is usual in Greek, the neuter plural subject (τὰ … ἐλεγχόμενα) takes a singular verb (φανεροῦται).

[65] The middle/passive participle φανερούμενον is thus taken as passive, "made visible," like the immediately previous use of the verb in 5:13 (see the preceding textual note). The KJV translates it as middle deponent (see Turner, *Syntax*, 55), "for whatsoever doth *make manifest* is light," or "whatever *illuminates* is light"—a translation that Moule, *Idiom Book*, 25, calls "a not very illuminating remark!" Barth, *Ephesians*, 2:573, n. 78, notes that φανερόω is not found in the middle deponent sense in Greek prior to the LXX or in the LXX.

it can transform its object into what it is, Paul returns to his foundational thought: the Ephesians themselves, who once "were darkness," have been turned into "light" (5:8) by the illumination of God's Word in Holy Baptism (1:18).[66] The first part of 5:14 thus forms a transition into the baptismal hymn that ends the unit on a decidedly Gospel note.

διὸ λέγει· ἔγειρε, ὁ καθεύδων, καὶ ἀνάστα ἐκ τῶν νεκρῶν, καὶ ἐπιφαύσει σοι ὁ Χριστός—The introductory formula διὸ λέγει, "therefore it says," might be understood to mean this is an OT quotation (see διὸ λέγει in Eph 4:8; James 4:6); but no such OT quotation can be located (hence the NA[27] margin's "unde?" "where?"). Presumably Paul is quoting an extrabiblical source sufficiently familiar to his addressees that he did not need to name it (just as he does in Acts 17:28). The hymn may be a paraphrase or interpretation of Is 60:1: "Arise, shine, for your light has come, and the glory of YHWH has risen upon you" (with an admixture of Is 9:1 [ET 9:2]; 26:19), but could hardly be called a quotation.[67] The content suggests it might be a liturgical piece, hymn, refrain, or versicle connected with the rite of Baptism.[68] It is addressed in the second person singular ("you"), as if to an individual candidate. It bears the marks of poetry (see "Structure and Rhetoric" in the commentary).

The verb καθεύδω, "to sleep," carries the metaphorical meaning of physical death, to be awakened later.[69] In divine perspective, death is merely a temporary "sleep" because of God's ability to bring back to life (1 Sam 2:6; Jn 5:21), either in the earthly ministry of Jesus[70] or on the Last Day.[71] For that reason Scripture also uses "awake(n)"

---

[66] Cf. Col 1:12–13; Heb 6:4; 10:32; and "Enlightened Eyes of Your Heart (1:18)" in the commentary on 1:15–23. Lincoln, *Ephesians*, 331, quotes the helpful paraphrase of J. B. Phillips (1958 ed.): "It is even possible (after all, it happened with you!) for light to turn the thing it shines upon into light also."

[67] Some church fathers believed it was an OT quotation (e.g., Hippolytus, *On Christ and Antichrist*, 65); others believed it came from an apocryphal writing, purportedly from Elijah or Jeremiah (e.g., Jerome, *Ephesians*, 3:5.14; Epiphanius, *Panarion*, 1:3.46.5); most thought it was an early hymn (e.g., Origen, *Catenae*; Theodoret, *Ephesians*, 5:14 [PG 82:544–45]). Clement of Alexandria, *Protrepticus*, 9:84.2, portrays the Lord himself as speaking it and follows it with three more lines: "The sun of resurrection, Begotten before the day-star, Who has given life with his own beams" (quoted in Greek and English in Bruce, *The Epistles to the Colossians, to Philemon, and to the Ephesians*, 377–78, including n. 45). These additional lines may be from the original hymn or from a later expansion of it. Jerome, *Ephesians*, 3:5.14, like Epiphanius, suggests it is a resurrection hymn addressed by Christ to Adam, whose skull was thought to be buried at the foot of the cross (see Bruce, *The Epistles to the Colossians, to Philemon, and to the Ephesians*, 376–77, n. 43). Understood as an allegorical interpretation of Baptism, this is not entirely off the mark.

[68] See Schnackenburg, " 'Er hat uns mitauferweckt': Zur Tauflehre des Epheserbriefes." 160–66.

[69] See καθεύδω, "to sleep," in the metaphorical sense of (temporary) death in, e.g., LXX Dan 12:2; Mt 9:24 ‖ Mk 5:39 ‖ Lk 8:52; 1 Thess 5:10. Likewise, see the synonym κοιμάομαι in the same sense in LXX 3 Kgdms 2:10; 11:43 (MT/ET 1 Ki 2:10; 11:43); Mt 27:52; Jn 11:11–12; Acts 7:60; 13:36; 1 Cor 7:39; 11:30; 15:6, 18, 20, 51; 1 Thess 4:13–15; 2 Pet 3:4. BDAG, s.v. καθεύδω, 2, misses the mark by placing Eph 5:14 and 1 Thess 5:6 into a category of spiritual indolence or indifference, a metaphorical category more appropriate for καθεύδω in Mt 13:25; 25:5; 26:40, 43, 45; Mk 13:36.

[70] Mt 9:24 ‖ Mk 5:39 ‖ Lk 8:52; Mt 27:52; Jn 11:11–12.

[71] LXX 3 Kgdms 2:10; 11:43 (MT/ET 1 Ki 2:10; 11:43); Dan 12:2; Acts 7:60; 13:36; 1 Cor 7:39; 11:30; 15:6, 18, 20, 51; 1 Thess 4:13–15; 5:10; 2 Pet 3:4.

for the resurrection of the dead, again, either by Jesus proleptically (Jn 11:11) or on the Last Day (Is 26:19; Dan 12:2; Ps 17:15; 1 Thess 5:10). In the present verse, the image of spiritual death as a kind of sleep is thus a double metaphor rooted in the earlier conviction that pagans were "dead in [their] trespasses and sins" (Eph 2:1, 5; cf. Col 2:13). It is entirely appropriate, therefore, that the divine response to this spiritual death/sleep is presented with vocabulary of resurrection that doubles as language of waking from sleep. ἔγειρε, the imperative of ἐγείρω (which has the basic sense of physical motion upward, "rise"), may accordingly be translated either as "wake up!" or "arise [from the prone position of death]!"[72] Like the words of Jesus, "Talitha cumi, ... little girl, ... *arise* [ἔγειρε]" (Mk 5:41), the words do what they say; they bring about the resurrection.[73] The dead have no ability to respond to the call on their own strength, but are given life by the divine Word.[74] The address of this verb to the baptismal candidate recalls the resurrection of Christ himself from the dead, with whom one is "coraised [συνεγείρω]" in Baptism (Eph 2:6; Col 2:12; 3:1). Baptism as death and resurrection is a standard Pauline image (Rom 6:1–11; Col 2:11–13).

The next clause renders the meaning of the preceding clause explicit: καὶ ἀνάστα ἐκ τῶν νεκρῶν, "and arise from the dead." The verb ἀνίστημι may carry the literal meaning of "stand up, rise up," but like ἐγείρω it frequently bears the extended meaning of "rise up from death,"[75] also for Christ himself.[76]

The hymn's third and final clause concludes with the verb ἐπιφαύσει, the future of ἐπιφαύσκω, a NT hapax meaning "shine upon" (cf. LXX Job 25:5; 31:26) or perhaps "begin to shine" in the sense of a rising star or the dawning sun (cf. LXX Job 41:10 [ET 41:18]). The future tense suggests a setting for this hymn within the baptismal rite at the moment of Baptism itself. Perhaps the congregation (or minister) sang it as an exhortation to the baptismal candidate to receive the gift of resurrection and divine light in the Sacrament. The image of Christ as a light shining on Christians is ubiquitous in the NT,[77] but might suggest here one's entrance into the eternal paradise, that heavenly Jerusalem, where Christ himself is the sun and light (Rev 21:23). The future tense, on the other hand, should not be taken to mean that the light of Christ begins to shine only *after* the sleeper has arisen. It is the light of Christ that brings about the rising and continues to shine upon the one who has thereby arisen.[78]

---

[72] Cf., e.g., Mt 8:25; 9:5; 10:8; Mk 5:41; Lk 7:14; 8:54.

[73] Cf. the command to the widow's son, "young man, arise!" (Lk 7:14), and to Lazarus, "come out!" (Jn 11:43); also Peter to Tabitha (Acts 9:40).

[74] Wallace, *Greek Grammar*, 491, is quite wrong to identify the imperatives in Eph 5:14 as conditional (i.e., "if you arise, Christ will shine on you").

[75] E.g., Mt 12:41; Mk 5:42; 12:23, 25; Jn 11:23–24; 1 Thess 4:16.

[76] E.g., Jesus' passion predictions: Mk 8:31; 9:9, 31; 10:34. Cf. also Lk 9:8, 19; 11:32; 16:31; 1 Thess 4:14.

[77] E.g., Lk 2:32; Jn 1:4–9; 3:19–21; 8:12; 9:5; 12:35, 46; Rev 1:16; cf. Is 42:6; 49:6; 60:1–3; Mal 3:20 (ET 4:2).

[78] Barth, *Ephesians*, 2:576, paraphrases the last line: "This (the awakening and rising of the dead) happens not on the ground of man's own power but because of the radiant Messiah himself."

The variant reading ἐπιψαύσεις τοῦ Χριστοῦ, "you will touch/attain to Christ" (D* b; MVict Ambst Chr^mss), is poorly attested and is less suited to the context. Its substitution was probably sparked by the rarity of the verb ἐπιφαύσκω.

Commentary

Structure and Rhetoric

This pericope serves, like the previous one (4:17–5:2), as a *refutatio* in Paul's argument.[79] While the pericopes from 2:1 to 4:16 presented a sequence of positive proofs[80] for the true unity of Jew and Gentile within the body of Christ on the basis of a common reception of his gifts, particularly in Baptism, the next two pericopes (4:17–5:2; 5:3–14) address the question of what unity the Gentile Christians still have with their pagan past and the Gentile world. They function like chapter 6 of Romans, in which, after demonstrating that justification is entirely by faith apart from the works of the law (Rom 1:18–5:21), Paul addresses and refutes the improper conclusion "What then shall we say? Shall we continue in sin that grace might abound?" (Rom 6:1). So also here Paul addresses the contention that Gentile Christians might continue to live their old lives (or return to them), all the while enjoying God's forgiveness in Christ. It is this unthinkable proposal that Paul decisively refutes.

The ancient chapter divisions (*kephalaia*) preserved in the inner margins of NA^27 encourage us to treat 5:3–21 as a unit. The insight that arises is that the positive encouragement to being "filled up in the Spirit" (5:18), to singing "psalms and hymns and songs of the Spirit" (5:19), to "giving thanks always … in the name of our Lord" (5:20) stands in stark contrast to the temptation to engage in false worship with the pagan world around (5:3–12). In this way we see that the admonitions of 5:3–12 are not simply moral prescriptions for leading a pure and God-pleasing life, but are warnings against false worship. (While accepting the wisdom of keeping the thought of this ancient chapter together, this commentary divides its discussion into two pericopes [5:3–14 and 5:15–21] to keep them manageable.)

This pericope (5:3–14) does not divide neatly into parts, though an overall thematic movement from darkness to light is discernible. Within this movement three stages are apparent—though there is some overlap from one stage to the next, 5:11 and 5:12 being transitional. Paul's description of pagan sexual immorality occupies the first three verses (5:3–5). Thereupon he identifies the temptation to return to these evil works as an unthinkable act of false communion (5:6–12). The metaphor (though it is more than just a metaphor) that emerges most prominently is the contrast of light and darkness. Perhaps for Paul this metaphor most emphatically illustrates the incompatibility of Christianity and paganism, of good and evil, of God's kingdom and the devil's realm. The

---

[79] See "Refutations" in "Structure and Rhetoric" in the introduction.

[80] See "Proofs" in "Structure and Rhetoric" in the introduction.

image of light dominates the final section (5:11–14), in which the work of light progresses from *exposing* evil deeds to *convicting* their doers to *converting* them to light. By closing off the unit with a hymn presumably from a baptismal rite (5:14), Paul turns from an argument in which the convicting and guiding functions of God's Law are prominent to one entirely filled with Gospel. He reminds the Ephesians in the end of who they are in Christ.

The division of the pericope into three units, however, is somewhat artificial—first, because Paul is not treating three distinct topics, and second, because his thought is guided by another pattern. The "then-now" antithesis that has featured strongly in previous pericopes[81] is now developed into a series of stark oppositions:

once darkness (5:8, 11)	now light (5:8, 9, 13, 14)
sexual immorality, uncleanness, lust (5:3, 5); shamefulness, foolish talk, coarse joking (5:4)	thanksgiving (5:4, 20); goodness, righteousness, truth (5:9); speaking to one another in psalms, hymns, songs of the Spirit (5:19)
foolish, unwise (5:4, 15, 17)	wise (5:15); understanding the Lord's will (5:17)
sons of disobedience (5:6)	children of light (5:8)
fruitless works of darkness (5:11)	fruit of the light (5:9)
things done in secret (5:12)	things exposed, revealed (5:11, 13, 14)
fellowship with works of darkness (5:7, 11)	exposing the works of darkness (5:11–14) fellowship with one another in the Spirit, speaking to one another with psalms (5:18–20)
sleeping, dead (5:14)	awake, arise (5:14)
false, pagan worship (5:3–12)	true, Spirit-filled worship (5:15–21)
anti-communion	Eucharist

The dominant antithesis is light and darkness. Not only is this a deeply biblical metaphor for God/Christ and the devil, for God's Word and sinful man's foolishness, but it sets down the principle of discontinuity. There is no halfway house between darkness and light, nor can this be viewed dualistically as a battle between two equal powers. Light triumphs over and dispels darkness. This gives the pericope a real air of optimism. Each element of the old life is exposed as fruitless, lifeless, withered, and powerless, while the new is fruitful, alive, and

---

[81] See "once/then" (ποτέ) and/or "now" (νῦν) in 2:2, 3, 11, 13; 3:5, 10; 5:8, 29 (cf. 2:4; 4:17). See the table contrasting "then" with "now" in "Structure and Rhetoric" in the commentary on 2:11–22.

productive. How, then, could anyone give up life in the kingdom of God for the old "life" among the "dead" (5:14)?

Within the above contrasts there is an apparent preference for groups of three (a pattern we have previously noted in Ephesians, particularly in 4:1–16). Three gives rhythm and presents each idea with completeness but without exhaustion. So, for example, 5:3–5 present the old, pagan behavior in three sets of three, in sentences that share a common structure. In each sentence the triplet is followed by a rejection:

> [3]But let sexual immorality and [καί] all uncleanness or [ἤ] lust
> *not* even be named … ,
> [4]nor shamefulness and [καί] foolish talk or [ἤ] coarse joking,
> which are *not* fitting. …
> [5]Every sexually immoral or [ἤ] unclean or [ἤ] lustful person (that is, an idolater)
> does *not* have an inheritance in the kingdom of Christ and God.

In 5:3 and 5:4 the end of each list is signaled by the shift in conjunction from καί to ἤ (for list structures, see the textual note on 4:11).[82] The shift from "and" to "or" probably has no other significance. In 5:5 the insertion of the phrase "that is, an idolater" obviates the need to mark the end of the list in a similar way. It is intriguing to ponder the possibility that Paul sees the one word εὐχαριστία, "thanksgiving" (5:4), as so weighty as to counterbalance this entire ninefold presentation of evil. Yet Paul has still more to say and presents the fruit of the light as threefold: "in all goodness and righteousness and truth" (5:9). He will also present the true worship of the baptized, the fruit of the Spirit, with three participles: "speaking … giving thanks … being subordinate" (5:18–21), and will present "speaking to one another" with three terms: "psalms and hymns and songs of the Spirit" (5:19). The larger unit (5:3–21; see above on the *kephalaia*) ends with a strong Trinitarian reference (5:18–20), and it is tempting to read the threefold patterning that is so prominent in the pericope as Trinitarian throughout, though this is probably to overinterpret it.

The final tightly structured element of this pericope (5:3–14) is the "hymn" of 5:14. It is introduced with a quotation formula, "therefore it says," but it cannot be found in the OT (unless it is understood as a paraphrase of Is 60:1). On what basis, then, is it understood as a baptismal hymn (as suggested in the last textual note on 5:14)? The poetic features are most obvious in the Greek,[83] and more obvious in English when a literal translation is given:

---

[82] The textual variants in 5:4 that substitute καί for ἤ, and ἤ for καί, simply misunderstand this patterning.

[83] For examples and analysis of poetry in the NT, see Ralph P. Martin, "Poetry in the NT," in *The International Standard Bible Encyclopedia* (ed. Geoffrey W. Bromiley; Grand Rapids: Eerdmans, 1986), 3:898–99; James L. Bailey and Lyle D. Vander Broek, *Literary Forms in the New Testament: A Handbook* (Louisville: John Knox, 1992), 76–82; Michael Peppard, "'Poetry,' 'Hymns' and Traditional Material' in New Testament Epistles or How to Do Things with Indentations," *Journal for the Study of the New Testament* 30 (2008): 319–42. This is an exceedingly underresearched topic in NT studies.

ἔγειρε, ὁ καθεύδων,	Get up, / O sleeper,
καὶ ἀνάστα ἐκ τῶν νεκρῶν,	and arise / from the dead,
καὶ ἐπιφαύσει σοι ὁ Χριστός.	and will shine upon you / the Christ.

The poem consists of three brief lines, each having a duple rhythm (1-2, 1-2, 1-2). Each line begins with a verb, which may be a Semitic feature (though the first two verbs, as imperatives, naturally come at the beginning), as is the parataxis of connecting the lines with a simple "and" (καί, like Hebrew ן). The first two lines end with the same sound, each created by the genitive plural ending -ων, -ōn. The two form "synthetic parallelism," describing the act of resurrection in the two stages of awaking ("get up") and arising. Finally, the poem develops a series of vivid images (sleeping, waking, resurrection, and light) into an extended metaphor without explanation—like all good poems. It is exegetes who belabor the obvious and try to explain poetry!

Darkness Has No Fellowship with Light (5:3–14)

In the previous pericope (4:17–5:2), Paul drew out the profound consequences of Holy Baptism for the Ephesians. It divided their lives into a "then" and a "now" (cf. 4:17).[84] In Baptism, they had stripped off the old Adam with his corrupt ways and had been clothed with the new man, Jesus Christ himself (4:22–24), as symbolized by the removal of everyday garments before the washing and the donning of clean white linen after the sacrament of rebirth.[85] Because of this profound change, it was unthinkable for them to return to their old lives. The consequences of the change could be described in terms of obedience to the Ten Commandments (4:25–31), but for the baptized there was a more powerful force driving their changed lives: their conformity to Jesus Christ, which led them to be imitators of God himself (5:1) in lives of forgiveness and love toward one another (4:32; 5:2). Thus, the logic of that pericope was internal to the community of believers. It portrayed the new life of the members of Christ's body, living no longer for themselves, but for each other.

In the present pericope, Paul revisits the theme of "once/then" and "now" (5:8), but with a sharper polemical edge. Two commandments of the Decalogue rise to prominence: the First (Ex 20:3–6; Deut 5:7–10) and the Sixth (Ex 20:14; Deut 5:18). The explanation for this focus can be found if one recalls the context of the Ephesian church (see "The City of Ephesus and Paul's Relationship to It" in the introduction). Ephesus was the location of one of the chief wonders of the ancient world, the monumental temple of Artemis, a study in classical excellence, whose marble columns spanned an area three or four times as large as the Athenian Parthenon. No Ephesian could ignore it. The story of Paul's clash

---

[84] See also "then" and/or "now" in 2:2, 3, 11, 13; 3:5, 10; 5:8, 29 and in "Structure and Rhetoric" immediately above.

[85] See "Stripping and Clothing (4:20–24)" in the commentary on 4:17–5:2.

with the silversmiths of Ephesus, whose business suffered greatly from Paul's success in preaching the true God, is recounted in Acts 19:21–41 and leads to his premature departure from the city.[86] "Great is Artemis of the Ephesians!" (Acts 19:28, 34), they cried.

It is difficult to determine the exact nature of her cult, since no ancient author describes it clearly. Matters are further confused by the fact that the ancient "Lady of Ephesus" was only later identified with the Greek goddess Artemis, twin sister of Apollo, the virgin hunter called Diana by the Romans. It is apparent that there was a fertility aspect to her cult, based on the legend that, having been born before her twin, she then assisted her mother with his delivery. Her followers therefore appealed to her for help with their own childbearing. But actual images of the Lady of Ephesus suggest that the fertility aspect of Artemis (the virgin) was more extreme in its Ephesian variety. Her statue portrays her chest ringed with dozens of extra breasts,[87] suggesting her own massive fertility and her ability to confer it on others. Without evidence it is impossible to speak with certainty, but it is a fair assumption that the sort of fertility rituals associated with other ancient cults were practiced also here. This probably included the services of sacred prostitutes in the temple precincts, who offered union with the deity and the promise of fertility through sexual relations with her worshipers.[88]

Sexual sin in this context is therefore even less a "sin outside oneself" than it might otherwise be misconstrued (cf. 1 Cor 6:18). A great danger lay in sexual immorality, far beyond the spiritual harm that all sin naturally bears. For the Ephesians, converted pagans, sexual immorality was a bridge back into idolatry. Playing with prostitutes was touching upon deep spiritual dangers. Paul's warning is akin to Peter's: "For the time that is past is sufficient for doing what the Gentiles want, wandering in sensuality, passions, drunkenness, orgies, drinking parties, and lawless idolatry" (1 Pet 4:3). The connection between sexual immorality and idolatry was intimate and obvious for such former pagans.[89] Two of the seven letters in Revelation refer to this danger. The letter to Thyatira

---

[86] See "Conflict with the Cult of Artemis Ephesia (Acts 19:21–41)" in "The City of Ephesus and Paul's Relationship to It" in the introduction.

[87] The more recent suggestion that they are bulls' testes or scrota still connects her cult with fertility. Some scholars see them as just decorative shells, but this seems an underinterpretation.

[88] See "The Cult of Artemis Ephesia" in "The City of Ephesus and Paul's Relationship to It" in the introduction. See also "Having Put Aside Idolatry (4:17–19)" in the commentary on 4:17–5:2.

[89] Tertullian, *Apology*, 15, writes:

> But if I add—it is what all know and will admit as readily to be the fact—that in the temples adulteries are arranged, that at the altars pimping is practised, that often in the houses of the temple-keepers and priests, under the sacrificial fillets, and the sacred hats, and the purple robes, amid the fumes of incense, deeds of licentiousness are done, I am not sure but your gods have more reason to complain of you than of Christians. (*ANF* 3:30)

might be construed as referring literally to a female false teacher who used her sexual appeal to lure Christians back into paganism:

> But I have [this] against you, that you tolerate the woman Jezebel, who calls herself a prophetess and teaches and deceives my servants to practice sexual immorality and eat food sacrificed to idols [πορνεῦσαι καὶ φαγεῖν εἰδωλόθυτα]. And I gave her time to repent, and she does not desire to repent from her sexual immorality [πορνείας]. Behold, I am casting her into a sickbed, and those who commit adultery [μοιχεύοντας][90] with her [I cast] into great tribulation, if they do not repent from her works, and her children I shall kill with death. (Rev 2:20–23; cf. Rev 2:14)

In our modern Western world, the connections and the dangers are no less acute. It would be a mistake to dismiss these warnings as inapplicable to our "mature" society, which, though no longer acting in the name of Artemis, is equally addicted to sexual immorality and has idolized the body with its desires.[91] Paul's contention was that even the act of speaking of such things had the potential to weaken the Ephesians' faith in the one true God and draw them back into the foul fellowship of demons, as also today a cavalier attitude toward immorality in the media and in our lives endangers our souls. For there is far more at stake here than morality. Or perhaps it is wiser to say that morality, or true obedience to God's Law, has a more profound motivation than is commonly assumed.[92]

Paul is concerned with the Ephesians' holiness—which is not merely a matter of behavior, but of their closeness to the holy God. God's holiness burns up anything that is not holy. Uncleanness separates people from God. Such OT language has not been rendered void by the obsolescence of the Jerusalem temple, but has been brought to its true goal in Christ. Paul has spoken of the church as the new, living temple, the dwelling place of God by his Spirit (2:19–22), and has introduced this very pericope with sacrificial language (5:2). Later Paul will present Christ as the one who washes us clean and makes us holy by the washing of Holy Baptism (5:26; cf. 1 Cor 6:11). The goal of this Sacrament is thus the true fulfillment of the temple, that we might be with God, to endure and

---

[90] The introduction of the term "adultery," which focuses on sexual sin by those married, probably alludes to the fact that these are *Christians* returning to paganism. Thus, as the bride of Christ (Eph 5:21–33), they are already betrothed (tantamount to marriage), and so their return to idolatry is adultery. The fact that the false teacher is a woman and the repeated sexual references to "sick*bed*," "sexual immorality," and "adultery" imply that there was literal sex involved in this apostasy from the true faith. (Cf. the discussion of πορνεία, "sexual immorality," in the first textual note on 5:3.)

[91] Contemporary socioeconomic entrapment in the sexual entertainment industry and the growing trade in human trafficking bear close resemblance to the ancient conscription of cult prostitutes. A vast difference from ancient fertility cults, whose worshipers typically desired a maximum of children, is the modern disdain for children, resulting in infanticide and the abortion of babies in utero. Yet these modern practices may in fact be further evidence of the idolatrous (demonic) nature of the modern cult of sexual immorality.

[92] Schlier, *Epheser*, 233: "The holiness of the members of Christ's body is, as we have seen, not established morally, but it has a moral side."

enjoy his holy presence without fear, by standing within the enveloping holiness of Jesus Christ.

Rhetorically, theologically, and pastorally, this pericope serves as a warning against returning to the deeds of the old life that would deny the Ephesian Christians the blessed enjoyment of God's presence. Within this purpose, Paul's proclamation of the Law certainly touches upon all three of its functions, as defined by the Formula of Concord and classical Lutheran theology.[93] That is to say, Paul aims to *prevent* them from returning to idolatry (first function); he *condemns* them (second and chief function) for speaking longingly of the pleasures of their old life (like Israel in the wilderness, Ex 16:3)[94] and would certainly bear down on them with the full weight of God's condemnation if they acted upon these desires by returning to the temple of Artemis.[95] The counterpart of such condemnation is the *exhortation* (third function) to expose and avoid evil works (5:7, 11–13), the commendation of "goodness and righteousness and truth" (5:9), and the positive admonition to worship the true God with thanksgiving (5:4, 18–21). But to get bogged down in a debate that sets the second and third functions of the Law in opposition, as if Paul were *only* condemning or *only* exhorting in such places as this is to miss the thrust of his argument. All three functions of the Law serve his intention of warning the Ephesians away from what will cause them great spiritual harm and directing them to what is wholesome in the Lord.

The pericope has, in fact, been gravely misunderstood by commentators who concentrate on the condemnation of one particular behavior that they believe lies at the heart of Paul's words. Since sleep is sometimes an image for spiritual lethargy or inattentiveness among Christians,[96] the call to awaken (5:14) has been interpreted as a present tense admonition, addressing the Ephesians as

---

[93] See, e.g., Formula of Concord, Article 6. See also "Epistolary Outline" in "Structure and Rhetoric" in the introduction and "Doctrine and Ethics, Gospel and Law? (4:1–16 in the Context of the Epistle)" in the commentary on 4:1–16.

[94] Schnackenburg, *Ephesians*, 230:

> More important for him is to remind the Christians of the novelty and different quality of their existence as Christians based on their Baptism, and to warn them of the danger of being dazzled by the glitter of a life of pleasure, giving heed to empty words (v. 6) and participating in 'unfruitful works' (v. 11) caused by passion.

[95] Luther, "Sermon for the Third Sunday in Lent, Ephesians 5:1–9":

> Hereby he [Paul] declares in dry words that the man who does not exhibit the fruits of faith is a heathen under the name of a Christian. Here is absolute condemnation in a word. The whoremonger is a denier of the faith; the unclean person is a denier of the faith; the covetous individual is a denier of the faith: all are rebellious, perjured and faithless toward God. (Lenker, 7:157; StL 12:456–57, § 15)

[96] Mt 26:40–41 (and parallels); Rom 13:11. 1 Thess 5:6 is probably not to be interpreted as Christian spiritual lethargy but, like Eph 5:14, as a reference to the spiritual death of unbelievers, contra BDAG, s.v. καθεύδω, 2. For "sleep" as death, see the second textual note on 5:14.

if they had fallen away and needed to be reborn.[97] In such a view, the passage is dealing with church discipline and exhorts the upright members of the church to exclude those who have fallen away, to have no fellowship with them.[98] This view is often buttressed by the claim that the concept of ἐλέγχω (5:11, 13) in the sense of "to convict" cannot be applied to unbelievers, who would pay no heed to the Word of God.[99] It is clear, however, that the primary meaning of ἐλέγχω in the context of the metaphor of light and darkness is to "expose" (as translated in 5:11, 13). Analogically, it refers to the work of a lighthouse that both lights up the perilous rocky shoal and warns ships away from it. The rocks are certainly thereby "convicted" as dangerous, but the main purpose is to protect the sailors from harm. The line of division in the text is between light and darkness, not between various shades of light; it is between Christians and pagans, not between faithful and unfaithful Christians.

There is indeed a legitimate application of the fellowship language in this text to the situation of church discipline (the denial of the Sacrament of the Altar to an apostate or unrepentant sinner), and even to the question of joint Communion between Christians of different confessions. Christians must not only be warned against shameful sexual words and deeds but also condemned when they enter into them.[100] But Paul's original purpose is deeper. As in 1 Corinthians (primarily chapters 6 and 10), Paul is drawing a line between paganism and Christianity, between the worship of idols (demons, 1 Cor 10:20–21; cf. 1 Tim 4:1) and the true God. The vocabulary of the text, including terms like συμμέτοχοι, "fellow partakers" (Eph 5:7; also 3:6), and συγκοινωνεῖτε, "have fellowship/be in communion with" (5:11), implies a stark contrast between two worshiping communities, two fellowships. Idolaters and unbelievers are not neutral figures in the spiritual world, but are part of a sort of "anti-communion" that stands with its sacrifices and temple meals and immoral bodily fellowship as a demonic imitation of the true communion of saints. As well as warning the Ephesian Christians away from this anti-communion, Paul points them back toward the true communion,[101] the place of thanksgiving (5:4,

---

[97] E.g., Schnackenburg, *Ephesians*, 228: "The sleeping in the second line, which was originally understood as the sleep of death, is now seen as a condition of forgetfulness and intoxication (cf. 1 Thess. 5.7)."

[98] E.g., Best, *Ephesians*, 495.

[99] Best, *Ephesians*, 492–94, raises this objection. Lincoln, *Ephesians*, 330, correctly counters that the entire passage is directed against the works of outsiders who are in darkness.

[100] Luther, "Sermon for the Third Sunday in Lent, Ephesians 5:1–9":

Unquestionably, among Christians there will always be some infirm one to fall; but we must labor diligently, correcting, amending and restraining. We must not suffer the offense to go unchallenged, but curtail and remedy it, lest, as remarked in the preceding lesson, the heathen stumble, saying: "Christians tolerate such vices among themselves; their conduct is not different from our own." (Lenker, 7:153; StL 12:453, § 6)

[101] See the textual note on 5:7 and the first textual note on 5:11, which consider connections to Holy Communion, the Sacrament of Christ's body and blood.

20), singing (5:19), and true spiritual fulfillment (5:18). It is a liturgical answer to a liturgical problem, true worship in place of false.

The classic biblical imagery of light and darkness presents itself to Paul as the cleanest exposition of these realities. It provides a means to show the Ephesians what they truly are. They are defined by what God has made them to be. Engaging in evil deeds involves a thorough denial of what God has made them in Baptism. They were dead in their trespasses and sins (2:1, 5); they were shrouded in the darkness of godlessness, hopelessness, fleshliness, idolatry, and slavery to the devil (2:2–3, 11–12; 4:17–19), but now they have been transformed into light. The light of Christ shone upon them when they were transformed in Holy Baptism, reborn as sons of God (5:13–14). The imperatives in the hymn, "get up" and "arise" (5:14), do not mean that the Ephesians are *now* asleep, but that they *had been* asleep (dead) before their Baptism, when that hymn was presumably sung to them for the first time. If our reconstruction of the origin and use of this hymn is on target (see the second textual note on 5:14), then it should be understood in the context of that sacramental action when they were definitively awakened and resurrected.

Nonetheless, while Baptism is a decisive past event for Christians, it is not an event that is merely done and gone. The Ephesians *are* baptized (present tense),[102] they "*are* light" (Eph 5:8), and they continue to shine against "the fruitless works of darkness" (5:11), to expose and convict them (5:11–12).[103] The baptismal act can be appealed to at all times not only as an exhortation to flee the old life and pursue the fruits of the new, but more importantly as a divine defense against the spiritual dangers of the world around us. In this way, an appeal to Baptism is an "encouragement,"[104] that is, an injection of courage that enables Christians to step forth along the path to heaven.[105]

---

[102] This present-tense aspect of Baptism is particularly prominent in Luther's thought; he writes in the Large Catechism, for example: "Thus we must regard Baptism and make it profitable to ourselves, that when our sins and conscience oppress us, we strengthen ourselves and take comfort and say: Nevertheless I am baptized; but if I am baptized, it is promised me that I shall be saved and have eternal life, both in soul and body" (LC 4:44 [*Triglotta*, 743]). Schnackenburg, *Ephesians*, 230: "Baptism is not simply a single act, but constantly bathes the whole life of the baptized in light."

[103] Luther, "Sermon for the Third Sunday in Lent, Ephesians 5:1–9":

While we were gentiles we knew not that all those things were sin, because of the darkness of unbelief, which prevented our knowing God. But now we have become a light in the Lord. That is, we have been so amply enlightened through Christ that we not only know God and what he desires, and understand what sin and wrong are, but we are also able to light others, to teach them what we know. (Lenker, 7:160; StL 12:459–60, § 21)

[104] Cf. the discussion of παρακαλῶ, "I encourage," in the first textual note and the commentary on 4:1.

[105] Schnackenburg, *Ephesians*, 228: "Hence it is still the best explanation that here a fragment from the baptismal liturgy is applied to the situation of those already baptized to remind them of the radiant life which has been granted to them in Baptism."

The imagery of darkness and light as representing the baptismal movement from paganism into the fellowship of the true God was instinctively grasped by the third-century author of the *Didascalia Apostolorum*:

> But to you of the People who have believed in Jesus we say: Learn how the Scripture bears witness to us and saith, *they have seen a great light*. You then who have believed in Him *have seen a great light*, even Jesus Christ our Lord; and they also shall see who are (yet) to believe in Him. But *they that sit in the shadow of death* are you who are of the Gentiles; for you were *in the shadow of death*, because you had set your hope on the worship of idols, and knew not God. But when Jesus Christ our Lord and Teacher appeared to us, *light rose upon you*, for you beheld and set your hope on the promise of the kingdom everlasting; and you have departed from the customs and practices of (your) former error, and no more serve idols as you were wont to serve them, but have already believed and been baptized in Him: and *a great light is risen upon you*.[106]

---

[106] *Didascalia Apostolorum*, 21, quoting Is 9:1 (ET 9:2); trans. Connolly, *Didascalia Apostolorum*, 186.

The Liturgy
of the Spirit-Filled Baptized

Translation

5 ¹⁵Therefore, watch carefully how you walk, not as unwise but as wise people,
   ¹⁶redeeming the time, for the days are evil.
¹⁷For this reason do not be foolish people, but understand what is the will
of the Lord.
¹⁸And do not get drunk with wine, in which is debauchery,
   but be filled up in the Spirit,
      ¹⁹speaking to one another in psalms and hymns and songs of the <u>Spirit</u>,
         singing and psalming with your heart to the Lord,
      ²⁰giving thanks always for all things in the name of our Lord
      <u>Jesus Christ</u> to [our] God and <u>Father</u>,
      ²¹being subordinate to one another in the fear of Christ:

Textual Notes

5:15 βλέπετε οὖν ἀκριβῶς πῶς περιπατεῖτε—The conjunction οὖν, "therefore," maintains a tight connection with the preceding pericope, as Paul now details the kind of walk that characterizes Christians who have given up their old pagan ways. "Therefore" draws out the significance of the quotation (5:14), meaning "since you have been enlightened through Holy Baptism."[1] The use of the verb βλέπω, "to see, look, watch," in the metaphorical sense of "pay close attention to, consider" is typical of the hortatory language of both Jesus and Paul.[2] The adverb ἀκριβῶς, "accurately, carefully," is not used elsewhere in the NT with βλέπω, but accompanies similar actions such as "search" (Mt 2:8), "follow" (Lk 1:3), "speak and teach" (Acts 18:25), and "know" (1 Thess 5:2).[3] In the majority of occurrences (particularly in early postapostolic literature), the adverb expresses the Christian emphasis on precise attention to teaching and listening to the Word of God. Thus, it is apparent how BDAG's explanation, "pert[aining] to strict conformity to a standard or norm,"[4] would be applicable to the present verse, for it is God's Word that forms the standard according to which one's walk is judged (Ps 119:105; cf. 2 Pet 1:19). Because God's Word is light and the baptized are enlightened, they are able

---

[1] Cf. Schlier, *Epheser*, 243; Barth, *Ephesians*, 2:577.

[2] Mt 24:4; Mk 4:24; 8:15; 12:38; 13:5, 9, 23, 33; Lk 8:18; 21:8; Acts 13:40; 1 Cor 1:26; 3:10; 8:9; 10:12, 18; 16:10; 2 Cor 10:7; Gal 5:15; Phil 3:2; Col 2:8; 4:17; cf. Heb 3:12; 12:25; 2 Jn 8.

[3] Cf. LXX Deut 19:18 (with ἐξετάζω); θ Dan 7:19 (ζητέω); *Barnabas*, 7:4 (προσέχω); Polycarp, *To the Philippians*, 3:2 (διδάσκω); *Shepherd of Hermas, Mandates*, 3:1.4; 4:3.7 (ἀκούω); *Shepherd of Hermas, Similitudes* 9:5.5 (γινώσκω); 9:6.3 (κατανοέω); 9:13.6 (ἐξετάζω).

[4] BDAG, s.v. ἀκριβῶς.

to see properly (see "Enlightened Eyes of Your Heart" in the commentary on 1:15–23). The verb περιπατέω, "to walk," is quite prominent in chapters 4 and 5 of Ephesians (4:1, 17; 5:2, 8, 15). In this latter part of the letter, Paul describes the new walk of the baptized (as in 2:10) and warns the Ephesians against returning to their old manner of life ("walk" in 2:2). The metaphor of "walking" includes the entire life of faith, confession, and obedience to God's Word and should not be reduced to the moralistic component of behavior alone.[5] In the present context, the Ephesians' walk includes how they worship the true God.

μὴ ὡς ἄσοφοι ἀλλ᾽ ὡς σοφοί—Like the metaphor of "walking," wisdom ("wise") is a concept with deep OT resonance. The two ideas often appear together,[6] as in the Colossians parallel that combines them so succinctly: "walk in wisdom toward outsiders, redeeming the time" (Col 4:5). Ephesians has placed a strong emphasis on true knowledge of God in Christ, as revealed through Paul as his apostle (1:9–10, 17–18; 3:1–13, 19; 4:13). But this is not mere knowledge of facts. Wisdom is the practical application of God's Word to one's faith and life.[7] It is the wisdom of God as conveyed through his Spirit (1:8, 17; 3:10), referring primarily to the revelation of Christ as the long-promised Redeemer of the world. It is a deep understanding of God's mind, a recognition of how his work and gifts in Jesus Christ affect every aspect of one's life. See the second textual note on 1:8.

Paul gives the listeners time to dwell on the idea by pairing σοφοί, "wise people," with its opposite, ἄσοφοι, "unwise (people)."[8] This pairing again evokes the contrast between their old Gentile lives and their new lives lived in Baptism.[9] It is the Gentiles who are "foolish" (5:4), inasmuch as foolishness is the denial of God (Pss 14:1; 53:2 [ET 53:1]). Paul reiterates the admonition two verses later with the synonym ἄφρονες, "foolish people" (5:17). A major goal of this writing has been to alleviate their ignorance by revealing the mystery and insight into God's plan that was granted to Paul as Christ's apostle (3:3, 5).

5:16 ἐξαγοραζόμενοι τὸν καιρόν, ὅτι αἱ ἡμέραι πονηραί εἰσιν—This verse expands the previous clause, explaining the manner of the Ephesians' walk. Thus, ἐξαγοραζόμενοι is a participle of manner dependent on the main verbal construction in 5:15: βλέπετε … πῶς περιπατεῖτε, "watch … how you walk, *redeeming* …" The

---

[5] Typical of the latter perspective is Bruce, *The Epistles to the Colossians, to Philemon, and to the Ephesians*, 378: "A further paraenetic paragraph now opens, setting out more general principles for Christian living." Not only does this distort the biblical meaning of "walk," but it makes little sense of the worship language that follows in 5:18–20.

[6] E.g., Prov 4:10–14; 8:1–9:18; 10:8–9; 12:15; 28:26; Eccl 2:14; 6:8; Hos 14:10 (ET 14:9); Baruch 3:23.

[7] E.g., Ps 119:65–67; Prov 1:2, 4, 7, 20, 22, 29. "All wisdom is the fear of the Lord, and in all wisdom is the accomplishment of the Torah [πᾶσα σοφία φόβος κυρίου, καὶ ἐν πάσῃ σοφίᾳ ποίησις νόμου]" (Sirach 19:20).

[8] The adjective with α-privative, ἄσοφος, "unwise," is a biblical hapax legomenon. It is, however, taken up by Clement in a verse that also quotes a phrase from Eph 4:18 by way of warning to Christians not to return to their former foolishness (*2 Clement*, 19:2).

[9] E.g., 2:1–5, 11–13, 19–22; 4:17–31; 5:3–14. See further "Structure and Rhetoric" in the commentary.

meaning of this verse may be simply "making the most of the time, because the days are evil" (RSV). The implication would be that in these dark and latter days, while we await the coming of our Lord Jesus, we should take advantage of any opportunity to walk in God's ways (5:15; cf. Gal 6:10).[10] It might mean the avoidance of worldly distractions (cf. 1 Cor 7:29–32). In this view, the καιρός ("time") is the "opportune moment" that occasionally slips in, an exception to the generally evil quality of the days. Or it may refer to the relative peace that the Christians were then experiencing, an opportunity for the kingdom to be advanced before the ever-more-evil days of oppression by the Roman Empire.

However, there are numerous difficulties with those interpretations. First, the previous verse has mandated the Christian *always* to walk in the way of God, not only when the occasional "opportunity" presents itself (thus, we have translated καιρός here as "time"). Nor is there any suggestion that Paul is talking about an opportune moment *for evangelism.*[11] Second, Paul does not say that the days are usually evil or are becoming evil but that they *are* evil. Thus, third, the common translations of ἐξαγοραζόμενοι (e.g., ESV: "making the best use of") makes little sense of the causal conjunction ὅτι ("because, for") and the explanation it introduces in the second half of the verse. How does "for the days are evil" provide a reason for the admonition to "make the most" of them?[12] The Christian's obligation is to flee evil, not use it. The words of the parallel Corinthian text, "the time has grown very short" (1 Cor 7:29), would fit this interpretation well; but this does not seem to be what Paul is saying here. In the perspective of Ephesians, the world is a hostile force against which the Christian is to do battle (6:10–17), as he stands firm "in the evil day" (6:13). The evilness of this age, of these latter days, is a biblical axiom; it is something from which we need deliverance.[13]

It is therefore worth reconsidering the meaning of ἐξαγοράζω. The linguistic parallel in LXX Dan 2:8, where the clause καιρὸν ὑμεῖς ἐξαγοράζετε means "you are trying to gain time [i.e., stall]," is scarcely applicable—unless perhaps it is translated as "buy time." Etymologically (and in common usage) ἐξαγοράζω relates to marketplace commerce, meaning "to buy up" something. Aside from the parallel to this text (Col 4:5), Paul uses the verb only twice more. In both cases it refers to the redemptive

---

[10] BDAG, s.v. ἐξαγοράζω, 2, offers the paraphrase "take advantage of any opportunity that comes your way," referring "to avoidance of anything that interferes with understanding of the Lord's will."

[11] Ephesians lacks the reference to "those outside" (Col 4:5), toward whom the Christian is to have speech that is "gracious" and "seasoned with salt" (Col 4:6). Those Colossian verses might well inform how a Christian confesses the faith within his vocation in the world.

[12] A *concessive* particle or participle meaning "even though" would be required to give this understanding.

[13] Gen 47:9; Pss 37:19 (LXX 36:19); 41:2 (ET 41:1; LXX 40:2); 49:6 (ET 49:5; LXX 48:6); 94:13 (LXX 93:13); Eccl 9:12; Jer 17:17–18; Amos 5:13; Micah 2:3; 2 Macc 1:5; Gal 1:4; 2 Tim 3:1; 2 Pet 3:3. Surely on the basis of Eph 5:15–16 Barnabas writes: "Since, therefore, the days are evil, and Satan possesses the power of this world, we ought to give heed to ourselves, and diligently inquire into the ordinances of the Lord" (*Barnabas*, 2:1 [*ANF* 1:137]; cf. *Barnabas*, 4:9; 8:6).

work of Christ, who "bought us out of" the curse of the Law (Gal 3:13; 4:5).[14] The metaphor refers to paying a purchase price to free a slave from his horrible plight, a Gospel picture Paul has already used in Ephesians (1:7). Like humans themselves, the days are not inherently or irredeemably evil, but are evil because of the intensive work of the evil one (6:11–12, 16).[15]

Perhaps, then, what Paul means is that, just as the Christian has been purchased and won out of the clutches of the devil by the innocent suffering and death of Jesus Christ (1 Pet 1:18–19; cf. SC, Apostles' Creed, Second Article), so the Christian as an agent of God redeems the present time—or more precisely, he takes up and uses it as a gift redeemed for him[16] by Christ. Paul offers this perspective as a robust contrast to conformity to the world and backsliding into the old Gentile life against which he has been warning. The conjunction ὅτι, "because," therefore expresses the reason why the καιρός, "time,"[17] in which one lives needs to be redeemed: since the days are evil. Salvation in Christ does not mean the Christian is immediately snatched from the grasp of this evil age, but that the age (the "time") is snatched by Christ and redeemed for the Christian's use. Thus, the paradox can be true that while the day of redemption still lies in the future (1:14; 4:30), Paul can nonetheless proclaim: "Behold, now is the favorable time [καιρός]; behold, now is the day of salvation" (2 Cor 6:2; cf. Eph 2:5, 8).

5:17 διὰ τοῦτο μὴ γίνεσθε ἄφρονες, ἀλλὰ συνίετε τί τὸ θέλημα τοῦ κυρίου—This sentence forms a perfect parallel to 5:15, reiterating that one's walk is to be directed by the wisdom given in God's Word, which reveals his will. ἄφρων (α-privative, "not," + φρόνημα, "mind, thinking") means "mindless, unthinking, foolish"[18] and parallels ἄσοφοι, "unwise" (5:15). Likewise, "understand what is the will[19] of the Lord" stands

---

[14] BDAG, s.v. ἐξαγοράζω, 3, offers as an alternative translation for Eph 5:16, "buy off," in the sense of satisfying the wrathful demands of the present evil days. This translation is supported by the only use of the verb in the Apostolic Fathers, referring to the martyrs who διὰ μιᾶς ὥρας τὴν αἰώνιον ζωὴν ἐξαγοραζόμενοι, "through one hour [of suffering] purchased eternal life" (*Martyrdom of Polycarp*, 2:3).

[15] Schlier, *Epheser*, 244. "When Paul says *the days are evil* [Eph 5:16] he does not mean that they are created evil or that they are by their nature evil. Rather he says this of the troubling events that occur in time" (Chrysostom, *Homilies on Ephesians*, 18:5.15–17, ACCS 8:190).

[16] The middle voice of ἐξαγοραζόμενοι may support this interpretation if it is understood as a true middle and not a deponent: "redeeming the time *for yourselves*" (see Wallace, *Greek Grammar*, 421).

[17] While καιρός often refers to a specific moment in time, an "opportunity," the proverbial distinction between καιρός, "moment," and χρόνος, "period of time," is not always observed in the NT (compare Eph 1:10 with Gal 4:4), even within Ephesians (compare 1:10; 2:12; 6:18). Nonetheless, the eschatological connotations of καιρός as the decisive end time (Rom 3:26; 8:18; 11:5; 13:11; 1 Cor 4:5; 7:29; 2 Cor 6:2; Gal 6:9; 1 Tim 2:6; 4:1; 6:15; 2 Tim 3:1; 4:3; Titus 1:3; 1 Pet 1:5; Rev 1:3; 22:10) are certainly appropriate to the present verse.

[18] The (substantival) adjective ἄφρων, "unthinking (person)," is especially frequent in OT Wisdom literature and forms a contrast with the wise child of God. It occurs seventy-four times in Proverbs, twenty-two times in Ecclesiastes, and eight times in Psalms (also eleven times in Sirach and eight times in the Wisdom of Solomon). In the NT it is prominent in 2 Corinthians (11:16 [twice], 19; 12:6, 11).

[19] The first-hand copyist of codex ℵ replaced θέλημα, "*will* (of the Lord)," with φρόνημα, "*mind* (of the Lord)." This variant strengthens the parallel with "walk … as *wise* people" (5:15), but

in parallel to "walk … as wise people" (5:15). The baptized have been transformed in such a way that they, unlike the people of the world around them, truly can understand the will of the Lord (Rom 12:2; Eph 5:10; 6:6; Col 1:9).[20] Where θέλημα, "will," appears elsewhere in Ephesians, it usually refers to the will of *God*, that is, the Father, who works out his plan of salvation through Jesus Christ, his Son (1:1, 5, 9, 11; 6:6; see the fifth textual note on 1:5). In the present context, "the Lord" could be a reference to *Christ*, as it is in 5:20 and probably in 5:19. All things considered, the will of God (the Father) is probably what Paul means, though the fact that the divine will is one within the persons of the Holy Trinity makes the decision less than critical. The textual variants here and in nearby verses indicate a general willingness to interchange God, Christ, and Lord where the distinction of divine persons is not at stake.[21]

5:18 καὶ μὴ μεθύσκεσθε οἴνῳ, ἐν ᾧ ἐστιν ἀσωτία, ἀλλὰ πληροῦσθε ἐν πνεύματι— The prohibition μὴ μεθύσκεσθε οἴνῳ, "do not get drunk with wine," is a legitimate application of the Law (cf. LXX Prov 23:31) which has clear parallels elsewhere in NT teaching.[22] It is no contradiction of the essential goodness of wine in God's creation[23] to condemn those who would abuse their bodies with excessive consumption and thereby weaken the will to oppose sin. Drunkenness was also connected with pagan worship, notably with the month-long festivities of Artemis Ephesia.[24] But there is no evidence that early Christians avoided wine entirely, nor that it would have been a practical lifestyle in a world offering few alternatives aside from water (which was often unsafe to drink). Indeed, wine was mandated in some drink offerings in OT liturgical worship,[25] and the abundance of wine is a prophesied feature of the messianic age,[26] a prophecy fulfilled in the central use of wine in the Lord's Supper,[27] which anticipates the heav-

---

is best explained as (unintentionally?) introducing antithetical parallelism *within* 5:17 via two words from the same root: ἄφρονες, "foolish [= not mindful]," and φρόνημα, "mind."

[20] Cf. Pss 40:9 (ET 40:8; LXX 39:9); 143:10 (LXX 142:10); Mk 3:35; Jn 9:31; Acts 22:14; Col 4:12; 1 Thess 4:3; 5:18; Heb 10:36; 1 Pet 2:15; 3:17; 4:2, 19; 1 Jn 2:17.

[21] A large number of manuscripts substitute θεοῦ, "God," for κυρίου, "Lord," in 5:17. One ancient manuscript, 𝔓[46], reads Χριστοῦ, "Christ," in place of κυρίου, "Lord." See similar variants in 5:10 (substituting "God" for "Lord"), in 5:21 (substituting "God" for "Christ"), and in 5:29 (substituting "Lord" for "Christ").

[22] Mt 24:49 ‖ Lk 12:45; Lk 21:34; Rom 13:13; 1 Cor 5:11; 6:10; 11:21; Gal 5:21; 1 Thess 5:7; 1 Tim 3:3; Titus 1:7; 1 Pet 4:3; Rev 17:2; 18:3.

[23] Ps 104:15; Mt 11:19; Lk 10:34; Jn 2:1–10; cf. Deut 28:39. "Wine was given to gladden us, not for intoxication" (Chrysostom, *Homilies on Ephesians*, 19:5.18, ACCS 8:191).

[24] Schwindt, *Das Weltbild des Epheserbriefes*, 110–11.

[25] E.g., Ex 29:40; Lev 23:13; Num 15:5, 7, 10; cf. the offering of bread and wine in Gen 14:18.

[26] Jer 31:12; Hos 2:24 (ET 2:22); Joel 2:19, 24; 4:18 (ET 3:18); Amos 9:13.

[27] Wine was not expressly mandated in the institution of the OT Passover, which focused instead on the lamb and unleavened bread (Exodus 12; cf. 1 Cor 5:7–8). Wine was probably added to the feast as a sign that the people had entered into the promised land—together with the shift from standing up (which, along with the unleavened bread, indicated the haste to leave the land of slavery [Ex 12:11]) to reclining (indicating feasting and leisure; see Mt 26:20; Mk 14:18; Jn 13:23, 28; cf. Mt 8:11; Mk 16:14; Lk 12:37; 13:29). Thus, the institution of the Lord's Supper with the "cup" of wine (Mt 26:27–28 and parallels; 1 Cor 10:16–17; 11:25–28) lends the Sacrament a decidedly NT character. The joyful use of wine (Ps 104:15) indicates that the people of God are no longer in the land of slavery (symbolized by the unleavened

enly banquet. Modern temperance movements have no support from this passage; it condemns not wine but drunkenness and calls it ἀσωτία, "debauchery, dissipation," which seems to be a natural consequence of drunkenness (Titus 1:6–7; 1 Pet 4:3–4).[28] The lifestyle of the prodigal son is depicted with the cognate adverb ἀσώτως: "living in reckless wastefulness" (ζῶν ἀσώτως, Lk 15:13).[29]

The question arises, however, why drunkenness is singled out in this text. The context of worship (5:19–20) might suggest an abuse of the Lord's Supper (1 Cor 11:20–22),[30] though Paul does not elaborate in this direction and ἀσωτία would seem too weak a label for such profanation. The imperative does not necessarily imply an existing problem, but merely states a general policy.[31] The warning may be suggested by the eschatological language of 5:16, in that the latter "time," in these evil "days," calls for sober attentiveness (Lk 21:34; Rom 13:13). But a deeper reason may be the close connection of drunkenness with the immorality that featured prominently in the previous pericope (Eph 5:3–5). The combination of immorality and idolatry, explained by the use of sacred prostitutes in pagan temples, is frequently extended in the NT to include drunkenness, which must have been just as prominent (Rom 13:13; 1 Cor 5:11; 1 Pet 4:3).[32] The desecration of the Jerusalem temple under Antiochus IV Epiphanes did not merely involve random acts of wildness, but comprised the deliberate importation of pagan practices into the holy place of YHWH with the intention of profaning it: "For the temple was filled with debauchery [ἀσωτία] and reveling by the Gentiles, who dallied with harlots and had intercourse with women within the sacred precincts, and besides brought in things for sacrifice that were unfit" (2 Macc 6:4 RSV). Thus, the admonition to avoid drunkenness continues Paul's warning against returning to the ways of the Gentile Ephesians' past.[33]

However, the contrast given in the second half of the verse, "but be filled up in the Spirit," suggests another reference might have been in Paul's mind. For it was on Pentecost in the temple that the disciples with their speaking in foreign languages were

---

bread), but are in the promised land. See Thomas M. Winger, "The Mandated Element of Wine," *Lutheran Theological Review* 21 (Academic Year 2008–2009): 9–14.

[28] The three NT appearances of ἀσωτία are in Eph 5:18; Titus 1:6; 1 Pet 4:4.

[29] The noun ἀσωτία with α-privative is a negated form of the verb σῴζω, "save," whose basic meaning is "to preserve." See BDAG, s.v. ἀσωτία. The adverb, then, refers to squandering dissipation.

[30] Schlier, *Epheser*, 246, 249–50.

[31] The present tense imperative should not be translated as "*stop* getting drunk with wine," as older grammars might suggest. It is simply Paul's normal tense for expressing policy commands: "*never* get drunk with wine." The counterpart in the second half of the verse is likewise a policy command: "but *always* be filled with the Spirit" (not, "*continue* to be filled with the Spirit"). See Wallace, *Greek Grammar*, 716–17, for a critique of the traditional interpretation of imperatives, and Voelz, *Fundamental Greek Grammar*, 200–2, for an analysis of NT usage.

[32] A specific reference to the Bacchanalia of the Dionysus cult is possible, but unnecessary, as those wine festivals were paralleled in many other pagan cults of the time. The tendency to profane worship with drunkenness was already noted and condemned in the OT (e.g., Lev 10:9; Is 28:7–8).

[33] See further "Structure and Rhetoric" in the commentary.

accused of drunkenness (which implied profaning the temple with pagan practices),[34] to which they responded that it was not wine but the Holy Spirit that had been poured out upon them (Acts 2:15–18).[35] If indeed Paul wrote Ephesians from prison in Caesarea, short weeks after being arrested in the temple during his Pentecost pilgrimage,[36] the recollection of the first Christian Pentecost could readily have influenced his thoughts.

The second half of this verse is typically translated as "be filled *with* the Spirit," as if the Spirit is the content, but this translation may be questioned. "Do not get drunk with wine [οἴνῳ]" involves a simple dative of means or instrument, "*by means of* wine." The grammar does not imply that wine is "filling up" the drinkers in such a way that the Spirit might materially take its place. Furthermore, the verb πληρόω normally takes a simple genitive for the contents.[37] While there are three or four NT examples of πληρόω with a simple dative for contents,[38] there are no examples outside the present verse of ἐν plus the dative for the contents of πληρόω.[39] Daniel Wallace has therefore suggested the phrase be taken as equivalent to a dative of means. He proposes this verse be understood as the culmination of the πληρόω language in Ephesians, noting particularly 3:19 and 4:10, and concludes: "Believers are to be filled *by* Christ *by means of* the Spirit *with* the content of the fullness of God."[40] One might even understand the phrase ἐν πνεύματι similarly to Paul's common use of "*in* Christ" in this letter (see the fifth textual note on 1:3), referring to the Spirit as the location *in* which the Christian reaches fulfillment (see 2:22; 3:5; 6:18).[41] This would be supported by the syntax of a parallel

---

[34] For the view that the disciples were in the temple on Pentecost, see the second textual note on 2:13.

[35] Cf. Eli the priest's incorrect supposition that Hannah was drunk with wine while she prayed in the temple (1 Sam 1:12–14).

[36] See "Paul's Trip to Jerusalem, Arrest, and Imprisonment (Acts 21:1–36)" in "The City of Ephesus and Paul's Relationship to It" in the introduction.

[37] E.g., πνεύματος ἁγίου, "filled *with* the Holy Spirit," in Acts 13:52. See also πνεύματος ἁγίου with the cognate verb πίμπλημι in Lk 1:15, 41, 67; Acts 2:4; 4:8; 9:17; 13:9 (similarly Sirach 48:12 [with ἐμπίπλημι]; Acts 4:31). Cf. the double accusative construction with ἐμπίπλημι in LXX Ex 31:3; 35:31.

[38] Wallace, *Greek Grammar*, 171, cites Lk 2:40; Rom 1:29; 2 Cor 7:4. He also points to the textual variant in Lk 2:40 that substitutes the genitive for the dative, indicating that the scribe was uncomfortable with the grammar (93, n. 62). Cf. Sirach 39:6.

[39] LXX Micah 3:8: ἐγὼ ἐμπλήσω ἰσχὺν ἐν πνεύματι κυρίου, "I will fill up with strength *in the Spirit* of the Lord," demonstrates that the ἐν πνεύματι construction can indicate something other than contents. Cf. the variant reading πεπληρωμένοι in Col 4:12. On the other hand, BDAG, s.v. πληρόω, 1 b, notes the superscription of Ignatius, *To the Smyrnaeans*, as a parallel: "filled *with* faith and love [πεπληρωμένη ἐν πίστει καὶ ἀγάπῃ]."

[40] Wallace, *Greek Grammar*, 375. BDAG, s.v. πληρόω, 1 b, notes the problem and suggests that meaning 3 might apply: "to bring to completion in/by the Spirit." Wallace's concern (94) is that this verse would seem to be the only NT example of a *command* to be filled with the Spirit (rather than a description). As such it has taken a prominent role among charismatics, who teach that Christians must seek extraordinary gifts of the Spirit beyond and/or apart from his indwelling through the work of Holy Baptism and the other divinely instituted means of grace (the Word in Scripture, preaching, absolution, and Lord's Supper).

[41] Cf. Mk 1:8; Rom 8:9; 14:17; 15:16; 1 Cor 12:3, 13; Rev 1:10; passim.

in Colossians, speaking of Christ, "you have been brought to fulfillment *in* him [ἐστὲ ἐν αὐτῷ πεπληρωμένοι]" (Col 2:10).[42]

On the other hand, the few uses of the simple dative with πληρόω are sufficient to cast doubt on the contention that ἐν plus the dative cannot express contents. The language of being filled with the Spirit (Acts 2:4) and the pouring out of the Spirit (Acts 2:16–18) upon the apostles at Pentecost (which event is evoked by the language of this verse) suggest that Paul might indeed be thinking of the Holy Spirit as the one who takes up residence in the baptized and fills him. This interpretation would also be supported by the characterization of John the Baptizer as one who (like a Nazirite) will "not drink wine" but instead "will be filled *with* the Holy Spirit [πνεύματος ἁγίου πλησθήσεται]" (Lk 1:15). As long as the Holy Spirit is properly understood as a divine person, not a substance, the difference between the two interpretations is minimal.[43]

In any case, the role of the Spirit in Paul's thought is clear: because they are baptized (5:14), the Ephesians are filled up *in* and *with* the Spirit, who makes them wise in the Word of God (5:15–17) and leads them to acts of worship and submission (5:19–21).

5:19 λαλοῦντες ἑαυτοῖς [ἐν] ψαλμοῖς καὶ ὕμνοις καὶ ᾠδαῖς πνευματικαῖς, ᾄδοντες καὶ ψάλλοντες τῇ καρδίᾳ ὑμῶν τῷ κυρίῳ—The participle λαλοῦντες is dependent on the imperative πληροῦσθε in the previous verse: "*be filled* with/by the Spirit … *in such a way that* you speak to one another …"[44] It is the Holy Spirit who gives rise to right worship. In line with Paul's preference in this chapter for groups of three,[45] he contrasts the false worship of pagans (5:3–5) with a threefold description of the right use of words in the Christian liturgy. This patterning suggests there might be no clear distinction between the three nouns for Christian song, though the question is intriguing for students of early Christian worship.

The first of the three nouns is ψαλμός, which can mean "song of praise" and therefore might be just another word for a Christian hymn. But with few exceptions, in the Greek OT ψαλμός refers to the hymnal of the OT, the book of Psalms.[46] Since the NT follows this usage in the clearest examples,[47] it is likely that references to ψαλμοί in

---

[42] Cf. "faithful is the Father in Jesus Christ to fulfill my petition [πιστὸς ὁ πατὴρ ἐν Ἰησοῦ Χριστῷ πληρῶσαί μου τὴν αἴτησιν]" (Ignatius, *To the Trallians*, 13:3).

[43] Schnackenburg, *Ephesians*, 237: "Christians should allow themselves to be filled *by* the Spirit (instrumental use of ἐν) and at the same time *with* him." Best, *Ephesians*, 508: "The Spirit is the real subject of the verb, 'Let the Spirit fill you' when you gather for worship."

[44] We therefore take the participles as adverbial/circumstantial, indicating manner, answering the question "how?" (with Schlier, *Epheser*, 246). Wallace, *Greek Grammar*, 639, concludes that the participles in 5:19–21 indicate result.

[45] For other verses in this chapter with a group of three items, see 5:3, 4, 5, 9, 14. See further "Rhythm" in "Orality and the Interpretation of the Epistles: A Brief Introduction" in the introduction.

[46] LXX 2 Kgdms 23:1 (MT/ET 2 Sam 23:1); seventy-two times in the Psalms; Is 66:20; Zech 6:14; Judith 16:1; 3 Macc 6:35.

[47] See ψαλμός, "psalm," in Lk 20:42; 24:44; Acts 1:20; 13:33. Cf. also ὑμνέω, "sing hymns/psalms" (Acts 16:25; Heb 2:12), which in the context of Mt 26:30 (‖ Mk 14:26) may refer to Jesus and the disciples singing the Hallel (Psalms 113–118), as the singing of these psalms after the meal was a traditional part of the Jewish Passover Seder. For early Jewish evidence

Christian worship refer to "psalms" (1 Cor 14:26 [where it occurs in the singular]; Col 3:16). The earliest patristic literature demonstrates that Christians sang the Psalms in their Divine Service.[48] It is not clear, however, that the cognate verb ψάλλω ("psalming," 5:19b) always refers specifically to psalm singing. Originally it referred to the "plucking" of the strings of an accompanying instrument (e.g., harp),[49] but came to refer more broadly to music making, with or without instruments.[50] There are therefore three possibilities for the meaning of the two participles ᾄδοντες and ψάλλοντες in the present verse: (1) they refer respectively to "singing" and "playing instrumental music (or accompanied singing)";[51] (2) they refer respectively to "singing [Christian] hymns" and "singing the OT psalms"; and (3) they are near synonyms with little distinction, "singing and making melody."

The second noun, ὕμνος, *hymnos*, is a religious song, from which the English word "hymn" is derived. The present verse and its parallel (Col 3:16) contain its only NT occurrences, though it is frequent in the LXX, where it often refers to the psalms of David.[52] The third noun, ᾠδή, is a near synonym with less explicitly religious

---

of the singing of psalms while the second temple still stood (as it did in Paul's day), see Emil Schürer, *The History of the Jewish People in the Age of Jesus Christ* (new English ed.; Edinburgh: T&T Clark, 1979), 2:303–4, including n. 41.

[48] Basil, Epistle 207:3, says this of the Christians: ἀντιψάλλουσιν ἀλλήλοις, "they sing psalms antiphonally with one another" (PG 32:764A; cf. *NPNF*[2] 8:247). *Apostolic Constitutions*, 2:57, and Augustine, Sermon 176:1, describe psalms sung in response to the Scripture readings. The *Church History* of Socrates, 6:8, claims that Ignatius of Antioch introduced the custom of antiphonal psalm singing, on the basis of a vision of heaven. The more mundane probability is that early Christians simply continued the practice of the temple and synagogue.

[49] LXX 1 Kgdms 16:16–17, 23; 19:9 (MT/ET 1 Sam 16:16–17, 23; 19:9); 4 Kgdms 3:15 (MT/ET 2 Ki 3:15); Pss 32:2 (MT/ET 33:2); 70:22 (MT/ET 71:22); 97:5 (MT/ET 98:5); 143:9 (MT/ET 144:9); 146:7 (MT/ET 147:7); 149:3. Cf. ψαλμός as "playing the harp" in LXX 1 Kgdms 16:18 (MT/ET 1 Sam 16:18); Job 21:12; 30:31; Amos 5:23.

[50] LXX 2 Kgdms 22:50 (MT/ET 2 Sam 22:50). Of forty-five occurrences of ψάλλω in LXX Psalms, the majority are a reference to the activity of singing the psalms themselves (e.g., LXX Pss 7:18 [ET 7:17]; 9:3, 12 [ET 9:2, 11]; 12:6 [MT/ET 13:6]). The other three NT occurrences (Rom 15:9; 1 Cor 14:15; James 5:13) are indeterminate.

[51] In support of the possibility that Paul had accompaniment with the harp in mind, see 1 Cor 14:7 (written from Ephesus); Rev 5:8 (written near Ephesus); and the imagery of Ignatius, *To the Ephesians*, 4:1: "For your justly renowned presbytery, worthy of God, is fitted as exactly to the bishop as the strings are to the harp. Therefore in your concord and harmonious love, Jesus Christ is sung." The seal of Polycrates, bishop of Ephesus in AD 190, included a harp. See John Foster, "The Harp at Ephesus," *Expository Times* 74 (1962–1963): 156, citing Clement of Alexandria, *The Instructor*, 3:11.

[52] E.g., LXX 2 Chr 7:6; Neh 12:46; 1 Macc 4:33; 2 Macc 1:30. The plural of ὕμνος is frequently used in the title of the canonical psalms (LXX Pss 53:1 [MT 54:1; ET superscription of Psalm 54]; 54:1 [MT 55:1; ET superscription]; 60:1 [MT 61:1; ET superscription]; 66:1 [MT 67:1; ET superscription]; 71:20 [MT/ET 72:20]; 75:1 [MT 76:1; ET superscription]) and the psalms of Solomon (superscription of Psalms of Solomon 10; 14; 16). Note also the combination of the verb ψάλλω and the noun ὕμνος in ὕμνον καινὸν ψάλατε τῷ θεῷ, "sing/psalm a new hymn to God" (Ps Sol 3:1). The cognate verb ὑμνέω likely refers to singing psalms (Mt 26:30 ‖ Mk 14:26; Acts 16:25; Heb 2:12); see the footnote that discusses these verses in the discussion on ψαλμός above.

associations, though it frequently appears coupled with ὕμνος in the LXX.[53] The combination of the three nouns in LXX Ps 66:1 (ἐν ὕμνοις· ψαλμὸς ᾠδῆς; MT 67:1; ET superscription)[54] further suggests that no significant distinction should be made.[55] In fact, it may be historically accurate to view "psalms and hymns and songs" as a category referring first and foremost to the canonical psalms as the hymnal of the early church; second, to other biblical canticles; and third, to newly written Christian hymns, of which there is some evidence in Ephesians itself (5:14).[56] Thus, Paul himself models the use of psalms (4:8) and hymns to edify the church in this very letter.

The adjective πνευματικαῖς, "spiritual," is not restrictive, implying that some Christian songs are "spiritual," while others (such as the aforementioned biblical psalms) are not. Neither does "spiritual" imply unintelligible "speaking in tongues,"[57] since they are addressed ἑαυτοῖς, "to one another," which implies the corporate edification that this letter has so often stressed. Nor is there any reason to believe it means only songs that are uttered ecstatically or spontaneously.[58] Inasmuch as the previous verse has spoken of the Holy Spirit as the one who fills all Christians (5:18) and thus enables them to sing, the adjective should best be understood as modifying all three nouns (ψαλμοῖς καὶ ὕμνοις καὶ ᾠδαῖς)[59] and indicating that they are all songs inspired by the Holy Spirit: "psalms and hymns and songs that are [all] of the Spirit."

This, then, informs the meaning of the phrase τῇ καρδίᾳ ὑμῶν, "in/with your heart," which refers not to internal, silent worship, but to the heart as the instrument of true worship inasmuch as the heart of the baptized is the dwelling place of the Spirit

---

[53] LXX 2 Chr 7:6; Pss 66:1 (MT 67:1; ET superscription of Psalm 67); 75:1 (MT 76:1; ET superscription of Psalm 76); 136:3 (MT/ET 137:3); 1 Macc 13:51.

[54] That Greek might be rendered literally as "in hymns; a psalm of a song." It translates the Hebrew words בִּנְגִינֹת מִזְמוֹר שִׁיר: in the superscription of Psalm 67. The first Hebrew word may mean "with stringed instruments," and the next two words stand in apposition as synonyms, "a psalm; a song."

[55] Lincoln, *Ephesians*, 346: "The three terms used here are best seen as another example of this writer's fondness for piling up synonyms. ... They are the three most common terms in the LXX for religious songs and occur there interchangeably in the titles of the psalms." See also ᾠδή and ὕμνος in Josephus, *Antiquities*, 7:305, and ὕμνος and ψαλμός in *Antiquities*, 12:323.

[56] Cf., e.g., Phil 2:5–11; Col 1:15–20; 1 Tim 3:16; Rev 4:11; 5:9–10, 12, 13; 14:3–4; 15:3–4. The Gospel canticles (Magnificat, Lk 1:46b–55; Benedictus, Lk 1:68–79; Nunc Dimittis, Lk 2:29–32), used in the daily office from earliest times, should probably be included in this category of "psalms and hymns and songs of the Spirit" as well. The book of Odes, found in most manuscripts of the LXX after the book of Psalms, is likely a Christian collection and gives evidence that such "hymnals" were produced in earliest times.

[57] In 1 Cor 14:15 Paul speaks of singing (ψάλλω) "with the Spirit ... and with my mind" in contrast to praying in a tongue (1 Cor 14:14).

[58] The comment that "the expression 'speaking to one another' [5:19] suggests an intimate, spontaneous atmosphere for worship" (MacDonald, *Colossians and Ephesians*, 318) is without support in the text. Stoeckhardt is likewise guilty of anachronism when he reads Pietism into the text, describing the third element as "those spiritual, lovely songs, ... which were heard in the homes of the Christians," and suggests that "speaking to one another" refers to prayer group gatherings and social "get-togethers" (*Ephesians*, 238).

[59] The fact that πνευματικαῖς is feminine and agrees properly only with the third noun, ᾠδαῖς, is no deterrent, inasmuch as "attributives ... which belong to two or more connected substantives customarily agree with the nearest" (BDF, § 135 [3]).

(1:18; 3:16–17).[60] The Spirit's role, furthermore, is always to direct the heart towards "the Lord" (τῷ κυρίῳ)—which, in view of the use of κύριος in the next verse (5:20), probably refers to Christ, the usual referent of κύριος in the NT (rather than God the Father; see also the textual note on 5:17).

There is no contradiction between λαλοῦντες ἑαυτοῖς, "speaking to one another,"[61] and the Christ-directed conclusion to the verse.[62] True praise is not simply language of adoration directed to God. Praise involves the proclamation of God's mighty, saving deeds to one another within the royal priesthood (1 Pet 2:9). God is most pleased (praised) when Christians tell each other what he has done. Thus, the great praise songs of the Christian liturgy (such as the Gloria in Excelsis and the Agnus Dei) consist largely of the proclamation of the Gospel.

5:20 εὐχαριστοῦντες πάντοτε ὑπὲρ πάντων—The participle εὐχαριστοῦντες (like λαλοῦντες in 5:19) is dependent on the imperative πληροῦσθε in 5:18: "*be filled* with/by the Spirit … *in such a way that* you give thanks always …" As the adverb πάντοτε, "always," indicates, thanksgiving for the gifts of God is the Christian's constant pleasure and duty (1 Thess 5:18; 1 Tim 4:4).[63] Thanksgiving is the ever-appropriate antithesis to the filthy talk of pagans (εὐχαριστία, 5:4). However, in light of the language of pagan idolatry in the earlier part of the chapter (5:3–5) and the context of the previous verse (5:19), it is likely that Paul has something more specific in mind: the corporate thanksgiving of the church gathered in the Divine Service. Because of the prominence of the verb εὐχαριστέω, "give thanks," in the NT accounts of the institution of the Lord's Supper,[64] the Sacrament of the Altar came to be called "the Eucharist," "the Thanksgiving" par excellence, in early Christendom, already from early postapostolic

---

[60] Cf. Rom 5:5; 2 Cor 1:22; 3:3; Gal 4:6. Best, *Ephesians*, 513: "It comes from the deepest level of existence and is not purely emotional ('hearty') froth but contains considerable intellectual content."

[61] This should not be translated as "speaking to *themselves*," as in the self-edificatory form of glossolalia (1 Cor 14:28). The overlap of meanings between ἑαυτῶν, "themselves/one another," and ἀλλήλων, "one another," is apparent from Eph 4:32; Col 3:13, 16 (see Turner, *Syntax*, 43; BDF, § 287). Paul might be describing antiphonal singing (cf. Ezra 3:11). Pliny the Younger, *Epistles*, 10:96.7, reports that "they [the Christians] voiced by alternation [*secum invicem*] a hymn to Christ as to a god."

[62] Contra Lincoln, *Ephesians*, 345: "Its [the first participial clause's] focus in fact is not on praise of God. … It is significant that much of what is taken to be hymnic in the Pauline corpus has a didactic and paraenetic function." This presents a false dichotomy. True praise is at the same time didactic. It is perhaps significant that the "teaching" phrase found in the parallel Colossian text, "teaching and admonishing one another in all wisdom" (Col 3:16), is absent here. This subtle shift orients the Ephesian text more firmly toward divine praise and perhaps evidences a greater stress on the work of the office of the ministry in Ephesians.

[63] Cf. 1 Cor 1:4; Col 1:3, 12; 4:2; 1 Thess 1:2–3; 2 Thess 2:13; Philemon 4. The Proper Preface in the Western liturgical rite begins "it is truly good, right, and salutary that we should at all times and in all places give thanks to You …" (e.g., *LSB Altar Book*, 145) and then proceeds to identify the unique aspects of saving history for which God is thanked at this particular celebration of the Lord's Supper at this time in the church year.

[64] See the discussion of the use of εὐχαριστέω and εὐλογέω in the Words of Institution in "The *Berakah* Prayer: Background and Parallels" in the commentary on 1:3–14.

times.[65] Thus, while Paul might not be saying narrowly, "celebrating the Lord's Supper," the thanksgiving prayers surrounding the Lord's Supper are probably the chief example of the εὐχαριστοῦντες, "giving thanks," that Paul has in mind (cf. 1 Cor 14:16–17). Such thanksgiving prayers would not only have referred to the Lord's Supper itself, but would have also included the many supplications and thanksgivings that comprise the (general) prayer of the church (cf. Phil 4:6; 1 Tim 2:1). Thus, in contrast to the foul language and drunken orgies of pagan worship, Paul directs the Ephesian Christians to a pattern of worship in the Holy Spirit that is Christ-centered and consists of the wholesome words of psalm-singing and sacramental thanksgiving.

ἐν ὀνόματι τοῦ κυρίου ἡμῶν Ἰησοῦ Χριστοῦ τῷ θεῷ καὶ πατρί—The formulaic conclusion to the verse, "in the name of our Lord Jesus Christ to [our] God and Father" gives the passage a Trinitarian frame with "Spirit" in 5:18, 19 and evokes the Trinitarian pattern of liturgical prayer with which Paul began the letter (1:3). The *Berakah* prayer (1:3–14) is a classic example of what Paul means by a prayer of thanksgiving. The distinct roles given to each divine person in this section demonstrate the contours of the Holy Trinity: the Holy Spirit inspires Christians to give thanks through the name of Christ to the Father (cf. Col 3:17). All Christian worship is in the name of Jesus.[66]

5:21 ὑποτασσόμενοι ἀλλήλοις …—Like the participles λαλοῦντες in 5:19 and εὐχαριστοῦντες in 5:20, the participle ὑποτασσόμενοι, "being subordinate," is one of manner and should be understood as dependent on the imperative πληροῦσθε in 5:18. The meaning is "*be filled* by/with the Spirit … *in such a way that* you are subordinate to one another …" This verse forms a bridge into the next section (5:21–6:9) and will be treated in greater detail there; see the textual notes and the commentary on 5:21 in the next pericope, 5:21b–33.

Commentary
Structure and Rhetoric

The basic structure of this pericope is a series of stark antitheses, whose oppositions continue the vital contrasts between the old pagan life and the new life of the baptized that have characterized Paul's language since as far back as chapter 2.[67] What began there as a contrast between "then" and "now"[68] was continued in the immediately preceding pericope (5:3–14) in oppositions of pagan versus Christian life based on darkness versus light.[69] It is, in fact, mis-

---

[65] Ignatius, *To the Ephesians* 13:1; Ignatius, *To the Philadelphians* 4:1; Ignatius, *To the Smyrnaeans* 7:1; 8:1. See also *Didache*, 9:1, 5; 10:7; 14:1; Justin Martyr, *First Apology*, 66:1; 67:5; Origen, *Against Celsus*, 8:57.20. This is synecdoche of a part for the whole; the entire Sacrament is referred to by the name of one prominent part or by its opening words.

[66] Mt 18:20; 1 Cor 5:4; 6:11; Phil 2:10; Col 3:17.

[67] See 2:1–5, 11–13, 19–22; 4:17–31; 5:3–14.

[68] See "once/then" (ποτέ) and/or "now" (νῦν) in 2:2, 3, 11, 13; 3:5, 10; 5:8, 29 (cf. 2:4; 4:17). See the table contrasting "then" with "now" in "Structure and Rhetoric" in the commentary on 2:11–22.

[69] See the table in "Structure and Rhetoric" as well as the section entitled "Darkness Has No Fellowship with Light" in the commentary on 5:3–14.

leading to separate the present pericope greatly from the previous one, except for the convenience of interpreting a more modest unit here. The language of περιπατέω, "to walk" (5:15), ties these verses tightly to the preceding (5:8).[70] So too does the expanded description of the Spirit-filled words of worship and thanksgiving (compare 5:19–20 with 5:3–5). The present pericope continues the antitheses of the previous one with a contrast of two ways of "walking" rooted in language of wisdom and worship:

"not" (μή, 5:15)	"but" (ἀλλά, 5:15)
"un-wise" (ἄ-σοφοι, 5:15a)	"wise" (σοφοί, 5:15b)
"the days are evil" (5:16b)	"redeeming the time" (5:16a)
"un-thinking, foolish" (ἄ-φρονες, 5:17a)	"understand … the will of the Lord" (5:17b)
"do not get drunk with wine" (5:18a)	"be filled up in the Spirit" (5:18b)

With the final opposition ("wine" versus "Spirit," 5:18) Paul shifts the balance toward the new life in the Spirit. Instead of continuing to attack the old life, he expands his description of the new with three statements in 5:19–21. Each begins with a Greek participle and unpacks what it means to "be filled up in the Spirit" (5:18):

[19]speaking [λαλοῦντες] to one another in ⸢psalms and hymns and songs⸣ of the Spirit,
    singing and psalming with your heart to the Lord,
[20]giving thanks [εὐχαριστοῦντες] always for all things in the name of our Lord Jesus Christ to [our] God and Father,
[21]being subordinate [ὑποτασσόμενοι] to one another in the fear of Christ

This unit is patterned in threes at multiple levels. First, there are three main participial clauses in 5:19–21, each of which is dependent on the imperative "be filled up" (5:18). Second, Paul uses three near-synonyms for songs, "psalms and hymns and songs" (5:19). It is possible, though difficult, to make distinctions among the three Greek terms in ψαλμοῖς καὶ ὕμνοις καὶ ᾠδαῖς, but Paul is probably more interested in the rhythm and pattern of the triad.[71] Third, in 5:19 he supplements the first participle (λαλοῦντες) with two more (ᾄδοντες καὶ ψάλλοντες) to make another threesome: "speaking … singing and psalming," the latter two participles being explanatory of the first. Finally, "of the Spirit" (5:19; see also "Spirit" in 5:18), together with the clause in 5:20, gives the unit an explicitly

---

[70] See also περιπατέω, "to walk," previously in 2:2, 10; 4:1, 17; 5:2, 8. See the first textual note on 2:2 and the third textual note on 4:1, as well as the relevant textual notes and the commentary on the other verses. The commentary on 4:17–5:2 is titled "The Baptismal Walk: Clothed in Christ."

[71] The author of Ephesians "never objects to using three words where one would suffice" (Best, *Ephesians*, 511).

Trinitarian pattern. It is by being filled with the Spirit that the baptized are able to give thanks to God the Father through the name of Jesus (5:20).[72] No doubt, then, the threefold patterns are intended by Paul as Trinitarian.[73]

The inclusion of 5:21 at the close of *this* pericope requires some explanation. The primary punctuation of NA[27] and most modern versions attach 5:21 to what follows. Various interpretations of the participle ὑποτασσόμενοι, "being subordinate," will be considered in the next pericope (5:21b–33), including the possibility that it stands independently of what comes before. The lack of a verb in 5:22 invites the attachment of 5:21 to what follows it. Some interpreters also note how 5:20 forms a sort of doxological termination to 5:3–20 or 5:15–20: "in the name of our Lord Jesus Christ to [our] God and Father." Full stop.[74]

However, two considerations favor the inclusion of 5:21 here. First, the natural grammatical interpretation of the three main participial clauses in 5:19–21 that flow in neat and parallel succession to the imperative πληροῦσθε, "be filled up" (5:18), is that they are all dependent upon it and belong together. The three participles describe three activities the Holy Spirit inspires ("speaking … giving thanks … being subordinate"). Second, by including 5:21 with the preceding, we follow the interpretation of the *kephalaia* (marked by numerals in the NA[27] inner margin), which represent the section divisions of the great fourth century AD manuscripts. By appending "being subordinate" (5:21) to the inspiration of the Spirit (5:18), the Christian's humble submission to God's order is rooted not just in the realm of Law (command) but also in the Gospel (gift). We submit because God has changed our hearts, has filled them with the Spirit; submission flows naturally from this regeneration.

Nevertheless, 5:21 certainly serves a dual purpose and will be taken as a hinge verse, both concluding the preceding unit (5:3–21 or 5:15–21) and serving as a heading for the three sections of *Haustafel* ("table of duties") that follow in 5:22–6:9. From 5:3 to the end of Ephesians, the pericopal divisions become decidedly murkier.

Watch Carefully How You Walk

In the final chapters of Ephesians the verb περιπατέω holds a prominent place, framing and permeating the three pericopes leading up to the present one (4:1, 17; 5:2, 8, 15; also 2:2, 10). This OT image is more significant than the vocabulary of exhortation (παρακαλέω, "encourage; exhort"), which occurs only twice in Ephesians (4:1; 6:22). While the second half of Ephesians cannot be summarized simplistically as "exhortation,"[75] if the full range and complex-

---

[72] See also the threefold κύριος, "Lord," in 5:17, 19, 20.

[73] For Paul's penchant for using groups of three throughout Ephesians, see "Rhythm" in "Orality and the Interpretation of the Epistles: A Brief Introduction" in the introduction.

[74] E.g., Lincoln, *Ephesians*, 338.

[75] See "Doctrine and Ethics, Gospel and Law? (4:1–16 in the Context of the Epistle)" in "Structure and Rhetoric" in the commentary on 4:1–16. See also "Epistolary Outline" in "Structure and Rhetoric" in the introduction.

ity of "walking" is considered, "the baptismal walk" might be a fair précis of these chapters.[76] The OT source of the image is further qualified and established by the "wisdom" language of 5:15–17. While the wisdom of God has been prominent in Ephesians (1:8, 17; 3:10; 5:15), together with the language of "knowledge" (1:9–10, 18; 3:1–13, 19; 4:13), Paul is not simply repeating his own words but drawing again on OT Wisdom literature, including the psalms to which he explicitly refers (5:19). The central tenet of that literature is perhaps best expressed by Ps 119:105, "your Word is a lamp to my feet and a light to my path," from which thought pattern Paul has drawn both the darkness/light contrast of the previous pericope (5:3–14) and the "walking" pattern of the present one.[77]

The transition from 5:14 to 5:15 through the verb βλέπετε, "watch!" (5:15) is thereby illuminated. Because the Ephesian Christians have become enlightened through Christ's shining upon them in Holy Baptism (5:14; cf. 1:18; 4:5), they are now able to see clearly how they should walk (5:15). Concretely, this means that God's Word has made them "wise" (5:15), and by the continual application of that Word they will be able to see what they should believe and do. They are no longer frozen on the spot by fear of the surrounding darkness, but through the light of the Word that first shone on them they can redeem the time, make their way through the dark world by shining that light and displacing the devil's lordship over the present evil days (5:16). The Word gives insight into the very mind of God, so that the Christian need not flail around blindly when seeking to follow his will (5:17). This determinedly Word-based view of the Christian life prompts Luther, in his early preaching on the text, to direct the Christian to the simple contents of the catechism:

> Then be careful to avail yourself of the present opportunity. Embrace it while he [God] is near, and faithfully consider what he requires of you. To ascertain this, go to the Creed and the Ten Commandments. They will tell you. Regulate your life by them. Be helped by the Lord's Prayer. Begin with yourself; then pray for the Church. Let it be your desire that God's name be everywhere sanctified and that your life conform to his will. If you are faithful in these things, assuredly you will walk wisely; you will avoid sin and do good.[78]

The inclusion of the Creed in Luther's exhortation reminds us that "to walk" begins with "to believe/trust." Walking in the light of the Lord's Word cannot be reduced to a pattern of behavior that is expected of those whom God has redeemed—a simplistic Gospel-Law sequence that we have rejected in

---

[76] The commentary on 4:17–5:2 is titled "The Baptismal Walk: Clothed in Christ."

[77] In addition to the OT language of "walking" (הָלַךְ), also relevant are the many terms for "way" and "path" that abound in the Psalms and Proverbs, particularly the theme of the two contrasting ways (e.g., Psalms 1; 119; Proverbs 1–9), the way of wisdom/righteousness/life/the Lord (Prov 3:17; 4:11; 6:23; 8:20; 10:29) and the way of folly/evil/death/Sheol (Prov 2:12–13; 4:14; 5:5; 7:27; 12:15).

[78] Luther, "Sermon for the Twentieth Sunday after Trinity, Ephesians 5:15–21," October 29, 1536, Lenker, 8:323; StL 12:929–30, § 13.

analyzing the letter's structure.[79] Inasmuch as the shining of Christ's light was introduced in the baptismal hymn (5:14) as the point of rebirth, "walking" in the light of God's Word is an allegory of the *entire* new life, viewed from the perspective of both faith and deeds. Neither may be separated from the other. The Christian life cannot be analyzed merely by the criterion of obedience to God's Law, as if wisdom were only the knowledge of what God expects us to do, and not the knowledge of his person and trust in him.[80] So also faith cannot be detached from continual repentance for sin and the resolve to fight against it, as if the Christian might consider himself above God's Law and plunge headlong into sin with the excuse that he is nonetheless forgiven (Romans 6).

The previous and present pericopes (5:3–14 and 5:15–21) therefore consist of both warning and exhortation from Paul. It is a twofold warning neither to return to the life that the Gentile Ephesians lived before Holy Baptism, consisting in idolatry, lust, and filthy talk (5:3–5), nor to join those currently outside the fellowship of Christ's body in worldly belief and behavior (5:5–13). And it is an exhortation to take up the Word of God as a beacon, both shining on the path in front of the Christian on his pilgrimage and illuminating the Christian's inner being. There it exposes disobedience, false belief, and despair and also nourishes faith and deeds, like the sun giving growth to the seedling of the Word's planting. In other words, the Christian's walk in the light of God is characterized both by trust in God engendered by his Word (cf. Pss 40:5 [ET 40:4]; 111:7; 119:42) and the desire to obey the precepts of his Law (cf. Pss 19:9 [ET 19:8]; 119:40, 104).

The elderly Luther, wearied both by the antinomians and by the lethargic Wittenberg Christians who took for granted the hard-fought knowledge of the Gospel, preached the Law with full force against those Christians who, like the rhetorical foes of Romans 6, would use the Gospel as a pretense to continue sinning:

> This Epistle [lesson, Eph 5:15–20] admonishes [us] that, after we have become Christians and have been enlightened with faith through the Word, we should live as Christians and beware of everything that might hinder and draw us away from Christian life. For it is not the case with a Christian that once he believes the Word and has been baptized into the Lord, who [shed His] precious [blood], we should live without a care according to our own pleasure, as if everything were all taken care of, snoring and slumbering away, [saying:] "I am baptized and have the Gospel. I will leave it at that and live without any care whatsoever"—as if he did not dare to do anything. That is not enough. This abomination has intruded more and more over time. We say, "But I am a Christian; I believe; I am baptized; and I can talk all about it too"—and we

---

[79] Again, see "Doctrine and Ethics, Gospel and Law? (4:1–16 in the Context of the Epistle)" in "Structure and Rhetoric" in the commentary on 4:1–16. See also "Epistolary Outline" in "Structure and Rhetoric" in the introduction.

[80] Already in the OT, the Wisdom literature emphasizes trust (faith) in the Lord as the key to walking in the right way/paths, e.g., Pss 26:1; 37:3–5; Prov 3:5–6.

become presumptuous and lazy spirits, who do not ripen but fall [from the tree] like wormy fruit.

"No," says Paul, "we were not called and baptized in order that we might be careless, lazy, negligent, and do nothing, even though you may say, 'I am a believer; I have the Gospel.'" Rather, he says: "You should take heed that you do not snore and sleep, as if you could be saved even with your presumption and dissolute life, [saying]: 'It will not do me any harm. I am a Christian; the remission of sins is such a great thing that now [sins] are no great matter.'"[81]

The Liturgy of the Spirit-Filled Baptized

In previous pericopes we have noted Paul's frequent recourse to "liturgical" language,[82] perhaps prompted by the protracted pastoral relationship Paul had with the Ephesians over the course of a three-year ministry.[83] Ephesus was a place where, more than any other, Paul would have baptized, absolved, preached, and presided at the Lord's Supper.[84] It was therefore unsurprising that the letter began with a *Berakah* prayer (1:3–14), which not only built on OT prototypes but also echoed eucharistic praying in early postapostolic literature.[85] So also his exuberant outburst of praise in response to the revelation of God's mysteries (3:20–21) resonates with the formal language of public prayer, while he frequently refers to his ongoing pastoral petitions for his flock (1:15–23; 3:14–19; cf. 6:18–20). It seems that when Paul thinks of the Ephesians, he pictures them as a congregation gathered around Word, Sacrament, and prayer. He imagines the reading of his letter slotting neatly into these public gatherings.

By calling the language of Ephesians "liturgical," we mean that it bears itself with the dignity of these reverential public gatherings around the holy things of God and is suffused with the substance of his gracious gifts. Paul does not simply envision the Christian life as a personal affair between the believer and God, nor is it just about conducting oneself through the world in accord with Scripture. God's Word, applied to the individual in Holy Baptism and speaking to him ever thereafter, leads the baptized into the liturgy.[86] The individual is

---

81 Luther, "Sermon for the Twentieth Sunday after Trinity, Ephesians 5:15–20," October 18, 1545, AE 58:295; WA 51:60–61.

82 In the introduction, see "Liturgical Context" in "Evaluation of the Case" in "Authorship," as well as "The Liturgical Context of the New Testament Epistles" in "Orality and the Interpretation of the Epistles: A Brief Introduction." See also the commentary on 1:1.

83 See "Paul and Ephesus in Acts" in "The City of Ephesus and Paul's Relationship to It" in the introduction.

84 For Baptism, see the textual notes and the commentary on, e.g., 1:13, 18; 2:5; 4:4–6, 22–24, 30; 5:7, 14, 26. For allusions to the Lord's Supper, see the textual notes and the commentary on, e.g., 1:7; 4:4; 5:3–20, 29–31; 6:18–24; this commentary perceives a eucharistic quality to the prayers in 1:3–14 and 3:14–21.

85 See the discussion in "The *Berakah* Prayer: Background and Parallels" in the commentary on 1:3–14.

86 Thus, we use the term λειτουργία, "liturgy," not in the derived and inaccurate modern sense of "order of service," which is more properly called "rite," but in the original Greek sense of the term that can properly occur only in the singular, as defined by Melanchthon in the Apology:

led by the Spirit of God into the fellowship of Christ's body, into communion with him and all his members. Paul's categories of thinking do not move simply in the domains of faith and works, but press on into the realm of worship. One might say that worship is the ultimate work to which the Spirit leads the baptized by his nourishment and inner motivation. But worship is also the place where faith itself is engendered and strengthened by God's continual giving of his Son through his Word and Christ's body and blood. It is heaven on earth for the baptized, a foretaste of the eschatological goal, a radical alternative to the darkness of the world and the godlessness of the old pagan life.

The divide of Ephesians into supposed doctrinal and ethical halves (debunked earlier[87]) is thus not only simplistic, unsupported by the linguistic evidence, and a confusion of the roles of Law and Gospel, but more significantly, perhaps, an analysis that would cut off Paul's argument before it reaches its goal. Consider the stark alternatives with which Paul began the previous unit:

> [3]But let not sexual immorality and all uncleanness or lust even be named among you, as is fitting for saints
> [4]nor shamefulness and foolish talk or coarse jokes, which are not fitting,
> but rather <u>thanksgiving</u>.
> [5]For know this with certainty: no sexually immoral or unclean or lustful person (that is, an <u>idolater</u>) has an inheritance in the kingdom of Christ and God. (5:3–5)

The shameful and foolish talk is not simply characterized as sinful or inappropriate for Christians, countered by a corresponding exhortation to wholesome talk. Rather, Paul paints it with the brush of idolatry—false worship—and offers the alternative of "thanksgiving" (εὐχαριστία, *eucharistia*, 5:4).

Eph 5:19–20, with "giving thanks" (εὐχαριστοῦντες), might well be understood as an expansion of that earlier exhortation (5:4). Where previously Paul merely pointed to the act of thanksgiving, in the wake of his rejoicing in the gifts of enlightenment and resurrection in Holy Baptism (5:14), he can now

---

But let us talk about the term "liturgy" [Greek: λειτουργία, as Melanchthon notes at the beginning of Ap 24:79]. It does not really mean a sacrifice but a public service [*publicum ministerium*; *Triglotta*, 411, translates the phrase as "the public ministry"]. Thus it squares with our position that a minister who consecrates shows forth the body and blood of the Lord to the people, just as a minister who preaches shows forth the gospel to the people, as Paul says (I Cor. 4:1), "This is how one should regard us, as ministers of Christ and dispensers of the sacraments of God [*dispensatores sacramentorum Dei*]," that is, of the Word [*evangelii*, "Gospel"] and sacraments; and II Cor. 5:20, "We are ambassadors for Christ, God making his appeal through us. We beseech you on behalf of Christ, be reconciled to God."

Thus the term "liturgy" [λειτουργία] squares well with the ministry [*ministerium*]. (Ap 24:79–81)

[87] Once again, see "Doctrine and Ethics, Gospel and Law? (4:1–16 in the Context of the Epistle)" in "Structure and Rhetoric" in the commentary on 4:1–16. See also "Epistolary Outline" in "Structure and Rhetoric" in the introduction.

root the exhortation in the fullness of the Holy Spirit, in whom the baptized now reside (5:18b). Because they are filled in and with the Holy Spirit, the Ephesian Christians can worship the Triune God rightly and from the heart. This includes the singing of psalms and canticles and hymns (5:19) in a kind of anti-drunkenness that arises not from "spirits" (an English double entendre that encompasses both wine and demons), but from the Holy Spirit.[88] Luther's boisterous take on the text captures the image Paul has in mind:

> That is to say: hear the Word and become inebriated with it, so that you sing—not indecent songs like peasants in the tavern—[but] those who are drunken [must] sing. You sing like this: "Blessed be the Lord [the Benedictus]," or the psalms, in which you give thanks to God. Praise God, so that it may resound to heaven [and] the devil may flee. Sing with your whole heart like those in the beer hall. Be inebriated in such a way that you sing in the name [of God]; that is fitting for you. [Sing] like the martyrs, those fine Christians [who said,] "You are leading me to prison, but it seems to me as if you were leading me to a dance."[89]

Ironically, for the average Christian not (yet) blessed with martyrdom, the songs of rejoicing Paul has in mind lead not *to* death but *from* death, from the death of Christ that leads to the prayers of thanksgiving centered on the reception of his body and blood in the meal the early church came to call "the Thanksgiving (Eucharist)."[90]

---

[88] Cf. "Eat, friends! Drink and be drunk with love!" (Song 5:1); cf. Mitchell, *The Song of Songs*, 872–73, including n. 197.

[89] Luther, "Sermon for the Twentieth Sunday after Trinity, Ephesians 5:15–20," October 18, 1545, AE 58:302; WA 51:67. Luther has in mind the stories of early martyrs who sang hymns all the way to their deaths. This sermon excerpt, incidentally, puts to lie the myth that Luther put sacred words to drinking songs. The devil's tunes are not borrowed but steadfastly shunned and replaced with holy songs. This principle was also observed in the early church, which refused to let the world's culture invade its worship or piety. Chrysostom, for example: "Do you wish to be happy? Do you want to know how to spend the day truly blessed? … Learn to sing psalms! Then you will see pleasure indeed. Those who have learned to sing with the psalms are easily filled with the Holy Spirit. But if you sing only the devil's songs you will soon find yourself filled with an unclean spirit" (*Homilies on Ephesians*, 19:5.19–21, ACCS 8:191–92).

[90] See the first textual note on 5:20.

The Gospel in God's Order:
The Bridegroom and the Bride

Translation

5   ... [21]being subordinate to one another in the <u>fear</u> of Christ:

> [22]wives to their own husbands as to the Lord,
>> [23]for the husband is the head of the wife as also Christ is head of the church,
>>> he himself [being] the Savior of the body;
>> [24]but as the church is subordinate to Christ,
> thus also wives to [their] husbands in all things.

> [25]Husbands, love [your] wives, just as also Christ loved the church and gave himself up for her,
>> [26]that he might sanctify her by cleansing [her] with the washing of water in the Word,
>>> [27]that he himself might present the church to himself as glorious,
>>>> not having a spot or wrinkle or any of such things,
>>>> but that she might be holy and without blemish.
> [28]Thus, husbands, too, ought to love their own wives as their own bodies. He who loves his own wife loves himself. [29]For no one ever hated his own flesh, but nourishes and cherishes it, just as also Christ the church, [30]for we are members of his body.

> [31]"For this reason a man will leave father and mother and cleave to his wife, and the two will become one flesh." [32]This mystery is great; but I say [it refers] to Christ and to the church.

> [33]In any case, every one of you also: let each love his own wife as himself, and let the wife respect/<u>fear</u> [her] husband.

Textual Notes

5:21 ὑποτασσόμενοι ἀλλήλοις—The arguments for attaching this participial clause to the imperative verb in 5:18 have been introduced previously[1] and are taken up again in this pericope in "Structure and Rhetoric." In this view, as adopted by the present commentary, willing subordination to one another within the body of Christ is first a gift of the Spirit, from which, second, a series of consequences may be derived. The clause is

---

[1]   For the inclusion of 5:21 at the end of the pericope 5:15–21, see "Structure and Rhetoric" in the commentary on 5:15–21.

therefore a "hinge," connecting the work of the Spirit (5:18–20) to the entire *Haustafel*,[2] "household table" or "table of duties," that follows (5:21–6:9).

The alternative view is that the participle ὑποτασσόμενοι should be understood as an independent imperatival construction introducing a new section: "be subordinate to one another …" Willing subordination is, in this view, more in the way of command than gift. Advocates argue that the verb is parallel to the imperatives in 5:25, 33; 6:1, 4, 5, 9. While participles are normally subordinate to a finite verb, it must be acknowledged that there are examples in the NT (and in secular Greek) of their independent use. 1 Peter is replete with independent participles that appear to be equivalent to imperatives (1 Pet 1:14; 2:18; 3:1, 7, 9; 4:8, 10). This imperatival usage of the participle may derive from the rabbis, who, either because of the nature of Hebrew grammar or perhaps because of a reluctance to trespass on the divine prerogative to issue commands, couched their injunctions in participial form.[3] It is true that NT examples seem restricted to the *Haustafeln*. Many of these participles, however, can be interpreted as dependent on a somewhat distant, preceding main verb. Note the use of the imperative ὑποτάγητε, "be subordinate" (1 Pet 2:13), followed later by the same participle as here in Eph 5:21, ὑποτασσόμενοι, "being subordinate" (1 Pet 2:18; see also 1 Pet 3:1). Thus, these participles that are usually interpreted as imperatival can easily be explained according to the normal rules of Greek syntax (see also 1 Pet 4:7–10; Heb 13:3–5).

Paul himself is fond of continuing the thought of a finite verb (including imperatives) with a long series of participles. Participles that appear to be independent are most often just an extension of this construction.[4] Though Paul can be very free in his inter-

---

[2] See "A Note on the Term *Haustafel*" in "Structure and Rhetoric" in this pericope.

[3] J. N. D. Kelly, *A Commentary on the Epistles of Peter and of Jude* (London: Black, 1969), 67–68: "This is not, as was once supposed, a Hellenistic grammatical development, but reproduces, as is now recognized, the rabbinic Hebrew practice of using participles to express, not direct commands, but rules of conduct and even religious precepts." (Kelly's subsequent conclusion that the NT tables of duties must be translations of Hebrew or Aramaic originals is unjustified.) See also Turner, *Grammatical Insights*, 165–68, who considers the practice to be a Semitism, but does not accept the notion of direct rabbinic influence on the NT texts. Moulton, *Prolegomena*, 180–83, considers it a Hellenistic development, but is probably wrong, as demonstrated in the exhaustive essay by David Daube, "Participle and Imperative in I Peter," in Edward Gordon Selwyn, *The First Epistle of St. Peter* (London: Macmillan, 1947), 467–88, who also rejects the idea that it is "an anacoluthon, regarding a convenient imperative such as ἐστέ as implied, or the like" (467). Daube points to copious rabbinic examples and roots their linguistic pattern in the Hebrew manner of using participles for habitual action—what is customary may easily be seen as obligatory: "The phrase 'it is not done' normally means 'it ought not to be done' " (472).

[4] BDF, § 468 (2). Most examples of supposedly independent participles are not thoroughly convincing and can easily be connected to previous finite verbs: e.g., in 2 Cor 9:10–13; Phil 1:29–30; Col 3:16–17. Such participles have imperatival connotation simply because they depend on imperatives, not because they are imperatival participles. BDF notes:

> Frisk, *op. cit.* 65f. explains all the cited cases of "imperatival" ptcps. as correctly subordinated. … In several instances, however, the ptcp. is more or less independent, so that it receives the meaning of an independent statement or exhortation acc. to the situation. The ptcp., accordingly, is on a par with other nouns (subst. and adj.), which also, without a verb, can have the value of a sentence in the popular, energetic, cliché-laden style. (Citing Hjalmar Frisk, "Partizipium und Verbum finitum im Spätgriechischen," *Glotta* 17 [1928]: 56–66)

change of finite verbs, participles, and adjectives (see Rom 12:1–17), recourse to the idea that a participle is fully independent ought to be taken only when simple dependence on a finite verb is impossible (see also Eph 3:17; 4:1; 5:18).[5] This is hardly the case in the present verse, in which the dependence of the participle ὑποτασσόμενοι ("being subordinate") on the imperative πληροῦσθε ("*be filled up* in the Spirit") in 5:18 is the simple solution. The participle thereby describes an activity that is moved by the Holy Spirit (5:18), rather than simply being a command.

The syntactical question, however, is often a smokescreen for an underlying theological shift. By detaching the participial clause from the preceding section (5:3–20) and attaching it (only) to what immediately follows (5:22–33), modern commentators try to blunt Paul's supposedly offensive and archaic language of husbandly headship and wifely submission.[6] They apply the clause "being subordinate/submitting to one another" directly and exclusively to the marriage relationship, as if to say that, while wives are to submit to their husbands, husbands are likewise to submit to their wives. "Mutual submission" is the banner.[7]

While this commentary does understand "being subordinate to one another" as a heading, it is seen as applying to the whole unit (5:21–6:9), not just the marriage relationship. But more significantly, *the meaning and usage of the verb ὑποτάσσω*

The most persuasive example of a truly independent participle is in 2 Cor 8:24 (where many manuscripts substitute the imperative). Wallace, *Greek Grammar*, 650–51, calls the imperatival participle "quite rare," restricting NT examples to, in addition to 2 Cor 8:24, Romans 12 and 1 Peter, cases that we have questioned above.

[5] Wallace, *Greek Grammar*, 651: "The basic rule here is simply this: If a participle can be identified as dependent (i.e., if it can at all be attached to a verb), it should be so considered." Robertson, *Grammar*, 1133–34: "In general it may be said that no participle should be explained in this way [as an independent participle] that can properly be connected with a finite verb."

[6] Sampley, *"And the Two Shall Become One Flesh,"* 117, goes so far as to say that "the author" has placed 5:21 at the head of the *Haustafel* (5:22–6:9) because he does not entirely agree with its contents! Thus, the idea of "mutual submission" is seen as a corrective to the traditional values it contains. Lincoln, *Ephesians*, 365–66, rightly questions why an author would include such a large amount of traditional material with which he disagrees; but Lincoln nonetheless argues that the author (in his view, not Paul) introduces the mutual submission language of 5:21 as a compatible counterpart to the hierarchical view espoused in the pericopes that follow: "Mutual submission coexists with a hierarchy of roles within the household." Unfortunately, Lincoln confuses submission (which cannot be mutual) with the attitudes of humility and gentleness incumbent upon all Christians equally (see 1 Pet 5:5). Best's comment reveals an ideology at work: "Mutual subordination is of course a necessary basis for democracy" (*Ephesians*, 518). The NT has no particular interest in promoting democracy.

[7] Mutuality is sometimes thought to be the necessary implication of ἀλλήλοις, "to one another." E.g., Alan G. Padgett, *As Christ Submits to the Church: A Biblical Understanding of Leadership and Mutual Submission* (Grand Rapids: Baker Academic, 2011), 41. Certainly this reciprocal pronoun (ἀλλήλων) can imply equal activity in a relationship (as in "be at peace with one another," Mk 9:50; cf. Jn 13:35; Rom 1:12; 15:5; Gal 5:13; Eph 4:2, 25, 32; James 5:16; 1 Pet 5:5). But it can also refer to a more diverse exchange of activities within a group of people in a context where mutuality is impossible or unlikely—see, e.g., Mt 24:10 (betraying one another is not mutual; some betray and some are betrayed); Lk 7:32 (not everyone played the flute to the others); Acts 19:38 (not everyone is charged); Gal 6:2 (burdens are not interchanged equally); Rev 6:4 (two people do not slay each other).

simply does not allow for the idea of mutual submission within a single relationship.[8]
ὑποτάσσω (ὑπό, "under," + τάσσω, "appoint, order, arrange") in biblical thinking presumes the singular preeminence of God, who sets all things in their proper place beneath him.[9] Greek speakers of Paul's day would hear a reference to τάξις, "order, rank," which has strong, hierarchical military connotations.[10] The cognate noun τάξις (or τάγμα) is used in the LXX of a "division of an army" or "ordered unit" heading into battle, each soldier taking his proper place behind the captain, and of the analogous orderly arrangement of the tribes of Israel around their standards.[11] Likewise, the priests and Levites are placed into orderly ranks for their temple service, each having a divinely assigned task.[12] The sense is that each individual has an appropriate place, just as the sun itself knows its job is to rise in the morning because God has given it this mandate (συντάσσω, LXX Job 38:12). Thus, "decently and in order [κατὰ τάξιν]" (1 Cor 14:40) does not simply mean the polite taking of turns, but refers to offices, ranks, and duties that are given by God.[13]

The compound verb ὑποτάσσω (the preposition ὑπό prefixed to τάσσω), literally, "to under-order" or (Latin) "sub-ordinate," thus means to give a rank or place in the divinely established order of things. The passive voice of the participle ὑποτασσόμενοι (5:21)[14] implies the divine Agent who creates the order. Thus, "being subordinated"

---

8   See, e.g., Wayne Grudem, "The Myth of Mutual Submission as an Interpretation of Ephesians 5:21," in *Biblical Foundations for Manhood and Womanhood* (ed. Wayne Grudem; Wheaton, Ill.: Crossway, 2002), 221–32; and in the same volume, Daniel Doriani, "The Historical Novelty of Egalitarian Interpretations of Ephesians 5:21–22," 203–20.

9   "God is not a God of confusion" (1 Cor 14:33). Cf. the use of τάσσω with God as the subject in LXX Gen 3:24; 2 Kgdms 7:11 (MT/ET 2 Sam 7:11); Job 14:13; Jer 5:22; Hab 1:12; Ep Jer 61; Acts 13:48; 22:10; Rom 13:1.

10 See *1 Clement* 37, quoted in "Subordination Is Not Demeaning, but God's Order for the Transmission of Blessings" in the commentary.

11 LXX Num 1:52; Judg 5:20; 2 Macc 8:22; 10:36; 13:21. See also ὑποτάσσω in 2 Macc 8:9, 22; τάσσω in LXX 2 Kgdms 23:23 (MT/ET 2 Sam 23:23); Lk 7:8.

12 LXX 1 Esdras 1:5, 15; Lk 1:8. Cf. τάσσω in LXX 1 Chr 16:4, 7; 2 Chr 31:2; 1 Esdras 1:15. That Jesus is "a high priest after the order [κατὰ τὴν τάξιν] of Melchizedek" (LXX Ps 109:4 [MT/ET 110:4]; Heb 5:6, 10; 6:20; 7:11, 17) means that he holds an analogously high rank in the priestly hierarchy. He is under no one but God the Father. Cf. Clement's application of the priestly ordering to the Christian ministry, *1 Clement*, 40:1–41:2.

13 Kleinig, "Ordered Community," 49: "This instruction [1 Cor 14:40] does not just insist that their worship should be orderly, which would mean that any order was acceptable. It implies that the service should be done according to an established order, God's order, the right pattern for speaking and hearing God's Word and for giving and receiving Christ's Body and Blood."

14 The present tense participle ὑποτασσόμενοι is nominative masculine plural; the form may be either *middle* or *passive* in voice. If it were understood as *middle*, one might translate it as "subordinating themselves" or "letting themselves be subordinated"; if taken as *passive*, it would be translated as "being subordinate(d)." BDAG, s.v. ὑποτάσσω, takes all non-active voice occurrences of the verb as passive (not middle). This decision is probably based on the fact that, in instances where middle and passive forms can be distinguished (i.e., the aorist and future), ὑποτάσσω invariably appears in passive form (Rom 8:20; 10:3; 1 Cor 15:28; Heb 12:9; James 4:7; 1 Pet 2:13; 3:22; 5:5). In some other instances, the context requires the passive (e.g., the demons "are [unwillingly] subjected" to the preachers [Lk 10:17, 20]). In the context of the present verse (Eph 5:21), the Holy Spirit (5:18) is the one who subordinates,

means "[willingly] taking the place given by God."[15] Within such an order, it is impossible simultaneously to hold both upper and lower ranks. "Mutual submission" is no submission at all.[16] In each NT example of the verb, it is quite impossible to run the relationship in reverse.[17] Within each relationship Paul discusses in this unit (5:21–6:9), one party holds the rank of head and another the rank of body; one leads and the other submits. Within this pericope it is significant that the verb ὑποτάσσω is used explicitly of the wife/church, but never of the husband/Christ.[18] The same is true in parallel passages that speak of the wife submitting to the husband, but never the reverse.[19]

The language, however, reflects more than just the nonegalitarian nature of ancient cultures. It is highly Christological. At the ascension of Christ, God "subordinated all things under his feet" (Eph 1:22; cf. Pss 8:7 [ET 8:6]; 110:1). This military image arises from the fact of Christ's victory over his enemies and their forced submission to his kingship (Phil 3:21; Heb 2:8; 1 Pet 3:22), language found originally in the campaigns of Israel's ancient kings to whom God subordinated all their enemies.[20] Christ's enemies are subjected to him involuntarily (Eph 1:20–22; Phil 2:10); Christians are subordinate

---

that is, puts wives into order underneath their husbands so that they are subordinate(d) (passive). Yet through the gracious gift of the Spirit, Christians accept such subordination *willingly* (in contrast to the demons). For the active of ὑποτάσσω with God as the subject and spiritual forces as the object, see 1:22.

[15] Note the distinction between the passive (first) and the active (second): "And all of you were humble in mind, not boastful in any way, *being subordinate* rather than *imposing subordination* [ὑποτασσόμενοι μᾶλλον ἢ ὑποτάσσοντες], giving more gladly than taking" (*1 Clement*, 2:1).

[16] Many commentators note the inherent contradiction, but fail to resolve it. E.g., Bruce, *The Epistles to the Colossians, to Philemon, and to the Ephesians*, 383: "While the household code is introduced by a plea for mutual submissiveness, the submissiveness enjoined in the code itself is not mutual." Likewise, Barth, *Ephesians*, 2:609; Best, *Ephesians*, 517. Even BDAG, s.v. ὑποτάσσω, 1 b β, tries to draw a distinction between the usual meaning, "recognition of an ordered structure" (5:22 [variant reading]; 5:24) and "submission in the sense of voluntary yielding in love" (5:21). The proposal of the latter distinct meaning in 5:21 would seem to arise from a preconception that it describes "mutual submission" and from a failure to recognize the verse's role as a heading for the entire *Haustafel* (5:21 through 6:9).

[17] Nordling, "Research Notes [on Eph 5:21]," 329–30, cites these uses of ὑποτάσσω, "to subordinate; (passive:) be subordinate":

The submission of Jesus to his parents (Luke 2:51); of demons to the disciples (Luke 10:17, 20); of citizens to the governing authorities (Rom 13:1; Titus 3:1; 1 Pet 2:13); of all things in the universe to Christ (1 Cor 15:27 [citing Ps 8:7 LXX (ET 8:6)]; Eph 1:22); of angels, authorities, and powers to Christ (1 Pet 3:22); of Christ to God the Father (1 Cor 15:28); of church members to their leaders (1 Cor 16:15–16; 1 Pet 5:5); of the church to Christ (Eph 5:24); of slaves to their masters (Titus 2:9; 1 Pet 2:18); of Christians to God (Heb 12:9; James 4:7); and of wives to their husbands (Col 3:18; Titus 2:4–5; 1 Pet 3:5).

[18] See ὑποτάσσω in 5:24 and the textual variants in 5:22. The verb φοβῆται, "let her fear [her husband]," in 5:33 is parallel to ὑποτάσσω in a way that the husband's ἀγαπάτω, "let him love [his wife]" (5:33), is not.

[19] Col 3:18; Titus 2:5; 1 Pet 3:1, 5.

[20] See ὑποτάσσω in LXX 1 Chr 22:18; 29:24; Pss 17:48 (MT 18:48; ET 18:47); 46:4 (MT 47:4; ET 47:3); 59:10 (MT 60:10; ET 60:8); 107:10 (MT 108:10; ET 108:9); 143:2 (MT/ET 144:2); Wis Sol 8:14; 3 Macc 2:13; see also Josh 10:24; 2 Sam 22:39.

to him as their Savior with a willing heart, as moved by the Holy Spirit (Eph 5:18). All proper submission is ultimately submission to God himself, who established the order and stands at its head,[21] and refusal to submit is an attitude that arises from a sinful heart in rebellion against God's Word (Rom 8:7; 10:3).

Likewise, then, when wives submit to husbands (Eph 5:21–24), children to parents (6:1–2), and slaves to masters (6:5–8), they recognize the headship of Christ himself over all that he has purchased and won; contrariwise, rejecting earthly headship is rejecting Christ himself. The divine order is for Christ to be the Savior and his people to be the saved: "but each in his own position/rank [ἐν τῷ ἰδίῳ τάγματι]: Christ the firstfruits, then those who are Christ's at his appearing" (1 Cor 15:23). To reject the divine order by refusing to submit to those who represent Christ is therefore to put oneself in place of the savior, to upset not just the order of creation but also the order of salvation; such rebellion holds theological kinship with Pelagianism. Indeed, as with the pagan worship Paul had rejected in 5:3–5, to usurp the role of Christ is an act of self-idolatry, a violation of the First Commandment (Ex 20:3; Deut 5:7).

ἐν φόβῳ Χριστοῦ—A brief note cannot do justice to the phrase "the fear of God/ the Lᴏʀᴅ,"[22] which stands behind these words, "in the fear of Christ." "Respect" alone falls short of what is meant by φόβος. This kind of "fear" is the prerogative of God; thus "the fear of Christ" confesses the identity of Jesus Christ with YHWH/the Lᴏʀᴅ, and therefore his divinity. "The fear of YHWH is the beginning of wisdom" (Prov 9:10).[23] Such "fear" is certainly the worshipful attitude of *reverence and awe* before the glory of God and may be identified with faith itself.[24] But it also includes the appropriate *fear of judgment* that an unholy creature ought to display before God's consuming holiness.[25]

In Luther's explanation of the Decalogue in the SC, "we should *fear and love* God" includes in the factors that drive the Christian to obey God: both fear of punishment and faith in his grace. The same factors are at work in this pericope concerning Christ. Although the phrase "the fear of Christ" is unique in the NT, fear and trembling frequently seize the witnesses of Christ's power in the NT.[26] But equally, Christ comforts his disciples with the message "do not fear" (e.g., Mt 14:27; 28:5, 10). They need not fear him as the holy and almighty God because he comes to them in grace as their Savior. A similar, though not identical, relationship between fear and love is at work in the present passage with respect to human relationships, including marriage. Barth comments: "Fear without love would be horrible. Just as God's love of man and man's

---

21 LXX Pss 36:7 (MT/ET 37:7); 61:2, 6 (MT 62:2, 6; ET 62:1, 5); 2 Macc 9:12; Rom 13:1; 1 Cor 15:27–28; Heb 12:9; James 4:7.

22 The textual variants here that substitute "fear of the Lord" or "fear of God" indicate how the phrase resonated with the earliest readers.

23 Cf. Deut 10:12, 20; Pss 5:8 (ET 5:7); 19:10 (ET 19:9); 111:10; Prov 1:7; 14:26–27; Job 28:28; 2 Cor 5:11; Col 3:22; 1 Pet 2:17; Rev 14:7.

24 E.g., Lk 1:50; Acts 9:31; 10:35; 13:16; Rev 19:5. Cf. Is 11:2–3, where "the fear of YHWH" characterizes the Messiah's own ministry and the Spirit who rests upon him.

25 Is 6:5; Lk 2:9; Rev 14:7; 15:4. See Schlier, *Epheser*, 252; Barth, *Ephesians*, 2:608, 662–68.

26 Mt 9:8; Mk 4:41; 5:15, 33; 9:32; 10:32; 11:18; 16:8; 2 Cor 5:11; Col 3:22.

responding love of God are the basis of the fear of God, so only the wife who is joined to her husband by love can fear her husband."[27]

In this pericope, such "fear of Christ" (tempered by love) serves as a pattern for the subordinate relationships of wives to husbands ("let the wife respect/fear," 5:33) and slaves to masters ("with fear," 6:5)—and implicitly also for children to their parents ("honor," 6:2). The precise nature of "fear" along the spectrum between "reverence" and "fear of punishment" depends on the particular relationship. The husband's Christlike love of his wife is to engender "fear" (5:33) that leans decidedly towards the reverential side of the term's meaning, while the slave might rightly have a "fear" (6:5) of punishment from his master—the addition of "trembling" (6:5) in the latter case marks a distinction between the two. With appearance of the noun φόβος here in 5:21 and the cognate verb φοβέω in 5:33, such "fear/reverence/respect" forms an *inclusio* around this pericope; the recurrence of the noun φόβος in 6:5 marks its thematic significance for the entire *Haustafel* (5:21–6:9). The point is that every relationship is transformed by discerning its typological character, the wife seeing her husband as Christ (thus "fearing" him), the husband seeing his wife as the church (thus "loving" her). So also the slave's obedience to his master "with fear and trembling" is rendered "as to Christ" (6:5; cf. "as to the Lord," 5:22). The transformative function of the phrase "in the fear of Christ" (5:21) parallels the expression "in the Lord/in him/in the Spirit."[28]

5:22 αἱ γυναῖκες τοῖς ἰδίοις ἀνδράσιν ὡς τῷ κυρίῳ—Here Paul introduces the first pairing in a series of three: wives to husbands (5:22–33), children to parents (6:1–4), and slaves to masters (6:5–9). The parallelism of these pairings, all of which refer to the domestic realm, as well as the inclusion of ἰδίοις, "their own" (5:22),[29] suggests that Paul means to speak specifically of wives and husbands, not women and men in general (see also the next textual note, on 5:23). Nonetheless, the subordination of the wife to the husband is rooted in the general headship of Christ over man and of man over woman to which Paul refers in the next verse (5:23; cf. 1 Cor 11:3; 14:34). The phrase ὡς τῷ κυρίῳ, "as to the Lord," does not merely set up an analogy ("as if, in the same way as").[30] Rather, this phrase, repeated verbatim in Eph 6:7 (cf. Eph 6:5; Col 3:23), is

---

[27] Barth, *Ephesians*, 2:667.

[28] See 2:21–22; 4:1, 17; 5:8; 6:1 (cf. Col 3:18). See also "in Christ" in the fifth textual note on 1:3.

[29] With this possessive "wives to *their own* husbands," Paul does not imply that some wives were submitting to the wrong husbands! Rather, in the ambiguity of Greek, in which ἀνήρ can mean either "man" or "husband," the possessive adjective ἴδιος is used to clarify which meaning is in mind: "women to their *own* men" means "wives to their husbands." Cf. 1 Cor 7:2; 14:35; Titus 2:5; 1 Pet 3:1, 5.

[30] Barth, *Ephesians*, 2:612, offers four possible interpretations of ὡς τῷ κυρίῳ: (1) it indicates the urgency of the wife's subordination, "because you fear the Lord"; (2) it describes the mode and extent: "with equally unlimited trust and in the same unrestricted manner" as to the Lord; (3) the husband may have "a typological, sacramental or eschatological role: he may be designated as the representative of Christ to his wife"; or (4) subordination to the husband is a mere training ground for the higher, supreme subordination to Christ. The third option is in accord with our commentary. Barth reveals his aversion to this option by suggesting that the husband would thereby take on an exclusive, mediatorial role in salvation, but that is a distortion of Paul's point; the husband is a *proclamation* of Christ, not a substitute for him.

equivalent to ἐν φόβῳ Χριστοῦ, "in the fear of Christ" (Eph 5:21), and ἐν κυρίῳ, "in the Lord" (Col 3:18). It means "when you submit to your husbands, *you are* submitting to the Lord." Its repetition emphasizes that Paul's final purpose is not to govern household relationships for their own sake, but to direct hearts and minds ever back to Christ, to unveil the eternal purpose of God that lies behind these divinely instituted earthly estates.

Since the verb ὑποτασσόμενοι, "being subordinate," has just been expressed in the previous verse (5:21), which serves as hinge between the two units of 5:3–21 and 5:21–6:9, Paul does not repeat it here. If a verb is to be supplied in translation, it is best to retain the participial mood (as in Titus 2:5; 1 Pet 3:1) to maintain the connection with the Spirit's work (Eph 5:18), rather than inserting an imperative.[31]

5:23 ὅτι ἀνήρ ἐστιν κεφαλὴ τῆς γυναικὸς ὡς καὶ ὁ Χριστὸς κεφαλὴ τῆς ἐκκλησίας, αὐτὸς σωτὴρ τοῦ σώματος—This verse introduces the (theo-)logical justification for Paul's prior statement that Christian wives are gifted by the Holy Spirit to take their subordinate place willingly. Paul points not to natural law, to the order of creation, or to the fall into sin (as in 1 Tim 2:1–15), but to the headship of Christ over his church. This flows out of the prior argumentation of the letter (1:21–23; 4:15; see the textual notes and the commentary on 1:22). God exalted Christ over all things to be the Head of the church for her sake. Christ's headship is the pattern to which the husband's headship is conformed in a typological manner, the earthly marriage relationship displaying an unseen heavenly reality.[32] As earlier (κεφαλή, 1:22; 4:15), the meaning of "head" here is clearly "authority,"[33] the counterpart of subordination—but this is a Christ-kind

---

[31] The second and third person plural imperatives (ὑποτάσσεσθε, ὑποτασσέσθωσαν) provided in the textual variants arise from a misunderstanding of the "pivot" role of 5:21. By inserting an imperative ("be subordinate!" or "let them be subordinate!"), rather than leaving the verse dependent on the preceding participle ("being subordinate," 5:21), the variants subtly change the meaning of the verse, breaking its dependence on the gift of the Spirit (5:18). Of course, Paul's use of ὑποτάσσεσθε, "be subordinate," in the same context in Col 3:18 demonstrates that the imperatival meaning is not wrong. But Colossians 3 has a significantly abridged *Haustafel* and lacks the sophistication of Ephesians—in Colossians subordination is not explicitly made a gift of the Spirit, as it is in Ephesians—a sign, perhaps, that Ephesians is Paul's later and more fully developed statement on the subject.

[32] Thus, Paul uses the words ὡς τῷ κυρίῳ, "as to the Lord" (5:22), and ὡς καὶ ὁ Χριστός, "as also Christ" (5:23), to set up the analogical relationship. Their meaning is not to define the husband's headship as if to say that he is the wife's head *in exactly the same way as* Christ is the church's head (contra Barth, *Ephesians*, 2:614). That would contradict the uniqueness of Christ's role as "the Savior of the body" (5:23). But neither is the analogy a mere comparison (with ὡς simply meaning "as"). The combination in 5:23, ὡς καί, "as also," can be stronger, forming a causal connection: "*because* the Messiah is the head of the church" (Barth, *Ephesians*, 2:613).

[33] The oft-suggested meaning of κεφαλή as "source" is used to blunt the force of Paul's argument by suggesting a simple reference to the creation of Eve from the side of Adam. That meaning is not only poorly supported in Greek literature but also makes no sense of the verb ὑποτάσσω, "to subordinate" (5:21, 24). While Adam was literally the source of Eve and Christ is certainly the source of his body's life (see 4:15–16), it is hard to see how the husband is the source of his wife's life. See Wayne A. Grudem, "Does κεφαλή ('Head') Mean 'Source' or 'Authority Over' in Greek Literature? A Survey of 2,336 Examples," *Trinity Journal* 6 (1985): 38–59; Grudem, "Appendix 1: The Meaning of Κεφαλή ('Head'): A Response to Recent Studies,"

of headship that does not tyrannize but rather sacrifices itself, as Paul's exposition will demonstrate.[34]

There is broad consensus for continuing in 5:23 (as in 5:22) to translate ἀνήρ as "husband" and γυνή as "wife." It is unfortunate, however, that in English we are unable to maintain the dual meanings of the Greek terms: "man/husband" and "woman/wife," respectively. As in 1 Corinthians 11 and 14, Paul appears to defend the subordination of wife to husband on the basis of a general subordination of woman to man[35] (the details of which must be worked out for every earthly relationship, as Paul does here for marriage). But his major concern is reiterated in the verse's final words: "he himself [being] the Savior of the body."[36] The wife cannot take on the role of head in the marriage because that would imply that the church can act as her own savior. The present argument is keenly focused on the Gospel. Paul moves very quickly from talking about husbands and wives to talking about Christ. σωτήρ, "Savior," is an extraordinarily common OT title for God;[37] its application to Christ is again an assertion of his divinity.[38]

---

in *Recovering Biblical Manhood and Womanhood: A Response to Evangelical Feminism* (ed. John Piper and Wayne A. Grudem; Wheaton, Ill.: Crossway, 1991), 425–68; and Joseph A. Fitzmyer, "*Kephalē* in I Corinthians 11:3," *Interpretation* 47 (1993): 52–59.

[34] Gibson, "Ephesians 5:21–33 and the Lack of Marital Unity in the Roman Empire," 176, elaborates on the countercultural nature of this headship:

> Though the husband is to be in a position of authority over his wife, it is a type of authority never seen before or since (apart from Christ). In every human οἰκονομία [ordered household], the κεφαλὴ ["head"] is a position of honor. Such a person is waited on by servants; every need of the κεφαλὴ is met by others. In the οἰκονομία of God [Eph 1:9–10; 3:3–10], however, the situation is reversed. The κεφαλὴ is the one who sacrifices.

[35] 1 Corinthians 11 expands the argumentation on which Paul appears to rely here: παντὸς ἀνδρὸς ἡ κεφαλὴ ὁ Χριστός ἐστιν, κεφαλὴ δὲ γυναικὸς ὁ ἀνήρ, κεφαλὴ δὲ τοῦ Χριστοῦ ὁ θεός, "the head of every man [husband?] is Christ, the head of woman [a wife?] is man [her husband?], and the head of Christ is God" (1 Cor 11:3). The generality of Paul's statement there is significantly diluted if man/woman are excluded and replaced with husband/wife, and it seems more likely that Paul is speaking of a general subordination of woman to man that arises from the order of creation. Note the reference to the Torah later in that letter: "let the women keep silence in the churches: for it is not permitted to them to speak; but let them be subordinate [ὑποτασσέσθωσαν], as also the Law says" (1 Cor 14:34).

[36] The referent of this final phrase would seem to be Christ alone (contra, e.g., Chrysostom, Theophylact, and Oecumenius, who spoke of the husband as his wife's savior [cf. Barth, *Ephesians*, 2:615, n. 25]), though the husband's actions are analogical—his acts of sacrificial love are like Christ's, but do not save his wife in an eternal sense. Thus, a reference to 1 Cor 7:16, in which a wife or husband's quiet testimony may lead to the spouse's salvation, is not apropos.

[37] The word occurs thirty-eight times in the LXX, often referring to God.

[38] See Lk 1:47; 2:11; Titus 2:13; 3:4, 6. Although "Savior of the body" (Eph 5:23) is a unique expression in the NT and is a somewhat mixed metaphor (can a body be lost? can a head redeem its body?), it is fully understandable in the context. There is no need to seek its meaning in Gnostic thought (contra Schlier, *Epheser*, 266–76). Nor does the phrase imply a preexistence of the church as an entity in a fallen state, for Ephesians clearly teaches that Christ brought the church (the new man) into existence by his work on the cross (2:15–16). Christ *has saved* the church, *remains* her Savior, and *will* finally rescue her from this present evil age.

5:24 ἀλλὰ ὡς ἡ ἐκκλησία ὑποτάσσεται τῷ Χριστῷ, οὕτως καὶ αἱ γυναῖκες τοῖς ἀνδράσιν ἐν παντί—The words that deal with the role of the wife (5:22–24) form a chiasm (see the translation), which is concluded in this verse. The adversative ἀλλά, "but," recalls us to consideration of the wife after a strong statement about Christ (5:23b).[39] It draws consequences from the divine marriage for the human relationship.

Significantly, Paul uses the *indicative* ὑποτάσσεται, "*is* subordinate," rather than an imperative.[40] Perhaps this should be understood as a customary present, "as the church [customarily, instinctively, by nature] submits to Christ." Thus, Paul does not so much *command* the wife to submit as simply *describe* the way things are for those who are filled with the Spirit (5:18): the wife willingly subordinates herself to her husband in everything. Her willing subordination is patterned on the subordination of the church to Christ, the contours of which have filled the previous chapters of Ephesians. The church receives Christ as her head (1:21–23), the cornerstone/keystone of her temple-like structure (2:20–21); she is rooted in his love (3:17–19), receives his many gifts (4:7–12), grows up toward him as he builds his body (4:15–16), lives in his love and forgiveness (4:32–5:2), and sings his praises (5:18–20).[41] The wife's subordination is like this.

The second half of this verse, οὕτως καὶ αἱ γυναῖκες τοῖς ἀνδράσιν ἐν παντί, lacks a verb. Paul expects the reader to make up the ellipse by supplying some form of the verb ὑποτάσσω. The simplest explanation is that the reader should repeat ὑποτάσσεται, "is subordinate," from the first half of the verse, changing its grammatical number to fit the plural subject, "wives" (i.e., ὑποτάσσονται, "are subordinate"). However, the chiastic structure we have noted above suggests that οὕτως καὶ αἱ γυναῖκες τοῖς ἀνδράσιν ἐν παντί, "thus also wives to [their] husbands in all things" (5:24b), is a parallel repetition (with minor variation) of αἱ γυναῖκες τοῖς ἰδίοις ἀνδράσιν ὡς τῷ κυρίῳ, "wives to their own husbands as to the Lord" (5:22). Paul returns to the statement he made at the beginning of the chiastic section. Thus, one might posit that the verb to be supplied here, as in 5:22, is the participle ὑποτασσόμενοι, "being subordinate," from 5:21. Whichever decision is taken, the important point to retain is that the entire *Haustafel* (5:21–6:9) is (theo-)logically dependent on the imperative πληροῦσθε, "*be filled up* in the Spirit" (5:18), even though Paul does not (and could not be expected to) maintain a syntactical structure of dependent participles through to the very end.

The final phrase, ἐν παντί, "in all/everything," again recalls the pattern of Christ's headship, under whom God has placed "all things" (πάντα, twice in 1:22), the Christ

---

[39] Lincoln, *Ephesians*, 372, suggests that the force of ἀλλά is "notwithstanding the difference" (i.e., that Christ is Savior in a way that the husband cannot be).

[40] ὑποτάσσεται is present middle/passive in form, to be understood as passive in voice, "the church *is subordinate(d)* to Christ." For the significance of the distinction between the middle and passive, see the footnote on ὑποτασσόμενοι in the first textual note on 5:21 above in this pericope.

[41] Lincoln, *Ephesians*, 372:

> The Church's subordination, then, means looking to its head for his beneficial rule, living by his norms, experiencing his presence and love, receiving from him gifts that will enable growth to maturity, and responding to him in gratitude and awe. It is such attitudes that the wife is being encouraged to develop in relation to her husband.

who himself fills "all things in all" (τὰ πάντα ἐν πᾶσιν, 1:23) and who "in all things" is preeminent (ἐν πᾶσιν, Col 1:18). One who chooses when and where to submit (or not to submit) to Christ has not truly acknowledged his headship; likewise, the wife's subordination must be unconditional to be true subordination.[42] For Christ himself withheld nothing when he sacrificed his very life for his bride (Eph 5:25).

5:25 οἱ ἄνδρες, ἀγαπᾶτε τὰς γυναῖκας—In light of the second person plural imperative ἀγαπᾶτε, "love!" the articular noun οἱ ἄνδρες, "the men/husbands," should be understood as vocative, "O men/husbands."[43] Paul addresses the men directly. An ancient reader might have expected Paul to balance the wives' obligation to submit with an exhortation to the husbands to "rule" well[44] or to "make" his wife submit.[45] The imperative ἀγαπᾶτε, "love," is therefore quite stunning.[46] This might explain the contrast in Paul's approach: while he addressed the wives indirectly in just three brief verses (5:22–24), Paul speaks directly to the husbands in at least six (5:25–30). One might deduce that the sacrificial love laid upon the husband is more complicated to explain—and more countercultural—than the wife's subordination. But when one notes that these latter verses are actually dominated by the proclamation of Christ's work rather than admonition to the husband, the real reason for the imbalance becomes clear: it is not that Paul has more to say to the husband, but that he is really concerned to unfold the "mystery" (5:32) of the Gospel of Christ, for which the role of the husband in marriage is a type. In this regard, Ephesians moves far beyond what the NT elsewhere says to the husband (Col 3:19; 1 Pet 3:7).

---

[42] Cf. ἐν πάσῃ ὑποταγῇ, "with *all* subordination" (1 Tim 2:11); ὑποτασσόμενοι ἐν παντὶ φόβῳ, "subordinating with *all* fear" (1 Pet 2:18); ὑπακούετε … κατὰ πάντα, "heed … *in all things*" (Col 3:20, 22).

[43] This is common for nouns with the article, since there is no vocative form of the article. See BDF, § 147; Turner, *Syntax*, 34–35. Cf. Eph 5:14. The article indicates that the men are being addressed as a class (Wallace, *Greek Grammar*, 229); cf. likewise τὰ τέκνα (6:1), οἱ πατέρες (6:4), οἱ δοῦλοι (6:5), οἱ κύριοι (6:9).

[44] Plutarch, for example, though writing with some tenderness, nevertheless speaks of ruling, not loving: "The husband should rule his wife not as a lord rules over his property but as the soul rules the body, sympathizing with her and fostering their growing together by a good attitude" (*Conjugalia Praecepta*, 33 [142E], quoted in Schnackenburg, *Ephesians*, 252).

[45] Note again Clement's careful distinction: "And all of you were humble in mind, not boastful in any way, being subordinate *rather than imposing subordination* [ὑποτασσόμενοι μᾶλλον ἢ ὑποτάσσοντες], giving more gladly than taking" (*1 Clement*, 2:1).

[46] The OT notes that some men loved their wives (e.g., Gen 24:67; 29:18, 20, 30; cf. Deut 21:15–16; Judg 16:4, 15); a man is exhorted to love divine wisdom (Prov 4:6) and be enthralled in love for his wife (Prov 5:18–19; cf. Song of Songs passim). Exhortations to the husband to love his wife are rare outside Christian literature in the ancient world, and the verb ἀγαπάω, "love," does not occur in Greco-Roman household codes (Lincoln, *Ephesians*, 374). This is a firm reminder that Paul's *Haustafel* (including the subordination of the wife) is not simply an accommodation to cultural norms of the day. Pseudo-Phocylides, 195–97, uses the weaker verb στέργω in commanding husbands to "feel affection" for their wives. Talmud, *Yebamoth*, 62b, says: "Our Rabbis taught: Concerning a man who loves his wife as himself, who honours her more than himself, who guides his sons and daughters in the right path and arranges for them to be married near the period of their puberty, Scripture says, *And thou shalt know that thy tent is in peace* [Job 5:24]" (Soncino ed.).

The variant reading that inserts ὑμῶν, "your," after τὰς γυναῖκας, "(the) wives," likely arose from a misunderstanding of the use of the article τάς with the meaning of a possessive pronoun.[47] Paul does not say, "men, love *the* women," but "husbands, love *your* wives."

καθὼς καὶ ὁ Χριστὸς ἠγάπησεν τὴν ἐκκλησίαν καὶ ἑαυτὸν παρέδωκεν ὑπὲρ αὐτῆς—The phrase καθὼς καί, roughly translated as "just as also," is particularly common in Paul.[48] It reflects his love of analogy and typology, and in the present verse it establishes such a relationship between the husband's love for his wife and Christ's for the church. The call to love is not an appeal to the emotion (which cannot be generated by an imperative), but a call to the husband's will to think and act in a loving way toward his wife; in the context of the analogy, he is to love not *as much as* but *in the way that* Christ loved.[49] There may also be a hint of causative meaning (cf. 1:4; 4:4, 32; 5:2),[50] suggesting that Christ's love for the church can generate the husband's love for his wife: "inasmuch as/since Christ loved the church." Christ's sacrificial act is both a model for and a source of the husband's love. This would be in accord with the way the love of God and the love of Christians for each other are related throughout Ephesians (most clearly in 5:1–2). Love is a major theme of the letter, as Paul draws the Ephesians into peace, unity, and brotherly love by proclaiming the love of God in Christ.[51]

The verb παραδίδωμι, "to hand over, betray," is commonly used in the Gospels (and Paul) to refer to the passion of Christ (e.g., Mk 9:31; 10:33; 14:41–44). Here Paul emphasizes the voluntary nature of Christ's self-sacrifice: "he gave himself up for her" without hope of personal reward; this, if anything, is the distinctive characteristic of the "love" called ἀγάπη (e.g., Eph 1:4; 2:4; 3:19; 5:2). This is what love in action looks like. In this context the preposition ὑπέρ carries both meanings of benefit and substitution: "for her sake" and "in her place." See the second textual note on 5:2.[52] This is a compact statement of the vicarious atonement. Note how quickly Paul moves away from admonishing the husband to proclaiming the Gospel, which is the main theme of the section.

5:26 ἵνα αὐτὴν ἁγιάσῃ καθαρίσας—The sacrificial language of the previous verse now intensifies with the explicit vocabulary of temple ritual (cf. Rom 15:16). The verbs ἁγιάζω, "sanctify," and καθαρίζω, "cleanse," reflect the movement from unclean and common to clean and holy (Lev 10:10) that was necessary before any person or thing

---

[47] Wallace, *Greek Grammar*, 215–16.

[48] Twenty-two of thirty-four occurrences of καθὼς καί in the entire Greek Bible are in Paul.

[49] This is the reason why the wife, who might be expected to have an emotional love for her husband, is not *commanded* to love. It is not her calling to sacrifice herself for her husband. In any case, in traditional societies where arranged marriages were common, love was not viewed as a necessary component of marriage.

[50] BDF, § 453 (2); BDAG, s.v. καθώς, 3; cf. 1 Cor 1:6; Phil 1:7; 2 Thess 1:3.

[51] Aside from the rest of this pericope, see also 1:4–6, 15; 3:17–19; 4:2, 15–16; 5:1–2; 6:23–24. The ἀγαπ- stem ("love, beloved") occurs twenty-two times in Ephesians. On a percentage basis, this ranks the letter behind only the Johannine epistles, Jude, and Philemon.

[52] The same two verbs as in 5:25b and the same preposition ὑπέρ were used in 5:2: ὁ Χριστὸς ἠγάπησεν ἡμᾶς καὶ παρέδωκεν ἑαυτὸν ὑπὲρ ἡμῶν.

could stand in the presence of the holy God without being destroyed (Eph 1:4).[53] In the OT sacrificial system, cleansing took place through ritual washings and through the daily rite of atonement by the blood of sacrifice. Holiness was conveyed from God to the people through contact with the "most holy" things (Ex 29:37).[54] In this way, what was common but unclean was made clean and what was clean but common was made holy. The two steps of "cleansing" and "sanctifying" correspond to the verbs in this verse.[55]

God's holy presence • light • life • heaven	sanctification ← cleansing			Satan and demons • darkness • death • hell
	holy and clean	common and clean	common and unclean	
	desecration → defilement			

The NT does not erase these old distinctions, but relocates them from the Jerusalem temple to the person of Christ (Jn 2:21). His priestly work is to cleanse and sanctify (Jn 13:8–11; Titus 2:14), by the power of his own blood (Heb 9:13–14; 1 Jn 1:7; Rev 1:5 [variant reading]) and through his Word (Jn 15:3; 17:17). Jesus himself is our righteousness and sanctification (1 Cor 1:2, 30). Thus, while the twofold movement of cleansing and sanctifying is maintained in the NT, they are compressed into one action in the person of Christ. It is therefore unlikely that the participle καθαρίσας ("cleansing"), though aorist, should be taken as indicating an action prior to the timeframe of the main verb (ἀγιάσῃ, "that *he might sanctify*"), as if Christ *first* cleansed "with the washing of water in the Word" and *then later* sanctified. Rather, as 1 Cor 6:11 suggests, the actions of washing, sanctifying, and justifying occur simultaneously in the sacramental action. The aorist participle καθαρίσας (Eph 5:26) therefore portrays an action simultaneous with the main verb ἀγιάσῃ, indicating the means, manner, or accompaniment: "that he might sanctify with/by cleansing."[56]

τῷ λουτρῷ τοῦ ὕδατος ἐν ῥήματι—The dative τῷ λουτρῷ indicates the means or instrument of the cleansing: "with the washing." Continuing the ritual language of the temple, the noun λουτρόν, "washing," evokes the cleansing baths (λούω) by which priests were prepared for service in the temple (Ex 29:4; 40:12; Lev 8:6; 16:4, 24), lepers

---

[53] With its total of sixteen occurrences of ἅγιος, "holy," and ἁγιάζω, "sanctify," Ephesians stands very close to Leviticus in a statistical ranking of holiness language in the Greek Bible. Most of the Ephesian occurrences are references to the Christians as ἅγιοι, "saints," those made holy through Holy Baptism. See particularly 1:1, 4; 2:19–21; 5:3, 26–27. Note, then, that the sanctification described here is passive sanctification, what is received as a gift, not active sanctification, the Christian's ongoing life of good works that later dogmaticians commonly refer to as sanctification.

[54] For the priests, see, e.g., Lev 6:10–11, 18–20 (ET 6:17–18, 25–27). For all Israel, see, e.g., Lev 19:1–8.

[55] See Kleinig, "Sharing in God's Holiness." The chart is adapted from p. 108. See also Kleinig, *Leviticus*, 1–13.

[56] See Voelz, *Fundamental Greek Grammar*, 260; Burton, *Moods and Tenses*, §§ 132–51; Wallace, *Greek Grammar*, 628–30; BDF, § 339 (1). Cf. Eph 1:20; 2:15.

were restored to the worshiping congregation of Israel (Lev 14:9), and other contractions of uncleanness were dealt with (Leviticus 15; 22:6). The implication is that this NT washing likewise incorporates people into the worshiping community of God (Eph 2:19); it also invites the imagery of a priesthood of all the baptized (1 Pet 2:1–10). It is through this washing that the Ephesians are able to stand in the presence of a holy God, like all Israel at Mount Sinai (Ex 19:10–11) and like the priests who served in the Holy Place (Exodus 29).

This is the only NT passage that explicitly connects "washing" with "the Word."[57] Yet, as in similar NT passages that combine water and the Spirit into one washing,[58] this is a clear and unmistakable reference to Holy Baptism,[59] constituted by the work of the Holy Spirit through the holy Triune name of God with the water (Mt 28:19). λουτρόν ("washing") occurs only once more in the NT, in another clear reference to Baptism (Titus 3:5), while Heb 10:22—using ὕδωρ, "water," and the verb λούω, "to wash"—unmistakably connects Christian Baptism to OT cleansing baths, and in Acts 22:16 the verb ἀπολούω, "wash away," is used of Baptism.[60]

At first glance, the prepositional phrase ἐν ῥήματι (which only occurs here in the NT) might be taken adjectivally to modify one of the two preceding nouns, indicating that either the "washing" or the "water" is "in the Word," but the syntax does not support this.[61] More likely it is formulaic, equivalent to "using the divine name" or "in accord with Christ's mandate."[62] But, as the frequent Ephesian expression "in Christ" identi-

---

57 But see 2 Ki 5:10, 13–14, in which the Word of God through the prophet gives Naaman's washing its cleansing power. Note also the connection of βαπτίζω with λουτρόν in Sirach 34:25. See also *Shepherd of Hermas, Visions*, 3.3.5: "I asked her, 'Why was the tower built upon the waters, O Lady?' She answered, '… It is because your life has been, and will be, saved through water. For the tower was founded on the word of the almighty and glorious Name, and it is kept together by the invisible power of the Lord' " (*ANF* 2:14).

58 Jn 3:5; cf. Mk 1:8, 10; Jn 1:33; 7:38–39; 1 Cor 12:13; Titus 3:5; Heb 10:22; 1 Jn 5:8; Rev 22:17.

59 Marius Victorinus: "Here we take *the church* to mean every believer and everyone who has received baptism. The believer is brought to faith by the washing in water and the invocation of the Word" (*Ephesians*, 2:5.25–26, ACCS 8:195–96).

60 Cf. Justin Martyr, *First Apology*, 61:3, 10, 12; 66:1; Justin Martyr, *Dialogue with Trypho*, 13:1; 14:1.

61 If the prepositional phrase ἐν ῥήματι were adjectival, one would expect it to have a definite article: τῷ λουτρῷ τοῦ ὕδατος τῷ ἐν ῥήματι, "the washing of water, the [washing that is] in the Word." Or the phrase would be "sandwiched," e.g., τῷ ἐν ῥήματι λουτρῷ τοῦ ὕδατος, "the in-the-Word washing of water," or τῷ λουτρῷ τοῦ ἐν ῥήματι ὕδατος, "the washing of the in-the-Word water" (which would support Luther's explanation in SC 4). As the words stand, however, the phrase ἐν ῥήματι appears to modify everything that precedes.

62 Moule, *Idiom Book*, 78, calls it "[ἐν] of accompaniment, attendant circumstances"; thus, he suggests this translation for ἐν ῥήματι: "perhaps *accompanied by the formula* (or is it instrumental?)." Cf. βαπτίζοντες αὐτοὺς εἰς with the Triune name in Mt 28:19; also ἐπὶ τῷ ὀνόματι Ἰησοῦ Χριστοῦ, "[baptized] in the name of Jesus" (Acts 2:38); ἐν τῷ ὀνόματι Ἰησοῦ, "in/at the name of Jesus" (Acts 3:6; 4:10; 10:48; Phil 2:10); ἐν τῷ ὀνόματι τούτῳ, "in this name" (1 Pet 4:16); τὸ καλὸν ὄνομα τὸ ἐπικληθὲν ἐφ᾽ ὑμᾶς, "the noble name that was called down upon you" (James 2:7); οἱ βαπτισθέντες εἰς ὄνομα κυρίου, "those who have been baptized into the name of the Lord" (*Didache*, 9:5; cf. *Didache*, 7:1–3). Chrysostom: "By what *word* is she *washed*? *In the name of the Father, and of the Son and of the Holy Spirit* [Mt 28:19]" (*Homilies on Ephesians*, 20:5.27, ACCS 8:196). The phrase is surely not a reference to the

fies a spiritual location, so here the preposition ἐν may also imply that the "washing of water" is wrapped in the Word of God, as Luther explains in the Small Catechism: "Baptism is not just plain water, but it is the water included [*gefasset*] in God's command and combined [*verbunden*] with God's word."[63] By anchoring the divine marriage in Baptism, Paul points the Ephesian Christians to the concrete, earthly locatedness of their union with God, which is therefore not merely eschatological but carried out in the present through his apostolic instruments.[64]

5:27 ἵνα παραστήσῃ αὐτὸς ἑαυτῷ ἔνδοξον τὴν ἐκκλησίαν, μὴ ἔχουσαν σπίλον ἢ ῥυτίδα ἤ τι τῶν τοιούτων—Although Baptism is certainly applied to individual Christians, Paul's language here is corporate. We are reminded of his earlier contention that there is truly only "one Baptism" (4:5)—the Baptism, death, and resurrection of Christ, into which all Christians are incorporated by their sacramental experience. The sacrificial language of the previous verse compels us to keep Christ's own Baptism and his passion an undivided whole (cf. Mk 10:38–39; Lk 12:50; Col 1:22; 1 Cor 1:13; Rom 6:3). Through these actions he has cleansed and sanctified his bride, the church. Thus, the presentation of the bride, though it has eschatological aspects (as worked out in the parable of the Ten Virgins, Mt 25:1–13), has already been accomplished in the atoning work of Christ.[65] The church is already now the bride of Christ (Mt 9:15; 22:1–14; Rev 19:7); she celebrates liturgically on earth the marriage feast of the Lamb (Rev 19:9) even though it reaches its full glory only in eternity (Rev 21:2). The Lord's Supper encapsulates the "now" and "not yet" aspects of the marriage of Christ and the church most beautifully; it is the "foretaste of the feast to come."[66] The past and future aspects of the presentation are accompanied by a present continuous sense, as Christ, through the ministry, presents the bride to himself with every individual Baptism (2 Cor

---

believer's own confession of faith (contra Bruce, *The Epistles to the Colossians, to Philemon, and to the Ephesians*, 388–89), for the whole emphasis of this passage is on the monergistic action of Christ. Nor should the water and the Word be separated, as if sanctification happens through one and cleansing through the other. Both "of water" and "in the Word" modify λουτρῷ, "washing."

63 SC 4:2 (*LSB* 325; *BELK*, 515; cf. *Triglotta*, 550).

64 Luther, "Second Wedding Sermon on Ephesians 5:22–33," StL 12:2020–22, §§ 5–9.

65 Contra, e.g., Bruce, *The Epistles to the Colossians, to Philemon, and to the Ephesians*, 389, and Barth, *Ephesians*, 2:628, 669, 678, who hold to an exclusively eschatological presentation. Mitchell, *The Song of Songs*, 51–53, emphasizes the "not yet" aspect of the NT marriage imagery (in contrast to the "now" emphasis in the OT), though he notes the tension that must be maintained between passages that speak of the church as betrothed to Christ, awaiting the consummation (e.g., Mt 25:1–13), and those that speak of the eschatological feast as already begun (e.g., Mt 9:15; 22:1–14; Rev 19:7–9). The term νύμφη, "bride," captures this tension well, in that it can refer to the woman both immediately before and immediately after the marriage ceremony. It is interesting that the church is called the γυνή, "wife," of Christ only at the very end (Rev 19:7; 21:9). However, it is not insignificant that Paul is addressing *husbands and wives* in Ephesians 5, not betrothed couples, when comparing them to Christ and the church.

66 *LSB* 955; cf. *LSB* 155: "This *is* the feast of victory for our God. ... For the Lamb who was slain *has begun* His reign" (emphasis added). Both © 1978 *Lutheran Book of Worship*; used by permission of Concordia Publishing House.

11:2).[67] The present verse, by maintaining the figure of marriage, suggests an analogy between Baptism and the ceremonial bath by which a bride was prepared for her wedding.[68] What is remarkable in Paul's presentation is that the groom himself prepares the bride for the wedding, by bathing, dressing, and adorning her—an action that would be entirely inappropriate at the human level.[69] Christ thus fills multiple roles in the ancient Jewish wedding: friend or guardian of the bride (cf. Song 3:6–8; 2 Cor 11:2), "friend of the bridegroom" (cf. Judg 14:20; 15:2, 6; Jn 3:29), and the bridegroom himself (Mt 9:15). Through this astonishing image, God's own actions in preparing Israel to be his bride (Is 60:9; Ezek 16:8–14) are evoked. Thus, it is "he [Christ] himself" (αὐτός) who presents (παραστήσῃ) the bride "to himself" (ἑαυτῷ) in all her radiance (cf. 2 Cor 4:14; 11:2; Col 1:22). There is no room here for synergism.

The nouns σπίλος, "spot," and ῥυτίς, "wrinkle," are rare.[70] That the bride has neither spot nor wrinkle is probably a reference to her youthful beauty. This is the physical side of ἔνδοξον, "glorious," which includes also the bride's clothing and jewelry.[71] Certainly an earthly bride is expected to come to her marriage with moral purity, which her outward splendor represents (παρθένον ἁγνήν, "pure virgin," 2 Cor 11:2). But in the case of this divine marriage, Paul emphasizes that her true spiritual holiness is a gift of the Bridegroom, just as God says to his child-bride Israel: "[It is] my splendor that I bestowed upon you" (Ezek 16:14; cf. Rev 19:8; 21:9–11).[72]

---

[67] Luther, "Second Wedding Sermon on Ephesians 5:22–33," StL 12:2021, § 6, compares the apostolic ministry to the role of the servant (the *Freier*, "suitor") who is sent to secure a bride for Isaac (Genesis 24).

[68] Evidence for the Jewish bridal bath is given in Str-B, 1:506. See Ruth 3:3; Ezek 16:9; 23:40. Non-Jewish cultures had similar traditions. The *Catechism of the Catholic Church* (Ottawa: Canadian Conference of Catholic Bishops, 1994), § 1617, draws the sacramental connection: "The entire Christian life bears the mark of the spousal love of Christ and the Church. Already Baptism, the entry into the People of God, is a nuptial mystery; it is so to speak the nuptial bath [cf. Eph 5:26–27] which precedes the wedding feast, the Eucharist."

[69] In ancient times, the bride's female family members and friends (cf. Song 1:4–5; 8:13) or servants would have prepared her, and her father or a friend of the groom would have presented her, though the customs likely varied, and there is little evidence to go on. See Best, *Ephesians*, 545; Barth, *Ephesians*, 2:678–79; Str-B, 1:500–17.

[70] Elsewhere in the Greek Bible, σπίλος, "spot, stain," appears only in 2 Pet 2:13, and the cognate verb σπιλόω, "to stain," only in Wis Sol 15:4; James 3:6; Jude 23. "Spot" might have a double reference to a disqualification from being an acceptable sacrifice; see ἄσπιλος, "spotless," and/or ἄμωμος, "without blemish," in 1 Pet 1:19; 2 Pet 3:14; see also ἄμωμος in the second textual note on Eph 5:27. The noun ῥυτίς is a biblical hapax legomenon, although it is attested in Classical Greek with the meaning "pucker, wrinkle" (LSJM).

[71] See Ezek 16:10–14; Ps 45:14 (ET 45:13); cf. Lk 7:25. In the messianic Psalm 45, the bride is called "all glorious [כָּל־כְּבוּדָּה; LXX: πᾶσα ἡ δόξα]" (Ps 45:14 [ET 45:13; LXX 44:14]), perhaps a reference to the splendor of her wedding garment, which is colorful and interwoven with gold. Adjectives formed with ἐν- often stand in parallel or contrast to ones formed with ἀ- (*alpha*-privative); see 1 Cor 4:10; 9:21 (cf. Rom 2:12); see also BDF, § 120 (2). Hence, ἔνδοξον, "glorious" (Eph 5:27), not only contrasts with the terms "spot" and "wrinkle," but also parallels the ἀ-privative term ἄμωμος, "without blemish" (see the next textual note).

[72] The verb παρίστημι, "present," here takes a double accusative: "that he might present *the church* [τὴν ἐκκλησίαν] ... as *glorious* [ἔνδοξον]" (cf. ὑμᾶς ... παρθένον ἁγνὴν παραστῆσαι, "to present *you* ... as a *pure virgin*," in 2 Cor 11:2). BDAG, s.v. παρίστημι, 1 c, suggests this for Eph 5:27: " 'present' becomes almost equivalent to ***make, render*.**" In other words, it is

ἀλλ' ἵνα ᾖ ἁγία καὶ ἄμωμος—With these words the verse returns to OT cultic language (see ἅγιος and ἄμωμος also in the fourth textual note on 1:4). An ordinary but beautiful earthly bride might be described as "without blemish,"[73] but "holy" says something that takes us beyond the ordinary bridal analogy. In addition to the bridal bath, therefore, there is a double reference to the washing by which priest and people are prepared to come into God's presence, as in 5:26. The term ἄμωμος, "without blemish," alludes to the cultic regulations of Leviticus, which stipulate, first, that a blemish disqualifies a man from service in God's presence as a priest (Lev 21:17–23). Thus, the church, as God's priestly people, must be holy and without blemish to dwell in his presence (1 Pet 2:9–10). Second, all sacrifices must be "without blemish"; the offering of a damaged or worthless animal is an affront to the Lord (Lev 22:20–25). Christ, by contrast, prepares the bride through the washing of Holy Baptism to be a perfect living sacrifice (Rom 12:1; 1 Pet 2:5)—not destroyed through the offering, but transformed from a profane and filthy existence into a holy and blameless people of God.[74]

As "holy" and "without blemish" are qualities of Christ himself (ἅγιος in Lk 1:35; 4:34; and passim; ἄμωμος in Heb 9:14; 1 Pet 1:9), this holy marriage involves an "exchange of goods" between the Bridegroom and the bride: all that is his becomes hers, and all that is hers (every spot and wrinkle) becomes his (Is 53:2–5; 2 Cor 5:21).

5:28 οὕτως ὀφείλουσιν [καὶ] οἱ ἄνδρες ἀγαπᾶν τὰς ἑαυτῶν γυναῖκας ὡς τὰ ἑαυτῶν σώματα—With the adverb οὕτως, "thus," Paul rounds off this section of the analogy involving Christ and the husband (5:25–30) with a concluding exhortation to the husband (5:28–30), just as he had spoken to the wife (5:24). Thus, 5:25–30 forms a unit, with words to the husband (5:25a, 28–29a) framing a proclamation of what Christ has done (5:25b–27). The verb ὀφείλουσιν (from ὀφείλω), "ought," which implies a debt, a moral obligation (cf. Rom 13:8), reminds us that even though the main point of the passage is a proclamation of the Gospel of Christ, the obligations laid upon husband and wife remain significant. The adverb οὕτως, "thus," means that the husband's obligation

---

Christ's work that makes her glorious. Like God's bride Israel, as imaged by Hosea's wife, the prostitute (Hos 1:2), or the sordid women who receive Jesus' love (Lk 7:36–50; Jn 4:18), the bride brings no comeliness of her own. With ἔνδοξος, "glorious," Paul may imply a reference to glory as an essential quality of God (e.g., LXX Is 24:15; 59:19; Dan 3:45; *1 Clement*, 43:2; 58:1). Thus, the holy and glorious bride looks divine. Cf. Eph 1:6, 17–18 and the third textual note on 1:17.

[73] Certainly, even in the marital analogy, "without blemish" can have a typological double meaning, as with the description of the bride in the Song of Songs: "there is no blemish in you [μῶμος οὐκ ἔστιν ἐν σοί]" (LXX Song 4:7). A blemish may result from old age or disease, as the healthy Judean youths in LXX Dan 1:4 are ἀμώμους, "without blemish." Thus, on the one hand, the king's bride is young and beautiful (physically "without blemish"). But as a type of the bride of Christ, the church, she is also given the gift of spiritual cleansing so that she is "without blemish" in God's eyes. See also the next textual note.

[74] The term for "blemish" in Song 4:7 is מוּם, regularly translated in the LXX as μῶμος. In one passage (Job 11:15), however, the LXX makes a fascinating exception: because of an apparent textual confusion between מוּם, "blemish," and מַיִם, "water," the LXX renders "you will lift up your face without blemish" as "your face will shine again as pure water [ὕδωρ καθαρόν]." With some caution, Sampley, *"And the Two Shall Become One Flesh,"* 49, therefore argues that "washing with water … that she might be holy and without blemish" (Eph 5:26–27) might involve a play on words between מוּם, "blemish," and מַיִם, "water."

to his wife is a conclusion drawn from the relationship of Christ to the church. We should, therefore, understand the words ὡς τὰ ἑαυτῶν σώματα, "as their own bodies," not as a simple comparison ("*in the same way* that they love their own bodies") but as a cause, "*since* they are their own bodies."[75]

With this conclusion, however, Paul introduces a major point that bears further explanation, forming the basis of the following verses (5:29–32). The identification of the wife with the husband's own body means that his obligation to love his wife is more intense than the general debt of love between Christians.[76]

ὁ ἀγαπῶν τὴν ἑαυτοῦ γυναῖκα ἑαυτὸν ἀγαπᾷ—This clause explains more precisely the previous phrase, "as their own bodies." Paul has previously identified the church as Christ's "body" (σῶμα, 5:23).[77] Soon he will identify the sexual act as a concrete expression of the union between husband and wife, their "one flesh" relationship (5:31). Here he identifies the foundational spiritual union that leads a man to consider his wife to be his very own body. She is not just *like* his own body, she *is* his own body; husband and wife have a unity that is every bit as real as the mystical union of the church with Christ through Baptism into him. Far from encouraging a selfish view of marriage (as if one ought to care more for oneself than for others),[78] Paul's words forbid a husband so to distance himself from his wife that he might consider himself more important than her. If God's children should love their neighbors (and even their enemies!) as themselves,[79] how much more a husband his wife.[80]

---

[75] Barth, *Ephesians*, 2:629–30, argues that the placement of καί before οἱ ἄνδρες (rather than before σώματα) requires this interpretation. In other words, the chief point of comparison is between Christ and husbands, not between the husbands' bodies and their wives. This, too, is the meaning of the parallel expression οὕτως καὶ αἱ γυναῖκες, "thus also wives," in 5:24. This argument is weakened if the omission of καί in א 𝔐, etc., is the original reading. The textual support for its inclusion is very strong, though it might have been inserted out of a desire to harmonize with 5:24 and to resolve the ambiguity of the comparison here.

[76] Rom 13:8; 15:1; 1 Jn 3:16; 4:11.

[77] Also 1:23; 2:16; 4:4, 12, 16; 5:30; cf. 3:6.

[78] "Paul does not depreciate the husband's love by measuring it with the stick of natural egotism and by subjecting the wife to her husband's untamed selfishness" (Barth, *Ephesians*, 2:630). "Paul's thought does not ascend from love of self to love for one's wife, and from there to love of Christ. Rather his logic goes in the opposite direction: from the love shown by Christ (vss. 25–27), he descends to the love shown for the wife, and he ends with the love of the husband for 'himself'" (Barth, 2:633).

[79] Lev 19:18; Mt 19:19; 22:39 (and parallels); Rom 13:9; Gal 5:14; James 2:8.

[80] Sampley, *"And the Two Shall Become One Flesh,"* 30–34, argues that Paul bases the admonition to love one's *wife* as oneself (Eph 5:28) on Lev 19:18's admonition to love one's *neighbor* as oneself, suggesting that OT and Jewish tradition had already made the equation of "wife" and "neighbor." As evidence, Sampley notes that the Song of Songs uses the feminine form of the noun "neighbor" (רַעְיָה; LXX: ἡ πλησίον) as a term of endearment for the bride (1:9, 15; 2:2, 10, 13; 4:1, 7; 5:2; 6:4). Since "neighbor" means "one near by," the point is that a man's wife is the one "nearest" and dearest to him and therefore is to be loved as his neighbor par excellence. Yet, as Best, *Ephesians*, 558, wryly observes: "Surely also there must be a distinction between the way a husband loves his wife and the way he loves his neighbour's wife." Thus, Paul is probably not *extending* Lev 19:18 to a husband's love for his wife, but making an argument from lesser to greater.

5:29 οὐδεὶς γάρ ποτε τὴν ἑαυτοῦ σάρκα ἐμίσησεν ἀλλὰ ἐκτρέφει καὶ θάλπει αὐτήν, καθὼς καὶ ὁ Χριστὸς τὴν ἐκκλησίαν—Paul's proverb-like assertion that "no one ever *hated* his own flesh" (ἐμίσησεν, a gnomic aorist[81]) perhaps strikes the modern reader as naïve in an age of bulimia, self-loathing, and suicidal depression. Some extreme ascetic practices in Christian history (such as self-flagellation) could also be raised in objection. One suspects such tragic self-hatred existed back in Paul's day—certainly asceticism did (Col 2:23)—even if it did not reach the level induced by our success- and celebrity-driven culture. His statement is perhaps hyperbolic ("*no* one *ever*"), but it expresses the natural desire for self-preservation that God has implanted in his creatures.[82]

For, as a general rule, people do try to "nourish" (ἐκτρέφω) their "flesh."[83] ἐκτρέφω occurs in the NT only here and in 6:4, but twenty-six times in the LXX, where it often refers to raising and feeding children. The second verb, θάλπω, "cherish," also can refer to caring for children (1 Thess 2:7) and conjures a tender image of a husband's relationship to his wife (cf. the young woman who cherishes so as to warm the aged King David: θάλπω, LXX 3 Kgdms 1:2, 4 [MT/ET 1 Ki 1:2, 4]). It would be wrong to suggest that Paul treats the wife as a child, since, first, he uses these two verbs of the man's care for his own body, and, second, the verbs are used for marriage and other relationships in extrabiblical Greek.[84] But it is certainly appropriate to think of the church as a tender young bride under Christ's mature and caring guardianship. There may even be a subtle nod to the NT teaching that the church is an infant, nourished and fed by Christ toward maturity.[85] The language is thus particularly appropriate to the heavenly side of the analogy, for Christ truly nourishes the church, even to the point of giving his very body and blood for her to eat, spreading a banquet before her.[86] Thus, both Baptism (5:26) and the Lord's Supper feature prominently in Christ's care for his bride, the church. Birth is followed up with feeding.

5:30 ὅτι μέλη ἐσμὲν τοῦ σώματος αὐτοῦ—This clarification of the terms of the analogy, "for we are members of his body," is scarcely necessary at this point in the letter,

---

[81] BDF, § 333 (1); Turner, *Syntax*, 73–74; Burton, *Moods and Tenses*, § 43. In this usage we see that the aorist (literally, "undefined") is often timeless. It can be translated with a general present tense in English: "no one ever hates …"

[82] "Every creature loves its like, and every person his neighbor; all living beings associate by species, and a man clings to one like himself" (Sirach 13:15–16 RSV).

[83] The shift from σῶμα, "body" (5:28), to σάρξ, "flesh" (5:29), may have been prompted by the fact that the latter noun is feminine and thus more neatly identifies with the wife; it is also the term used in Gen 2:24, which Paul quotes in Eph 5:31. Generally σάρξ is interchangeable with σῶμα. See 1 Cor 6:16; 15:39–40; 2 Cor 4:10–11. Compare 2 Cor 12:7 to Gal 6:17.

[84] See BDAG, s.v. ἐκτρέφω, 1, with its reference to Aesop. Best, *Ephesians*, 550, quotes the language of an ancient marriage contract: θάλπειν καὶ τρέφειν καὶ ἱματίζειν αὐτήν, the husband is "to cherish and nourish and clothe her [his wife]" (citing Friedrich Preisigke, *Wörterbuch der griechischen Papyrusurkunden* [Berlin: Selbstverlag der Erben, 1925], 1:665; see the similar marriage contract in Moulton-Milligan, s.v. θάλπω; cf. Moulton-Milligan, s.v. τρέφω).

[85] Eph 4:14–16; 1 Thess 2:7; 1 Pet 2:2; cf. Mt 11:25; 1 Cor 3:1.

[86] Ps 23:5; Mt 26:26–29; Jn 4:32–34; 6:53–58; 10:9, 27–28; 21:15–17; Rev 2:7. Cf. Justin Martyr, *First Apology*, 66:1.

in which the church as Christ's "body" has featured significantly.[87] But perhaps the unique application of the "head" and "body" image to marriage (5:23, 28) prompts Paul to repeat the point—and to make an explicit identification of the two major images for the church in this letter: the church that has been called Christ's wife/bride is now also called his body. Although Paul has used biological language of Christians as joints and ligaments within Christ's body (4:15–16) and has called Christians "members [μέλη] of one another" (4:25), this is the only place in Ephesians where he explicitly identifies Christians as "members" (μέλη) of Christ's body (but he does so elsewhere, e.g., 1 Cor 6:15; 12:27).

The image may have been prompted by consideration of Gen 2:24, which Paul will quote in the next verse (Eph 5:31). The church as Christ's bride consists of members of his body because she has been formed from his side (Jn 7:38; 19:34; 1 Jn 5:6),[88] just as Eve was drawn forth from Adam's (Gen 2:21–23).[89]

5:31 ἀντὶ τούτου καταλείψει ἄνθρωπος [τὸν] πατέρα καὶ [τὴν] μητέρα καὶ προσκολληθήσεται πρὸς τὴν γυναῖκα αὐτοῦ, καὶ ἔσονται οἱ δύο εἰς σάρκα μίαν— There are two intriguing aspects to the way Paul uses this quotation of Gen 2:24. First, he inserts it into the discussion without any citation formula (such as "Scripture says" or "it says," as in Eph 4:8; 5:14). This may simply mean that Paul believes the passage is so familiar that no introduction is needed. But it may also suggest that the passage has been so organically incorporated into the context of Eph 5:31 that it is not purely a quotation of the OT. This impression is reinforced by a second fact: while Paul appears to be following the LXX, he quotes the passage with variations that on the surface appear to be minor, but may actually be quite significant.[90] It is Paul's habit to quote OT pas-

---

[87] See σῶμα in 1:23; 2:16; 4:4, 12, 16; 5:23, 30; cf. 3:6.

[88] Augustine, *Tractates on John*, 9:10, comments on Jn 2:6:

And since the Lord has enlightened us through the apostle, to show us what we were in search of, by this one sentence, "The two shall be one flesh; a great mystery concerning Christ and the Church" [Eph 5:31–32]; we are now permitted to seek Christ everywhere, and to drink wine from all the water-pots. Adam sleeps, that Eve may be formed [Gen 2:21–23]; Christ dies, that the Church may be formed. When Adam sleeps, Eve is formed from his side; when Christ is dead, the spear pierces His side [Jn 19:34], that the mysteries [*sacramenta*, "Sacraments"] may flow forth whereby the Church is formed. (*NPNF*[1] 7:66–67; PL 35:1463)

[89] "Just as Eve was fashioned from Adam, so were we from Christ the Lord. We are buried with him in baptism. We rise with him. We eat his body and drink his blood [in the Eucharist]" (Theodoret, *Ephesians*, 5:30, ACCS 8:198). The textual variant in Eph 5:30 that inserts the words "of his flesh and of his bones" from Gen 2:23, though probably not original to Paul, confirms that scribes picked up on the allusion to Eve's creation from Adam's side.

[90] In comparing Eph 5:31 with LXX Gen 2:24, one notes these differences:

1. The preposition ἀντί replaces ἕνεκεν, with no difference in meaning (BDF, § 208 [1]; Moule, *Idiom Book*, 71).

2. The LXX includes the possessive pronoun αὐτοῦ, "his," after "father" and "mother," faithfully reproducing the original Hebrew possessive suffixes, while Ephesians omits them.

3. The Hebrew definite articles on "father" and "mother" are represented in the LXX, but are omitted in some manuscripts (B D* F G) of Eph 5:31. The uncertainty expressed by the brackets in NA[27], [τὸν] ... [τήν], despite the weak attestation for the omission, arises

sages in such a way that their fulfillment in Christ is highlighted (see the textual notes on 4:8). Thus, it may be that through these variations from the LXX Paul wishes to express more clearly the application of the text from Genesis to Christ and the church (see Eph 5:32). It is possible, then, that Paul's introductory words, ἀντὶ τούτου, "for *this* reason" (which differ slightly from the LXX), have a meaning and referent in the present context that goes beyond their original context in Gen 2:23–24; that is, they may refer back to *Paul's* previous statement "we are members of his [Christ's] body" (Eph 5:30), which gives a deeper reason why "a man will leave father and mother and cleave to his wife" (5:31).[91] In other words, all human marriages take place not simply because Eve was created from Adam but because of and in order to point to Christ's marriage to the church (5:32; see below).

More important than the state of the text are the two chief reasons Paul introduces it. First, the text may be viewed as the foundation of Rabbi Paul's "midrash," his exposition of the Torah. Although the mystery of Christ has been revealed to him as an apostle in the line of prophets (Eph 3:1–13), he remains rooted in the written Word and its exposition. Second, the text is the divine institution of marriage and for this reason serves as Paul's starting point. In this way he follows our Lord (Mt 19:5; Mk 10:7–8).

In the extended analogy between earthly marriage and the divine marriage of Christ and the church, Paul finds significance in the parallel actions of "leaving" and "cleaving." The referent of the former is not obvious, though Paul probably had in mind the incarnation and/or the humiliation of Christ, by which the Son of God left ("descended," 4:9–10) his heavenly Father to seek out his earthly bride.[92] The verb καταλείπω, "leave" (Eph 5:31), is used of Jesus' departure from his earthly family as he begins his ministry (Mt 4:13). The related verb ἐγκαταλείπω is used when in death Jesus is "forsaken"

---

from the fact that scribes would be more likely to bring the text in line with the LXX than out of line.

The quotation of Gen 2:24 in Mt 19:5 ‖ Mk 10:7–8 has similar minor variations. The inclusion of οἱ δύο, "the two," in Eph 5:31 suggests Paul is indeed following the LXX, since the original Hebrew simply has a plural verb: וְהָיוּ, "and they will be." Likewise, the noun ἄνθρωπος in the quotation indicates Paul's dependence on the LXX, since he has heretofore used ἀνήρ (5:22–25, 28; also in 5:33).

[91] See Barth, *Ephesians*, 2:639: "Why has it been written, 'A man will leave … be joined … become one' [Gen 2:24]? And the answer is given: Because in that great event in which the Messiah proved to be 'savior of his body,' the church ([Eph 5:]23), all that was said of Adam and Eve in Gen 2 was fulfilled!"

[92] "From heav'n He came and sought her To be His holy bride" (*LSB* 644:1; cf. *LSB* 556:5). Cf. J. Jeremias, "νύμφη, νυμφίος," *TDNT* 4:1105. Jerome (*Ephesians*, 3:5.32 [PL 26:535]) and Augustine (*Tractates on John*, 9:10) identified the father as God the Father and the mother as the heavenly Jerusalem or as Judaism, respectively. Augustine writes:

He left his Father in the sense that, when he was in the form of God he … emptied himself, assuming the form of a slave. … That means that he left the Father, not by deserting him or withdrawing from him but by coming to humanity in a lowly form in which he temporarily divested his glory with the Father. (ACCS 8:198)

Lincoln, *Ephesians*, 380; Best, *Ephesians*, 556; and Schnackenburg, *Ephesians*, 255, are oddly opposed to an allegorical interpretation of "leaving." While the distinction between a father and a mother may not be an intended part of the typology, it is not far-fetched to see a reference to the incarnation in the language of "leaving."

by his Father for the sake of his bride (Mt 27:46). On more than one occasion, Jesus distances himself from any claim that his mother (and brothers) might have over him, devoting himself exclusively to his mission (Mt 12:46–50; Jn 2:3–4; cf. Mk 3:21); in this way he might be said to have "left his mother," as he did at the cross (Jn 19:26–27). The "cleaving" is clearly the marriage itself. προσκολληθήσεται, "he shall be joined to," is a future[93] passive that might imply God as the active agent, i.e., "God will join the man to his wife," but is more likely passive simply because this is an intransitive use of the verb προσκολλάω, thus meaning "he shall cleave to."[94] "Cleaving" to God is OT language for true faith in him that already then evoked a marriage-like relationship between God and his people.[95]

The interpretative problems in the second half of the verse are more suited to a commentary on Genesis, but can be summarized here: What is the precise referent of "and the two will become one flesh"? Is this a quasifigurative statement of the spiritual, emotional, or mystical union between husband and wife that is the essence of marriage, and thereby an explanation of "cleave to"? Or does it refer to the sexual union that is subsequent to the marital union proper, serving as an expression and consummation of the union brought about by the Word of God? The former interpretation might be supported by the previous context, in which the husband is exhorted to view his wife as his own flesh—a perspective that would apply to every moment of the married life and not simply to the moment of the sexual union. Thus, Christ draws the conclusion "so they are no longer two but one flesh" (Mt 19:6). The latter interpretation would be supported by Paul's statement that one who joins himself to a prostitute becomes "one body" with her (1 Cor 6:16), which surely cannot mean that they are married—indeed, the immorality of the act follows precisely from the fact that they are *not* married. The most satisfactory interpretation takes both points into account: that through marriage

---

[93] The future tense should not be interpreted as eschatological, that is, as implying that the union of Christ and his bride, the church, is entirely in the future. The future tense comes from the text quoted, which has the identical verb; προσκολληθήσεται in LXX Gen 2:24 might be called "gnomic" (BDF, § 349 [1]; cf. Rom 3:20; 5:7; 7:3), i.e., it is a proverbial convention referring to all marriages subsequent to Adam and Eve's. The LXX faithfully reproduces the original Hebrew, which uses an imperfect (יַעֲזָב־) for any man in future generations who "*will* leave" his parents, followed by a perfect with *waw* consecutive (וְדָבַק), meaning "and [then] he *will* cleave to" his wife. In such a verbal sequence, the perfect with *waw* consecutive takes on the time frame or aspect of the preceding verb and thus is translated as future tense.

[94] BDAG, s.v. προσκολλάω: "to adhere to closely, *be faithfully devoted to, join* w. dat." This lexicon makes the marriage bond unduly subjective, however, when it says "of the *attachment felt* by a husband for his wife" (emphasis added). There is no indication in Gen 2:24 that the bond consists of emotion. Nor does the marriage bond dissolve simply because a spouse's feeling of attachment weakens.

[95] See דָּבַק, "cleave, cling to" (the verb in Gen 2:24), with reference to God in Deut 4:4; 10:20; 11:22; 13:5 (ET 13:4); 30:20; Josh 22:5; 23:8; 2 Ki 18:6; Jer 13:11; Pss 63:9 (ET 63:8; LXX 62:9); 119:31 (LXX 118:31). In many of these verses, the LXX translates the verb with κολλάω or προσκολλάω; see also LXX Deut 6:13; Ps 72:28 (MT/ET 73:28). Josh 23:12 combines both the theological and the human dimensions when it warns the Israelites against "cleaving to" (דָּבַק) the remaining Canaanites and intermarrying with them, for such human marriages ensnare God's people in idolatry and join them to false gods, as happened to Solomon (דָּבַק in 1 Ki 11:2; cf. 2 Ki 3:3).

the husband and wife are one body, one flesh, and that the sexual union is the most intimate consequence and expression of that mystical union. Through marriage a new family has been formed, a new flesh and blood kinship.[96] In both respects, mystical and fleshly, the marriage of a man and a woman is like the relationship between Christ and the church, for it is a union effected by God through his Word that is so intimate as to be called "one body" (4:4), "one flesh" (5:31 in light of 5:32). The NT uses such language of both Holy Baptism and the Lord's Supper, the Sacraments by which the Christian is joined with Christ in his death and resurrection and united to his very body and blood.[97]

5:32 τὸ μυστήριον τοῦτο μέγα ἐστίν—The meaning of this clause was unhappily rendered by the KJV as "this is a great mystery." It is more accurately translated as "this mystery is great."[98] Paul is not saying that it is something that is simply beyond our comprehension, though that is one aspect of μυστήριον, "mystery." But as Paul has previously used this key term in Ephesians (1:9; 3:3, 4, 9; later, 6:19), a μυστήριον is something that was once *hidden* in the mind of God, yet has now been *disclosed* through the revelation of Jesus Christ to his apostolic messengers.[99] As the content of the mystery in Paul's usage is always Jesus Christ, the application of the term to holy marriage implies also that *Christ* was once hidden in marriage and is now visible. Paul's purpose in the words leading up to the biblical quotation in 5:31 has been to demonstrate this very thing, to disclose the typological nature of marriage, showing how it teaches Christ's sacrificial love for the church and the church's corresponding submission to his

---

[96] Gordon J. Wenham, *Genesis* (Waco: Word, 1987), 1:71:

"They become one flesh" [Gen 2:24]. This does not denote merely the sexual union that follows marriage, or the children conceived in marriage, or even the spiritual and emotional relationship that it involves, though all are involved in becoming one flesh. Rather it affirms that just as blood relations are one's flesh and bone (cf. *Comment* on v 23), so marriage creates a similar kinship relation between man and wife. They become related to each other as brother and sister are.

[97] E.g., Jn 6:53–58; Rom 6:1–4; 1 Cor 10:16; 11:23–29; 12:13; Gal 3:26–29. Again, Theodoret comments: "Just as Eve was fashioned from Adam, so were we from Christ the Lord. We are buried with him in baptism. We rise with him. We eat his body and drink his blood [in the Eucharist]" (*Ephesians*, 5:30, ACCS 8:198). Schlier, *Epheser*, 280, draws a similar twofold sacramental connection. Nonetheless, it is not defensible to distinguish the mystical from the sexual union in such a way as to align one with each Sacrament, Baptism as the mystical/marital union and the Lord's Supper as the fleshly union. While there are clear allusions to both Sacraments in this unit, such an interpretation might be labeled "allegorizing"—i.e., it seeks a higher degree of correspondence between the individual details of the type and antitype than the author of the text likely had in mind.

[98] Scharlemann, "The Pastoral Office and Divorce, Remarriage, Moral Deviation," 146:

Unhappily the New King James Bible has not corrected the old reading, "This is a great mystery." The Greek word order can only mean: "This mystery is a big one"; namely, God's redeeming activity is somehow reflected and to be seen in a very special way when "the husband loves his wife as himself, and the wife respects her husband" (v. 33), and when both do so with Christ and His church as their paradigm.

[99] See especially the first textual notes and the commentary on 1:9 and 3:3. Preaching on Eph 5:32, Luther defines a "mystery" as "a hidden, secret thing, which is understood in the Spirit, only through faith and according to the Word, not through reason or by sight" ("Second Wedding Sermon on Ephesians 5:22–33," StL 12:2023, § 11). He proceeds to explain that it is in the water and Word of Holy Baptism that the mystery is unfolded.

saving work. The mystery is "great" not because it is unusually difficult, but because its content (the Gospel of Jesus Christ) is so significant (cf. 1 Tim 3:16).

Most Old Latin translations[100] and the Vulgate rendered μυστήριον as *sacramentum*,[101] which means "sacred/holy thing." Although most early church fathers did not thereby draw the conclusion that marriage was a "Sacrament" in the same sense as Baptism and the Eucharist,[102] this verbal correspondence ultimately lent support to the inclusion of marriage among the seven Sacraments of the Roman (and Orthodox) Church—though enumerations of the Sacraments varied widely until the twelfth century (Peter Lombard).[103] When the Augsburg Confession failed to enumerate the seven Sacraments in Article 13, the Roman Confutation objected. The Apology responded with little interest in a precise enumeration of the Sacraments, but expressed a concern to maintain what was instituted in Scripture. The Apology distinguishes marriage, instituted at creation, from the Sacraments that were instituted later by Christ in the NT and are "testimonies of grace and of the forgiveness of sins" (Ap 13:14). Yet, because marriage is instituted by God, the Apology is willing to call marriage a Sacrament in the broad sense (Ap 13:15). The assertion that marriage has "certain promises" pertaining "to physical life and not strictly to the New Testament" (Ap 13:14) confesses accurately the essential nature of marriage as applicable to all people, whether Christian or not, and its "of this world" nature.[104] Marriage does not in and of itself confer sav-

---

[100] A few have *mysterium* or *ministerium*.

[101] Later Christian writers, who identify marriage as a Sacrament simply by citing this verse in its Vulgate translation, make a basic linguistic error. They assume, first, that Jerome used the term *sacramentum* in its later dogmatic sense; and, second, they read that dogmatic meaning back into the underlying Greek term μυστήριον, as if it meant "Sacrament" in the NT. In a sense, the argument of the translation of μυστήριον itself distracts from the real interpretative issues in the passage. Schlier, *Epheser*, 276, argues that marriage is to be regarded as sacramental not because μυστήριον has been translated as *sacramentum* but because Paul views earthly marriage as the *Nachvollzug*, "representation, type," of the heavenly marriage of Christ and the church.

[102] That is, a "Sacrament" in the sense of something that is holy in itself and that sanctifies or makes holy. See Schnackenburg, *Ephesians*, 332–34.

[103] Peter Lombard, *Sentences*, 4:2.1. The Council of Florence (1439) was the first to enumerate the seven Sacraments officially (*Decree for the Armenians*, quoted in Denzinger, §§ 1310–27). This was repeated by Trent (Denzinger, §§ 1800–1801). Schnackenburg, *Ephesians*, 334, n. 17, points most helpfully for further detail to Ralph J. Lawrence, *The Sacramental Interpretation of Ephesians 5:32 from Peter Lombard to the Council of Trent* (Washington, D.C., 1963; originally an S.T.D. dissertation, Catholic University of America, 1963); and E. Schillebeeckx, *Marriage: Human Reality and Sacred Mystery* (New York: Sheed & Ward, 1965), 111–17. Schnackenburg, *Ephesians*, 335, notes that even though Trent enumerated marriage with the Sacraments, there remained significant differences of opinion among the participants in the council. The final pronouncement merely says that Paul in Eph 5:25, 32 "*indicates* (innuit) the grace which Christ earned for us through his death which completes the natural love, secures the insoluble unity and sanctifies the partners in the marriage" (Schnackenburg, 335; see Denzinger, § 1799).

[104] Schnackenburg, *Ephesians*, 335–36, quotes the Roman Catholic scholar Schillebeeckx, whom he says "level-headedly gives his opinion":

> The reaction of the Reformation which refused to accept the *sacramentality* of marriage was not, if we go to the root of the matter, a denial of the holy character of married life but rather a protest against the extension of ecclesiastical jurisdiction in

621

ing faith or righteousness upon its recipients. But there is more that can be said on the basis of Paul's words. Paul discloses the "mystery" (Eph 5:32) to the baptized, so that the "enlightened" (1:18) can see something in marriage that is deeper than what the unbeliever experiences: the proclamation of the Gospel of Christ.[105] Luther, even while denying that marriage is a Sacrament, can call it an "outward allegory" of Christ and the church.[106] In this sense we can speak of "*holy* matrimony"[107] and view it as a sign of the Gospel to be received by faith. Thus, if it is not a Sacrament in the proper sense, it is nevertheless sacramental.[108] Luther offered the following prayer at the marriage of Caspar Creuziger and Apollonia Gunterode (Easter 1536):

> Lord God, who created man and wife and appointed them to the estate of marriage, who furthermore did bless them with the fruits of the body, and thereby did signify [*bezeichnet*] the Sacrament of your dear Son, Jesus Christ, and the church, his bride: we entreat your boundless goodness that you would

---

> a matter which was held to be essentially "worldly," although it was conceded that it must be lived "in the Lord." (As quoted in the English translation of Schnackenburg's commentary; cf. Schillebeeckx, *Marriage*, 316)

[105] Luther, "Second Wedding Sermon on Ephesians 5:22–33," StL 12:2019, § 2, proclaims:

> For although even the heathen have held the estate of marriage to be praised and honored against whoring and adultery, nevertheless they have not known about this high honor, that God holds it so highly that he has intertwined himself into it and through it united himself with us. Therefore they have been unable to hold it so high and gloriously as Christians, who know that Christ himself is our Bridegroom and they (as members of Christendom, his bride) belong to this spiritual marriage.

[106] Luther, *The Babylonian Captivity of the Church* (1520), AE 36:94–95:

> Therefore, a sacrament is a mystery, or secret thing, which is set forth in words, but received by the faith of the heart. Such a sacrament is spoken of in the passage before us: "The two shall become one. This is a great sacrament" [Eph. 5:31–32], which they understand as spoken of marriage, whereas Paul himself wrote these words as applying to Christ and the church, and clearly explained them himself by saying: "I take it to mean Christ and the church" [Eph. 5:32]. See how well Paul and these men agree! Paul says he is proclaiming a great sacrament in Christ and the church, but they proclaim it in terms of man and a woman! If such liberty in the interpretation of the sacred Scriptures is permitted, it is small wonder that one finds here anything he pleases, even a hundred sacraments.

> Christ and the church are, therefore, a mystery, that is, a great and secret thing which can and ought to be represented in terms of marriage as a kind of outward allegory. But marriage ought not for that reason to be called a sacrament.

[107] "Holy Matrimony" is the title of the rite in, e.g., *LSB Agenda*, 64.

[108] Schnackenburg, *Ephesians*, 256, maintains the tension between what he calls the Roman Catholic and Protestant views: "Just as the Church is not freed from her existence in the world, so is the worldliness of marriage not called into question; and yet if the Christian marriage is lived in the manner required, as a meeting of love and subordination in love, it is also constantly summoned from a compulsive connection with the world in its limitations and referred to the area of salvation in Christ–Church." Schnackenburg (256, n. 59) illustrates the Roman Catholic position from Michael Schmaus, *Katholische Dogmatik* (Munich: Hueber, 1952), 4/1:622: "Marriage is to a certain extent an epiphany of the bond between Christ and Church. The fellowship of Christ with the Church has an effect on the fellowship between man and woman. This is filled with the life exchanged between Christ and the Church." This is a fair summary of what Paul is saying here. See also "Is Marriage an Allegory, a Type, a Sacrament, a Prophetic Sign, an Analogy, or What?" in Mitchell, *The Song of Songs*, 67–97.

not let this your creation, order, and blessing be frustrated or destroyed, but be preserved among us graciously, through Jesus Christ, our Lord. Amen.[109]

ἐγὼ δὲ λέγω εἰς Χριστὸν καὶ εἰς τὴν ἐκκλησίαν—The introductory words, ἐγὼ δὲ λέγω, "but I say," are emphatic and express a contrast. Perhaps Paul implies that his interpretation of the text is different from that of his contemporaries.[110] In this way he follows Christ's pattern in the Sermon on the Mount ("you have heard that it was said … ; but I say," e.g., Mt 5:21–22). Christ, as the author of Scripture, has the right to interpret it authoritatively. Paul speaks as Christ's apostle and writes under divine inspiration; thus, he can rightly claim to know the true meaning of Scripture because he has the mind of Christ (1 Cor 2:16; 7:25, 40) and has received a revelation of the mysteries (Eph 3:3).

The Spartan grammar of this clause makes little sense if it is translated word-for-word: "but I say to Christ and to the church."[111] The KJV, "but I speak concerning Christ and the church" (cf. NIV), might be understood to say that Paul is talking about the mystery of Christ and the church *rather than* about marriage. Paul's intention, however, is to relate the two things. One might, therefore, interpret Paul's meaning as "but I say that *marriage* refers to Christ and to the church." One could even say more precisely that the *first marriage* (that of Adam and Eve) refers to Christ and the church.[112] However, as these words follow so closely on the heels of the quotation of Gen 2:24 in Eph 5:31

---

[109] Luther, "Second Wedding Sermon on Ephesians 5:22–33," StL 12:2031.

[110] If the analogy to Christ is primary, Paul would be contrasting his interpretation with that of the rabbis. However, he may also be referring to various Greek notions that humanity was originally created androgynous before the separation of Eve from Adam and that salvation entailed the restoration of androgyny. Were such ideas prominent in Asia Minor at this time, as they would be among Gnostics and Encratites in later centuries? See the references in Lincoln, *Ephesians*, 382–83, e.g., *Gospel of Thomas*, logion 22, and Philo. NT references to anti-sexual ascetic tendencies may be related to this false teaching (1 Cor 7:5; 1 Tim 4:3). Adherents of this false teaching may have claimed Jesus' words in Lk 20:34–36 or Paul's in Gal 3:28 in support of their views. Barth, *Ephesians*, 2:644–45, argues that Gnosticizing interpretations of Christ and the church are dependent on Ephesians 5 and not vice versa.

[111] BDAG, s.v. λέγω, 2 e, suggests the translation "interpret with reference to." Unfortunately there is no precise parallel to this use of λέγω εἰς in the Greek Bible. Closest is Δαυὶδ γὰρ λέγει εἰς αὐτόν, "for David says concerning him [Christ]" (Acts 2:25). See also καὶ τοῦτο οὐκ εἰς ταύτας τὰς ἡμέρας λέγω, "and this I do not say [with reference] to these days" (*Shepherd of Hermas, Similitudes*, 9:26.6).

[112] Jerome comments:

The same allegorical interpretation applies both to Christ and to the church, that Adam is to prefigure Christ and Eve the church. For *the last Adam was made a lifegiving spirit* [1 Cor 15:45]. Just as the whole human race is born from Adam and his wife, so the whole multitude of believers has been born of Christ and the church. (*Ephesians*, 3:5.31, ACCS 8:198)

And he says:

Even all that is said of Adam and Eve is to be interpreted with reference to Christ and the church. (*Ephesians*, 3:5.32, ACCS 8:199)

As Jerome quite rightly supports his comments with a cross-reference to Paul (1 Cor 15:45), the Adam-Christ typology is easily demonstrated (cf. Rom 5:12–21), even in Ephesians (4:24). The Eve-church typology is not explicit in Paul (cf. Revelation 12), but might be a natural interpretation of the present passage.

(and the demonstrative pronoun τοῦτο, "this [mystery]," earlier in 5:32, refers to something immediately preceding), it is more likely that Paul is referring specifically to the exegesis of that passage; it contains a mystery.[113]

The full meaning of Gen 2:24 was not clear until Christ came. Now, by the revelation of the mystery, we see that it was never just about marriage; its deeper meaning was always about Christ's leaving the Father and cleaving to the church. The referent of "the mystery" is therefore Gen 2:24 itself,[114] a mysterious passage that has now been made clear. The meaning of Paul's words, then, is this: "but I say [that Gen 2:24 refers] to Christ and to the church" or "but I disclose the mystery of Gen 2:24 as being Christ and the church." The staggering import of Paul's words is a thoroughgoing reversal of the manner in which the symbolism of marriage is typically expressed. Paul does not simply say that the relationship of Christ to the church is *like* marriage. Rather, the apostle teaches that God *first* had Christ in mind and *then* instituted marriage to reflect what he would ultimately do.[115] In other words, earthly marriage reflects Christ and the

---

[113] Schlier, *Epheser*, 262, paraphrases: "*Ich* deute (die Stelle) auf Christus und die Kirche ['I point (the passage) to Christ and the church']," and says that Paul sees a *typos* in the passage. The use of μυστήριον to refer to an OT Bible passage needing interpretation in light of Christ is unparalleled in the NT, though the implication of Eph 3:5 is that the mystery was hidden in the OT, and Peter indicates that the prophets probed their own writings, seeking their messianic meaning (1 Pet 1:10–12). The usage can be found in early church fathers, including Justin Martyr, *Dialogue with Trypho*, 44, 78. It is also characteristic of Qumranic exegesis, where the Aramaic equivalent רז, "secret, mystery," is used (see Bruce, *The Epistles to the Colossians, to Philemon, and to the Ephesians*, 394–95). Barth, *Ephesians*, 2:643, demonstrates that this is the most common patristic interpretation of Eph 5:32 (Chrysostom, Theodore of Mopsuestia, Theodoret, Jerome), prior to its medieval use as a proof text for the "Sacrament of marriage." Markus N. A. Bockmuehl, *Revelation and Mystery in Ancient Judaism and Pauline Christianity* (Tübingen: Mohr, 1990), 204:

> Most plausible, and consistent with the practice not only of the New Testament, but also e.g. of Qumran, Philo, and the Rabbis, would seem to be the idea that we are dealing here with an *exegetical* mystery: a deeper (in this case either allegorical or prophetic) meaning of a Scriptural text which has been elicited by means of some form of inspired exegesis. In other words, the deeper meaning of Gen 2:24 points typologically to Christ and the church.

[114] "Since an exhortatory conclusion regarding marital life is drawn from the text and its exposition, μυστήριον refers to the text and not to the institution of marriage itself. The μυστήριον is thus the allegorical meaning of the OT saying, its mysteriously concealed prophecy of the relation of Christ to the ἐκκλησία ['church']" (G. Bornkamm, "μυστήριον," *TDNT* 4:823).

[115] Schnackenburg, *Ephesians*, 254: Eph 5:32 "is not a belated re-interpretation of the quotation which originally related to the creation of man and woman so that marriage is only in retrospect interpreted according to the relationship of Christ and the Church. Rather it must be seen from the outset as a key to the understanding which the author wishes to give to the quotation." Voelz, *What Does This Mean?* 259–60, speaks of the overall relationship of OT history to God's plan of redemption:

> We may say, then, that **what happened in the OT**, either "ordinarily" or in the special historical "visitations" of God, **happened because of the future**. That is to say, **what happened in Israel's history was determined by the future**, by what would happen in the Age to Come/ὁ μέλλων αἰών. … **Things happened in Israel's history, OT people experienced what they experienced, because of what God *would do* in the Age to Come**—which age invaded history proleptically, and manifested its shape and form, in the Christ-event.

church, not the other way around.[116] Once this is clear, it is quite in accord with Paul's words to speak of marriage itself as a mystery, as it was instituted for the very purpose of displaying Christ to the world.[117]

5:33 πλὴν καὶ ὑμεῖς οἱ καθ᾽ ἕνα—Each of the three sections of this pericope (5:22–24, 25–30, 31–32) has centered on Christ and the church as the true meaning of the marital mystery. Yet, at the conclusion of each preceding section (to wives in 5:24; to husbands in 5:28–30), Paul has also consistently returned to the implications of the mystery for the conduct of marriage in this world. So also here in 5:33 he concludes the entire pericope with a recapitulation of his words to husbands and wives, reminding them that their marriage ought to be lived in accord with the Christological image. πλήν is adversative ("but, however"), yet can be used to draw a discussion to a close by returning to a significant point: "in any case."[118] Thus, Paul returns to the consequences of Christ's relationship to the church for the interaction of husband and wife in marriage. The mystical meaning of the text does not preclude its literal meaning. The phrase ὑμεῖς οἱ καθ᾽ ἕνα, literally "you [plural] one by one,"[119] encompasses all husbands and wives, leaving no room for evading the Word of God, as if one could claim to confess the Gospel of Christ without living one's marriage in accord with it. Neither can one claim that only some marriages are reflections of the heavenly pattern. Paul then summarizes his previous teaching with a distinct exhortation to each of the two partners in the marriage.

ἕκαστος τὴν ἑαυτοῦ γυναῖκα οὕτως ἀγαπάτω ὡς ἑαυτόν, ἡ δὲ γυνὴ ἵνα φοβῆται τὸν ἄνδρα—The third person imperative ἀγαπάτω, "let him love," addressed to "each" husband, mandates him to love his wife as himself. Thus, "love" is the summary of the husband's role in marriage. It is somewhat surprising, then, that Paul does not

---

[116] Weinrich, "'It Is Not Given to Women to Teach': A *Lex* in Search of a *Ratio*," 23:

> In Ephesians 5 Paul's point is not that Christ's love for his Bride, the Church, is patterned after what was to be the case between Adam and Eve in the Garden. Rather, it is in view of Christ's love for his Bride, the Church, that husbands are to love their wives and that wives are to be subject to their husbands as to their head. The true marriage was not that marriage in the Garden. The true marriage is that between Christ and the Church. All other marriages (including that first one in the Garden)—and this is true the more marriages are blessed by love—are faint images and icons of that Marriage of the Lamb with his Bride, the Church.

[117] Lincoln, *Ephesians*, 381, denies that "mystery" refers to marriage at all, averring that it refers only to the Christ-Church relationship. If true, then Paul's statement would be tautological: "but I say that the relationship of Christ and the church refers to Christ and the church." Or, if the "mystery" is the OT passage, then, by Lincoln's analysis, Paul would be saying that Gen 2:24 refers *only* to Christ and the church and *not* to human marriage. Neither interpretation is satisfactory. Nevertheless, Lincoln arrives at the insightful conclusion: "It was because the Church was Christ's body which was one with him, a relationship which was the model for human marriage, that wives could be seen in terms of their husbands' bodies."

[118] BDAG, s.v. πλήν, 1 c; BDF, § 449 (2); cf. 1 Cor 11:11; Phil 3:16; 4:14; Rev 2:25. This use of πλήν is parallel to ἀλλά in Eph 5:24 and οὕτως in 5:28.

[119] The preposition κατά is used distributively ("individually," Moule, *Idiom Book*, 60; cf. BDAG, s.v. κατά, B 3 a). The article with a prepositional phrase οἱ καθ᾽ ἕνα is equivalent to a noun, "the [husbands and wives] as individuals" (see Turner, *Syntax*, 15). Note also that the third person singular imperatives that follow—ἀγαπάτω, "*let* each [husband] *love*," and φοβῆται, "*let* the wife *respect/fear*"—place the obligation squarely on each individual (Wallace, *Greek Grammar*, 486).

summarize the wife's role with the passive of ὑποτάσσω, "be subordinate," with which he had begun and concluded the section addressed to her (5:22–24; ὑποτάσσω is implied in 5:22 [cf. 5:21] and expressed in 5:24). Instead he introduces[120] the verb φοβέομαι, saying, "Let the wife respect/fear [her] husband."[121] Rhetorically, this forms an *inclusio* around the pericope, inasmuch as he began by calling for submission to one another "in the fear [φόβος] of Christ" (5:21). He thereby indicates that he has drawn the pericope to a close. But he also indicates subtly the nature of the wife's subordination to her husband. Unlike that of children and servants, it is not best characterized with the verb ὑπακούω, "heed/obey" (6:1, 5; but see the textual notes on it there). Nor is this fear characterized, as in the case of servants, as "fear and trembling" (6:5). But it is an attitude of "fear" toward the husband that should be interpreted in accord with the fear of the Lord that introduces the pericope and is a major theme (5:21). While the wife's attitude toward her husband is best characterized as "respect/honor" rather than "fear of punishment,"[122] we retain "fear" as an alternate translation so that the reader might note the parallel to "the fear of Christ" that is implied.[123] In NT teaching, fear and submission to authority are closely related and mutually interpretive.[124] Sarah feared Abraham by calling him κύριος, "lord, sir," an act that Peter describes as "submitting" (the passive of ὑποτάσσω) and "heeding" (ὑπακούω, 1 Pet 3:5–6).

Commentary

Structure and Rhetoric

The latter chapters of Ephesians are no longer characterized by the clear and concise pericopes of its first four chapters. The question of whether 5:21 should be attached to the preceding or following unit is one aspect of the larger structural issue.[125] The absence of any conjunction in or around 5:21 is a strong

---

[120] This is the sole occurrence of the verb φοβέομαι in Ephesians.

[121] The subjunctive form of the verb in the clause ἵνα φοβῆται, "that she should fear," is equivalent to an imperative. See BDAG, s.v. ἵνα, 2 g; BDF, § 387 (3); Turner, *Syntax*, 95; Moule, *Idiom Book*, 144; Wallace, *Greek Grammar*, 477; Zerwick, *Biblical Greek*, § 415. Contra Barth, *Ephesians*, 2:648, who denies that Paul uses ἵνα clauses this way (cf. 2 Cor 8:7–8) and who prefers to translate with "may she fear."

[122] Kleinig, "Ordered Community," 56: "In a society where wives were often expected to serve their husbands sexually and to use their sexual assets to gain what they wanted, the apostles merely urge wives to 'respect' their husbands (Eph. 5:33) and to be fearless in doing what is good, without using their sexuality to manipulate their husbands (I Pet. 3:1–7)."

[123] Lincoln, *Ephesians*, 384–85:

This fear certainly includes having respect, but is stronger than this, though not the fear of a slave [Eph 6:5]. ... In the case of human relations, as we noted with the notion of subordination also, fear involves observance of the appropriate authority structures. ... Since the fear of Christ ([Eph 5:]21) is believers' appropriate response to his overwhelming love and power, the wife's fear is her appropriate response to her husband's headship exercised in self-sacrificial love.

Barth, *Ephesians*, 2:648–50, 662–68, presents a lengthy defense of "fear."

[124] Rom 13:3–7; Eph 6:5; 1 Pet 2:18; 3:1–2.

[125] See Nordling, "Research Notes [on Eph 5:21]," for an exegetical examination consonant with our own.

hint that Paul is not moving into a completely new section.[126] In the commentary on the preceding pericope (5:14–21) and in the first textual note on 5:21 in this pericope, we have considered the evidence that 5:21 should be considered, first, as a hinge verse that belongs to both pericopes and, second, as a heading to the large unit that follows (5:21–6:9).[127] Indeed, there are good reasons to view as much as 5:3–6:9 as one large unit, perhaps even to reach farther back and include 4:17–5:2 in the same.

Rhetorically, by 4:16 Paul has concluded the *probatio* section containing the "proofs,"[128] the positive points of his argumentation in favor of the unity of Jew and Gentile within the church on the basis of a common Baptism into Christ Jesus (2:1–4:16). From 4:17 through 6:9 Paul moves into the rhetorical category of *refutatio*, or "refutations,"[129] considering objections to his argument such as the syncretistic pagan enticement: "if Christ has overcome all hostile powers and has forgiven your sins, you may therefore return to the practices of your former pagan existence without fear." We have compared this argument to Paul's logic in Romans,[130] in whose sixth chapter he considered the horrific proposition "What then shall we say? Should we continue in sin so that grace might abound?" and replied, "May it never be!" (Rom 6:1–2). Because of the specific features of the Ephesian religious environment (specifically the temple of Artemis), sexual immorality was "intimately" connected with idolatry, a fact that helped us understand 5:3–14 not simply as an ethical exhortation to avoid impurity but especially as a rejection of a possible return to pagan worship. With the baptismal hymn of 5:14 serving as a critical juncture in the argument, Paul proceeds in 5:15–21 to describe the alternative to pagan worship: the Spirit-filled liturgy of the baptized.

So, having rejected the simplistic division of Paul's letters into "doctrinal" and "ethical" halves,[131] we must consequently be wary of the temptation to read the present pericope as a purely ethical admonition to structure household relationships in a Christian manner.[132] If the words beginning in 5:21 are properly tied to the preceding, there are strong grounds for placing them into the category of "worship" rather than "ethics." In contrast to the false worship of the pagan Greek life (5:3–13), Paul describes a new life in the Spirit which

---

[126] Wallace, *Greek Grammar*, 651.

[127] See also Sampley, *"And the Two Shall Become One Flesh,"* 10.

[128] See "Proofs" in "Structure and Rhetoric" in the introduction.

[129] See "Refutations" in "Structure and Rhetoric" in the introduction.

[130] For this comparison to Romans 6, see "The Rhetoric: Refutation" in the commentary on 4:17–5:2; "Structure and Rhetoric" in the commentary on 5:3–14; and "Watch Carefully How You Walk" in the commentary on 5:15–21.

[131] See "Doctrine and Ethics, Gospel and Law? (4:1–16 in the Context of the Epistle)" in "Structure and Rhetoric" in the commentary on 4:1–16.

[132] Lincoln, *Ephesians*, 389, e.g., writes: "Paraenesis is his primary concern, and in the end the Christological and ecclesiological formulations serve that purpose. The focus of the pericope is believers' conduct." The present writer's contention is precisely the opposite.

not only consists of "psalms and hymns and songs of the Spirit" (5:19) but also includes the daily worship of submitting to the vocation God has given in every earthly relationship (5:21–6:9). The shift is not, therefore, from *God's* work to *man's* work, but from God's work in *Baptism* to God's work in *worship*, understood most broadly as embracing the entire Christian life.[133] Here again Ephesians parallels Romans, in which Paul subordinates his so-called "ethical admonitions" (chapters 12–16) to the heading: "I therefore encourage you, brothers, on account of the mercies of God, to present your bodies as a sacrifice [that is] living, holy, well-pleasing to God—your spiritual worship [λογικὴν λατρείαν]. And do not be conformed to this age ..." (Rom 12:1–2). The first part of Rom 12:1 is echoed in Eph 5:1–2. The final phrase of Rom 12:1, whose very difficult adjective λογικός has been rendered as "rational, reasonable" or "spiritual," would seem to root this new "worship" in the inner transformation of the Christian through the indwelling of the Holy Spirit, as also in Eph 5:18. The Christian worships God in everyday life because the Spirit produces such worship as a fruit.

The worship that Paul describes in the present unit of Ephesians bears all the marks and full contours of the Lutheran theology expounded in Articles 4 and 24 of the Apology of the Augsburg Confession.[134] It includes receiving in faith the gifts of God that he has located in marriage, family, and workplace; discerning their proclamation of Jesus Christ; praising him by extolling these gifts; and honoring him by submitting to the roles he has given rather than holding up self-chosen works (Ap 15:25–26). While the delivery of the gifts of the forgiveness of sins, life, and salvation in the Divine Service of Word and Sacrament is unique, the Christian must not erect a barrier between that liturgy and the rest of his life. In Baptism the dividing wall between worship and everyday life, between the sacred and the profane, is broken down. By binding 5:21–6:9 intimately to what precedes, Paul confesses the holiness of marriage, family, and all of life.[135]

---

[133] See Grothe, *The Justification of the Ungodly*, 620–24; also "Worship, Not Ethics," 632–36.

[134] "It is easy to determine the difference between this faith and the righteousness of the law. Faith is that worship [λατρεία] which receives God's offered blessings; the righteousness of the law is that worship which offers God our own merits. It is by faith that God wants to be worshiped, namely, that we receive from him what he promises and offers" (Ap 4:49). "The woman [in Lk 7:47] came with the opinion concerning Christ that with Him the remission of sins should be sought. This worship is the highest worship of Christ. Nothing greater could she ascribe to Christ. To seek from Him the remission of sins was truly to acknowledge the Messiah. Now, thus to think of Christ, thus to worship Him, thus to embrace Him, is truly to believe" (Ap 4:154 [*Triglotta*, 163, where it is numbered as Ap 3:33]). "But let us talk about the term 'liturgy' [λειτουργία]. It does not really mean a sacrifice but a public service [*publicum ministerium*; *Triglotta*, 411, translates the phrase as 'the public ministry']. Thus it squares with our position that a minister who consecrates shows forth the body and blood of the Lord to the people, just as a minister who preaches shows forth the gospel to the people, as Paul says (I Cor. 4:1)" (Ap 24:79–80).

[135] Martin Franzmann, *Romans* (Concordia Commentary; St. Louis: Concordia, 1968), 216: "The new worship comprehends the whole life of the new man in a sense and in a depth in which the worship of an ancient Israel could not yet comprehend it."

Paul expresses this intimate connection between worship in the Spirit and the so-called *Haustafel*[136] through the use of a participle, ὑποτασσόμενοι, "being subordinate" (5:21), rather than breaking off at 5:20 and starting a new section with a conjunction and finite verb. While there is some NT evidence for the view that such a participle might be translated as an imperative (i.e., "submit!"), recourse to such an explanation should be taken only when one cannot locate a preceding finite verb on which it might depend (see the first textual note on 5:21 in this pericope). In the present case, the participle is easily and naturally interpreted as dependent on the imperative in πληροῦσθε ἐν πνεύματι, "be filled up in the Spirit" (5:18). It appears that Paul has again shown his fondness for groups of three, describing the results of being filled in/with/by the Spirit with three participles:

> [18]be filled up in the Spirit,
>> [19]speaking [λαλοῦντες] to one another in psalms and hymns and songs of the Spirit,
>>> singing and psalming with your heart to the Lord,
>> [20]giving thanks [εὐχαριστοῦντες] always for all things in the name of our Lord Jesus Christ to [our] God and Father,
>> [21]being subordinate [ὑποτασσόμενοι] to one another in the fear of Christ:

This is the grammatical structure that binds the participle in 5:21 to what comes before. It implies that subordination to one another within the body of Christ should be understood as a gift of the Spirit and a part of the worship he inspires. Rhetorically, therefore, this pericope cannot be separated from the refutation that precedes (4:17–5:21).

At the same time, the absence of a verb in the next verse (5:22) presses the participle ὑποτασσόμενοι in 5:21 into double duty. In order to make sense of 5:22, one must fill the ellipse by repeating the participle: "wives [being subordinate] to their own husbands as to the Lord." Yet, the very meaning of the verb ὑποτάσσω, "to subordinate; (passive:) be subordinate," forbids us to continue with the corollary "and husbands being subordinate to their own wives" (see the first textual note on 5:21 in this pericope). This means that "being subordinate to one another" (5:21) cannot on *semantic* grounds be a heading just for the subunit on marriage (5:22–33). Paul is *not* saying "be subordinate to one another in marriage, wives to their husbands and husbands to their wives." This is a necessary conclusion, despite the *syntactical* reality that Paul gives up the structure of dependent participles and introduces indicative verbs starting in 5:25.[137] For mutual subordination (or submission) *within a single relationship*

---

[136] See "A Note on the Term *Haustafel*" in "Structure and Rhetoric" in this pericope.

[137] Although the finite verb ὑποτάσσεται, "is subordinate," appears already in 5:24, that verb has "the church" as its subject and appears in a clause giving a comparison. The first finite verb with one of the human subjects of the *Haustafel* as its subject is ἀγαπᾶτε, "husbands, *love* [your] wives" (5:25). In 5:24b, where the clause οὕτως καὶ αἱ γυναῖκες τοῖς ἀνδράσιν ἐν

is not really subordination. Subordination inherently means that one party is above the other in a hierarchy of office, vocation, or authority (though not necessarily in power, intelligence, or value; see below). Thus, if we are to avoid a contradiction between the "mutual submission" of 5:21 and the asymmetrical marriage relationship Paul subsequently describes in 5:22–33, we are compelled to understand 5:21 as a heading to the entire unit that follows, 5:21–6:9.

What Paul means, then, is this: *the spiritual blessing of "being subordinate to one another in the fear of Christ" (5:21) requires one to discern in each relationship who is the Christ figure and who is the church figure and to order the relationship accordingly.* To live according to this discernment is part of the liturgy of the baptized,[138] one's "living sacrifice" (Rom 12:1). It enables the Christian to worship God by being Christlike, or to worship God by submitting to Christ in the appropriate way in every walk of life. What Paul is doing is identifying for us the Christ-church typology that elevates the Christian view of life above the secular principles of the *Haustafel*.[139] The lines of typology are disclosed in the structure of the larger unit, in which each relationship is placed into parallel with that of Christ and the church.

We can, therefore, extend the participial structure (above) by highlighting Paul's expansion of the third participle ("being subordinate," 5:21):

be filled up in the Spirit … (5:18)
<ul><ul>being subordinate to one another in the fear of Christ (5:21)</ul></ul>
- wives to their own husbands as to the Lord (5:22)
- children, heed your parents in the Lord (6:1)
- slaves/servants, heed your fleshly lords/masters (6:5)

Being subordinate is therefore not only "taking one's place in the order" (according to the semantics of the term), but also recognizing Christ in the person placed above. In each of these three primary relationships, there is also a reciprocal obligation for the *super*ordinate figure to discern his own likeness to the Lord and to view his *sub*ordinate as an image of the church:

- husbands, love [your] wives just as also Christ loved the church and gave himself up for her (5:25)
- fathers, do not provoke your children to anger, but raise them in the discipline and instruction of the Lord (6:4)
- lords/masters, do the same things to them … knowing that … there is no partiality with him [the Lord] (6:9)

παντί, "thus also wives to [their] husbands in all things," has no verb, one might still provide the participle ὑποτασσόμενοι, "being subordinate," from 5:21, which was dependent on the preceding imperative πληροῦσθε, "*be filled up* in the Spirit" (5:18). Beginning in 5:25 Paul gives up the *syntactical* pattern of dependent participles, though the content remains *(theo-) logically* dependent on that gift of the Spirit.

[138] The commentary on 5:15–21 is titled "The Liturgy of the Spirit-Filled Baptized."

[139] For secular counterparts to the biblical tables of duties, see "A Note on the Term *Haustafel*" in "Structure and Rhetoric" in this pericope.

The resulting pattern of typology reorders every relationship in the image of our redemption:

Christ		husbands		fathers/parents		lords/masters	
loves *sacrifices* ↓	↑ *submits* *fears*	*love* *sacrifice* ↓	↑ *submit* *fear*	*discipline* *instruct* ↓	↑ *heed* *honor*	*treat well* *do not* *threaten* ↓	↑ *heed* *fear*
church		wives		children		slaves/servants	

It is important to note that, while Paul aligns a figure in each relationship with Christ or the church, he does not flatten the various vocations, but uses distinct verbs to describe the appropriate actions. Thus, while children and servants are called upon to *heed* their superordinates, wives are charged to *be subordinate willingly*. Likewise, the duties of each Christ figure are tweaked in accord with the relationship—masters, for example, are not asked to sacrifice themselves for their servants, but merely to be *Godlike* in showing no partiality and *Gospel-oriented* in avoiding threats.

Finally, a few comments about the structure of 5:21–33 are called for. This pericope dealing with the marriage relationship is marked out by an *inclusio* formed by "fear" (the noun φόβος in 5:21; the verb φοβέομαι in 5:33). Second, the pericope itself can be broken down into a sequence of parts, beginning with words to the wife, followed by words to the husband, then addressing marriage as a whole, and finally returning to the husband and the wife (thus forming a chiasm):

> "in the <u>fear</u> of Christ" (5:21)
>> wives (5:22–24)
>>> husbands (5:25–30)
>>>> marriage (5:31–32)
>>> husband (5:33a)
>> wife (5:33b)
> "and let the wife <u>fear</u> [her] husband" (5:33b)

Interpreting the pericope as a single large chiasm, however, results in a rather imbalanced arrangement in which the "center" (5:31–32) falls perilously close to the end and 5:33b is seen as doing double duty. It may be more sensible to analyze the pericope in three sections, with a recapitulation of the first two parts marking the close:

1. Wives (5:22–24)
2. Husbands (5:25–30)
3. Marriage (5:31–32)
   Recapitulation: husbands, wives (5:33)

Within each of the three main sections there is a persistent reference back to Christ and the church. In the first (5:22–24) this comparison forms the center of a chiasm:

A   wives [being subordinate] to their own husbands as to the Lord (5:22)
  B   the husband is the head of the wife as also Christ is the head of the church (5:23)
  B'   as the church is subordinate to Christ (5:24a)
A'   thus also wives [being subordinate] to [their] husbands in all things (5:24b)

The point of this careful patterning appears to be to reinforce at each point the parallelism of Christ to the husband and the church to the wife.[140] Indeed, it is vital to note that the relationship of Christ to the church invades every section of the pericope to the point that one might say—as Paul does (5:32)—that *it is really about Christ and the church.*

A Note on the Term *Haustafel*

The present unit of Ephesians (5:21–6:9) is often referred to as a *Haustafel.* The term is generally attributed to Luther (see, e.g., SC, section 3, "Table of Duties"), though he is probably only responsible for popularizing this particular German expression. Rather than "table of duties," it is better rendered as "domestic order." Its origin lies in the Greek term οἰκονομία (see the first textual note on 1:10, where it is translated as "administer"). Other NT units that fall into the category of *Haustafeln* include Col 3:18–4:1; 1 Tim 6:1–2; Titus 2:1–3:7; 1 Pet 2:11–3:22; 5:1–5.[141] Various commentators discuss the biblical pattern and secular parallels in the ancient world.[142] Lincoln quotes Aristotle:

> Now that it is clear what are the component parts of the state, we have first of all to discuss household management; for every state is composed of households. … The investigation of everything should begin with its smallest parts, and the primary and smallest parts of the household are master and slave, husband and wife, father and children; we ought therefore to examine the proper constitution and character of each of these three relationships, I mean that of mastership, that of marriage … , and thirdly the progenitive relationship.[143]

Though the NT writers may have included such traditional material for apologetic reasons—to counter claims that Christianity was disrupting social

---

[140] Sampley, *"And the Two Shall Become One Flesh,"* 103–8, observes that the pericope alternates between husbands/wives and Christ/church, with a Greek particle of comparison marking the shift at each point: ὡς ("as," 5:23b), οὕτως ("thus," 5:24b), καθώς ("just as," 5:25b), οὕτως ("thus," 5:28a), καθώς ("just as," 5:29c), with the conclusions marked by ἀντὶ τούτου ("for this reason," 5:31), δέ ("but,"5:32), and πλήν ("in any case," 5:33). He describes this pattern as ABABABA.

[141] In the Apostolic Fathers, see *Didache,* 4:9–11; *Barnabas,* 19:5–7; *1 Clement,* 21:6–8; Ignatius, *To Polycarp,* 4:1–6:1; Polycarp, *To the Philippians,* 4:2–6:3.

[142] See Lincoln, *Ephesians,* 355–61; Bruce, *The Epistles to the Colossians, to Philemon, and to the Ephesians,* 161–63; Best, *Ephesians,* 519–27; MacDonald, *Colossians and Ephesians,* 159–69; Sampley, *"And the Two Shall Become One Flesh,"* 18–30; David L. Balch, *Let Wives Be Submissive: The Domestic Code in 1 Peter* (Chico, Calif.: Scholars, 1981); and Timothy G. Gombis, "A Radical New Humanity: The Function of the *Haustafel* in Ephesians," *Journal of the Evangelical Theological Society* 48 (2005): 317–30.

[143] Aristotle, *Politics,* 1:1253b (trans. H. Rackham, LCL), quoted in Lincoln, *Ephesians,* 357.

order[144]—what is crucial for understanding Ephesians 5 is how Paul's teachings *differ*: "modifications or additions are frequently indicative of the author's special concerns."[145] The expanded treatment of marriage (5:21–33) in the Ephesian *Haustafel* (5:21–6:9) likely relates to the letter's emphasis on the church's one-body unity with Christ and does not necessarily imply that there was a problem with marriage in Ephesus. This passage is distinguished from secular parallels by its the Christological references and use of the OT.[146]

Taking One's Place in God's Order

Marriage in the Ancient World: The Countercultural Nature of Paul's Words

Every pastor who has conducted a wedding can attest to the great anxiety that is engendered by the reading of Ephesians 5 or the use of traditional marriage vows based upon it. In the last half century particularly, the church has been under siege from a society that views the biblical teaching with contempt, and those faithful pastors who still teach a distinction of roles within the marital relationship find themselves ever more lonely as their ranks on the church's ramparts steadily thin. But the worldly portrayal of the church as clinging stubbornly to an outdated and unfashionably conservative view of marriage is open to serious objection. It is darkly humorous to quote the observation of the Lutheran commentator George Stoeckhardt from more than a hundred years ago: "These words … may not seem palatable to modern ears, but no pastor should stoop to surrender these words for the sake of pleasing the whims of our modern generation."[147] Did Paul in Ephesians 5 simply parrot uncritically the misogynist sentiments and patriarchal structures of his cultural context? Is the headship of the husband to be doffed and laid aside like the culturally contingent head coverings of 1 Corinthians 11?[148] Or were his words as countercultural in the first-century Greco-Roman Empire as they are today?

---

[144] So MacDonald, *Colossians and Ephesians*, 161–62, 337–38; Lincoln, *Ephesians*, 358.

[145] Sampley, *"And the Two Shall Become One Flesh,"* 23.

[146] Sampley, *"And the Two Shall Become One Flesh,"* 25.

[147] Stoeckhardt, *Ephesians*, 248. The original German text was published in 1910.

[148] Lincoln, *Ephesians*, 392–94, argues passionately that the contemporary church should not repeat the conclusions of the author of Ephesians, but should "attempt to do something similar in their own setting—to bring to bear what they hold to be the heart of the Christian message on the marriage conventions of their time" (393). Lincoln challenges the equation of the husband with Christ and the wife with the church, arguing that one could easily reverse this. He concludes that "mutual loving submission" would be the best contemporary appropriation. Best, *Ephesians*, 530–31, believes that the wife is associated with the church simply because ἐκκλησία ["church"] is feminine in Greek; "otherwise in non-sexist days there appears no reason why the church should not be regarded as masculine" (531).

Neither of those positions fully absorbs the nature of Paul's argumentation on the basis of creation, inter-Trinitarian relationships, the soteriological relationship of God/Christ to mankind, and the unfailingly feminine conception of God's people throughout Scripture; these arguments, pursued in the commentary, urge us to accept the authoritative apostolic teaching of Ephesians 5 as universally applicable to all subsequent ages of humanity's sojourn on earth.

633

Certainly Paul was not a social revolutionary, and his words concerning marriage, family life, and slavery demonstrate that he was not primarily concerned with the agendas of various liberationists today. Yet, there is evidence within the NT itself that Paul was not simply reiterating the social norms he had inherited. His measured advocacy of remaining single and temporary celibacy within marriage in view of the impact of Christ and his imminent return (1 Corinthians 7) was not entirely consistent with Rabbinic Judaism's unwavering commitment to marriage[149] and likely puzzled Greeks and Romans, who saw marriage as a civic duty and were at the same time generally libertine in their sexual lives.[150] While his teachings on the headship of the husband and the subordination of the wife would have raised few eyebrows in the ancient world, his exhortation to the husband to love his wife and sacrifice his very life for her finds few parallels in ancient thinking and demonstrates that while the ink was still wet on the papyrus, Paul's words were already somewhat countercultural.

Our exegesis has shown that Paul is not simply repeating classical opinions like that of Aristotle, although Ephesians 5 has sometimes been misinterpreted along these lines:

> Hence it is manifest that all the persons mentioned have a moral virtue [ἠθικὴ ἀρετή] of their own, and that the temperance [σωφροσύνη] of a woman and that of a man are not the same, nor their courage [ἀνδρεία] and justice [δικαιοσύνη], as Socrates thought, but the one is the courage of command [ἀρχική], and the other that of subordination [ὑπηρετική], and the case is similar with the other virtues.[151]

Paul's line of argumentation does not proceed from judgments about the fitness of man to lead and of woman to follow. He offers no commentary on the strength or weakness of either sex. He does not repeat ancient opinions, so offensive to modern ears, that describe a wife as the husband's sexual slave, as his plaything, or merely as fertile soil for the implantation and nurture of children. In fact, it would be a mistake to suggest that there was even a universal cultural opinion on marital relations to which Paul might have conformed himself. For there were

---

Barth's assessment of the passage is strikingly different from those of Lincoln and Best: "A greater, wiser, and more positive description of marriage has not yet been found in Christian literature" (*Ephesians*, 2:715).

[149] George Foot Moore, *Judaism in the First Centuries of the Christian Era: The Age of the Tannaim* (Cambridge, Mass.: Harvard University Press, 1958), 2:119:

> Marriage was regarded not only as the normal state, but as a divine ordinance. ...

> Celibacy was, in fact, not common, and was disapproved by the rabbis, who taught that a man should marry at eighteen, and that if he passed the age of twenty without taking a wife he transgressed a divine command and incurred God's displeasure.

[150] MacDonald, *Colossians and Ephesians*, 14: "Among the strongest challenges to Greco-Roman social order put forward by some early Christians was their determination to remain unmarried in a society where such efforts elicited mixed reactions at best." See also MacDonald, 338–39.

[151] Aristotle, *Politics*, 1:1260a (trans. H. Rackham, LCL); see also Aristotle, *Politics*, 1:1254b; 1:1259b.

as many marriage customs in ancient times as there were societies, and the legal rights and responsibilities of men and women varied enormously.[152] A Roman married woman, for example, could be legally subordinate to her father or her husband—not both at the same time—or even legally independent.[153] Thus, in Ephesus there would have been different opinions on what made a good marriage: "In the ancient world a variety of concepts co-existed with or followed upon one another regarding the position of women and the order and purpose of marriage. … Certainly the Ephesians knew of more than one custom-sanctioned or literally documented, traditional or revolutionary, attitude to women and marriage."[154] It is time once and for all to set aside the myth that Ephesians 5 is the meek repetition of the hidebound traditions of a patriarchal, misogynist era.

Mutual Love and Service within the Christian Community

What, then, is the norm by which Paul challenges and redevelops the traditional elements of marriage for application to Christian lives? Surely it is the Gospel, for the sacrificial love of Christ for the church as his bride is the dominant theme of this pericope. The crucial question, however, is whether (or to

---

[152] See "The Position of Women and Marriage at Paul's Time" in Barth, *Ephesians*, 2:655–62. Among the contrasting views cited by Barth are the following:

> "We have courtesans (*hetairai*) for our pleasure, prostitutes (i.e. young female slaves) for daily physical use, wives to bring up legitimate children and to be faithful stewards in household matters" [Pseudo-Demosthenes (ca. 340 BC), *Against Neaera*, 122]. … According to rabbinic tradition, R. Judah or R. Meir (both ca. A.D. 150) enjoined every Jewish man to say the following three blessings every morning: (I thank the Lord) "that he did not make me a Gentile, … a woman, … a boor" [Tosefta, *Berakoth*, 7:18; Talmud, *Menahoth*, 43b]. (*Ephesians*, 2:655–56)

> At a given period in Sparta women possessed two-thirds of the land. In Rome and Athens, and in some cases even among the Jews, they could obtain a divorce without losing the financial assets they had brought into marriage. Among the Pythagoreans women enjoyed equal rights with men, and the Therapeutae [a Jewish sect] described by Philo appear to have held women in similar esteem. In Plato's *Republic* they bear political, educational, and military privileges and duties that are essentially equal to men's, though commensurate to the lesser physical strength of the female sex. (*Ephesians*, 657)

[153] See Gibson, "Ephesians 5:21–33 and the Lack of Marital Unity in the Roman Empire." In Paul's day divorce was common and successful marriages were on the decline (Gibson, 166–67). In contrast to Judaism, both Roman and Greek women could initiate divorce against their husbands and had considerably more independence (163). Paul's proclamation of wifely subordination could therefore have been quite countercultural:

> Therefore this statement by Paul to wives would have been understood by them as meaning they were to enter into a type of marriage in which a wife submitted to her husband rather than her father, and that she was not to follow the trend of the "New Woman" in allowing her newly achieved emancipation to lead her to adopt an independent identity separate from her husband. In the new οἰκονομία [ordered household] of God, she should favor a relationship with her husband that promoted unity, rather than obstructed it. (Gibson, 175)

[154] Barth, *Ephesians*, 2:658–59. The notion that Ephesus was a bastion of feminism (such that Paul's comments on the role of women in Ephesians 5 and 1 Timothy 2 should be restricted to situations where women are exalting themselves over men) is carefully deconstructed by Baugh, "A Foreign World: Ephesus in the First Century."

what extent) the Gospel breaks down order in the Christian community. Some NT evidence might suggest that it does. Paul admonishes Christians in a similar context "not to think more highly of oneself than is necessary," to "be devoted to one another in brotherly love," and to "be thinking the same thing toward one another" (Rom 12:3, 10, 16; cf. Rom 15:5; Phil 2:2). Christians are to look not only to their own interests but also to the interests of others (Phil 2:4). Tracing the language of ἀλλήλων, "one another," repeatedly turns up such admonitions. Paul calls for there to be no division in the body, but for the members to care equally for one another (1 Cor 12:25). He explains that Gospel freedom is not to be used to gratify the flesh, but to serve one another (Gal 5:13) and to "bear one another's burdens" (Gal 6:2). The Spirit leads Christians to bear "with one another in love" (Eph 4:2), to " 'speak truth with his neighbor,' for we are members of one another" (Eph 4:25, quoting Zech 8:16), and likewise to be kind, tenderhearted, and forgiving to one another (Eph 4:32). Paul prays that the Lord would make the Thessalonians "abound in love for one another" (1 Thess 3:12).

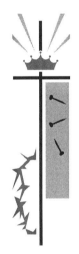

The admonition to mutual service and love is rooted in Christ himself as the prototype. He did not think more highly of himself than others, but humbled himself, taking the form of a slave (Phil 2:7). Like a slave he stripped and bent down to wash his disciples' feet (Jn 13:4–5). He called on his disciples to show a similar attitude of servanthood,[155] even though they were to become the apostolic foundation of the church.[156] Paul gladly took up the name of δοῦλος, "slave/servant," for himself (e.g., Rom 1:1; Phil 1:1; Titus 1:1, the same term for the "slaves" in Eph 6:5–8). And yet there is a clear distinction between humility and subordination. Jesus does not trade offices with the disciples when he washes their feet; to the contrary, he firmly rejects Peter's objection, averring that it is necessary for him to wash Peter's feet and not the other way around (Jn 13:6–9). For it is Jesus' *office* to wash them clean. Jesus does not *subordinate* himself to the disciples, but carries out his *superordinate* office as Savior in an attitude of humble servanthood.[157] Paul, likewise, maintains the obligation of the Christian community to submit to their pastoral leaders (1 Cor 16:16; 1 Thess 5:12–13) even while Peter admonishes the pastors to exercise their authority in a non-tyrannical manner (1 Pet 5:2–3).

Peter's subsequent words are enormously helpful in demonstrating that subordination and mutual humble service within the Christian community need not be collapsed into one another: "likewise, you who are younger, be subordinate to the presbyters; and all of you, clothe yourselves with humility toward one another, for God 'opposes the proud, but gives grace to the humble' " (1 Pet 5:5, quoting Prov 3:34).[158] The order cannot be reversed; the presbyters do not sub-

---

[155] Mt 20:26; Mk 10:43; Lk 22:26; Jn 13:14–17.

[156] Mt 16:18; Gal 2:9; Eph 2:20; Rev 21:14.

[157] Contra Best, *Ephesians*, 517.

[158] Clement also quite happily combines mutual humility with asymmetrical order: "And all of you were humble in mind, not boastful in any way, being subordinate rather than imposing

ordinate themselves to the young men, yet they are included in the admonition to be humble to one another. Likewise, the above-quoted language of brotherly love and harmony in Romans 12 is followed by Paul's favored image of the church as Christ's body (Rom 12:4–5), in which he delineates the unique roles that each part has. Mutual love and humility do not erase the distinctive functions (Rom 12:4). God's order remains, though the gifts differ and are to be exercised according to God's giving of them (Rom 12:6–8). So also in Ephesians, the admonitions to peace, bearing with one another, and forgiving one another (4:1–3; 4:32–5:2) do not erase the distinctiveness of the pastoral office established as a gift of the ascended Christ (4:11)—in fact, one of the chief functions of the office is to ensure the harmonious working of the body with all its members (4:12–16). Nor do those earlier words imply that "being subordinate to one another" (5:21) must entail erasing the distinctive roles, offices, and orders within the Christian community and Christian households.

Paul, then, must have something else in mind when he speaks of subordination to one another. The oxymoron of "mutual submission" is neither consistent with the semantics of ὑποτάσσω, "to subordinate; (passive:) be subordinate" (5:21, 24; also 1:22), nor with the content of the subunits that follow 5:21 (5:22–32; 6:1–4, 5–9). Those commentators who wish to trump 5:22–33 with 5:21 and accuse Paul of inconsistency in his view of marriage[159] must contend with the fact that 6:1–9 is equally incompatible with their interpretation. That is to say, the relationships of parents and children, masters and servants/slaves, are clearly not invertible and are even more difficult to reconcile with a purported mutual submission. Surely what Paul means to say is this: *"within each of your God-given relationships (the following three[160] being the chief examples thereof), it is the work of the Spirit in you that you worship God by willingly taking the subordinate role with respect to each person whom God has placed over you or by serving as God's instrument to deliver his gifts of care and protection to those placed under you."*

Since Paul's *Haustafel* describes the relationship between husband and wife typologically, as an image of Christ and the church, one might assume that it addresses only the ideal situation in which both husband and wife are Christian. To a certain extent this is true. Only Christians can render God-pleasing worship. Marriage functions best as a presentation of the Gospel when both parties carry out their divinely appointed roles in accord with Paul's words. When one party violates the pattern, the marital situation becomes more complicated. Is

---

subordination [ὑποτασσόμενοι μᾶλλον ἢ ὑποτάσσοντες], giving more gladly than taking" (*1 Clement*, 2:1).

[159] For example, Schnackenburg, *Ephesians*, 245: "Hence if certain anthropological-social ideas of that time creep in in the exhortation to wives (cf. vv. 22 f.), this is a contemporary limitation which does not question the fundamental claim on all Christians to be subordinate to one another."

[160] That is, (1) husbands and wives (5:21–33); (2) parents and children (6:1–4); and (3) masters and slaves (6:5–9).

the wife to submit to her husband *only* when he is Christlike? Is the husband to love his wife *only* if she willingly submits to him? On the one hand, even if only one spouse is Christian, that spouse's submission to his or her God-given role in the marriage (as head or subordinate) is a God-pleasing act of worship. With respect to the proclamation of the Gospel in such an asymmetrical marriage, Paul's advice in 1 Cor 7:12–16 is apropos. If a non-Christian man consents to live with his Christian wife (or vice versa), the wife's submission to her unbelieving husband as to Christ or the husband's Christlike love of his unbelieving wife is a unilateral proclamation of the Gospel that may have salvific impact on the other spouse (1 Cor 7:16). In this case, one must stress that Paul's respective encouragements to love and to be subordinate are not conditional, but express the calling one has from God (cf. 1 Cor 7:17, 24).

On the other hand, Paul in Ephesians 5 simply does not address the very real possibility (faced in his day as much as ours) that the husband might be abusive toward his wife, that he might forbid her to practice the Christian faith or compel her to join him in false worship, that he might betray her sexually or compel her to join him in immoral sexual practices. While a wife might view such marital suffering in light of Christ's call to take up one's cross and follow him (Mt 16:24 and parallels), the way of the cross does not extend to disobedience against God, who must be obeyed rather than men (Acts 5:29). The subordination Paul describes is not absolute, but is governed by "the fear of Christ" (Eph 5:21), which implies the priority of submission to the Lord. So also the call for a wife to be subordinate does not mean that she must endure abuse from a husband who had promised and is obligated under God to care for her physical well-being (Eph 5:25, 28; cf. Ex 21:10–11). In such cases, marital separation may be the wisest, safest, and most God-pleasing course of action.

Certainly Peter admonishes Christians to endure unjust suffering even as Christ did (1 Pet 2:18–25); yet it is significant that those words come in the portion of his *Haustafel* that is directed to citizens and slaves, not to husbands and wives—though even the latter must contend with Peter's concluding admonition not to "return evil for evil or reviling for reviling" (1 Pet 3:9) and may be comforted by his reminder that "even if you should suffer for righteousness' sake, [you are] blessed" (1 Pet 3:14; cf. Mt 5:10–12). And although divorce is contrary to God's original will for mankind and is never the *necessary* consequence of adultery—forgiveness is a central component of the typological relationship Paul describes—Christ himself acknowledges that adultery is such a fundamental violation of the marital relationship that it may legitimately lead to the dissolution of the marriage (Mt 5:32; 19:9; cf. 1 Cor 6:16). Thus, Paul's depiction of a properly ordered Christian marriage may be tempered by the realities of sinful relationships between people corrupted by the fall.

Subordination Is Not Demeaning, but God's Order for the Transmission of Blessings

To be fair to those who stumble at the thought of superordination and subordination within the body of Christ, one must acknowledge that modern Westerners often view subordination as not a humble but a humiliating act, not honorable but demeaning.[161] We must stress that Paul does not at all suggest that wives, children, or servants are less valuable or are inferior by nature to their superordinates. Inasmuch as children are to honor and heed their parents throughout their lives, not only when they are young, they may quickly become stronger, more vigorous, more intelligent, richer, and more powerful than their parents—and yet they remain subordered. Likewise, servants may be stronger, smarter, or more honorable than their masters, and yet they are ordered under them, remaining their servants. So also wives may certainly be superior to their husbands in any number of ways, but are both obligated and gifted by the Spirit to submit to their place in the order with respect to their husbands.[162]

In fact, it is important to stress that in each ordered relationship the *subordinate* person is the valuable one, in the sense that the *superordinate* person's office is instituted for the sake of those for whom they care. That is to say, it is the servants' valuable work that the master manages; it is the welfare of the children that is paramount in a family. And just as civil law is properly most concerned with protecting the wife as the precious bearer of children and the one who normally is more physically vulnerable, so also Ephesians 5 lays the greater burden on the husband to love and care for his dear wife, even at the expense of his own life. So also Christ does not assert his superiority, but gives up the glories of heaven and lays down his life for the sake of the church, his precious bride!

The clearest biblical illustration of these important distinctions is Jesus' voluntary submission to his parents (expressed with the same verb that is in Eph 5:21, 24): "and he went down with them and came to Nazareth, and he was being *subordinate* to them [ἦν ὑποτασσόμενος αὐτοῖς]" (Lk 2:51). In no way does this text imply that Jesus was inferior to his parents in value or ability—as graphically illustrated by the immediately preceding story of him amazing the temple teachers and baffling his parents with his words. But it was their office to nurture and raise this Child and his office to receive their devoted care.

The ordering implied by the verb "being subordinate" (the passive of ὑποτάσσω, Eph 5:21, 24) is not the ranking of items according to their innate qualities or accomplishments, like a bestseller list or a sports league table. It

---

[161] Kleinig, "Ordered Community," 45–46: "Most people equate subordination with destructive subservience to authoritarian leaders, enforced servitude to power-mongers, and a disabling sense of inferiority in a hierarchy of domination. It bespeaks all that we abhor most."

[162] So also Kleinig, "Ordered Community," argues that the restriction of the pastoral office to men by divine mandate does not demean women or imply that they are less competent or less valuable. It is simply not their place in God's order.

is, rather, bound up with the nature of ἐξουσία, "authority."[163] Paul aligns the vocabulary of subordination and authority in admonishing the Romans to submit to the government (even though it was at the time a pagan and authoritarian state and therefore not *morally* superior): "Let every person *be subordinate* to the *authorities* who are above one [ἐξουσίαις ὑπερεχούσαις ὑποτασσέσθω], for there is no *authority* [ἐξουσία] except from God, and those that exist are *set in order* [τεταγμέναι] by God" (Rom 13:1). The centurion at Capernaum dared in faith to make a comparison between his own authority over his soldiers and Jesus' authority over sickness and death: "For also I am a man *ordered under authority* [ὑπὸ ἐξουσίαν τασσόμενος], having soldiers under me; and I say to this one, 'Go,' and he goes, and to another, 'Come,' and he comes, and to my servant, 'Do this,' and he does it" (Lk 7:8).

Christ can use the same kind of language of his own place in the order with respect both to God the Father (above him) and to his apostles (beneath him): "All *authority* in heaven and on earth has been given to me [ἐδόθη μοι πᾶσα ἐξουσία]; therefore, when you go, make disciples of all nations by baptizing them in the name of the Father and of the Son and of the Holy Spirit" (Mt 28:18–19). Here Christ teaches that he submits to the authority of the Father— yet only a heterodox Trinitarian theology or Christology would permit one to conclude that the Son is inferior by nature to the Father. It is not only a part of Christ's state of humiliation that he submits to the Father's will but also a part of the internal ordering of the persons of the Holy Trinity,[164] among whom there is nevertheless full equality of eternity, power, knowledge, and deity. Thus, Paul

---

[163] For this reason it is critical to distinguish "power" and "authority" when translating the NT vocabulary. ἐξουσία is not about the power or ability to do something, but the mandate or "authority" that is given and by which one acts legitimately. Thus, a thug may have the "power" to kidnap, but a police officer has the "authority" to arrest. Both involve detaining a person against his will, but only the latter is legitimate. The police officer may not even have the superior "power" needed to overwhelm a criminal who is bigger, stronger, or more heavily armed; but the criminal may nevertheless submit to the officer's authority.

In Ephesians the noun ἐξουσία, "authority," appears in 1:21; 2:2; 3:10; 6:12, but in reference to spiritual authorities (including evil ones, 2:2; 6:12), not to the proper exercise of God-given human authority.

[164] The latter assertion is, admittedly, a point on which even Lutheran dogmaticians have differed. Luther and Chemnitz themselves offered divergent opinions as to whether the subordination of the Son is related to his human nature, his state of humiliation, or his eternal personal relationship to the Father. Often the dogmaticians are guilty of confusing submission with inferiority (see, e.g., Martin Chemnitz, *The Two Natures in Christ* [trans. J. A. O. Preus; St. Louis: Concordia, 1971], 275). Luther locates the Son's submission *prior* to his state of humiliation in his great hymn "The Son obeyed His Father's will, Was born of virgin mother; and God's good pleasure to fulfill, He came to be my brother" (*LSB* 556:6). The NT evidence for the Son's submission to the Father seems broader than simply in his state of humiliation or even his incarnation; see particularly 1 Cor 15:28, but also Mt 26:39; Jn 3:35; 4:34; 5:30; 6:38; 12:49; 13:3; 1 Cor 15:24; Heb 10:7, 9. The Son's exaltation to the right hand of God itself implies an ordering (Eph 1:20; cf. Acts 2:33). Eph 2:18 teaches that even now the Son's role is to be the vehicle of access to the Father. For further discussion, see John W. Kleinig, "The Subordination of the Exalted Son to the Father," *Lutheran Theological Review* 18 (Academic Year 2005–2006): 41–52.

can align the subordination of wife to husband with that of the Son to the Father without in any way demeaning the subordinated figures:[165]

παντὸς ἀνδρὸς ἡ κεφαλὴ ὁ Χριστός ἐστιν, κεφαλὴ δὲ γυναικὸς ὁ ἀνήρ, κεφαλὴ δὲ τοῦ Χριστοῦ ὁ θεός.

The head of every man is *Christ*, and [the] head of [the/his] woman/wife is the *man/husband*, and [the] head of Christ is *God*. (1 Cor 11:3)[166]

This is nothing other than a "hierarchy," an ordering of offices:

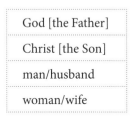

God [the Father]

Christ [the Son]

man/husband

woman/wife

It is vitally important, then, to ask *why* the Son submits to his Father's will. The answer, of course, is that he might gain our salvation.[167] Thus, the ordering of offices includes both Law and Gospel elements. This is not simply a chain of command, but a chain of transmission of blessings.[168] When husbands and wives take their proper roles, the marriage is a blessing to both.[169] Not only does the subordination of wife to husband (5:21–33), child to parent (6:1–4), and servant to master (6:5–9) act typologically to proclaim the Gospel relationship of the church to Christ (see below), but also in and of themselves these relationships, properly ordered, are a blessing of God for the Christian church and her members. "Subordination presupposes the primacy of community over individuality, the need for communal solidarity for the wellbeing of each person."[170] This is a countercultural ideal, both then and now. Instead of independence, the ideal is dependence. Servants and masters, children and parents, wives and

---

[165] Lockwood, *1 Corinthians*, 365: "It must be conceded that it is no more demeaning for a woman to be subject to a man than it is for the man to be subject to Christ, and for Christ to be subject to God the Father."

[166] In each of the last three clauses of Paul's sentence, the word κεφαλή ("head") comes first. But the use of the definite article on "Christ" (ὁ Χριστός), "man" (ὁ ἀνήρ), and "God" (ὁ θεός) indicates that they are the subjects of the verb "is" (ἐστιν)—they are probably placed last in each clause for emphasis. In accord with Colwell's Rule, the predicate nominative κεφαλή ("[the] head") may be definite even without the article; and according to Apollonius' Canon, the genitive noun (γυναικός, "of [the/his] woman/wife") attached to it may also be definite, even without the article. See Wallace, *Greek Grammar*, 5, 239–40, 242–43.

[167] Luther sings: "God said to His beloved Son: 'It's time to have compassion. Then go, bright jewel of My crown, And bring to all salvation' " (*LSB* 556:5).

[168] Kleinig, "Ordered Community," 58.

[169] Chrysostom, *Homilies on Ephesians*, 20:5.33, ACCS 8:200: "God's purpose in ordering marriage is peace. One takes the husband's role, one takes the wife's role, one in guiding, one in supporting. If both had the very same roles, there would be no peace. The house is not rightly governed when all have precisely the same roles. There must be a differentiation of roles under a single head."

[170] Kleinig, "Ordered Community," 45.

husbands are in one way or another totally dependent on each other—and to be dependent is *better* than to be independent, even as it is better to be saved than to be responsible for saving oneself (and inevitably fail!). Thus, Paul asks us to submit *joyfully* to those whom the Father has given to care for us.[171] And Paul invites those to whom God has committed headship to receive it with both joy and humility, with the spirit of self-sacrifice, recognizing that it is not given on the basis of merit nor for the sake of domination, but that the head might be an instrument of his blessing.

As the earliest interpreter of Paul, Clement of Rome is best situated to expound the joys of a well-ordered community:

> [37:1]Let us then, men and brethren, with all energy act the part of soldiers, in accordance with His holy commandments [προστάγμασιν]. [2]Let us consider those who serve under our generals, with what order [εὐτάκτως],[172] obedience [ἐκτικῶς],[173] and submissiveness [ὑποτεταγμένως] they perform the things which are commanded them. [3]All are not prefects, nor commanders of a thousand, nor of a hundred, nor of fifty, nor the like, but each one in his own rank [ἐν τῷ ἰδίῳ τάγματι] performs the things commanded [τὰ ἐπιτασσόμενα] by the king and the generals. [4]The great cannot subsist without the small, nor the small without the great. There is a kind of mixture in all things, and thence arises mutual advantage. [5]Let us take our body for an example. The head is nothing without the feet, and the feet are nothing without the head; yea, the very smallest members of our body are necessary and useful to the whole body. But all work harmoniously together, and are under [ὑποταγῇ] one common rule for the preservation of the whole body.
>
> [38:1]Let our whole body, then, be preserved in Christ Jesus; and let every one be subject [ὑποτασσέσθω] to his neighbour, according to the special gift bestowed upon him.[174]

Five Essential Characteristics of Subordination in Ephesians

The structure of subordination taught in 5:21–6:9 stands therefore at the conclusion of a careful sequence of biblical teachings. Subordination is, *first*, built into creation itself. Paul alludes, for example, to the formation of woman from the side of man (Eph 5:29–30; cf. Gen 2:21–23) and appeals directly to the divine institution of marriage in Genesis (Eph 5:31, quoting Gen 2:24).[175] The

---

[171] Kleinig, "Ordered Community," 46: "Subordination involves our willing acceptance of our given communal leaders and our whole-hearted cooperation with them because they are our leaders. We are subordinate to those who are our heads, because they occupy an office over us, a divinely instituted position of leadership in our community. We are subordinate to them in their office."

[172] εὐτάκτως is better translated as "with *good* order."

[173] ἐκτικῶς is better translated as "with habitual ease, fluency."

[174] *1 Clement* 37:1–38:1 (*ANF* 1:15; verse numbers added).

[175] Cf. 1 Cor 11:8; 14:34; 1 Tim 2:8–15. The similarity of these two letters to Ephesians with respect to the role of women derives not only from their common Pauline authorship but perhaps also from the fact that 1 Timothy was written *to* (Timothy in) Ephesus and 1 Corinthians *from* Ephesus. See "Paul's Sermon to the Ephesian Pastors (Acts 20:15–38; cf. 1 Timothy)" in "The City of Ephesus and Paul's Relationship to It" in the introduction.

subordination of children to parents is supported by a quotation of the Fourth Commandment (Eph 6:2, quoting Ex 20:12), which is an affirmation of natural law (cf. the reference to creation in Ex 20:11). In this respect, the subordination structure taught in Ephesians is also of the left-hand kingdom; as a pattern built into creation, it is applicable to all people, whether they are Christians or not, whether they acknowledge God's order or not.

At the same time it is important to recognize that Paul is alluding here to only one aspect of the order of creation, namely, the order of marriage in the household. Put another way, the wife's submission to her husband cannot be extrapolated into the broad generalization that all women are subordinate to all men all the time as part of "*the* order of creation."[176] It is helpful to recall the threefold distinction made in the *Book of Concord*, derived from Luther and entirely traditional in its makeup, between the ecclesiastical, domestic, and civil estates.[177] Ephesians 5–6 is concerned specifically with the domestic estate, and its description of the subordination of wife to husband—though consistent with the broader scriptural teaching on the relationship of men and women— is unique to the marital union.

Certainly Paul also teaches a structure of subordination within the ecclesiastical estate, including the necessity of the flock to submit to the authority of their shepherd.[178] Within the ecclesiastical estate there is also a subordination of women to men that takes its most visible shape in the restriction of the pastoral *office* to men and is also evident in the broader prohibition of women even carrying out the *functions* of proclaiming God's Word and exercising its

---

[176] Kleinig, "Ordered Community," 51–53, on the basis of Scripture, distinguishes different subordinate relationships within the order of the household, the order of the government, and the order of the church (with further differentiation in the order of the church triumphant, the angelic order, and the order of the Holy Trinity). He maintains that each of the three earthly orders (household, government, and church) involves a separate set of relationships for men and women that cannot be universalized (53):

> Three things are worth noting from this data. First, the New Testament does not teach that there is a general universal order of creation. Second, it does not speak of the general subordination of all women to all men but only their subordination in particular relationships, according to their station, such as wives to husbands. There is therefore no theological reason why women cannot be leaders in government. Third, subordination means different things in different contexts and different relationships. While a woman may not speak as teacher in the liturgical assembly, she may question her husband at home (I Cor. 14:33–35) and teach younger women to be good wives and mothers (Tit. 2:3–5).

[177] Lutheran theology traditionally identifies these three estates (*Stände*) as the ones instituted by God, sometimes calling them the *Lehrstand*, *Nährstand*, and *Wehrstand* ("teaching estate," "nourishing estate," and "defending estate"). In Luther, see, e.g., AE 7:312; 22:405; 37:364–65; 41:154–64. In the *Book of Concord*, see, e.g., AC 16:5; Ap 16:3, 5; SA 2:4.7; 3:11.1; LC 1:126, 206–8; 4:20; FC Ep 12:12; FC SD 12:17.

[178] Though the subordination of the laity to the ministry does not belong in a domestic code, it is implied by the teaching of Ephesians 4 (see especially 4:11–12). It is common NT and early patristic teaching: 1 Cor 16:16; cf. Heb 13:17; 1 Pet 5:5; *1 Clement*, 1:3; 57:1–2; Ignatius, *To the Ephesians*, 2:2; 5:3; Ignatius, *To the Magnesians*, 2:1; 3:1; 13:2; Ignatius, *To the Trallians*, 2:1–2; 13:2; Ignatius, *To Polycarp*, 6:1; Polycarp, *To the Philippians*, 5:3.

authority in the divine service.[179] Paul also teaches the need for Christians to submit to civil authorities (Rom 13:1–8; cf. 1 Pet 2:13–14). But it is notable that Paul does not distinguish the roles of men and women in the civil estate. That is to say, he makes no claim that women may not hold a superordinate position within government.[180] It is also highly significant that the civil order *does not* feature in Ephesians. In this way Paul stands apart from secular *Haustafeln* in ancient times that viewed the domestic estate as a microcosm of the political.[181] For it is neither the order of creation nor the political sphere but the church that is the primary model for Paul's words to husband and wife in Ephesians 5.

Paul's genius in Ephesians is to move beyond the order of creation to make an appeal that is uniquely heard by the baptized.[182] This is not the first occurrence of subordination in the letter. For subordination is, *second*, defined by the order that flows out of Christ's redemptive work. In his resurrection and ascension Christ subordinated all spiritual forces, defeating and disarming them. When God exalted him, he placed every rank of angelic being, whether good or evil, beneath the feet of Christ, whom he seated at his right hand (1:20–22; 3:10; 4:8–10; cf. 6:12). Like the order of creation, this involved an involuntary subordination; the demons had no choice but to acknowledge Christ's headship. This victory, too, was achieved for the benefit of all; but it was especially for his body, the church, who receive the spoils of the battle (1:22–23; 2:6).

---

[179] The admonition for women to be silent in the church (1 Cor 14:34) and the prohibition against their teaching or having authority over men, asserted in the context of public worship (1 Tim 2:8–15), preclude the ordination of women; but Paul does not explicitly say that women may not be ordained into the pastoral office. Rather the logic is as follows: because women are prohibited from carrying out the *functions* that are distinctive of the office, therefore they may not hold the *office*. The prohibition of women's ordination is a consequence of the broader principle. This means, by corollary, that it is illogical to permit women to carry out the *functions* of the office (proclaiming God's Word and giving out the Sacraments in the Divine Service), while arguing that one is still honoring the apostolic prohibition against their holding the *office*.

[180] Christians have differed in their response to this question over the centuries, though there are countless examples of women ruling in Christian countries. Sixteenth-century Britain provides a well-known case study. Fearful of a return to civil war if the two female offspring of his first two marriages were the only claimants to his throne, Henry VIII pursued four more wives mostly in the desire to produce a male heir. In the event, after the brief reign of Edward the child king, both Mary and Elizabeth were (grudgingly) accepted as legitimate monarchs. Mary, the Roman Catholic, however, relinquished her father's title "Supreme Head of the Church of England" and restored the papacy; Protestant Elizabeth took the title "Supreme Governor" of the Church of England instead. Thus, while the theologians were able to justify the reign of a woman in the civil realm and could stomach the queen as "governor" of the church, they could not accept the notion that a woman might take the Christlike role of the church's "head."

[181] See the quotation of Aristotle in "A Note on the Term *Haustafel*" in "Structure and Rhetoric" in this pericope. See also MacDonald, *Colossians and Ephesians*, 337.

[182] For Baptism in Ephesians, see especially the textual notes and the commentary on 1:13, 18; 2:5; 4:4–6, 22–24, 30; 5:7, 14, 26. See also "Baptism and the Spirit" in "Purpose and Themes" in the introduction; "Baptism in the Prologue" in the commentary on 1:3–14; "Enlightened Eyes of Your Heart (1:18)" in the commentary on Eph 1:15–23; and "Creedal, Baptismal Unity" in the commentary on 4:1–16.

In this way the teaching of subordination begins to take on a Gospel aspect. As far as the church is concerned, subordination is, *third*, transformed by Christ's work to have higher significance than it does in the civil realm. While the Stoics could speak of order as that which is "fitting" (i.e., in accord with natural law)—language which Paul could sometimes coopt (Eph 5:3–4; Col 3:18)—Paul prefers to speak of order "in … Christ/the Lord" (5:21; 6:1) and of submission "as to Christ/the Lord" (5:22; 6:5, 7). With such phrases the so-called *Haustafel* is moved out of the realm of ethics and away from its contemporary cultural parallels. As Bruce comments:

> While many of the ethical emphases in these Christian summaries can be paralleled from Jewish and Stoic sources, to say that the addition of such a phrase as "in the Lord" ([Col 3:]18, 20) "Christianizes them in the simplest possible way" [W. K. L. Clarke] is to say everything, for such an addition introduces a difference in kind and not merely in degree. Here is a new and powerful dynamic:
>
> > *This is the famous stone*
> > *That turneth all to gold* [George Herbert].[183]

Traditional human relationships are thereby not just put on a more sure footing by the Christian faith, but they also take on a typological, evangelical, and Christological character.

Within the realm of the Gospel, subordination is no longer just imposed, no longer simply a given. Because it is, *fourth*, a gift of the Spirit (5:18), Christians are enabled to submit to the order willingly. Christian subordination can, therefore, be clearly distinguished from the defeated posture of the demons and from the servile fear of the abject and weak.[184] As a willing act of those who have been filled with the Spirit in Holy Baptism, Christian subordination is, *fifth*, an act of worship. For this reason it is not simply declared by Paul as a de facto condition (i.e., "you are subordinate"), but is encouraged[185] by participles and imperatives that appeal to the pattern of Christ and the church.

It is in these five crucial ways that Paul's teaching on subordination departs radically from the superficially similar *Haustafeln*[186] of the ancient world. Here, too, not only in his view of marriage itself, Paul is not a mere product of his

---

[183] Bruce, *The Epistles to the Colossians, to Philemon, and to the Ephesians*, 162, quoting W. K. Lowther Clarke, *New Testament Problems: Essays, Reviews, Interpretations* (London: SPCK, 1929), 159, and George Herbert, *The Elixir*. The quotation from Herbert's poem actually refers to the prayer phrase "for thy sake," but makes Bruce's point.

[184] Barth, *Ephesians*, 2:609, distinguishes voluntary Christian subordination "(a) from the 'subjection' of the creatures 'to futility' (Rom 8:19[–20]), (b) from the present and future 'subjugation' of principalities and powers to the feet of Christ (I Cor 15:25–27; Eph 1:21–22), and (c) from loss of all power and from exposure to ridicule (Col 2:15)."

[185] Kleinig, "Ordered Community," 55: "The moral philosophers in antiquity did not call on wives, children, and slaves to be subordinate, because they had no choice but to submit to their superiors. In contrast, the call for subordination by Paul and Peter arises from their equality [that of wives, children, and slaves] before God."

[186] See "A Note on the Term *Haustafel*" in "Structure and Rhetoric" in this pericope.

times for whom the modern church ought to apologize, but is a "critic" through the lens of the Gospel.

> When the apostles Peter and Paul teach subordination, they do not thereby sanction the social, political, economic status quo, but, in fact, acknowledge how riddled it is with sin and the abuse of power. They do not propose a social or political agenda for the reformation and transformation of a society by the behaviour of its lower classes. Nor do they reinforce cultural roles or stereotypical patterns of behaviour in marriage, family life, and society at large. Instead, they show how Christians can already now, by faith, live with God as citizens of heaven within the earthly orders of a fallen world, because Christ has transformed the whole human life cycle from the womb to the tomb by His incarnation and His exaltation. Christ does not abolish the old divinely instituted orders of family and government to free His disciples from life in community, but He redeems these orders so that they can accomplish their proper purpose.[187]

Holy Matrimony and the Gospel

The preceding section endeavored to rethink subordination in biblical terms, to shift our understanding of the divinely mandated structure of human existence away from modern prejudices rooted in egalitarianism that would view order only in terms of oppression and devaluation. God's order is a gift and may be received as such and cherished joyfully by the Christian whose will has been transformed by the indwelling Spirit. Thus, though we shall highlight the fundamentally Gospel orientation of this pericope (below), as the revelation of God's will for human thoughts, words, and deeds this text also contains a clear word of *Law*. Abiding by this word of Law carries the promise of a well-ordered marriage in which the delivery of God's blessings can be found. For Christians, though we fail to live up to its standard and our marriages constantly need God's forgiveness, this Law is nevertheless a joy to fulfill, particularly since its fulfillment entails conformity to Christ. The majority of ancient commentators focus in this way on what the pattern of Christ and the church means for the Christian practice of marriage.[188] A fine representative of this pattern of exegesis is Chrysostom:

> Have you noted the measure of obedience? Pay attention to love's high standard. If you take the premise that your wife should submit to you, as the church

---

[187] Kleinig, "Ordered Community," 57–58.

[188] The conclusions drawn by Schnackenburg in his survey of the fathers include the following:

> (1) The writers of the early Church without exception took the quotation in v. 31 to refer directly to human marriage and then only in a second step referred the "great mystery" to Christ and the Church; (2) The Fathers, who look back to the divine establishment of marriage on the morning of Creation, make no basic difference between a "natural marriage" and Christian marriage; (3) the marriage established by God is regarded as good and holy in the repulsing of other conceptions, especially in Gnosticism; ([4]) considerable consideration is given to the figurative character of marriage in relationship to Christ and the Church, but it is evaluated in various ways. (*Ephesians*, 332)

submits to Christ, then you should also take the same kind of careful, sacrificial thought for her that Christ takes for the church. Even if you must offer your own life for her, you must not refuse. Even if you must undergo countless struggles on her behalf and have all kinds of things to endure and suffer, you must not refuse. Even if you suffer all this, you have still done not as much as Christ has for the church. For you are already married when you act this way, whereas Christ is acting for one who has rejected and hated him. So just as he, when she was rejecting, hating, spurning and nagging him, brought her to trust him by his great solicitude, not by threatening, lording it over her or intimidating her or anything like that, so must you also act toward your wife. Even if you see her looking down on you, nagging and despising you, you will be able to win her over with your great love and affection for her.[189]

This concern for the husband and wife's behavior toward one another, with Christ and the church as a pattern, is certainly present in the text. Though for Paul it is a *secondary* focus of his teaching, he is careful at each stage of his proclamation of Christ to remind the married couple that there are implications for the way they treat each other (5:24, 28, 33). As even ancient writers like Chrysostom noticed, Paul reserves the greater extent of his admonitions for the husband in his responsibility to love and sacrifice himself for his wife. Yet Paul does not shrink from admonishing the wife to submit to her husband. In this Paul is thoroughly consistent with NT teaching.[190]

However, despite the prominence of the word "obey" in traditional marriage rites,[191] our analysis of ὑποτάσσω (whose passive is translated as "be subordi-

---

[189] Chrysostom, *Homilies on Ephesians*, 20:5.25, ACCS 8:195.

[190] 1 Cor 11:3; 14:34; Col 3:18; Titus 2:5; 1 Pet 3:1, 5.

[191] Our English rites almost universally derive from the *Book of Common Prayer* (1549, 1552, 1559, and 1662). In the 1549 rite, the husband is asked in the declaration of intent "Wilt thou *loue* [love] her, *coumforte* [comfort] her, honor, and kepe her in sickenesse and in health? And forsaking all other kepe thee only to her, so long as you both shall liue?" The respective questions to the wife are "Wilt thou *obey* him, and *serue* [serve] him, loue, honor, and kepe him in sickenes and in health? And forsaking al other kepe thee onely to him, so long as you bothe shall liue?" Emphasis added. In the vows, the husband likewise pledges "to loue and to cherishe," while the wife vows "to loue, cherishe, and to obey." See *The First and Second Prayer Books of Edward VI* (London: Prayer Book Society, 1999), 253–54. According to Diarmaid MacCulloch, *Thomas Cranmer: A Life* (New Haven: Yale University Press, 1996), 420–21, the phrases in the vows that expressed the distinct roles of husband and wife respectively were added by Thomas Cranmer to the medieval Sarum rite that he was revising for the *Book of Common Prayer*. The Sarum rite, whose marriage order dates to the fourteenth century and includes vows in English (that the couple might understand what they were saying), contained its own distinctive admonition to the bride, that she promise to be "bonere and boxsom, in bedde and atte bord." Cranmer was perhaps aware that the phrase "bonere and boxsom" (i.e., "bonair and buxom," meaning "meek and compliant") was archaic and that the accompanying reference "in bedde [in bed] and atte bord [at table]" was a little racy. This may have been the reason he borrowed the words "obey him, and serve him" from the Sarum rite's preceding Latin question of consent (*obedire & seruire*) and substituted them in his English rite's questions to the bride. See Kenneth Stevenson, *Nuptial Blessing: A Study of Christian Marriage Rites* (London: SPCK, 1982), 79.

In the liturgical heritage of LCMS Lutheranism, Cranmer's vows were loosely followed, including the word "obey," in the agendas that accompanied the *Evangelical Lutheran Hymn-Book* (rev. ed.; St. Louis: Concordia, 1912); *The Lutheran Hymnal* (St. Louis: Concordia,

nate" in 5:21, 24) has demonstrated that "being subordinate" is not adequately or comprehensively rendered with the vocabulary of obedience.[192] Obedience may be a consequence of subordination, but is not its immediate meaning.[193] It is interesting to note that in 6:1–9 the more usual verb ὑπακούω, "heed, obey," is applied to children (6:1) and slaves (6:5),[194] but it does not occur here in chapter 5 with reference to wives. Thus, while Paul *could* have called on wives to "heed, obey," it appears that he made a deliberate choice to use the passive of ὑποτάσσω, "be subordinate."[195]

This, too, was a countercultural move for Paul. Giving orders and obeying them is an ancient conception of the marital relationship of husband and wife that Paul does not adopt in toto. Hellenistic Judaism often calls for wives to obey their husbands, while the use of Paul's vocable ὑποτάσσω for the relationship is rare.[196] Likewise, Plato, quoting Homer, says: "Each one gives law to his

---

1941); and *Lutheran Worship* (St. Louis: Concordia, 1982). See, respectively, *Liturgy and Agenda* (St. Louis: Concordia, 1917), 342; *The Lutheran Agenda* (St. Louis: Concordia, n.d. [194-]), 37, 45, 49; *Lutheran Worship: Agenda* (St. Louis: Concordia, 1984), 122. Unfortunately, they removed the unique obligation laid upon the husband to "comfort" (either by removing "comfort" altogether or by including it in the vows of both the bridegroom and the bride), thus suggesting that only the wife had a distinctive role. Luther's *Traubüchlein*, "Marriage Booklet," appended to the Small Catechism, contains none of this language as it has no vows. The LCMS German agenda gave distinctive duties to husband and wife, respectively: "sie lieben, ehren, nähren und ihr vorstehen ['love, honor her, nourish, and lead her']"; "ihn lieben, ehren, ihm folgig und gehorsam sein ['love, honor him, be following and obedient to him']" (*Kirchen-Agende für Evang.-Luth. Gemeinden ungeänderter Augsburgischer Confession* [St. Louis: Barthel, 1866], 25). Tracing the origin of this language is beyond the scope of this commentary. The 2006 *LSB Agenda* (67–68), following Ephesians 5 more closely, introduced into the bride's vows the language "submit to him as the Church submits to Christ" and gave the husband the unique duty to "nourish and cherish her as Christ loved His body, the Church, giving Himself up for her." The Christological imaging is thus made explicit in this new rite.

[192] As translations of ὑποτάσσω, particularly in the present context, "to obey," "to submit," and "to be subject" are inadequate if they imply a servile or debased act of passive submission to the will of another rather than a willing acceptance of an order. See Kleinig, "Ordered Community," 50, n. 13.

[193] G. Delling, "ὑποτάσσω," *TDNT* 8:41. Stoeckhardt's interpretation is therefore not faulty for its old-fashioned ring, but because it misinterprets the verb: "And just so in wedlock the man is lord and head, he decides, he determines, he commands. Naturally, then, it is the duty of the wife to hearken, to follow, and to submit to the man's demands" (*Ephesians*, 241). Paul nowhere in this passage speaks of a husband who "commands" or issues "demands."

[194] See the second textual note on 6:1 for the meaning of ὑπακούω, which is not always simply "obey."

[195] Kleinig, "Ordered Community," 51: "Surprisingly, the call for subordination of a Christian wife to her husband does not focus on her obedience to him, but on her respect for him as her head (Eph. 5:22, 33; I Pet. 3:2). Its purpose is for her to receive his love (Eph. 5:24–27), and, if she is married to an unbeliever, to gain his conversion (I Pet. 3:1–2)." The use of ὑπακούω, "heed, obey," for Sarah's response to Abraham (1 Pet 3:6) is an exception to this linguistic pattern—though Paul would certainly agree that obedience is a component of wifely subordination.

[196] Lincoln, *Ephesians*, 367.

children and to his wives."[197] And Aristotle asserts: "The male is by nature fitter to command than the female."[198] The distinction between such ancient thinkers and Paul was often lost on Christian commentators in ancient times. Aquinas, for example, might be mistaken for Aristotle when he writes: "The relation of a husband to his wife is, in a certain way, like that of a master to his servant, insofar as the latter ought to be governed by the commands of his master."[199] But though Paul draws certain parallels between the three relationships of marriage (5:21–33), family (6:1–4), and servanthood (6:5–9), obedience is not the chief thought.

What the three hold in common is rather the way in which they are all conformed to the pattern of Christ's relationship with the church. And it is here that the distinction between subordination and obedience is most critical. Subordination may entail obedience,[200] but to equate the two is to shift the meaning significantly and to distort the typology of Christ and the church. If marriage is adduced by Paul as an image of Christ and the church—or vice versa—then to identify obedience as its chief characteristic is to forfeit the Gospel. That is to say, if obedience is the chief way in which the wife operates toward her husband, then by way of Paul's analogy it would also be the chief way in which the church operates toward Christ. The church's (and therefore also the individual Christian's) chief duty would then be to *obey* Christ. This is to formulate the relationship entirely in the way of the Law. Once again, it is certainly true that the Christian (and the church) is obligated to obey Christ; to deny this is to deny his Lordship, his headship, his very divinity. Yet the church's chief modus operandi in her relationship with her divine Bridegroom is *faith*. For the church, subordination to Christ means relinquishing the act of redemption to him, allowing him to be the Savior rather than seeking in any synergistic or Pelagian manner to save herself (an effort that would surely fail).

Paul's ultimately *Gospel* orientation in this pericope is clear from a number of features. First, the very balance of his language is decidedly weighted toward the work of Christ for the church. It is not simply that Paul has more to say to the husband than to the wife when he allots three verses to the latter (5:22–24) and six to the former (5:25–30). More significantly, the words to the husband are utterly dominated by proclamation of the saving work of Christ. Even the words to the wife are predicated on the central declaration that Christ is the Savior of the body (5:23). Second, Paul's overriding concern to preach

---

[197] Plato, *Laws*, 3:680b–c, quoting Homer, *Odyssey*, 9:114–15, quoted in Barth, *Ephesians*, 2:611, n. 12.

[198] Aristotle, *Politics*, 1:1259b, quoted in Barth, *Ephesians*, 2:611, n. 12.

[199] Thomas Aquinas, *Commentary on Saint Paul's Epistle to the Ephesians* (trans. Matthew L. Lamb; Albany, N.Y.: Magi, 1966), 217 (on Eph 5:22; lecture 8), quoted in Barth, *Ephesians*, 2:708.

[200] "Someone in the marriage relationship has the responsibility for decision and direction. In the 'order' that God has designed, the husband has been given that burden" (Scharlemann, "The Pastoral Office and Divorce, Remarriage, Moral Deviation," 146).

Christ through marriage (not vice versa) is proclaimed by his urgent clarification near the conclusion of the unit "but I say [it refers] to Christ and to the church" (5:32)—which might be translated as "but I am speaking of Christ and the church [i.e., not chiefly about marriage]." Thus, for Paul "the marriage bond is an exhibit and a constant reminder, on the level of the obvious and visible, of God's agenda at work in history; namely, to bring the totality of all things under the headship of Jesus Christ (Eph. 1:10)."[201] Paul's ultimate goal is not to order earthly relationships, but to preach the Gospel. Finally, the logic of Paul's presentation is significant: despite his appeal to the creation of Eve from the side of Adam and the institutional mandate for marriage in Genesis (Eph 5:29–32; cf. Gen 2:21–24), Paul's argument with respect to Christian marriage is not essentially *derived from* the order of creation. In fact, Paul argues in completely the opposite fashion: from Christ and the church backwards to the order of creation. That is to say, the order of creation, including the institution of marriage for all time and for all people, was set in place so that it might stand as a perpetual proclamation of the Gospel.[202]

This salvation-historical perspective ought to remind us that Paul's view of marriage as an image of the Gospel does not originate within his creative mind, but is rooted in the way of God with his people Israel in the OT. Though marriage language is not used in the Torah's account of Sinai, the Rabbinic Judaism of Paul's day celebrated that making of the covenant as a marriage between God and his people.[203] In preparation for their meeting God at Sinai, the children of Israel were required to be consecrated through the washing of water and clothed in clean robes (Ex 19:10, 14)—baptismal language that is also evocative of the preparation of a bride (of Jerusalem in Ezek 16:9–10; of

---

[201] Scharlemann, "The Pastoral Office and Divorce, Remarriage, Moral Deviation," 146.

[202] Weinrich, " 'It Is Not Given to Women to Teach': A *Lex* in Search of a *Ratio*," 22–23:

> The "order of creation" is not transformed in the "order of redemption" but is rather illuminated in the "order of redemption." … It is not that Christ was a male human person because in the "order of creation" God had given headship and authority to the man, Adam. Rather, God who created humankind in order that He might have communion with it in and through His Word gave the headship of humanity to the man, Adam, **in view of** the eschatological goal of humanity which is Christ and His Church. Because in the final purpose and telos of God for the world the man Jesus Christ was to be the Head of His Body, the Church (which relates to Christ as Bride to Bridegroom), God in the beginning gave Adam to be head to Eve.

[203] See, e.g., the rabbinic midrash *Song of Songs Rabbah*, quoted at some length in Jacob Neusner, *Israel's Love Affair with God: Song of Songs* (Valley Forge, Pa.: Trinity Press International, 1993). See also Kirby, *Ephesians: Baptism and Pentecost*, 99–100, 148–49. E. Stauffer, "γαμέω," *TDNT* 1:654, has further rabbinic references. The view of Pentecost as the celebration of all the covenantal promises of God was promulgated by the *Book of Jubilees*. The fact that the Decalogue begins with "you shall have no other gods" (Ex 20:3; Deut 5:7) and ends with "you shall not covet your neighbor's wife" (Ex 20:17; Deut 5:21) might be seen as forming a thematic *inclusio* depicting the Ten Commandments as a marriage covenant; certainly in its context God speaks of himself as a "jealous" God (קַנָּא, Ex 20:5; 34:14; Deut 5:9; etc.), just as a husband "is jealous" (קַנָּא, Num 5:14, 30). See Mitchell, *The Song of Songs*, 43.

the church in Eph 5:26–27).[204] It may, in fact, be Paul's recent celebration of Pentecost at the temple, shortly before his arrest (Acts 20:16; 1 Cor 16:8), that brought the marriage of God and his people to mind in the writing of this letter.[205] Later OT language is more explicit. The marriage of God to his people is vividly depicted by way of allegory in the messianic Psalm 45, which compares it to the marriage of the king to a princess, and the extended allegory of the Song of Songs.[206] The prophet Isaiah is replete with language of Israel as the Lord's bride, particularly in the image of holiness as pure clothing and splendid jewelry: "I will rejoice exuberantly in YHWH. My soul will indeed exult in my God, because he clothed me in garments of salvation. In a robe of righteousness he covered me, as a bridegroom dresses like a priest with a beautiful headdress and as a bride adorns herself with her jewels" (Is 61:10; cf. Is 49:18; 62:5; Jer 2:32; Ezek 16:8–14). Because Israel is his bride, the Lord will always redeem her from harm (Is 54:4–8; 62:4–5; Jer 2:2–3). Often it is Israel's *unfaithfulness* that is the focus of the image: she is a bride whom the Lord sends away (Is 50:1), a whore (Is 1:21; Jer 2:20) and an adulteress (Ezek 16:15–48; 23:2–49),[207] as is famously depicted by God's command to Hosea to marry a prostitute.[208] Yet the Lord promises to restore the marriage through the forgiveness of her sins "in that day" (Hos 2:18–23 [ET 2:16–21]) of eschatological restoration (Jer 33:11; Ezek 16:52–63)—a clear messianic promise. Perhaps the most extensive and vivid of all portrayals of the marriage of God to Israel fills the sixteenth chapter of Ezekiel, a text which gives crucial background imagery for Ephesians 5.

Judaism thought of the coming messianic age as the final renewal of the covenant, when the true marriage feast would take place.[209] Jesus' use of marriage parables (Mt 22:1–14; 25:1–13) and his reference to himself as the Bridegroom (Mt 9:15; cf. Jn 3:29) demonstrate that he saw himself as the true fulfillment of these expectations. The provision of copious amounts of wine at the Cana wedding may be viewed as Jesus' pronouncement that the messianic marriage feast had begun (Jn 2:1–11). Paul saw his apostolic ministry as facilitating

---

[204] The *Mekilta* on Ex 19:10 changes the text from "consecrate them today" to "betroth them today" (quoted in Kirby, *Ephesians: Baptism and Pentecost*, 99).

[205] See "Paul's Trip to Jerusalem, Arrest, and Imprisonment (Acts 21:1–36)" in "The City of Ephesus and Paul's Relationship to It" in the introduction.

[206] Mitchell, *The Song of Songs*, 58: "In our opinion, Eph 5:21–33 is the closest biblical parallel to the Song and also is the passage that sheds the most light on the proper hermeneutical approach to the Song."

[207] Hence the OT expression "to whore [זָנָה] after other gods" (Judg 2:17; see also, e.g., Ex 34:15–16; Deut 31:16; Judg 8:33; 1 Chr 5:25).

[208] Hos 1:2–3; 2:3–3:5 (ET 2:1–3:5); cf. Jer 3:6–10; 4:30; Ezekiel 23. Mitchell, *The Song of Songs*, 44: "It is striking that *marriage itself is a prominent element in the ministries of several prophets* [Is 8:3–4; Ezek 24:16–27; Hosea 1–3]. *The marriage of these prophets is a prophetic sign, a proclamation of Law and Gospel.*" See also his "Antonymous Texts with Adulterous Language" (62–64).

[209] E. Stauffer, "γαμέω," *TDNT* 1:654.

the marriage, presenting the virgin bride to Christ (2 Cor 11:2).[210] The church is feminine not simply because of the gender of the Greek noun ἐκκλησία ("church") but also because she is always the bride (e.g., Rev 21:2, 9; cf. 1 Pet 5:13; 2 Jn 1, 13).[211] She is also feminine as the birthmother of believers (Is 66:7–13; Gal 4:26).[212] She is the woman who gives birth to the child in the wilderness—an image that rolls together Israel, Mary, and the church (Revelation 12). The anti-church is a prostitute precisely in contrast to the church as bride (Revelation 17–18). The final word of the NT is the invitation of the Bridegroom to his bride, the church, to join him in the eternal feast of heaven (Rev 22:17; cf. Rev 19:7–9; 21:2, 9).

From this biblical survey it is amply clear that Paul neither invented the marriage allegory nor borrowed it from secular sources.[213] It is likewise clear that Paul could not have run the allegory as a simple one-way equation in order to encourage certain behaviors in Christian marriages on the basis of Christ and the church as an illustration. For Paul, the marriage allegory is chiefly a vehicle for the proclamation of the Gospel of Jesus Christ. Paul is the friend of the Bridegroom (akin to a best man or, better in modern terms, the father of the bride), who presents the church to Christ in holy marriage (2 Cor 11:2). Ephesians 5 not only contains a most remarkable restoration of the original institution and purposes of marriage as a blessing to man and wife in this life, but it also transcends the earthly blessings by revealing the mystery of the Gospel hidden in every marriage, if husband and wife would have the eyes of faith to discern it. For, each day as the husband loves his wife in a thoroughly self-sacrificing way, he proclaims Jesus Christ to her and likewise to himself as

---

[210] Paul's advocacy of the single life in view of the imminent return of Christ (1 Cor 7:26–35), paralleled by God's command to Jeremiah to remain single in view of the impending destruction of Jerusalem (Jer 16:1–4), gives evidence that he saw the *eternal, eschatological* marriage of Christ to his church as the goal toward which all earthly marriages point. Thus, on the cusp of eternity, earthly marriage fades away (cf. Mt 22:30). While Paul might have remained single himself in light of his role as a third party in bringing the bride to Christ (2 Cor 11:2), his example cannot be used to promote an enforced celibacy among clergy in light of his advocacy that the minister be "the husband of one wife" (1 Tim 3:2; Titus 1:6) and his warning against those who would forbid marriage (1 Tim 4:3).

[211] Nonetheless, this is just an image, and the church is clearly not confined to women (Gal 3:28) any more than the church's depiction as 144,000 *male* virgins (Rev 14:3–4), the use of the term "brother" (passim), and the adoption to *sonship* (e.g., Rom 8:15, 23; Eph 1:5) would imply that the church is restricted to men.

[212] See Lessing, *Isaiah 56–66*, 484–88; Das, *Galatians*, 477–511, titles his commentary on Gal 4:21–31 "A Tale of Two Birthing Movements." Cyprian, *The Unity of the Catholic Church*, 6, expresses the classic Christian image: "One cannot have God as Father who does not have the church as mother" (PL 4:519).

[213] On the use of nuptial imagery in the Bible in general, see Mitchell, *The Song of Songs*, 40–66; Schlier, *Epheser*, 264–76. Barth, *Ephesians*, 2:617–18, gives persuasive evidence that the image of head and body for marriage is original to Paul, and not borrowed from contemporary authors. It is not rooted in patriarchalism, which was, in any event, on the wane in Greco-Roman culture. "There is as yet no proof that Paul repeated a generally accepted contemporary opinion, and that he contributed to it no more than a few more or less penetrating Christian phrases" (2:618).

he puts to death the old man and emerges in the image of Christ. And each day, as she submits to his love, as she entrusts herself to him, as she respects his headship, she learns ever more the nature of faith and sees the contours of Christ's redeeming sacrifice in the Christlike figure God has placed into her life.[214] In this way marriage is for the Christian couple a very holy thing.[215]

---

[214] Luther asks the bride not only to view her husband as her head but also to think "my husband is a picture of the true, exalted Head, Christ, for whose sake I will honor him, and do what is pleasing to him." To the bridegroom Luther likewise says: "In the same way the husband should love his wife from the heart for the sake of the exalted love that he sees in Christ, who gave himself up for us" ("Second Wedding Sermon on Ephesians 5:22–33," StL 12:2030, §§ 26–27).

[215] While it is necessary to maintain the distinction between marriage and the Sacraments instituted by Christ as confessed in Ap 13 (see the discussion above), we can rejoice to find a great measure of exegetical agreement with the following words from Vatican II:

> For as God of old made Himself present to His people through a covenant of love and fidelity, so now the Savior of men and the Spouse of the Church comes into the lives of married Christians through the sacrament of matrimony. He abides with them thereafter so that, just as He loved the Church and handed Himself over on her behalf, the spouses may love each other with perpetual fidelity through mutual self-bestowal. (*Gaudium et spes* [Pastoral Constitution on the Church in the Modern World], Article 48 [*The Documents of Vatican II* (ed. Walter M. Abbott; New York: Guild, 1966), 251; quoted in Schnackenburg, *Ephesians*, 337])

Order "in the Lord":
Parents/Children, Masters/Slaves

Translation

5 ... [21]**being subordinate to one another in the fear of Christ:** ...

6   [1]**Children, heed your parents in the Lord, for this is righteous.**
        [2]**"Honor your father and mother"—which is the first commandment
        with a promise—** [3]**"that it may be well with you and you will be long-
        lived on the earth."**

        [4]**And fathers, do not provoke your children to anger,
        but raise them in the discipline and instruction of the Lord.**

        [5]**Slaves, heed your fleshly lords/masters with fear and trembling in the
        sincerity of your heart, as to Christ,**
            [6]**not with eye-service, as if pleasing men,
            but as slaves of Christ, doing the will of God from the soul,**
            [7]**serving with a good attitude as to the Lord and not to men,**
            [8]**knowing that if one should do anything good, he will receive it back
            from the Lord, whether [he is a] slave or free.**

        [9]**And lords/masters, do the same things to them, giving up threatening,
        knowing that both their Lord and yours is in heaven, and there is no
        partiality with him.**

Textual Notes

6:1   τὰ τέκνα—In striking contrast to other ancient household orders that are chiefly concerned with free male adults, Paul directly addresses[1] the subordinate figures of "children" (and later "slaves" in 6:5–8). Their fitting response to their parents' authority is not merely assumed, but encouraged—thus, it is seen as a fruit of the Spirit (5:18) that is worked through the regenerate will.[2] The children are addressed as *believers*. Since the letter was disseminated through public reading in the Divine Service,[3] we must

---

[1]   The articular noun τὰ τέκνα is nominative, but stands for the vocative, "O children" or "you children." See οἱ ἄνδρες in the first textual note on 5:25. See also οἱ πατέρες in 6:4; οἱ δοῦλοι in 6:5; and οἱ κύριοι in 6:9.

[2]   The imperatives in 6:1, 4, 5, 9 are interpreted as subordinate to the imperative πληροῦσθε, "*be filled up* in the Spirit," in 5:18 and to the subsequent clause that serves as a heading to 5:21–6:9, "being subordinate to one another in the fear of Christ" (5:21). See "Structure and Rhetoric" in the commentary below.

[3]   See "Liturgical Context" in "Evaluation of the Case" in "Authorship" in the introduction. See also "The Liturgical Context of the New Testament Epistles" in "Orality and the Interpretation of the Epistles: A Brief Introduction" in the introduction.

also conclude that children were participants in the assembled liturgical community. While this is theologically significant for issues such as infant Baptism, one must also note that "children" includes those of all ages whose parents remain alive. This was particularly relevant to ancient societies in which extended families living under one roof was the norm. Although marriage entails the husband "leaving" father and mother and "cleaving" to his wife in a new family (Gen 2:24, quoted in, e.g., Mt 19:5; Eph 5:31), it does not break the original order. It may no longer be their primary relationship, but children remain subordinate to their parents throughout their lives.[4] Where the orders of marriage and parenthood come into conflict, the divine institution of marriage requires the husband to love his wife and his wife to submit to him above all others. As with all human orders, however, obedience to God takes precedence over even these fundamental relationships (Mt 19:29; Mk 10:29–30; Lk 18:29–30).

ὑπακούετε—The key term describing the response of children (and slaves in 6:5) is the verb ὑπακούω. Whereas Paul previously addressed wives with the passive of ὑποτάσσω, "be subordinate" (5:24, as in 5:21), he subtly shifts the character of the subordination with the new verb here.[5] Traditionally translated as "obey," the choice of ὑπακούω implies that Paul is imposing a more subservient role upon children (and slaves) than upon wives; this is fitting in light of the uniqueness of each relationship.[6] However, although the English word "obey" has an etymological heritage similar to that of ὑπακούω, in modern English usage "obey" no longer carries the *aural* flavor of its origins: "to listen to."[7] ὑπακούω, likewise, derives from ὑπό, "under," and ἀκούω, "to listen," implying a "subordination of the ear." The sense of "obey, do what one is told" is a subcategory of meaning that is appropriate when the word that is heard is a command.[8] But ὑπακούω can also be the appropriate response to a word of promise, in which context the best translation might be "trust, believe."[9] Or in response to a word of

---

4   Mt 15:3–6 ‖ Mk 7:9–13; Rom 1:30; 1 Tim 5:1–4; 2 Tim 3:2. Cf. "O son [τέκνον], help your father in his old age, and do not grieve him as long as he lives; even if he is lacking in understanding, show forbearance; in all your strength do not despise him" (Sirach 3:12–13 RSV).

5   In Ephesians ὑπακούω appears only in 6:1, 5.

6   The distinction between the passive of ὑποτάσσω ("be subordinate," 5:21, 24) for wives and ὑπακούω ("heed," 6:1, 5) for other relationships is not maintained consistently in the NT; see 1 Pet 3:6, in which Sarah "heeded [ὑπήκουσεν]" Abraham. Nevertheless, the present investigation suggests that the translation "obey" either for the passive of ὑποτάσσω or for ὑπακούω is too narrow for the marriage relationship (see also the first textual note on 5:21 and the sections "Five Essential Characteristics of Subordination in Ephesians" and "Holy Matrimony and the Gospel" in the commentary on 5:21–33). Note that in LXX Gen 16:2 Abram "heeded [ὑπήκουσεν]" Sarai's entreaty that he father a child from her servant. Thus, ὑπακούω is not the same as "be subordinate."

7   "Obey" comes from the Old French *obeir*, which itself derives from the Latin *oboedire*, which derives from *ob*, "to," and *audire*, "to listen."

8   E.g., Mt 8:27; Mk 1:27; Lk 17:6; Rom 6:12, 16. The word of command may even entail reception of a gift, such as Abraham's heeding of the Lord's "command" to go to (and acquire) the promised land (Heb 11:8). In such a case, "obey" overlaps considerably with "receive."

9   The combination of ὑπακούω with the indirect object πίστις or εὐαγγέλιον should therefore not be translated as "obey the faith," but "believe the faith," or "give the appropriate hearing that is faith." See ὑπακούω with πίστις in Acts 6:7; Heb 11:8; and ὑπακούω with εὐαγγέλιον in Rom 10:16; 2 Thess 1:8; cf. Rom 6:16–17; Phil 2:11–12. See also ὑπακοὴ πίστεως, not "the obedience of faith," but "the appropriate hearing that is faith" (Rom 1:5;

instruction, it may mean "listen, learn."[10] In response to a request, it may mean "grant, answer."[11] In other words, ὑπακούω in general terms means "give the appropriate hearing," and the best translation may depend on its object:[12]

ὑπακούω					
"subordinate one's hearing to, listen appropriately, heed the message"					
Message	Law	Gospel	instruction	warning	request
Response	"obey"	"trust"	"learn"	"heed"	"grant"

In the present verse, where no message is expressed, a neutral translation like "heed" is best. What is meant by ὑπακούω is clarified subsequently by the imperative of τιμάω, "honor" (τίμα, 6:2),[13] and by the parental delivery of "the discipline and instruction of the Lord" (6:4). In other words, children "heed" their parents not only when they obey their commands but also when they trust them, learn from them, and believe what they are taught "in the Lord."[14] If the subordinate relationship of children to parents is to mirror that of the church to Christ (see the commentary on 5:21–33), it is surely broader than obedience, for Christ "became the cause of eternal salvation to all who heed [ὑπακούουσιν] him" (Heb 5:9; cf. 1 Pet 1:2).

τοῖς γονεῦσιν ὑμῶν—The noun οἱ γονεῖς, "parents" (γονεύς occurs only in the plural in biblical literature), derives from the verb γίνομαι, thus meaning "those who bring [their children] into existence." In the Greek Bible, it appears mostly in the later books of the LXX and in the NT. There is no equivalent collective term in the Hebrew OT, which prefers to speak of "father and mother."[15] The orderly, submissive relationship

---

16:26; cf. Rom 15:18; 16:19; 2 Cor 10:5–6; 1 Pet 1:13–14, 22). Prov 29:12 gives the opposite: "believes [מַקְשִׁיב; LXX: ὑπακούοντος] unjust talk." In Ignatius, *To the Ephesians*, 20:2, εἰς τὸ ὑπακούειν ὑμᾶς τῷ ἐπισκόπῳ καὶ τῷ πρεσβυτερίῳ, "that you heed the bishop and the presbytery," means in context not merely to "obey" them but to "receive" their gifts, the Lord's Supper in unbroken unity. Cf. Deut 17:12: "not to heed" (לְבִלְתִּי שְׁמֹעַ; LXX: τοῦ μὴ ὑπακοῦσαι) the priest at the altar.

[10] BDAG, s.v. ὑπακούω, 1: "to follow instructions." See 2 Thess 3:14: "heed our message through this letter [ὑπακούει τῷ λόγῳ ἡμῶν διὰ τῆς ἐπιστολῆς]"; cf. Prov 2:2; 8:1; Is 29:24.

[11] Thus, ὑπακούω can mean "to answer a knock at the door, open" (Acts 12:13); "hear a request [positively]" (e.g., LXX 2 Kgdms 22:42 [MT/ET 2 Sam 22:42]; Esth 3:4; Job 5:1; 9:16; 14:15; Song 3:1; 5:6; *1 Clement*, 39:7).

[12] Most English versions therefore misrepresent the OT expression שָׁמַע בְּקוֹל (LXX: ἀκούω or a cognate such as ὑπακούω + φωνῆς), literally, "to hear by the voice (of someone)," by indiscriminately rendering it as "obey." The translation takes on significant theological significance when used of *God's* voice. Inasmuch as the Word of God may be Law and/or Gospel, a more neutral translation such as "heed/listen to [God's] voice" would be preferable. See, e.g., Gen 22:18; 26:5; Deut 26:14, 17; 30:2; Judg 2:2; Jer 3:13, 25. See Winger, "The Priesthood of All the Baptized," 12–15. Also instructive are those passages in which God "heeds" the voice of men (answers their prayers), which surely should not be translated as "obey" (Gen 30:6; Num 21:3; Deut 1:45; Josh 10:14; Judg 13:9; 1 Ki 17:22).

[13] See further the textual note on 6:2–3.

[14] The teacher speaking in Sirach says: "Listen [ἀκούσατε] to me your father, O children; and act accordingly [οὕτως ποιήσατε], that you may be kept in safety [σωθῆτε]" (Sirach 3:1 RSV).

[15] The participle of הָרָה, "to conceive," is feminine singular in reference to a mother in Hos 2:7 (ET 2:5) and Song 3:4, but appears in the masculine plural in Gen 49:26 in reference to "parents." הוֹרָה has become the Modern Hebrew term for "parent."

of children to parents is assumed by the OT, which prescribes death by stoning to the unruly son (Deut 21:18–21; cf. Ex 21:17). Such disobedience is taken most seriously in that it brings evil into the midst of the holy people Israel, and presumably because it mirrors rebellion against God himself. The unspeakable evil of children betraying their own Christian parents is part of the suffering that is brought by the radical Gospel (Mt 10:21; Lk 21:16; cf. Lk 18:29–30). Disobedience to parents takes a striking place in Paul's list of Gentile rebellion against God's Law (Rom 1:30; cf. 2 Tim 3:2). By dramatic contrast, the submission of the Child Jesus to his parents is the perfect fulfillment of the Law (Lk 2:51). His submission to the will of his eternal Father is a "heeding" that brought salvation (Heb 5:8; cf. Phil 2:8).[16] For this reason the child's "heeding" of parents can serve as a picture of the Gospel.

This raises the intriguing thought that, while Christ does not take the role of a wife but only the husband (Eph 5:22–33), he does fulfill both sides of the subsequent relationships in this pericope. First (6:1–4), children submit to parents as the church does to the Lord, yet Christ is also the model of true sonly submission to the heavenly Father. Second (6:5–9), slaves are to submit to their fleshly lords/masters as the church submits to Christ, her Lord, yet Christ took on the form of a slave (Phil 2:7) and gave the greatest pattern of faithful service in his state of humiliation and submission to the Father's will.[17]

ἐν κυρίῳ—The phrase ἐν κυρίῳ, "in the Lord," lifts Paul's admonition above a secular *Haustafel*.[18] It modifies both the verb ὑπακούετε, "heed," and the noun τοῖς γονεῦσιν, "parents," so that the action of heeding is distinguished from the obedience enjoined on children by countless secular authors and so that the parental objects are identified as images of Christ.[19] Part of a long line of "in Christ" phrases that has characterized Ephesians (see the fifth textual note on 1:3), it implies that ordinary earthly relationships have been transformed by one's Baptism into Christ (cf. 2:21, 22; 4:1, 17; 5:8; 6:10, 21). The implication is that the children should heed their parents not simply because their parents gave them birth or have been set over them with authority, nor because they fear punishment,[20] but because their parents are earthly representatives

---

[16] "The Son obeyed His Father's will, Was born of virgin mother; And God's good pleasure to fulfill, He came to be my brother" (*LSB* 556:6).

[17] See also "Subordination Is Not Demeaning, but God's Order for the Transmission of Blessings" in the commentary on 5:21–33.

[18] "Household order"; see "A Note on the Term *Haustafel*" in "Structure and Rhetoric" in the commentary on 5:21–33.

[19] However, Paul probably does not mean by this phrase to restrict what *kind* of parents are to be heeded: "your *parents-in-the-Lord*" (as if only *Christian* parents need be heeded or, even more remotely, as if the phrase referred to "*spiritual* fathers [pastors]"). If Paul wished to say that, he would probably have placed the prepositional phrase inside the article-noun sandwich: τοῖς ἐν κυρίῳ γονεῦσιν ὑμῶν, "the in-the-Lord parents of you," as he later defines earthly masters as τοῖς κατὰ σάρκα κυρίοις, "the according-to-the-flesh lords/masters" (6:5). At the same time, the phrase *limits* and *qualifies* obedience to parents by subordinating it to faithfulness to God (see the first textual note on 6:1).

[20] Luther's distinction between servile and filial fear is helpful: "The servile fear is indissolubly connected to secret hatred—the one who is caught in it flees the parents in his heart and fears their punishment more than angering them. The filial fear battles the hatred and comes

of God himself. Thus, to heed parents is to heed God.[21] The significance of the phrase "in the Lord" (6:1) is emphasized by Paul's use of seven additional phrases with a similar import in the pericope: "of the Lord" (6:4), "as to Christ" (6:5), "of Christ" (6:6), "of God" (6:6), "as to the Lord" (6:7), "from the Lord" (6:8), and "both their Lord and yours" (6:9). The omission of ἐν κυρίῳ in some significant early manuscripts (B D* F G b) and some church fathers is difficult to explain;[22] the possibility that it was added by harmonization to Eph 5:22 and Col 3:20 is even more difficult, since it is not really parallel to either. The strength of early witnesses favors its inclusion, and it certainly encapsulates well the thought of the passage and of Ephesians as a whole. (If Paul did not write it here, he certainly could have.)

τοῦτο γάρ ἐστιν δίκαιον—The meaning of δίκαιος here is "righteous," in accord with God's will (Acts 4:19; 2 Thess 1:6) and in conformity with his Law (Rom 2:13; 7:12).[23] This understanding is attested by the immediate quotation of the Fourth Commandment (Ex 20:12; Deut 5:16) in Eph 6:2–3. As a word of Law, this statement both guides and condemns the hearers, the children who strive to heed their parents, but find that their actions fall short of God's demands. However, just as Christ is the only truly obedient Child, so also he is the one who is truly "righteous" on behalf of the unrighteous (Mt 27:19; Lk 23:47; Acts 3:14; 1 Pet 3:18). Thus, true righteousness is available by faith in him (Rom 1:17; 3:25; Gal 3:11) and through Baptism into him (Eph 4:24). His obedience leads to our righteousness (Rom 5:19). Again, the earthly relationship serves as a picture of the Gospel, the imperfectly righteous submission of children pointing to the higher and better righteousness of the Son of God.

6:2–3 τίμα τὸν πατέρα σου καὶ τὴν μητέρα, ἥτις ἐστὶν ἐντολὴ πρώτη ἐν ἐπαγγελίᾳ, ἵνα εὖ σοι γένηται καὶ ἔσῃ μακροχρόνιος ἐπὶ τῆς γῆς—The mandate for children to "heed" (ὑπακούετε, 6:1) their parents is grounded in the Word of God with the mandate to "honor" (τίμα) them.[24] Paul's citation of the Fourth Commandment is a complex conflation of the two foundational sources in the Pentateuch:

---

near in love; it fears saddening the parents more than their punishment" (Peters, *Commentary on Luther's Catechisms*, 1:211).

[21] See also the wife's subordination to her husband "as to the Lord" (5:22) in the commentary on 5:21–33. Once again, if parents command what is contrary to God's will, they cease to be representatives of God to their children and should not be heeded.

[22] Lincoln, *Ephesians*, 395, postulates that Marcion, the earliest witness, might have removed ἐν κυρίῳ to avoid connecting Christ the Lord to the OT commandment. Best, *Ephesians*, 564, counters that it would be more like Marcion to omit the commandment itself.

[23] Cf. BDAG, s.v. δικαιοσύνη, 3 c: "uprightness as determined by divine/legal standards." Contra BDAG, s.v. δίκαιος, 2, "right, fair, equitable" (e.g., Lk 12:57; Phil 4:8). G. Schrenk, "δίκαιος," *TDNT* 2:188, contends (in line with our interpretation): "The phrase … in relation to the obedience of children does not mean only the 'right and fitting' of natural law; it means that which corresponds to the righteous divine order enjoined by the commandment." Josephus, *Antiquities*, 6:165; 8:208, defines δίκαιος as obedience to God's commands.

[24] Luther understands "honor" to imply that parents represent God: "For it is a far higher thing to honor than to love one, inasmuch as it comprehends not only love, but also modesty, humility, and deference as to a majesty there hidden" (LC 1:106 [*Triglotta*, 611]). Melanchthon, *Catechesis puerilis* (1540), expands on these ideas: "Honor, therefore, encompasses these three elements: first, acknowledgment of God's presence and of God's work and ordination;

MT Exodus 20:12

כַּבֵּד אֶת־אָבִיךָ וְאֶת־אִמֶּךָ
לְמַעַן יַאֲרִכוּן יָמֶיךָ
עַל הָאֲדָמָה
אֲשֶׁר־יְהוָה אֱלֹהֶיךָ נֹתֵן לָךְ׃

Honor your father and your mother
that your days may be prolonged
on the land
which YHWH your God is giving to you.

LXX Exodus 20:12

τίμα τὸν πατέρα σου καὶ τὴν μητέρα,
<u>ἵνα εὖ σοι γένηται,</u>
<u>καὶ</u> ἵνα μακροχρόνιος γένῃ
ἐπὶ τῆς γῆς <u>τῆς ἀγαθῆς,</u>
ἧς κύριος ὁ θεός σου δίδωσίν σοι.

Honor your father and mother
<u>that it may be well with you</u>
<u>and</u> that you may be long-lived
on the <u>good</u> land
which YHWH your God is giving you.

MT Deuteronomy 5:16

כַּבֵּד אֶת־אָבִיךָ וְאֶת־אִמֶּךָ
כַּאֲשֶׁר צִוְּךָ יְהוָה אֱלֹהֶיךָ
לְמַעַן יַאֲרִיכֻן יָמֶיךָ
וּלְמַעַן יִיטַב לָךְ עַל הָאֲדָמָה
אֲשֶׁר־יְהוָה אֱלֹהֶיךָ נֹתֵן לָךְ׃

Honor your father and your mother,
as YHWH your God commanded you,
that your days may be prolonged
<u>and that it may be well with you</u> on the land
which YHWH your God is giving to you.

LXX Deuteronomy 5:16

τίμα τὸν πατέρα σου καὶ τὴν μητέρα σου,
ὃν τρόπον ἐνετείλατό σοι κύριος ὁ θεός σου,
<u>ἵνα εὖ σοι γένηται,</u>
<u>καὶ</u> ἵνα μακροχρόνιος γένῃ ἐπὶ τῆς γῆς,
ἧς κύριος ὁ θεός σου δίδωσίν σοι.

Honor your father and your mother,
as the LORD your God commanded you,
<u>that it may be well with you</u>
<u>and</u> that you may be long-lived on the land
which the LORD your God is giving to you.

Paul's rendering is closest to the LXX of Exodus. He omits Deuteronomy's unique clause "*as the LORD your God commanded you*" (italicized), but includes the clause "<u>that it may be well with you</u>" (underlined), which LXX Ex 20:12 itself had borrowed from MT/LXX Deut 5:16. Yet what is notable is that Paul makes three significant changes to the LXX text.

---

second, the kind of obedience by which we, from our heart, attribute the praise of wisdom and justice to parents and magistrates; third, clemency in covering their disadvantages and sins" (quoted in Peters, *Commentary on Luther's Catechisms*, 1:210–11, n. 195, citing Johann Michael Reu, ed., *Quellen zur Geschichte des kirchlichen Unterrichts in der evangelischen Kirche Deutschlands zwischen 1530 und 1600* [Gütersloh: Bertelsmann, 1904], 1.2.2:32.13). See also Luther's threefold definition in LC 1:109–11.

659

First, he inserts the comment ἥτις ἐστὶν ἐντολὴ πρώτη ἐν ἐπαγγελίᾳ, "which is the first commandment with a promise."[25] This is perhaps not technically true, as the Decalogue includes the promise of "steadfast love to thousands" (Ex 20:6; Deut 5:10) in the so-called "prologue," which follows the First Commandment. Likewise, the Third Commandment includes a promise of blessing when it says that the Lord "blessed" the Sabbath (Ex 20:11; cf. Deut 5:14). Yet neither of these two earlier promises is directly attached to the fulfillment of a specific commandment. And there may be a yet simpler explanation. In common Christian usage the Decalogue is abridged in such a way that this is indeed the first promise to appear. Paul's statement may be evidence that the Jews were accustomed to a similar abridgement.[26]

Second, Paul replaces the second purpose clause containing a subjunctive clause (ἵνα μακροχρόνιος γένῃ, "that you *may* be long-lived") with a simple future indicative (ἔσῃ μακροχρόνιος, "you *will* be long-lived"). This apparently insignificant change transforms the promise from *probability* to *reality*. The OT promise of long life in the land of Israel was contingent on faithfulness to the covenant.[27] Paul is so confident of the Lord's blessing on his Gentile Christian readers that he steps up the promise to the indicative ἔσῃ, "you will be."[28]

Third, Paul omits the final clause, referring to the land: "which the LORD your God is giving to you." Paul's motivation for this change may be clarified by comparison with Luther's Catechisms. In the German text of the Small Catechism, Luther abbreviates the commandment considerably: "You shall honor your father and your mother" (SC 1:7). The official Latin translation adds the clause "that you may be long-lived on earth."[29] But neither version includes the words that Paul also omits, referring

---

[25] Since the definite article is not used with ἐντολή, one might translate this as "a preeminent commandment with a promise" (see Schlier, *Epheser*, 281; Best, *Ephesians*, 567). However, it is normal practice in Greek to omit the article in predicate position, and the same phrase in Mk 12:28 clearly means "*the* first commandment" (cf. Mt 22:36). See Moule, *Idiom Book*, 113. The use of ἐν to mean "with" in the sense of "accompanied by" is unusual, but is the only sensible interpretation of this phrase. Compare Mk 1:23 with Lk 4:33; cf. 1 Macc 4:6; 1 Cor 4:21. See Wallace, *Greek Grammar*, 372, explaining a possible use of ἐν: "Thing Possessed: *with* (in the sense of *which possesses*)" (i.e., the commandment "possesses, has" a promise); cf. Wallace, 151.

[26] It is perhaps significant that every other citation of the Fourth Commandment in the NT abridges it (Mt 15:4; 19:19; Mk 7:10; 10:19; Lk 18:20). Only Paul includes the promise.

[27] This promise is repeated frequently in Deuteronomy, often in connection with the entire body of the Law, not simply the Fourth Commandment: see Deut 4:40; 5:33–6:2; 11:8–9; cf. Deut 17:18–20; 22:7; 25:15.

[28] The future indicative *may* be equivalent to ἵνα plus the subjunctive (Burton, *Moods and Tenses*, § 198; Turner, *Syntax*, 100), but the fact that Paul *changes* the wording of a commandment suggests he intends to change the meaning. See BDF, § 369 (3).

[29] See *BELK*, 508. With the exception of slight variations in the use of "Dein," "your," the text of the commandment in the Large Catechism (Preface; 1:104) is identical to that in the Small, with the same distinction between the German and the Latin (*BELK*, 555, 587). That Luther was well aware of the biblical text of the Fourth Commandment and that he deliberately modified it for inclusion in the Catechisms can be deduced by comparing the above text with the translation of Ex 20:12 in his 1545 Bible: "Du solt deinen Vater und deine Mutter ehren, Auff das du lang lebest im Lande, das dir der HERR dein Gott gibt" (WA DB 8:263), "… in the land that the Lord your God is giving to you."

to the *land* that God is giving to the Israelites. When Luther expounds the command-ment in the Large Catechism, he follows Paul (citing Ephesians 6) in noting the promise attached to it: "Auf daß Du langes Leben habst im Lande, da Du wohnest ['that you may have long life in the land where you dwell]" (LC 1:131).[30] But his paraphrase is highly significant. Luther cannot say to his German audience that the Lord has given them a specific piece of promised land, as God once did to Israel.[31] Likewise, St. Paul omits the clause when addressing the Ephesian Gentiles, to whom God had not prom-ised a specific piece of land.[32]

The consequence is profound: Christians are given to enjoy not just one speck of land, but the entire earth and its fruits, in accord with the original promise of creation. In Christ the promise made to Abraham and his heirs is applied to all who share his righ-teousness by faith: they will inherit the world (Rom 4:13). He is King David's greater Son, who extends the kingdom of God far beyond the land of Israel (Ps 2:8). This prom-ise has both eschatological and temporal aspects. The promise is completely fulfilled only in eternity, when a new heaven and a new earth will be provided to the children of God;[33] for now, suffering Christians are comforted by the promise that their recompense is in heaven (Mt 5:12). But we are not just strangers in a foreign land. God's created order still carries the blessings that God placed into it for those who use it rightly here and now (Eph 6:8; 1 Tim 4:8). These blessings of the Law, diminished by the world's sinfulness, are enriched for those who are in Christ, who has redeemed the world (2 Cor 5:19) and calls upon us consequently to redeem the present time (Eph 5:16).

6:4 καὶ οἱ πατέρες, μὴ παροργίζετε τὰ τέκνα ὑμῶν—Paul turns his attention from children to "fathers."[34] Certainly, in light of his use of "parents" (6:1) and "your father and mother" (6:2), this admonition could be understood to include also mothers (cf. Heb

---

[30] *BELK*, 594. The citation of Eph 6:2–3 is in LC 1:133.

[31] Later Jewish tradition would likewise omit the promise of the land in the citation of this com-mandment after the loss of the Holy Land. In the rabbis and Philo (*On the Special Laws*, 2:261–62), the promise of long life is sometimes applied to eternity. See Str-B, 3:614–15. Since Paul speaks of an eternal inheritance (Eph 1:14; 3:6; Col 3:24), some commentators (e.g., Schlier, *Epheser*, 282, following Jerome and Aquinas) have applied this promise like-wise to eternal life gained through Christ. But Paul's retention of the words ἐπὶ τῆς γῆς, "on the earth," suggests he did not mean to exclude long life on earth in the present age, even if the promise would only reach its ultimate fulfillment in the new earth of the age to come.

[32] The logic is similar to Luther's in *How Christians Should Regard Moses* (1525), AE 35:165:

That Moses does not bind the Gentiles can be proved from Exodus 20[:1], where God himself speaks, "I am the Lord your God, who brought you out of the land of Egypt, out of the house of bondage." This text makes it clear that even the Ten Commandments do not pertain to us. For God never led us out of Egypt, but only the Jews. The sectar-ian spirits want to saddle us with Moses and all the commandments. We will just skip that. We will regard Moses as a teacher, but we will not regard him as our lawgiver—unless he agrees with both the New Testament and the natural law. Therefore it is clear enough that Moses is the lawgiver of the Jews and not of the Gentiles. He has given the Jews a sign whereby they should lay hold of God, when they call upon him as the God who brought them out of Egypt. The Christians have a different sign, whereby they conceive of God as the One who gave his Son, etc.

[33] Is 65:17; 66:22; 2 Pet 3:13; Rev 21:1.

[34] The nominative οἱ πατέρες is used for the vocative. See the first textual note on 6:1.

11:23). However, Paul may have narrowed his address for good reasons beyond simple brevity. First, as the husband is the head of the wife (Eph 5:23), he is ultimately the responsible party in the order of the household, the *paterfamilias*. The OT consistently holds fathers accountable for obeying or violating the commandments of God and for holding to the true worship of YHWH.[35] Second, Paul addresses the father as the representative of God. Just as in the marriage analogy (5:22–33), it is the male figure that represents Christ to a female, churchly bride, so here the figure who is typological of both Christ and God the Father in the parental relationship is naturally the father. Third, fathers in general are more inclined to harshness with their children than mothers, and so are the natural recipients of Paul's admonition.

The verb παροργίζω (παρά, "beyond," + ὀργή, "anger") means to "make intensely angry, provoke to anger." Its only other NT occurrence is in a LXX quotation (Rom 10:19, quoting Deut 32:21); in the LXX it almost always refers to provoking God to anger through disobedience or idolatry (e.g., Deut 4:25). Its use here is therefore part of the ongoing analogy of divine relationships with family relations (cf. Sirach 3:16). As the husband was exhorted to exercise his headship with sacrificial love (Eph 5:25), so now the father is warned not to abuse his authority through excessively severe discipline, partiality, unreasonableness, or unjust condemnation; he is to exercise his fatherhood as God does (cf. 6:9). He is to treat his children not as property but as fellow members of the body of Christ. The present imperative prohibition does not imply that the activity is a particular problem in Ephesus that must stop (i.e., "fathers, stop provoking your children to anger"), but is simply a policy command (*"never* provoke …").[36] The cognate noun παροργισμός, "state of being provoked to anger," occurred in Eph 4:26. ὀργή, "anger," was named in a catalogue of sins that are to be put away within the body of Christ (4:31). Thus, anger is identified with the old Adam, the former way of life that has been drowned in Baptism (4:22).

ἀλλὰ ἐκτρέφετε αὐτὰ ἐν παιδείᾳ καὶ νουθεσίᾳ κυρίου—Following the rhythmic pattern of negatives coupled with positives in this letter ("do not … but do …"; see particularly 4:25–5:21), Paul now encourages fathers to act as blessings to their children in the way that God has given them to do. The verb ἐκτρέφω, "to nourish," occurs in the NT only here and in 5:29, where it compared a man's care of his own body to Christ's care for his bride, the church (who is a tender young bride under Christ's mature and caring guardianship). Its twenty-six occurrences in the LXX often refer to raising and feeding children.

It is a father's calling to provide παιδεία, "discipline," to his children (Heb 12:7), which may include painful correction and punishment (Heb 12:11; see also Prov 13:24; 23:13–14). A παιδευτής, "instructor," must παιδεύω, "discipline," his pupils (Heb 12:9–10; see παιδεύω also in Lk 23:16; 2 Cor 6:9). But here the noun παιδεία is doubly modified so that "corporal punishment" does not appear to be its chief reference. First, it is accompanied by νουθεσία, which is "instruction" rooted in God's Word (cf.

---

[35] Gen 48:15; Deut 13:7 (ET 13:6); Josh 24:2; Judg 2:17; 1 Ki 15:12; 2 Ki 15:9; 17:41; Jer 16:11; etc.

[36] See Wallace, *Greek Grammar*, 717, 725; Voelz, *Fundamental Greek Grammar*, 202.

1 Cor 10:11). It is "setting right the mind" through teaching, reproof, or warning.[37] Second, it is the discipline "of the Lord." Thus, the emphasis is more on the *teaching* duties of the father as a παιδευτής, "instructor" (Rom 2:20; cf. Acts 7:22; 22:3; Titus 2:12), who not only gives instruction from and about the Lord (Prov 2:1–5; *1 Clement*, 21:8) and his wisdom (Sirach 1:27) through his Word (2 Tim 3:16), but does so also in his stead (Prov 3:11; Heb 12:9).[38] To *discipline* is to make a *disciple*, that is, to put the Lord's *teachings* into the child.[39] Paul's admonition is that the medium and the message ought to coincide, that the teaching be done with gentleness (2 Tim 2:25) and love (Rev 3:19), as God himself does.

6:5 οἱ δοῦλοι—It is again countercultural for Paul to address the δοῦλοι, "slaves," directly,[40] rather than just the masters (cf. 1 Cor 7:21; Col 3:22). Paul speaks to the slaves as "saints and faithful ones in Christ" (1:1), as fellow baptized children of God. The word δοῦλος occurs 496 times in the Greek Bible, 126 of which are in the NT. Together with its cognates,[41] it stakes out a massive semantic territory, corresponding to slavery's pervasive social role in ancient times. The modern rejection of slavery as an abhorrent evil[42] has unalterably colored our reception of the translation "slave," which today is separated by a vast chasm from the term "servant." The chasm was narrower in ancient times, making it difficult to decide on the most suitable translation.[43] There were so many different patterns of slavery in antiquity that it cannot be painted with one brush, though some generalizations are applicable to the NT context.

On the one hand, a δοῦλος, "slave," stood in stark contrast to an ἐλεύθερος "free (man)." "Property" is an essential component of its meaning.[44] Slaves could be treated with an inhuman viciousness whose mere description leads the modern reader to avert

---

[37] Note the coupling of the cognate verb νουθετέω with διδάσκω, "to teach," and σοφία, "wisdom" deriving from the Word of God, in Col 1:28; 3:16. It is not at all certain that νουθετέω should be translated as "admonish" in these passages; it may simply mean "instruct."

[38] G. Bertram, "παιδεύω," *TDNT* 5:624.

[39] In Latin, *discipulus*, "student, disciple," is derived from *disciplina*, "teaching, discipline," giving us the corresponding English vocabulary. In Greek the noun μαθητής, "student, disciple," is derived from the verb μανθάνω, "to learn." The Greek term παῖς, "child, servant," is related to παιδεία, "discipline, teaching," but is not used explicitly of a "student, disciple" in the NT.

[40] The nominative οἱ δοῦλοι is used for the vocative. See the first textual note on 6:1.

[41] Its cognates include δουλεύω, "to be a slave"; δούλη, "female slave"; δουλόω, "to enslave"; and σύνδουλος, "fellow slave."

[42] Despite the banning of the slave *trade* in the British Empire in 1807, the abolition of the *practice* there in 1833, and its abolition in the United States in 1865, it was estimated in 2003 that as many as twenty-seven million people remain in some form of slavery in the world (Nordling, *Philemon*, 39, quoting Andrew Cockburn, "21st-Century Slaves," *National Geographic* 204.3 [September 2003]: 8). More recent estimates speak of thirty million slaves today, more than in any prior era of world history.

[43] BDAG, s.v. δοῦλος, 1, comments parenthetically: " 'Servant' for 'slave' is largely confined to Biblical transl. and early American times [s. OED s.v. servant, 3a and b]; in normal usage at the present time the two words are carefully distinguished."

[44] Louw-Nida, § 87.76, defines δοῦλος as "one who is a slave in the sense of becoming the property of an owner (though in ancient times it was frequently possible for a slave to earn his freedom)—'slave, bondservant.' "

the eyes.[45] On the other hand, slavery in the Greco-Roman world was different in key ways from the American experience that arose out of the British trade in African slaves (and other modern imperial practices). First, while many ancient societies (including Israel) restricted slavery to foreigners,[46] it was not based on race (or skin color) as a biological characteristic. Second, in ancient societies slaves could be highly educated and hold relatively high social positions.[47] One might add that Greco-Roman slaves of above-average competence could reasonably expect eventual manumission from their owners if they wished to make the transition from slave to free.[48] In comparison to modern examples, slaves were more likely to be well-treated and valued (Lk 7:2–3; 12:37) and to hold positions of stewardship (trust and responsibility) in an ancient household.[49] They could own property and other slaves,[50] be responsible for money and property, and be in debt (Mt 18:23–35; in fact, these "servants/slaves" of the king might be called government "ministers"[51]). For this reason, one is tempted to translate δοῦλος as "servant."[52]

Yet the fundamental contrast in the Bible between δοῦλος and ἐλεύθερος, "slave" and "free," favors the former as the preferred translation.[53] For δοῦλος takes on a significant *typological* role in the proclamation of the Gospel of freedom (see particularly

---

[45] See "A World Not Our Own" in Nordling, *Philemon*, 39–44.

[46] See Lev 25:39–46. But the Torah also stipulated that if an Israelite did acquire a Hebrew slave, the slave's servitude was limited to six years, for in the seventh year he was to be manumitted at no cost and supplied with sustenance for his freed life (Ex 21:2; Deut 15:12–14). See "Slavery Viewed Typologically" in the commentary.

[47] See "Two Significant Differences between Ancient and Modern Slavery" in Nordling, *Philemon*, 68–85.

[48] See Nordling, *Philemon*, 46–58, 84–85; Lincoln, *Ephesians*, 417. There was an increase in the ease and frequency of manumission in the first century AD. Manumission might have taken place after ten or twenty years of service, when the slave reached the age of thirty, when his owner died, or when his freedom was purchased (by himself or another), but not all slaves would have jumped at the chance to be suddenly responsible for their own welfare. "Self-sale" into slavery by free men for the sake of its benefits was also nothing unusual (Nordling, 94–96) and is evidence that not all ancients agreed with the Greeks (and modern Americans) that freedom was the highest good. See *1 Clement*, 55:2.

[49] Mt 24:45–51; 25:14–30; Lk 12:41–48. Nordling, *Philemon*, 78–82, argues that most of the people called οἰκονόμος, "steward"; παιδαγωγός, "tutor, guardian"; or ἐπίτροπος, "manager," in the NT were probably slaves—though the fact that slavery was less common among the Jews, who were forbidden to enslave their fellow Jews (Lev 25:39–46; cf. Ex 21:2; Deut 15:12–14), suggests caution in making this assumption.

[50] Nordling, *Philemon*, 82. Lincoln, *Ephesians*, 416–17: "Slaves of Greek owners could own property, including their own slaves, and could obtain permission to take other employment in addition to their duties as slaves."

[51] See BDAG, s.v. δοῦλος, 2 b α.

[52] Louw-Nida, § 87.81 (s.v. σύνδουλος): "In some languages there is a very strong negative connotation in any word meaning 'slave,' for it may suggest 'vile person' or even 'foreigner,' since in a number of areas only foreigners were made slaves. It may therefore be necessary to use a term for slave which is more or less equivalent to 'servant,' 'one who works without pay,' 'one who must work without pay,' or 'bondservant.'"

[53] This is the common view of the contrast between slavery and freedom in the Greco-Roman world:

> The distinctive feature of the self-awareness of the Greek is the thought of freedom. The Greek finds his personal dignity in the fact that he is free. Thus his self-awareness stands out sharply from anything which stands under the concept δουλεύειν ["to be/

Gal 3:28–4:9). The intercession of Paul with Philemon on behalf of Onesimus the slave serves as an allegory of the Gospel, Christ Jesus interceding with the Father on behalf of humanity.[54] All Christians are likewise "slaves" of God, purchased and won from slavery to sin and the devil by the blood of Christ to be his slaves.[55] To be God's δοῦλος is not to work for him as a free agent, but to be owned by him, body and soul.[56] This language is rooted in the OT predilection for calling the Israelite believer God's עֶבֶד, particularly in the context of worship.[57] Paul the apostle, inasmuch as he has been captured by Christ and bound to his service, also sees himself and his pastoral colleagues not simply as "servants" but also as "slaves of Christ/God."[58] Ultimately, slavery is an image of Christ himself, who relinquished his freedom, submitted himself to the Father's will, and took on the form of a slave to accomplish our redemption (Mk 10:43–45; Jn 13:4–5; Phil 2:7).[59] For crucifixion was a form of punishment generally reserved for slaves and foreigners (Phil 2:8).[60]

ὑπακούετε τοῖς κατὰ σάρκα κυρίοις—For the verb ὑπακούω, see the second textual note on 6:1. To "heed" is to "subordinate the ears"—not only to obey the master's orders (Rom 6:16) but also to listen to his warnings, instructions, mandates, and

---

serve as a slave"]. For where there is δουλεύειν human autonomy is set aside and an alien will takes precedence of one's own. (K. H. Rengstorf, "δοῦλος," *TDNT* 2:261)

[54] See, e.g., Luther's "Preface to Philemon" (1522, 1546), AE 35:390:

What Christ has done for us with God the Father, that St. Paul does also for Onesimus with Philemon. For Christ emptied himself of his rights [Phil. 2:7] and overcame the Father with love and humility, so that the Father had to put away his wrath and rights, and receive us into favor for the sake of Christ, who so earnestly advocates our cause and so heartily takes our part. For we are all his Onesimus's if we believe.

[55] Lk 2:29; Jn 8:33–36; Acts 2:18; Rom 6:16–20; 7:1–4; 1 Cor 7:21–23; 1 Pet 1:18–19; 2:16; 2 Pet 2:19.

[56] "Hence we have a service which is not a matter of choice for the one who renders it, which he has to perform whether he likes or not, because he is subject as a slave to an alien will, to the will of his owner" (K. H. Rengstorf, "δοῦλος," *TDNT* 2:261).

[57] E.g., Lev 25:42, 55; Pss 113:1; 135:1; Is 56:6; 63:17; cf. Rev 2:20; 7:3; 15:3; 19:5; 22:3. The use of δοῦλος in the NT for God's people is particularly significant when one considers the translational habits of the LXX: "When παῖς is used for עֶבֶד in the sense of slave it denotes a natural relationship which cannot be materially contested, whereas when δοῦλος is used the primary thought is that of illegality and essential unreason of the service rendered. Thus, the word group is used in the LXX for the bondage of the Israelites in Egypt (Ex. 14:5 etc.)" (K. H. Rengstorf, "δοῦλος," *TDNT* 2:266). In other words, δοῦλος in the LXX means someone who has been captured into slavery and thus serves in the NT for both slavery to sin and slavery to God.

[58] Rom 1:1; 2 Cor 4:5; Gal 1:10; Phil 1:1; Col 4:12; 2 Tim 2:24; Titus 1:1; cf. Mk 10:44; Acts 16:17; James 1:1; 2 Pet 1:1; Jude 1; Rev 1:1. This usage may connect to the designation of the OT prophets as God's "slaves" (MT: עֲבָדִים, LXX [usually] and NT: δοῦλοι, e.g., Jer 7:25; 26:5; Ezek 38:17; Zech 1:6; Rev 10:7; 11:18).

[59] In light of the previous note on LXX usage, it is interesting that the LXX of Isaiah usually uses παῖς, not δοῦλος, for YHWH's עֶבֶד, "Servant" (παῖς in LXX Is 42:1; 49:6; 50:10; 52:13; but δοῦλος in LXX Is 49:3, 5). Perhaps the translators viewed this "Servant" as willingly entering into this role. The other slaves of YHWH (Moses, Joshua, etc.) are normally, though not exclusively, called δοῦλος (e.g., LXX Josh 24:29; 1 Ki 8:53; cf. Rev 15:3).

[60] See "Theological Implications of Slavery in the New Testament" in Nordling, *Philemon*, 109–39; Martin Hengel, *Crucifixion* (trans. John Bowden; London: SCM, 1977), 51–63.

promises. It is in the nature of a δοῦλος to be subordinate to his master's authority without question (Mt 8:9); he is ordered under his master (Mt 10:24; Jn 13:16; Titus 2:9 with ὑποτάσσω). The careful attribute τοῖς *κατὰ σάρκα* κυρίοις, "the *in-the-flesh* lords/masters,"[61] reminds both slave and master that both are subject to a higher Lord in heaven (6:9). The implication is that Paul is addressing both slave and master as *Christians*. Even though all slaves are subject to their masters, the baptized recognize a deeper truth in their relationship: that in heeding their earthly lords, the slaves are giving honor to their heavenly Lord. Thus, Paul can speak of slaves in their obedience giving glory to God's name (placed on them in Baptism) and his doctrine (1 Tim 6:1–2), demonstrating thereby their faith (Titus 2:9–10). Even where the master may not be a Christian (as might be implied by the abuse considered in 1 Pet 2:18–25), slaves are to submit and thereby be conformed to the suffering of Christ (1 Pet 2:21). But where the master is a fellow Christian, to "heed" him may also include receiving the teachings of God from him as the *paterfamilias*.[62]

μετὰ φόβου καὶ τρόμου ἐν ἁπλότητι τῆς καρδίας ὑμῶν ὡς τῷ Χριστῷ—It is natural to enjoin "fear/respect" (φόβος) upon the slave as the appropriate attitude to his master (1 Pet 2:18). But the attitude of "fear" ought not be correlated to the secular principle of the master's ability to punish the slave; it is part of the typology. Just as wives are to "fear/respect" their husbands (Eph 5:33; cf. 1 Pet 3:1–2), just as children are to "honor" their parents (Eph 6:2), so also when slaves show "fear" to their masters they are participating in the church's submission to Christ as God himself.[63] The second noun, τρόμος, etymologically connected to its English translation "trembling," is regularly coupled with φόβος in the Greek Bible. It is the appropriate attitude owed to God and his earthly representatives (such as Noah, Israel, or Titus).[64] The additional modification, ἐν ἁπλότητι τῆς καρδίας ὑμῶν, "in the sincerity of your heart" (Eph 6:5), stands parallel to the admonition in the next verse to avoid "eye-service" (Eph 6:6; cf. Col 3:22). The "heart" in Jewish thinking is the seat not of emotions but of the will or the mind (cf. Mt 15:18–20). It is the seat of faith and the place into which the light of God's

---

[61] Cf. τὰ ἔθνη ἐν σαρκί, "Gentiles in the flesh" (2:11). See BDF, § 272. The phrase κατὰ σάρκα is a common way of distinguishing the way of the Law, this world, or sight from the way of the Gospel and faith: Rom 4:1; 8:4–5, 12–13; 9:3, 5; 1 Cor 10:18; 2 Cor 5:16; Gal 4:23, 29; etc. In this context "flesh" does not have the connotation of "sinful."

[62] In ancient societies, it would be most common for the entire household to be baptized into the Christian faith with their master/father (cf. Acts 16:15, 31–34; 18:8; 1 Cor 1:16; 16:15). Slaves might at first have been unwilling recipients of the things of God, but were nevertheless blessed by receiving them from their earthly lords. Note Philo's depiction of the Jewish household in *Hypothetica: Apology for the Jews*, 7:14: "Any of them whom you attack with inquiries about their ancestral institutions can answer you rapidly and easily. The husband seems competent to transmit knowledge of the laws to his wife, the father to his children, the master to his slaves" (quoted in Lincoln, *Ephesians*, 398). But it was not inevitable that slaves would embrace their master's religion, and the NT itself gives evidence of slaves becoming Christian apart from their masters (1 Pet 2:18–20). Roman law during the Principate "became more tolerant about slaves' participation in other cults, and there was considerable freedom for slaves to practice their own religion" (Lincoln, *Ephesians*, 419).

[63] See the second textual note on 5:21 in the pericope 5:21b–33.

[64] LXX Gen 9:2; Ex 15:16; Deut 2:25; 11:25; Pss 2:11; 54:6 (MT 55:6; ET 55:5); Is 19:16; Dan 4:37; Judith 2:28; 15:2; 1 Macc 7:18; 4 Macc 4:10; 1 Cor 2:3; 2 Cor 7:14–15; Phil 2:12; cf. Mk 5:33.

Word shone when the slaves were baptized and where it continues to shine.[65] While a worldly attitude of formal obedience, even with an unwilling heart, might serve a slave adequately, Paul's call for honesty of the heart emphasizes that the slave's work is only a good work in God's eyes if it proceeds from faith.[66] Likewise, worship is only acceptable to God if it proceeds from the sincerity/faith of the heart (1 Chr 29:17). Thus, Paul emphasizes again the master's typological role, saying ὡς τῷ Χριστῷ, "as to Christ." This means not simply "*as if* you were serving Christ [contrary to fact]," but "*because* you are serving Christ."[67]

6:6 μὴ κατ᾽ ὀφθαλμοδουλίαν ὡς ἀνθρωπάρεσκοι—The rhythm of "not this, but that" has been characteristic of Paul's language in this part of the letter (see particularly 4:25–5:21; 6:4). It is the rhetorical strategy of *refutatio*.[68] Paul rejects one possible interpretation of the Christian life in favor of what is true and right. ὀφθαλμοδουλία, "eye-service," was not just an hypothetical temptation for slaves, but a very common strategy of survival. This term, found only here and in Col 3:22 (thus, perhaps coined by Paul), may imply that the slave works only when his master is looking. But in light of the contrast with "sincerity of the heart" (Eph 6:5), it more likely implies a service that is external, formalistic, and lacking honesty, but most important, lacking *faith*. It is the sacrifice of Cain in comparison with Abel's (Heb 11:4). ἀνθρωπάρεσκος is another rare term; it occurs five times in the LXX and only here and in Col 3:22 in the NT. Combining ἄνθρωπος, "man," and the verb ἀρέσκω, "to please," it denotes a "pleaser of man"[69] and implies an obsequious, fawning behavior that seeks the earthly master's praise without concern for pleasing God, who sees the heart (Lk 16:15; 18:14).

ἀλλ᾽ ὡς δοῦλοι Χριστοῦ ποιοῦντες τὸ θέλημα τοῦ θεοῦ ἐκ ψυχῆς—Paul surely does not simply mean "as [literal] slaves who belong to Christ." Rather, he develops the analogical language of the passage by explicitly tying the earthly institution of slavery to its theological equivalent. These literal slaves are not to view their earthly relationships as definitive of their personhood, value, or self-identity, but they are to see themselves together with all the baptized as those whom Christ has purchased and won: slaves owned by Christ and in his service (1 Cor 7:22; see the first textual note on Eph 6:5). To be a slave is to obey whatever enslaves you (Rom 6:16; Eph 2:3)—hence it is inherent in their new relationship as *God's* slaves that they must work his works, do his will (cf. Mt 7:21; 12:50; Lk 12:47). This is to be slaves like Christ, who came to do the Father's will (Jn 4:34; 5:30; 6:38). It is only through him that Christians can do the same (Heb 13:20–21). ἐκ ψυχῆς, "from the soul" or "from one's very being,"[70] stands

---

[65] See the textual notes on 1:18; "Enlightened Eyes of Your Heart (1:18)" in the commentary on 1:15–23; and the textual notes on 5:14.

[66] In some passages ἁπλότης, "innocence, sincerity," especially when it is "of the heart," is a virtual synonym for the righteousness of faith: 1 Macc 2:37, 60; Wis Sol 1:1; 2 Cor 11:3. This may be its meaning in Rom 12:8.

[67] See the textual note on Eph 5:22 and the first textual note on 5:28; cf. Col 3:22.

[68] See "Refutations" in "Structure and Rhetoric" in the introduction.

[69] Cf. LXX Ps 52:6 (MT 53:6; ET 53:5); Ps Sol 4, superscription; Ps Sol 4:7, 8, 19; Gal 1:10; 1 Thess 2:4; *2 Clement*, 13:1; Ignatius, *To the Romans*, 2:1.

[70] BDAG, s.v. ψυχή, 2 c, suggests what here (in light of 6:5) is a redundant translation: "from the heart, gladly."

in parallel to "sincerity of the heart" (Eph 6:5) and again implies the works and worship that proceed from faith. The sense is the same as the summary of the commandments: "you shall love the LORD your God with all your heart [καρδία] and with all your soul [ψυχή] and with all your might" (LXX Deut 6:5 and similar verses).

6:7 μετ' εὐνοίας δουλεύοντες ὡς τῷ κυρίῳ καὶ οὐκ ἀνθρώποις—Yet another rare term,[71] εὔνοια probably does not imply the emotion of "affection" (as in many examples in the Apostolic Fathers), but rather the more etymological sense of "good mind," hence, "good attitude, willingness."[72] This is a further explication of and somewhat synonymous with the preceding expressions "sincerity of the heart" (6:5) and "from the soul" (6:6). The summary of the commandments as love for the Lord with all one's "heart" and "soul" is sometimes extended by the noun διανοία, "mind" (Mt 22:37; Mk 12:30; Lk 10:27; cf. LXX Josh 22:5). By using the related noun here, εὔνοια, "good mind," Paul clearly wishes to evoke that summary in his words to the slaves, again both implying and verbally expressing that their service to their earthly masters is "to the Lord."

6:8 εἰδότες ὅτι ἕκαστος ἐάν τι ποιήσῃ ἀγαθόν, τοῦτο κομίσεται παρὰ κυρίου εἴτε δοῦλος εἴτε ἐλεύθερος—Though the emphatic upfront positioning of ἕκαστος, "each one," complicates the word order,[73] the first clause clearly forms the protasis of a present general conditional statement (ἐάν + the subjunctive ποιήσῃ): "knowing that each person, *if ever he should do* anything good, then …" This epistle hitherto has carefully placed good works in their proper position in the way of salvation, entirely excluding them from the factors that make one "saved" (2:8–9) and shifting their place to the *consequences* of God's new creation in Christ (2:10). We are God's ποίημα, "workmanship"; we are κτισθέντες, "created" (passive), *by God*, who himself has prepared "good works" ahead of time and placed us into them (2:10). It would be entirely against the run of play if Paul were to relinquish this pattern now and suggest to the Ephesian slaves that their good works *intrinsically* and on their own *merit* deserved a payment by way of reward. For this reason, first, he couches the language of doing good in a conditional sentence, in the subjunctive, not promising that they *will* do good, but admitting that they *may*. Second, the emphasis of the apodosis does not lie on the verb κομίσεται, "he will receive it back"[74] (which in any case does not imply a reward that is *earned* by the recipient[75]), but on the One who rewards: παρὰ κυρίου, "from the Lord."

---

[71] The noun εὔνοια is a NT hapax legomenon. See also the two rare terms discussed in the first textual note on 6:6.

[72] BDAG, s.v. εὔνοια, 2. As an emotion, affection cannot be elicited on command, and one wonders whether it would be strictly necessary for a slave to show affection to his master.

[73] Note the massive confusion this peculiar word order caused in the manuscript variants.

[74] In form κομίσεται is the future middle indicative of κομίζω, whose middle means "to come into possession of someth[ing], … *get (for oneself), receive*" (BDAG, s.v. κομίζω, 3). Its implied subject is ἕκαστος, "each one," and its direct object is the neuter demonstrative pronoun τοῦτο, "this," translated as "it," whose antecedent is the neuter ἀγαθόν, something "good." For other passages where the middle of κομίζω means "to receive, get (back), obtain," see, e.g., LXX Gen 38:20; Mt 25:27; Heb 10:36; 11:19; 1 Pet 1:9; 5:4. In the active voice it can mean "to bring" (1 Esdras 4:5; 9:39–40; Lk 7:37).

[75] The Colossian parallel (Col 3:24) to Eph 6:8 inserts the key term κληρονομία, "inheritance [from the Lord]"; an inheritance is never earned, but simply received. Cf. the parable of the

In the context of the previous verses, Paul's point is that the slaves ought not to be subordinate to their masters merely to be rewarded in this life and only by their *earthly* masters; but in faith they should commit themselves entirely to *God*, trusting him to provide them with what is needed, in this world and the next (Mt 5:12; 6:1; Lk 6:35; 2 Cor 5:9–10). Indeed, the implication of *God's* reward is that, despite what the eyes see in this life (cf. ὀφθαλμοδουλία, Eph 6:6), there is an eschatological treasure awaiting God's children (cf. 1:14).[76] Paul does *not* suggest thereby that there is *no* reward for obedience in this life; on the contrary, whereas a slave has no right to expect a reward from an earthly master to whom he simply *owes* his service, God is a *gracious* God who rewards both slave and free equally (Gal 3:28; Col 3:11), sometimes in accord with what they have done (Mt 16:27; Rom 2:6), sometimes despite it (Ps 103:10), but always as he alone sees fit (1 Cor 12:11). The slave can expect to be treated like a free man (and the free man like a slave!).

6:9 καὶ οἱ κύριοι, τὰ αὐτὰ ποιεῖτε πρὸς αὐτούς, ἀνιέντες τὴν ἀπειλήν—The noun οἱ κύριοι, "lords,"[77] clearly means the "masters, owners" of the slaves in this context. It is unfortunate that the English language no longer uses the same term for earthly "lords" as for the heavenly "Lord," on which Greek wordplay the typology of this section relies (cf. 1 Pet 3:6).[78] Paul's admonition, "do the same things to them," cannot be taken literally, as if the masters are to behave toward their slaves in *exactly* the same way as the slaves to their masters (cf. the oxymoron of "mutual submission"). It is rather a form of shorthand into which we should insert the phrase *mutatis mutandis*, "changing what needs to be changed." It refers chiefly to the phrase "doing the will of God from the soul" (6:6), with the details modified according to the masters' office. In other words, in carrying out their role as masters, they are not to treat their slaves as if only to please men (whether the slave or an observer), but "with fear and trembling" (toward their heavenly Lord; cf. 6:5), they are to carry out their vocation from the faith in their hearts

---

workers in the vineyard (Mt 20:1–16), as discussed in Gibbs, *Matthew 11:2–20:34*, 990–93. A μίσθος, "reward, recompense" (Mt 20:8), may simply be "in place of" something else and may be a gift (LXX Gen 15:1) or a punishment (LXX Is 40:10; Ezek 29:19; 2 Macc 8:33; Rev 22:12). Because Paul is mandated by Christ to preach the Gospel and does not do it as his own choice, his "reward" (μίσθος) is simply that he can present the Gospel "free of charge" (1 Cor 9:17–18). "Reward" (μίσθος) is connected to "righteousness" and "faith" in the way of gift, not merit (LXX Prov 11:18, 21; Is 62:11; Wis Sol 5:15; Sirach 2:8; 11:22; 51:30; Rom 4:4). The "prophet's reward" (Mt 10:41–42) is not a *quid pro quo* payment in return for giving the prophet a drink, but the overwhelming, undeserved gift that bursts through when one receives a prophet: the message he brings from the Lord, and he who receives the one sent by Christ receives Christ himself (Mt 10:40). Note the meaning of the parable of the workers in the vineyard: no matter how much or little each worked, the "reward" is the same (Mt 20:1–16).

[76] "He does not make this-worldly promises to them but points directly to the world to come. … In this way he raises up and soothes their wounded souls. … Their brief earthly submission is for a time only" (Chrysostom, *Homilies on Ephesians*, 22:6.5–8, ACCS 8:204).

[77] The nominative οἱ κύριοι is used for the vocative. See the first textual note on 6:1.

[78] The choice of κύριος, "lord," seems deliberate on Paul's part, since he could have used the common term δεσπότης, "master" (1 Tim 6:1–2; Titus 2:9; 1 Pet 2:18). Though δεσπότης can also be used of God (Lk 2:29; Acts 4:24; 2 Pet 2:1; Jude 4; Rev 6:10), it is a far less common translation of יהוה or אֲדֹנָי than is κύριος in the Hebrew-based portions of the LXX, hence δεσπότης would have been a less natural way to speak of God.

as an act of worship to God and service to others. *Noblesse oblige*, "nobility obligates," is how British lords (in the language of their Norman forebears) articulated the way in which the superordinate person is to serve not himself but the community for whose sake he administers his estate.

The circumstantial participle ἀνιέντες (from ἀνίημι) briefly describes the manner in which the master is to exercise his authority (cf. the words to fathers in 6:4): "easing up, giving up" τὴν ἀπειλήν, "threatening" (cf. Acts 16:26, where ἀνίημι refers to the "loosening" of prison chains). It was a perpetual temptation for masters to resort to force to bring about obedience when words failed (Prov 29:19; cf. Job 19:16), or even to abuse the faithful slave (Sirach 7:20; 33:31). Here Paul perhaps repents of his own prior abuse of authority, his "threatening" against the disciples of Christ (ἀπειλή, Acts 9:1). God's Law calls high and low to repentance.

εἰδότες ὅτι καὶ αὐτῶν καὶ ὑμῶν ὁ κύριός ἐστιν ἐν οὐρανοῖς—While the slaves are encouraged to heed the Lord God through their master as his earthly representative (6:5), the earthly lords themselves are not simply encouraged to act *like* the Lord above, but themselves to submit to their heavenly Lord. Once again the straightforward typology of 5:22–33, in which the husband corresponds to Christ and the bride to the church, is complicated by multiple lines of analogy (cf. fathers/children in 6:1–4 and slaves in 6:5–8, in both of which Christ appears in multiple roles). The masters are not only types of Christ in his *Lordship* over the church but also in his *submission* to the heavenly Father. For Christ himself not only exercised authority over the church but also joined his disciples in addressing God as "*our* Father" (Mt 6:9), "my Father and your Father," and "my God and your God" (Jn 20:17). Perfect submission is found only in him. By calling the masters to acknowledge that they stand with their slaves under the same heavenly Lord, he is asking them to view their slaves as brothers and sisters in Christ.[79]

καὶ προσωπολημψία οὐκ ἔστιν παρ᾿ αὐτῷ—The noun προσωπολημψία (πρόσωπον, "face," + λαμβάνω, "to receive")[80] is the very human failing of judging the value of another person by his appearance and treating him accordingly, i.e., "partiality." The classic illustration is James' depiction of the congregation that offers the best seat to the rich man and the worst to the poor one (James 2:1–9, with προσωπολημψία in James 2:1). To show partiality is not only to pervert the justice defined in God's

---

[79] "You shall not command with bitterness your male slave or female slave, those who hope in the same God, lest you should not fear the God who is above both; for he came to call [people] not according to their outward appearance [κατὰ πρόσωπον], but [those] upon whom the Spirit worked preparation" (*Barnabas*, 19:7).

[80] The compound forms προσωπολημπτέω, προσωπολήμπτης, and προσωπολημψία, appear to be Christian creations on the basis of the LXX expression πρόσωπον λαμβάνω. See BDAG, s.vv. προσωπολημπτέω and πρόσωπον, 1 b α. The LXX expression, in turn, translates the Hebrew idiom נָשָׂא פָּנִים, literally, "lift up a face," but usually meaning "show partiality" (e.g., Lev 19:15; Deut 10:17; Mal 2:9, all translated by the LXX with πρόσωπον λαμβάνω; see the Hebrew idiom in the same sense also in Job 13:8; 32:21; 34:19; Prov 18:5). The Hebrew idiom can also mean "be favorable toward" (Gen 32:21 [ET 32:20]; Deut 28:50; Mal 1:8–9) or "grant a request" (Gen 19:21; 1 Sam 25:35).

Law[81] but also to depart from the image of God, who shows no partiality, as a defining characteristic of his just and gracious nature (Deut 10:17; 2 Chr 19:7; Job 34:19; Gal 2:6), condemning all equally under the Law (Rom 2:11; 1 Pet 1:17) and redeeming all without discrimination. "There is no partiality with God" is so proverbial that Paul can even omit "with God" (Col 3:25) and expect his audience to know what he means! The impartiality of God features prominently in the movement of the Gospel from Jew to Gentile without the requirement of fulfilling the ceremonial features of the Law (Acts 10:34). Christ, too, shows his divine nature in refusing to show partiality, but being just and gracious to all (Lk 20:21). Thus, the master conforms to the image of God, whom he represents, when he puts away partiality.

Commentary
Structure and Rhetoric

The place of this pericope in the logic and argumentation of Ephesians is explained in detail in "Structure and Rhetoric" in the commentary on 5:21–33. Eph 6:1–9 is really a continuation of the same "household order" or *Haustafel*[82] unit (5:21–6:9), separated in this commentary for manageability, but not to be divided in interpretation. Since 4:17 Paul has been in the rhetorical mode of *refutatio*,[83] answering the objections of those who would misinterpret the Gospel as implying that Christians could continue in the practices of their old pagan life. Thus, 4:17–5:14 rejected pagan worship and its morality and, via the hinge of Holy Baptism (4:22–24; 5:14), taught the new worship in the Spirit (5:15–20). The command "be filled up in the Spirit" (5:18) was modified by three participles, the third of which, "being subordinate" (5:21), serves as a hinge and title for the entire unit that follows (5:21–6:9). Thus, "being subordinate to one another in the fear of Christ" (5:21) is a gift of the Holy Spirit whose implications for each of the three standard relationships in the household order are explained in the pericopes that follow:

> be filled up in the Spirit … (5:18)
> > being subordinate to one another in the fear of Christ (5:21)
> > > • wives to their own husbands as to the Lord (5:22)
> > > • children, heed your parents in the Lord (6:1)
> > > • slaves/servants, heed your fleshly lords/masters (6:5)

This is not "mutual submission" (everyone submitting to everyone else), but appropriate submission. In each relationship, one person is *superordinate* and another is *subordinate*.[84]

---

[81] Lev 19:15; Deut 16:19; Job 13:10; Prov 24:23; Sirach 35:12; 1 Tim 5:21; *Barnabas*, 19:4; *Didache*, 4:3.

[82] See "A Note on the Term *Haustafel*" in "Structure and Rhetoric" in the commentary on 5:21–33.

[83] See "Refutations" in "Structure and Rhetoric" in the introduction.

[84] See the first textual note on 5:21 in the pericope 5:21b–33.

The "order" corresponds in many ways to the traditional structures of ancient societies, which Paul does not fundamentally overturn. The traditional nature of the language suggests Paul is not addressing any particular problem with disorder or rebellion in the Ephesian church. While some wives and some slaves might have misunderstood equality in the Gospel as implying that they should no longer submit to their earthly superordinates,[85] it is difficult to imagine that Christian children became particularly rebellious against their parents because of the Gospel. Yet, Paul's argument is not simply traditional. At significant points in the argument, he demonstrates that he is proceeding not from nature or culture but from the Word of God (5:31; 6:2–3) and the Gospel of Christ (5:23–30). But most telling is the eightfold repetition in 6:1–9 of submission to Christ via the mostly synonymous phrases "in the Lord" (6:1), "of the Lord" (6:4), "as to Christ" (6:5), "of Christ" (6:6), "of God" (6:6), "as to the Lord" (6:7), "from the Lord" (6:8), and "both their Lord and yours" (6:9) (the same and similar phrases pervade 5:21–33). These phrases are the golden thread in the tapestry, and their overwhelming frequency in such a short section indicates that Paul is not merely including the Christological analogy as one factor in shoring up the traditional household order. Rather, *the Christological analogy is the chief point of the pericope.* Although Paul does not delve so deeply into the details of the Gospel as he did in the previous section on marriage (5:22–33), the repetition of phrases like "as to the Lord" serves notice that the reader should continue to read this pericope through Gospel glasses. Thus, the two sections on children/fathers (6:1–4) and slaves/masters (6:5–9) should be understood as continuing the Christ/church analogy that was so explicit in the treatment of marriage:

Christ		husbands		fathers/parents		lords/masters	
loves *sacrifices* ↓	↑ *submits* *fears*	*love* *sacrifice* ↓	↑ *submit* *fear*	*discipline* *instruct* ↓	↑ *heed* *honor*	*treat well* *do not* *threaten* ↓	↑ *heed* *fear*
church		wives		children		slaves/servants	

However, in comparison to the previous pericope, the lines of analogy are not entirely consistent. In the exposition of marriage, Christ was unalterably identified with the husband and the church with the wife, corresponding to the well-established biblical "metaphor" by which marriage had regularly described God's relationship to his people.[86] But the relationship of children to fathers is complicated by the complexity of Trinitarian relationships. That is, while the submission of children to their fathers is like the submission of Christians to

---

[85] For women, see 1 Cor 11:2–16; 14:34–38; 1 Tim 2:8–15. For slaves, see 1 Tim 6:1–2.

[86] See "Holy Matrimony and the Gospel" in the commentary on 5:21–33. The fact that this relationship is not invertible demonstrates that the maleness of God is not merely a figure of speech that could easily be rephrased. Because God *is* the Father, because Christ *is* a man, God cannot be represented by the bride in the heavenly marriage.

Christ, it is also like the submission of Christ, the Son of God, to his Father. Thus, Christ is not only represented by earthly parents, to whom children submit, but Christ is also the perfect Son, who both models true submission and forgives the failure to conform to his model. It is, after all, natural for earthly fathers to represent God the Father, and Paul specifically emphasizes God's Fatherhood over all people/things in this epistle (3:14–15; 4:6). Likewise, in the relationship of slaves to their lords/masters, Paul emphasizes that heeding masters is not only *like* heeding Christ the Lord, but since lords/masters are put in their office by God and represent him, heeding them *is* heeding Christ the Lord. All those baptized into Christ have died to their former master (sin) and become slaves of Christ.[87] Yet it is also true that Christ "took the form of a slave" (Phil 2:7) and heeded his Father's plan to the point of suffering a slave's death on the cross (Phil 2:8). Thus, Christ is also the greatest model of true slavery and the one whose true and full obedience rendered satisfaction for every Christian slave's failure to be like him.

With its treatment of the three basic household relationships, Ephesians is consistent with other *Haustafeln*[88] in the NT. However, there are some notable differences. First, its unique strength is the extended treatment of marriage as a presentation of the Gospel of Christ. This is a significant expansion on the otherwise similar *Haustafel* in Colossians (3:18–4:1).[89] Second, just as Col 3:22–4:1 has an expanded treatment of the slave/master relationship, so also here Paul's words to the slaves occupy a greater proportion of the pericope than his words to any other party. One might hypothesize that this is influenced by the situation of Onesimus, the runaway slave,[90] who was most likely present with Paul during the writing of this letter and who was sent back to his master in the company of Tychicus, who was bearing Colossians, Philemon, and Ephesians.[91] It was important for Paul to explain the impact of the Gospel on slaves. Third, whereas in the previous pericope Paul addressed himself at greater length to the superordinate figure (the husband in 5:25–30), here Paul's words to the subordinate figures (children, slaves) predominate. It may be that, having treated the Christological nature of the superordinate's role at such length, Paul did not feel the need to repeat himself here; it may also be that children and slaves

---

[87] These points will be fleshed out in the commentary below.

[88] German plural for "household orders"; see "A Note on the Term *Haustafel*" in "Structure and Rhetoric" in the commentary on 5:21–33.

[89] This commentary has mostly refrained from drawing conclusions about the literary relationship between Colossians and Ephesians. One might conclude from the extended treatment of marriage, however, that Ephesians is a later expansion of Colossians. It is difficult to imagine why Paul would write Ephesians first and then later omit this marvelous Gospel analogy from Colossians. See further "Relationship to Colossians" in the introduction.

[90] Sampley, *"And the Two Shall Become One Flesh,"* 21, following John Knox, *Philemon Among the Letters of Paul: A New View of Its Place and Importance* (rev. ed.; New York: Abingdon, 1959), 36–45.

[91] Col 4:7–9, 17; Eph 6:21; Philemon 2, 10, 23. See the setting deduced in "Location and Date of Writing" and in "Relationship to Colossians" in the introduction.

were more likely than parents and masters to misunderstand the implications of the Gospel.[92]

In comparison to the previous section on marriage (5:22–33), which was extended by its lengthy treatment of the saving work of Christ, the present part (6:1–9) of the unit (5:21–6:9) is compact and balanced, its structure readily discernible:

> 6:1–3   Children, heed your parents in the Lord.
> 6:4   Fathers, raise your children in the instruction of the Lord.
> 6:5–8   Slaves, heed your masters as Christ himself.
> 6:9   Masters, treat your slaves according to God's will, since you have the same Lord.

Children and Parents

The *Haustafel*[93]

The authority of parents and the obedience of children are universal precepts of household codes in the Greco-Roman world.[94] Much can be said about the supreme legal authority that a father held over his children in the Roman world.[95] Fathers had authority over the life or death of their children until they themselves departed this world, and children were to honor and obey their parents in all things. Dionysius of Halicarnassus expressed astonishment and admiration at the virtually unlimited authority of the Roman father in comparison to his Greek tradition.[96] Jewish tradition, while not granting the harshest rights

---

[92] Schlier, *Epheser*, 283–84. Some critical commentators have suggested that the concentration on the subordinate figure in 6:1–9 is evidence of the institutionalization of Christianity in a post-Pauline period (cf. 1 Tim 6:1–2; Titus 2:9–10, which say nothing at all to masters; such critics view both Ephesians and these Pastoral Epistles as non-Pauline). Yet such interpretations are part of a circular argument involving the supposed marks of "incipient Catholicism," not objective conclusions drawn from the text itself. The explanations we have considered here are sufficient. (See further the two sections titled "Incipient Catholicism," the first in "Arguments against Pauline Authorship" and the second in "Evaluation of the Case," both in "Authorship" in the introduction.)

[93] See "A Note on the Term *Haustafel*" in "Structure and Rhetoric" in the commentary on 5:21–33.

[94] The data are summarized in Best, *Ephesians*, 562–64; Lincoln, *Ephesians*, 398–402. Basic classical texts include Aristotle, *Nicomachean Ethics*, 9:2; Plutarch, *Moralia*, 479–80; Dionysius of Halicarnassus, *Roman Antiquities*, 2:26.1–4.

[95] See Lincoln, *Ephesians*, 398–402. Dionysius of Halicarnassus, *Roman Antiquities*, 2:26.4, writes: "The law-giver of the Romans gave virtually full power to the father over his son, whether he thought proper to imprison him, to scourge him, to put him in chains, and keep him at work in the fields, or to put him to death" (quoted in Lincoln, *Ephesians*, 398). One must not, however, assume that Roman fathers were generally so callous as to treat their sons in this manner (nor indeed their wives or slaves).

[96] Dionysius of Halicarnassus, *Roman Antiquities*, 2:26.1. Greeks, he says, limited a father's authority over his son to the time of his youth, ending three years after attaining maturity or when he got married.

In other cases, Greek fathers kept their authority until they attained the age of sixty. But Roman fathers retained it until their death. See Lincoln, *Ephesians*, 399.

of Roman law to fathers, did not vary greatly in its view of parental authority.[97] The OT did not flinch from advocating the "rod" in the father's hand and prescribed severe punishment, including stoning, for obdurately disobedient children.[98] It is, in fact, "striking" that Paul does *not* appeal to the fathers to use corporal punishment to force obedience.

While Paul's *Haustafel* proceeds from the same assumption of parental authority as other ancient writers, it is not his mildness that distinguishes him from them. Other writers advocated a light hand for parents and masters, some from the pragmatic standpoint that harshness does not always achieve what is intended, some from the "humanitarian" perspective that acknowledged the personhood of children and slaves.[99] Paul's thought is consonant in many respects with his Greek and Roman contemporaries, but it is misleading to think that he merely re-presents their thoughts with a light Christian dressing. His starting point is entirely different: the Word of God. For him, first, marriage and family are institutions of God himself, such that Paul can allude to the creation of woman from the side of man (Eph 5:29–30; cf. Gen 2:21–23) and appeal directly to the divine institution of marriage (Eph 5:31, quoting Gen 2:24). Thus, second, it is not merely nature, but God himself who placed fathers and mothers over children. Third, although obedience to God's Law in the household order entails certain earthly rewards—as indeed all created beings may enjoy the blessings placed by God into his creation—the baptized child of God seeks and finds a deeper blessing in what God has established and given. By recognizing in family life the gracious disposition of his heavenly Father, the Christian discovers that the divinely ordered family, like marriage itself, can be a vehicle of the Gospel.

Paul's *Haustafel*, therefore, despite its legal appearance, is more concerned with promise and blessing than with obedience, reward, and punishment. What is crucial is that he sees God at work in the institution of marriage and family. Parents are to be honored and children cared for because they are set in order by God and convey his gifts. In this perspective Paul is rooted in the OT itself. His appeal to the Fourth Commandment (Ex 20:12; Deut 5:16) as "the first commandment with a promise" (Eph 6:2–3) is not unique. Other Jewish theologians had appealed to the promise inherent in this commandment, and the intertestamental *Haustafel* preserved in Sirach bears great similarity to Paul's:

> [1]Listen to me your father, O children; and act accordingly, that you may be kept in safety. [2]For the Lord honored the father above the children, and he confirmed the right of the mother over her sons. [3]Whoever honors his father atones for sins, [4]and whoever glorifies his mother is like one who lays up treasure. [5]Whoever honors his father will be gladdened by his own children,

---

[97] E.g., Philo, *On the Decalogue*, 111–20; Philo, *On the Special Laws*, 2:224–41; Josephus, *Against Apion*, 2:206.

[98] Ex 21:17; Deut 21:18–21; Prov 13:24; 19:18; 23:13–14; 29:15, 17; Sirach 7:23; 30:1–13.

[99] See references in Best, *Ephesians*, 568; Lincoln, *Ephesians*, 406–7.

and when he prays he will be heard. ⁶Whoever glorifies his father will have long life, and whoever obeys the Lord will refresh his mother; ⁷he will serve his parents as his masters. ⁸Honor your father by word and deed, that a blessing from him may come upon you. ⁹For a father's blessing strengthens the houses of the children, but a mother's curse uproots their foundations. (Sirach 3:1–9 RSV)

The First and Fourth Commandments

But Paul's appeal to the promise contained in the Fourth Commandment (Ex 20:12; Deut 5:16) is not an end in itself. All the commandments stem from the First (Ex 20:3; Deut 5:7).[100] To violate any commandment is to lack the fear, love, and trust of God. To steal, for example, is to refuse to trust that God has provided everything one needs for this body and life. To commit adultery is to reject God's provision of a wife or husband, thus, to reject God. So also, to obey the Fourth Commandment is to obey the First, for by heeding father and mother, children are acknowledging and trusting the God who placed their parents over them.

Yet Paul's Jewish contemporaries saw a unique relationship between the Fourth and the First Commandments. While the distinction between the two tables of the Law is rooted in the fact of their having been given to Moses on two tablets,[101] the Scriptures are not definitive in drawing a line between the two tables. The summary of the Law draws it between the love of God and the love of neighbor (Mt 22:37–40), on which basis Luther and the Western tradition have placed the Fourth Commandment into the Second Table. This distinction makes sense and may be supported by Christ's words (Mt 19:18–19). But Paul does not include the Fourth Commandment in his summary of the Second Table (Rom 13:9), and in this he may have been following Jewish tradition which (perhaps on the basis of Lev 19:2–4), included the Fourth Commandment in the *First* Table.[102]

---

[100] See Luther, LC 1:48, 324–25.

[101] See, e.g., Ex 31:18; 32:15; 34:1, 4; Deut 4:13; 10:1–5.

[102] In Jewish numbering, the introductory sentence, "I am the Lord your God …" (Ex 20:2) was counted as the first "word," so that "honor your father …" was the fifth "word" of the Decalogue, and it concluded the First Table. Thus, Philo comments: "Having then now philosophized in this manner about the honour to be paid to parents, he closes the one and more divine table of the first five commandments [θειοτέρᾳ πεντάδι]. And being about to promulgate the second [table] which contains the prohibitions of those offences which are committed against men, he begins with adultery, looking upon this as the greatest of all violations of the law" (Philo, *On the Decalogue*, 121 [trans. Yonge, *The Works of Philo*]). However, in *On the Special Laws*, 2:261, Philo considers the commandment to honor parents to be inferior to the first four commandments, since it deals with mortals. Jerome, *Ephesians*, 3:6.1, and Ambrosiaster, *Ephesians*, 6:3.2 (ACCS 8:202), represent the later Christian tradition that included this commandment in the Second Table since, as Ambrosiaster noted, it "pertains to humans."

The Fourth Commandment thus occupies a hinge position, a pivot point between the tables of the law.[103] Parents are not simply one's neighbors, but one's own flesh and blood, and the originators of one's flesh and blood. This observation leads Paul's Jewish contemporaries to emphasize the role of parents as agents of God, co-creators, and participants in God's ongoing governance of creation. Josephus, for example, comments on the Fourth Commandment:

> The law ordains also, that parents should be honored immediately after God himself, and delivers that son who does not requite them for the benefits he hath received from them, but is deficient on any such occasion, to be stoned. It also says, that the young men should pay due respect to every elder, since God is the eldest of all beings.[104]

Philo, likewise:

> For parents themselves are something between divine and human nature, partaking of both; of human nature, inasmuch as it is plain that they have been born and that they will die; and of divine nature, because they have engendered other beings, and have brought what did not exist into existence: for, in my opinion, what God is to the world, that parents are to their children; since, just as God gave existence to that which had no existence, they also, in imitation of his power, as far at least as they were able, make the race of mankind everlasting.[105]

Such statements are consistent with Paul's choice of the Greek term γονεύς, "progenitor," for parents, his modification of the command with the phrase "in the Lord,"[106] and his appeal to what is "righteous" on the basis of the Torah (6:1). In this respect, Paul's words to children are radically different from secular *Haustafeln* of the day.[107]

Parents in God's Stead

The correlation of the First and the Fourth Commandments[108] has a number of consequences. First, children learn to know God through the gracious care that their parents provide. Luther preaches on the Fourth Commandment:

---

[103] Despite Luther's abiding by the traditional Western division of the tables, his interpretation of the Fourth Commandment in the Large Catechism is not so different from the Jewish tradition:

> The Fourth Commandment occupies a key position between the two Tables. It already deals with our actions toward people, which is why it belongs to the Second Table. However, from these people it lifts up the men who, by virtue of God's ordering, are placed before and over us and sets them between us and God. On them rests the majesty of God's ordering in creation and by the Word; thereby they share in God's fatherly majesty itself. (Peters, *Commentary on Luther's Catechisms*, 1:192–93)

[104] Josephus, *Against Apion*, 2:206 (trans. Whiston, *The Works of Josephus*).

[105] Philo, *On the Special Laws*, 2:225 (trans. Yonge, *The Works of Philo*).

[106] See the explanation in the fourth textual note on 6:1.

[107] Other differences from secular parallels are observed in "A Note on the Term *Haustafel*" in "Structure and Rhetoric" in the commentary on 5:21–33.

[108] See Peters, *Commentary on Luther's Catechisms*, 1:194–97.

God is known and nicely copied in the image of the parents. ... For God entrusts father and mother with the office of taking care of the children. There one can see as in a mirror how God is disposed toward us, namely, as a father's heart is to the children, so God's heart is disposed toward you.[109]

Second, it means for children not only that honor is *owed* to parents as God's representatives but also that to honor parents *is* to honor God himself. It is therefore an act of worship. Although Paul does not speak to the children about the role of the "heart" and mind ("soul," "attitude") as he does to slaves in 6:5–7, we may fairly assume those words are applicable. Paul addresses children as persons who are capable of hearing the Word of God and responding to it. He thereby treats them as believers, on the basis of their Baptism, and calls them to worship God from the faith of their heart by heeding their God-given parents. This conclusion prompts Luther to exalt the honoring of parents above all the self-chosen works of monasticism and medieval ceremonial law:

Notice how great, good, and holy a work is here assigned children, which is, alas! utterly neglected and disregarded, and no one perceives that God has commanded it, or that it is a holy, divine Word and doctrine. (LC 1:112 [*Triglotta*, 613])

Even almsgiving and all other works for our neighbor are not equal to this. For God has exalted this estate of parents above all others; indeed, he has appointed it to be his representative on earth. (LC 1:126)

Here we see Luther drawing the inevitable third conclusion: *parents stand in the place of God himself.*

We must, therefore, impress it upon the young that they should regard their parents as in God's stead, and remember that however lowly, poor, frail, and queer they may be, nevertheless they are father and mother given them by God. They are not to be deprived of their honor because of their conduct or their failings. Therefore we are not to regard their persons, how they may be, but the will of God who has thus created and ordained. (LC 1:108 [*Triglotta*, 611])

In this light we can understand the horrific (and probably rarely used) OT penalty of stoning prescribed for rebellion against parents (Ex 21:17; Deut 21:18–21). For if parents are God's representatives on earth, then to rebel against them is to reject God himself. Luther preaches: "Other than against God, I cannot commit a greater sin than to sin against a power instituted by Him, which indeed is God's honor."[110]

Although Paul does not delve into such details in this pericope, one must also note the *limit* that the First Commandment places on the Fourth. The Fourth orders parents *under* God, and when honoring God conflicts with honoring parents, the former takes precedence:

---

[109] Luther, "Sermon on Exodus 20," October 29, 1525, WA 16:489.16, 490.7–10 (trans. Peters, *Commentary on Luther's Catechisms*, 1:196).

[110] Luther, "Sermon on Exodus 20," November 5, 1525, WA 16:506.4–5 (trans. Peters, *Commentary on Luther's Catechisms*, 1:195).

… so that if God's Word and will are in force and being accomplished, nothing shall be esteemed higher than the will and word of parents; yet so that it, too, is subordinated to obedience toward God and is not opposed to the preceding commandments. (LC 1:116 [*Triglotta*, 615])

Thus, the apostles, when forbidden by the Jewish authorities to preach the Gospel of Christ, aver that they must obey God rather than men (Acts 4:19–20; 5:29). And Christ himself sets aside the priority of fleshly family relationships when they conflict with the Gospel (Mt 4:22; 8:21–22; 10:35–37; 12:46–50; and parallels). Family and government authorities who are unfaithful to God in carrying out their vocation can no longer claim to be representing him, but will be liable to his judgment. When such authorities disobey God and become, tragically, agents of the devil, to heed and follow them in their disobedience is no longer divine worship but false worship, falling under the condemnation of idolatry in the First Commandment (Ex 20:3–5; Deut 5:7–9).

To Teach the Word of the Lord

Neither Paul's nor Luther's conception of parents as representatives of God is static. Parents do not simply sit still and accrue honor from their children on this basis, even though honor is always due to them. But Paul is clear in his mandate that children are obligated to heed their parents chiefly because the parents have the duty of teaching them the Word of the Lord. This is the implication of the vocabulary Paul carefully chooses in commanding the fathers to "raise them in the discipline and instruction of the Lord [ἐκτρέφετε αὐτὰ ἐν παιδείᾳ καὶ νουθεσίᾳ κυρίου]" (6:4). This mandate is rooted in the OT, which placed primary responsibility on fathers for the nurture of children in the Word and will of God.[111] The Jews took this mandate seriously, as evidenced by Josephus' claim: "Our principal care of all is this, to educate our children well; and we think it to be the most necessary business of our whole life to observe the laws that have been given us, and to keep those rules of piety that have been delivered down to us."[112]

The vocabulary of nourishing, disciplining, and instructing in the fear of the Lord and in his Word is carried on and explicated in the Apostolic Fathers:

You shall not remove your hand from your son or from your daughter, but from their youth you shall teach them the fear of God [διδάξεις τὸν φόβον τοῦ θεοῦ]. (*Didache*, 4:9)

Let your children be partakers of the discipline that is in Christ [τῆς ἐν Χριστῷ παιδείας]. (*1 Clement*, 21:8)

---

[111] See, e.g., Gen 18:19; Deut 4:9–10; 6:7; 11:19; 32:46; Ps 78:5. The entire book of Proverbs is largely phrased as a father teaching divine wisdom to his son, thus, "hear, my son, the instruction of your father" (Prov 1:8, with further addresses to "my son" throughout the book); see also Prov 22:6.

[112] Josephus, *Against Apion*, 1:60 (trans. Whiston, *The Works of Josephus*).

Next, [teach] your wives [to walk] in the faith given to them and in love and purity, tenderly loving their own husbands in all truth and loving all [others] equally in all chastity, and to train up their children in the knowledge and fear of God [τὰ τέκνα παιδεύειν τὴν παιδείαν τοῦ φόβου τοῦ θεοῦ]. (Polycarp, *To the Philippians*, 4:2)

What emerges is a thoroughly Christian picture of the household, with the father (and mother) instructing the children in the Word of God, treating them as fellow believers, as baptized children of God worthy of all love and nurture, not as slaves but as free in Christ.[113]

The Promise

This means that, although Paul proceeds from the Law of God as *command*, we should take seriously his insistence that it is the *promise* in the Law that is vital. On the one hand, obedience to the Law of God brings the results that God built into his creation. That is to say, God's Law is not arbitrary, as if it were to be obeyed simply because God says so, regardless of whether there is any benefit. On the contrary, because God is the Creator, he has designed his world in such way that the Law serves as a sort of "user's guide" to deriving the benefits that he placed in it. So Luther can locate the Fourth Commandment's promise in the present life and world: "He [God] not only declares that it [honoring parents] is well pleasing to Him, and that He has joy and delight therein; but also that it shall be for our prosperity and promote our highest good; so that we may have a pleasant and agreeable life, furnished with every good thing."[114] In this respect the Law differs from the Gospel. For while the Gospel bestows blessings apart from worthiness on those who are unable to fulfill God's requirements and despair of self-help, the Law connects its blessings to its fulfillment: "do this, and you will live" (Lk 10:28). Nor is the delivery of the Law's blessings arbitrary, but it is connected to the sphere of life to which that commandment pertains. In other words, obeying the Fourth Commandment brings blessings within family life, not necessarily outside it. Heeding parents delivers the blessings that are located in the parents. If the father says, "Eat," the blessing of obedience is to receive the food and be nourished (not to become rich, for example). Thus, the Fourth Commandment entails the promise of long life on this earth, a life full of the blessings that fathers and mothers bring.

Yet the delivery of the Law's gifts in a fallen world is hampered by a variety of consequences of sin. Jerome expresses what is the common experience of many in this world, who would doubt the blessings of the Law: "For there

---

[113] Thus, Chrysostom's explanation, while at first sounding entirely secular, in fact is rooted in the Gospel that views the child as fundamentally free (Gal 3:28–4:7): "*Do not make your children angry* [Eph 6:4]. So many parents do this. They do this by depriving them of their portion of the inheritance and their promises, by oppressing them with burdens, by treating them not as though they were free but as slaves" (*Homilies on Ephesians*, 21:6.4, ACCS 8:203).

[114] LC 1:132 (*Triglotta*, 619). Peters, *Commentary on Luther's Catechisms*, 1:191: "Luther emphasizes unabashedly this earthly walk of ours at the place assigned to us by God."

surely have been many who, even while being obedient to their parents, died abruptly. Others who have been irreverent to their parents have reached extreme old age."[115] His response is to seek a spiritualized interpretation of the promise attached to the Fourth Commandment:

> Rightly interpreted the command looks for the land that the Lord promises to Israel. It is offered to those who have left the spiritual Egypt. It calls us to patience as we traverse the vast and terrible wilderness of this life, as we overcome great challengers whom the Lord strikes down and as we enter into the Judea that flows with milk and honey.[116]

This spiritualizing is faulty if it proposes eternal blessings as an alternative to earthly ones, if it robs the Law entirely of its gifts in this life. If this were Paul's meaning, he could have abbreviated his citation of the commandment even farther by removing entirely any mention of "the earth" (Eph 6:3).

But Jerome's recognition that there is a higher, eternal reward entailed in the promise of God, that holds the Christian's gaze as he walks the path of this life and looks beyond its trials and tribulations, is certainly consistent with Paul. For when children honor their Christian parents, they receive, as we have noted, "the discipline and instruction of the Lord" (6:4)—and this brings with it an eternal blessing. Thus, hidden in the concrete, earthly promise of the Fourth Commandment is an eternal gift. And the gift is available because of the Law's fulfillment in Christ. By heeding parents "in the Lord" (6:1), children receive Christ's blessings. And so, just as we cautiously accepted a sacramental aspect to marriage insofar as it serves as a vivid picture of the Gospel to those who are equipped by God's Word to see it,[117] so also can we view parents as a quasi-sacramental sign, an outward enfleshment of the very gifts and promises of God in Christ.[118]

Likewise, one cannot hear of a promise attached to children in the Lord without recalling the promise that "to such as received him, he gave authority

---

[115] Jerome, *Ephesians*, 3:6.1, ACCS 8:203.

[116] Jerome, *Ephesians*, 3:6.1, ACCS 8:203.

[117] See the first textual note on 5:32 and "Holy Matrimony and the Gospel" in the commentary on 5:21–33.

[118] Peters, *Commentary on Luther's Catechisms*, 1:209–10, writes on the basis of Luther:

> "This is why you [children] should be glad in your heart and thank God that He has chosen you and made you worthy to do such precious, pleasing works for Him" [LC 1:117]. ... As we are in the midst of rushing toward death, we are permitted to achieve the insurmountable certainly that the invisible Creator God Himself has put us on this place, has given us "living parents" [LC 1:125], and has placed them near our heart by means of His commandment. His commandment thereby becomes our breathing space of the life of grace before His face. As we bow before our parents, we directly and immediately bow before Him. ... By doing so, the parents become a sacrament for us, a bodily sign of invisible grace. As we face them, our trusting heart at the same time faces the eternal God in His word-like condescension itself. Concretely obeying the parents, however, only becomes a sacramental sign of saving grace and of the Creator's blessing where God's previous election of grace has met us and where His Holy Spirit has created our heart anew.

to become children of God [τέκνα θεοῦ], those who believed in his name, who were born not of blood nor of the will of the flesh nor of the will of man, but from God" (Jn 1:12–13). The thought of Galatians 3–4 underlies much of Ephesians, particularly the fundamental statement "for in Christ Jesus you are all sons of God [υἱοὶ θεοῦ], through faith; for as many of you as have been baptized into Christ have put on Christ" (Gal 3:26–27). On the basis of this baptismal rebirth, Paul draws the conclusion "there is not Jew or Greek, there is not slave or free, there is not male and female, for you are all one in Christ Jesus" (Gal 3:28). Paul then proceeds to proclaim the Gospel on the basis of the contrast between slavery and sonship. Those who are sons receive the inheritance (Gal 3:29), are adopted by God himself (Gal 4:5), so that they can speak to God through the Spirit with Christ as "Father" (Gal 4:6) and be heirs in his household (Gal 4:7). Already in Ephesians Paul has spoken of Christians as "children" of God (5:1, 8) who bear a striking resemblance to their Father in forgiving and loving one another. So also here "children" evokes all the Gospel blessings of those who are incorporated into the Son of God and through him are made to be God's children.[119]

Slaves and Lords/Masters

The Societal Role of Slavery and Its Transformation through God's Order

To present a thorough and balanced depiction of slavery in classical antiquity is beyond both the scope of this commentary and the competence of its author, who makes no claims of being a trained classicist. One who can make such a claim is John Nordling, whose commentary on Philemon in this Concordia Commentary series offers an incomparable treatment of slavery both as a social reality and a theological concept in Scripture.[120] Certainly, a basic understanding of the institution is necessary to dispel common misunderstandings that arise, at least in the English-speaking Western world, from the British and American history of slavery. Nordling suggests two major ways in which slavery in the Greco-Roman world differed from the Anglo-American experience: first, while many ancient societies (including Israel) restricted slavery to foreigners,[121] it was not based on race (or skin color) as a biological characteristic; second, in ancient societies slaves could be highly educated and hold relatively high social positions.[122]

---

[119] Cf. υἱοθεσία, "adoption as sons" (1:5; cf. Rom 9:4). For sonship as a metaphor of the Gospel (and more than a metaphor, a reality in Christ), see also Mt 5:9; Lk 20:36; Rom 8:14–19, 21, 29; Phil 2:15; 1 Jn 3:1–2, 10; 5:2.

[120] See Nordling, *Philemon*, 39–139. See also Lincoln, *Ephesians*, 415–20; MacDonald, *Colossians and Ephesians*, 159–69; Deterding, *Colossians*, 170–76.

[121] See the first textual note on 6:5.

[122] See "Two Significant Differences between Ancient and Modern Slavery" in Nordling, *Philemon*, 68–85.

Modern readers of the Bible can enter into the minds of its original audience only if they recognize the vastly greater extent and integration of slavery into its world. It is estimated that fully one-third of the population of Greece and Italy was enslaved in the NT era.[123] It was an inextricable part of the social order. It is hard for modern minds to comprehend that no known ancient writer ever proposed the abolition of slavery[124] (although in 1 Cor 7:21 Paul encouraged a slave to gain his freedom if he had the opportunity to do so). Certainly Paul was not alone in calling for kind treatment of slaves, and though they were viewed as property, not all influential figures viewed them as subhuman. Seneca's call for decent treatment of slaves proceeds from precisely the opposite claim:

> "These people are slaves." No: they are human beings. "These people are slaves." No: they are those with whom you share your roof. "These people are slaves." No: when you consider how much power Chance [*fortuna*] can exert over you both, they are fellow-slaves. … I don't want to let myself go on this vast topic, and give you a homily on how to treat your slaves: we behave toward them in a proud, cruel and insulting fashion. The sum of what I wish to preach is this: treat those whose status is inferior to your own in the same manner as you would wish your own superior to treat you.[125]

Contemporary Jewish sources contain similar admonitions (Sirach 4:30; 7:20–21; 33:31). Philo exhorts masters to grant slaves the Sabbath rest and to keep their own muscles in shape by doing the slaves' work for them![126] He sounds like Paul when he writes: "Cease, therefore, ye who are called masters, from imposing harsh and intolerable commands on your slaves, which break the strength of the body by their compulsion, and compel the souls to faint even before the bodies."[127] Such admonitions presume, of course, that slave owners could be harsh or even brutal, and there is no escaping this reality.[128] Yet an old shoe is a comfortable shoe, and the very pervasiveness and success of slavery was in great part owing to a pragmatic approach on the part of masters and slaves that led to cooperation and making the most of the status quo. Nordling warns us against the modern presumption (often based on fiction and film, not history) that slavery was universally despised and despicable:

> There is plenty of evidence that suggests that ancient slavery was not quite the uniformly horrible thing so many today simply assume that it was. In fact, we believe it can be shown that slavery served necessary and even salubrious

---

[123] Lincoln, *Ephesians*, 417.

[124] Lincoln, *Ephesians*, 415. Philo goes so far as to designate slaves an indispensable part of society (*On the Special Laws*, 2:123).

[125] Seneca, *Epistles*, 47, quoted in Lincoln, *Ephesians*, 416.

[126] Philo, *On the Special Laws*, 2:66–68. The presumption of his admonition is that the masters are Gentiles who would be permitted to work on the Sabbath while allowing their Jewish slaves to rest.

[127] Philo, *On the Special Laws*, 2:90 (trans. Yonge, *The Works of Philo*); cf. *On the Special Laws*, 3:137–43.

[128] See "A World Not Our Own" in Nordling, *Philemon*, 39–44.

functions for nearly everyone in ancient society, and not just for the pampered elites. This last point is worth pondering because, on the whole, the NT presents slavery as a vocation in which typical Christians could honorably serve God, their master, and many others in ancient society.[129]

Modern attitudes to slavery arise not simply from an aversion to abuse and brutality, for, even if it could be demonstrated that a slave was well treated, the modern observer would object to slavery on principle. That principle is *freedom*. A slave, even when warmly embraced as a beloved household servant, was still *property* by very definition. And the value placed on freedom is not purely modern; the Greeks prized it above all else, though they distinguished various facets of freedom.[130] The Greeks themselves owned slaves (primarily foreigners, of course), and it is evident that for them as a people freedom meant the ability to govern themselves democratically without the oppression of foreign powers—though it must again be noted that democratic rights in Greece were vastly restricted in comparison to modern states. Modern people who presume a priori that the Bible simply *must* be opposed to slavery and advocate the liberation of slaves often overlook two crucial realities of Greco-Roman law and custom: first, that manumission was a very real possibility for most slaves;[131] and, second, that many slaves, if offered the chance, would and did decline it (cf. Ex 21:5–6; Deut 15:16–17) because of the stress and difficulty of making a new, self-sufficient life for themselves.[132] In addition, as there were various "levels" of freedom, manumission might have entailed only the recognition of self-determination, but might not have relieved the slave of significant responsibilities and debts to his former owner.[133]

Thus, modern readers must reckon with the fact that slavery (particularly in the Christian household context that Paul was addressing) sometimes offered a comfortable life that was preferable to any available alternative. It was, furthermore, an evolving institution. In the early days of Rome's worldwide conquests, most slaves were foreigners, soldiers conquered in battle who were enslaved

---

[129] Nordling, *Philemon*, 43. Again:

> It seems fairer to conclude that while ancient masters lived in a world quite unlike our own, most were not complete monsters. To be sure, both masters and slaves were sinful human beings who had ample opportunity to display the depravity of fallen human nature. Nevertheless, as they strove to better themselves in this world, they generally interacted within the boundaries of what was considered fair and equitable. (58)

[130] Lincoln, *Ephesians*, 417: "Greek law defined four elements of freedom—freedom to act as one's own legal person, freedom from being seized as property, freedom to earn a living in the way one wanted, and freedom of movement, including the right to live where one wished. But to establish freedperson status only the granting of the first of these was necessary."

[131] See Nordling, *Philemon*, 46–58, 84–85; Lincoln, *Ephesians*, 417. There was an increase in the ease and frequency of manumission in the first century AD. Manumission might have taken place after ten or twenty years of service, when the slave reached the age of thirty, when his owner died, or when his freedom was purchased (by himself or another).

[132] See Nordling, *Philemon*, 56–57.

[133] Lincoln, *Ephesians*, 417.

rather than put to the sword and conscripted residents of vanquished territories. Such foreigners would have been more likely to long for freedom. By the first century AD, however, most slaves no longer came from war or piracy, but from household births. They were born into their social class, trained for their particular jobs, and Roman law kept pace by guaranteeing them more humane treatment than their foreign-born forebears had received. Manumission was for many of these household servants a somewhat unattractive option.[134] Nordling notes that the institution was, in the end, useful to both master and slave:

> In fact, we have now seen how slaves, freedmen, and freedwomen alike often "used" masters to get what *they* needed and wanted out of life: room and board, clothing, gainful employment, *peculium* [a monetary fund], upward social mobility, legal representation, and so forth. Hence "mutual interdependence" would seem to be an accurate way of categorizing the relationship that existed between vast numbers of masters and slaves in antiquity, not just the domination-submission model assumed by so many today.[135]

The preceding survey is not meant, of course, to suggest that the reader make a positive moral judgment on what was certainly a deplorable abuse of human dignity and a departure from God's good intention for humanity in his creation. Here we concur with the judgment of Chrysostom, who himself was in no position to abolish slavery:

> Society arrangements, like laws made by sinners, acknowledge these distinctions of classes. But we are all called to accountability before the law of the common Lord and Master of all. We are called to do good to all alike and to dispense the same fair rights to all. God's law does not recognize these social distinctions. If anyone should ask where slavery comes from and why it has stolen into human life—for I know that many are keen to ask such things and desire to learn—I shall tell you. It is avarice that brought about slavery. It is acquisitiveness, which is insatiable. This is not the original human condition. Remember that Noah had no slave, nor Abel nor Seth nor those after them. This horrid thing was begotten by sin. It does not come from our earliest ancestors. We pay our ancestors no respect by blaming them. We have insulted nature by this system.[136]

But before the abolitionist arguments of the nineteenth century are brought to bear on Paul, before it is assumed that he simply *must* have called for all Christian masters to free their slaves and for all slaves to rebel against their masters, it is important to understand these crucial differences.[137] Once this anachronistic assumption is set aside, though, one can discern some significant

---

[134] Lincoln, *Ephesians*, 418: "Many slaves in the Greco-Roman world enjoyed more favorable living conditions than many free laborers."

[135] Nordling, *Philemon*, 58–59.

[136] Chrysostom, *Homilies on Ephesians*, 22:6.9, ACCS 8:206.

[137] Lincoln, *Ephesians*, 416: "Modern readers need to free themselves from a number of assumptions about first-century slavery, including the assumptions that there was a wide separation between the status of slave and freedperson, that all slaves were badly treated, and that all who were enslaved were trying to free themselves from this bondage."

criticisms of the institution even in the positive words of Eph 6:5–9. For, first, Paul neither here nor elsewhere in his writings uses the term δοῦλος, "slave," in a pejorative or scornful manner.[138] Unlike even some of his Jewish contemporaries, Paul does not speak of slavery as necessary or useful; nor does he speak to slaves as if addressing a less valuable form of humanity or a lower social class. Those who hold a subordinate place in the order are, for Paul, neither less valuable nor necessarily less capable.[139]

Second, in contrast to many contemporary *Haustafeln*, Paul does not speak only to the masters as the responsible (moral) party. He addresses the slaves directly, indeed first (6:5–8). He treats them (as Seneca would encourage) as human beings capable of acting in accord with good advice or against it, for their own well-being, in integrity and faithfulness—or not. From a purely practical standpoint and in line with what we have noted above about the earthly blessings that flow from obedience to God's order, Paul's admonitions to slaves were an entreaty for them to take advantage of the possible blessings to be found in their vocation by locating themselves on the positive side of the twofold pattern of slave-master relations in the ancient world:

1. On the one hand, slaves who were lazy, disobedient, disrespectful or who otherwise did not live up to the master's trust (as evidenced in many of the Gospel parables cited above) usually had to endure stormy and unhappy relationships with their respective masters: perpetual humiliations, demotions, beatings, and worse.

2. On the other hand, slaves who did their best for the master and his interests and were hardworking, honest, and resourceful, usually found themselves on the master's good side, appreciated his rewards, and could enjoy an astonishing degree of independence and autonomy—even as slaves.[140]

Paul's complementary words to the masters, "do the same things to them" (6:9), could equally be viewed as a strategy for mutual prosperity and as good, solid advice on how to get the best service out of a slave.

But, of course, there is something else going on here. The qualification of masters as τοῖς κατὰ σάρκα κυρίοις, "the in-the-flesh lords/masters" (6:5), together with the conclusion that "both their Lord and yours is in heaven" (6:9), frames the address to slaves and masters with the reminder that earthly slavery is not the ultimate determinant of their status. Both slave and master are in service to a higher authority, to God, "who is over all and through all and in all" (4:6). This is a baptismal reality (4:5) for both (on the assumption that

---

[138] K. H. Rengstorf, "δοῦλος," *TDNT* 2:271: "It thus follows that in the NT the δοῦλος is the classical picture of bondage and limitation. This being so, it is the more remarkable that he is never spoken of in the disparaging and contemptuous fashion common in the Greek and Hellenistic world. ... The δοῦλος is never despised or rejected [in the NT] simply because he is a slave."

[139] See the first textual note on 5:21 and "Five Essential Characteristics of Subordination in Ephesians" in the commentary on 5:21–33.

[140] Nordling, *Philemon*, 59.

master and slave are both Christians). Like the whole congregation in Ephesus, like Jews and Gentiles, like men and women, they have been made one with each other through a common death to sin and resurrection to divine new life in Holy Baptism (e.g., 2:13–18; 4:4–5; cf. Gal 3:26–28). All this is evoked by Paul's reference to the impartiality of God (Eph 6:9), the One who does not "look upon faces."

This is why, for Paul, it matters not whether slavery is overturned in this world or continues. It is a platitude to repeat that Paul is not a social revolutionary; but it is he who defines himself as a preacher of the *Gospel*.[141] Is a slave's status before God improved if he becomes free? Is a master's eternal, spiritual lot diminished if he is sold into slavery? Paul's attitude to social status in this world is entirely ambivalent. He is concerned about a much greater kind of slavery, fervently desiring that all hearts be rescued from slavery to Satan, sin, and death, and become enslaved to Christ (Rom 6:16–22; cf. Jn 8:34–36). Thus, he can tell slaves:

> [20]Let each one remain in the vocation in which he was called [ἐν τῇ κλήσει ᾗ ἐκλήθη]. [21]Were you a slave when you were called? Let it not matter to you. But if, on the other hand, you are able to become free, make use of it instead [μᾶλλον χρῆσαι]. [22]For the slave who was called in the Lord is a freedman of the Lord. Likewise, the free man who was called is a slave of Christ. [23]You were purchased at a price; do not become slaves of men. [24]Brothers, in whatever [state] he was called, let each one remain—with God. (1 Cor 7:20–24)

These words bear some careful thought. On the one hand, Paul seems to embrace both slavery and freedom in the noun κλῆσις, "vocation" (derived from the verb here, καλέω, "call"; this is, in fact, the passage on which Luther most prominently based his theology of vocation). The implication is that even being a slave can be a calling from God, a place in which one can serve God and do good works for the neighbor. There is, therefore, no reason why the converted slave should necessarily seek to escape his position.[142] On the other hand, the phrase "make use of it instead" (μᾶλλον χρῆσαι) implies a certain preference for the road of manumission.[143] Paul backs up this preference by speaking of the Corinthians' redemption in Christ in terms evocative of manumission (1 Cor 7:23). If they are truly free in Christ—which is an eternal reality not dependent on their earthly status as slave or free—it is consistent with their status to be free of enslavement

---

[141] Rom 1:15; 15:20; 16:25; 1 Cor 1:17; 9:16; Col 1:23; 2 Tim 1:10–11; etc.

[142] Some Christians even sold themselves into slavery to provide food and aid to others (*1 Clement*, 55:2).

[143] As he does with Philemon, Paul may have occasionally pressed Christian masters to free their slaves, when possible. MacDonald, *Colossians and Ephesians*, 164, infers this from Paul's words to the Colossian masters: "When the *paterfamilias* is exhorted to treat his slaves fairly and justly in [Col] 4:1 this would presumably include the granting of manumission in due course as a reward for faithful service, but there are no immediate demands placed on masters to grant manumission, and slaves owe them unquestioning obedience."

to men.[144] But most importantly, their relationship to God in Christ has already transformed the status of both slave and master in this world, for they are now "in the Lord" and "with God." This is truly revolutionary.

Slavery Viewed Typologically

Nonetheless, Paul's primary word to slaves and masters is not that they should seek an earthly escape from their lot, but that their attitudes should be reoriented in the Lord—the slave seeing his master as an earthly representative of God, and the master acting toward his slave as Christ did for the church. The early Apostolic Fathers drew out the explicitly typological language of Paul's words:

> You shall be subordinate to masters as to a type of God, in modesty and fear [ὑποταγήσῃ κυρίοις ὡς τύπῳ θεοῦ ἐν αἰσχύνῃ καὶ φόβῳ]. (*Barnabas*, 19:7)

> And you slaves, be subordinate to your masters as to a type of God [ὑποταγήσεσθε τοῖς κυρίοις ὑμῶν ὡς τύπῳ θεοῦ], in modesty and fear. (*Didache*, 4:11)

This reinterpretation itself would be enough to quell calls for liberation through unlawful or violent means, to dampen a desire for social upheaval on Christian principles. But Paul's more urgent message is that such earthly relationships cannot have any effect on one's relationship with God, which is what matters ultimately. For in Christ "*there is*" (ἔνι) neither slave nor free (Gal 3:28; Col 3:11); ἔνι is *present* tense and indicative, not imperative (cf. also 1 Cor 12:13). True freedom is a freedom of the heart, a hidden quality that no earthly lord can take away. A slave who seeks earthly freedom at the expense of his master is living to himself, not to the Lord, when the baptized are given to do the opposite (Rom 14:7–8; 2 Cor 5:15). A slave who is insubordinate to his master on the basis that the latter is a fellow Christian not only injures the earthly prospects of the Gospel by damaging its reputation but also rebels against the God whom his master represents (1 Tim 6:1–2).[145]

---

[144] The Apostolic Fathers are replete with evidence that the first generation after Paul drew this conclusion from his writings. *Shepherd of Hermas, Similitudes*, 1:8, encourages Christians to buy "afflicted souls" rather than land (trans. Kirsopp Lake, LCL). Ignatius is led to warn: "Do not despise either male or female slaves, neither let them be puffed up, but rather let them serve as slaves all the more, to the glory of God, that they may obtain from God a better freedom. Let them not long to be set free at common expense [ἀπὸ τοῦ κοινοῦ], that they be not found to be slaves of desire" (*To Polycarp*, 4:3 [trans. adapted from *ANF* 1:94]). MacDonald, *Colossians and Ephesians*, 163, explains: "Here what was at issue was not the individual master granting manumission to a slave, but rather the expectation that the church would purchase the freedom of slaves from funds out of its common chest." Ignatius' words of warning are evidence that the practice was happening. His admonition that they not be "slaves of desire" implies that by longing for freedom at the expense of others they would merely be exchanging one kind of slavery for another (coveting money and freedom, they would become slaves to them).

[145] Although Paul does not express the obverse point with reciprocal words to the master, either here or in 1 Timothy 6, one might infer that Christian masters ought not take advantage of their Christian slaves. That is to say, they ought not assume that their slaves must serve without

Slavery does not enter into Ephesians in isolation from its companions in the *Haustafel*, and we would do Paul a grave injustice if we treated his words merely from a sociological perspective. Just as marriage (5:22–33) became an *evangelischer Ansatz*, a "launching pad of the Gospel,"[146] so also fatherhood and sonship (6:1–4) invited the reader to enter through the doorway into Paul's treasure house of Gospel analogies conveyed by that basic human relationship. Slavery, too, serves as an opportunity for Paul to draw back the veil of "mystery" (5:32) to disclose that the earthly master is a representative of the Lord God himself and the earthly slave is subordinate to him in the way of Christ to the church. Although Paul does not explicitly identify the slave's submission to his master with the church's submission to Christ nor the master's leadership with Christ's sacrificial love for the church, the context of the pericope within the *Haustafel* as a whole invites the reader to draw such implications. If slavery were a subject restricted to the household orders in Paul's writings, this step might be deemed unjustified. But it bears considering that slavery is a deep-rooted and consistent framework for proclaiming God's salvation in both Testaments.

In the OT, as has been noted, slavery was not outlawed, but it was carefully circumscribed.[147] The people of Israel could purchase slaves from foreigners (Lev 25:44–45).[148] They could also take captive foreigners defeated in war to serve as their slaves or take their women as wives.[149] Post-exodus Israelites, while subduing the peoples surrounding the promised land, frequently did so, often at God's explicit command.[150] Yet the enslavement of their fellow Israelites was strictly forbidden (Lev 25:39–46), and even during the time of civil war in the divided kingdom it merited the wrath of God (2 Chr 28:8–11). The provision that Israelites could retain fellow Hebrews as slaves for a period of six years but must release them in the seventh (Ex 21:1–11; Deut 15:12–14) seems contradictory to Leviticus 25. It is likely, however, that Exodus with its limited period of "slavery" was simply restricting a form of "indentured servanthood"

---

reward, purely out of love, or necessarily go beyond the call of duty simply because they are fellow Christians. The masters, in imitation of their heavenly Father, ought to love their fellow Christians unconditionally.

[146] This translation of Werner Elert's characteristic German phrase *evangelischer Ansatz* gets at its meaning perhaps more fundamentally than Walter Hansen's "impact of the Gospel," which misses Elert's view of the Gospel as the *starting point* and the *driving force* in Luther's theology. See Elert, *The Structure of Lutheranism* (trans. Walter A. Hansen), xix, 11–13, and passim.

[147] Here we treat only the Mosaic Law's provisions for slavery, not the widespread reality of slavery in the pre-Sinai period and in surrounding nations not bound by God's Law. Abraham, for example, had many slaves in his household and at one point even considered one to be his heir (Gen 15:2–3), though such slaves were probably foreigners (cf. Gen 17:12–13, 27).

[148] Cf. Philo, *On the Special Laws*, 2:123, who notes that the Law allows for enslaving foreigners since slaves are "indispensable property" (trans. Yonge, *The Works of Philo*).

[149] Num 31:9; Deut 20:14; 21:10–14.

[150] Judg 5:30; 1 Sam 4:9; 2 Sam 12:29–31; 1 Ki 9:15, 20–22.

for the purpose of paying off a debt.[151] The underlying reality of indentured servanthood is admitted in the regulation of Israelites serving rich foreigners living in Israel, yet even here the term is limited. While foreigners could be enslaved permanently and passed on as possessions to Israelite children (Lev 25:45–46), if a poor Israelite became an indentured servant, he had to be released in the Year of Jubilee (Lev 25:39–40). If he sold himself to a rich sojourner, it was the duty of his relatives to try to purchase his freedom; in addition, the sojourner was admonished to treat him as a servant, not a slave; and he was in any case to be released in the Jubilee Year (Lev 25:47–54).

The fundamental reason for these rules was quite simple and repeated like a litany: the Israelites had been slaves in Egypt, and God had redeemed them from slavery at great cost; they were therefore never to fall back into slavery or enslave each other (Lev 25:38–39, 42, 55; Deut 15:15; Jer 34:13). Their God had not simply set them free, but he had purchased and won them *for himself*. Israel, his firstborn son (Ex 4:22–23; Hos 11:1), was also *God's slave*. "For it is to me that the sons of Israel are slaves [עֲבָדִים], *my* slaves [עֲבָדָי], whom I brought forth out of the land of Egypt; I am YHWH your God" (Lev 25:55). The exodus is the paradigmatic saving event of the OT. It is God's magnificent, monergistic act on which he bases his claim over the Israelites as his people and which gives him the right to establish the covenant (Ex 19:4–6; 20:2). Israel's worship constantly refers back to the exodus as the basis of the people's praise (e.g., Psalms 78; 135; 136). Egypt, correspondingly, is an everlasting and pervasive symbol of all the enemies of God's people (e.g., Isaiah 19). From the exodus, two complementary views of slavery emerged: the Israelites were God's slaves, and therefore, they could not be the slaves of any other.

Yet the meaning of the exodus was more than practical or even just symbolic. Egypt was not just Israel's prototypical *earthly* enemy but also represented all her *spiritual* enemies. Egypt symbolized the oppression and slavery of sin, death, hell, and the devil. We have seen this correspondence already in Ephesians as Paul applied Ps 68:19 (ET 68:18), which in its original context referred to the rescue of Israel from Egypt and her implantation onto Zion's heights, to Christ's Easter victory over sin, death, and the devil, and his glorious ascension to heaven (Eph 4:8). The evangelist Luke assumes and invites this comparison by using the term "exodus" (ἔξοδος, *exodos*, literally, "a road out," commonly translated as "departure") to refer to Jesus' upcoming passion

---

[151] Cf. 2 Ki 4:1; Neh 5:5, 8. Consider also Jacob's seven-year labor for each of his brides from Laban in Gen 29:18–30. Isaac Mendelsohn, *Slavery in the Ancient Near East* (Oxford: Oxford University Press, 1949), 32–33, notes the similar provision of a three-year period for debtors to be indentured as slaves in the Code of Hammurabi, § 117. Note that the purpose of the provisions in Ex 21:1–11 and Deut 15:12–14 is not to *allow* a form of Hebrew-to-Hebrew slavery, but to *limit* its damage by providing a specific timeframe for the servant's release, allowing him (if he was already married when he became a slave) to take his wife and children with him into freedom, and requiring the master to provide him with enough goods to make a fresh start. When Israel failed to grant such freedom, freeing their slaves in the sixth year only to buy them back, God severely punished them (Jer 34:8–22).

in his account of the transfiguration conversation between Jesus, Moses, and Elijah (Lk 9:31). Peter likewise calls his departure from this life into eternity an "exodus," a crossing into the promised land (ἔξοδος, 2 Pet 1:15). And Paul calls Christ himself our πάσχα, our "Passover" (1 Cor 5:7).

This paradigmatic use of the exodus stands behind the NT's pervasive language of slavery to sin.[152] Sin is the Egypt in which humanity stands in bondage and in which Christians stood before their baptismal crossing brought them into the promised land. The equations made by the NT texts are consistent and obvious:

- Egypt represents slavery to sin, death, and the devil.

- As Israel was God's firstborn son whom God rescued by killing the firstborn of Egypt, so by the sacrifice of Jesus, God's firstborn Son, he rescues us as Christ's brothers and sisters.

- Christ is our Passover Lamb, by whose blood we are redeemed from slavery and rescued from death (Eph 1:7; 2:13; also 1 Cor 1:30; Heb 9:14; 1 Pet 1:18–19; 1 Jn 1:7). See the third textual note on Eph 1:7.

- The Lord's Supper is our Passover meal, in which we eat the true Passover Lamb, bring to remembrance Christ's "exodus" (Lk 9:31), and are saved from death by his blood (1 Cor 10:16; 11:23–25).

- Holy Baptism is our crossing of both the Red Sea (Exodus 14–15) and Jordan River (Joshua 3–4; cf. Mt 3:13; Eph 4:5), leading us out of oppression and into the promised land (1 Cor 10:1–4; 12:13).

- Through this rescue we are no longer slaves to sin, but slaves of Christ, of God, and of righteousness (Eph 6:6; also Lk 2:29; Acts 2:18; Rom 6:18, 22; 14:18; 1 Cor 7:22; 1 Pet 2:16).

- This "slavery" to Christ is really true freedom (Jn 8:35–36; 15:15).

The wholesale conscription of exodus language in the service of the Gospel is the driving force in that most beautiful sentence in the German language, Luther's explanation of the Second Article in the Small Catechism:

> I believe that Jesus Christ, true God, begotten of the Father from eternity, and also true man, born of the virgin Mary, is *my Lord*, who has *redeemed* me, a lost and condemned person, *purchased* and won me from all sins, from death, and from the power of the devil; not with gold or silver, but with His holy, precious *blood* and with His innocent suffering and death, *that I may be His own* and live under Him in His kingdom and *serve Him* in everlasting righteousness, innocence, and blessedness just as He is risen from the dead, lives and reigns to all eternity.[153]

Here Luther most forcefully identifies the *Lordship* of Christ not with the Law (his ability to give orders and our duty to obey), but with the Gospel: he is our Lord because he has paid the price to redeem us out of slavery. Although we are called into his service and are his slaves, it is first a movement from death into

---

[152] Jn 8:33–34; Rom 6:16–20; 7:1–4; 2 Pet 2:19.

[153] SC 2:4 (*LSB* 322–23; emphasis added).

life, from sin into righteousness, and from hell into heaven. "Slavery" itself is redefined when the Master is Christ.[154]

This is the message of Galatians 3–5, the greatest Pauline exposition of slavery as a Gospel motif. Paul speaks of the Law as a παιδαγωγός, a kind of "slave-tutor" (Gal 3:24) preparing Israel for the coming of Christ. To be under the Law's tutelage was to experience a kind of slavery (Gal 3:23). But with the coming of Christ and our Baptism into him (Gal 3:25–27), we have become "sons of God" (Gal 3:26). This is true because through faith, in Baptism, we have become "clothed with Christ" (Gal 3:27) so that when God looks at us he sees only Christ; we are sons by being in the Son. The result is that, from the divine perspective, there can no longer be any talk of Jew or Greek, slave or free, male and female (Gal 3:28). In the succeeding verses, Paul skillfully weaves together the analogies of slavery and freedom, adoption and sonship, inheritance and promise, all rooted in the promises made to Abraham and the "allegory" of Hagar and Sarah (Gal 4:1–7, 21–31). The conclusion he draws is this: "for freedom Christ has set us free; therefore stand fast and do not again submit to a yoke of slavery" (Gal 5:1).

Thus, while Paul's Gospel message does not consist of a call for the *literal* release of slaves, it declares the *true, spiritual* release of all slaves to sin in Christ. It has been argued that this message would have been particularly attractive to slaves, and there is some evidence in the NT that slaves formed a substantial portion of the early Christian congregations (1 Cor 1:26–28).[155] Those who were "non-persons" in the eyes of the world became the very sons of God in the church.[156] This was a joyful message to slaves—even to children and women, who fared scarcely better under ancient law. But Paul's message, to

---

[154] K. H. Rengstorf, "δοῦλος," *TDNT* 2:264, notes that the employment of slavery language for man's relationship with a deity was unique and derives from the OT rather than from Greek classical literature: "Within the Gk. concept of God there is in fact no place for this word group as an expression of religious relationship and service. It is a distinctive feature of the Greek attitude to the gods that gods and men may be bound by family relationships." But the Bible uses both kinds of relationships, family and slavery, and Paul combines them to great effect in this section of Ephesians (5:21–6:9). Ultimately, both analogies derive from Christ, for he is Husband (5:22–33) and Son (1:2–3; cf. 6:1–4), Lord (e.g., 1:2–3, 7; 4:5) and slave (cf. 6:5–8), as also God is both his Father and ours (1:2–3; 3:14–15; 4:6), both his Lord and ours (6:9).

[155] This supposition is supported by the very presence of so many household orders in the NT that speak to slaves (besides Eph 6:5–9, see Col 3:22–4:1; 1 Tim 6:1–2; Titus 2:9–10; 1 Pet 2:18). Nordling, *Philemon*, 115, who quotes Celsus from Origen, *Against Celsus*, 3:44: "Later pagans opined that educated persons could not possibly be Christians for that religion appealed only to 'foolish, dishonorable and stupid' people—indeed to 'slaves [ἀνδράποδα], women, and little children.'"

[156] Nordling, *Philemon*, 67:

They believed and were baptized, and hence they passed from "non-person" to fully enfranchised status in God's sight by the *faith* that had been wrought in them by the Gospel. That which was true in the first century A.D. is true still *today*. It is in the baptismal and *eschatological* sense that all the diverse Christians are no longer Jew, Greek, slave, free, male, or female [Gal 3:27–28].

repeat, is not aimed in a liberationist manner merely at the slaves of this world. The slavery that concerns Paul is that which bound all the Gentiles to whom he preached the Gospel, those enslaved by the spirit of the air and the elemental forces of this world (Eph 2:1–2; 6:12), over whom Christ has triumphed by his death, resurrection, and ascension, whom God has placed as a footstool under his feet (1:21–22; 3:10). The slavery that concerns Paul is the oppression of the flesh and its sinful desires, which dragged down even (especially!) the Jews, who were in possession of God's written Law (Eph 2:3; cf. Rom 7:9). The recognition of the deeper, truer slavery explains why Paul should say "whether [he is a] slave *or free*" (Eph 6:8; cf. Gal 3:28; Col 3:11). It is socially understandable that Paul might explicitly note that *slaves* receive freedom through the Gospel. But to those who believe themselves to be *free* and yet are bound by unseen bonds, the message is just as liberating—and perhaps more striking (cf. Jesus' words to the Jews in Jn 8:31–36).

Indeed Christ, the freest of the free, the Creator of both master and slave, the Lord of the Torah, gave up his freedom for the sake of the enslaved world. All claims from mankind to be "free" (Jn 8:33) founder on the fact of Christ's forsaking freedom for us. Just as the Pharisees who claimed to see were truly blind because they claimed to see and yet did not believe in Christ (Jn 9:39–41), so also the Jews who claimed to be free children of Abraham were truly slaves because they also did not believe in Christ (Jn 8:39–47). Neither slave nor free can claim to be anything in the face of a Creator who gave up freedom to be their slave. When Peter speaks to Christian slaves who (it appears) are in service to abusive, non-Christian masters, he cites Christ's own slavery as the paradigm: "for to this you were called, because even Christ suffered for you, leaving behind a pattern [ὑπογραμμόν] for you, that you should follow in his footsteps" (1 Pet 2:21). Nordling notes how the slave could draw comfort from this conformity to Christ in suffering:

> *Christ's* submissive suffering and death is presented in [1 Pet] 2:21–25 as the epitome of the kind of undeserved suffering experienced by *the slaves* in [1 Pet] 2:18–20. In other words, *Christ is revealed here as the Slave par excellence*, as the innocent Sufferer upon whom even the most wretched slave in the original situation might well have depended, and as *the exemplar of the entire suffering and persecuted church in fidelity to Christ.*[157]

---

[157] Nordling, *Philemon*, 124. Markus Barth, *Ephesians*, 2:757–58, vividly draws the same Christological comparison:

> When Paul speaks to the slaves [in Eph 6:5–8], he speaks not only of "fear and trembling," "obedience," and "service." He also appeals to their "wholeheartedness" … and to their knowledge of the Lord's fairness. … He shows them their dignity as laborers in the Lord's employment, which cannot be questioned or abrogated even by cruel or pagan masters, and which must not be belied by doing poor work and offering cheap lip service. Again, it is only on the basis and after the model of the Servant-Messiah that Paul expects the enthusiastic acceptance of subordinate positions (Philip 2:3–11). … It is an expression of the freedom of those who, just like Paul, are "prisoners" (3:1; 4:1) of the Messiah Jesus and engaged in His service.

Yet even here, Christ is not merely an example for slaves (or free) to emulate. Peter does not tell the slaves to endure suffering in the way Christ did, following his example. Rather, he simply notes that suffering is that to which they have been called *because they are in Christ*. Peter then uses the slave's suffering as a "launching pad of the Gospel," not simply presenting Christ as one who suffered like us and with us, but *for us*. Commenting on this verse Luther writes: "The chief article and foundation of the gospel is that before you take Christ as an example, you accept and recognize him as a gift, as a present that God has given you and that is your own."[158]

The same approach to Christ's slavery characterizes Paul's great *Carmen Christi* ("Song of Christ," Phil 2:5–11). What appears in the beginning to be a simple call to emulate Christ in one's humble attitude toward others within the body of Christ quickly turns out to be something quite different. Christ took on the form of a slave not as an example for us to emulate, but in order to accomplish something that we could not: to die a slave's death on the cross in our place and for our benefit (Phil 2:6–8). In vindication of and by way of stamping his approval on Christ's self-offering, God the Father glorified him, exalted him, and bestowed on him the highest and most praiseworthy name (Phil 2:8–11).

This pattern of self-sacrifice and exaltation runs through Ephesians likewise. It is not our imitation of Christ's humble service that counts for anything, since our works are worthless (2:1–3, 8–9). Rather, if we have been united with Christ through Baptism (1:4–7; 4:4–6), then God will raise us up and seat us with him in the highest heavenly places (1:18–23; 2:4–7). Since we are one body with him (2:13–22; 4:15–16; 5:30), wherever he goes, we go. Thus, we who were slaves have been made free because the One who became a slave for us was vindicated, glorified, and exalted by God the Father for us and with us. It is impossible to read Paul's words to slaves and master ("slaves of Christ," 6:6; "both their Lord and yours is in heaven," 6:9) without recalling the entire way of salvation that the image of slavery and redemption conveys.

The Application of Paul's Words on Slavery

We now have the resources to answer the question "what is the contemporary application of the household code's words to slaves?" First, Christian readers in the Western world must not make the mistake of assuming that there are no Christian slaves today who might hear Paul's words in the way of their original audience. Slavery persists in many corners of the world, in which it is estimated that thirty million people still live in some form of forced service.[159] Unfortunate baptized children of God who find themselves in this condition may apply Paul's words more literally to themselves than can the rest of us. Second, those who are not slaves may nevertheless read the Gospel from Paul's words,

---

[158] Luther, "A Brief Instruction on What to Look for and Expect in the Gospels" (1521), AE 35:119.

[159] See the footnote on this topic in the first textual note on 6:5.

understanding that they were slaves to sin who have been freed by Christ. The words of Romans 6–8, in which Paul contemplates the freedom wrought by Baptism into Christ's death and the ensuing struggle against sin's attempts to reassert its lordship, are a classic example of this application.

But may we adapt the pattern of masters and slaves to the workplace relationship of employer and employee? The Lutheran instinct to recognize authority—wherever it is rightly used as authority stemming from God—might encourage us to do so. Thus, John Nordling, in writing on Philemon, concludes:

> We propose that, in the main, the relationship between masters and slaves in the NT and between Christians and persons of greater or lesser station in the world (as Luther articulated this in his doctrine of vocation) is essentially the same. …
>
> Let modern Christians see themselves in this picture, then, and not simply dismiss such passages of God's Word as outmoded relics of an earlier age.[160]

At a practical level this application is sound and useful. Employers ought not be harsh with their workers. Employees ought not work as if only to please men in the way of "eye-service" (6:6), but ought to see their work as pleasing to God insofar as it is in accord with his will and good for the neighbor. Such attitudes and actions are natural outcomes of Christian love and are worship of God as good works that proceed from faith.

However, while there are superficial similarities between the two situations, the modern workplace relationship of employer-employee is fundamentally different from the master-slave relationship. First, the crucial, defining factor of *ownership* is missing. The employee exchanges his labor for the employer's payment by way of a freely entered contractual arrangement. Second, because the employer does not own the employee, the nature of the relationship is entirely different: for the employee is only temporarily in the workplace, may have multiple "bosses," and may frequently move from one job to another. It is, consequently, quite difficult to see the employer as a representative of God.[161] Comparing the free, contractual relationship of employer-employee to the relationship of the baptized with God seriously skews the picture of the Gospel away from divine monergism. Paul's inclusion of slavery in the *Haustafel* does not add to it the additional layer of "workplace," but derives from the fact that slaves were part of the household.[162] They had no choice in receiving their master, just as children do not choose their parents and subjects do not choose their monarch. Parents and kings are gifts of God, and the slave is called upon to

---

[160] Nordling, *Philemon*, 138–39; original emphasis removed.

[161] This we maintain, notwithstanding the NT's application of this language to civil government (Jn 19:11; Rom 13:1). Citizens of a country or subjects of a realm do not come and go from the authority of their government or monarch like employees who punch the clock or change jobs. They live under civil authority perpetually, so long as they remain in that "kingdom."

[162] When Luther derives the authority of masters from parents (LC 1:141–42), he is making the same assumption, for in medieval Europe most work was domestically based.

view his master under the same rubric. The difficulty, then, in applying slavery language to the modern workplace is that the typological argument that is so fundamental to Paul's words cannot easily be applied. The modern preacher cannot expect his hearers to see the workplace as an ongoing proclamation of the Gospel in the way Paul preaches marriage and home in Ephesians 5 and 6.

Ephesians 6:10–24

Conclusion

Ephesians 6:10–17

Epilogue: The Armor of God: Baptismally Enclosed in Christ

Translation

6 **¹⁰**Finally, be strengthened in the Lord, that is, in his mighty strength.
¹¹Let yourselves be clothed with the <u>full armor</u> of God so that you may be able to <u>stand</u> against the devil's schemes.
¹²For our struggle is not against blood and flesh,
but against the rulers,
against the authorities,
against the world powers of this darkness,
against the spiritual forces of evil in the heavenly places.
¹³For this reason take up the <u>full armor</u> of God, that you may be able to <u>withstand</u> in the evil day, and so, having accomplished all things, to <u>stand</u>.

¹⁴<u>Stand</u>, therefore, having belted your waist with truth,
and having clothed yourselves with the breastplate of righteousness,
¹⁵and having shod your feet with the preparation of the Gospel of peace,
¹⁶among all these things having taken up the shield of faith, with which you will be able to extinguish all the flaming arrows of the evil one;
¹⁷and receive the helmet of salvation,
and the short sword of the Spirit, which is the Word of God.

Textual Notes

6:10 τοῦ λοιποῦ—The adjective λοιπός, "remaining," is often used adverbially, with or without the article, most often in the accusative (λοιπόν). In the only other biblical occurrence of the articular genitive form here, τοῦ λοιποῦ, it carries the classical sense of a genitive of time with χρόνου understood, "for the rest of time, henceforth."[1] The accusative (τὸ) λοιπόν may have the same meaning.[2] But in the context of 6:10 it seems more likely that τοῦ λοιποῦ should be understood with the derived logical meaning of "finally, in conclusion."[3] It introduces the *peroratio* or epilogue (6:10–17), the sum-

---

[1] Gal 6:17; cf. *Shepherd of Hermas, Similitudes*, 9:11.3. See BDF, § 186 (2); Turner, *Syntax*, 235; Moule, *Idiom Book*, 39. Some commentators believe Paul is preparing his audience for an impending, *future* conflict (e.g., Barth, *Ephesians*, 2:759–60; Schlier, *Epheser*, 289).

[2] E.g., 1 Cor 7:29; 2 Tim 4:8. See BDAG, s.v. λοιπός, 3; BDF, § 451 (6); Turner, *Syntax*, 336.

[3] It is therefore equivalent to (τὸ) λοιπόν in 2 Cor 13:11; Phil 3:1; 4:8; 1 Thess 4:1; 2 Thess 3:1. See Moule, *Idiom Book*, 161. For this reason many manuscripts substitute τὸ λοιπόν in Eph 6:10, either because scribes believed it to be grammatically more correct than the genitive τοῦ λοιποῦ or because it is much more common in Paul. In all of these parallel passages, Paul adds ἀδελφοί (μου), "(my) brothers," which likely explains the insertion of ἀδελφοί μου by many of the same manuscripts in the present verse (Best, *Ephesians*, 589). Or it may be added by influence of liturgical reading; see Zuntz, *The Text of the Epistles*, 176.

ming up of the argument that leads into the epistolary conclusion (6:18–24).[4] It does *not* introduce a new or additional argument.[5]

ἐνδυναμοῦσθε ἐν κυρίῳ καὶ ἐν τῷ κράτει τῆς ἰσχύος αὐτοῦ—The present imperative ἐνδυναμοῦσθε is passive[6] and is from ἐνδυναμόω, "to strengthen." Such passives formed from transitive verbs without a stated subject *may* be understood as active intransitives,[7] in which case one would translate the imperative as "be strong." However, the prepositional phrases that follow imply that the agent, the one who strengthens, is "the Lord." We have therefore translated the imperative as a divine passive: "be strengthened." Paul is not calling upon the Christian to seek a strength within, but to find it in God and where he has promised to give it. "I can do all things *in him who strengthens me* [ἐν τῷ ἐνδυναμοῦντί με]" (Phil 4:13).[8]

In this summation of the letter's message, the phrase ἐν κυρίῳ, "in the Lord" (Eph 6:10), recalls all that Paul has said about what it means to be joined to Christ in Holy Baptism (see the fifth textual note on 1:3; cf. 2 Tim 2:1). The language of "being strengthened in the Lord" also evokes the Lord's equipping of his warriors in the OT.[9] The phrase καὶ ἐν τῷ κράτει τῆς ἰσχύος αὐτοῦ, "that is,[10] in his mighty strength" (τῆς ἰσχύος is a genitive of quality)[11] recalls Paul's prayer that the Ephesians, having had the eyes of their hearts enlightened (in Baptism),[12] would know more deeply "what is the surpassing greatness of his power [δυνάμεως] for us who believe, according to the working of his mighty strength [τοῦ κράτους τῆς ἰσχύος αὐτοῦ]" (1:19; cf. Col 1:11). It is God's power that stands behind Paul's ministry (Eph 3:7), the Spirit who strengthens the baptized (3:16), and God who has the power to do all things (3:20). This provides the perspective for the Christians' entry into spiritual battle: not looking to their own ability to fight, but to the strength of the Lord. The language is reminiscent of the famous charge to Joshua before entering into the promised land to do battle with its illicit occupants: "be strong and courageous" (חֲזַק וֶאֱמָץ; LXX: ἴσχυε καὶ ἀνδρίζου; Josh 1:6, 7, 9, 18).

6:11 ἐνδύσασθε τὴν πανοπλίαν τοῦ θεοῦ—The form ἐνδύσασθε is an aorist middle imperative of ἐνδύω, whose middle means "to clothe oneself, put on" (cf. 4:24; 6:14). In

---

[4] See "Conclusion (ἐπίλογος, *Peroratio*)" in "Structure and Rhetoric" in the introduction, as well as "Structure and Rhetoric" in the commentary below.

[5] Perhaps (τὸ) λοιπόν may introduce a new argument in 1 Cor 4:2; 7:29; Phil 3:1.

[6] To take the middle/passive form as a middle reflexive, "strengthen yourselves," would be contrary to the context since the strengthening occurs ἐν κυρίῳ καὶ ἐν τῷ κράτει τῆς ἰσχύος αὐτοῦ, "in the Lord, that is, in *his* mighty strength."

[7] See Voelz, *Fundamental Greek Grammar*, 144–45; BDAG, s.v. ἐνδυναμόω, 2 b.

[8] Cf. Rom 4:20; 1 Cor 16:13; 2 Cor 12:9; 2 Tim 2:1; 1 Pet 4:11; *1 Clement*, 55:3.

[9] ἐκραταιώθη Δαυιδ ἐν κυρίῳ θεῷ αὐτοῦ, "David was strengthened in the Lord, his God" (LXX 1 Kgdms 30:6 [MT/ET 1 Sam 30:6]); κατισχύσω αὐτοὺς ἐν κυρίῳ θεῷ αὐτῶν, "I shall make them strong in the LORD, their God" (LXX Zech 10:12); "God, who equipped me with strength" (Ps 18:33 [ET 18:32]); see also Ps 18:40 (ET 18:39).

[10] The καί is epexegetical, "that is," since "be strengthened in the Lord" is explained by "in his mighty strength."

[11] See τοῦ κράτους τῆς ἰσχύος αὐτοῦ (Eph 1:19); ἐν κράτει ἰσχύος (LXX Is 40:26); ἐν τῷ κράτει τῆς ἰσχύος μου (θ Dan 4:30); cf. ἐν ἰσχύι κράτους μου (LXX Dan 4:30).

[12] See "Enlightened Eyes of Your Heart (1:18)" in the commentary on 1:15–23.

light of the divine passive ἐνδυναμοῦσθε in the previous verse, one might expect a passive here, "be clothed [by God]." Paul could have used a passive imperative to express this. However, the *middle* voice of ἐνδύω is by far the most common usage in Greek, whether one clothes oneself or is clothed.[13] It is sometimes appropriate to translate middle imperatives as permissive; thus, we translate with "let yourselves be clothed with."[14] Certainly in this allegorical context one need not press for consistency in every detail, and it is entirely possible to translate the imperative as "clothe yourselves" or "put on" without offending against the monergism of God. But the permissive middle gets at the *theological* sense of the pericope, which stresses the armor, strength, and defense provided by the Lord.

None of the actions in this unit may be counted as the Christian's contribution to winning the battle. It is the Lord's battle and his victory on our behalf. Thus, one might imagine God putting the armor on the Christian, dressing him as a parent does a child.[15] Earlier in Ephesians, Paul has said that the Christian has "put off … the old man" and "put on the new man" (4:22, 24),[16] an evocation of Holy Baptism as the moment when one is clothed with Christ (cf. Rom 13:14; Gal 3:27; see the first textual note on Eph 4:24). The recurrence of this clothing vocabulary invites us to consider the armor of God as the baptismal robe (cf. Rev 19:14). The Ephesians are pointed to the armor that has already been given to them (cf. Rom 13:12; 1 Thess 5:8).[17]

---

[13] In the context of a traditional (or upper class) household with servants, one might say, "The mistress dressed for dinner," even though her servant did the work. The middle voice does not necessarily stress that the grammatical subject is the actor but that "the action is performed with special reference to the subject" (Smyth, *Greek Grammar*, § 1713 [p. 390], quoted approvingly in Wallace, *Greek Grammar*, 415). See the discussion of ἐνδύσασθαι in the first textual note on 4:24.

[14] BDF, § 317; Wallace, *Greek Grammar*, 425–27. Cf. "arise and let yourself be baptized and washed" (Acts 22:16)—the Baptism was not performed by Paul on himself, but by Ananias (Acts 9:17–18). Cf. "until you are clothed [ἐνδύσησθε—aorist *middle* subjunctive] with power from on high" (Lk 24:49); "you let yourselves be washed [ἀπελούσασθε]" (1 Cor 6:11); "that all the world should let themselves be registered [ἀπογράφεσθαι]" (Lk 2:1). Cf. Rom 13:14 and Grothe, *The Justification of the Ungodly*, 709.

[15] In 1 Cor 15:53–54, the clothing of the mortal body with immortality is expressed with the aorist *middle* infinitive ἐνδύσασθαι; yet clearly the dead body does not "clothe itself" but "is clothed." Judg 6:34 is most interesting: "and the Spirit of YHWH clothed [לָבְשָׁה] Gideon, and he sounded the trumpet/horn, and the Abiezrites were called together after him." Codex Alexandrinus of the LXX translates with the active verb ἐνέδυσεν, the Spirit "clothed" him, but Vaticanus renders it with the active verb ἐνεδυνάμωσεν, "strengthened," thus equating the same two verbs (ἐνδύω and ἐνδυναμόω) whose middle forms appear in Eph 6:10–11: ἐνδυναμοῦσθε, "be strengthened" (6:10), and ἐνδύσασθε, "be clothed" (6:11).

[16] These are also middle voice verbs, ἀποθέσθαι in 4:22 and ἐνδύσασθαι in 4:24, which could be translated as permissive or passive. Cf. LXX Jer 26:4 (MT/ET 46:4); Col 3:12.

[17] Contra Best, *Ephesians*, 590–91: "Believers are not automatically equipped with armour; indeed at the beginning when they became Christians they will not have realised the true nature of the struggle in which they were involved." Indeed, Paul's point is precisely that Christians have already been given the armor, but *they may be unaware why they needed such heavy armor until the nature of the battle is described to them*. Thus, the imperative, "let yourselves be clothed with," does not imply that Christians have no armor until they respond to the command, but rather points them to what is already theirs and bids them see its use.

The noun πανοπλία (πᾶς, "whole,"[18] + ὅπλον, "weapon") refers to "the complete equipment of a heavy-armed soldier,"[19] including both armor and weapons.[20] In the NT πανοπλία is used only in this pericope and in Lk 11:22 (referring to weapons and armor of the strong man whom Jesus disarms). It is rare in the Greek rendition of the OT.[21] OT accounts of warfare seldom use a Hebrew collective noun that would include both armor and weaponry, but often enumerate the weapons.[22] The Greek term πανοπλία is, however, common in the intertestamental literature of the LXX and is used of God's own armor in Wis Sol 5:17 and Sirach 46:6. The genitive in πανοπλίαν τοῦ θεοῦ, "full armor of God," implies not only that the armor is *supplied* by God but also that it is the armor *worn* by God himself into battle, his personal armor (e.g., Is 59:17). See the commentary for further discussion.

πρὸς τὸ δύνασθαι ὑμᾶς στῆναι πρὸς τὰς μεθοδείας τοῦ διαβόλου—The infinitival clause πρὸς τὸ δύνασθαι ὑμᾶς, "so that you may be able,"[23] indicates the *purpose* of the armor. Just as Christians have no strength in themselves, but receive it "in" and from the Lord (6:10), so it is the Lord's armor that makes them able to stand in battle.[24] The verb ἵστημι, "to stand," appears only three times in Ephesians, all in this pericope (6:11, 13, 14). The related compound verb ἀνθίστημι (ἀντί + ἵστημι), "to withstand," occurs only once in Ephesians, in 6:13. These two verbs set the scene of the battle. Paul does not describe an offensive, by which the Ephesians are encouraged to storm the enemy's position. Rather, he envisions the enemy's final assaults on the army of Christ,

---

[18] It may not be incidental that Paul chooses the compound form beginning with πᾶς, "all," for πᾶς occurs more frequently in Colossians and Ephesians as a percentage of total words than in any other NT book. The overwhelming completeness and perfection of God's work for us is a major theme of the letter. See "The *Berakah* Prayer (1:3–14) as Prologue" in the commentary on 1:3–14.

[19] BDAG, s.v. πανοπλία, 1.

[20] Barth, *Ephesians*, 2:793–95, argues that, because some typical pieces are missing from the armor and weapons described in this passage, the implication of πανοπλία must be "*splendid* armor," emphasizing the quality, not the number, of the weapons. His logic falters, however, when he suggests that because God has other weapons ascribed to him in the OT, the Christian's armor here is incomplete. It is "full armor" because God promises that it is all the Christian needs. This is not to deny that the baptismal robe is splendid (cf. Ps 3:4 [ET 3:3], in which God's shield about us is his glory), and Barth is correct to emphasize that this armor has not only military but also "moral or psychological" value.

[21] For the canonical Hebrew books, πανοπλία appears in translation only in LXX 2 Kgdms 2:21 (MT/ET 2 Sam 2:21; armor taken as plunder) and LXX Job 39:20, which departs from the MT (but cf. the weaponry in Job 39:21–23).

[22] Phrases like כְּלֵי מִלְחַמְתּוֹ, "his instruments of war" (Deut 1:41), come close to πανοπλία. Cf., e.g., Judg 9:54; 18:11, 16–17; 1 Sam 8:12; 14:1, 6; 17:38; 2 Sam 1:27; 1 Ki 20:11; 22:34; 2 Ki 3:21; 7:15; 1 Chr 10:9–10; 12:34, 38 (ET 12:33, 37); Is 8:9; Jer 21:4; 46:4; 51:3, 20; Ezek 23:12; 32:27; 38:4.

[23] The verb δύναμαι is deponent, i.e., it has no active form: the present *middle* infinitive (δύνασθαι, 6:11), future *middle* indicative (δυνήσεσθε, 6:16), and aorist *passive* subjunctive (δυνηθῆτε, 6:13; the passive voice is used for the aorist tense) forms in this pericope have an active, intransitive meaning, "be able."

[24] "The phrase, 'Put on ... armor *in order to be* able,' indicates, therefore, that just as clothes make the man so arms make the soldier" (Barth, *Ephesians*, 2:762).

whose members take their stand[25] in the Lord's territory. Because Christ has already triumphed over the enemy (Eph 1:20–23; 2:5–6; 3:10; 4:8; Col 2:15), there is no need for the church to attack, but simply to stand firm[26] while Christ continues to defend his people against the mortally wounded foe's fading forays (1 Pet 5:8).[27] The order to "stand" that pervades 6:11–14 does not imply that Christian soldiers are given a special *tactic* by which they are able to defend themselves, but rather teaches them that the battle is the Lord's. They are to stand back and watch him win the victory for them (cf. הִתְיַצְּבוּ, "stand firm!" in Ex 14:13 in the context of Ex 14:13–14, 30–31; and הִתְיַצְּבוּ עִמְדוּ, "stand firm! stand!" in 2 Chr 20:17).

The phrase πρὸς τὰς μεθοδείας τοῦ διαβόλου, "against the schemes of the devil,"[28] identifies the danger more literally than does the ensuing battle imagery. Though his fate is sealed, the devil is not without resources. His chief weapon against the church is false doctrine, a crafty, "deceitful scheming [τὴν μεθοδείαν τῆς πλάνης]" (4:14),[29] designed to lead the children of God away from the truth by attacking it from within (cf. 2 Tim 2:25–26). He also seeks to divide the body of Christ by inciting sinful anger (Eph 4:26–27). While fleshly human beings are the devil's instruments in such cases, Paul warns that the true battle is against the spiritual forces that stand behind them (6:12; cf. 2 Cor 10:4). On the meaning of διάβολος, "devil," see the textual note on Eph 4:27.

6:12 ὅτι οὐκ ἔστιν ἡμῖν ἡ πάλη πρὸς αἷμα καὶ σάρκα—Originally the noun πάλη denoted a "wrestling match." The related verb παλαίω, "to wrestle," is used of Jacob and God in LXX Gen 32:25–26 (ET 32:24–25).[30] Wrestling was an image ready to

---

[25] This is a military image. Cf., e.g., Polybius: "[Philip] gave the Aetolians an interval in which to make a stand, to take precautionary measures, and to prepare for the future" (*Histories*, 4:61); "[centurions,] such as in the face of superior numbers and overwhelming pressure will die in defence of their post" (*Histories*, 6:24; both trans. Shuckburgh, *The Histories of Polybius*).

[26] Cf. Rom 5:2; 11:20; 14:4; 1 Cor 10:12; 15:1; 16:13; 2 Cor 1:24; Gal 5:1; Phil 1:27–28; 4:1; Col 4:12; 1 Thess 3:8; 2 Thess 2:15; Jude 24.

[27] By way of contrast, Xenophon, *Anabasis*, 1:10.1, reports: "Then the head of Cyrus and his right hand were cut off. But the King, pursuing Ariaeus, burst into the camp of Cyrus; and Ariaeus and his men no longer stood their ground [οὐκέτι ἵστανται], but fled through their own camp to the stopping-place from which they had set out that morning" (trans. Carleton L. Brownson, LCL). Where the leader has failed, his army cannot hold their ground. Cf. Judg 2:13–14; Rev 6:15–17.

[28] The preposition πρός (here and in 6:12) means "against" in the sense of facing oneself "toward" a particular hostility (see BDAG, s.v. πρός, 3 d α; Turner, *Syntax*, 4). The plural form τὰς μεθοδείας τοῦ διαβόλου, "the *schemes* of the devil" (6:11) may be equivalent to the singular τὴν μεθοδείαν, "scheming," in 4:14 by way of *pluralis poeticus* (Turner, *Syntax*, 27–28). In light of the military context, Best, *Ephesians*, 592, suggests the translation "stratagems," though that is perhaps not negative enough.

[29] Luther: "Deep guile and great might Are his dread arms in fight" (*LSB* 656:1); "and he comes against us not with force, but with cunning, that is, with lies (John 8 [:44])" ("Sermon for the Twenty-first Sunday after Trinity," October 25, 1545, AE 58:304–5; WA 51:68). Chrysostom: "The devil never openly lays temptation before us. He does not mention idolatry out loud. But by his stratagems he presents idolatrous choices to us, by persuasive words and by employing clever euphemisms" (*Homilies on Ephesians*, 22:6.11, ACCS 8:207–8). See also the names of the demons in *Testament of Solomon*, 34, quoted below.

[30] Paul elsewhere uses terms for athletic competitions like wrestling (ἀγών, "struggle, conflict, fight," and ἀγωνίζομαι, "to strive, struggle, fight") as an image of the Christian life and of his

hand, as it was common in the games of Asia Minor, particularly in Ephesus. Pausanius relates a story of an Ephesian wrestler who won repeated victories in Olympia until it was revealed that he had six magical words, the "Ephesia Grammata," written on his ankles, intended to invoke the power of the gods.[31] Once these were removed, he lost three successive matches.[32] Paul may be evoking this story and implying that the name of the Lord is a far more potent amulet, able to defeat even the spiritual forces that the Grammata represented.

In the present context, however, the πάλη Paul has in mind is a military battle, a metaphorical application of the term already present in pre-Christian literature.[33] Thus, πάλη need not imply only a close-in, hand-to-hand fight, especially in light of the "flaming arrows" hurled by the enemy (6:15). With this language Paul reminds the listener that, although Christ has won the victory, the fight is not over so long as Christians remain in this age. The Christian may fight an internal battle against the desires of the "flesh."[34] There is also an external battle brought on by the visible enemies of the Christian church: false teachers (4:14; 6:11) and oppressive governments (Revelation 13), pagan neighbors and the enticements of the old Gentile life (Eph 2:1–2; 5:3–12). But Paul insists that these "blood and flesh" (6:12)[35] figures are not the *real* enemy. He

---

ministry: 1 Cor 9:25; Phil 1:30; Col 1:29; 2:1; 4:12; 1 Thess 2:2; 1 Tim 4:10; 6:12; 2 Tim 4:7 (cf. Lk 13:24; Jn 18:36; Heb 12:1). These terms had already been be used metaphorically of a battle (e.g., 2 Macc 8:16; 10:28; 14:18; 15:9). Victor C. Pfitzner, *Paul and the Agon Motif: Traditional Athletic Imagery in the Pauline Literature* (Leiden: Brill, 1967), 159, emphasizes the characteristics of the wrestling image when he paraphrases Paul: "Our battle against the powers of darkness is not like the contest of the wrestler, for he can easily come to grips with his opponent." But Paul does not say "it is not a πάλη, 'wrestling match,'" but rather "our πάλη, 'struggle,' is not against blood and flesh." The contrast lies in the opponents, not the game. Chrysostom, *Baptismal Instructions*, 9:29, apparently draws upon the present verse when he pictures the thirty-day catechumenate before Baptism as preparations for a lifelong wrestling match with the devil:

> After baptism we are going to strip for the combat against him [the wicked demon]; he will be our opponent in the boxing bout and the fight. Let us learn, during this time of training, the grips he uses, the source of his wickedness, and how he can easily hurt us. Then, when the contest comes, we will not be caught unaware nor be frightened, as we would be if we were to see new wrestling tricks; because we have practiced among ourselves and have learned all his artifices, we will confidently join grips with him in the combat. (Trans. Paul W. Harkins, *ACW* 31:141)

[31] For the Ephesia Grammata, see "The Temple of Artemis Ephesia" in "The City of Ephesus and Paul's Relationship to It" in the introduction.

[32] Arnold, *Power and Magic*, 15, 116–17. The story is cited by Eustathius of Thessalonica, *Commentary on Homer*, 19:247.

[33] BDAG, s.v. πάλη; H. Greeven, "πάλη," *TDNT* 5:721. There is no reason to believe that Paul was uncomfortable with the language of war, which he uses in, e.g., Rom 7:23; 1 Cor 14:8; 2 Cor 10:3–5; Gal 5:17; 1 Tim 6:12; 2 Tim 2:3; 4:7.

[34] E.g., Romans 6–8; 1 Cor 15:50; 2 Cor 7:1; Gal 5:13–24; Eph 2:3.

[35] It is ironic (part of the theology of the cross) that while the enemy is not made of "blood and flesh," it is through "blood and flesh" that Christ wrought his victory (Heb 2:14; cf. Jn 6:53–56). The order "blood and flesh" is of no particular significance, as it varies in such expressions; see "flesh and blood" in Sirach 14:18; 17:31; Mt 16:17; 1 Cor 15:50; Gal 1:16. There is no reason why Greek should be as formulaic with this expression as English is.

has just been named (διάβολος, the "devil," 6:11), and now Paul will elaborate on the spiritual forces that are allied with this "ruler of the authority of the air" (2:2).

ἀλλὰ πρὸς τὰς ἀρχάς, πρὸς τὰς ἐξουσίας, πρὸς τοὺς κοσμοκράτορας τοῦ σκότους τούτου, πρὸς τὰ πνευματικὰ τῆς πονηρίας—Of the four terms used here, only the first two, ἀρχή, "ruler," and ἐξουσία, "authority," appeared in Paul's earlier list (Eph 1:21; cf. Eph 3:10; Col 2:15). The third, κοσμοκράτωρ, literally, "world ruler,"[36] is a biblical hapax legomenon. The fact that Paul varies the list here in his summation confirms our earlier judgment that the terms should not be identified in any systematic way with particular orders of evil angels; they simply illustrate the diversity of the evil one's demonic subordinates (see the first textual note on 1:21). The summary phrase τὰ πνευματικὰ τῆς πονηρίας, literally, "the spiritual entities of evil,"[37] makes this very point. Whether worshiped as gods among the pagans, appeased as spirits of the earth and air, or admitted into the soul's inner sanctum through possession or trance, these demons (1 Cor 10:20) are the enemy's shock troops who inspired fear and reverence among the Ephesian Gentiles before they were rescued from their grasp by that magnificent change of lordship: Baptism into Christ, who "triumphed over them by [the cross]" (Col 2:15). Thus, Paul's warning that the battle is not against blood and flesh is not meant to frighten the Ephesians, but to provide fair warning of where the real danger lies and to encourage them to treat their fellow human beings as victims in need of rescue. To call these demons τοὺς κοσμοκράτορας τοῦ σκότους τούτου, "the world

---

[36] The term κοσμοκράτωρ originated in astrological texts referring to the heavenly bodies (i.e., the gods behind them) as determinative of human affairs (BDAG, s.v. κοσμοκράτωρ; Lincoln, *Ephesians*, 444; Schnackenburg, *Ephesians*, 273–74). It was later used of pagan deities and even the Roman emperor (Bruce, *The Epistles to the Colossians, to Philemon, and to the Ephesians*, 405). Irenaeus, *Against Heresies*, 1:5.4, refers to the devil as κοσμοκράτωρ. The *Testament of Solomon*, 34 [8:1–4] (cf. 72 [18.2]), a text datable to the first–third centuries AD and probably written in Ephesus, uses the same language:

> And I glorified God afresh who gave me this authority, and ordered another demon to come before me. And there came seven spirits, females, bound and woven together, fair in appearance and comely. And I Solomon, seeing them, questioned them and said: "Who are ye?" But they, with one accord, said with one voice: "We are of the thirty-three elements of the cosmic ruler [κοσμοκράτωρ] of the darkness." And the first said: "I am Deception." The second: "I am Strife." The third: "I am *Klothod*, which is battle." The fourth: "I am Jealousy." The fifth: "I am Power." The sixth: "I am Error." The seventh: "I am the worst of all, and our stars are in heaven. Seven stars humble in sheen, and all together. And we are called as it were goddesses. We change our place all together, and together we live, sometimes in *Lydia*, sometimes in *Olympus*, sometimes in a great mountain." (Trans. F. C. Conybeare, "The Testament of Solomon," *Jewish Quarterly Review* 11.1 [October 1898]: 24)

[37] With τῆς πονηρίας as an adjectival genitive, this could be translated as "evil spiritual forces." Schnackenburg, *Ephesians*, 274, n. 17: "The Genitive τῆς πονηρίας characterizes the spirits in general as wicked and leading astray to evil, cf. similar semitizing Genitives in 1.13; 2.2, 3, 12, 15; 4.24; 5.6." It is interesting that in the OT an "evil spirit" (רוּחַ modified by רָעָה) is always sent by God (Judg 9:23; 1 Sam 16:14–16, 23; 18:10; 19:9). In the NT an "evil spirit" (πνεῦμα modified by πονηρός) is always in opposition to God's kingdom and associated with the devil (Mt 12:45; Lk 7:21; 8:2; 11:26; Acts 19:12–13, 15–16). The consciousness of the devil's work perhaps became more acute in the intertestamental period (cf. Tobit 6:8), though the message of both Testaments is that no evil spirit acts without God's sufferance (e.g., Job 1–2; Mt 8:31–32).

powers of this darkness," is not to cede territory to their control, but to confine their power to this world and its age (cf. 1 Cor 2:6–8; Eph 2:2), and also to locate them in that spiritual darkness where all evil lingers (Eph 4:18; 5:11–12; Col 1:13)[38] and from which the baptized have been removed by enlightenment (Eph 1:18; 5:8, 14; see the first textual note and the commentary on 1:18). In contrast to these powers limited to this cosmos (κοσμοκράτωρ, *cosmo-crator*), God is the "*all* powerful, almighty" (παντοκράτωρ, *panto-crator*, Nicene Creed).

ἐν τοῖς ἐπουρανίοις—This distinctive Ephesian phrase (1:3, 20; 2:6; 3:10; 6:12) refers to "heavenly places" which have consequences for "heavenly matters." In the present context this is not "heaven" as the place of the blissful enjoyment of God's presence (which takes place "far above all the heavens," 4:10), but the "lower heavens" as the realm of spiritual battle (cf. "the ruler of the authority of the air," 2:2).[39] Paul does not work with a simple "three story" view of the universe (heaven-earth-hell), and even his more complicated cosmology should not be interpreted spatially (as if spirits were definitively located in between earth and God). Rather, with such language Paul wishes to lift our eyes to see the true nature of the battle that is being waged on a grand, cosmic, and spiritual scale. Yet, Christians need not fear these forces as if they were "above" them, for through Baptism into Christ we are already seated with Christ in the heavenly places, with these enemies under our feet (1:20–22; 2:6). See the fourth textual note on 1:3 and "Christ's Victorious Ascension to God's Right Hand (1:20–23)" in the commentary on 1:15–23.

6:13 διὰ τοῦτο ἀναλάβετε τὴν πανοπλίαν τοῦ θεοῦ, ἵνα δυνηθῆτε ἀντιστῆναι—The logical connector διὰ τοῦτο, "on account of this," refers to Paul's unveiling of the true nature of the battle (6:12). When contemplating the evil spiritual forces arrayed against them, the Ephesians can finally understand the need for the armor and weapons with which God equipped them in Holy Baptism. The verb ἀναλάβετε, "take up," suggests the image of a quartermaster who presents the soldier with his provision of equipment.[40]

---

[38] Here "darkness" does not refer to a feature of the natural world as such, as if in contrast to the heavens (contra Schnackenburg, *Ephesians*, 274), but a characteristic of the world insofar as it is dominated by evil spiritual creatures. The association of evil forces with darkness in a cosmic battle is a notable feature of the Qumran literature: e.g., 1QM 13; 16:11–16; 17:5–9; 1QS 3:18–25. This is not to suggest Qumran's influence on Paul, but to note a common appropriation of OT imagery (see the first textual note on 1:18).

[39] The idea that evil spiritual forces could be battling in "heaven" puzzled many patristic commentators (Best, *Ephesians*, 594–95). Jerome, e.g., writes: "It is indeed impious to suppose that the spirits of wickedness in the heavens occupy the same heaven of which God says, *It is my throne* [Is 66:1]" (*Ephesians*, 3:6.11, ACCS 8:209). Some therefore interpreted ἐν τοῖς ἐπουρανίοις as "in heavenly matters"; others, following Origen (*Ephesians*, on Eph 6:12), interpreted it in light of Eph 2:2 as a reference to a lower level of heavenly places (Best, *Ephesians*, 595). But the presence of evil spirits in heavenly places is attested in the OT (e.g., 1 Ki 22:21–22; Job 1:6–12; 2:1–7), and it was not at all foreign to Jewish or early Christian thinking, as demonstrated by M. Jeff Brannon, *The Heavenlies in Ephesians: A Lexical, Exegetical, and Conceptual Analysis* (London: T&T Clark, 2011), 186–98.

[40] This "provisioning" is one possible meaning of τὸν καταρτισμὸν τῶν ἁγίων, literally, "the outfitting of the saints" (4:12). The use of ἀναλαμβάνω, "take up," with weapons or armor is common (e.g., Deut 1:41; Judith 6:12; 2 Macc 10:27; Herodotus, *Histories*, 3:78.2; Josephus, *Antiquities*, 4:88; 20:110).

This first half of 6:13 repeats the content of 6:11 with slight variations in vocabulary: ἵνα δυνηθῆτε for πρὸς τὸ δύνασθαι ὑμᾶς, both meaning "so that you may be able";[41] and ἀντιστῆναι, "withstand, stand against,"[42] for στῆναι, "to stand." The sentence thus forms an *inclusio* that draws the first subunit (6:10–13) to a close and prepares for the allegorical description of the armament in the ensuing verses.

ἐν τῇ ἡμέρᾳ τῇ πονηρᾷ—"In the evil day" extends the battle image.[43] The adjective πονηρός, "evil," reminds us of the spiritual enemies who have been characterized by the noun πονηρία, "evil" (6:12), and anticipates the great "evil one" (ὁ πονηρός) who fires flaming arrows at the saints (6:16). The military image of standing firm implies a watchfulness for the enemy's attack, that evil moment when he launches his offensive. Should the "evil day" therefore be viewed as *future* from the perspective of Paul's writing to the Ephesians?[44] Or does it refer to the present time,[45] inasmuch as he has already declared that "the days *are* evil" (αἱ ἡμέραι πονηραί εἰσιν, 5:16) and the "spirit" (the devil) is "*now* [νῦν] working" (2:2)?[46] In keeping with NT eschatology in general, a combination of the two is likely:[47] the "day" of battle has already begun, but it will only get worse (1 Cor 7:26, 29) and will culminate in an all-out battle when the devil will show his true colors and the Lord will be manifestly just in destroying him (2 Thess 2:6–8; Rev 19:11–21; 20:7–10).[48] See the textual note on Eph 5:16.

---

[41] The aorist *passive* subjunctive δυνηθῆτε, is deponent. Thus, it is not "that you may be enabled [by God]"—though that is theologically and contextually true—but simply "that you may be able" (intransitive active). See the footnote on δύναμαι in the second textual note on 6:11.

[42] The verb ἀνθίστημι refers to "withstanding" or "resisting" the devil also in James 4:7; 1 Pet 5:9. In LXX Dan 10:13 it refers to the demonic prince of the kingdom of Persia "opposing" and "withstanding" the preincarnate Son of God until the angel Michael came to his aid in the battle (see Steinmann, *Daniel*, 501–4).

[43] See the graphic battle imagery "on the day" in the War Scroll, 1QM 1:10–13.

[44] Schlier, *Epheser*, 292–93, and Kirby, *Ephesians: Baptism and Pentecost*, 144, identify it as a day of great tribulation just before the parousia. Jerome (*Ephesians*, 3:6.13, ACCS 8:209) points to LXX Ps 40:2 (MT 41:2; ET 41:1): "in the evil day the Lord will deliver him [ἐν ἡμέρᾳ πονηρᾷ ῥύσεται αὐτὸν ὁ κύριος]." Cf. "in the evil day [ἐν ἡμέρᾳ πονηρᾷ]" (LXX Jer 17:17–18); and "the Day of YHWH" (Is 13:6, 9; Jer 46:10; Ezek 13:5; 30:3; Joel 1:15; 2:1, 11; 3:4 [ET 2:31]; 4:14 [ET 3:14]; Amos 5:18–20; Obad 15; Zeph 1:7, 14; cf. Zech 14:1). The overwhelming number of NT references see this "day" as Christ's second coming: "the day of the Lord (Jesus)" (1 Cor 5:5; 2 Cor 1:14; 1 Thess 5:2; 2 Thess 2:2; 2 Pet 3:10); "the day of Christ" (Phil 1:10; 2:16); "his day" (Lk 17:24); and especially "that day" (Mt 7:22; 24:36; 26:29; Lk 10:12; 2 Thess 1:10; 2 Tim 1:12, 18; 4:8; cf. Rom 2:16; 1 Thess 5:4; 2 Thess 2:3).

[45] So, e.g., Bruce, *The Epistles to the Colossians, to Philemon, and to the Ephesians*, 406.

[46] Cf. "the present evil age" (Gal 1:4). "The day of the Lord" is inaugurated by the first advent of Christ (Mal 3:23 [ET 4:5]; Jn 8:56; Acts 2:20); "that day" is the passion of Christ and the Easter time of the church (Jn 14:20; 16:23, 26; 20:19). For Christians, "the ends of the ages have come" (1 Cor 10:11).

[47] E.g., Barth, *Ephesians*, 2:765, 804–5; Schnackenburg, *Ephesians*, 276 (though he views the future day as vague, not definite); Best, *Ephesians*, 596; and Lincoln, *Ephesians*, 446: "The readers are to realize that they are already in the evil days (cf. 5:16), but that these will culminate in a climactic evil day, when resistance will be especially necessary." Paul has already said that Christ has triumphed over these spiritual forces "not only in this age but also in the one to come" (1:21).

[48] Fischer, *Tendenz und Absicht*, 165–66, discerns a tension between the focus on an eschatological battle in the present pericope and the insistence of the earlier parts of the letter that the

καὶ ἅπαντα κατεργασάμενοι στῆναι—Many interpreters take ἅπαντα κατεργασάμενοι, "having accomplished all things," as a reference to putting on the armor of God: i.e., "and when you have got yourself completely dressed in armor, then stand ready for battle."[49] Certainly Paul's repeated use of "stand/withstand" (στῆναι here, as in 6:11; ἀντιστῆναι in 6:13a; στῆτε in 6:14) is somewhat ambiguous.[50] Yet, to interpret the final clause of 6:13b in this way would make it a simple repetition of 6:13a, which has already described donning the armor to be able to "withstand." The conjunction καί with κατεργασάμενοι, an aorist temporal participle (typical of a narrative sequence), describes an action *subsequent*[51] to "the evil day"[52] and *prior* to the final standing.[53] Thus, it is more likely that with this clause Paul looks to the *outcome* of the battle: the Christian will remain standing.

It would be contrary to context to understand the verb κατεργασάμενοι, "having accomplished [all things]," as implying that the soldiers themselves have worked the victory.[54] It means no more than "when all is done and dusted" and emphasizes the result more than the cause.[55] What matters is what Christ has accomplished for the Christians and through them (Rom 15:18). At the end of "the evil day" (Eph 6:13), when God has worked victory for his people, they will stand above the ruin while all others lie in death and destruction.[56] To remain standing is itself a triumph (Lk 21:36). The image is more

---

battle has already been decisively won by Christ (see, e.g., 1:20–23; 4:8–10). He postulates that the eschatological elements arise from traditional baptismal catechetical material that exhorted the candidates to see their Baptism as "die Ausrüstung für den apokalyptischen Endkampf ['equipping for the apocalyptic final battle']" (166). Fischer proposes that in Ephesians the apocalyptic perspective, paralleled in the Qumran War Scroll, was then supposedly modified for a Hellenistic audience, which did not work with such a "temporal dualism," by adding elements appropriate to a present and ongoing battle. If one sets aside Fischer's hypothesis about the evolution of the tradition, his analysis provides some insight into Paul's own eschatological thinking here. Paul does not believe that the battle will only be fought in the future, but that it has already occurred and has ongoing consequences.

49 E.g., Lincoln, *Ephesians*, 446; Schnackenburg, *Ephesians*, 276; MacDonald, *Colossians and Ephesians*, 345; Barth, *Ephesians*, 2:765–66.

50 See the second textual note on 6:11 and the first textual note on 6:13.

51 The καί introduces a *consecutive* action: "and so …"; see BDF, § 442 (2).

52 See the second textual note on 6:13.

53 For the eschatological "standing," see the first textual note on 6:13.

54 Thus, we do not necessarily accept that κατεργάζομαι here means "overpower, subdue, conquer" (BDAG, s.v. κατεργάζομαι, 4; e.g., 1 Esdras 4:4), a meaning that is not otherwise attested in Paul's writing but is sometimes suggested for this verse (e.g., Schlier, *Epheser*, 293). The victorious outcome of the battle can be viewed as "accomplished" without positing a different meaning for the verb (cf. Chrysostom's homily on this verse [*Homilies on Ephesians*, 22:6.13]).

55 Cf. Rom 5:3; 7:15; 2 Cor 7:10–11; 9:11; James 1:3.

56 Cf. Stoeckhardt, *Ephesians*, 257. In the last editions of his German Bible (1545–1546), Luther paraphrases Paul's final clause, "and so, having accomplished all things, to stand" (6:13), by inserting the military image of "holding the field": "auff das ir … Widerstand thun, und alles wol ausrichten, *und das Feld behalten*, müget ['so that you … may withstand and accomplish everything well *and hold the field*']" (WA DB 7:208–9, including the footnotes). This is reminiscent of his battle hymn: "das feld mus er behalten ['he (Christ) holds the field forever']" (WA 35:456; *LSB* 656:2).

military[57] than judicial (standing before God's judgment in innocence),[58] though it certainly leads to the eternal enjoyment of God's blessed presence.[59]

6:14 στῆτε οὖν—With the conjunction οὖν, "therefore," Paul places a minor break into the flow of the text, dividing it into two subunits. Eph 6:10–13 paints the larger picture, placing the full armor on the Christian, standing him in the midst of the battle, and envisioning its triumphant outcome; then 6:14–17 delves into the details of the pieces of armor that have been given. Thus, the imperative στῆτε, "stand," should be understood not as a new and subsequent action, but as a reiteration of the initial call to stand firm in the face of the devil's attacks (see the second textual note on 6:11).

περιζωσάμενοι τὴν ὀσφὺν ὑμῶν—Paul proceeds to portray six articles of armor, in two groupings of three (6:14–15 and 6:16–17). The first four are introduced by aorist participles of manner[60] that describe the way in which the Christian warrior stands: περιζωσάμενοι, ἐνδυσάμενοι, ὑποδησάμενοι, and ἀναλαβόντες, "having belted … having clothed … having shod … having taken up" (6:14–16). περιζώννυμι in the middle voice means "to wrap/fasten something around [περί] oneself"; since "truth" is wrapped around the "waist" like a belt, the participle is rendered as "having belted."[61] The traditional translation, "girding the loins," is not clearly understood today. It reflects Hebrew idioms that refer to the action of catching together the folds of a robe in a belt, or "hiking up" a long robe around the middle of the body to make it easier to run, travel, work, or fight.[62] The noun ὀσφῦς refers to the midsection of the body: either to the "waist," where a belt is worn (e.g., Mt 3:4), or to the "loins" as the genital area (referring

---

[57] See Lev 26:37; Josh 1:5; 7:12–13; 10:8; 23:9; Dan 8:4, 7; 11:16. In the Peloponnesian War, in response to the overwhelming forces of Athenians who wished the Melians to surrender without a fight, their envoys defiantly proclaimed: "But we know that the fortune of war is sometimes more impartial than the disproportion of numbers might lead one to suppose; to submit is to give ourselves over to despair, while action still preserves for us a hope that we may *stand erect* [στῆναι … ὀρθῶς]" (Thucydides, *History of the Peloponnesian War*, 5:102 [translation from Thucydides, *The Peloponnesian War* (London: Dent, 1910)]; emphasis added). "To escape all these things" and "to stand before the Son of Man" (Lk 21:34–36) seem to describe standing in victory, not judgment.

[58] For "standing" before God in judgment (either to be acquitted or to be damned), see, e.g., Nah 1:6; Ezra 9:15; Pss 1:5; 5:6 (ET 5:5); 76:8 (ET 76:7); Rom 14:10; 1 Cor 10:12; Rev 20:12 (cf. Rom 14:4).

[59] Schlier, *Epheser*, 293: "ein in Ewigkeit vor Gott stehen können ['to be able to stand before God in eternity']"—which implies not the moment of judgment but the ongoing experience of God's blessed company that results from the victory achieved. See Jer 15:19; Dan 7:10; Prov 12:7; Rom 14:4; Rev 7:9; 14:1; 15:2.

[60] These aorist participles are also temporal, e.g., "*after* having girded the loins." But the temporal sequence is not the main point, which is rather to describe the Christians' condition of armored readiness. Wallace, *Greek Grammar*, 624, notes helpfully that the *temporal* implication of a participle is only the first component of its meaning. The interpreter must also look for a "more specific semantic value."

[61] The part of the body to be "girded, wrapped" is put in the accusative (τὴν ὀσφὺν ὑμῶν, "your waist"); the garment is indicated by the preposition ἐν (ἐν ἀληθείᾳ, "with truth"). See BDAG, s.v. περιζώννυμι, 2 c.

[62] E.g., Ex 12:11; 1 Ki 18:46; 2 Ki 4:29; 9:1; Jer 1:17.

to reproductive ability or manly power, e.g., LXX Gen 35:11; Acts 2:30; Heb 7:5, 10).[63] The expression περιζώννυμι + ὀσφῦς is common in the OT with a literal meaning.[64] In the present verse, the imagery refers figuratively to readiness for action.[65] In light of the "army of God" context, Paul may have been alluding quite specifically to the preparation of Israel for the exodus from Egypt: "In this manner you shall eat it: with your belt fastened [αἱ ὀσφύες ὑμῶν περιεζωσμέναι], your sandals on your feet [cf. Eph 6:15], and your staves in your hand; and you must eat it in haste. It is the LORD's Passover" (LXX Ex 12:11). The belt fastened around the waist provides a place for the sword,[66] and perhaps this is what one should imagine here.[67] The Israelites exited Egypt not just as travelers but as God's army, his "hosts" (Ex 12:17; Numbers 2), equipped by him for battle.[68] In Paul's day, Roman soldiers wore their distinctive belt as a mark of vocation, even apart from their full armor; it signaled to the public that they were soldiers.[69]

ἐν ἀληθείᾳ—The identification of "truth" with the belt is likely drawn from the messianic prophecy of Is 11:5: "righteousness [צֶדֶק; LXX: δικαιοσύνη, 'with righteousness'] shall be the belt [אֵזוֹר; LXX: ἐζωσμένος, 'belted'] of his waist [מָתְנָיו; LXX: τὴν ὀσφὺν αὐτοῦ], and truth/faithfulness [הָאֱמוּנָה; LXX: ἀληθείᾳ, 'with truth'] the belt [אֵזוֹר; LXX: εἰλημένος, 'bound'] of his loins [חֲלָצָיו; LXX: τὰς πλευράς, 'his sides']."[70] The prophet places "truth" in parallel with "righteousness," as in Eph 6:14, suggesting they form hendiadys: the Messiah's "righteous truth" or "true righteousness" (cf. 2 Cor

---

[63] BDAG, s.v. ὀσφῦς.

[64] LXX Ex 12:11; 2 Kgdms 20:8 (MT/ET 2 Sam 20:8); 3 Kgdms 21:32 (MT/ET 1 Ki 21:32); 4 Kgdms 1:8 (MT/ET 2 Ki 1:8); Is 32:11; Jer 1:17; Ezek 44:18; Dan 10:5; cf. Prov 31:17. Girding the loins with sackcloth is a sign of mourning (e.g., Gen 37:34; 2 Sam 3:31) or humility in a plea for mercy (1 Ki 20:31–32).

[65] As also in Lk 12:35; cf. LXX Job 38:3; 40:7; Lk 17:8; 1 Pet 1:13.

[66] 2 Sam 20:8; Eph 6:17; cf. 1 Ki 2:5; Neh 4:12 (ET 4:18). A. Oepke, "ζώννυμι κτλ.," *TDNT* 5:303:

The Roman legionary also wore above his armour a broad leather belt studded with metal which with its hanging ends, issuing in strong metal strips, protected the lower body. … In many cases this belt serves also as a sword-belt, while in others the sword, or more rarely the dagger, is carried in a special strap running over the right or left shoulder.

[67] Cf. the military imagery of the armed soldier in, literally, "the belt of his loins is not loosed" (Is 5:27) and "strengthen the loins," i.e., dress for battle (Nah 2:2 [ET Nah 2:1]). It is probably pressing the details too firmly to argue that because this belt is mentioned first, it cannot be the outer sword harness, but must be a leather apron worn under the armor like breeches (A. Oepke, "ζώννυμι κτλ.," *TDNT* 5:303, 307).

[68] See περιζώννυμι in LXX Ps 17:33, 40 (MT Ps 18:33, 40; ET 18:32, 39).

[69] See D'Amato, *Arms and Armour of the Imperial Roman Soldier*, 20–24, 98–101, 212. D'Amato, notes:

Cingulum was the true name of the belt of the Roman soldier. It was used between the first century BC and the second century AD to indicate an indispensable part of military equipment, the belt, as an insignia that commanded respect and which designated a man who was subject to military discipline. To take the belt (*cingi*) was synonymous with being a soldier; to be deprived of it (*discingi*) meant to be reduced in rank." (20)

[70] This is the first in a series of allusions to three major passages of Isaiah: to Is 11:5 and Is 59:17 in Eph 6:14; to Is 52:7 in Eph 6:15; and again to Is 59:17 in Eph 6:17.

6:7; Eph 4:24; 5:9). This allusion to Is 11:5 is the first clue that the armor Paul has in mind is Christ's very own (see the preincarnate Christ in Ezek 1:27; 8:2).[71] Although Christians are to "speak truth" to one another (Eph 4:25; cf. 4:15), the truth that is their defensive armor is Christ's truth, indeed Christ himself, in whom is the "truth" (4:21) and who *is* the truth (Jn 14:6),[72] who was placed upon them through the baptismal "Word of truth" (1:13; cf. 4:24). Truth is the logical weapon to be wielded against the διάβολος, the "devil" or "slanderer," who schemes to deceive with his lies (6:11).

καὶ ἐνδυσάμενοι τὸν θώρακα τῆς δικαιοσύνης—The second piece of armor is likewise introduced by an aorist participle of manner that describes the Christians' stand: ἐνδυσάμενοι, "having clothed yourselves."[73] A θώραξ is a protective covering for the chest in combat, a "breastplate."[74] It protects the body's most vital organs and thus is the principal piece of armor. In the Greco-Roman period there were solid or segmented breastplates made of laminated leather or metal (bronze, copper, or iron) in use, as well as more flexible coats of chain mail or metal scales.[75] Elsewhere Paul identifies the breastplate with "faith and love" (1 Thess 5:8), perhaps envisioning these virtues as the Christian's best occupation in these last days. In Ephesians, Paul appears to draw more directly on OT language of the armor that God himself wore in battle against his

---

[71] The high belt or sash is also evocative of the high priest's vesture, and righteousness is the clothing of a king, priest, or elder in the gate (Barth, *Ephesians*, 2:767, 797, referencing Is 11:4–5; Ex 28:15–30; Job 29:14; Sirach 27:8; Baruch 4:20). The depiction of Christ in Revelation alternates between priest (Rev 1:13) and warrior (Rev 1:15–16). His victory is won not by literal battle but by his priestly and sacrificial work. Thus, if it were not for the military context in Eph 6:10–17, one might see an allusion to the priestly robes that were designed to cover the groin modestly when the priests ascended to the altar (Ex 28:42–43; Lev 6:3 [ET 6:10]; 16:4; Ezek 44:18; cf. 1 Chr 15:27; Rev 15:6; *Testament of Levi*, 8:1–10). One might then recognize in this clothing a priesthood of all the baptized.

[72] Contra, e.g., Lincoln, *Ephesians*, 448: "It is probable that truth here refers to an element of character and activity to be demonstrated by the readers." Similarly, MacDonald, *Colossians and Ephesians*, 345: "a virtue that believers must demonstrate"; Bruce, *The Epistles to the Colossians, to Philemon, and to the Ephesians*, 408: "ethical qualities"; Stoeckhardt, *Ephesians*, 258: "moral integrity." On the contrary, Schnackenburg, *Ephesians*, 277, writes: "It is the expression for the equipment given to the Christian through grace," though he includes "uprightness and holiness … given and demanded by God." In the context of the divine armor given to the Christian to defend him in battle, it is unlikely that the Christian's own virtues are in mind. Schlier, *Epheser*, 295, including n. 3, is more emphatic in denying that the Christian's own uprightness is in Paul's mind and quotes Vilmar approvingly: "Above all, church members must possess as a weapon the Truth that appeared alive and bodily, which once stood before Pilate [Jn 18:37], which from the beginning stood against the liar" (August Friedrich Christian Vilmar, *Praktische Erklärung des Neuen Testaments*, vol. 2 [Gütersloh: Bertelsmann, 1880], 316). Best, *Ephesians*, 599, similarly calls it "God's truth, doctrinal truth, the gospel."

[73] The aorist middle participle ἐνδυσάμενοι (from ἐνδύω; cf. ἐνδύσασθε in 6:11) could be translated as permissive, "having let yourselves be clothed," but though this rightly conveys the meaning, it is cumbersome. See the first textual note on 6:11 and the second textual note on 6:14.

[74] BDAG, s.v. θώραξ, 1. Cf. 1 Sam 17:5; 1 Ki 22:34; 2 Chr 26:14; Neh 4:10 (ET 4:16); Jer 46:4 (LXX 26:4); Ezek 38:4; 1 Macc 3:3; 6:2, 43; Rev 9:9, 17.

[75] A. Oepke, "θώραξ," *TDNT* 5:308–9. See also D'Amato, *Arms and Armour of the Imperial Roman Soldier*, 38–43, 49–52, 122–44, 159–60, 191–92.

enemies.[76] The identification of the breastplate with God's righteousness can be found in Is 59:16–17 and Wis Sol 5:17–18.[77] The quality of δικαιοσύνη, "righteousness," is therefore not the Christian's own righteous acts, but the passive righteousness God has bestowed upon him through Christ (e.g., Rom 3:22),[78] which protects against all spiritual enemies (Rom 8:38–39). The identification of "righteousness" with clothing is well established in the Bible (Job 29:14; Ps 132:9; Is 61:10; Rev 19:8) and in early apostolic literature[79] and is a key component of the baptismal imagery of this text. To put on Christ is to put on his righteousness (Gal 3:27; Eph 4:24).[80]

6:15 καὶ ὑποδησάμενοι τοὺς πόδας—A third aorist participle of manner,[81] "having shod," rounds out the first grouping of armor (6:14–15). The verb ὑποδέω, literally "to bind under," suggests that what is put on the feet are sandals (Acts 12:8), the minimum protection the foot requires (2 Chr 28:15; Mk 6:8–9). They are part of a traveler's necessary preparation and again evoke the exodus—the Israelites wore "sandals" (Ex 12:11) that were miraculously preserved throughout the forty years (Deut 29:4 [ET 29:5]). However, since the noun σανδάλιον is absent here, the verb may simply refer to "putting on footwear"—which leaves open the possibility of a reference to military shoes

---

[76] See further "The Old Testament" in "Sources of Paul's Armor Imagery" in the commentary.

[77] "He [YHWH] put on righteousness as a breastplate [ἐνεδύσατο δικαιοσύνην ὡς θώρακα]" (LXX Is 59:17). "He [the Lord] will put on righteousness as a breastplate [ἐνδύσεται θώρακα δικαιοσύνην]" (Wis Sol 5:18).

[78] "Passive righteousness" refers to the righteousness of Christ received by the Christian passively, purely as a gift, through Baptism into Christ and through the instrumental means of faith in Christ. Best, *Ephesians*, 599, notes the significance of the context and interprets righteousness as we have: "It is difficult to see the gospel of peace (v. 15), salvation (v. 17) and the word of God (v. 17) as human activities. Thus it is better to take righteousness here as that justifying righteousness which is the foundation of Christian existence." Barth, *Ephesians*, 2:796, astutely notes: "In the context of the book of Isaiah, 'righteousness' means help, salvation, and peace for the downtrodden. No one except the Messiah can and will establish it among his people and the nations. It is a gift of God."

[79] Polycarp, *To the Philippians*, 4:1:

"But the beginning of all evils is the love of money" [cf. 1 Tim 6:10]. Knowing, therefore, that "we brought nothing into the world, so we have nothing to carry out" [cf. 1 Tim 6:7], let us arm ourselves with the armor of righteousness [ὁπλισώμεθα τοῖς ὅπλοις τῆς δικαιοσύνης], and let us teach each other, first, to walk in the instruction of the Lord.

Shepherd of Hermas, Mandates, 12:2.4:

As for you, then, put on [ἔνδυσαι] the desire of righteousness [τὴν ἐπιθυμίαν τῆς δικαιοσύνης]; and arming yourself [καθοπλισάμενος] with the fear of the Lord, resist [ἀντίστηθι] them [evil desires]. For the fear of the Lord dwells in good desire. But if evil desire should see you armed [καθωπλισμένον] with the fear of God, and resisting [ἀνθεστηκότα] it, it will flee far from you, and it will no longer appear to you, for it fears your armor [τὰ ὅπλα σου].

[80] As with other pieces of armor in this description, the "breastplate" may also be connected to a part of the high priest's distinctive clothing: the jeweled "ephod," the "breastplate of judgment" (Ex 28:15–35; 39:8–21). See Barth, *Ephesians*, 2:769.

[81] For the four aorist participles of manner in 6:14–16, see the second textual note on 6:14.

or boots.[82] The Roman soldier was equipped with leather boots,[83] sometimes armored with metal strips, for support in marching and protection in battle. There is also evidence of shoes with nails driven through the soles to help the soldier "stand firm."[84] This is probably the military allusion Paul has in mind. Gleaming (i.e., metal-armored) boots are part of Christ's own armor (Rev 1:15; 2:18; cf. Dan 2:33) and are conveyed to the Christian through him.

ἐν ἑτοιμασίᾳ τοῦ εὐαγγελίου τῆς εἰρήνης—The figurative meaning Paul assigns to the "preparation" (ἑτοιμασία) with footwear is "the Gospel of peace." This is the third clear allusion in this pericope to Isaiah (cf. Is 11:5; 59:17 in Eph 6:14), through whom God promised a future messenger to bring the good news of return from exile, which itself would be a proleptic experience of the messianic age: "how beautiful upon the mountains are *the feet of him who brings good news, who announces peace* [LXX: πόδες εὐαγγελιζομένου ἀκοὴν εἰρήνης], who brings good tidings, who announces salvation, who says to Zion, 'Your God reigns' " (Is 52:7; cf. Nah 2:1 [ET 1:15]; Rom 10:15). Paul has already emphasized that the One who accomplished this peace is Christ, who on his cross reconciled men to God and to each other (Eph 2:14–17) and who "himself is our peace" (2:14). Paul saw this as a fulfillment of Isaiah's prophecy of "peace, peace" (Is 57:19). The meaning of the phrase ἐν ἑτοιμασίᾳ τοῦ εὐαγγελίου, "with the preparation of the Gospel,"[85] is therefore that the Christian is prepared for battle by *receiving* the Gospel from Christ through his messengers. It is ironic, but the Christian's best defense in battle is the knowledge that peace has already been attained! "Nothing is more precious than peace, by which all war, both in heaven and earth, is brought to an end."[86] "Have no fear, beloved, the victory is already won. This is the good news."[87]

---

[82] Even sandals could be military footwear; see ὑποδήματα in Xenophon, *Anabasis*, 4:5.14; Josephus, *Wars*, 6:85. See also Josh 5:15; 1 Ki 2:5; Is 5:27; cf. Is 9:4 (ET 9:5).

[83] "The legionary wears the *caliga*, a low half-boot with a strong sole and open leather work above" (A. Oepke, "ὑποδέω," *TDNT* 5:311). See also D'Amato, *Arms and Armour of the Imperial Roman Soldier*, 56, 222–24.

[84] Josephus, referring to a Roman soldier in the precincts of the Jerusalem temple: "For as he had shoes [ὑποδήματα] all full of thick and sharp nails [ἥλοις], as had every one of the other soldiers, so when he ran on the pavement of the temple, he slipped, and fell down upon his back with a very great noise, which was made by his armor" (*Wars*, 6:85 [trans. Whiston, *The Works of Josephus*]).

[85] The genitive τοῦ εὐαγγελίου, "of the Gospel," may be taken as objective ("God provided the Gospel to us"), subjective ("the Gospel prepared us"), or even appositional ("the preparation that is the Gospel"). But the idea that it means "Christians must be ready to proclaim the Gospel of the peace of God" (Stoeckhardt, *Ephesians*, 258) is unsupportable from the grammar. Best, *Ephesians*, 599–600, carefully disposes of this interpretation. Thus, this phrase should not be understood as a call for Christians to *spread* the Gospel of peace, as preachers are mandated to do in Rom 10:15 (contra, e.g., Schnackenburg, *Ephesians*, 278). The Gospel of peace in the present context is not an offensive weapon, but a part of the defensive armor that enables Christians to stand firm in battle. In modern Greek ἑτοιμασία means "equipment," which is its implication here (BDAG, s.v. ἑτοιμασία); cf. LXX Nah 2:4 (ET 2:3). For ἑτοιμασία as God's "provision" (what he provides), see LXX Pss 9:38 (MT/ET 10:17); 64:10 (MT 65:10; ET 65:9).

[86] Ignatius, *To the Ephesians*, 13:2 (*ANF* 1:55).

[87] Chrysostom, *Homilies on Ephesians*, 24:6.14–17, ACCS 8:211.

6:16 ἐν πᾶσιν ἀναλαβόντες τὸν θυρεὸν τῆς πίστεως—The list of six articles of armor is divided in half by the phrase ἐν πᾶσιν, "among all," together with the recapitulation of the main verb ἀναλαμβάνω, "take up" (6:13), in the form of the fourth aorist participle of manner:[88] ἀναλαβόντες, "having taken up." The absolute expression ἐν πᾶσιν, "in all things," occurs frequently in the NT as a summary statement[89] and is typical of Ephesians (also 1:23; 4:6), which uses πᾶς, "all," more frequently than any other NT book save Colossians.[90] Although Paul does not include every conceivable piece of armor, the six he chooses constitute the main items of a πανοπλία, "*full* armor" (6:11, 13). Thus, rather than translating ἐν πᾶσιν as "beyond all these things, moreover,"[91] we suggest "among all these things,"[92] meaning that the shield is another part of the complete armament; indeed, the expression may highlight "faith" (πίστις) as the preeminent piece of armor, as a factor in using all the others, or, like the shield itself, as the piece that envelopes the Christian soldier.[93]

The noun θυρεός denotes a "long oblong shield" whose name derives from θύρα, "door."[94] Polybius describes the robust construction of this heavy defensive implement in the Roman panoply:

> … a large shield [θυρεός, *scutum*], the surface of which is curved outwards, its breadth two and a half feet, its length four feet—though there is also an extra sized shield in which these measures are increased by a palm's breadth. It consists of two layers of wood fastened together with bull's-hide glue; the outer surface of which is first covered with canvas, then with calf's skin, on the upper and lower edges it is bound with iron to resist the downward strokes of the sword, and the wear of resting upon the ground. Upon it also is fixed an iron boss, to resist the more formidable blows of stones and pikes, and of heavy missiles generally.[95]

---

[88] For the four aorist participles of manner in 6:14–16, see the second textual note on 6:14.

[89] 2 Cor 11:6; Phil 4:12; Col 1:18; 3:11; 1 Tim 3:11; 2 Tim 2:7; 4:5; Titus 2:9–10; Heb 13:18; 1 Pet 4:11.

[90] Paul employs πᾶς fifty-two times in Ephesians. As a percentage of the total number of words in the book, the occurrences in Ephesians are exceeded only by those in Colossians. See "The *Berakah* Prayer (1:3–14) as Prologue" in the commentary on 1:3–14.

[91] This translation is implied by the textual variant for ἐν πᾶσιν that has ἐπί plus the dative (cf. Col 3:14). See BDF, § 235 (3).

[92] Moule, *Idiom Book*, 78, suggests "*in the midst of everything*, i.e. *in all circumstances*" (Robertson, *Grammar*, 589, similarly); yet it seems simpler to seek the referent of πᾶσιν in the items of armor.

[93] Schlier, *Epheser*, 296: "In any case, faith appears as the indispensable weapon. … Faith is the presupposition of righteousness, of truth, of peace as manners of Christian existence."

[94] BDAG, s.v. θυρεός; A. Oepke, "θυρεός," *TDNT* 5:312. See also D'Amato, *Arms and Armour of the Imperial Roman Soldier*, 25–32, 49, 101–9, 184, 205–6.

[95] Polybius, *Histories*, 6:23 (trans. Shuckburgh, *The Histories of Polybius*, which includes the editorial insertion of Latin terms). See also the fuller quote of Polybius in "The Roman Soldier" in "Sources of Paul's Armor Imagery" in the commentary.

Though this is the only NT occurrence of the term, it is common in the LXX, where it often accompanies a term for a "spear."[96] Paul's inclusion of "shield" but not "spear" is another indication that he is concerned with *defensive* weaponry only.[97] This long shield that protects the whole body[98] in a defensive position must be distinguished from the more maneuverable "buckler," the small round shield that enables a soldier to attack with a long sword.[99] In the OT, ceremonial shields were made of bronze or gold,[100] but the working shield was made of wood.[101] Of all the weapons in this passage it is the shield that has the most deeply established figurative meaning in the OT: YHWH himself is his people's "shield."[102] So also is his "salvation" (2 Sam 22:36) and his "gracious favor" (Ps 5:13 [ET 5:12]). This may be the reason why in the LXX a shield is included only once among the items of God's own armor[103]—for he himself is the shield. Thus, the gift of the shield bestows divine strength on the Christian soldier: "on that day YHWH will shield [יָגֵן; LXX: ὑπερασπιεῖ] the inhabitants of Jerusalem so that the weakest among them on that day will be like David and the house of David will be like God, like the Angel of YHWH, [who goes] before them" (Zech 12:8). In light of this, πίστις, "faith," ought not be understood as something that the Christian contributes to the battle as a personal quality.[104] Whether Paul has in mind *fides qua creditur*

---

[96] See θυρεός in, e.g., LXX Judg 5:8 (B); 2 Kgdms 1:21 (MT/ET 2 Sam 1:21); 2 Chr 12:9; and with "spear" in LXX 1 Chr 12:9, 35 (ET 12:8, 34); 2 Chr 14:7 (ET 14:8); 25:5; 26:14; Neh 4:10 (ET 4:16); Ps 45:10 (MT 46:10; ET 46:9).

[97] In the OT, God could fire flaming missiles in attack (Deut 33:2; Pss 7:14 [ET 7:13]; 21:10 [ET 21:9]; Is 4:4; 66:15–16; cf. Heb 12:29), but here the Christian is only defended against them. The full armor does not include a bow and arrows nor a spear.

[98] Polybius, *Histories*, 2:30.2–3, remarks on the ineffectiveness of Gallic shields that were not quite large enough to protect the whole body from the Roman javelins raining down upon them.

[99] 2 Chr 23:9; Pss 35:2 (LXX 34:2); 91:4 (LXX 90:4); Jer 46:3 (LXX 26:3); Ezek 23:24; 38:4; 39:9. The distinction between צִנָּה as a "large shield" for the whole body and מָגֵן as a "small shield" is not always clear in the OT. The LXX usually translates צִנָּה with θυρεός, "long shield," and מָגֵן most often as ὅπλον, "weapon," but sometimes with other words, including ἀσπίς, "small round shield"; ὑπερασπιστής, "one holding up a round shield"; and πέλτη, "small leather shield." Josephus describes the distinction made among Roman soldiers: "Those footmen also that are chosen out of the rest to be around the general himself, have a lance [λόγχη] and a buckler [ἀσπίς, 'small round shield']; but the rest of the foot soldiers [φάλαγξ] have a spear [ξυστόν] and a long shield [θυρεός ἐπιμήκης]" (*Wars*, 3:95 [translation adapted from Whiston, *The Works of Josephus*]). The small round shield was also wielded by Roman cavalrymen; see D'Amato, *Arms and Armour of the Imperial Roman Soldier*, 49.

[100] Bronze: 1 Ki 14:27; 2 Chr 12:10. Gold: 2 Sam 8:7; 1 Ki 10:16–17; 14:26; 1 Chr 18:7; 2 Chr 9:15–16; 12:9.

[101] Thus, in Ezek 39:9 the shields can be burned up. Because ancient shields were made of perishable material, archaeologists have found none in Palestine. See *IDB* 4:824, § 4 a.

[102] See "shield" in, e.g., Gen 15:1; Deut 33:29; 2 Sam 22:3, 31; Pss 3:4 (ET 3:3); 5:13 (ET 5:12); 7:11 (ET 7:10); 18:3, 31 (ET 18:2, 30); 28:7; 33:20; 35:2; 59:12 (ET 59:11); 84:10, 12 (ET 84:9, 11); 115:9–11; 119:114; 144:2; Prov 2:7; 30:5.

[103] "He will take holiness as an invincible buckler" (λήμψεται ἀσπίδα ἀκαταμάχητον ὁσιότητα, Wis Sol 5:19)—note that this is the small round shield used in offensive action. God goes on the attack (Ps 35:1–2).

[104] Contra Lincoln, *Ephesians*, 449; but with A. Oepke, "θυρεός," *TDNT* 5:314; Schnackenburg, *Ephesians*, 278; Schlier, *Epheser*, 296. Barth, *Ephesians*, 2:773, goes so far as to equate the

or *fides quae creditur*—"faith" as trust in God or "the faith" as the body of Christian teaching (see the second textual note on 2:8)—what matters is that this crucial defense against the devil is a gift of God. "By (the) faith" he defends us and enables us to stand firm (Col 1:23). By faith the saints of old "extinguished the power of fire, escaped the edges of the sword, were made strong in weakness, became mighty in war, put foreign armies to flight" (Heb 11:32–34).

ἐν ᾧ δυνήσεσθε πάντα τὰ βέλη τοῦ πονηροῦ [τὰ] πεπυρωμένα σβέσαι—Because the long shield was typically made of wood, even if covered with layers of leather, an effective tactic practiced in Roman times was to dip arrows[105] in pitch, set them alight, and land them on the enemy's shield to set it ablaze in his hand.[106] If it penetrated the shield it might kill the soldier; if not, it at least forced him to throw the shield away and caused great panic in the ranks.[107] In defense against this tactic, soldiers would sometimes soak their shields in water overnight before a battle.[108] Inasmuch as an ordinary dry shield would not "extinguish … the flaming arrows of the evil one" (6:16).[109] Paul may have had this tactic in mind. If so, then it affirms the baptismal flavor of the passage. Soaked in this sacramental water, Christians are resistant to the devil's attacks.[110] Their baptismal forgiveness is a preemptive defense against his temptations to sin and accusations of wrongdoing. By being dipped in this baptismal water, they are given

---

shield with God's own faithfulness, which stands not in opposition to man's faith, but is its source and strength.

[105] The neuter noun βέλος, derived from βάλλω, could refer to any kind of projectile or missile that might be launched from a machine or catapult. The use of a shield in defense, however, suggests arrows, not siege engines.

[106] A. Oepke, "θυρεός," *TDNT* 5:314, n. 10. The OT also refers to fiery arrows or missiles (Ps 7:14 [ET 7:13]; Prov 26:18; LXX Job 41:21 [ET 41:29]). So also Thucydides, *History of the Peloponnesian War*, 2:75.5; Herodotus, *Histories*, 8:52; Livy, *History*, 21:8.10–12; Diodorus Siculus, *Bibliotheca historica*, 20:96; and Qumran, 1QH 2:25–26; 10:23–26.

[107] Livy, *History*, 21:8.12.

[108] Lincoln, *Ephesians*, 450, and Barth, *Ephesians*, 2:772, make this assertion on the basis of Thucydides, *History of the Peloponnesian War*, 2:75.5. That text describes a framework of wood with bricks behind it and covered with leather to protect workers from fiery arrows (πυρφόροις οἰστοῖς) during a siege. Unfortunately, it does not speak of soaking shields in water. Best, *Ephesians*, 601, also describes this tactic, but his classical references do not refer to it either. Whether the tactic is explicitly described in classical texts, it seems a likely practice. Josephus, *Wars*, 3:173, describes the use of fresh ox hides thrown over the wooden extensions to the Jerusalem walls during the Roman siege so that missiles other than rocks would slide off them "and the fire that was thrown would be quenched by the moisture that was in them" (trans. Whiston, *The Works of Josephus*).

[109] As A. Oepke, "θυρεός," *TDNT* 5:314, protests. σβέσαι is the aorist infinitive of σβέννυμι, "extinguish, put out" (BDAG, s.v. σβέννυμι, a); cf. "who through faith … *extinguished* the power of fire" (Heb 11:33–34); also Mt 12:20; 25:8; Mk 9:48.

[110] Cf. Luther's exclamation "I am baptized!" (LC 4:44). Chrysostom, *Baptismal Instructions*, 2:24, interprets 6:16 baptismally: "Next after this, in the full darkness of the night, he [the priest] strips off your robe and, as if he were going to lead you into heaven itself by the ritual, he causes your whole body to be anointed with that olive oil of the spirit, so that all your limbs may be fortified and unconquered by the darts which the adversary aims at you" (trans. Paul W. Harkins, *ACW* 31:52).

divine protection.[111] Though Paul does not elsewhere call the devil "the evil one," the title is common elsewhere in the NT.[112] The evil one's "flaming arrows" (6:16) may be identified with his deceitful "schemes" (6:11; cf. 4:14) and the ongoing work of his evil spiritual forces (6:12).

6:17 καὶ τὴν περικεφαλαίαν τοῦ σωτηρίου δέξασθε—In line with the passive imperative "be strengthened" (6:10), the middle imperative "let yourselves be clothed" (6:10), and the mild verb ἀναλαμβάνω, "take up" (6:13, 16), the passive meaning of the verb δέξασθε, "receive" (not "grasp"), ought to be noted.[113] The verb highlights the gift nature of the armor. The noun περικεφαλαία, "helmet," is common in the LXX in military texts;[114] in the NT it occurs only figuratively (also 1 Thess 5:8). As its etymology implies, it goes "around [περί] the head [κεφαλή]" to protect this vital part of the body (Roman helmets could include cheek and neck guards, sometimes masks or visors).[115]

When "helmet" is figurative, the item associated with it varies.[116] Here with σωτήριος,[117] "salvation," it would appear that Paul again[118] has God's own armor in mind: περιέθετο περικεφαλαίαν σωτηρίου ἐπὶ τῆς κεφαλῆς, "he put a *helmet of salvation* upon his head" (LXX Is 59:17; cf. Wis Sol 5:18). Likewise, in the OT God himself is frequently declared to be his people's "salvation."[119] In contrast to spiritualizing ten-

---

[111] On this divine protection, see "The Old Testament" in "Sources of Paul's Armor Imagery" in the commentary. Cf. the legend of Achilles being given divine protection by being dipped in the River Styx.

[112] Mt 13:19, 38; 1 Jn 2:13–14; 3:12; 5:18–19. A possible exception in Paul is 2 Thess 3:3, in which πονηροῦ may be either neuter, "evil," or masculine, "the evil one"; cf. Mt 5:37; 6:13 (the Seventh Petition of the Lord's Prayer); Jn 17:15.

[113] Though it is a middle deponent imperative, the underlying meaning of the verb is passive. See Voelz, *What Does This Mean?* 121–22, who contrasts δέχομαι, "receive," with κρατέω, "take, grasp," both of which are taxonomically subordinate to the general term λαμβάνω, "get"; see also Schnackenburg, *Ephesians*, 279, n. 36. Lincoln, *Ephesians*, 450, is wrong to claim that the earlier participles (see the second textual note on 6:14) had implied human cooperation prior to this verb's shift into the language of divine gift.

[114] 1 Sam 17:5, 38, 49; 2 Chr 26:14; Jer 26:4; Ezek 27:10; 38:4, 5; 1 Macc 6:35.

[115] See D'Amato, *Arms and Armour of the Imperial Roman Soldier*, 32–38, 49, 109–21, 158–59, 184–91. Roman helmets were generally made of bronze (33, 111), occasionally iron (35). Elaborate Greek-style helmets were adopted by Roman officers and elite soldiers as status symbols (36).

[116] In Wis Sol 5:18 the helmet is κρίσιν ἀνυπόκριτον, "impartial justice"; in 1 Thess 5:8 it is ἐλπίδα σωτηρίας, "the hope of salvation"; in Ignatius, *To Polycarp*, 6:2, it is "faith."

[117] The usual NT term for "salvation" is the feminine noun σωτηρία. Note that in the present verse we have the neuter form of the adjective σωτήριος used as a noun, τὸ σωτήριον, literally, "the saving thing." This neuter usage appears elsewhere in the NT only in Lk 2:30; 3:6; Acts 28:28, but is common in the LXX (136 times). See Moule, *Idiom Book*, 96; Turner, *Syntax*, 14. As Eph 6:17 is the sole Pauline usage of the substantivized neuter form, it probably derives from the LXX reference (Is 59:17). Paul uses σωτήριος only one other time, as a feminine adjective in Titus 2:11.

[118] See also the fourth textual note on 6:14 and "The Old Testament" in "Sources of Paul's Armor Imagery" in the commentary. This is the fourth time Paul has made a major allusion to a passage of Isaiah in these verses (previously, to Is 11:5 and Is 59:17 in Eph 6:14 and to Is 52:7 in Eph 6:15).

[119] See, e.g., σωτηρία, "salvation," in LXX Pss 17:3 (MT 18:3; ET 18:2), 47 (MT 18:47; ET 18:46); 34:3 (MT/ET 35:3); 36:39 (MT/ET 37:39); Is 33:2, 6; 45:17; 46:13; Jer 3:23; τὸ

dencies in modern Christianity's use of the term, in biblical usage the implication of σωτηρία is "deliverance from danger or death";[120] this implies a salvation that applies to both body and soul. In the context of battle this means a safe outcome for the Christian. But while in 1 Thess 5:8 the helmet is the *"hope* of salvation," Ephesians speaks of a salvation that has already been accomplished and bestowed, for the baptized are already in a saved condition (ἐστε σεσῳσμένοι, 2:8). The "helmet of salvation" means that one leads surely and certainly to the other: because Christians have *already* died, risen, and ascended with Christ in Holy Baptism, the outcome of the battle for them is assured: Christ will return on the Last Day to raise their bodies and rescue them from the battle.

καὶ τὴν μάχαιραν τοῦ πνεύματος, ὅ ἐστιν ῥῆμα θεοῦ—The final element of the baptismal armor, "the sword of the Spirit," has so captured Christian imagination that it serves as the motto for St. Paul in Christian art: *Spiritus gladius*. The sword is often explained as the only piece of offensive weaponry in the list,[121] though this assertion calls for some scrutiny. In the Greek Bible there are two common nouns for "sword": ῥομφαία and μάχαιρα. The former (not used in Ephesians) is the "large and broad sword" originally used by non-Greek peoples (barbarians).[122] It is the common LXX translation for חֶרֶב, especially when a great weapon is in mind.[123] This is an offensive weapon, designed to be swung at the enemy in an aggressive attack. Figuratively, this sword often represents the Lord's judgment.[124] By corollary, the Lord takes up the sword to win victory for his people by destroying their enemies (Pss 17:13; 35:3). When the

---

σωτήριον, "salvation," in LXX Pss 9:15 (ET 9:14); 19:6 (MT 20:6; ET 20:5); 20:2, 6 (MT 21:2, 6; ET 21:1, 5); 69:5 (MT 70:5; ET 70:4); Is 51:5–6; and σωτήρ, "Savior," in LXX Ps 64:6 (MT 65:6; ET 65:5); Is 17:10; 62:11.

[120] See BDAG, s.v. σωτηρία, 1. See σωτηρία and cognate words in Rom 5:9; 10:9–10, 13; 13:11; Phil 2:12; 1 Thess 5:9; cf. LXX Joel 3:5 (ET 2:32); Mt 10:22; Heb 9:28; 1 Pet 1:5.

[121] E.g., Lincoln, *Ephesians*, 451; Stoeckhardt, *Ephesians*, 262–63; Arnold, *Power and Magic*, 120–21. Luther likewise:

> This [the sword of the Spirit] is the last, but it is the strongest and the right weapon for smiting the devil and overcoming him. For it is not enough to have defended ourselves against the enemy, and to be able to stand against him when he attacks us, so that we are not defeated; that is called defence. We must also be able to take the offensive—that is, to pursue the enemy, and put him to flight. Similarly, here it is not enough to ward off the devil with faith and hope as our shield and helmet, but we must draw the sword, hit back at him, hunt him down, and make him flee, thus gaining the victory for ourselves. And that sword, he says, is the Word of God. ("Sermon on the Christians' Armor and Weapons, Ephesians 6:10–17," October 20, 1532, *Day by Day We Magnify Thee*, 387; StL 9:855; WA 34/2:405)

[122] BDAG, s.v. ῥομφαία. Plutarch, *Aemilius Paulus*, 18:3, describes fearsome Thracians advancing with "heavy iron-headed swords [ῥομφαῖαι]" on their right shoulders.

[123] E.g., the cherub's flaming sword (Gen 3:24); the Angel of YHWH's sword (Num 22:23; Josh 5:13; 1 Chr 21:12, 16, 27, 30; cf. Susannah 59); the instrument for executing enemies of God and his people (Ex 32:27; Josh 6:21; 8:24); Gideon's sword (Judg 7:14); Goliath's sword (1 Sam 17:51); cf. Joshua's sword (Sirach 46:2); Judas Maccabeus' sword (1 Macc 3:3). ῥομφαία appears 236 times in the LXX.

[124] See especially Ezekiel 21. See also, e.g., Ex 5:3; 22:23 (ET 22:24); Is 27:1; 34:5–6; cf. Gen 3:24; 2 Chr 20:9; Ezra 9:7; Pss 7:13 (ET 7:12); 78:62; Is 49:2; 66:16; Jer 43:11; 44:13; Lam 2:21; Ezek 5:2, 17; 14:17, 21; Hos 14:1 (ET 13:16); Amos 4:10; 7:9; 9:4, 10; Judith 8:19; 11:10; 1 Macc 9:73; 2 Macc 15:16; Sirach 26:28; 39:30; passim.

Lord fights for Israel, he declares that victory is attained "not by *your* sword or by *your* bow" (Josh 24:12).[125] In the LXX the great sword, the offensive weapon, is thus a central component of God's own weaponry: "he will sharpen severe wrath for a sword [ὀργὴν εἰς ῥομφαίαν]" (Wis Sol 5:20). In Revelation the Son of Man is pictured figuratively with this long sword proceeding from his mouth (Rev 1:16; 2:12),[126] by which he wages war and executes judgment like YHWH and his Angel (Rev 2:16; 19:15, 21; cf. Rev 6:8). The same vision connects the Son of Man with the Word of God (Rev 19:13), thus continuing the OT image by which a sword proceeding from the mouth represents God's Word.[127] It is instructive that, with one exception (Lk 2:35), the ῥομφαία ("long sword") in the NT is always the sword by which God wages war.

The distinction between ῥομφαία and the term in Eph 6:17, μάχαιρα, is not always clear (the LXX can use either one to translate חֶרֶב),[128] and μάχαιρα is frequently used as an offensive weapon of war, including in contexts of God's wrath and victory.[129] However, the LXX often uses μάχαιρα for a smaller weapon or tool, a "short sword," dagger, or knife (sometimes for מַאֲכֶלֶת).[130]

The safest conclusion is that, though the LXX does not carefully distinguish between ῥομφαία and μάχαιρα, the latter (the term in Eph 6:17) *can* be used of a smaller tool or weapon, while the former *cannot*. This corresponds to classical usage[131] and to a distinction made by Josephus with reference to long and short swords in Roman

---

[125] Cf. Pss 44:4 (ET 44:3); 45:4 (ET 45:3); Hos 1:7.

[126] The LXX is inconsistent again by rendering the sword proceeding from the Servant of YHWH's mouth with μάχαιρα in Is 49:2. This passage and Is 11:4 form the basis of the imagery in Revelation, to which Paul likely alludes here and in 2 Thess 2:8.

[127] The imagery of a sword representing words or breath is common: Word of God: Is 49:2; Hos 6:5; Wis Sol 18:15–16; Heb 4:12; words of men: Ps 56:5 (LXX [MT 57:5; ET 57:4]); Prov 5:3–4; 12:18; 25:18. A midrash on Ps 45:4 (ET 45:3), "gird your sword on your thigh," suggests that the sword is the Torah (Str-B, 3:618, 687–88).

[128] Note the use of both translations for חֶרֶב to refer to the Angel of YHWH's sword in the very same narrative context (Num 22:23, 31). Compare also Judg 19:29 in Codex Alexandrinus and the remaining manuscript tradition, each choosing a different Greek word. Likewise, compare the sword of Goliath: ῥομφαία in LXX 1 Kgdms 17:51 (MT/ET 1 Sam 17:51) and μάχαιρα in LXX Ps 151:7. And note the choice of μάχαιρα for חֶרֶב and τομίς, "knife," for מַאֲכֶלֶת when the two appear together (LXX Prov 30:14).

[129] E.g., "the sword of the LORD" (LXX Is 34:5–6); the sword of the Angel of the LORD (LXX Num 22:31); cf. LXX Gen 31:26; 34:25; 48:22; Ex 15:9; 22:23 (ET 22:24); Lev 26:25; Deut 32:41; passim. Note also the use of τὸ ἐγχειρίδιον, "dagger," for God's sword (LXX Ezek 21:8 [ET 21:3]).

[130] Abraham's dagger (LXX Gen 22:6); flint knives (LXX Josh 5:2–3); Ehud's short sword (LXX Judg 3:16); a household knife (LXX Judg 19:29 [Alexandrinus]); a sword concealed in Joab's hand (LXX 2 Kgdms 20:10 [MT/ET 2 Sam 20:10]).

[131] "μάχαιρα ... is very common from the time of Hom[er], first in the sense of 'knife.' ... As a weapon from the time of Hdt. [Herodotus]: 'small sword,' to be distinguished from the sword proper (ἡ ῥομφαία) 'dagger,' 'sabre' " (W. Michaelis, "μάχαιρα," *TDNT* 4:524).

weaponry[132] and so may represent a common distinction in Paul's day.[133] The "short sword" (Latin: *gladius*) that was the normal weapon of a Roman soldier corresponds to the Greek term μάχαιρα; it was used for both offensive and defensive purposes in close fighting.[134] In the NT some occurrences of μάχαιρα refer to a soldier's weapon; but the possession of the instrument by ordinary people implies a small weapon.[135] In the present context of defensive weaponry, it is therefore likely that Paul chose μάχαιρα because he had in mind a "short sword" used primarily for close battle,[136] to parry the blows of an advancing opponent.[137] Just as Christ defended himself from Satan with the Word of God (Mt 4:1–11), so also it is the Christian's defense.[138] For we know that God has already used the Word to defeat the devil.[139]

---

[132] "The footmen are armed with breastplates [θώρακες] and headpieces [κράνη], and have swords [μαχαιροφοροῦντες] on each side; but the sword [ξίφος] which is upon their left side is much longer than the other, for that on the right side is not longer than about nine inches [σπιθαμή, 'handspan']" (Josephus, *Wars*, 3:93–94 [translation adapted from Whiston, *The Works of Josephus*]).

[133] Thus, BDAG, s.v. μάχαιρα, 1, gives the definition "a relatively short sword or other sharp instrument, *sword*, *dagger*." LSJM offers similar definitions for classical usage (e.g., Herodotus, *Histories*, 6:75; Xenophon, *On the Art of Horsemanship*, 12:11; Xenophon, *Hellenica*, 3:3.7).

[134] See D'Amato, *Arms and Armour of the Imperial Roman Soldier*, 12–20, 80–97, 153–56. The cavalryman's sword, primarily an offensive weapon, was necessarily longer (49, 182–83), so also the sword of the auxiliaries (153). The longer sword was traditionally associated with barbarians, though Roman troops at the far reaches of the empire sometimes borrowed them and by the second century AD they came into general use (87–88).

[135] Mt 26:47–55; Lk 22:36, 38, 49; Jn 18:10–11.

[136] E.g., Xenophon, *Cyropaedia*, 1:2.13:

But if it is necessary to make a military expedition anywhere, those who have been thus educated take the field, no longer with bow and arrows, nor yet with spears, but with what are termed "weapons for close conflict"—a corselet about their breast, a round shield upon their left arm (such as Persians are represented with in art), and in their right hands a sabre [μάχαιρα] or bill [κοπίς, "curved knife"]. (Trans. Walter Miller, LCL)

[137] E.g., "In that place they [the Hellenes] defended themselves with swords [ἀλεξομένους μαχαίρῃσι], if they still had them, and with hands and teeth" (Herodotus, *Histories*, 7:225.3).

[138] The Jewish philosopher Philo, *On Dreams*, 1:103, 108, recognized the power of speech in general as a defensive weapon given by God to all people:

In much the same manner, speech [λόγος] has been given to man by God, as the most excellent of gifts; for in the first place, it is a defensive weapon [ὅπλον ἀμυντήριον] against those who would attack him with innovations. For as nature has fortified all other animals with their own appropriate and peculiar means of defence, by which they are able to repel those who attempt to injure them, so also has it bestowed upon man that greatest defence and most impregnable protection of speech, with which, as with a panoply [πανοπλία], every one who is completely clothed, will have a domestic and most appropriate bodyguard; and employing it as a champion, will be able to ward off all the injuries which can be brought against him by his enemies. …

For, as neighing is the peculiar attribute of a horse, … so also is speaking, and speech itself, the peculiar property of man: for this is what man has received above all other animals as his peculiar gift, as a protection [ἔρυμα], a bulwark [περίβλημα], and panoply [πανοπλία], and wall of defence [τεῖχος]; he being, of all living creatures, the most beloved by God. (Trans. Yonge, *The Works of Philo*)

[139] Luther: "One little word can fell him [the devil]" (*LSB* 656:3).

Note that while some previous genitives in this pericope have been appositional (e.g., "the helmet *of salvation*" in 6:17 means "salvation *is* the helmet"), "the sword *of the Spirit*" does not mean that the Spirit *is* the sword. Paul identifies the sword with the ῥῆμα θεοῦ, "Word of God," suggesting that the genitive τοῦ πνεύματος, "of the Spirit," is *qualitative*: the sword is given its effectiveness, its "cutting edge," by the Spirit,[140] with whom God's Word is intimately bound.[141] The ῥῆμα θεοῦ, "Word of God," is that Gospel word (Rom 10:8; 1 Pet 1:25) by which the soldier in the church has been baptized (Eph 5:26) and granted faith in Christ by the Spirit (Eph 1:13; cf. Rom 10:17).[142]

Commentary

Structure and Rhetoric

Epilogue/*Peroratio*

While the adverbial expression τοῦ λοιποῦ, "finally" (6:10), does not always mark the conclusion of an epistle, at this point in Ephesians, this is clearly its function (see the first textual note on 6:10). Paul has completed his positive arguments or "proofs" (2:1–4:16) and his refutations of the counter-arguments (4:17–6:9).[143] In the course of these refutations, he has developed a thorough, positive assessment of the Gospel's impact on the relationships in which Christians find themselves (5:21–6:9). Now, rather than introducing a new argument or treating an additional topic, he draws the epistle to a grand conclusion (6:10–17). In classical rhetorical terms this is his *peroratio* or epilogue, the summation of the oration. (The formal epistolary conclusion follows in 6:18–24.)

Rhetoric is primarily the art of public *speaking*, and evidence of its impact on NT documents reminds us that they were meant to be read aloud.[144] George Kennedy has shown that many recorded sermons or speeches in the NT display rhetorical arrangement, frequently concluding with an epilogue.[145] Paul's epistles, originally meant to be proclaimed in the liturgy to the gathered

---

[140] Lincoln, *Ephesians*, 451. Schlier, *Epheser*, 298, calls it a "genitive of quality and author [source]." The neuter relative pronoun in the clause ὅ ἐστιν, "which is," does not mean that the *Spirit* (neuter, τὸ πνεῦμα) is the Word of God, but refers in a general way to the preceding phrase, "the sword of the Spirit" (even though μάχαιρα is feminine; cf., e.g., Eph 5:5; Col 3:14; 2 Thess 3:17). See BDF, § 132 (2); Burton, *Moods and Tenses*, § 295. It is possible that the pronoun ὅ is neuter by attraction to the predicate noun ῥῆμα (see BDF, § 132 [2]), but since ὅ ἐστιν is a formulaic expression in Koine Greek, this explanation is unnecessary.

[141] 2 Sam 23:2; Jn 3:34; 6:63; Acts 4:31; 10:44; 16:6; 1 Cor 2:4, 13; Eph 1:13; 1 Thess 1:5–6; Heb 6:4–5.

[142] A distinction between the noun for "word" here, ῥῆμα (68 times in the NT), and the more common noun λόγος (330 times) ought not be stressed; a comparison of the present text with, e.g., LXX Is 11:4; Mt 4:4; Lk 3:2; Jn 8:47; Heb 4:12; 6:5; 11:3 suggests the terms are interchangeable.

[143] See "Proofs" and "Refutations" in "Structure and Rhetoric" in the introduction.

[144] See "Orality and the Interpretation of the Epistles: A Brief Introduction" in the introduction.

[145] Throughout *New Testament Interpretation through Rhetorical Criticism*, Kennedy notes epilogues in speeches: Mt 7:21–27 (the Sermon on the Mount); Jn 14:25–31; 16:29–33 (portions of the Farewell Discourse); Acts 3:26; 7:54–56; 13:38–39; 19:40; 20:32–35 (among the

congregation,[146] show similar oral rhetorical patterning. Epilogues appear at the conclusion of briefer units within his epistles[147] and frequently can be discerned at the close of a letter.[148] Many of these epilogues contain substantial parallels to 6:10–17 in form and content. See, for example, the following:

- "stand firm in the Lord" (στήκετε ἐν κυρίῳ, Phil 4:1)
- "finally, brothers" (τὸ λοιπόν, ἀδελφοί, Phil 4:8; cf. 2 Cor 13:11; 2 Thess 3:1)
- "fight the good fight of the faith" (ἀγωνίζου τὸν καλὸν ἀγῶνα τῆς πίστεως, 1 Tim 6:12; cf. 2 Tim 4:1–8)

Chrysostom comments: "This is the rhetoric Paul always employs when he is about to conclude his discourse."[149]

Aristotle describes most succinctly what was expected: "The epilogue is composed of four parts: to dispose the hearer favorably towards oneself [the speaker] and unfavorably towards the adversary; to amplify [the arguments pro] and depreciate [the arguments con]; to excite the emotions of the hearer; to recapitulate."[150] This penultimate pericope of Ephesians (6:10–17) does not (and should not be expected to) execute all four functions in equal measure.[151] The epilogue could vary according to the situation or the rhetorical tradition:

> At the end of a speech there is commonly an epilogue; in classical theory its primary functions are to recapitulate the points the speaker has made and to arouse the emotions of the audience toward action, but in a short speech recapitulation may not be necessary and a coolly rational summary may be inimical to the orator's objective. Greek oratory, as seen for example in the speeches of Demosthenes, tends to reach its emotional climax near the

---

speeches of Acts). (See Kennedy, 49, 82, 84, 119, 122, 125, 132, 133.) Acts 20:32–35, as it comes from a speech of Paul to the Ephesian pastors, is a highly relevant example.

[146] See "Liturgical Context" in "Evaluation of the Case" in "Authorship" in the introduction, as well as "The Liturgical Context of the New Testament Epistles" in "Orality and the Interpretation of the Epistles: A Brief Introduction" in the introduction. See also "The Liturgy of the Spirit-Filled Baptized" in the commentary on 5:15–21.

[147] E.g., 1 Cor 12:27–31; 13:13; 15:51–58 (epilogues to those chapters); 2 Cor 7:2–16 (epilogue to the first part of the letter). The use of "finally" at an earlier point in an epistle may mark such an epilogue, or it may introduce the final topic in a series of proofs (Phil 3:1; 1 Thess 4:1).

[148] E.g., Rom 15:14–33; Gal 6:11–18; Phil 4:1–20; 1 Thess 5:12–24; 2 Thess 3:1–16; 1 Tim 6:11–16; 2 Tim 4:1–8; Philemon 17–22. The precise limits of these epilogues are often debatable, and often the formal elements of a letter are confused (quite understandably) with the rhetorical functions of its concluding sections. Jewett, "Following the Argument of Romans," identifies Rom 15:14–16:27 as the epilogue, thus including the formal epistolary conclusion. In analyzing the conclusion of Philippians (4:1–20), Davis, *Oral Biblical Criticism*, 133–38, mixes content categories (e.g., "Paraenesis") with formal epistolary categories (e.g., "Pseudo-Thanksgiving") and fails to identify the rhetorical function of the section as an epilogue.

[149] Chrysostom, *Homilies on Ephesians*, 22:6.10, ACCS 8:207.

[150] Aristotle, *Rhetoric*, 3:19.1 (trans. John Henry Freese, LCL).

[151] Lincoln, *Ephesians*, 432: "There is no particular reason why *all* these factors should be found in this conclusion, but they can provide a convenient point of comparison, and the writer does appear to have fashioned his own version of them."

middle of a speech and end quietly and thoughtfully; Roman oratory, as seen in Cicero, is more often passionate at the end.[152]

At the close of Ephesians we do not find a "coolly rational summary" of the facts, but a passionate exhortation designed to stir up the listeners' faith.[153] Paul's epilogue begins with a warning that exposes the very real danger posed by the evil spiritual forces arrayed against the Ephesians.[154] The chief message, however, is not fear, but comfort.[155] Paul proclaims the consequences of Christ's victory (so richly detailed earlier in the letter) and encourages the Ephesians to believe that they are well protected against the enemy's assaults when they are enveloped in the baptismal armor of the Divine Warrior, Christ.

The battle imagery is the clearest reminder that this epilogue is not akin to the closing arguments of a defense attorney. It is far more like the epideictic rhetoric of a general exhorting his troops before they go into battle. This is a kind of speech well illustrated in classical literature;[156] but it differs to the extent that the speaker believes the victory has quite literally already been won. For God is the true Warrior, and his troops must not believe that they can conquer the enemy by their own strength (see OT examples below). Thus, while the battle imagery and the depiction of the enemy's evil strength lend tension and urgency to the epilogue, this general's speech offers ultimate *comfort* to his troops. Whether Paul was aware of the rhetoric of the Qumran War Scroll or not, he might well have approved of its eschatological language:

> Then the High Priest shall rise, with the [Priests], his brethren, and the Levites, and all the men of the army, and he shall recite aloud the Prayer in Time of War [written in the Book] of the Rule concerning this time, and also all their Hymns. He shall marshal all the formations there, as is [written in the Book of War], and the priest appointed for the Day of Revenge by the voice of all

---

[152] Kennedy, *New Testament Interpretation through Rhetorical Criticism*, 48. Cf. Quintilian, *Institutio oratoria*, 6:1.1: "There are two kinds of peroration, for it may deal either with facts or with the emotional aspect of the case" (trans. Harold Edgeworth Butler, LCL).

[153] Although Paul is not seeking applause, Quintilian's description of the epilogue is close to the mark: "It is at the close of our drama that we must really stir the theatre, when we have reached the place for the phrase with which the old tragedies and comedies used to end, 'Friends, give us your applause'" (*Institutio oratoria*, 6:2.52 [trans. Harold Edgeworth Butler, LCL]).

[154] Luther: "Christ has indeed conquered [him]. But this enemy is not to be despised, for he is the prince of this world and has powerful princes in the world on his side" ("Sermon for the Twenty-first Sunday after Trinity," October 25, 1545, AE 58:306; WA 51:70).

[155] Schnackenburg, *Ephesians*, 270:

> The insertion of the battle-metaphor [into the structure of Ephesians] is in keeping with his endeavour to immunize his Christian readers against the influences of their pagan environment and to activate them to a more determined realization of a Christian existence. For this it is necessary to hold before their eyes the ever-present danger to their salvation but also to remind them of God's power effective in them.

[156] E.g., Thucydides, *History of the Peloponnesian War*, 2:89; Xenophon, *Cyropaedia*, 1:5; Polybius, *Histories*, 3:63 (see more examples in Lincoln, *Ephesians*, 433). Lincoln describes the rhetorical features of these speeches and in comparison notes about Eph 6:10–17, "this battle speech has rhetorical force but is restrained rather than overindulgent" (434).

his brethren shall go forward to strengthen the [hearts of the fighting men]. Speaking, he shall say:

Be strong and valiant; be warriors! Fear not! Do not be [confused and do not let your hearts be afraid!] Do not be fearful; fear them not! Do not fall back … for they are a congregation of wickedness and all their works are in Darkness; they tend towards Darkness. …

[Be brave and] strong for the battle of God! For this day is [the time of the battle of] God against all the host of Belial, [and of the judgment of] all flesh. The God of Israel lifts His hand in His marvellous [might] against all the spirits of wickedness. [The hosts of] the warrior "gods" gird themselves for battle, [and the] formations of the Holy Ones [prepare themselves], for the Day [of Revenge] … XVI … For the God of Israel has called out the sword against all the nations, and He will do mighty deeds by the saints of His people.[157]

Luther is attuned to this rhetoric as he preaches on the text:

And he [Paul] acts like a pious and true field marshal, who gives a battlefield speech to his people who are arranged in battle formation and admonishes them to stand fast and to defend themselves boldly and confidently; so it may well be called an army speech [*Heerpredigt*] for Christians. For he shows here that those who are baptized into Christ and would cling to him must and should be warriors and must always be armed with their weapons and armor, and that the Christian estate is not an idle estate, nor an estate of peace and security, but that it is a matter of always being on the field of battle and waging war, and applying one's whole self to it.[158]

Preaching on another great NT battle text, Luther places such a speech into the mouth of Christ, who stands on the battle plain with his troops:

Therefore he [Christ] here warns and musters his soldiers, saying, "You are in my army and under my flag; see to it that you are on the look-out for the enemy, ready to defend yourselves against his angels, for he is never far away from you." As long as you do that, you need have no fear. For we belong to a Lord who has angels Himself and power enough, and is called the Lord of hosts and the true victor over the dragon, and He stands by us, even fights for us, so that the devil and all his angels will fall down and be cast out. For the Word of the Lord abides for ever.[159]

Nevertheless, Paul's epilogue to Ephesians is not merely "rhetoric" (in the modern and historically inaccurate sense of the term). He not only builds up the Ephesians' courage and strengthens their faith with his brilliant peroration, but he also recapitulates the major teachings of the epistle:

---

[157] 1QM 15:4–16:3 (trans. Vermes, *The Complete Dead Sea Scrolls in English*; the bracketed material and most of the ellipses are in Vermes).

[158] Luther, "Sermon on the Christians' Armor and Weapons, Ephesians 6:10–17," October 20, 1532, StL 9:812; WA 34/2:372.

[159] Luther, "Sermon for the Feast of St. Michael, Revelation 12:7–12," September 29, 1544, *Day by Day We Magnify Thee*, 381; WA 49:583–84.

Ephesians 6:10–17	Body of Ephesians
ἐνδυναμοῦσθε … ἐν τῷ κράτει τῆς ἰσχύος αὐτοῦ, "be strengthened … in his mighty strength" (6:10)	"what is the surpassing greatness of his power [δύναμις] for us who believe, according to the working of his mighty strength [τοῦ κράτους τῆς ἰσχύος αὐτοῦ]" (1:19; cf. 3:7, 16, 20)
ἐν κυρίῳ, "in the Lord" (6:10)	ἐν Χριστῷ, "in Christ" (1:1, 3 and passim); ἐν αὐτῷ, "in him" (1:4 and passim); ἐν (τῷ) κυρίῳ, "in the Lord" (1:15; 2:21; 4:1, 17; 5:8; 6:1, 21)
ἐνδύσασθε, "let yourselves be clothed" (6:11); ἐνδυσάμενοι, "having clothed yourselves" (6:14)	ἐνδύσασθαι τὸν καινὸν ἄνθρωπον, "that you have put on the new man" (4:24; cf. 2:15; 3:16; 4:22)
τὰς μεθοδείας τοῦ διαβόλου, "the devil's schemes" (6:11)	τὴν μεθοδείαν τῆς πλάνης, "deceitful scheming" (4:14)
πρὸς τὰς ἀρχάς, πρὸς τὰς ἐξουσίας … ἐν τοῖς ἐπουρανίοις, "against the rulers, against the authorities … in the heavenly places" (6:12)	ἐν τοῖς ἐπουρανίοις ὑπεράνω πάσης ἀρχῆς καὶ ἐξουσίας καὶ δυνάμεως καὶ κυριότητος, "in the heavenly places, far above every ruler and authority and power and lordship" (1:20–21; cf. 1:3, 20; 2:6; 3:10)
πρὸς τοὺς κοσμοκράτορας τοῦ σκότους τούτου, "against the world powers of this darkness" (6:12)	κατὰ τὸν αἰῶνα τοῦ κόσμου τούτου, "according to the age of this world" (2:2); ἐσκοτωμένοι τῇ διανοίᾳ ὄντες, "being darkened in their understanding" (4:18; cf. 5:8, 11–12)
τὰ πνευματικὰ τῆς πονηρίας, "the spiritual forces of evil" (6:12); ἐν τῇ ἡμέρᾳ τῇ πονηρᾷ, "in the evil day" (6:13); τὰ βέλη τοῦ πονηροῦ [τὰ] πεπυρωμένα, "the flaming arrows of the evil one" (6:16)	αἱ ἡμέραι πονηραί εἰσιν, "the days are evil" (5:16)
ἐνδύσασθε τὴν πανοπλίαν τοῦ θεοῦ, "let yourselves be clothed with the full armor of God" (6:11); ἀναλάβετε τὴν πανοπλίαν τοῦ θεοῦ, "take up the full armor of God" (6:13)	τὸν καταρτισμὸν τῶν ἁγίων, "the outfitting of the saints" (4:12)
περιζωσάμενοι τὴν ὀσφὺν ὑμῶν ἐν ἀληθείᾳ, "having belted your waist with truth" (6:14); ἐνδυσάμενοι τὸν θώρακα τῆς δικαιοσύνης, "having clothed yourselves with the breastplate of righteousness" (6:14)	ἐστιν ἀλήθεια ἐν τῷ Ἰησοῦ, "the truth is in Jesus" (4:21); τὸν κατὰ θεὸν κτισθέντα ἐν δικαιοσύνῃ καὶ ὁσιότητι τῆς ἀληθείας, "created according to God's [likeness] in true righteousness and holiness" (4:24; cf. 4:25; 5:9)

Ephesians 6:10–17	**Body of Ephesians**
τοῦ εὐαγγελίου τῆς εἰρήνης, "the Gospel of peace" (6:15)	εὐηγγελίσατο εἰρήνην, "he proclaimed the Gospel of peace" (2:17; cf. 1:2; 2:14–15; 4:3)
τὸν θυρεὸν τῆς πίστεως, "the shield of faith" (6:16)	τῇ γὰρ χάριτί ἐστε σεσῳσμένοι διὰ πίστεως, "for by grace you have been saved through faith" (2:8; cf. 1:15; 3:12, 17; 4:5, 13)
τὴν περικεφαλαίαν τοῦ σωτηρίου, "the helmet of salvation" (6:17)	χάριτί ἐστε σεσῳσμένοι, "by grace you have been saved" (2:5; cf. 1:13; 2:8; 5:23)
τὴν μάχαιραν τοῦ πνεύματος, "the short sword of the Spirit" (6:17)	πνεῦμα σοφίας, "the Spirit of wisdom" (1:17; cf. 1:13; 2:18, 22; 3:5, 16; 4:3–4, 30; 5:18)
ὅ ἐστιν ῥῆμα θεοῦ, "which is the Word of God" (6:17)	τῷ λουτρῷ τοῦ ὕδατος ἐν ῥήματι, "with the washing of water in the Word" (5:26; cf. 1:13)

Paul thus reaches far back into his letter, roaming far and wide[160] in his earlier teaching to construct the armor of God from the elements he has been carefully assembling. The pieces of armor do not arise out of the blue; but, as they allude to the letter's prior argumentation, they remind the hearers of what they have been taught and help them apply the teaching to their present situation in the spiritual battle.

Outline and Limits of the Pericope

The pericope appears to fall into two sections:

1. The first half (6:10–13) describes the gift of armor in general terms and exposes the true nature of the great spiritual battle that requires the Christian to be so well defended.
2. The second half (6:14–17) pursues the allegorical details of the armor, identifying the gifts of God in Christ that constitute the Christian's protection in the battle.

The midpoint of the pericope is marked by the repetition of the verb ἵστημι, "stand," which appears at the end of 6:13 (στῆναι, "to stand [firm]") and again

---

[160] The chart of evidence demonstrates that Best is quite wrong to presume Paul draws only on the first half of the letter: "If this is the letter's *peroratio* we should see it then in the light of 1.3–3.21 rather than of 4.1–6.9, for it does not exhort readers to fight against dishonesty or sexual indulgence but returns to the supernatural nature of Christian existence as set out in 1.3–3.21" (*Ephesians*, 585). Best's error lies more deeply in his presumption that the "ethical" half of the letter (chapters 4–6) has no real connection to its "doctrinal" half (chapters 1–3). He fails to see that "dishonesty" and "sexual indulgence" are spiritual problems related to the hostile attacks of the evil one.

at the beginning of 6:14 (στῆτε οὖν, "stand, therefore"). The emphatic repetition of this verb highlights "stand!" as the pericope's central thought.[161]

The first half (6:10–13) is further marked out by the chiastic repetition of the exhortation to put on the armor (6:11, 13). In our opinion, the first half of the pericope describes the entire battle from beginning to end, with the final verb στῆναι, "to stand [firm]" (6:13), referring to the soldier's standing victoriously at the end of the battle on the Last Day; then Paul returns to the details of the armor in the second half of the unit. Some commentators see this "standing" (6:13) as the result of the outfitting *before* battle.[162] While this interpretation is unobjectionable, it seems rhetorically weak for Paul to refer three times to the act of standing *before* battle; his encouragement is far stronger if he can point his hearers to the image of their sure and certain victory at the end of the day.

In the second half of the pericope, Paul describes six pieces of armor. While the inclusion of prayer (6:18) would bring the number to a round, Spiritual seven, there are stronger arguments against including prayer in the armor (see below). The first three pieces of armor are grouped together grammatically by the use of Greek participles joined by καί, "and." They refer to the foundational garments of belt, breastplate, and boots ("belted ... breastplate ... shod," 6:14–15). The phrase "among all these things" (ἐν πᾶσιν at the beginning of 6:16) then breaks the sequence before the addition of the "shield," which is the first item to be given a more elaborate allegorical explanation: "with which you will be able to extinguish all the flaming arrows of the evil one" (6:16). The final two elements are connected to the imperative δέξασθε, "receive" (6:17). "The helmet of salvation" (6:17), like the first three items in the list, is given a simple allegorical identification. The final element, "the short sword of the Spirit," is, like the shield, given an extended description as "the Word of God" (6:17). These irregularities in the list could be interpreted to mean that "the shield of faith" and "the sword of the Spirit" held particular significance in Paul's mind.

There is at least one significant argument in favor of extending the pericope's limits to 6:20 and including prayer as a seventh piece of armor—the interpretation taken by most commentators on Ephesians. For 6:18–20 is indeed *grammatically* dependent on what precedes; it contains no main verb, but is (apparently) subordinated to the preceding by the participle προσευχόμενοι, "praying."[163] Certainly the repetition of "Spirit" in 6:17 and 6:18 ties the sections together.

---

[161] The verb ἵστημι, "to stand," occurs in 6:11, 13, 14, and the related compound verb ἀνθίστημι, "to withstand," appears in 6:13. Since these are the only instances of these verbs in the whole of Ephesians, their concentration here emphatically conveys the pericope's central idea.

[162] E.g., Barth, *Ephesians*, 2:766, who finds it unlikely that Paul would speak of the victory in 6:13 and then return to the preparations in 6:14.

[163] See the first textual note and the commentary on 6:18 for possible grammatical explanations of this participle.

However, four arguments against including prayer among the elements of the divine armor are more compelling. First, Paul does not identify prayer with a piece of armor, as he does with all six preceding items. He does not, for example, compare prayer to a javelin that is launched at the enemy. In fact, 6:18–20 entirely lacks battle imagery. Second, while each of the six preceding items is drawn from OT depictions of God's armor (see "The Old Testament" in "Sources of Paul's Armor Imagery" below), there is no mention of prayer in those OT texts. Indeed, prayer, as an activity of the Christian oriented toward God (though inspired by God's Spirit), differs qualitatively from the six items of armor, for they are conspicuously gifts of God bestowed upon the Christian: God's own righteousness, his salvation, his Word, and so forth. Third, the petitions of the prayers are unrelated to the preceding context. For example, Paul does not exhort the Ephesians to pray for God's help in their battle, but rather "concerning all the saints" (6:18) and for Paul himself to be given boldness to preach the Gospel in his imprisonment (6:19). Finally, a comparison with the Colossian parallel is most persuasive. The armor of God image is entirely absent from Colossians 4, which proceeds directly from the *Haustafel*'s concluding words about slaves and masters (Col 3:22–4:1; parallel to Eph 6:5–9) into an admonition to prayer (Col 4:2–4; parallel to Eph 6:18–20). Since Colossians includes the admonition to prayer but not the armor of God, one must conclude that Paul did not intend prayer to be considered a piece of the armor.

As we have argued and shall elaborate below, the overall thrust of Paul's exhortation is that the Christian should stand firm and allow God to win the victory. The armor is thus primarily *defensive*. Any interpretation that includes prayer as the Christian's *offensive* weapon perpetuates a misinterpretation of the pericope that would see the Christian as a synergistic battle companion of God.[164] Nevertheless, if prayer is properly understood as the Christian's admission of his own insufficiency, as an act of submission to God's will, as a cry for help when the Christian cannot help himself, then there need be no thoroughgoing objection to considering prayer part of the Christian's battle armor. God's protective gifts and the Christian's ceaseless prayer are inseparable companions in this spiritual war.[165]

Misreadings of This Popular Text

The inclusion of prayer in the armor of God is but one element of a popular approach to this pericope that sees the armor as partly or mostly *offensive*.

---

[164] Best, who considers prayer to be the Christian's own work, is himself is puzzled: "… (b) vv. 13–17 describe how God equips them [believers] so that they can defend themselves; … (c) vv. 18–20 deal with something believers must do on their own, pray and keep alert. The relation of this last section to the first two [6:11–12 and 6:13–17] is not immediately obvious. … It is possible, but unlikely, that prayer is set out as another piece of armour" (*Ephesians*, 589).

[165] Schnackenburg, *Ephesians*, 268: "The battle of the Christians against the powers of evil is not possible without prayer and constant alertness, prayerful vigilance impossible without God's armour and constant battle."

In such a view, the Christian's mandate from God is to take the battle to the devil, to attack the sinful world around us with the Gospel, to storm the devil's stronghold. Such an approach might be supported by Jesus' words to Peter that "on this rock I will build my church, and the gates of hell will not prevail against her" (Mt 16:18).[166] Likewise, Christ's observation at the end of the seventy preachers' mission, "I saw Satan fall like lightning from heaven" (Lk 10:18), indeed implies that the Gospel's impact on the world includes the devil's defeat. However, those words to the preachers of the Gospel are distinct from Paul's exhortation to the baptized in Ephesus. In Ephesians it is the devil and his forces that are attacking the Christians (2:2) and Christ who has taken the offensive against them (1:20–21; 4:8). In the present pericope, the verbs are defensive: "to stand against the devil's schemes" (6:11); "to withstand in the evil day, and so … to stand [firm]" (6:13). It is the devil who attacks with "flaming arrows" (6:16). And, as we shall illustrate below, in comparison with standard descriptions of ancient armor, Paul's list of the Christian's armor omits references to major offensive weapons such as arrows, javelins, and the long sword.

Paul's exhortation to the Ephesians is "to stand [firm]" (6:11, 13, 14) despite the devil's onslaught, in the knowledge that God's armor will protect them from harm. But what does this defensive posture mean for the Christian's hope? For how long must he hold on? Ephesians, scarcely bound by a thoroughgoing "realized eschatology" (as is often thought), displays the full spectrum of Paul's typical "now–not yet" tension. Though the battle is depicted as already underway in these evil days (5:16), it will not continue unabated. On the one hand, Paul warns that the battle will *intensify* as "the evil day" (6:13) approaches, rendering the strength of the divine armor ever more significant. But, on the other hand, the Christian has the additional confidence of knowing that the Lord will soon appear to end the war, like the proverbial cavalry appearing over the hill. Yet an interpreter would make a second grave mistake who would assume that the Christian church were left to fight the battle *alone*, as an old revival hymn presumes:

> "Hold the fort, for I am coming,"
>   Jesus signals still;
> Wave the answer back to heaven
>   "By Thy grace we will."[167]

---

[166] In an ancient city, the "gates" were the primary defensive fortification against attackers. Therefore Christ's words imply that the church is attacking the devil's stronghold (not vice versa, as it is commonly understood). See Gibbs, *Matthew 11:2–20:34*, 821–22. It is also possible that this verse refers to the release of God's people from the prison-house of sin and death achieved by Christ's Easter victory. See Peter Burfeind, "The Harrowing of Hell: Filling in the Blanks," *Logia* 18.1 (Epiphany 2009): 5–14.

[167] Refrain of "Hold the Fort" by Philip D. Bliss (1870), a popular revivalist hymn in the late nineteenth and early twentieth centuries (quoted in the two articles cited here). Jon D. Vieker, " 'What a Friend We Have in Jesus': Missouri Lutherans Encounter Revivalism and the Gospel Song," *Logia* 17.2 (Eastertide 2008): 26, quotes a critical review of the hymn published in *The Lutheran Witness*, 10.3 (July 7, 1891): 22:

We saints below neither wait for Christ to win the battle nor fight the fight for him. Christ is not an absent Warrior.[168] This is not the perspective of Ephesians. Instead, it proclaims that Christ has already won the battle, that God has raised him to the heavenly throne and put our spiritual enemies under his feet (1:20–23), that we have already been elevated to heaven with him (2:5–6). Nor indeed is Christ's victory partial, as if it depended on our holding the ground that he has won at such great price,[169] or even as if Christ expected us to gain more ground for him.[170] This is not the perspective of the Paul who wrote "by grace you have been saved through faith; and this is not from yourselves; it is the gift of God" (2:8). This salvation does not consist merely in being set on the right path, enrolled in the right army, tasked with preserving a hard-fought victory; but it includes the ultimate gift of emerging from the battle alive and unscathed.

The "gift of God" (2:8) perspective of Ephesians permeates the present pericope. It would be a mistake, then, third, to view these items of armor as a spiritual shopping list for the Christian to seek out and appropriate for himself.[171] The pericope is certainly replete with imperatives such as "take up the

---

Here the fort means the Church, and it is implied in this song that we poor sinners are left alone in it, by ourselves, to fight against and ward off the devil, till Christ gets here from heaven; for you see the song commands to "wave the answer back to heaven" where it takes for granted Christ is, as in opposition to His being on earth!

This false view, consistently carried out, leads to the separation of Christ's divine nature from His human nature.

[168] Luther preaches on the basis of Revelation 12:

For He [Christ] is the God who is a Prince of war and a true Duke who leads His regiment in battle, not in heaven above among the holy spirits where there is no need of battle, but here on earth in His Church. Yes (even though He is seated at the right hand of the Father) He is Himself with His warriors leading them against the enemy, whom no human power and weapons can withstand, resisting and restraining him with His Word, which He has given to His men. ("Sermon for the Feast of St. Michael, Revelation 12:7–12," September 29, 1544, *Day by Day We Magnify Thee*, 430; WA 49:580)

[169] Contra, e.g., Lincoln, *Ephesians*, 442–43: "The decisive victory has already been won by God in Christ, and the task of believers is not to win but to stand, that is, to preserve and maintain what has been won. … Believers must appropriate what has already been gained for them and do so against continuing assaults, and this is not automatic."

[170] Contra, e.g., Arnold, *Power and Magic*, 120:

The flow of the context also reveals that the author conceives of "standing" in offensive terms [!]. The author does not explicitly state that the readers need to regain old ground given to the enemy (cf. 4:27) and capture new ground currently held by the enemy, but this is the implication of the context. The offensive aspects of the resistance can be summarized as developing conduct governed by Christian ethics and maintaining the mission which Paul himself had inaugurated.

[171] If the gifts are the divine qualities of Christ, then they are already bestowed *in toto* on the Christian in his Baptism, as Christ is a person who cannot be divided. Thus, the Christian need not seek these qualities anywhere else. Although the Christian life involves a continual *strengthening* of these gifts through the means of grace, to seek "more righteousness" or "more truth" or "more faith" or "more salvation" suggests they are measurable human qualities rather than objective gifts of God. If they are human abilities that succeed or fail on the basis of their strength or size, then such weapons will have no hope of opposing a demonic

full armor of God" (6:13) and "stand" (6:14). But the unit is introduced with the *passive* imperative "be strengthened in the Lord, that is, in his mighty strength" (6:10). This theme interprets what follows; it is not the Christian's strength, but the Lord's that counts. The Lord provides the armor, with which the Christian is "clothed" (6:11, permissive middle: "let yourselves be clothed"). Just as no raw recruit in the army would claim to provide his own arms when he is mustered, so the Christian merely receives (6:17) what he is given from the Lord.[172] "Passive," of course, refers to *source* of the strength, not to its exercise. The Christian is certainly active in the battle, holding up the shield of faith and wielding the sword of God's Word. A defensive understanding of the pericope does not imply that the Christian may forsake the gifts that are given for his defense, as if God will defend him *apart from means*. But the weapons operate with and depend on the Lord's strength, not our own. And the tactics of battle must follow the Lord's plan and mandates, not our own.

Finally, then, if the battle is the Lord's, if Christ is still with us, if he has won the victory, if the arms are given by God, then it would be a mistake to presume that the outcome of the battle is uncertain.[173] To the contrary, the Christian's great comfort, his ability "to withstand in the evil day" (6:13), derives from his knowledge that the enemy has already been decisively defeated and that Christ already reigns in triumph at the Father's right hand (1:20). This is the basis of Paul's dramatic exhortation.

The Nature of the Battle

The Christian life is frequently depicted in the NT as a battle, and Paul is particularly fond of the image. He admonishes the Romans on the basis of their Baptism into the death of Christ no longer to present their "members" (μέλη) to sin as "weapons of unrighteousness" (ὅπλα ἀδικίας), but to present them to God as "weapons of righteousness" (ὅπλα δικαιοσύνης, Rom 6:13; cf. 2 Cor 6:7)—note the parallel between the "weapons" or "arms" (ὅπλα, *hopla*) and the "full armor" (πανοπλία, *pan* + *hoplia*) of our text. The metaphor compares the newborn Christian to a soldier who is captured and conscripted into the conquering army, bringing his weapons and armor into the service of his new

---

foe. The call to seek bigger or better weapons for battle will inevitably introduce doubt that what has already been received is sufficient. The Gospel is opposed to doubt.

[172] Schnackenburg, *Ephesians*, 280:

> The impressive metaphor ... has no moralizing tendency but is meant in the first place to show the Christians the protection provided for them by God and encourage them to stand fast amid the temptations and struggles of the world. In this respect the Christian paraclesis differs from comparable uses of the familiar metaphor in the non-Jewish environment.

[173] Contra Fischer, *Tendenz und Absicht*, 165, who assumes that the supposedly traditional material found in this pericope differs in eschatological perspective from the rest of the letter: "The text has an essentially different eschatology than appears elsewhere in Ephesians. For Ephesians the typical expressions are that the powers have already been overcome for the church's sake, while here the decisive battle yet awaits."

general. The language of this text makes clear the *spiritual* nature of the battle: one fights either for sin or for God. For this reason the weapons must have not fleshly but divine power; they are not puny toys for toy soldiers, but have the strength of a great siege engine that can destroy castle walls (2 Cor 10:3–4). Paul sees himself in his apostolic office as a soldier for God (1 Cor 9:7; cf. Phil 2:25; Philemon 2), who by the sunset of his life has "fought the good fight" (2 Tim 4:7) and encourages his successor to do the same (1 Tim 1:18; 2 Tim 2:3–4).[174] But in light of the spiritual battle against the forces of darkness into which every Christian is thrust by Baptism into Christ, Paul enlists all the baptized into God's army, exhorting, "Let us be clothed with the weapons/armor of light" (ἐνδυσώμεθα τὰ ὅπλα τοῦ φωτός, Rom 13:12; the same verb for "be clothed" as in Eph 6:11, and *hopla* comparable to *pan* + *hoplia* in Eph 6:11). Yes, the divine armor image is scarcely unique to Ephesians. Paul has already formed the image *in nuce* with Romans (written shortly after his Ephesian ministry) and with his even earlier letter to the Thessalonians:

> ἡμεῖς δὲ ἡμέρας ὄντες νήφωμεν ἐνδυσάμενοι θώρακα πίστεως καὶ ἀγάπης καὶ περικεφαλαίαν ἐλπίδα σωτηρίας.

> But since we are of the day, let us be sober, having let ourselves be clothed with the breastplate of faith and love, and with the hope of salvation as a helmet. (1 Thess 5:8)

Here Paul associates his favored trio, the divine gifts of faith, hope, and love (1 Cor 13:13), with the Christian's armament.

Yet, the divine warfare imagery is broader than these texts about weapons and armor. One ought also consider the significant prophetic texts describing the spiritual battle between good and evil angels that parallel and perhaps also direct the earthly manifestations of the divine war (Dan 10:13, 20–21; 12:1).[175] Likewise, the NT draws back the veil to expose the demonic instigator of Judas' betrayal our Lord (Lk 22:3; Jn 13:2) and the true spiritual enemies of Paul (2 Cor 11:14–15). So also John's Revelation shows a battle in the heavenly places, in

---

[174] Luther preaches on 6:10–17:

> Christendom must also have people who can beat down their adversaries and opponents and tear off the devil's equipment and armour, that he may be brought into disgrace. But for this work powerful warriors are needed, who are thoroughly familiar with the Scriptures and can contradict all false interpretations and take the sword from false teachers—that is, those very verses which the false teachers use and turn them round upon them so that they fall back, defeated. But as not all Christians can be so capable in defending the Word and articles of their Creed, they must have teachers and preachers who study the Scripture and have daily fellowship with it, so that they can fight for all the others. Yet each Christian should be so armed that he himself is sure of his belief and of the doctrine and is so equipped with sayings from the Word of God that he can stand up against the devil and defend himself, when men seek to lead him astray, and so can help to fight the battle for the maintaining of true doctrine. ("Sermon on the Christians' Armor and Weapons, Ephesians 6:10–17," October 20, 1532, *Day by Day We Magnify Thee*, 385; StL 9:820; WA 34/2:378–79)

[175] Luther: "One devil has Saxony, [another] the Mark [Brandenburg], [another] the Turks" ("Sermon for the Twenty-first Sunday after Trinity," October 25, 1545, AE 58:305; WA 51:69).

which the captain of the Lord's forces, Michael, engages and defeats the age-old foe (Revelation 12), a battle that perhaps simultaneously describes the prehistoric expulsion of the rebellious evil angels from heaven and Christ's defeat of the same on the cross. The image of the Christian church as God's army, with the office of the ministry providing its commanding officers, is taken up with vigor by the apostolic fathers, who draw heavily on Paul's inspiring exhortation in this pericope.[176]

But who are the enemies in this divine war? In the letter to the Ephesians, there are plenty of human adversaries that might be in contention for this role. Jews and Gentiles were in conflict with each other over their respective places in God's kingdom (Acts 19:8–10, 33; 20:3; Eph 2:1–22).[177] Those baptized by Apollos were perhaps in conflict with those brought in later through the Pauline mission (Acts 18:24–19:7; Eph 4:1–6).[178] There are hints of false teaching (Acts 20:29–30; Eph 4:14),[179] and the danger of compromising truth for the sake of love is exposed (4:15, 25). There are natural conflicts between sinful Christians within the community of the faithful (4:25–32). Pagan neighbors entice Christians to return to their old way of life (5:3–12). Paul's *Haustafel* addresses the roots of conflict between husbands and wives, parents and children, masters and slaves (5:21–6:9). And the record of Acts adds that Paul had come into conflict both with practitioners of magic (Acts 19:11–20) and with the idolatrous worshipers of Artemis (Acts 19:21–41).[180]

But the message of Paul's epilogue is that these visible foes are not the *true* enemy and that what one sees is not the real battle. These interpersonal fights might be viewed as merely minor squabbles that can be resolved through compromise, dialogue, and love. But Paul avers that such feigned resolutions would merely hide the actual adversary and allow him to become even more dangerous: "for our struggle is not against blood and flesh, but against the rulers, against the authorities, against the world powers of this darkness, against the spiritual forces of evil in the heavenly places" (6:12). This is indeed a *spiritual* battle. Fellow human beings are not the enemy, but the victims and the tools of the enemy.

---

[176] *1 Clement*, 37; Polycarp, *To the Philippians*, 4:1; *Shepherd of Hermas, Mandates*, 12:2.4.

[177] See "Conflict with the Jews (Acts 19:8–10)" in "The City of Ephesus and Paul's Relationship to It" in the introduction.

[178] See "Conflict over Baptism and the Spirit (Acts 18:24–19:7)" in "The City of Ephesus and Paul's Relationship to It," as well as "Baptism and the Spirit" in "Purpose and Themes," both in the introduction.

[179] Luther, in preaching on this text, identifies the Qur'an; the Turks; the pope and his court; and such heretics as the Anabaptists, Sacramentarians, Arians, and Macedonians as agents of devils in this spiritual battle ("Sermon for the Twenty-first Sunday after Trinity," October 25, 1545, AE 58:310; WA 51:74).

[180] See "Conflict with Jewish Exorcists and Pagan Magicians (Acts 19:11–20)" and "Conflict with the Cult of Artemis Ephesia (Acts 19:21–41)" in "The City of Ephesus and Paul's Relationship to It" in the introduction.

Christians should beware the scheming of the devil (6:11, 16), one who uses deceit (Jn 8:44), manipulative words (1 Cor 2:4), and flattery (1 Thess 2:5) to disguise his evil intent. He uses spiritism, astrology, magic, and pagan idolatry with their promise of great power to attract his followers, as the Gentile Ephesian Christians had once experienced (Acts 19:11–41; Eph 2:1–2; 4:17; 5:3–11).[181] He masquerades as an angel of light (2 Cor 11:14) and needs to be exposed for what he is.[182] And it is for this reason that the elements of the Christian's armor and weaponry are associated consistently with weapons of the *Spirit* rather than with human strength or wisdom. It is only by *God's* truth, righteousness, Gospel peace, faith, salvation, and Word that the enemy's attacks will be thwarted. For it is by these gifts that the baptized are immersed in Christ himself, who takes on the devil as the church's Champion[183] and has won ultimate victory over the spiritual forces (1:20–23; 2:5–6; 3:10; 4:8). In striking Gospel irony, these enemies who are not made of blood and flesh are defeated by the flesh and blood of the divine Man Jesus Christ, crucified and risen to unite all people in himself (2:13–18; cf. Heb 2:14; Jn 6:53–56).

The theme of Paul's *peroratio* (Eph 6:10–17), the spiritual nature of the battle and the source of the church's victory and strength, is perhaps best paraphrased by Luther's famous hymn:

> Though devils all the world should fill,
> All eager to devour us,
> We tremble not, we fear no ill;
> They shall not overpow'r us.
> This world's prince may still
> Scowl fierce as he will,
> He can harm us none.
> He's judged; the deed is done;
> One little word can fell him. (*LSB* 656:3)

Sources of Paul's Armor Imagery

The Roman Soldier

Because Paul was in prison when he wrote this letter,[184] many commentators have assumed that he derived the details of the armor from the model of a Roman soldier-guard.[185] While this may be a natural assumption with some merit, there

---

[181] See "Polytheism," "The Temple of Artemis Ephesia," and "The Cult of Artemis Ephesia" in "The City of Ephesus and Paul's Relationship to It" in the introduction.

[182] Luther's 1545 sermon on this text includes an extended exposé, using the Ten Commandments as a template, of the devil's work behind the scenes of this world ("Sermon for the Twenty-first Sunday after Trinity," October 25, 1545, AE 58:303–12; WA 51:67–76).

[183] Luther: "Here there are two lords, Christ and the devil, who do battle day and night" ("Sermon for the Twenty-first Sunday after Trinity," October 25, 1545, AE 58:306; WA 51:70).

[184] See "Paul's Imprisonment" in "Location and Date of Writing" in the introduction.

[185] This view has been most influentially promulgated by A. Oepke, "πανοπλία," *TDNT* 5:301, who thinks that such Roman imagery is foremost in Paul's mind (while not entirely excluding the OT as a secondary source). Luther, e.g., simply assumes that Paul is referring to a Roman soldier, though he comments humorously: "Today, this would be a wretched armament; the

are factors that qualify it. First, the depiction of Paul's lengthy (two-year) incarceration in Caesarea, during which he frequently had conversational meetings with the governor and the king, suggests he was not guarded by heavily armed, battle-ready Roman soldiers (he was held in "Herod's praetorium," Acts 23:35). He was arrested primarily for his own protection (Acts 21:32; 23:27), and his judges repeatedly determined that he was innocent (Acts 25:18, 25; 26:32), so it is unlikely that he would have been treated as a dangerous prisoner. The picture changes little if Rome was the place of the letter's origin.[186] Although he was at one point in the company of the Praetorian guard (Phil 1:13), he was mostly under house arrest with the ability to welcome visitors, guarded by just one soldier (Acts 28:16–31). It is unlikely that such a guard would have carried the "full armor" (πανοπλία, Eph 6:11, 13) described in this pericope, including such items as the door-like "shield" (θυρεός) that protected the soldier from head to foot in battle.[187] On the other hand, inasmuch as Paul's depiction omits the chief offensive battle weapon, the javelin, the more lightly equipped soldier-guard would have resembled Paul's description to a certain extent. Like any citizen of the Roman world (including the Ephesians themselves[188]), Paul would have sometimes seen Roman legions marching by in full battle array, and shortly before his lengthy imprisonments began, he was escorted to Caesarea by a fearsome cohort of two hundred foot soldiers, seventy horsemen, and two hundred spearmen[189] (Acts 23:23).

Thus, it is probably enough to say that the constant contact Paul had with Roman soldiers during his arrest and imprisonment *prompted* him to develop his allegory of the Christian's full armor, even if the details did not fully correspond to the soldiers by whom he was guarded. Ancient literature contains a number of depictions of Roman soldiers,[190] the most extensive and significant being that of Polybius, which is worth reading in full:

---

guns have changed everything" ("Sermon for the Twenty-first Sunday after Trinity," October 25, 1545, AE 58:304; WA 51:68).

[186] See "Rome?" in "Location and Date of Writing" in the introduction.

[187] Best, *Ephesians*, 587: "The individual items are conventional and would have been known to anyone in the ancient world; there is no need then to imagine Paul, if he is the writer, drawing the imagery from the Roman soldier guarding him; a soldier guarding an individual would not in any case have needed the large shield of v. 16."

[188] Scharlemann, "Secret," 342, refers to pillars in Ephesus on which Roman armor was depicted.

[189] The meaning of the term δεξιολάβος is highly uncertain; the Vulgate renders it *lancearios*, from which the English translation "spearmen" derives. It is thought that Jerome would know as well as any modern scholar. But since all Roman soldiers carried the *pilum*, "javelin/spear," as a basic weapon, it has been suggested that δεξιολάβοι (literally, "those who take with the right hand") could refer to "slingers" (i.e., of projectiles), "archers," "men leading horses," or simply "lightly armed auxiliary soldiers." See BDAG, s.v. δεξιολάβος; C. K. Barrett, *A Critical and Exegetical Commentary on the Acts of the Apostles* (International Critical Commentary; London: T&T Clark, 1998), 2:1077–79.

[190] The term πανοπλία, "full armor," was not exclusively Roman and occurs regularly in texts that describe a soldier's heavy battle armor: e.g., Thucydides, *History of the Peloponnesian War*, 3:114.1 ("three hundred sets of full armor"); Isocrates, *Speeches*, 16:29 ("so distinguished himself in the perilous actions of the campaign that he was crowned and received a full suit

The second rank, the *Hastati*, are ordered to have the complete panoply [πανοπλία, "full armor"]. This to a Roman means, first, a large shield [θυρεός, *scutum*], the surface of which is curved outwards, its breadth two and a half feet, its length four feet—though there is also an extra sized shield in which these measures are increased by a palm's breadth. It consists of two layers of wood fastened together with bull's-hide glue; the outer surface of which is first covered with canvas, then with calf's skin, on the upper and lower edges it is bound with iron to resist the downward strokes of the sword [τῶν μαχαιρῶν], and the wear of resting upon the ground. Upon it also is fixed an iron boss [σιδηρᾶ κόγχος, *umbo*], to resist the more formidable blows of stones and pikes, and of heavy missiles generally. With the shield they also carry a sword [μάχαιρα, *gladius*] hanging down by their right thigh, which is called a Spanish sword. It has an excellent point, and can deal a formidable blow with either edge, because its blade is stout and unbending. In addition to these they have two pila [ὑσσοί, "javelins"], a brass helmet [περικεφαλαία χαλκῆ], and greaves [προκνημίς, *ocreae*, "shin armour"]. Some of the pila are thick, some fine. Of the thicker, some are round with the diameter of a palm's length, others are a palm square. The fine pila are like moderate sized hunting spears, and they are carried along with the former sort. The wooden haft of them all is about three cubits [ca. four and a half feet or one and a half meters] long; and the iron head fixed to each half is barbed, and of the same length as the haft. They take extraordinary pains to attach the head to the haft firmly; they make the fastening of the one to the other so secure for use by binding it half way up the wood, and riveting it with a series of clasps, that the iron breaks sooner than this fastening comes loose, although its thickness at the socket and where it is fastened to the wood is a finger and a half's breadth. Besides these each man is decorated with a plume of feathers, with three purple or black feathers standing upright, about a cubit [ca. one and a half feet or half a meter] long. The effect of these being placed on the helmet, combined with the rest of the armour [τοῖς ἄλλοις ὅπλοις], is to give the man the appearance of being twice his real height, and to give him a noble aspect calculated to strike terror into the enemy. The common soldiers also receive a brass plate, a span square, which they put upon their breast and call a breastpiece [καρδιοφύλακα, *pectorale*], and so complete their panoply [καθόπλισις, "armor"]. Those who are rated above a hundred thousand asses, instead of these breastpieces wear, with the rest of their armour, coats of mail [ἀλυσιδωτοὺς … θώρακας, *loricae*]. The *Principes* and *Triarii* are armed in the same way as the *Hastati*, except that instead of pila they carry long spears [δόρατα, *hastae*].[191]

Josephus describes the armor of Roman soldiers, like those who attacked Jerusalem in the war of AD 66–73, in similar terms:

[93]When, after this, they are gone out of their camp, they all march without noise, and in a decent manner, and everyone keeps his own rank, as if they were going to war. The footmen are armed with breastplates [θώρακες] and

of armor from his general" [trans. George Norlin, LCL]). Cf. LXX 2 Kgdms 2:21 (MT/ET 2 Sam 2:21); Judith 14:3; 1 Macc 13:29; 2 Macc 3:25; 10:30; 11:8; 15:28; Wis Sol 5:17; Lk 11:22.

[191] Polybius, *Histories*, 6:23 (trans. Shuckburgh, *The Histories of Polybius*, which includes the editorial insertion of Latin terms). See also Polybius, *Histories*, 3:62.5; 4:56.3.

headpieces [κράνη], and have swords [μαχαιροφοροῦντες] on each side; [94]but the sword [ξίφος] which is upon their left side is much longer than the other, for that on the right side is not longer than about nine inches [σπιθαμή, "handspan"]. [95]Those footmen also that are chosen out of the rest to be around the general himself, have a lance [λόγχη] and a buckler [ἀσπίς, 'small round shield']; but the rest of the foot soldiers [φάλαγξ] have a spear [ξυστόν] and a long shield [θυρεός ἐπιμήκης], besides a saw and a basket, a pickaxe, and an axe, a thong of leather, and a hook, with provisions for three days; so that a footman has no great need of a mule to carry his burdens. [96]The horsemen have a long sword on their right sides [μάχαιρα μὲν ἐκ δεξιῶν μακρά], and a long pole in their hand; a shield [θυρεός] also lies by them obliquely on one side of their horses, with three or more darts that are borne in their quiver, having broad points, and not smaller than spears. They have also headpieces [κράνη] and breastplates [θώρακες], in like manner as have all the footmen.[192]

One notes from these two passages, first, that both the elements of equipment given to a Roman soldier and the terminology used (in Greek and Latin) could vary significantly.[193] Thus, it is not possible to make a firm decision as to whether Paul modeled his Christian soldier directly on a Roman soldier. Yet there is enough similarity that certain conclusions may be drawn. First, each element chosen by Paul is indeed present in these depictions and so might have been observed by him personally. Second, these extensive descriptions enable us to discern which common elements of a Roman soldier's heavy weaponry are *not* part of Paul's picture: a javelin/spear/lance for throwing or thrusting (ὑσσός, λόγχη, δόρυ, ξυστόν; Latin terms include, from lighter to heavier, *pilum, graesum,* and *hasta*), greaves/shin armor (προκνημίς), and a long sword (ξίφος, ῥομφαία). The omission of the greaves may not be significant, as Paul does not treat every detail of the armor. But the omission of the javelin/spear[194] (the definitive weapon of the ancient Greek *phalanx* and the Roman foot soldier) and the long sword surely betrays a deliberate shift in emphasis from offense to defense.[195] Without these two crucial weapons, the foot soldier could

---

[192] Josephus, *Wars*, 3:93–96 (translation adapted from Whiston, *The Works of Josephus*); cf. the Romans putting on armor and massing in the Fortress Antonia to withstand the Jewish mobs in Josephus, *Antiquities*, 20:110.

[193] See D'Amato, *Arms and Armour of the Imperial Roman Soldier*, xi–xiv, who emphasizes that the equipment and clothing of the Roman army varied considerably by time and place as the soldiers preserved older weapons and adapted what was available locally. The main thesis of his study is to demonstrate this diversity.

[194] Ignatius' allegorizing of love as a spear (*To Polycarp*, 6:2) is an exception to this pattern. For further information on the javelin/spear, see D'Amato, *Arms and Armour of the Imperial Roman Soldier*, 6–12, 48, 67–80, 152–53, 182, 200–204.

[195] This is a better explanation than Oepke's, who claims these elements are missing simply because the picture is of close, hand-to-hand combat:

The absence of the spear cannot be explained archaeologically, but no effort was made to be complete, and in any case it would be hard to give a separate interpretation for the lance as compared with the sword. The demons fight artfully from a distance (βέλη ["arrows"], v. 16). The believer, however, must fight hand to hand (πάλη ["struggle"], v. 12). Hence no *pilum* [the Roman foot soldier's "javelin/spear"] is needed. ("πανοπλία," *TDNT* 5:301)

not advance against his enemy and would have no choice but to stand firm and rely on his armor. Furthermore, while the enemy is apparently in possession of a bow and arrow with which to hurl flaming arrows (6:16), Paul grants no such weapon to the Christian for retaliation, but asks him to be satisfied with blocking and extinguishing these attacks.

Details from a marble relief depicting the Parthian Campaign (AD 161–166), made after the death of Emperor Lucius Verus (AD 169), originally located in Ephesus, now in the Ephesus Museum, Vienna. The relief attributes the Roman victory to Artemis Ephesia.

Photos: © 2014 Thomas M. Winger.

A soldier defends himself with a full-length shield, a short sword in his right hand,
a dagger in his left; the attacking soldier has a helmet, boots, a short sword, and a shield.

A soldier defends himself with a shield and a short sword.

Emperor Lucius Verus in a splendid muscled breastplate and belt.

The Old Testament

If Paul's selectivity was governed by his overwhelmingly *defensive* perspective on the Christian's position in battle, are there additional factors that led him to choose precisely these six pieces of armor and weapons? It is at this point that the Roman source must give way, first, to the Christian gifts that Paul wishes to depict, and, second, to the OT passages in which he finds them already depicted as pieces of armor.[196] Considering the number of battles in Israel's history, it is no surprise to find frequent descriptions of weapons and armor in the OT. In fact, if Paul had never seen a Roman soldier, he would have had ample material in the OT from which to fashion his allegory (as we do today to understand it). While Hebrew seldom employs a term that would be equivalent to "full armor" ($\pi\alpha\nu o\pi\lambda\acute{\iota}\alpha$) and that would encompass both weapons and armor, in OT accounts of warfare there are frequent enumerations of a soldier's weapons.[197] These items usually do not differ greatly from what we have already seen among the Romans. Defensive pieces included a small or large shield (2 Sam 1:21; 8:7; Jer 46:3), a helmet (Ezek 23:24; 27:10), body armor (1 Sam 17:38; Jer 46:4), greaves (1 Sam 17:6), and shoes (Is 9:4 [ET 9:5]). Offensive weapons included the sword (Judg 8:10), spear (Judg 5:8; 1 Sam 17:45; 18:11), bow (2 Sam 1:22), arrow (Jer 51:11), and sling (1 Sam 17:40).[198] The depiction of Goliath gives a fairly complete picture:

> [5]A helmet of bronze was on his head, and he was clothed with body armor of scales, and the weight of the body armor was five thousand shekels, [and it was] bronze. [6]Greaves of bronze were on his legs, and a javelin of bronze [was slung] between his shoulders. [7]The wooden shaft of his spear was like a weaver's beam, and his spear's head [weighed] six hundred shekels, [and it was] iron. And the bearer of his body shield went before him. (1 Sam 17:5–7)[199]

Goliath's armor was clearly exceptional, both because of his unusual size and because of his status as the Philistines' champion. His armor must have been not only extremely valuable but also visually stunning; it contributed to

---

[196] Lincoln, *Ephesians*, 435–36:

> Certainly the term $\pi\alpha\nu o\pi\lambda\acute{\iota}\alpha$ "full armor," would have brought to mind for Gentile readers in western Asia Minor the suit of armor of the Roman soldier. But the writer is not concerned with an accurate or detailed description of such armor. As we have seen, he omits some key terms and includes other more general equipment, and in this his ultimate focus is on the Christian realities to which he desires to point. For this purpose he is aided more by his knowledge of OT imagery than by his observation of Roman soldiers.

[197] See the first textual note on 6:11. The Greek term $\pi\alpha\nu o\pi\lambda\acute{\iota}\alpha$, "full armor," is common in the intertestamental literature of the LXX and is used of God's own armor in Wis Sol 5:17; Sirach 46:6.

[198] A. Oepke, "$\pi\alpha\nu o\pi\lambda\acute{\iota}\alpha$," *TDNT* 5:296.

[199] Cf. similar descriptions: "And Uzziah prepared for them, for all the army: shields, spears, helmets, body armor, bows, and stones for slinging" (2 Chr 26:14). "Arrange buckler and shield, and advance for battle! Harness the horses; mount, O horsemen! Take your stand with helmets, polish the spears, put on the body armor!" (Jer 46:3–4).

the mystique of the unconquerable hero, pressed to the front of the army in the hope of intimidating the enemy to surrender. Here we learn, then, that armor in the ancient world could hold more than just a pragmatic function. This role becomes all the more apparent when we read of King Saul and the young David:

> [38]Then Saul clothed David with his armor. He put a helmet of bronze on his head and clothed him with body armor. [39]David belted his sword over his armor. He tried to walk, for he had not tested [the wearing of armor]. Then David said to Saul, "I am not able to walk with these, for I have not tested." So David removed them from himself. [40]Then he took his staff in his hand and chose for himself five smooth stones from the wadi and put them in the shepherd's equipment which he had, in the pouch. His sling was in his hand, and he approached the Philistine. (1 Sam 17:38–40)

Both Saul's and David's motives are usually interpreted pragmatically. While Saul perhaps had little interest in protecting David's life, he was concerned that David should have some hope of success against Goliath, since the outcome of the battle depended on it. David, then, refused the armor because it was too large and heavy for him to manage, and he was unskilled in its use.

But there is more going on here. The rivalry between Saul and David had already begun.[200] Saul's attempt to clothe David in his own armor and weapons may have been an attempt to take some credit for the victory—for just as Goliath's armor was part of the mystique of his champion character, so Saul may have believed that his armor would lend David his own legendary power in battle. If David won with Saul's sword, the crowds might chant, "Saul's sword has won the victory!" But the narrative is insistent that "there was no sword in the hand of David" (1 Sam 17:50). Thus, there may be a similar motive in David's refusal. By choosing not to wear Saul's armor, he was refusing to allow Saul to claim the impending victory. And by approaching Goliath without any armor, carrying only a sling and five smooth stones as his weapon, David displayed a complete disdain for human strength and demonstrated that he was relying completely on God to give him the victory:

> [45]Then David said to the Philistine, "You are coming against me with a sword and with a spear and with a javelin, but I am coming against you in the name of YHWH of hosts, the God of the battle lines of Israel, whom you have mocked. [46]This day YHWH will deliver you into my hand, and I will strike you down, and I will remove your head from upon you. And I will give the corpses of the camp of the Philistines this day to the birds of the air and to the wild beasts of the earth, and all the earth will know that there is a God for Israel, [47]and all this assembly will know that it is not with a sword or with a spear that YHWH saves. For the war belongs to YHWH, and he will give you into our hand." (1 Sam 17:45–47; cf. 1 Sam 17:37)

On the one hand, Saul's attempt to equip David with his own armaments displays the typical ancient belief that the weapons and armor of a great, legendary

---

[200] The Lord had already rejected Saul and anointed David as king (1 Samuel 15–16).

warrior conveyed their strength to the one who took them up.[201] Such legends are familiar to modern ears from the Arthurian tales of the sword Excalibur, or the elven swords and armor that strike terror into the orcs of Tolkien's Middle Earth. And yet there is more to the story—for David refused the weapons of the great warrior Saul in order to face Goliath "naked," as it were. He is clothed only with the righteousness and strength of the name of the God who alone saves. In fact, in contrast to the glorious campaigns of the mature David, this story highlights the weakness, youth, and inexperience of this young boy—for this is a God who gives strength to the weak, exalts the lowly, and brings triumph through the unlikely.[202]

Paul, then, in appealing to the "armor of God" (Eph 6:11, 13), is alluding to the classical belief that a champion's armor brought strength and victory to those who wore it. But he goes farther, for this is not just the armor of an ordinary human champion. First, God clothes the Christian with *divine* strength (Eph 6:10; cf. 2 Cor 10:4). Thus, the "armor of God" (Eph 6:11, 13) is not merely given *by* God, but is endued with *his own* power. God himself defends his people. We have noted that God is frequently described in the OT as his people's armor, most often as their "shield"[203] and their "fortress" or "refuge."[204] Second, we might rightly conclude then that the armor of God *is* God himself. Baptized into Christ, the Christian is clothed with God, enwrapped in him as in a breastplate, shielded behind him, enclosed within his battlements.

---

[201] "In this connection we might mention Odin's helmet as a cap of invisibility, also the invincibility of Achilles and Siegfried, the former by virtue of the armour forged by Hephaistos, the latter by virtue of the sword Balmung" (A. Oepke, "πανοπλία," *TDNT* 5:297). The making of Achilles' elaborate shield, helmet, breastplate, and greaves, as requested by his goddess mother Thetis from the god Hephaestus, is described in Homer's *Iliad*, 18:127–44, 187–201, 368–616, and their bestowal on Achilles is depicted in *Iliad*, 19:1–24. This divine gift was necessitated by a most significant plot point in the *Iliad*: since Achilles had fallen out with Agamemnon and refused to fight any longer for the Greeks, he had given his armor to his friend Patroclus. The armor of the great, undefeatable warrior was expected to protect him. Unfortunately, the Trojan leader Hector mistook Patroclus for Achilles, killed him, and stripped him of the armor. Armed with his new, divine armor, Achilles later took revenge on Hector. Here ends Homer's account, but later legends add that after Achilles' eventual death in battle, his divine armor was bestowed on Odysseus, who later gave it to Achilles' son. (Note that the legend of invulnerability bestowed on Achilles by being dipped in the River Styx was added much later.) The learned apostle Paul would certainly have known these myths, as would his Ephesians readers. The bronze-headed spear that supposedly belonged to Achilles was on display in the temple of Artemis in Phaselis, on the south coast of Asia Minor, in Paul's day.

[202] Cf. Judith, who goes forth to defeat Holofernes, commander of the Syrian army, as she trusts only in the Lord. In fact, she delights in her weakness, praying: "Behold their pride, and send thy wrath upon their heads; give to me, a widow, the strength to do what I plan. By the deceit of my lips strike down the slave with the prince and the prince with his servant; crush their arrogance by the hand of a woman" (Judith 9:9–10 RSV).

[203] See the first textual note on 6:16.

[204] See, e.g., Pss 14:6; 18:3 (ET 18:2); 31:3–5 (ET 31:2–4); 46:2, 8, 12 (ET 46:1, 7, 11); 59:10, 17, 18 (ET 59:9, 16, 17); 61:4–5 (ET 61:3–4); 62:3, 7–9 (ET 62:2, 6–8); 71:3; 91:2; 142:6 (ET 142:5); 144:2; 2 Sam 22:2–3.

But when one traces the details of Paul's allegory in the OT, an even more remarkable picture appears. For this is not simply a defense *provided by* God; *it is the armor that God himself has worn in battle*. In Isaiah 59 God looks out upon the world and sees great wickedness, oppression, and unrighteousness. Israel is full of apostates; his own people disobey him; their enemies persecute them; and there is no human champion, no savior, no judge to raise up and render ultimate justice. So God himself takes up the call to arms:

> [16]He saw that there was no man, and he was appalled that there was no intercessor; so his own arm worked salvation for him, and his own righteousness was what supported him. [17]He put on righteousness as a breastplate [LXX: ἐνεδύσατο δικαιοσύνην ὡς θώρακα], and a helmet of salvation [LXX: περικεφαλαίαν σωτηρίου] on his head; he put on garments of vengeance for clothing and wrapped himself in zeal as a cloak. (Is 59:16–17)[205]

Here is the root not only of the pieces of armor that Paul chooses but also their allegorical meaning. From this passage it is clear that the "righteousness" which defends the Christian like a breastplate (Eph 6:14) is not his own, but God's righteousness. "The helmet of salvation" (6:17) is likewise God's act of rescue. The allegory is extended in the apocryphal Wisdom of Solomon, in which God comes to the rescue of the righteous and "takes care of them" (Wis Sol 5:15 RSV):

> [17]The Lord will take his zeal as his whole armor [πανοπλία], and will arm [ὁπλοποιήσει] all creation to repel his enemies; [18]he will put on righteousness as a breastplate [ἐνδύσεται θώρακα δικαιοσύνην], and wear impartial justice as a helmet; [19]he will take holiness as an invincible shield, [20]and sharpen stern wrath for a sword [ὀργὴν εἰς ῥομφαίαν], and creation will join with him to fight against the madmen. (Wis Sol 5:17–20 RSV)

Though these two texts are the most extended images of the Warrior God, there are others that fill out the picture by ascribing to YHWH in battle a sword (Is 34:5–6; Ezek 21:8–10 [ET 21:3–5]; Ps 7:13 [ET 7:12]), bow and arrows (Ps 7:13–14 [ET 7:12–13]; Hab 3:9), and a spear (Hab 3:11).

These elements of God's armor and weaponry highlight a significant difference between the OT depiction of the Warrior God and Paul's depiction of the Christian's armor. For in contrast to Paul's image, YHWH's weaponry includes fearsome *offensive* weapons. The Lord strides forth to attack his enemies. God is the great Warrior who wins the battle on behalf of his people. The apocryphal Sirach's depiction of Israel's battle under Joshua's leadership, while calling Joshua "mighty in war" (Sirach 46:1 RSV), highlights again the true source of his strength:

> [5]He [Joshua] called upon the Most High, the Mighty One, when enemies pressed him on every side, [6]and the great Lord answered him with hailstones of mighty power. He hurled down war upon that nation, and at the descent of Beth-horon he destroyed those who resisted, so that the nations might know

[205] For an exposition of this passage in relation to Eph 6:10–17 (as well as 1 Thess 5:8), see "Reflections" in the commentary on Is 59:1–21 in Lessing, *Isaiah 56–66*, 206–8.

his armament [πανοπλία, "full armor"], that he was fighting in the sight of the Lord. (Sirach 46:5–6 RSV)

The armor, therefore, that brings the Lord God great victory in battle is the very same armor that is given to the Christian, who thereby participates in the benefits of God's work. The elimination of the offensive weapons in Paul's allegory, however, teaches that the victory has already been achieved and that the Christian need only be defended from the final fading assaults of enemy. But how does the Christian inherit this great armor? A bridge between God and man is needed, and here Isaiah's prophetic words again come into play. For God first clothes his own messianic Son in his armor. The Messiah fights for his people as God himself:

> He shall judge the poor in righteousness and adjudicate in uprightness for the meek of the earth; and he shall strike the earth with the rod of his mouth [LXX: τῷ λόγῳ τοῦ στόματος αὐτοῦ, "with the *word* of his mouth"], and with the spirit/breath of his lips [LXX: ἐν πνεύματι διὰ χειλέων] he shall put to death the wicked. (Is 11:4)

This association of the Messiah with the Divine Warrior is, of course, dogmatically significant in demonstrating that the Messiah is divine. But it also sets the stage for the NT's claim that Jesus of Nazareth is YHWH himself, that the Christ who fulfilled these OT prophecies is the Son of God, the Divine Warrior, who won the ultimate victory for God's people. The vision of the Messiah granted to John in his Revelation draws an unmistakable connection with the prophecy of Isaiah:

> [13]And in the midst of the lampstands was one like a Son of Man, clothed with a long robe and belted with a golden girdle [ζώνην χρυσᾶν] round his breast; [14]his head and his hair were white as white wool, [white] as snow; his eyes were like a flame of fire, [15]his feet were like burnished bronze [χαλκολιβάνῳ], refined as in a furnace, and his voice was like the sound of many waters; [16]he had in his right hand seven stars, and from his mouth issued a sharp two-edged sword [ῥομφαία δίστομος], and his face was like the sun shining in full strength. (Rev 1:13–16)

St. Jerome draws it all together:

> From what we read of the Lord our Savior throughout the Scriptures, it is manifestly clear that the whole armor of Christ is the Savior himself. It is he whom we are asked to *put on*. It is one and the same thing to say *Put on the whole armor of God* and "Put on the Lord Jesus Christ." Our belt is truth and our breastplate is righteousness. The Savior is also called both *truth* and *righteousness* [cf. Jer 23:6; Jn 14:6]. So no one can doubt that he himself is that very belt and breastplate. On this principle he is also to be understood as the *preparation of the gospel of peace*. He himself is the *shield of faith* and the *helmet of salvation*. He is the *sword of the Spirit*, because he is the Word of

God, living and efficacious, the utterance of which is stronger than any helmet and sharp on both sides.[206]

The Battle Is the Lord's

If the battle of David with Goliath is an apt illustration of divine armor in OT thinking, the Passover and exodus from Egypt are, as a whole, even more instructive. And since the Jews observed Pentecost liturgically as a remembrance of Mount Sinai and the giving of the covenant to the people whom God had just redeemed from slavery in Egypt, these events would have been fresh in Paul's mind after celebrating Pentecost in Jerusalem shortly before writing Ephesians from prison.[207] The exodus account uses distinctly militaristic imagery for Israel's preparations and departure from Egypt. The Israelites are to eat the Passover meal not reclining as for a leisurely feast (what would become the custom after entering the promised land), but "with your loins girded [i.e., with your belt fastened], your sandals on your feet, and your staff in your hand. And you shall eat it in haste" (Ex 12:11). This looks like either pilgrims preparing for travel or soldiers ready to march. While the former seems obvious, later language suggests the latter is also true. They are called "YHWH's hosts" (צִבְאוֹת יְהוָה) that is, his "armies" (Ex 12:41; see also Ex 12:17, 51). They have the fearsome strength of "six hundred thousand men on foot" (Ex 12:37). They go up from the land of Egypt "organized for battle" (Ex 13:18)[208] and are later pictured in the wilderness as encamped around the tabernacle in orderly military design, by "rank and file," as legions aligned with each tribe's flag (Numbers 2).

Though the Israelites plundered the Egyptians of silver and gold jewelry (Ex 12:35–36), they did not take their weapons and armor, but marched forth in plain traveling clothes without the typical provisions for war. In some senses they looked like an army, while in others they did not. For YHWH's army is unique: *they do not fight for him, but he fights for them.* They were able to march forth from Egypt because God had already defeated the Egyptians with the ten plagues and particularly by killing their firstborn (Ex 13:15). It was by his "strong hand" that the Lord brought them out (Ex 13:3, 14, 16). Though they were a mighty host, God kept them away from battle, lest they turn tail and flee back to Egypt (Ex 13:17). When Pharaoh's hard heart led him to pursue them into the wilderness, God commanded the Israelites to make camp with the sea behind them, "up against a wall," as it were, luring the Egyptians into a trap (Ex 14:1–9). Fearing the worse, aware that they were not equipped to do battle

---

[206] Jerome, *Ephesians*, 3:6.11, ACCS 8:208.

[207] See "Paul's Trip to Jerusalem, Arrest, and Imprisonment (Acts 21:1–36)" in "The City of Ephesus and Paul's Relationship to It" in the introduction, as well as "Location and Date of Writing" in the introduction.

[208] The term חֲמֻשִׁים is difficult. In form a Qal passive participle, it would literally mean "to be fiftied" and would imply organization in companies of fifty soldiers (cf. Josh 1:14).

with Pharaoh's army, the Israelites cried out to the Lord for help. And through Moses God answered with these crucial words of promise:

> [13]Do not fear, stand firm [הִתְיַצְּב֥וּ; LXX: στῆτε], and see the salvation of YHWH, which he will work for you today. For those whom you see today, the Egyptians, you shall never see them again forever. [14]YHWH will fight for you, and you yourselves are to be silent. (Ex 14:13–14)

It is these words that most clearly explain what Paul means with his repeated exhortation to the Ephesians to "stand [firm]" (6:11, 13, 14). For this is not a mere battle strategy, a trick to lure the enemy in for the kill. It is rather a command borne of the conviction that the Lord himself will fight for us, that the Christian's role is to stand firm and watch him win the victory, to entrust oneself completely to the Lord's strength.[209]

The Egyptians who were sinking in the mud and drowning drew the correct conclusion from their predicament: "Let us flee from before Israel, for YHWH fights for them against the Egyptians" (Ex 14:25). What terror this must have struck in their hearts, to know that the unconquerable, almighty God was their enemy! Throughout the history of Israel, this message was repeated in battle after battle. On the famous day when the sun stood still, the Lord killed more Amorites by hailstones than the swords of Israel struck down (Josh 10:11).[210] Sirach comments about this event that God wished the nations "to know his [Joshua's] full armor [πανοπλία], that his war was in the sight of the Lord" (Sirach 46:6). In other words, the hailstones demonstrated that the true victorious Warrior fighting on Israel's behalf was God. In the conquest of the promised land, it was always the Lord who won the battles for his people, as Joshua reminded Israel in his latter years: "And you have seen all that YHWH your God has done for your sake to all these nations before you, for it is YHWH your God who has fought for you" (Josh 23:3; cf. Josh 21:44; 23:5, 9). It was not by human sword or bow (Josh 24:12). Human mathematics therefore fail in calculating the odds of victory: "One man of you puts to flight a thousand, for it

---

[209] Cf. "be watchful, *stand* in the faith, be courageous [literally, 'be manly'], be strengthened [γρηγορεῖτε, στήκετε ἐν τῇ πίστει, ἀνδρίζεσθε, κραταιοῦσθε]" (1 Cor 16:13).

[210] God's victory raining down from heaven is depicted even more graphically in Maccabees:

> [28]Just as dawn was breaking, the two armies joined battle, the one having as pledge of success and victory not only their valor but their reliance upon the Lord, while the other made rage their leader in the fight.

> [29]When the battle became fierce, there appeared to the enemy from heaven five resplendent men on horses with golden bridles, and they were leading the Jews. [30]Surrounding Maccabeus and protecting him with their own armor and weapons [πανοπλίαι, "full armors"], they kept him from being wounded. And they showered arrows and thunderbolts upon the enemy, so that, confused and blinded, they were thrown into disorder and cut to pieces. (2 Macc 10:28–30 RSV)

> Cf. the angelic warrior who later came in answer to prayer: "and there, while they were still near Jerusalem, a horseman appeared at their head, clothed in white and brandishing weapons [πανοπλία, 'full armor'] of gold [ἐν λευκῇ ἐσθῆτι πανοπλίαν χρυσῆν κραδαίνων]" (2 Macc 11:8 RSV).

is YHWH your God who fights for you, as he promised you" (Josh 23:10). For this reason God commands Gideon to *reduce* the size of his army when facing the Midianites: "The people who are with you are too great for me to give the Midianites into their hand, lest Israel boast against me, saying, 'My own hand has saved me'" (Judg 7:2). So, via a series of artifices, the original thirty-two thousand soldiers were reduced to three hundred—and even then the victory came not by their swords, but by the Lord's sending confusion into the enemy camp so that they slew each other (Judg 7:22).[211]

The pattern continues through the history of Israel, so that when they are unfaithful to God their enemies defeat them, and when they worship him rightly and trust in his protection he defeats their enemies. This perspective is especially prominent in King David's reign. The battles are not his own; he is merely a participant in the Lord's war (1 Sam 18:17; 25:28). Thus, he can pray to God:

> [1]Contend, O YHWH, with those who contend with me; war against those who war against me! [2]Take hold of buckler [מָגֵן; LXX: ὅπλον] and large shield [צִנָּה; LXX: θυρεός], and arise as my help! [3]Draw the spear [LXX: ῥομφαία, "long sword"] and javelin against those who pursue me! Say to my soul, "I am your salvation!" (Ps 35:1–3 [LXX 34:1–3])

Here we again see that the armor and weapons are the Lord's and that he takes up the great offensive weapons to gain victory on David's behalf. Israel should not look to worldly allies like Egypt (Is 31:1–2), because God goes forth into battle for his people like a mighty man (Is 42:13). Thus, Paul's words to the Ephesians are best understood in light of such promises as God once made to his people under King Jehoshaphat:

> You will not need to wage war in this [battle]. Stand firm [הִתְיַצְּבוּ], stand [עִמְדוּ], and see the salvation of YHWH on your behalf, O Judah and Jerusalem. Do not be afraid, and do not be terrified. Tomorrow go out against them, and YHWH will be with you. (2 Chr 20:17)

The presence of God with his people is therefore the greatest comfort. If God is on their side, no one can harm them, for no one who opposes God can succeed (Acts 5:39).[212] In the midst of the spiritual battle that encompasses all the bap-

---

[211] Cf. Judith 9:11: "For thy power depends not upon numbers, nor thy might upon men of strength" (RSV). So also Judas Maccabeus cries out as his small group of warriors approaches the large Syrian army:

> [18] ... It is easy for many to be hemmed in by few, for in the sight of Heaven there is no difference between saving by many or by few. [19]It is not on the size of the army that victory in battle depends, but strength comes from Heaven. ... [22]He [God] himself will crush them before us; as for you, do not be afraid of them. (1 Macc 3:18–19, 22 RSV)

[212] Luther preaches on Eph 6:10–17:

> Thus, he [Paul] wishes herewith to give us great courage that, even if we must spend our whole lives in this world in battle and strife, and suffer everything to rage and storm against us, nevertheless this does not happen for our sake but for God's sake, and therefore the battle is not ours but God's own, and we stand in his service, and can take all the more certain comfort that he will not leave us, but that he will most faithfully stand by us and help, so that we will not labor in vain, but that he will mightily win

tized and that particularly frightened Christians like the Ephesians who were surrounded by idol-worshipers, Paul's concluding exhortation is to stand firm and see the salvation of their God.

Baptism as Armor

The great mystery of Ephesians 6 is that God bestows his own armor on his people. The medium of the great gift is first Jesus Christ, God's Champion, who is depicted by the OT and the NT as clothed in the same armor as YHWH, wielding his ferocious long sword against his people's enemies (Is 11:4–5; 59:16–17; Rev 1:13–16; 19:11–15). But Ephesians takes this one step farther by arguing that, since the Christian is mystically "in Christ,"[213] this armor is bestowed on everyone baptized into him.[214] The conclusion that Paul has Holy Baptism in mind is suggested, first, by the great Galatian summary statement that makes explicit what could be the thesis of Ephesians:

ὅσοι γὰρ εἰς Χριστὸν ἐβαπτίσθητε, Χριστὸν ἐνεδύσασθε.

For as many of you as have been baptized into Christ have put on Christ. (Gal 3:27)

One who has been baptized into Christ is therefore "in him" wherever he is and in whatever he has done. Ephesians is profuse in portraying the implications:

- "In Christ/him," Christians are chosen (just as Christ is God's Elect One) to be holy, faithful, and blameless (like Christ) before God (1:1, 3–4).

- Through Baptism, Christians are adopted as sons of God, like Christ (1:5).

- By the blood of Christ, those baptized into Christ have their sins forgiven (1:7).

- In Christ, the baptized share in his eternal inheritance ("in whom," 1:11).

- Through Baptism, those in Christ are sealed with the promised Holy Spirit ("in whom," twice in 1:13).

---

the victory through us. ("Sermon on the Christians' Armor and Weapons, Ephesians 6:10–17," October 20, 1532, StL 9:822; WA 34/2:380)

[213] See the fifth textual note on 1:3 and "Baptism in the Prologue" in the commentary on 1:3–14.

[214] Luther is one of the rare interpreters who draws a connection between Baptism and the Christian's armor:

For he [Paul] shows here that those who are baptized into Christ and would cling to him must and should be warriors and must always be armed with their weapons and armor. ("Sermon on the Christians' Armor and Weapons, Ephesians 6:10–17," October 20, 1532, StL 9:812; WA 34/2:372; see the fuller quotation in "Epilogue/*Peroratio*" in "Structure and Rhetoric" above)

But Paul is speaking chiefly about diabolical works in the First Table, that is, the Spaniards and the Turks [Papist and Muslim armies], the worst devils, who assail the doctrine. The household estate and the worldly estate do not lead to heaven. There must be pastors, preachers, and Baptism, who reveal the kingdom of heaven through the Word and Baptism. ("Sermon for the Twenty-first Sunday after Trinity," October 25, 1545, AE 58:309; WA 51:73)

For we are called by Christ and already enrolled (in Baptism) in the army which shall fight under Christ against the devil. ("Sermon for the Feast of St. Michael, Revelation 12:7–12," September 29, 1544, *Day by Day We Magnify Thee*, 430; WA 49:579–80)

- In and with Christ, the baptized are raised above all spiritual foes (1:20–23).
- "With Christ" and "in Christ," the baptized have died, risen, ascended, and been seated in heaven (2:5–6; 4:8–10; cf. Rom 6:3–5).
- "In Christ," all Christians are peacefully united with each other and with God, built together into a spiritual temple (2:13–22).
- In and through Christ, the baptized have open access to the throne of God ("in whom," 3:12).
- In Christ, we may call God our Father (3:14–15).
- In Christ, the baptized are one body, united in the Spirit under one Father (4:1–6).
- In Christ, the baptized have already put off the old, corrupt man and been clothed with the new man, re-created in God's image and with his righteousness (4:22–24).
- In Christ, the baptized walk in God's love and forgive one another (4:32–5:2).
- In the Lord, the baptized are awakened and enlightened (5:8–14; cf. 1:18).
- And baptized into Christ, the church is made one flesh with him as a beloved bride, cleansed, washed, and made glorious (5:25–33).

"In the Lord" (6:10) ought therefore to be taken quite literally, for the Christian who has been baptized into Christ is thereby clothed and wrapped with Christ as if putting on a garment (Rom 13:14; Gal 3:27; Col 2:9–12). It is this concrete realization that prompted Paul to speak of the one baptized into Christ as possessing a divine armor (Rom 13:12; Eph 6:10–17; 1 Thess 5:8). The image is equivalent to (or a development of) the common NT image of the righteousness of Christ as a (white) robe or garment.[215] Here, the baptismal robe is Christ himself[216] with all his weapons and defenses. Early evidence that we should read this armor baptismally[217] is found in Ignatius' paraphrase of the pericope:

> Be pleasing to him whom you serve as a soldier [στρατεύεσθε], from whom you also receive your wages: let none of you be found a deserter; *let Baptism remain as your arms*, faith as your helmet, love as your spear,

[215] Cf. Mt 22:11–12; 1 Cor 15:53–54; Col 3:9–12; 1 Pet 5:5; Rev 3:5, 18; 4:4; 6:11; 7:9, 13–14; 19:8, 14; 22:14.

[216] Chrysostom, *Baptismal Instructions*, 2:11, 25, 27, makes this identification explicit on the basis of Gal 3:27:

> We put off the old garment, which has been made filthy with the abundance of our sins; we put on the new one, which is free from every stain. What am I saying? We put on Christ Himself. *For all you*, says St. Paul, *who have been baptized into Christ, have put on Christ. ...*

> Instead of the man who descended into the water, a different man comes forth, one who has wiped away all the filth of his sins, who has put off the old garment of sin and has put on [ἐνδυσάμενος, or "clothed himself with"] the royal robe. ...

> Since they have put on [ἐνδεδύμενοι, or "clothed themselves with"] Christ Himself, wherever they go they are like angels on earth, rivaling the brilliance of the rays of the sun. (Trans. Paul W. Harkins, *ACW* 31:47, 52, 53)

[217] Modern commentators rarely discern or accept the connection of the divine armor with Baptism. Lincoln, *Ephesians*, 440, notes with some skepticism the view of Fischer, *Tendenz und Absicht*, 165–66, who sees a tension between eschatological perspectives in the pericope and argues from this tension that the more apocalyptic material originated in baptismal catechesis in which Baptism was viewed as armor to protect believers in the end-time battle.

endurance as your full armor [τὸ βάπτισμα ὑμῶν μενέτω ὡς ὅπλα, ἡ πίστις ὡς περικεφαλαία, ἡ ἀγάπη ὡς δόρυ, ἡ ὑπομονὴ ὡς πανοπλία].[218]

Writing these words on his way to his martyrdom, Ignatius exhorts his audience not to flee in the face of their terrifying enemies, but to embrace the battle, knowing that Christ will defend them. Thus, his warning against desertion is equivalent to Paul's admonition to "stand" firm and "withstand" (Eph 6:11, 13, 14).

This is not the first military metaphor in the epistle, which has frequently referred to Christ's work as a war against our spiritual enemies.[219] In fact, the way to the divine armor was carefully prepared by a suggestive phrase included among the gifts the risen Christ works through the pastoral office, words that might be rendered as "the equipping [for battle] of the holy [troops]" (τὸν καταρτισμὸν τῶν ἁγίων, 4:12). This implies that the giving of divine armor occurs through the ministry of Word and Sacrament.[220] The connection of the baptismal robe with divine armor is suggested also by the intriguing vision of John, in which Christ (himself clothed in the divine virtues of our text and wielding God's offensive weapons) leads a host arrayed in white as a Captain followed by his army:

> [11]And I saw heaven opened, and behold, a white horse! And he who sits upon it is called Faithful and True [πιστὸς καὶ ἀληθινός], and in righteousness [ἐν δικαιοσύνῃ] he judges and makes war [πολεμεῖ]. [12]And his eyes are like a flame of fire, and on his head are many diadems, [and] he has a name inscribed which no one knows except he himself, [13]and he is clothed [περιβεβλημένος] in a robe having been dipped [βεβαμμένον, baptized?] in blood, and his name is called "The Word of God [ὁ λόγος τοῦ θεοῦ]." [14]And the armies [τὰ στρατεύματα] of heaven, clothed [ἐνδεδυμένοι] in fine linen, white [and] pure, follow him on white horses. [15]And from his mouth issues a sharp long sword [ῥομφαία ὀξεῖα] so that with it he may smite the nations,

---

[218] Ignatius, *To Polycarp*, 6:2; emphasis added. Other early church fathers and baptismal rites frequently connect Baptism with the Christian soldier's armor, alluding to this text. Chrysostom, for example (referring specifically to prebaptismal anointing):

> As if you were a combatant chosen for the spiritual arena, the priest [that is, the bishop] anoints you on the forehead with the oil of the spirit and signs you [with the sign of the cross], saying: "So-and-so is anointed in the name of the Father, and of the Son, and of the Holy Spirit." …

> Next after this, in the full darkness of the night, he strips off your robe and, as if he were going to lead you into heaven itself by the ritual, he causes your whole body to be anointed with that olive oil of the spirit, so that all your limbs may be fortified and unconquered by the darts which the adversary aims at you. (*Baptismal Instructions*, 2:22, 24 [trans. Paul W. Harkins, *ACW* 31:51–52; quoted in Cabié, "Christian Initiation," 41])

[219] E.g., 1:19–23; 2:1–5, 14–16; 3:10; 4:8–10.

[220] Luther: "He has not only angels but also His officials here on earth, like bishops and pastors, who maintain the Church with the pure doctrine and with Baptism" ("Sermon for the Twenty-first Sunday after Trinity," October 25, 1545, AE 58:306; WA 51:70).

and he will shepherd/rule them with a rod of iron, and he himself will tread the wine press of the fury of the wrath of God the Almighty. (Rev 19:11–15)[221]

Observe the remarkable parallels of language with Eph 6:10–17, Christ himself being armed with faith(fulness), truth, righteousness, and the Word of God.

Indeed, it is worth noting that the specific items Paul lists in his catalog of armor, far from being arbitrary, are a summary collection of so much that he has previously said about God's gifts in Holy Baptism. This epilogue/*peroratio* thereby forms a neat *inclusio* around the epistle as it energetically expands the concise introductory statement of Paul's prologue:

> … in whom also you, having heard the <u>Word</u> of <u>truth</u>, the <u>Gospel</u> of your <u>salvation</u>, in whom, having also <u>believed</u>, you were sealed with the promised <u>Holy Spirit</u>. (1:13)

This "sealing," as suggested in the commentary there,[222] might well be interpreted as the branding of a soldier who is thereby marked as belonging to one particular king and army.[223] The underlined terms in 1:13 introduce *in nuce* the various gifts of God that form the Christian's baptismal armor and are fleshed out in the epistle before being summarized here in the epilogue/*peroratio*. Thus, the interpreter should not necessarily look for a direct point of comparison between each piece of armor and each divine gift (as if, e.g., "truth" [6:14] is somehow like a belt), but ought through this collection of terms in 6:10–17 recall all of God's gifts that Paul has proclaimed in this letter.

The act of clothing the soldier recalls, most basically, the image of putting off the old man and putting on the new:

> [You were taught in him …] [22]that you have <u>put off</u> with regard to [your] former way of life <u>the old man</u> who was being corrupted by deceitful lusts, [23]and that you were being renewed in the spirit of your mind, [24]and that you have <u>put on the new man</u> who has been created according to God's [likeness] in <u>true righteousness and holiness</u>. (4:22–24)

Here again the key terms "truth,"[224] "righteousness," and "holiness" are associated with being clothed in Christ. A close look at the six pieces of armor discloses that each item is a *divine* virtue bestowed on the Christian by baptismal incorporation into Christ:

---

[221] Cf. Judg 6:34, in which the Spirit of YHWH "clothed" Gideon for battle. Peter also uses military language for our union with Christ: "Since therefore Christ suffered in the flesh, arm yourselves [ὁπλίσασθε] with the same mind" (1 Pet 4:1).

[222] See the fifth textual note on 1:13 and "Baptism in the Prologue" in the commentary on 1:3–14. See also "Baptism and the Spirit" in "Purpose and Themes" in the introduction.

[223] Cf. George Kitchin's hymn "Lift High the Cross": "All newborn soldiers of the Crucified Bear on their brows the seal of Him who died" (*LSB* 837:3; © 1974 Hope Publishing Co., 380 South Main Pl., Carol Stream, IL 60188; used by permission; all rights reserved). "Newborn" evokes the new birth of Baptism, in which the sealing is acted out with the sign of the cross on the forehead.

[224] The noun ἀλήθεια, "truth," is translated adjectivally in 4:24: "true."

1. "Truth" (6:14), the first item in the divine armor, in addition to its prominent place in 1:13 and 4:24, has recurred frequently in the letter as a fundamental quality of Christ conferred on Christians (4:21; 5:9; see also 4:15).

2. "Righteousness" (6:14), pictured as a breastplate, is regularly associated with clothing in biblical imagery[225] and thus carries deep baptismal resonance (prominently in 4:24).

3. "The Gospel of peace" (6:15), which was already connected with footwear in Is 52:7, is at the core of Paul's description of Christ's work on the cross (Eph 2:13–17), which the Christian has joined through Baptism (Rom 6:3; Col 2:12), and "peace" is a major fruit of Baptism as it draws the church into unity (Eph 4:1–6; "the unity of the Spirit in the bond of peace," 4:3).

4. Closely associated with the Gospel of peace is "the shield of faith" (6:16). "Faith," which is always in Jesus (1:1, 15), stands at the center of the trio "one Lord, one faith, one Baptism" (4:4), and, as a good held in common, works for the unity of Christ's body (4:13; cf. 1 Cor 12:13).

5. The "salvation" (6:17) that is the Christian's helmet recalls those key Ephesian texts proclaiming that the Christian who is united with Christ in his death, resurrection, and ascension is thereby "saved" by grace (2:5–8). This "Gospel of … salvation" is connected to the Christian through baptismal sealing (1:13; cf. Titus 3:5; 1 Pet 3:21).

6. The "Word" and "Spirit" (6:17) that are connected to the final piece of armor, the short sword,[226] are the most explicitly baptismal items of all, as Paul has declared that Christ cleansed and washed his bride by "the washing of water in the Word" (5:26).

These linguistic and thematic ties to the prologue and body of the letter are compelling evidence that Paul intended a baptismal allusion in his allegory of the divine armor.

The rhetorical force of Paul's concluding words, though they include a stark depiction of the vile strength of the evil enemies arrayed before us (6:11–13, 16), is not the inducement of fear. In fact, it is quite the opposite. By depicting the great strength of the enemy, Paul teaches the Ephesians to value the even greater strength of their divine defenses. His epilogue is, on the one hand, an admonition to return ever again to the Word of God, to immerse oneself in it, and thereby to find a refuge against the devil.[227] Though the battle is the Lord's,

---

[225] E.g., Job 29:14; Ps 132:9; Is 59:17; 61:10; Eph 4:24; Rev 19:8.

[226] See the second textual note on 6:17.

[227] Thus, Luther admonishes and encourages the Christian:

Not only do we need God's Word daily as we need our daily bread; we also must use it daily against the daily, incessant attacks and ambushes of the devil with his thousand arts.

If this were not enough to admonish us to read the Catechism daily, there is God's command. That alone should be incentive enough. Deut. 6:7, 8 solemnly enjoins that we should always meditate upon his precepts whether sitting, walking, standing, lying down, or rising, and keep them before our eyes and in our hands as a constant token and sign. Certainly God did not require and command this so solemnly without good reason. He knows our danger and need. He knows the constant and furious attacks and

he works not only *for* but *through* his soldiers, who are active in his battle. But it is also a message of great comfort, an encouragement to rejoice in the manifold gifts of Holy Baptism that defend the Christian in the gray and latter days of the devil's final assaults.

A Warrior *Priest*?

The most obvious and indisputable metaphor in the Ephesian epilogue is military, alluding to contemporary Roman soldiers, but more deeply dependent on OT exodus, holy war, and Divine Warrior themes. The interpreter may find the foregoing exposition exhaustive of the imagery. But the reader may wish to consider cautiously the possibility that the clothing Paul here describes also bears similarity to the vesture of the *high priest* in the OT.[228] If the armor is Christ's armor, the clothing may also be seen as Christ's vesture as the great High Priest, as the NT proclaims him the fulfillment of all that office meant.[229] The belt (or sash), breastplate, and helmet of Ephesians 6 correspond to elements of the high priest's clothing, in addition to the enveloping robe that covered up his sinfulness with God's righteousness.[230] Before these garments were put on, the high priest Aaron and his sons, the priests, were washed with water; afterward Aaron was anointed with oil to indicate his consecration for office by the Holy Spirit.[231] Christ, too, was washed and anointed for his high office (Mt 3:13–17 and parallels; Acts 4:26; 10:38), and he promised the apostles that by the Spirit's anointing they would be "clothed with power from on high" (Lk 24:49), a promise fulfilled on Pentecost. In Ephesians Paul implies that Baptism is a continuation of these actions by asserting that the Christians have received an anointing of the Spirit (1:13; 4:30) and washing of water in the Word (5:26). What is Christ's is also given to those who are in him.

It is therefore quite appropriate when Peter calls those who have been baptized "a royal priesthood" (1 Pet 2:9; cf. 1 Pet 1:22–23; 2:2) to speak of "a priesthood of the baptized."[232] For they are able to approach God in his holy place because they have first been washed (Heb 10:19–22)—just as the people

---

assaults of the devil. So he wishes to warn, equip, and protect us against them with good "armor" against their "flaming darts," and with a good antidote against their evil infection and poison. O what mad, senseless fools we are! We must ever live and dwell in the midst of such mighty enemies as the devils, and yet we despise our weapons and armor, too lazy to give them a thought! (LC, Preface, 13–15)

[228] Barth, *Ephesians*, 2:766–69, understands the "belt" (6:14) as a mark of high office and suggests the "breastplate" (6:14) might resemble the high priest's "breastplate of judgment" (Ex 28:15–30; 39:8–21). He contends that πανοπλία does not mean "*full* armor" but "*splendid* armor" (2:761, 793–95), emphasizing not its military but its glorious symbolic character.

[229] Heb 2:17; 3:1; 4:14–15; 5:5, 10; 6:20; 7:26; 8:1; 9:11, 25–26; 13:11–12.

[230] Exodus 28; cf. Lev 8:6–10; 16:4; 1 Chr 15:27; Ezek 44:17–19; Sirach 45:6–12.

[231] Ex 29:4–9; 30:18–21; 40:11–15; Lev 8:6–10; 16:4.

[232] See Winger, "The Priesthood of All the Baptized."

Israel needed to be washed before they could approach God (Ex 19:10).[233] Perhaps, then, as in the depiction of God's people as a pilgrim army in Exodus,[234] we should view the soldiers of Ephesians 6 as *priestly* warriors or an army of priests—which ought not be considered a contradiction in terms if one remembers that God fights for his army and has no need of mighty men.[235] In Paul's day there was already an apocryphal tradition that made a similar allegory connecting divine virtues to elements of priestly garb:

> And I saw seven men in white raiment saying to me, Arise, put on the robe of the priesthood, and the crown of righteousness, and the breastplate of understanding, and the garment of truth, and the diadem of faith, and the tiara of miracle, and the ephod of prophecy. And each one of them bearing each of these things put them on me, and said, From henceforth become a priest of the Lord, thou and thy seed for ever. And the first anointed me with holy oil, and gave to me the rod of judgment. The second washed me with pure water, and fed me with bread and wine, the most holy things, and clad me with a holy and glorious robe. The third clothed me with a linen vestment like to an ephod. The fourth put round me a girdle like unto purple. The fifth gave to me a branch of rich olive. The sixth placed a crown on my head. The seventh placed on my head a diadem of priesthood, and filled my hands with incense, so that I served as a priest to the Lord.[236]

The reader may decide whether Paul had in mind such a dual referent. But so rich and varied is the metaphor of divine armor that pilgrim, warrior, and priest scarcely exhaust the biblical depictions of the baptized life and its gifts in Christ.[237]

---

[233] Judith washed, anointed, and reclothed herself before entering into battle with Holofernes—implying that she saw herself as a holy warrior whose strength was found not in herself but in her consecration to YHWH (Judith 10:1–4).

[234] See "The Battle Is the Lord's" in the commentary above, as well as the second textual note on 6:14 and the first textual note on 6:15.

[235] Again, see "The Battle Is the Lord's" in the commentary above.

[236] *Testament of Levi*, 8:1–10 (*ANF* 8:14). This text is usually dated to the second century BC. Feeding "with bread and wine" in a Jewish document is probably evocative of Melchizedek (Gen 14:18) as well as of the showbread which only the priests could eat (Lev 24:5–9; Mk 2:26); but in a Christian context it is intriguingly suggestive of the Lord's Supper.

[237] Barth, *Ephesians*, 2:769–70: "The fact that according to this exposition Eph 6:14 mixes war imagery with judgment symbolism is not strange. The same conflation occurs also in the OT, in Qumran and apocalyptic literature."

Epistolary Conclusion: Fellowship in Prayer, Commendation, and Blessing

Translation

6 ¹⁸**With every prayer and petition be praying at every opportune time in the Spirit,**
giving full attention to this with all persistence in petition concerning all the saints
¹⁹**and for me, that to me might be given the message [to speak] in the opening of my mouth,**
to make known with boldness the mystery of the Gospel,
²⁰**for which I am acting as an ambassador in chains,**
that I may be emboldened by it to speak [it] boldly, as I must.
²¹**And so that you, too, may know my circumstances, how I am getting along,**
Tychicus, the beloved brother and faithful minister in the Lord, will make everything known to you,
²²**whom I have sent to you for this very purpose,**
that you may know our circumstances and [that] he may comfort your hearts.
²³**Peace be to the brothers and love with faith from God the Father and the Lord Jesus Christ.**
²⁴**Grace be with all those who love our Lord Jesus Christ in incorruptibility. [Amen.]**

Textual Notes

6:18 διὰ πάσης προσευχῆς καὶ δεήσεως προσευχόμενοι—The near synonyms προσευχή, "prayer," and δέησις, "petition," appear together frequently. In the LXX they are coupled twenty-two times, arguably always in the context of public worship.[1] In the NT, the pair refers to public, liturgical prayers of the gathered congregation (1 Tim 2:1; also Acts 1:14 [variant reading]) or to prayers rendered in an official capacity for the whole church (1 Tim 5:5). While the present verse (like Phil 4:6) makes no explicit reference to this context, it is a fair conclusion from such parallels and from the phrase "concerning all the saints" (Eph 6:18) that Paul is referring to the Prayer of the Church in the Divine Service (though what Paul writes is certainly also applicable to the Christian's private prayers). Similar NT passages are replete with synonyms for

---

[1] Most interesting is the use of the couplet in Solomon's public prayer in the temple at its dedication (a total of eight times in LXX 3 Kgdms 8:38, 45, 54 [MT/ET 1 Ki 8:38, 45, 54]; 2 Chr 6:19, 29, 35, 39; 1 Macc 7:37; cf. Mt 21:13). The pair is also used in God's response to Solomon's prayer (LXX 3 Kgdms 9:3 [MT/ET 1 Ki 9:3]). Ten couplets are in the psalms (Pss 6:10 [ET 6:9]; 16:1 [MT/ET 17:1]; 38:13 [MT 39:13; ET 39:12]; 54:2 [MT 55:2; ET 55:1]; 60:2 [MT 61:2; ET 61:1]; 85:6 [MT/ET 86:6]; 87:3 [MT 88:3; ET 88:2]; 101:1 [MT 102:1; ET 102, inscription]; 101:18 [MT 102:18; ET 102:17]; 142:1 [MT/ET 143:1]). The three remaining couplets refer to public prayer for God's people (Jer 11:14; Baruch 2:14; Dan 9:17; see also θ Dan 9:3).

prayer,[2] suggesting that a distinction between the synonyms ought not be finely pressed, but that multiple terms for prayer encourage its comprehensiveness.[3] If a distinction is sought, προσευχή might be seen as the more general term for "prayer" (which comprehends petition, praise, confession, and thanksgiving), while δέησις would denote a specific "request" or "need."[4] Turner suggests that δέησις as an entreaty to God is "peculiarly Christian,"[5] which leads to an English translation like "petition" or "supplication." The apparent redundancy of διὰ … προσευχῆς … προσευχόμενοι, literally, "through … prayer … praying," might be understood as a Semitic intensive (equivalent to an infinitive absolute), "pray earnestly," but is in any case not unusual Greek (cf. Phil 1:4; James 5:17). While it may be impossible for an English translation to reflect the alliteration of the three particular Greek words that have an initial π (πάσης προσευχῆς … προσευχόμενοι), ours includes three English words with alliteration on "p" ("prayer … petition … praying").

If one follows the NA[27] editors, who place a full stop at the end of 6:17 and capitalize Διά at the start of 6:18, the sentence beginning here has no main (finite) verb, but only a sequence of two participles (προσευχόμενοι … ἀγρυπνοῦντες). This observation has persuaded many commentators that 6:18–20 is dependent on the preceding section and that its admonition to prayer is part of the armor of God.[6] But one conclusion does not necessarily follow from the other.[7] On the one hand, there are persuasive

---

2. Together with προσευχή, "prayer," and δέησις, "petition," the nouns εὐχαριστία, "thanksgiving," and ἔντευξις, "intercession," occur almost indiscriminately in passages describing public prayer (Phil 4:6; Col 4:2; 1 Tim 2:1; cf. Eph 1:16); see also ἱκετηρία, "supplication" (Heb 5:7). For προσευχή, "prayer," as a major function of the gathered congregation, see also Acts 2:42; 12:5; 16:13, 16; Rev 8:3–4.

3. The same may be said for the meaning of πάσης, which might be rendered as "*all* prayer," "the *whole* prayer," or "*every* prayer." See Moule, *Idiom Book*, 94, who rejects the traditional view that πᾶς without the article *must* mean "every" and yet offers the translation "with every possible prayer" for this verse.

4. Marius Victorinus posits the following distinction, which notably assumes the context of public worship: "It is a prayer when we speak the praises of God and recount his great works and when we give thanks and worship him. It is a petition when we pray to God either to pardon our sins or to offer his grace to us" (*Ephesians*, 2:6.18; ACCS 8:213).

    The compound noun προσευχή comes from εὐχή (derived from the verb εὔχομαι), "prayer, vow, wish," which may be a simple declamation. The noun δέησις, "entreaty," and the verb from which it is derived, δέομαι, "to request," are related to δέω, "to need, bind," thus referring to a request for something needed.

5. Turner, *Christian Words*, 342.

6. Schlier, *Epheser*, 298 (cf. 300): "Certainly also prayer in verses 18ff. is *materially* to be reckoned with the equipping with arms [*Waffenrüstung*] as the seventh weapon, but it is no longer *formally* included in the presentation of the equipping" (emphasis added). Otherwise it is mostly older commentators and preachers (as noted by, e.g., Barth, *Ephesians*, 2:777; Bruce, *The Epistles to the Colossians, to Philemon, and to the Ephesians*, 411) who speak of prayer as a weapon.

7. Lincoln, *Ephesians*, 451, makes the participles dependent on the main (finite) verb στῆτε, "stand" (6:14), rather than the intervening main (finite) verb δέξασθε, "receive" (6:17). Nonetheless, he perceptively argues: "But prayer is not the seventh piece of spiritual armor as some claim. … The military metaphors are limited to vv 14–17." Best, *Ephesians*, 604, likewise connects 6:18–20 to 6:10–17 yet sees prayer not as another weapon, but as "the attitude in which the weapons are to be used." Similarly Schnackenburg, *Ephesians*, 281.

contextual reasons to reject the view that prayer should be counted as a seventh piece of armor.[8] At the same time, the function of the participles is open to some debate. One might agree that they are *syntactically* dependent on an available main verb in the preceding context (στῆτε, "stand," 6:14, or δέξασθε, "receive," 6:17). We have argued elsewhere in this commentary that participles ought to be pinned to a finite verb if at all possible.[9] Even if this is true, the contextual evidence we have discussed would still suggest that 6:10–17 and 6:18–20 are *semantically* and *rhetorically* distinct. In other words, while loosely continuing the preceding grammatical structure, Paul turns to a new subject with 6:18.

An alternative grammatical explanation is that the participle προσευχόμενοι be understood as fully independent, equivalent to a finite verb, and therefore interpreted as a mild imperative: "be praying."[10] This interpretation is supported by the imperative that Paul uses in the close Colossian parallel (τῇ προσευχῇ προσκαρτερεῖτε, "be persistent in prayer," Col 4:2), which clearly marks the beginning of a new topic.

ἐν παντὶ καιρῷ—Does this mean "at every moment" (i.e., continually), "at every opportunity" (i.e., whenever you have the chance), or "at every proper time" (i.e., at the traditional hours of prayer)? The only explicit verbal parallel in the NT favors the first interpretation (Lk 21:36). Continual prayer in the Spirit is indeed a NT injunction.[11] But if this verse's vocabulary suggests public prayer, it is unlikely that Paul has in mind continual conscious and vocalized prayer. The second and third possible translations are suggested by the usual connotation of καιρός as "opportune moment" (which Christ has redeemed for our use; see the textual note on Eph 5:16). It is likely that Paul himself maintained the three Jewish hours of prayer (morning, noon, and afternoon/evening; see the third textual note on 1:16),[12] using those opportunities to pursue a disciplined intercession for the saints under his apostolic care.[13] As he prayed for them (1:16), he might be asking the Ephesians to remember him, likewise, in their regular daily prayer.[14] But if public prayer is in mind, and since the reading of this epistle in the liturgy might have

---

[8]   See "Outline and Limits of the Pericope" in "Structure and Rhetoric" in the commentary on 6:10–17.

[9]   E.g., in 3:17; 4:2–3, 25; 5:21. See especially the first textual note on 5:21 and "Structure and Rhetoric" in the commentary on 5:21–33. Wallace, *Greek Grammar*, 651: "The basic rule here is simply this: If a participle can be identified as dependent (i.e., if it can at all be attached to a verb), it should be so considered."

[10] For the evidence that a participle can have imperatival force, see the first textual note on 5:21 in the pericope 5:21b–33.

[11] Lk 18:1; Rom 8:26–27; 12:12; Col 4:2; 1 Thess 5:17.

[12] Ps 55:18 (ET 55:17); Dan 6:11, 14 (ET 6:10, 13); 9:21; Judith 12:5–7; 13:3. See also the practice of the apostles in Acts 3:1; 10:9 (cf. Acts 10:2–3, 30). More extensive prayer, seven times a day plus midnight, is noted in Ps 119:62, 164, which influenced later pious Christian and monastic practice.

[13] Rom 1:9–10; 1 Cor 1:4; Phil 1:3–4; Col 1:3–4; 1 Thess 1:2; 2 Thess 1:3, 11; 2:13; 2 Tim 1:3; Philemon 4; cf. Acts 6:4; Col 4:12.

[14] Cf. similar requests in Rom 15:30–32; Phil 1:19; Philemon 22; and more general requests in 2 Cor 1:11; 1 Thess 5:25; 2 Thess 3:1–2.

been followed by the Prayer of the Church in the Divine Service, it is even more likely that Paul is requesting the congregation to pray for him at every liturgical gathering.[15]

καιρός (6:18) is modified by the adjective πᾶς, "all, every," the second of the four occurrences of this adjective in this verse. Not only is the frequent use of πᾶς typical of the letter,[16] but in this context its use indicates the ongoing and comprehensive character of the prayer to which Paul directs the Ephesians (cf. Phil 1:3–4; 4:6). This verse therefore parallels the public, liturgical "giving thanks always [πάντοτε] for all things [πάντων]" (5:20) that Paul has identified as a gift of the Holy Spirit (5:18).

ἐν πνεύματι—This brief prepositional phrase is pregnant with meaning. It refers not to the human spirit as the source or location of prayer, but to God's Spirit: "together with the Holy Spirit," "immersed in the Spirit," "as moved by the Spirit." Nor does it imply a preference for spontaneous prayer over fixed forms, but merely identifies prayer as the Spirit's domain.[17] All access to the Father, opened up by the Son's work, is mediated and inspired by the Spirit (2:18; 3:5; 5:18). Paul's own prayers in Ephesians have been consistently Trinitarian, bearing the marks of careful, deliberate construction (1:3; 1:3–14 as a whole; 1:16–17; 3:14–17; 5:18–20).

καὶ εἰς αὐτὸ ἀγρυπνοῦντες—The participle ἀγρυπνοῦντες, "giving full attention," is subordinate to προσευχόμενοι and describes the manner of "praying." The verb ἀγρυπνέω, "to be alertly concerned about, *look after, care for*,"[18] is connected to the act of prayer by our Lord in his Little Apocalypse: ἀγρυπνεῖτε δὲ ἐν παντὶ καιρῷ δεόμενοι ἵνα κατισχύσητε, "be alert at every moment, praying that you may be strengthened" (Lk 21:36; cf. Mk 13:33). It is also reminiscent of Christ's words to the disciples in Gethsemane to "watch and pray" (γρηγορεῖτε καὶ προσεύχεσθε, Mt 26:41). Paul thus speaks for the Lord by repeating his own words, directing the Ephesians ever back to the occupation Christ enjoined on his waiting flock.[19] The admonition thus has an eschatological ring, encouraging Christians to wait for Christ's return in a certain manner (1 Pet

---

[15] See "The Liturgical Context of the New Testament Epistles" in "Orality and the Interpretation of the Epistles: A Brief Introduction" in the introduction, as well as "Liturgical Context" in "Evaluation of the Case" in "Authorship" in the introduction. Acts 2:42 demonstrates that public prayer was a major element of regular liturgical gatherings (cf. 1 Tim 2:1).

[16] See the discussion of the adjective πᾶς, "all, every" (which occurs fifty-two times in Ephesians), in "The *Berakah* Prayer (1:3–14) as Prologue" in the commentary on 1:3–14.

[17] Lk 10:21; Rom 8:15–16, 26–27; 15:30; 1 Cor 14:16; Gal 4:6; Eph 5:18–20; Jude 20; cf. Sirach 39:6.

[18] BDAG, s.v. ἀγρυπνέω, 2. Barth, *Ephesians*, 2:779, argues that ἀγρυπνέω, which means etymologically "to pass a sleepless night," can refer to a servant-like attitude, but not to a soldier's watchfulness (which would normally be γρηγορέω). If this distinction is valid (which is questionable in the NT, especially in light of Col 4:2), it is further evidence that prayer is not being treated as a weapon. Certainly its regular NT association with prayer renders a military connotation unnecessary (Best, *Ephesians*, 606).

[19] So also Polycarp, *To the Philippians*, 7:2: "Let us return to the word which has been handed down to us from the beginning; 'watching unto prayer' [1 Pet 4:7], and persevering in fasting" (*ANF* 1:34).

4:7). With the phrase εἰς αὐτό, Paul refers back to the preceding clause (Eph 6:18a), the activity of prayer as the focus of their attention: "to this."[20]

ἐν πάσῃ προσκαρτερήσει καὶ δεήσει—The noun προσκαρτέρησις is a biblical hapax legomenon meaning "firm persistence in an undertaking or circumstance."[21] The cognate verb προσκαρτερέω, "be busily engaged in, persevere in," is so regularly connected with prayer, public worship, and the ministry that it might be considered a Christian technical term.[22] "Persistence and petition" is puzzling. The καί may be epexegetical: "Persistence in what? In petition." The construction may be Semitic, as Hebrew can use conjoined nouns to express an adjectival relationship: "persistent petition."[23]

περὶ πάντων τῶν ἁγίων—The adjective πᾶς, "all," has now occurred four times in one verse.[24] This is typical of Ephesians, in which Paul's liturgical exuberance often extends to hyperbole. However, there is a literal side to the totality of this exhortation. Prayer may not be diminished or restricted in its scope. As Paul has first prayed for the saints in Ephesus (1:1–23; 3:14–21), he now asks these saints to pray for all the saints, that is, for the baptized everywhere in the catholic church, the body of Christ. Only after this request is he willing to append a petition for himself (6:19). Thus, he sets the pattern for Christian prayer: for all, for others, and lastly for oneself. For "saints," see the fourth textual note on 1:1.

6:19 καὶ ὑπὲρ ἐμοῦ—No distinction should be made between περί, "concerning" (used of the saints in 6:18), and ὑπέρ, "for," used here of "me."[25] Paul likely alternates the prepositions for purely stylistic reasons. Since Paul would be included in "all the saints" (6:18), καί might be understood as meaning *and in particular* for me."[26]

ἵνα μοι δοθῇ λόγος—The conjunction ἵνα, "that," introduces the content of the prayer.[27] The aorist *passive* subjunctive verb δοθῇ (from δίδωμι), "might be given," implies God as the giver; to him the prayer is directed, and from him the λόγος will come. Although commonly translated as "word," λόγος has a fuller and more dynamic

---

[20] Here the reflexive pronoun αὐτός simply takes the place of the third person personal pronoun, meaning "it" or "this [that I just mentioned]." In NT Greek αὐτός is beginning to infringe on οὗτός, "this." See BDAG, s.v. αὐτός, 2 a and 2 b α. Cf. εἰς αὐτό in Acts 27:6.

[21] BDAG, s.v. προσκαρτέρησις.

[22] Acts 1:14; 2:42, 46; 6:4; 8:13; Rom 12:12; Col 4:2; Polycarp, *To the Philippians*, 7:2.

[23] See, e.g., the two pairs of nouns in Is 30:15: בְּשׁוּבָה וָנַחַת תִּוָּשֵׁעוּן, "in repentance and in rest ['restful/trusting repentance'] you shall be saved," and בְּהַשְׁקֵט וּבְבִטְחָה תִּהְיֶה גְּבוּרַתְכֶם, "in quietness and in trust ['quiet trust'] shall be your strength."

[24] See the second textual note on 6:18.

[25] In the context of prayer, the prepositions περί and ὑπέρ are interchangeable and indicate the person(s) for whose benefit or on whose behalf the prayer is rendered. See BDAG, s.v. περί, 1 f; s.v. ὑπέρ, A 1 a α; BDF, § 229 (1); Turner, *Syntax*, 270; Moule, *Idiom Book*, 63; Wallace, *Greek Grammar*, 363; Zerwick, *Biblical Greek*, § 96. Compare Lk 22:32 with Acts 8:24, and Col 1:3 with Col 1:9. Cf. Heb 5:1, 3.

[26] Barth, *Ephesians*, 2:779, translates with "especially for me," citing Abbott, *The Epistles to the Ephesians and to the Colossians*, 188.

[27] ἵνα indicates the object or content of the prayer also in 1:17; 3:16, each time also with a form of δίδωμι, "give." See Turner, *Syntax*, 129, which considers ἵνα to be epexegetical rather than final (purpose).

sense than simply a single word written on a page or spoken. It means "message," "speech," or even "preaching." Paul is praying that the Spirit would give him "something to say" when he opens his mouth, as Christ himself promised the Spirit would do when the apostles would be hauled before kings and councils (Mt 10:17–20; Acts 9:15).

ἐν ἀνοίξει τοῦ στόματός μου—The passiveness of Paul's preaching is reiterated by this expression, "in the opening of my mouth." The prayer implies a desire to speak not his own words, but the Lord's. As an apostle (like a prophet), his mouth is but an instrument of God, and only God can give success to his speaking (cf. Col 4:3: "that God would open to us a door for the Word").[28] There is therefore an intimate connection between proclamation and praise, which likewise is only God-pleasing if it is initiated by him: "O Lord, open my lips, and my mouth will declare your praise."[29] Paul's prayer that only the Lord's words of grace would proceed from his mouth stands in opposition to the destructive talk prompted by sin (4:29).

ἐν παρρησίᾳ—The prayer that Paul might speak "with boldness" has two implications. First, it expresses the God-given confidence with which the prisoner Paul confesses the Lord's Gospel for which he is on trial (Acts 28:31; Eph 6:20; Phil 1:14–20).[30] Second, it evokes the boldness of access to the very throne of God that the justified have been granted on the basis of Christ's work and in the Spirit, which leads to confidence before him on the Day of Judgment.[31] This confidence is a quality of Christ himself,[32] appropriated by the believer through incorporation into him in Holy Baptism. As this happens through the apostolic ministry, there is a certain double entendre to Paul's words: the message is proclaimed with boldness and grants boldness to those who receive it. Such boldness even in the midst of suffering characterizes Christ, his suffering apostle, and the Christian who bears his cross. "Then the righteous man will stand with great confidence [ἐν παρρησίᾳ πολλῇ ὁ δίκαιος] in the presence of those who have afflicted him, and those who make light of his labors" (Wis Sol 5:1 RSV).

γνωρίσαι τὸ μυστήριον τοῦ εὐαγγελίου—This infinitival clause expresses the consequent purpose of the preceding petition: the prayer is for the message to be given *so that* Paul might "make known the mystery of the Gospel." This is the apostolic mandate

---

[28] Cf. Moses and Aaron (Ex 4:12, 15); Jeremiah (Jer 1:9); Ezekiel, who was otherwise mute (Ezek 3:27; 29:21; 33:22); and Daniel (Dan 10:16). The Lord can even open the mouth of an ass to be his prophetic instrument (Num 22:28)!

[29] These are the opening versicles of Matins and Vespers, from Ps 51:17 (ET 51:15; see *LSB* 219, 229). Cf. the Spirit-inspired worship of Eph 5:18–20; the opening of Zechariah's mouth to praise God (Lk 1:64); and Wisdom's opening the mouth of the dumb (Wis Sol 10:21; Sirach 15:5; 39:6).

[30] Such boldness in speaking is the distinctive mark of an apostle, to whom Christ has given the authority to speak by the power of the Holy Spirit: Acts 2:29; 4:13, 29, 31; 2 Cor 7:4; Philemon 8; cf. 1 Tim 3:13. See further "Paul's Imprisonment" in "Location and Date of Writing" in the introduction.

[31] Eph 2:18; 3:12 (see the textual notes on those verses); cf. Rom 5:2; 2 Cor 3:12; Heb 4:16; 10:19, 35; 1 Jn 2:28; 3:21; 4:17; 5:14.

[32] Jn 7:26; 11:14; 16:25, 29; 18:20; Col 2:15 (cf. Jn 7:4; 10:24).

(see 3:3–6, 9), which Paul's imprisonment has only made more urgent.[33] On "mystery," see the first textual note on 1:9.

6:20 ὑπὲρ οὗ πρεσβεύω ἐν ἁλύσει—The verb πρεσβεύω means "to be an ambassador/envoy."[34] Its sister noun πρεσβεία, "ambassadorial envoy, delegation," occurs in two parables of our Lord that depict the "diplomatic relations" between God and his people in the age before Christ's return (Lk 14:32; 19:14; cf. 2 Macc 4:11). These words are cognate to the comparative πρεσβύτερος, "elder," since an ambassador was usually appointed from the ranks of elder statesmen.[35] There is therefore a connection between Paul's ambassadorial image and the office of the ministry,[36] for which πρεσβύτερος is the most common NT term.[37] In the only other NT occurrence of the verb πρεσβεύω, Paul says of himself and his co-author Timothy: "Therefore, we are ambassadors for Christ [ὑπὲρ Χριστοῦ οὖν πρεσβεύομεν], [in the belief][38] that God is exhorting through us; we entreat you for Christ's sake, be reconciled to God" (2 Cor 5:20). With these words Paul expresses richly the meaning of his office: (1) he represents Christ, carrying his authority; (2) God speaks through him; and (3) he is an agent of God in effecting a reconciliation of the world to God through the proclamation of the Gospel. Thus, the verb πρεσβεύω carries the freight of ἀπόστολος, "apostle" (see the first textual note and the commentary on 1:1). Paul's appeals to his office thus frame the epistle (1:1; 6:20).

The addition of ἐν ἁλύσει, "in chains,"[39] adds a tragic poignancy to the statement. The reference to chains may be partly metaphorical (meaning "imprisoned"), as Paul may not have been literally chained during the full length of his Caesarean and

---

[33] See further "Paul's Imprisonment" in "Location and Date of Writing" in the introduction.

[34] BDAG, s.v. πρεσβεύω. For ministers acting as ambassadors to effect divine reconciliation between churches, see Ignatius, *To the Philadelphians*, 10:1; Polycarp, *To the Philippians*, 13:1.

[35] BDAG, s.v. πρεσβεύω, cites Herodotus and other authors for the verb's primary sense "be older" or "in the first rank." In the LXX, cognate words can mean "right of the firstborn" (πρεσβεῖον, Gen 43:33); "old age" (πρεσβεῖον, 3 Macc 6:1; cf. Ps 70:18 [MT/ET 71:18]); or "ambassadorial delegation" (πρεσβευτής, 2 Chr 32:31; 1 Macc 13:21; 14:21–22, 40; 15:17; πρεσβεία, 2 Macc 4:11).

[36] In Philemon 9 Paul calls himself πρεσβύτης νυνὶ δὲ καὶ δέσμιος Χριστοῦ Ἰησοῦ, usually translated as "*an old man* and now also a prisoner of Christ Jesus." However, it is possible that πρεσβύτης should be understood as πρεσβευτής, "ambassador"—either because of an early copying mistake or simply because the two terms were somewhat interchangeable. See Nordling, *Philemon*, 230.

[37] The translation of πρεσβύτερος as "elder," though literally correct, can be misleading in a modern Protestant context in which "elder" usually indicates a lay office in a congregation. It is better to render the term as "presbyter" or "priest"—the English term "priest" (like the German *Priester*) is derived from πρεσβύτερος, not the Latin *sacerdos* or the Greek ἱερεύς. See the fifth textual note on 4:11. The noun πρεσβύτερος is used for the incumbents of the pastoral office at Ephesus (Acts 20:17). See also the "presbyters" in, e.g., Acts 14:23; 15:2, 4, 6; 1 Tim 5:17, 19; Titus 1:5; James 5:14; 1 Pet 5:1, 5; and the apostle John as "the presbyter" in 2 Jn 1; 3 Jn 1. See also τὸ πρεσβυτέριον, "the body of presbyters" or perhaps "the office of presbyter" in 1 Tim 4:14.

[38] See Smyth, *Greek Grammar*, § 2078, for this interpretation of ὡς plus a participle.

[39] The singular noun ἅλυσις can be a collective, hence the plural translation "chains." Paul refers to wearing "this chain" in Acts 28:20 (cf. Acts 21:33); 2 Tim 1:16. Cf. Paul's other references to imprisonment in Eph 3:1, 13; 4:1; 2 Tim 2:9.

Roman imprisonments.[40] Yet he was literally chained on a number of occasions, when first arrested and when brought out for interview or trial (Acts 21:33; 26:29; 28:20). To imprison an ambassador is to violate the principle of diplomatic immunity and sever relations with the one who sent him.[41] The world stands in a broken relationship with God, whom people have rejected by rejecting his messengers (Lk 10:16). For any ordinary ambassador, to be imprisoned means his mission has failed. But not so for Paul. Through his ensuing trial he hopes to defend and proclaim the Gospel of Christ and thereby effect reconciliation of the world to God. Far from lamenting his sufferings, Paul rejoices in them (Col 1:24), as they have given him this great opportunity.[42]

ἵνα ἐν αὐτῷ παρρησιάσωμαι—The verb παρρησιάζομαι, "to speak freely, openly, fearlessly," is cognate to παρρησία, the "boldness" with which Paul expected to make the Gospel known (see the fourth textual note on 6:19). Such boldness is a defining characteristic of apostolic preaching inasmuch as the apostles could appeal to the mandate of Christ and had received the power of the Spirit.[43] The *reason* for the boldness, which may also be the *object* of the free speech, is given by the preposition ἐν:[44] "by *it*." The Gospel itself gives him the boldness to speak the Gospel.[45]

ὡς δεῖ με λαλῆσαι—This ὡς clause may refer to either the *act* or the *manner* of speaking, "*since* it is necessary for me to speak" or "*how* it is necessary for me to speak [i.e., boldly]." The former is certainly true and would entail a reference to Paul's mandate from Christ, who commissioned Paul to proclaim this Gospel (e.g., Acts 26:15–18). In his earlier discussion of his imprisonment, Paul emphasized strongly that he preaches to the Gentiles because Christ gave him a revelation of the mystery and mandated him to preach it (Eph 3:1–8). For Paul such preaching is a necessity (1 Cor 9:16). His imprisonment fulfills the necessity of his journey to Rome with the Gospel (Acts 19:21). However, ὡς is not normally used with a causative meaning, but rather introduces a point of comparison or the manner in which an action proceeds.[46] Thus, Paul probably means that the Ephesians are to pray that he might speak the Gospel *boldly*, as it is *necessary* for him to speak it this way (cf. Col 4:4). This is in accord with the revelation of

---

[40] See further "Paul's Imprisonment" in "Location and Date of Writing" in the introduction.

[41] "Custom and law forbid the infliction of harm on human ambassadors. So would it not be presumptuous and rash to bring on the ambassadors of God not only harm but death?" (Ambrosiaster, *Ephesians*, 6:20.3, ACCS 8:215).

[42] Barth, *Ephesians*, 2:782, even suggests that Paul might be making an ironic allusion to the pompous chains worn around the neck by ambassadors as a mark of office.

[43] παρρησιάζομαι regularly marks apostolic preaching: Acts 9:27–28; 13:46; 14:3; 19:8; 26:26; 1 Thess 2:2 (cf. Acts 18:26).

[44] BDAG, s.v. παρρησιάζομαι, 1. Cf. LXX Ps 11:6 (MT 12:6; ET 12:5); Acts 9:27–28; 1 Thess 2:2. Note the textual variant (𝔓[46] B 1739. 1881) that substitutes the neuter pronoun αὐτό, "it" (perhaps following Col 4:4), for the prepositional phrase ἐν αὐτῷ, which would make the Gospel the direct object of the verb (see the next footnote).

[45] The referent of αὐτῷ, if taken as neuter, is therefore τὸ μυστήριον τοῦ εὐαγγελίου, "the mystery of the Gospel" or simply "the Gospel" (6:19). It is also possible that αὐτῷ is masculine, so that Paul is praying to be emboldened "in/by *him*," that is, "in Christ." While that phrase is a prominent theme in Ephesians (see the fifth textual note on 1:3), there is no reference to Christ in the immediate context.

[46] BDAG, s.v. ὡς, 1 and 2.

the mystery: the Gospel is not a secret that remains hidden to all outside a small circle of initiates, but an open proclamation to the world (Eph 3:8–10).

6:21 ἵνα δὲ εἰδῆτε καὶ ὑμεῖς τὰ κατ᾽ ἐμέ, τί πράσσω, πάντα γνωρίσει ὑμῖν—The wording of this commendation of Tychicus (6:21–22) is nearly identical to its Colossian parallel (Col 4:7–8), suggesting that only a brief time intervened between Paul's composition of the two letters and that Tychicus carried both to their destinations on the same trip.[47] The first five words to the Ephesians, ἵνα δὲ εἰδῆτε καὶ ὑμεῖς, are the most significant departure from Colossians. By writing "and so that *you, too*, may know," Paul is (consciously or not) building on what he has previously written to their neighboring church.[48]

The remainder of the text of 6:21 through 6:22 has a "boilerplate" character,[49] expressing the normal duty of the letter carrier to convey information not contained in the letter because it was either confidential, personal, or too complicated for writing. The situation of Paul's imprisonment has lent urgency to the need for him to explain his personal "circumstances" (τὰ κατ᾽ ἐμέ),[50] which is reflected by the parallel wording in the other Captivity Letters, Col 4:7–8 (as noted) and Phil 1:12: "I want you to know, brothers, that my circumstances [τὰ κατ᾽ ἐμέ] have really served the advancement of the Gospel." The expression τί πράσσω (Eph 6:21), in view of his imprisonment, should not be taken literally ("what I am doing"), but means "how I am getting along."[51] Thus, γνωρίζω, "to make known," which has been a key term for the disclosure of the Gospel mystery in Ephesians (1:9; 3:3, 5, 10; 6:19), carries here the more pedestrian meaning of bringing news. Yet, as the goal is that the Ephesians would pray for Paul, this is

---

[47] See "Fellowship through the Apostolic Emissary (6:21–22)" in the commentary. See also "Location and Date of Writing" and "Relationship to Colossians" in the introduction.

[48] Schlier, *Epheser*, 305–6. Baur, *Paul*, 2:43, drew this connection a century earlier. This interpretation takes the clause as strong evidence that Colossians was written first. Not all commentators who hold to Pauline authorship of both letters would concur. Barth, *Ephesians*, 2:809, and Bruce, *The Epistles to the Colossians, to Philemon, and to the Ephesians*, 414, contend that Paul is simply thinking of other churches that would have heard the news—but this does not explain why Paul includes the words to the Ephesians but not to the Colossians. Best, *Ephesians*, 613, suggests that the supposedly unknown author of Colossians cleaned up the redundancy in Ephesians by removing this clause. Lincoln, *Ephesians*, 464–65, takes the καί as merely emphasizing the pronoun ὑμεῖς, "you," just as κἀγώ in 1:15 emphasizes "I" without implying that anyone else is involved. Schnackenburg, *Ephesians*, 288, n. 5, notes that καί often has a vague position and function in Ephesians (1:13, 15; 2:3; 4:17). The textual variants indicate some confusion among the copyists over its function in the present verse.

[49] The sentence has a rough and ready oral quality to it, suggesting that it was rather casually dictated at the end of a long session. It is unusual for a purpose clause with ἵνα to *precede* the main clause (Turner, *Syntax*, 344), and the phrase τὰ περὶ ἡμῶν, "our circumstances" (6:22), is redundant after τὰ κατ᾽ ἐμέ, "my circumstances" (6:21).

[50] Paul uses the identical phrase, τὰ κατ᾽ ἐμέ, "my circumstances," in Phil 1:12; Col 4:7. See BDAG, s.v. κατά, B 6. Cf. Acts 24:22; 25:14.

[51] BDAG, s.v. πράσσω, 3. This usage would be akin to modern expressions like "How do you do?" "Comment ça va?" and "Wie geht's?" Barth, *Ephesians*, 2:809, translates with "the state of my affairs" to indicate that it is Paul's arrest and trial (cf. Acts 24:22; 25:14), not his personal welfare, that is primary.

more than news: by inviting them into his suffering he exercises the fellowship of the body of Christ.

Τυχικὸς ὁ ἀγαπητὸς ἀδελφὸς καὶ πιστὸς διάκονος ἐν κυρίῳ—In addition to being named in the concluding commendation in Ephesians (6:21) and Colossians (4:7), Tychicus appears three more times in the NT (Acts 20:4; 2 Tim 4:12; Titus 3:12). We read that Paul might send Tychicus to Titus in Crete (Titus 3:12).[52] At the end of his third missionary journey, after leaving Ephesus and spending three months in Greece, Paul was accompanied on his return journey to Syria by a crew of assistants drawn from the various places he had founded churches: "Sopater the Berean … ; and of the Thessalonians, Aristarchus and Secundus; and Gaius of Derbe, and Timothy; and the Asians, Tychicus and Trophimus" (Acts 20:4). Presumably they remained with Paul until he arrived in Jerusalem, for "Trophimus the Ephesian," at least, was seen with him there, featuring in the charges raised against him by the Jews (Acts 21:29). Paul later tells Timothy that he has sent Tychicus to Ephesus (2 Tim 4:12). This may be the very trip on which Tychicus carried the letters to the Ephesians, to the Colossians, and to Philemon.[53]

To call Tychicus "beloved brother" (Eph 6:21) is to call him a Christian, one not simply beloved of Paul, but loved by God (6:23).[54] But to add "faithful minister" is to place him alongside Paul in the office of the holy ministry (see the first textual note on 3:7).[55] To be "faithful" (6:21) to his Lord's mandate and gifts is the chief requirement laid on a minister.[56] The phrase ἐν κυρίῳ, "in the Lord," likely modifies both preceding

---

[52] The dating of this trip is unclear. Reicke, *Re-examining Paul's Letters*, 68–73, 110–13, would have Paul write to Titus from Troas (Acts 20:4–6) or Miletus (Acts 20:17), shortly before heading back to Jerusalem at the end of his third missionary journey. Since Tychicus ends up in Jerusalem with Paul, Reicke, 70, concludes that Paul sent Artemas to Crete instead of Tychicus (cf. Titus 3:12). Those who would date Titus much later (after a supposed release of Paul from Roman imprisonment) have no difficulty with Tychicus' movements in this verse.

[53] Reicke, *Re-examining Paul's Letters*, 80. He argues that, since Timothy is Paul's co-author of Colossians (1:1), but is not mentioned in Ephesians, Timothy may have departed for Mysia between the writing of the two letters; subsequently, Paul wrote to him there (2 Tim 4:13). The "onomastica" (lists of names) of Philemon 23–24 and Col 4:7–18 correspond closely to 2 Tim 4:10–12, 20, suggesting that 2 Timothy might have been written shortly after Ephesians. A difficulty with placing 2 Timothy into Paul's Caesarean imprisonment, however, is that in the same letter Paul says he left Trophimus ill in Miletus (2 Tim 4:20; cf. Acts 20:15), which would preclude him from being in Jerusalem with Paul (Acts 20:4; 21:29) at the same time. Reicke does not address or resolve this conflict. If Reicke is wrong and 2 Timothy was written somewhat later than Ephesians and from Rome (as Johnson, *The First and Second Letters to Timothy*, 319, concludes from 2 Tim 1:17), then Paul may have left Trophimus ill at Miletus on his way *to* Rome. Reicke, 79, suggests that the minor difficulties in sorting out the names is a mark of verisimilitude, for a forger would do a better job of harmonizing their whereabouts.

[54] Cf. 1 Cor 15:58; Phil 4:1; Col 4:9; 1 Thess 1:4; 3:2; 2 Thess 2:13; 1 Tim 6:2; Philemon 16; James 1:16, 19; 2:5.

[55] Cf. διάκονος, "minister," in 1 Cor 3:5; 2 Cor 3:6; 6:4; Phil 1:1; Col 1:23, 25; 1 Thess 3:2 (variant reading); 1 Tim 4:6. Note that Paul calls Epaphras "our beloved fellow slave, who is a faithful minister of Christ for your sake [τοῦ ἀγαπητοῦ συνδούλου ἡμῶν, ὅς ἐστιν πιστὸς ὑπὲρ ὑμῶν διάκονος τοῦ Χριστοῦ]" (Col 1:7) and Philemon "our beloved fellow worker [τῷ ἀγαπητῷ καὶ συνεργῷ ἡμῶν]" (Philemon 1); and Peter writes of "our beloved brother Paul" (2 Pet 3:15).

[56] Mt 24:45; 25:21, 23; Lk 12:42; 16:10; 19:17; 1 Cor 4:2, 17; Heb 3:5.

phrases: thus, Tychicus is not Paul's brother by blood, but "in the Lord"; and he is not a representative of any earthly master, but a "faithful minister in the Lord."[57] The full phrase constitutes Paul's commendation of Tychicus as his delegate and means "you can trust what he will say as coming from me—indeed, from the Lord" (cf. 1 Cor 4:17).

6:22 ὃν ἔπεμψα πρὸς ὑμᾶς εἰς αὐτὸ τοῦτο, ἵνα γνῶτε τὰ περὶ ἡμῶν—The epistolary aorist[58] ἔπεμψα, "I have sent," which might be translated as "I *am sending*," indicates that Tychicus carries some authority as Paul's delegate. The terms of authority are specified by the rest of the sentence, to which the phrase εἰς αὐτὸ τοῦτο, "for this very purpose,"[59] points: he is to convey information about Paul's circumstances. The expression with a plural pronoun, τὰ περὶ ἡμῶν, "*our* circumstances,"[60] is somewhat out of character for this letter, in which previously Paul has not mentioned any cowriter or colleagues. This inconsistency may either be owing to Paul's casual repetition of the conclusion from Col 4:7–8, or it may reflect the fact that he was not alone in his captivity.[61]

καὶ παρακαλέσῃ τὰς καρδίας ὑμῶν—The hearts of the Ephesians may have been troubled because of a twofold sense of guilt over Paul's arrest: that he was suffering for preaching the Gospel to the Gentiles and that one of their own members, Trophimus, was the trigger for his arrest (Acts 21:27–29).[62] Paul has previously allayed their fears by explaining that he preaches to the Gentiles because of Christ's mandate (Eph 3:1–13), and so his afflictions are for their benefit and for their glory (3:13). It is this message that Tychicus is to reinforce by comforting their hearts (6:22). On παρακαλέω, "to encourage, comfort," see the first textual note on 4:1. On the metaphorical meaning of the "heart," see the first textual note on 1:18. The dispatch of representatives from Paul to build up the churches under his care reminds us that the apostolic ministry does not end with the imprisonment or death of the apostles, but continues in their successors in the office of the ministry. For, ultimately, the ministry is not about the individual man,

---

[57] In the parallel text (Col 4:7) the additional attribute σύνδουλος, "fellow slave," separates διάκονος, "minister," from ἐν κυρίῳ, "in the Lord," confirming the view that the latter phrase modifies all preceding terms. If not for the addition of "in the Lord," one might argue that διάκονος, "minister," simply means "delegate *of Paul* in the matter of carrying the letter and delivering his news."

[58] The verb is written in the aorist because the sending will be in the past by the time the recipients read the letter. Cf., e.g., Acts 23:30; Phil 2:28; Col 4:8; Philemon 12. See BDF, § 334; Burton, *Moods and Tenses*, § 44; Turner, *Syntax*, 73; Moule, *Idiom Book*, 12; Wallace, *Greek Grammar*, 562–63. In Eph 3:3 the significance of the aorist προέγραψα is debatable.

[59] BDAG, s.v. αὐτός, 1 g, suggests for the phrase αὐτὸ τοῦτο the translation "just this." The phrase used here, εἰς αὐτὸ τοῦτο (cf. Rom 9:17; 13:6; 2 Cor 5:5; Col 4:8), is equivalent to the adverbial phrases τοῦτο αὐτό (2 Cor 2:3) and αὐτὸ τοῦτο (2 Pet 1:5), meaning "for this very reason/purpose."

[60] BDAG, s.v. περί, 1 i. Cf. Lk 24:19, 27; Acts 23:11; 28:15, 31; Phil 1:27; 2:19–20. In Acts 23:15; 24:10 the phrase τὰ περί with other pronouns is used of the charges laid against Paul. Josephus, *Antiquities*, 2:60, uses it of charges laid against Joseph by Potiphar's wife.

[61] Compare the list of characters in Col 4:7–14 with Philemon 23–24. By the time of 2 Timothy, Paul would write "Luke alone is with me" (2 Tim 4:11).

[62] See "Paul's Trip to Jerusalem, Arrest, and Imprisonment (Acts 21:1–36)" in "The City of Ephesus and Paul's Relationship to It" in the introduction.

but about the Lord whom he represents, the Christ who alone can give true comfort to the troubled hearts of Christians like these Ephesians (cf. 2 Thess 2:16–17).

6:23 εἰρήνη τοῖς ἀδελφοῖς καὶ ἀγάπη μετὰ πίστεως ἀπὸ θεοῦ πατρὸς καὶ κυρίου Ἰησοῦ Χριστοῦ—A final greeting is typical of ancient letters, but with Paul it carries additional pastoral and liturgical functions.[63] This sentence, which is unlike any other final greeting of Paul's, is largely parallel to the opening words of Ephesians (1:1–2), forming an *inclusio* around the letter. Together with 6:24, the *inclusio* is even partly chiastic:

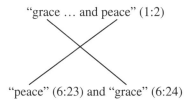

"grace … and peace" (1:2)

"peace" (6:23) and "grace" (6:24)

The Greek noun εἰρήνη, "peace," as a translation of the common Jewish greeting *shalom*, has taken on new meaning in light of Christ's uniting work on the cross (2:13–17; 4:3; 6:15), all of which is here recalled. Peace, as a gift from God, has reconciled Jew and Gentile, both to God and to one another.[64] The horizontal and vertical dimensions of peace are expressed in this blessing (6:23) respectively by "brothers" and "God the Father," and the combination of "love" and "faith."[65] The use of ἀδελφός, "brother," hitherto not applied to the Ephesians, is surely equivalent to Paul's opening address τοῖς ἁγίοις … καὶ πιστοῖς, "to the saints and faithful ones" (1:1).[66] As in 6:21, "brother" means Christian (the only other concluding blessing to address "brothers" is Gal 6:18). The noun ἀγάπη, "love," is unusual in Paul's final greetings,[67] but, as it is thematic of Ephesians (occurring ten times; see the textual notes on it in 1:4, 15; 6:24), it is not surprising in the closing words. As the prepositional phrase with ἀπό, "from," indicates, "peace" and "love" are not manmade, but are gifts from God the Father through Jesus Christ (cf. 2:4; 5:2).

The addition of μετὰ πίστεως, "with faith," is more puzzling.[68] There is no equivalent in Paul's other concluding blessings. The explanation for this combination of "love"

---

[63] See "Fellowship in Benediction (6:23–24)" in the commentary.

[64] Barth, *Ephesians*, 2:817, including n. 37, notes the significance in Ephesians of peace with God and peace between Jew and Gentile, which "take the central place which 'justification' and 'faith' have in other Pauline epistles. … Only here is 'peace' not just one element of preaching among others, but *the* substance of the gospel, 2:17; 6:15."

[65] Cf. the words of the post-Communion collect "in faith toward You and in fervent love toward one another" (*LSB* 201), composed by Luther on the basis of medieval examples for his German mass (1526), AE 53:84; see Reed, *The Lutheran Liturgy*, 381–82.

[66] In fact, 𝔓46 reads ἁγίοις, "saints," in place of ἀδελφοῖς, "brothers."

[67] In Paul's final greetings, ἀγάπη, "love," is found elsewhere only in 1 Cor 16:24, where it is Paul's "love," and 2 Cor 13:13 (ET 13:14), where it is God the Father's. Note also the connection of "love" and "peace" in 2 Cor 13:11: "and the God of love and peace will be with you."

[68] BDAG, s.v. μετά, A 2 f, offers this explanation for this use of the preposition: "to show a close connection betw[een] two nouns, upon the first of which the main emphasis lies." Cf. 4:2. However, it is not at all obvious that "love" has priority over "faith" in this verse. In fact,

and "faith" may be found in Paul's opening prayer, which arose from reports brought to him of the Ephesians' "faith in the Lord Jesus and love toward all the saints" (1:15; cf. 3:17), and in his opening address to the Ephesians as "faithful ones in Christ Jesus" (1:1).[69] Certainly "faith" has also been prominent in the letter's body.[70] Thus, in his final greeting Paul calls down the Lord's blessing upon them, that they might *continue* in these three thematic divine gifts: "peace," "love," and "faith." Such triplets are typical of Paul's style in Ephesians.[71]

6:24 ἡ χάρις μετὰ πάντων τῶν ἀγαπώντων τὸν κύριον ἡμῶν Ἰησοῦν Χριστόν— Although Paul's final greetings vary widely, his letters typically end with some variant of the basic formula ἡ χάρις μεθ᾽ ὑμῶν, "grace be with you" (Col 4:18; 1 Tim 6:21; 2 Tim 4:22). "Grace" occurs in the benediction of all thirteen epistles. Most also begin with such a blessing (see the first textual note on Eph 1:2). There is no greater gift than to receive the undeserved favor of God, and this grace has been a prominent theme in Ephesians.[72]

To refer to his addressees as "those who love our Lord Jesus Christ" is, however, almost completely unique. On the one hand, it is not unexpected, as "love" is a major theme of this letter. In Ephesians the verb ἀγαπάω normally refers to God "loving" mankind in Christ, though this is also seen as the inspiration and pattern for mutual love within the body of Christ (1:6; 2:4; 5:2, 25, 28, 33). The noun ἀγάπη most often refers to God's "love" for mankind (1:4; 2:4; 3:17, 19; 5:2; 6:23) and sometimes to Christian "love" for one another (1:15; 4:2, 15, 16). But nowhere does Ephesians speak of our love for God prior to this verse, and the normal expression of our relationship with Christ is "faith"[73] or "believe."[74] The closest parallel lies in the words immediately prior to the final greeting of 1 Corinthians: "If anyone does not love the Lord, let him be accursed.

Barth, *Ephesians*, 2:811, reverses BDAG's judgment, saying that the expression gives priority to "faith" over "peace" and "love" by putting it last! The preposition μετά may simply be used to bind "faith" with "love" (cf. Gal 5:6) and to distinguish this word pair from "peace." Chrysostom comments: "This love is always *with faith*, for there is no good in love without faith. Love cannot even exist without faith" (*Homilies on Ephesians*, 24:6.23, ACCS 8:216).

[69] Best, *Ephesians*, 618, contends that, as peace and love "belong as terms to the same semantic field denoting God's beneficent attitude towards people," therefore faith must also refer to *God's* attitude, his covenant faithfulness. This argument is not entirely coherent. First, unlike love and faith, "peace" is not a verbal noun, but describes a state of being. Second, while in Ephesians "love" is primarily God's attitude to mankind, Paul also emphasizes the Christian's consequent loving response to others. Finally, "faith" has been used mostly as *fides qua creditur* ("the faith by which it is believed"), i.e., the Christian's trust in God, and occasionally as *fides quae creditur* ("the faith which is believed"), the body of doctrine, but never for God's faithfulness toward mankind (see the second textual note on 2:8). To introduce it at this point in the letter would be unprecedented and unexpected.

[70] See "faith" (πίστις) or "believe" (πιστεύω) in Eph 1:13, 15, 19; 2:8; 3:12, 17; 4:5, 13; 6:16 (cf. πιστός, "faithful," in 1:1; 6:21).

[71] See the triads cited in "Rhythm" in "Orality and the Interpretation of the Epistles: A Brief Introduction" in the introduction.

[72] See χάρις, "grace," in 1:2, 6–7; 2:5, 7–8; 3:2, 7–8; 4:7, 29; and here in 6:24.

[73] See πίστις in 1:15; 2:8; 3:12, 17; 4:5, 13; 6:16, 23.

[74] See πιστεύω in 1:13, 19.

O Lord, come! [εἴ τις οὐ φιλεῖ τὸν κύριον, ἤτω ἀνάθεμα. μαράνα θά]" (1 Cor 16:22). The double formula of anathema and invitation has been interpreted as a statement of Communion fellowship, which means that those who love the Lord are the baptized, catechized, faithful, and orthodox members of the church.[75] "Those who love our Lord" (Eph 6:24) may then be equivalent to "those who walk by this rule [κανόνι]," upon whom Paul invokes the blessing "peace be upon them, and mercy, even upon the Israel of God" (Gal 6:16), and perhaps also corresponds to "those who love us in the faith [τοὺς φιλοῦντας ἡμᾶς ἐν πίστει]" (Titus 3:15). As a designation of the faithful community of God, it is also rooted in the OT formulae for "those who love God."[76] Paul's use of the formula here indicates an awareness that the letter was being read in the Divine Service and would be followed by the Lord's Supper, in which only "those who love our Lord" would participate.[77]

ἐν ἀφθαρσίᾳ—The final uncontested words of the epistle are puzzling. The noun ἀφθαρσία, "incorruptibility" (α-privative, "not," + φθείρω, "to corrupt"), refers in all other scriptural occurrences to a quality of the future life, the eternal endurance of the resurrected body.[78] This derives from the common usage of φθείρω for the corruption wrought in this world by human sin and God's judgment against it.[79] Thus, it is unlikely that in the present verse the phrase ἐν ἀφθαρσίᾳ would modify adverbially the articular participle τῶν ἀγαπώντων so as to mean something like "those *whose love* for the Lord is *undying*."[80] It would be peculiar for Paul to make his closing benediction conditional on the strength of a certain quality (love) in the recipients and thus at the very end of

---

[75] Robinson, "Traces of a Liturgical Sequence in 1 Cor. 16:20–24," 39, breaks down the final words of 1 Corinthians into versicles and responses. One might postulate that "O Lord, come!" was an acclamation expressing faith in both the real presence of Christ's body and blood in the Sacrament of the Altar and in his return on the Last Day (to which the Sacrament points).

[76] See the forms of אָהֵב, "to love," in, e.g., Ex 20:6; Deut 5:10; 6:5; 7:9; 10:12; 13:4 (ET 13:3); 19:9; 30:6, 16, 20; Judg 5:31; Pss 97:10; 145:20; Dan 9:4 (cf. Ps 122:6). See also ἀγαπάω in Tobit 14:7; Pss Sol 4:25; 6:6 (cf. Tobit 13:14); and in the NT, ἀγαπάω in Rom 8:28; 1 Cor 2:9; 8:3; 2 Tim 4:8; James 1:12; 2:5; 1 Pet 1:8; 1 Jn 4:20–21; 5:2.

[77] See "The Liturgical Context of the New Testament Epistles" in "Orality and the Interpretation of the Epistles: A Brief Introduction" in the introduction. See also Robinson, "Traces of a Liturgical Sequence in 1 Cor. 16:20–24," 39; Sasse, "Selective Fellowship," 53–54; Winger, "Orality as the Key to Understanding Apostolic Proclamation in the Epistles," 214–17; Schnackenburg, *Ephesians*, 291; Schlier, *Epheser*, 311.

[78] BDAG, s.v. ἀφθαρσία. See Rom 2:7; 1 Cor 15:42, 50, 53–54; 2 Tim 1:10. See also 4 Macc 9:22; 17:12; Wis Sol 2:23; 6:18–19. The adjective ἄφθαρτος, "incorruptible," has similar connotations: 1 Cor 9:25; 1 Cor 15:52; 1 Pet 1:4, 23; 3:4.

[79] See φθείρω, "to corrupt" (passive: "be corrupted"), in LXX Gen 6:11; Is 24:3–4; 54:16; Jer 13:9; Ezek 16:52; Hos 9:9. By contrast, the verb is negated in Deut 34:7 (Moses' vigor did not abate) and in Dan 2:44; 7:14, which refer to the Messiah's eternal kingdom that shall never be destroyed. In the NT, see φθείρω in 1 Cor 3:17; 2 Cor 11:3.

[80] Many English translations adopt this interpretation (e.g., ESV, NIV, NRSV, RSV). Abbott, *The Epistles to the Ephesians and to the Colossians*, 191, and Best, *Ephesians*, 620, also argue for this interpretation. Ignatius, *To the Romans*, 7:3, "incorruptible love [ἀγάπη ἄφθαρτος]" might be cited in support, but his grammar is different, and in context he clearly refers to eternal life. Moule, *Idiom Book*, 197, suggests a double entendre: "The last words of Ephesians, ἐν ἀφθαρσίᾳ, may be intended to mean both *sincerely* (in incorruption) and *eternally* (in incorruptibility)."

his epistle to cast the Lord's grace into doubt.[81] That interpretation is rendered yet more unlikely by the location of the prepositional phrase so far distant from the participle.[82]

A second possible interpretation is no more satisfactory: that ἐν ἀφθαρσίᾳ modifies adjectivally the preceding proper name Ἰησοῦν Χριστόν, as if to say "our Lord Jesus Christ *who is now in incorruptible [glory]*."[83] If this were meant, Paul would likely have written τὸν ἐν ἀφθαρσίᾳ, "*the one* in incorruptibility." Most commentators therefore prefer to connect the prepositional phrase with χάρις, indicating the eternal effectiveness and fruit of God's "grace" (cf. 2:7).[84] But an even greater distance separates the phrase ἐν ἀφθαρσίᾳ from the noun χάρις.[85]

Therefore it may be best simply to understand ἐν ἀφθαρσίᾳ as a supplementary phrase that modifies the entire blessing and describes the resulting state of those who love the Lord. It stands in opposition to what they once were. Those who have been baptized have put off "the old man *who was being corrupted* [τὸν φθειρόμενον] by deceitful lusts" (4:22). In Baptism they have already died and risen to new life; in their continuing reception of his life-giving, resurrected body and blood at the altar, they are already enjoying the blessings of the resurrected life; they are thus "in incorruptibility" (6:24; cf. Jn 5:24; 1 Jn 3:14). The only other occurrences of the prepositional phrase ἐν ἀφθαρσίᾳ in biblical or early postapostolic literature carry the same eschatological reference to the incorruptibility of the age to come.[86] The phrase therefore conveys a Spirit-wrought[87] locatedness of the baptized that is similar to "the saints and faith-

---

[81] Barth, *Ephesians*, 2:814: "The imposition of a condition upon the saints would spoil the tone of this letter, for it would have Ephesians conclude with an expression of the author's doubt as to the readers' election and good faith."

[82] Five Greek words (τὸν κύριον ἡμῶν Ἰησοῦν Χριστόν) intervene between τῶν ἀγαπώντων and ἐν ἀφθαρσίᾳ.

[83] Cf. 1 Tim 1:17. Support for this might also be found in *2 Clement*, 20:5, which describes Christ as "the Savior and Prince of incorruptibility [τὸν σωτῆρα καὶ ἀρχηγὸν τῆς ἀφθαρσίας]."

[84] Schnackenburg, *Ephesians*, 291; Schlier, *Epheser*, 311–12. Lincoln, *Ephesians*, 467–68: "Both grace and immortality are seen as blessings from God that the writer desires to be conferred on his readers. The combination of grace with immortality is an appropriate one, allowing for each notion to color the other." Bruce, *The Epistles to the Colossians, to Philemon, and to the Ephesians*, 416, including n. 114, asserts that it is common in Ephesians for a word or a phrase to be modified by a word that follows ἐν used in a "comitative" sense, citing 3:12; 4:19; 6:2. Lincoln argues similarly, citing 2:7; 3:12; 6:2. (Bruce also cites 1:4, 8, where this commentary has argued that the prepositional phrase goes instead with the verb that *follows*.) Barth, *Ephesians*, 2:814, argues that ἐν is equivalent to "and" or "together with," and quotes Robinson, *Ephesians*, 200: "Grace together with blessed immortality."

[85] Nine Greek words (μετὰ πάντων τῶν ἀγαπώντων τὸν κύριον ἡμῶν Ἰησοῦν Χριστόν) intervene between ἡ χάρις and ἐν ἀφθαρσίᾳ.

[86] "Thus also the resurrection of the dead. It [the body] is sown in corruption [ἐν φθορᾷ]; it is raised in incorruptibility [ἐν ἀφθαρσίᾳ]" (1 Cor 15:42). "I bless you that you have counted me worthy of this day and this hour, that I should receive a share in the number of [your] martyrs, in the cup of your Christ, [with a view] to the resurrection of eternal life, both of soul and body, in the incorruptibility [ἐν ἀφθαρσίᾳ] of the Holy Spirit" (*Martyrdom of Polycarp*, 14:2; cf. *Martyrdom of Polycarp*, 17:1; 19:2).

[87] "Such life and incorruption [ἀφθαρσίᾳ] this flesh can partake of, when the Holy Spirit is joined to it. No one can utter or speak 'what the Lord hath prepared' [1 Cor 2:9] for His elect" (*2 Clement*, 14:5 [*ANF* 7:521]).

ful ones *in Christ Jesus* who are *in Ephesus*" (Eph 1:2), with which the epistle began. Paul's final words are therefore a promise.[88]

[ἀμήν]—The textual evidence for the inclusion of "amen" as the original reading at the end of the epistle is weak (even though the majority of later manuscripts include it). It is absent in the earliest manuscripts (e.g., 𝔓⁴⁶ ℵ* A B), but added by correctors and included in the Western and Byzantine traditions (e.g., ℵ² D 1739ᶜ 𝔐 it). A concluding "amen" is found with undivided attestation in only one Pauline epistle (Gal 6:18).[89] In all remaining epistles it appears in one part of the manuscript tradition, but is absent from some of the earliest manuscripts.[90] There is little consistency between the different Pauline epistles within each manuscript, suggesting that the preference of the copyist was not the major factor.[91] The same pattern is evidenced in the Catholic Epistles, in which the concluding "amen" always occurs in some part of the manuscript tradition, but is only undisputed in one instance.[92]

What conclusion should be drawn from this evidence? Although it is not impossible that Paul could have added "amen" to his benediction (as he concludes his doxology with "amen" in 3:21), it is more likely that he did not. "Amen" is present in at least *some* manuscripts at the end of *every* NT epistle; in the Pauline epistles and in most of the Catholic Epistles, it is present in the *majority* of later manuscripts (often signified by 𝔐). The persistence of "amen" in the manuscript tradition suggests that in public liturgical reading the congregation was accustomed to respond to the blessing with an "amen," from which custom it crept into the manuscripts themselves. "Amen" is a word of faith, by which the recipients of the blessing acknowledge God's gift and thank him for it. It is therefore a fitting response for any reader/hearer of Ephesians today and a fitting conclusion to this epistle of grace.

For "amen" in doxologies and its OT background, see the last textual notes on 1:14 and 3:21.

---

[88] So also Ignatius writes to the same Ephesian churches that incorruptibility is a gift: "For this reason the Lord received the ointment [μύρον] upon his head, that he might breathe incorruptibility into his church [ἵνα πνέῃ τῇ ἐκκλησίᾳ ἀφθαρσίαν]" (*To the Ephesians*, 17:1). It is unclear in context whether Ignatius is referring to Jesus' literal anointing by the woman (Mt 26:7) or to his Baptism (to which Ignatius explicitly refers shortly afterwards [*To the Ephesians*, 18:2]).

[89] In Rom 16:27 there is an undisputed "amen" at the end of the doxology, but the placement of the doxology within the book of Romans is notoriously complicated.

[90] 1 Cor 16:24; 2 Cor 13:13; Eph 6:24; Phil 4:23; Col 4:18; 1 Thess 5:28; 2 Thess 3:18; 1 Tim 6:21; 2 Tim 4:22; Titus 3:15; Philemon 25 (cf. Rom 15:33).

[91] E.g., even in the early manuscripts 𝔓⁴⁶ and ℵ, "amen" comes and goes, though the late Majority tradition (𝔐) always includes it. By the time of the later Majority manuscripts, "amen" loses its character as a liturgical response to a blessing and simply appears as the conclusion to the book, even in the four Gospels and Acts.

[92] Jude 25 has an uncontested "amen," but this is at the conclusion of a doxology. Among the remaining Catholic Epistles only 2 Pet 3:18 has strong textual evidence in favor of the originality of "amen."

Commentary

Structure and Rhetoric

The neat and inarguable pericopal divisions that characterized the early chapters of Ephesians have faded into a succession of rather fuzzy lines in its later parts. Whether the pericope that begins at 4:17 is marked by 4:32 or 5:2 as its conclusion, and whether 5:21 belongs to the preceding (5:3–21) or following (5:21–6:9), have been tricky questions to resolve. One thing leads to the next in Paul's mind, and so it may be best to recognize that he has now settled into a more continuous flow of thought. Both 5:1–2 and 5:21 are bridges that belong partly to what precedes and partly to what follows.

The same may be said for 6:18–20, the subject of much structural debate. We have contended (with the majority of modern commentators) that the "prayer" which serves as the subject of these verses ought not be considered part of the armor of God (see "Structure and Rhetoric" in the commentary on 6:10–17). Thus, 6:18–20 is distinct *semantically* from 6:10–17. These verses (6:18–20) treat a different subject, even though they are linked by the common work of the Holy Spirit. Yet most modern commentators still connect 6:18–20 to the preceding pericope (6:10–17) because of the not insignificant *syntactical* connection between them.[93] For 6:18–20 does not contain a finite (main) verb. Its introductory participle προσευχόμενοι, "praying" (6:18), though it could be understood independently as imperatival, "be praying!" is probably dependent grammatically on a finite verb in the preceding verses: either στῆτε, "stand" (6:14), or δέξασθε, "receive" (6:17).[94] The ensuing confusion is illustrated by the ambiguous editorial layout in NA[27], which places a minor division between 6:17 and 6:18, while punctuating 6:18–20 as an independent sentence, and yet places a major division between 6:20 and 6:21 (this is easier to see than to explain!).

Departing from majority opinion, this commentary proposes that it is more helpful to consider 6:18–20 together with the verses that *follow*, as being part of the epistle's conclusion (6:18–24). For while Paul has perhaps continued the

---

[93] Lincoln, *Ephesians*, 430–31, admits that 6:18–20 *appears* to move on to a new subject, but engages in a struggle to find a thematic connection with the armor of God because he believes the syntax demands it.

[94] For the dependence of participles on a finite verb, see the grammatical evidence in the first textual note on 5:21 and "Structure and Rhetoric" in the commentary on 5:21–33. See also the discussion in the first textual note on 6:18. The two choices are summarized by BDF, § 468:

> (1) Paul is fond of continuing a construction begun with a finite verb by means of co-ordinated participles, sometimes in a long series. ... (2) Related to this type of anacoluthon and probably arising from it is the peculiar use of a participle in place of a finite verb and without any connection to one, usually in a long series and in an imperatival sense; it is common in Paul and even more so in Peter. ... ἐστέ may be supplied throughout.

These two choices are illustrated, respectively, by (1) "... praying ..." in ESV and (2) "Pray ..." in RSV.

See Moulton, *Prolegomena*, 180–82 for an extended discussion of the "imperatival participle" (choice 2).

grammar of the preceding pericope, he has really moved on to a new (though related) *subject*. This decision is buttressed by a consideration of the section's *rhetorical* function, for prayer requests such as this (cf. Col 4:2) typically belong to the epistolary conclusion. The evidence for this contention emerges from an examination of letter-writing patterns in antiquity and in Paul.

Greco-Roman letters, on the one hand, conclude in a remarkably consistent manner, with thousands of examples scarcely deviating from the following formula:

1. greetings, often including the names of friends and family members (sometimes absent in earlier Greek letters, but common in Roman ones)
2. a wish for the recipient's good health
3. a farewell formula, almost always ἔρρωσο, "be strong/well!" (from ῥώννυμι), or εὐτύχει, "prosper!"[95]

The rhetorical function of this concluding pattern was clearly to strengthen the relational ties between the sender and the recipient(s).

Paul's pattern, while superficially similar (if one would equate his greetings and blessing with the above), differs quite remarkably.[96] He does not speak specifically of his recipients' physical health, though he is certainly concerned with their spiritual well-being. The near-universal words of farewell do not appear in any of Paul's letters, even the ostensibly private ones. In place of this brief, formulaic conclusion, Paul weaves a complex and varied end to his letters from any number of the following elements:

1. disclosure of his travel plans and reference to those of the recipients
2. request for prayer for him and his mission
3. final words of exhortation
4. bestowal of peace
5. commendation of the letter carrier as his representative; sometimes commendation of other travelers
6. greetings from those with him and to those with the recipients
7. expressions of closed Communion: the holy kiss, invitation, and exclusion
8. reference to the procedure of dictation (amanuensis)
9. a few words in his own hand ("large letters") to function as a seal or signature
10. admonition to read the letter publicly
11. doxology
12. blessing[97]

---

[95] Doty, *Letters in Primitive Christianity*, 39; Nordling, *Philemon*, 313–16. See examples in Stowers, *Letter Writing in Greco-Roman Antiquity*, passim.

[96] Doty, *Letters in Primitive Christianity*, 39–40: "Pauline and other primitive Christian letters are less bound to the closing conventions of the Hellenistic letters than to any other formulaic portion: neither the health wish nor the Greek word of farewell is found in Pauline letter closings; rather, a benediction or doxology appears, serving the same functions."

[97] This twelvefold listing is our own. But compare the brief (and inadequate) analysis in Doty, *Letters in Primitive Christianity*, 39–43.

Paul's Epistolary Conclusions

	Rom	1 Cor	2 Cor	Gal	Eph	Phil	Col	1 Thess	2 Thess	1 Tim	2 Tim	Titus	Philemon
1. Travel plans	15:22–29	16:1–9	13:10			(4:14–18)					4:9, 12–13, 20–21a	3:12–13	22
2. Prayer request	15:30–32				6:18–20	(4:6, 10–14)	4:2–4 (4:18)	5:25	3:1–2		(4:16–18a)		22
3. Exhortation		16:13–16	13:11a	6:12–15, 17		4:8–9a	4:5–6		3:13	6:17–21a		3:14	20–21
4. Peace	15:33		13:11b	6:16	6:23	4:7, 9b		5:23–24	3:16				
5. Commendation	16:1–2	16:10–12, 17–18	(8:16–24)		6:21–22	2:19–30 4:18	4:7–9						10–18
6. Greetings	16:3–23	16:19–20a	13:13			4:21–22	4:10–15, 17				4:10–13, 19, 21b	3:15a–b	23–24
7. Closed Communion	16:16–20a	16:20b, 22	13:12	6:16	6:24			5:26	3:14–15		4:14–15	3:15b	
8. Amanuensis	16:22												
9. "My own hand"		16:21		6:11			4:18a		3:17				19
10. Read publicly							4:16	5:27					
11. Doxology	16:25–27					4:19–20				6:15–16	4:18b		
12. Blessing	16:20b	16:23–24	13:14	6:18	6:24	4:23	4:18b	5:28	3:18	6:21b	4:22	3:15c	25

Note: the material in lighter shading is somewhat dislocated from the rest of the epistle's conclusion; parentheses indicates verses that only partially serve the indicated function.

Departing so greatly from the Greco-Roman norm, Paul appears to have established a new Christian rhetoric,[98] imitated by the other NT writers and the early postapostolic fathers.[99] See "Paul's Epistolary Conclusions."

Although the order of elements varies naturally (as Paul likely did not consciously work from a fixed outline), his conclusions fall into four main sections, each with a unique function:

1–3. Paul refers to his own situation and that of his recipients. By noting his travel plans and those of his closest associates, he reminds his recipients that the letter is a substitute for his personal presence (which would be more desirable).[100] His personal circumstances, particularly (in his Captivity Letters) his imprisonment for the Gospel,[101] explain both his inability to travel to them and his deep desire to receive their prayers.

4–7. The sending of the letter carrier, who most often was a minister serving as Paul's authorized delegate, together with other Christian travelers, gave opportunity to express personally and concretely (incarnationally!) the fellowship he had with his children and brothers in the faith throughout the world. The bestowal of peace, the kiss of peace, and the exhortations to practice closed Communion (condemnation and invitation) allude to the sacramental context into which the letter brought Paul's presence. Thus, the naming of brothers and sisters in the faith with their greetings, when examined in context, should be understood not merely like their secular counterparts, but as an exercise of church fellowship.

8–10. While it is likely that Paul used a secretary (amanuensis) to carry out the difficult work of placing ink onto papyrus, he indicates in his conclusion that the words are his very own by taking pen in hand and writing the final words in his own amateur hand ("large letters"). This was not only necessitated by the danger of forgery (2 Thess 2:2), but provided him with a further opportunity

---

[98] The chart demonstrates visually the diversity in Paul's conclusions and puts to lie Lincoln's conclusions: "In comparison with Paul's letters, Ephesians has reduced the closing elements to a minimum. … In Pauline conclusions there is, however, a set sequence of the major items—hortatory remarks, wish of peace, greetings, and grace-benediction. Whatever elements may be added or omitted, this sequence does not vary" (*Ephesians*, 462–63).

[99] "Paul had a certain way of concluding his letters, as both he himself and the entire church apparently recognized. Hence, if the apostle John in Revelation and the writer to the Hebrews were not deliberately *mimicking* Paul's characteristic way of concluding a letter, it seems certain that at least the *apostolic nature* of the grace formula was understood and appreciated already during the NT era" (Nordling, *Philemon*, 317–18).

[100] Heikki Koskenniemi argued that the primary purpose of the Hellenistic letter was to maintain personal contact, thus "die ἀπουσία zur παρουσία machen ['turning absence into presence']" (*Studien zur Idee und Phraseologie des griechischen Briefes bis 400 n. Chr.* [Helsinki: Suomalainen Tiedeakatemia, 1956], 38). Robert Funk developed this idea in his *Parables and Presence*:

> Paul regarded his apostolic presence (in Greek: *parousia*) to his congregation under three different but related aspects at once: that of the letter, that of the apostolic emissary, and that of his own personal presence. All three are media through which Paul made his apostolic authority effective in the churches. The underlying theme is therefore the apostolic *parousia*—the presence of apostolic authority and power—of which the travelogue in the narrow sense is only one element. (81)

[101] See further "Paul's Imprisonment" in "Location and Date of Writing" in the introduction.

to enter the recipients' liturgical gathering. These are his own words and are to be read aloud to the congregation as if they were hearing his own voice.

11–12. Finally, Paul replaces the secular greeting and farewell with a blessing from the Lord. This is his apostolic mandate and prerogative.

What emerges from this analysis is that *Paul's primary concern in the conclusion of his letters is to establish his personal presence among the recipients in the liturgical gathering.* This means, first, that the request for prayer (Eph 6:18–20), paralleled explicitly in or near this location in five other epistles and alluded to in two more, is most certainly to be included in the epistle's closing section. Aside from this structural conclusion, the above-noted patterns suggest Paul is referring to public prayer of the gathered congregation and that his request is part of his desire to exercise his fellowship with them. Second, and more generally, this analysis suggests that there is far more going on in Paul's conclusions than simply his following epistolary convention or fulfilling polite necessities. The rhetorical function of the conclusion is directly related to the setting for which the epistle was written and in which it was to be read. By expressing his desire to be with them, appealing for their prayers, commending the letter carrier as his representative, giving and receiving the greetings of Christian brothers, Paul enters into their Divine Service to be present with them,[102] gives and receives the holy kiss from a great distance, and demonstrates that by the common reception of Christ's holy body and blood, Paul and his addressees are one body nonetheless. With this in mind one should hear his final blessing—the only element found in every epistle without exception—as the very voice of the apostolic minister, speaking for Christ as if presiding in their midst from the altar.

It may therefore be somewhat surprising that Paul does not include any greetings in Ephesians. Indeed, most commentators have highlighted this omission as evidence that this letter was *not* written to Ephesus, but must be a circular letter intended for a more general audience (see "Addressees" in the introduction).[103] After all, how could Paul fail to name anyone in a congregation where he had served for three years?[104] The evidence presented here in

---

[102] Writing to the Corinthians about the need to excommunicate (i.e., separate from the Holy Communion) an impenitent sinner, Paul writes quite explicitly of his presence with them in the Divine Service: "For I myself, though absent [ἀπών] in body but present in spirit [παρὼν δὲ τῷ πνεύματι, or 'by the Spirit'] … : when in the name of our Lord Jesus you and my spirit are gathered together [συναχθέντων ὑμῶν καὶ τοῦ ἐμοῦ πνεύματος] with the power of our Lord Jesus …" (1 Cor 5:3–4; cf. Mt 18:20).

[103] E.g., Lincoln, *Ephesians*, lx–lxi: "The lack of personal greetings reinforces this picture of the author as having no intimate connection with his readers."

[104] For the duration of his ministry there, see "Paul and Ephesus in Acts" in "The City of Ephesus and Paul's Relationship to It" in the introduction. Schnackenburg, *Ephesians*, 288: "If he omits the list of greetings, the letter cannot be intended for the congregation at Ephesus in which Paul was active over a long period and knew many Christians personally." Best, *Ephesians*, 612: "AE [the unknown author of Ephesians] may not have known enough about Paul in prison to create a true scenario. If Paul is the author then it may be that he has been held for so long

chart form demonstrates, however, that this interpretation of the evidence may be completely inverted. For which church receives the largest list of greetings from Paul? Romans, a church which he did not found and had never even visited![105] Next comes the rather long list of greetings in Colossians, a church he did not found and may never have visited. In writing twice to Corinth, where Paul had served a lengthy pastorate, Paul does not name a single person *in Corinth*, but merely gives a general greeting and names the people who are *with him*.[106] Finally, Paul does not greet anyone by name at the close of Galatians, Philippians, or 1 and 2 Thessalonians, places where he himself had founded churches and frequently visited. (The Pastoral Epistles and Philemon, as written to individuals, may be excluded from this discussion.)

Thus, it would be incorrect to assume that Paul greets a lot of people by name because he knows the congregation well. The opposite is more likely the case.[107] He greets many people by name in congregations where those may be the only people he knows; that is, *such greetings function to establish a personal relationship where none may yet exist*. When writing to the Romans with the expressed desire of procuring their support for his proposed mission to the far West, Paul names those Romans whom he has come to know from their travels in the East. When writing to congregations he had founded and perhaps served at length, it was unnecessary for Paul to attempt to establish a relationship in this way, by naming individuals. In fact, there would have been a great danger in doing so: to name the few would be to risk offending the many. Where he had been pastor to everyone, it would have been improper to single out "favorites." This is the experience of wise pastors even today, who have great difficulty deciding how to keep contact with their former parishioners without creating offense and division. In the case of Ephesians, like the other churches where Paul had served for a lengthy time as pastor, he may well have decided the wiser course was to name no one.

With the absence of a lengthy list of greetings, what remains is a conclusion that falls into three basic divisions:

1. the exercise of fellowship in prayer (6:18–20)
2. the exercise of fellowship through sending an apostolic delegate (6:21–22)
3. the exercise of fellowship through giving his apostolic blessing (6:23–24)

---

as a prisoner in close confinement that he has lost touch with his local Christian community and so has no greetings to send from them."

[105] The old critical conjecture, that the greetings in Romans 16 were originally meant for Ephesus, is based on this misconception. For a careful refutation see Reicke, *Re-examining Paul's Letters*, 64–65. Today this hypothesis has been largely abandoned.

[106] Guthrie, *New Testament Introduction*, 413–14, notes correctly that Paul's normal practice is to send greetings by name *from* people rather than *to* people. He speaks for his colleagues when expressing church fellowship.

[107] See Black, "The Peculiarities of Ephesians and the Ephesian Address," 62–64; Dahl, "The Particularity of the Pauline Epistles as a Problem in the Ancient Church," in *Studies in Ephesians*, 172. Deterding, *Colossians*, 7, arguing along the same lines as the present author, cites the lengthy greetings in Colossians 4 as evidence that Paul was writing to a congregation he did not personally found.

Fellowship in Prayer (6:18–20)

Prayer has featured prominently in Ephesians. It is one of only three NT epistles to begin with a formal *Berakah* prayer, patterned on OT, temple, and synagogue models (1:3–14; cf. 2 Cor 1:3–4; 1 Pet 1:3–9). Longest and most elaborate of the three, Paul's opening prayer in Ephesians is a typical pious Jewish response to the revelation of a great mystery from God—in this case, the disclosure of salvation for Jew and Gentile alike in Jesus Christ, as he later explains (3:1–13). The very act of explaining it leads him again to bend his knee in prayer and doxology (3:14–21). Paul's opening prayer (1:3–14) is followed by his bold claim that he always remembers the Ephesians in his prayers (1:15–23)—a reference to his apostolic duty to intercede for the flock throughout the world that the Lord had put under his care (see the textual notes on 1:16). Most likely Paul carried out this duty at the traditional hours of prayer (at the very least, morning, noon, and afternoon/evening, with the possible addition of the third and ninth hours, if they are distinct from the former). Prayer is also implied repeatedly in the letter, as he calls for "thanksgiving" (εὐχαριστία, 5:4) and "giving thanks" (εὐχαριστέω, 5:20), coupled with the Spirit's inspiration of psalms, hymns, and songs of the Spirit (5:18–20). While noting, therefore, that prayer is a significant theme of the letter, we can also see a pattern emerging that is brought to completion by Paul's concluding words of prayer.

First, there is a clear correspondence between Paul's opening prayers for the Ephesians (1:3–14, 15–23) and his closing call for them to pray for him (6:18–20). The letter is enwrapped in prayer by way of *inclusio*; it gives the letter its structure. *Second*, the rhythm of prayer is instructive. Paul prays for them in order to teach them how to pray for him and for others, just as our Lord prayed for his disciples (John 17) and taught them (and us) how to pray (Lk 11:1–4). Paul does not pray for himself, but for them, asking them in turn to intercede for him. Thus, while Paul considers prayer part of his apostolic duty for those under his care, he also sees prayer as a priestly, intercessory task. The priesthood of all the baptized stand before God through Jesus, their High Priest, to beg for help for their brothers and sisters in Christ. Like Christ, they pray principally for others, and the body of Christ is built up as each member is bound to the other through intercessory prayer (4:15–16). *Third*, while private prayer neither can nor ought to be excluded, the language and context of Ephesians places a greater emphasis on the corporate Prayer of the Church in the Divine Service. The language of the opening *Berakah* prayer greatly parallels not only temple and synagogue prayers but also the eucharistic praying of the early church (e.g., *Didache*, 9:1–10:7). And Paul's language of thanksgiving parallels the *Berakah* prayer's opening, while following on from a clear description of public worship: εὐχαριστοῦντες πάντοτε ὑπὲρ πάντων ἐν ὀνόματι τοῦ κυρίου ἡμῶν Ἰησοῦ Χριστοῦ τῷ θεῷ καὶ πατρί, "giving thanks always for all things/people in the name of our Lord Jesus Christ to [our] God and Father" (Eph 5:20; cf. 1:3). Note how ὑπὲρ πάντων, "for all things/people" (5:20), parallels περὶ πάντων τῶν ἁγίων, "concerning all the saints" (6:18). Thus, it is appropriate

to conclude that Paul's final call for prayer for all Christians and particularly for him is directed to the congregation gathered for the reading of his letter (cf. Col 4:16); it is a request that they remember him in the Prayer of the Church.

A digression into the history of public prayer in the Christian church would take this commentary too far afield. Suffice it to say, however, that a rather sweeping generalization might be instructive for the present passage: (1) in earliest times, intercession for the whole church was not a separate act, but a component of eucharistic praying;[108] (2) the medieval canon of the mass[109] submerged these intercessions beneath its sacrificial language for the Eucharist and its invocation of the saints; (3) when Luther therefore removed the canon of the mass from the eucharistic portion of the liturgy, the way was paved for subsequent Lutheran Church orders to introduce the Prayer of the Church as a distinct element occurring prior to the Sacrament.[110] One cannot derive a detailed order of service from the following text, but the earliest NT description of what baptized Christians did in worship connects public prayer very closely to the Lord's Supper: "And they were devoting themselves to the teaching of the apostles and to the communion in the breaking of the bread and to the prayers" (Acts 2:42).[111]

---

[108] This is easily demonstrable by surveying the early rites in Jasper and Cuming, *Prayers of the Eucharist*.

[109] "Canon of the mass" refers to the order (κανών, "rule") of praying between the Sanctus and the Agnus Dei in the medieval Western rite of the liturgy (still used by Roman Catholics). It is the distinctively Roman Catholic form of "Eucharistic Prayer" or "anaphora"—more general terms that can refer to any substantial historical pattern of prayer at the Sacrament. The canon included prayers of praise and thanksgiving, but also intercessions for and to the saints, as well as language that suggested the body and blood of Christ were offered up to God the Father by the priest as a propitiatory sacrifice. It included the Words of Institution and the Lord's Prayer—the only portions that Luther's reform retained. For the text of the Roman canon, see Reed, *The Lutheran Liturgy*, 721–28; and Jasper and Cuming, *Prayers of the Eucharist*, 163–66. See also Luther's critique of the canon in "The Abomination of the Secret Mass," 1525, AE 36:307–28; WA 18:22–36.

[110] Lutherans are inclined to view the general prayer as a bridge from the Service of the Word to the Service of the Sacrament, rather than as a component of eucharistic praying itself. This interpretation deserves reevaluation. Nonetheless, one should note that in Lutheran rites, prayers have always remained attached to the Lord's Supper. The Proper Preface offers praise and thanksgiving to God for his gifts of salvation in Christ. The Lord's Prayer was/is universal. And a post-Sanctus prayer akin to a *Berakah* was common at least in the Scandinavian rites. But for the most part, perhaps from fear that the Lord's Supper might be viewed sacrificially, Lutherans have excluded *intercession* from eucharistic praying and restricted it to the earlier Prayer of the Church. This pattern was established by Luther's decision in his 1523 Latin rite to remove the canon of the mass (AE 53:25–26). Some helpful historical background is found in Reed, *The Lutheran Liturgy*, 315–19.

[111] ἦσαν δὲ προσκαρτεροῦντες τῇ διδαχῇ τῶν ἀποστόλων καὶ τῇ κοινωνίᾳ, τῇ κλάσει τοῦ ἄρτου καὶ ταῖς προσευχαῖς. The comma placed after κοινωνίᾳ in NA[27] encourages a distinction between τῇ κοινωνίᾳ ("the communion") and τῇ κλάσει τοῦ ἄρτου ("the breaking of the bread") that is probably incorrect, given the NT usage of the terms. In light of the absence of a καί between the two, the second dative is more likely means or instrument: "the communion that takes place by means of breaking break." In the oral culture of NT times, the καί structure is a more reliable indicator of semantic grouping than hypothetical punctuation (which would have been absent in the autograph and is lacking in the early manuscripts). See Winger, "Orality as the Key to Understanding Apostolic Proclamation in the Epistles," 216.

The same conclusion arises from the *Didache*, whose eucharistic prayer has intercession for the whole church embedded within it:

> Even as this broken *bread* was scattered over the hills, and was gathered together and became one, so let Thy Church be gathered together from the ends of the earth into Thy kingdom; for Thine is the glory and the power through Jesus Christ for ever. (*Didache*, 9:4 [*ANF* 7:380])

> Remember, Lord, Thy Church, to deliver it from all evil and to make it perfect in Thy love, and gather it from the four winds, sanctified for Thy kingdom which Thou hast prepared for it; for Thine is the power and the glory for ever. (*Didache*, 10:5 [*ANF* 7:380])

Likewise, Ignatius places great stress on the symbolic value of the body of Christ praying with one voice through the liturgical leadership of the holy ministry:

> [1]As therefore the Lord did nothing without the Father, being united to Him, neither by Himself nor by the apostles, so neither do ye anything without the bishop and presbyters. Neither endeavour that anything appear reasonable and proper to yourselves apart; but being come together into the same place [ἐπὶ τὸ αὐτό], let there be one prayer, one supplication, one mind, one hope, in love and in joy undefiled [μία προσευχή, μία δέησις, εἶς νοῦς, μία ἐλπὶς ἐν ἀγάπη, ἐν τῇ χαρᾷ τῇ ἀμώμῳ]. There is one Jesus Christ, than whom nothing is more excellent. [2]Do ye therefore all run together as into one temple of God, as to one altar, as to one Jesus Christ, who came forth from one Father, and is with and has gone to one. (*To the Magnesians*, 7:1–2 [*ANF* 1:62])

That Ignatius is thinking of public prayer in connection with the Lord's Supper is suggested by his use of Paul's phrase ἐπὶ τὸ αὐτό, "into/at the same place" (1 Cor 11:20), and by the location at the "one altar." There is significant convergence of vocabulary between Ignatius' passage and Ephesians, including an emphasis on "one," "one hope" (4:4), "in love" (1:4; 3:17; 4:2, 15, 16; 5:2), "blameless" (1:4; 5:27), and particularly the use of the same two Greek terms for public prayer as used in Eph 6:18: προσευχή, "prayer," and δέησις, "petition, supplication." This suggests that Ignatius, whose own letter to the Ephesians was demonstrably influenced by Paul (see "Ignatius to the Ephesians" in "Addressees" in the introduction), was also influenced by Paul's letter in his own language of public, eucharistic prayer.[112]

---

[112] The connection of prayer to the rite of Communion is also evident in the second-century writings of Justin Martyr, *First Apology*, 65–66 (trans. Jasper and Cuming, *Prayers of the Eucharist*, 28–29). Note also the developed explanation of the closed Communion practices that are only hinted at in Paul:

> When we have ended the prayers, we greet one another with a kiss.

> Then bread and a cup of water and (a cup) of mixed wine are brought to him who presides over the brethren, and he takes them and sends up praise and glory to the Father of all in the name of the Son and of the Holy Spirit, and gives thanks at some length that we have been deemed worthy of these things from him. When he has finished the prayers and the thanksgiving, all the people give their assent by saying "Amen." "Amen" is the Hebrew for "So be it."

Paul's request for prayer is therefore not merely a formality, a Christianized sort of farewell, but is one significant part in a cohesive whole that forms the conclusion of his letters. The prayers, the greetings, the kiss of peace, the words of invitation and exclusion, and the apostolic blessing parallel what was happening in the Service of the Sacrament in which Paul's letter was being read. He calls for prayer because he knows his addressees will be offering it and asks that he be included.

There is, however, another function of this request yet to be considered. Paul explicitly asks his recipients to pray for him in the conclusion of six epistles:

- **Rom 15:30–32**—Paul requests prayers (1) that he be delivered from his enemies in Judea; (2) for the success of his offering for the famine-plagued saints in Jerusalem; and (3) that he may come to the Romans and be refreshed by their company.
- **Eph 6:18–20**—Paul requests prayers that he be able to speak the Gospel with boldness during his imprisonment and trials.[113]
- **Col 4:2–4**—Paul requests prayers that a door be opened during his imprisonment for a bold confession of the Gospel.
- **1 Thess 5:25**—"Brothers, pray for us." No specifics are given.
- **2 Thess 3:1–2**—Paul requests prayers (1) that "the Word of the Lord may run ahead and be glorified" and (2) that he might be delivered from wicked men.
- **Philemon 22**—Paul requests prayers that he might be graciously given to them, i.e., that he might be released from prison and be able to travel to Colossae to meet the saints who gather at Philemon's house church.[114]

A pattern emerges. Paul does not request prayers for his personal welfare, for his own health or prosperity. He prays, first, for the success of the Gospel. Second, he prays that God would thwart the evil plans of his enemies that would obstruct the proclamation of that Gospel. And third, he prays that his present trials as a prisoner for the Gospel would be turned into an opportunity to proclaim Christ and earn freedom for that message to be preached freely throughout the world. The same motivation lies behind Paul's indirect calls for prayer in those passages where he discloses to his recipients his suffering in chains (Phil 4:6, 10–14; 2 Tim 4:16–18a).

And when the president [presider] has given thanks and all the people have assented, those whom we call deacons [διάκονοι, "assistant ministers"] give to each of those present a portion of the bread and wine and water over which thanks have been given, and take them to those who are not present.

And we call this food "thanksgiving [εὐχαριστία, Eucharist]"; and no one may partake of it unless he is convinced of the truth of our teaching, and has been cleansed with the washing for forgiveness of sins and regeneration, and lives as Christ handed down.

Hippolytus, *Apostolic Tradition*, 21 (ca. A.D. 200), makes the same connection: "And when they have prayed, they shall give the kiss of peace" (trans. Jasper and Cuming, 37).

[113] See further "Paul's Imprisonment" in "Location and Date of Writing" in the introduction.

[114] The Greek pronouns in Philemon 22 rendered as "your" (ὑμῶν) and "to you" (ὑμῖν) are plural and thus refer to the other saints in addition to Philemon. Philemon 1–2 indicates that a church met in his house.

Thus, by requesting prayers for him in his capacity as a suffering servant of the Gospel, Paul is inviting the Christian church in all places to participate in his mission. God heard the early Christians' prayers and allowed Paul to carry his message to Rome, even granting him the freedom to receive visitors and proclaim the Gospel openly for two years (Acts 28:30–31). Despite his fetters, the Word was free (2 Tim 2:9). Even some of his guards were persuaded by the Gospel, and his boldness in preaching while imprisoned emboldened others (Phil 1:12–20). Paul attributes this success to their prayers (Phil 1:19). Thus, like the Philippians' financial support of his mission (Phil 1:5; 4:15), which Paul calls κοινωνία, "communion/fellowship" (Phil 1:5), and κοινωνέω, "to have communion/fellowship" (Phil 4:15), to pray as the body of Christ for God's blessing on Paul's apostolic ministry is to exercise their *communion/fellowship* with him in Christ.

Finally, we cannot entirely ignore the way in which the call to prayer (6:18–20) does indeed flow naturally from the armor of God (6:10–17). In addition to the syntactical connection created by the use of a dependent participle,[115] the naming of the Holy Spirit in 6:17 and 6:18 forms a hinge between the two pericopes.[116] If prayer is not a weapon, it certainly is the appropriate accompaniment to spiritual warfare. Prayer expresses the Christian's sense of utter dependence on God, his realization that victory comes not from his own efforts, but is a divine gift. Thus, the comprehensiveness of language with which Paul describes this prayer in 6:18—the fourfold repetition of πᾶς, "every, all," and the two synonyms "prayer and petition"—is not entirely attributable to the context of the general prayer in public worship. Prayer ought to be the continual occupation of Christians in these evil latter days (5:16; 6:13). While this does not necessarily mean the unceasing utterance of conscious prayer, it may include the liturgical practice of all-night prayer vigils, well-attested in the Bible and in the early church.[117] Thus, the concluding admonition to all-encompassing and constant prayer lends the passage an *eschatological urgency* as the Ephesians are called upon to spend the final days of this age in rapt concentration on the impending return of Christ.

Watch and pray [γρηγορεῖτε καὶ προσεύχεσθε]. (Mt 26:41)

---

[115] See the discussion of προσευχόμενοι, "praying," in the first textual note on 6:18.

[116] Lincoln, *Ephesians*, 451–52: "The close link between the material on prayer and what has preceded, through the participles and διά, 'through,' underlines the spiritual nature of believers' combat."

[117] Schnackenburg, *Ephesians*, 282; Schlier, *Epheser*, 301; Best, *Ephesians*, 606. The verb ἀγρυπνέω (6:18), used here by Paul in the sense of "paying close attention to," literally means "to stay awake all night" (LXX Ps 126:1 [MT/ET 127:1]; cf. ἀγρυπνία in 2 Cor 6:5; 11:27). Literally staying awake to pray is Jesus' admonition in Gethsemane (Mt 26:40–41; Mk 14:37–38) and is part of many parables (Mt 24:42–43; 25:13; Lk 12:37). Jesus himself prayed all night (Lk 6:12), as have faithful supplicants like Nehemiah (Neh 1:6; 4:3 [ET 4:9]), psalmists (Ps 42:4, 9 [ET 42:3, 8]), Anna (Lk 2:37), Paul (Acts 16:25; 1 Thess 3:10), faithful widows (1 Tim 5:5), and the saints in heaven (Rev 7:15; cf. Rev 4:8).

Watch; keep alert [βλέπετε, ἀγρυπνεῖτε]; for you do not know when the time [ὁ καιρός] will come. (Mk 13:33)

Be alert at every moment, praying that you may be strengthened [ἀγρυπνεῖτε δὲ ἐν παντὶ καιρῷ δεόμενοι ἵνα κατισχύσητε]. (Lk 21:36)

[11]In addition to this, you know the time [τὸν καιρόν], that the hour has already come for you to wake from sleep. For salvation is nearer to us now than when we first believed. [12]The night is far advanced; the day has come near. Therefore let us put off the works of darkness and put on the armor of light [τὰ ὅπλα τοῦ φωτός]. (Rom 13:11–12)

Fellowship through the Apostolic Emissary (6:21–22)

Although it is not explicitly stated, Tychicus was surely the bearer of Paul's letter to the Ephesians, together with Colossians and Philemon[118] and perhaps an additional letter to the Laodiceans.[119] He was accompanied by the runaway slave Onesimus, returning to his master (Col 4:7–9; Philemon 10). A sensible analysis of the geography would suggest that Tychicus visited Colossae first and then traveled down the valleys of the Lycus and Meander Rivers on the main thoroughfare to Ephesus.[120] It is not at all obvious to modern readers, accustomed to public postal services and email, that Paul's commendation of Tychicus as the bearer of news between the two parties should be connected to his carrying the letter. Though in the ancient Roman world the only formal postal service was reserved for official correspondence of the empire, Paul could have sent the letter by a paid courier.[121] However, a comparison with other ancient examples suggests that when a letter contains such a commendation as this, the one commended is the letter carrier himself.

There were, in fact, "letters of commendation"[122] whose sole purpose was to commend the letter carrier as one who would carry out an action on behalf of the one who sent him or who would convey a message too secret, delicate, or complicated to put into writing. This appears to be the very earliest form of Greek letter, logical in a time when written communication was distrusted and was thoroughly subordinated to the oral.[123] There were also brief commendations

---

[118] See "Location and Date of Writing" and "Relationship to Colossians" in the introduction.

[119] Paul mentions a letter "from Laodicea" (Col 4:16), which may be a distinct, but lost letter of Paul's, or may refer to Ephesians itself, a copy of which could have gone to Laodicea before being sent on to the Colossians. There was considerable debate about this letter in the early church, and forgeries later circulated under this title; see "Evidence from the Fathers" in "Addressees" in the introduction.

[120] See Reicke, *Re-examining Paul's Letters*, 131–32.

[121] See Klauck, *Ancient Letters and the New Testament*, 60–65.

[122] συστατικαὶ ἐπιστολαί (2 Cor 3:1).

[123] This reflects the historical roots of the term ἐπιστολή, which was, as David Aune, notes, "an *oral* communication sent by messenger (Herodotus 4.10.1; Thucydides 7.11.1)" (*The New Testament in Its Literary Environment*, 158). In this early form it might well be translated as "message, communiqué." See LSJM, s.v. ἐπιστολή, 1: *"anything sent by a messenger, message, order, commission, whether verbal or in writing."*

within a longer letter by which the writer authorized the letter carrier to expand upon the letter's contents.[124] Ancient rhetorical handbooks gave instructions and examples of these practices, which are well illustrated by the following:

> To Julius Domitius, military tribune of the legion, from Aurelius Archelaus, his *beneficarius*, greeting. I have recommended my friend Theon to you before, and now *I ask you, lord, to look upon him as if he were myself.* He is truly a man worthy of your love. He left his loved ones, property, and business to follow me and through it all he has seen to my safety. I ask you therefore to allow him into your company; *he can tell you about our activities.* Whatever he says about me is the truth. I have loved the man […] may you and your household be happy and in good health, lord. *When you read this letter imagine that I am speaking to you.* Farewell.[125]

The three emphasized sentences encapsulate superbly both the role of the letter carrier and the purpose of the letter: the writer would much prefer to be present in person; by designating the letter carrier as his representative, he brings his presence to the recipients in an inferior, but significant way. Through the letter carrier, they not only learn about the author's circumstances and receive his instructions, but they also hear his very voice.

J. A. T. Robinson has insightfully observed that, in contrast to the common opinion of critical scholars, the Gospels (and other NT writings) were produced not because the apostles had died (so that a subsequent generation would seek to harness their reputation by imitating their voice), but because they could not be everywhere at once.[126] The NT writings carried the apostolic presence to the entire Christian world—and also through time, preserving their living voice even after they passed into glory.[127] As illustrated above, the desire to be present with the recipients is a key theme in ancient letters.[128] So also we find

---

[124] See Doty, *Letters in Primitive Christianity*, 10–11; "Letters of Mediation" in Stowers, *Letter Writing in Greco-Roman Antiquity*, 153–65; Aune, *The New Testament in Its Literary Environment*, 166–67; and Winger, "Orality as the Key to Understanding Apostolic Proclamation in the Epistles," 289–305.

[125] *P.Oxy.* 32, second century AD (trans. Stowers, *Letter Writing in Greco-Roman Antiquity*, 157; emphasis added).

[126] Robinson, *Redating the New Testament*, 346. See also E. Earle Ellis, "New Directions in Form Criticism," in *Jesus Christus in Historie und Theologie: Neutestamentliche Festschrift für Hans Conzelmann zum 60. Geburtstag* (ed. Georg Strecker; Tübingen: Mohr, 1975), 304–9; and Reicke, *The Roots of the Synoptic Gospels*, passim.

[127] Note, for example, the *present tense* verbs in 1 Jn 1:1–5. John views his testimony in writing as his living voice for the church everywhere and at all times. See Schuchard, *1–3 John*, 40–43.

[128] This was not only a feature of letters of commendations but also of what Stowers calls "letters of friendship" (see Stowers, *Letter Writing in Greco-Roman Antiquity*, 58–70). Jerome, for example, writes to Florentius (AD 374): "Wishing to do the best I can, as I cannot come in person I send you a letter instead; and thus, though absent in the body, I come to you in love and in spirit" (Letter 5 [*NPNF*[2] 6:7; quoted in Stowers, 69]). A fourth-century AD letter parody opens with these words: " 'Thou hast come! well hast thou done!' You have indeed come, even though absent, by means of your letter. … With my soul I behold you as though you were present, and am with you when absent, and nothing is enough to quench my insatiate

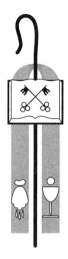

in Paul's letters the frequently agonized desire to be present with his flock, for which his letter was a mere substitute.[129] Thus, he expresses to Timothy that his epistle is a substitute for his presence: "These things I write to you while hoping to come to you soon; but if I delay, [I write] that you may know how one ought to conduct oneself in the house of God" (1 Tim 3:14–15). And he writes to the Corinthians *as if he were present* with the gathered congregation:

> [3]For I myself, though absent [ἀπών] in body but present in spirit [παρὼν δὲ τῷ πνεύματι, or "by the Spirit"], have already judged the one who has done this, [working from the presupposition that] I am really present [ὡς παρών]: [4]when in the name of our Lord Jesus you and my spirit are gathered together [συναχθέντων ὑμῶν καὶ τοῦ ἐμοῦ πνεύματος] with the power of our Lord Jesus, [5][my judgment is] to hand such a one over to Satan … (1 Cor 5:3–5)

> Let such a one consider this, that what we are in word through letters when absent [τῷ λόγῳ δι᾽ ἐπιστολῶν ἀπόντες] such we are in deed when present [παρόντες τῷ ἔργῳ]. (2 Cor 10:11)[130]

Writing to the Philippians, the sending of his emissary gives occasion for Paul to express his own desire to burst his bonds and come to them:

> [23]I hope therefore to send him [Timothy] just as soon as I see how my circumstances will fare, [24]and I am persuaded in the Lord that also I myself will swiftly come. (Phil 2:23–24)

Such expressions shed light on Paul's frequent references to his travel plans (see the chart "Paul's Epistolary Conclusions" above), which, far from being purely informative, exercise the rhetorical function of conveying his desire to be with his recipients.[131]

Paul's commendations, as most clearly evident here in Ephesians, contain two essential elements: (1) he sets forth the credentials of the emissary by identifying his personal relationship with Paul, his faithfulness as a brother Christian, and often his official status as a fellow minister of Christ; and (2)

---

desire" (trans. Wilmer Cave Wright, *The Works of the Emperor Julian* [LCL], Letter 77; quoted in Stowers, 65). So also "the letter of consolation" (Stowers, 143), as Demetrius' handbook illustrates: "Since I did not happen to be present to comfort you, I decided to do so by letter" (quoted in Stowers, 144).

[129] Funk, *Parables and Presence*, 84–85, 92–94, contends for a hierarchy, in which Paul's letters are inferior to his personal presence. Margaret Mitchell, "New Testament Envoys," 642–43, avers that sometimes Paul's letters were *more effective* than his personal presence (cf. 2 Cor 1:23; 10:1, 9–10; 12:20–21) and that he chose in each situation whether to come in person, write a letter, or send an envoy. This argument is moot, however, in the case of the Prison Letters, as Paul had no such choice.

[130] Cf. Phil 1:27; Col 2:4–5; 2 Thess 3:14.

[131] In the terminology of speech-act theory, while the *illocutionary* force is to inform his recipients of his travel plans, the *perlocutionary* force is to express his heartfelt desire to be with them. When Paul unfolds his travel plans, Paul also seeks support for his mission trips and for the collection for the poor saints in Jerusalem (Rom 15:22–29; 1 Cor 16:1–9; 2 Cor 9:1–5). Disclosing his travel plans to Philemon may be meant to urge compliance with his desire to have Onesimus freed into his service (Philemon 13–22). To the Corinthians Paul's travel plans were expressly a warning (2 Cor 13:10).

he details the task given to the emissary, which most often includes conveying news about Paul.[132]

> For this reason I sent you Timothy, who is my beloved child and faithful in the Lord [μου τέκνον ἀγαπητὸν καὶ πιστὸν ἐν κυρίῳ], who will remind you of my ways in Christ, just as I teach everywhere in every church. (1 Cor 4:17)

> And we sent Timothy, our brother and God's coworker [τὸν ἀδελφὸν ἡμῶν καὶ συνεργὸν τοῦ θεοῦ] in the Gospel of Christ, to establish you and encourage you in your faith. (1 Thess 3:2)

Some commendations lack any mention of a mandated task and may indicate that the letter carrier has business of his (or her) own to conduct. Similarly, in some cases Paul commends a group of people who may be traveling with the letter carrier or arriving separately (1 Cor 16:12; 2 Cor 8:23; Phil 2:19–24). In these cases, Paul is exhorting the churches, nevertheless, to treat these Christian travelers as they would treat him:[133]

> [1]I commend to you our sister Phoebe, a representative [διάκονος] of the church in Cenchreae, [2]that you may receive her in the Lord [in a way] worthy of the saints and help her in whatever matter she may need from you; for she has been a benefactor [προστάτις] of many and [especially] of myself. (Rom 16:1–2)

> [10]When Timothy comes, see that he is at ease among you; for he is accomplishing the work of the Lord, as also I am. [11]So let no one despise him. Help him on his way in peace, that he may come to me, for I am expecting him with the brothers. (1 Cor 16:10–11)

> As for Titus, he is my partner [κοινωνός] and fellow worker [συνεργός] for your benefit. And as for our brothers, they are representatives of the churches [ἀπόστολοι ἐκκλησιῶν], the glory of Christ. (2 Cor 8:23)

> I have considered it necessary to send to you Epaphroditus my brother and fellow worker and fellow soldier, and your representative and servant to my need [τὸν ἀδελφὸν καὶ συνεργὸν καὶ συστρατιώτην μου, ὑμῶν δὲ ἀπόστολον καὶ λειτουργὸν τῆς χρείας μου]. (Phil 2:25)[134]

---

[132] Cf. Stowers, *Letter Writing in Greco-Roman Antiquity*, 156:

> Kim has identified three parts to Paul's commendations: (1) An "introduction" that includes a petition and the phrase "concerning my child" in reference to the one being commended; (2) the "credentials," where Paul praises, or presents credentials, or, as in papyrus letters, recommends the person by describing the person's relationship to himself; (3) the "desired action," where Paul states what he wants the recipient to do.

See Chan-Hie Kim, *Form and Structure of the Familiar Greek Letter of Recommendation* (Missoula, Mont.: Society of Biblical Literature, 1972), 126–35.

[133] Paul admonishes Philemon concerning Onesimus, the slave: "Therefore, if you hold me as a partner [κοινωνόν], receive him as me [προσλαβοῦ αὐτὸν ὡς ἐμέ]" (Philemon 17). Surely Paul does not mean that Philemon is to *heed* Onesimus as one bringing a message from Paul, but rather that Philemon is to *treat* Onesimus kindly, as he would treat Paul himself. Commendations come in various forms.

[134] Phil 2:19–30 contains an extended commendation of both Timothy and Epaphroditus. Further references to letters of commendation are found also in Acts 9:2; 18:27; 1 Cor 16:3, 17–18; 2 Cor 3:1–2; perhaps 1 Thess 5:12–13. The entirety of 3 John might be considered a letter of commendation for Demetrius. Philemon is a letter of commendation for Onesimus.

One way of expressing the relationship between Paul and his emissaries might be to borrow the language of apostleship, for just as Paul was sent by the Lord to speak and do only what Christ gave him to speak and do as his representative, so the emissary was sent by Paul with such distinct authority.[135] Thus, ἀπόστολος, *apostolos*, together with διάκονος, *diaconos*, and λειτουργός, *leitourgos*, can be used in both a narrow sense (to refer to one of the twelve apostles or to someone holding a permanent office as a representative of Christ) and in a broad sense (to refer to a representative of an apostle or a church).[136] What distinguishes the two is the *external entailments*:[137] Paul is "apostle of Christ Jesus through the will of God" (ἀπόστολος Χριστοῦ Ἰησοῦ διὰ θελήματος θεοῦ, Eph 1:1), but other men may be thought of as apostles of Paul. Timothy and Titus carry out this role in a regular and distinctive manner. They are Paul's emissaries par excellence.[138] They, especially Timothy, are most highly commended (2 Cor 8:16–17, 23; Phil 2:19–24) and represent him in choosing and ordaining pastors (1 Tim 3:1–13; Titus 1:5–9). But there can also be ἀπόστολοι ἐκκλησιῶν, "apostles/ambassadors/delegates of the churches" (2 Cor 8:23). Epaphras can be an ἀπόστολον καὶ λειτουργόν, "representative and servant," sent by the Philippians to minister to Paul's needs (Phil 2:25). And Phoebe can serve as a διάκονον τῆς ἐκκλησίας τῆς ἐν Κεγχρεαῖς, perhaps "deaconess" (*diaconos* is certainly not "minister"), but more likely "official representative of the church in Cenchreae" (Rom 16:1).[139]

Thus, the purpose of Eph 6:21–22 is to establish the credentials of Tychicus to serve as Paul's representative to the Ephesians (as he is in Col 4:7–8 to the Colossians) in order to bring news of Paul's circumstances, to comfort their hearts thereby (cf. Eph 3:13), and to interpret any of his teaching in the letter that bears further explanation. A comparison of the commendation with

---

[135] Doty, *Letters in Primitive Christianity*, 37, comments: "We also gain a sense of the importance of his emissaries or letter carriers: they receive authority to convey the letters, to expand upon them, and to continue Paul's work" (see also 16, 30, 45–46).

[136] In the early fathers, the use of the noun ἀπόστολος, *apostolos*, for a general messenger/envoy quickly faded, likely in consciousness of its having become a technical term in the Christian church for the apostles and was replaced in such contexts by the perfect passive participle ὁ ἀπεσταλμένος, "the one sent" (see, e.g., *1 Clement*, 65:1).

[137] On "external entailments," see Voelz, *What Does This Mean?* 188–90.

[138] See Mitchell, "New Testament Envoys in the Context of Greco-Roman Diplomatic and Epistolary Conventions: The Example of Timothy and Titus."

[139] The extent to which Phoebe, as authorized letter carrier, could also serve as Paul's *representative* to the Romans, is debatable given both the legal customs of the ancient world and Paul's stated, dominically informed view that women may not teach publicly in the church (1 Cor 14:34–35; 1 Tim 2:11–12). There are no ancient examples of women serving as authorized letter carriers. Yet in the NT women were patrons of churches in their homes (Rom 16:3–5; 1 Cor 16:19; Col 4:15; perhaps Acts 16:15), Chloe could send a delegation to Paul (1 Cor 1:11), and Priscilla could work with her husband, Aquila, to teach Apollos (Acts 18:26). Thus, there is no particular reason to doubt that Phoebe could hold a limited role as letter carrier. But note that, in contrast to his words concerning (male) letter carriers in other passages, Paul does not here give Phoebe a task to carry out on his behalf.

Colossians displays its formulaic character—this is the longest verbatim agreement between the two letters—while the minor differences (underlined) hint at the likelihood that Colossians was written before Ephesians:[140]

Colossians 4:7–8	Ephesians 6:21–22
[7]τὰ κατ᾽ ἐμέ πάντα γνωρίσει ὑμῖν Τύχικος ὁ ἀγαπητὸς ἀδελφὸς καὶ πιστὸς διάκονος <u>καὶ σύνδουλος</u> ἐν κυρίῳ, [8]ὃν ἔπεμψα πρὸς ὑμᾶς εἰς αὐτὸ τοῦτο, ἵνα γνῶτε τὰ περὶ ἡμῶν καὶ παρακαλέσῃ τὰς καρδίας ὑμῶν.	[21]<u>ἵνα δὲ εἰδῆτε καὶ ὑμεῖς</u> τὰ κατ᾽ ἐμέ, <u>τί πράσσω,</u> πάντα γνωρίσει ὑμῖν Τύχικος ὁ ἀγαπητὸς ἀδελφὸς καὶ πιστὸς διάκονος ἐν κυρίῳ, [22]ὃν ἔπεμψα πρὸς ὑμᾶς εἰς αὐτὸ τοῦτο, ἵνα γνῶτε τὰ περὶ ἡμῶν καὶ παρακαλέσῃ τὰς καρδίας ὑμῶν.
[7]My circumstances, everything he will make known to you, Tychicus, the beloved brother and faithful minister <u>and fellow slave</u> in the Lord, [8]whom I have sent to you for this very purpose, that you may know our circumstances and [that] he may comfort your hearts.	[21]<u>And so that you, too, may know</u> my circumstances, <u>how I am getting along,</u> everything he will make known to you, Tychicus, the beloved brother and faithful minister in the Lord, [22]whom I have sent to you for this very purpose, that you may know our circumstances and [that] he may comfort your hearts.

One must recall that Paul's letters to the Christians in Ephesus and Colossae have been spurred partly by *his* circumstances and partly by *theirs*—and their circumstances include their response to his! Paul has received news from their quarter via their emissary and pastor Epaphras (Col 1:7; 4:12). Through him Paul "heard of" the "faith" and "love," both of the Ephesians (Eph 1:15) and of the Colossians (Col 1:3–4, 7–8). But through him Paul also must have learned how they had reacted to the news of his imprisonment. The charges raised by the Jews against Paul that led to the near riot in the temple and his arrest for his own protection were doubly connected to the Ephesians: first, the Jews claimed that Paul was "teaching everyone everywhere against the people [the Jews] and the Torah and this place" (Acts 21:28), that is, that he was permitting Gentiles to enter into God's kingdom without going through the way of the Jewish ritual; and second, "they had previously seen Trophimus *the Ephesian* in the city with him, whom they supposed Paul had brought into the temple" (Acts 21:29), thus violating the division between Jew and Gentile.[141]

---

[140] See the textual notes on 6:21–22, as well as "Relationship to Colossians" in the introduction.

[141] See further "Paul's Trip to Jerusalem, Arrest, and Imprisonment (Acts 21:1–36)" in "The City of Ephesus and Paul's Relationship to It" in the introduction.

On hearing the tragic news of Paul's arrest, then, it is quite likely that the Ephesian Christians would have felt a double sense of guilt: that he was suffering for preaching the Gospel to them and that one of their own members was the trigger. Paul has previously explained at great length that such fears are groundless, inasmuch as he preaches to the Gentiles because Christ mandated him to do so (3:1–13), and so his afflictions are for their benefit and for their glory (3:13). It is this message that Tychicus is to reinforce by comforting their hearts (6:22). And by joining with the Ephesians in public worship as he reads and explains Paul's letter, Tychicus would become the instrument for reestablishing and exercising the Christian fellowship they had with Paul in the body of Christ. When Tychicus then communed with them, he did so as Paul's representative, reminding them that by the body and blood of Christ held in common, they were not truly separated from their apostolic father.

Fellowship in Benediction (6:23–24)

Paul's final words to the Ephesians are purest Gospel. While other NT writers follow Paul to a greater or lesser extent, sometimes ending their letters on a rather peculiar note (e.g., 1 Jn 5:21), and while Paul himself is not completely consistent in choosing the elements of his epistolary conclusions, at this one point he never varies: he ends with a blessing. The Pauline benedictions are not long, and it is convenient to see them in one glance:

ὁ δὲ θεὸς τῆς εἰρήνης μετὰ πάντων ὑμῶν, ἀμήν. (Rom 15:33)	The God of <u>peace</u> be with you all. Amen. (Rom 15:33)
ὁ δὲ θεὸς τῆς εἰρήνης συντρίψει τὸν σατανᾶν ὑπὸ τοὺς πόδας ὑμῶν ἐν τάχει.	The God of <u>peace</u> will crush Satan under your feet soon.
ἡ χάρις τοῦ κυρίου ἡμῶν Ἰησοῦ μεθ' ὑμῶν. (Rom 16:20)	The <u>grace</u> of our Lord Jesus Christ be with you. (Rom 16:20)
[23]ἡ χάρις τοῦ κυρίου Ἰησοῦ μεθ' ὑμῶν. [24]ἡ ἀγάπη μου μετὰ πάντων ὑμῶν ἐν Χριστῷ Ἰησοῦ. (1 Cor 16:23–24)	[23]The <u>grace</u> of the Lord Jesus be with you. [24]My love be with you all in Christ Jesus. Amen. (1 Cor 16:23–24)
καὶ ὁ θεὸς τῆς ἀγάπης καὶ εἰρήνης ἔσται μεθ' ὑμῶν. (2 Cor 13:11) ἡ χάρις τοῦ κυρίου Ἰησοῦ Χριστοῦ καὶ ἡ ἀγάπη τοῦ θεοῦ καὶ ἡ κοινωνία τοῦ ἁγίου πνεύματος μετὰ πάντων ὑμῶν. (2 Cor 13:13 [ET 13:14])	And the God of love and <u>peace</u> will be with you. (2 Cor 13:11) The <u>grace</u> of the Lord Jesus Christ and the love of God and the communion of the Holy Spirit be with you all. (2 Cor 13:13 [ET 13:14])

εἰρήνη ἐπ᾽ αὐτοὺς καὶ ἔλεος καὶ ἐπὶ τὸν Ἰσραὴλ τοῦ θεοῦ. (Gal 6:16) ἡ χάρις τοῦ κυρίου ἡμῶν Ἰησοῦ Χριστοῦ μετὰ τοῦ πνεύματος ὑμῶν, ἀδελφοί· ἀμήν. (Gal 6:18)	Peace be upon them and mercy, even upon the Israel of God. (Gal 6:16) The grace of our Lord Jesus Christ be with your spirit, brothers. Amen. (Gal 6:18)
[23]εἰρήνη τοῖς ἀδελφοῖς καὶ ἀγάπη μετὰ πίστεως ἀπὸ θεοῦ πατρὸς καὶ κυρίου Ἰησοῦ Χριστοῦ. [24] ἡ χάρις μετὰ πάντων τῶν ἀγαπώντων τὸν κύριον ἡμῶν Ἰησοῦν Χριστὸν ἐν ἀφθαρσίᾳ. (Eph 6:23–24)	[23]Peace be to the brothers and love with faith from God the Father and the Lord Jesus Christ. [24]Grace be with all those who love our Lord Jesus Christ in incorruptibility. (Eph 6:23–24)
καὶ ἡ εἰρήνη τοῦ θεοῦ ἡ ὑπερέχουσα πάντα νοῦν φρουρήσει τὰς καρδίας ὑμῶν καὶ τὰ νοήματα ὑμῶν ἐν Χριστῷ Ἰησοῦ. (Phil 4:7) καὶ ὁ θεὸς τῆς εἰρήνης ἔσται μεθ᾽ ὑμῶν. (Phil 4:9) ἡ χάρις τοῦ κυρίου Ἰησοῦ Χριστοῦ μετὰ τοῦ πνεύματος ὑμῶν. (Phil 4:23)	And the peace of God, which passes all understanding, will keep your hearts and your minds in Christ Jesus. (Phil 4:7) And the God of peace will be with you. (Phil 4:9) The grace of the Lord Jesus Christ be with your spirit. (Phil 4:23)
ἡ χάρις μεθ᾽ ὑμῶν. (Col 4:18)	Grace be with you. (Col 4:18)
αὐτὸς δὲ ὁ θεὸς τῆς εἰρήνης ἁγιάσαι ὑμᾶς ὁλοτελεῖς ... (1 Thess 5:23–24) ἡ χάρις τοῦ κυρίου ἡμῶν Ἰησοῦ Χριστοῦ μεθ᾽ ὑμῶν. (1 Thess 5:28)	And the God of peace himself will sanctify you wholly ... (1 Thess 5:23–24) The grace of our Lord Jesus Christ be with you. (1 Thess 5:28)
αὐτὸς δὲ ὁ κύριος τῆς εἰρήνης δῴη ὑμῖν τὴν εἰρήνην διὰ παντὸς ἐν παντὶ τρόπῳ. ὁ κύριος μετὰ πάντων ὑμῶν. (2 Thess 3:16) ἡ χάρις τοῦ κυρίου ἡμῶν Ἰησοῦ Χριστοῦ μετὰ πάντων ὑμῶν. (2 Thess 3:18)	Now may the Lord of peace himself give you peace through every time in every way. The Lord be with you all. (2 Thess 3:16) The grace of our Lord Jesus Christ be with you all. (2 Thess 3:18)
ἡ χάρις μεθ᾽ ὑμῶν. (1 Tim 6:21)	Grace be with you. (1 Tim 6:21)
ὁ κύριος μετὰ τοῦ πνεύματός σου. ἡ χάρις μεθ᾽ ὑμῶν. (2 Tim 4:22)	The Lord be with your [singular] spirit. Grace be with you [plural]. (2 Tim 4:22)
ἡ χάρις μετὰ πάντων ὑμῶν. (Titus 3:15)	Grace be with you all. (Titus 3:15)
ἡ χάρις τοῦ κυρίου Ἰησοῦ Χριστοῦ μετὰ τοῦ πνεύματος ὑμῶν. (Philemon 25)	The grace of the Lord Jesus Christ be with your spirit. (Philemon 25)

We have noted that Paul's double blessing in Eph 6:23–24, by concluding with "peace" (6:23) and then "grace" (6:24), forms a chiastic *inclusio* with the letter's opening blessing of "grace … and peace" (1:2). This letter is not unique in this pattern. Every Pauline letter begins with a benedictory greeting of "grace … and peace"; every letter ends with a blessing that bestows God's *grace* upon his flock. But seven (more than half) precede this final blessing with the *Pax Domini*, the giving of the Lord's *peace*. Ephesians is unique only to the extent[142] that it places the two concluding blessings into immediate succession,[143] while in all other letters with a final blessing of "peace," there are greetings, commendations, exhortations, or other literary formalities that intervene before "grace."[144]

Curiosity seeks an explanation for this consistency of form. Why the giving of both "peace" and "grace"? Certainly, the parallel to his opening blessing (1:2) provides a satisfactory answer; the Hebrew *shalom* is again combined with the Greek *greeting/grace*.[145] It is also typical of Ephesians to be liturgically redundant, and with this double blessing Paul manages to sum up the letter's theme with the key terms "peace … love … faith … grace … love" (6:23–24).[146] However, the context suggested by the greetings, the kiss of peace, and the language of closed Communion invites the reader to hypothesize about possible liturgical explanations. Just as the medieval Western rite, inherited by Lutherans, connects the giving of the Lord's peace intimately to the moment

---

[142] Some commentators argue that Ephesians is also unique in using the third person plural ("the brothers … all those who love" rather than the plural "you") for the blessing. This feature is certainly unusual in a strictly formal sense (the only other NT example is Rev 22:21). It has been interpreted as giving the blessing "a certain aloofness (Barth), solemnity (Ernst) and impersonality" (Best, *Ephesians*, 617), though Barth notes: "The distance is not to be exaggerated, for those blessed are still called 'brothers' and people who 'love the Lord' " (*Ephesians*, 2:815). (For "solemnity," see Josef Ernst, *Die Briefe an die Philipper, an Philemon, an die Kolosser, an die Epheser* [Regensburg: Pustet, 1974], 403.) Most interpret it as evidence that this is a circular letter—but there is no reason why this should be the case, as the only explicitly circular letters in the NT end with a *second* person plural blessing (Gal 6:18; 1 Pet 5:14; the blessing of peace in Gal 6:16 is third person plural). It may be better to view the third person expression "grace be with all who love the Lord …" as a contraction of the greetings and language of closed Communion found in other epistles, and perhaps even a quotation of familiar language from an early Christian liturgical rite.

[143] The resultant, apparently double blessing has been interpreted as (1) making a distinction between Paul's fellow workers ("brothers," 6:23) and the rest of the church ("all those … ," 6:24) and (2) representing a formal blessing through the amanuensis (6:23) followed by a second in Paul's own hand (6:24). See E. Earle Ellis, "Paul and His Co-workers," *New Testament Studies* 17 (1970–1971): 445–51, cited by Bruce, *The Epistles to the Colossians, to Philemon, and to the Ephesians*, 415, n. 108. In light of the rather consistent pattern in the rest of Paul's letters and the common use of "brothers" for all Christians, this explanation is unjustified.

[144] Rom 16:20 might appear to be parallel to Eph 6:23–24 in this regard, but Rom 16:20a does not constitute a *blessing* with "peace"—that was back in Rom 15:33.

[145] See the first textual note on 1:2 for an explanation of how the apostle transforms the common Greek "joyful greetings" (χαῖρε, χαίρετε, or χαίρειν) into "grace" (χάρις).

[146] Barth, *Ephesians*, 2:816.

of holding forth the Lord's body and blood to the gathered faithful,[147] so also the most ancient of Eastern rites include an apostolic blessing of peace in the Service of the Sacrament. Likewise, the oldest Eastern rites often use Paul's benediction to introduce the Sacrament: "The grace of the Lord Jesus Christ and the love of God and the communion of the Holy Spirit be with you all" (2 Cor 13:13 [ET 13:14]).[148]

This raises, of course, a certain "chicken and egg" question: did the earliest rites draw these words from Paul, or did Paul get them from existing liturgical practice? It is intriguing to consider the possibility of a little of both. That is, as Paul enters into the Ephesian congregation's Divine Service with his letter, he may have consciously chosen to quote or paraphrase the very sorts of blessings that were spoken in the liturgy at that point, taught by him in his own ministry among the Ephesians perhaps, or drawing on the common practice of apostolic Christianity. At the same time, the inspired Pauline forms of these blessings, recognized by the early church as so very appropriate to the context of the Sacrament, likely gave consistency to the formulations used at this point in the early rites. The point is that by blessing the brethren with "peace," "love," "faith," and "grace" (6:23–24), Paul was probably alluding to the words of peace that were part of the expression of Communion fellowship in the earliest rites.

---

[147] "P: The peace of the Lord be with you always. C: Amen." See, e.g., *LSB* 197. Luther gives the following explanation in his 1523 revision of the Latin mass:

> But immediately after the Lord's Prayer shall be said, "The peace of the Lord," etc., which is, so to speak, a public absolution of the sins of the communicants, the true voice of the gospel announcing remission of sins, and therefore the one and most worthy preparation for the Lord's Table, if faith holds to these words as coming from the mouth of Christ himself. On this account I would like to have it pronounced facing the people, as the bishops are accustomed to do, which is the only custom of the ancient bishops that is left among our bishops. (AE 53:28–29)

[148] In some older forms of the Preface dialogue, "the Lord be with you," which opens the Service of the Sacrament (e.g., *LSB* 194), is expanded to "the *peace of* the Lord be with you." See, for example, *The Liturgy of Saints Addai and Mari* (trans. Jasper and Cuming, *Prayers of the Eucharist*, 42), which derives from Edessa, Syria, and reflects early practice prior to the dominance of the Byzantine rite (material in angle brackets has been supplied by the translators from other manuscripts of the same document):

> *Priest:* Peace be with you.
>
> *Answer:* And with you and your spirit.
>
> *Priest:* The grace of our Lord <Jesus Christ and the love of God the Father, and the fellowship of the Holy Spirit be with us all now and ever world without end>.
>
> *Answer:* Amen.
>
> *Priest:* Up with your minds [= *sursum corda*, "lift up your hearts," in the Latin rite].
>
> *Answer:* They are with you, O God [= *habemus ad Dominum*, "we have them with the Lord," in the Latin rite].

From here the rite continues with the Preface and the Sanctus. The following early Eastern rites also begin the Preface with 2 Cor 13:13 (ET 13:14): *The Liturgy of Saint James* (Jasper and Cuming, 90), *The Apostolic Constitutions* (Jasper and Cuming, 104), *The Byzantine Liturgy of St. Basil* (Jasper and Cuming, 116), and *The Liturgy of St. John Chrysostom* (Jasper and Cuming, 131). Many later, dependent rites could also be cited.

Thus, the "peace" is the final piece in the puzzle that included the kiss of peace, the greetings, and the invitations to and exclusions from the Supper. Peace, a gift of God, had the effect of reconciling brothers and sisters to each other as both prerequisite and consequence of communing together. "Grace," its counterpart, was the gift of God that reconciled them to himself, in Christ, merited by his atoning work, and bestowed by the Holy Spirit's working in the Gospel delivered through Word and sacramental gifts. With these final words Paul takes again his old position at the Ephesian sacramental table (cf. 1 Cor 10:21) and speaks the Lord's blessing from the place where the Lord's gifts are given out. He enters again into the Ephesians' fellowship.

As in the introductory blessing (1:2) and the doxologies (1:3; 3:21), Paul uses no verb to bestow the "grace" or "peace" in these blessings (6:23–24). This is the most common NT pattern, as can be seen from the chart above, in which only one blessing includes such a verb: the optative δῴη, "may he give," in 2 Thess 3:16. Where no verb is present in Greek it is natural to supply the copula in the indicative: "is." This might suggest that Paul's "blessings" are merely statements of fact: the Ephesians *do have* peace and grace from God. However, as blessings and doxologies in the Greek Bible sometimes include indicative verbs and sometimes optatives (see the first textual note on 1:3), one cannot exclude either verbal aspect from their interpretation. In other words, *in his apostolic blessing, Paul expresses what is true, prays that it may be true, and makes it true by his speaking.* Where optatives occur in the LXX, they are often translations of the Hebrew jussive (e.g., Num 6:24–26).[149] These jussives and optatives are not mere wishes, but are chosen by the inspired biblical writers as the best grammar to express the reality of a divine blessing: through such human words God actually confers his gifts. As God commanded the priests to bless the people with his words, so Paul is God's instrument for conveying this final word of blessing. When the Ephesians—indeed, all Christians who receive his letter—hear Paul, they hear the One who sent him (Lk 10:16; Acts 26:16–18; 2 Cor 5:20). As this Lutheran commentary on Paul draws to a close, it is fitting to give Luther the final word:

> But this blessing is more than an empty sound of words or some verbal wish in which one person tells and wishes another person good things, as when I say: "May God grant you pious and obedient children." These words are nothing more than wishes with which I give nothing to the other person but only desire something eagerly for him, and it is a blessing that depends entirely on events and is uncertain. But this blessing of the patriarch Isaac [Gen 27:29] states facts and is sure to be fulfilled. It is not a wish; it is the bestowal of a good thing—the bestowal with which he says: "Take these gifts which I am promising you verbally." For it is one thing when I say: "I would wish you

---

[149] In Num 6:24–26, the verbs יָאֵר ("make shine," Num 6:25) and וְיָשֵׂם ("and give," Num 6:26) are jussive both in form and meaning; and the other four verbs, while indistinguishable in form, are jussive in meaning. See Joüon, § 114 g, n. 1. The LXX appropriately translates all six Hebrew verbs with the Greek optative mood.

to have a strong and healthy body, and to be gifted with fine talents," where the Word by which you get these things does not follow. It is another thing when I offer you a bag of money and say: "Take the thousand guldens I am presenting to you," or when Christ says to the paralytic (Matt. 9:6): "Take up your bed and go home." According to an ordinary blessing, He would say: "Would that you were well and in full possession of your strength!" But the sickness would not be removed. Nor would a restoration of his strength ensue. Therefore it is only a verbal blessing.

In Holy Scripture, however, there are real blessings. They are more than mere wishes. They state facts and are effective. They actually bestow and bring what the words say. We also have blessings of this kind in the New Testament through Christ's priesthood, which is our blessing when I say: "Receive the absolution of your sins." If I said: "Would that your sins were forgiven you; would that you were pious and in God's grace!" or "I wish you grace, mercy, the eternal kingdom, and deliverance from your sins," this could be called a blessing of love. But the blessing of a promise, of faith, and of a gift that is at hand is this: "I absolve you from your sins in the name of the Father and of the Son and of the Holy Spirit; that is, I reconcile your soul to God, remove from you God's wrath and displeasure, put you in His grace, and give you the inheritance of eternal life and the kingdom of heaven." All these things have the power to grant you forgiveness immediately and truly if you believe, for they are not our works; they are God's works through our ministry. Accordingly, they are not blessings that express wishes; they are blessings that have the power to bestow. When I baptize you in the name of the Father and of the Son and of the Holy Spirit, it is just as if I were saying: "I am snatching you from the hands of the devil and bringing you to God, and I am doing this truly and in fact."[150]

---

[150] Luther, *Lectures on Genesis*, on Gen 27:29, AE 5:140–41. Cf. Peter Brunner, *Worship in the Name of Jesus* (trans. Martin H. Bertram; St. Louis: Concordia, 1968), 136.

Index of Subjects

807

Greek (language), 6, 10, 13–17, 34, 42,
54–55, 71–73, 89, 105, 136, 154–56,
167, 173–74, 179, 183, 193, 197, 204,
207–8, 211, 216, 220, 239–40, 243,
249, 259, 281, 286, 294, 311, 314,
336–37, 372, 391, 397, 400, 421, 432,
440, 444, 449–51, 456, 462, 470, 496,
513, 527, 537, 566, 591, 595, 599–
601, 604, 606, 613, 669, 713, 719, 737

Greeks, 6, 98, 121, 127, 141–44, 202, 240,
249, 272–73, 281, 320, 330, 335, 372,
717, 742. *See also* Gentiles; Paganism;
World, ancient
culture of, 202, 255, 258, 271–74, 346,
429, 635, 663–64, 674–75, 684,
686, 717–18
literature or rhetoric of, 148, 179, 192,
197, 257, 271, 297, 425, 546, 605,
722–23
philosophy or religion of, 55, 60, 101,
103–6, 135, 314, 318, 320, 346,
369, 390, 483, 573, 623

Greeting. *See also* Salutation
at conclusion of epistle, 26, 48, 57, 89,
119, 149–50, 176–77, 766, 772,
775–76, 780, 790, 792
as liturgical, 174
at opening of epistle, 11–12, 21, 26,
88, 94, 123, 131, 135, 148, 173,
326
as personal, 91–92, 774–76

Grief, 390, 528–29, 546–47

Growth, 336–37, 472–73, 475–76, 498,
594, 607

Guard, 781

Guide
Law as, 152, 477

Guns, 735

Gunterode, Apollonia, 622

Gut, 532

Guthrie, Donald, 33, 63, 138

Hades, 444–47. *See also* Hell

Hadrian, 103

Hagar, 191, 692

Hagia Sophia, 102

Hail, 746

Hall of Tyrannus, 114

Hallel, 586

Hamann, Henry, 460–61, 495

Hand, 230, 737

"Hand over," 488, 509, 534, 536–37, 609

Hand, right, 244–45, 260–61, 265–66,
268, 303–4, 306, 369, 442, 448, 491,
640, 644, 731. *See also* Ascension;
Authority; Session

Handbook, 8, 13, 148, 150–58, 175, 257,
335, 783–84

Handwriting, 772–74, 790

Hannah, 585

Hapax legomena, 36, 49–53, 204, 289, 342,
580, 613, 705, 759
of NT, 243, 284, 318, 362, 371, 397,
462, 470, 509, 516, 523, 554, 565,
568, 611, 668

Haplography, 236

Harbor, 97

Hardening, 508–9

Harmony, 336, 487. *See also Concordia*;
Unity

Harnack, Adolf von, 22, 42

Harp, 587

Harris, Horton, 66–67

Harrowing of hell, 443–46, 491–93, 729.
See also Descent of Christ into hell

Harshness, 662

Hasmoneans, 320, 346

Hatred, 284, 321, 616, 657

Hauptpfarrer, 364

Haustafel, 21, 135, 478, 592, 599–600, 602,
604–5, 607–8, 629–33, 638, 644–45,
654, 657, 671, 673–76, 686, 689, 728,
733

Head, 45, 249, 605, 617, 642
covering of, 633

Headlam, Arthur C., 34

Headpiece, 720

Headship, 62–63. *See also Haustafel*
of Christ, 3, 39, 68, 70, 131, 201, 244,
248–52, 254, 269–76, 432–34, 473,
475, 479, 497, 500, 602, 604–5,
630–53
of husband, 600, 602–9, 630–53, 663

Healing, 264, 462

Health, 148–49, 772, 780, 793

Hearer, 8, 13–14, 18, 495

811

Theater, 97, 99, 117, 142

Thecla, 76

Theme, 52, 159, 180, 202, 220, 441, 523,
783
in Ephesians, 14–15, 46, 50, 58–59,
63, 69–70, 129, 138–48, 181, 198,
200, 203, 215, 220–21, 226, 239,
255, 259, 263, 275, 280, 286, 298,
325, 327, 336, 338, 340, 342–43,
358, 362, 378, 389, 417, 421, 428,
432, 446, 462, 480, 483, 488, 521,
524, 551, 560, 562, 572, 593, 609,
626, 635, 702, 731, 734, 753, 762,
767, 774, 777, 790

Theology of Ephesians, 26, 38–44, 55–68

Therapeutae, 635

Thessalonians (people), 32, 88, 636, 764

Thessalonians, First, 22, 25, 59, 75, 87, 92,
118, 150, 168, 256–57, 259, 476, 776

Thessalonians, Second, 25, 48, 59, 75, 92,
150, 168, 193, 257, 776

Thessalonica, 100

Thetis, 742

Thief, 525

Thinking, 239, 395

Thought, 273, 285, 305, 706
of Ephesians, 38–44, 55–68

Thracians, 718

Threats, 631, 670

Three, 481. *See also* Triad

Throne, 289–90, 306, 448

Thug, 640

Thyatira, 573–74

Tiberius, 103

Time, 200–201, 238, 290, 312, 397, 581

Timothy (person), 9, 92, 110, 117–20, 126,
136, 140, 168, 176, 311, 355, 357,
368, 430, 453–57, 470, 494, 534, 761,
764, 784–86

Timothy, First, 44, 46, 54–55, 70–71, 105,
118–20, 211, 256, 456, 642

Timothy, Second, 25, 122, 126, 168, 257,
765

Title, 84, 168

Titus (book), 26, 55, 193, 211

Titus (person), 26, 55, 176, 666, 764,
785–86

Tobias, 529

Tobit (person), 529

Tolkien, J. R. R., 742

Tomb of Jesus, 228

Tongue as language, 588

Topic, 49

Topoi. *See* Commonplaces

Torah, 7–8, 43, 73, 128–29, 281, 285, 319,
323, 346, 385–86, 441, 536, 538, 606,
618, 658, 677, 693, 719

Tower, 308, 611

Tradition, 346–47, 486

Tradition, oral, 3–5, 167, 198, 310. *See also*
Orality

Trafficking, 574

Trajan, 93, 100, 117, 435

Trallians, 82

Trans-Anatolian highway, 98

Transcendence
of God, 251, 437

Transfiguration, 187, 192, 239, 548, 691

Transitus, 407

Translations of Scripture, 458–59, 464, 474,
500–501, 513

Transliteration, 404

Treachery, 281, 509

Treatise, 10

Tree, 416, 526, 562

Trembling, 522, 603–4, 626, 666, 669, 693

Trespass, 281

Triad, 14, 217, 260, 571, 586, 591–92, 629,
767

Trial, 762–63

Tribe, 272, 338, 601, 745

Tribulation, 374

Trickery, 471, 482

Trinity, 14, 112–13, 149, 159, 184, 186,
192, 205, 209, 211, 213, 217, 219,
238, 260, 327, 337, 351, 378, 390–91,
432, 435, 481, 486–87, 533, 571, 583,
592, 633, 640, 643, 672, 779, 793

Triumph. *See* Victory

Troas, 93, 110, 136, 764

Trophimus, 121, 126–27, 142, 181, 237,
319, 322, 345, 348, 354, 374, 380,
483, 764, 787

Index of Passages

22:21–22, 706
22:34, 702, 711

2 Kings
1:8, 517, 710
1:13, 390
3:3, 619
3:15, 587
3:21, 702
4:1, 690
4:29, 709
5:7, 288
5:10, 611
5:13–14, 611
7:15, 702
9:1, 709
15:9, 662
17:10, 543
17:16, 246
17:41, 662
18:6, 619
18:19, 372
18:22, 372
19:28, 522
20:3, 562
20:19, 526
22:8–10, 8
23:1–3, 8
23:7, 556
25:17, 334

1 Chronicles
5:25, 556, 651
10:9–10, 702
12:9 (ET 12:8), 715
12:34 (ET 12:33), 702
12:35 (ET 12:34), 715
12:38 (ET 12:37), 702
15:27, 547, 711, 753
16:4, 258, 601
16:7, 601
16:13, 187
16:22, 557
16:27, 192
16:28–29, 417
16:34, 526
16:36, 182, 258, 404
18:7, 715
21:12, 718
21:16, 718
21:27, 718
21:30, 718
22:18, 602
23:25, 338

23:30, 258
24:5, 202
24:7, 202
24:31, 202
25:3, 258
25:8, 202
25:9, 202
26:13, 202
26:14, 202
26:27, 465
29:1, 465
29:10, 182
29:11–13, 417
29:12, 393
29:15, 328
29:17, 667
29:20, 389
29:24, 602

2 Chronicles
1:12, 393
2:10–11 (ET 2:11–12), 215
2:11 (ET 2:12), 183
5:13, 526
6:4, 183
6:13, 390, 409
6:19, 755
6:29, 755
6:32, 316
6:35, 755
6:39, 755
6:41, 547
7:3, 526
7:6, 587–88
9:8, 183
9:15–16, 715
11:15, 507
12:9, 715
12:10, 715
13:12, 272
14:7 (ET 14:8), 715
17:5, 393
17:7–9, 179
18:1, 393
18:16, 455
19:7, 671
20:9, 718
20:17, 703, 747
20:18, 389
23:9, 715
25:5, 715

26:14, 711, 715, 717, 740
28:8–11, 689
28:15, 712
29:31, 327
30:18, 526
30:27, 338
31:2, 601
31:20, 562
32:27, 393
32:31, 761

Ezra
3:11, 258, 589
4:12–13, 463
4:16, 463
5:3, 463
5:9, 463
5:11, 463
6:12, 338
6:13, 357
6:14, 463
7:27, 183
9:5, 390, 409
9:7, 718
9:8, 240
9:13, 294
9:15, 709
10:2, 315

Nehemiah
1:6, 781
2:4, 390
4:3 (ET 4:9), 781
4:10 (ET 4:16), 711, 715
4:12 (ET 4:18), 710
5:5, 690
5:8, 690
8:1–3, 8
8:6, 404
8:18, 8
9:3, 8
9:5, 183
9:6, 288
9:17, 286
9:19, 282
9:30, 23
9:33, 471
12:24, 258
12:46, 587

Esther
1:4, 393
3:4, 656

847

18:17, 57
18:20, 338, 422,
   447–48, 590, 775
18:23–35, 664
18:34, 509
19:5, 618, 655
19:6, 619
19:9, 638
19:17, 431
19:18, 525
19:18–19, 676
19:19, 615, 660
19:28, 180, 289
19:29, 208, 655
20:1–16, 669
20:8, 669
20:18–19, 536
20:23, 296
20:25–28, 497
20:26, 363–64, 366,
   636
20:28, 195, 364
20:34, 532
21:4, 7
21:13, 755
21:16, 463, 469
21:26, 333
21:33, 318
21:33–46, 208
21:35, 450
21:42, 334
22:1–14, 275, 328, 428,
   547, 612, 651
22:4, 296
22:11–12, 749
22:14, 187
22:30, 652
22:36, 323, 660
22:37, 668
22:37–40, 541, 676
22:38–40, 323
22:39, 615
22:44, 245
23:8, 457
23:9, 436
23:12, 429
23:32, 439
24:1, 465
24:2, 321
24:3, 248
24:4, 579
24:8, 375
24:9, 374
24:10, 600

24:11, 333
24:15, 357
24:21, 374
24:22, 187
24:24, 187, 333, 557
24:29, 246, 374
24:31, 187
24:36, 707
24:42–43, 781
24:45, 764
24:45–51, 664
24:49, 583
25:1, 466
25:1–13, 275, 328, 612,
   651
25:2–8, 554
25:5, 567
25:6, 466
25:8, 716
25:11–12, 247
25:13, 781
25:14–30, 664
25:15, 450
25:21, 764
25:23, 764
25:27, 668
25:29, 9
25:31, 392
25:32, 456
25:34, 189, 202, 208,
   296
25:34–46, 557
25:37–40, 296
25:40, 366
26:2, 536
26:7, 770
26:15–16, 536
26:20, 583
26:21–25, 536
26:26, 214
26:26–27, 214
26:26–29, 493, 616
26:27, 214
26:27–28, 583
26:28, 113, 196, 314
26:29, 707
26:30, 586–87
26:31, 456
26:39, 389, 640
26:40, 567
26:40–41, 575, 781
26:41, 758, 781
26:42, 192
26:43, 567

26:45, 567
26:45–48, 536
26:61, 321
26:64, 245
26:65, 531, 546
26:67, 449
27:2–4, 536
27:9, 7
27:18, 536
27:19, 658
27:26, 536
27:28–29, 517
27:31, 546, 548
27:35, 546, 548
27:45–46, 238
27:46, 183, 619
27:51, 319, 350
27:52, 567
27:59–60, 548
27:66, 228
28:5, 603
28:10, 603
28:16–20, 57, 223, 361,
   382, 452, 493
28:17, 449
28:18, 179, 266, 336
28:18–19, 640
28:19, 112–13, 144,
   391, 520, 611
28:19–20, 172, 180,
   206, 326, 338, 360,
   387, 499, 511–12
28:20, 248, 323, 431,
   447–48, 493, 495

Mark
1:4, 113, 145, 196
1:6, 517
1:8, 112, 512, 585, 611
1:10, 113, 611
1:11, 187, 192, 194,
   199
1:15, 200, 206
1:19, 463
1:23, 660
1:27, 655
1:40, 390
1:41, 532
2:19–20, 275
2:26, 754
3:5, 508
3:14–19, 391
3:21, 619
3:27, 492
3:28, 359

875

889

893